# When We Were Young

## A Baby-Boomer Yearbook

### RITA LANG KLEINFELDER

PRENTICE HALL GENERAL REFERENCE

*New York  London  Toronto  Sydney  Tokyo  Singapore*

For my family and friends
who shared
those years with me
and
for my husband David
who loved and supported me
through their re-creation.

PRENTICE HALL GENERAL REFERENCE
15 Columbus Circle
New York, New York, 10023

Library of Congress Cataloging-in-Publication Data

When we were young : a baby-boomer yearbook / Rita Lang
Kleinfelder.
p.    cm.
Includes bibliographical references and index.
ISBN 0-671-84747-3
1. United States—Civilization—1945—Chronology.
2. Civilization, Modern—1950—Chronology.   I. Title.
E169.12.K54   1993
973.92—dc20                                              92-572

Designed by Irving Perkins Associates
Manufactured in the United States of America

First Edition

# Acknowledgments

Heartfelt thanks to my agent Diane Cleaver for her belief in my idea and for her confidence and support through the difficult times.

My thanks and gratitude to Gerard Helferich, my editor, for his skillful advice and endless patience, and to Prentice Hall for their commitment.

Marilyn L. Robinson contacted hundreds of companies and organizations in a search for photographs. As well, she verified and expanded my research on the Nobels, compiled the lists of Sports Winners, wrote up my TV Program list, proofread, and, through everything, inspired me with her good cheer and enthusiasm. My eternal gratitude.

Thanks to Barbara Mah for volunteering to type up New Movies, Sports Winners, TV Programs, and other lengthy lists. Fortunately, our friendship survived those countless hours at the keyboard.

My sister Irene Walton organized my New Words research and helped with borderline songs from her era. Thank you for that and the encouragement over the years.

The Edmonton Public Library deserves a special acknowledgment. The purchasing department went after requested volumes, the magazine staff lugged out back issues and microfilm, and the reference librarians offered unfailing assistance in tracking down those elusive bits of information.

Thanks to William Kurmey, at the University of Alberta, for his invaluable tips on indexing.

And without the skills of my chiropractor, Dr. Donald J. Bradley, months and years at the computer would have been impossible.

Last, but hardly least, my love to my husband, David, for his assistance with Sports, input on other questions and problems, and, most of all, for putting up with my doubts and insecurities.

# PHOTOGRAPH CREDITS

# Contents

# Preface

*Through the sheer weight of their numbers, baby-boomers have shaped our culture for 45 years. As infants, we made a monster best-seller of Dr. Spock's book on child care. As children, we demanded Davy Crockett caps, transistor radios, and Barbie dolls. And, in the late 1960s, we politicized campuses and created the hippie culture.*

*Today, baby-boomers look back at their youth with mixed emotions, fondly remembering classic TV shows, early rock music, and the Hula Hoop, but recalling the Vietnam War and Watergate with bitterness and regret.*

*When We Were Young returns to those yesterdays, the years that shaped our lives and changed our world forever.*

## 1947–1975

While 1946 marked the beginning of the baby boom, 1947 witnessed the greatest single-year population spurt in U.S. history and marked a watershed between the aftermath of World War II and the onset of the Cold War.

In turn, 1975 signaled the end of an era, the last Apollo mission, the Watergate convictions, and the final withdrawal from Vietnam.

To give the reader a sense of immediacy, the book is written in the present tense with the terms of the day. Beijing is Peking, for instance, and African-Americans are called Negroes through the early 1960s. The Russia of our youth must remain the sole exception. With recent political developments, confusion could only be avoided by referring to the USSR (Union of Soviet Socialist Republics) and the Soviet Union.

## HOW TO USE THE BOOK

Each chapter begins with a summary introduction and covers the same topics. In this way, the reader can move comfortably from one year to the next or skip from chapter to chapter for a subject of special interest.

A topic, under any one year, may omit one or more subsections.

**News.** Events appear in chronological order; items difficult to pin down to a specific day or month are discussed last as *More news.*

At the end of each year's News, the reader will find general obituaries. The cross-reference 'See News' denotes earlier extensive coverage under the person's death date. Generally, an omission of nationality means the individual was American.

**Beginnings and Endings.** News (the first airplane hijacking, the opening of Disneyland), Records, establishment of Government Departments and Agencies, New Products and Businesses, and Fads.

**Science and Technology.** News, Other Discoveries, Developments, and Inventions, and Obituaries.

**The Arts.** Coverage includes fine arts, opera, dance, drama, and symphonic music, with a selection of New On and Off Broadway Productions, Tony Awards, News, and Obituaries.

**Words.** A selection of New Books, News, Cartoons and Comics, *Time* Man of the Year (the person who, for good or bad, exerted the greatest influence on that year), New Words and Phrases which became prominent or were coined over that and the previous year (reprinted with permission from editions of the *Britannica Book of the Year*, copyrighted 1947 to 1976, by Encyclopaedia Britannica, Inc., Chicago, Illinois), and Obituaries.

**Fashion.** Haute Couture, News, Color and Materials, Clothes, Accessories, Hair and Cosmetics, and Obituaries.

**Popular Music.** Number 1 and Number 2 Hits (title/title means a two-sided hit; artist/artist means two versions; See 1955 for a full explanation of Billboard selections), Grammy Awards (1958 on, under the year of production), News, New Recording Artists, and Obituaries. [Note: December releases, which take weeks to reach Number 1 or Number 2, are listed under the following year.]

**Movies.** A selection of New Releases (title, director, color or black/white print, actors; memorable films, but not necessarily box-office hits) Academy Awards, News, the annual lists of Top Box Office Stars and Newcomers (reprinted with the permission of Quigley Publishing Company, Inc.), Top Moneymaker, Flop of the Year, Quote of the Year, and Obituaries.

**Television and Radio.** New Prime-Time TV Programs (first and last episodes, actors, and type of show), Emmys (from 1949 on, the major categories listed vary over the years according to the Academy designation), News, TV Commercials, Memorable Radio Programs End, and Obituaries.

**Sports.** Winners (in each major sport), Last Season (retiring athletes), News, Records, What They Said, and Obituaries.

## *Appendix*

**Acronyms.** After the first mention, the text refers to many organizations and government departments by their acronym or abbreviation only. The full term accompanies each acronym or abbreviation in this alphabetical list.

## *Select Bibliography*

Since hundreds of books were used in researching this book, the bibliography includes only the most important titles. Those suggested for browsing are asterisked. Some of the books are no longer in print, but may be available at your local library.

# 1947

---

*Although victorious in W.W.II, Britain and France are devastated by the years of battle. Only the United States and the Union of Soviet Socialist Republics (USSR) emerge as economic powers, and each threatens the other from opposite ends of the political spectrum. The Soviets, determined to prevent another German invasion, move into bordering Eastern European states. The Americans, faced with expanding Communism, abandon isolationism and embrace the Marshall Plan.*

*With aid to Europe priming the economy, U.S. manufacturers are once again able to produce consumer goods. But the construction industry staggers under the housing demands of thousands of returning veterans and their young families.*

*Headline news in 1947 includes the Texas City disaster, the deaths of Henry Ford and gangsters Al Capone and Bugsy Siegel. Princess Elizabeth marries a member of the Greek royal house, Jackie Robinson breaks baseball's color barrier, Thor Heyerdahl rafts across the Pacific, and Howard Hughes flies the Spruce Goose. Edwin Land introduces the Polaroid camera, Raytheon rents the first microwave oven, and Christian Dior drops women's skirts to within a foot of the floor.*

## NEWS

**January 1.** With the end of W.W.II, the victorious Allies (United States, Great Britain, France, and the USSR) divided Nazi Germany into four zones of occupation. The Big Four, at the Potsdam Conference later that year, pledged a united Germany, but, in the two years since, Moscow has resisted all attempts at reunification rather than risk another war with Germany. Instead, the Soviets have established a Communist state in their eastern zone and siphoned off millions of dollars in reparations.

The frustrated Americans and British, convinced that only a healthy Germany can contribute to its own economic rehabilitation, today merge their zones economically. In effect, they divide Germany into eastern and western halves and set its future course within Europe.

**January 1.** The Atomic Energy Act of 1946 removes control of the powerful new form of energy from the army and places it in the hands of a civilian agency, the Atomic Energy Commission. The AEC will continue to meet the needs of the military, while placing increased emphasis on peaceful applications. All fissionable materials and most production facilities are to remain government owned.

**January 1.** With the agreement of all parties, the Labour government in Great Britain establishes a welfare state, with the nationalization of the coal mines. To assume responsibility for areas such as industry, health, education, housing, and working conditions, the government will nationalize other industries as well; private companies will receive compensation.

**January 3.** The 80th Congress convenes with 245 Republicans and 187 Democrats in the House and 51 Republicans and 45 Democrats in the Senate. Last year's midterm elections gave the Republicans control of both houses for the first time in 16 years and, for the first time since Woodrow Wilson's second administration, one party holds the presidency while the other holds the majorities in Congress. New to the Senate is Joseph McCarthy (R., Wisc.); new to the House are Richard Nixon (R., Calif.) and John F. Kennedy (D., Mass.).

**January 19.** In Soviet-occupied Poland, the Communists and their allies, the Socialists, gain a majority through rigged elections. Despite Western diplomatic protests, the Communists will dominate that government by the end of 1948 and Poland will become the third "People's Democracy." Stalin, determined to secure his western border, has already seen to the election of Communist-dominated governments in Albania and Bulgaria.

---

*Statistics:* A 1945 Gallup poll revealed 38 percent of Americans viewed the Soviet Union as "aggressive"; a poll this year shows 66 percent consider the Communist nation a threat.

---

**January 24.** Continuing protests by white liberals force Ottawa to cancel the planned deportation of Japanese-Canadians. During W.W.II, authorities moved over 20,000 Japanese-Canadians into detention camps. The federal government, toward the end of the war, offered internees assistance to return to Japan. Some 10,500 accepted, but, once the war ended over 6,000 chose to remain in Canada. Ottawa refused them permission and a

1946 legal challenge found in favor of the government decision.

**January 25.** Gangster Al "Scarface" Capone dies of syphilis. Capone controlled the Chicago underworld in the 1920s and, during Prohibition bootleg wars, probably ordered more than 300 murders. Yet the mobster eluded prosecution until 1932 when agents nailed him for tax evasion. Capone was paroled in 1939 for good behavior, but with his mind already damaged by disease, retired to Florida.

**January 26.** Grace Moore, the internationally famous American opera, radio, and screen star, dies in a plane crash in Copenhagen, Denmark. At least 26 other civilian air crashes this year will take a total of 643 lives, with 53 being the greatest number lost in a single accident; 96 will survive in 8 different crashes.

**January 29.** The United States, after many years of special friendship with China, formally terminates its mediation efforts between Chinese Nationalists and Communists. In 1911, Sun Yat-sen led a successful revolution against the Manchu dynasty, rulers of China since 1644, but his new government failed to establish its authority. Following Sun Yat-sen's death in 1925, General Chiang Kai-Shek finally won the struggle for power. He established a centralized Nationalist government in 1928, then conducted a series of campaigns against the Communist revolutionaries. The Communists eventually fled to northwestern China in 1934. During that harrowing Long March, in which thousands died, Mao Tse-tung emerged as their leader.

After the Japanese surrender at the end of W.W.II, the Nationalists and Communists both sought control of resource-rich Manchuria, and civil war broke out. The United States moved to reinforce Chiang Kai-shek, while American envoy General George C. Marshall tried, for 12 months, to reconcile the two governments.

With the announcement today, Washington publicly condemns both Nationalist and Communist extremists for the ongoing conflict.

**Early 1947.** A Bedouin boy, searching for a stray animal, discovers ancient parchments hidden in a cave. The Dead Sea scrolls expand scholars' knowledge of early Judaism and reveal that the Bible did not develop as a whole text. Through the remainder of the decade and into the early 1950s, scrolls will be found in 10 more caves.

**February 10.** The Allied nations (United States, Canada, Britain, France, and the USSR) and the former Axis powers (Italy, Finland, Romania, Bulgaria, and Hungary) formally terminate their state of war. The peace treaties are relatively mild since all five defeated nations made peace before the end of the war, then fought against their former ally, Germany. Italy suffers the greatest loss, with its North African colonies and part of its national territory going to Yugoslavia and Greece. (Because the issue of German reunification remains unresolved, that country is not part of the agreement.)

**February 13.** After 28 years of oil exploration in western Canada, Imperial Oil strikes it rich, near Leduc in central Alberta. An additional 30 wells, drilled by the end of the year, turn the farming community into an important oil field and save a province almost bankrupted by the Depression of the 1930s. Further exploration uncovers huge reserves of natural gas.

**February 14.** Britain announces its decision to place the Palestine issue before the United Nations. The British conquered Palestine at the close of W.W.I. With their declared support for the establishment of a Jewish national home, the League of Nations gave Britain a mandate to administer the former Turkish territory. But following W.W.II, London was torn by its pledge to the Jews and a need for Arab support in the Middle East. As both Zionist and Arab leaders reject its latest plan of partition, Britain admits failure.

In May, as the United Nations wrestles with the problem, Iraq's delegate, Fadhil Jamali, comments on the movement of Jewish refugees into Palestine. "The trouble with you Americans is that you think it is a case of a people without a homeland moving into a land without a people" (*Time*, May 19, 1947).

**March 12.** In a major foreign policy address to a joint session of Congress, President Truman proposes that the United States abandon its traditional stance of nonintervention to help Greece and Tur-

key recover from the war and strengthen their resistance to Communism.

Britain, since liberating Greece from the Nazis in 1944, has provided the Loyalists with military and economic aid to fight the Greek Communist resistance movement. But last month, the financially exhausted British secretly urged Washington to take on the responsibility. Truman states, "I believe that it must be the policy of the United States to support free peoples who are resisting attempted subjugation by armed minorities or by outside pressures."

Congress gives the president a standing ovation and later passes a $400-million aid bill. Yet there is some fear that a policy of "containment" will divide the world into spheres of influence. In Rome, *Time* magazine correspondent Emmet Hughes describes European reaction to the Truman Doctrine: "Everywhere, racing tongues and typewriters, trying to articulate racing hopes and fears, greeted the dramatic appearance of the U.S. in the center of the world arena with some hysteria, much hyperbole, great hope—and a perceptible shudder" (*Time*, March 24, 1947).

HARRY S. TRUMAN
Born: May 8, 1884, Lamar, Missouri, eldest of 2 boys and 1 girl
Education: Night classes at Kansas City Law School, 1923–1925
Military Service: U.S. Army in W.W.I
Marriage: Bess Wallace, June 28, 1919
Children: (Mary) Margaret (b.1924)
Previous Occupations: farmer, haberdasher, judge, senator
Position Before Taking Office: Vice-President
Legal Residence When Elected: Missouri

**March 14.** The government of the Philippines signs a 99-year treaty with the United States, guaranteeing American military and naval bases in the islands. The Philippines, conquered by the Spanish in 1565 and ceded to the United States after the 1898 Spanish-American War, just won its independence in July of last year.

**March 21.** Congress approves the first proposed constitutional amendment in 14 years, the 22nd, which limits the president to two full terms in office. As well, if a vice-president serves more than two years of a president's unfinished term, he may only be elected to one more term (Truman is exempt). Following President Roosevelt's four terms (1933–1945), the 22nd Amendment reflects a belief that this powerful office should not be occupied by one person indefinitely.

Of the 2,000 constitutional amendments proposed in the United States since 1789, only 26 have received the two-thirds majority needed in both Houses for submission to the states for ratification: 21 have been approved, 4 have been rejected, and 1 on child labor is pending.

The 36th state will ratify the 22nd Amendment on February 26, 1951, making Franklin Delano Roosevelt the first and last president to serve more than two terms.

**March 22.** As postwar relations with the Soviet Union have deteriorated, the American government has moved against the threat of Communist infiltration. Approximately 800 federal employees have been fired on "disloyalty charges" following secret investigations, and a dozen states have banned the Communist party from the electoral ballot. President Truman, in an attempt to protect federal employees from unfounded accusations and prevent Congress from instituting more stringent measures, issues Executive Order 9835.

No federal employee may belong to or sympathize with Communist organizations and the Federal Bureau of Investigation (FBI) will investigate all employees through "loyalty" boards. But, when Republicans brand the investigations a whitewash, the measure simply feeds the rising tide of anti-Communist paranoia.

**March 24.** The House Committee on Un-American Activities (HUAC), created in 1938 to investigate German-American associations for pro-Nazism, begins hearings on proposals to restrict Communist activities. HUAC hears from former ambassador to Russia, William Bullit (1933–1936), that the American Communist party is an agency of Moscow, intended to weaken the United States

for Soviet attack. FBI Director J. Edgar Hoover agrees that the Communists are "a fifth column if there ever was one," but advises against outlawing the party since the "Reds" will only go underground.

The Committee ignores his advice and on April 1 asks Attorney General Tom Clark to begin prosecuting Communists as unregistered foreign agents. Officially, HUAC can only suggest appropriate alterations to any law.

**March 25.** In Illinois, an explosion rocks a Centralia coal mine, trapping 142 men in a four-mile-long tunnel. Only 31 survive, making this the worst American mine disaster since 1928, when 195 miners died in an explosion at Mather, Pennsylvania. An investigation uncovers numerous safety violations reported over many years; in 1948 the Centralia Coal Company will be fined $1,000 for willful neglect.

**March 31.** An evaluation of the U.S. separate school system reveals that, while Negroes make up 10–11 percent of the nation's population, they lack proportional representation in the professions: 1,000 out of 176,000 American lawyers are black; 8,000 of 400,000 nurses are black; and there is only 1 Negro doctor for every 4,000 blacks, while Caucasians have a 1:950 ratio. The United Negro College Fund ordered the study, reportedly not to attack or defend the system, but to determine the size of the problem.

**March 31.** The military draft, established by the Selective Service Act of 1940, ends, making the United States the only major world power without peacetime conscription.

A week later Washington discloses some W.W.II statistics: 15 percent of the 1940 American population was enlisted in the Armed Forces; the war cost $340 billion, or 87.5 percent of the entire national wealth (20 times U.S. costs in W.W.I); and, unlike W.W.I, when 70 percent of the indebtedness of other countries to the United States was for war goods, 90 percent of W.W.II indebtedness to the United States is for rehabilitation and reconstruction funds provided over the past two years.

**April 15.** Former Auschwitz Commandant Rudolf Hoess is hanged today on the site of the concentration camp in Poland. During his trial, Hoess admitted to exterminating 3 million Jews.

**April 16.** "Let us not be deceived—we are today in the midst of a cold war." American millionaire and adviser to U.S. presidents, Bernard Baruch, coins the phrase at a speech in the South Carolina Legislature.

**April 16.** In Texas City, Texas, fire breaks out on the moored French freighter *Grandcamp.* As fire fighters battle the blaze, the cargo of ammonium nitrate fertilizer explodes, killing everyone on the vessel and docks. A chain reaction detonates the nearby Monsanto chemical plant, demolishes most of the business district, and sets off fires throughout the rest of the city. With most of the fire-fighting equipment destroyed and the water supply knocked out, the situation quickly becomes desperate. When a second shipload of nitrates blows up after midnight, many people flee, leaving the city to burn itself out.

The worst disaster in U.S. history kills at least 561 (likely more, since migrant laborers worked the dock area) and seriously injures some 3,000. The causes? The cargo of ammonium nitrate, formerly used by the army for explosives, was packed in highly flammable plastic containers. Unaware of the danger, the crew smoked on board. Once fire broke out, the ship's officers, fearing water damage to the cargo, failed to fight the blaze aggressively through the night. And finally, authorities hesitated over towing the ship away from the dock area; the order came just five minutes before it exploded. Lawsuits follow, but the last action will not be settled until 1953, when the total payout will reach $17 million.

**April 21.** On her 21st birthday, Princess Elizabeth of Great Britain, heir to the throne, speaks on the radio to her people. "I declare before you all that my whole life, whether it be long or short, shall be devoted to your service and the service of our great imperial family to which we all belong."

**May 3.** Following last month's parliamentary elections, the Japanese constitution goes into effect. On August 14, 1945, five days after the detonation of a second atomic bomb over Japan, Tokyo accepted the Allied terms of surrender. American troops landed two weeks later and have occupied the country since. Still, General Douglas MacArthur, su-

preme commander in Japan for the Allied Powers, has pushed for some measure of independence for this potentially valuable ally. As well, today, he allows the Japanese to display their Rising Sun flag for the first time since the end of the war.

**May 25.** Anastasio Somoza García seizes the government of Nicaragua in a bloodless coup. U.S. influence in the country dates from 1912 when continuing social and political unrest prompted Washington to send in the Marines to protect American interests. The Americans withdrew following the establishment of an elected government in 1933; Somoza overthrew that government on January 1, 1937. His presidential term of office had expired earlier this year.

**June 5.** Secretary of State George C. Marshall (appointed in January to replace the ill James Byrnes) outlines a long-range policy of aid to Europe and Asia, in a speech at Harvard University. He suggests that, if the Europeans together take the initiative of drawing up a comprehensive recovery program, America, with more than half the world's industrial capacity and shipping, will provide the financial support.

Washington hopes to strengthen U.S. ties with Western Europe and combat the spread of Communism, but Moscow accuses the United States of planning to split Europe into Eastern and Western blocs by imposing an economic dictatorship over the continent. The Soviets withdraw from the program, forcing other Eastern European countries to follow.

Sixteen Western European nations submit a proposal for $16.4–$22.4 billion of aid over four years. Truman reduces the amount to $17 billion in grants and loans, and presents the Marshall Plan to Congress on December 19.

**June 16.** When the Republican-dominated House and Senate cut income taxes to fulfill a campaign promise, Truman vetoes the bill. He insists that, with employment and income at record high levels, any budget surplus should be applied to debt retirement. (The national debt skyrocketed from $16.1 billion in 1930, through the Depression and the war, to $269.4 billion in 1945.) The House fails by two votes to muster the two-thirds majority needed to override the veto. In August, the administration reduces the debt by over $11 billion, the first downturn in 17 years.

> *Statistics*: One-third of U.S. families earn between $2,500 and $5,000.

**June 23.** Congress passes the Taft-Hartley Labor-Management Relations Act over the veto of President Truman. Widespread antilabor sentiment grew last year, when 4,985 strikes, three times the previous yearly high, slowed the U.S. economy.

The act forbids the closed shop (meaning that a worker does not have to join a union) and sympathy strikes, introduces an 80-day "cooling off" period before a strike or lockout, authorizes government injunctions where strikes "imperil the national health or safety," and bars unions from contributing to political campaigns. The act's most controversial clause proves to be section 9(h), which requires union officers to file affidavits disclaiming any connection with Communism. Labor vows to fight for a repeal of the legislation.

**June 24.** While flying his two-seater plane to Portland, 32-year-old Idaho businessman Kenneth Arnold sees nine saucerlike objects streaking over the Cascade Range at "1,200 mph in formation, like the tail of a kite." Despite additional ground reports from more than 30 states and Canada over the next two weeks, psychiatrists label the sightings mass hallucination or suggestibility. The air force calls them a possible "prank of nature." The public, for the first time, dubs the phenomena "unidentified flying objects" or "UFOs."

**July 18.** A new U.S. Presidential Succession Act provides in the absence of a vice-president that the presidency will go to the speaker of the House, then to the president pro tempore of the Senate, the secretary of state, and finally Cabinet members according to rank. President Truman, who recommended the change soon after assuming office in April 1945, believes the speaker of the House—elected first by his constituents then chosen by his peers—best represents selection by the people. Under the act of 1886, the secretary of state headed the list.

**July 26.** Acting on a presidential recommendation, Congress reorganizes the antiquated American defense setup to provide a military foundation for Cold War diplomacy. The National Security Act regroups the Armed Forces into a national military establishment with executive departments of the army, navy, and air force and secretaries for each. (The air force will be created from the Army Air Corps, while the navy retains its air arm and the Marine Corps.) A U.S. secretary of defense will oversee all branches; James Forrestal, as the first secretary, is sworn in on September 17.

The National Security Act also establishes the National Security Council (NSC), to advise the president on policies relating to national security, and the Central Intelligence Agency (CIA), to coordinate and analyze foreign intelligence reports for the president, to whom the agency is solely responsible. To avoid conflict with the FBI and to protect the privacy of American citizens, the CIA is to have "no domestic security functions."

**August 15.** For 346 years Britain has ruled the Indian subcontinent as a single country. But, as the Indian people fought for their independence, Moslems demanded a country separate from the Hindus. London, faced with a potential civil war, agreed.

The Indian Independence Act partitions the subcontinent into the predominantly Hindu Dominion of India and the mainly Moslem state of Pakistan, with its two parts bracketing India on the east and west. Although the Moslem League and the All-India Congress endorsed the political division, the failure to clearly separate Hindus and Moslems has provoked rioting in both countries. By mid-September, an estimated 4 million people are on the move from one country to the other, and the disruption and bloodshed will continue into 1948.

**August 31.** Soviet pressure has discredited the non-Communist postwar government of Hungary. In today's elections, the Hungarian Communists become the largest single party with 21.6 percent of the vote. And another Eastern European country quietly disappears behind what Winston Churchill in 1946 labeled the "Iron Curtain."

**September 1.** The American Civil War ended 82

years ago but, according to *Time*, 12 southern states continue to pay out more than $3 million yearly in pensions to fewer than 100 Confederate veterans and some 5,000 widows. Still, the women must wait until 1958 before a forgiving Congress will finally declare them eligible for veterans' benefits.

**September 2.** The first U.S. postwar defense agreement, the Rio de Janeiro Pact calls for the peaceful settlement of disputes in the Western Hemisphere and action against aggressors. But the American nations (except Nicaragua and Ecuador) make no provision for a joint military force, and the United States finds itself responding unilaterally to crises in the Western Hemisphere.

**September 25.** Chief War Crimes prosecutor Joseph Keenan announces in Tokyo that, after thorough investigation, "no evidence was available to support the charge that the Emperor [Hirohito] participated in the conspiracy" leading to war in the Pacific. Hirohito will not be tried as a war criminal.

**October 1.** The U.S. housing industry, slowed by the Great Depression, ground to a halt under wartime restrictions. Last spring, William Levitt used an assembly-line system to throw up 2,000 identical Cape Cod houses on his Long Island properties. When the canny businessman set the price under $7,000 with no down payment, hundreds of desperate veterans and their new wives lined up at the sales office. The first families move in today.

Eventually the project will expand to 17,447 homes and a second development will mushroom in Pennsylvania. Although denounced by many as a "social cancer," Levittowns will offer working people a chance to own a home—white working people, that is. Blacks are excluded from this American dream.

**October 3.** In Germany, the U.S. military government exempts an estimated 500,000 former Nazis from trial to hasten the end of denazification proceedings.

**October 5.** In the first televised broadcast from the White House, President Truman urges Americans to voluntarily conserve food to increase food exports to a recovering Europe. An unusually harsh European winter, followed by summer drought, has caused heavy crop losses.

When a 12-car Friendship Train leaves Los Angeles for a cross-country collection, the people of America respond with generosity; the train entering New York on November 10 has grown to 266 cars filled with food.

Asked if the United States will receive any credit for its foreign aid, President Truman responds, "We're not doing this for credit. We are doing this because it's right and necessary" (*Time*, October 27, 1947).

---

*Statistics*: The farming population in the United States continues to decline, dropping from 29.9 percent of the total population in 1920, to 23 percent in 1940, and 19.3 percent this year.

---

**October 5.** In reaction to the Marshall Plan, nine European Communist parties, at a secret conference in Warsaw, establish a Communist Information Bureau. Cominform will coordinate party activities throughout Europe and provide a united front against the "dollar imperialism" of the United States.

**October 10.** The first contingent of American war dead returns home. Of the 313,000 W.W.II U.S. fatalities, an estimated 200,000 will be buried at the request of next of kin in private or military cemeteries. Meanwhile, the American Graves Registration Service continues searching for 17,126 missing GIs.

**October 29.** President Truman's Committee on Civil Rights, established late last year following a number of racial murders, releases a historic report on discrimination in the United States. The committee recommends a complete program to protect civil rights and end segregation: a federal antilynching bill; the elimination of poll taxes to provide equal voting opportunities; the removal of racial housing restrictions; the withholding of federal grants to those practicing discrimination; the creation of a permanent federal commission on civil rights; and the reorganization of the civil rights division of the Justice Department. The government begins to prepare supporting legislation for some of the recommended measures.

**November 20.** Princess Elizabeth marries Lt. Philip Mountbatten (now the Duke of Edinburgh) in Westminster Abbey. With wartime shortages still very evident, the Royal family wanted a simple ceremony, but the British people demanded much more, an occasion to help them forget their hardships and find something steady in their lives again. Over one million people line the streets for the wedding procession. The occasion unknowingly marks the last gathering of European royalty, as several monarchies will fall in the coming years.

**November 29.** Acting on the recommendation of a commission of inquiry, the U.N. General Assembly approves, 33–13, the division of Palestine into Arab and Jewish states, with both to achieve full independence by October 1, 1948. The decision grants a homeland to the survivors of the Holocaust, but, with no provision for implementation, hostilities immediately break out between Jews and Arabs. At least 150 die over the next week, and Washington embargoes all American arms shipments to the Middle East.

**December 15.** In the second significant advance on the civil rights front this year, the President's Commission on Higher Education urges the complete elimination of educational segregation and recommends that all future federal aid include a provision forbidding the discriminatory use of funds.

**December 23.** President Truman pardons 1,523 Americans who evaded the W.W.II draft.

**December 30.** Romanians force young King Michael, the last reigning monarch in Eastern Europe, from the throne and establish a "People's Republic." Since Soviet "liberation" at the end of W.W.II, Michael had used his constitutional powers to fight Communist domination.

## Obituaries

**Stanley Baldwin** (August 3, 1867–December 13, 1947). In 1936, the third-term prime minister informed King Edward VIII that Wallis Simpson, a twice-divorced American, would not be acceptable as the Queen of England, prompting Edward to abdicate.

**R. B. Bennett** (July 3, 1870–June 26, 1947). Canadian prairie farmers, unable to afford gas during the Depression years, dubbed their horse-drawn automobiles "Bennett buggies" after the unpopular Conservative prime minister (1930–1935).

**Al Capone** (January 17, 1899–January 25, 1947). *See* News.

**Christian X** (September 26, 1870–April 20, 1947). The beloved Danish king (1912–1947) was held under house arrest during W.W.II for defying the Nazi occupation force. His son ascends the throne as Frederick IX.

**William Durant** (December 6, 1861–March 18, 1947). With the Buick patent in hand, he purchased the Cadillac and Oldsmobile companies and two others in 1908 to form General Motors (GM); Chevrolet was added in 1915. Durant was pushed out of the company in 1920 and later became a real estate broker.

**George II** (July 20, 1890–April 1, 1947). The king of Greece (1922–1924 and 1935–1947) is succeeded by his brother Paul.

**Paul Percy Harris** (April 19, 1868–January 27, 1947). The founder of the Rotary Club (1905) saw the organization expand into more than 70 countries.

**Frances Folsom Preston** (July 21, 1864–October 29, 1947). When 49-year-old Grover Cleveland wed 21-year-old Frances, he became the first U.S. president to marry while in office. She remarried after his death in 1908.

**Anna Sage** (circa 1889–April 1947). In 1934, "the woman in red" identified gangster John Dillinger to waiting FBI agents, who gunned him down outside Chicago's Biograph movie house. Deported two years later for running a brothel, she claimed the bureau never paid her the promised reward money.

**Benjamin "Bugsy" Siegel** (February 28, 1906–June 20 1947). Reportedly, the Chicago syndicate executed the colorful West Coast mobster for dipping into gambling revenues.

**Victor Emmanuel III** (November 11, 1869–December 28, 1947). Crowned as Italy's third king in 1900, Victor Emmanuel lost favor in 1922 after surrendering power to the Fascists. Last year, in a belated effort to save the monarchy, he abdicated in favor of his son Umberto. Just one month later, the Italian people overwhelmingly voted for a republican form of government.

**Andrew Volstead** (October 31, 1860–January 20, 1947). In 1919, the Republican representative authored the Prohibition Act, which became the 18th Amendment to the Constitution; it was repealed in 1933.

## BEGINNINGS AND ENDINGS

### News

**January 3.** The Canadian Citizenship Act requires the term *Canadian*, rather than *British subjects*, in legal and other documents—80 years after Confederation—and recognizes a woman's right to determine her own nationality rather than automatically assuming the nationality of her non-Canadian husband.

**February 7.** The House and Senate Press Gallery admit a Negro journalist, Percival L. Prattis of the Negro magazine *Our World* in New York.

**March 25.** On the United Nations' first anniversary, John D. Rockefeller III presents an $8.5 million check to Secretary-General Trygve Lie for the purchase of a 6-block river tract north of 42nd Street. The generous gift ends a 15-month search for a site.

**April 29.** The U.S. Post Office issues the Air Letter, a single sheet of paper that can be folded into a stamped envelope.

**May 8.** The International Monetary Fund (IMF), a specialized U.N. agency chartered in 1945, conducts its first piece of business. The World Bank,

*The first U.S. president to visit Canada as a state occasion, Harry S. Truman waves to an Ottawa crowd with Prime Minister William Lyon Mackenzie King.*

created at the same time, began advancing loans to member governments last year.

**June 17.** Pan American Airways inaugurates the first round-the-world airline service. The $1,700 flight will take 13 days (4 days, 5 hours, 32 minutes in the air) to return to New York.

**June 20.** An act of Congress establishes the Everglades National Park as a refuge for endangered plants and animals. By 1960, additional parcels of land will make the Everglades the country's third largest park behind Yellowstone and Mt. McKinley.

**June 27.** Ford Motors grants the auto industry's first pension plan (years of employment × 1 percent of pay). The average 30-year worker will receive $77 a month upon retirement.

**July.** To guard against a Japanese invasion of Alaska during W.W.II, the United States and Canada built a 1,500-mile supply route from Dawson Creek, British Columbia, through the Yukon to Fairbanks at a cost of $140 million to $150 million. This month, the Alaskan Highway opens to commercial freight. Next summer, the roadway will see its first tourists.

**July 18.** Promoted to colonel, Florence Blanchfield is the first woman to receive a commission in the U.S. Army. As Superintendent of Army Nurses, she was instrumental in securing full military rank for the women.

**November 3.** Canada removes the last wartime control on food (sugar and molasses).

**More news.** Oral Roberts, a 29-year-old Oklahoma faith healer, broadcasts over two radio stations this year. He starts up a ministry in 1948 and within 12 years his Pentecostal Holiness Church will attract 2 million members.

• Cleveland's WEWS-TV hires the nation's first news anchorwoman, Dorothy Fuldheim. The sponsoring beer company, at first reluctant, remains loyal to the program for 18 years.

• The Federal Communications Commission (FCC) grants the first citizens band, or CB, radio license. The voice radio communication covers 40 frequencies, with Channel 9 reserved for emergency use and Channel 19 for motorists and truck drivers.

## Records

**February 2.** Snag, in the Yukon, reports the lowest recorded temperature in North America. When the thermometer mercury drops below the last line at −80 degrees, the temperature must be recorded as −81 degrees Fahrenheit; an unofficial guess places the low at −83.

**June 19.** Reaching 623.8 mph, an Army Lockheed P-80R Shooting Star jet recaptures the world speed record for the United States after 24 years.

**August 10.** William P. Odum completes an around-the-world flight from Chicago in 73 hours, 5 minutes, 11 seconds, shattering the only previous solo flight time of 186 hours set by Wiley Post in 1933. But, as Odum fairly points out, his plane

*With their first appearance in the December issues of* Charm, True Story, *and* Mademoiselle, *the Toni Twins establish comparative demonstration as a classic form of advertisement.*

never flew under 330 mph, while Post's averaged 127 mph.

The exhausted Odum, who lost his automatic pilot over Asia, woke at one point over the Rockies to find himself flying straight at the top of Mt. Logan. He claims not to have felt sleepy since.

## *Government Departments and Agencies*

**May 31.** Price Administration officially closes. The office managed 13 rationing programs and stabilized prices and residential rentals over the past five years.

**July 27.** The Housing and Home Finance Agency (HFFA) is established to deal with the enormous housing shortage.

## *New Products and Businesses*

Monosodium glutamate (MSG), a powder that enhances the flavor of meat, is sold under the Ac'cent label.

Brothers-in-law Burton "Butch" Baskin and Irvine Robbins merge their small chains of ice-cream stores in southern California. Baskin-Robbins's 100-plus flavors immediately find a market. Franchised next year, the company will be selling enough ice cream by 1975 to fill 800 million cones annually.

Procter & Gamble introduces Tide, the first hard-water detergent.

# SCIENCE AND TECHNOLOGY

## *News*

**February 21.** Dr. Edwin Land, age 37, demonstrates the revolutionary Polaroid Land Camera. Film develops inside the camera and produces a sepia-toned print within one minute. Model 95 goes on sale for $90 in Boston later this year.

**March 6.** In a three-month exploration of the Antarctic, Admiral Richard E. Byrd and the U.S. Navy Expedition discovered 10 new mountain ranges and 5 offshore islands and mapped some 845,000 square miles (over one-third never seen before). Officially described as a scientific expedition, the mission was largely undertaken to strengthen U.S. claims to the Antarctic and to provide navy personnel with extreme weather training.

**March 9.** Following the discovery of a rich oil field during W.W.II, the first offshore drilling rig is set up in the Gulf of Mexico. This year, a record 35,000 wells are drilled in the United States, but production only meets domestic requirements.

**March 13.** Since fewer than 50 percent of Americans use a toothbrush, the American Dental Association recommends that dentists apply a sodium fluoride solution to children's teeth during routine dental treatments. The value of fluoridation was first recognized in the 1800s, and the first trials with fluoridated water took place in 1915. But, with this recommendation, the controversy over the chemical's effectiveness and safety begins in earnest.

**April 7.** The Public Health Service (PHS) reports the life expectancy of white Americans at 66 years, versus 57 for Negroes. The latter have a 33 percent higher death rate, largely because of the greater prevalence of pneumonia, tuberculosis, and other diseases, and because many medical facilities refuse to treat them. Only 124 Negro hospitals exist at this time.

**April 29.** In an attempt to prove that pre-Incan Indians of South America settled Polynesia, anthropologist Thor Heyerdahl and his five-man crew sail westward from Peru on a balsa raft. The *Kon-Tiki* lands on a Polynesian reef on August 7. The 32-year-old Norwegian's story of his voyage becomes required reading in many schools.

**May 29.** At the University of Chicago, chemistry Professor Willard Frank Libby announces that radiocarbon, or Carbon-14, atoms in organic matter decay at a uniform rate. Measuring the amount of radioactive carbon will fix the age of human, animal, and plant remains. For his discovery, Libby will win the 1960 Nobel prize in chemistry.

**Summer.** This summer, the Mark II begins to give erroneous information. (Howard Aiken's Mark I was the first American programmable computer). A navy investigation discovers a dead moth beside the faulty relay. The insect is taped into the log book with the notation, "First actual bug found."

Later, when programmers must explain delays, Grace Hopper and her colleagues say they are "debugging" the machine.

**August 29.** The AEC announces the completion of a new atomic power plant at the Los Alamos Scientific Laboratory in New Mexico. With plutonium rather than uranium fuel, the "fast reactor" utilizes neutrons to produce energy at a slow, steady rate rather than explosively.

**September 3.** An expedition from the Canadian Mines and Resources Department reports that in the last 40 years the magnetic North Pole has moved 200 miles farther north, to Prince of Wales Island. There it shifts constantly in a 50-mile ellipse.

**September 3.** For the past year, the uranium pile at Oak Ridge, Tennessee, has produced radioactive isotopes for sale to American institutions. Today, President Truman announces that the AEC will furnish other countries with radioisotopes for biological and medical research. The USSR and 29 other nations file applications within days. Over the next year, 15 out of 21 qualifying nations receive shipments.

**September 28.** Dutch and American laboratories simultaneously announce the successful synthesis of vitamin A.

**October 7.** Dr. Hilde Bruch of Columbia University makes the newspapers when he announces that recent studies show overeating, not glandular disturbances, causes obesity. Fewer than 1 in 200 overweight people have a glandular problem.

**October 14.** In a secret flight, 24-year-old test pilot Chuck Yeager breaks the sound barrier in a rocket-propelled Bell X-1. When *Aviation Week* breaks the story in December, Air Force Secretary Symington attempts to block publication. The attorney general informs him that prosecution in peacetime would be impossible, and Symington finally confirms the historic event on June 10, 1948.

**November.** At the 32nd National Hotel Exposition, the Raytheon Company of Waltham, Massachusetts, creates a sensation with its microwave oven. (The effect was accidentally discovered when Percy LeBaron Spencer realized that signal-transmission microwaves had melted a chocolate

bar in his pocket.) The company plans to rent the ovens to the catering trade at $5 a day.

**November 2.** Howard Hughes takes the Hughes H.2 Hercules on a one-mile test flight. Designed during the metal shortages of the war, the wooden eight-engine seaplane is the world's largest aircraft, with a wingspan of 320 feet. But the Pentagon rejects Hughes's design and the eccentric millionaire puts the "Spruce Goose" into permanent storage.

**More news.** Eric Leaver and G. R. Mounce patent AMCRO (automatic machine control by recorded operation). A lack of capital in Canada forces the inventors to look south, but American manufacturers resist the concept. Never fully developed, the articulated hand-arm machine remains a forerunner of later factory robotics.

• Forty-seven-year-old Hungarian-British physicist Dennis Gabor forms the theoretical basis of holography. At this time, however, no form of light exists that could produce the three-dimensional image. With the later development of the laser, holography will bring Gabor the 1971 Nobel prize in physics.

## Other Discoveries, Developments, and Inventions

Tubeless tires, from B. F. Goodrich, which reseal themselves

Electromatic speed meter capable of clocking cars

First successful launch of a missile from a moving platform, a German V-2 captured at the end of the war

First major U.S. aerosol food product, aerated real whipped cream from Reddi-Wip

Varifocal, or "zoom," lens for TV, and 16-mm and 35-mm cameras

Piston core sampler for ocean-floor drilling

Canadian de Havilland Beaver, a bush plane developed in response to a questionnaire

Robot-piloted USAF airplane

Concentrated frozen orange juice from Florida

Disposable plastic baby bottle which, as the milk flows out, collapses as a result of a vacuum

Remote-controlled TV camera from the navy

Standardized film speeds from the American Standards Association (ASA ratings)

First military transport helicopter, the Piasecki HRP-1 Rescuer

## *Obituaries*

**Henry Ford** (July 30, 1863–April 7, 1947). With no professional training in engineering, the car manufacturer built his first vehicle in 1896, established the Ford Motor Co. in 1903, and settled on the Model T design by 1908. Before the design was abandoned in 1927, some 15 million Tin Lizzies had rolled off the assembly line and his concepts of mass production had transformed American industry.

Ford retired in 1918, leaving his son Edsel in charge. When Edsel died in 1943, Henry returned to the company for two years, then turned over control to his grandson, Henry Ford II. Led by the patriarch, the family has donated large sums of money to the philanthropic Ford Foundation.

**Frederick Gowland Hopkins** (June 20, 1861– May 16, 1947). The British biochemist discovered vitamins in 1906.

**Max Planck** (April 23, 1858–October 4, 1947). Along with Einstein, the German scientist revolutionized physics. His fundamental quantum theory earned him the Nobel prize in 1918.

**Almroth Edward Wright** (August 10, 1861– April 30, 1947). The British scientist saved thousands of lives with his typhoid vaccine.

*Note:* Technology relating to a specific subject, such as TV and Radio, will be found in that section.

## THE ARTS

**January 10.** *Finian's Rainbow*, with Ella Logan, David Wayne (725 performances before closing).

**March 13.** *Brigadoon*, with David Brooks, Marion Bell (685 perfs.).

**October 9.** *High Button Shoes*, with Phil Silvers, Nannette Fabray (727 perfs.).

**December 3.** *A Streetcar Named Desire*, with Marlon Brando, Jessica Tandy, Kim Hunter, Karl Malden (855 perfs.).

## *Tony Awards*

Formed in 1917 to assist war relief, the American Theatre Wing was headed by Antoinette Perry during W.W.II. In her memory, the Wing this year creates the Tony (her nickname) to honor Broadway performances and productions.

Actor (Dramatic)—José Ferrer, *Cyrano de Bergerac*
Actress (Dramatic)—Ingrid Bergman, *Joan of Lorraine*; Helen Hayes, *Happy Birthday*
Play—no award

## *News*

**August 24.** Largely a music festival, the first Edinburgh International Festival of Music and Drama nonetheless attracts "fringe" companies that perform their dramas in church halls and on improvised stages.

**October 23.** Julie Andrews makes her stage debut at age 12 in a revue at the London Hippodrome.

**November 12.** Dutch courts convict artist Han van Meegeren of forgery. His paintings in the style of Vermeer and Pieter de Hooch had been widely hailed, and at least one sold for more than $500,000. But van Meegeren will never enter prison; he dies of a heart attack shortly after the trial.

**More news.** For the 1946–1947 season, art auction sales in New York totaled more than $6 million. In London, top prices included $52,000 for Rembrandt's *Self-Portrait* and $44,000 for a Velázquez. Gainsborough's *View of the Mouth of the Thames* brought $16,000.

## WORDS

Saul Bellow, *The Victim*
John Gunther, *Inside U.S.A.*
A. B. Guthrie, *The Big Sky*
Laura Hobson, *Gentleman's Agreement*
Malcolm Lowry, *Under the Volcano*
James A. Michener, *Tales of the South Pacific*

Jean Paul Sartre, *The Age of Reason*
John Steinbeck, *The Pearl*; *The Wayward Bus*
Hugh Trevor-Roper, *The Last Days of Hitler*
Frank Yerby, *The Vixens*

## News

**January 28.** The *Bay Psalm Book*, the first book printed in the American colonies, fetches $150,000 at a New York auction, the highest price ever paid for a single volume.

**August 4.** Abraham Lincoln's papers are made public. When his son Robert Lincoln died in 1926, at the age of 83, he bequeathed his father's papers to the Library of Congress providing the 194 volumes remain under lock and key for 21 years. Supposedly, Robert Lincoln feared that Albert Beveridge, then senator from Indiana, would use the documents to attack the Lincoln family. Yet a scholarly examination reveals nothing sensational, and historians suggest that the son may have wanted to avoid the anticipated flood of requests from Americans seeking a presidential letter to their family.

**August 18.** Dr. T. M. Pearce of the University of New Mexico predicts the atomic age will turn English into a language of acronyms (such as AEC for the Atomic Energy Commission).

**September 16.** In Philadelphia, the seven-car Freedom Train begins a cross-country exhibit of 100 important U.S. documents. The sponsoring American Heritage Foundation has refused to stop in any town that limits Negroes' access to the display.

**More news.** In 1900 no U.S. magazine circulated more than 500,000 copies. This year, 38 periodicals sell more than 1 million.

• Ten million adult Americans are illiterate and between 20 percent and 33.3 percent of school children fail to meet the reading standards of their grade.

• A total U.S. college enrollment of 2.5 million students includes 1 million veterans attending under the G.I. Bill of Rights.

• In the *Pocket Book of Baby and Child Care* (1946), pediatrician Dr. Benjamin Spock creates a relaxed tone with his opening words: "Trust your-self. You know more than you think you do." Millions of new middle-class mothers choose his common-sense approach over the previous child-care standard, *Psychological Care of Infant and Child* (1928), which advised, "Never, never kiss your child. Never hold it on your lap." Eventually Spock's landmark book will become an all-time best-seller, second only to the Bible.

## Cartoons and Comics

**December.** Fox Features brings out the first confession comic book with a romance theme, *Sunny, America's Sweetheart*. The title folds after a year.

**More news.** After 13 years, artist Milton Caniff leaves *Terry and the Pirates* to debut another comic strip, *Steve Canyon*.

## TIME *Man of the Year*

George C. Marshall

## New Words and Phrases

across the board
baby-sit
blackmarketing
bubble gum
chain reaction
flying saucer
hot rod
launderette
lay-up (in basketball)
pipe line (a channel of information, communication)
police state
to sideline (a player)
spot check
strip (a row of restaurants on a highway)
watchdog commission

## Obituaries

**Willa Cather** (December 7, 1876–April 24, 1947). One of the nation's most honored writers, Cather is best remembered for her novel *My Antonia* (1918).

**Hugh Lofting** (January 14, 1886–September 26, 1947). His classic Dr. Doolittle books, begun during W.W.I in letters home to his children, were largely written in the 1920s.

**Charles Nordhoff** (February 1, 1887–April 12, 1947). He and James Hall coauthored the famous *Bounty* trilogy: *Mutiny on the Bounty* (1932; made into a popular film), *Men Against the Sea* (1933), and *Pitcairn's Island* (1934).

**Baroness Emmuska Orczy** (1865–November 12, 1947). The novelist's daredevil hero, *The Scarlet Pimpernel* (1905), appeared in 12 more novels.

**Lloyd Osbourne** (c. 1874–May 22, 1947). As a 12-year-old boy, Lloyd asked his stepfather to write a story without girls. Robert Louis Stevenson used a map drawn by his stepson to produce his first successful novel, *Treasure Island* (1881).

# FASHION

## Haute Couture

In a dramatic departure from functional wartime styles, French designer Christian Dior eliminates shoulder pads and drops skirts to within 12 inches of the floor. Suit jackets fit tightly through the bodice, then flare out from the waist over a straight skirt or an exceptionally wide skirt taking yards of material. (With fabric shortages, Britain considers barring production.) Evening skirts are shortened to emphasize the ankle and leg.

*Life* magazine dubs the curvaceous designs the "New Look," but critics describe them as a throwback to the 1860s. (Dior rigidly tailors and corsets his models with padded bras, a new waist cincher, and padded hips.) Most men agree with actor Jimmy Stewart's assessment: "Long dresses are going to interfere with a very fine hobby" (*Time*, July 21, 1947). But, after years of wartime austerity, women enthusiastically embrace the more feminine styles.

The hugely successful Dior line—his very first collection—revitalizes the fashion industry and introduces the concept of a single-event collection.

## News

**November 20.** British couturier Norman Hartnell creates a magnificent satin gown for the royal wedding, embroidering some 10,000 tiny American seed pearls into flowers.

Princess Elizabeth's trousseau consists mainly of New Look fashions.

**More news.** On July 5, 1946, at a Paris press gathering, couturier Jacques Heim introduced the "atome," or world's smallest bathing suit. Just four days earlier, the United States had exploded an atomic bomb over a tiny Pacific atoll, and inevitably Heim's creation was named after Bikini. A craze in Europe this year, the suit appears in America in a more modest version.

• In Switzerland, Heberlein Patent Corp. introduces nylon stretch yarn for ski pants. Interest in Helanca yarn will gradually spread around the world.

• Medical experts, puzzled at the number of women with damaged incisors, find that repeated use of the front teeth to open bobby pins abrades enamel.

## Colors and Materials

With the revival of European industry, the United States once again imports fabrics. But postwar inflation drives the price of British woolens 116 percent over 1939 costs, while cottons, with continuing tropical shortages, skyrocket 340 percent.

## Accessories

Cultured pearls and long chains of pearl beads, à la the 1920s, capture the market.

Flat-heeled ballet shoes remain popular. For the shorter evening length, "naked" sandals are built up to decorate the leg.

The New Look renews the hat industry. In the fall, berets and pillboxes win favor while the more daring wear fezzes trimmed with feathers and veils.

# POPULAR MUSIC

"Near You"—Francis Craig's Band; vocal: Bob Lamm

"Ballerina"—Vaughn Monroe & His Band

"Heartaches"—Ted Weems & His Orchestra

"Peg o' My Heart"—Harmonicats

"Smoke, Smoke, Smoke (That Cigarette)"—Tex Williams & His Band the Western Caravan

"Chi-Baba, Chi-Baba (My Bambino Go to Sleep)"/"When You Were Sweet Sixteen"—Perry Como

"Linda"—Ray Noble Orchestra featuring Buddy Clark

"Too Fat Polka"—Arthur Godfrey

"The Anniversary Song"—Al Jolson

"Open the Door, Richard"—Dusty Fletcher

"Almost Like Being in Love" (from the film *Brigadoon*)

"Zip-A-Dee-Doo-Dah" (from the film *Song of the South*)

"Here Comes Santa Claus"—Gene Autry

## News

**This year.** A film biography of composer Joe E. Howard brings back his song "I Wonder Who's Kissing Her Now." With its renewed popularity, Harold Orlob goes to court. In 1909, Orlob sold the song to Howard, who published the number under his own name—a perfectly acceptable practice in those days. Orlob, who wants no compensation, wins the case and the right to see his name published as co-composer.

• Last year, manufacturers offered the first magnetic tape recorder for home use, but consumers found it too complicated to use and far too expensive at $229.50. This year, a simpler Sears radio-phonograph combination sells for $169.50.

• Billy Eckstine's three-year-old band folds and the singer launches a new career as a solo performer.

• Lyricists Dusty Fletcher and John Mason use a 1930s–1940s comedy routine for the title of their song "Open the Door, Richard." The phrase becomes part of the American vocabulary.

## New Recording Artists

Vic Damone
Frankie Laine
Sarah Vaughan

## Obituaries

**Walter Donaldson** (February 15, 1893–July 15, 1947). A top writer of popular songs in the 1920s, his hits included "Yes Sir, That's My Baby" (1925) and "Love Me or Leave Me" (1928).

**Bert Kalmar** (February 10, 1884–September 18, 1947). The lyricist, who collaborated mainly with composer Harry Ruby, wrote the words for "Who's Sorry Now?" (1923) and "I Wanna Be Loved By You" (1928), among others.

**Georg von Trapp** (1880–May 30, 1947). Baron von Trapp, his wife Maria, and 10 children fled the Nazi occupation of Austria in 1938. (The movie *The Sound of Music* will chronicle the family's experience.) The Trapp Family Singers settled in the United States and have since made some 700 appearances.

# MOVIES

*The Bachelor and the Bobby-Soxer* (d. Irving Reis; bw)—Cary Grant, Shirley Temple, Myrna Loy

*Body and Soul* (d. Robert Rossen; bw)—John Garfield, Lilli Palmer

*Crossfire* (d. Edward Dmytryk; bw)—Robert Young, Robert Mitchum, Robert Ryan, Gloria Grahame

*Dark Passage* (d. Delmer Daves; bw)—Humphrey Bogart, Lauren Bacall, Agnes Moorehead

*A Double Life* (d. George Cukor; bw)—Ronald Colman, Shelley Winters

*The Farmer's Daughter* (d. H. C. Potter; bw)—Loretta Young, Joseph Cotten, Ethel Barrymore, Charles Bickford

*The Fugitive* (d. John Ford; bw)—Henry Fonda, Dolores Del Rio, Pedro Armendariz

*Gentleman's Agreement* (d. Elia Kazan; bw)—Gregory Peck, Dorothy McGuire, John Garfield, Celeste Holm, Anne Revere

*The Hucksters* (d. Jack Conway; bw)—Clark Gable, Deborah Kerr, Ava Gardner, Sidney Greenstreet

*Kiss of Death* (d. Henry Hathaway; bw)—Victor Mature, Brian Donlevy, Coleen Gray, Richard Widmark

*Life with Father* (d. Michael Curtiz; color)—William Powell, Irene Dunne, Elizabeth Taylor

*Miracle on 34th Street* (d. George Seaton; bw)—Edmund Gwenn, Maureen O'Hara, John Payne, Natalie Wood

*Monsieur Verdoux* (d. Charles Chaplin; bw)—Charles Chaplin, Martha Raye, Isobel Elsom

*My Favorite Brunette* (d. Elliott Nugent; bw)—Bob Hope, Dorothy Lamour, Peter Lorre

*Nightmare Alley* (d. Edmund Goulding; bw)—Tyrone Power, Coleen Gray, Joan Blondell

*Odd Man Out* (British, d. Carol Reed; bw)—James Mason, Robert Newton, Kathleen Ryan

*Possessed* (d. Curtis Bernhardt; bw)—Joan Crawford, Raymond Massey, Van Heflin

*Road to Rio* (d. Norman Z. McLeod; bw)—Bob Hope, Bing Crosby, Dorothy Lamour

## Academy Awards

**March 13.** In 1927, Hollywood founded the Academy of Motion Picture Arts and Sciences in an attempt to overcome the industry's scandalous reputation and to legitimize films as an art form. The first awards, presented on May 16, 1929, honored motion picture achievements during 1927–1928.

Each year, branch members vote for their peers—actors choose actors—while the full membership selects the best picture. Winners pledge not to sell their Oscars, except back to the Academy.

Jack Benny hosts this year's ceremonies in Hollywood. Setting off the festivities, Ronald Reagan, president of the Screen Actors Guild, narrates a series of clips taken from Oscar-winning movies.

The scenes run backward and upside down on the screen behind him.

**Best Picture**—*The Best Years of Our Lives*
**Best Actor**—Fredric March (*The Best Years of Our Lives*)
**Best Actress**—Olivia de Havilland (*To Each His Own*)
**Best Director**—William Wyler (*The Best Years of Our Lives*)
**Best Supporting Actor**—Harold Russell (*The Best Years of Our Lives*)
**Best Supporting Actress**—Anne Baxter (*The Razor's Edge*)
**Best Song**—"On the Atchison, Topeka and Santa Fe" from *The Harvey Girls*

Harold Russell receives a Special Award as well "for bringing hope and courage to fellow veterans through his appearance." The ex-paratrooper, acting in his first role, lost both hands in a W.W.II training exercise.

## News

**February 23.** The *New York Times* notes that, just five years ago, no American movie house offered popcorn and most sold their candy through vending machines. Today, an estimated 85 percent sell both across the counter. And one large theater chain in the West sends young women, dressed in evening gowns, up and down the aisles with trays of candy during intermission.

**June 11.** King George VI knights Laurence Olivier for his services to the British stage and cinema.

**August 11.** Figures released today show that last year's top Hollywood salary went to 31-year-old Betty Grable ($299,333).

**August 21.** Radio-Keith-Orpheum (RKO) hires a helicopter to shoot two chase sequences: a speeding car and convicts escaping through a wheat field. This first use of a helicopter for motion picture filming saves the studio $10,000 in production costs.

**October 20.** Last May, the House Un-American Activities Committee held closed hearings in

Hollywood to investigate Communist subversion in U.S. films. Influential witnesses named dozens of friends and colleagues with left-wing sympathies.

In public hearings opening today in Washington, HUAC questions more cooperative witnesses. But Chairman J. Parnell Thomas, under pressure from movie mogul Samuel Goldwyn, calls a halt on October 31. The committee failed to prove the Communist doctrine has reached theater screens, yet studio executives refuse work to known Communists and an industry blacklist names those merely under suspicion.

Before the adjournment, ten of 19 subpoenaed or unfriendly witnesses, mainly writers, had appeared. Because they refused to answer the question, "Are you or have you ever been a member of the Communist party?", the courts eventually find the "Hollywood Ten" guilty of contempt of Congress. All serve some time in prison.

**October 22.** In New York, the movie version of the racy novel *Forever Amber* collects record first-day receipts ($25,308).

**More news.** With *Dark Delusion*, Metro-Goldwyn-Mayer (MGM) ends one of Hollywood's most entertaining and successful film series, *Dr. Kildare* (1938–1947). The last six pictures featured crusty old Dr. Gillespie, played by Lionel Barrymore, the only actor to appear throughout the series.

| Top Box Office Stars | Newcomers |
| --- | --- |
| Bing Crosby | Evelyn Keyes |
| Betty Grable | Billy DeWolfe |
| Ingrid Bergman | Peter Lawford |
| Gary Cooper | Janis Paige |
| Humphrey Bogart | Elizabeth Taylor |
| Bob Hope | Claude Jarmon, Jr. |
| Clark Gable | Janet Blair |
| Gregory Peck | Macdonald Carey |
| Claudette Colbert | Gail Russell |
| Alan Ladd | Richard Conte |

### Top Money-Maker of the Year

*The Best Years of Our Lives* (1946; bw)—Fredric March, Myrna Loy, Teresa Wright, Dana Andrews

### Obituaries

**Ernst Lubitsch** (January 29, 1892–November 30, 1947). The German-born director, one of the first from Europe to earn Hollywood's respect, is best remembered for *Ninotchka* (1939) and *Heaven Can Wait* (1943).

**Grace Moore** (December 5, 1901–January 26, 1947). *See* News.

## TELEVISION AND RADIO

### Radio

The age of radio began on November 15, 1926, with the founding of the National Broadcasting Company (NBC). Twenty-one years later, NBC has been joined by the Columbia Broadcasting System (CBS), the American Broadcasting Company (ABC), and the Mutual Broadcasting System (MBS). And Americans, with a flick of a dial, can laugh at the antics of Jack Benny and "Fibber McGee and Molly," thrill to the adventures of "Superman" and "The Shadow," or cry with soap operas like "Ma Perkins." Imagination creates another whole world just from the voices and sound effects.

### Television

Television was invented independently in 1925 by Charles Francis Jenkins in the United States and John Logie Baird in Scotland. Within three years, GE and RCA demonstrated the first home sets. But prohibitive costs during the Great Depression, and then World War II, effectively ended the development of this fledgling industry.

Still, in 1941, the Federal Communications Commission authorized the broadcast of commercial television. Five years later, on April 13, the age of television was finally inaugurated when the DuMont Television Network connected a New York and a Washington station by cable. But, with continuing material shortages and a raging controversy over a color receiver, manufacturers produced just 6,476 TV sets in 1946. This year, 178,571 roll off the assembly line with screen sizes ranging from

7 to 20 inches; the majority are 10-inch table models. The cost varies from $225 to $2,500, plus a minimum $45 antenna installation fee.

All four networks—ABC, CBS, NBC, and DuMont—currently broadcast 25–30 hours of live programming each week. (ABC temporarily closes down during the year to finance the construction of new stations.) For cities outside AT&T's coaxial cable, DuMont offers the kinescope, a grainy picture made by filming the program off a TV monitor.

Yet, despite growing pains, television evolves over this year and the next from experimental technology to an established broadcasting service.

### New Prime-Time TV Programs

"Kraft Television Theatre" (May 7, 1947–
   October 1, 1958; Drama Anthology)
"Mary Kay & Johnny" (November 18, 1947–
   March 11, 1950; Situation Comedy)—Mary
   Kay Stearns, Johnny Stearns
"Meet the Press" (November 20, 1947–August
   29, 1965; Interview)—*Note:* The program
   will move to Sunday afternoon in 1965.
"Small Fry Club" (March 11, 1947–June 15,
   1951; Children's)—Host: Bob Emery

### News

**January 3.** The telecast of the opening session of Congress marks the first pictorial broadcast of any congressional event.

**January 20.** Lee De Forest, whose invention of the audion tube in 1907 was basic to the transmission of sound over air, writes to the National Association of Broadcasters (NAB) on the 40th anniversary of his invention. "This child of mine has been resolutely kept to the average intelligence of 13 years . . . as though you and your sponsors believe the majority of listeners have only moron minds. Nay, the curse of his commercials has grown consistently more cursed, year by year." This year, 93% of U.S. households own radios.

**March 11.** The first network series designed for children and the first broadcast five days a week, "Small Fry Club" appears on at least two stations

this fall (accurate records disappear when the DuMont network folds).

**March 18.** The FCC rules in favor of the black-and-white very-high-frequency (VHF, channels 1–13) system, in effect giving commercial TV full approval. Station applications begin pouring in.

**May 7.** Through the early years of TV, a single sponsor is very common and many programs include the product name in their title. Tonight, the first "Kraft Television Theatre" promotes Imperial Cheese. Within three weeks, the new product sells out in New York City. This proof of television's reach and a rapidly expanding audience draws considerable business interest.

**June 16.** The first nighttime TV news show, "News From Washington" with anchor Walter Compton, debuts on the DuMont network. As well this year, "CBS Evening News" introduces Douglas Edwards.

**June 27.** A Washington outlet joins NBC's New York, Philadelphia, and Schenectady stations. The network televises an average 28 hours per week; 23 have the same announcer, Bob Stanton.

**July 6.** Allen Funt's "Candid Microphone" debuts on ABC radio. The program offers a payment of up to $15 to badly embarrassed individuals, while an angry person might receive $25. The show is canceled next year partly because many believe the "candid" moments are rigged.

**September 30.** For the first time, millions of baseball fans watch the World Series from the best seat in the house, in front of a TV set. An estimated audience of 3.8 million see the Yankees take their 11th championship. Afterward, retailers report a sharp increase in TV sales.

**November 21.** Television networks fly in newsreels from yesterday's royal wedding in London—four days faster than movie theater newsreels.

**November 30.** Hooperatings, the radio audience measurement in wide use since 1935, rates the top 10 programs (in order): "Bob Hope," "Jack Benny," "Fibber McGee & Molly," "Charlie McCarthy," "Amos 'n' Andy," "Fred Allen," "Red Skelton," "Radio Theatre," "Mr. District Attorney," "Truth or Consequences."

**More news.** Prominent entertainers take over the

role of master of ceremonies on musical-record radio shows as national networks promote the "disc jockey" (DJ) type of program.

• The first all-black programming station, WDIA in Memphis, takes to the airwaves early this year. By 1958, between 50 and 60 radio stations offer black programming, but the majority remain white-owned. As well, this year, the first all-Spanish U.S. radio station (KCOR) begins broadcasting, in San Antonio.

• The juvenile adventure serial "Buck Rogers in the Twenty-Fifth Century" ends after 15 years on the radio. Buck and villain Killer Kane fight through most of the last episode.

• On the DuMont network, wrestlers confront each other before and after the matches. Fans soon recognize the regulars, including Gorgeous George with his peroxide blond hair.

• "Hour Glass," the first hour-long variety series, leaves the air after just one year.

# SPORTS

## Winners

### Baseball

World Series—New York Yankees (AL), 4 games; Brooklyn Dodgers (NL), 3 games
Player of the Year—Joe DiMaggio (New York Yankees, AL); Bob Elliott (Boston Braves, NL)
Rookie of the Year—Jackie Robinson (Brooklyn Dodgers, NL)

### Football

National Football League (NFL) Championship—Chicago Cardinals 28, Philadelphia Eagles 21
College Bowls (January 1, 1947)—
Rose Bowl, Illinois 45, UCLA 14
Cotton Bowl, Arkansas 0, LSU 0
Orange Bowl, Rice 8, Tennessee 0
Sugar Bowl, Georgia 20, North Carolina 10
Heisman Trophy—John Lujack (Notre Dame, QB)

Grey Cup—Toronto Argonauts 10, Winnipeg Blue Bombers 9

### Basketball

Professional—Last year, with collegiate players coming out of the Armed Forces, owners of large sports arenas organized an 11-team Basketball Association of America. The BAA quickly moved to draw athletes away from the nine-year-old National Basketball League (NBL), the most successful of the early leagues.
National Collegiate Athletic Association (NCAA) Championship—Holy Cross 58, Oklahoma Univ. 47

### Tennis

U.S. National—Men, Jack Kramer (vs. Frank Parker); Women, Louise Brough (vs. Margaret Osborne)
Wimbledon—Men, Jack Kramer (vs. Tom Brown); Women, Margaret Osborne (vs. Doris Hart)

### Golf

Masters—Jimmy Demaret
U.S. Open—Lew Worsham
British Open—Fred Daly

### Hockey

Stanley Cup—Toronto Maple Leafs, 4 games; Montreal Canadiens, 2 games

### Ice Skating

World Championship—Men, Dick Button (U.S.); Women, Barbara Ann Scott (Canada)
U.S. National—Men, Dick Button; Women, Gretchen Merrill
Canadian National—Men, Norris F. Bowden; Women, Marilyn Ruth Take

### Kentucky Derby

Jet Pilot—Eric Guerin, jockey

*Athlete of the Year (chosen by Associated Press sports editors)*

Male—Johnny Lujack (Football); Female—
    Mildred (Babe) Didrikson Zaharias (Golf)

*Last Season*

(Aubrey) Dit Clapper (Hockey)
Bill Cowley (Hockey)
Rick Ferrell (Baseball)
Hank Greenberg (Baseball)
Al Lopez (Baseball)
Mel Ott (Baseball)
(Walter) Babe Pratt (Hockey)
(Charles) Red Ruffling (Baseball)

## News

**February 1.** Barbara Ann Scott becomes the first North American woman to win the world figure skating championship. When she returns home to Ottawa, 70,000 cheering fans welcome her at the train station.

**April 9.** Holding Leo Durocher to account for "an accumulation of unpleasant incidents . . . detrimental to baseball," Commissioner Albert "Happy" Chandler suspends the Brooklyn Dodgers' manager for the entire season. Rumor associates Durocher with gamblers.

**April 10.** After a year with the farm team in Montreal, Jackie Robinson signs with the Brooklyn Dodgers. He is the first official Negro player in the major leagues since the 1880's (earlier in this century, some light-skinned blacks passed as Cuban or Indian).

To help him deal with the pressure and outright hostility, team president Branch Rickey sets up a "how-to-handle-Robinson" committee in each city and gives Jackie a list of do's and don'ts: ignore insults, accept no endorsements or social invitations, avoid flattery, and leave by a secret exit. When the St. Louis Cardinals threaten to strike, National League President Ford Frick tells them, "If you do this you are through, and I don't care if it wrecks the league for 10 years. You cannot do this, because this is America."

*Baseball great Jackie Robinson.*

Robinson not only survives, he hits .297 and leads the league in stolen bases. By the end of the season four other Negroes sign major league contracts.

**June 24.** In the first defense of his welterweight title, black boxer Ray Robinson (Walker Smith) knocks out Jimmy Doyle in the eighth round. The next day, Doyle dies of his injuries. The fatality—the first in a modern championship bout—leads to nationwide reform in verbal and physical examinations.

*Note:* Walker Smith borrowed Ray Robinson's fighting license for his first contest, then kept the name for himself.

**October 13.** To support the players' pension, the National Hockey League (NHL) holds the first All-Star game. The game's top players defeat the defending Stanley Cup champions, the Toronto Maple Leafs, 4–3.

**December 5.** Jersey Joe Walcott floors heavyweight champion Joe Louis in the first and again in the fourth round, but loses the fight on a split decision. Louis, disappointed with his performance, tells Walcott, "I'm sorry, Joe," and promises a rematch in 1948. In their second bout, the champ settles the controversy by knocking out Walcott in the 11th round.

**More news.** Jackie Robinson wins baseball's first Rookie of the Year award. Beginning in 1949, a rookie will be selected from each league.

• This year, NHL statistician Alan Roth approaches the Brooklyn Dodgers. He asks owner Branch Rickey if it would be helpful to know whether a batter hits better against a right-handed or a left-handed pitcher. Roth is hired as baseball's first statistician.

## Records

**This year.** Outfielder Ted Williams leads the American League in batting, home runs, and runs batted in. The Boston Red Sox's second Triple Crown (he won his first in 1942), matches the record set by Rogers Hornsby in 1922 and 1925.

## *Obituaries*

**Josh Gibson** (December 21, 1912–January 20, 1947). Baseball's greatest home run hitter retired last year from the Negro Baseball Leagues. Gibson is credited with 960 HR, but, since recordkeeping was inconsistent during his 17-year career, he may have hit many more.

**Man O' War.** The $5,000 race horse won 20 out of 21 races in a brief career from 1919 to 1920. Retired to stud, the stallion sired 383 foals, many of whom became famous in their own right. In 1950, Man O' War will be overwhelmingly voted the greatest horse of the first half of the 20th century.

**Manuel (Manolete) Rodriguez** (July 5, 1917–August 28, 1947). Gored in the thigh, Spain's most famous bullfighter died from shock and loss of blood. He had retired after a 13-year career, but his adoring fans brought him back.

# 1948

When push comes to shove, Americans simply fly over the problem. Moscow blockades Berlin to drive the Allies out of Soviet-occupied Germany. The United States and Britain, to avoid a war and yet safeguard the remainder of Europe, mount an around-the-clock airlift of food and supplies.

With this battle of wills and a United Nations deadlock over atomic energy, the major powers reverse their postwar disarmament and initiate a worldwide search for uranium. Washington, remembering the bitter lesson of Pearl Harbor, allots huge sums for defense and imposes the first permanent draft in U.S. history.

As well, this year, in the United States, the Chicago Daily Tribune prints "Dewey Defeats Truman" before the president posts a surprise victory, and the Supreme Court rules against the teaching of religion in schools. In other parts of the world, the formation of Israel ignites a war with adjoining Arab nations. South Africans elect the National party on an apartheid platform, an assassin strikes down Mohandas Gandhi, and Britain celebrates the birth of Charles, Princess Elizabeth's first child.

Other events and discoveries include the RCA long-playing phonograph record, the first missile guidance system, demonstrations of the transistor and xerography, the development of Orlon, and the first nonstop commercial flight across the Atlantic. In California, few motorists notice a new hamburger stand opened by Maurice and Richard McDonald.

## NEWS

**January 1.** Signed by 23 nations, the General Agreement on Tariffs and Trade (GATT) reduces artificial trade barriers, particularly those formed during the protectionist years of the Depression. The accord affects approximately half the world's trade.

**January 13.** The Presidential Air Policy Commission, established last July, sets January 1, 1953, as A-day, the date when other nations will possess atomic weapons in quantity. Before the end of the month, the Joint Committee on Atomic Energy gives weapons development priority over civilian research. In April, Congress increases the number of air force groups to 70 and appropriates funds to stabilize and strengthen the aircraft industry. Plants, closed since the end of W.W.II, reopen and employment reaches a peacetime high.

**January 30.** A Hindu extremist assassinates Mohandas Gandhi. Last year, the revered spiritual leader (called Mahatma, or "man of pure soul") led

India to independence, but the Hindu-Moslem partition resulted in bloodshed. To win a "reunion of hearts," the 78-year-old fasted earlier this month until worried religious leaders guaranteed peace among their followers. His death deals a terrible blow to their tentative agreement.

On January 31, millions line the streets of Delhi to watch the funeral procession and the Hindu cremation. His assassin, Vinayak Gadse, will be hanged next year.

**February 2.** In support of last year's historic report, Truman presents Congress with a 10-point civil rights program that includes measures against lynching and poll taxes. Democratic congressmen from the South attack the proposals and, before the end of the month, adopt a resolution against the inclusion of a strong civil rights plank in the 1948 party platform.

---

*Statistics:* A nationwide Gallup poll in July shows that 42 percent of Americans favor racial segregation in public transportation while 49 percent favor integration. In the South, the percentage of those in favor jumps to 84 percent.

---

**February 21.** In Czechoslovakian 1946 parliamentary elections, Communists won 114 of 300 seats and a dominant role in the ruling coalition. But today, faced with increasing popular discontent and upcoming elections, the government seizes control of the country in a bloodless coup.

Within days, Foreign Minister Jan Masaryk commits suicide or is murdered. May elections offer a single Communist slate and, in June, a revised constitution establishes a repressive Stalinist regime.

**March 8.** In a case brought by an atheist parent (McCollum v. Board of Education, Illinois), the U.S. Supreme Court finds (8–1) the teaching of religion in public schools unconstitutional. Some states, in interpreting the decision, discontinue all religion classes while others permit off-premises instruction.

**March 17.** Inviting other countries to join, the

foreign ministers of Britain, Belgium, France, the Netherlands, and Luxembourg sign a 50-year treaty of military aid and economic and social cooperation. The Brussels Pact notifies the Soviet Union of their intent to resist any further Communist advance. President Truman immediately pledges U.S. assistance.

**April 2.** The Revenue Act removes 7.4 million Americans from the tax rolls. Truman, who unsuccessfully vetoed the bill, had argued that inflation, heavy defense and foreign aid expenditures, and a $250-billion national debt preclude tax reductions. Next year, the government will collect $5 billion less from individual income taxes.

---

*Statistics:* With retail prices at their highest level since 1929, a new Ford sedan sells for $1,236 and a Chevrolet convertible costs $1,750. Automobile workers receive about $1.60 an hour while construction workers— the highest hourly wage earners in the United States—receive $2.10.

---

**April 3.** Prompted by the Communist coup in Czechoslovakia, Congress has overwhelmingly approved the Foreign Assistance Act, earmarking funds for the European Recovery Program or Marshall Plan. Over the next four years, in an unprecedented peacetime offering, the United States will distribute some $12 billion. The 16 Western European nations will liberalize trade through the Organization for European Economic Cooperation (OEEC), and, as their gross national products increase by 15–25 percent, American industry will prosper.

**April 30.** In Colombia, United States and Latin American delegates create the Organization of American States (OAS). The Charter of Bogota aims to strengthen the peace and security of the Western Hemisphere and to encourage economic development. Congress will take until 1951 to ratify the charter; it will go into effect late that year.

**May 3.** In *Shelley v. Kramer*, the Supreme Court finds restrictive racial covenants unenforceable in the sale of property. This landmark decision, for the first time, bars state and federal courts from enforcing private acts of discrimination against a citizen.

**May 14.** With the expiration of the British mandate over Palestine, Israel proclaims its independence. (Chaim Weizmann becomes provisional president and David Ben-Gurion becomes prime minister until elections in 1949 confirm their positions.) The Arab nations, which last year rejected a United Nations partition, immediately invade Israel from the north, east, and south.

Truman, against the advice of State Secretary Marshall, grants Israel diplomatic recognition. Whether the president, as some claim, was concerned for those who survived Nazi persecution or, as others believe, with domestic politics, his decision sets the course for U.S.-Arab relations.

> *Statistics:* Almost three-fourths of the 700,000 Arabs in Israel have already fled, as Jews, mainly survivors of the Holocaust, continue to arrive; Jewish immigration reaches 100,000 by the end of 1948.

**May 17.** The United Nations Atomic Energy Commission suspends discussions on international control of the atomic bomb. The United States has recommended the establishment of an international agency to produce fissionable materials, inspect sites, and punish violators. Once this agency gains control, the United States will surrender all bombs.

The Soviets, claiming this plan would give the Americans a monopoly, demands that the bombs be destroyed first and the Security Council assume control. Since the Soviets could veto any council decisions, the two superpowers remain at an impasse.

**May 17.** The AEC announces the completion of three atomic tests at Eniwetok in the Marshall Islands. The atoll was chosen for more extensive testing because prevailing winds will carry radioactive particles "harmlessly" out over open seas.

For two earlier tests, in 1946, the Americans moved 160 islanders off Bikini atoll, in the U.S.

Pacific Trust Territory, then dropped a bomb onto a group of 75 U.S. ships, 4 battleships, and 2 airplane carriers, and detonated a second below the surface of the lagoon. Although scientific evaluation of the area earlier this year found the remaining target ships and marine plants and animals radioactive, the military maintains that all 42,000 servicemen and civilians present for the tests, including those drenched with radioactive water, are "free of contamination."

**May 26.** In South Africa, after a bitter election campaign, the National party defeats the coalition United-Labour government. The Nationalist apartheid platform (in Afrikaans *apartheid* means "apartness") promises to uphold the predominant position of whites by physically separating the races. The defeated coalition, led by Jan Christian Smuts, had promised to give blacks some measure of authority.

When Winston Churchill hears of Smuts's defeat, he remarks, "A great world statesman has fallen and with him his country will undergo a period of anxiety and perhaps temporary eclipse."

**June 18.** As Moscow drags out negotiations on a German peace treaty, the United States, Britain, and France announce their intention to consolidate their separate occupation zones into a federal state. The Soviets, charging the West with strengthening western Germany for a future attack on the USSR, halt all surface traffic to Berlin. (With Germany's defeat, Stalin agreed to divide the important city—deep in the Soviet occupation zone—and to guarantee access.) On the 23rd, railway traffic is stopped and electrical power cut off.

To save Germany and avoid a military confrontation, the Allies decide to airlift supplies to the city of 2.5 million behind the Iron Curtain. Beginning on the 28th, a plane lands every three minutes round the clock with food, fuel, clothing, and raw materials. The U.S. Air Force (USAF) makes about two-thirds of the flights, the British the rest.

An agreement reached at the end of August breaks down over implementation and the Soviets use their veto to block discussion in the United Nations. By September, 4,000 tons of supplies arrive in Berlin each day.

**June 24.** With only volunteer enlistment, U.S. Armed Forces have been fully extended to occupy Europe, Japan, and Korea, and to maintain garrisons in the Pacific and Caribbean. The Selective Service Act, signed today, provides for the registration of all American men between 18 and 25, and the induction of 19- to 25-year-olds for 21 months of service. In the first year, the army expands by over 200,000 men.

Since the act fails to ban segregation, Truman establishes a Commission on Equality of Treatment and Opportunity in the armed services.

**June 24.** At the first televised convention, the Republicans renominate Thomas E. Dewey of New York as their presidential candidate; Dewey was defeated by Roosevelt in 1944. Earl Warren wins the vice-presidential nomination.

**June 25.** The Displaced Persons Act authorizes the admission of 205,000 European refugees to the United States over the next two years. But, with its stated preference for farmers and people from the Balkans or eastern Poland, President Truman criticizes the act as "flagrantly discriminatory" against Jews and Catholics. The restrictions will be removed in June 1950, and 415,000 displaced persons, or DPs, as many Americans call them, will eventually enter the country.

**June 28.** Cominform expels Yugoslavia and accuses President Tito of nationalist deviation from Marxism-Leninism and of hostility to the Soviet Union. Tito countercharges Moscow with suppressing criticism, shattering the myth that Communist parties in Eastern Europe function independently of the Kremlin. In the years ahead, Tito will refuse to take sides in the Cold War, preferring instead to develop ties between Yugoslavia and other nonaligned nations.

**July 15.** In the early hours of the morning, the Democratic National Convention nominates Harry S. Truman and Alben Barkley as presidential and vice-presidential candidates.

When the convention, in a close vote, adopted a strong civil rights platform, the Mississippi delegation and half the Alabama delegation walked out in protest. Within days, "Dixiecrats" from 13 states form the States' Rights Democrats and nominate

Governor J. Strom Thurmond of South Carolina as their presidential nominee.

In another major defection, the Progressive party nominates Henry Wallace, a former member of the Roosevelt cabinet and opponent of the Cold War. No one expects either Thurmond or Wallace to win, but most believe their candidacies will cost Truman the election.

**July 15.** General John Joseph Pershing, commander in chief of the American expeditionary force in W.W.I, dies at the age of 87. He insisted that American soldiers fight as a unit and, at one point, commanded 2.5 million U.S. troops. During W.W.II, Chief of Staff General George C. Marshall frequently consulted Pershing, who then bore the nation's highest military rank, general of the armies of the United States; the only other soldier to hold the same rank was George Washington.

**July 26.** Despite the split in the Democratic party, President Truman acts on his civil rights platform with two executive orders: a declaration of policy to gradually eliminate segregation in the armed services and a proposal to set up a fair employment policy in federal bureaus.

**August 15.** President Syngman Rhee, age 73, elected in a U.S.-sponsored election, proclaims the Republic of Korea in the capital of Seoul. Just 25 days later, the Soviets establish the Korean People's Democratic Republic under the leadership of Korean-born Red Army Captain Kim Il-Sung.

In 1945, the Allies ended 35 years of Japanese rule over Korea. It was agreed that, until a unified and independent government could be established, the United States would occupy Korea south of the 38th parallel and the Soviet Union would occupy the northern half. But East–West negotiations broke down and the United States placed the issue before the United Nations in late 1947. The Soviets rejected the subsequent proposal for democratic elections.

At the end of this year, the United Nations General Assembly recommends, 48–6, that the government of South Korea be recognized as the only legitimate Korean government. North Korea ignores the resolution and claims sovereignty over the entire country.

**Fall.** After flying supplies into blockaded Berlin, Lt. Gail Halvorson, USAF, gives some German children two sticks of gum. Their excitement amazes him, and he promises to drop candy from his plane the next day. As goodies continue to fall from the sky, the children lose their wartime fear of planes and Halvorson is dubbed the "Candy Bomber."

**October.** During the presidential campaign, the complacent Republicans intentionally avoid issues. Truman, on the other hand, campaigns vigorously to overcome serious party defections. Underfinanced—radio stations regularly cut him off in midspeech for nonpayment—the president travels over 31,000 miles, stopping in big cities and at tiny railroad junctions, to speak to some 12 million people. He blasts "the do-nothing, good-for-nothing" GOP Congress and calls those farmers and workers who plan to vote Republican "ingrates." As election day nears, the president draws enthusiastic and ever-larger crowds.

**November 2.** Defying predictions of a Republican landslide, Harry S. Truman wins 49.5 percent of the popular vote and 303 votes from the electoral college. He carried the West and the farm belt, and won labor support with his promise to repeal the Taft-Hartley Act, and drew the Negro vote with his civil rights platform (blacks knew Truman had taken a huge risk and felt obliged to support him). Thomas Dewey garners 45 percent, but just 189 electoral votes. Thurmond takes 3 percent and 39 votes.

Possibly because of a low voter turnout, the Democratic vote failed to splinter. The party regains control of the House with 262 seats; the Republicans win 171 and the American Labor party 1. In the Senate, the Democrats take 54 and the Republicans 42. Still, Congress remains conservative and continues to plague Truman during his second administration.

Newcomers to the Senate include Hubert Humphrey (D., Minn.) and Lyndon Baines Johnson (D., Texas). Punsters refer to the senator from Texas as "Landslide Johnson" because of his questionable 87-vote win in the Democratic senatorial primary. But analysts, who believe both party machines carried out fraudulent practices, conclude Johnson likely knew nothing of last-minute entries on the voter list or lost ballots.

**November 15.** Louis St. Laurent succeeds William Lyon Mackenzie King as leader of the Liberal party and prime minister of Canada.

**November 30.** Jewish and Arab commanders sign a full cease-fire in Jerusalem. Last May, the United Nations appointed Count Folke Bernadotte to mediate in the Arab-Israeli War in Palestine. The 53-year-old Swedish diplomat persuaded both sides to accept a cease-fire, but worked in vain to establish a lasting truce. Two months ago, Jewish extremists assassinated Bernadotte, probably for proposing Arab refugees return to Israel. The United Nations released his peace plan posthumously and chose American Ralph Bunche as his successor.

**December 10.** The United Nations General Assembly adopts the Declaration of Human Rights, 48–0 (abstainers include the Soviet Union and its satellites, plus Saudi Arabia and the Union of South Africa). The delegates give Eleanor Roosevelt a standing ovation for her part in drafting the document.

While not binding in international law, colonies will use the bill in their fight for independence, and nations of influence will refer to it in their condemnation of overt racial discrimination and, later, the violation of human rights.

**December 31.** Over 661,000 W.W.II POWs have been released this year, and an additional 101,000 should be repatriated from France, Yugoslavia, Poland, and Czechoslovakia by the end of January. Yet, more than three years after the end of the war, the Soviet Union officially continues to hold 410,000 German POWs; unofficial estimates run as high as 1,977,000.

The United States, Belgium, Luxembourg, and Britain freed their prisoners in 1947, yet not all the men returned home. In recovering nations, able-bodied POWs are an economic asset. In France alone, over 80,000 former enemy soldiers have signed one-year work contracts.

**December 31.** A federal court has ordered Oklahoma to admit blacks to university courses not offered in Negro institutions. In an attempt to forestall further court decisions, a Southern Governors' conference proposes a segregated regional plan of higher educational facilities. Congress offers no endorsement, but the state leaders proceed with their plans.

**More news.** When Harry S. Truman moved into the White House, he found the wooden interior dangerously close to collapse. The decision was made to gut the interior for reconstruction, using as much of the original material as possible in rebuilding. The president has ordered a balcony for the second-floor level of the south portico, but the Fine Arts Commission rejects the architectural design. Truman, who considers the back porch an American institution, fires the director and proceeds with the project. Renovations will be completed in 1952, and in the years ahead, presidential families will make the porch their favorite spot.

### Obituaries

**Edward Beneš** (May 28, 1884–September 3, 1948). The Czechoslovakian nationalist leader, who directed his government-in-exile during the Nazi occupation, served as president until this year's coup.

**Edward Joseph Flanagan** (1886–May 15, 1948). In 1917, the U.S. Roman Catholic monsignor, who believed "there is no such thing as a bad boy," founded Boys Town in Omaha. Spencer Tracy's Oscar-winning portrayal of Flanagan, in *Boys Town* (1938), made the priest world famous.

**Mohandas Gandhi** (October 2, 1869–January 30, 1948). *See* News.

**Anna Jarvis** (May 1, 1864–November 24, 1948). Following her mother's death on May 9, 1905, she held a yearly memorial service and encouraged other sons and daughters to do the same. Congress voted to recognize Mother's Day in 1913.

**Mohammed Ali Jinnah** (December 25, 1876–September 11, 1948). The revered Moslem leader proposed the separation of Pakistan from India as an independent Moslem state. As Pakistan's first governor general, he was the first nonwhite to hold a vice-regal position in a British dominion.

**John Joseph Pershing** (September 13, 1860–July 15, 1948). *See* News.

**Edith Kermit Carow Roosevelt** (August 16, 1861–September 30, 1948). The second wife and widow of Theodore Roosevelt, the 26th U.S. president, was first lady from 1901 to 1909.

## BEGINNINGS AND ENDINGS

### News

**January 12.** The American Red Cross inaugurates a blood program. In two years, 550 chapters in 35 states will collect 400,000 pints of blood.

**March.** During the war, reduced grain crops limited farm livestock as well as brewing and distilling. This month, Washington removes all restrictions on the liquor industry; a tight feed supply prevents any increase in animal stock.

**March 10.** Off the California coast, two American FJ-1 Fury fighters make the first jet plane landings on an aircraft carrier.

**March 15.** The United States initiates air parcel service with 21 European and African countries (then adds South America and the Pacific before year's end). On September 1, the U.S. Post Office sets up an identical domestic service.

**April 7.** The United Nations establishes the World Health Organization (WHO), its ninth specialized agency.

**April 28.** Air France completes the first nonstop commercial flight between Paris and New York—16 hours, 1 minute on a propeller-driven plane.

**April 30.** The U.S. Mint replaces the Liberty walking half-dollar, in circulation since 1916, with the Franklin-Liberty Bell.

**June 16.** Hong Kong police become suspicious after finding spent bullets in the wreckage of a Catalina flying-boat. An informant hospitalized with the sole survivor, Wong-yu Man, learns that his gang of bandits attempted the first aerial hijacking, to ransom the passengers. The plane crash took 26 lives.

**July 1.** Doubling its subway fare to 10 cents, New York is the last major American city to abandon the nickel ride.

**July 1.** President Truman dedicates Idlewild International Airport in New York City. Constructed at a cost of $80 million, the world's largest commercial airport sprawls over 4,900 acres.

**July 14.** Landing in Nova Scotia, six Royal Air Force de Havilland Vampires complete the first jet crossing of the Atlantic. A few days later, 16 U.S. Air Force Shooting Stars make the crossing from west to east.

**August 22.** Protestant and Orthodox church delegates from 44 countries meet in Amsterdam for the first assembly of the World Council of Churches. The Roman Catholic and Russian Orthodox churches boycott the meeting.

> *Statistics:* At the beginning of the year, an 11-nation Gallup poll of religious beliefs recorded the highest percentage of believers in Brazil (96 percent) and the lowest in France (66 percent). In the United States, 94 percent professed to believe in God.

**September 4.** At age 68, Queen Wilhelmina of the Netherlands ends her 50-year reign, abdicating in favor of her 39-year-old daughter Juliana.

**September 13.** Maryland elects Margaret Chase Smith, the first Republican woman to win a full Senate term. (Hattie Wyatt Caraway became the first Democratic Senator in 1932.)

**October 11–22.** In their final communiqué, the nine nations of the British Commonwealth simply refer to it as *the Commonwealth.* India, Ceylon, and Pakistan, attending their first conference, had expressed a desire to drop the term *British.*

**November 14.** Princess Elizabeth gives birth to the future king of the British Empire, Charles Philip Arthur George.

**November 29.** Condemned to menial labor by India's upper caste, some 40 million "untouchables" live in abject poverty. Today, finishing a crusade begun by Mohandas Gandhi, the Constituent Assembly abolishes the practice of untouchability in any form. The new law proves difficult to enforce.

**More News.** This year, Moscow closes the Bering Strait border, ending the shared aboriginal lifestyle of the Inuit and their Siberian relatives.

## Records

**April 21.** Canadian Prime Minister William Lyon Mackenzie King surpasses Sir Robert Walpole's record as the longest-serving prime minister under the British Crown: 21 years, 5 months, 5 days (1921–1930, except for 4 months in 1926, and 1935 to 1948). King resigns on November 15, but stays on as a member of parliament.

## Government Departments and Agencies

**January 27.** The Voice of America (VOA), established in 1942 to penetrate Nazi censorship in Europe, becomes a permanent agency of the State Department. VOA short-wave transmitters broadcast conflicting views, a mixed sample of American culture, and news to countries around the world.

## New Products and Businesses

Just before the end of the year, the McDonald brothers open a hamburger stand in San Bernardino, California. Maurice and Richard efficiently serve precooked food rather than preparing to order. Their limited menu includes 15-cent hamburgers (4 cents more for cheese), 10-cent soft drinks, 20-cent milk shakes, and 5-cent coffee.

In September, Soichiro Honda uses $7,000 in capital to incorporate his two-year-old Honda Technical Research Institute as the Honda Motor Co.

Armour and Company in Chicago introduces Dial, the world's first deodorant soap.

The Adidas athletic shoe manufacturer is founded in West Germany.

Campbell Soup Co. brings out V-8 Cocktail Vegetable Juice.

Nestlé's Quik chocolate powder for milk competes with Ovaltine.

> *Statistics:* Since 1946, U.S. candy consumption has risen from an annual 17.3 pounds per capita to 19 pounds. While several leading chocolate bars now sell for 10 cents, 85 percent remain at 5–7 cents.

Pepsi Cola is sold in cans for the first time.

On April 8, the major aviation companies in Denmark, Norway, and Sweden merge as Scandinavian Airlines.

Cadillac adds rounded tailfins, a profile inspired by the Lockheed P-38 Lightning fighter plane. This first postwar change in body style is poorly received.

# SCIENCE AND TECHNOLOGY

## News

**January 27.** International Business Machines (IBM) demonstrates the Selective Sequence Electronic Calculator (SSEC). Virtually obsolete upon completion, with its 12,000+ vacuum tubes and over 20,000 electromechanical relays, the publicly displayed SSEC nonetheless creates a lasting image of what a computer looks like—room-sized with flashing lights.

**February.** Astronomer Gerard Kuiper, using a 2–3-minute exposure, photographs a fifth body orbiting the planet of Uranus. (The first two were discovered in 1787 and the second two in 1851.) But, rather than name the satellite after a god or spirit, Kuiper breaks with tradition and chooses Miranda, the human heroine of Shakespeare's *Tempest*.

**February 6.** The U.S. Army announces the successful test of an electronic guidance system in a German V-2 rocket. (The Nazis simply aimed rather than guided their invention.)

**April 15.** A privately sponsored Antarctic expedition, led by explorer Finn Ronne, returns to the United States after a year. From the information gathered, the 23-member group concludes that Antarctica is a single continent, not two islands as previously believed.

**June.** By the end of this month, the AEC tallies 3,136 shipments of radioactive isotopes to medical, educational, industrial, and research institutions in 33 states. The program began on August 2, 1946.

**June 3.** After 20 years of work, the Hale telescope is dedicated at the Mount Palomar Observatory. In 1928, astronomer George Hale convinced the Rockefellers to donate $6.55 million for the huge 200-inch telescope—twice the size of the biggest in existence. Hale died in 1938.

**June 14.** The Universal Pictures Building in New York City boasts the first elevator with electronic controls. With its gradual adoption, the mechanical innovation from Otis Elevator Co. will put thousands of elevator operators out of work.

**June 30.** Bell Telephone Laboratories demonstrates the transistor, an invention of company physicists John Bardeen, age 40, Walter H. Brattain, age 46, and William Shockley, age 38. A fraction of the size of tubes, the solid transistor requires no vacuum, seldom needs replacing, uses little energy, and, unlike radio vacuum tubes, needs no warm-up time. For their revolutionary invention, the Bell scientists will share the 1956 Nobel prize in physics.

**July 20.** Lederle Laboratories reports the development of aureomycin chlortetracycline, the first broad-spectrum antibiotic. Next year, the sulfa drug will be declared effective against whooping cough.

**August.** The automobile industry celebrates the production of the 100 millionth American car. With 50 million cars scrapped and some 10.5 million sold in other countries, 39.5 million autos remain in use.

Other nations have manufactured 24 million cars to date, but the number exported to the United States has remained at an annual 1,500. This year, however, with demand exceeding supply, Americans import 21,977 autos; the majority come from Britain.

**October 22.** In the late 1930s, Chester F. Carlson discovered a duplicating process using powder. He produced the first true images two years later, then patented the process in 1940. Some 20 companies rejected Carlson's idea before the nonprofit Memorial Battelle Institute, in Columbus, Ohio, signed an agreement to develop xerography (Greek for "dry writing").

In 1947, Battelle brought in Haloid, a small photo company in Rochester, New York. Today, Haloid presents a public demonstration at the Optical Society's annual meeting—10 years to the day after Carlson produced his first copy.

**More news.** Belgian astronomer Georges Lemaître theorized in 1927 that the universe was formed when a huge mass (the "cosmic egg") exploded, sending matter hurtling into space; the still-receding galaxies were taken as evidence of his theory. Supporter George Gamow calls it the "big bang."

This year, Thomas Gold, Fred Hoyle, and other astronomers argue that, if the "big bang" theory were so, all galaxies would be the same age and space would have opened up between them. Rather than a one-time event, their "steady-state theory" suggests that as galaxies separate new matter forms in the vast spaces between, expanding the universe at a constant rate.

• Biochemist Karl A. Folkers uses bacterial response and chromatography to isolate vitamin $B_{12}$. British scientists independently achieve the same result. Their work completes the isolation of all 13 essential vitamins.

• American mathematician Norbert Wiener explores the control functions in animals and machines in his book *Cybernetics*, the first important study to look closely at computers.

• The USSR places the Mikoyan-Gurevich MiG-15 in service. In its first extensive combat use, during the Korean War, the craft will surpass Allied fighters in climb, ceiling, and high-altitude turns.

---

*Statistics:* The number of U.S. births attended by a physician has risen from 55.8 percent to 85.6 percent since 1940.

---

## Other Discoveries, Developments, and Inventions

> First camera with interchangeable lenses and reflex focusing, from Victor Hasselblad in Sweden
>
> Four-wheel drive civilian vehicle from Land-Rover in Britain
>
> Stainless steel pin to repair bone fractures

## Obituaries

**Harry Brearley** (1871–July 14, 1948). The Englishman applied his discovery of stainless steel to cutlery in 1914.

**Charles W. Nash** (January 28, 1864–June 6, 1948). The U.S. automobile manufacturer merged his Nash Motors with Kelvinator in 1937.

**Orville Wright** (August 19, 1871–January 30, 1948). On December 17, 1903, at breezy, sandy-hilled Kitty Hawk, North Carolina, Ohio bicycle manufacturers Orville and Wilbur Wright completed the first powered, sustained, and controlled airplane flight. Orville flew their fabric biplane first, a distance of 120 feet. Wilbur, in the last flight of four on that day, traveled 852 feet in 59 seconds. Two years of improvements extended the distance to 24 miles.

Following his brother's death from typhoid in 1912, Orville constructed what was probably the first wind tunnel. Much of the remainder of his life was spent defending the Wright claim to the invention of the airplane. Later this year, as per his wishes, the plane returns to the United States from England, where it has been on display, and goes to the Smithsonian.

## THE ARTS

**February 18.** *Mister Roberts*, with Henry Fonda, David Wayne, Robert Keith (1,157 perfs.)

**October 11.** *Where's Charley?* with Ray Bolger, Allyn Ann McLerie (792 perfs.)

**December 30.** *Kiss Me Kate*, with Alfred Drake, Patricia Morrison (1,077 perfs.)

## Tony Awards

Actor (Dramatic)—Henry Fonda, *Mister Roberts*; Paul Kelly, *Command Decision*; Basil Rathbone, *The Heiress*

Actress (Dramatic)—Judith Anderson, *Medea*; Katharine Cornell, *Antony and Cleopatra*; Jessica Tandy, *A Streetcar Named Desire*

Actor (Musical)—Paul Hartman, *Angel in the Wings*

Actress (Musical)—Grace Hartman, *Angel in the Wings*

Play—*Mister Roberts*

## News

**February 11.** The Soviet Communist Central Committee rebukes Sergei Prokofiev, Dimitri Shostakovich, and Aram Kachaturian for work that "strongly smells of the spirit of current modernistic bourgeois music of Europe and America." The composers promise to correct their mistakes.

**May 29.** *Oklahoma!*, Broadway's longest-running show, closes after 2,248 performances.

**More news.** The two-year-old Ballet Society becomes the New York City Ballet. Under choreographer George Balanchine, the company quickly gains an international reputation.

## Obituaries

**Franz Lehár** (April 30, 1870–October 24, 1948). The Hungarian-born composer is best remembered for his operetta *The Merry Widow* (1905).

# WORDS

Albert Camus, *The Plague*

Dale Carnegie, *How to Stop Worrying and Start Living*

Lloyd C. Douglas, *Big Fisherman*

Frank B. Gilbreth and Ernestine Gilbreth Carey, *Cheaper by the Dozen*

Graham Greene, *The Heart of the Matter*

Alfred C. Kinsey et al., *Sexual Behavior in the Human Male*

Norman Mailer, *The Naked and the Dead*

Alan Paton, *Cry the Beloved Country*

Harold Robbins, *Never Love a Stranger*

## News

**January.** Released this month, *Sexual Behavior in the Human Male* creates a storm of controversy. The researchers conclude, for instance, that males reach their sexual peak at 18 years of age, while females sexually mature in their mid-30s. But many scientists question a sample—based on just 5,300 of 12,000 conducted interviews, all white, generally college-educated, and largely from the northeastern United States. Still, the Kinsey report (named after research director Alfred Charles Kinsey) remains on the best-seller list for more than a year, suddenly making sexuality an appropriate topic of conversation.

**January.** The *Philadelphia Inquirer* becomes the first U.S. newspaper to broadcast facsimile editions. Some 20 years in development, the new medium transmits text over FM radio waves to a recorder.

**January 7.** The periodicals *United States News* (1933) and *World Report* (1946) merge as *U.S. News and World Report*.

**November 20.** A scholar at the University of Chicago announces the discovery of a fragment of *Thousand and One Nights*. Dated at A.D. 800–1,000, the tales may be the oldest paper book in existence.

**More news.** The five leading U.S. publishers of 1948 are Macmillan (with 466 titles), Doubleday (369), Harper (245), McGraw-Hill (222), and Grosset & Dunlap (162).

• Norman Mailer's first book, *The Naked and the Dead*, stands out in a passel of W.W. II novels. Other first novels this year include *The Young Lions* by Irwin Shaw and *Raintree County* by Ross Lockridge.

## Cartoons and Comics

**April.** New this month, the comic book *Little Audrey* continues publication until 1957. A second title, *Little Audrey and Melvin*, will run from 1962 to 1973.

**May 10.** Psychiatrist Nicholas Dallis, age 36,

writes the story line for the new comic strip *Rex Morgan, M.D.*

**October 4.** The American Municipal Association reports that 50 U.S. cities have banned comic books dealing with sex or crime, but the U.S. Supreme Court has invalidated a similar New York statute.

**More news.** *Pogo* debuts in the *New York Star* (when the newspaper folds next year Walt Kelly moves over to the *New York Post*). Within six years, the cartoonist's revolutionary mix of humor, slapstick, and satire will make the comic strip one of the world's most popular. Kelly later describes his Okefenokee Swamp opossum as "the reasonable, patient, soft-hearted, naive, friendly little person we all think we are."

In Canada, James Simpkins introduces *Jasper the Bear* in *Maclean's* magazine. The federal government later uses the friendly creature on bear-warning posters.

### TIME *Man of the Year*

Harry S. Truman

### New Words and Phrases

airdrop, airlift
copter
cybernetics
expressway
kingmaker
LP (Columbia Records trademark for long-playing record album)
Mothball Fleet (the inactive part of the Navy)
to profile (someone)
radiation sickness
spelunker
tele, telesee (short for television)
thruway (an express highway)
TV

### Obituaries

**John Robert Gregg** (June 17, 1867–February 23, 1948). The American was just 21 years old when he invented the Gregg shorthand system.

# FASHION

### Haute Couture

The extravagance of the New Look gives way to more natural lines. Unpadded skirts draw excessive pleating to the back, for a more interesting "walkaway" look, while jackets pare down for a trim silhouette.

*Stanley Marcus and Neiman-Marcus house models with samples of the New Look.*

### News

**December 1.** E. I. du Pont de Nemours (U.S.) unveils the synthetic fiber Orlon. Over a 1.5-year exposure test, the new material lost just 23 percent of its strength while natural fibers nearly disintegrated. But, with few workable dyes, two years will pass before the first Orlon clothes appear on the market.

• Industry statistics show that the state of New York, with over 40 percent of the industry's more than 1 million workers, produces over half the country's garments.

• American designer Mainbocher creates the British Girl Guide uniform.

### Clothes

The tank coat gives way to the belted greatcoat and fitted styles, some with small shoulder capes.

Along with the resurrection of the empire-waist evening dress, designers introduce a new silhouette for late afternoon and evening, the lamp-shade. The line fits tightly to midthigh, then abruptly flares out.

### Accessories

With only 12 inches of visible leg, the wedge shoe of the 1930s and 1940s surrenders to finer, higher heels and lighter ankle-strapped sandals. The reappearance of straps brings back little buttons that were rationed during the war.

Some women wear knee-high stockings with the longer skirts.

Patent leather returns in belts and hand-size bags.

Jewelry shrinks to a bare minimum.

To finish their look, many women choose a stole—fur, tweed, wool, jersey, stenciled leopard—or a little fur jacket.

### Hair and Cosmetics

Women hark back to the soft curls or small-cap shapes of the 1920s. During the war, few could afford professional haircuts or permanent waves; most wore their hair long, or rolled up and over the forehead.

Some manufacturers attempt to revive interest in facial beauty patches with boxes of 100 assorted black silk hearts, circles, stars, diamonds, and other shapes.

## POPULAR MUSIC

"Buttons & Bows"—Dinah Shore
"Twelfth Street Rag"—Pee Wee Hunt & His Orchestra
"Mañana (Is Soon Enough for Me)"—Peggy Lee
"A Tree in the Meadow"—Margaret Whiting
"Nature Boy"—Nat King Cole
"Now Is the Hour"—Bing Crosby
"I'm Looking Over a Four Leaf Clover"—Art Mooney & His Orchestra
"You Can't Be True Dear"—vocal: Jerry Wayne; organist: Ken Griffin
"On a Slow Boat to China"—Kay Kyser Orchestra; vocal: Harry Babbitt & Gloria Wood/ Benny Goodman Orchestra; vocal: Al Hendrickson
"Woody Woodpecker"—Kay Kyser Orchestra
"All I Want for Christmas Is My Two Front Teeth"—Spike Jones & His City Slickers
"It's a Most Unusual Day"—Jane Powell
"Once in Love with Amy"—Ray Bolger
"Red Roses for a Blue Lady"—Vaughn Monroe & Guy Lombardo & His Royal Canadians

### News

**June 21.** Columbia Records unveils a 12-inch unbreakable vinyl disc that spins on the turntable at $33^1/_3$ revolutions per minute (rpm). Inventor Peter Goldmark, who will receive no royalties, wanted to overcome the time limitations of the 78 rpm, a mere $3^1/_2$–4 minutes on each side of the 12-inch classical-music disc and still less on the popular 10-inch version. The revolutionary long-playing record (LP) will hold 45–50 minutes of music on its microgrooves.

**October 29.** Columbia raises the price of its 78 rpm's from 75 cents to 79 cents.

**December.** Radio Corp. of America (RCA) Victor introduces a 7-inch 45-rpm record with up to 5 minutes of playing time on each side. The company initially assigns a color for each type of music: red for classical, midnight blue for semiclassical, and black for pop.

Reportedly, RCA rejected Columbia's offer to share the 33–1/3 technology. Both disc formats increase the quality of reproduction, but existing record players can handle just one speed.

**December 14.** The American Federation of Musicians and 13 major record producers sign a 5-year agreement, providing for a welfare fund financed by 1–2½ percent royalties on each disc sold. During the 11½-month strike preceding the agreement, the union barred members from performing in recording studios.

**December 25.** A poll by *Down Beat* magazine lists Duke Ellington's band as the most popular in the nation.

**More news.** eden ahbez, a Brooklyn yogi who believes that only deities' names merit capitalization, leaves a song at the stage door of a California theater for Nat King Cole. The popular singer finds a hit with "Nature Boy."

• Most radio and record studios have now installed reel-to-reel tape machines. The new technology permits editing and makes taped performances indistinguishable from live ones.

• Early in the year, organist Ken Griffin records a 1935 German tune as an accompaniment for ice skaters. The popularity of "You Can't Be True, Dear" prompts publisher Dave Dreyer to dub in vocalist Jerry Wayne. With a top 10 placement in the charts, the tune becomes the first superimposed recording to find success.

*New Recording Artists*

Doris Day (solo)
Patti Page
Kay Starr (solo)

## Obituaries

**Frederick Allen (Kerry) Mills** (February 1, 1869– December 5, 1948). The U.S. composer, musician, author, and music publisher was best known for his tune "Meet Me in St. Louis, Louis" (1904).

# MOVIES

*Abbott and Costello Meet Frankenstein* (d. Charles Barton; bw)—Bud Abbott, Lou Costello, Lon Chaney Jr., Bela Lugosi

*Call Northside 777* (d. Henry Hathaway; bw)— James Stewart, Lee J. Cobb

*Command Decision* (d. Sam Wood; bw)—Clark Gable, Walter Pidgeon, Van Johnson

*Easter Parade* (d. Charles Walters; color)—Fred Astaire, Judy Garland, Ann Miller, Peter Lawford

*Fort Apache* (d. John Ford; bw)—Henry Fonda, John Wayne, Shirley Temple, Ward Bond, John Agar

*Hamlet* (British, d. Laurence Olivier; bw)— Laurence Olivier, Eileen Herlie, Jean Simmons

*I Remember Mama* (d. George Stevens; bw)— Irene Dunne, Barbara Bel Geddes, Oscar Homolka, Ellen Corby

*Johnny Belinda* (d. Jean Negulesco; bw)—Jane Wyman, Lew Ayres, Charles Bickford, Agnes Moorehead

*Key Largo* (d. John Huston; bw)—Humphrey Bogart, Lauren Bacall, Lionel Barrymore, Claire Trevor, Edward G. Robinson

*The Naked City* (d. Jules Dassin; bw)—Barry Fitzgerald, Don Taylor

*Oliver Twist* (British, d. David Lean; bw)— Robert Newton, Alec Guinness, Kay Walsh, John Howard Davies

*The Paleface* (d. Norman Z. McLeod; color)— Bob Hope, Jane Russell

*Red River* (d. Howard Hawks; bw)—John Wayne, Montgomery Clift, Joanne Dru, Walter Brennan, John Ireland

*The Red Shoes* (British, d. Michael Powell; color)—Anton Walbrook, Moira Shearer

*The Search* (d. Fred Zinnemann; bw)— Montgomery Clift, Ivan Jandl, Aline MacMahon, Jarmila Novotna, Wendell Corey

*Sitting Pretty* (d. Walter Lang; bw)—Clifton Webb, Robert Young, Maureen O'Hara

*The Snake Pit* (d. Anatole Litvak; bw)—Olivia

de Havilland, Leo Genn, Mark Stevens, Celeste Holm

*State of the Union* (d. Frank Capra; bw)—Spencer Tracy, Katharine Hepburn, Adolphe Menjou, Van Johnson

*The Three Godfathers* (d. John Ford; color)—John Wayne, Pedro Armendariz, Harry Carey, Jr.

*The Time of Your Life* (d. H. C. Potter; bw)—James Cagney, William Bendix, Wayne Morris, Jeanne Cagney

*The Treasure of the Sierra Madre* (d. John Huston; bw)—Humphrey Bogart, Walter Huston, Tim Holt, Alfonso Bedoya

*Unfaithfully Yours* (d. Preston Sturges; bw)—Rex Harrison, Linda Darnell

## Academy Awards

**March 20.** Dick Powell and Agnes Moorehead host the ceremonies at the Shrine Auditorium in Los Angeles. For the first time, the Academy specifically honors a foreign-language film as part of the Special Awards category.

Best Picture—*Gentleman's Agreement*
Best Actor—Ronald Colman (*A Double Life*)
Best Actress—Loretta Young (*The Farmer's Daughter*)
Best Director—Elia Kazan (*Gentleman's Agreement*)
Best Supporting Actor—Edmund Gwenn (*Miracle on 34th Street*)
Best Supporting Actress—Celeste Holm (*Gentleman's Agreement*)
Best Song—"Zip-A-Dee-Doo-Dah" from *Song of the South*
Special Award—*Shoeshine* (Italian) (*Note:* Not all special awards are listed.)

A preaward poll of voting members named Rosalind Russell the sure choice for best actress and Loretta Young the least likely to win. When Young reaches the stage, she demands to see the name in the envelope before accepting her Oscar.

## News

**May 11.** In a record cash deal Howard Hughes pays nearly $9 million for RKO, the studio that produced the classic Fred Astaire-Ginger Rogers musicals. The eccentric oil millionaire immediately begins to make his presence felt.

**October 30.** In Hollywood, the RKO board of directors accepts a voluntary Justice Department agreement to separate their theater properties from company production and distribution. Other major studios fall into line.

Two Supreme Court rulings this year effectively end the motion-picture monopoly: One prohibits affiliated theater owners from bargaining together to secure competitive advantages, while the second bans the practice of tying admission prices to the exhibition of copyrighted films.

**More news.** Studios save on film set costs with the increased use of new construction materials—strippable adhesive wallpaper, temporary flooring, and plastics for breakaway glass, building columns, and tree trunks.

• Lee Strasberg takes over the directorship of the year-old Actor's Studio. His "Method" technique of acting, used by such young students as Marlon

*Humphrey Bogart and Lauren Bacall in* Key Largo, *the last and best of their four films together.*

Brando, Paul Newman, Joanne Woodward, and James Dean, will exert enormous influence on the American stage and screen.

• In her first film role, Doris Day sings "It's Magic" in *Romance on the High Seas*. The song becomes a popular hit.

• In *Fast and Furry-ous*, animators Chuck Jones and Mike Maltese parody chase films with their new cartoon characters—the Road Runner and the Coyote.

• At the age of 44, Johnny Weissmuller makes his 12th and last Tarzan film, *Tarzan and the Mermaids*. The former Olympic swimming champion—regarded as the most dominant swimmer in sports history—debuted in 1932 in the first Tarzan talkie. He will switch to *Jungle Jim* pictures and, next year, Lex Barker will take over as the King of the Jungle.

| Top Box Office Stars | Newcomers |
|---|---|
| Bing Crosby | Jane Powell |
| Betty Grable | Cyd Charisse |
| Bud Abbott & | Ann Blyth |
| Lou Costello | Celeste Holm |
| Gary Cooper | Robert Ryan |
| Bob Hope | Angela Lansbury |
| Humphrey Bogart | Jean Peters |
| Clark Gable | Mona Freeman |
| Cary Grant | Eleanor Parker |
| Spencer Tracy | Doris Day |
| Ingrid Bergman | |

## Top Money-Maker of the Year

*The Road to Rio* (1947)

## Quote of the Year

Werewolf Lon Chaney, Jr., confesses, "You don't understand. Every night, when the moon is full, I turn into a wolf."

Lou Costello, misunderstanding, quips, "You and 50 million other guys!"

(*Abbott and Costello Meet Frankenstein*, original screenplay by Robert Lees, Frederic I. Rinaldo and John Grant.)

## Obituaries

**Sergei Eisenstein** (January 23, 1898–February 11, 1948). One of the greatest innovators in the history of motion pictures, the Soviet director remains best remembered for his silent films *October: Ten Days That Shook the World* (1928) and *Potemkin* (1925).

**D(avid) W(ark) Griffith** (January 22, 1875–July 23, 1948). Cecil B. DeMille called the pioneer director and producer "the master of us all." Griffith originated the full-length silent feature and developed the close-up, high- and low-angle shots, the fade-in and fade-out, the moving camera, and other film techniques. Yet his sound films appeared dated, and he found little employment through the 1930s and 1940s. His most celebrated picture, the Civil War epic *The Birth of a Nation* (1915), has earned an estimated $48 million to date, but Griffith dies in relative obscurity.

**Louis Lumière** (October 5, 1864–June 6, 1948). With his brother Auguste, the "father of motion pictures" ingeniously combined the ideas and inventions of others to construct the first successful camera-projector, demonstrated to the paying public on December 28, 1895.

**Fred Niblo** (January 6, 1874–November 11, 1948). He directed *Blood and Sand* (1922), with Rudolph Valentino, *The Three Musketeers* (1922), with Douglas Fairbanks, and *Ben Hur* (1926), among others.

# TELEVISION AND RADIO

## New Prime-Time TV Programs

"Arthur Godfrey's Talent Scouts" (December 6, 1948–July 21, 1958; Talent)—Host: Arthur Godfrey

"Break the Bank" (October 22, 1948–January 15, 1957; Quiz)—Host: Bert Parks

"Candid Camera" (August 1948–September 1950; October 1960–September 1967; Humor)—Host: Allen Funt

"The Ed Sullivan Show" (June 20, 1948–June 6, 1971; Variety)—Host: Ed Sullivan. *Note:* The show will be called "Toast of the Town" until 1955.

"Kukla, Fran & Ollie" (November 29, 1948–August 31, 1957; Children's)—Hostess: Fran Allison

"Lucky Pup" (August 23, 1948–June 23, 1951; Children's)

"The Milton Berle Show" (June 8, 1948–June 1956; Comedy Variety)—Milton Berle

"The Original Amateur Hour" (January 18, 1948–September 26, 1960; Talent)—Emcee: Ted Mack. *Note:* The show will appear on Sunday afternoon 1960–1970.

"The Perry Como Show" (December 24, 1948–June 12, 1963; Musical Variety)

"Philco TV Playhouse" (October 3, 1948–October 2, 1955; Drama Anthology)—*Note:* Between 1951 and 1955, the program will alternate on NBC with "Goodyear TV Playhouse."

"Studio One" (November 7, 1948–September 29, 1958; Drama Anthology)

"Wrestling" (July 30, 1948–March 5, 1955)—Various networks and times

## News

**This year.** A major source of entertainment during the Great Depression, radio became all the more important over the war years with the shortage of newsprint. Peace has brought enormous expansion with 500 new stations in 1946 and 400 last year. This year, 94.2 percent of American families own at least one radio. At the same time, television emerges from its interim period, with number of sets in U.S. homes jumping to 350,000 in the first six months of the year.

**March 18.** On the verge of a major program expansion, the fledgling TV networks finally reach an agreement with the American Federation of Musicians to allow the live broadcast of music. Just two days later, CBS transmits the first live symphony concert.

**March 21.** "Stop the Music" premieres on ABC radio. Host Bert Parks dials random telephone numbers until someone identifies the song. The appeal of immediate cash prizes flattens the competition;

Fred Allen drops from his top 10 perch to 38th and Edgar Bergen leaves the air for a season. The cheaper quiz show has arrived.

**October.** The FCC, in a controversial decision, lowers the wattage requirement for radio stations from 250 to 10. The commission hopes that campus stations will later add power to serve a wider area, but few do and the FM spectrum becomes unexpectedly crowded.

**April 14.** In the first public showing of television theater, moviegoers at the Paramount Theatre in New York watch boxing matches from Brooklyn. The elapsed time from punch to screen is 66 seconds.

**Spring.** With Daylight Savings Time this year, NBC and CBS begin recording their radio programs for later broadcast out west. (ABC and Mutual first recorded programs in 1946.) But each 16 inch disc costs $8, and NBC, along with ABC, soon switches to magnetic tape recorders. The new technology, brought in from Germany at the end of the war, costs just $4.50 for each half-hour show.

**May 6.** The FCC reserves channel 1 for the military.

**June 8.** Milton Berle hosts the first "Texaco Star Theatre." After a summer of rotating emcees, he takes over the show. Obviously a visual comedian—half a dozen radio shows all fared poorly—his zany costumes and slapstick will sell more TV's than manufacturers' ads.

**June 20.** On his variety show, Ed Sullivan proves to be a very different kind of host. Chosen for his skills as a producer, the *New York Daily News* columnist brings on unknown comedians Dean Martin and Jerry Lewis, composers Rodgers and Hammerstein, and a singing fireman for the first "Toast of the Town"—all for under five hundred dollars. Jack Gould of the *New York Times* describes the network's choice of emcee as "ill-advised." Sullivan's "matter-of-factness and his tendency to introduce friends in the audience add up to little sparkling entertainment."

**July 15.** Party campaign organizers, taking note of enormous TV sales over the past year, arrange an 18-station broadcast of both conventions. This evening, a common pool camera focuses on the Democratic podium; President Truman appears in a white suit, a color he was told would look good on the small screen.

**July 26.** Pianist Bob Howard is the first black artist to host a network TV series, a 15-minute musical show on CBS.

**August 10.** Producer-host Allen Funt switches from radio to television. Off and on over the next 19 years, he will gleefully tell victims, "Smile! You're on Candid Camera."

**September 30.** Overwhelmed with requests for new stations, the FCC freezes TV licensing. With 37 stations in 22 cities and 86 others granted permits, cross-station interference requires a study of frequency allocations.

**October 3.** On the first NFL telecast, Joe Hasel gives the play-by-play of a 41–10 Washington Redskin victory over the New York Giants. Only ABC, the NFL radio broadcaster as well, considers football worth covering.

**December 24.** Perry Como premieres in the 15-minute "Chesterfield Supper Club." His program will expand to one hour in 1955, and remain one of the most popular shows through to 1963. The singer will then continue with "Kraft Music Hall" specials for another four years.

**November 29.** "Kukla, Fran and Ollie" quickly becomes one of the most successful of the hand-puppet shows. During live broadcasts, actress Fran Allison chats with Punch-like Kukla or Oliver J. Dragon (voiced by creator Burr Tillstrom), in addition to singing a song or visiting with other players in the Kuklapolitan Playhouse, including Beulah Witch.

Competition from shows like "Captain Video" will push "Kukla" into a daytime slot from 1954 to 1957. It will be revived in 1961–1962 and syndicated in 1965.

**More news.** As TV goes national, time changes create a monumental problem—a live broadcast at 7:00 P.M. EST appears at 4:00 P.M. PST. For the West Coast, the only alternative is local programming or a kinescope recording straight from the TV screen. And even with improvements "kines" (pronounced "kinnies") remain grainy.

## TV Commercials

**Ajax.** The first professionally animated commercial, Ajax's three little pixies promote the "foaming cleanser" in the first popular TV jingle.

## Memorable Radio Programs End

> The American School of the Air (February 4, 1930)
> Hop Harrigan (August 31, 1942)
> The Hour of Charm (January 3, 1935)
> Information Please (May 17, 1938)
> The Land of the Lost (October 9, 1943)

# SPORTS

## Winners

### Baseball

World Series—Cleveland Indians (AL), 4 games; Boston Braves (NL), 2 games
Player of the Year—Lou Boudreau (Cleveland Indians, AL); Stan Musial (St. Louis Cardinals, NL)
Rookie of the Year—Alvin Dark (Boston Braves, NL)

### Football

NFL Championship—Philadelphia Eagles 7, Chicago Cardinals 0
College Bowls (January 1, 1948)—
  Rose Bowl, Michigan 49, USC 0
  Cotton Bowl, Southern Methodist 13, Penn State 13
  Orange Bowl, Georgia Tech 20, Kansas 14
  Sugar Bowl, Texas 27, Alabama 7
Heisman Trophy—Doak Walker (Southern Methodist, HB)
Grey Cup—Calgary Stampeders 12, Ottawa Rough Riders 7

### Basketball

NCAA Championship—Kentucky 58, Baylor 42

## Tennis

U.S. National—Men, Pancho Gonzalez (vs. Eric Sturgess); Women, Margaret du Pont (vs. Louise Brough)

Wimbledon—Men, Robert Faulkenburg (vs. John Bromwich); Women, Louise Brough (vs. Doris Hart)

## Golf

Masters—Claude Harmon
U.S. Open—Ben Hogan
British Open—Henry Cotton

## Hockey

Stanley Cup—Toronto Maple Leafs, 4 games; Detroit Red Wings, 0 games

## Ice Skating

World Championship—Men, Dick Button (U.S.); Women, Barbara Ann Scott (Canada)

U.S. National—Men, Dick Button; Women, Gretchen Merrill

Canadian National—Men, Wallace E. Diestelmeyer; Women, Barbara Ann Scott

## Kentucky Derby

Citation—Eddie Arcaro, jockey

## Athlete of the Year

Male—Lou Boudreau (Baseball); Female—Fanny Blankers-Koen (Track and Field)

## Last Season

Syl Apps (Hockey)
Toe Blake (Hockey)
Bryan Hextall (Hockey)
Joe Medwick (Baseball)
Barbara Ann Scott (Figure Skating)

# News

**January 30–February 8.** Some 700 athletes from 28 nations gather at St. Moritz, Switzerland, for the first Olympics in 12 years (W.W. II's losers—Germany, Italy, and Japan—are not invited). The leaders Sweden and Norway each win 4 gold, 3 silver, and 3 bronze. Americans collect their first golds ever in two events: 18-year-old Dick Button's in figure skating and Gretchen Fraser's in skiing. Canada's ice hockey team and figure skater Barbara Ann Scott bring home gold medals for their country.

**February 20.** Knocked down by heavyweight contender Ezzard Charles, Sam Baroudi dies 10 hours later. With this fatality and others, the National Boxing Association rules that following a knockdown a boxer must take an eight-second count before resuming the match.

**March 11.** Reginald Weir is the first black to play in a U.S. national tennis tournament. He is eliminated in the second round.

**June 13.** His voice hoarse with throat cancer, Babe Ruth thanks the nearly 50,000 fans who have come out to honor him at Yankee Stadium. The former baseball great left the team in 1935, played briefly with the Boston Braves, and coached for the Brooklyn Dodgers in 1938. The Yankees retire Ruth's No. 3 and send his uniform to Cooperstown's Baseball Hall of Fame.

**July 29–August 14.** Despite generally poor weather, British spectators witness several outstanding performances at the Summer Olympics: a win from the youngest decathlete ever, 17-year-old American Bob Mathias; a record time in the 10,000 meters from underrated Czech runner Emil Zátopek; and a record-breaking four gold medals from Fanny Blankers-Koen, in the 100-meter and 200-meter sprints, 80-meter hurdles, and 400-meter relay (the 30-year-old Dutch athlete holds world records in the long jump and high jump, but Olympic rules limit her to three individual events). The United States, with a sweep of the swimming events, places first overall, with 38 gold medals.

**August 13.** Satchel Paige, a legendary pitcher in the Negro Leagues, makes his major league debut and shuts out the White Sox 5–0. In his next start, for the Cleveland Indians, Paige throws another shutout. The phenomenally durable pitcher (his

*With victories in the Preakness, Belmont, and Kentucky Derby (pictured here), Citation and jockey Eddie Arcaro capture racing's most coveted prize—the Triple Crown.*

mother says he is 44) finishes the year with a 6–1 record and a 2.48 ERA.

---

*Statistics:* This year, the combined total attendance for all organized baseball climbs to 63.8 million, an increase of 3.6 million over 1947.

---

**September 21.** Title holder Tony Zale fails to answer the 12th-round bell and French boxer Mar-

cel Cerdan becomes the first non-American middleweight champion of the century.

**October 4.** With the same win-loss record, the Cleveland Indians and the Boston Red Sox meet in the AL's first postseason playoff. Indians' player-manager Lou Boudreau hits two home runs to lead his club to its first pennant in 28 years.

**November 30.** With the drain of talent to the majors, the Negro National League dissolves. The 10-team Negro American League remains as the only segregated association in baseball.

**More news.** At the beginning of the 1948–1949 season, the Basketball Association of America all but finishes the National Basketball League by picking up four of the best NBL franchises, including Minneapolis with star George Mikan.

## Records

**October 10.** The fifth game of the World Series at Cleveland Municipal Stadium draws a record 86,288 fans.

## What They Said

To suggestions he might be named Rookie of the Year, Satchel Paige responds, "Twenty-two years is a long time to be a rookie."

## Obituaries

**George Herman "Babe" Ruth** (February 6, 1895– August 16, 1948). While a phenomenally successful pitcher—1.75 ERA in 1916 and 29 consecutive scoreless innings in that year's World Series— Ruth's power hitting caused the Red Sox to convert him to an outfielder. In 1919, he set a major league record of 29 home runs. And when Boston traded him to the Yankees in 1920, the "Sultan of Swat" shattered his own record with 54 HR.

Over the succeeding years, Ruth rewrote the record books, averaging 50 homers a year between 1926 and 1931 and chalking up an enormous 60 in 1927, leading the league in RBIs for six seasons, setting an all-time single-season walk record, and so on. With seven league pennants and four World Series championships, Yankee Stadium became known as "The House That Ruth Built."

The highest-paid player of his era, the Babe was known off the field as a carouser (roommate Ping Brodie reportedly said, "I don't room with him. I room with his suitcase") as well as a soft touch who volunteered time to needy children.

While his body lies in state at Yankee Stadium, 100,000 fans come out to pay one last tribute to the "Bambino."

# 1949

*East-West scorekeeping in 1949 leaves most observers dizzy. The Allies establish NATO, outlast the Berlin blockade, and form West Germany to block further Communist expansion in Europe. But the Soviets counterbalance all gains in one stroke—their first detonation of an atomic bomb. Worse still for the West, Communists establish a People's Republic in the most populous nation on earth, China.*

*Suddenly faced with the very real possibility of a third world war, Americans in at least 26 states require an oath of loyalty from public officials. And a federal jury sends U.S. Communist leaders to jail for advocating the forceful overthrow of the government.*

*For black Americans, Truman's Fair Deal is the most momentous event of the year. Confident with reelection, he puts forward the first major civil rights legislation since Reconstruction.*

*The United States enters the space age, and introduces the first long-distance dial telephone service. William Faulkner wins the Nobel prize in literature, George Orwell writes* Nineteen Eighty-Four, *and author Margaret Mitchell dies following a car accident.*

*Kids are more interested in Silly Putty, the new Oreo cookie, and the first telecasts of "Hopalong Cassidy" and "The Lone Ranger," over the new coaxial cable.*

## NEWS

**January 1.** In 1947, the Maharaja of Kashmir ignored his subjects' wishes and joined with Hindu India rather than Moslem Pakistan. An undeclared war over the strategic northwestern state ends today with most of the disputed territory left within India. But Pakistan continues to reject the Maharaja's act of accession, and fighting will break out again in 1965 and 1971.

**January 5.** President Truman uses his annual State of the Union message to introduce the first major civil rights bill since Reconstruction. The Fair Deal program calls for an end to discrimination against blacks in voting rights and jobs, access to education and public facilities, as well as the establishment of the Civil Rights Commission and a Civil Rights Division in the Department of Justice. Truman's progressive legislative program also includes a national health insurance program, aid to the elderly, more federal housing, and a higher minimum wage.

**January 10.** Defense, or Cold War, costs account for fully one-third of the estimated $41.8 billion annual budget—the largest peacetime budget in American history. By the end of the 1950 fiscal year, the U.S. deficit reaches $3.1 billion and the national debt, which results from deficit spending, rises to $4.3 billion by December. Until 1949, the Truman administration had completed three successive years of debt reduction.

**January 20.** Harry S. Truman and Alben W. Barkley are inaugurated as the president and vice-president of the United States in an elaborate Washington ceremony. (The Republican Congress, expecting a Dewey victory, had provided generous funds.)

In his address, President Truman proposes four guidelines for U.S. foreign policy: support for the United Nations; continuation of the Marshall Plan; military aid to nations to fight Communist aggression; and the sharing of scientific advances and industrial programs with underdeveloped nations. Point Four, signaling the beginning of U.S. technical assistance to Third World countries, arouses great interest at home and abroad. Unfortunately, initial funds of $34 million fail to meet expectations.

**February 24.** Israel and Egypt sign an armistice to end nine months of alternating battles and truces. U.N. mediator Ralph Bunche, who receives the 1950 Nobel peace prize for his work, negotiates a further peace agreement between Israel and Trans-Jordan on April 3, and Syria on July 20.

The settlements give Israel 21 percent more land than originally allotted under the 1947 partition, but make no provisions for the thousands of Arabs who have fled or been expelled (most of the Palestinian refugees went to Jordan or Gaza). The Arab governments, normally quarrelsome, now unite against the Jewish nation.

**March 31.** Newfoundland enters the Dominion of Canada as the 10th province. In a 1948 referendum, 78,323 Newfoundlanders voted for confederation while 71,334 chose self-government, a difference of less than 5 percent. A 1950 election picks Joey Smallwood as the province's first premier.

**April 4.** The United States, Canada, Britain, and nine Western European nations pledge mutual defense against aggression and cooperation in military training and strategic planning. The North

Atlantic Treaty Organization (NATO), while necessary to counter the growing Soviet threat, completes the division of Europe into Eastern and Western blocs.

Membership in the alliance ends American isolationism and, for the first time, commits the United States to the defense of other nations in advance of war. Following ratification, Congress approves the Mutual Defense Assistance Act to provide the 11 pact nations with massive military aid.

**April 14.** In Nuremberg, the last American war crimes tribunal sentences 19 former German officials and military leaders to prison terms of 4 to 25 years. Altogether the United States has sentenced 459 Nazis to death, imprisoned 1,110, and acquitted 304.

Although information on trials in the Soviet Union and other Communist nations remains sketchy, at least 10,000 have been tried, with a conviction rate of 80 percent.

In 1965, Germany will extend the 20-year statute of limitations on war criminals to 1969 then again to 1979.

**April 18.** Eire becomes the Republic of Ireland. Granted independence in 1921 as a dominion of the British Empire, Eire became a sovereign state within the Commonwealth under a new constitution in 1937. Today, allegiance to the British Crown officially ends.

Next month, the British House of Commons passes a bill allowing Northern Ireland (the nine northern counties of Ulster) to remain in the United Kingdom.

**May 5.** Ten Western European nations establish the Council of Europe to prevent a recurrence of European nationalism, to safeguard common heritages, and to further human rights. The Consultative Assembly, with no powers, will make recommendations to the Committee of Ministers. West Germany will become a full member in 1951, and other nations will join through the 1950s and 1960s.

**May 12.** In Japan, American occupation continues to shift away from punitive measures. General Douglas MacArthur unilaterally terminates Japanese war reparations and reopens stock exchanges to encourage economic recovery. Then, in July, to give the Japanese greater autonomy in local affairs, he orders the dissolution of the Allied military government by year's end.

From the end of the war to mid-1949, U.S. civilian relief supplies to Japan have amounted to $1.26 billion.

**May 23.** With Allied agreement on all questions relating to the formation and control of a West German state, a new constitution creates the Federal Republic of Germany, with Bonn as the capital. Parliamentary elections, on August 14, produce a coalition government, with Christian Democrat Konrad Adenauer, age 73, as the nation's first chancellor.

Comprising some two-thirds of the old Germany, the new nation faces overwhelming social problems including a shortage of housing, high unemployment, and a flood of returning POWs and refugees from Eastern Europe. The Marshall Plan will extend much-needed aid by the end of the year.

**June 7.** The Soviets continue to withdraw troops from North Korea while strengthening the North Korean People's Army. The U.S. joint chiefs of staff, while aware of the buildup, still believe that aid will make South Korea's prospects for survival "favorable."

President Truman, who wants to cut back military spending, withdraws occupational forces—the last U.S. troops depart today—and urges Congress to appropriate $150 million in economic aid. He calls Korea a testing ground for democracy "matched against the practices of Communism." The request will not be approved until late in the year.

**June 7.** The House passes the Central Intelligence Act of 1949, authorizing the secret operation of the Central Intelligence Agency with exemptions from regular audits and civil service regulations. With only four nay votes, the act passes under the suspension of rules, without debate or public explanation.

**June 20.** The Reorganization Act becomes effective. A bipartisan Commission, under the direction of former president Herbert Hoover, recommended the president be given greater direct authority to consolidate the executive branch for both efficiency and economy. (In 20 years, the number of civil servants has mushroomed from 570,000 to over 2 million.) A second commission will sit from 1953 to 1955 under Dwight Eisenhower.

In 1958, a private study will conclude that 72 percent of the first commission's suggestions were fully or partially implemented—including the organization of a Joint Chiefs of Staff and the creation of a Department of Health, Education, and Welfare—and 64 percent from the second. Hoover later states that his commissions probably saved the government some $10 billion annually.

**June 27.** In parliamentary elections, Louis St. Laurent leads the governing Liberal party to the largest majority in Canadian history, taking 193 of 262 seats in the House of Commons.

**August 5.** Since 1947, when civil war erupted in China, Truman has provided only limited assistance to Chiang Kai-shek. The Nationalists would need American troops to overthrow the Communists; and the president refuses to make that commitment.

Today, a State Department White Paper reveals that the Nationalists have virtually wasted $2 billion in U.S. aid while failing to bring about basic reforms. As a result, aid is terminated, and Washington will concentrate on halting the expansion of Communist doctrine into other Asian nations. Republicans and many voters criticize the administration for "losing" China to the Communists.

**August 5.** Ecuador's worst earthquake in modern times destroys over 50 towns, killing more than 6,000 people, injuring another 20,000, and leaving 100,000 homeless.

**August 10.** An amended National Security Act reorganizes the National Military Establishment into the Department of Defense, increases the authority of the secretary, and appoints a chairman to the Joint Chiefs of Staff; General Omar Bradley is the first. The 1947 legislation had produced interservice rivalry.

**September 6.** In Camden, New Jersey, Howard Unruh goes berserk and shoots 13 people in 12 minutes. When he surrenders, the 28-year-old claims people had been laughing at him behind his back. "I'm no psycho," he says. "I have a good mind." Unruh, who won marksmanship ratings in the service, later claims he would have killed more people but ran out of ammunition. Never tried for murder, the former war hero receives a life sentence in an asylum for the criminally insane.

**September 17.** In Toronto Harbor, at 2:30 A.M., a passenger discovers a fire on board the excursion ship *Noronic*. A critical eight minutes pass as he and a crew member attempt to put out the flames. Feeding on wood-framed cabins, wooden decks, and other flammable materials, the inferno roars through the corridors. With no sprinkler system on board, at least 118 die and many others are seriously burned.

**September 23.** The leaders of the United States, Britain, and Canada announce the detection of a Soviet nuclear explosion (a USAF plane accidentally discovered radioactive debris while flying over the Pacific). Two days later, Moscow confirms an August 29 blast as part of a large-scale operation to construct mines, canals, and roads in Siberia.

The Communists' possession of "the bomb" accelerates the U.S. defense program. In Europe, Charles de Gaulle responds by calling for a French atomic weapons program. He claims that the United States "is neither obliged nor prepared to participate in the direct and immediate defense of our continent."

**September 29.** A U.S. jury convicts Japanese-American Iva Toguri D'Aquino of treason. Caught in Japan at the outbreak of World War II, D'Aquino became one of several radio announcers who, as Tokyo Rose, broadcast a mix of propaganda and music to U.S. servicemen in the Pacific. But she worked only under duress and refused to renounce her American citizenship.

Trial officials intimidated and bribed witnesses and the judge called for a guilty verdict, but the jury finds the 34-year-old innocent of eight overt acts of treason and guilty on just one count of attempting to undermine U.S. morale. D'Aquino will serve six and a half years in prison.

**September 30.** The Soviets officially ended the Berlin blockade on May 12, but the United States and Britain continued to fly in supplies until today.

Over the 328 days, pilots delivered 2.3 million tons of supplies in more than 277,000 flights; 48 airmen died.

The Soviets suffer a total defeat and, by trying to drive the Allied powers out of Berlin, replace the Germans as the common Western enemy.

**October 1.** As the Nationalists flee to the offshore island of Formosa, the Communists proclaim the People's Republic of China in Peking. Mao Tsetung becomes chairman and Chou En-lai premier and foreign minister. The Kremlin immediately extends diplomatic recognition.

The leaders of the new nation face the worst summer floods of this century. Thousands have drowned, 20 million have been left homeless, and, with the resulting food shortages, 4,700 starve to death in Shanghai alone.

**October 7.** In a political response to the creation of West Germany, the Soviets create the German Democratic Republic. No elections are held. Bonn declares East Germany illegal and claims that the Federal Republic has responsibility for all Germans.

**October 14.** A federal jury, at the end of a nine-month trial, finds 11 top American Communist leaders guilty of advocating, on orders from Moscow, the forceful overthrow of the U.S. government. Ten men receive 5-year prison terms, the other 3 years; all receive fines of $10,000. The verdict, in effect, bans the Communist party in the United States.

**October 16.** A cease-fire is announced in the Greek Civil War. With liberation from the Nazis, the Communist underground and many other Greeks resisted the return of their exiled king (the British founded the monarchy in 1832 with a Bavarian king). When the monarchists won the 1946 elections, civil war broke out.

During the three-year conflict, 29,000 Communists and 15,000 Royalists died in battle, but, for most Greeks, the 4,200 civilian dead leave the bitterest memories. The Communists executed 3,500 and, on their flight to Communist countries north of Greece, abducted another 28,000, many children.

**October 19.** General MacArthur announces the completion of U.S. war crimes trials in the Far East.

Altogether, the Allied nations have convicted 4,200 Japanese of war crimes, executed 720, and sentenced the rest to terms of varying lengths. Some 2,500 remain in prison.

**November 1.** In the worst civil aviation disaster in U.S. history, a Bolivian test pilot accidentally rams an Eastern Airlines Douglas plane with his P-38 fighter above the Washington, D.C., airport. He survives, but the 55 on board the commercial flight are killed.

*Eleanor Roosevelt holds a poster of the Declaration of Human Rights in Spanish, ready for distribution in November. The United Nations passed the landmark document late last year.*

**November 6.** In East Germany, an explosion in a uranium mine kills an undetermined number of miners. A fire brigade officer, who escapes from the Eastern zone in early December, says the death toll reached 3,700. The Soviets claim one miner died.

**December 2.** The British Parliament accedes to Canada's request and revises the British North America Act, giving Canada the power to amend all matters except those relating to provincial rights (such as property and civil rights), languages, and minority rights in education.

**December 27.** Indonesia gains independence from the Netherlands. When the Dutch attempted to forcibly reimpose their 350-year colonial rule at the end of W.W.II, sharp criticism from the United Nations brought them to the negotiation table. The United States of Indonesia will be an independent federation of 16 states, united with the Netherlands as an equal partner. Sukarno becomes the first president. Next year, the federation will be abandoned in favor of a unitary state dominated by Java.

## Obituaries

**James Forrestal** (February 15, 1892–May 22, 1949). Appointed Navy secretary in 1944, Forrestal became the first secretary of defense under the National Security Act of 1947. Strongly anti-Communist, he advised a Cold War military buildup and strove to coordinate the three services. But the pressures of the job proved too much and the exhausted secretary resigned on March 28. While hospitalized, he jumped from a window to his death.

**Prince Louis II** (July 12, 1870–May 9, 1949). The 29th ruler (1922–1959) of the tiny principality of Monaco is succeeded by his grandson, Prince Rainier III.

## BEGINNINGS AND ENDINGS

### News

**January 11.** San Diego's first recorded snowfall comes in the midst of a two-week cold spell.

**January 20.** For the first time, Negroes attend official inaugural events in Washington, as Harry S. Truman begins his first full term as president.

**March 2.** The U.S. Air Force's Lucky Lady II completes the first nonstop flight around the world. The B-50 refueled four times in midair during the 94-hour, 1-minute journey. (One tanker crashed north of Manila, killing all nine crewmen.) Strategic Air Command Lt. Gen. Curtis LeMay, upon greeting Capt. James Gallagher and his crew at Fort Worth, claims the United States can now drop an atomic bomb "any place in the world."

**March 17.** With voter approval, South Carolina becomes the last state to legalize divorce.

**April 2.** Tonight, crowds marvel at London's street lamps and advertising signs, relit after 10 years. Nighttime blackout, instituted in 1939 to thwart Nazi bombers, was continued after the war to conserve electricity for a recovering economy.

**April 29.** Four American charter companies receive authorization to schedule the first regular freight flights to compete with mail-passenger lines.

**May 7.** The first bomb explosion on a commercial airplane kills 13 en route to Manila. Crispin Vergo, who wanted to collect a relative's life insurance, is convicted of the crime.

**May 11.** Siam officially becomes Thailand (Land of the Free).

**June 3.** Wesley A. Brown, age 22, is the first black American to graduate from the U.S. Naval Academy at Annapolis.

**August 9.** Lt. J. L. Fruin is the first American airman to use an ejection seat in an emergency. He abandons his disabled McDonnell Banshee over South Carolina and survives.

**August 22.** Released from government wardship, the Saginaw-Chippewas of Michigan and the Stockbridge-Munsees of Wisconsin are the first American Indian tribes to gain full control over their affairs.

**August 23.** KKK members from six southern states form the Knights of the Ku Klux Klans of America and elect an "imperial emperor." The Knights estimate membership at 265,000 nationwide.

**August 31.** The Grand Army of the Republic holds its 83rd and last encampment. Only 6 of the 16 surviving veterans, who fought for the Union in the American Civil War (1861–1865), were able to attend.

**October 12.** President Truman names Eugenie Anderson, age 40, to represent the U.S. in Denmark. She is the first American woman ambassador.

**October 25.** The first jet airliner, a British Overseas Airway (BOAC) de Havilland Comet, flies 2,980 miles from London to Tripoli in a record 6 hours, 38 minutes—100 mph faster than the swiftest propeller plane.

---

*Statistics:* Plasters and lathers collect the country's highest weekly wage—$83.13.

---

**October 26.** An amendment to the Fair Labor Standards Act of 1938 raises the minimum hourly wage from 40 cents to 75 cents.

**November 18.** The first U.S. vice-president to marry in office, Alben W. Barkley, weds Carleton S. Hadley. The 71-year-old Barkley was widowed in 1947; Hadley, also widowed, is 38.

**December 2.** London transfers final legal authority for Canadian civil cases to the Supreme Court in Ottawa. The right to hear appeals in Canadian criminal cases was transferred in 1933.

**December 25.** United Nations International Children's Emergency Fund (UNICEF) chooses Jitka Samkova's colorful painting of children dancing around a maypole for the agency's first Christmas card. Because her school had no paper, the 7-year-old Czechoslovakian used a piece of glass.

**More news.** The International Ice Patrol, established after the *Titanic's* fatal collision with an iceberg in 1912, for the first time conducts its entire patrol by air.

• Billy Graham, who began his evangelical career in 1944 with the Youth for Christ movement, bursts on the national scene with an eight-week tent revival in Los Angeles. The dramatic young preacher claims over 3,000 converts during his campaign, including a gangster and an alcoholic radio actor.

• Domestic airlines introduce coach service— lower fares and less emphasis on frills. Experts view the innovation as an important step toward mass air transport.

## New Products and Businesses

General Mills and Pillsbury market prepared cake mixes.

Oreo cookies make their first appearance.

Charles Lubin, a 44-year-old Chicago baker, names a refrigerated cheesecake after his daughter, Sara Lee.

This year, the Allies return the Volkswagen factory to German control. Prototypes appeared in the late 1930s, but then war broke out. Two of the odd-looking automobiles sell in the United States.

## Memorable Ad Campaigns

In New York, at the Waldorf-Astoria, the first GM "Motorama" features cars of the future, current production models, and other glitzy displays. Over the next 12 years, each of eight Motoramas draws an estimated 2 million people.

## Fads

Almost unknown at the beginning of the year, the Argentine card game canasta enthralls an estimated 10 million Americans and pushes three rule books onto the best-seller list.

During W.W.II, General Electric (GE) chemists accidentally created a synthetic with no practical use. Advertiser Peter Hodgson discovers that the rubbery substance bounces, stretches slowly or snaps into pieces, and picks up images when pressed onto printed matter. He packages "Silly Putty" in plastic eggs and sells 30 million worldwide over the next five years.

Pay $1 to join, bring in two new members, and after 12 days collect $2,048 in turn from the Pyramid club. The feverish craze dies a natural death when people realize the mathematical impossibility of finding recruits to add to the pot.

# SCIENCE AND TECHNOLOGY

## News

**January 6.** The National Bureau of Standards announces the development of an "atomic" clock. Using the vibrations of ammonia atoms, the timepiece will lose or gain no more than one second in 3 million years.

**January 7.** Drs. Daniel Pease and Richard Baker have produced the first photograph of a gene, magnified 120,000 times.

**February 25–27.** A report, presented at a meeting sponsored by the American Cancer Society and the National Cancer Institute, links the rapid rise in the incidence of lung cancer, over the past 25 years, to cigarette smoking.

**May.** The AEC confirms the loss of 1.05 ounces of U-235 at the Argonne National Laboratory. In the ensuing public uproar, authorities deliberately steal two bars to check security; the theft goes undetected. The missing bottle is later found in a garbage dump, but questions remain over possible discrepancies in the inventory.

**May 3.** *Viking I*, a 45-foot experimental navy rocket, takes the United States into the space age with a respectable 50-mile altitude. Engineering data from each subsequent flight improves the next generation. The last *Viking* will be launched on February 4, 1955.

**May 30.** Dr. Edward C. Kendall of the Mayo Clinic, in his presentation to the Seventh International Congress on Rheumatic Diseases, reports that a hormone from the adrenal glands of cattle and the natural pituitary hormone ACTH have both proven effective in treating arthritis. Advances over the next year will substantially lower the costs of manufacturing the former, *cortisone*.

**Spring.** Studies reveal small quantities of DDT in cow's milk, and farmers are warned not to use the insecticide on dairy cows or in dairy barns.

**June 20.** At the University of Chicago, Dr. Gerard Kuiper confirms the discovery of a 2nd moon orbiting Neptune. Nereid is the 30th moon found in our solar system.

**August 16.** Attached to a cable, a 7,000-pound benthoscope takes 48-year-old Otis Barton down to a record depth of 4,500 feet in the Pacific. The previous deep-sea mark of 3,028 feet was made in a bathysphere off Bermuda in 1934.

**August 21.** John W. Mauchly and John Presper Eckert, Jr., demonstrate BINAC (Binary Automatic Computer).

In 1946, the two scientists constructed the first U.S. electronic stored-program computer, largely to compute army ballistic firing tables. ENIAC (Electronic Numerical Integrator and Calculator), with 18,000 vacuum tubes, required 15,000 square feet and, legend has it, the massive machine dimmed the lights of Philadelphia when it was turned on. BINAC, made for Northrop Aircraft, contains just 700 tubes, but is said to be three times faster.

**August 29.** Cancer patients at the University of Illinois receive treatment from a 22-million-volt betatron, the first atom-smasher built as a medical device. The radiation penetrates deeper than conventional x-rays without harming surface tissue.

**August 31.** In the fight for appropriations, a navy Banshee jet flew to 48,846 feet to take the highest-altitude man-made photo yet. The Department of Defense suppresses the picture, but somehow a copy of clearly recognizable Washington targets ends up on the wall of a local bar.

---

*Statistics:* Ten years ago the average bomber weighed some 20,000 pounds when empty. Today, at least one bomber in production weighs 150,000 pounds.

---

**October 7.** Dr. George D. Ludwig of the Naval Research Medical Institute in Washington, D.C., reports that his animal experiments with ultrasound suggest that surgeons could use the technology to locate gallstones and other foreign matter within the human body. Currently, ultrasound is used to detect flaws in metals.

**October 17.** The first long-distance dial telephone call connects New York and San Francisco in 12 seconds.

**October 28.** A storm-detector radar scope begins operations in the midst of Signal Corps Laboratories, Fort Monmouth, New Jersey. Unlike wartime radar, this instrument is designed to provide six to eight hours advance warning of approaching weather systems.

**December 26.** Albert Einstein attempts to unify the basic theories of gravitation and electromagnetism with four mathematical equations. The great scientist concedes it will be difficult to test his extension of the theory of relativity. He will revise his unified field theory in 1953.

**More news.** William Cumming Rose demonstrates that humans require eight "essential" amino acids in their diet, and that the body can use them to compensate for any other deficiencies.

• In Canada, Murray Barr discovers a deviation in the nuclei of the normal female cell which makes it distinguishable from the normal male cell—a dark spot on one of the two X chromosomes. Cellular diagnosis of sex, through the Barr body, will later be used to determine the sex of athletes.

• American astronomer Fred Lawrence Whipple suggests that comets are essentially dirty snowballs of ice or ammonia ice and silicate dust and gravel. The sun's heat explosively vaporizes the dust, forming the comet's haze and tail. Other astronomers readily accept his theory.

## Other Discoveries, Developments, and Inventions

Wheel clamp used to immobilize Denver's illegally parked cars, later called the Denver Boot

Nonmagnetic compass for polar navigation from the navy and the Bureau of Standards

Heat-resistant ceramic from the USAF for use in jet and rocket engines

First zigzag stitch, in the Italian Necchi sewing machine

Wire-strand recorder for 30-second telephone messages

Key ignition replacing the button ignition, in some Chrysler models

Eye-level reflex focusing, in the 35-mm Contax "S", from Zeiss-Ikon

Dramamine for motion sickness

Gas-turbine electric locomotive which enters service in 1952–1953

Urine test for pregnancy

## Obituaries

**Friedrich Bergius** (October 11, 1884–March 30, 1949). During his career, the German Nobel chemist discovered the processes for producing sugar from wood and synthetic oil from coal.

**Leonarde Keeler** (October 30, 1903–September 20, 1949). The American criminologist invented the polygraph, or lie detector, in 1923.

**Edward Thorndike** (August 31, 1874–August 9, 1949). An educator and pioneer in experimental animal psychology, he developed the maze and puzzle box as standard testing devices.

# THE ARTS

February 10—*Death of a Salesman*, with Lee J. Cobb, Mildred Dunnock, Arthur Kennedy, Cameron Mitchell (742 perfs.)

April 7—*South Pacific*, with Mary Martin, Ezio Pinza, Juanita Hall (1,925 perfs.)

December 8—*Gentlemen Prefer Blondes*, with Yvonne Adair, Jerry Craig, Carol Channing (740 perfs.)

## Tony Awards

Actor (Dramatic)—Rex Harrison, *Anne of the Thousand Days*

Actress (Dramatic)—Martita Hunt, *The Madwoman of Chaillot*

Actor (Musical)—Ray Bolger, *Where's Charley?*

Actress (Musical)—Nanette Fabray, *Love Life*

Play—*Death of a Salesman*

Musical—*Kiss Me Kate*

Note: In 1947 and 1948, male Tony winners received a scroll and cigarette lighter and female winners received a scroll and compact. This year, the Tony becomes an official medallion.

## News

**October 9.** The Sadler's Wells Ballet from London opens its first North American tour in New York at the Metropolitan Opera House (the Met). The *Herald-Tribune* describes 30-year-old Margot Fonteyn as "a ballerina among ballerinas."

**More news.** *Death of a Salesman* is the first play to win the Pulitzer prize, the Critics Circle Award, and the Tony.

• Pierre Auguste Renoir's *Young Bather* sells for $10,500 while Degas's *Ballet School* fetches $25,000.

## Obituaries

**Richard Strauss** (June 11, 1864–September 8, 1949). In later years, the German composer abandoned experimental rhythms and harmonies for more conservative forms. His first great opera, *Salome* (1905), and *Der Rosenkavalier* (1911) remain his best-known works.

# WORDS

Nelson Algren, *The Man with the Golden Arm*
A. B. Guthrie, *The Way West*
George Orwell, *Nineteen Eighty-Four*
Harold Robbins, *The Dream Merchants*
Frank Yerby, *Pride's Castle*

## News

**February 24.** The 2,500 subscribers to *New Colophon*, the book collector's quarterly, pick Eugene O'Neill as the American writer most likely to be called "great" in the year 2000. Placing 2nd through 10th are Sinclair Lewis (just two points behind), Robert Frost, Ernest Hemingway, Carl Sandburg, John Steinbeck, T. S. Eliot, George Santayana, and Edna St. Vincent Millay.

**June 13.** The chilling portrayal of totalitarianism in George Orwell's novel *Nineteen Eighty-Four* introduces a new phrase to the Western world: "Big brother is watching you."

**December 29.** *Time* magazine names Winston Churchill "Man of the Half-Century." In a United Press (UP) poll, editors place the British politician fourth behind Franklin D. Roosevelt, Adolf Hitler, and Thomas Edison.

**More news.** This year, one of the five existing manuscript copies of Lincoln's "Gettysburg Address" fetches the highest auction price for a single work—$54,000.

• In his *Zoo* books, Clare Barnes, Jr., hilariously captions bird and animal photos to poke fun at typical types in the office, at home, on campus, and in politics. *White Collar Zoo* and *Home Sweet Zoo*, along with three books on canasta, capture the year's top spots on the best-seller list.

## Cartoons and Comics

**June 24.** Millions of Americans eagerly check their newspapers today for the long-overdue marriage of heavyweight boxing champ "Joe Palooka" (1928) and his fiancée, cheese heiress Ann Howe. Writer Hammond Fisher sent out engraved invitations to the comic-strip wedding, and Chief Justice Vinson and General Omar Bradley, among others, readily accepted.

**More news.** A series of confession titles, including *My Love Life* from Fox Features and *Sweetheart Diary* from Fawcett Publications, establishes a new trend in comic books.

## TIME *Man of the Year*

Winston Churchill

## New Words and Phrases

afterburner (a ram-jet booster engine)
automation
beefcake (exposure of men's chests)
bikini
bonus player (in baseball)
chucks (teenage slang for something humorous)
community college
disposable income
freeze-drying
guppy (a snorkel submarine)
neo-Nazism
no-day [work] week (euphemism for a strike)
paramilitary
parlay (to exploit something with marked success)

pitch-out (in football)
reactor
simulcast (simultaneous radio and television transmission)
Titoism (Yugoslavian Marshal Tito's advocacy of a Communism that places national interests above international, or specifically Soviet, concerns)
Veep (from VP, vice-president of the United States)
welfare state
wetback (illegal Mexican immigrant)

In addition, teenagers introduce a new all-purpose phrase: "How _____ can you get?" Some of the fill-ins include "stupid" and "frantic." This year, youngsters replace last year's "terrific" with "wizard."

## Obituaries

**(William) Hervey Allen** (December 8, 1889–December 28, 1949). His immensely popular novel, the 1,000-page *Anthony Adverse* (1933), launched a trend toward historical romances.

**Clifford Berryman** (April 2, 1869–December 11, 1949). The dean of political cartoonists, after 40 years at the *Washington Post*, Berryman will likely be remembered instead for originating the Teddy bear in his lampoons of President Theodore Roosevelt. He never made any money from his idea.

**Margaret Mitchell** (November 8, 1900–August 16, 1949). With millions of copies sold, a Pulitzer, and the movie, *Gone With the Wind* (1936) brought the American author fame and wealth. (Reportedly, she wrote the last chapter first, the first chapter next, and the rest in no particular order.) Mitchell, who burned another manuscript before *Gone With the Wind*, never wrote another book. Struck down by an automobile, on August 11, she dies from her injuries.

**Robert Ripley** (December 25, 1893–May 27, 1949). After his first *Believe It or Not* book won national recognition in 1929, various artists ghosted his daily panels to newspapers around the world.

# FASHION

## Haute Couture

Further refining the straight line of the New Look, designers ease the transition from fuller skirts by adding pleats, hip bows, or panels of matching or contrasting fabrics. (Pencil-slim skirts, with only the slit length or style varying, remain in vogue through the next decade.)

With fewer wealthy customers in war-ravaged Europe, Dior, Fath, and Schiaparelli travel to New York to sell their high-priced collections to manufacturers. This amazing innovation gives American women the latest in high fashion.

## News

**June.** "Gorgeous Gussy" Moran plays at Wimbledon in a fitted short dress. When matching lace-edged panties become visible during play, sports photographers lie on their stomachs to shoot Ted Tinling's daring design. Once the clamor dies down, the public readily accepts fashion in tennis.

**More news.** This year, stores offer numerous markdown sales and American women finally leave wartime clothing shortages behind.

## Colors and Materials

Textured fabrics for softer daytime styles— tweeds, thick fleeces, chinchilla cloth, wools with small floral or geometric patterns—all but eliminate flat materials. Velvet makes a strong comeback in evening wear.

As new fibers become more readily available, manufacturers increasingly use rayon suiting for menswear. Hand-washable dress materials, looking like crepe, worsted, and seersucker, need little ironing, and women love quick-drying nylon underwear.

## Clothes

One of the year's biggest hits, the overblouse falls below the belt or gathers at the waist with an elastic band or drawstring.

An extension of the straight look harks back to the 1920's chemise dress, with narrow shoulder straps or strapless, no waistline and few darts, trimmed with beads, embroidery, and/or fringe.

Above-the-waist interest centers on sleeves (dropped shoulders) and necklines (extreme oval décolletage with boned brassiere).

Teenage girls wear rolled-up jeans and flat, ballet-style slippers.

With the millions of postwar babies in the United States, women's magazines feature mother-daughter matching dresses and playsuits.

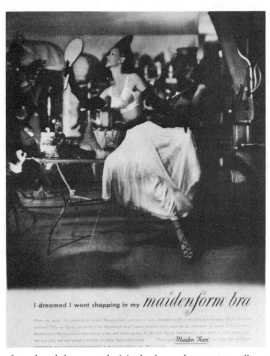

I dreamed I went shopping in my *maidenform bra*

*Introduced this year, the Maidenform ad campaign will run for twenty years with changing "I Dreamed I . . ." captions.*

## Accessories

Fur, pigskin, and alligator accessories meet the emphasis on texture.

To match shorter hairstyles, milliners create small dinner caps, in velvet and satin with dangling jewels or feathers, and a jockey cap with the brim worn over one ear.

Women like elasticized ankle boots, often in soft leather.

### Hair and Cosmetics

Hairstyles emphasize short, straight cuts.

For the first time, Brylcreem tells men, "A little dab'll do ya."

## POPULAR MUSIC

"Riders in the Sky"—Vaughn Monroe

"Some Enchanted Evening"/"Bali Ha'I"—Perry Como

"I Can Dream, Can't I?"—Patty Andrews & Gordon Jenkins & His Orchestra

"You're Breaking My Heart"—Vic Damone

"That Lucky Old Sun"—Frankie Laine

"Cruising Down the River"—Russ Morgan & His Orchestra & the Skylarks

"A Little Bird Told Me"—Evelyn Knight & the Stardusters

"Slippin' Around"—Margaret Whiting & Jimmy Wakely

"Mule Train"—Frankie Laine

"Baby, It's Cold Outside"—Esther Williams & Ricardo Montalban

"Dear Hearts and Gentle People"—Bing Crosby

"Diamonds Are a Girl's Best Friend"—Carol Channing

"Rudolph the Red-Nosed Reindeer"—Gene Autry

"Far Away Places"—Bing Crosby with the Ken Darby Choir

"Again"—Vic Damone

### News

**October.** In Cambridge, Massachusetts, record store owner William Schwann types a 26-page listing of new releases—the first record catalog.

**More news.** Capitol joins RCA Victor in releasing 45 rpm records, but most companies follow Columbia's lead and issue LPs. As phonograph manufacturers scramble to adapt, Columbia and Philco offer a special turntable and arm for existing machines ($29.95).

• Jazz musician George Shearing forms a quintet. In 1952, the group records what will become his best-known composition, "Lullaby of Birdland."

• In 1943, *Oklahoma!* was the first Broadway sound track to be sold in a complete boxed set. This year, the Rodgers and Hammerstein musical appears as an LP; sales will reach 2 million.

• Charlie Parker, in *Down Beat* magazine, describes bop as "trying to play clean and looking for the pretty notes." Small jazz bands continue to search for the offbeat as bop music surges in popularity.

• A radio station in Omaha pioneers the Top 40 format (*see* Television and Radio).

### New Recording Artists

Ames Brothers

Fats Domino

Tennessee Ernie Ford

Burl Ives

B. B. King

Dean Martin

### Obituaries

**Buddy Clark** (July 26, 1912–October 1, 1949). The big band singer, because he often sang on radio and records without credit, remained relatively unknown until the 1940s. He died in a plane crash.

**Huddie (Lead Belly) Ledbetter** (January 20, 1889–December 6, 1949). Ledbetter spent 12 years in prison for crimes of violence and frequently worked away from music. Still, with his unique voice, his skill with a 12-string guitar, and his compositions, such as "Cotton Fields" and "Goodnight Irene," the black performer played a major role in reviving the American folk song.

## MOVIES

*Adam's Rib* (d. George Cukor; bw)—Spencer Tracy, Katharine Hepburn, Judy Holliday, Tom Ewell, David Wayne

*Adventures of Don Juan* (d. Vincent Sherman;

color)—Errol Flynn, Viveca Lindfors, Robert Douglas

*The Adventures of Ichabod and Mr. Toad* (Disney; color; animated)—Voices: Bing Crosby (Ichabod narrator); Basil Rathbone (Mr. Toad narrator)

*All the King's Men* (d. Robert Rossen; bw)—Broderick Crawford, John Ireland, Mercedes McCambridge

*The Bicycle Thief* (Italian, d. Vittorio De Sica; bw)—Lamberto Maggiorani, Enzo Staiola

*Champion* (d. Mark Robson; bw)—Kirk Douglas, Marilyn Maxwell, Arthur Kennedy

*The Hasty Heart* (d. Vincent Sherman; bw)—Ronald Reagan, Patricia Neal, Richard Todd

*The Heiress* (d. William Wyler; bw)—Olivia de Havilland, Montgomery Clift, Ralph Richardson

*Kind Hearts and Coronets* (British, d. Robert Hamer; bw)—Alec Guinness, Dennis Price, Valerie Hobson, Joan Greenwood

*A Letter to Three Wives* (d. Joseph L. Mankiewicz; bw)—Jeanne Crain, Ann Sothern, Linda Darnell, Kirk Douglas, Paul Douglas

*On the Town* (d. Stanley Donen, Gene Kelly; color)—Gene Kelly, Frank Sinatra, Jules Munshin, Vera-Ellen, Betty Garrett, Ann Miller

*Pinky* (d. Elia Kazan; bw)—Jeanne Crain, Ethel Barrymore, Ethel Waters

*Sands of Iwo Jima* (d. Allan Dwan; bw)—John Wayne, John Agar

*The Set Up* (d. Robert Wise; bw)—Robert Ryan, Audrey Totter

*She Wore a Yellow Ribbon* (d. John Ford; color)—John Wayne, Joanne Dru, Ben Johnson, John Agar

*So Dear to My Heart* (Disney; d. Harold Schuster; color)—Burl Ives, Beulah Bondi, Bobby Driscoll

*Take Me Out to the Ball Game* (d. Busby Berkeley; color)—Frank Sinatra, Esther Williams, Gene Kelly, Betty Garrett

*The Third Man* (British, d. Carol Reed; bw)—Joseph Cotten, Orson Welles, Alida Valli, Trevor Howard

*Tight Little Island* (British title: *Whiskey Galore*) (d. Alexander Mackendrick; bw)—Basil Radford, Catherine Lacey

*Twelve O'Clock High* (d. Henry King; bw)—Gregory Peck, Hugh Marlowe, Gary Merrill, Dean Jagger

*White Heat* (d. Raoul Walsh; bw)—James Cagney, Virginia Mayo, Edmond O'Brien, Margaret Wycherly

### Academy Awards

**March 24.** When the financially strapped studios cut back their funding for this year's Oscars, the Academy must hold the ceremonies in its own small theater. The lack of seats creates an uproar in the industry. Actor Robert Montgomery hosts. For the first time, the Academy includes costume design in the award categories.

Best Picture—*Hamlet*
Best Actor—Laurence Olivier (*Hamlet*)
Best Actress—Jane Wyman (*Johnny Belinda*)
Best Director—John Huston (*The Treasure of the Sierra Madre*)
Best Supporting Actor—Walter Huston (*The Treasure of the Sierra Madre*)
Best Supporting Actress—Claire Trevor (*Key Largo*)
Best Song—"Buttons and Bows" from *The Paleface*
Special Award—*Monsieur Vincent* (French)

Britain dominates the awards, as *Hamlet* (the first British-made film to win best picture) and *The Red Shoes* together collect six Oscars.

Walter Huston and John Huston become the first father and son to win Oscars. Upon accepting his, Walter Huston comments, "Many, many years ago, I raised a son and I said to him, 'If you ever become a writer or director, please find a good part for your old man.'"

### News

**March.** With box-office receipts down, studios fire lower-level personnel, eliminate long-term contracts for their stars, and demand greater production efficiency to meet higher postwar set-construction costs. Yet none of the solutions addresses the problem uncovered by last month's *Fortune* entertainment survey: 38 percent of respondents believe Hollywood is producing fewer good movies than two or three years ago.

**May 27.** Glamor queen Rita Hayworth marries Aly Khan, the oldest son of the Aga Khan, spiritual leader of some 15 million Ismaili Moslems. Their courtship and divorces have kept the tabloids busy. The actress gives birth before the end of the year. Their daughter will become the center of a custody battle after the famous couple separate in 1951.

**June 22.** Fire destroys the 30-year-old western saloon lot at Universal-International. With a floor built to support over two dozen men on horseback, the saloon appeared in almost 1,000 Westerns with such famous cowboys as Tom Mix, Hoot Gibson, John Wayne, James Stewart, and Gary Cooper.

**September 10.** Some 750 theater owners (65 percent of the nation's seating capacity) open a four-day convention in Los Angeles. Although concession profits continue to grow, most owners glumly predict admission prices will climb no higher than the current national average of 40.2 cents.

**November.** The world's first newsreel theater in 1929, the Embassy in New York switches from an all-news-and-shorts program to feature films. TV coverage has drawn away the audience.

**December 19.** New York Police Sergeant P. K. Leitner receives a state employee award for suggesting that drive-in theaters face their screens away from highways to cut down on traffic accidents.

**December 21.** Deanna Durbin marries director Charles Henri David and retires to France. Signed by Universal Pictures in 1936, the 14-year-old Canadian-born singer captured the hearts of America with her fresh appeal and beautiful soprano voice. Reportedly, her first feature film, *Three Smart Girls* (1936), saved Universal from bankruptcy.

Over the years, the biggest fan club in the world happily watched Deanna mature into romantic leads and become the Armed Forces sweetheart. And, while her recent films have proved less successful, Durbin is still at the peak of her career.

**More news.** Roland Winters stars in *Sky Dragon*, the last of 43 Charlie Chan films. From 1931 to 1941 at 20th Century-Fox and 1944 to 1949 at Monogram, Winters and two other actors played the Oriental detective with the countless wise sayings.

• United Productions of America (UPA) introduces Mr. Magoo in the cartoon "Ragtime Bear." Actor Jim Backus provides the voice for the nearsighted little man.

• Following the success of last year's *Easter Parade*, MGM planned a second film for Fred Astaire and Judy Garland. But, as Garland continues to struggle with personal problems, the studio hires Ginger Rogers to star in *The Barkleys of Broadway*. Astaire and Rogers last danced together in the RKO musical *The Story of Vernon and Irene Castle* (1939).

• Poor Gerald McBoing Boing, unable to speak, he utters the strangest sounds. Robert Cannon created the little boy from a story by Dr. Seuss. The cartoons will remain popular through the 1950s.

| *Top Box Office Stars* | *Newcomers* |
|---|---|
| Bob Hope | Montgomery Clift |
| Bing Crosby | Kirk Douglas |
| Bud Abbott & | Betty Garrett |
| Lou Costello | Paul Douglas |
| John Wayne | Howard Duff |
| Gary Cooper | Pedro Armendariz |
| Cary Grant | Dean Stockwell |
| Betty Grable | Wanda Hendrix |
| Esther Williams | Wendell Corey |
| Humphrey Bogart | Barbara Bel Geddes |
| Clark Gable | |

### Top Money-Maker of the Year

*Jolson Sings Again* (1949) (d. Henry Levin; color)—Larry Parks, Barbara Hale

### Quote of the Year

"Made it, Ma. Top of the world!"

James Cagney, a gangster with a mother fixation, reaches the top of an oil tank in the climactic *White Heat* shootout. (Screenplay by Ivan Goff and Ben Roberts; based on a story by Virginia Kellogg.)

## Obituaries

**Wallace Beery** (April 1, 1886–April 15, 1949). A major MGM star for nearly 20 years, the veteran actor made some 250 pictures and won the 1931–1932 best actor Oscar for *The Champ*. In later years, he usually played lovable rogues.

**Frank Morgan** (June 1, 1890–September 18, 1949). The stage and screen actor appeared in scores of movies, but most film goers remember him as the Great Oz in *The Wizard of Oz* (1939).

**Bill "Bojangles" Robinson** (May 25, 1878–November 25, 1949). Although he never took a lesson, the "King of Tap Dancers" created ingenious steps like the stair tap routine in pictures like *The Little Colonel* (1935), with Shirley Temple. Tributes pour in and an estimated 8 million line New York streets to pay their last respects, but Mr. Bojangles, always a soft touch, died in relative poverty.

**Sam Wood** (July 10, 1884–September 22, 1949). The director of 70 films, including *A Night at the Opera* (1935) and *Goodbye, Mr. Chips* (1939), considered *For Whom the Bell Tolls* (1943) his best work.

## TELEVISION AND RADIO

### New Prime-Time TV Programs

"Arthur Godfrey and His Friends" (January 12, 1949–April 28, 1959; Musical Variety)—Host: Arthur Godfrey

"The Big Story" (September 16, 1949–June 28, 1957; Drama Anthology)

"Captain Video and His Video Rangers" (June 27, 1949–April 1, 1955; Children's) Richard Coogan, Al Hodge, Don Hastings, Hal Conklin

"Fireside Theatre" (April 5, 1949–May 1958; Drama Anthology)

"Ford Theatre" (October 7, 1949–July 10, 1957; Drama Anthology)

"The Fred Waring Show" (April 17, 1949–May 30, 1954; Musical Variety)—Fred Waring and His Pennsylvanians

"The Goldbergs" (January 10, 1949–October 19, 1954; Situation Comedy)—Gertrude Berg

"Hopalong Cassidy" (June 24, 1949–December 23, 1951; Western)—William Boyd, Edgar Buchanan

"The Lone Ranger" (September 15, 1949–September 12, 1957; Western)—Clayton Moore (1949–1952; 1954–1957), John Hart (1952–1954), Jay Silverheels. *Note:* After 1957, the program will appear during the day or around dinnertime.

"Mama" (July 1, 1949–July 27, 1956; Comedy/Drama)—Peggy Wood, Judson Laire

"Man Against Crime" (October 7, 1949–August 19, 1956; Detective)—Ralph Bellamy (1949–1954), Frank Lovejoy (1956)

"Mr. I Magination" (May 29, 1949–April 13, 1952; Children's)—Paul Tripp

"Paul Whiteman's TV Teen Club" (April 2, 1949–March 28, 1954; Talent)

"Quiz Kids" (March 1, 1949–November 1953; January 1956–September 1956; Quiz/Panel)

"Stop the Music" (May 1949–April 1952; September 1954–June 1956; Quiz/Audience Participation)—Emcee: Bert Parks

"This Is Show Business" (July 15, 1949–September 11, 1956; Variety)—Emcee: Clifton Fadiman

"Twenty Questions" (November 26, 1949–May 3, 1955; Quiz/Panel)

"The Voice of Firestone" (September 1949–June 1959; September 1962–June 1963; Music)

### Emmy Awards 1948 (January 25, 1949)

The National Academy of Television Arts and Sciences presents the first Emmys for outstanding programs, performers, and productions in television broadcasting.

Most Popular Television Program—"Pantomime Quiz Time"

Most Outstanding Television Personality—Shirley Dinsdale and her puppet Judy Splinters

### News

**This year.** The FCC freeze instituted in 1948 continues to hold television at the verge of major expansion. During the delay, the networks have refined their broadcasting techniques and formats while one-station cities have found themselves in the enviable position of a four-network choice of programs.

**January 11.** The Midwest coaxial cable connects with the East Coast network and, for the first time, live network programming reaches one-fourth of the nation's population.

**January 20.** An audience of 10 million for the first televised presidential inauguration exceeds the number of Americans in attendance at all other inaugurations since George Washington.

**January 31.** With the continuing popularity of radio soaps, NBC follows the same 15-minute format with the first episode of "These Are My Children." (The DuMont Network premiered television's first soap opera on October 2, 1946: "Faraway Hill.") The magazine *Television World*, in its review, says, "There is no place on television for this type of program; a blank screen is preferable."

**March 24.** Described by some as "cheesecake with violence," Roller Derby calls on women to use any and every means to skate past their rivals, including hair-pulling and wrestling. The ABC version debuts tonight and, as the sport takes on the proportions of a fad, the program occupies much of the Saturday evening telecast by May.

**April 9.** Milton Berle hosts the first telethon. The 14-hour program raises $1.1 million for cancer research.

**May 5.** Time-Life produces television's first documentary series, "Crusade in Europe" (ABC).

**June 2.** The FCC ends the wartime prohibition against radio editorializing with the admonition to present all sides of controversial issues.

**June 26.** Fred Allen, master of the ad-lib, broadcasts his last radio show. He and Jack Benny carried a mock feud through 13 years, the longest-running gag in the history of comedy.

**June 27.** One of the most popular kids' programs, "Captain Video" uses his scientific genius to protect the universe against evil villains. But success proves a mixed blessing for star Al Hodge. Typecast as a 6'2" space hero, he will find little work after the show ends in 1955.

**August 19.** The FCC bans radio and television prize-shows, but a federal district court restrains the commission. Still the question of legality pushes many of the 38 programs off the air. Networks turn to celebrity panel shows, and by 1954, when the Supreme Court overturns the ruling, the giveaway craze will have passed—for the moment.

**September.** A Los Angeles hit, the 15-minute "Time for Beany" is the first children's program syndicated to other stations via kinescope. Bob Clampett creates all the wonderful puppets—innocent, wide-eyed Beany, who meets his boyhood friend Cece the Sea Serpent in a stormy sea, uncle Captain Horatio K. Huffenpuff, and the dastardly Dishonest John (D.J. for short) with the "Nya ha ha!" laugh every fan imitates. Kids clamor for Beany caps with a propeller on top and other character merchandise. The show will win three Emmys before the last episode airs in mid-1955.

**September 15.** Many radio programs never make the transition to television because their visual images fail to live up to the listener's imagination. But, with General Mills bankrolling $1 million for 52 filmed episodes, "The Lone Ranger" is an unqualified success.

An upright, patriotic hero, he never kills a bad guy. And Clayton Moore, the star through most of the program's run, refuses to remove his mask rather than risk disillusioning his young fans.

Next season, three NBC stations, capitalizing on the Western ratings bonanza, finance the production of "The Cisco Kid."

**Fall.** The Park Sheraton is the first U.S. hotel to place a TV in every room at no extra charge.

**November.** DuMont expands into the daytime hours with fashion and cooking shows. Jack Gould, of the *New York Times*, wryly comments, "The idea of a nation of housewives sitting mute before the video machine when they should be tidying up the premises or preparing the formula is not something to be grasped hurriedly. Obviously it is a matter fraught with peril of the darkest sort." But the programming innovation fails to pan out and daytime television will fight a bad reputation for years to come.

**More news.** TV sales skyrocket during the year,

with an estimated 250,000 sets installed every month. With advertising opportunities opening up, sponsors costs double from $1,000 to $2,000 for an evening. Still, many manufacturers reap enormous benefits without the expense of commercials. Puppets and cowboy outfits, just like those seen on the program, rank high in Christmas toy sales.

• At WOR, Mutual's key New York station, the program vice-president continues his innovative campaign to replace all standing microphones and their tangle of cords with overhead mikes.

• KOWH in Omaha pioneers the disc jockey radio format—a limited number of records played over and over, limited DJ patter, an hourly news break, and jingles for identification.

### Memorable Radio Programs End

"Captain Midnight" (September 30, 1940)
"The Eddie Cantor Show" (September 13, 1931)
"Kay Kyser's Kollege of Musical Knowledge" (1938)
"The Kraft Music Hall" (June 26, 1933)

# SPORTS

## Winners

### Baseball

World Series—New York Yankees (AL), 4 games; Brooklyn Dodgers (NL), 1 game
Player of the Year—Ted Williams (Boston Red Sox, AL); Jackie Robinson (Brooklyn Dodgers, NL)
Rookie of the Year—Roy Sievers (St. Louis Browns, AL); Don Newcombe (Brooklyn Dodgers; NL)

### Football

NFL Championship—Philadelphia Eagles 14, Los Angeles Rams 0
College Bowls (January 1, 1949)—
Rose Bowl, Northwestern 20, California 14
Cotton Bowl, Southern Methodist 21, Oregon 13

Orange Bowl, Texas 41, Georgia 28
Sugar Bowl, Oklahoma 14, North Carolina 6
Heisman Trophy—Leon Hart (Notre Dame, E)
Grey Cup—Montreal Alouettes 28, Calgary Stampeders 15

### Basketball

NCAA Championship—Kentucky 46, Oklahoma A&M 36

### Tennis

U.S. National—Men, Pancho Gonzalez (vs. Ted Schroeder); Women, Margaret du Pont (vs. Doris Hart)
Wimbledon—Men, Ted Schroeder (vs. Jaroslav Drobny); Women, Louise Brough (vs. Margaret du Pont)

### Golf

Masters—Sam Snead
U.S. Open—Cary Middlecoff
British Open—Bobby Locke

### Hockey

Stanley Cup—Toronto Maple Leafs, 4 games; Detroit Red Wings, 0 games

### Ice Skating

World Championship—Men, Dick Button (U.S.); Women, Aja Vrzanova (Czechoslovakia)
U.S. National—Men, Dick Button; Women, Yvonne Sherman
Canadian National—Men, Roger Wickson; Women, Suzanne Morrow

### Kentucky Derby

Ponder—Steve Brooks, jockey

### Athlete of the Year

Male—Leon Hart (Football)
Female—Marlene Bauer (Golf)

## News

**February 7.** Last year, Joe DiMaggio received an enormous raise, from $43,750 to $70,000. (When veterans returned from war, U.S. law required them to receive the same pay as before their service.) Today, the Yankees raise his salary to $90,000—the highest in baseball history. (Only the Babe received more because he collected 10 percent of the gate receipts at exhibition games.)

**March 1.** Joe Louis retires from the ring after nearly 12 years as heavyweight champion of the world. In his 25 title bouts, only three fighters went the distance with the Brown Bomber—Tommy Farr, Arturo Godoy, and Jersey Joe Walcott.

On June 22, black boxer Ezzard Charles outpoints Walcott to take over the vacated title under the National Boxing Association. Louis will come out of retirement next year, but Charles will win on points to gain recognition from New York State.

**April 20.** At Bay Meadows, a 17-year-old jockey brings home his very first winner and collects a $10 fee. Willie Shoemaker is destined to become racing's most winning jockey.

**Summer.** The 17 teams of the BAA and NBL merge to form the National Basketball Association (NBA). The number of franchises will drop to 11 next season, then consolidate at 10 in early 1951.

**September 13.** Largely to provide competition for Mildred (Babe) Didrikson Zaharias, the Ladies Professional Golf Association (LPGA) is formed in New York. Wilson golf equipment, her sponsor, agrees to pay the bills.

**December 9.** The 3-year-old All-American Conference merges with the NFL. With a 13-club circuit, the league eliminates the East and West divisions and forms National and American conferences.

**December 12.** NL baseball owners agree to turn on their stadium lights when afternoon games run into darkness and agree to continue play past the 12:50 A.M. curfew to break a tie. AL owners, on the other hand, will turn on the lights only during important series at the end of the season.

**More news.** In a major rule change, the NHL eliminates the assessment of a penalty shot when a goalie commits an infraction. Instead, as with penalized forwards and defensemen, the team will play short-handed. Also this season, the league begins painting ice surfaces white.

## Records

**February 10.** Philadelphia Warrior Joe Fulks sets an NBA record with a remarkable 63 points against the Indianapolis Jets. With no time limit on ball possession, many games finish with fewer points.

**April 16.** The Toronto Maple Leafs defeat the Detroit Red Wings to collect a record third consecutive Stanley Cup.

## What They Said

On June 16 in the first round of his title defense, Marcel Cerdan rips a muscle in his left shoulder. Gamely hanging on, the Frenchman tells his manager, "If you stop the fight I will kill myself." But with Cerdan unable to lift his arm, the manager throws in the towel at the end of the 9th. American Jake LaMotta becomes the new middleweight champion of the world.

## Obituaries

**Marcel Cerdan** (July 22, 1916–October 28, 1949). Returning to the United States for a rematch against Jake LaMotta, Cerdan dies in a plane crash. In 100 matches, the French boxer lost two and was disqualified in two others.

**Tom Longboat** (July 4, 1887–January 9, 1949). A champion long-distance runner from the Six Nations Reserve in Ontario, Longboat was one of the most celebrated athletes in the pre-W.W.I era.

**Bobby Walthour** (January 1, 1878–September 1, 1949). This American cyclist held virtually every record during his racing career, and twice won world championships while holding the U.S. title. He retired in 1929 after fracturing his collarbone for the 29th time.

# *1950*

At the half-century, the world is polarized into Communist and non-Communist camps. The White House plans to build a bigger and better bomb, offers Paris aid in Indochina, and, at midyear, takes a stand against Communism in Korea. Senator Joseph McCarthy captains the search for Reds under government beds.

Domestic news includes the first vote on the Equal Rights Amendment (ERA), an attempt on the president's life, a Supreme Court decision permitting witnesses' use of the Fifth Amendment, and a new FBI list of the "Ten Most Wanted Criminals."

Surgeons perform the first kidney transplant and Haloid brings out the first photocopying machine. George Bernard Shaw, Al Jolson, and Edgar Rice Burroughs pass away. The first NBA Championship goes to the Minneapolis Lakers and Althea Gibson becomes the first black woman to win at Wimbledon. Top songs include "Frosty the Snowman" and "Peter Cottontail," and the year produces several movie classics: All About Eve, Harvey, Cinderella, Rio Grande, and Sunset Boulevard. But, with the prevailing political climate, Hollywood institutes a devastating blacklist.

## NEWS

**January 14.** The United States makes the final diplomatic break with the People's Republic of China, recalling all State Department personnel.

**January 17.** Seven men break into the Boston Brink's Express Company shortly after 7:00 P.M., tie up the employees, and escape with $1.2 million in cash and $1.5 million in money orders. Over the next six years, the FBI spends over $129 million trying to catch the robbers. Then, just days before the statute of limitations expires, a gang member confesses. Two of the 10 implicated die before coming to trial while the other 8 receive life sentences.

The informer, Specs O'Keefe, is released in 1960; only $50,000 of the take is recovered.

**January 21.** Alger Hiss is convicted of perjury and sentenced to five years in prison. In 1948, self-confessed Communist Whittaker Chambers told HUAC that Hiss, while working for the State Department in the 1930s, held Communist party membership and passed him secret papers for the Soviets.

Hiss, former advisor to President Roosevelt and current president of the Carnegie Endowment for International Peace, sued for slander. But Chambers produced incriminating documents, including some reputedly typed on Hiss's own typewriter. With the statute of limitations expired on 1930s espionage, Hiss was indicted for perjury.

Although some question the fairness of the trial and even Hiss's guilt, the sensational proceedings fuel Americans' growing fears of Communism. The man most responsible for pursuing Chambers' charges and bringing Hiss to trial was Richard Nixon.

**January 25.** In the first vote since the proposal was put forward in 1923, the Senate passes the ERA. The senators accepted the proposal only after an amendment guaranteed the retention of those special protections already accorded women by law.

---

*Statistics:* The *Wall Street Journal* reports the number of women working or looking for jobs has increased over the past 10 years, by an estimated 24 percent. In a count of working wives, the number has jumped 90 percent.

---

**January 29.** France grants independence to Vietnam, Laos, and Cambodia within the French Union. Bao Dai, former emperor of Annam, heads the independent government of Vietnam in Saigon.

During W.W.II, Japan occupied the French Indochinese states in Southeast Asia. An independence movement sprang up, and Ho Chi Minh led the Vietnam Doc Lap Dong Minh, or Vietnam Independence League (Vietminh for short), in proclaiming a Vietnamese republic. Postwar negotiations with the French failed and a colonial war broke out in 1946.

Moscow and Peking, rejecting continued French authority in Indochina, recognize Ho Chi Minh's regime as Vietnam's legal government. Just a week later, President Truman reverses America's traditional support for nationalist movements to recognize the "independent" states. Analysts view the U.S. decision as a reaction to last year's Communist victory in China.

**January 31.** Truman, pushed by the Berlin blockade, worldwide Communist gains, and the recent Soviet nuclear test, orders the AEC to develop the hydrogen bomb—a weapon expected to be 100

to 1,000 times more powerful than the bomb dropped on Hiroshima. The American people, anxious to maintain nuclear superiority, fully support the president's decision.

**February 9.** First-term Senator Joseph McCarthy, disliked by his colleagues and facing certain defeat in the 1952 election, grasps at an opportunity for public attention. Speaking before the Women's Republican Club in Wheeling, West Virginia, McCarthy holds up what he claims is a list of 205 known Communists currently working in the State Department. (His evidence is a three-year-old letter written by former Secretary of State James Byrnes stating that tenure may be denied to unnamed state employees on various grounds, including drunkenness.)

Two days later, McCarthy's 205 "security risks" become 57 "card-carrying Communists" then, in the Senate on the 20th, 81 "cases" of questionable loyalty. Whatever the numbers, the senator refuses to produce names; he has found his cause. The Senate unanimously approves a Foreign Relations Committee investigation of his charges.

**February 14.** The USSR and Communist China sign a 30-year treaty of aid, friendship, and mutual defense. The Sino-Soviet Agreement creates a new international balance of power.

**March 12.** A charter plane, returning to Wales from a rugby match in Belfast, jackknifes at the Cardiff airport and flips over, killing 80 in the world's worst aviation disaster to date. The three surviving passengers include two brothers-in-law who sat in different sections of the aircraft.

**May 4.** The Soviet Union announces that all 1,939,163 German POWs have now been released. In response West Germany charges that hundreds of thousands remain in captivity. And the United States, just days later, demands that Moscow account for 300,000 missing Japanese POWs.

In December, over Soviet bloc opposition, the U.N. General Assembly calls for an investigation.

**May 8.** Following reports of a pact between China and North Vietnam, the United States accedes to French requests for military aid in the Far East. The White House decision, whether taken to appease Paris over the resurgence of Germany or to halt Communism in Asia, sets the course for American policy in Indochina.

In July, with the conflict in Korea further threatening Vietnam's stability, the Truman administration sends a Military Assistance and Advisory Group (MAAG) to Saigon.

**May 9.** The Canadian House of Commons defeats a motion to outlaw the Communist party (147–32). Less than a week later, Venezuela becomes the 15th country to ban Communism in national politics.

**May 26.** A five-man Senate committee, chaired by Estes Kefauver, launches a 15-month investigation into organized crime. As the panel moves across the country, a fascinated American public watches some 600 witnesses questioned on television. ("Taking the Fifth" becomes part of everyday language.) When the hearings end, an exposed Mafia faces the added scrutiny of the FBI for Hoover finally acknowledges the existence of the criminal organization.

**June 5.** In two unanimous rulings, the Supreme Court invalidates segregation practices in two southern universities and in southern railway dining cars. In November, the Interstate Commerce Commission (ICC) will order all southern railroads to abolish separate dining car facilities in interstate travel. But the justices, by referring to the equal protection clause of the 14th Amendment in their decision, fail to alter the 1896 "separate-but-equal" doctrine laid down in *Plessy v. Ferguson*—the basis for most segregation in the South.

**June 9.** The Population Registration Act—apartheid's first key enabling law—completes a stormy passage through the South African House and Senate. Each citizen must be racially classified—white, black, or colored (mixed race). Those no longer officially "white" face the loss of their jobs, forced separation from their children, and arrest for their marriage to a white person.

A second major apartheid law, the Group Areas Act, passes in July despite rioting. It sets up a uniform system for the racial separation of residential and occupational areas.

And, to prevent further opposition, the government pushes through the Suppression of Communism Act, which provides such a broad definition that virtually any organization, publication, or individual can be labeled subversive.

**June 25.** The North Korean People's Army invades South Korea at dawn. President Truman, despite the exclusion of Korea from the U.S. perimeter of defense, refers the issue to the United Nations.

When the Communists ignore the call for withdrawal, the Security Council brands North Korea the aggressor and, on the 27th, imposes military sanctions for the first time. The historic resolution passes only because the Soviets, boycotting the United Nations over the continued presence of Nationalist China, are not present to cast their veto.

On the 29th, President Truman tells the American people that the United States is supporting a police action, not fighting a war. The next day, he authorizes the transfer of ground troops from Japan, gives the air force permission to bomb north of the 38th parallel, and orders the Seventh Fleet to move between Formosa and Communist China. The first American soldiers land in South Korea on July 1.

Although Korea marks the first mobilization of the United Nations, to the outside world, the conflict looks like an American war. The command is unified under the United States, with General Douglas MacArthur commander in chief, and Americans account for 85 percent of foreign troops. (South Korean soldiers make up 60 percent of the force.)

**July 18.** Following its investigation, a Senate subcommittee reports that Senator Joseph McCarthy, in "the most nefarious campaign of half-truths and untruth in the history of the Republic," has failed to prove that any State Department employee is a Communist.

Nonetheless, conservatives support McCarthy, and Americans, reeling under the shock of spy trials and the war in Korea, accept his oversimplified explanations. The senator continues to move from one sensational accusation to another, never stopping long enough to answer denials.

**July 22.** The Census Bureau reports that since 1940 the population of the United States has risen nearly 19 million, to 150,520,198 (later revised to

154,233,000) and has shifted westward. Oregon, Washington, and California show a net gain of over 50 percent, while 11 southeastern states gained just 7.7 percent.

**August 15.** The second severest earthquake in history, measuring 8.6 on the Richter scale, leaves 5 million homeless, destroys crops, and damages agricultural land in a remote area on the Indian-Tibetan border. But because of the sparse population, the death toll remains relatively low, at 600–1,500.

**August 25.** As a looming rail strike threatens defense production, Truman seizes control of the railroads under a 1916 emergency war measure. (This invocation marks the president's third rail seizure since 1946 and the fifth by the White House since 1918.) The union calls off the strike as the Army takes over supervision.

**September 15.** Post-W.W.II demobilization and factory closures left the United States ill-prepared for the North Korean invasion. To prevent a total rout of the South Korean Army, General Mac-Arthur was forced to dispatch poorly trained and

*A U.S. infantryman, grief-stricken over the loss of his buddy in Korea, is comforted while a medical corpsman fills out casualty tags.*

underequipped U.S. occupation troops from Japan. Predictably, by the end of August, the outnumbered U.N. force had fallen back to Pusan, with 6,000 American and 70,000 South Korean casualties.

Today, after 48 hours of air strikes and offshore shelling, Americans and South Koreans land behind enemy lines at Inchon on the west coast. Supported by strikes at other ports, the U.N. force takes the offensive and the Eighth Army charges out of Pusan. Barreling northward, the Allies retake Seoul by the 25th.

On October 1, as the U.N. force approaches the 38th parallel, MacArthur calls for North Korea's unconditional surrender. The Communists refuse. The Truman administration abandons its policy of containment, and the general orders his troops to cross the border.

**September 19.** Communist aggression in Europe and the Far East has accelerated the rehabilitation of West Germany. In June, the fledgling nation joined the Council of Europe as a free and equal partner. Today, NATO, at a meeting in New York, agrees to end the "state of war" with Bonn and warns Moscow that an attack on West Germany would be viewed as an "attack upon themselves."

**September 23.** Concern over recent spy trials— Klaus Fuchs in Britain and Hiss and Judith Coplon in the United States—has generated the Internal Security, or McCarran, Act. The legislation requires the registration of Communist and Communist-front groups, bars Communists from federal and defense jobs, denies them passports, and provides for internment camps in a national emergency. Truman denounced the measure as "a mockery of the Bill of Rights," but Congress overrides his veto.

**October 7.** Communist China invades Tibet. More than 250 years ago, a prophesy foretold four disasters in Tibet heralded by a comet: A mountain would move, the Tsangpo River would be thrown from its course, the country would be "overrun by terror," and the line of Dalai Lamas would come to an end.

In 1948, a comet appeared. Last year, an earthquake moved a mountain and turned aside the Tsangpo. Today, the Communist Chinese cross the border. To forestall the last prophesy, the Tibetans hurriedly install their underage Dalai as head of state.

The isolated nation looks to the United Nations for help, but the international body, fearful that further intervention in the Far East would trigger a world war, rejects the appeal.

Next May, Peking forces Tibet to formally accept Communist control. Thousands of Chinese settlers surge in, and a campaign of cultural genocide levels temples and libraries and destroys religious works of art and some 6,000 monasteries. By 1975, an estimated 1 million Tibetans will die under Chinese occupation.

**October 15.** Truman meets with MacArthur on Wake Island to discuss military progress in Korea. The general assures the president that China will not enter the war and he promises victory by Thanksgiving. Truman accepts his assessment and approves an advance to within a few miles of the Chinese border.

The Americans and South Koreans reach their goal by the end of the month, but MacArthur has underestimated Peking. When he orders an "end-the-war" effort on November 24, Chinese troops—already in place—launch a massive counteroffensive. U.N. soldiers fight desperately, but hundreds of thousands of Chinese "volunteers" surge forward, ignoring their losses. The Allies fall back as the Communists retake all the hard-won U.N. territory and recapture Seoul.

On the 30th, the United Nations demands that China withdraw, but the Soviets veto the ultimatum. Meanwhile, Truman confirms the U.S. commitment to South Korea and threatens to use atomic weapons, if necessary, to prevent Chinese forces from conquering the beleaguered nation.

**November 1.** Two Puerto Rican nationalists try to shoot their way into Blair House, the president's temporary residence during White House renovations. The more experienced gunman, Griselio Torresola, fatally wounds Private Leslie Coffelt before agents gun him down. The second would-be assassin, Oscar Collazo, fires nine shots, but manages to shoot just one guard in the leg. Neither penetrates the outer ring of security.

Since Truman strongly supports Puerto Rican rights to self-determination, a suggested connection with the Nationalist uprising in Puerto Rico, on October 30, appears doubtful. In fact, investigation reveals the gunmen hatched their plot only the week before.

Collazo receives the death penalty, but the president commutes his sentence to life.

**November 7.** The Democrats retain control of Congress in mid-term elections, but the Republicans win enough seats to block Truman's Fair Deal legislative program.

During the campaign, Republicans accused the administration of being "soft on Communism." Richard Nixon, for one, relied on this tactic to defeat Democratic Representative Helen Gahagn Douglas in California. He distributed 500,000 pink leaflets falsely tying her voting record to that of "a notorious Communist-line congressman." In response, the small Southern California newspaper *The Independent Review* printed the caption "Tricky Dick" above Nixon's picture; the epithet sticks.

*Statistics:* Currently, 52 of 74 countries grant women full political equality. In 12 of the other 22 nations, including Switzerland, women are denied the right to hold public office.

**November 22.** Locked brakes force the 6:09 train to halt just two miles outside Penn Station, in New York City. The 6:13, with no warning of trouble ahead, rams into the last car of the 6:09, killing 78 people and injuring over 200.

In a disastrous year for U.S. railways, 152 passengers are killed and another 888 injured in the first nine months. Over the same period in 1949, only 1 passenger died.

**November 23.** The United States, Britain, and Canada agree to release secret data on the design, construction, and operation of "low-power" nuclear reactors. The information will not assist rival nations with military applications of atomic energy, but will enable universities and private industry to build reactors for research purposes.

**November 25–28.** Blanketing the northeastern quarter of the United States, snowstorms hit Connecticut, Massachusetts, and Vermont the hardest. At least 295 people die and damages reach $400 million.

**November 28.** Britain, Canada, Australia, India, New Zealand, Ceylon, and Pakistan set up the Colombo Plan to raise the living standards of 570 million South and Southeast Asians and to counteract the appeal of Communism (effective June 30, 1951). The six-year program will be extended and other countries will join, including non-Commonwealth nations such as the United States and Japan.

**December 11.** With reference to the Fifth Amendment, the Supreme Court holds (8–0) that witnesses may refuse to testify about Communist activities if they plead the answers would incriminate them. (Under the 1940 Alien Registration, or Smith Act, passed in the days leading up to American entry into W.W.II, a person faces prosecution for advocating or teaching the necessity of overthrowing the U.S. government or for belonging to or knowing the purpose of such an organization.) Next year, the court will rule that witnesses claiming the Fifth need not explain how their testimony would incriminate them.

**December 12.** To reduce costs and strengthen nuclear security, the AEC moves the U.S. nuclear test program from the Pacific to the sparsely populated desert area of Nevada. President Truman has approved a series of low-yield tests.

The commission has recommended underground detonations rather than risk fallout blowing southeast over Utah. But the Defense Department wants above-ground testing in order to give American forces practical field experience. Today, the AEC agrees.

> *Statistics:* A *New York Herald Tribune* article, on December 31, estimates that the USSR has stockpiled 24 nuclear weapons.

**December 16.** In October, the National Production Authority ordered manufacturers to give priority to defense orders. Now, as the United States faces possible war with China, President Truman proclaims a state of emergency and places the country on a wartime footing. He creates an Office of Defense Mobilization, to coordinate various government activities, while the Economic Stabilization Agency moves to impose new wage and price controls.

> *Statistics:* On December 7, the ninth anniversary of Pearl Harbor, a Gallup poll reports that 55 percent of Americans believe that W.W.III has already begun.

## *Obituaries*

**Evangeline Booth** (December 25, 1865–July 17, 1950). The daughter of William Booth, the founder of the Salvation Army, made the Army an American institution during her 30 years as commander. Booth then served as general of the international movement from 1934 to 1939.

**Hattie Wyatt Caraway** (February 1, 1878–December 21, 1950). When Senator Thaddeus Caraway died in 1931, Arkansas Democrats appointed his widow to hold the office until the next election. She chose to contest the seat and won, becoming the first woman elected to the U.S. Senate. Caraway lost to J. William Fulbright in 1944.

**Gustav V** (June 16, 1858–October 29, 1950). The longest reigning monarch in Swedish history (1907–1950) led his country in maintaining neutrality during both world wars. His eldest son, Gustav VI Adolf, succeeds him at the age of 66.

**William Lyon Mackenzie King** (December 17, 1874–July 22, 1950). Elected leader of the Canadian Liberal party in 1919, upon the death of Wilfrid Laurier, King served as prime minister for most of the 1920s and again from 1935 to 1948. A skillful politician, he established Canada's independence from Britain during W.W.II and held the country together when French-Canadians resisted conscription. Yet, unknown to the voters, King made decisions on the basis of secret communications with his dead mother, dead politicians, and even his dead dogs.

Jan Christian Smuts (May 24, 1870–September 11, 1950). The soldier and politician, who served as prime minister of South Africa from 1919 to 1924 and from 1939 to 1948, gained worldwide stature through his prominent role in founding the League of Nations and the United Nations.

Henry Lewis Stimson (September 21, 1867–October 20, 1950). As secretary of war during W.W. II, Stimson recommended that the United States drop atomic bombs on Japan. In a written explanation of his decision in 1947, he argued that an invasion would have taken 300,000 American lives and the United States had no extra bombs to use for threatening demonstrations.

# BEGINNINGS AND ENDINGS

## News

March 14. The FBI issues its first list of the "Ten Most Wanted Criminals" in the United States. Their photographs appear in newspapers, magazines, and post offices across the country. Over the next two decades, "Most Wanted" publicity will lead to about 15 arrests annually. The numbers will drop drastically in the 1970s when fugitive radicals disappear into an organized underground.

March 16. A butter shortage forces Congress to repeal the 64-year tax on oleomargarine. Still, under pressure from dairies, legislators require distinct packaging and triangular restaurant servings to avoid confusion with butter. State taxes remain in effect.

April 18. To curtail a mounting deficit, the U.S. postmaster general cuts mail delivery to once a day.

May 3. The Communist Chinese government outlaws polygamy and the sale of women.

May 3. The Association of American Physicians admits Dr. Helen B. Tausig, the group's first female member.

May 5. King Phumiphol (or Bhumibol) Adulyadej, the 23-year-old grandson of King Chulalongkorn of King and I fame, is crowned in Thailand as Rama IX.

May 29. The Royal Canadian Mounted Police (RCMP) ship St. Roch journeys from the west coast through the Panama Canal to Halifax to complete the first circumnavigation of North America. During World War II, to assert Canadian sovereignty and to secure the Arctic, the same ship traversed the Northwest Passage both ways (1940–1942 and 1944).

July 26. The Senate approves a one-house legislature for Guam and grants the 28,000 islanders American citizenship. The Pacific island was ceded to the United States at the end of the Spanish-American War in 1898.

August 12. The AEC and the U.S. Defense Department issue a 438-page handbook on The Effects of Atomic Weapons. This first nonclassified publication on nuclear weaponry tells worried Americans, "In the considered opinion of many who have made observations of atomic explosions, the fallout in the case of a low air burst might be an inconvenience, but it would not, in general, represent a real danger."

August 21. In New York City, 450 members of the U.N. Secretariat move into their new office building overlooking the East River. The 39-story structure was designed by an international board of architects.

August 24. Edith S. Sampson is the first Negro appointed to a U.S. Assembly delegation to the U.N.

October 20. With admission to the American Nurses' Association, the 41-year-old National Association of Colored Graduate Nurses votes to disband in the New Year.

November 8. In the first jet-to-jet dogfight, U.S. Shooting Stars stave off an attack over Korea by Soviet-made MiG-15s. The Americans report no losses and one enemy aircraft downed.

November 19. The American Red Cross will no longer tag blood with the donor's race.

November 29. Twenty-five Protestant denominations and 4 Eastern Orthodox churches, representing 71 percent of American non-Catholic Christians, form the National Council of Churches of Christ.

More news. Entrepreneur Ralph Schneider enlists 27 New York restaurants for his Diners Club.

His credit card is the first to act as a middleman, collecting payments for a group of businesses.

• Ottawa enfranchises 5,000 Eskimos of voting age.

• Canada and the United States erect a weather station at the northern tip of Ellesmere Island. Just 500 miles from the North Pole, Alert is the world's northernmost permanent habitation.

### Government Departments and Agencies

**December 1.** An executive order establishes an independent Federal Civil Defense Administration. Within two weeks, a new code of air-raid signals requires a 3-minute siren to mark a red alert. Communities without sirens must use horns or whistles.

### New Products and Businesses

New foodstuffs this year include Sugar Pops, Minute Rice, and the first concentrated milk.

Clairol introduces the revolutionary Miss Clairol hair color, which requires half the standard application time.

In 1937, a chemist working with sodium cyclohexyl sulfamate noticed his cigarette tasted sweet. This year, Abbott Labs in Britain introduces the sweetener sucaryl sodium for diabetics.

As Europe slowly recovers from the war, Gerard Blitz sets up holiday tents on the Spanish island of Majorca. He calls his camp Club Med.

Ferdinand Porsche manufactures his first Model 356. The car's body will remain basically unchanged through to 1964.

### Fads

"Hopalong Cassidy" first appeared on New York television as early as 1945, then went national in 1949. This year, the silver-haired cowboy and his horse Topper draw as many as 300,000 fans at a personal appearance. Children clamor for black Hoppy hats, shirts, guns and holsters, and other merchandise. (Reportedly,

the demand creates a national shortage of black dye.) Actor William Boyd, who owns all rights to his edited films, collects 5 percent.

## SCIENCE AND TECHNOLOGY

### News

**February 6.** The Defense Department announces that the navy has successfully test fired "Mighty Mouse," the first air-to-air rocket for use in aerial combat.

**March 30.** Bell Telephone Laboratories disclose the development of the phototransistor. Still in the experimental stage, the transistor will operate by light rather than electric current.

**April 17.** Army Chemical Corps Chief General Anthony McAuliffe discusses the development of "nerve gases" and other bloodless weapons to destroy the will of the enemy while preserving cities and industrial centers. He maintains that the Soviet Union is conducting the same research.

**April 18.** In the first international jet-transport flight in North America, Canada's Avro carrier arrives in New York after a record 59-minute, 56-second flight. But Avro abandons production of the aircraft to concentrate on the CF-100 Canuck jet fighter.

**May 5.** A special commission of the U.S. Armed Forces Epidemiology Board reports that antihistamine drugs offer no help in preventing or treating the common cold. Nonetheless, sales of the drugs this year mount to $100 million.

**May 26.** The 13-year-old Aransas National Wildlife Refuge, in Texas, witnesses the first hatching of a rare whooping crane in captivity. But the chick disappears and most of the other 21 young hatched during this decade will be lost to natural predators.

**June 2.** With the new Mount Palomar telescope, Professor Gerard Kuiper makes the first accurate measurements of the planet Pluto. A diameter of no more than 3,600 miles and a mass one-tenth the size of Earth explains the planet's dimness.

**June 9.** Upjohn Pharmaceutical Co. announces that a 2-million-volt electron accelerator has sterilized antibiotics, the first practical use of an atom smasher.

**June 17.** In a 45-minute operation at a Chicago hospital, Dr. Richard Lawler performs the first transplant of a kidney from one human to another.

**July 2.** Newspapers announce the discovery of the ocean's greatest depth—34,440 feet—in the Cape Johnson Deep off the east coast of the Philippines.

**October 17.** Elizabeth L. Hazel, age 63, and Rachel Brown, age 50, announce their discovery of the first safe fungicide. A derivative of the streptomycin family, nystatin is heralded as the greatest breakthrough in antibiotics since the discovery of penicillin in 1928. The women, who named the drug after their employer, the New York State Institute of Health, decline lucrative offers from pharmaceutical companies and patent the drug through a nonprofit research organization, refusing all royalties.

**October 22.** Yale Observatory completes a 23-year project to catalog some 128,000 stars between 30 degrees south of the celestial equator and 30 degrees north. Those visible outside these latitudes were measured by observatories in England and South Africa.

**October 27.** Drs. J. C. Callaghan and W. G. Bigelow from the University of Toronto describe their experimental work with an "electrical artificial pacemaker." Electrodes, inserted through an incision, have been used to revive the hearts of animals.

**More news.** Unlike other ballpoint pens, the Paper-Mate neither leaks nor smudges. With hundreds given away, sales will rise from $300,000 in the first year to $19 million in 1953.

• The U.S. Time Corp. introduces an inexpensive watch with bearings made from a hard new alloy. By 1962, one out of every three watches sold in the United States will be a Timex.

• The Haloid Co. of Rochester manufactures the first copying machine to use xerography. The company will later adopt the trade name Xerox.

• Two Oldsmobile models replace the two-piece windshield (separated by a center metal strip) with a one-piece unit.

*Statistics*: The first true automatic transmission was introduced in 1940, but wartime production intervened. Some 1.5 million automatic cars manufactured this year fail to keep up with demand.

• At a scientific symposium this year, geneticist Barbara McClintock hypothesizes—in direct opposition to current theories—that genes can pass from cell to cell. Her talk is poorly received (partly because she is a woman) and, over the next 20 years, few show interest in her papers.

In the late 1960s and early 1970s, research will show that "jumping" genes explain how bacteria develop a resistance to antibiotics or why a new plant or animal species suddenly emerges. Eventually, scientists acknowledge McClintock's work as one of the greatest discoveries in genetics.

## Other Discoveries, Developments, and Inventions

Squeeze plastic bottles for toiletries

Underwater camera with fins and rudder, the 35-mm French Eclair Aquaflex

Rolodex address file, from New Yorker Arnold Neustadter

Black-and-white Polaroid print to replace the 1947 sepia print

Radio paging service—Aircall—in New York City

GE robot mechanism for handling radioactive materials

First gas-turbine automobile, from Rover

F-86 U.S. sweep-wing fighter

## Obituaries

**Karl Guthe Jansky** (October 22, 1905–February 14, 1950). While working for Bell Telephone on the problem of ship-to-shore radio static, Jansky found, by 1932, that weak static emanated from the constellation Sagittarius. His findings made front-page news, but Jansky never pursued his theory. With better instrumentation over the years, astronomers have learned to interpret radio-wave emission. In his honor, the unit of strength was named the jansky.

**Ransom E. Olds** (June 3, 1864–August 26, 1950). The automobile pioneer, who gave his name to the Oldsmobile and later the Reo (his monogram), started America's first car factory in 1899.

## THE ARTS

**January 5**—*The Member of the Wedding*, with Ethel Waters, Julie Harris, Brandon de Wilde (501 perfs.)
  **October 12**—*Call Me Madam*, with Ethel Merman (644 perfs.)
  **November 24**—*Guys and Dolls*, with Robert Alda, Isabel Bigley, Vivian Blaine, Sam Levene (1,200 perfs.)

### Tony Awards

  Actor (Dramatic)—Sidney Blackmer, *Come Back, Little Sheba*
  Actress (Dramatic)—Shirley Booth, *Come Back, Little Sheba*
  Actor (Musical)—Ezio Pinza, *South Pacific*
  Actress (Musical)—Mary Martin, *South Pacific*
  Play—*The Cocktail Party* by T. S. Eliot
  Musical—*South Pacific*

### News

**February 2.** Lauritz Melchior ends his 24-year career at the Metropolitan Opera House following a contractual argument with the incoming general manager, Austrian-born Rudolf Bing. The tenor will continue to sing in films and operettas.
  **May 18.** Some 1,400 villagers participate in the famous 18-hour *Oberammergau Passion Play*. The first in 16 years, the play has been held every 10 years since 1634, except in times of war.
  **November 17.** When the female lead in Mozart's *Don Giovanni* suffers from food poisoning, soprano Roberta Peters steps in. Amazingly, the 20-year-old's Met debut marks her first appearance on stage.

**More news.** A. Perrottet and E. Stroecklin place the audience in the center of their patented revolving stage.
  • An increasing number of large hotels convert lobby space into profitable stores, coffee shops, and restaurants. As well, with more Americans vacationing by car, many downtown hotels offer guests a parking space in a garage.

### Obituaries

**Julia Marlowe** (August 17, 1866–November 12, 1950). Before retiring in 1924, the English-American actress played in more Shakespearean dramas before more people than any other stage actor in history.
  **Vaslav Nijinsky** (February 28, 1890–April 8, 1950). With his dramatic technique and extraordinary agility, the Russian was called the greatest male dancer of all time. He appeared in *The Specter of the Rose* and choreographed the sensational *Rite of Spring* and *Afternoon of the Faun*. But, tragically, Nijinsky never reached artistic maturity. He was committed to an asylum in 1918 with acute schizophrenia.
  **George Bernard Shaw** (July 26, 1856–November 2, 1950). One of the most influential figures in modern literature, the British critic, novelist, and playwright won the 1925 Nobel prize in literature. (But Shaw refused a peerage, claiming to have already conferred the Order of Merit on himself.) Many of his more than 50 plays have become classics of the Western theater, including *Major Barbara* (1905), *The Doctor's Dilemma* (1906), and *Pygmalion* (1912).
  **Kurt Weill** (March 2, 1900–April 3, 1950). The German-American composer remains best known for the bitter, satirical *Threepenny Opera* (with text by Bertolt Brecht). Updated versions, in 1952 and 1954, will produce the song "Mack the Knife."

## WORDS

  Ray Bradbury, *The Martian Chronicles*
  Paul Brickhill, *The Great Escape*
  Gwen Bristow, *Jubilee Trail*

Graham Greene, *The Third Man*

Giovanni Guareschi, *The Little World of Don Camillo*

John Hersey, *The Wall*

Thor Heyerdahl, *Kon-Tiki: Across the Pacific by Raft*

Haywood Patterson, *Scottsboro Boy*

Henry Morton Robinson, *The Cardinal*

Nevil Shute, *A Town Like Alice*

## News

**March 31.** *Scientific American* announces that the AEC ordered 30,000 copies of the April issue burned. Reportedly, an article by Cornell physicist Hans Bethe contained technical information on the H-bomb.

**October 16.** *Life* magazine compares an 1898 poll of 1,440 Minnesota and California children with one taken this year in five U.S. cities. The question? "What person of whom you have heard or read would you like most to resemble?"

Last century's list included George Washington, John Whittier, Anne Sullivan Macy, Julius Caesar, Abraham Lincoln, Clara Barton, Christopher Columbus, Jim Corbett, William Jennings Bryan, Queen Elizabeth I, Napoleon Bonaparte, and Louisa May Alcott.

In 1950, students most admire General Douglas MacArthur, Florence Nightingale, Vera-Ellen, Doris Day, Abraham Lincoln, Clara Barton, Franklin D. Roosevelt, Joe DiMaggio, Babe Ruth, Roy Rogers, Sister Elizabeth Kenny, and Louisa May Alcott.

A professor who took a similar poll two years ago finds nothing wrong with idealizing accomplishments of "muscle, brawn, and brain." But, he says, the addition of movie actors is "possibly a less reassuring trend."

**More news.** Louis L'Amour, age 42, writes his first book, *Westward the Tide*. In the years ahead, the American novelist will become the world's best-selling author of Westerns.

• The only known copy of Robert Frost's first book, *Twilight* (1894), fetches $3,500 at an auction. Booksellers describe the high price as "astonishing."

In a publishing innovation, Simon & Schuster simultaneously releases a hardcover and lower-priced paperback edition of a novel, *The Cardinal*.

## Cartoons and Comics

**October 2.** The United Features Syndicate picks up *Li'l Folks* by 27-year-old Charles Schulz, then renames the strip *Peanuts*. (The cartoonist hates the name.) From an initial placement in 8 newspapers, *Peanuts* syndication will mushroom to 400 dailies before the end of the decade.

**More news.** Educational Comics (later Entertaining Comics [EC]) launches a new comic book trend with a series of well-written and artfully drawn titles: *Weird Fantasy*, *Crypt of Terror*, and *The Vault of Horror*.

• Mort Walker introduces the comic strip *Beetle Bailey*.

## TIME **Man of the Year**

The U.S. Fighting Man

## New Words and Phrases

air coach (an airliner with inexpensive seats)
apartheid
bopera (a nightclub specializing in bop music)
captive audience
femineered (designed by a woman)
fire fight (close-range rifle fighting)
glamourlovely (a beautiful, buxom woman)
guilt by association
heliport
litterbug
McCarthyism
nerve gas
rat pack (from California, teenagers who roam about at night victimizing people)
theater-in-the-round

## Obituaries

**Edgar Rice Burroughs** (September 1, 1875–March 19, 1950). Critics pan Burroughs as a pulp-fiction writer, but Tarzan ranks with Dracula and Sherlock Holmes as one of popular fiction's most enduring characters. At his death, Burroughs's 50 or more Tarzan novels have sold millions of copies, a Tarzan comic strip appears in 200 newspapers, and Tarzan movies have been shown worldwide.

**Edna St. Vincent Millay** (February 22, 1892– October 19, 1950). The foremost American woman poet of the 1920s and 1930s will appear old-fashioned by the 1970s. Millay's first long poem, "Renascence," will remain one of her best-known works.

**George Orwell** (June 23, 1903–January 21, 1950). Ironically, in the early years of the Cold War, the British novelist's left-wing satirization of totalitarian society in *Animal Farm* (1945) and his prophesy of totalitarianism in *Nineteen Eighty-Four* (1949) are widely used to condemn the USSR and any American with leftist sympathies.

**Rafael Sabatini** (April 29, 1875–February 13, 1950). One of this century's most widely read authors, the Italian-born writer mastered the historical novel in *The Sea Hawk* (1915), *Captain Blood* (1922), and others.

# FASHION

## The 1950s

With women dressing alike and girls copying their mothers, couturiers wield enormous clout. Each occasion calls for different clothes, but always a dress or skirt. Women only wear slacks or calf-length pedal-pushers for play.

As some 12 million war babies reach their teens during this decade, their clamor for more youthful fashions will foretell the enormous fashion upheaval ahead in the 1960s.

## Haute Couture

Designers hold to the fitted look while some feature tunics and flared three-quarter-length coats.

## News

**This year.** With the outbreak of the Korean War, large government orders and civilian panic buying drive up the cost of raw and finished materials. The overheated market forces textile manufacturers to ignore the government's voluntary price freeze.

Italian aristocrat Marchese Pucci di Barsento opens the couture house Emilio. Pucci clinging chemises, at-home robes, scarves, and resort shirts will become status symbols during the decade.

## Colors and Materials

Fashionable women adopt a black-and-white color scheme. A Spanish influence highlights black-accented reds, yellows, and other bold colors as well as ball fringe, trimmings, beads, and gems.

Dominant fabrics include transparent chiffons and organdies, all shades of gray tulle, and velvets, particularly velveteen.

## Clothes

Designers attempt a 1920s revival, but only the waistless chemise succeeds. Cut straight from armhole to flank, the dress silhouette allows women to create their own waist—high or low, tight or loose. An evening version usually flares out stiffly near the hemline.

Tailored gingham blouses are new this spring. In the summer, with little air conditioning available, women choose sleeveless blouses and dresses.

A handsome male model wearing an eye-patch brings attention to the Hathaway shirt.

## Accessories

Bags, belts, and shoes promote two colors or two textures, but patent leather remains the standard.

Fox furs enjoy a huge revival while fabric stoles match dresses.

Big, glittery rhinestone jewelry—intentionally fake—is worn anytime, anywhere.

Quite small hats perch farther forward. The number of men wearing hats continues to decrease.

## Hair and Cosmetics

Short hair gives way to longer tresses and a few women wear chignons.

Makeup sales rise dramatically as women copy Parisian "doe eyes," using pencil, mascara, and shadow to extend and emphasize the eyes.

## POPULAR MUSIC

"Goodnight Irene"/"Tzena Tzena Tzena"— Gordon Jenkins & His Orchestra with the Weavers

"Third Man Theme" (Instr.)—Anton Karas/ Guy Lombardo & the Royal Canadians

"Mona Lisa"—Nat King Cole

"Music! Music! Music!"—Teresa Brewer

"Harbor Lights"—Sammy Kaye & His Orchestra

"The Thing"—Phil Harris

"Chattanoogie Shoe Shine Boy"—Red Foley

"Rag Mop"/"Sentimental Me"—Ames Brothers

"Play a Simple Melody"/"Sam's Song"—Bing & Gary Crosby

"Bewitched, Bothered & Bewildered"—Bill Snyder & His Orchestra

"Bibbidi-Bobbidi-Boo"—Perry Como

"Enjoy Yourself (It's Later Than You Think)"— Guy Lombardo & His Royal Canadians

"Frosty the Snowman"—Gene Autry

"La Vie en Rose"—Edith Piaf

"Peter Cottontail"—Merv Shiner/Gene Autry

"If I Knew You Were Comin' I'd've Baked a Cake"—Eileen Barton

"All My Love"—Patti Page

"My Foolish Heart"—Billy Eckstine/Gordon Jenkins Orchestra

## News

**This year.** Through the late 1940s, various stores and businesses introduced recorded music to perk up their employees and increase their efficiency and job attitude. This year, the 12-year-old Muzak Corp. confirms, from a survey of some 35,000 workers, that programs must be specially planned to be accepted by employees.

• *Down Beat* lists the most popular male vocalists as Billy Eckstine, Perry Como, Frankie Laine, Frank Sinatra, Louis Armstrong, and Mel Tormé. The most popular females are Sarah Vaughan, Ella Fitzgerald, Doris Day, Kay Starr, Peggy Lee, Billie Holiday, Patti Page, Jo Stafford, and Fran Warren.

• Conceding defeat in the war of phonograph speeds, RCA releases LP records. Still, the company's smaller 45 rpm has established itself as the best format for jukeboxes and next year Columbia will adopt the 7-inch disc.

• After 12 years in the business, Teresa Brewer scores her first million-seller, "Music, Music, Music." She is 19.

• "Goodnight, Irene," a Huddie Ledbetter song adapted by John Lomax, remains at No. 1 for 13 weeks, a record unsurpassed over the next quarter century.

### New Recording Artists

Teresa Brewer
Eddie Fisher
Mitch Miller & His Orchestra
Guy Mitchell
Les Paul & Mary Ford

## Obituaries

**George Gard (Buddy) De Sylva** (January 27, 1896–July 11, 1950). The prolific lyricist, who is usually identified with Lew Brown and Ray Henderson, counted "April Showers" (1921), "California, Here I Come" (1924), and "The Birth of the Blues" (1926) among his hits.

**Al Jolson** (March 26, 1886–October 23, 1950). Enormously successful in vaudeville, the singer-actor was the obvious choice for the second talkie, *The Jazz Singer* (1927). He divided his time between film and stage during the 1930s, but during the war concentrated on entertaining U.S. troops. In the

1940s, two autobiographical films (using his dubbed-in voice) gave Jolson a second career.

A tremendous crowd pleaser, he would finish an emotional tune and promise the audience, "You ain't heard nothin' yet!" His hits included "Sonny Boy" and the trademark "Toot, Toot Tootsie, Goo' Bye."

The show-biz legend died of a heart attack after returning from a U.S. services tour in Korea.

**Harry Lauder** (August 4, 1870–February 26, 1950). Knighted in 1919 for his wartime entertainment work, the Scottish music-hall comedian and singer toured the world. His simple compositions included "Roamin' in the Gloamin" (1911).

## MOVIES

*All About Eve* (d. Joseph L. Mankiewicz; bw)—Bette Davis, Ann Baxter, George Sanders, Celeste Holm, Gary Merrill, Marilyn Monroe

*The Asphalt Jungle* (d. John Huston; bw)—Sterling Hayden, Louis Calhern, Jean Hagen, James Whitmore, Sam Jaffe

*Born Yesterday* (d. George Cukor; bw)—Judy Holliday, Broderick Crawford, William Holden

*Broken Arrow* (d. Delmer Daves; color)—James Stewart, Jeff Chandler, Debra Paget

*Cinderella* (Disney; color; animated)—Voices: Ilene Woods (Cinderella); Eleanor Audley (Stepmother); Verna Felton (Fairy Godmother)

*Cyrano de Bergerac* (d. Michael Gordon; bw)—José Ferrer, Mala Powers

*Father of the Bride* (d. Vincente Minnelli; bw)—Spencer Tracy, Joan Bennett, Elizabeth Taylor

*The Gunfighter* (d. Henry King; bw)—Gregory Peck, Helen Westcott, Jean Parker, Karl Malden

*Harvey* (d. Henry Koster; bw)—James Stewart, Josephine Hull, Victoria Horne

*In a Lonely Place* (d. Nicholas Ray; bw)—Humphrey Bogart, Gloria Grahame, Frank Lovejoy

*King Solomon's Mines* (d. Compton Bennett; color)—Deborah Kerr, Stewart Granger, Richard Carlson

*The Men* (Reissue title: *Battle Stripe*) (d. Fred Zinnemann; bw)—Marlon Brando, Teresa Wright, Everett Sloane

*Rio Grande* (d. John Ford; bw)—John Wayne, Maureen O'Hara, Ben Johnson, Harry Carey, Jr., Victor McLaglen

*Sunset Boulevard* (d. Billy Wilder; bw)—Gloria Swanson, William Holden, Erich von Stroheim

*Three Came Home* (d. Jean Negulesco; bw)—Claudette Colbert, Patric Knowles, Florence Desmond, Sessue Hayakawa

*Three Little Words* (d. Richard Thorpe; color)—Fred Astaire, Red Skelton, Vera-Ellen, Arlene Dahl

*Treasure Island* (Disney, d. Byron Haskin; color)—Bobby Driscoll, Robert Newton

*Winchester '73* (d. Anthony Mann; bw)—James Stewart, Shelley Winters, Dan Duryea

### Academy Awards

**March 23.** In an attempt to placate the industry, the studios agree once again to fund the Oscars. The ceremonies are held in the 2,812-seat RKO Pantages Theatre in the heart of Hollywood. Veteran stage and recent screen actor Paul Douglas hosts.

Best Picture—*All the King's Men*

Best Actor—Broderick Crawford (*All the King's Men*)

Best Actress—Olivia de Havilland (*The Heiress*)

Best Director—Joseph L. Mankiewicz (*A Letter to Three Wives*)

Best Supporting Actor—Dean Jagger (*Twelve O'Clock High*)

Best Supporting Actress—Mercedes McCambridge (*All the King's Men*)

Best Song—"Baby, It's Cold Outside" from *Neptune's Daughter*

Special Award—*The Bicycle Thief* (Italian)

Two Hollywood legends never before honored by the Academy receive Special Awards tonight. Oscar salutes producer-director Cecil B. DeMille for his distinguished 37-year career and Fred Astaire "for his unique artistry and his contributions to the technique of musical pictures."

Mercedes McCambridge's role in *All the King's Men* is the first debut performance to win an Oscar.

## News

**February.** Ending a 2¹/₂-year government antitrust suit, Technicolor agrees to license 92 patents royalty-free and 60 others on a reasonable basis. The settlement includes the company's 1932 invention, the three-strip color separation camera.

**February 22.** A half-century *Variety* poll names Irving Thalberg best producer, D. W. Griffith best director, Greta Garbo best actress, Charlie Chaplin best actor, and *Gone With the Wind* (1939) best picture.

**March 14.** Senator Edwin C. Johnson launches a congressional attack against actress Ingrid Bergman, calling her the "apostle of degradation." Last year, movie fans were outraged by her extramarital affair with Italian film director Roberto Rossellini. Hounded into exile by the press, Bergman bore his son in Rome last month. Her American career destroyed, she remains in Europe and marries Rossellini.

**May 6.** At age 18, actress Elizabeth Taylor marries Conrad Hilton, Jr., son of the hotelier. She will seek a divorce before the end of the year.

**May 26.** *Film Daily* estimates that U.S. movie attendance has dropped over the past two years from 90 million per week to 70 million, which is the lowest average since 1934, at the height of the Depression.

With ticket sales plummeting, some 3,000 theaters have closed. Hollywood blames the expanding television industry, even though theaters in areas outside broadcast range have also reported losses. At year's end, motion picture insiders bitterly quip, "Buy Christmas seals and help stamp out TV."

**September.** As blacklisting grips Hollywood, Monogram Studios shelves a film on Hiawatha, afraid that a movie about an Indian peacemaker might be viewed as Communist propaganda.

Worried studio executives rely on security advisers and anti-Communist publications to ferret out leftist sympathizers. Last June, American Business Consultants, publishers of the weekly newsletter *Counterattack*, issued *Red Channels: The Report of Communist Influence in Radio and Television*. The consultants had culled HUAC files, the Justice Department's subversive list, and various other state and local files for suspect entertainers—Pete Seeger, Orson Welles, Lee J. Cobb, Zero Mostel, Lee Grant, and 146 others. Although no attempt was made to verify charges, the publishers will remove a name only if the individual joins or works for a pro-American organization or makes a full public confession before HUAC.

Grant, her teacher an admitted Communist and her husband suspect, will fight a successful five-year court battle to have her name deleted. But the studios maintain their blacklists and she will be unable to find a decent job until the late 1960s.

**December 16.** In California, 22-year-old Shirley Temple marries television executive Charles Black and announces her retirement.

In 1934, the 6-year-old singer-dancer with the curls and dimples made her first movie. Two years later, she topped the box-office list, then held onto the spot for another four years as a multimillion-dollar industry churned out Shirley Temple dolls, dresses, coloring books, and other merchandise. But unlike Deanna Durbin, who started in movies as a teenager, Temple was unable to sustain her appeal past childhood.

**More news.** Although film exhibitors leave Marlon Brando off the list of cinema newcomers, his debut as a W.W.II paraplegic in *The Men* receives critical acclaim. A young black actor destined for fame also debuts this year, playing a slum area doctor in *No Way Out*—Sidney Poitier.

• The 12-year Blondie series, with Penny Singleton as Blondie and Arthur Lake as Dagwood Bumstead, ends with the 28th film, *Beware of Blondie*.

• This year, Gloria Swanson and Bette Davis give their most memorable performances, in parts originally intended for other actresses. The 51-year-old Swanson, out of films since 1941, is cast as the aging actress in *Sunset Boulevard* after Mae West, Mary Pickford, and Pola Negri turn down the script. And Davis wins her role in *All About Eve* when Claudette Colbert cracks a vertebra.

• Columbia Pictures pays writer Garson Kanin $1 million for rights to his Broadway show *Born Yesterday*—the first million-dollar property. Reportedly, Kanin named an "impossibly high" figure because of a long-running feud with production chief Harry Cohn.

• Walt Disney follows his brother Roy's advice and uses accrued British royalties (frozen by postwar monetary restrictions) to make four films in Britain. *Treasure Island* is the studio's first live-action picture without an animated sequence.

| Top Box Office Stars | Newcomers |
| --- | --- |
| John Wayne | Dean Martin and Jerry |
| Bob Hope | Lewis |
| Bing Crosby | William Holden |
| Betty Grable | Arlene Dahl |
| James Stewart | Ruth Roman |
| Bud Abbott & | Vera-Ellen |
| Lou Costello | John Lund |
| Clifton Webb | William Lundigan |
| Esther Williams | Dean Jagger |
| Spencer Tracy | Joanne Dru |
| Randolph Scott | James Whitmore |

### Top Money-Maker of the Year

*Samson and Delilah* (1949) (d. Cecil B. DeMille; color)—Victor Mature, Hedy Lamarr.

### Quote of the Year

"Fasten your seatbelts. It's going to be a bumpy night."

Bette Davis comments on clashing egos at the party in *All About Eve*. (Screenplay by Joseph L. Mankiewicz; based on a radio play and short story by Mary Orr.)

### Obituaries

**Sidney Grauman** (March 17, 1879–March 5, 1950). The U.S. theatrical producer originated the floodlit, gala premiere, and, at his Chinese theater, created a hall of fame for movie stars' hands and footprints.

**Walter Huston** (April 6, 1884–April 7, 1950). The Canadian-born actor, who won an Oscar for his role in *Treasure of the Sierra Madre* (1948), was long identified with the tune "September Song" from his one Broadway musical, the 1938 *Knickerbocker Holiday*.

**Emil Jannings** (July 26, 1886–January 2, 1950). In 1928, the American-born German actor won the first best actor Academy Award for *The Way of All Flesh*. Still, his best-known role remains the professor destroyed by Marlene Dietrich in the German film *The Blue Angel* (1930).

## TELEVISION AND RADIO

### New Prime-Time TV Programs

"Armstrong Circle Theatre" (June 6, 1950–August 28, 1963; Dramatic Anthology)

"The Arthur Murray Party" (July 20, 1950–September 6, 1960; Musical Variety)—Kathryn Murray, Arthur Murray, The Arthur Murray Dancers

"Beat the Clock" (March 23, 1950–February 16, 1958; Quiz/Audience Participation)—Emcee: Bud Collyer

"Beulah" (October 3, 1950–September 22, 1953; Situation Comedy)—Ethel Waters (1950–1952), Louise Beavers (1952–1953)

"The Colgate Comedy Hour" (September 10, 1950–December 25, 1955; Variety)—Eddie Cantor, Martin & Lewis, Donald O'Connor, Abbott & Costello

"Football" (ABC; October 1950–January 1951; September 1953–December 1953; October 1957–December 1957; August 1959–October 1959; September 1970–    )

"The Gene Autry Show" (July 23, 1950–August 7, 1956; Western)—Gene Autry, Pat Buttram

"The George Burns and Gracie Allen Show" (October 12, 1950–September 22, 1958; Situation Comedy)—George Burns, Gracie Allen, Bea Benaderet

"The Jack Benny Show" (October 28, 1950–September 1965; Comedy)—Jack Benny, Eddie "Rochester" Anderson, Don Wilson, Dennis Day, Mary Livingston

"Lux Video Theatre" (October 2, 1950–September 12, 1957; Dramatic Anthology)

"Robert Montgomery Presents" (January 30, 1950–June 24, 1957; Dramatic Anthology)—Host: Robert Montgomery. *Note:* Title varies week to week according to sponsor, e.g., "Your Lucky Strike Theater."

"What's My Line" (February 16, 1950–September 3, 1967; Quiz/Audience Participation)—Moderator: John Daly; Panelists: Arlene Francis, Dorothy Kilgallen, Bennett Cerf

"You Asked for It" (December 29, 1950–September 27, 1959; Audience Participation)

"You Bet Your Life" (October 5, 1950–September 21, 1961; Quiz/Audience Participation)—Emcee: Groucho Marx; Announcer: George Fenneman

"Your Hit Parade" (July 10, 1950–April 1959; Music)

"Your Show of Shows" (February 25, 1950–June 5, 1954; Comedy Variety)—Sid Caesar, Imogene Coca, Carl Reiner

## Emmy Awards 1949 (January 27, 1950)

The Academy differentiates between best "live" and best "kinescoped" performers and programs for this one year only.

Best Live Show—"The Ed Wynn Show" (CBS)

Best Kinescope Show—"Texaco Star Theater" (NBC)

Best Children's Show—"Time for Beany"

Most Outstanding Live Personality—Ed Wynn ("The Ed Wynn Show," CBS)

Most Outstanding Kinescope Personality—Milton Berle ("Texaco Star Theater," NBC)

## News

**This year.** Entering the second year of the six-month FCC freeze, half the country is buying hundreds of thousands of TV sets while the other half has yet to see a single program. The networks, limited by an established market, begin to feel the squeeze. Hardest hit, ABC cuts 20 percent from its budget during the winter.

**January 30.** With his drama showcase "Robert Montgomery Presents," the actor becomes the first Hollywood star to defect to the small screen.

**February.** With few cable links between the East and Midwest, the networks argued against an NBC monopoly of their joint connection for the new 2½-hour "Saturday Night Revue." As a result, the FCC has pushed NBC into televising the first hour, "The Jack Carter Show," from Chicago and the second hour and a half, "Your Show of Shows" with Sid Caesar and Imogene Coca, from New York.

Until this time, entire programs have been sustained by network money, single sponsorship, or inserted commercials at the local level. The restrictions imposed on "Saturday Night Revue" give rise to 15-minute segment sponsorship, likely an inevitable development with the rising costs of production.

**February.** TV viewers on the West Coast receive kines of live New York productions, but Easterners, unused to the poor resolution of monitor recordings, generally ignore rebroadcasts from Los Angeles.

This month, the New York "Silver Theater" moves out West and overcomes this disadvantage with the multicam system. By positioning three film cameras like regular TV cameras, the director achieves the flow of a live broadcast while gaining the advantages of editing. An average live broadcast requires five days of preparation and rehearsals; a filmed program needs three.

**February 2.** On "What's My Line," panelists use the catchphrase "Is it bigger than a breadbox?" to question the unusual occupation or product of contestants. TV's longest-running quiz show will be syndicated from 1968 to 1975; on the last program, host John Daly will be the guest celebrity.

**February 28.** C. E. Hooper Inc. sells the

national radio and television Hooperatings to A. C. Nielsen. To gather TV data, Nielsen places an Audimeter in some 1,200 homes nationwide. The daily viewing record from each "little black box," plus written logs in other households, picks "Texaco Star Theater" as the No. 1 show for 1950–1951.

**April.** Every day at 5:30 Buffalo Bill asks, "Say, kids . . . What time is it?" And an excited peanut gallery yells back, "It's Howdy Doody time!"

Since its premiere, on December 27, 1947, "Howdy Doody" has climbed the children's ratings to reach the top this month. With the prerecorded voice of nonventriloquist Bob Smith (Buffalo Bill), the freckle-faced puppet enchants children with new words like "thingamajig." Clarabell the Clown, who never speaks, uses a sour horn to answer "no" and a sweeter note to say "yes."

The vocal audience cheers or boos various real and wooden characters like Princess Summerfall Winterspring, Flub-a-Dub, Chief Thunderthud, Ugly Sam, and the crotchety Mayor Phineas T. Bluster.

Howdy makes a fortune for Smith's merchandising company—games, comic books, puddings, shovel sets—while one premium offer, early in the decade, draws some 750,000 letters.

**April 9.** Bob Hope portrays a gun-toting cowboy on "Star Spangled Revue." The first major radio comic to appear on TV, he readily adapts to the rapid-fire delivery demanded by the new medium.

**May 29.** NBC originates the informal talk show with "Broadway Open House." Jerry Lester hosts the one-hour program three nights a week, Morey Amsterdam the other two. Regulars perform skits, dances, and songs, and celebrities are encouraged to drop in.

**June 4.** At the Boston University graduation ceremonies, President Daniel Marsh tells seniors, "If the television craze continues with the present level of programs, we are destined to have a nation of morons."

**July 23.** Gene Autry, the first singing cowboy actor, branches out from movies and radio into television. With bumbling sidekick Pat Buttram and Champion, his chestnut stallion, Autry fights the badmen of the West. But his video character

abandons flashy embroidered outfits for Levis and plain shirts.

**August 19.** ABC pioneers children's Saturday-morning programming with "Animal Clinic," a show on the care and training of pets. But executives pay little attention to the concept and by mid-decade most ABC Saturday-morning programs will disappear.

---

*Statistics:* A survey conducted at a Connecticut junior high school finds the average student watches 27 hours of TV every week— three-quarters of an hour less than the time spent in school.

---

**September 9.** One of the first TV shows to be canceled in midseason, "The Hank McCune Show" leaves a terrible legacy—the sitcom laugh track.

**September 11.** W.W.II veterans Ed Kemmer and Lyn Osborn head the TV-radio cast of the Los Angeles-based "Space Patrol." Moved to Saturday mornings in mid-1952, the weekly space opera generates some $40 million in spin-off merchandise sales by September of that year. The show will end in early 1955.

**September 25.** NBC scores a success with the musical-variety "Kate Smith Show," the first major program scheduled in the afternoon.

**October 1.** After playing Hopalong Cassidy in more than 60 "B" Westerns, actor William Boyd was typecast. Touring with circuses by the mid-1940s, he readily agreed to join promoter Toby Anguish and buy all rights to his films.

Edited for television, "Hopalong Cassidy" was first broadcast in Los Angeles in 1948. A positive response prompted NBC to pick up the half-hour shows, reedit them, and tack on additional narration by the deep-voiced star. Within a month of today's national debut, Hoppy carries a 34.8 audience share.

White-haired since the age of 19, Boyd luckily avoids age comparisons during personal appearances with his horse Topper. A merchandising bonanza and further filmed episodes (1952–1954) make the handsome TV cowboy the first pop hero of the second half of the century.

**October 2.** The sci-fi thriller "Tom Corbett, Space Cadet" benefits from the technical advice of

YOUR HOST OF THE AIRWAVES
*The Coca-Cola Company presents*
EDGAR BERGEN with CHARLIE McCARTHY-CBS 8 p.m. EST every Sunday
*And every day . . . wherever you travel, the familiar red cooler is your*
HOST OF THE HIGHWAYS . . . HOST TO THE WORKER in office
and shop . . . HOST TO THIRSTY MAIN STREET the country over.

*In their 13th year on radio, ventriloquist Edgar Bergen and his pal Charlie McCarthy remain one of the top 10 evening programs.*

German-rocket authority Willy Ley and the likable personality of star Frankie Thomas. Fans eagerly join the Space Cadet Club, eat Kellogg's cereals for a Cadet ring, or buy any of 50 merchandise items, including a tie that glows in the dark. The last episode will be televised on June 25, 1955.

**October 11.** After nine months of hearings, the FCC chooses the CBS color television system. RCA quickly obtains a restraining order against the controversial decision.

In 1947, the FCC authorized start-up for television manufacture, suspended during the war, but waffled over the incompatible CBS color method and the inferior adaptable RCA system. As a result, three years later, some 5 million American homes

(estimates range up to 10 million) own TV sets incapable of receiving a CBS color broadcast.

**October 12.** The husband and wife comedy team of George Burns and Gracie Allen move to television. Reportedly, Burns describes their show as having "more plot than a variety show and not as much as a wrestling match."

**More news.** Since youngsters are likely to control the family's single set, early-evening programming continues to target their tastes. But this season, children's broadcasts begin moving into late afternoon.

• Catering to the burgeoning TV industry, manufacturers offer furniture with casters for rearrangement.

### *Memorable Radio Programs End*

"Blondie" (July 3, 1939)
"Burns and Allen" (February 15, 1932)
"Dr. I.Q., the Mental Banker" (June 10, 1939)
"The Fred Waring Show" (1932)
"Jack Armstrong, the All-American Boy" (July 31, 1933)
"Today's Children" (May 15, 1933)
"The Tom Mix Ralston Straightshooters" (September 25, 1933)

## SPORTS

### *Winners*

*Baseball*

World Series—New York Yankees (AL), 4 games; Philadelphia Phillies (NL), 0 games
Player of the Year—Phil Rizzuto (New York Yankees, AL); Jim Konstanty (Philadelphia Phillies, NL)
Rookie of the Year—Walt Dropo (Boston Red Sox, AL); Sam Jethroe (Boston Braves, NL)

*Football*

NFL Championship—Cleveland Browns 30, Los Angeles Rams 28

College Bowls (January 1, 1950)—
  Rose Bowl, Ohio State 17, California 14
  Cotton Bowl, Rice 27, North Carolina 13
  Orange Bowl, Santa Clara 21, Kentucky 13
  Sugar Bowl, Oklahoma 35, LSU 0
Heisman Trophy—Vic Janowicz (Ohio State,
  HB)
Grey Cup—Toronto Argonauts 13, Winnipeg
  Blue Bombers 0

*Basketball*

NBA Championship—Minneapolis Lakers, 4
  games; Syracuse Nationals, 2 games
NCAA Championship—CCNY 71, Bradley 68

*Tennis*

U.S. National—Men, Art Larsen (vs. Herb
  Flam); Women, Margaret du Pont (vs. Doris
  Hart)
Wimbledon—Men, J. Edward "Budge" Patty
  (vs. Frank Sedgman); Women, Louise
  Brough (vs. Margaret du Pont)

*Golf*

Masters—Jimmy Demaret
U.S. Open—Ben Hogan
British Open—Bobby Locke

*Hockey*

Stanley Cup—Detroit Red Wings, 4 games;
  New York Rangers, 3 games

*Ice Skating*

World Championship—Men, Dick Button
  (U.S.); Women, Aja Vrzanova
  (Czechoslovakia)
U.S. National—Men, Dick Button; Women,
  Yvonne Sherman
Canadian National—Men, Roger Wickson;
  Women, Suzanne Morrow

*Kentucky Derby*

Middleground—Bill Boland, jockey

*Athlete of the Year*

Male—Jim Konstanty (Baseball)
Female—Mildred (Babe) Didrikson Zaharias
  (Golf)

*Last Season*

Frank Brimsek (Hockey)
Bill Durnan (Hockey)
Alexander Wojciechowicz (Football)

## News

**February 7.** With a new $125,000 contract, Ted
Williams of the Boston Red Sox becomes baseball's
highest-paid player.

**February 15.** In an AP poll, sports writers and
broadcasters choose the athletes of the half century:
Babe Ruth, baseball; Jim Thorpe, football; George
Mikan, basketball; Jack Dempsey, boxing; Bill
Tilden, tennis; Johnny Weismuller, swimming;
Jessie Owen, track and field; Man O' War, thor-
oughbred racing. As well, the voters select Jim
Thorpe as the greatest male athlete and Mildred
Didrikson Zaharias as the greatest female athlete.

**April 18.** Although professional baseball introduced night games in 1935, clubs have continued to
play their opening games during the day. This season, in the first nighttime opener, the St. Louis
Cardinals beat the Pittsburgh Pirates 4–2 on
homers by Red Schoendienst and Stan Musial.

**April 24.** The Boston Celtics draft the NBA's
first black player, all-star Charles Cooper.

**May 12.** The American Bowling Congress ends
its membership restriction to white males only. On
June 5, the Women's Congress passes the same resolution.

**June 11.** In February of last year, Ben Hogan
suffered a fractured pelvis, collarbone, and left ankle in a near-fatal car crash. Doctors believed he
might never walk again, but the gritty golfer rebuilt
his strength and began to work out. Just 10 months
later he reached a playoff in the Los Angeles Open.
Today, in extra holes, Hogan wins the U.S. Open.
Sportswriters name him "Golfer of the Year."

**July 16.** Uruguay edges Brazil 5–4 in Rio to win

the World Cup. In the late 1920s, Jules Rimet and Henri Delauney, leading figures in French soccer, planned a series of matches to provide international competition for professional players. First held in 1930, the Cup was halted in 1938 by the oncoming war.

**August 29.** Althea Gibson becomes the first black woman to compete in a national tennis tournament, with her entry at the West Side Tennis Club in Forest Hills. Wimbledon champion Louise Brough eliminates her, but not easily: 6–1, 3–6, 9–7.

**November 25.** Rain on top of yesterday's record snowfall turns the Grey Cup into the "Mud Bowl." The hometown Toronto Argonauts, with better ball control, defeat Winnipeg 13–0. But after the game, quarterback Al Dekdebrun displays the thumb tacks taped to his passing hand. The fiasco finally forces the league to buy a tarpaulin.

## Records

**June 8.** Hammering the St. Louis Browns 29–4, the Boston Red Sox set a one-game major league scoring record. Fortunately for the Browns, the baseball game is in Boston.

**August 8.** American Florence Chadwick swims the English Channel in 13 hours, 20 minutes—a record time for women. Next year, with an England-to-France crossing, she becomes the first woman to swim the channel in both directions.

**October 7.** The Yankees' sweep of the Phillies is baseball's lowest-scoring World Series—16 runs. The previous record of 18 was set in 1905 by the Giants and Athletics.

## Obituaries

**Grover Cleveland (Pete) Alexander** (February 26, 1887–November 4, 1950). As one of baseball's most successful pitchers, the right-hander posted a career 373 wins and 208 losses despite problems with alcohol and epilepsy. His record of 30 or more victories in three successive seasons (1915–1917) still stands (Alexander's games usually took just 90 minutes). He left the majors in 1930, but continued to pitch in sideshows and touring teams until the age of 51.

# 1951

*In Korea, sons, brothers, and husbands die fighting for obscure hills quickly reclaimed by the other side. Truce talks produce just a brief cease-fire at the end of the year.*

*The Truman administration, faced with threats on all fronts, signs a peace treaty with Japan, allows West Germany to manufacture military goods, and, without prior notice, begins a series of aboveground atomic tests in the continental United States. And when the president fires General MacArthur for planning an attack on China, the nation literally erupts in protest.*

*With the wartime economy, sports provides a welcome relief. In a stellar year for boxing, a number of classic bouts include Robinson-LaMotta, Saddler-Pep, Walcott-Charles, and Robinson-Turpin. Ford Frick takes over as baseball commissioner, the St. Louis Browns send 3'7" Eddie Gaedel to the plate, Bob Feller throws his third no-hitter, the Giants sign Willie Mays, the Yankees add Mickey Mantle, and the great Joe DiMaggio retires at the end of the year.*

## NEWS

**January 15.** President Truman submits the largest peacetime budget in U.S. history—$71.5 billion. With U.S. involvement in Korea, 73 percent goes to "major national security programs."

**January 18–21.** In New Guinea, the "extinct" volcano Mt. Lamington blows off its entire north face. Clouds of dust and steam pour down the slopes, suffocating at least 5,000 people and destroying 20 villages and nearby sugar plantations.

**January 27.** The AEC gives no advance warning of the first atomic test at Frenchman's Flat, just 75 miles outside of Las Vegas. People in the city see the flash, hear the roar, and experience the vibrations and blast of air. The commission confirms the test

three days later. On the 28th, a second, more powerful, detonation is observed from 200 miles away.

Next month, scientific instruments in the East note a measurable increase in radiation, and experts speculate that winds have carried radioactive particles across the country. In response, the AEC states, "No levels of radiation have been found anywhere, which could conceivably produce any damage to humans, to animals, or to water supply."

**February 6.** In New Jersey, the engine and five cars of the Broker Special cross a temporary wooden overpass safely, then the bridge collapses. The remaining cars crash down onto the roadbed below, killing 85 people. Authorities charge the construction company and Pennsylvania Railroad officials with manslaughter, but the train engineer finally admits he crossed at twice the posted speed.

**March 14.** Pushed south by Chinese forces late last year, the United Nations troops regrouped in January and launched a counteroffensive. Today, the Americans and South Koreans reoccupy Seoul then steadily shift their front lines northward almost to the 38th parallel. When a new Communist drive fails in late April, the war loses its unusual mobility and settles into a conservative pattern of limited combat and artillery exchanges.

On March 27, George Marshall, in his first formal news conference as Defense Secretary, expresses amazement at the public and congressional lack of interest in mobilization (66% of Americans, in a January poll, favored pulling out of Korea "as fast as possible"). Marshall warns Americans to expect 10 years of tense relations with the Soviet Union.

---

*Statistics:* In 1951, U.S. Armed Forces number 2.9 million, double their strength 9 months ago. As well, the Navy returns over 250 vessels to active duty from the "mothball fleet," while the Air Force adds 28 groups, for a total of 90.

---

**March 29.** After a highly publicized trial, a jury finds Ethel and Julius Rosenberg guilty of selling U.S. atomic secrets to the Russians during World War II. Judge Irving Kaufman hands down the death penalty—the first for peacetime espionage, arguing that possession of the bomb gave Moscow the confidence to support the North Korean war effort.

**April 4.** In September 1950, President Truman ordered four additional U.S. divisions to Europe. With gains in midterm elections, the Republicans attacked the administration's link with Western Europe. The Senate, after hearing testimony from NATO commander General Eisenhower, and Defense Secretary Marshall, approves a "fair share" contribution of ground forces to NATO. But in failing to demand prior congressional approval for further White House commitments abroad, the Senate gives future presidents scope to involve the United States in Vietnam.

**April 7.** In Indochina, Ho Chi Minh orders his Communist forces to switch from regular military tactics to guerrilla warfare.

**April 11.** Truman stuns the nation by firing Douglas MacArthur. The general, continuing to speak out against U.S. policy in Korea, had threat-

*The president begins his day—here at 6:32 A.M.—with a brisk walk. Truman, who often conducts curbside interviews, has been known to leave Secret Service agents trailing behind.*

ened to attack coastal China and had written the House Minority leader, "There is no substitute for victory," even if it meant using atomic weapons.

Truman replaces MacArthur with Lt. Gen. Matthew Ridgway so there will be "no doubt or confusion as to the real purpose and aim of our policy. . . . World peace is more important than any individual." But the dismissal creates an uproar. Letters and telegrams pour into the White House, running 20–1 for MacArthur, and Republicans threaten presidential impeachment.

On the 19th, the 71-year-old general addresses a respectful joint session of Congress. "Like the old soldier of the ballad, I now close my military career and just fade away." The next day, an estimated 3 million New Yorkers cheer his ticker-tape parade.

But the Chiefs of Staff support the White House

decision and the controversy eventually dies down. Still, the dispute will cost the Democratic party dearly in next year's election.

**April 18.** France, Germany, Italy, the Netherlands, Belgium, and Luxembourg establish the European Coal and Steel Community. Last year, French Foreign Minister Robert Schuman proposed pooling Western European coal and steel production to reduce the possibility of another Franco-German war. Britain, resisting the concept of supranational authority, decides not to join what will later evolve into the European Economic Community.

**April 24.** Under the threat of expanding Communism, the Defense Department announces a major policy reversal. Formosa will now rank with Western Europe in priority for the shipment of U.S. arms and ammunition. A military advisory group is established next month and Congress receives a request for some $307 million in military aid.

**June 19.** Following the outbreak of war in Korea, Congress extended the Selective Service Act until July 1951. The Universal Military Training and Service Act, effective today, extends Selective Service to July 1, 1955, lowers the draft age from 19 to $18^{1}/_{2}$ years (but to be drafted only after the 19–26 pool is exhausted), lengthens training and active service to 2 years, and sets 6 years as the reserve call-up period. As well, college students may be deferred after passing a test.

With the existence of nuclear weapons, the United States can no longer count on months to prepare for war. The military training program adds more than 1 million men to the U.S. Armed Forces this year, bringing the total to 3.5 million.

---

*Statistics:* With a spotty radar network covering strategic air approaches, the U.S. Aircraft Warning Service looks for 500,000 volunteer plane spotters.

---

**July 10.** On June 23, Soviet U.N. representative Jacob Malik proposed armistice talks in Korea. (North Korean radio abruptly changed the "Drive the enemy into the sea" slogan to "Drive the enemy to the 38th parallel.") The United States responded positively, and preliminary talks open today at Kaesong, a town under Communist control.

The Communists, concerned more with political than military objectives, soon abandon their insistence on full U.N. withdrawal to concentrate on achieving a line of demarcation and the return of all POWs. But the North Koreans will suspend the often bitter discussions on August 23 over alleged violations of their territory.

**July 12.** After two months of heavy rains, a four-day storm saturates the Kansas River Basin in the most devastating flood in U.S. history. At least 41 people die, 500,000 are left homeless, and property and crop damages mount to $1 billion. Several businessmen unsuccessfully sue the Weather Bureau for an erroneous forecast.

**July 16.** When King Leopold recently returned from his 6-year exile, some 500,000 Belgians took to the streets to protest his quick wartime surrender to the Nazis. He abdicates today in favor of his 19-year-old son Baudouin.

**July 20.** King Abdullah ibn Hussein of Jordan is assassinated. His son Prince Talial, under treatment in Switzerland for a nervous breakdown, eventually ascends the throne. Talial has a 16-year-old son, Hussein.

**August 14.** At dedication ceremonies for the Washington headquarters of the American Legion, Truman attacks the anti-Communist campaign that has chipped away at basic American freedoms. Although McCarthy is never mentioned by name, no one questions the president's target. "Slanders, lies, character assassination—these things are a threat to every single citizen everywhere in this country. . . . It is the job of all of us—of every American who loves his country and his freedom—to rise up and put a stop to this terrible business." Afterward, the Legion's national commander tells reporters he certainly will not lead his organization against the senator.

**August 30.** Washington signs a mutual defense pact with the Philippines. Two days later, a common defense treaty with Australia and New Zealand (ANZUS) further defines American policy in the Far East. For the two former British colonies,

ANZUS establishes a foreign policy independent of London.

**September 4.** The one millionth U.S. soldier killed since the Battle of Lexington in 1775 dies in Korea.

**September 8.** After more than a year of negotiations, 48 nations sign a peace treaty ending the war with Japan. (The USSR and other Communist nations refuse.) The Japanese regain full sovereignty and suffer no reparations, but lose all overseas possessions.

To the many signatories bitter over the defeated nation's quick economic recovery, President Truman says, "The United States has not forgotten Pearl Harbor or Bataan and many of the other nations represented here have similar memories that will not be easily erased. The new Japan will not find the world entirely friendly or trusting. It will have to keep on working to win the friendship and trust of other peoples."

With the formal end to Allied occupation, Tokyo and Washington sign a mutual security pact allowing American troops to remain in Japan indefinitely.

**October 19.** President Truman signs a proclamation ending the state of war with Germany, 9 years, 10 months, and 8 days after President Roosevelt signed the declaration. (The document has no effect on Allied military occupation of Germany.) Britain, Canada, Mexico, and Luxembourg ended their state of war with Germany in July.

**October 22.** Greece and Turkey join NATO, extending the defense organization's security guarantee across the Mediterranean to the Middle East.

**October 25.** The United States and North Korea agree on the creation of a neutral zone at the village of Panmunjom, and truce talks resume after a two-month suspension. Delegates negotiate a 30-day cease-fire but, with no further progress, fighting resumes on December 27.

**October 25.** Defeated in 1945 in the first postwar election, 77-year-old Winston Churchill and his Conservative party return to power with an 18-seat parliamentary majority. The new government faces difficult conditions as food supplies in Britain reach an 11-year low.

**November 1.** To overcome the serviceman's fear of atomic weapons, the United States Army conducts the first simulated nuclear warfare maneuver at Yucca Flat, Nevada. Some 5,000 men from the army, navy, and air force crouch in trenches 6 miles away, covering their heads for protection against the force and heat of the blast.

After the 21-kiloton explosion, they walk through to the test site. If the radiation badges worn by some show an excessive dose, the men brush each other down with brooms. (Still, the badges fail to measure the radioactive dust in the air or drinking water.) The soldiers wear their regular uniforms; AEC personnel wear protective clothing.

**November 8.** During the year, U.S. defense production has equaled the highest levels of W.W.II. To guarantee supplies of materials, the National Production Authority further restricts civilian manufacturing. Auto makers, for instance, are forbidden to retool for major style changes.

**December 4.** To counteract racism, an executive order implements the nondiscrimination clauses in government contracts. In response to criticism from the South, Truman points out that such clauses have been mandatory for nearly 10 years. The president appoints a federal commission to supervise compliance, but the NAACP maintains that the body lacks the power of enforcement.

**December 21.** An explosion rocks a section of New Orient Mine No. 2 in West Frankfort, Illinois, killing 119 of 281 miners. Six months ago, federal inspectors recommended that older sections of the mine be closed off to prevent methane gas seepage. Not required by law to obey, the Wilmington & Franklin Coal Co. chose to ignore the recommendation. Next year, Congress will authorize inspectors to close down a dangerous mine.

**More news.** Shockingly ill-prepared for Nazi aggression, the nations of Western Europe organize against a possible Soviet invasion. With the help of the CIA and the British secret service, NATO develops a secret paramilitary network with stockpiled weapons and explosives ("Gladio" in Italy, "Red Fleece" in Belgium, "Rose in the Wind" in France.) During the decade, more countries will join the clandestine operation.

## Obituaries

**Joseph Clovese** (circa 1844–July 13, 1951). The last surviving Negro veteran of the Civil War deserted his plantation master to join up as a drummer boy. He later enlisted in a Negro unit.

**Will Keith Kellogg** (April 7, 1860–October 6, 1951). The accidental discovery of corn flakes in the early 1900s formed the basis of his cereal empire. In 1930, he founded the philanthropic W. K. Kellogg Foundation, which has thus far spent $32 million.

**Nellie McClung** (October 20, 1873–September 1, 1951). As one of the Famous Five, the Canadian author and suffragette embarked on a decade-long legal battle to convince the British Privy Council (at that time Canada's highest court) that women were legally "persons" under the British North America Act. On October 18, 1929, the court ruled in their favor.

**Philippe Pétain** (April 24, 1856–July 23, 1951). As vice premier of France in 1940, the old soldier capitulated to the Nazis then headed the collaborationist Vichy government. He was tried for treason in 1945 and sentenced to death, but de Gaulle commuted his sentence to life imprisonment.

# BEGINNINGS AND ENDINGS

## News

**January 16.** Ending the use of "recruit," the U.S. Army gives all new soldiers the rank of private.

**March 28.** In the first such arrangement with a noncountry, the United States agrees to honor U.N. stamps for local deliveries.

**May 15.** AT&T becomes the first corporation in the world to count one million stockholders.

**May 26.** In 1,000 centers across the United States, 175,000 young men take the nation's first test for draft deferment. On March 31, President Truman had authorized draft exemption for students with a high scholastic standing or a passing mark on the aptitude test.

**May 29.** Flying a single-engine converted P-51, 41-year-old Charles Blair, Jr., completes the first solo flight across the North Pole. He took 10 hours and 29 minutes to fly from Norway to Alaska.

**July 23.** The Supreme Headquarters Allied Powers in Europe (SHAPE) is established 15 miles west of Paris. Commander Gen. Eisenhower points out that SHAPE is the first international military effort created to "preserve peace and not to wage war."

**November 29.** The first underground nuclear test is held, at Frenchman Flat in Nevada. Witnesses see debris rise in two columns and a cloud form above the test site.

**December 27.** Cincinnati takes delivery of the nation's first right-hand-drive automobile designed for mail delivery.

**More news.** In Britain new black-and-white zebra crossings require drivers to stop if a pedestrian steps off the curb.

## New Products and Businesses

Earl Tupper sells his temperature-resistant, food storage containers directly to householders. Within three years, 19,000 salespeople are holding in-home Tupperware parties.

---

*Statistics*: While Americans eat just 1 percent fewer calories than 30 years ago, per capita consumption of flour has dropped 27 percent.

---

Gerber Products Co. begins adding MSG to its baby foods.

On October 1, the Japanese establish their first national overseas airline, Japan Airlines (JAL).

This year, the American hotel industry notes a significant trend. Many resorts that previously stayed open for either the summer or winter months now accept reservations year-round.

# SCIENCE AND TECHNOLOGY

## *News*

**June 14.** Dedicated today at the Census Bureau in Philadelphia, UNIVAC (Universal Automatic Computer) is the first general-purpose electronic computer manufactured for commercial sale. John W. Mauchly and John Eckert designed the computer, but a shortage of funds forced them to sell the patent to Remington Rand. In 1963, UNIVAC will be retired and placed on display at the Smithsonian.

**June 23.** A report presented to the American Astronomical Society suggests that radiation outbursts from the edge of the sun may cause the disturbances noted in the earth's ionosphere.

**September 29.** At the Mt. Wilson Observatory in California, Seth Nicholson sights the 12th moon of Jupiter. He discovered another Jupiter satellite in 1914 and two more in 1938.

**October 9.** Researchers from the Hines Veterans Hospital and the University of Illinois use normal blood vessels from other parts of the body to replace hardened leg arteries.

**November.** A clinic of the Ontario Cancer Foundation is the first to use the cobalt "bomb" for radiation treatment. The patient is briefly exposed

*Students participate in New York City's first atomic bomb safety drill.*

when a window opens at the end of the 3.5-ton lead-lined steel tube.

**November 10.** An 18-second conversation between the mayors of Englewood, New Jersey, and Alameda, California, inaugurates telephone coast-to-coast direct-dial service.

> *Statistics:* New York and other large U.S. cities double the cost of a phone call, from 5 cents to 10 cents.

**December 5.** The Holger Nielsen method of artificial respiration (back-pressure, arm-lift) officially replaces the method of prone pressure used in the United States for the past 24 years. The Danish technique is already used throughout Europe.

**More news.** Tired of washing diapers, American Marion Donovan cuts up a shower curtain to make the Booter disposable diaper. When manufacturers reject the concept as too expensive, she finances production herself and eventually sells the company for $1 million.

> *Statistics:* Since 1920, the infant mortality rate has dropped from 85.8 per 1,000 live births to 29.2 per 1,000.

• Johns Hopkins Hospital in Balitmore experiments with group psychotherapy. Patients reportedly help each other in solving emotional problems.

• In his book *Numbers in Color*, Belgian educator Emile-Georges Cuisenaire teaches children how to count by matching a single color to a set length (1–10 centimeters). Schools throughout the world will adopt Cuisenaire rods.

• After test irradiation (24–40 hours), milk remains sterile for three weeks.

• Chrysler offers power steering in Crown Imperial sedans and convertibles. (Francis Wright's mechanism was used in U.S. armored vehicles during W.W. II. The 1926 patent has expired.) Reportedly, the hydraulic system requires one-fifth of the effort demanded by conventional steering.

• Cornell University adopted the army's intensified method of language instruction in 1946. Spoken exercises, including inexpensive records in a language lab, make up one-third of the lessons. This year's positive evaluation assures widespread adoption.

• With tiny Mini-Max batteries from National Carbon, Kalart produces a compact power pack for flash photography. In 1937, American flash-lamp sales totaled 6.5 million; this year, 400 million are purchased.

• Stanford physicist Edward Ginzton uses electronic means to set the speed of light at 186,280 miles per second. Earlier, less precise methods established the speed at 186,272 miles per second.

## Other Discoveries, Developments, and Inventions

Antibiotic neomycin, which offers dramatic treatment for urinary tract infections
Valeteria, or automatic clothes-pressing unit
Kalashnikov assault rifle in the USSR
Squeezit plastic bottles for food and household items

## Obituaries

**Ferdinand Porsche** (September 3, 1875–January 30, 1951). The German designer emphasized simplicity of operation and maintenance in creating the Volkswagen in 1933. But the auto pioneer dies before the Volk auto, or "people's car," becomes an international success story.

**Lincoln Ellsworth** (May 12, 1880–May 26, 1951). The polar explorer claimed more than 300,000 square miles of territory for the United States during his 1935 flight over the Antarctic.

## THE ARTS

February 3—*The Rose Tattoo*, with Maureen Stapleton, Eli Wallach (306 perfs.)
March 29—*The King and I*, with Gertrude Lawrence, Yul Brynner (1,246 perfs.)
October 24—*The Fourposter*, with Jessica Tandy, Hume Cronyn (632 perfs.)

November 1—*Top Banana*, with Phil Silvers (350 perfs.)

## Tony Awards

Actor (Dramatic)—Claude Rains, *Darkness at Noon*

Actress (Dramatic)—Uta Hagen, *The Country Girl*

Actor (Musical)—Robert Alda, *Guys and Dolls*

Actress (Musical)—Ethel Merman, *Call Me Madam*

Play—*The Rose Tattoo*

Musical—*Guys and Dolls*

## News

**February 16.** Lotte Lehmann, one of the greatest singers of the German repertory, retires just before her 63rd birthday. The soprano moved to the United States when the Nazis came to power.

**October 26.** U.S. immigration authorities refuse to admit French composer-conductor Emmanuel Rosenthal because the woman accompanying him is not his wife.

**November 7.** In Washington, new management at the National Theater eliminates racial segregation to end a 2½-year boycott by the Actors' Equity Association.

**November 12.** Last year Celia Franca, principal dancer and ballet-mistress of England's Metro Ballet, accepted an invitation to found a company in Toronto. Today the National Ballet of Canada gives its first public performance—in the auditorium of an Eaton's department store.

## Obituaries

**Fanny Brice** (October 29, 1892–May 29, 1951). A Ziegfeld Follies' singer and comedienne, Brice introduced her most famous character—little Baby Snooks—on radio in the late 1930s. Her early life and second marriage to gambler Nicky Arnstein will be portrayed in the 1960s musical *Funny Girl*.

**Sigmund Romberg** (July 29, 1887–November 9, 1951). One of the great names in musical theater, the Hungarian-born composer remains best known for the operettas *Maytime* (1917), *The Student Prince* (1924), and *The Desert Song* (1926).

**Arnold Schoenberg** (September 13, 1874–July 13, 1951). The Austrian-American's innovative 12-tone system, created between 1914–1924, produced strident, often grating, compositions that outraged contemporary audiences. But Schoenberg, along with Igor Stravinsky, revolutionized 20th-century music.

## WORDS

Rachel Carson, *The Sea Around Us*

James Jones, *From Here to Eternity*

Pär Fabian Lagerkvist, *Barrabas*

Catherine Marshall, *A Man Called Peter*

James A. Michener, *Return to Paradise*

Nicholas Monsarrat, *The Cruel Sea*

J. D. Salinger, *The Catcher in the Rye*

Herman Wouk, *The Caine Mutiny*

## News

**August 13.** The longest teletype channel in the world (9,000 miles) delivers an Associated Press (AP) report directly from New York to newspaper subscribers in Tokyo.

Two months ago, AP began using a teletypesetter to send the main news to U.S. afternoon papers. (The tape, run through linecasting machines, automatically sets the type.) This trunk service is extended in November to morning papers.

**More news.** After hardcover publishers reject Harry Bennett's account of his years with Henry Ford, a paperback company puts *We Never Called Him Henry* on the best-seller list. The book's astonishing success makes several established writers reconsider softbound publication. Currently, paperbound reprints of hardcover originals sell for 25 cents.

• Just before the onset of the Great Depression, the inflated rare book market saw an annotated *Queen Mab* (1813), by Percy Bysshe Shelley, sell for $68,000. A 1951 auction fetches just $8,000.

## Cartoons and Comics

**March.** Inspired by his 5-year-old son and a remark by his wife Alice—"Your son is a menace!"—

30-year-old Henry (Hank) Ketcham creates the comic strip *Dennis the Menace.*

**More news.** Imitations of EC horror titles create widespread controversy, with their emphasis on sex and violence.

• This year, Classics Illustrated switches to a major distributor and replaces line-drawn covers with paintings. With marketing savvy (as 15-cent books rather than 10-cent comics) and their unassailable content, Classics prospers as other series fold. The line was started in October 1941, by Gilberton Co., with *The Three Musketeers.* Owner Albert L. Kanter wanted to expose children to the great works of literature. Each issue still advises: "Don't miss the enjoyment of reading the original, obtainable at your school or public library."

### TIME *Man of the Year*

Mohammed Mossadegh

### New Words and Phrases

Air-Evac (air evacuation of wounded soldiers)
brainwashing
bug (slang for a lottery)
chicken (dangerous game in which two teenagers drive cars straight toward each other; the one who turns aside is "chicken")
fly-past (British ceremonial parade of planes)
frogman
ground zero (the point directly under a nuclear explosion)
hard core (the crucial or essential part)
influence peddler
paramedic
petrochemical
to quarterback (to direct)
roadblock
roll-forwards—price increases
target date
whomp

### Obituaries

**Dorothy Dix** (November 18, 1861–December 16, 1951). By the end of her career, an estimated 60 million Americans followed Dix's syndicated column for the lovelorn.

**Lloyd C. Douglas** (August 27, 1877–February 13, 1951). One of the most popular novelists of his day, the Lutheran minister remains best known for *The Robe* (1942).

**André Gide** (November 22, 1869–February 19, 1951). A leading French writer in this century—essays, poetry, fiction, drama, criticism—Gide won the 1947 Nobel prize for literature.

**James Norman Hall** (April 22, 1887–July 5, 1951). The American writer wrote the Bounty trilogy with Charles Nordhoff.

**William Randolph Hearst** (April 29, 1863–August 14, 1951). A dominant figure in U.S. journalism for more than 50 years, the newspaper magnate relied on mass appeal—characterized by some as sensationalism—to build a media empire.

**Sinclair Lewis** (February 7, 1885–January 10, 1951). His remarkable sense of American life in five enormously successful novels—*Main Street* (1920), *Babbitt* (1922), *Arrowsmith* (1925), *Elmer Gantry* (1927), and *Dodsworth* (1929)—brought Lewis the 1930 Nobel prize in literature. (He was the first American to receive the prize.) Critics regard his later novels as lesser works.

## FASHION

### Haute Couture

Designers raise skirt lengths to 13–15 inches from the ground, crop long sleeves well above the wrist, highlight the bosom with a draped, empire line, and emphasize the waist with fuller skirts (some over crinolines and petticoats). Still, most women opt for the straight silhouette in suits and dresses.

### News

**March 21.** In 1941, John Whinfield of the Calico Printers Association in England developed the world's first polyester fibers. Du Pont, which obtained exclusive U.S. rights in 1946, unveils Dacron today at a press conference. The new synthetic—after 67 days of wear, an on-the-spot dunking in a swimming pool, and a machine washing—needs no ironing. The first Dacron suits will appear next year, and the drip-dry fabric will revolutionize shirts and trousers.

**More news.** Inflated by the Korean War, the raw wool market bottoms out. Consumers reject high-priced clothing, mills wait for prices to stabilize, and many factories cut back to part-time.

• After extensive research, the U.S. Armed Forces adopts specialized clothing including cold-weather garments with layered dead-air space for warmth.

## Colors and Materials

Texture plays a major role this year with the emphasis on pure silks and light bulky wools.

The high price of woolens and worsteds and the shortage of tropical fabrics give synthetics (largely rayons and acetates) an increasing share of the market.

Color eclipses black—including the inevitable black dinner dress—and gray replaces the standard navy-blue or black suit.

## Clothes

A revival of interlinings and featherboning creates a firm "body" for dresses.

Women show interest in separate skirts and blouses, with individual tastes reflected in unusual fabric combinations.

With more living rooms centering around the TV set, separates promote "at-home" fashions.

Women spurn long evening dresses for short styles in rich, often embroidered, fabrics.

Throughout the decade, trim high-waisted slacks end just above the anklebone; the more expensive ones are lined. Still, girls usually choose pedal-pushers.

Both full and fitted coats display large, picturesque pockets and collars.

## Accessories

Many women abandon cotton gloves for fast-drying nylon, even though the synthetic fabric proves hotter.

Pearls or scarves fill out the neckline of jackets too tight to allow a blouse underneath.

Hats remain petite but continue to migrate on the head, usually perching at the front, side, or back. Evening styles add a contour veil with glittering jewels. Crazy beach hats, costing $6–$20, add ornaments on top—burros and riders, little chairs, tables, brooms.

Long daytime shoes, with pointed, closed toes, sit on narrow heels. Jewel-covered strip sandals appear at night.

## Hair and Cosmetics

Some women downplay their eyes with natural brows and lighter makeup, but doe eyes remain in vogue for much of the first half of the decade.

At the end of the year, the poodle cut brings back short hair. But teenagers pull their hair back into an elastic band and "pony tail" enters the American vocabulary.

## Obituaries

**Charles Nessler** (c. 1873–January 22, 1951). The Swiss inventor gave his first lecture on the theory of the permanent wave in 1905. Four years later, he replaced electric irons with a machine. Nessler immigrated to the United States in 1915 and charged $120 for a perm before selling out in 1928. He also invented false eyelashes.

# POPULAR MUSIC

"Because of You"—Tony Bennett
"The Tennessee Waltz"—Patti Page
"Too Young"—Nat King Cole
"How High the Moon"—Les Paul & Mary Ford
"Cold, Cold Heart"—Tony Bennett
"Be My Love"—Mario Lanza
"If"—Perry Como
"Come On-a My House"—Rosemary Clooney
"My Heart Cries for You"/"The Roving Kind"—Guy Mitchell
"It's No Sin"—Eddy Howard/Four Aces
"Hello, Young Lovers"—Gertrude Lawrence

"In the Cool, Cool of the Evening"—Bing Crosby

"The Loveliest Night of the Year"—Mario Lanza

"Mockin' Bird Hill"—Les Paul & Mary Ford

"On Top of Old Smokey"—Weavers

"My Truly, Truly Fair"—Guy Mitchell

"Jezebel"—Frankie Laine

"Tell Me Why"—Four Aces

## News

**This year.** Al Alberts organized the Four Aces in 1949. This year, the group scores its first hit with "It's a Sin."

• Ross Bagdasarian composes the music and his cousin, playwright William Saroyan, writes the lyrics on a dare. The Armenian dialect makes "Come On-a My House" a novelty hit.

• Jazz pianist Dave Brubeck forms his first quartet. By 1958, Paul Desmond, Joe Morello, and Gene Wright will make up the classic Brubeck quartet.

• Two recording techniques revolutionize the music industry in 1951. Les Paul and his wife Mary Ford use multitrack voices and guitar on "Mockin' Bird Hill." Patti Page, in her smash hit "Tennessee Waltz," harmonizes with her own voice in a pre-recorded independent melody.

*Statistics:* $33^1/_3$'s capture 30 percent of record sales this year.

• Songwriter Carl Sigman adds lyrics to "Melody," an instrumental piece written and published in 1912 by Charles Gates Dawes, a future vice-president of the United States (1925–1929). Tommy Edwards records the song as "It's All in the Game."

*New Recording Artists*

Tony Bennett
Ray Charles
Rosemary Clooney
Clovers
Four Aces
Mario Lanza
Johnnie Ray

## Obituaries

**Henry W. Armstrong** (July 22, 1879–February 28, 1951). The composer and his lyricist Richard Girard sold their rights to "Sweet Adeline" (1903) for $5,000. The barbershop favorite has thus far earned $2 million.

**Eddy Duchin** (April 1, 1909–February 9, 1951). His sweet piano style and good looks made Duchin's orchestra one of America's most popular. He died of leukemia.

**Herman Hupfeld** (February 1, 1894–June 8, 1951). His best known composition remains "As Time Goes By" (1931), the song featured in the 1943 movie *Casablanca.*

**Egbert A. Van Alstyne** (March 5, 1882–July 9, 1951). His more than 500 popular songs included "In the Shade of the Old Apple Tree" (1905) and "That Old Girl of Mine" (1912).

## MOVIES

*The African Queen* (d. John Huston; color)—Humphrey Bogart, Katharine Hepburn

*Alice in Wonderland* (Disney; color; animated)—Voices: Kathryn Beaumont (Alice); Ed Wynn (Mad Hatter); Sterling Holloway (Cheshire Cat)

*An American in Paris* (d. Vincente Minnelli; color)—Gene Kelly, Leslie Caron

*A Christmas Carol* (British, d. Brian Desmond Hurst; bw)—Alastair Sim

*Cry, the Beloved Country* (British, d. Zoltan Korda; bw)—Canada Lee, Charles Carson, Sidney Poitier

*The Day the Earth Stood Still* (d. Robert Wise; bw)—Michael Rennie, Patricia Neal, Hugh Marlowe

*Death of a Salesman* (d. Laslo Benedek; bw)—Fredric March, Mildred Dunnock, Kevin McCarthy, Cameron Mitchell

*The Desert Fox* (d. Henry Hathaway; bw)—James Mason, Cedric Hardwicke, Jessica Tandy, Luther Adler

*Detective Story* (d. William Wyler; bw)—Kirk Douglas, Eleanor Parker, William Bendix, Lee Grant

*The Enforcer* (d. Bretaigne Windust; bw)—Humphrey Bogart, Zero Mostel

*The Lavender Hill Mob* (British, d. Charles Crichton; bw)—Alec Guinness, Stanley Holloway, Sidney James, Alfie Bass

*People Will Talk* (d. Joseph L. Mankiewicz; bw)—Cary Grant, Jeanne Crain

*A Place in the Sun* (d. George Stevens; bw)—Montgomery Clift, Elizabeth Taylor, Shelley Winters

*Quo Vadis?* (d. Mervyn LeRoy; color)—Robert Taylor, Deborah Kerr, Peter Ustinov, Leo Genn

*Rashomon* (Japanese, d. Akira Kurosawa; bw)—Toshiro Mifune, Machiko Kyo

*The Red Badge of Courage* (d. John Huston; bw)—Audie Murphy, Bill Mauldin, John Dierkes

*Show Boat* (d. George Sidney; color)—Kathryn Grayson, Howard Keel, Ava Gardner, Joe E. Brown, Marge and Gower Champion, William Warfield

*Strangers on a Train* (d. Alfred Hitchcock; bw)—Farley Granger, Robert Walker

*A Streetcar Named Desire* (d. Elia Kazan; bw)—Vivien Leigh, Marlon Brando, Kim Hunter, Karl Malden

*The Thing* (d. Christian Nyby; bw)—Kenneth Tobey, James Arness, Margaret Sheridan, Robert Cornthwaite

## Academy Awards

**March 29.** This year, the Special Awards change to Honorary and Other Awards. The host is Fred Astaire.

Best Picture—*All About Eve*

Best Actor—José Ferrer (*Cyrano de Bergerac*)

Best Actress—Judy Holliday (*Born Yesterday*)

Best Director—Joseph L. Mankiewicz (*All About Eve*)

Best Supporting Actor—George Sanders (*All About Eve*)

Best Supporting Actress—Josephine Hull (*Harvey*)

Best Song—"Mona Lisa" from *Captain Carey, USA*

Honorary Awards—Louis B. Mayer *The Walls of Malapaga* (Franco-Italian)

Broadway dominates this year's awards, as José Ferrer, Judy Holliday, and Josephine Hull receive Oscars for re-creating their original stage roles. (Ferrer, investigated by HUAC for his alleged Communist sympathies, was not expected to win.)

Glamorous Marlene Dietrich, climbing the stage stairs to present an Oscar, nearly stops the show as a knee-high slit in her evening gown reveals her legendary legs.

## News

**February 9.** A *New York Times* photo shows the mysterious Greta Garbo receiving her American citizenship. In 1925, the 20-year-old Swedish actress arrived in Hollywood. Just 16 years later, after 24 U.S. films, she retired an international star.

**July 5.** *Time* discontinues the 16-year-old "March of Time" newsreels, to concentrate on television and occasional theatrical films.

**August 6.** Warner Bros. celebrates the 25th anniversary of John Barrymore's *Don Juan*, the first partially synchronized sound film. (The first picture with full sound, *The Lights of New York*, was produced in 1928. *The Jazz Singer*, generally believed to be the earliest, only included songs and sporadic dialogue.)

**More news.** The Automobile Manufacturers Association reports that, since the end of W.W.II, 2,100 drive-in theaters have opened in the United States.

• Biblical spectacle *Quo Vadis* costs some $7 million to make, but enormous box-office receipts guarantee a series of Hollywood copycat epics throughout the 1950s.

• Various American agencies reach an agreement on the release of *Oliver Twist* (1948). The British motion picture, barred for the anti-Semitic depiction of the character Fagin, will be shown without the offending scenes.

| Top Box Office Stars | Newcomers |
|---|---|
| John Wayne | Howard Keel |
| Dean Martin & | Thelma Ritter |
| Jerry Lewis | Shelley Winters |
| Betty Grable | Frank Lovejoy |
| Bud Abbott & | Debra Paget |
| Lou Costello | David Brian |
| Bing Crosby | Piper Laurie |
| Bob Hope | Gene Nelson |
| Randolph Scott | Dale Robertson |
| Gary Cooper | Corinne Calvet |
| Doris Day | |
| Spencer Tracy | |

## Top Money-Maker of the Year

*David and Bathsheba* (1951) (d. Henry King; color)—Gregory Peck, Susan Hayward, Raymond Massey

## Quote of the Year

"Nature, Mr. Allnut, is what we are put into this world to rise above."

Katharine Hepburn puts Humphrey Bogart in his place in *The African Queen*. (Screenplay by James Agee and John Huston; based on the novel by C. S. Forester)

Reportedly, during the filming, director John Huston promised the actress that, before she went into the water, gunshots would scare away any crocodiles. Hepburn responded, "What about the deaf ones?"

## Obituaries

**Warner Baxter** (March 29, 1891?–May 7, 1951). The Hollywood leading man was best known for his Oscar-winning performance as the Cisco Kid, in the Western *In Old Arizona* (1929).

# TELEVISION AND RADIO

## New Prime-Time TV Programs

"Goodyear TV Playhouse" (October 14, 1951–September 12, 1960; Drama Anthology)

"I Love Lucy" (October 15, 1951–June 1957; Situation Comedy)—Lucille Ball, Desi Arnaz, Vivian Vance, William Frawley

"The Red Skelton Show" (September 30, 1951–August 29, 1971; Comedy Variety)—Red Skelton, David Rose and His Orchestra

"The Roy Rogers Show" (December 30, 1951–June 23, 1957; Western)—Roy Rogers, Dale Evans, Pat Brady, Trigger, Bullet

"Schlitz Playhouse of Stars" (October 5, 1951–March 27, 1959; Dramatic Anthology)

"Strike It Rich" (July 4, 1951–January 12, 1955; Quiz/Audience Participation)

"Watch Mr. Wizard" (May 26, 1951–February 19, 1955; Children's)—Don Herbert. *Note:* In 1955, the program will move to Saturday morning where it remains until June 27, 1965.

## Emmy Awards 1950 (January 23, 1951)

Used inconsistently over the next 25 years, the term "Best" will be employed here for convenience.

Best Dramatic Show—"Pulitzer Prize Playhouse" (ABC)

Best Variety Show—"The Alan Young Show" (CBS)

Best Children's Show—"Time for Beany"

Best Actor—Alan Young ("The Alan Young Show," CBS)

Best Actress—Gertrude Berg ("The Goldbergs," CBS)

Most Outstanding Personality—Groucho Marx ("You Bet Your Life," NBC)

## News

**March 3.** Despite continuous time-slot changes, "Watch Mr. Wizard" will run for the next 21 years. Educator-scientist Don Herbert uses Ping-Pong balls to demonstrate chain reaction or a hypodermic syringe to illustrate the principles of a hydraulic lift in some 6,000 experiments. During the 1955–1956 season, an estimated 100,000 children will join 5,000 fan clubs across the United States, Canada, and Mexico.

**March 18.** Comedian Milton Berle signs the industry's longest contract, a 30-year deal that reportedly runs into seven figures.

**April 15.** "The Adventures of Wild Bill Hickock" is the first TV show based on a genuine frontier hero. With his palomino Buckshot and sidekick Andy Divine (as Jingles), Guy Madison becomes an idol for modern-day children.

In 1953, episodes of Hickock will be cobbled together in the first theatrical spin-off from a television series.

**June.** General Foods drops "The Goldbergs" after co-star Philip Loeb is blacklisted for alleged left-wing sympathies. The comic actor declared under oath that he was not a Communist, but the taint of controversy makes advertisers leery. Unable to find work, Loeb will commit suicide in 1955.

**Summer.** The cancellation of "Mr. I Magination" produces a deluge of phone calls and letters. CBS rethinks its decision—the first case of public demand bringing back a show—but a new January time slot, opposite "Roy Rogers" and "Space Patrol," spells the end for the program's simple tales of time travel.

**June 22.** After 1,000 complaints in 72 days, the FCC urges TV stations to air less crime and nudity, and fewer advertisements.

---

*Statistics:* A Cincinnati University survey finds that 92 percent of 694 teachers favor the use of television in the classroom.

---

**July 9.** For years, Freeman Gosden and Charles Correll have portrayed "Amos 'n' Andy" on radio. The characters are Negro, the actors white. To cash in on the television boom, Gosden and Correll have conducted a much publicized hunt for a black cast. Debuting tonight, "Amos 'n' Andy" outrages the NAACP, which condemns TV for portraying of Negroes as "amoral, semiliterate, lazy, stupid, dishonest, and scheming."

**September 3.** With today's debut of the 15-minute "Search for Tomorrow," CBS quickly takes the lead in daytime soaps. (Actress Mary Stuart will become the first daytime star to have her pregnancy written into the script.) "Love of Life" premieres three weeks later.

**September 4.** President Truman's speech at the Japanese peace conference, in San Francisco, marks the first coast-to-coast transmission over the 107 stations of the transcontinental microwave system. With no further need for a western production center, most Chicago-based productions are phased out. And the competition for air time quickly pushes up the cost of advertising.

**September 29.** On May 28, the U.S. Supreme Court upheld the right of the FCC to approve the CBS color system over the competitive RCA television transmission. Today, in the first exhaustive test, CBS broadcasts a football game between the universities of Pennsylvania and California. But the *New York Times*, finds the color "erratic in quality and far from true."

For that reason and others, Americans refuse to give up their black-and-white sets. Thus CBS readily agrees when the Truman administration asks the network to cease color transmissions during the war emergency. Industry insiders regard the network's decision as the end of incompatible color.

**September 30.** With a western cable hookup, Los Angeles receives the first direct broadcasts out of New York. The shows include NBC's debut of "The Red Skelton Show" and "The Fred Waring Show" on CBS.

**October 4.** Four years of pooled coverage end as the World Series becomes the exclusive property of NBC.

**October 15.** A Detroit mobile unit travels to Windsor, Ontario, to make the first international coast-to-coast telecast. Bud Lynch, announcing the arrival of Princess Elizabeth and the Duke of Edinburgh, describes the royal couple as "the heiress presumptive to the throne and her sailor husband."

**October 15.** Comedienne Lucille Ball, coming off a three-year radio run on "My Favorite Husband," agrees to a CBS situation comedy, providing that the show is filmed in Los Angeles and co-stars her husband, Cuban bandleader Desi Arnaz. Their agent suggests a pay cut to please the sponsors; Desi adds the proviso that he and Lucy own 100 percent of the show. The network agrees.

Desilu productions hires 39-year-old Vivian Vance to play the middle-aged wife of 64-year-old

William Frawley. (Vance must agree to remain 20 pounds overweight for the role.) Fred and Ethel are best friends to up-and-coming nightclub performer Ricky and his zany wife Lucy. A prime-time smash hit, "I Love Lucy" creates the mold for TV sitcoms. And CBS will later pay nearly $5 million to buy back the show's 179 episodes.

**November 18.** In the debut episode of the Sunday documentary "See It Now," host Edward R. Murrow claims, "No journalistic age was ever given a weapon for truth with quite the scope of this fledgling television." The program will move to prime time in 1952.

**December 30.** "The Roy Rogers Show" co-stars his wife Dale Evans ("Queen of the West"), Pat Brady as the comic sidekick Sparrow Biffle, and, more importantly for the kids, Rogers's beautiful palomino Trigger, Evans's buckskin Buttermilk, Bullet the "Wonder Dog," and Nellybelle the trick jeep.

A singer first, Rogers broke into movies in the 1930s. And despite, or perhaps because of, the flashy extremes of his dress, he has been the top money-maker in Western films since 1943. The action carries over to his TV series and, with a wholesome life on and off screen, the cowboy star draws hundreds of thousands of kids to his fan clubs during the 1950s.

After the show ends on NBC in 1957, CBS will rerun the episodes on Saturday morning from 1961 to 1964.

**More news.** The first automobile TV rests at the back of the front seat on a wide floor. Controls are found in the armrest, and the trunk sports an antenna.

• With an estimated audience of 30 million, the Kefauver Commission rivals World Series television ratings. The networks plan to capitalize on the unexpected daytime audience and increase the number of crime dramas in prime time.

• Hollywood refuses to sell movies to its rival. The networks, faced with unfilled air time, produce their own live plays. Since one series could theoretically present all of Shakespeare's works in a single season, producers and directors encourage young dramatists like Rod Serling, Paddy Chayevsky, and Gore Vidal.

And, with live presentations, young actors gain an incomparable opportunity to hone their skills.

### TV Commercials

Anheuser-Busch—The brewery's Clydesdale team makes its first appearance.

### Memorable Radio Programs End

"The Adventures of Superman" (February 12, 1940)

"The American Album of Familiar Music" (1931)

"Can You Top This?" (December 9, 1940)

"The Colgate Sports Newsreel" (October 8, 1939)

"Mr. District Attorney" (April 3, 1939)

"The Screen Guild Theatre" (January 8, 1939)

"We, the People" (October 4, 1936)

## SPORTS

### Winners

#### Baseball

World Series—New York Yankees (AL), 4 games; New York Giants (NL), 2 games

Player of the Year—Yogi Berra (New York Yankees, AL); Roy Campanella (Brooklyn Dodgers, NL)

Rookie of the Year—Gil McDougald (New York Yankees, AL); Willie Mays (New York Giants, NL)

#### Football

NFL Championship—Los Angeles Rams 24, Cleveland Browns 17

College Bowls (January 1, 1951)—
Rose Bowl, Michigan 14, California 6
Cotton Bowl, Tennessee 20, Texas 14
Orange Bowl, Clemson 15, Miami 14
Sugar Bowl, Kentucky 13, Oklahoma 7

Heisman Trophy—Dick Kazmaier (Princeton, HB)

Grey Cup—Ottawa Rough Riders 21, Saskatchewan Roughriders 14

## Basketball

NBA Championship—Rochester Royals, 4
  games; New York Knickerbockers, 3 games
NCAA Championship—Kentucky 68, Kansas
  State 58

## Tennis

U.S. National—Men, Frank Sedgman (vs. Vic
  Seixas); Women, Maureen Connolly (vs.
  Shirley Fry)
Wimbledon—Men, Richard Savitt (vs. Ken
  McGregor); Women, Doris Hart (vs. Shirley
  Fry)

## Golf

Masters—Ben Hogan
U.S. Open—Ben Hogan
British Open—Max Faulkner

## Hockey

Stanley Cup—Toronto Maple Leafs, 4 games;
  Montreal Canadiens, 1 game

## Ice Skating

World Championship—Men, Dick Button
  (U.S.); Women, Jeanette Altwegg (Britain)
U.S. National—Men, Dick Button; Women,
  Sonya Klopfer
Canadian National—Men, Peter Firstbrook;
  Women, Suzanne Morrow

## Kentucky Derby

County Turf—Conn McCreary, jockey

## Athlete of the Year

Male—Dick Kazmaier (Football)
Female—Maureen Connolly (Tennis)

## Last Season

(James) Cool Papa Bell (Baseball)
Joe DiMaggio (Baseball)

# News

**January.** A college basketball scandal rocks the nation this month when a CCNY player reports the
offer of a bribe. The follow-up investigation implicates almost the entire squad as well as players from
LIU and NYU. Eventually, three students go to jail
and nine others receive suspended sentences. The
judge blames the coaches and college administrators.

**February 14.** The referee stops the fight in the
13th round rather than let Jake LaMotta take any
more punishment, and Sugar Ray Robinson becomes the first welterweight boxer to win a middleweight championship. He briefly loses his title to
British and European champion Randy Turpin,
then regains it in September.

**February 25–March 8.** Nations in the Pan
American Union agreed to hold athletic games in
1942, to foster better relations in the Western
Hemisphere and to provide international competition between Olympiads, but war intervened. In
1946, general political instability forced a second
cancellation.

This year, Buenos Aires hosts the first Pan American Games. Unfortunately, with the one-year
proximity to the Olympics, many athletes, particularly U.S. athletes, will choose not to attend.

**March 2.** In the first NBA All-Star game,
10,000 fans watch the East defeat the West, 111–
94, in Boston Gardens.

**March 12.** A. B. "Happy" Chandler is dismissed.
During his six-year term, baseball's second commissioner broke the game's color bar by overriding the
owners' 15–1 vote against signing Jackie Robinson.
Chandler's action most likely played some part in
his dismissal.

**July 14.** With a win in the Gold Cup, Citation
becomes the first thoroughbred racehorse to earn
more than $1 million. In just four years, his owners
have collected $1,085,760 on 32 firsts, 10 seconds,
2 thirds, and 1 unplaced.

**July 18.** Jersey Joe Walcott knocks out heavyweight champion Ezzard Charles in the seventh. The
37-year-old Walcott—the oldest fighter to win the
title—is greeted with a 2.5-mile parade in his hometown of Camden, New Jersey. Next June, the champ
will successfully defend his title in a rematch.

**August 19.** This year, owner Bill Veeck holds
Bat Day in the St. Louis stadium and in one crazy

stunt lets some 1,000 fans decide strategy for his last-place Browns by flashing "Yes" and "No" cards (the fans beat the Athletics 5–3).

Today, the Browns' owner sends in 3'7" Eddie Gaedel to pinch hit against the Tigers. As expected, the stunned Detroit pitcher fails to find the strike zone. Number 1/8 goes to first on a walk and a pinch runner steps in. (Supposedly, Veeck told the miniature batter if he so much as tried to swing, a rifleman on the roof would pick him off.)

But Baseball's smallest player has made his first and last appearance. Just two days later, American League President Will Harridge bans all midgets.

**September 20.** Major league owners choose Ford C. Frick as commissioner. A former sportswriter, pioneer of nightly radio sports, and NL president since 1934, Frick is regarded as a resourceful advocate of the sport. His salary is $65,000 a year.

**October 3.** On August 9, a third straight victory over the Giants moved the Dodgers up 12½ games in the race for the pennant. But their loud locker-room celebration proved premature. The humiliated second-place Giants won an astounding 38 of their final 45 games to pull dead even.

In a 3-game pennant play-off, each team has won one game. Today, in the classic payback, Bobby Thomson hits "the shot heard round the world." With men on second and third, in the bottom of the ninth, the lanky third baseman slams a home run off Dodger pitcher Ralph Branca to give the Giants the National League title.

**October 26.** Rocky Marciano ends Joe Louis's attempted comeback with a knockout (KO) in the eighth. During his career, the Brown Bomber lost just 3 bouts and knocked out five heavyweight champions—Max Schmeling, Jack Sharkey, Primo Carnera, Max Baer, and Jimmy Braddock.

**More news.** This year, 20-year-old Willie Mays joins the Giants and 19-year-old Mickey Mantle signs with the Yankees. Fans ignite a decade-long rivalry between two of the sport's premiere players.

• A Brooklyn bowling alley installs one of the first automatic pin setters. Players like the quicker setup, and the recreational sport will enjoy a renaissance.

## Records

**July 1.** Cleveland Indian Bob Feller becomes the first pitcher in the modern era to throw three no-hitters.

**October 10.** Joe DiMaggio sets a major league record with his 51st World Series appearance. But the season's final game marks the end for the Yankee Clipper; he retires in December at age 37.

DiMaggio's career, like many others, was split by the war. Each season of the first half (1936–1942) saw a .300 batting average and 100 RBI. And, in 1941, he enthralled the nation with a magical 56-game hitting streak. But after losing three prime years, his second career (1946–1951) has been plagued with injuries and the effects of age. Yet, ever the consummate professional, DiMaggio has led the Yankees to four World Championships since 1947.

With defensive fielding (a lone error in 1947), power hitting (361 HR with half in the toughest ballpark for right-handers), just 369 strikeouts, and a constant work ethic, Joe DiMaggio is, in the opinion of many, the greatest player in the history of the game.

**December 9.** Los Angeles Rams quarterback Bob Waterfield kicks a record five field goals against Detroit Lions.

**This year.** George Connor of the Chicago Bears is the first NFL player named All-Pro on both offense and defense. He will repeat this remarkable achievement in 1952 and 1953.

## What They Said

On April 7, Ben Hogan finally captures the only major golf title to elude him, the Masters. He says, "If I never win another, I'll be satisfied. I have had my full share of golfing luck."

## Obituaries

**Eddie (Edward Trowbridge) Collins** (May 2, 1887–March 25, 1951). Batting titles were scarce in Ty Cobb's era, but the durable second baseman (1906–1930) hit a lifetime .333 with 3,311 RBI. In later years, as general manager and vice-president of the Boston Red Sox, Collins made one scouting trip; he brought back Bobby Doerr and Ted Williams.

# 1952

After Richard Nixon explains away a slush fund, war-weary Americans gladly sweep the Eisenhower ticket into office.

Internationally, King George VI dies, Canada falls victim to the world's first serious nuclear accident, and Britain declares a Kenyan state of emergency against the Mau Mau.

Americans make the first airplane landing at the North Pole and the British launch the first jet passenger service. Surgeons perform the first open-heart surgery, manufacturers introduce transistorized hearing aids, and Buckminster Fuller creates the geodesic dome.

Bookstores sell the tragic story of Anne Frank in an English translation of A Diary of a Young Girl, and Ernest Hemingway's The Old Man and the Sea is published in a magazine. TV networks offer new programs like "Dragnet," "Our Miss Brooks," and "The Guiding Light." Actor Ronald Reagan marries Nancy Davis and Hollywood creates 3-D to bring audiences back to the theaters.

For black Americans, 1952 marks the first year since 1882 without a lynching.

## NEWS

**February 6.** King George VI of Great Britain dies of lung cancer at the age of 56.

When Edward VIII abdicated in 1936 to marry Wallis Simpson, his next youngest brother became head of a badly shaken monarchy. But the new monarch and his queen, Elizabeth, gained the love and respect of their people, working hard at royal duties and loyally staying in London throughout heavy German bombing. Following the war, he oversaw the establishment of the British Commonwealth and the beginnings of the welfare state.

His eldest daughter returns from a tour abroad and, on February 8, takes her oath of office as Queen Elizabeth II.

**Early this year.** In an unpublished policy paper on Southeast Asia (Burma, Thailand, Indochina, Malaya, and Indonesia), the National Security Council states, "The loss of any single country would probably lead to relatively swift submission to or an alignment with Communism by the remaining countries of this group."

To prevent Communist expansion in Asia, the Middle East, and Europe, the study recommends that the United States give France military and financial aid for Indochina, assist in the development of Vietnamese armed forces. If China

*Three queens mourn their king: Queen Elizabeth II, his daughter; Dowager Queen Mary, his mother; and Queen Mother Elizabeth, his widow.*

should attack Vietnam, the response must be a counterattack. To ensure success, the government should "make clear to the American people the importance of Southeast Asia to the security of the United States."

---

*Statistics*: Since the end of W.W.II, U.S. foreign aid has totaled $38.1 billion in credits and grants. Recipients have repaid about $3 billion.

---

**February 20.** President Truman issues regulations requiring 8,000 conscientious objectors to give two years of national service.

---

*Statistics*: In August, the FBI reports having tracked down nearly 20,000 draft evaders since the passage of the 1948 Selective Service Act.

---

**March 3.** Ceded to the United States following the Spanish-American War of 1898, Puerto Rico became an American possession—not part of the United States but not independent either. Puerto Rico opposed this status and, in 1911, Washington granted American citizenship to the island's residents.

Today, the people of Puerto Rico overwhelmingly ratify a constitution giving the island Commonwealth status as a self-governing territory under U.S. control. President Truman signs the constitution on July 3.

**March 10.** Fulgencio Batista, who directly or indirectly ruled Cuba from 1933 to 1944, regains control in a military coup. Washington recognizes his government on March 27, after he pledges support for U.S. foreign policy.

**March 21–22.** A cluster of tornadoes devastates six states from Missouri to Alabama in one of the nation's 10 worst disasters. Over 200 die, 2,500 are injured, and 3,500 homes destroyed.

**April 1.** The USAF announces that all combat aircraft will be equipped to carry atomic weapons.

**April 8.** To prevent a nationwide strike, President Truman orders the federal seizure of U.S. steel mills. But the owners take legal recourse, and, on June 2, the Supreme Court finds that the president exceeded his constitutional authority. Truman releases the mills, and the workers walk out. With White House mediation, a settlement is reached in late July.

The strike slowed the war effort only temporarily, but constitutional experts believe the controversy redefined the powers of the presidency and the courts.

**April 26.** During night maneuvers in the mid-Atlantic, the aircraft carrier *Wasp* turns into a strong wind to land the last flight of planes, but the

*Hobson* fails to compensate. The minesweeper rams the bow of the carrier, breaks in two, and sinks within four minutes. Only 61 of 236 men survive. An inquiry places full blame on skipper Lt. Commander Tierney for giving the fatal order. He died in the tragic collision.

**May 26.** Pending a treaty, the United States, Britain, and France sign a peace contract with the German Federal Republic, ending Allied occupation and promising NATO protection. Still, the three retain military rights in West Germany, and Bonn must contribute to troop maintenance. (Under a separate pledge, the United States and Britain agree to maintain forces in Europe indefinitely.)

The next day, West Germany and five other European nations attempt to create a Defense Community and a joint army to counterbalance the Soviet military presence in Eastern Europe. But the French National Assembly will refuse to ratify the treaty and the opportunity for European integration will be stillborn.

**June 27.** The McCarran-Walter Immigration and Nationality Act drops racial barriers, but retains the quota system, which is based on the national origins of the existing U.S. population. (Early British immigration gives Britain a quota of 65,000 while a small Asian population gives each Asian-Pacific country a quota of 100 with a total limit of 2,000.) As well, under the new selective system, immigrants with superior education or needed skills receive top priority.

Truman labeled the bill "discriminatory," but Congress overrides his veto today. Later, an investigative commission upholds the president's judgment, branding the act as unworkable and a threat to sound foreign relations and national security.

**July 10.** Korean truce talks enter their second year of secret sessions. The major stumbling block remains the Communist demand for the forcible repatriation of all POWs. Only 70,000 of 170,000 Chinese and North Korean prisoners want to return home.

**July 11.** The Republicans nominate Dwight Eisenhower and Richard M. Nixon as their presi-

dential and vice-presidential candidates. Nixon's "Tricky Dick" reputation is overshadowed by the practicalities of his tough anti-Communist stance and the geographical balance that his California riding brings to the ticket.

**July 23.** In Egypt, the military overthrows the corrupt government of King Farouk (his seven-month-old son succeeds him but never reigns). General Mohammed Naguib will head the revolutionary government until 1954, when Gamal Abdel Nasser will assume the premiership, then the presidency.

**July 26.** President Truman announced on March 29 that he would not run for reelection. Today, at the Democratic Convention, Governor Adlai Stevenson of Illinois is nominated on the third ballot, the first presidential nominee to be drafted since James Garfield in 1880. Senator John Sparkman of Alabama is chosen as his running mate.

In accepting, Stevenson tells the delegates the party must "talk sense to the American people. Let's tell them the truth, that there are no gains without pains."

**August 4.** Rapid growth in the nuclear energy industry produces the Western world's first known uranium claim-staking rush. Through tomorrow, some 300 prospectors file claims in northern Saskatchewan. Their finds and others during the decade ahead will make this Canadian province the world's leading producer of uranium.

**August 27.** Upon his return from Alaska, General Omar Bradley confirms that radar protects the northwestern air approach to the United States. In September, Washington announces that a huge air base, under construction at Thule in northwestern Greenland, will cover the northeastern corridor. The estimated cost is $263 million.

**September 10.** Last September, the West German Parliament voted unanimously to pay reparations for Nazi Germany's "unspeakable crimes." Today, Bonn agrees to pay Israel $822 million, largely to cover the new nation's costs in absorbing displaced Jews. Next year, the West German will pass legislation to pay a further $952 million to victims of Nazi persecution.

*Statistics:* A World Jewish Congress census counts 11,672,000 Jews in 17 countries—6.4 million fewer than before W.W.II.

**September 18.** The *New York Post* uncovers an $18,000 slush fund set up by California oilmen for Richard Nixon. Eisenhower, while publicly refusing to support or condemn his running mate, privately warns him he must come out "clean as a hound's tooth."

In desperation, Nixon gives an emotional 30-minute speech on national television, on the 23rd. Detailing his early life, war record, and continuing fight against Communism, he concedes the fund exists but claims the money was only used "to pay for political expenses that I did not think should be charged to the taxpayers of the United States." (Nixon fails to point out that the electoral system requires politicians to cover their personal expenses.) The Republican nominee admits receiving one gift, a little cocker spaniel his children call Checkers, and says, "Regardless of what they say about it, we're gonna keep it."

The day after the "Checkers" speech, when thousands of Americans offer their support in telegrams and letters, Eisenhower embraces a "completely vindicated" Nixon.

**October.** During the election campaign, Republican supporters boast "I Like Ike" (a phrase used by the Democrats in 1947 in an attempt to draft the general), while scornfully branding Adlai Stevenson an "egghead." Stevenson, with typical wit, pokes fun at the GOP ploy with a parody of Marx— "Eggheads unite! You have nothing to use but your yolks."

**October 3.** Some 50 miles off the northwest Australian coast, Britain detonates its first atomic bomb. Entry into the nuclear club cost the recovering nation an estimated $560 million. The Society of Friends (Quakers) warns that the test will provoke other nations "to redouble their efforts to rearm."

**October 8.** Outside London, the Perth Express speeds into the back of a waiting commuter train.

Just seconds later, another express plows into the wreckage. An inquiry blames the Perth-London engineer, who either ignored or failed to see a warning signal. He died in the crash, along with 111 others.

**October 16.** At the first All-Union Communist Party Congress since 1939, delegates in Moscow replace the ruling Politburo with a Presidium. The party's governing group consists of 25 full and 11 alternate members; Premier Joseph Stalin is chairman.

**October 21.** Britain declares a state of emergency in Kenya and dispatches troops to the colony to combat the terrorist Mau Mau (Hidden Ones). Kikuyu tribesmen created the secret organization to drive whites and their native farm laborers from tribal lands.

Next March, a massacre of 150 Kikuyu will finally turn the tribe against them. Within two months, Kenyan courts will sentence six Mau Mau leaders, including Jomo Kenyatta, to seven years in prison.

**October 31.** About 35 miles east of Eniwetok proving ground, the U.S. detonates the world's first thermonuclear, or hydrogen, bomb. (A smaller device was tested in the spring of 1951.) The massive explosion obliterates the small coral island.

News of the test leaks out through servicemen's letters home, and President Eisenhower will finally acknowledge the detonation in early 1953. But the military edge lasts less than a year; the Soviets will conduct their own experiment next August.

**November 4.** Voters turn out in record numbers to elect the first Republican president in 20 years. Dwight D. Eisenhower and Richard Nixon carry 39 of the 48 states in a landslide victory, with 442 electoral votes.

Analysts had predicted that Truman's dismissal of MacArthur and recent Democratic scandals over "gifts" and influence peddling would translate into Republican gains. But the party manages to acquire only narrow control of Congress, and several prominent members lose their seats (including Senator Henry Cabot Lodge, to young Democrat John F. Kennedy).

At Truman's suggestion, White House representatives meet with Eisenhower's advisors to provide—for the first time in American history—an orderly and informed transfer of power.

**November 4.** An earthquake off Siberia's Kamchatka Peninsula, at 8.5 on the Richter scale, is one of the most violent in recorded history. A tidal-wave alert prevents injury in Hawaii where the largest of four waves reaches 13 feet.

**November 10.** U.N. Secretary-General Trygve Lie resigns. Since 1950, when the superpowers failed to agree on his successor, the Communists have refused to deal with Lie because of his support for the Korean police action. More recently, many censured his ready compliance with Washington's demands for the dismissal of any American U.N. employee suspected of leftist sympathies.

**December 5–9.** When a warm-air mass traps tons of coal smoke and sulfur dioxide over London, England, water condensation produces a lethal fog. The black, poisonous fumes kill some 4,000 people; another 8,000 later suffer respiratory failure. In 1956, the Clean Air Act will ban the burning of untreated coal.

**December 12.** At the Chalk River research reactor, in Ontario, an employee unintentionally releases almost 1 million gallons of radioactive water in the world's first serious nuclear accident. Three U.S. Naval officers, including Jimmy Carter, disassemble the damaged core in a 1½-minute operation. (They receive the maximum annual recommended radiation dosage.) There are no fatalities.

**December 20.** The U.N. General Assembly adopts an International Convention on the Political Rights of Women, guaranteeing women the right to vote and the right to hold public office.

**December 20.** A transport plane taking servicemen home for Christmas crashes at Larson Air Force Base in the state of Washington, killing 87 passengers and crew and severely crippling some of the 44 survivors. Over the last 1½ months, 300 people have died in nine military airplane accidents.

**December 22.** The U.N. General Assembly adopts a Uruguayan-Bolivian resolution confirming the right of nations to nationalize industries and

*U.S. soldiers crouch in a trench behind an atomic test. In the coming years, at least 210,000 men will become nuclear veterans.*

raw materials without compensation to private investors. Only Britain, New Zealand, South Africa, and the United States vote against the proposal.

**December 23.** Yielding to pressure, the AEC transfers to the Pentagon military radiological responsibility during atomic tests. Under commission authority, trenches were dug six to seven miles from ground zero. Now servicemen—without protective clothing—observe detonations from as close as two miles. As well, the Pentagon raises the maximum allowable radiation dosage to 6 roentgens, almost double the AEC personnel limit.

**More news.** An executive directive changes the Armed Forces Security Agency into the National Security Agency (NSA). Employing over 20,000 people, the intelligence organization protects American codes and gathers foreign intelligence information by monitoring all international telephone calls to and from the United States. (During the 1960s and early 1970s, other government agencies will convince the NSA to monitor antiwar activists and criminals.)

Several years will pass before Washington even acknowledges the agency's existence. A creation of the White House rather than Congress, NSA will maintain complete secrecy and be more or less immune to congressional review.

## Obituaries

**John Dewey** (October 20, 1859–June 1, 1952). One of the most influential American thinkers of this century, he made his greatest impact in education, where the pragmatic Dewey philosophy emphasized "learning by doing."

**George VI** (December 14, 1895–February 6, 1952). *See* News.

**Hugh Herndon** (October 3, 1904–April 5, 1952). In 1931, he and Clyde Pangborn (October 28, 1894–March 29, 1958) made the first nonstop flight across the Pacific—41 hours, 13 minutes in a single-engine monoplane.

**Wilfrid Reid "Wop" May** (March 20, 1896–June 21, 1952). A hero in his day, the Canadian pilot made 8 kills in W.W.I, in 1929 flew diphtheria serum to an isolated Alberta community—700 miles at minus 30° in an open cockpit—later pioneered aerial search-and-rescue techniques, and helped establish the first Arctic mail run.

**Maria Montessori** (August 31, 1870–May 6, 1952). The Italian educator won international renown for her emphasis on individual initiative over formal instruction.

**Vittorio Emanuele Orlando** (May 19, 1860–December 1, 1952). The respected Italian politician was the last surviving Big Four leader from the Versailles Peace Conference ending W.W.I.

**Eva Perón** (May 7, 1919–July 26, 1952). In 1946, within months of their marriage, the beautiful, unknown actress had orchestrated Juan Perón's election to the presidency of Argentina. She cultivated her own political following by winning for women the right to vote and by championing the poor. (The Eva Perón Foundation established thousands of hospitals, orphanages, and old-age homes for her *los descamisados*, or "shirtless ones.") For impoverished Argentineans, Evita attains near sainthood upon her death from cancer. Buried at trade union headquarters, her body will be spirited away by the military following the 1955 coup and hidden in Italy for 15 years.

**Chaim Weizmann** (November 27, 1874–November 9, 1952). An eminent chemist, the Russian-born Jew devoted his life to the cause of Zionism. He served as Israel's first president.

# BEGINNINGS AND ENDINGS

## News

**January.** An Old Age Security Pension provides $40-per-month for all people 70 and over who have been Canadian residents for at least 10 years. Previously, seniors received $20 after a strict means test. (A 1973 amendment will grant indexed quarterly increases.)

**January 24.** The prime minister of a British dominion names his choice for governor general, but Buckingham Palace appoints. Royal approval of Vincent Massey, the first native-born governor general of Canada, is interpreted by many as overdue recognition of a distinct Canadian nation.

**February 21.** The International Civil Aviation Organization issues an air-to-ground communications code for international airports. Words are assigned to each letter of the alphabet, so BTZ becomes Bravo Tango Zulu.

**April 21.** British Overseas Airways inaugurates the world's first jet passenger service, with a 4¾-hour round-trip flight from London to Rome. On May 2, BOAC establishes the first regularly scheduled commercial route, a 23-hour, 38-minute flight from London to Johannesburg.

**May.** Eleven transatlantic airlines inaugurate low-fare flights to Europe.

**May 3.** Alaska Air Command reports the first successful landing at the North Pole, a USAF ski-and-wheel-equipped C-47.

**July 1.** The AEC approves the formation of a radiation laboratory at Livermore, California. Over the coming years, intense competition between Livermore and Los Alamos will give top priority to atmospheric nuclear tests.

**September.** Pope Pius, concerned about the decreasing number of women choosing a vocation, authorizes some changes in the traditional nun's habit.

**December 30.** The Tuskegee Institute reports

that 1952 was the first year without a lynching since the earliest records in 1882.

**More news.** The army establishes the elite Special Forces to train in guerrilla warfare and counterinsurgency. The group adopts distinctive green berets but, in the mid-1950s, must give up the "too foreign" headgear.

### New Products and Businesses

Kellogg's introduces two new cereals, Sugar Smacks and Sugar Frosted Flakes.

Procter & Gamble brings out Gleem toothpaste.

Using cyclamates, Kirsch Beverages of Brooklyn produces the first successful sugar-free soft drink—No-Cal Ginger Ale.

---

*Statistics*: Due to high liquor taxes, more illegal than legal whiskey was made in the United States last year.

---

M. and R. Dietetic Labs in Columbus, Ohio, produces Pream, a powdered instant cream for coffee.

Palmer Paint Co. of Detroit uncovers a gigantic market of amateur artists for its paint-by-number pictures.

The draftsman at Balton Sign Co. adds "Holiday Inn" to the sign sketch for a new motel in Memphis. Owner Kemmons Wilson likes the catchy name. Within eight years, 280 Holiday Inns will be constructed in the United States, Canada, and Puerto Rico.

Sears, Roebuck and Co. partners with the Toronto mail-order house Simpson Ltd. to open a chain of Simpson-Sears retail stores across Canada.

### Fads

In the early 1930s, Alfred Butts invented a crossword game with wooden tiles. Entrepreneur James Brunot took over marketing in 1947 and changed the name from Criss-Cross to Scrabble. This year, when his production facilities fail to meet the huge demand, he sells out to Selchow & Righter. The Scrabble fad wanes in 1953, but the game will remain a perennial favorite.

This spring, male students carry out daring panty raids on women's dormitories in American colleges and universities. Authorities put an end to the expeditions when they eventually get out of hand.

Over 90 products promise freshness with the addition of green chlorophyll, including gum, cough drops, deodorants, socks, and toilet paper. The rage will die out late next year when scientists find nothing to support advertising claims.

## SCIENCE AND TECHNOLOGY

### News

**February 17.** Bonn University medical authorities confirm the effective treatment of rheumatism, sciatica, lumbago, and mild arthritis with ultrasound waves.

**June.** To avoid the hype and inevitable letdown following each new polio "cure," Dr. Jonas Salk secretly injects inactive strains of the polio virus into 161 youngsters at a Pennsylvania home for the handicapped. Just 2–3 weeks later, blood samples show the presence of polio antibodies.

**September 2.** At the University of Minnesota, a medical team carries out the first successful open-heart surgery, lowering five-year-old Jackie Johnson's body temperature to 79 degrees Fahrenheit to slow the flow of blood. Afterward, a 40-minute hot bath restores her circulation.

**September 11.** Dr. Charles Hufnagel at the Georgetown University Hospital fits the first plastic heart valve into a 30-year-old woman.

**November 13.** Paul Zoll of Harvard reports the first use of electric shock to treat cardiac arrest. In two instances, needles inserted into the flesh on each side of the chest conducted an impulse to the heart.

**December 1.** Scandalized U.S. newspapers report that Danish surgeons have transformed George

Jorgensen, Jr., into a woman. The 26-year-old former U.S. Army clerk, who assumes the name Christine, has undergone castration and plastic surgery for psychological relief. Jorgensen capitalizes on the notoriety to sing in nightclubs and play several minor roles on stage.

**December 25.** In Paris, a mother gives one of her kidneys to her son in the first human transplant of an organ from a living donor. But his body rejects the kidney, and he dies of uremia 33 days later.

**December 29.** The Sonotone hearing aid, introduced today, is the first consumer product to use transistors. Bell Labs, in a tribute to Alexander Graham Bell—a teacher of the deaf as well as the inventor of the telephone—has granted free use of the transistor to hearing aid manufacturers.

**More news.** U.S. chemist Stanley Lloyd Miller, working on his Ph.D. this year, adds an "atmosphere" of methane, ammonia, and hydrogen to pure, sterile water. After passing through an electrical charge for a week, he finds organic compounds and some simple amino acids—the components of proteins. His work suggests that life began on earth with the discharge of lightning through an oxygen-poor atmosphere.

• Grace Murray Hopper and her staff at Remington produce a computer "compiler" to carry out basic repetitive work. Previously, programmers had to write full machine instructions for each new software package.

• Virginia Apgar, age 43, takes five measurements at birth to check an infant's health: pulse, reflexes, respiration, color, and muscle tone. The Apgar score will often reveal prenatal problems and birthing injuries previously undetected.

---

*Statistics:* With the millions of babies born since the end of the war, the United States suffers its worst polio epidemic—57,244 new cases this year. The previous high was 42,033 in 1949.

---

• Joshua Lederberg learns that viruses can transmit genetic material from one cell to another. Since viruses could be deliberately used to introduce genetic changes, transduction represents an important step toward genetic engineering.

• American architect and inventor Buckminster Fuller creates the geodesic dome. Using aluminum or other lightweight materials and waterproof plastic, he combines 4-faced triangular pieces into 20-faced forms that, when connected, resemble part of a sphere. In 1953, Ford Motors places a geodesic dome on top of the Rotunda Building, in Dearborn Michigan, and the military adopts Fuller's invention for radar installations and shelters.

• An experimental 5-inch portable TV updates RCA applications of the transistor. At this time, each transistor costs $15–$25 to produce. RCA points out that the 21-cent vacuum tube initially cost $12.

• Robert Wallace Wilkins used Reserpine to treat high blood pressure, but noticed the drug sedated without putting the patient to sleep or impairing alertness. A welcomed alternative to barbiturates, Reserpine is quickly adopted and becomes known as a "tranquilizer."

## Other Discoveries, Developments, and Inventions

Air-conditioning unit in 1953 Cadillacs and Oldsmobiles

Tinted windshield glass, which fades out near the bottom, automatic headlamp dimmer, automatic overdrive

Movie Mite, the first 8-mm sound-on-film projector

Three-color traffic light in New York City eliminating the 3.5-second dark period between the red and green

## Obituaries

**Elizabeth Kenny** (September 20, 1886–November 30, 1952). Refusing to immobilize polio victims with casts and splints, the Australian nurse instead stimulated and reeducated paralyzed muscles. She traveled to the United States in 1940 and, with American Medical Association approval, set up the

Sister Kenny Institute in Minneapolis to train nurses and physiotherapists in her technique.

## THE ARTS

May 16—*New Faces of 1952*, with Robert Clary, Carol Lawrence, Ronny Graham, Eartha Kitt, Alice Ghostley, Paul Lynde (365 perfs.)

June 25—*Wish You Were Here*, with Patricia Marland, Jack Cassidy (598 perfs.)

October 29—*Dial M for Murder*, with Maurice Evans (552 perfs.)

November 20—*The Seven Year Itch*, with Tom Ewell, Vanessa Brown (1,141 perfs.)

### Tony Awards

Actor (Dramatic)—José Ferrer, *The Shrike*

Actress (Dramatic)—Julie Harris, *I Am a Camera*

Actor (Musical)—Phil Silvers, *Top Banana*

Actress (Musical)—Gertrude Lawrence, *The King and I*

Play—*The Fourposter*

Musical—*The King and I*

### News

**May 21.** Lillian Hellman denies being a Communist but, fearful of incriminating others, refuses to inform HUAC of her past beliefs. The most accomplished female playwright of her time, she says, "I cannot and will not cut my conscience to fit this year's fashions."

**November 25.** For her 80th birthday tribute in 1947, Queen Mary requested something by Agatha Christie on the radio. The novelist responded with a 30-minute play called *Three Blind Mice*. Since-expanded for the theater, *The Mousetrap* opens tonight in London with Richard Attenborough and his wife Sheila Sim. The murder mystery will still be running in 1975.

### Obituaries

**Gertrude Lawrence** (July 4, 1898–September 6, 1952). Equally at home in musical or straight comedy, the British actress recently achieved one of her greatest successes in *The King and I*.

## WORDS

Thomas B. Costain, *The Silver Chalice*

Daphne du Maurier, *My Cousin Rachel*

Ralph Ellison, *The Invisible Man*

Edna Ferber, *Giant*

Anne Frank, *The Diary of a Young Girl*

Ernest Hemingway, *The Old Man and the Sea*

Marie Lyons Killilea, *Karen*

Bernard Malamud, *The Natural*

Norman Vincent Peale, *The Power of Positive Thinking*

John Steinbeck, *East of Eden*

Amy Vanderbilt, *Complete Book of Etiquette*

Kurt Vonnegut, Jr., *Player Piano*

E. B. White, *Charlotte's Web*

### News

**March 11.** Newspapers report the sale of the most valuable Shakespearean collection in private hands—73 volumes of folios and quartos. Dr. Abraham S. Wolf Rosenbach received more than $1 million from Swiss banker Martin Bodmer.

**March 31.** Generoso Pope, Jr., buys the *National Enquirer* (1926) for $75,000. Announcing his intention to drop its Democratic partisanship, the 25-year-old maintains that his weekly will never become a tabloid.

**September 1.** Ernest Hemingway's *The Old Man and the Sea* appears first in this week's issue of *Life* magazine. (The author receives $30,000.) Expanded from an 18-year-old *Esquire* piece, the novella wins a Pulitzer prize.

**November 29.** Only the third authorized Protestant revision in 341 years, the Revised Standard Version of the Old Testament has sold an astounding 1.6 million copies in 8 weeks. (*Gone With the Wind*, in 1936, set the previous record with 1 million sales in six months.)

**December 4.** A West German court upholds Adolf Hitler's will leaving his estate to the Nazi party and German State. The Führer's sister, Paula Wolf, and a Swiss publisher had sought publication rights to dinner conversations recorded during Hitler's years in power. Wolf will die penniless in 1960.

**More news.** Although experts continue to debate the exact year of publication, the world celebrates the 500th anniversary of the Gutenberg Bible. Fewer than 50 copies remain of this first substantial work from a printing press.

• Protestant clergyman Norman Vincent Peale, one of the first to relate religion to psychiatry, scores an enormous hit with *The Power of Positive Thinking.* The book will stay on the best-seller list for over 175 weeks.

• Paperback binders substitute a du Pont synthetic resin for animal glue and speed up production 100 percent. But while paperbacks account for 36 percent of output, at 25 cents each, they garner just 7.8 percent of $602.5 million total sales.

• Five years ago, a Dutch publisher released *A Diary of a Young Girl.* Translated into English this year, Anne Frank's personal journal tells North American readers of the Nazi persecution of Jews.

## Cartoons and Comics

**August.** Fans buy the first issue of the satirical comic book *MAD.*

**More news.** Nicholas Dallis and Dan Heilman debut the comic strip *Judge Parker.*

## TIME Man of the Year

Queen Elizabeth II

## New Words and Phrases

bafflegab (unintelligible language used in government communications)
bamboo curtain (the "Iron Curtain" of Communist China)
clanks (jitters, nervousness)
crash job (one calling for the greatest possible speed)
creeping (used as an adjective)
cronyism

downgrade
hot rodder
miniaturization
pony tail
printed circuit
Teleprompter
telethon
walkie-lookie (a hand-held television camera)
whirlybird (a helicopter)

*Note:* A song by Al Hoffman and Dick Manning injects the phrase "Takes Two to Tango" into everyday speech.

# FASHION

## Haute Couture

In a year of transition, couturiers use crepe and chiffon to slim and soften stiffened skirts. Dior, with new developments in metallurgy, introduces a sharply pointed stiletto heel.

## News

**February.** Hubert de Givenchy, age 25, opens a couture house in Paris. Critics praise his understated, elegant styles for their "spirit of youth."

**More news.** This year, Gucci leather goods of Italy make their first appearance in the United States.

## Colors and Materials

Fashion again focuses on fabric with poodle cloth, the leading coat material, and silk, dominant in dresses. Chiffon, silk crepe, and oriental gauzes are favored for softer lines.

The wool market stabilizes by midyear, but "miracle fabrics" continue to gain in popularity (manufacturers turn out 15 million pairs of rayon trousers and just 6.7 million wool, the reverse of five years ago). As well, both men and women demand more natural-synthetic blends for better wearability.

## Clothes

Abandoned by designers, full skirts nonetheless remain popular with girls. Yet, teenagers also like the sheath, fitted closely from bust to hip, and cinched in with a wide belt.

Marilyn Monroe's well-publicized dimensions bring back the "sweater girl." Pointed bras, with circle-stitched cups and underneath wire support, achieve the desired effect. (Quite unexpectedly, the physical demands of this formidable display improve posture.) The gaudy pullovers flaunt beads, sequins, embroidery, even rhinestones.

Last year's plunging neckline shallows out into a wide arc.

With new fabrics and processes, all-over permanently pleated dresses appear on the market.

Spectators at the Olympics spot a German skier wearing pants made of a stretch-wool fabric called Helanca. Within 10 years, the manufacturer will sell 120,000 pair annually.

This year, with sport shirts outselling dress shirts two to one, manufacturers run off 8 million sports coats (compared to 800,000 in 1940). The figure drops back 10 percent in 1953.

## Accessories

Women like flat shoes, or "flatties," particularly the narrow-banded mule sandal from Italy.

The stole remains the most popular all-round accessory—fur, wool, satin, tulle.

Jewelry becomes louder and bulkier with multistrand pearls and large-loop earrings.

Milliners reshape the small hats of recent years into higher, pointed styles and relocate them in more extreme positions. During the day fashionable women don pointed turbans or helmets to conceal their hair then at night top their outfits with jeweled caps, veiled pillboxes or, following the accession of Elizabeth II, tiaras.

## Hair and Cosmetics

Many return to soft waves or long bobs. The tight curls of the less-than-flattering poodle cut demanded either a permanent or 125 pincurls every night along with a biweekly trim. Some women imitate Mamie Eisenhower's long bangs.

# POPULAR MUSIC

"Cry"/"The Little White Cloud That Cried"—Johnnie Ray

"Blue Tango" (Instr.)—Leroy Anderson Orchestra

"Wheel of Fortune"—Kay Starr

"Auf Wiederseh'n Sweetheart"—Vera Lynn

"You Belong to Me"—Jo Stafford

"I Went to Your Wedding"/"You Belong to Me"—Patti Page

"Why Don't You Believe Me"—Joni James

"Here in My Heart"—Al Martino

"Glow Worm"—Mills Brothers

"It's in the Book"—Johnny Standley

"High Noon (Do Not Forget Me, Oh My Darling)"—Frankie Laine

"I Saw Mommy Kissing Santa Claus"—Jimmy Boyd

"Lawdy Miss Clawdy"—Lloyd Price

"A Guy Is a Guy"—Doris Day

"Kiss of Fire"—Georgia Gibbs

"Slow Poke"—Pee Wee King

"Wish You Were Here"—Eddie Fisher

"Half as Much"—Rosemary Clooney

"Delicado"—Percy Faith

## News

**This year.** In the past six years, all but 4 of 162 million sellers were produced by the Big Six record companies—RCA, Columbia, Decca, Capitol, MGM, and Mercury.

• British lyricist Tommie Connor, who wrote the English words for the German song "Lili Marlene," pens "I Saw Mommy Kissing Santa Claus." Toward

Christmas, 12-year-old Jimmy Boyd's rendition sells an unprecedented 700,000 copies in just 10 days.

Until this year, Muzak had transmitted recorded music from central studios through wire-line networks to offices and industrial plants. Now, long-playing magnetic tape units make it possible to sell programs far from metro centers. As more supermarkets convert to self-service, many look to Muzak to create a friendlier atmosphere for their customers.

• This year's novelty records include the hit "Radio Bloopers." Radio-TV producer Kermit Schafer, who coined the term "blooper," puts out a series of blooper albums and writes a daily column.

• Cowboy singer and movie star Tex Ritter sings the theme for the film *High Noon*. But when preview audiences show no interest in the music, Ritter refuses to record the song for general release. Composer Dimitri Tiomkin convinces Frankie Laine to do the job.

*New Recording Artists*

Four Lads
Bill Haley & His Comets
Joni James
Steve Lawrence
Al Martino
Lloyd Price

## Obituaries

**Nat Ayer** (1887?–September 19, 1952). The British-American composer remains best known for his international hits "Oh You Beautiful Doll" (1911) and "If You Were the Only Girl in the World" (1916).

**Raymond Egan** (November 14, 1890–October 13, 1952). The Canadian-American songwriter wrote such hits as "Ain't We Got Fun?" (1921) and "Sleepy Time Gal" (1925).

**Fletcher Henderson** (December 18, 1897–December 29, 1952). One of the great pop innovators, the jazz musician organized his own orchestra and composed for himself and others.

# MOVIES

*The Bad and the Beautiful* (d. Vincente Minnelli; bw)—Lana Turner, Kirk Douglas, Walter Pidgeon, Dick Powell, Gloria Grahame

*Come Back, Little Sheba* (d. Daniel Mann; bw)—Burt Lancaster, Shirley Booth

*The Crimson Pirate* (d. Robert Siodmak; color)—Burt Lancaster, Nick Cravat

*The Greatest Show on Earth* (d. Cecil B. DeMille; color)—Betty Hutton, Cornell Wilde, Charlton Heston, Dorothy Lamour, Gloria Grahame, James Stewart

*High Noon* (d. Fred Zinnemann; bw)—Gary Cooper, Grace Kelly, Lloyd Bridges, Katy Jurado

*Ivanhoe* (d. Richard Thorpe; color)—Robert Taylor, Joan Fontaine, Elizabeth Taylor, George Sanders

*Limelight* (d. Charles Chaplin; bw)—Charles Chaplin, Claire Bloom, Buster Keaton

*The Lusty Men* (d. Nicholas Ray; bw)—Susan Hayward, Robert Mitchum, Arthur Kennedy

*The Man in the White Suit* (British, d. Alexander Mackendrick; bw)—Alec Guinness, Joan Greenwood, Cecil Parker

*Monkey Business* (d. Howard Hawks; bw)—Cary Grant, Ginger Rogers, Charles Coburn, Marilyn Monroe

*Moulin Rouge* (d. John Huston; color)—José Ferrer, Colette Marchand, Zsa Zsa Gabor

*Pat and Mike* (d. George Cukor; bw)—Spencer Tracy, Katharine Hepburn

*The Quiet Man* (d. John Ford; color)—John Wayne, Maureen O'Hara, Barry Fitzgerald, Victor McLaglen, Ward Bond

*Singin' in the Rain* (d. Gene Kelly, Stanley Donen; color)—Gene Kelly, Donald O'Connor, Debbie Reynolds, Jean Hagen, Cyd Charisse

*Son of Paleface* (d. Frank Tashlin; color)—Bob Hope, Jane Russell, Roy Rogers

*The Story of Robin Hood* (Disney, d. Ken Annakin; color)—Richard Todd, Joan Rice

*Sudden Fear* (d. David Miller; bw)—Joan Crawford, Jack Palance

*In their seventh and possibly best film together, sports promoter Spencer Tracy readies athlete Katharine Hepburn in* Pat and Mike. *Babe Didrickson Zaharias makes a guest appearance in the film, which mirrors her athletic career.*

*Viva Zapata!* (d. Elia Kazan; bw)—Marlon Brando, Jean Peters, Anthony Quinn

## Academy Awards

**March 20.** Danny Kaye hosts.

Best Picture—*An American in Paris*
Best Actor—Humphrey Bogart (*The African Queen*)
Best Actress—Vivien Leigh (*A Streetcar Named Desire*)
Best Director—George Stevens (*A Place in the Sun*)
Best Supporting Actor—Karl Malden (*A Streetcar Named Desire*)
Best Supporting Actress—Kim Hunter (*A Streetcar Named Desire*)
Best Song—"In the Cool, Cool, Cool of the Evening" from *Here Comes the Groom*
Honorary Awards—Gene Kelly; *Rashomon* (Japanese)

*A Streetcar Named Desire* becomes the first film to win three of the four acting awards, and some in-

siders believe only a sentimental vote for Humphrey Bogart prevented a complete sweep.

Since only two musicals have ever won best picture, the choice of *An American in Paris* stuns Hollywood. Critics point to the number of Academy voters who work for MGM.

## News

**March 4.** Actor Ronald Reagan marries actress Nancy Davis in California. The marriage is Davis's first, Reagan's second. He was previously married to actress Jane Wyman.

**May 26.** Reversing a 1915 decision, the U.S. Supreme Court guarantees the constitutional rights of free speech and free press to motion pictures and denies cities and states the right to censor or bar a film because it is sacrilegious.

**Midyear.** Warner Bros. and 20th Century-Fox announce the discontinuation of "B" pictures, once the mainstay of Hollywood. Studio executive Jack L. Warner claims a single $3-million picture is better business than three $1-million films.

*Business Week* reports the movie industry is keeping close tabs on TV subsidiaries set up by Columbia, Monogram, Republic, and Universal-International. Studio executives have begun to realize, with only 14 million TVs in the United States (largely in the northeast and north central regions and around Los Angeles), broadcasting expansion across the country may open a vast new Hollywood market.

**September 30.** With attendance down almost 50 percent since 1947, studio moguls use technology to compete with free TV. Opening today, the first Cinerama feature projects three simultaneously shot films horizontally across a huge curved screen—3 times the average width and 1 1/2 times as high. The realistic roller-coaster ride and other short subjects, in *This Is Cinerama*, amaze audiences, and the movie's enormous success clinches a permanent place for the wide-screen format.

**November 26.** Hollywood introduces a second, even more dramatic innovation, 3-D. To view *Bwana Devil*, with Robert Stack and Barbara Britton, moviegoers wear 10-cent throwaway glasses with polarized lenses. While hardly a new technique—filmmakers have experimented with 3-D since the turn of the century—three-dimensional images intrigue more sophisticated postwar audiences. Total first-week receipts of $95,000 break all records.

**More news.** In winning an Honorary Oscar and the Venice Grand Prix, director Akira Kurosawa's *Rashomon* opens the West to a wealth of Japanese films.

• According to the Department of Commerce, the average 1952 Hollywood movie costs $900,000 to produce, while most theaters charge 47 cents admission. Moviegoers generally spend 6 cents on refreshments at indoor theaters and 20 cents at drive-ins.

• The title *Mara-Maru* disgusts Japanese distributors, and Warner Bros. quickly recalls the picture. *Mara-Maru* is the name of star Errol Flynn's treasure ship, but in Japanese *mara* means "feces." The studio changes the title, deletes all shots of the ship's name, and returns the film to Tokyo.

| Top Box Office Stars | Newcomers |
| --- | --- |
| Dean Martin & | Marilyn Monroe |
| Jerry Lewis | Debbie Reynolds |
| Gary Cooper | Marge & Gower |
| John Wayne | Champion |
| Bing Crosby | Mitzi Gaynor |
| Bob Hope | Kim Hunter |
| James Stewart | Rock Hudson |
| Doris Day | Audie Murphy |
| Gregory Peck | David Wayne |
| Susan Hayward | Forrest Tucker |
| Randolph Scott | Danny Thomas |

## Top Money-Maker of the Year

*The Greatest Show on Earth*

## Quote of the Year

"It's no good. I've got to go back. They're making me run. I've never run from anybody before."

Marshall Gary Cooper explains to his bride,

Grace Kelly, why he must return to their dusty little western town for a shoot-out at *High Noon*. (Screenplay by Carl Foreman; based on a short story by John W. Cunningham.)

## Obituaries

**William Fox** (January 1, 1879–May 8, 1952). He combined film production, leasing, and exhibition to form Fox Film Corp in 1915. With early stars such as Tom Mix and Theda Bara, the company grew into a $200-million enterprise before its collapse in 1930. Five years later, the firm merged with 20th Century Pictures.

**John Garfield** (March 4, 1913–May 21, 1952). James Dean and Marlon Brando later copy Garfield's tough, cynical character, from the wrong side of the tracks. Critics regard *Body and Soul* (1947) and *Force of Evil* (1948) as the best performances of his 14-year career. The actor suffered a fatal heart attack and friends blame HUAC and the industry blacklist for hastening his death.

**Canada Lee** (May 3, 1907–May 9, 1952). One of the few black American actors to achieve prominence, Lee played the lead role in the British film *Cry, the Beloved Country* (1951).

**Hattie McDaniel** (1895?–October 26, 1952). McDaniel made some 300 films from the early 1930s until her death from cancer. A best supporting Oscar for her role as "Mammy" in the classic *Gone With the Wind* (1939) made her the first black performer to win an Academy Award.

## TELEVISION AND RADIO

### New Prime-Time TV Programs

"The Adventures of Ozzie & Harriet" (October 3, 1952–September 3, 1966; Situation Comedy)—Ozzie Nelson, Harriet Nelson, David Nelson, Eric (Ricky) Nelson

"Dragnet" (January 3, 1952–September 1959; Police)—Jack Webb, Ben Alexander (1955–1959)

"Four Star Playhouse" (September 25, 1952–September 27, 1956; Drama Anthology)—

Regulars: David Niven, Charles Boyer, Dick Powell, Ida Lupino

"I Married Joan" (October 15, 1952–April 6, 1955; Situation Comedy)—Joan Davis, Jim Backus

"I've Got a Secret" (June 19, 1952–April 1967; Quiz/Audience Participation)—Host: Garry Moore (1952–1964), Steve Allen (1964–1967)

"The Jackie Gleason Show" (September 20, 1952–June 1955; Comedy Variety)—Jackie Gleason, Art Carney, Audrey Meadows, Joyce Randolph

"Life Is Worth Living" (February 12, 1952–April 8, 1957; Religious Talk)—Bishop Fulton J. Sheen

"Masquerade Party" (July 14, 1952–September 16, 1960; Quiz/Audience Participation)

"Mr. Peepers" (July 3, 1952–June 12, 1955; Situation Comedy)—Wally Cox, Marion Lorne

"My Little Margie" (June 16, 1952–August 24, 1955; Situation Comedy)—Gale Storm, Charles Farrell

"Our Miss Brooks" (October 3, 1952–September 21, 1956; Situation Comedy)—Eve Arden, Gale Gordon, Robert Rockwell, Dick (Richard) Crenna

"The Red Buttons Show" (October 14, 1952–May 13, 1955; Comedy Variety)—Red Buttons

"See It Now" (April 20, 1952–July 5, 1955; Documentary)—Host: Edward R. Murrow. *Note:* An irregularly scheduled program from fall 1955, the last episode will be broadcast July 7, 1958.

"This Is Your Life" (October 1, 1952–September 3, 1961; Testimonial)—Host: Ralph Edwards

## Emmy Awards 1951 (February 18, 1952)

Best Dramatic Show—"Studio One" (CBS)

Best Variety Show—"Your Show of Shows" (NBC)

Best Comedy Show—"The Red Skelton Show" (NBC)

Best Actor—Sid Caesar ("Your Show of Shows," NBC)

Best Actress—Imogene Coca ("Your Show of Shows," NBC)

Best Comedian or Comedienne—Red Skelton ("The Red Skelton Show," NBC)

## News

**January 3.** With scripts based on Los Angeles police files, actor Jack Webb begins a seven-year TV run with the radio show "Dragnet." As Sergeant Joe Friday, he introduces police jargon and routines to the small screen. Fans across the country are soon humming, "DUM DE DUM DUM."

**January 14.** In New York, the first "Today" show opens with Chicago radio personality Dave Garroway sitting in front of a row of clocks and teletype machines. Only a single sponsor signs up for the first program, but NBC's two hours of news and interviews builds a lasting audience. Garroway will stay until 1961, John Chancellor will fill in for a year, then Hugh Downs will take over the daytime show.

**March.** With extensive TV coverage of Eisenhower's write-in victory in New Hampshire, the networks demonstrate their ability to cover news as well as, or better than, established radio and newsreel reporters. That state's primary now becomes a national barometer for the presidency.

**March 1.** In response to the growing criticism of television sex and violence, the NAB adopts a voluntary code: Shows will not sympathize with evil; degrade honesty, goodness, and innocence; ridicule figures of lawful authority; or fail to punish lawbreakers. (Alfred Hitchcock will now come on at the end of each of his programs to describe the terrible fate of any unpunished character.) Nearly 80 of the 108 stations have pledged compliance.

**April 13.** After 3 1/2 years of deliberation, the six-month TV licensing freeze finally ends. The FCC expands the current VHF band from 400 to 620 stations and makes 1,400 stations available on the ultra high frequency spectrum by opening up 70 channels (14 to 83). And, in an innovative step, the commission reserves 242 channels (largely UHF) for noncommercial educational television.

But since present TV sets lack the UHF capability, applicants battle over VHF allocations. In a year, commercial TV mushrooms from 108 VHF stations to 200, with another 200 under construction. The expansion hammers the last nail in the coffin of prime-time radio.

**June 19.** The first guest on "I've Got a Secret" confesses to a fear of mice. The contestant? Horror film star Boris Karloff. For the next 15 years, four celebrity panelists each get 30 seconds to guess the truth. Regulars include Bill Cullen, Faye Emerson, Jayne Meadows, Henry Morgan, and Betsy Palmer.

**June 30.** A radio soap since 1937, "The Guiding Light" debuts on CBS in the typical 15-minute television format. The cast continues to broadcast on radio, at a different time, for another four years. Star Charita Bauer will still be with the show in 1975.

**July 11.** The Republican National Convention, which ends tonight, was broadcast on all three networks to an estimated audience of 70 million. CBS introduces new anchor Walter Cronkite and Westinghouse makes a star of Betty Furness. She becomes the decade's most trusted spokesperson.

A postconvention television sales boom fails to materialize. Surveys show 80 percent of those polled in Boston already own a set, 76 percent in Philadelphia, and 71 percent in New York. The *New York Times* concludes, "The television set, in short, now ranks with the electric box, radio set, and telephone. It's a household fixture."

**September 1.** "Art Linkletter's House Party" debuts on daytime television. The 40-year-old emcee and ad-libber extraordinaire, who already appears in "People Are Funny," will develop still more shows. (Next year, in the periodical *Current Biography*, a former college classmate says, "He was the long-playing record of his day, and you could get him started without a needle.")

**September 6.** The Canadian Broadcasting Corporation (CBC) televises from its first station, in Montreal. Toronto begins telecasts two days later.

**September 23.** Richard Nixon, one of the first politicians to understand the campaigning poten-

tial of television, appears on screen to explain his actions, in the "Checkers" speech (see the News). Eisenhower's advisers, as well, have successfully manipulated broadcasts to show their candidate at his best. During the final two weeks, the first presidential ads flood the airwaves—20-second network spots costing $600 each.

**October 1.** Host Ralph Edwards tells his shocked guests, "This Is Your Life" as old friends, teachers, and others appear from the past. The first guest is 73-year-old pioneer Laura Marr Stone. Those who learn of the secret broadcast beforehand never receive their tribute; Joe Louis is one.

**October 3.** Ozzie and Harriet Nelson make an effortless transition from radio to television. Their family comedy holds a special appeal for younger viewers. By the time the program leaves the air, in 1966, son Ricky Nelson will be an established rock star.

**October 5.** After 11 years on radio, "Inner Sanctum Mysteries" leaves listeners with one of the medium's most vivid images—a slowly creaking door and a "Good niii-iiight. . . . Pleasant dreeeaams."

**November 15.** CBS dedicates its $12 million Television City in Hollywood. Later this year, NBC opens a facility in Burbank. The success of filmed series, such as "I Love Lucy" and "Dragnet," and the coast-to-coast cable linkup have pushed the networks into California production.

**December 30.** Called to a press conference by Bing Crosby Enterprises, Los Angeles news people watch a video recorder capture a demonstration on magnetic tape, then play it back on a standard TV monitor. The technology is expected to be available in 1954. A 15-minute show will cost about $80 to tape; currently, a kinescope costs $600.

---

*Statistics:* The U.S. television system transmits 525 lines to the inch, sharper than the British 450 lines, but less clear than the 625-line resolution adopted by most European countries and the 819 lines used by France and Monaco.

**More news.** This year, 20 Mule Team Borax sponsors the Western "Death Valley Days." (Borax is mined in the valley.) Stanley Andrews will host the program for 12 years, then Ronald Reagan (3), Robert Taylor (2), and Dale Robertson (3). The 20-year syndicated program never receives a network slot.

## TV Commercials

Timex—In one of the live torture tests, John Cameron Swayze attaches a Timex watch to an outboard engine propeller, but the timepiece slips off in the water. Later recovered, and still running, the flub makes the point.

Gillette—Sharpie the parrot tells sports fans, "Look Sharp! Feel Sharp! Be Sharp!" with Gillette razor blades.

Ford Motors—Their cartoon dog becomes the first identifiable character to be merchandised in spin-off products, including the Ford Dog doll bank.

## Memorable Radio Programs End

"The Adventures of Ozzie and Harriet" (October 8, 1944)
"Big Sister" (September 14, 1936)
"Big Town" (October 19, 1937)
"Double or Nothing" (September 29, 1940)
"The Green Hornet" (January 31, 1936)
"I Love a Mystery" (1939)
"Inner Sanctum Mysteries" (January 7, 1941)
"The Mysterious Traveler" (1943)

# SPORTS

## Winners

### Baseball

World Series—New York Yankees (AL), 4 games; Brooklyn Dodgers (NL), 3 games
Player of the Year—Bobby Shantz (Philadelphia Athletics, AL); Hank Sauer (Chicago Cubs, NL)

Rookie of the Year—Harry Byrd (Philadelphia Athletics, AL); Joe Black (Brooklyn Dodgers, NL)

### Football

NFL Championship—Detroit Lions 17, Cleveland Browns 7
College Bowls (January 1, 1952)—Rose Bowl, Illinois 40, Stanford 7
  Cotton Bowl, Kentucky 20, Texas Christian 7
  Orange Bowl, Georgia Tech 17, Baylor 14
  Sugar Bowl, Maryland 28, Tennessee 13
Heisman Trophy—Billy Vessels (Oklahoma, HB)
Grey Cup—Toronto Argonauts 21, Edmonton Eskimos 11

### Basketball

NBA Championship—Minneapolis Lakers, 4 games; New York Knickerbockers, 3 games
NCAA Championship—Kansas 80, St. John's 63

### Tennis

U.S. National—Men, Frank Sedgman (vs. Gardnar Mulloy); Women, Maureen Connolly (vs. Doris Hart)
Wimbledon—Men, Frank Sedgman (vs. Jaroslav Drobny); Women, Maureen Connolly (vs. Louise Brough)

### Golf

Masters—Sam Snead
U.S. Open—Julius Boros
British Open—Bobby Locke

### Hockey

Stanley Cup—Detroit Red Wings, 4 games; Montreal Canadiens, 0 games

### Ice Skating

World Championship—Men, Dick Button (U.S.); Women, Jeanette Altwegg (Britain)

U.S. National—Men, Dick Button; Women, Tenley Albright

Canadian National—Men, Peter Firstbrook; Women, Marlene E. Smith

*Kentucky Derby*

Hill Gail—Eddie Arcaro, jockey

*Athlete of the Year*

Male—Bob Mathias (Track & Field, Football)
Female—Maureen Connolly (Tennis)

*Last Season*

(Walter) Turk Broda (Hockey)
Lou Boudreau (Baseball)
Dick Button (Figure Skating)
(John) Black Jack Stewart (Hockey)
Clyde Turner (Football)
Bob Waterfield (Football)

## News

**February 19.** At the New York Athletic Club Games in Madison Square Garden, judges declare Don Gehrmann the winner in a close mile race. But after an examination of the photographed finish, Fred Wilt is awarded first place. Under a recent rule, the Amateur Athletic Union (AAU) permits the use of an official photo "if needed." The option now becomes a "must" in doubtful outcomes.

**February 14–25.** Norway places first overall at the Olympics in Oslo. The Americans, in their best winter showing thus far, finish second with golds from Andrea Mead in giant and regular slalom and Dick Button in figure skating. In his last year as an amateur, Button executes the first triple jump. The Canadians collect the gold in ice hockey, for the sixth time in seven Olympics.

**February 20.** The Class C Southwestern International League authorizes Emmett L. Ashford as an umpire. He is organized baseball's first black official.

**July 16.** Avery Brundage, president of the U.S.

Olympic Committee since 1929, is elected president of the International Olympic Committee (IOC). He is the first American to hold that office.

**July 19–August 3.** The Summer Olympic Games in Helsinki draw 4,925 athletes from 69 nations, including the USSR following a 40-year absence. In this first Cold War competition, the Soviets lead until the final day, when the Americans sweep ahead with an amazing 111 points. (At first *Pravda* reports a national victory, but a few days later concedes a fictitious tie.)

Outstanding individual performances include American Bob Mathias, who breaks his own decathlon record for an unprecedented second gold medal, and Czech Emil Zátopek, who wins the 5,000-meter race, the 10,000-meter, and the marathon.

Five U.S. boxing golds include one for 17-year-old middleweight Floyd Patterson. Swede Ingemar Johansson, on the other hand, is disqualified in the second round of his gold-medal heavyweight bout; he failed to throw a single punch.

**September 23.** Rocky Marciano knocks out defending heavyweight champion Jersey Joe Walcott in the 13th round of their title match. In a return bout next May, Walcott will go down at 2:25 of the first round.

**October 7.** At the Montreal Forum, Danny Gallivan broadcasts his first NHL game. In the years ahead, he will originate such words as "spinarama" and "cannonading" shot.

**More News.** This year, General Manager Branch Rickey slots 17 untried youngsters into the Pirates roster in an attempt to build a pennant team. But the "Rickey Dinks" post a whopping 112 losses and finish 54½ games out of first place. For eight of the players, 1952 marks their only year in the majors.

## Records

**December 30.** Apprentice jockey Tony DeSpirito brings home his 389th win of the year, erasing the mark of 388 set by Walter Miller in 1906.

## What They Said

"If I owned a newspaper, I'd blow that picture up to 6 or 8 columns," says an unsympathetic Commissioner Frick. The photo shows umpire Art Passarella's disputed safe call in the 5th game of the World Series.

The *New York Times* follows Frick's advice. Next day, the reproduced photograph clearly shows Yankee Johnny Sain's foot on first base as Gil Hodges stretches for the ball—still several feet away. The recharged Dodgers scored a run in the top of the 11th and won the game 6-5.

## Obituaries

**John Cobb** (December 2, 1899–September 29, 1952). The British racer is killed when his jet-propelled boat breaks up on Loch Ness; he held the world's water and land speed records.

**Wilbur Frank Henry** (October 31, 1897–February 7, 1952). In 1923, John Heisman described the Canton Bulldog as "the greatest punt blocker the game has ever known." And that year, Henry kicked a 94-yard punt, which will remain unsurpassed until 1969. The Football Hall of Fame later picks him as All-Pro for the 1920s.

# *1953*

A Republican sits in the Oval Office for the first time in 24 years. But Eisenhower, unlike his predecessors, refuses to interfere with the legislative process ("I don't feel like I should nag them"). Instead, he concerns himself with larger issues such as the conclusion of a Korean armistice.

The White House finally acknowledges the 1952 hydrogen bomb test. George C. Marshall wins the Nobel peace prize and Earl Warren is named chief justice of the Supreme Court.

International headline news includes the first successful scaling of Mt. Everest, the coronation of Queen Elizabeth II, the appointment of Dag Hammarskjöld as Secretary-General, the violent suppression of anti-apartheid demonstrations in South Africa, and the death of Joseph Stalin.

On the entertainment scene, Ben Hogan becomes the first golfer to win the Masters and the British and U.S. Opens in a single year. Playboy magazine appears on the newsstands. Hollywood brings out the first CinemaScope films and Charlie Chaplin, under scrutiny for "subversive" tendencies, leaves the United States for Europe. "Superman" debuts on TV and the entire country keeps an excited baby watch on Lucille Ball.

## NEWS

**January 2.** After an 18-month investigation, a Senate Privileges and Elections Subcommittee charges Joseph McCarthy with being "motivated by self-interest" in certain political and personal activities, but does not try to remove him from his seat.

Easily reelected last November, McCarthy now assumes the chair of the Senate Permanent Investigating Subcommittee of the Government Operations Committee. With broad authority to scrutinize government activities at all levels, he initiates hearings on the role of Communism in agencies and departments such as the CIA, the State Department, and the VOA. (During 1953–1954,

HUAC investigates Communism in entertainment while the Senate Internal Subcommittee looks at education.)

McCarthy meets no resistance from Eisenhower. The newly elected president believes in an Oval Office of limited powers and intends to avoid dissension within his party.

**January 7.** In his last State of the Union Address, Truman confirms that the United States has developed a hydrogen bomb and warns Moscow that war would mean certain ruin. Yet, despite his administration's strategic success, the president leaves the White House under a cloud. News stories of influence-peddling by friends and associates have undermined his authority while personal attempts to control McCarthyism met with either public fear or disapproval. Last month's Gallup poll gave Truman a 31-percent approval rating.

**January 15.** Quick thinking averts a disaster when the brakes fail on the Federal Express bound for Washington's Union Station. The engineer sounds warning blasts, the crew evacuates the front coaches, and the alerted station master clears the waiting room. Plowing full speed through shops and newsstands, the locomotive and first coach collapse through the waiting room floor into the baggage room below. Only 41 people are injured.

**January 20.** Dwight D. Eisenhower and Richard M. Nixon are inaugurated as president and vice-president of the United States. The first soldier-president since Ulysses S. Grant (1869–1877), Eisenhower states that America must strive for peace. "We must be ready to dare all for our country. For history does not long entrust the care of freedom to the weak or the timid."

The new president's Cabinet clearly reflects his political orientation, with lawyers such as John Foster Dulles as secretary of state, and Charles Erwin Wilson (president of GM) as secretary of defense. Wags quickly dub the cabinet "eight millionaires and a plumber." Odd man out is Secretary of Labor Martin Durkin, former president of the International Plumbers' Union. But Durkin resigns by September, charging Eisenhower with failing to keep his promise to revise the hated Taft-Hartley Act.

DWIGHT D. EISENHOWER

Born: Oct. 14, 1890, Denison, Texas, 3rd of 7 sons

Education: U.S. Military Academy (1911–1915)

Military Service: Supreme commander of the Allied Expeditionary Forces (1944–1945), commander of U.S. occupation forces in Europe (1945), U.S. Army chief of staff (1945–1948), supreme commander of NATO forces (1950–1952)

Marriage: Mamie (Mary Geneva) Doud, July 1, 1916

Children: David (b.1917–d.1921), John (b.1923)

Previous Occupations: Army officer

Legal Residence When Elected: New York

**January 31–February 1.** Hurricane-force winds push a midnight high tide over dikes in the Netherlands, flooding some 400,000 acres of reclaimed land and drowning over 1,800 people. Another 300 people drown along the British coast.

**February 6.** As U.S. inflation continues to drop, the Eisenhower administration risks removing wage controls and most consumer price ceilings. The price index rises steadily, but it peaks in mid-October without the expected runaway increases. Business enters a boom period that will extend through most of Eisenhower's tenure in the White House.

---

*Statistics:* Since 1942 per capita state taxes have increased from $29.50 to $68.04 annually.

---

**February 19.** The South African Parliament crushes the civil disobedience campaign against apartheid. (During 1952, over 8,000 blacks and coloreds were arrested, and authorities dealt severely with several riots.) The Public Safety Act empowers the government to declare a state of emergency and authority to summarily arrest and detain any person. And five days later an amendment to the Criminal Law makes passive resistance a serious offense.

As well, this year, to discourage "false expectations," the Separate Amenities Act allows local white governments to bar blacks from buses, swimming pools, libraries, and other public facilities without provision for equal black facilities. And the Bantu Education Act separates black students from whites and places black schooling under the Department of Native Affairs with new educational directives.

**March 6.** Moscow announces the death of Joseph Stalin, the undisputed leader of the USSR since 1928. In those years, he turned his predominantly agricultural nation into one of the world's greatest powers. But at what cost.

In the early 1930s, a government-induced famine took the lives of hundreds of thousands of Ukrainian farmers when they resisted collectivization. And, throughout his regime, the paranoid and neurotic Stalin used political terrorism to eliminate any opposition to one-party rule. Altogether an estimated 20 million people died under his dictatorship; at his death, labor camps still hold 12 million. (Not surprisingly, when he suffered his brain hemorrhage on March 1, high-level officials withheld medical aid for more than 12 hours.)

Before the end of the month, the Politburo forces the new premier Georgi Malenkov to surrender the post of party secretary to a group that includes Nikita Khrushchev.

**March 31.** The U.N. Security Council recommends Dag Hammarskjöld, age 47, as successor to Secretary-General Trygve Lie. The Soviet Union had vetoed the nomination of Canadian Lester B. Pearson.

**April 11.** Negotiators at the Korean truce talks reach a settlement on the exchange of sick and wounded prisoners—605 U.N. soldiers, including 149 Americans, for 6,030 North Koreans and Chinese. Returning American POWs tell of North Korean torture and brainwashing techniques; as many as 1,500 captive U.N. soldiers may have died of ill treatment. Talks resume on the 26th, but negotiations continue to stall over the question of prisoner repatriation.

**April 21.** Last week, the Eisenhower administration, "on highest considerations of national security," convinced the Justice Department to drop proceedings against five oil companies for participation in an international cartel. Today, the department files a civil antitrust suit.

In 1960, a consent judgment will require the firms to refrain from fixing prices, dividing markets, or allocating output—for 25 years.

**April 27.** Abolishing the controversial Truman Loyalty Review Board, Eisenhower establishes three-member security boards for each government agency and department. By October, when the president directs that anyone refusing to testify on the grounds of self-incrimination be fired, the stricter guidelines account for 863 dismissals and 593 resignations.

In late October, former Soviet intelligence officer Ismael Akhmedov Ege will undermine any remaining opposition to the program with his testimony before a Senate subcommittee. He will claim that 20–25 Communist spy networks may be currently operating in the United States.

**May 11.** In late afternoon, as people work at their desks, a twister cuts a 5-block wide swathe through downtown Waco, Texas, killing at least 114 people.

In June, a cluster of tornadoes kills 113 people outside Flint, Michigan. The next day, the worst twister in New England's history takes 92 lives.

Over the first six months of the year, 130 tornadoes kill 420 people throughout the United States, well above the yearly average of 150 twisters and 222 deaths.

**May 19.** At Yucca Flat, Nevada, an accident with the test shot named "Harry" sends excessive fallout east. The town of St. George, Utah, receives a dose of 6,000 millirems in one day. The Atomic Energy Commission sets the maximum level at 1,900 millirems, yet authorities broadcast, "There is no danger." This dirty detonation follows on last month's "Simon," the nation's first 50-kiloton bomb. Afterward, for miles around the site, the radiation count reached record levels.

During the spring, the AEC explodes 11 bombs in 80 days.

**May 29.** Edmund Hillary of New Zealand and Tensing Norgay of Nepal are the first men to climb Mt. Everest, the world's highest peak. Reaching the summit at 11:30 A.M., the two stop for just 15 minutes. The 34-year-old New Zealander takes off his oxygen mask for pictures, and the 42-year-old Nepalese climber leaves behind a Buddhist offering of bars of chocolate and packages of biscuits as well as the flags of Britain, Nepal, and the United Nations.

Upon their return Hillary describes the pinnacle as "a symmetrical, beautiful snow cone," but at that extreme height the view was "unspectacular."

The British expedition required 362 porters and

10,000 pounds of baggage for the 80-day ascent from Nepal (10 previous expeditions had approached from the Tibet side). The group offers the feat as a coronation gift for Queen Elizabeth. Buckingham Palace announces the achievement on June 1, and the Queen knights Hillary on June 6.

**June 2.** Queen Elizabeth II is crowned by the Archbishop of Canterbury at Westminster Abbey. Representatives from most nations of the world attend the 2½-hour ceremony, while the people of the Commonwealth and British colonies hold their own day-long celebrations.

The millions lining the route for a glimpse of Elizabeth in her four-ton gilded coach, refuse to let heavy rains dampen the festive atmosphere. Afterward, at Buckingham Palace, the new Queen makes six balcony appearances, until midnight.

Unlike her son, four-year-old Prince Charles, Elizabeth was not destined for the throne. Only when her Uncle Edward abdicated in 1936 and her father George became king, did she become heir.

**June 14.** The State Department, in response to an attack by Senator Joseph McCarthy, has purged all its overseas books and materials by "Communists, fellow travelers, et cetera." In a speech today at Dartmouth College, Eisenhower warns graduates not to join the book burners. "Don't think you are going to conceal faults by concealing evidence that they ever existed," he says.

Afterward the president explains that he opposes the removal of non-Communist books simply because they are controversial. The comments, widely interpreted as an attack on McCarthy, are Eisenhower's first public criticism of the senator.

**June 17.** An East Berlin protest against increased construction quotas quickly escalates into a nationwide workers' strike. East Germans deeply resent the forced collectivization of agriculture and poor working conditions under Communism. When local police fail to control the rioting, Soviet troops move in and declare martial law. At least 38 Berliners die.

But food shortages persist, and President Eisenhower promises relief. In late July, on the first day of the U.S. program, over 100,000 East Ger-

mans defy authorities and cross over into West Germany. Their food packages include lard, flour, four cans of condensed milk, and 2 pounds of dried peas or beans. In one and a half months, the Americans hand out 4 million free parcels.

**June 18.** Flying out of Tokyo to Korea, the pilot of a huge USAF C124 Globemaster reports "one engine out . . . returning to field." Just minutes later, the four-engine double-decker lies burning in a rice paddy, and 129 American servicemen die in the world's worst air crash. The air force grounds all C124's, but the cause of the crash is never discovered.

**June 19.** Julius and Ethel Rosenberg walk to the electric chair in Sing Sing Prison after the U.S. Supreme Court, for the seventh and last time, refuses to hear their appeal.

Scientists claim David Greenglass, the man who allegedly provided the Rosenbergs with atomic information, was incapable of transmitting the complex scientific data. The White House has received hundreds of thousands of letters from around the world asking for a stay of execution. But Eisenhower, convinced the couple deliberately betrayed the nation, has denied clemency. (The attorney general offered to reduce the sentence to life with an admission of guilt; the Rosenbergs refused.) Their co-conspirators all received jail terms.

Justice Hugo Black, in dissenting with the Supreme Court decision, wrote, "There may always be questions as to whether these executions were legally and rightfully carried out."

**June 22.** On the eve of the 44th Annual NAACP Convention, Executive Secretary Walter White announces the organization's abandonment of the "separate but equal" philosophy for "total integration." On the 27th, delegates call on Eisenhower to fulfill his campaign promise to eliminate Negroes' "second-class citizenship."

**July 26.** Fidel Castro, a 26-year-old lawyer and son of a sugar planter, leads 170 followers in an attack on the Moncada barracks in Cuba. At least 69 soldiers die, but the coup attempt fails. The Batista government imprisons the rebels, rounds up hundreds of political suspects, and suspends constitutional guarantees. Freed in 1955 as part of a general amnesty, Castro will leave Cuba to organize a guerrilla campaign.

**July 27.** Finally conceding the issue of prisoner repatriation, the North Koreans sign an armistice. (U.N. representatives omit the traditional handshake.) International analysts believe the recent turmoil surrounding Stalin's death, and Eisenhower's hint that he might use nuclear weapons provided the Communists with the needed incentive to end the three-year war. The exchange of 12,763 U.N. and 74,000 Communist POWs begins in early August.

South Korea gains 12,000 square miles above the 38th parallel and a 2½-mile-wide demilitarized zone divides the two nations in an uneasy truce. But critics charge that the cost was too high. South Korea lost 1.3 million people (the majority civilians), while North Korea lost more than 500,000, and the Chinese Communists 900,000–1 million. American losses reached 33,629 killed in action and 20,617 dead of injuries or disease; 103,327 were wounded. U.N. forces from 15 other nations suffered losses of 3,360.

Supporters claim the war kept South Korea out of Communist hands and maintained the integrity of the United Nations through "effective collective security." Most people concede the first point, but many challenge the second. Since South Korea and the United States contributed 95 percent of U.N. troops, the force could hardly be described as an international effort.

**August 8.** Soviet Premier Malenkov announces that the United States no longer has a monopoly on the hydrogen bomb. Four days later, American scientists detect a hydrogen bomb explosion in Siberia. Washington soon responds by authorizing the development of intercontinental ballistic missiles.

**August 13.** President Eisenhower establishes a 15-member Government Contract Committee to ensure compliance with Truman's executive order requiring no discrimination in government contracts.

**August 16.** Shah Mohammed Riza Pahlavi flees Iran after failing to dismiss Mohammed Mossadegh. The premier acquired dictatorial powers after lead-ing the government in nationalizing the British-controlled oil industry in 1951. But a CIA-engineered coup ousts Mossadegh on the 19th and the shah returns to power.

Within weeks, Washington grants Iran $23.4 million for technical and military projects—the largest Point Four expenditure to one country—and another $45 million for emergency economic aid. Mossadegh, sentenced to prison and then house arrest, will die in Tehran in 1967.

**September 26.** After two years of negotiations, Spain agrees to allow the construction of American military bases on Spanish soil in return for U.S. economic and military aid. The pact ends the isolation of the right-wing Franco government and clears the way for Spain to join the United Nations in 1955.

**September 30.** Following the death of Supreme Court Chief Justice Frederick M. Vinson on September 8, Eisenhower nominates 62-year-old Earl Warren. The president wants someone relatively young, "a man whose reputation for integrity, honesty, middle-of-the-road philosophy, experience in government [and] in the law were all such as to convince the United States that [he] had no ends to serve except the United States and nothing else." Warren has served as the attorney general of California (1929–1943) and governor of that state since 1943.

**October 1.** South Korea and the United States sign a mutual defense treaty in Washington. Two months later, an economic rehabilitation agreement provides Seoul with $628 million in U.S. aid for 1954. In turn, Communist China cancels the North Korean war debt and grants $317 million in aid.

**October 26.** Over the spring and summer, about 4,300 of 11,000 sheep died while grazing near the Nevada nuclear test site. The government, blaming bad weather and poor forage, refuses to compensate the ranchers. A six-month investigation will exonerate the Atomic Energy Commission, but a study made years later will prove that radioactive grass killed the animals.

**December 11.** George C. Marshall receives the Nobel peace prize for the post-W.W. II European aid plan that bears his name. He is the first professional soldier to win the award.

**December 12.** Adlai Stevenson charges that the "four freedoms" of the Roosevelt administration have given way to "four fears" under the Republicans: fear of economic depression, fear of Communism, fear of ourselves, and fear of freedom itself. Stevenson praises Ike personally, but in reference to the president's reluctance to speak out he adds, "I only wish President Eisenhower could speak for the Eisenhower administration."

**December 29.** In his semiannual report, Defense Secretary Charles Wilson predicts that even with the end of the Korean War the United States faces high defense costs and compulsory military service "for many years to come." But he warns that an excessive defense buildup could endanger American economic health.

By next June, the national debt will rise to $274.3 billion.

## Obituaries

**Carol II** (October 16, 1893–April 4, 1953). Forced to abdicate in favor of his son Michael in 1940, Romania's playboy king fled with his longtime mistress and never spoke to his son again.

**Mary** (May 26, 1867–March 24, 1953). The queen of Great Britain during the reign of George V (1910–1936) became the dowager queen mother upon the accession of her son Edward in 1936.

**Abd ul-Aziz Ibn Saud** (1880–November 9, 1953). The Arab sheik defeated rivals in the early 1920s and, on January 8, 1926, declared himself "king of the Hejaz and Nejd and its dependencies." Six years later, the country was renamed Saudi Arabia in his honor. By the time of his death, the oil concession granted to Aramco in 1933 had made him the first of the wealthy Arab rulers.

**Joseph Stalin** (December 21, 1879–March 5, 1953). *See News.*

**Robert A. Taft** (September 8, 1889–July 31, 1953). The son of the 27th president of the United States, the Senate majority leader served as a spokesman for conservative Republicans during his 15 years in the Senate. After a failed third bid for the presidential nomination, in 1952, "Mr. Republican" campaigned hard for Eisenhower and strongly supported him in the early months of his administration.

**Jonathan M. Wainwright** (August 23, 1883– September 2, 1953). In 1942, with General MacArthur ordered to Australia, Wainwright assumed command of all U.S.-Filipino forces. Hopelessly outnumbered, and with their ammunition exhausted, he surrendered to the Japanese at Corregidor. Wainwright was awarded the Congressional Medal of Honor and promoted to the rank of general; he retired in 1947.

# BEGINNINGS AND ENDINGS

## News

**January.** The New York Curb Exchange assumes the name American Stock Exchange. (Stocks were last traded from the curb in 1921.)

**March 3.** A Canadian Pacific Comet plummets to the ground on takeoff at the Karachi airport in Pakistan, killing 11 in the first fatal crash of a commercial jet liner.

**March 5.** When a Polish Air Force lieutenant lands in Denmark and applies for political asylum, Western powers get their first look at an operational MiG-15 fighter jet.

**March 11.** Mexican women gain the right to vote.

**May 2.** King Hussein I formally assumes the throne of Jordan while Faisal II is installed in Iraq. The British-educated cousins both turned 18 this year.

**May 15.** The first McDonald's franchise opens in Phoenix, Arizona.

**May 22.** Shangri-la, the presidential hideaway in Maryland, is renamed Camp David in honor of President Eisenhower's father and grandson.

**June 11.** For the first time, Harvard Law School awards a bachelor degree to a woman. (In the past, the school accepted only female masters students.)

**June 18.** The revolutionary council of Egypt abolishes the monarchy and proclaims a republic. (The royal house was founded in 1805 by

Mohammed Ali, an Albanian soldier in the Turkish army, who set himself up as viceroy.)

**August 7.** Although Ohio joined the Union in 1803, Congress never formally voted for admittance. This year, a tongue-in-cheek resolution was presented to settle "some little confusion." Eisenhower affixes his signature today.

**September 12.** John F. Kennedy, age 36, weds Jacqueline Lee Bouvier, age 24. The marriage of the senator and the former newspaper photographer is regarded as one of the year's most brilliant matches.

**September 16.** Washington conducts a nationwide test of the Conelrad system. During an air raid, "control of electromagnetic radiation" will broadcast information to the public over the radio without giving enemy planes a constant signal to fix on.

**October 6.** UNICEF becomes a permanent agency of the United Nations. The name changes to the U.N. Children's Fund, but the acronym UNICEF remains the same.

**October 6.** The U.S. Post Office inaugurates New York-Chicago air service for regular 3-cent mail. When the planes cut delivery time by 11½ hours, the post office will expand air service along the West Coast and the Eastern Seaboard within the year.

**November 29.** American Airlines inaugurates the first regular nonstop transcontinental flight, between Los Angeles and New York.

---

*Statistics:* In 1929, transcontinental service—a mixed journey by plane and train—took 48 hours. In 1940, a three-stop plane trip took 14 hours. This year, the standard time is 7 hours, 15 minutes.

---

**December 15.** In 1951, President Truman ordered stricter controls on government security information. Today, a second executive order applies uniform standards of "confidential," "secret," and "top secret" to all national defense material.

**More news.** This year, France shuts down the 99-year-old penal colony on Devil's Island. With the

brutal conditions and escape all but impossible, only some 2,000 of the 70,000 men imprisoned there ever returned.

## Government Departments and Agencies

**April 1.** A joint resolution creates Health, Education, and Welfare. The new cabinet-rank department incorporates the Food and Drug Administration (FDA) and much of the Federal Security Agency. Oveta Culp Hobby is HEW's first secretary.

**August 1.** With staff in dozens of countries, the United States Information Agency (USIA) will use books, films, and other media to foster a better understanding of the United States and its policies.

## New Products and Businesses

Pepsi-Cola and Schweppes agree to cross market their products in the United States and Britain. But FDA restrictions on the word *tonic* force the British to rename their product Schweppes Quinine Water.

The Buena Vista Cafe in San Francisco introduces Irish Coffee. Columnist Stanton Delaplane, who discovered the mix of whisky, coffee, cream, and sugar in Ireland, gave the recipe to the cafe owners.

The Seeman Brothers of New York market the first instant iced tea, White Rose Redi-Tea.

At this year's Motorama, GM receives an enthusiastic response to the experimental Corvette. To capitalize on the publicity, the auto maker opts for a quicker-to-manufacture fiberglass body. The first Big Three sports car since the end of the war, the Corvette sells for $3,513. Next year, a fiberglass top will offer weather protection.

## Fads

With the merchandise spin-off, *Life* magazine carries a 4-page spread of Roy Rogers toy guns, hats, vests, pajamas, lunch boxes, and TV chairs.

Toy railroads, increasingly popular since W.W.II, peak at Christmas. By 1955, sales will be down 33 percent.

# SCIENCE AND TECHNOLOGY

## News

**April 25.** In this month's issue of *Nature*, British geneticist Francis Crick and American genetic researcher James Watson announce one of the century's most important discoveries—the double-helix structure of the deoxyribose nucleic acid molecule.

DNA, found in all living cells, codes genetic information for the transmission of inherited traits. The Crick-Watson model breaks that code, explaining how chromosomes duplicate during cell division and how information is stored. Further research will confirm their findings.

Maurice Wilkins will share in their Nobel prize, but Rosalind Franklin will never receive credit. She deduced the staircase structure, and Watson utilized her x-ray diffraction photos without permission. She will die of cancer in 1958.

**May 6.** Dr. John H. Gibbon, at Jefferson Medical College in Philadelphia, performs the first successful open-heart surgery using a heart-lung machine. The result of decades of cooperative invention, the device takes over essential functions during the 26-minute operation. The 18-year-old female patient was born with a hole in her heart.

**May 25.** The U.S. military tests the YF-100A Super Sabre—the first combat aircraft capable of sustained supersonic-level flight.

**June.** Dr. Warren Snyder Reese reports the successful implantation of a plastic lens in the eyes of 16 cataract patients. The surgical procedure was developed by British physician Harold Ridley.

**June 1.** In the experimental treatment of stomach ulcers, medical researcher E. A. Marshall finds that antacid chemicals reduce the effect of digestive juices on the stomach wall.

**September 3.** By comparing American and foreign eating habits, a University of Minnesota study shows that fat intake, not calories, causes the higher cholesterol levels linked to coronary disease.

**September 17.** A team of New Orleans doctors completes the first successful surgical separation of Siamese twins. Two-month-old Carolyn Anne and Catherine Anne Mouton were joined at their lower intestines and by spinal bone structure.

**November 21.** The British Museum of Natural History announces that chemical tests have uncovered a "most elaborate and carefully prepared hoax."

In 1912, lawyer and amateur geologist Charles Dawson sent the museum the remains of a skull reportedly found in a gravel pit near Piltdown, Sussex. Dr. Arthur Woodward, a leading expert on early man, conducted further excavations with Dawson, then pieced together bone fragments to form the skull of a 500,000-year-old half-man half-ape. Hailed as the first firm evidence of the theory of evolution, *Eoanthropus dawsoni* made its discoverer famous.

In fact Piltdown Man is a 50,000-year-old human cranium was added to the stained jawbone and tooth of a modern ape, to create a phony "missing link." The fraud will never be solved, but Dawson, who died in 1916, will remain the prime suspect. Swanscombe Man will be reclassified as the oldest human ancestor.

**December 17.** At Fort George Meade, 24 miles northeast of Washington, the army is reportedly installing the nation's first battery of surface-to-air (SAM) missiles. Tracked on radar, the Nike-Ajax missiles will be guided to the enemy planes at a speed of 1,500 mph.

**More news.** Eric Rath loads his well-worn truck onto a freighter for the Florida-Puerto Rico run to save loading costs at both ends. By 1957, major ports will clear dock areas for trucks and plan new berths for the burgeoning container industry.

• One-fourth the size of the earlier SSEC and 25 times faster, the IBM 701 is the company's first production computer. It was designed principally for scientific calculations.

• German chemist Karl Ziegler uses atmospheric pressure, rather than the traditional 30,000 pounds per square inch, to produce stronger, more resistant polyethylene. His catalytic process opens a new era for plastics.

• Edward F. Knipling first theorized in 1938 that sterilization could control insect populations. Now director of the Department of Agriculture's research division, he conducts the first field tests this year off the coast of Florida.

Under Knipling, the DOA shifts insect control from conventional chemical poisons to biological and other selective means. He will retire in 1973 after implementing what some scientists consider the most original thought of the 20th century.

• American inventor Robert H. Abplanalp develops a plastic valve for aerosol cans. With the cost reduction, manufacturers will use spray cans, first developed in the 1920s, for countless products. Abplanalp becomes a millionaire at least a hundred times over.

• Graduate student Eugene Aserinsky detects the first physical evidence of dreaming. A person whose eyes moved under the eyelids during sleep remembers a dream if awakened; with no eye movement nothing can be recalled. The phenomenon is named rapid eye movement, or REM.

• Audrey (automatic digit recognizer), from Bell Telephone Labs, can recognize 10 numbers spoken into the mouthpiece. Although it must be readjusted for each new speaker, the device is regarded as the first step in the development of machines capable of obeying spoken commands.

## Other Discoveries, Developments, and Inventions

Thermostat on an electric frying pan
Portable clock-radio with long-life batteries
Hydraulic-lift ambulance for large airplanes
Photographic type-composing machine
Automatic paint dispenser for custom mixing thousands of colors
U.S. long-range artillery for atomic weapons
Tetracycline, which will become one of the world's most widely prescribed antibiotics

## Obituaries

**Chester I. Hall** (circa 1888–December 6, 1953). In his 24 years at GE, the inventor was awarded 139 patents, including the pop-up toaster and the car-engine thermostat.

**James Lewis Kraft** (1874–February 16, 1953). The Mennonite cheese peddler founded the Kraft Foods Corp. in 1909. Seven years later, he developed a processing method to dramatically extend the shelf life of cheese.

**Robert Millikan** (March 22, 1868–December 19, 1953). The U.S. physicist received the 1923 Nobel prize for determining the electric charge of an electron. Two years later, he named the radioactive rays emanating from outer space "cosmic rays."

## THE ARTS

February 19—*Picnic*, with Ralph Meeker, Janice Rule, Paul Newman, Kim Stanley, Eileen Heckart, Arthur O'Connell (477 perfs.)

February 25—*Wonderful Town*, with Rosalind Russell, Edith (Edie) Adams (559 perfs.)

May 7—*Can-Can*, with Gwen Verdon, Lilo, Peter Cookson, Hans Conried (892 perfs.)

September 30—*Tea and Sympathy*, with Deborah Kerr, John Kerr, Leif Ericson (712 perfs.)

October 15—*The Teahouse of the August Moon*, with John Forsythe, David Wayne, Paul Ford (1,027 perfs.)

November 5—*The Solid Gold Cadillac*, with Josephine Hull (526 perfs.)

December 3—*Kismet*, with Alfred Drake, Joan Diener, Richard Kiley (583 perfs.)

### Tony Awards

Actor (Dramatic)—Tom Ewell, *The Seven Year Itch*

Actress (Dramatic)—Shirley Booth, *Time of the Cuckoo*

Actor (Musical)—Thomas Mitchell, *Hazel Flagg*

Actress (Musical)—Rosalind Russell, *Wonderful Town*

Play—*The Crucible*

Musical—*Wonderful Town*

### News

**July 13.** In Ontario, Alec Guinness and Irene Worth perform *Richard III* and *All's Well That Ends*

*Well* in a tent. The sparse facilities and small salaries, drawn by founder Tom Patterson, artistic director Tyrone Guthrie, and guest star Alec Guinness, ensure success for the first Stratford Festival.

**More news.** A lighting technique patented in Britain by A. M. Low and T. C. Arnold projects light through liquids or fluid film to achieve a colored effect. (Psychedelic rock shows in the 1960s will make use of the concept.)

• Although the play contains no cohernet dialogue, *Waiting for Godot* brings Samuel Beckett international fame. The Irish-born dramatist writes mainly in French, and this English translation comes a year later.

## Obituaries

**Kathleen Ferrier** (April 22, 1912–October 8, 1953). The beloved British contralto dies of cancer.

**James Earle Fraser** (November 4, 1876–October 11, 1953). One of this century's best-known American artists designed the buffalo-head nickel and sculpted the weary Indian on horseback, *The End of the Trail.*

**Eugene O'Neill** (October 6, 1888–November 27, 1953). The playwright won 3 Pulitzers, for *Beyond the Horizon* (1920), *Anna Christie* (1921), and *Strange Interlude* (1928) (in 1957 *Long Day's Journey into Night* wins a fourth), and the 1936 Nobel prize in literature. Yet O'Neill's experimental forms and autobiographical subjects have limited his impact on American theater.

**Sergei Prokofiev** (April 23, 1891–March 8, 1953). Most Westerners know the Soviet composer for his fairy-tale orchestral suite, *Peter and the Wolf.*

## WORDS

James Baldwin, *Go Tell It on the Mountain*
William S. Burroughs, *Junkie*
Jacques Cousteau, *The Silent World*
Simone de Beauvoir, *The Second Sex*
Nikos Kazantzakís, *Zorba, the Greek*
Alfred Kinsey, *Sexual Behavior in the Human Female*

James A. Michener, *The Bridges at Toko-Ri*
B. F. Skinner, *Science and Human Behavior*
Leon Uris, *Battle Cry*

## News

**June 25.** The American Library Association and the American Book Publishers Council, denouncing State Department attempts to limit literary expression in U.S. libraries abroad, adopt a manifesto on the freedom to read. The next day, President Eisenhower supports their action.

**August 20.** Dr. Alfred Kinsey and 13 collaborators report the findings from 6,000 interviews in *Sexual Behavior in the Human Female.* For instance, 50 percent of the female subjects had engaged in premarital sex (half with their fiancés) while 26 percent had conducted extramarital affairs. As with the Kinsey report, critics charge the sample is too small to be statistically trustworthy.

**September 18.** Dismissing a complaint against a book club, the Federal Trade Commission (FTC) reverses a five-year-old ban against the use of "free" in describing goods given with the purchase of other merchandise.

**December.** With a background in editing and advertising, 27-year-old Hugh Hefner invests $10,000 in a magazine for male swingers. The first issue of *Playboy* features nude calendar photos of Marilyn Monroe on the cover and inside as "Sweetheart of the Month." The next cover sports Arthur Paul's stylized logo of "the playboy of the animal world"—the bunny rabbit.)

In the early issues, Hefner relies heavily on reprinted material, but his basic concept—nude women and racy cartoons—proves so successful that *Playboy* survives its first year without advertising.

**More news.** Enormously popular upon initial release, in 1942, *The Robe* tops the fiction list again with this year's movie tie-in.

*Statistics:* Over the past 12 years, the average retail price of a hardcover novel has risen from $2.58 to $3.29.

• Adolf Hitler's personal copy of *Mein Kampf* fails to draw the reserve price of $11,000 at a London public auction and the item is returned unsold to its owner.

## Cartoons and Comics

**November.** In 1941, a 5,000-year-old Egyptian wizard revealed the magic behind the word SHAZAM! (S = Solomon's wisdom, through to M = Mercury's speed) to Billy Batson, and the skinny newsboy turned into "Captain Marvel." With the comic book's popularity ("Shazam!" became an everyday expression of surprise), *Superman's* publisher, National, sued for copyright infringement. This month, after years of litigation, Fawcett cancels *Captain Marvel.* Ironically, National will revive the character in 1973.

## TIME *Man of the Year*

Konrad Adenauer

## New Words and Phrases

book burning
concussion grenade
cookout
count-down
drag strip
egghead
girlie magazine
lure girl (a female secret agent)
MASH (Mobile Army Surgical Hospital)
name-dropper
PNP (powerful new person)
red carpet
skygirl (an airline stewardess)
split-level (type of home)
sportoon (a cartoon about sports)
telegraph (to hint at something to come)
wumgush (nonsense)

The slogan "Ban the Bomb" enters usage in the United States. Also, linguists comment on the new sexual connotation given to some baseball terms—getting to first base, a home run, and so on.

## Obituaries

**Marjorie Kinnan Rawlings** (August 8, 1896–December 14, 1953). *The Yearling* (1938) remains the American novelist's best-known work.

**Dylan Thomas** (October 27, 1914–November 9, 1953). Regarded as the finest poet of his generation, the Welshman often gave readings using his expressive voice to convey the aural richness of his verse. He died suddenly of acute alcoholism during a U.S. speaking tour.

# FASHION

## Haute Couture

An abrupt rise in skirt lengths during the year—to $15\frac{1}{2}$ inches off the floor—rouses considerable controversy. The nipped waistline of the last two years relaxes and designers introduce a sleek sheath and a semifitted suit. To soften the silhouette, some add a wide folded or cuffed neckline.

Several prominent designers, including Adrian, Lilly Dache, and Schiaparelli, add men's clothing to their collections.

## News

**June 2.** Norman Hartnell, designer of Princess Elizabeth's wedding gown, creates a magnificent coronation robe. Embroidered symbols for England (rose), Scotland (thistle), Ireland (shamrock), and Wales (leek) on the skirt in order of precedence. On the lower half, the flower of each Commonwealth country nestles around a Tudor rose to form a garland. Opals, topaz, rubies, and amethysts bejewel the entire robe.

**More news.** In the United States, the Flammable Fabrics Act bans the use of some fabrics for certain clothing, such as brushed rayon or acetate for children's garments.

## Colors and Materials

Influenced by the pageantry of Queen Elizabeth's coronation, the fashion world highlights brilliant, jewel-like colors.

Charcoal gray succeeds beige as the most popular daytime neutral.

## Clothes

Skirts, full or slim, display a smooth and slender hipline and backswept effect.

The jeweled sweater fad continues, but the fashion world acknowledges separates as an established element.

With the elegant feminine mood set by couturiers, slacks and at-home pants taper to the ankle and occasionally mold to the knee. Long, tailored shorts sell in linen, raw silk, or fine flannel.

To fulfill the silhouette of the 1950s, Warner's creates a long girdle with bra called the "Merry Widow" (named after a 1952 MGM film). Back laced, front hooked, or zipped up, the foundation brutally takes in 2–3 inches. (Actress Lana Turner reportedly says, "I'm telling you, the Merry Widow was designed by a man. A woman would *never* do that to another woman.") Other companies turn out imitations, but by mid decade Warner's annually sells 6 million.

Fashion observers note the growing popularity of jeans and casual slacks with men and women.

In the first fashion fad for men in years, the American male wears Bermuda walking shorts everywhere—in the office, on the patio, even with a dinner jacket in the evening.

## Accessories

Women reject the new seamless stockings with their poor shape and tendency to snag.

Wide necklines call for multi-strand pearls or soft scarves.

Rising hemlines focus attention on shoes again.

Both stacked and stiletto heels win favor while manufacturers offer a wide range of colors and materials for at-home clothes.

## Hair and Cosmetics

For the more flattering, easier-to-maintain Italian haircut, short, casual layers brush forward around the face.

# POPULAR MUSIC

"Vaya Con Dios"—Les Paul & Mary Ford

"Song from Moulin Rouge (Where Is Your Heart?)"—Percy Faith & His Orchestra; vocal: Felicia Sanders

"How Much Is That Doggie in the Window"—Patti Page

"Don't Let the Stars Get in Your Eyes"—Perry Como

"Till I Waltz Again with You"—Teresa Brewer

"Rags to Riches"—Tony Bennett

"You You You"—Ames Brothers

"I'm Walking Behind You"—Eddie Fisher

"I Believe"—Frankie Laine

"April in Portugal"—Les Baxter & His Orchestra

"Ebb Tide"—Frank Chacksfield Orchestra

"Crying in the Chapel"—Rex Allen

"Your Cheatin' Heart"—Hank Williams

"No Other Love"—Perry Como

"Eh, Cumpari,"—Julius LaRosa

"I Love Paris"—Les Baxter & His Orchestra

"Baubles, Bangles and Beads"—Peggy Lee

## News

**April 29.** Columbia Records retails a three-speed portable phonograph for $29.95.

---

*Statistics:* The number of turntables in the United States has risen from 8 million in 1946 to 24 million this year.

**July 15.** A report to the National Association of Music Merchants confirms that 1952 record sales exceeded $200 million—78's account for 52 percent of sales, 45's for 28 percent, and LP's 19 percent.

**More news.** *Billboard* magazine's chart of hits includes the first rock 'n' roll song, "Crazy, Man, Crazy," with Bill Haley & His Comets (Essex Records).

• Singer Tony Williams forms a new black group, the Platters. Clyde McPhatter leaves the Dominoes and organizes the Drifters. But after a 1954–1956 stint in the Armed Forces, McPhatter will leave the group for a solo career.

• Robert Wright and George "Chet" Forrest plunder the music of Russian composer Aleksandr Borodin for their musical *Kismet*. The Polovtsian Dances, from the opera *Prince Igor*, form the basis of their *Stranger in Paradise* while *And This Is My Beloved* and *Baubles, Bangles, and Beads* rely heavily on themes from Borodin's *String Quartet No. 2*.

*New Recording Artists*

Drifters
Flamingos
Marty Robbins

**Obituaries**

**Fred Ahlert** (September 19, 1892–October 20, 1953). The famous composer of the 1920s and 1930s wrote such hits as "Walkin' My Baby Back Home" (1930) and "I'm Gonna Sit Right Down and Write Myself a Letter" (1935).

**Peter De Rose** (March 10, 1900–April 23, 1953). The U.S. composer, who produced his best-known songs during the 1930s, wrote "Deep Purple" (1933) and "Wagon Wheels" (1934).

**Hank Williams** (September 17, 1923–January 1, 1953). One of the greatest country and western (CW) stars, the Alabaman singer-songwriter pioneered the honky-tonk style. His songs, many with lyrics purchased from others, tore at the emotions of his biggest fans, poor white Southerners. Hoping for a comeback after the Opry fired him last year, Wil-

liams died of heart failure (probably caused by heavy drinking and an addiction to painkillers for a birth defect).

# MOVIES

*The Band Wagon* (d. Vincente Minnelli; color)—Fred Astaire, Cyd Charisse, Oscar Levant, Nanette Fabray, Jack Buchanan

*The Big Heat* (d. Fritz Lang; bw)—Glenn Ford, Gloria Grahame, Alexander Scourby, Lee Marvin

*The Captain's Paradise* (British, d. Anthony Kimmins; bw)—Alec Guinness, Yvonne De Carlo, Celia Johnson

*The 5,000 Fingers of Dr. T* (d. Roy Rowland; color)—Peter Lind Hayes, Mary Healy, Tommy Rettig, Hans Conried

*From Here to Eternity* (d. Fred Zinnemann; bw)—Burt Lancaster, Deborah Kerr, Montgomery Clift, Frank Sinatra, Donna Reed, Ernest Borgnine

*Genevieve* (British, d. Henry Cornelius; color)—John Gregson, Dinah Sheridan, Kenneth More, Kay Kendall

*It Came from Outer Space* (d. Jack Arnold; bw; 3-D)—Richard Carlson, Barbara Rush

*Julius Caesar* (d. Joseph L. Mankiewicz; bw)—James Mason, Marlon Brando, John Gielgud, Deborah Kerr, Greer Garson

*Kiss Me Kate* (d. George Sidney; color)—Kathryn Grayson, Howard Keel, Ann Miller

*Lili* (d. Charles Walters; color)—Leslie Caron, Mel Ferrer, Jean-Pierre Aumont

*Mogambo* (d. John Ford; color)—Clark Gable, Ava Gardner, Grace Kelly

*Mr. Hulot's Holiday* (French, d. Jacques Tati; bw)—Jacques Tati

*The Naked Spur* (d. Anthony Mann; color)—James Stewart, Janet Leigh, Ralph Meeker, Robert Ryan

*Peter Pan* (Disney; color; animated)—Voices: Bobby Driscoll (Peter); Hans Conried (Captain Hook)

*Roman Holiday* (d. William Wyler; bw)—Gregory Peck, Audrey Hepburn, Eddie Albert

*Shane* (d. George Stevens; color)—Alan Ladd, Jean Arthur, Van Heflin, Jack Palance, Brandon de Wilde

*Stalag 17* (d. Billy Wilder; bw)—William Holden, Don Taylor, Otto Preminger, Robert Strauss

*War of the Worlds* (d. Byron Haskin; color)—Gene Barry, Ann Robinson

*The Wild One* (d. Laslo Benedek; bw)—Marlon Brando, Mary Murphy, Robert Keith, Lee Marvin

## Academy Awards

**March 19.** When several movie studios once again withdraw financial support, a desperate Academy accepts an NBC broadcast bid of $100,000 to save the Oscars.

In these first televised ceremonies, Bob Hope hosts in Hollywood and Conrad Nagel in New York.

Best Picture—*The Greatest Show on Earth*
Best Actor—Gary Cooper (*High Noon*)
Best Actress—Shirley Booth (*Come Back, Little Sheba*)
Best Director—John Ford (*The Quiet Man*)
Best Supporting Actor—Anthony Quinn (*Viva Zapata!*)
Best Supporting Actress—Gloria Grahame (*The Bad and the Beautiful*)
Best Song—"High Noon (Do Not Forsake Me, Oh My Darlin')" from the film of the same name
Honorary Awards—Harold Lloyd; Bob Hope; *Forbidden Games* (French)

Gary Cooper becomes the third actor to win two Oscars (Spencer Tracy won in 1937 and 1938 and Fredric March in 1931–1932 and 1946). Cooper and Anthony Quinn, working together on location in Mexico, are absent from the ceremonies, as is John Ford. For the fourth time, the legendary director fails to collect his Oscar. Still, the largest audience in TV's short history is dazzled by the sight of so many Hollywood stars.

An Oscar for the song "High Noon" marks the end of a cinema era. Previously, nominated tunes were sung as part of the movie plot. But, with the near death of the small musical, songs will now largely be sung in the opening credits or as incidental music.

## News

**April 15.** British-born Charlie Chaplin has surrendered his reentry permit to the U.S. Justice Department. The silent screen comedian, who went abroad last fall, recently received notification that Immigration would investigate his alleged subversive tendencies before allowing him to return to the United States. On April 17, in London, the 64-year-old Chaplin claims that the persecution of "powerful reactionary groups" makes it impossible for him to work in America. He vows never to return and this October, sells his Hollywood movie studio for $650,000.

**September 16.** In obvious competition with Cinerama, 20th Century-Fox premieres *The Robe*, the first motion picture in CinemaScope. The process, using a lens invented by Frenchman Henry Chrétien in the late 1920s, compresses and distorts images during filming, then spreads the frames out on a screen two and a half times the normal size. This simpler, clearer wide-screen format, with stereophonic sound, is an instant hit with moviegoers.

**More news.** Cartoonist Walter Lantz, the creator of Woody Woodpecker, introduces the penguin Chilly Willy to the screen. The woebegone little creature will continue his quest for food and shelter until 1973, when Lantz closes his studios.

• Referring to the standards of the Hays Code, the Motion Picture Association of America (MPAA) refuses to approve *The Moon Is Blue*—the first film to use the words *virgin* and *pregnant*.

In 1922, Hollywood scandals forced studio bosses to create the Motion Picture Producers and Distributors of America. The MPPDA, under the leadership of lawyer and politician Will H. Hays, initially coordinated industry policies and practices. Then, in 1930, the Hays Office created a production code to enforce strict self-censorship and to reestablish public confidence in Hollywood films (effective July

1, 1931). The MPDDA became the MPAA in the mid-1940s, and Hays retired, but the code has remained in effect. Director Otto Preminger, refusing to knuckle under, distributes *The Man Is Blue* himself. Some states ban exhibition, but the movie's financial success spells the end for self-regulation.

• His career foundering, singer Frank Sinatra begs for the dramatic role of Angelo Maggio in *From Here to Eternity*. Finally his wife, actress Ava Gardner, intercedes, and Sinatra gets the part. In a spectacular comeback, he wins an Oscar and goes on to make 10 more films over the next three years.

• With a lead role in the 3-D movie *House of Wax*, Vincent Price becomes an international star of horror films. In the same picture, a future box-office star, Charles Buchinsky, plays Price's mute assistant. He will later change his name to Charles Bronson.

• Over the past two years, the number of movies filmed in color has increased from 23 percent to 42.7 percent of total releases.

| Top Box Office Stars | Newcomers |
| --- | --- |
| Gary Cooper | Janet Leigh |
| Dean Martin & | Gloria Grahame |
| Jerry Lewis | Tony Curtis |
| John Wayne | Terry Moore |
| Alan Ladd | Rosemary Clooney |
| Bing Crosby | Julie Adams |
| Marilyn Monroe | Robert Wagner |
| James Stewart | Scott Brady |
| Bob Hope | Pier Angeli |
| Susan Hayward | Jack Palance |
| Randolph Scott | |

### Top Money-Maker of the Year

*The Robe* (1953) (d. Henry Koster; color)—Richard Burton, Jean Simmons, Victor Mature

### Obituaries

**Nigel Bruce** (February 4, 1895–October 8, 1953). The British-American actor is best remembered for his definitive portrayal of the bumbling Dr. Watson in the Sherlock Holmes movies and radio program (1938–1945).

**William Farnum** (July 4, 1876–June 5, 1953). One of the highest-paid and most popular matinee idols of the silent era, Farnum took on character parts with the introduction of sound.

## TELEVISION AND RADIO

### New Prime-Time TV Programs

"Coke Time with Eddie Fisher" (April 29, 1953–February 22, 1957; Music)—Eddie Fisher, Freddy Robbins

"The Danny Thomas Show" (September 29, 1953–September 1964; Situation Comedy)—Danny Thomas, Jean Hagen (1953–1956), Marjorie Lord (1957–1964), Rusty Hamer, Angela Cartwright

"General Electric Theater" (February 1, 1953–September 16, 1962; Drama Anthology)—Host/Star: Ronald Reagan (1954–1962)

"The Life of Riley" (January 1953–August 22, 1958; Situation Comedy)—William Bendix, Marjorie Reynolds, Wesley Morgan

"The Loretta Young Show" (September 20, 1953–September 10, 1961; Drama Anthology)—Hostess/Star: Loretta Young

"Name That Tune" (June 29, 1953–October 19, 1959; Quiz/Audience Participation)—Emcee: George de Witt (1955–1959)

"Omnibus" (October 4, 1953–March 31, 1957; Culture)—Host: Alistair Cooke. *Note:* The program will continue on Sunday afternoon until May 10, 1959.

"Private Secretary" (February 1, 1953–September 10, 1957; Situation Comedy)—Ann Sothern, Don Porter, Ann Tyrrell

"The U.S. Steel Hour" (October 27, 1953–June 12, 1963; Drama Anthology)

"You Are There" (February 1, 1953–October 13, 1957; Documentary Drama)—Reporter: Walter Cronkite

## Emmy Awards 1952 (February 5, 1953)

Best Dramatic Program—"Robert Montgomery
    Presents" (NBC)
Best Variety Program—"Your Show of Shows"
    (NBC)
Best Situation Comedy—"I Love Lucy" (CBS)
Best Children's Program—"Time for Beany"
Best Actor—Thomas Mitchell
Best Actress—Helen Hayes
Best Comedian—Jimmy Durante
Best Comedienne—Lucille Ball ("I Love Lucy,"
    (CBS)

## News

**January.** NBC revives "The Life of Riley". (An
earlier TV version of the radio show failed to catch
on.) With a five-year run, the sitcom's title enters
the American vocabulary as the ultimate expression
of a lazy, inactive life style.

**January 7.** A *Radio-Television Daily* poll names
Arthur Godfrey as the top radio personality and
Bishop Fulton J. Sheen as tops for TV.

**January 19.** Afraid her absence would spell the
end for their series, Lucille Ball and Desi Arnaz
have written her pregnancy into the script. A
priest, minister, and rabbi attended the filming of
the first episode. When asked if they found anything
objectionable, the three said in near unison,
"What's questionable about having a baby?" They
never changed a word, but CBS requested that
*pregnant* be replaced with *expectant.*

The hilarity of early episodes and the publicity
campaign have built viewer anticipation to fever
pitch. Lucille Ball enters the hospital today for a
cesarean section; coincidentally, tonight the birth
episode draws an estimated 44 million, or 70 percent, of the U.S. television audience. The baby, a
boy in both real life and make-believe, receives
truckloads of gifts from generous fans.

In March, Lucy and Desi sign the biggest contract in TV history, an $8-million "I Love Lucy"
agreement through 1955. Their spin-off merchandise also sells well, including Lucy dolls

*In the top-rated "I Love Lucy," comedienne Lucille Ball
usually performs some screwball stunt in each episode.*

and aprons, Ricky smoking jackets, furniture, jewelry, and baby items.

**January 19.** A 66-mile microwave relay between
Buffalo and Toronto is the first TV link between the
United States and Canada.

**February 9.** Financially troubled ABC receives
FCC permission to merge with United Paramount
Theaters. The commission had questioned a deal
that gave a theater chain ownership of a TV network. With the injection of money and Hollywood
know-how, the network will sign some $4 million
worth of new business over the next month.

**February 9.** A hero to generations of kids, "Superman" first appeared on radio on February 12,
1940, just a few months after the first Action
Comic. When the program ended in 1951, filming
began on the TV series. The first episode, held back
pending the release of the movie *Superman and the
Mole Men* (1951), airs today.

Early in the filming, a pulley broke and a hospitalized George Reeves refused to fly on a wire again. A special hydraulic unit lifts and lowers Superman now in front of moving backgrounds. But, during the first two years, Reeves and the producer become alarmed over the number of children leaping out of windows. In 1955, the actor will sternly tell his young audience, "No one, but no one, can do the things Superman does. And that goes especially for flying!"

**February 10.** The initial success of "Romper Room" prompts a network offer, but creator Bert Claster decides to remain with syndication. His wife Nancy, with her nursery school background, selects and trains each new teacher, and Claster provides a trunk of props and a steady supply of scripts. The women then entertain preschoolers from their local television station. By 1969, the kindergarten show will appear in 103 U.S. cities.

**April 3.** The first issue of *TV Guide* sports a photograph of Desi Arnaz, Jr. By the end of the first year, the pocket-size publication circulates 1.5 million copies every week.

**May 25.** KUHT in Houston becomes the nation's first educational television station.

**June 2.** Newsreels flown across the Atlantic allow CBC (Canada) and ABC to broadcast the coronation of Elizabeth II, eight hours after the ceremony.

**June 15.** For the company's 50th anniversary, Ford Motors purchased the same time slot from all three networks and spent an unprecedented sum of $500,000 on a one-hour special (a 30-minute Arthur Godfrey program typically costs $2,500). Edward R. Murrow narrates various film clips and Mary Martin and Ethel Merman stop the show with a medley of 31 songs (later released as a 45-rpm).

**October 19.** A huge personality on radio, Arthur Godfrey readily adapted his folksy style to TV. With the backup of a solid supporting cast, his two shows have topped the ratings. But Godfrey demands absolute loyalty and virtual subservience from his employees. Singer Julius LaRosa recently overstepped the bounds, hiring his own agent and signing an independent recording contract, and tonight the boss fires him on the air.

LaRosa never becomes a big success story, despite press and public support, but next season, Godfrey will drop out of the top 10. He never wins back his following and will leave the air in 1959.

**October 20.** CKSO-TV, Canada's first privately owned television station, begins operations in Sudbury, Ontario.

**December 16.** For the first time, the White House releases a complete press conference tape to radio networks.

**December 17.** On March 25, CBS acknowledged it would be "economically foolish" to force the industry to accept a color system incompatible with the black-and-white TV sets already in 23 million American homes. RCA immediately organized the first coast-to-coast compatible color broadcast on November 3, a program starring Nanette Fabray.

With the CBS surrender and the success of last month's telecast, the FCC—in a rare change of heart—today approves the RCA system. NBC schedules color programs over the Christmas holidays and, on December 30, Admiral Corp. offers the first compatible color TVs—$1,175 each.

---

*Statistics*: 99 percent of TV stations carry network affiliations: NBC accounts for 56.3 percent, CBS 26.2 percent, and ABC 19 percent. By 1969, total affiliation will drop to 84 percent and the network share will even out to 31.9 percent for NBC, 28.7 percent for CBS, and 23.6 percent for ABC.

---

**More news.** This year, CBC carries the first broadcast of "Hockey Night in Canada."

• For the first time since the Great Depression, radio revenues take a downward turn, dropping from $473.1 million in 1952 to $450.4 million. TV revenues, on the other hand, continue to escalate, jumping from last year's $235 million to $324 million.

## TV Commercials

Campbell's Soups—Campbell's Kids, created in 1904, disappeared in the hard-sell market of the thirties. Reintroduced in 1947, the chubby-cheeked boy and girl advertise for "Lassie."

## Memorable Radio Programs End

"The Aldrich Family" (July 2, 1939)
"The Cavalcade of America" (October 9, 1935)
"Dr. Christian" (November 7, 1937)
"The Judy Canova Show" (July 6, 1943)
"Lum and Abner" (April 1931)
"Meet Corliss Archer" (1943)
"The Quiz Kids" (June 28, 1940)
"The Red Skelton Show" (October 7, 1941)
"This Is Your FBI" (April 6, 1945)

# SPORTS

## Winners

### Baseball

World Series—New York Yankees (AL), 4 games; Brooklyn Dodgers (NL), 2 games
Player of the Year—Al Rosen (Cleveland Indians, AL); Roy Campanella (Brooklyn Dodgers, NL)
Rookie of the Year—Harvey Kuenn (Detroit Tigers, AL); Jim Gilliam (Brooklyn Dodgers, NL)

### Football

NFL Championship—Detroit Lions 17, Cleveland Browns 16
   College Bowls (January 1, 1953)—
   Rose Bowl, USC 7, Wisconsin 0
   Cotton Bowl, Texas 16, Tennessee 0
   Orange Bowl, Alabama 61, Syracuse 6
   Sugar Bowl, Georgia Tech 24, Mississippi 7
Heisman Trophy—John Lattner (Notre Dame, HB)
Grey Cup—Hamilton Tiger-Cats 12, Winnipeg Blue Bombers 6

### Basketball

NBA Championship—Minneapolis Lakers, 4 games; New York Knickerbockers, 1 game

Rookie of the Year—Don Meineke (Fort Wayne Zollner Pistons)
NCAA Championship—Indiana 69, Kansas 68

### Tennis

U.S. National—Men, Tony Trabert (vs. Vic Seixas); Women, Maureen Connolly (vs. Doris Hart)
Wimbledon—Men, Vic Seixas (vs. Kurt Nielsen); Women, Maureen Connolly (vs. Doris Hart)

### Golf

Masters—Ben Hogan
U.S. Open—Ben Hogan
British Open—Ben Hogan

### Hockey

Stanley Cup—Montreal Canadiens, 4 games; Boston Bruins, 1 game

### Ice Skating

World Championship—Men, Hayes Alan Jenkins (U.S.); Women, Tenley Albright (U.S.)
U.S. National—Men, Hayes Alan Jenkins; Women, Tenley Albright
Canadian National—Men, Peter Firstbrook; Women, Barbara Gratton

### Kentucky Derby

Dark Star—Henry Moreno, jockey

### Athlete of the Year

Male—Ben Hogan (Golf)
Female—Maureen Connolly (Tennis)

### Last Season

Johnny Mize (Baseball)
Chuck Rayner (Hockey)
Arnold Weinmeister (Football)

## News

**January 11.** The Dallas Texans receive NFL approval to transfer to Baltimore. The team will be called the Baltimore Colts.

**February 15.** Tenley Albright becomes the first American to win the World Figure Skating Championship. This year, the 17-year-old also wins the North American and U.S. championships.

**February 20.** Anheuser-Busch, the St. Louis brewery, pays Fred Saigh $3.75 million for the Cardinals baseball team and farm system.

**March 17.** NL owners approve the transfer of the Boston Braves to Milwaukee—baseball's first major-league relocation in 50 years. The move follows an 80-percent drop in attendance in Boston over the last four years. In Milwaukee, the team sets a league attendance record with 1,826,397 tickets sold.

**May 2.** The favorite Native Dancer loses to longshot Dark Star in the Kentucky Derby. The second-place finish marks Dancer's only loss in 22 races, but with a recurring foot ailment he will be retired to stud next year.

**July 10.** With a win in the British Open, Ben Hogan becomes the first golfer to sweep the British tournament, the U.S. Open, and the Masters in a single year.

**September 7.** In tennis, 18-year-old Maureen Connolly becomes the first woman to win the Grand Slam—Wimbledon, the French and Australian titles, and today's U.S. National. (Fans fondly call the diminutive player "Little Mo.") Only one other player has accomplished the same feat, fellow American Don Budge in 1938.

**September 8.** World Series contenders agree to the first price increases in many years. Box seats will sell for $10, reserved seats for $7, and bleachers for $2.

**September 29.** AL owners allow last-place St. Louis Browns to move to Baltimore. With a 52-year win-loss percentage of .433, attendance had dwindled to less than 4,000 per game. The business syndicate, which paid nearly $2.5 million for Bill Veeck's controlling interest, will rename the club the Orioles.

**November 9.** In a case brought by a former minor league owner and two ex-players, the U.S. Supreme Court upholds a 1922 ruling that organized baseball is "not within the scope of the federal antitrust laws." The justices conclude that "evils" within organized sports will have to be corrected by Congress.

**December 1.** Following his demand for a multi-year contract, the Brooklyn Dodgers fire Chuck Dressen and hire Walter Alston. Alston will continue to manage on one-year contracts as the Dodgers capture seven pennants and four World Series by 1975.

**More news.** In 1933, swimmer Henry Meyer refined and popularized the butterfly. He maintained that the stroke conformed to the written rules and should be allowed in competition. Swimming authorities finally accept his argument and classify the butterfly apart from the breast stroke.

## Records

**October 5.** Second baseman Billy Martin drives in the winning run in the bottom of the ninth and the Yankees become the first baseball team to win five consecutive World Series.

**This year.** Jockey Willie Shoemaker, age 22, brings home an astounding 485 winners. His 1,683 mounts included 302 second-place finishes and 210 third.

• Amateur and professional boxing reports an all-time high of 22 deaths.

## What They Said

NHL scoring champion for the last two years, 24-year-old Gordie Howe once again leads the league. Since the Detroit forward is at his best when challenged, opposition teams believe, "The best defense against Howe is to treat him courteously." (*Time* Mar. 2)

## Obituaries

**James Jeffries** (April 15, 1875–March 3, 1953). The heavyweight champion retired in 1905, but was persuaded to return to the ring five years later to fight Negro champion Jack Johnson. Jeffries was knocked out in the 15th round—the only defeat of his career.

**(Charles Augustus) Kid Nichols** (September 14, 1869–April 11, 1953). One of the top pitchers of the 19th century, the durable right-hander posted 30 or more victories in seven consecutive seasons—a record that still stands.

**Jim Thorpe** (May 28, 1888–March 28, 1953). Perhaps the greatest male athlete of this century, Thorpe played baseball, basketball, lacrosse, and hockey, and excelled at football and track and field.

Of mixed Indian blood, he trained at the Carlisle Indian School in Pennsylvania (in existence from 1879–1918) under renowned coach Glen "Pop" Warner. In 1911, Thorpe led his football squad to 11 victories in a 12-game season; in one memorable contest, he scored all 18 points—a touchdown and four field goals.

In 1912, the young man astounded the world by winning both the pentathlon and decathlon at the Olympics. But the following year the Olympic Committee stripped him of his medals for accepting money to play off-season baseball (a common practice among athletes at the time).

After playing part-time with the Giants baseball team, Thorpe returned to football in 1920. He helped found the American Professional Football Association, which became the NFL in 1921, and played for several teams before retiring in 1929. An alcoholic, Thorpe eventually died of a heart attack.

**(William Tatem) Bill Tilden II** (February 10, 1893–June 5, 1953). Voted the greatest tennis player of the half century, Tilden dominated the sport during the 1920s. He was the first American to win at Wimbledon, was a seven-time U.S. champion, and a member of the U.S. Davis Cup team from 1920 to 1929. "Big Bill" turned professional in 1930 and continued to play until he was nearly 50 years old.

# 1954

Two decisions hold enormous long-term consequences for the United States. In May, the Supreme Court rules that segregated schools deny American citizens equal protection under the 14th Amendment. With the abolition of all-Negro Armed Forces units as well this year, black Americans finally begin to break free of institutionalized racial separation.

Then, following the French defeat in Vietnam, the Eisenhower administration offers aid directly to Saigon. U.S. support will eventually allow the Diem regime to reject the Geneva agreement and reunification with North Vietnam.

Americans hail the development of a polio vaccine. With the postwar baby boom, the number of cases has risen steadily. As well, in science and technology, Texas Instruments produces the silicon transistor and researchers show dramatic evidence of a connection between smoking and lung cancer.

Of a more frivolous nature, Coco Chanel makes a comeback, the first transistor radios sell for $49.95, the Thunderbird appears on U.S. highways, newsstands carry the new Sports Illustrated, comic book publishers adopt a censorship code, and more radio shows disappear under the onslaught of TV programs like "Adventures of Rin Tin Tin," "Lassie," and "Father Knows Best."

## NEWS

**January 12.** With the enormous costs of both conventional forces and atomic weapons, the Eisenhower administration opts for a nuclear arsenal. As Secretary of State John Foster Dulles explains today, the best way to deter aggression is "to depend primarily upon a great capacity to retaliate instantly, by means and at places of our own choosing."

But the voters and America's allies worry that "massive retaliation" as a military deterrent might force the United States to turn a local incident into a nuclear war. The president declares that the United States will never be the first to use the H-bomb.

By the end of the year, Washington trims over $2 billion from defense costs and accelerates manpower cuts.

**February 18.** London reports that Britain is now producing atomic weapons. Next February 17, the British government will announce its intention to build the H-bomb "as a deterrent to war."

**March 1.** Puerto Rican nationalist Lolita Lebron and three accomplices open fire from the House gallery, wounding five members of Congress. In

Puerto Rico, police quickly round up nationalist and Communist leaders.

American courts sentence the would-be assassins (all of the wounded recover) to life terms and, in the months ahead, convict 13 more nationalists.

**March 1.** At Bikini Atoll, in the South Pacific, the atomic test shot Bravo yields double the anticipated power. Prevailing winds blow the huge cloud of radioactive debris toward the Marshall Islands, the island of Rongerik, and a Japanese fishing boat. No warning was given.

The army pronounces the 28 U.S. soldiers on Rongerik in good health and refuses to provide medical care. Yet the people of Bikini are evacuated and Japan receives $2 million in damages when a Japanese fisherman dies seven months later. (Next year, the AEC will report that Bravo contaminated a 7,000-square-mile area.)

In July, the U.N. upholds the right of the United States to conduct nuclear tests in its Pacific Trust Territory.

**March 8.** Less than nine years after the end of W.W.II, the United States and Japan sign a Mutual Defense Assistance Pact. Washington hopes that Japanese rearmament, in return for U.S. economic and military aid, will fill the power vacuum in Asia and prevent the further spread of Communism. Before the end of the year, the American Navy begins training Japanese pilots.

**March 13.** In Caracas, at the 10th Inter-American Conference, the United States successfully sponsors a resolution barring Communism from the Western Hemisphere (only Guatemala opposes, while Argentina and Mexico abstain). But, at the same time, the Latin American nations call for an end to European colonialism in the Americas; the United States abstains in protest.

**April 22.** The Army-McCarthy hearings begin in Washington. Late last year, Senator McCarthy turned his attention to the American Army, charging officers with shielding Communists. When he discredited Army Secretary Robert Stevens, the humiliated service struck back, accusing McCarthy of seeking preferential treatment for a recently inducted aide. The senator countercharged the army with blackmail because of his recent investigation

of Signal Corps operations. When both sides refuse to back down, the Senate opens McCarthy's subcommittee to the public, and the senator relinquishes his chair.

ABC and DuMont, with little daytime programming, televise the full hearings. Many Americans get their first close look at the controversial senator, his long-winded arguments, constant interruptions ("point-of-order" briefly becomes a catch phrase), and personal attacks. Army Counsel Joseph Welch, in comparison, uses soft-spoken logic. And when the 63-year-old eloquently defends his young assistant from McCarthy's accusations—"Have you no sense of decency, sir?"—spectators unexpectedly burst into applause.

The hearings end June 17 without resolution, but for many that spontaneous moment of appreciation for Welch has marked the beginning of the end of McCarthyism.

**May 7.** The French surrender at Dien Bien Phu. The Indochinese War has cost France billions of dollars and the lives of some 50,000 soldiers. General Henri Navarre, sent out last year to win a definitive victory, believed that in a classic military battle superior French equipment and strategy would defeat a peasant army. He placed a fortified camp deep in Vietminh territory and waited. But North Vietnamese General Giap ignored the script, hauled artillery into the hills above the camp, and on March 13 laid siege.

In the desperate weeks since, the French asked the United States for military assistance. Washington is already covering 78 percent of the war costs. President Eisenhower explained to the American people that the fall of Vietnam could mean the loss of Southeast Asia: But the "domino theory" failed to bring the British into a coalition.

Three days after the fall of Dien Bien Phu, Eisenhower directs Dulles to draft a congressional resolution authorizing the commitment of U.S. troops. Although the Joint Chiefs of Staff evaluate Indochina as "devoid of decisive military objectives," they recommend the use of atomic weapons if the Chinese invade.

But as the military situation deteriorates, the

bitter French National Assembly refuses further action and the White House decides that the moment of intervention has passed.

---

*Statistics:* A June Gallup poll shows 72 percent of Americans disapprove of sending troops to Indochina. Almost half believe that the United States would have nothing to gain.

---

**May 17.** In a historic decision, the Supreme Court unanimously overrules state rights and finds that segregated schools deprive Negro Americans of the equal protection guaranteed by the 14th Amendment.

Southern communities have long ignored the "separate but equal" doctrine in their schools, allocating an average $4 for every white student and just $1 for every Negro one. When Oliver Brown attempted to redress this inequality and register his daughter Linda in an all-white Topeka school, she was refused admittance.

The NAACP, under the leadership of Thurgood Marshall, argued Brown's case and three others all the way to the Supreme Court, despite opposition from some Negroes who feared that a negative ruling would slow the fight for racial equality. Today, in *Brown* v. *Board of Education*, the justices instruct those states with compulsory segregation (17 and the District of Columbia) and those with permissive segregation (4) to comply "with all deliberate speed."

NAACP branch offices immediately petition local school boards, and just two weeks later the National Education Association (NEA) endorses integration. But, with no court timetable for compliance, many states move to circumvent the law, some by creating "state-subsidized" private schools. And Southern governors at a November conference promise to use "every proper prerogative" to uphold state control of school policy.

Still, legal experts believe the Supreme Court, in finding separate facilities "inherently unequal,"

condemns all forms of segregation by implication. Other favorable rulings are anticipated.

**May 26.** A huge explosion rips through the third deck of the aircraft carrier U.S.S. *Bennington* off Rhode Island, killing 103 men and injuring 200. Later, several officers claim to have smelled hydraulic oil; in 1953, vaporized hydraulic fuel ignited a deadly explosion that took 37 lives on the *Leyte* in 1953. The *Bennington* tragedy is the second worst noncombatant disaster in U.S. naval history; only a 1942 collision involving the *Ingraham* killed more men (218).

**June.** Prominent business leaders in Indianola, Mississippi, establish a White Citizens' Council to preserve white political power. Other councils will sprout up throughout the South over the next few years. Members will use their influence to push through segregation laws and to economically punish supporters of integration or black voting rights.

**June 29.** At the end of a four-week hearing, the AEC finds Dr. J. Robert Oppenheimer, director of the secret Manhattan Project during W.W.II, guilty of prewar Communist associations and later opposition to the H-bomb. The panel votes 4–1 against reinstating his security clearance. Defended by the scientific community, Oppenheimer comes to symbolize the American repression of intellectual freedom during the Cold War.

**July 21.** In Switzerland, world powers sign the Geneva Accords ending the eight-year Indochina War and transferring French sovereignty to governments in Laos, Cambodia, and Vietnam. The agreement temporarily partitions Vietnam (roughly along the 17th parallel, with a five-mile-wide Demilitarized Zone [DMZ] as a buffer), prohibits foreign military use of Vietnamese territory, and calls for reunification elections no later than July 1956.

Under Chinese and Soviet pressure, the victorious Vietminh settled for just half at the negotiating table. The Democratic Republic of Vietnam, under 64-year-old Ho Chi Minh, is to govern the North while the French-backed government of Bao Dai, with Ngo Dinh Diem as premier, will govern the State of Vietnam in the South. Both the United States and South Vietnam refuse to sign the peace treaty, but Washington pledges not to upset the terms of the accord.

**August 5.** Iran reaches a 25-year oil-production agreement with an international consortium (five of the eight companies are American) for 50 percent of net profits. Industry nationalization, carried out in 1951, failed for lack of markets. Once Tehran settles on compensation for earlier lost properties and oil rights, Washington grants the Middle East nation $42 million.

**August 12.** The United Nations formally withdraws from Korea, ending the police action begun in 1950. Earlier this year, the U.S. Defense Department, on the basis of intelligence research and other data, charged the USSR with having engineered the conflict.

**August 16.** American ships begin evacuating North Vietnamese, mostly Catholics concerned for their religion under Communist rule. Eventually, "Operation Passage to Freedom" relocates some 900,000 people to the South. The refugees form an important political base for the fledgling Saigon government.

**August 17.** Under the Atomic Energy Act of 1946, all fissionable materials and most production facilities must be government owned. Eisenhower has asked Congress for an amendment permitting private ownership of nuclear power. After two weeks of debate, Congress agrees providing that companies surrender all atomic patents.

**August 20.** Before the settlement of the Indochina War, Eisenhower sent American agents into North Vietnam to undermine the Communist government through paramilitary operations and political-psychological warfare. Today, against the advice of the Joint Chiefs of Staff and the American intelligence community, the president approves an NSC recommendation that the United States bypass Paris and give aid directly to Vietnam. In 1955, Washington will distribute $200 million without the U.S.-buy rule.

**August 24.** The Communist Control Act deprives the U.S. Communist party of "the rights, privileges, and immunities attendant upon legal bodies" and penalizes Communist-action groups that fail to register under the Subversive Activities Control Act. The legislation stops short of making party membership a crime.

**September 8.** The Southeast Asia Defense Treaty (SEATO), or Manila Pact, pledges the United States, Britain, France, Australia, New Zealand, Philippines, Thailand, and Pakistan to mutual defense against Communist aggression within the treaty area and South Vietnam, Laos, and Cambodia (barred by the Geneva Accords from joining any military alliance). State Secretary Dulles had pushed for a defense pact to support treaties with Korea, Japan, and Formosa.

Effective February 1955, the alliance in the end will have little impact on Asia. All the members except Thailand and Pakistan already have security agreements with the United States, and India and Indonesia opt for neutralism. Since the organization, unlike NATO, has no unified military command, Washington will continue to deal unilaterally with crises in the SEATO area.

**September 26.** In Japan, the worst of 15 powerful typhoons this year destroys at least 1,000 small craft in Hakodate Bay and capsizes the harbor ferry *Toya Maru*, drowning 1,172 passengers (including at least 40 Americans). Altogether, nearly 1,600 people die.

**October 5–18.** Hurricane Hazel, the most severe storm in North American history, rages up from the Caribbean, killing an estimated 600 to 1,200 people, including 95 in the United States.

The U.S. Weather Bureau predicts the storm will fade before hitting Canada. Ontario Chief Meteorologist Fred Turnbull believes otherwise, but his broadcasted warnings go unheeded. Hazel hits Toronto on the 16th and within 12 hours dumps 4 inches of rain on the already swollen rivers. Meandering creeks become torrents, and 3,000 people flee for their lives; 81 die.

**October 30.** The U.S. Armed Forces report the abolition of all-Negro units. The impetus for integration came from President Truman's Commission on Equality of Treatment and Opportunity in the Armed Services (established in 1948) and from the realities of the Korean battlefield. Since 1949, the number of black officers and enlisted men has doubled, with the greatest increase coming in the army.

**October 31.** In Algeria, the Front de la Libération Nationale (FLN) revolts against French rule. France colonized the territory between 1830 and 1860 and, by the turn of the century, had denied most political rights to the Arab population. In 1947, Paris promised the Moslem people a role in politics and gradual control, but colonial authorities continue to stall. When the French military responds violently, new recruits flock to the heavily outnumbered FLN.

**November 2.** Unusually close midterm elections see the Democrats regain narrow control of Congress. Sam Rayburn and Lyndon Johnson head the House and Senate.

**November 15.** Implementing Eisenhower's "Atoms for Peace" plan, the United States, Canada, Britain, France, Australia, and South Africa agree to distribute fissionable material to less developed nations. The U.N. agency will hopefully short-circuit the inevitable development of weapon technologies. Other nonnuclear nations, as well as the USSR, are encouraged to join.

**November 20.** Washington and Ottawa announce construction plans for DEW, a Distant Early-Warning Line of radar stations above the Arctic circle. Currently the two nations rely on several radar systems: fixed stations off the northeast coast of the United States; transport planes and naval picket vessels; the Pinetree Line, completed this year, along the U.S.-Canada border; and the Mid-Canada Line south of Hudson Bay.

**November 30.** At a televised celebration in Westminster Hall, both Houses of Parliament and some 2,000 guests commemorate Winston Churchill's 80th birthday. The first British prime minister so honored, Churchill claims, "I have never accepted what many people have kindly said—namely that I inspired the nation [during the Second World War]. . . . It was the nation and the race dwelling all round the globe that had the lion heart. I had the luck to be called upon to give the roar."

**December 2.** A mutual defense treaty with Nationalist China completes a series of Asian-American alliances. The United States pledges to retaliate against a Communist attack on Formosa, but does not guarantee protection for offshore islands.

**December 2.** The U.S. Senate votes to "condemn" Joseph McCarthy on a variety of counts following charges of abuse of power by Republican Ralph Flanders and Independent Wayne Morse.

The fifth investigation of the senator had recommended formal censure on two counts. The Senate bitterly debated the issue before splitting 67–22 for the lesser condemnation. Nonetheless, the decision marks just the third such verdict in American history.

When Eisenhower compliments the committee, McCarthy makes his final, fatal mistake and attacks the president personally for being "soft" on Communism.

He chairs his last Subcommittee hearing on January 3. Nearly five years of vicious McCarthy accusations, which have ruined uncounted careers and lives, failed to uncover one Communist.

**More news.** For the first time, the United States records more than 4 million births in one year—an estimated 4,076,000. The postwar baby boom will top 4 million annually for the next 10 years.

## Obituaries

**Émilie Dionne** (May 28, 1934–August 6, 1954). The world's first quintuplets to survive birth—Émilie, Yvonne, Annette, Cécile, and Marie—were removed from their northern Ontario farmhouse by the Canadian government and exhibited in a specially built nursery complex. Before the girls returned to their home at the age of 10, some 3 million people visited. In 1953, the famous quints decided to live separate lives. Émilie, a postulant at a nunnery, died of suffocation following an epileptic seizure.

**Arthur Garfield Hays** (December 12, 1881–December 14, 1954). An expert on civil liberties, the American lawyer defended Sacco and Vanzetti and the Scottsboro Boys, and had served as general counsel for the American Civil Liberties Union (ACLU) since 1923.

**Robert H. Jackson** (February 13, 1892–October 9, 1954). Appointed to the Supreme Court in 1941, Jackson took leave after the war to serve as U.S. chief counsel at the Nuremberg war trials. A moderate, he found Truman's seizure of the steel mills unconstitutional and upheld the separation of church and state.

**George "Machine Gun" Kelly** (July 17, 1895–July 17, 1954). The infamous gangster likely never fired a gun. Reportedly, Kelly's wife fabricated his bloodthirsty reputation. He died in prison.

**Agnes Macphail** (March 24, 1890–February 13, 1954). Elected in 1921, the first female member of the Canadian House of Commons championed the poor and underprivileged and founded the Elizabeth Fry Society of Canada to promote prison reform. She sat in Parliament for 19 years.

**Mary Terrell** (September 23, 1863–July 24, 1954). Born in the year Lincoln issued the Emancipation Proclamation, the lifelong crusader against racial discrimination was a charter member and the first president of the NAACP. In 1953, she headed a committee demanding the enforcement of a 75-year-old law against racial discrimination in Washington, D.C., restaurants. Negroes finally began to integrate Terrell's city this year.

## BEGINNINGS AND ENDINGS

**January 14.** Nash-Kelvinator Corp. and Hudson Motor Car Co. merge to form American Motors Corp., the fourth largest auto manufacturer in the United States. AMC production moves from Detroit to Kenosha, Wisconsin.

**February 15.** The Defense Department finishes construction of an "underground Pentagon" beneath Raven Rock Mountain in Frederick County, Maryland. The huge bomb shelter cost $35 million.

**March 30.** Canada's first subway opens in Toronto—4.6 miles.

**April 24.** Employed by Civil Air Transport in the Dien Bien Phu airlift, 32-year-old USAF veteran Paul Holden becomes the first American casualty in the Indochina War. He is severely wounded in the arm and thigh when anti-aircraft fire hits his C-119 Flying Boxcar.

**May 24.** Veterans Day replaces Armistice Day, the November 11 commemoration of W.W.I since 1928.

**June.** With the introduction of Super Constellations, Trans-Canada Air Lines (TCA) eliminates the need for a stopover (at Iceland) on westbound transatlantic flights.

**June 14.** The United States holds the first nationwide civil defense test as a precaution against atomic attack.

**June 14.** President Eisenhower signs a bill modifying the pledge of allegiance to the flag. "One nation, indivisible" becomes "one nation under God," indivisible."

**July 4.** Britain terminates the last continuing W.W.II rationing program, ending 14½ years of limits on meat consumption.

**July 13.** Electronic Associates rents an Analog computer to Princeton University, the first computer put into operation on a commercial basis.

**August 17.** The stockholders of Studebaker Corp. (1902) and Packard Motor Car Co. (1899)—the last independent car manufacturers—agree to merge as Studebaker-Packard Corp. A revitalization at best, further financial losses will force the company to close the U.S. plant in 1963 and the Canadian operation—the last—in 1966.

---

*Statistics:* Of the 2,500 different firms that participated in the development of the American automobile, only 6 remain.

---

**August 17.** The Vatican gives American priests the option of using English instead of Latin in the sacraments of baptism, matrimony, and extreme unction. (Clergymen in France, Germany, Italy, China, and some missionary areas earlier received permission to use the local language.)

**October 25.** Jean Drapeau, age 37, is elected mayor of Montreal. As one of the longest-serving mayors in North America, he will turn the river port into a thriving metropolis.

**November 12.** The immigration processing station at Ellis Island is closed down after 62 years. In 1956, President Eisenhower will order General Services not to sell the New York harbor island, the "gateway to America" for an estimated 20 million immigrants.

**November 15.** Scandinavian Airlines establishes the first regularly scheduled flight over the North Pole—Los Angeles-Copenhagen. An experimental run in 1952, from Los Angeles to Copenhagen, knocked four hours off the route through New York.

**More news.** During W.W.II, the Armed Forces used the military alphabet—Able, Baker, etc.—to name typhoons and hurricanes. (Before the war, meteorologists employed unwieldy latitude-longitude sightings.) This year, the U.S. Weather Service begins assigning 26 preselected female names in alphabetical order.

### New Products and Businesses

After 14 successful years with M&M's, Mars adds all-brown peanut M&M's to its candy line.

New to America this year, English miniature Matchbox cars are packaged in small cardboard boxes.

Sherwood "Shakey" Johnson and his partner Edward Plummer open Shakey's Pizza Parlor in Sacramento. They will franchise in 1958.

In competition with the Corvette, Ford introduces the two-seater Thunderbird for $2,950. The auto maker describes the model as a "personal car," and buyers like the sporty look. First-year sales reach 16,155.

When a single hamburger stand in San Bernardino orders eight milk shake machines, Ray Kroc decides to investigate. The 52-year-old salesman, amazed at the production level, offers to act as the restaurant's exclusive national agent. He opens his first McDonald's franchise next year, in Des Plaines, Illinois.

The Northland Mall—the world's largest shopping center—opens in Detroit with 100 stores.

*Statistics:* In 1955, the American retail industry counts 1,000 shopping centers with another 2,000 under construction or in the planning stages.

## SCIENCE AND TECHNOLOGY

### News

**February 16.** Geologists from Harvard and the University of Wisconsin have discovered the first evidence of plant life on earth more than 1 billion years ago.

**February 23.** School children in Pittsburgh receive the first mass polio immunization shots. With government certification of Salk's vaccine, in late March, some 440,000 elementary students in 44 states, 3 areas of Canada, and part of Finland are immunized; another 210,000 are injected with a test placebo. Volunteers for the largest U.S. peacetime mobilization ever include 20,000 doctors, 40,000 nurses, and 50,000 school teachers.

Although three American scientists receive a Nobel prize this year for devising better ways to detect polio virus in tissue cultures, neither Salk nor later Albert Sabin will receive a Nobel for their vaccines.

*Statistics:* This year's new polio cases are the third highest on record—40,000, with about half paralytic.

**March 9.** At the Pennsylvania State College of Optometry, Dr. John O'Neill reports the development of the first cornea-size plastic contact lenses. Contacts date back to Adolf Fick in 1887, but the German physician only had glass to work with.

**April 5.** Dr. R. G. Bunge reports the first successful artificial insemination of women with stored frozen semen.

**June 21.** Epidemiologists present dramatic evi-

*General Dynamics Electric Boat Division launches the U.S.S. Nautilus on January 21. The world's first nuclear submarine, built at a cost of $55 million, will set out on its first sea trial in January 1955.*

dence that lung cancer occurs 3 to 9 times more often in smokers than in nonsmokers; among heavy smokers the rate is 5 to 16 times higher.

Following the announcement, cigarette sales fall off, but within weeks the number of smokers rises again, to an estimated 60 percent of American men and 30 percent of women.

**August 5.** The B-52, in its first flight, exceeds all USAF expectations. Modernized over the years, the intercontinental aircraft will eventually achieve a range of 12,000 miles. Production of the strategic bomber will end in 1962.

**December.** With 1,500 leased over the next 15 years, the IBM 650 becomes the first mass-produced computer. It rents for $3,000 to $4,000 per month.

**December 23.** In the first successful kidney transplant from a live donor, Ronald Herrick receives the organ from his twin brother, Richard, in Boston.

**More news.** Texas Instruments in California introduces the first practical silicon transistor. The earlier germanium transistors have dropped in price, but, unable to function well at high temperatures, they will give way to silicon by the 1960s.

*Boeing wheels out the Dash 80 for a test flight on July 15. With further development, the 707 will first fly commercially in late 1957; it will quickly become the standard long-range jetliner.*

• American Ernest Robert Sears achieves a breakthrough in wheat genetics, showing that specific chromosomes can be manipulated to produce high-yield, drought-resistant hybrids.

• Vincent Du Vigneaud is the first to synthesize a hormone, the simple protein oxytocin.

### Other Discoveries, Developments, and Inventions

Gas turbine-powered automobile, the XP-21 Firebird from GM

Traveling sidewalk between the Erie and H&M Jersey City railroad stations

USAF rocket-driven sled, on rails, to study rapid deceleration

Wraparound windshield, to reduce blind spots, in Buicks, Cadillacs, and Oldsmobiles

Chlorpromazine, the first antipsychotic drug

Solar battery from Bell Telephone Labs

Adhesive-backed vinyl Con-Tact paper (59 cents a yard)

Instant nonfat dry milk from Carnation, after 40 years of experimentation

Artillery range finder, from American Locomotive

### Obituaries

**Jacques Brandenberger** (1873–July 13, 1954). While living in France in 1908, the Swiss-born chemist invented cellophane. He sold the U.S. commercial rights to du Pont in 1919.

**Samuel J. Crumbine** (September 17, 1862–July 12, 1954). The "frontier doctor," in fighting for better sanitation, invented the flyswatter in 1905 and succeeded in outlawing the common drinking cup in trains, hotels, and schools (which subsequently led to the invention of the paper cup).

**David Fairchild** (April 7, 1869–August 6, 1954). The U.S. government botanist vastly increased agricultural output through the introduction of some 200,000 plants, including Japanese rice and Mexican cotton.

**Enrico Fermi** (September 29, 1901–November 28, 1954). History credits the Italian-American physicist, more than anyone else, with creating the atomic bomb. By bombarding atoms with neutrons, Fermi produced artificial radioactivity, an achievement that brought him the 1938 Nobel Prize. He refused to return to Fascist Italy, immigrated to the United States, and, two years later, joined the team of scientists working on the bomb. On December 2, 1942, it was Fermi who completed the first nuclear chain reaction, marking the birth of the atomic age. An American citizen since 1945, he died of cancer.

**Kokichi Mikimoto** (January 1858–September 21, 1954). In the 1890s, the merchant placed irritants in oysters and produced the first cultured pearls. He amassed a fortune from his discovery.

**John Daniel Rust** (September 6, 1892–January 20, 1954). The U.S. inventor developed the basic principles of the mechanical cotton picker in 1927. The machine entered mass production in the late 1940s.

**Gideon Sundback** (April 24, 1880–June 21, 1954). Whitcomb Judson invented a crude zipper in the early 1890s, but Sundback perfected the slide fastener and its means of manufacture. The Swedish-American's 1914 patent expired in 1931.

**Wallace Turnbull** (October 16, 1870–November 26, 1954). The Canadian first tested his variable pitch propeller in 1927. The blade adjustment, for take-off and level flight, was hailed as the most significant invention in the history of aeronautics.

## THE ARTS

January 20—*The Caine Mutiny Court-Martial*, with Lloyd Nolan, Henry Fonda, John Hodiak (415 perfs.)

May 13—*The Pajama Game*, with John Raitt, Janis Paige, Eddie Foy, Jr., Carol Haney (1,063 perfs.)

September 30—*The Boy Friend*, with Julie Andrews (485 perfs.)

November 4—*Fanny*, with Ezio Pinza, Florence Henderson, Walter Slezak (888 perfs.)

December 8—*The Bad Seed*, with Patty McCormack, Nancy Kelly, Eileen Heckart (332 perfs.)

### Tony Awards

Actor (Dramatic)—David Wayne, *The Teahouse of the August Moon*
Actress (Dramatic)—Audrey Hepburn, *Ondine*
Actor (Musical)—Alfred Drake, *Kismet*
Actress (Musical)—Dolores Gray, *Carnival in Flanders*
Play—*The Teahouse of the August Moon*
Musical—*Kismet*

### News

**April 4.** Arturo Toscanini resigns as conductor of the NBC Symphony Orchestra (1937–1954) at the age of 87.

**November 10.** Dedicated at Arlington, the Iwo Jima Memorial Monument reenacts Joe Rosenthal's celebrated photo of the W.W.II flag-raising. Felix de Weldon sculpted the 32-foot-high bronze figures that honor all marine war dead.

**December 22.** The U.S. Mint admits to the accidental release of 3 million rare Liberty Head silver dollars, valued at $2–$17 each.

### Obituaries

**Charles Ives** (October 20, 1874–May 19, 1954). After his death, Ives will come to be regarded as the most important American composer of this century. His *Third Symphony* won the 1947 Pulitzer.

**Henri Matisse** (December 31, 1869–November 3, 1954). The renowned French artist used color and form to express emotion in various media.

**Oscar Straus** (March 6, 1870–January 11,

1954). The Austrian-American composed 50 operettas, but he is best remembered for *The Chocolate
Soldier* (1908).

## WORDS

Harriette Arnow, *The Dollmaker*
Pierre Boulle, *The Bridge Over the River Kwai*
Adelle Davis, *Let's Eat Right to Keep Fit*
Ian Fleming, *Casino Royale*
William Golding, *Lord of the Flies*
Mac Hyman, *No Time for Sergeants*
Evan Hunter, *The Blackboard Jungle*
Morton Thompson, *Not as a Stranger*
J. R. R. Tolkien, *The Two Towers*
J. R. R. Tolkien, *The Fellowship of the Ring*

### News

**August 16.** Time-Life, Inc., launches *Sports Illustrated.* The magazine's first "Sportsman of the Year"
is Roger Bannister.

**September 21.** Despite TV's growing popularity,
the Brooklyn Public Library's annual report indicates that circulation has topped 8 million books for
the first time since the Depression. In London, the
British Library Association claims TV has actually
increased reading levels.

**More news.** Several new paperback lines, with
their more literary content, are priced close to $1.

### Cartoons and Comics

**October 27.** Under the threat of censorship from
the Senate Subcommittee on Juvenile Delinquency,
publishers move to self-regulate the comic book
industry. Issued today, the Comics Code Authority
forbids: plots depicting the "unique details" of a
crime; the use of profanities, obscenities, or the
words *terror* or *horror*; depraved or gruesome cover
art; and the sympathetic treatment of criminals or
undignified portrayal of law officers. Good must
always triumph over evil. The publishers describe
their code as "the most stringent . . . in existence
for any communications media."

**More news.** Writer Mort Walker and artist Dik

Browne introduce the comic strip *Hi and Lois.* As
well, this year Bradley Anderson debuts *Marma-
duke.*

### TIME *Man of the Year*

John Foster Dulles

### New Words and Phrases

belt (to sing loudly)
desegregation
do-it-yourself
dragster
fall-out (particles falling from the atmosphere,
    specifically those originating in atomic blasts)
goof (a mistake; to make a mistake)
hard sell
punk out (to quit)
scifi (science fiction)
sonic boom
VTO (aircraft vertical take-off)
windfall profits

### Obituaries

**Robert Capa** (October 22, 1913–May 25, 1954).
With his motto "the closer the better," the renowned photographer captured the first dramatic
close-ups of battle. (The *New York Times* says the
Hungarian-American free-lancer "made veteran
combat troops blink in uneasy disbelief.") Capa was
killed by a land mine outside of Hanoi.

**Colette (Sidonie Gabrielle Colette)** (January 28,
1873–August 3, 1954). Perhaps the leading French
woman writer of this century, Colette captured the
emotions of love and evoked the life of the senses in
more than 50 novels and scores of short stories.

**James Hilton** (September 9, 1900–December
20, 1954). The best-selling British novelist saw five
of his books turned into movies, including *Lost
Horizon* (1933) and *Goodbye Mr. Chips* (1934).

**George McManus** (January 23, 1884–October
22, 1954). His comic strip *Bringing Up Father* was
syndicated to 750 newspapers worldwide and was
made the subject of several radio shows and films.

# FASHION

## Haute Couture

Paris finally abandons the austere pointed bustline, tiny waist, and full skirts of the New Look. The new softer, straighter silhouette deemphasizes the bust, relaxes the waistline, and places belts, sashes, or drapery at the hip.

## News

**February 5.** With perfect timing, Coco Chanel leaves retirement to launch a comeback. Critics reject the 1920s and 1930s styles, but her simple, practical clothes—the "little black dress," blouses with bows, easy-fitting pastel suits with collarless, braid-trimmed cardigan jackets—are a tremendous success. By the end of the decade, every fashionable woman will have at least one classic Chanel suit in her wardrobe.

**More news.** The House of Worth in Paris, just four years short of its centenary, accepts a takeover bid from Paquin. The first to present gowns on live models, Worth set the fashion standard for American and European high society for 50 years.

• Levi Strauss & Co. enters the sportswear business with Lighter Blues® casual slacks.

• On October 27, 1938, du Pont foretold the end of silk stockings with the announced development of a group of synthetic polymers named nylons. When the first nylon stockings appeared across the United States, on May 15, 1940, retailers reported near riots.

But war soon diverted the new fiber to military usage (largely in parachutes) and women returned to rayon, cotton, or wool stockings. Since the war, production has slowly gathered steam until, this year, a total of 672 million pairs of nylons account for 95 percent of the hosiery market.

## Colors and Materials

The return of patterned fabrics, particularly flowers, marks the beginning of a fashion revolution.

A silken shimmer dominates textile manufacture with satin-backed suitings, shiny coat fabrics, and silk worsteds for dresses.

Couturiers seldom use "miracle fibers" in outer garments, but young people love Orlon sweaters and any fabric incorporating nontarnishable Lurex metallic strands for sparkle.

## Clothes

Designers emphasize the "costume look" with overblouses made for specific suits and dresses matched or blended with coats.

The colorful, chunky Italian sweater appears on the scene, with wide armholes, large polo neck or turtleneck, and sometimes a practical hood.

Smart and easy-to-care-for permanent pleating spreads to sportswear, particularly tennis skirts.

Three-quarter-length and seven-eighth-length coats fall straight from the shoulder.

Slacks shorten, shorts lengthen, and buckles appear at the back of both.

A cotton T-shirt dress, with crew neckline and a belt at the waist, is a summer favorite.

The jumper, recut to adult lines, enjoys a resurgence. Many sell with companion blouses or jackets.

Work-shirt sales decline—down 15 percent over the first six months—as men switch to lighterweight cotton sport shirts.

Young men back from the Korean War make their own fashion statement on college campuses—Bermuda shorts, gray flannels, reversible loud vests, button-down shirts, sports jackets threaded with Lurex, and 1½-inch-wide ties.

## Accessories

Longer necklaces—particularly the 60-inch bead rope—flatter sweaters. The new Pop-it beads allow for length changes.

Gloves and the clutch or envelope bag finish outfits.

Chanel's reentry into high fashion brings back the beret.

For men, the shoe industry introduces a low-top, two-eyelet style and new leathers—embossed, meshlike, or perforated.

### Hair and Cosmetics

During the first years of this decade, teenage boys wear a duck-tail or flattop haircut while most men opt for the crew cut.

Max Factor introduces Erace, a flesh-colored makeup stick for concealing dark circles under the eyes.

## POPULAR MUSIC

"Hey There"/"This Ole House"—Rosemary Clooney

"Little Things Mean a Lot"—Kitty Kallen

"Wanted"—Perry Como

"Oh, My Papa (Oh, Mein Papa)"—Eddie Fisher

"Sh-Boom (Life Could Be a Dream)"—Crew-Cuts

"Mr. Sandman"—Chordettes

"I Need You Now"—Eddie Fisher

"Make Love to Me!"—Jo Stafford

"That's Amore"—Dean Martin

"Secret Love"—Doris Day

"Hernando's Hideaway"—Archie Bleyer & His Orchestra

"Home for the Holidays"—Perry Como

"Papa Loves Mambo"—Perry Como

"Shake, Rattle & Roll"—Bill Haley & His Comets

"Three Coins in a Fountain"—Four Aces

"Young at Heart"—Frank Sinatra

"The Naughty Lady of Shady Lane"—Ames Brothers

"Stranger in Paradise"—Tony Bennett/Four Aces

### News

**May 1.** White disc jockey Alan Freed plays black rhythm and blues (R&B) records from independent labels on his late-night Cleveland radio show, "Moondog Rock 'n' Roll Party." Tonight, in Newark, New Jersey, he holds his first rock 'n' roll dance

outside his home base. The Clovers, the Harptones, Muddy Waters, and others perform as thousands are turned away at the door.

**July.** At Sun studio in Memphis, a local boy cuts his first record, "That's All Right (Mama)" and "Blue Moon of Kentucky." Elvis Presley is 19 years old.

**July 17–18.** Optimistic organizers hope Dizzy Gillespie, Oscar Peterson, Ella Fitzgerald, and other performers will draw about 5,000 people to the first Newport Jazz Festival. Attendance at the two-day event reaches 7,000.

**September.** The big labels use any available singer, usually a former big band vocalist, to record their version of the newest hit. But young white audiences, tired of bland pop tunes, are tuning in to Negro radio stations and buying that music at Negro record stores.

In an attempt to recover that lost trade, record companies have begun to cover black R&B hits with white artists—the Crew-Cuts on the Chords' "Sh-Boom," Bill Haley on Joe Turner's "Shake, Rattle and Roll," the McGuire Sisters on the Moonglows' "Sincerely." But cover versions just delay the inevitable. Alan Freed gains wider exposure with his move to WINS-Radio in New York this month, and disc jockeys across the country are encouraged to follow his example.

---

*Statistics:* This year, Americans buy a record 225 million records and for the first time 78's account for less than 50 percent of the dollar volume. As a result, Mercury and RCA Victor no longer send 78 rpm demos to radio stations.

---

**More news.** Muzak develops a self-contained operating system for office and industry music. About the size of a desk, the 16-hour playback machine uses a synchro-clock to start and stop the music at a predetermined hour.

• Records are presented in more elaborate and expensive packaging. Even at $25 or more, two such albums lead in sales volume, including Bing Crosby's greatest hits.

• Nat King Cole signs a two-year exclusive contract with the Sands Hotel. With guaranteed access to all of the hotel's facilities, Cole becomes the first black performer to cross the Las Vegas color barrier.

• The mambo, an advanced Cuban form of the rhumba, has gained in popularity in the five years since its introduction. This year, the cha-cha-cha appears as a variation.

• Canadian singer Hank Snow remains on the CW charts for 52 weeks, through this year and next, with "I Don't Hurt Anymore."

• Eddie Fisher, age 26, whose career was interrupted by military service, is the nation's No. 1 singing idol with two big hits.

• Motorola produces the first high-fidelity record players while Philco manufactures the first phonograph without a radio.

### New Recording Artists

LaVern Baker
Sammy Davis, Jr.
McGuire Sisters
Platters
Elvis Presley
Andy Williams

## Obituaries

**Louis Silvers** (September 6, 1889–March 26, 1954). The Hollywood musical director's popular compositions included "April Showers" (1921).

## MOVIES

*Bad Day at Black Rock* (d. John Sturges; color)—Spencer Tracy, Robert Ryan, Anne Francis, Dean Jagger, Walter Brennan

*The Barefoot Contessa* (d. Joseph L. Mankiewicz; color)—Humphrey Bogart, Ava Gardner, Edmond O'Brien

*Beat the Devil* (d. John Huston; bw)—Humphrey Bogart, Gina Lollobrigida, Jennifer Jones, Peter Lorre

*The Bridges at Toko-Ri* (d. Mark Robson; color)—William Holden, Fredric March, Grace Kelly, Mickey Rooney

*Broken Lance* (d. Edward Dmytryk; color)—Spencer Tracy, Robert Wagner, Jean Peters, Richard Widmark, Katy Jurado

*The Caine Mutiny* (d. Edward Dmytryk; color)—Humphrey Bogart, José Ferrer, Van Johnson

*Carmen Jones* (d. Otto Preminger; color)—Dorothy Dandridge, Harry Belafonte, Pearl Bailey

*The Country Girl* (d. George Seaton; bw)—Bing Crosby, Grace Kelly, William Holden

*The Dam Busters* (British, d. Michael Anderson; bw)—Richard Todd, Michael Redgrave

*Dial M for Murder* (d. Alfred Hitchcock; color; 3-D)—Ray Milland, Grace Kelly, Robert Cummings

*Doctor in the House* (British, d. Ralph Thomas; color)—Dirk Bogarde, Kenneth More, James Robertson Justice

*Executive Suite* (d. Robert Wise; bw)—William Holden, June Allyson, Barbara Stanwyck, Fredric March

*The Glenn Miller Story* (d. Anthony Mann; color)—James Stewart, June Allyson

*The High and the Mighty* (d. William A. Wellman; color)—John Wayne, Claire Trevor, Laraine Day, Robert Stack

*Hobson's Choice* (British, d. David Lean; bw)—Charles Laughton, Brenda de Banzie, John Mills

*Johnny Guitar* (d. Nicholas Ray; color)—Joan Crawford, Sterling Hayden, Mercedes McCambridge, Scott Brady

*On the Waterfront* (d. Elia Kazan; bw)—Marlon Brando, Lee J. Cobb, Rod Steiger, Karl Malden, Eva Marie Saint

*Rear Window* (d. Alfred Hitchcock; color)—James Stewart, Grace Kelly, Raymond Burr, Thelma Ritter, Wendell Corey

*River of No Return* (d. Otto Preminger; color)—Robert Mitchum, Marilyn Monroe, Tommy Rettig

*Sabrina* (d. Billy Wilder; bw)—Humphrey Bogart, William Holden, Audrey Hepburn

*Seven Samurai* (Japanese, d. Akira Kurosawa; bw)—Toshiro Mifune, Takashi Shimura

*A Star Is Born* (d. George Cukor; color)—Judy Garland, James Mason, Jack Carson

*Them!* (d. Gordon Douglas; bw)—James Whitmore, Edmund Gwenn, Joan Weldon, James Arness

*20,000 Leagues Under the Sea* (d. Richard Fleischer; color)—Kirk Douglas, James Mason, Paul Lukas, Peter Lorre

## Academy Awards

**March 25.** Donald O'Connor hosts in Hollywood, while Fredric March is the master of ceremonies in New York.

Best Picture—*From Here to Eternity*
Best Actor—William Holden (*Stalag 17*)
Best Actress—Audrey Hepburn (*Roman Holiday*)
Best Director—Fred Zinnemann (*From Here to Eternity*)
Best Supporting Actor—Frank Sinatra (*From Here to Eternity*)
Best Supporting Actress—Donna Reed (*From Here to Eternity*)
Best Song—"Secret Love" from *Calamity Jane*

*From Here to Eternity* ties the eight-Oscar record set by *Gone With the Wind* in 1939. Walt Disney sets a new one-year individual record—four Oscars (a cartoon, a two-reel short, and two documentaries).

NBC infuriates winners and TV viewers alike by cutting to commercials in the middle of acceptance speeches, and when the show runs over the allotted two hours, the director gives William Holden just enough time for a terse "Thank you."

## News

**January 18.** The U.S. Supreme Court upholds the 1952 ruling guaranteeing freedom of speech to motion pictures. Yet the failure to rule all censorship unconstitutional only confuses the 6 states and 50 cities currently censoring movies.

**Midyear.** After a glut of 3-D films—60 over two years—the craze fades. Moviegoers have found the flimsy cardboard glasses a nuisance and literally a headache with the polarized lenses. The few remaining 3-D pictures are released as conventional prints.

CinemaScope, on the other hand, is a huge international success. Studios rent the special camera lenses from 20th Century-Fox, and some 9,000 U.S. theaters switch to CinemaScope screens and equipment by the end of the year.

**Summer.** Drive-ins follow the bigger-is-better trend and increase their screen width to 100 feet.

**July 12.** A Los Angeles Superior Court dismisses a 1951 damage suit brought by 23 blacklisted actors and writers, ruling that Hollywood studios acted within their rights in denying employment to those who refused to testify before HUAC.

**October 18.** In *Gene Autry and Roy Rogers v. Republic Pictures*, the U.S. Supreme Court finds motion picture producers have the right to determine the medium of exhibition. The cowboy stars had opposed the lease of their pre-1948 features to commercial TV.

• Three years in the making, the first British feature-length cartoon, *Animal Farm*, reaches theaters.

*Marilyn Monroe with her new husband, former New York Yankees star Joe DiMaggio. The actress will file for divorce nine months later.*

• To counteract the appeal of CinemaScope, Paramount releases *White Christmas* in VistaVision. The larger negative, reduced for projection, provides a sharper, clearer image on a more normally proportioned screen (1.85 to 1).

• *Doctor in the House*, the story of students at the end of their medical training, spawns six more films, through to 1970, and a television series.

• Over three months, RKO shoots *The Conqueror* just outside of St. George, then hauls back 60 tons of rock and desert sand for additional studio scenes. In later years, that area of Utah will be identified as a radioactive hot spot from the Nevada atomic tests. A statistically high number of the film's cast and crew will die from cancer, including director Dick Powell and actresses Agnes Moorehead and Susan Hayward. John Wayne is the star of the movie.

• Concentrating on epics and spectaculars, the studios put out 25 percent fewer motion pictures this year. In recognition of the serious downturn, the Theater Owners of America and Columbia Pictures each set up funds for independent film production.

• For the first time, color movies equal or surpass (depending on the source) the number of black-and-white films. Surprisingly, the trend temporarily reverses—back down to 48.6 percent in 1955, then 43 percent in 1956—before climbing still higher.

• In 1939, Rhett Butler's famous line—"Frankly, my dear, I don't give a damn"—finally broke the screen taboo against swear words. This year, *On the Waterfront* reaches a second cinema landmark with the previously forbidden "Go to hell."

| *Top Box Office Stars* | *Newcomers* |
| --- | --- |
| John Wayne | Audrey Hepburn |
| Dean Martin & | Maggie McNamara |
| Jerry Lewis | Grace Kelly |
| Gary Cooper | Richard Burton |
| James Stewart | Pat Crowley |
| Marilyn Monroe | Guy Madison |
| Alan Ladd | Suzan Ball |
| William Holden | Elaine Stewart |
| Bing Crosby | Aldo Ray |
| Jane Wyman | Cameron Mitchell |
| Marlon Brando | |

## Top Money-Maker of the Year

*White Christmas* (1954) (d. Michael Curtiz; color)—Bing Crosby, Danny Kaye, Rosemary Clooney, Vera-Ellen

## Quote of the Year

Girl: "What are you rebelling against?"
Johnny: "Whaddya got?"

Marlon Brando sets the pattern for troubled young bikers in *The Wild One*. (Screenplay by John Paxton; from a short story by Frank Rooney)

## Obituaries

**Lionel Barrymore** (April 28, 1878–November 15, 1954). The first of the famous Barrymores to abandon the theater for film, in 1925, Lionel won the 1930–1931 best actor Oscar for *A Free Soul*. Partially paralyzed in 1938 by arthritis and a leg injury, Barrymore continued to perform from a wheelchair. The veteran actor made some 250 films with MGM, but movie fans remember him best as old Mr. Potter, the skinflint in *It's a Wonderful Life* (1946).

**Sydney Greenstreet** (December 27, 1879–January 18, 1954). The British-American stage actor became a star "fat man" with his first screen role—the ruthless Kasper Guttman in *The Maltese Falcon* (1941). He created his other most memorable role in *Casablanca* (1943).

**Will(iam) H. Hays** (November 5, 1879–March 7, 1954). Appointed the first MPPDA president in 1922, Hays devised a strict code of production do's and don'ts, by 1930, to keep film censorship within the industry. The "czar" of Hollywood retired in 1945, but he lived to see the Hays Code breached by *The Moon Is Blue* in 1953.

# TELEVISION AND RADIO

## New Prime-Time TV Programs

"The Adventures of Rin Tin Tin" (October 15, 1954–August 28, 1959; Western)—Lee Aaker, James Brown, Joe Sawyer

"Caesar's Hour" (September 27, 1954–May 25, 1957; Comedy Variety)—Sid Caesar, Carl Reiner, Howard Morris, Nanette Fabray

"December Bride" (October 4, 1954–September 1959; Situation Comedy)—Spring Byington, Frances Rafferty, Dean Miller

"Father Knows Best" (October 3, 1954–September 1960; Situation Comedy)—Robert Young, Jane Wyatt, Elinor Donahue, Billy Gray, Lauren Chapin

"The George Gobel Show" (October 2, 1954–June 5, 1960; Comedy Variety)—George Gobel

"Lassie" (September 12, 1954–September 12, 1971; Family Adventure)—Tommy Rettig (1954–1957), John Provost (1957–1964), June Lockhart (1958–1964) Paul Martin (1958–1964)

"The Lineup" (October 1, 1954–January 20, 1960; Police Drama)—Warner Anderson, Tom Tully (1954–1959), Marshall Reed (1955–1959)

"People Are Funny" (September 19, 1954–April 2, 1961; Quiz/Audience Participation)—Emcee: Art Linkletter

"Tonight" (September 27, 1954–January 25, 1957; Talk/Variety)—Host: Steve Allen

"Walt Disney" (October 27, 1954–  ; Family Anthology)—Host: Walt Disney (1954–1966) *Note:* The original title "Disneyland" becomes "Walt Disney Presents" in 1958, "Walt Disney's Wonderful World of Color" in 1961, and "The Wonderful World of Disney" in 1969.

## Emmy Awards 1953 (February 11, 1954)

Best Dramatic Show—"The United States Steel Hour" (ABC)

Best Variety Program—"Omnibus" (CBS)

Best Situation Comedy—"I Love Lucy" (CBS)

Best Children's Program—"Kukla, Fran and Ollie" (NBC)

Best Actor in a Series—Donald O'Connor ("Colgate Comedy Hour," NBC)

Best Actress in a Series—Eve Arden ("Our Miss Brooks," CBS)

Most Outstanding Personality—Edward R. Murrow ("See It Now," CBS)

## News

**January 1.** The Tournament of Roses parade marks the first prolonged NBC color telecast where neither movement nor lighting can be controlled. At this point, 22 cities have received the RCA-compatible color equipment. While reviews describe the results as "exceedingly good," viewers must draw their shades to prevent light from washing the colors on the screen.

**January 3.** Bing Crosby appears in his first TV special. Still, 10 years will pass before "Der Bingle" accepts a weekly series.

**March 9.** Edward R. Murrow becomes the first major journalist to launch a full-scale attack on the politics of Joseph McCarthy. Clips and commentary demonstrate the senator's browbeating tactics, his slandering, and his uncouth social habits. The "See It Now" broadcast prompts an outpouring of calls and telegrams, 10–1 in support of Murrow, although thoughtful critics question the ultimate influence of television. His courageous stand, supported by CBS, is later credited with bringing about the senator's downfall.

**May 30.** CBC radio broadcasts "The Investigator," a play about a man investigating heaven. The parallels with McCarthyism raise positive and negative reaction in the United States.

**June 6.** A telecast from the Vatican inaugurates the eight-nation Eurovision network. Up to 20 million people watch the pope as he urges networks to be selective in their programming.

**September 7.** The FCC requires radio and TV stations to offer equal treatment to all legally qualified candidates for the same political office and to charge them the going commercial rates.

**September 11.** Lee Ann Meriwether, age 19, of San Francisco, is named Miss America in the first nationally televised beauty pageant.

**September 12.** Incredibly brave and smart, Lassie puts up with endless dim-witted owners—

"What is it, girl?"—in seven different TV versions over the next 20 years.

**September 27.** Broadcast just in the New York area since June 1953, Steve Allen moves "Tonight" to an NBC weeknight slot. A composer and marvelous ad-libber, he interacts with regulars, guests, members of the audience, even people on the street.

But, with a prime-time series in the summer of 1956, Allen will cut back to a Wednesday–Friday schedule and comic Ernie Kovacs will sit in as permanent Monday–Tuesday host in October. Allen will leave the show in January 1957.

**October 15.** The great-great-grandson of the original movie Rin-Tin-Tin, who died in 1932, is one of several German shepherds playing the star in the TV adventure series. A formula program—a dog, a boy, and the cavalry—Rinty becomes wildly popular. After five years in prime time, the ABC program will move to the late afternoon schedule through 1961.

**October 21.** Barry Nelson plays the first James Bond in a production of "Casino Royale" on the CBS *Climax* drama anthology. Peter Lorre plays a Soviet agent.

**October 27.** CBS and NBC turned down the deal, but ABC agreed to invest in Disneyland and pay $50,000 per episode for a Walt Disney television series. With a unique programming philosophy, Disney sends the network 21 episodes for scheduling throughout the year, rather than fall back on summer reruns. ABC telecasts "Disneyland" at the half-hour to edge out rival shows.

The first broadcast features "Plane Crazy" (1928), Mickey Mouse's first starring film, and a preview of upcoming shows and attractions at the theme park still under construction. (Right from the beginning, Disney wisely shoots all programs in color.) The December hit show (see below) ensures immediate success for the series, but the overall blend of action stories, comedy, real-life adventure, animals, and animation are what turn Walt Disney and his show into an American institution.

**November 1.** The first transistor radio, the pocket-size Regency, runs on a power cell and costs $49.95. Consumers describe the radio's sound as high-pitched and tinny.

**December 15.** As the first episode airs tonight, Disney filmmakers are killing Davy Crockett off in the third. But Fess Parker, dressed in buckskins and a coonskin hat, turns the real-life American frontiersman into a cult phenomenon. Pleas pour in to save Davy from his inevitable fate at the Alamo.

Rather than deny history, Disney films the pioneer's younger years for "The Legends of Davy Crockett," a river race against Mike Fink and battles with river pirates. The series makes a star of Parker and revives the career of his partner Buddy Ebsen.

---

*Statistics:* Only 1 percent of U.S. households own color TV sets, but NBC and CBS together transmit 68 hours of color programming this year.

---

**December 16.** For the first time in the industry's short history, television profits exceed radio's—$68 million to $55 million.

**December 26.** "Who knows . . . what evil . . . lllurks . . . in the hearts of men? The Shadow knows!" For 24 years, the Shadow remained invisible to right wrongs, protect the innocent, and punish the guilty. (Orson Welles played the Shadow until 1938.) The radio program has its final broadcast today.

**More news.** The White House adds actor-producer Robert Montgomery to the presidential staff as a special adviser in visual communications.

• United Press expands coverage with a regional audio service for radio-news operations. National within four years, the feed helps those stations wishing to remain independent of network affiliation. Twenty years will pass before AP offers the same service.

• "General Electric Theater," in its second season, hires a host, actor Ronald Reagan. He will remain with the program until it leaves the air in 1962.

• Food reflects the growing influence of television

in American homes. Along with new snacks, shoppers bring home Swanson frozen TV dinners. National sales of the novelty product immediately take off.

## Television Commercials

Hamm's Beer—Introduced this year, the trademark bear becomes one of the most recognized advertising figures in the United States.

Westinghouse—In a legendary moment in early television, Betty Furness simply cannot open a Westinghouse refrigerator door during a live broadcast.

## Memorable Radio Programs End

"The Amos 'n' Andy Show" (August 19, 1929)
"Beulah" (1945)
"The Bing Crosby Show" (September 2, 1931)
"The Bob Hope Show" (September 27, 1938)
"The Falcon" (July 3, 1945)
"Let's Pretend" (1939)
"Mary Margaret McBride" (1934)
"Mr. Keen, Tracer of Lost Persons" (October 12, 1937)
"The Shadow" (August 1930)
"Sky King" (October 28, 1946)
"Stars Over Hollywood" (1941)
"The Theatre Guild on the Air" (September 9, 1945)
"Twenty Questions" (February 2, 1946)

# SPORTS

## Winners

### Baseball

World Series—New York Giants (AL), 4 games; Cleveland Indians (NL), 0 games
Player of the Year—Yogi Berra (New York Yankees, AL); Willie Mays (New York Giants, NL)
Rookie of the Year—Bob Grim (New York Yankees, AL); Wally Moon (St. Louis Cardinals, NL)

### Football

NFL Championship—Cleveland Browns 56, Detroit Lions 10
College Bowls (January 1, 1954)—
Rose Bowl, Michigan State 28, UCLA 20
Cotton Bowl, Rice 28, Alabama 6
Orange Bowl, Oklahoma 7, Maryland 0
Sugar Bowl, Georgia Tech 42, West Virginia 19
Heisman Trophy—Alan Ameche (Wisconsin, FB)
Grey Cup—Edmonton Eskimos 26, Montreal Alouettes 25

### Basketball

NBA Championship—Minneapolis Lakers, 4 games; Syracuse Nationals, 3 games
Rookie of the Year—Ray Felix (Baltimore Bullets)
NCAA Championship—La Salle 92, Bradley 76

### Tennis

U.S. National—Men, Vic Seixus (vs. Rex Hartwig); Women, Doris Hart (vs. Louise Brough)
Wimbledon—Men, Jaroslav Drobny (vs. Kenneth Rosewall); Women, Maureen Connolly (vs. Louise Brough)

### Golf

Masters—Sam Snead
U.S. Open—Ed Furgol
British Open—Peter Thomson

### Hockey

Stanley Cup—Detroit Red Wings, 4 games; Montreal Canadiens, 3 games

### Ice Skating

World Championship—Men, Hayes Alan Jenkins (U.S.); Women, Gundi Busch (West Germany)
U.S. National—Men, Hayes Alan Jenkins; Women, Tenley Albright

Canadian National—Men, Charles Snelling; Women, Barbara Gratton

*Kentucky Derby*

Determine—Ray York, jockey

*Athlete of the Year*

Male—Willie Mays (Baseball)
Female—Mildred (Babe) Didrickson Zaharias (Golf)

*Last Season*

Sid Abel (Hockey)
Doug Bentley (Hockey)
Max Bentley (Hockey)
Joe Fulks (Basketball)
Joe Garagiola (Baseball)
Mildred (Babe) Didrickson Zaharias (Golf)

## News

**January 1.** Rice University fullback Dicky Moegle sprints down the field in a 95-yard touchdown (TD) run at the Cotton Bowl. Frustrated Alabama fullback Tommy Lewis jumps off the bench and stops him with a flying tackle. The referee picks up the ball and carries it to the Alabama goal line for a touchdown.

**March 7.** The Soviets upset the Canadians, 7–2, in Stockholm to capture their first world ice hockey championship.

**April 12.** With his victory over Ben Hogan, in an 18-hole play-off at Augusta, Sam Snead joins Jimmy Demaret as a three-time winner of the Masters (1949, 1952, 1954).

---

*Statistics:* Golfer Bob Toski, with wins in four major tournaments, heads this year's list of money winners—$65,819. Patty Berg tops the LPGA with $16,011.

---

**May 6.** At the Empire Games in Vancouver, John Landy looks back over his left shoulder as Roger

*Roger Bannister runs the first sub-4-minute mile.*

Bannister surges past on the right in the final yards of the mile race. His 3:58:8 time and Landy's 3:59:6 break a historic sports barrier—the 4-minute mile. Bannister, a 25-year-old English medical student, retires later this month after running just 15 one-mile races.

**May 7.** In testimony before a House Armed Services subcommittee, Army personnel chief General Herbert Powell concedes that Willie Mays was assigned to Fort Eustis during his army service to play baseball (with the club in the physical training department). The general absolves the Giants center fielder of any part in the "shenanigans."

**July 12.** The Major League Baseball Players Association is established to represent players in policy-making negotiations with club owners.

**July 20.** Her horse, frightened by a cement truck, crushes Maureen Connolly's leg against the vehicle, breaking a bone and badly gashing the muscles and tendons. The 20-year-old tennis star, who had successfully defended her French and Wimbledon titles earlier this year, will never compete again.

**September 9.** The first person to swim across

Lake Ontario, Canadian Marilyn Bell reaches Toronto from Youngstown, New York. Radio announcers on both sides of the border kept listeners up to date during the plucky 16-year-old's 20-hour, 56-minute crossing. Next year, she will become the youngest swimmer to cross the English Channel.

**More news.** To speed up the game, the NBA introduces the 24-second clock, requiring teams to shoot within 24 seconds of gaining possession of the ball. As well this year, the NBA attempts to cut back excessive fouling; if a team compiles more than six personal fouls in a quarter, the opposing team receives a bonus foul shot.

• The NHL requires teams to wear white uniforms at home and colored uniforms on the road. Referees and linesmen will wear black-and-white vertically striped shirts.

• This year, 20-year-old Hank Aaron joins the Milwaukee Braves.

## Records

**February 13.** Furman guard Frank Selvy scores 100 points in a 149–95 basketball victory over Newberry, shattering the previous NCAA individual record of 73.

**May 2.** Cardinals outfielder Stan Musial hits a record 5 home runs in a doubleheader against the New York Giants. The Cards win the first game 10–3, but even with the heroics of Stan the Man the Giants win the second, 9–7.

## What They Said

At Empire Stadium on May 6, marathoner James Peters staggers onto the track a full 20 minutes ahead of the next runner. Exhausted, he falls again and again as teammates spur him on. Outraged at the cruelty, spectators yell, "Take him out!" Finally, believing he has reached the finish line, the British runner collapses—20 yards short. On his return home, the wan Peters tells reporters, "I wouldn't have cared if I had died if I had won the race for England."

## Obituaries

**Oscar Charleston** (October 12, 1896–October 6, 1954). Generally regarded as the greatest player of the Negro Leagues, the outfielder possessed a strong throwing arm, incredible speed, and an unerring ability to judge a fly ball. Age forced him to move to first base, but continued success at the plate gave him a lifetime average as high as .376 (from available statistics).

**Lionel Conacher** (May 24, 1902–May 26, 1954). Canada's outstanding athlete of the half-century excelled at several sports. He won the national light-heavyweight boxing title and an Ontario wrestling title before the age of 18, scored three touchdowns for the Toronto Argonauts in their 1921 Grey Cup win, played with the provincial lacrosse champs, was part of the 1926 championship Toronto Triple-A baseball team, and played professional hockey for 12 years. He then entered politics. The Liberal MP died of a heart attack while playing softball against the press corps.

**Charles (Gus) Dorais** (July 2, 1891–January 4, 1954). The 5'7" quarterback, with Knute Rockne, legitimized the forward pass in a 1913 Notre Dame victory over the unbeaten Army team.

**Hugh Duffy** (November 26, 1866–October 19, 1954). In 1894, the outstanding Boston outfielder established a single-season batting average of .438—a record that still stands. And with 18 HR and 145 RBI that year, Duffy won baseball's first Triple Crown. He never approached those statistics again.

**(Walter) Rabbit Maranville** (November 11, 1891–January 5, 1954). Just a 5'5" clown on the field, Maranville nonetheless remains first among shortstops in putouts (5,139), third in assists (7,534), and second in total chances (13,124). He played his entire 22-year major league career with the Braves.

**Glen (Pop) Warner** (April 5, 1871–September 7, 1954). Over a 44-year career, the legendary football coach outpointed opponents 8,795 to 2,810 with 312 wins, 32 ties, and 104 losses. But more importantly, his many innovations—the huddle, headgear, the spiral punt, hidden ball, reverse, full extended body block—shaped the modern game.

# *1955*

"Nobody is mad at nobody," trumpets Life magazine this summer. Ike, at the height of his popularity, settles Communist Chinese claims to offshore islands with a veiled threat of nuclear weapons and at the Geneva summit he completes promising talks with a more cooperative Soviet leadership. A lessening of tensions gives Americans a chance to reevaluate their widespread loyalty boards.

Prosperous parents indulge the first of the baby-boomer fads, buying TVs for the kids to watch Davy Crockett. For themselves, they want to see Marshal Dillon, Ralph Kramden, and Alfred Hitchcock in this season's new shows. Teens, meanwhile, flock to movie theaters for Blackboard Jungle and East of Eden and to record stores for some 18 rock 'n' roll hits, including "Maybellene," "Earth Angel," and "Rock Around the Clock."

Newspapers carry a new advice column by Ann Landers, the DuMont television network folds, and Walt Disney opens a huge amusement park south of Los Angeles. And, with all the postwar babies entering school, the supply of teachers falls short by almost 150,000.

## NEWS

**January 28.** With China and Taiwan (formerly Formosa) battling over offshore islands, Eisenhower has asked for congressional authority to protect the Nationalists from Communist attack. Today, a vaguely worded resolution grants that discretionary power while avoiding a specific commitment to force.

The situation fails to improve. Finally, in April, an exasperated Eisenhower will hint that the United States might use nuclear weapons if drawn into another war. Before the end of the month, Chou En-lai will agree to negotiate to reduce tensions in the area.

Much more than a negotiating ploy, the presi-

dent's threat will in fact rest on a Pentagon plan to bomb Communist coastal bases even though experts anticipated the atomic explosions would kill millions of civilians.

**February 8.** Soviet leaders remove Georgi Malenkov from the premiership and renounce his emphasis on consumer goods over heavy industry. Nikolai Bulganin takes over the vacant position, but First Secretary Nikita Khrushchev emerges as the most powerful figure in the USSR.

**February 12.** The U.S. MAAG takes over command of the South Vietnamese Army from France.

**March 1.** House and Senate conferees increase congressional salaries by $7,500 annually. From 1789, pay rose from $6 a day (while in attendance) to $3,000 a year in 1856, $10,000 in 1925, dropped back briefly to $8,663 during the Depression, then rose again to $10,000. Over the past 19 years, salaries jumped 50 percent, to $15,000.

**April 5.** Winston Churchill, age 80, resigns as British prime minister and leader of the Conservative party. He recommends Foreign Secretary Anthony Eden as his successor, and the party will formally elect Eden later this month. Churchill, who remains in the House, is the longest-serving British MP in history and the last surviving politician to have served under Queen Victoria.

**May 5.** The Federal Republic of Germany, covering two-thirds of the former German state, becomes a sovereign nation, with the deposition of the 1954 Paris pacts. West Germany formally enters NATO on the 9th and the United States quickly extends military funding.

The Soviets, in a last-ditch attempt to block rearmament, had called for talks on German reunification. Bonn rejected the offer. Accordingly, on September 20, Moscow grants sovereignty to East Germany. The Allied powers and West Germany refuse to recognize the Communist nation.

---

*Statistics:* Nobel physicist Cecil Powell estimates that the United States has stockpiled 4,000 nuclear weapons and the Soviet Union 1,000.

---

**May 14.** In response to West German participation in NATO, the USSR signs the Warsaw Pact with Poland, Czechoslovakia, Hungary, Bulgaria, Romania, Albania, and East Germany. The 20-year mutual defense treaty provides for the creation of a unified military command under Soviet authority. In reality, Warsaw troops will guard the Iron Curtain and ensure that member nations follow the Communist line.

**May 15.** The USSR joins the United States, Britain, and France in signing an Austrian peace treaty. The settlement reestablishes pre-1938 borders, claims no reparations, and commits Austria to

permanent neutrality. Austrians will regain their sovereignty on July 27, and occupation troops will withdraw by October.

**May 31.** Reinforcing last year's *Brown* decision, the Supreme Court finds segregation in public education unconstitutional and declares that "all provisions of federal, state, or local law requiring or permitting such discrimination must yield to this principle." School districts must desegregate "within a reasonable time" or prove the need for a delay (local animosity is not a valid reason). Lower federal courts will enforce the order.

The four border states—Delaware, Maryland, Missouri, and West Virginia—have already begun to comply, but the Deep South—Georgia, South Carolina, Mississippi, and Louisiana—declare complete opposition to the ruling. The other affected states remain noncommittal.

At this crucial moment, Eisenhower fails to swing moderate Southern whites behind the court decision. Certainly the president moves to end discrimination in areas under federal control, such as veterans' hospitals, but he never publicly approves or disapproves of the decision.

**June 2.** President Tito and Premier Bulganin sign a declaration of friendship and cooperation in Belgrade, ending the seven-year feud between Yugoslavia and the Soviet Union. Reportedly, as a precondition, Tito demanded the abolition of Cominform. The organization will be dissolved on April 17, 1956.

**June 15–17.** "Operation Alert" runs a three-day mock H-bomb drill in 53 U.S. cities. Evaluations of the exercise show 8.5 million Americans died, but evacuation saved 2.5 million, even with just an hour's warning. Authorities believe a greater time margin, with the completed DEW Line, will substantially increase the number saved.

**July 18.** In the first Big Four meeting since the end of W.W.II, President Eisenhower, Prime Minister Sir Anthony Eden of Britain, Premier Nikolai Bulganin of the USSR, and Premier Edgar Faure of France gather in Geneva to discuss East-West tensions. Eisenhower, in an astonishing disarmament plan, suggests the four powers exchange complete military blueprints and allow periodic aerial inspections as a deterrent against surprise attack. The British and French greet his proposal with enthusiasm, but the Soviets counter with a step-by-step plan for weapons reduction.

Although the meeting achieves nothing concrete, for a few brief months the "Spirit of Geneva" buoys the world with optimism. At a second foreign ministers' meeting in the fall, the Soviets will show little change in attitude.

**August 8.** The United States joins the USSR and 70 other nations in Geneva for the first International Conference on the Peaceful Uses of Atomic Energy. Eisenhower's Atoms for Peace Plan forms the basis of the agenda. (The AEC has already concluded Atoms for Peace agreements with 27 countries.)

**August 9.** With Communism less aggressive on the world scene and the Democrats threatening to examine past dismissals, Eisenhower agrees to a bipartisan investigation of the entire security program. Between May 1953 and September 1954, 3,002 security risks were dismissed from federal positions.

**August 11.** Sweeping out of the Caribbean, Hurricane Diane combines with remnants of Hurricane Connie to batter the already saturated East Coast. (In Stroudsburg, Pennsylvania, the water level rises 30 inches in 15 minutes, drowning 50.) Altogether some 200 people die and damage soars to $1.5 billion, making Diane the most expensive storm in American history. Within a week, the Weather Bureau announces it is examining hurricane warning procedures.

**August 28.** Two white men kidnap 14-year-old Emmett Till, a Northern black boy visiting Mississippi, after he supposedly whistles at a white woman. His body is recovered four days later, mutilated and shot through the head. Emmett's mother insists on an open-casket funeral so all the world can see what happened to her son.

The NAACP keeps the story in the news, but an all-white, male jury acquits the woman's husband and brother-in-law; the body was "too badly decomposed" to identify. Still, the horror of the crime and the surrounding controversy convince many whites to push ahead on civil rights.

---

*Statistics*: In January of this year, the Tuskegee Institute reported that no lynchings had occurred in the United States for three years.

---

**September 9–13.** Konrad Adenauer travels to Moscow to reestablish diplomatic links with the USSR. The West German chancellor insists on tying the talks to German POWs. The Soviets, acknowledging that they still hold 9,626 "war criminals," later in the month approve a decree for the soldiers' unconditional release.

**September 18.** The British Foreign Office announces that, in May 1951, diplomats Guy Burgess and Donald Maclean defected to the Soviet Union. This belated confirmation follows the newspaper publication of an article by an ex-Soviet spy, who maintains that the KGB recruited Burgess and Maclean at Cambridge and had received classified information from them for some time.

**September 19.** Following a civilian-supported military coup, Argentine dictator Juan Perón flees to Paraguay. During his nine years in power, Perón won over the people by creating Latin America's first labor movement, nationalizing foreign industries, and establishing a place for Argentina in the Third World bloc. But after his idolized wife, Evita, died in 1952, Perón became increasingly dictatorial, and the tide of opposition overwhelmed his still large following.

**September 24.** President Eisenhower suffers a mild heart attack. Two days later, on Monday, the stock market sees its heaviest losses to date—$14 billion in one day. But Vice-President Nixon opposes any move to make him acting president. After nearly seven weeks of treatment, Eisenhower is discharged from Denver's Army Hospital and returns to Washington.

**October 14.** U.S. banks increase the prime lending rate from 3.25 percent to 3.5 percent, its highest level in 25 years. Money experts point to heavy demand for loans and the shortage of lendable money.

**October 18.** When President Bao Dai of Vietnam dismisses Ngo Dinh Diem, American backing gives the premier authority to call for a national referendum.

Last April, in a brief civil war, Ngo Dinh Diem's supporters defeated those of Bao Dai. The victory persuaded the Eisenhower administration to continue to support him in office.

On October 23, Diem will receive overwhelming approval (the Pentagon describes 98.2 percent as "too resounding"). He deposes Bao Dai, and on the 26th he will proclaim South Vietnam an independent republic and himself president.

**November 7.** In the first extension of the *Brown* decision, the Supreme Court unanimously bans racial segregation in publicly financed parks, playgrounds, golf courses, and swimming pools.

**November 21.** To prevent Communist expansion into the Middle East, the U.S. secretary of state engineers a defense agreement among the northern Moslem nations of Iraq, Iran, Turkey, and Pakistan. But the Baghdad pact raises alarm and resentment from Africa to India (Egypt objects to Iraq becoming the center of Arab politics and turns to the Soviets for military equipment). As a result, the Americans refrain from formally joining the alliance and simply offer members military and economic aid.

**November 25.** Responding to recent Supreme Court decisions and an NAACP case against 13 railway companies, the Interstate Commerce Commission rules that racial segregation on interstate buses and trains and in terminals must end next year. But the ICC ruling leaves enforcement of the decree to the carriers and state law.

**December 1.** In Montgomery, Alabama, Rosa Parks is arrested for refusing to give up her bus seat to a white man. Upon the request of black community activists, she agrees to make the arrest the basis of a major civil rights action.

Some 40,000 people organize over two days, hold a one-day bus boycott, then, on the night of the 5th, gather to decide whether to continue. The keynote speaker is a charismatic new preacher in the community, asked to head the campaign—Martin Luther King, Jr. The people vote to continue.

Initially, the boycotters ask for a more humane system of segregation. When city authorities refuse,

they decide to push for integration. Montgomery whites respond with violence, but King calls on his people to love, not hate. And, despite pressure, the buses remain empty for a second month as the blacks of Montgomery car pool or walk.

King's group files a federal suit against the unconstitutionality of bus segregation. When the white community charges 80 black leaders under an old antiboycott law, the civil rights boycott—the longest ever—finally attracts the attention of the national press.

**December 14.** A five-year U.N. deadlock over the admission of new members breaks today with the acceptance of a Soviet compromise. Japan and Outer Mongolia are excluded, while 16 nations are admitted: Albania, Austria, Bulgaria, Cambodia, Ceylon, Finland, Hungary, Ireland, Italy, Jordan, Laos, Libya, Nepal, Portugal, Romania, and Spain. The total membership now stands at 76.

## *Obituaries*

**Chief Iron Hail** (circa 1857–November 1955). The Native American was the last survivor of the Battle of Little Big Horn, in 1876. General George Custer and 264 men of the Seventh Cavalry died there.

**Frank Hamer** (1884–July 11, 1955). During his career, first with the Texas Rangers then the Highway Patrol, the legendary lawman was wounded 20 times in some 50 gun battles and 4 ambushes. In 1934, he and others tracked Bonnie and Clyde for 102 days, before cornering and killing the notorious couple on May 23.

**Jane Herveux** (circa 1890–January 15, 1955). In 1909, the French-born aviation pioneer became the first woman to fly an airplane solo.

**Herbert Sherman Houston** (November 23, 1866–May 15, 1955). The American editor and publisher founded the U.S. and International Chambers of Commerce.

**Cordell Hull** (October 2, 1871–July 23, 1955). As state secretary under Franklin Delano Roosevelt, for an unprecedented (and unduplicated) 11 years, Hull garnered congressional support for the creation of the United Nations. For this work, he received the Nobel peace prize in 1945.

Oscar Mayer (March 29, 1859–June 12, 1955). At age 14, the Bavarian immigrated to the United States. By the time of his death, Oscar Mayer had made his name a household word for prepared meats.

Walter White (July 1, 1893–March 21, 1955). Acknowledging his fraction of Negro blood in order to fight racism in the American South, the crusader organized rallies, wrote books, worked with presidents Roosevelt and Truman, and, through his efforts to obtain a federal antilynching law, almost eliminated lynching.

## BEGINNINGS AND ENDINGS

### News

February 24. Robbins Mills, American Woolen Co., and Textron American, Inc., incorporate as the first U.S. business conglomerate—Textron American.

April 1. Effective today the U.S. Post Office will no longer deliver unaddressed material. Advertisers, quickly adjusting, mark their mail "Occupant."

April 5. Elected mayor of Chicago, Richard Daley will become one of the longest-serving and most visible mayors in the country.

July 11. The USAF Academy, created by Congress on April 1, 1954, receives the first class of cadets at Lowry Air Force Base in Denver, Colorado. In 1958, the Academy will transfer to permanent quarters north of Colorado Springs.

July 17. Walt Disney dedicates Disneyland south of Los Angeles "to the ideals, the dreams, and the hard facts which have created America." Opening day fulfills the industry's worst predictions—rides break down, food stands run out of supplies, a gas leak closes two theme lands—but Disney, who has risked everything he owns, quickly resolves all problems. Just seven weeks later, the giant amusement park welcomes its one millionth guest.

August 13. A Continental Can-American Can Co. contract with the United Steel Workers of America establishes the first guaranteed annual wage in any major industry. Supplemented unemployment benefits will give laid-off workers 65 percent of their regular pay for up to 52 weeks.

October. Chicago's O'Hare Airport, named after America's greatest W.W.II naval hero Edward 'Butch' O'Hare, opens to domestic traffic. By 1961, O'Hare will be the world's busiest airport.

December. When a Sears Flyer misprints Santa's telephone number, children reach Colonel Harry Shoup on a top secret line at Continental Air Defense Command in Colorado Springs. Incapable of disappointing excited youngsters, the father of four starts a military Christmas tradition with his impersonation of jolly old St. Nick.

The Command, later NORAD, will offer a prerecorded broadcast of Santa while fighter pilots standing by at the North Pole use radar to "track" Santa's trip.

December 5. The American Federation of Labor (AFL), with 10 million members in 109 unions, and the Congress of Industrial Organizations (CIO), with 5.7 million in 32 unions, merge after a 20-year split. Elected president, George Meany heads the largest national labor federation in the Western world, the AFL-CIO.

More news. With $12.4 billion in sales, GM becomes the first corporation to report an annual net income of more than $1 billion.

• Almost 20 years after railways first piggybacked loaded motor trucks, the first highway trailers ride the rails.

• L. Ron Hubbard, age 42, founds the Church of Scientology with his best-selling book *Dianetics: The Modern Science of Mental Health*. He believes counseling clears the brain of past traumas and allows people to achieve their free and immortal spirit. Hubbard later admits tying his concepts to religion simply to gain access to prisons, hospitals, and other institutions. As a result, many look on his church as little more than a cult.

### Records

This year. U.S. auto makers produce 7,920,186 cars, shattering the 1950 record by more than 1 million. (Imports total 57,115.)

## New Products and Businesses

The first postwar Japanese products appear on the U.S. market. Americans soon equate "Made in Japan" with junk.

Kellogg's introduces Special K breakfast cereal.

Coca-Cola switches from a 6-ounce to a 10-ounce bottle.

## Memorable Ad Campaigns

Kellogg's adds cartoon character Tony the Tiger to "They're G-R-Reat!," a campaign for Sugar Frosted Flakes which began in 1951.

Competing for a limited market, auto makers follow GM's lead and 'present' new designs. The unveiling of 'This Year's Model' quickly becomes an annual event.

*The Sears mail-order catalog offers a variety of Davy Crockett merchandise, including the popular raccoon caps. Some 10 million hats sell before this fad wanes.*

Rainbow Crafts creates the modeling compound Play-Doh for the enormous influx of baby-boomers in North America's nursery schools.

## Fads

Between December 1954 and February of this year, Walt Disney televised three episodes of "Davy Crockett, King of the Wild Frontier." By the time Disney rebroadcasts the programs in April, Crockett mania has engulfed America.

Merchandisers sell $100 million worth of 3,000 different items—coonskin hats, leather jackets, bicycles, bedspreads, lunch buckets, jigsaw puzzles. The craze fades in the fall, then plummets when a fourth episode in November puts the heroic frontiersman in a mere raft race.

# SCIENCE AND TECHNOLOGY

## News

**March 3.** The New York State Health Department informs hospitals that the high incidence of blindness in premature babies results from the administration of oxygen following birth, a routine first introduced around 1940.

**April 16.** With an official stamp of approval, the 1955 polio vaccine program gets under way. Some 6.5 million children receive a vaccination by September. Follow-ups find the attack rate down one-fourth to one-third among those vaccinated. The chairman of the AMA describes Salk's discovery as "one of the greatest events in the history of medicine."

**July 29.** As the U.S. contribution to the International Geophysical Year, the National Academy of Sciences and the National Science Foundation announce plans for an artificial satellite. Next day, the Soviets disclose similar intentions.

Although few perceive the projects as a race, Washington and Moscow make decisions at this

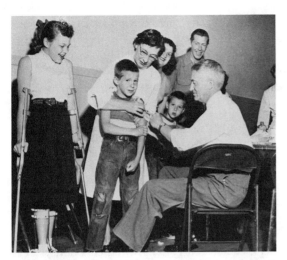

*In San Diego, 6-year-old Michael Urnezis receives one of the last polio shots in the nation's first mass inoculation. His 12-year-old sister Joanne, an earlier victim of the disease, looks on.*

time that guarantee a second-place finish for the United States. The Americans, waiting for smaller warheads, defer work on intercontinental ballistic missiles (ICBM) and deny satellite scientists access to the rocket technology. The Soviets, on the other hand, give their space program the huge rockets developed to carry their primitive bombs.

**August 3.** California scientists report that they have traced photosynthesis, the process by which green plants turn solar energy into sugars, starches, fats, and proteins, and give off oxygen. To follow the path, the researchers introduced synthetic carbon dioxide from a carbon isotope.

**September 8.** Following studies by the National Geographic Society, astronomers theorize that a 200,000-square-mile blue-green area of Mars may contain plant life. The announcement produces intense speculation.

**October 4.** In the first commercial use of solar power, Bell completes a telephone call on a rural circuit in Georgia.

**October 18.** Berkeley scientists announce the creation of the antiproton. After some 20 years of supposition, the negative particle confirms the existence of antimatter.

**October 22.** Three doctors report the use of transplants and plastic substitutes to restore normal blood flow to patients with hardened arteries.

**October 25.** Demonstrated at a press conference in New York, the Tappan electronic range uses microwaves to cook a five-pound roast in 30 minutes, broccoli in 4.5 minutes, bacon in 90 seconds, and eggs in 22 seconds. The range will sell next year for $1,200.

**More news.** Late this year, the United States commissions the world's first guided missile cruiser, the *Boston*. And, in another link in the nation's defense system, a man-made island and radar tower are towed 100 miles off the New England coast.

• Spanish-born biochemist Severo Ochoa synthesizes ribonucleic acid (RNA). Since RNA controls cell growth, Ochoa's achievement marks an enor mous step toward deciphering the genetic code. He will share the 1959 Nobel prize with Arthur Kornberg.

• IBM begins the development of the model 704, the first computer with a programming language (4,096 words, later expanded to 32K words).

• At Cambridge University, a team of researchers works out the chemical structure of vitamin $B_{12}$, then quickly begins work on its synthesis.

• A new field ion microscope, developed by German-American physicist Erwin Mueller, offers a clearer image of all atoms on the surface of a specimen. He developed the first field electron microscope in 1936 and, 15 years later, modified it to operate with ions.

## Other Discoveries, Developments, and Inventions

Hydropneumatic suspension in the French Citroen ID-19 and, in the United States, sealed beam headlights and torsion bar suspension

*Statistics:* In the late 1940s, only one in four new cars had automatic transmission. This year, 69 percent are automatics.

Miltown, one of the first tranquilizers, later found to be addictive

Industrial-quality synthetic diamonds from GE

Fast 35-mm Ektachrome from Kodak

Experimental automaticket in 60 New York Central railroad stations

15-inch sun-powered automobile model from GM

Crystallization of an animal virus

## Obituaries

**Hubert Booth** (July 4, 1871–January 14, 1955). In 1901, the British inventor came up with the vacuum cleaner.

**Albert Einstein** (March 14, 1879–April 18, 1955). Perhaps the greatest theoretical physicist of all time, Einstein was known to the general public for his General Theory of Relativity (1915). But he made other major contributions, including pioneer work in quantum theory, for which he received the 1921 Nobel prize.

When Hitler came to power, in 1930, Einstein was lecturing in California; he chose to remain in the United States and became an American citizen in 1940. A pacifist all his life, the renowned physicist ironically alerted the White House in 1939 to the possibility of an "extremely powerful" weapon, the atom bomb. Throughout the remainder of his life, Einstein advocated a socialist world government and total disarmament.

**Alexander Fleming** (August 6, 1881–March 11, 1955). The Scottish bacteriologist discovered penicillin in 1928. He realized its implications, but left the development to colleagues. Howard Florey and Ernest Chain produced the prototype and shared a Nobel prize with Fleming in 1945. (Gladys Hobby, who purified the antibiotic at Columbia University in 1940, was the first to treat a patient with an injection. It was in full-scale production within two years.) Asked once why he never patented the drug, Fleming replied, "It never occurred to me."

**Calvin Hooker Goddard** (October 30, 1891–February 22, 1955). In the late 1920s, the U.S. Army officer originated the branch of criminology known as forensic ballistics.

**Louis Thurstone** (May 29, 1887–September 29, 1955). His studies led to the development of personality and aptitude tests.

## THE ARTS

February 24—*Silk Stockings*, with Hildegarde Neff, Don Ameche, George Tobias, Julie Newman (477 perfs.)

March 2—*Bus Stop*, with Kim Stanley, Albert Salmi, Elaine Stritch (478 perfs.)

March 24—*Cat on a Hot Tin Roof*, with Barbara Bel Geddes, Ben Gazzara, Mildred Dunnock, Pat Hingle, Burl Ives (694 perfs.)

April 21—*Inherit the Wind*, with Paul Muni, Ed Begley, Tony Randall (806 perfs.)

May 5—*Damn Yankees*, with Gwen Verdon, Stephen Douglass, Ray Walston (1,019 perfs.)

October 5—*The Diary of Anne Frank*, with Joseph Schildkraut, Susan Strasberg (717 perfs.)

October 13—*Will Success Spoil Rock Hunter?*, with Orson Bean, Jayne Mansfield, Walter Matthau (441 perfs.)

October 20—*No Time for Sergeants*, with Andy Griffith, Roddy McDowall (796 perfs.)

### Tony Awards

Actor (Dramatic)—Alfred Lunt, *Quadrille*
Actress (Dramatic)—Nancy Kelly, *The Bad Seed*
Actor (Musical)—Walter Slezak, *Fanny*
Actress (Musical)—Mary Martin, *Peter Pan*
Play—*The Desperate Hours*
Musical—*The Pajama Game*

### News

**January 7.** The first black American to sing a major role at the Met, Marian Anderson appears as Ulrica in Verdi's *Masked Ball*. Toscanini has said of the 31-year-old contralto, "A voice like hers comes only once in a century."

**April 5.** Herbert von Karajan, age 47, succeeds the late Wilhelm Furtwaengler as conductor of the Berlin Philharmonic. In U.S. concerts later this year, the orchestra will receive critical acclaim.

**September 20.** In 1928, Germans Kurt Weill and Bertolt Brecht staged a modern version of John Gay's 18th-century *Beggar's Opera*. A Broadway adaptation flopped in the early 1930s, but last year Marc Blitzstein's translation of *The Threepenny Opera* received good reviews in a limited run. His version opens tonight in Greenwich Village with Lotte Lenya, Weill's wife, re-creating her role as the prostitute Jenny. The play's long run (2,600 perfs.) and the popularity of "Mack the Knife" will spur the growth of Off-Broadway productions.

**September 24.** A $450 painting purchased last year by Chicago art dealer Hanns Teichert is identified as an original Leonardo da Vinci *Madonna and Child*, worth $1 million.

**November 9.** A Van Gogh painting of a vase of flowers fetches $37,000 at a New York auction.

**November 21.** On the 50th anniversary of her stage debut—at the age of five—Broadway renames the New York Fulton Theatre in honor of Helen Hayes. She wryly comments, "An actress's life is so transitory—suddenly you're a building."

**More news.** Master photographer Edward Steichen examines the work of 257 documentary photographers from 68 countries in organizing *The Family of Man*. The Museum of Modern Art chronicle of life from birth to death will show worldwide to some 9 million people, and millions more will buy the book.

### Obituaries

**Robert E. Sherwood** (April 14, 1896–November 14, 1955). The American author won four Pulitzers including two for his plays *Idiot's Delight* (1936) and *Abe Lincoln in Illinois* (1938).

## WORDS

James Baldwin, *Notes of a Native Son*
Patrick Dennis, *Auntie Mame*

Ian Fleming, *Live and Let Die; Moonraker*
Thomas E. Gaddis, *Birdman of Alcatraz*
Graham Greene, *The Quiet American*
John Gunther, *Inside Africa*
MacKinlay Kantor, *Andersonville*
Anne Morrow Lindbergh, *Gift from the Sea*
Vladimir Nabokov, *Lolita*
John O'Hara, *Ten North Frederick*
Harold Robbins, *79 Park Avenue*
J. R. R. Tolkien, *The Return of the King* (volume 3 of the *Lord of the Rings* trilogy)
Leonard Wibberley, *The Mouse That Roared*
Sloan Wilson, *The Man in the Grey Flannel Suit*
Herman Wouk, *Marjorie Morningstar*

### News

**February 3.** In a publishing innovation, Pocket Books inserts advertising into its paperbacks. The four promotions include one for *Time* magazine.

**March 2.** The U.S. Post Office refuses to deliver *Pravda* and *Izvestia*, the leading Soviet newspapers, to American subscribers.

**June 16.** The Universal Copyright Convention goes into effect following ratification by the 12th nation, Monaco. To receive protection in member nations, a writer need copyright a work only domestically. Publications will bear the symbol © and the name of the copyright proprietor.

**October 5.** A Defense Department press release on military travel allowances inadvertently discloses the whereabouts of many U.S. and British overseas bases. Alert reporters prevent publication of the classified information.

**October 16.** Esther Pauline Friedman Lederer, age 37, launches her advice column in the *Chicago Sun-Times*. Within two years, Ann Landers' column will be syndicated to 100 dailies.

**More news.** The best-known writers of the "beat generation," Jack Kerouac, William Burroughs, and Allen Ginsberg, relate their alienation from society in improvisational prose and poetry. But Americans, on the whole, are more fascinated with their drab bohemian clothes, colorful language ("crazy" for great), and use of marijuana.

• Given the go-ahead by the director of the Guinness brewing firm, journalists Ross and Norris McWhirter compile their collection of way-out information into the *Guinness Book of Superlatives*. Although the book is an instant hit, the twin brothers will revise the text next year and so set the standard for future annual editions of the *Guinness Book of Records*.

## Cartoons and Comics

**January.** By forcing publishers to cancel dozens of titles, the restrictive Comics Code Seal of Approval (effective this month) brings the Golden Age of Comics to an end. The industry will take nearly a decade to recover.

**More news.** Alfred E. Neuman appears on the cover of *MAD* (issue No. 21) as a write-in candidate for president. The cartoon character dates back to the early 1900s, but *MAD* gives him a name. His "What—me worry?" will become a catchphrase. This year, the comic book switches to a larger, magazine format to escape the restrictive code.

### TIME *Man of the Year*

Harlow Curtice (American business leader)

## New Words and Phrases

automated
beercasting (beer advertising on radio and TV)
brush fire war
certified mail
church key (a bottle opener, especially for beer)
classic car (an automobile manufactured between 1925 and 1942)
cue card
demolition derby
fish stick
junk mail
oillionaire (a millionaire from oil)
open occupancy (real estate open to any race)

option (a football play)
rock-and-roll
second banana (a supporting comic)
smust (a combination of smoke and dust)
summit (top-level)
UFO (unidentified flying object)
urban legend (modern folktale)

## Obituaries

**James Agee** (November 27, 1909–May 16, 1955). The American poet and critic had concentrated on screenplays since 1948, turning out *The African Queen* (1951) and others. His posthumously published novel *Death in the Family* will win a Pulitzer.

**Dale Carnegie** (November 24, 1888–November 1, 1955). The American writer and lecturer developed courses in public speaking and personality development, but was best known for his enormously popular book, *How to Win Friends and Influence People* (1936).

**Hammond Fisher** (September 24, 1900–December 27, 1955). Cartoonists hired for his comic strip *Joe Palooka* (1928) included, in the early days, Al Capp. Recently, in a continuing feud, the mentally unbalanced Fisher took Capp to court on falsified charges of artistic obscenity. The Society of Cartoonists expelled Fisher; he then committed suicide.

**Thomas Mann** (June 6, 1875–August 12, 1955). Winner of the 1929 Nobel prize for literature, Mann was one of the few German authors of this century to attain international stature. He left Germany under the Nazi regime and took up American citizenship in 1944.

# FASHION

## Haute Couture

The semifitted sheath, this year's favorite silhouette, suggests sexy, graceful lines under a high round bosom, long bodice, and accented hipline. Normally proportioned suits and dresses widen at the shoulders with spread collars, puffed sleeves, and elaborate back blousing.

## News

**February 18.** Imperial Chemical Industries (ICI) begins licensing world rights to the polyester fiber Terylene.

**April 18.** Celanese announces the commercial readiness of 50 fabrics made of Arnel, a triacetate fiber.

**More news.** The word *cleavage* is introduced, in the mid-1950's, to describe the sight of well-endowed actresses, like Marilyn Monroe and Jayne Mansfield, in low-cut dresses.

• With husband Alexander, Mary Quant opens her own shop in Chelsea, London. Frustrated in her attempts to find young fashions, she turns to design.

One of her first items is a small, white plastic collar to brighten a dress or sweater. With enthusiastic customer response, Quant creates colorfully patterned dresses and experiments with balloon dresses and knickerbockers.

• During the war, Levi's® jeans were reserved for defense workers. But as sales rose into the early 1950s, the company was forced to abandon the wholesaling of other firm's goods.

This year, Levi adds zippers. With Marlon Brando (*The Wild One*) and James Dean (*Rebel Without a Cause*) both wearing jeans in their films, sales take off.

• The United States reports the highest annual shoe production ever—576,973,000 pairs, or nearly 40 percent of the world's total.

## Colors and Materials

An Oriental influence pairs brilliant colors in offbeat combinations.

Manufacturers weave fur, angora, or cashmere hairs into deluxe woolens. For day clothes, soft lightweight wools forgo the textured look of recent years for distinct patterns.

## Clothes

Designers stay with the ensemble coat and matching dress or two-piece long-jacketed suit and overblouse. Different-weight fabrics in the same color or pattern link the pieces.

Every teenage girl wants a full-circled poodle skirt with an appliquéd cutout (a poodle with a furry tail and rhinestone eyes and collar, or maybe a hot rod) near the hemline. Lots of petticoats underneath, a white shirt, small neckerchief, and saddle shoes with bobby sox complete the outfit. As well, teens favor sweater sets, Peter Pan collars, and tweed skirts or jumpers.

Some teenage boys and young men emulate Marlon Brando's movie attire—black boots, leather belt with outsized metal buckle, black leather motorcycle jacket—while others copy James Dean—haircut, pack of smokes rolled up in a T-shirt sleeve.

## Accessories

In keeping with the Oriental mood, stores sell beaded and embroidered Turkish slippers in deep colors.

College girls wear black leotards with a plaid skirt or jumper.

Nylon stretch socks finally give wives and mothers a respite from darning their men's woolen hose.

Against this year's vertical silhouette, jewelry becomes outsized and hats grow to the size of a vegetable bowl.

Longer, slimmer gloves bunch down to meet above-wrist sleeves.

Heel height drops a half inch and stores once again carry the classic pump with open toe. The industry introduces the ripple sole for cushioning.

## Hair and Cosmetics

Cosmetics and toiletries mushroom with an astounding 250 new trademarks.

More women add eye shadow to their makeup cache.

With back combing and brushing, hair puffs out into bouffant styles.

## POPULAR MUSIC

With the beginning of the rock 'n' roll era, the yearly list of No. 1 and No. 2 hits will be drawn from the *Billboard* charts used by Joel Whitburn in *The Billboard Book of Top 40 Hits*.

The songs are listed according to the number of weeks each holds No. 1 and stays in the top 40. For instance, "Cherry Pink and Apple Blossom White" and "Sincerely" both topped the 1955 chart for 10 weeks, but the former remained in the top 40 for 26 weeks while the latter dropped out after 21 weeks. Not all No. 2 songs are listed in any given year and sheer numbers—particularly in later years—require that some hits be left out.

"Cherry Pink and Apple Blossom White" (Instr.)—Perez Prado & His Orchestra

"Sincerely"—McGuire Sisters

"(We're Gonna) Rock Around the Clock"—Bill Haley & His Comets

"Sixteen Tons"—Tennessee Ernie Ford

"Love Is a Many Splendored Thing"—Four Aces

"The Yellow Rose of Texas"—Mitch Miller Orchestra & Chorus

"Ballad of Davy Crockett"—Bill Hayes

"Autumn Leaves" (Instr.)—Roger Williams

"Let Me Go, Lover!"—Joan Weber

"Dance With Me, Henry"—Georgia Gibbs

"Hearts of Stone"—Fontane Sisters

"Unchained Melody"—Les Baxter & Orchestra & Chorus

"Learnin' the Blues"—Frank Sinatra

"Ain't That a Shame"—Pat Boone

"The Crazy Otto (Medley)" (Instr.)—Johnny Maddox & the Rhythm Masters

"Moments to Remember"—Four Lads

"I Hear You Knocking"—Gale Storm

"Ko Ko Mo (I Love You So)"—Perry Como

"Melody of Love" (Instr.)—Billy Vaughn & His Orchestra

## News

**January.** Early this month, RCA drops the retail price of an LP from $6 to $4. Other companies follow suit and within six months the industry reports album sales up by as much as 40 percent. With 50 minutes of playing time, an LP costs about 8 cents per minute. The 78-rpm, in the 12-inch classical format, sells for $1.50, or about 21 cents per minute.

**January 14–15.** In the greatest advance sale for a dance promotion, over 15,000 people purchase tickets for Alan Freed's first Rock 'n' Roll Party in New York City. Fats Domino, the Drifters, the Clovers, Joe Turner, the Moonglows, and others perform.

**January 31.** RCA chairman David Sarnoff announces the development of a music synthesizer. Prepunched holes, a revolving paper roll, electronically imitate any known or imaginable musical tone or combination of tones. Although the device only produces a series of single tones, a whole orchestra can be simulated by recording each synthesized sequence.

**Summer.** Columbia Records becomes the first of the old-line companies to organize a record club.

**November 22.** During 1954 and 1955, young Elvis Presley has recorded about a dozen songs in Memphis. A regional artist at best, his rockabilly style receives some exposure when disc jockey Bill Randle spins the records at Cleveland's WERE. The enormous response prompts several companies to bid for Presley's contract and his manager Colonel Tom Parker negotiates an unprecedented deal with RCA Victor for $35,000. (Only one year remains on the contract, but RCA receives exclusive rights to all of Elvis's recordings for three years.) Apparently, Sam Phillips of Sun studio believed Carl Perkins would be the bigger star.

**More news.** After fairly good initial sales, "Rock Around the Clock" shoots to No. 1 following the release of the Hollywood film *Blackboard Jungle*. (It plays during the opening credits.) The first song to successfully mix CW and R&B, Haley's smash hit marks the beginning of the rock era. Before the end of the year, some 18 rock singles will place high on the charts.

• R&B makes a dramatic crossover to the *Billboard* top 50 with the number of black acts rising from last year's 3 percent to 10 percent this year. Fats Domino leads the way with his first national hit. (His 22 million sales, through to the 1960s will rank him right behind the Beatles.) Chuck Berry's "Maybellene" sets the mold for guitar bands, and the Penguins and Platters offer white groups "doo wop" harmonizing (named after a favorite chant), with a single lead voice and three to four backup singers.

• On more than 20 different labels, Davy Crockett songs sell an estimated 7 million copies in less than six months.

• Mercury Records wanted to sign the Penguins, but manager Buck Ram refused permission until the company agreed to sign another of his groups as well. The Penguins put out "Earth Angel," their first and only hit. The Platters, on the other hand, will go on to become the decade's most successful vocal group with four No. 1 hits and 16 gold records.

• In a *Billboard* poll, DJ's pick Frank Sinatra as top male singer and Doris Day as top female vocalist.

*New Recording Artists*

Harry Belafonte
Chuck Berry
Pat Boone
Dells
Etta James
Little Richard
Roger Williams

## Obituaries

**Charlie (Bird) Parker** (August 29, 1920–March 12, 1955). Endless improvisations on his saxophone made Yardbird one of the most influential figures in the development of bop. Shortly after he arrived in Harlem in 1939, Parker became a drug addict. An alcoholic as well, his body had little resistance to pneumonia. He made few recordings, but fans' tapes of his renditions and compositions will make them modern jazz standards.

**Andrew B. Sterling** (August 26, 1874–August 11, 1955). The lyricist's hits included "Meet Me in St. Louis, Louis" (1904) and "Wait Till the Sun Shines Nellie" (1905).

## MOVIES

*Blackboard Jungle* (d. Richard Brooks; bw)—Glenn Ford, Anne Francis, Sidney Poitier

*East of Eden* (d. Elia Kazan; color)—James Dean, Julie Harris, Raymond Massey, Jo Van Fleet

*Guys and Dolls* (d. Joseph L. Mankiewicz; color)—Marlon Brando, Jean Simmons, Frank Sinatra, Vivian Blaine

*I'll Cry Tomorrow* (d. Daniel Mann; bw)—Susan Hayward, Richard Conte, Eddie Albert, Jo Van Fleet

*Lady and the Tramp* (Disney; color; animated)—Voices: Barbara Luddy (Lady); Larry Roberts (Tramp); Peggy Lee (Darling and others)

*The Ladykillers* (British, d. Alexander Mackendrick; color)—Alec Guinness, Katie Johnson, Cecil Parker, Herbert Lom, Peter Sellers

*Love Me or Leave Me* (d. Charles Vidor; color)—Doris Day, James Cagney, Cameron Mitchell

*The Man from Laramie* (d. Anthony Mann; color)—James Stewart, Arthur Kennedy

*Marty* (d. Delbert Mann; bw)—Ernest Borgnine, Betsy Blair

*Mister Roberts* (d. John Ford, Mervyn LeRoy; color)—Henry Fonda, James Cagney, Jack Lemmon, William Powell

*My Sister Eileen* (d. Richard Quine; color)—Betty Garrett, Janet Leigh, Jack Lemmon

*The Night of the Hunter* (d. Charles Laughton; bw)—Robert Mitchum, Shelley Winters, Lillian Gish

*Oklahoma!* (d. Fred Zinnemann; color)—Gordon Macrae, Shirley Jones, Rod Steiger, Gloria Grahame

*Picnic* (d. Joshua Logan; color)—William Holden, Kim Novak, Rosalind Russell, Susan Strasberg, Arthur O'Connell

*Rebel Without a Cause* (d. Nicholas Ray; color)—James Dean, Natalie Wood, Sal Mineo

*The Rose Tattoo* (d. Daniel Mann; bw)—Anna Magnani, Burt Lancaster

*The Seven Year Itch* (d. Billy Wilder; color)—
Marilyn Monroe, Tom Ewell
*Summertime* (d. David Lean; color)—Katharine
Hepburn, Rossano Brazzi
*To Catch a Thief* (d. Alfred Hitchcock; color)—
Cary Grant, Grace Kelly

## Academy Awards

**March 30.** Bob Hope hosts the award ceremonies in
Hollywood and Thelma Ritter presides in New
York. Earlier this year, the Academy announced the
Oscar nominees on a live telecast from Romanoff's
restaurant in Hollywood; not considered a success,
the experiment will never be repeated.

Best Picture—*On the Waterfront*
Best Actor—Marlon Brando (*On the Waterfront*)
Best Actress—Grace Kelly (*The Country Girl*)
Best Director—Elia Kazan (*On the Waterfront*)
Best Supporting Actor—Edmond O'Brien (*The
Barefoot Contessa*)
Best Supporting Actress—Eva Marie Saint (*On
the Waterfront*)
Best Song—"Three Coins in the Fountain" from
the film of the same name
Honorary Awards—Danny Kaye; Greta Garbo;
*Gate of Hell* (Japanese)

*On the Waterfront* ties the eight-Oscar record set
by *Gone With the Wind* in 1939 and equaled by *From
Here to Eternity* in 1954.

The Academy honors the legendary Greta
Garbo, 14 years after her last film, but the elusive
actress is a no-show.

## News

**July.** With some 15,000 indoor theaters and 4,300
drive-ins, the United States reaches a ratio of one
theater seat to every 42 Americans.

**July 18.** Howard Hughes, breaching the unwritten Hollywood edict to ignore television, sells the
entire RKO library—*King Kong* (1933), *Citizen
Kane* (1941), the Astaire-Rogers films—to General

Teleradio Inc. for a reported $15–$25 million. The
first of the 740 pictures will reach the small screen
early next year. Hughes acquired controlling interest in RKO in 1948. His aggressive interference
quickly put the studio in the red and, by 1953,
production ceased. This past March, Hughes
bought up the remaining company stock with a
$23-million personal check.

**December 6.** Once again, the MPAA withholds
the seal of approval from an Otto Preminger film.
*The Man With the Golden Arm*, starring Frank Sinatra, Kim Novak, and Darren McGavin, deals with
drug addiction, a subject forbidden under the code.
UA resigns from the association in protest and releases the film, to sensational reviews.

**More news.** Warner Bros. animation studio introduces "The Fastest Mouse in All of Mexico"—in
*Speedy Gonzales*. His favorite victim remains Sylvester the Cat.

• With the Davy Crockett craze, Disney splices
three one-hour TV episodes into a 93-minute feature film. The picture's enormous popularity warrants a sequel.

• Critical and commercial successes, *The Blackboard Jungle* and *Rebel Without a Cause* portray teen
problems and their love of rock 'n' roll. But many
parents resent the clear depiction of juvenile delinquency, and Britain will ban *The Blackboard Jungle*
for 11 years.

• Movie producer Mike Todd films *Oklahoma!* in
Todd-AO, a 65-mm-wide negative (three and a half
times the 35-mm area) run at 30 frames per second
(rather than 24) to reduce screen flicker. The film's
stereophonic soundtrack plays over surround and
behind-the-screen speakers. The Todd-AO format
will eventually become the industry standard.

• With his co-star getting most of the fan mail,
Donald O'Connor decides to quit Universal's popular *Francis* series. In six films since 1950, the actor
played a rather dense West Point cadet pushed into
trouble by Francis the Talking Mule (whose voice is
provided by actor Chill Wills). One more Francis
movie, in 1956, will star Mickey Rooney.

The series director Arthur Lubin, later creates a
talking horse for television—"Mr. Ed."

## Top Money-Maker of the Year

*Cinerama Holiday*

## Flop of the Year

*The Silver Chalice*
In this expensive disaster, 29-year-old Paul Newman debuts as a Greek sculptor in Roman times.

## Quote of the Year

"Captain, it is I—Ensign Pulver—and I just threw your stinking palm tree overboard. Now, what's all this crud about no movie tonight?"

With the death of *Mister Roberts* (played by Henry Fonda), Jack Lemmon finally confronts the tyrannical captain, James Cagney. (Screenplay by Frank S. Nugent and Joshua Logan; based on the play by Thomas Heggen and Joshua Logan and the novel by Thomas Heggen.)

## Obituaries

**Theda Bara** (July 20, 1890–April 7, 1955). Admirers coined the word *vamp* to describe the sensational femme fatale in *A Fool There Was* (1915). But post-W.W.I audiences found Hollywood's first sex star too melodramatic, and in 1926 she disappeared from the screen.

**James Dean** (February 8, 1931–September 30, 1955). In his three major roles—*East of Eden*, *Rebel Without a Cause*, and *Giant*—Dean portrayed a very modern kind of hero, a sensitive outsider who relied on his own inner strength. A cult forms around this appealing persona and some deny that Dean really died at the wheel of his new silver Porsche. Only once before have movie fans turned a screen star into an American icon—Rudolph Valentino in the 1920s.

Actor James Dean in Giant, *his third and final starring role.*

**Carmen Miranda** (February 9, 1909–August 5, 1955). Known for her flamboyant costumes and elaborate headgear, the dynamic Brazilian singer, dancer, and actress made 14 films in the 1940s before the big-band musical died out.

# TELEVISION AND RADIO

## New Prime-Time TV Programs

"The Adventures of Robin Hood" (September 26, 1955–September 22, 1958; Adventure)—

Richard Greene, Bernadette O'Farrell (1955–1957)

"Alfred Hitchcock Presents" (October 2, 1955–September 6, 1965; Suspense Anthology)—Host: Alfred Hitchcock. *Note:* In 1962, an expanded program becomes "The Alfred Hitchcock Hour."

"The Bob Cummings Show" (January 2, 1955–September 15, 1959; Situation Comedy)—Bob Cummings, Rosemary DeCamp, Ann B. Davis, Dwayne Hickman

"Cheyenne" (September 20, 1955–December 1962; Western)—Clint Walker

"Gunsmoke" (September 10, 1955–September 1, 1975; Western)—James Arness, Milburn Stone (Doc), Amanda Blake (1955–1974), Dennis Weaver (Chester, 1955–1964), Ken Curtis (Festus, 1964–1975), Glen Strange (Sam, the Bartender, 1962–1974)

"The Honeymooners" (October 1, 1955–September 1956; Situation Comedy)—Jackie Gleason, Art Carney, Audrey Meadows, Joyce Randolph

"The Lawrence Welk Show" (July 2, 1955–September 4, 1971; Music)—Lawrence Welk

"The Life and Legend of Wyatt Earp" (September 6, 1955–September 26, 1961; Western)—Hugh O'Brien

"The Millionaire" (January 19, 1955–September 28, 1960; Drama Anthology)—Marvin Miller, Paul Frees (voice of Mr. Tipton)

"The Phil Silvers Show" (September 20, 1955–September 11, 1959; Situation Comedy) Phil Silvers, Harvey Lembeck, Herbie Faye, Paul Ford

"The $64,000 Question" (June 7, 1955–November 2, 1958; Quiz/Audience Participation)—Emcee: Hal March

## Emmy Awards 1954 (March 7, 1955)

Best Dramatic Series—"The United States Steel Hour" (ABC)

Best Variety Series—"Disneyland" (ABC)

Best Situation Comedy Series—"Make Room for Daddy" (ABC)

Best Children's Program—"Lassie" (CBS)

Best Actor in a Series—Danny Thomas ("Make Room for Daddy," ABC)

Best Actress in a Series—Loretta Young ("The Loretta Young Show," NBC)

## News

**January 7.** The opening of Parliament is televised in Canada for the first time.

**January 19.** The networks pool their cameras for the first filmed presidential press conference. The 33 minutes are edited to 28½.

**March 7.** Mary Martin sails over an NBC soundstage just nine days after *Peter Pan* closed on Broadway. The enormous success of the Monday night "Producer's Showcase"—a record 33–50 percent of Americans tune in—finally dents sponsor resistance to the TV spectacular.

**March 7.** Steve Allen emcees the first televised Emmys. NBC will carry the annual broadcast through to 1966, when the networks will establish a rotation system.

**May.** DuMont—the first of the Big Four—ceases operations at its annual stockholders' meeting. The TV network, in an attempt to draw affiliates, had funded a New York production center just as the industry began to shift westward to Hollywood. By October, DuMont stations will carry only a couple of sporting events.

**June 7.** Last year the Supreme Court voided the 1949 FCC ban against quiz shows. Tonight, CBS launches the first big-prize show, "The $64,000 Question." From the $8,000 question on, contestants answer from a soundproof booth (allowing audience members to scream their heads off). Success, as usual, prompts a spate of similar programs.

**July 2.** *TV Guide* remarks, "The [summer] program lacks the necessary sparkle and verve to give it a chance against any really strong competition." But TV viewers love the mix of old-fashioned music, and "The Lawrence Welk Show" will remain on the air for 16 years. Following cancellation, the orchestra leader will take his close-knit group of performers into successful syndication.

**August 13.** After the unexpected death of the

host in 1954, "Smilin' Ed McConnell and His Buster Brown Gang" finished out the season with reruns. Today, the series returns to Saturday mornings as "Andy's Gang." Squeaky-voiced host Andy Devine talks with the puppet Froggy the Gremlin and others and dramatizes the filmed stories of Gunga Rama and his elephant Teela. Buster Brown Shoes will remain the sole sponsor until the program ends in 1960.

**September.** In response to the outstanding success of ABC's "Disneyland," CBS premieres three early evening kids' programs: "The Adventures of Robin Hood," "Sergeant Preston of the Yukon," and "The Adventures of Champion," replaced in February by "My Friend Flicka."

---

*Statistics:* By October, the number of TV sets in the United States reaches an estimated 33.5 million.

---

**September.** In Britain, the BBC finally receives some competition with the inauguration of commercial television. Initially reliant on American film series, British TV will be exporting quality series to the United States within five years.

**September 10.** Radio's "Gunsmoke" offered the TV show a ready-made audience, but CBS draws more viewers with a hard-bitten look at the American West. The show will reach No. 1 in the ratings by the 1957–1958 season, then remain there for four seasons. (Reportedly, each week a number of American men strap on their guns to face Marshal Dillon at the beginning of the show. At least one shoots himself in the foot.)

**September 19.** Frank Sinatra sings "Love and Marriage" during the musical adaptation of Thornton Wilder's *Our Town.* The tune will become the first popular number to win an Emmy.

**September 28.** NBC carries the first color telecast of a World Series game. (The Yankees beat the Dodgers 6–5.) This season, the number of color broadcasts rises dramatically. In October, for instance, NBC weekly coverage expands to 37 hours—excluding sports events—compared to 7 hours in October 1954. A new 21-inch RCA receiver contributes much to the increase. The set requires just 26 electron tubes rather than the 36 in earlier versions.

**September 29.** During the first season of "Sergeant Preston," Quaker Oats offers kids a unique premium—a legal deed to one square inch of Yukon territory. The cereal company paid the Canadian government $10,000 for 19.1 acres outside Dawson—the equivalent of 21 million of these tiny plots. Eventually, Ottawa will reclaim the land for $37 in back taxes.

**October 3.** To challenge the "Today" show's grip on the preschool time slot, ABC introduces Bob Keeshan as "Captain Kangaroo" (named after the enormous pockets in his coat). The gentle-voiced 28-year-old, who originated Clarabell the Clown on "Howdy Doody," interacts with a number of puppets—Mr. Moose, Miss Worm, Homer the dog, and teaches his little fans how to make simple things. As well, Mr. Green Jeans (Hugh "Lumpy" Brannum) introduces a variety of real-life animals.

In 1958, the show will receive the first of three Peabody Awards—"the only genuine children's program on network television, certainly the only one which puts the welfare of the children ahead of that of the sponsor." Over the years, Keeshan will need less and less makeup and padding to enter his character, but the show will still be enthralling young viewers 20 years from now.

**October 3.** Wearing their mouse ears and club sweaters, host Jimmie Dodd and 24 Mouseketeers cheerily spell out the club song—M-I-C, K-E-Y, M-O-U-S-E. The group of youngsters, including Johnny Crawford, Annette Funicello, and Paul Petersen (only nine remain throughout), sing, dance, and perform skits in two quarter-hour segments. The other half-hour includes Disney cartoons, a "Mickey Mouse Club Newsreel," and daily themes like Friday's "Talent Round-Up" for amateur performers.

The *New York Times* review predicts the Disney production will never woo kids away from established programs, but an estimated 10 million American children faithfully tune in this year, each and every day. (At its peak in popularity, Disney sells 26,000 pairs of mouse ears weekly.) The show will end on September 25, 1959, but a reedited half-hour version will be shown between 1962 and 1965.

**October 15.** "Fury" is a hit Saturday-morning series on NBC. Over the first four seasons, the stallion and his friend Joey average a 17.8 audience share—better than many prime-time shows. After the last program in 1966, Joey's adoptive father, Peter Graves, will find even greater success in "Mission: Impossible."

**November 3.** Using the scatter system, NBC bounces a signal off an airplane to make the first overseas broadcast in television history—from Havana to Miami.

In another technological advance this year, MIT successfully transmits UHF radio waves. The over-the-horizon signals require 20,000 times the power and 30 times the antenna size used in the present microwave radio relay system.

**December 10.** Saturday-morning programming adds the first network animated series, "Mighty Mouse Playhouse." (Artist Isidore Klein, partial to mice, premiered the tiny superhero in "The Mouse of Tomorrow" in 1942. Super Mouse became Mighty Mouse seven films later.) CBS paid cartoonist Paul Terry $3.5 million for his studio and assets.

Supporting characters in this first episode, those mischievous magpies Heckle and Jeckle will be pulled next year for their own series.

**More news.** FCC authorization for multiplex broadcasting gives FM radio a boost. Now, a second and third program may be transmitted simultaneously on the same channel.

• ABC signs an exclusive contract with Warner Bros. and over the next three years their collaboration produces a number of popular Westerns, including "Cheyenne" and "Wyatt Earp" this year, "Colt .45," "Maverick," and "Sugarfoot" in 1957, and "The Rifleman" in 1958. However, ABC will continue to trail in the network ratings.

• According to A. C. Nielsen polls, the greatest number of radio listeners prefer "Lux Radio Theatre" on winter evenings and "Dragnet" during the summer. "Ma Perkins" remains the daytime favorite year round.

• This year, local programmers introduce pre-1948 Warner Bros. cartoons, including Daffy Duck

and Porky Pig, under the umbrella title "Looney Tunes."

• One of radio's most lingering memories ends with the last episode of "The Whistler." (Composer Wilbur Hatch once guessed that just 1 person in 20 could whistle his melody.) Bill Forman played the lead through most of the run.

• To compete against baseball broadcasts, NBC introduces *Monitor* to weekend radio. The 40-hour mix offers sports, news, comedy skits, interviews, and on-the-scene reports. But major-market stations refuse to experiment and the feed will eventually cut back to 16 hours. In January 1975, *Monitor* will quietly leave the air.

### Memorable Radio Programs End

"Bobby Benson and the B-Bar-B Riders" (1949)
"The Hallmark Hall of Fame" (June 10, 1948)
"The Jack Benny Program" (May 2, 1932)
"Just Plain Bill" (September 19, 1932)
"The Lone Ranger" (January 30, 1933)
"Lux Radio Theatre" (October 14, 1934)
"Nick Carter, Master Detective" (April 11, 1943)
"The Roy Rogers Show" (November 21, 1944)
"Sergeant Preston of the Yukon" (June 12, 1947)
"Space Patrol" (1950)
"Stella Dallas" (June, 1938)
"True Detective Mysteries" (October 1, 1944)
"The University of Chicago Round Table" (October 1933)
"The Whistler" (1947)

# SPORTS

### Winners

#### Baseball

World Series—Brooklyn Dodgers (NL), 4 games; New York Yankees (AL), 3 games
Player of the Year—Yogi Berra (New York Yankees, AL); Roy Campanella (Brooklyn Dodgers, NL)
Rookie of the Year—Herb Score (Cleveland Indians, AL; Bill Virdon (St. Louis Cardinals, NL)

## Football

NFL Championship—Cleveland Browns 28, Los Angeles Rams 14
College Bowls (January 1, 1955)—
  Rose Bowl, Ohio State 20, USC 7
  Cotton Bowl, Georgia Tech 14, Arkansas 6
  Orange Bowl, Duke 34, Nebraska 7
  Sugar Bowl, Navy 21, Mississippi 0
Heisman Trophy—Howard Cassady (Ohio State, HB)
Grey Cup—Edmonton Eskimos 34, Montreal Alouettes 19

## Basketball

NBA Championship—Syracuse Nationals, 4 games; Fort Wayne Zollner Pistons, 3 games
Rookie of the Year—Bob Pettit (Milwaukee Bucks) NCAA Championship—San Francisco 77, La Salle 63

## Tennis

U.S. National—Men, Tony Trabert (vs. Kenneth Rosewall); Women, Doris Hart (vs. Patricia Ward)
Wimbledon—Men, Tony Trabert (vs. Kurt Nielsen); Women, Louise Brough (vs. Beverly Fleitz)

## Golf

Masters—Cary Middlecoff
U.S. Open—Jack Fleck
British Open—Peter Thomson

## Hockey

Stanley Cup—Detroit Red Wings, 4 games; Montreal Canadiens, 3 games

## Ice Skating

World Championship—Men, Hayes Jenkins (U.S.); Women, Tenley Albright (U.S.)
U.S. National—Men, Hayes Jenkins; Women, Tenley Albright
Canadian National—Men, Charles Snelling; Women, Carole Jane Pachl

## Kentucky Derby

Swaps—Willie Shoemaker, jockey

## Athlete of the Year

Male—Howard Cassady (Football)
Female—Patty Berg (Golf)

## Last Season

Maureen Connolly (Tennis)
Ray Dandridge (Baseball)
Bill Mosienko (Hockey)
Milt Schmidt (Hockey)

## News

**March 17.** Yesterday, NHL President Clarence Campbell suspended scoring leader Maurice Richard for the remaining three games of the season. The Montreal Canadien attacked Boston Bruin Hal Laycoe in a game on the 13th then took a punch at a linesman.

Tonight at the Forum, outraged fans shower Campbell with peanuts and programs. And when an exploding tear-gas bomb clears the building, a mob pours down Montreal's main avenue looting stores. On the radio the next day, Rocket Richard pleads for calm, telling his fans, "I will take my punishment."

At the end of the season, teammate Bernie Geoffrion wins the Art Ross Trophy with 75 points. Richard, who tallied 74, will never again come this close to the scoring title.

**May 12.** Chicago Cub Sam Jones gets his no-hitter over Pittsburgh the hard way, loading the bases on walks before striking out the side in the ninth. He is the first black pitcher to throw a major league no-hitter.

**May 30.** While none of the other drivers is seriously injured, Bill Vukovich dies in a four-car pileup at the Indianapolis 500. The winner of the 1953 and 1954 Indys is the first driver killed in a championship auto race.

**June 11.** When the lead car suddenly cuts for the pit, during the grueling 24-hour Le Mans, French driver Pierre Levegh swerves, clips several other cars, and slams into a wall. His Mercedes engine rips loose and hurtles into the crowd along with a flying rear axle and burning gasoline. He dies along with 82 spectators in the worst accident in auto racing history. Later some witnesses claim that Levegh prevented a worse tragedy by avoiding even denser crowds. But the working people of Paris believe he chose to hit the spectators rather than another driver.

**August 31.** Earlier this year, Swaps beat the favorite Nashua in the Kentucky Derby. Today, in a two-horse match, Nashua collects the $100,000 purse. Next year, the four-year-old's lifetime earnings of $1,288,565 will surpass the record set by Citation.

**September 21.** Rocky Marciano runs his unbeaten string to 49 with a ninth-round KO of light-heavyweight champion Archie Moore. (Marciano was dropped, in the second round, for only the second time in his career.) Some 61,000 watch the bout at Yankee Stadium while another 350,000 flock to 133 theaters across the country.

**October 4.** The Brooklyn Dodgers come back from a 2–0 deficit to capture their first World championship. In five previous series, "The Boys of Summer" lost each time to the Yankees.

**October 24.** The Boxing Hall of Fame is dedicated at Madison Square Garden. The board of directors votes in 15 pioneer prize-fighters, including heavyweight John L. Sullivan. An old timers' committee chooses 6, including heavyweight Jack Johnson, and the moderns elect 3—Jack Dempsey, Joe Louis, and Henry Armstrong.

**December 9.** After 30 months in retirement, Sugar Ray Robinson challenges Carl (Bobo) Olson for the middleweight crown. When he knocks out Olson in the second, Robinson becomes the first fighter to return to the ring and win back a title, as well as the first to capture the middleweight championship three times.

**More news.** The Athletics move to Kansas City. Following the team's last-place finish in 1950, Philadelphia Athletics' owner Connie Mack was forced into retirement by his children. In 1954, they sold the club.

## Records

**March 23.** Blackhawk Bill Mosienko scores a third-period hat trick on New York Ranger goalie Lorne Anderson in 21 seconds—6:09, 6:20, and 6:30—with both teams at full strength. Chicago wins 7–6.

**July 23.** In England, Donald Campbell pilots his speedboat *Bluebird* to 202.32 mph, almost 25 mph faster than the previous record. (Several men have died attempting to break the 200-mph "water barrier.") By 1959, the British racer will reach 275 mph.

**September 19.** Cubs shortstop Ernie Banks sets a major league record with his fifth grand-slam HR of the season. Baltimore's Jim Gentile will equal his feat in 1961.

## What They Said

At Denver's Cherry Hills Country Club, a vacationing Eisenhower sights TV sportscaster Dizzy Dean. The president asks, "Diz, for a man that plays golf as well as you do, how can you permit yourself to get so overweight?" The former major league pitcher replies, "Well, Mr. President, I'll tell ya. I was on a diet for 25 years—now that I'm making some money I'm gonna eat good." (*Sports Illustrated* September 5).

## Obituaries

**Clark Griffith** (November 20, 1869–October 27, 1955). A top pitcher of his era (1891–1914), Griffith invented the screwball (with Christy Mathewson). As the vice-president of the Players' Association in 1900, he led the first universal players' strike largely to help his friend Ban Johnson set up a rival American League. And as the Cincinnati manager, Griffith brought in Armando Marsans, the first Cuban player to find success in the major leagues.

From 1912 to 1920, Griffith purchased a controlling interest in the Washington Senators. With that team, he made his major contribution to the game—the development of the relief pitcher. One of his last innovations was the speed gun, introduced in 1946 to generate fan interest in visiting fastball pitcher Bob Feller. In recent years, nephew and adopted son Cal Griffith has assumed responsibility for the team.

**(Johannes P.) Honus Wagner** (February 24, 1874–December 6, 1955). The first players elected to the Baseball Hall of Fame in 1936 were Ty Cobb, Babe Ruth, Walter Johnson, Christy Mathewson, and Honus Wagner.

In his 17 years with Pittsburgh, Wagner played every position except catcher, but excelled as a shortstop. He once threw a runner out with his hand caught up in a back pocket reaching for tobacco. (Reportedly, Wagner wanted no part of the famous tobacco company baseball card because he would appear to condone cigarette smoking.) He established a lifetime batting average of .329 and was high on the hits, triples, and stolen-base lists. Wagner left professional baseball in 1917, played semipro for several years, then worked as a Pirate coach from 1933 to 1951. At his death, Branch Rickey praises Wagner as the greatest player he ever saw.

**Denton True (Cy) Young** (March 29, 1867–November 4, 1955). Early on, a young catcher judged Young's blistering pitches "as fast as a cyclone." Reporters shortened the description to Cy.

Over a 21-year career in the AL and NL, the durable right-hander posted a staggering 511 wins, most completed games (751), and most innings pitched (7,356). He tossed more than 30 victories in 5 seasons, 3 no-hitters, and a perfect game for Cleveland against the Athletics on May 5, 1904. Legend has it, Young was so intent on defeating left-hander Rube Waddell he realized the game was perfect only when teammates congratulated him.

His arm never wore out; he retired at the age of 44 simply because an increasingly stout build had slowed his recovery time on bunts.

# 1956

The Soviets invade Hungary, the British and French invade Egypt, and the North Vietnamese bitterly watch Saigon hold illegal elections. Moscow ignores international condemnation, Paris and London yield to pressure and withdraw, and Hanoi, by the end of the decade, will turn its conflict with the South Vietnamese into a civil war.

Still, amidst the turmoil, Britain dedicates the world's first full-scale nuclear power station and the Soviets participate in their first Summer Olympics. Grace Kelly marries Prince Rainier III of Monaco. And the first transoceanic telephone cable connects Scotland with Newfoundland.

At home, Americans bring Eisenhower and Nixon back for a second term. The Montgomery bus boycott, founded on Martin Luther King's gospel of nonviolence sparks the civil rights movement. Ford Motors goes public and IBM agrees to sell rather than lease its computers to settle a lengthy antitrust suit. As well the first enclosed shopping center opens and Congress authorizes the first interstate freeway.

My Fair Lady and Long Day's Journey into Night open on Broadway. Elvis Presley scores his first hit single and co-stars in his first film. Bob Feller, George Mikan, and Jackie Robinson retire, Connie Mack dies, and Floyd Patterson becomes the new heavyweight champion of the world.

## NEWS

**January.** This year, in a Cold War competition for the goodwill of developing countries, the Soviets target new nations in Asia, Africa, Latin America, and the Middle East, providing more than $1 billion in foreign aid credits. The Eisenhower administration, in turn, offers $337 million in development funds and $1 billion in military aid. Domestic critics brand the program as an attempt to buy friendship.

**February 3.** Using a Supreme Court order, Autherine Lucy registers as the University of Ala-bama's first Negro student. But, as some 1,000 people riot in protest, the Board of Trustees suspends the 26-year-old woman for "her own safety." She files a suit charging, among other things, that university officials have deliberately permitted the demonstrations.

To the whites who advise gradualism, Lucy's counsel Thurgood Marshall replies, "Maybe you can't override prejudice overnight, but the Emancipation Proclamation was issued in 1863, 90 odd years ago. I believe in gradualism and I also believe that 90 odd years is pretty gradual."

On the 29th, when a federal judge orders Lucy's

*United Nations Secretary-General Dag Hammarskjöld (left) during his current six-week tour visits with King Hussein of Jordan on January 25.*

reinstatement, the trustees expel her for "false" and "scandalous" charges against the university.

**February 14.** At the 20th Soviet Communist Party Congress, First Secretary Khrushchev declares that Communism must follow "peaceful co-existence" in confronting Western ideology or face "the most devastating war in history. There is no third alternative."

Khrushchev, determined to become absolute ruler of the USSR, deliberately sets out in his seven-hour speech to destroy the legend of Joseph Stalin. He condemns "the cult of the individual" and charges the former dictator with misrule and a number of crimes.

Khrushchev achieves the power he craves, but de-Stalinization in apparently sanctioning non-Soviet routes to socialism gives satellite nations free rein to challenge unpopular Communist leaders.

**March 5.** The Supreme Court extends the 1954 public school ruling to tax-supported colleges, thus effectively banning segregation in all public institutions of higher learning.

**March 5.** In South Vietnamese elections supporters of President Ngo Dinh Diem win 112 of 123 seats in the country's first National Assembly. Within days, the pro-Western government formally notifies SEATO that it considers the Geneva Accords nonbinding.

The agreement, which ended the Indochina War in 1954, had promised the victorious North Vietnamese that full elections within two years would reunite the North and South under one leader. The Americans, who like the South Vietnamese never signed the agreement, support Saigon's decision. (Eisenhower will later reveal that his administration believed Ho Chi Minh would win at least 80 percent of the vote.)

On October 26, South Vietnam will promulgate a new constitution giving broad powers to the country's first president, Diem.

**March 11.** Every senator and representative from the former Confederate states—except Lyndon Johnson from Texas and Estes Kefauver and Albert Gore from Tennessee—sign a manifesto pledging to use "all lawful means" to overturn the 1954 Supreme Court ruling on desegregation. Their stand, in effect, legitimizes opposition to integration throughout the South.

**March 30.** On Kamchatka Peninsula, in the USSR, the extinct volcano Mt. Bezymianny stuns experts by literally blowing its top. The largest single volcanic eruption of the 20th century, Bezymianny levels trees up to 25 miles away and expels enough ash and rock to cover the city of Paris to a depth of 49 feet. No one lives close enough to hear the explosion, but scientists observe an air wave circling the earth one and a half times.

**May.** The Geneva Accords specified that the United States could station no more than 342 personnel in South Vietnam. This month, the Eisenhower administration sends an additional 350 people, supposedly to help South Vietnam recover equipment abandoned by the French.

**June 5.** Objecting to American control of a trans-Canada pipeline, the Tory opposition and the Co-operative Commonwealth Federation (CCF) began a filibuster last month on the authorization bill. Since delay will postpone project start-up until next year, the Liberal government today imposes closure, a seldom-used parliamentary device to limit debate. The bill passes, 148–52, the next day.

The petroleum and gas pipeline will be completed in October 1958. But public reaction to one of the most controversial issues in Canadian political history will contribute to the government's defeat in the next general election.

**June 9.** In the second major medical incident of his presidency, Eisenhower undergoes an operation for acute ileitis (inflammation of the lower portion of the small intestine). He returns to the White House on July 15.

**June 28.** Polish workers attack government and party buildings in Poznan to protest economic and social conditions under the Communist regime. The militia suppresses the riot, but only with a heavy loss of life (estimates range from 200 to 500).

To prevent widespread rebellion, the party appoints Wladyslaw Gomulka as first secretary. He will end collectivization and regains internal political control but, convinced that deviation from Marxist doctrine would threaten stability, will stop short of true reform.

**June 29.** With more and more people driving to work and taking automobile holidays, the Federal Aid Highway Act authorizes the construction of the first U.S. interstate freeway. The 42,500-mile system gobbles up huge tracts of land, changing the face of America. By the target completion date in 1972, the budget will have risen from the projected $33.5 billion to over $70 billion; work will still be under way in 1975.

**June 30.** A TWA Constellation and a United DC-7 collide in midair over the Grand Canyon, in broad daylight and clear skies. All 128 people on board both planes die in the first commercial air disaster to kill more than 100 people.

---

*Statistics:* Last month a Pan Am DC-7 set a distance record for a nonstop commercial flight, flying 4,800 miles from Miami to Paris in 14 hours.

---

**July 25.** Just before midnight, in heavy fog off Nantucket Island, the Swedish liner S.S. *Stockholm* drives 30 feet into the side of the Italian liner *Andrea Doria*. Water pours into the huge hole. Yet somehow the liner manages to stay afloat until rescue ships remove the 1,600 passengers and crew.

Most of the fatalities, 5 on the *Stockholm* and 52 on the *Andrea Doria*, occurred during the collision. The stricken ship sinks the next day while the *Stockholm* limps into port.

Each shipping company sues the other, but by mutual consent both will drop all legal action in early 1957. To prevent a similar tragedy, maritime radar undergoes improvements and two-man watches become mandatory in the wheelhouse.

**August 7.** In the city of Cali, just after midnight, seven army trucks of dynamite, ammunition, and gasoline explode near the railway terminal, killing over 1,100 people. The Colombian government charges political sabotage, but the cause of the disaster is never determined.

**August 16.** At the Democratic National Convention in Chicago, Adlai Stevenson wins the presidential nomination on the first ballot. When Stevenson declines to choose a running mate, Senator Estes Kefauver defeats Senator John F. Kennedy in a close second ballot.

**August 22.** The Republican National Convention in San Francisco renominates Dwight Eisenhower and Richard Nixon. Some delegates, concerned that Eisenhower might not survive a second term, started a "dump Nixon" campaign. But the president, realizing the issue would split the party, killed the move by refusing his support.

**September 29.** Nicaraguan president Anastasio Somoza dies of gunshot wounds suffered in an assassination attempt eight days ago. A virtual dictator since 1935, Somoza had worked with the CIA to intervene in the affairs of neighboring countries. Following his death, the Nicaraguan Congress unanimously elects his eldest son, Luis Somoza Debayle.

**October 4.** *Southern School News* reports that Southern and border states have desegregated 797 school districts since the 1954 *Brown* decision, placing 319,184 Negro children in schools beside 2 million white children. Still, the vast majority of blacks, an estimated 2.4 million, remain in segregated schools.

Tennessee called out the National Guard to integrate the Clinton school district, but Alabama, Florida, Georgia, Louisiana, Mississippi, North Carolina, South Carolina, and Virginia have failed to desegregate a single school. At the same time, those states have enacted evasive legislation.

**October 14.** Campaigning in California three days ago, Pennsylvania Governor George Leader suggested Richard Nixon be retired to an offshore island. Following a critical outburst from his political opponents, the Democratic governor responds, "What is there about Nixon that makes even his supporters think of Alcatraz as a retirement home for him?" Leader insists he meant Treasure Island or the Seal Rocks.

**October 19.** The USSR and Japan end the state of war that has existed between them since August 8, 1945. Japanese reparations stop, diplomatic relations are reestablished, and all Japanese POWs are to be released (Tokyo estimates that 11,000 remain, but Moscow admits to holding just 1,200).

With the Soviets no longer exercising their veto, the General Assembly formally admits Japan to the United Nations on December 18.

**October 23.** De-Stalinization and the recent Polish uprising encourage Hungarians to protest the hardships brought on by a bad harvest and the installation of Stalinist Erno Gero as head of the Communist party. Today, thousands of men and women join students in demanding the formation of a new government under former premier Imre Nagy (1953–1955).

The next day, the party asks Nagy to head a coalition. He promises, in a radio broadcast, to extend democratization, raise living standards, and develop an independent Hungarian Communist party. On the 25th, Janos Kadar replaces Gero as party leader. But, when Soviet tanks and Hungarian police kill an estimated 170 protesters, the popular revolt spreads across the nation and Nagy

informs the Soviet ambassador that Hungary will denounce the Warsaw Pact.

On November 4, Soviet troops move in. An overwhelming force of eight divisions (seven armored) attacks Budapest and other key cities as Kadar replaces Nagy as premier.

Hungarians broadcast SOS pleas for military rescue. (European-based U.S. radio programs have talked of "liberating the captive nations.") But the Western nations, involved in the Suez Crisis, merely condemn the Soviet Union in the United Nations, 55–8. An estimated 10,000 to 25,000 die during the Hungarian Revolution and almost 200,000 eventually become refugees.

**October 29.** Israel invades the Sinai peninsula and the Gaza strip. Britain and France, with the right to intervene under the Tripartite Declaration of 1950, send bombers against Egypt within two days.

In June, Egypt assumed defense of the Suez Canal under an agreement with London. On July 26, President Gamal Nasser nationalized the canal and refused safe passage to Israeli ships. The British and French, dependent on canal income and afraid Egypt might cut their petroleum supply line, held secret talks with the Israelis.

The United Nations adopts a Canadian resolution on November 4 to send in a U.N. force, but Britain and France abstain and the next day drop paratroopers into the canal zone.

With the Soviets threatening intervention, the Americans, already angry at their rash Allies, vote with the Communists. London and Paris, buckling under U.N. pressure and worldwide hostility, agree to withdraw, and the U.N. peacekeeping force moves in on November 15.

A pivotal event in modern times, the Suez Crisis completely alters international and Middle East power structures. The Big Four become the Big Two as Britain and France lose their status as major world players. Nasser's prestige increases dramatically in the Arab countries, making him a power in the Middle East for years to come. But, perhaps more significantly, the United Nations gains immense credibility by defusing the potential for widespread war.

*President Dwight Eisenhower and first lady Mamie campaign for a second term in the White House.*

**November 6.** Despite his illnesses, Eisenhower wins 41 states and 457 electoral votes to defeat Adlai Stevenson for the second time. Still, as in 1952, Ike proves far more popular than the rest of his party, and the Democrats retain their majorities in the House and Senate. Only once before—in 1848, when Zachary Taylor was elected—has the president's party failed to win either house of Congress.

**November 18.** NATO envoys stalk out of a Kremlin reception when Khrushchev labels Britain and France "fascist" and "bandits" for attacking Egypt (the USSR, on the other hand, "had Hungary thrust upon us"). The first secretary cries out, "Whether you like it or not, history is on our side. We will bury you!"

**December 2.** According to the NEA, a shortage of teachers and classrooms deprived some 840,000 children of full-time instruction in the past school year. With continuing high birth rates, the U.S. association sees no remedy in sight.

**December 21.** For the first time in Montgomery

history, blacks ride at the front of the bus with whites.

On Nov. 13, the Supreme Court found the city's bus segregation unconstitutional. Yesterday, U.S. marshals served the Montgomery transit company with a federal injunction.

In the years ahead, black Americans will look back on Montgomery's year-long boycott as the grassroots beginning of the civil rights movement.

**More news.** This year, a prosperous United States, with only 6 percent of the world's population, produced 40 percent of the world's goods and services, purchased 15 percent of the imports, and accounted for 20 percent of the exports. The average American salary was 50 percent higher than in 1929, even after making allowances for tax and price increases.

## Obituaries

**Alben William Barkley** (November 24, 1877–April 30, 1956). One of the most effective orators of his time, Truman's running mate received much of the credit for the Democratic party's unexpected presidential victory in 1948. During his term in office, Barkley's 10-year-old grandson coined the term Veep.

**William (Billy) Bishop** (February 8, 1894–September 11, 1956). Canada's greatest W.W.I ace shot down 72 enemy planes in over 170 air engagements. His many decorations included the Victoria Cross, Britain's highest military honor.

**Ernest King** (November 23, 1878–June 25, 1956). Chief of U.S. naval operations during W.W.II, King's global strategy was largely responsible for the destruction of the Japanese fleet.

**Samuel James Seymour** (1860–April 13, 1956). As a child of five, he heard the shot, saw the president slump forward, and watched the assassin jump to the stage. Seymour was probably the sole remaining witness to the assassination of Abraham Lincoln.

*Note:* A West German court officially confirms the death of Adolf Hitler, by suicide, on April 30, 1945.

# BEGINNINGS AND ENDINGS

## News

**January 17.** One of the last giant companies in private hands, Ford goes public in the most sensational stock distribution ever—10.2 million shares.

**April 28.** San Antonio, Texas, becomes the first southern city to integrate all public facilities when city schools allow unsegregated swimming.

**July 16.** Ringling Brothers and Barnum & Bailey Circus perform their last show under a canvas tent. Rising costs and union disputes put an end to the long tradition.

**July 30.** President Eisenhower signs an act establishing "In God We Trust" as the motto of the United States. The phrase, which must be added to all new coins and currency, first appeared on bronze 2-cent pieces in 1864.

**October 8.** On opening day, 40,000 visitors flood the first enclosed, climate-controlled shopping center, outside Minneapolis. Grouping 50 stores around a 300-foot garden, the $20-million mall promises, "Every Day Will Be a Perfect Shopping Day."

**October 16.** With the issuance of a federal court order, the Grand Army of the Republic becomes defunct. (The Union Army's last Civil War veteran, Albert Woolson, died in August.) The Smithsonian Institution receives the remainder of its property.

**October 24.** In Syracuse, the Presbyterian Church in the United States ordains its first woman minister, 31-year-old Margaret E. Towner.

**November 20.** In the first aircraft landing at the South Pole, two U.S. Navy planes drop off a construction team to build a scientific observation post.

**December 1.** An experimental unit of 38 helicopters, equipped with howitzers and rocket launchers, replaces the last U.S. combat mule unit—the Fourth Field Artillery Battalion (Pack). Three days later, the army announces that electronic communication devices have made messenger pigeons obsolete.

**December 14.** At their convention in Ottawa, the Progressive Conservatives elect Saskatchewan MP John Diefenbaker, age 61, as party leader. Ill health forced George Drew (1948–1956) to resign in September.

**December 17.** The helicopter company New York Airways hires Perry H. Young, the first Negro crew member on any American airline.

**More news.** With the installation of ERMA (electronic recording machine, accounting), the Bank of America becomes the first U.S. financial institution to complete daily banking tasks with a computer.

• Either a scientist or a beekeeper imports the aggressive African bee into Brazil this year. Some of the insects will escape into the wild in 1957.

## Records

**March 10.** Peter Twiss pilots the British research plane *Fairey Delta II* to a top mark of 1,132 mph, shattering the U.S. record of 824 mph set last August.

## New Products and Businesses

When a new highway diverted traffic from his restaurant, Harland Sanders sold out. This year, at the age of 66, he hits the road with his fried chicken recipe. With 600 franchises sold over the next nine years, Sanders will adopt the dress of a Kentucky colonel to create his own trademark.

Other new franchises this year include Midas Muffler and the Burger King restaurants.

Procter & Gamble sells Crest toothpaste nationally and introduces Comet cleanser.

S. C. Johnson Company introduces Raid House & Garden Insecticide, the first insect spray for the home. (According to company legend, H. F. Johnson at first dismissed his son Sam's idea because the product contained no wax.)

The British firm Wilkinson Sword introduces long-life stainless-steel razor blades.

Five years ago, Bette Nesmith first relied on white, water-based paint to cover typing errors. With other harried typists clamoring for her correction fluid, she tries selling her Mistake Out to

*This fall the new Bel Air two-door Chevrolet sells for $2,338. Despite the small number of cars manufactured, the '57 Chevy becomes a classic presence on the American road.*

several manufacturers. They all pass. Nesmith, convinced of its marketability, works on a kitchen formula and next year will produce a renamed Liquid Paper. In 1958, a press release in *The Office* magazine will elicit 500 inquiries.

### Fads

Young kids sport "Captain Midnight" decoder rings while teenage girls put their boyfriend's high school rings on a gold chain around their necks.

## SCIENCE AND TECHNOLOGY

### News

**January 25.** IBM ends a four-year antitrust suit with an agreement to license patents and to sell, rather than rent, tabulators and electronic computers.

**March 19.** The U.S. Surgeon General claims that over the past 10 years early diagnosis, surgery, and radiation therapy, have increased the cancer rate of cure from 15 percent to more than 50 percent.

*Statistics:* Two years ago, 10 percent of cigarettes were filtered. Now, in an attempt to allay fears of lung cancer, 30 percent are.

**May 23.** With two fingers and a thumb on each hand, GE's Yes-Man duplicates the actions of a master machine operated by a human. The dexterous robot will perform jobs for the military in radioactive work areas.

**June 4.** Last month, the U.S. Naval Research Lab in Washington, D.C., installed a radiometer. The instrument quickly picked up continuous radio waves from Venus. Since thermal energy or heat creates the waves, scientists today report the planet's surface temperature is too hot to support life as we know it.

**June 21.** The AEC announces the discovery of the neutrino by Frederick Reines and Clyde Cowan at the Los Alamos Lab. American physicist Wolfgang Pauli hypothesized the existence of the atom particle in 1931 and Fermi named it in 1932,

On September 14, the University of California radiation lab will announces the discovery of the antineutron, an oppositely charged counterpart of the neutron.

**July 23.** A 10-year PHS study shows that fluoridated water reduces dental cavities by approximately 60 percent. This conclusive evidence, obtained from two locations in the United States and one in Canada, scientifically establishes the value of fluoridation.

*Statistics:* On October 1, 1955, 1,115 U.S. communities with a population of 22.09 million fluoridated their water supplies.

**August 1.** Dr. J. H. Tjio of Spain reports that humans have 46 chromosomes, not 48 as previously believed. Dr. Frazer Roberts of England confirms the research.

**August 7.** The Mechanics and Farmers Savings Bank, in Bridgeport, Connecticut, opens the first remote-controlled banking unit. Customers drive up, a teller communicates via a TV hookup, and air pressure takes or returns money through a delivery tube.

**August 22.** After 29 years of experimentation, Bell Telephone introduces a visual telephone, still pictures transmitted by telephone cable to a 2-inch by 3-inch screen. But, with a single image requiring up to 125 telephone connections, Bell drops the idea.

**September 25.** Ceremonies in New York, London, and Ottawa inaugurate the first transoceanic telephone cable (from Scotland to Newfoundland). Previously, calls were transmitted to Europe by radio, but with atmospheric interference and delays of up to 10 hours service was far from satisfactory. The $40-million cable, unaffected by weather, carries three times more calls, up to 36.

**October 1.** By the end of 1955, 7 million American school children had received the Salk polio vaccine. Now, with allotment controls lifted, the National Foundation for Infantile Paralysis begins a nationwide campaign to vaccinate everyone under the age of 35. This year, the number of polio cases drops to 15,000.

**October 9.** A *New York Times* article discusses a shunt for hydrocephalus, the dangerous buildup of brain fluid suffered by thousands of infants each year. The device, invented by the father of a recent victim, drains the fluid into the veins leading from the head; 57 of 68 babies treated are still alive. Surgeons call it "a fairy tale come true."

**October 17.** Although the first controlled, self-sustaining nuclear reaction occurred on December 2, 1942, at the University of Chicago, peaceful atomic energy has remained largely experimental. Today, at Calder Hall in England, the first full-scale nuclear power station begins producing electricity.

After the war, British industrial development threatened to outstrip coal production. Rather than rely on oil imports, London promoted atomic power. Still, most of the 28,000 kilowatts from this prototype station will go to the Windscale Plutonium Factory for military production.

**November 11.** The Convair B-58, the first supersonic bomber, makes a successful test flight in the United States. Innovations include a separate escape capsule for each member of the three-man crew, and fuel and armament pods which jettison when empty. The first squadrons will become operational in 1960.

**November 17.** The *New York Times* reports on the work of Dr. Narinder Singh Kapany, at the University of Rochester's Institute of Optics. With hair-thin strands of optical glass, he hopes to create a gastroscope to see inside the human stomach. He calls the new field fiber optics.

**December.** Herbert Friedman announces that instrument readings taken in a navy rocket show that solar flares emit x-rays. Traveling at the speed of light, their arrival causes radio blackouts on Earth. In 1958, after further studies, the American astronomer will conclude that the sun's corona produces x-rays as well.

**December 8.** A 48.5-foot Viking rocket tests successfully at Patrick Air Force Base in Florida. It is a scale model of the 72-foot Vanguard rocket that will launch the first U.S. satellite.

---

*Statistics:* Electronics becomes the country's fifth largest industry, with $11.5 billion in sales and a work force of 1.5 million; in 1939, with sales mostly in radios, the industry ranked 49th.

---

**More news.** With a grant from Planned Parenthood, Dr. Gregory Pincus began work in 1951, with Dr. M. C. Chang, on an oral contraceptive. Dr. John Rock tested the synthetic progesterones in a Massachusetts fertility clinic. This year, in large-scale field tests in Puerto Rico, Haiti, and elsewhere, women receive the first birth control pill.

• Arthur Kornberg, at the Washington University School of Medicine, announces the synthesis of

DNA. (An incorrect nucleotide sequence leaves the genetic material biologically inactive.) He will receive the 1959 Nobel prize in medicine and physiology for his work.

• Civilian aircraft under development include three jets—Boeing 707, Douglas DC-8, Convair 880 Golden Arrow—and two turboprops—Electra and Fairchild Friendship. By the end of the year, only the Boeing, the first jet transport, and the Fairchild complete test flights. Orders for piston-engine craft, mostly DC-6's and DC-7's, far out-number orders for jets.

> *Statistics*: Before W.W.II, airplanes carried just 5 percent of the total number of train passengers. This year, the airlines pull even with the railroads.

• With admissions nearly doubled since 1940, mental patients this year occupy more hospital beds than all other patients combined.

• For the first time, liquefied natural gas is produced on an industrial scale. The United States will export the gas to Britain, in 1959, in a specially converted tanker.

## Other Discoveries, Developments, and Inventions

Test of the Rolls-Royce Vertijet, the first aircraft able to shift from vertical to horizontal flight
Test flight of the French Mach 2 fighter Mirage
Motorized go-carts, in Los Angeles
Electric stamp vendors, in New York City

## Obituaries

**Hiram Bingham** (November 19, 1875–June 6, 1956). The American senator and explorer directed the Yale archeological expedition of 1911 that discovered the ancient Incan city of Machu Picchu, hidden in the Andes some 7,000 feet above sea level.

**Clarence Birdseye** (December 9, 1886–October

9, 1956). His 300 patents included the "Quick Freeze Machine," which produced better-tasting frozen food.

**William Boeing** (October 1, 1881–September 28, 1956). The aviation pioneer founded Pacific Aero Products in 1916; 13 years later it became the Boeing Airplane Co.

**Anton Carlson** (January 29, 1875–September 2, 1956). The Swedish-American physiologist contributed to a better understanding of almost every organ and system in the human body, including the origin of hunger pangs and the causes of diabetes.

**Charles Fairey** (May 5, 1887–September 30, 1956). The British aircraft designer invented the wing flap and developed the *Fairey Delta II*, the first aircraft to fly at more than 1,000 mph.

**Irène Joliot-Curie** (September 12, 1897–March 17, 1956). Daughter of Pierre and Marie Curie, the discoverers of radium, Joliot-Curie was herself a renowned scientist. With her husband Frederic Joliot, she received the Nobel prize in 1935 for the discovery of induced, or artificial, radioactivity. Her subsequent research on the neutron bombardment of uranium proved fundamental to the discovery of nuclear fission by Otto Hahn in 1938. Like her mother before her, Irène died of leukemia brought on by prolonged exposure to radiation.

**Alfred Kinsey** (June 23, 1894–August 25, 1956). The U.S. biologist became internationally famous in 1948 with his unprecedented study, *Sexual Behavior in the Human Male*.

**Joseph Le Prince** (August 8, 1875–February 10, 1956). During the construction of the Panama Canal and later in the United States, the British-American sanitary engineer pioneered the fight against malaria and yellow fever. While in Panama, he and his superior Dr. William Crawford Gorgas made a perilous canoe trip through the canal, two years before the passage of the first official ship.

**Charles Edward Taylor** (circa 1869–January 30, 1956). The gifted mechanic was chief designer and builder of the first successful airplane, the Wright brothers' 1903 *Flyer*.

**Preston Tucker** (September 21, 1903–December 26, 1956). Only 49 Tucker automobiles were manufactured before the automaker was indicted for fraud. Cleared of all charges in 1950, Tucker was unable to restart his company.

## THE ARTS

March 15—*My Fair Lady*, with Rex Harrison, Julie Andrews, Stanley Holloway, Kathleen Nesbitt (2,717 perfs.)

October 31—*Auntie Mame*, with Rosalind Russell (639 perfs.)

November 7—*Long Day's Journey into Night*, with Fredric March, Florence Eldridge, Jason Robards, Jr., Bradford Dillman, Katharine Ross (390 perfs.)

November 15—*Li'l Abner*, with Peter Palmer, Edith (Edie) Adams, Charlotte Rae, Stubby Kaye, Julie Newmar, Tina Louise (694 perfs.)

November 29—*Bells Are Ringing*, with Judy Holliday, Sydney Chaplin, Jean Stapleton (924 perfs.)

### Tony Awards

Actor (Dramatic)—Paul Muni, *Inherit the Wind*
Actress (Dramatic)—Julie Harris, *The Lark*
Actor (Musical)—Ray Walston, *Damn Yankees*
Actress (Musical)—Gwen Verdon, *Damn Yankees*
Play—*The Diary of Anne Frank*
Musical—*Damn Yankees*

### News

**January 1.** Queen Elizabeth installs ballerina Margot Fonteyn as a dame commander of the Order of the British Empire.

**October 29.** Maria Callas debuts at the Metropolitan Opera in the leading role of *Norma*. A child of Greek immigrants, the soprano trained in Europe and made her American debut earlier this year in Chicago.

**October 31.** Under royal charter, the 25-year-old Sadler's Wells Ballet becomes The Royal Ballet.

### Obituaries

**Bertolt Brecht** (February 10, 1898–August 14, 1956). An important German poet and dramatist, Brecht is best known in the West for *The Threepenny Opera*.

**Jackson Pollock** (January 28, 1912–August 11, 1956). The American artist pioneered abstract expressionism in the mid-1940s and, at the end of that decade, outraged purists by dripping swirls of color onto the canvas. Pollock had returned to more conventional techniques before his death in an automobile accident. In 1960, one of his canvases will sell for $100,000.

## WORDS

Nelson Algren, *A Walk on the Wild Side*
Morey Bernstein, *The Search for Bridey Murphy*
Ian Fleming, *Diamonds Are Forever*
Allen Ginsberg, *"Howl," and Other Poems*
Graham Greene, *The Quiet American*
Billie Holiday, *Lady Sings the Blues*
Kathryn Hulme, *The Nun's Story*
John F. Kennedy, *Profiles in Courage*
Alistair MacLean, *H. M. S. Ulysses*
Grace Metalious, *Peyton Place*
Nicholas Monsarrat, *The Tribe That Lost Its Head*
William Whyte, *The Organization Man*

### News

**June 19.** The Library Services Act appropriates $7.5 million for rural America. To receive funds, a state must submit a plan for extended services to towns with fewer than 10,000 people.

**December 20.** *Colliers* ceases publication after 68 years. (The final installment of the magazine's serial story runs in the *Saturday Evening Post*.) *Woman's Home Companion* (1871) also shuts down this year.

**More news.** The poem "Howl" is found "not without redeeming social significance" in an obscenity trial. The notoriety pushes poet Allen Ginsberg to the forefront of the counterculture.

• Pauline Esther Phillips starts "Dear Abby," an advice column for the McNaught Syndicate. Abigail Van Buren is the twin sister of Ann Landers.

• In his book *The Search for Bridey Murphy*, Morey Bernstein relates how under hypnotism housewife Ruth Simmons "remembered" a former life in 19th-century Ireland. Although skeptics question her parents' and foster-parents' Irish background, amateur hypnotism becomes the rage at parties this year.

• Americans are scandalized by the sordid goings-on in *Peyton Place*—teen abortion, suicide by hanging, merciless town gossip. Over the next 12 years, the story of a fictional New England town will sell almost 10 million copies and inspire a movie and prime-time TV series.

When Hugh Hefner persuades subscription manager Janet Pilgrim to pose for his magazine, her nude photo layout inspires a "Playmate of the Month" feature.

## Cartoons and Comics

**September–October.** The revival of the Flash, in DC Showcase Comics No. 4, marks the first step toward a Silver Age of comics.

**October.** With an unpaid contribution to New York's weekly *Village Voice*, Jules Feiffer introduces psychoanalysis to cartoons. His work will be nationally syndicated by 1958.

## Time Man of the Year

The Hungarian Freedom Fighter

## New Words and Phrases

automatic (a type of play in football)
brainstorming
brinkmanship
fishyback (moving a truck trailer by ship)
head shrinker
hero sandwich
industrial park
steel band (a musical band using oil drums)
tranquilizer

zigzag eating (shifting the fork to the other hand)

After five years of work at the Saskatchewan Hospital, Drs. Humphry Osmond and John Smythies theorize that schizophrenics suffer hallucinations because of the mescaline-like chemicals produced by their bodies. Interested in their research, author Aldous Huxley suggests *phanerothyme* (*phaneros*, "evident," *thymos*, "soul") as a name for the new drugs. In the end, Osmond's suggestion wins out—*psychedelic* (revealing the psyche).

Chuck Berry's song title "Roll-Over Beethoven" becomes a hip phrase.

A Los Angeles advertising agency answers each telephone call with, "Good morning. Carson/Roberts. Have a happy day." When the salutation is added to company products, such as stationery, crests, and beach towels, others quickly take it up. By the 1960s, the phrase will evolve into "Have a good day."

## Obituaries

**Walter de la Mare** (April 25, 1873–June 22, 1956). The British poet's verse conveyed a clear sense of childhood.

**H(enry) L(ouis) Mencken** (September 12, 1880–January 29, 1956). From 1910 through the 1930s, the editor and author launched controversial attacks on prudery, fundamentalism, mediocre literature, and the American middle class. He retired in 1948.

**A(lan) A(lexander) Milne** (January 18, 1882–January 31, 1956). The British author and playwright created the classic children's stories of Christopher Robin and Winnie the Pooh.

**Clarence E. Mulford** (February 3, 1883–May 10, 1956). When his 28th novel took Hopalong Cassidy to the age of 60, the 58-year-old American novelist stopped writing rather than kill him off.

**Alexander Raymond** (October 2, 1909–September 6, 1956). One of the most versatile and influential of American cartoonists, Raymond created four outstanding comic strips: *Flash Gordon*, *Jungle Jim*, *Rip Kirby*, and *Secret Agent X-9*. He died in a car accident.

# FASHION

## Haute Couture

Strongly influenced by the pre-W.W.I styles of *My Fair Lady*, couturiers soften the silhouette with clinging or floating fabrics, high waistlines, deeply pleated full skirts, and feminine trim such as roses and ribbons.

## News

**This year.** ICI introduces the first full range of bright, wash-fast dyes for cellulose fabrics. Previously, manufacturers could only produce fabrics like artificial silk in limited colors.

• The top magazine model of the decade, Suzy Parker makes thousands of dollars in the days when models never sign exclusive contracts. More than beautiful, Parker possesses the uncanny ability to look right in any clothes, in any situation.

• This year, the famous 65-year-old House of Paquin closes in Paris. Mme. Paquin, the first important woman in haute couture, died in 1936.

## Colors and Materials

Along with crepe for day dresses and chiffon for evening, the new clinging line stirs an interest in knits.

Materials display an even stronger Oriental influence with jeweled and embroidered metallic brocades and exotic color combinations, such as emerald green with sapphire blue.

Stylized colored flowers on a colored background is an interesting pattern innovation this year.

With the mink coat emerging as the new status symbol, fur trim appears on street dresses, tailored suits, and evening clothes.

## Clothes

The industry copies Chanel's comfortable jersey cardigan suits.

Fabric coats often flare out at the shoulders into a cape. Knitted coats and bulky coat sweaters become popular sports and daytime fashions.

The new fullness requires no petticoats, but young girls continue to use them—the more the better—to bell out their skirts. Petticoats often run stockings, some cause a rash, and many must be dry-cleaned or washed by hand.

Teenage girls team Dad's shirt with rolled-up jeans while boys try for the Ivy League look of sports blazer and peaked cap. Both wear jeans with either black-and-white saddle oxfords or penny-loafers, although some guys opt for white bucks.

A tailored cut eliminates much of the informality of men's sports jackets. All-year suits tend toward lighter-weight wools.

## Accessories

Manufacturers offer stiletto shoes with increasingly pointed toes.

Once again hats move forward over the brow. Dior popularizes the waterproof sou'wester.

Long, slim handbags add an outside pocket.

Eight-button gloves outsell the shorter length for day wear.

## Hair and Cosmetics

Teenage girls wear their hair in a ponytail while many women prefer the upswept style or chignon of *My Fair Lady*. Young guys go for Elvis Presley's oily ducktail and sideburns.

Sales of women's hair spray and men's shaving cream skyrocket as aerosol containers revolutionize the cosmetics industry.

# POPULAR MUSIC

"Don't Be Cruel"/"Hound Dog"—Elvis Presley

"Singing the Blues"—Guy Mitchell

"Heartbreak Hotel"—Elvis Presley

"The Wayward Wind"—Gogi Grant

"The Poor People of Paris" (Instr.)—Les Baxter & His Orchestra

"Memories Are Made of This"—Dean Martin

"Rock and Roll Waltz"—Kay Starr

"My Prayer"—Platters

"Love Me Tender"—Elvis Presley

"Lisbon Antigua" (Instr.)—Nelson Riddle

"I Almost Lost My Mind"—Pat Boone

"The Green Door"—Jim Lowe

"Moonglow & Theme from *Picnic*" (Instr.)— Morris Stoloff

"The Great Pretender"—Platters

"Hot Diggity (Dog Ziggity Boom)"—Perry Como

"I Want You, I Need You, I Love You"—Elvis Presley

"No, Not Much"—Four Lads

"Blue Suede Shoes"—Carl Perkins

"Honky Tonk (Parts 1 & 2)" (Instr.)—Bill Doggett & Chorus

"Whatever Will Be, Will Be (Que Será, Será)"— Doris Day

"Canadian Sunset" (Instr.)—Hugo Winterhalter Orchestra & Chorus

"Blueberry Hill"—Fats Domino

"Just Walking in the Rain"—Johnnie Ray

## News

**January.** Until this year, the six major record companies dominated the top 50 with former band singers, such as Perry Como, Frank Sinatra, and Doris Day. The emergence of rock 'n' roll revolutionizes the industry.

Teenagers, no longer willing to accept white versions of R&B hits, push black artists onto the charts. (The Platters are the first black group to reach No. 1.) By the end of the year, 25 different labels place hits in the top 50.

**March.** A jury of classical musicians, including Artur Rubinstein, awards 16-year-old classical pianist Neil Sedaka a two-year scholarship to the Juilliard School of Music.

**April.** Singer Gene Vincent travels to Los Angeles for a Capitol Records Elvis-sound-alike contest and wins with his own composition "Be-Bop-A-Lula." With the Bluecaps, one of the first pop groups, Vincent reaches No. 7 with the song.

**April 10.** In Birmingham, Alabama, six men leap over the footlights and assault singer Nat King Cole in front of an all-white audience. The police, on hand because of the White Citizens' Council campaign against "decadent" Negro music, quickly arrest the culprits. Cole receives a standing ovation, but he cancels the concert for a visit to the doctor. Later, he performs a second concert for black patrons.

**April 21.** Bill Haley & His Comets peak at No. 15 with their next release, "Razzle Dazzle." Young people, more sophisticated with their increased exposure to black artists, now find Haley's group uninteresting, vocally and musically. Another performer, 10 years younger, better looking, and with a much better voice, makes the fledgling rock 'n' roll music big business. Today, Elvis Presley's "Heartbreak Hotel" reaches No. 1—his first hit single and the first record ever to make all three song charts— Pop, R&B, and CW. For 25 of the next 37 weeks, Elvis tops the charts with seven smash hits. Teens, clamoring for his records, force RCA to use competitors' manufacturing facilities to meet the demand. And DJ's, virtually unaware of him last year, pick Presley as the top male vocalist of 1956.

*The young Elvis Presley.*

**December 3.** Dropping by Sun studios, Elvis meets up with Johnny Cash, Carl Perkins, and Jerry Lee Lewis. For 2½ hours, the rock 'n' rollers harmonize in a session of gospel. None of their record companies will ever release an LP, but bootleg copies of the "Million Dollar Quartet" supposedly exist.

**More news.** Annie Mae Bullock, age 16, joins Ike Turner's band and changes her name to Tina Turner.

• Convinced the song will flop, Doris Day refuses to record more than one take of "Whatever Will Be, Will Be."

• Following the lead of Columbia Records, three other large companies set up a Record of the Month plan. Their extensive advertising increases record-player sales, but clubs soon evolve into little more than a means of distribution for the big labels.

• Buffalo DJ Dick Biondi is fired for playing a Presley record.

• At 13 years of age, Frankie Lymon becomes rock 'n' roll's first teenage star. His "Why Do Fools Fall in Love," recorded with the Teenagers, reaches No. 6.

*New Recording Artists*

James Brown
Johnny Cash
Coasters
Diamonds
Eydie Gorme
Roy Orbison

## Obituaries

**Tommy Dorsey** (November 19, 1905–November 26, 1956). The trombonist formed popular dance bands with his brother Jimmy, the saxophonist, until a violent quarrel split them up in 1935. Tommy's orchestra peaked in the early 1940s, but an estimated 100 million record sales made his swing style an important influence in popular music. The brothers reconciled in 1953 and had since appeared together on TV.

**Albert Von Tilzer** (March 29, 1878–October 1, 1956). An important songwriter from the early 1900s into the 1920s, Von Tilzer is best remembered for a single collaboration with Jack Norworth—"Take Me Out to the Ball Game" (1908).

**Victor Young** (August 8, 1900–November 10, 1956). The influential composer's hits included "Sweet Sue," "Stella by Starlight," and "Around the World in Eighty Days" and he wrote and arranged the scores for more than 300 films.

## MOVIES

*Anastasia* (d. Anatole Litvak; color)—Ingrid Bergman, Yul Brynner, Helen Hayes

*Around the World in Eighty Days* (d. Michael Anderson; color)—David Niven, Cantinflas, Shirley MacLaine, Robert Newton

*Bus Stop* (d. Joshua Logan; color)—Marilyn Monroe, Don Murray, Arthur O'Connell

*Carousel* (d. Henry King; color)—Gordon Macrae, Shirley Jones, Cameron Mitchell

*The Court Jester* (d. Norman Panama; color)—Danny Kaye, Glynis Johns, Basil Rathbone

*Forbidden Planet* (d. Fred M. Wilcox; color)—Walter Pidgeon, Anne Francis, Leslie Nielsen

*Friendly Persuasion* (d. William Wyler; color)—Gary Cooper, Dorothy McGuire, Anthony Perkins

*Giant* (d. George Stevens; color)—Elizabeth Taylor, Rock Hudson, James Dean

*The Harder They Fall* (d. Mark Robson; bw)—Humphrey Bogart, Rod Steiger, Jan Sterling

*The Invasion of the Body Snatchers* (d. Don Siegel; bw)—Kevin McCarthy, Dana Wynter

*The King and I* (d. Walter Lang; color)—Deborah Kerr, Yul Brynner

*Lust for Life* (d. Vincente Minnelli; color)—Kirk Douglas, Anthony Quinn

*Richard III* (British, d. Laurence Olivier; color)—Laurence Olivier, Ralph Richardson, Claire Bloom, John Gielgud, Cedric Hardwicke

*The Searchers* (d. John Ford; color)—John

Wayne, Jeffrey Hunter, Vera Miles, Ward Bond, Natalie Wood

*The Seventh Seal* (Swedish, d. Ingmar Bergman; bw)—Max von Sydow, Gunnar Björnstrand

*Somebody Up There Likes Me* (d. Robert Wise; bw)—Paul Newman, Pier Angeli

*The Teahouse of the August Moon* (d. Daniel Mann; color)—Marlon Brando, Glenn Ford, Machiko Kyo, Eddie Albert, Paul Ford

*The Ten Commandments* (d. Cecil B. DeMille; color)—Charlton Heston, Yul Brynner, Anne Baxter, Edward G. Robinson

*Written on the Wind* (d. Douglas Sirk; color)—Rock Hudson, Lauren Bacall, Robert Stack, Dorothy Malone

## Academy Awards

**March 21.** In a historic first, Academy acting members nominate a performer posthumously, James Dean for *East of Eden.*

Three months after her engagement to Prince Rainier of Monaco, Grace Kelly presents an Oscar in her last public appearance as an actress.

Jerry Lewis hosts in Hollywood while actress Claudette Colbert and director Joseph L. Mankiewicz co-host in New York.

Best Picture—*Marty*

Best Actor—Ernest Borgnine (*Marty*)

Best Actress—Anna Magnani (*The Rose Tattoo*)

Best Director—Delbert Mann (*Marty*)

Best Supporting Actor—Jack Lemmon (*Mister Roberts*)

Best Supporting Actress—Jo Van Fleet (*East of Eden*)

Best Song—"Love Is a Many-Splendored Thing" from the film of the same name

Honorary Award—*Samurai, the Legend of Musashi* (Japanese)

The big story of the evening is *Marty*. This first American picture made from a TV play takes best picture, best actor, and best director, and Paddy Chayefsky wins an Oscar for his screenplay.

## News

**April 19.** Grace Kelly marries Prince Rainier III of Monaco in a religious ceremony. The 1,500 press members covering the elaborate Monte Carlo ceremony outnumber the guests and dignitaries.

Kelly is Monaco's second American princess. In 1889, widowed Prince Albert married 31-year-old Alice Heine, an American widow of French aristocracy. The couple had no children, and the prince's offspring by his first wife inherited the title.

**June 29.** Actress Marilyn Monroe marries playwright Arthur Miller.

**December 11.** A revised MPAA censorship code discourages racial slurs and the glorification of crime, but allows scenes dealing with abortion, prostitution, the kidnapping of children, and the sale and use of narcotics. Still, the treatment must stay "within the limits of good taste." The revisions were likely prompted by last year's controversy over *The Man with the Golden Arm*.

**More news.** Elvis Presley, with a seven-year 20th Century-Fox contract, appears this year in *Love Me Tender* starring Richard Egan and Debra Paget.

• Columbia Pictures finishes the last Hollywood movie serial—*Blazing the Overland Trail* (15 episodes).

From the serials' first appearance in 1912, their cliff-hanger endings thrilled audiences. Although never polished productions, serials occasionally introduced new talent (John Wayne) or tried out new story lines (space travel). But postwar union demands had cut further into budgets and studios simply phased out production.

• Producer Mike Todd uses 44 well-known actors and actresses in small roles to glamorize his film *Around the World in 80 Days*. He calls the brief appearances "cameos."

• This year, Hollywood puts out the first music films strictly for teenagers. In addition to the popular *Rock Around the Clock*, youngsters see *Shake, Rattle and Roll* with Fats Domino, Joe Turner, and the star, a young Touch [Mike] Connors. *Rock,*

*Rock, Rock!* features teenager Tuesday Weld in her first film (Connie Francis dubs her songs) and Chuck Berry, LaVern Baker, and Frankie Lymon and the Teenagers singing "I'm Not a Juvenile Delinquent."

• Japan's first science fiction film is retitled *Godzilla, King of the Monsters* for North American release. Embassy Pictures has spliced in 20 minutes of Canadian actor Raymond Burr "interacting" with other characters. The radioactive dinosaur will spawn endless sequels.

• To increase concession sales, New Jersey theater owner James Viccary flashes "Eat Popcorn" and "Drink Coca-Cola" on screen for 1/3,000 of a second during the movies. But reporters find that subliminal advertising fails to plant the idea in their minds.

• Comedy stars Dean Martin and Jerry Lewis bitterly end their 10-year partnership. In 16 films, since 1949, Lewis's zany clowning constantly interrupted Martin's crooning. Few insiders believe the singer will make it on his own.

• A starring role in *And God Created Woman* turns French actress Brigitte Bardot, age 22, into the silver screen's new sex kitten, guaranteeing a place for French films in U.S. theaters.

| Top Box Office Stars | Newcomers |
| --- | --- |
| William Holden | Rod Steiger |
| John Wayne | Jeffrey Hunter |
| James Stewart | Natalie Wood |
| Burt Lancaster | Dana Wynter |
| Glenn Ford | Tim Hovey |
| Dean Martin & | Yul Brynner |
| Jerry Lewis | George Nader |
| Gary Cooper | Joan Collins |
| Marilyn Monroe | Sheree North |
| Kim Novak | Sal Mineo |
| Frank Sinatra | |

## Top Money-Maker of the Year

*Guys and Dolls* (1955)

## Obituaries

**Edward Arnold** (February 18, 1890–April 26, 1956). One of Hollywood's foremost character actors remains best remembered for his starring role in *Diamond Jim* (1935).

**Henri Chrétien** (February 1, 1879–February 7, 1956). The French scientist demonstrated his wide-angle lens in 1937, but 16 years passed before 20th Century-Fox made the first CinemaScope film. Hollywood acknowledged his technical contribution with a special award in 1954.

**Alexander Korda** (September 16, 1893–January 24, 1956). Sir Alexander was a leading movie producer in the United States and Europe, as well as at home in Great Britain. His productions included *The Scarlet Pimpernel* (1935) and *The Third Man* (1949).

**Bela Lugosi** (October 20, 1888–August 16, 1956). With his definitive portrayal of Dracula in 1931, the Hungarian-born actor reached the height of his career. Lugosi, according to his wishes, is buried in his Dracula cape.

**Robert Newton** (June 1, 1905–March 25, 1956). The fine British actor is best known to Americans for his role as Long John Silver in Walt Disney's movie *Treasure Island* (1950).

# TELEVISION AND RADIO

## New Prime-Time TV Programs

"Circus Boy" (September 23, 1956–September 11, 1958; Adventure)—Mickey Braddock, Noah Beery, Jr.

"Dick Powell's Zane Grey Theater" (October 5, 1956–July 1961; Western Anthology)—Host: Dick Powell

"The Dinah Shore Chevy Show" (October 5, 1956–May 12, 1963; Musical Variety)—Dinah Shore. *Note:* The show is broadcast as a monthly special the first year, then on a rotating basis from 1961.

"The Ford Show" (October 4, 1956–June 29, 1961; Musical Variety)—Tennessee Ernie Ford. *Note:* The name refers to Ford Motor Co.

"The Gale Storm Show" (September 29, 1956–

March 24, 1960; Situation Comedy)—Gale Storm, ZaSu Pitts, Roy Roberts, Jimmy Fairfax

"Playhouse 90" (October 4, 1956–January 21, 1960; Drama Anthology)

"The Steve Allen Show" (June 24, 1956–June 1960, September 1961–December 1961; Comedy Variety)—Steve Allen, Louis Nye

"To Tell the Truth" (December 18, 1956–May 22, 1967; Quiz)—Host: Bud Collyer

## Emmy Awards 1955 (March 17, 1956)

Best Dramatic Series—"Producers Showcase" (NBC)

Best Variety Series—"The Ed Sullivan Show" (CBS)

Best Comedy Series—"You'll Never Get Rich" (CBS)

Best Children's Series—"Lassie" (CBS)

Best Actor in a Series—Phil Silvers ("You'll Never Get Rich," CBS)

Best Actress in a Series—Lucille Ball ("I Love Lucy" CBS)

## News

**January 28.** On the program "Stage Show," bandleaders Tommy and Jimmy Dorsey introduce a young country-rock singer out of Memphis. This is Elvis Presley's first appearance on television.

**March.** An 11-year-old Brenda Lee makes her television debut on ABC's "Ozark Jubilee"; she soon becomes a program favorite.

**March 17.** During the past season, Milton Berle lost his audience to "You'll Never Get Rich," the first time in eight years he failed to win his time slot. Today, Mr. Television announces his retirement.

Berle will return in 1958 for a single unsuccessful season but, trapped by his 30-year contract, must remain with NBC. Finally, in 1965, he will accept a 40-percent cut to obtain his release.

**April 2.** CBS debuts the first daily 30-minute TV soap operas—"As the World Turns" and "The Edge of Night." Unlike the action-packed radio soaps, these programs will rely on visual impact to show character development. "As the World Turns" will hold No. 1 in daytime programming from 1959 to 1971.

**April 14.** The videotape recording introduced by Bing Crosby Enterprises, in 1952, suffered from poor resolution. Today, Ampex Corp. demonstrates a single 14-inch reel machine with a picture comparable to live television, ready for commercial use. CBS orders three at $75,000 each.

**August 13.** NBC brings in Chet Huntley and David Brinkley as co-anchors for the Democratic convention in Chicago. Impressed with their performance, the network gives the pair a nightly newscast in October. By 1958, the show becomes "The Huntley-Brinkley Report" with their signature sign-off "Goodnight, Chet" . . . "Goodnight, David".

**September.** Last fall, Jackie Gleason discarded the variety part of his show to extend "The Honeymooners" comedy segment into a half-hour program with himself, Art Carney, Audrey Meadows, and Joyce Randolph. (Meadows, whose two brothers are lawyers, obtained a residual contract on all reruns, forever, rather than the usual five. Gleason's deal includes a generous percentage of rerun profits.)

As part of the agreement, the network accepted a half-hour program from Gleason's production company. But, by leading off the hour slot, the weaker "Stage Show" lost the audience before "The Honeymooners" reached the screen. Early in 1956, CBS convinced the comic to reverse the order, but it was too late to save the Kramdens and the Nortons.

Gleason returns to the hour-long variety format and "The Honeymooners" finishes in September after filming just 39 episodes.

**September 9.** Elvis Presley appears on "The Ed Sullivan Show" and sings "Don't Be Cruel," "Love Me Tender," "Ready Teddy," and "Hound Dog." (Sullivan is in the hospital following a serious automobile accident and actor Charles Laughton makes the introduction.)

A record 80 percent of the TV viewing audience tunes in, but many parents are embarrassed by Elvis the Pelvis's gyrations. (John Lardner wrote, in the July 16 issue of *Time*, that "what Elvis acts like is a lovesick outboard motor.") Nonetheless, the young singer receives an unprecedented $50,000 for this appearance and two later ones on the show.

**September 10.** The old salt was introduced to the funnies in 1929 and four years later told movie audiences, "I Yam What I Yam." Today, New York and Chicago TV stations show the first of 234 "Popeye the Sailor" cartoons. By 1960, he will be gulping spinach on 150 stations across the country.

**September 30.** With the DuMont shutdown, CBS picks up Sunday NFL games. Wider coverage generates greater interest in the game.

**October 11.** Rod Serling's *Requiem for a Heavyweight* debuts on the new live anthology, "Playhouse 90." The outstanding drama, starring Jack Palance, Keenan Wynn, and Ed Wynn, wins an Emmy as the best single performance of the year. "Playhouse 90" quickly becomes the standard against which all other television dramas are judged.

**November 3.** CBS pays $225,000 for a first-time showing of the 1939 Hollywood classic *The Wizard of Oz*.

**November 5.** "The Nat King Cole Show" marks the first prime-time network series headlined by a major black performer. Initial poor ratings scare off some sponsors and others refuse to risk the wrath of Southern viewers. NBC sustains the 15-minute program, and name performers—black and white—appear for next to nothing, but Cole will be canceled on December 17, 1957.

**December 18.** Panelists on the new quiz show "To Tell the Truth" try to match a life history to one of three contestants. Each round ends with the command, "Will the real . . . please stand up!" Regulars include Kitty Carlisle and Tom Poston. When the show enters syndication in 1969, Garry Moore will replace host Bud Collyer.

**More news.** All the major movie studios sell or lease films to the networks: MGM releases 725, Warner Bros. 750, RKO 740, 20th Century-Fox 390, and Columbia 104. Although the films predate August 1, 1948, their unprecedented ratings strike a mortal blow to the more expensive, local live programming.

• Since 1953, the number of educational TV stations has increased from 1 to 20.

• Of the 123 series broadcast this year, 101 are half-hour programs, 20 are 1-hour, and 2 are 1½-hour. The types of programs include 29 domestic shows, 21 comedies, 16 quiz shows, 16 musical-variety programs, 10 action-adventure, and 7 Westerns.

• Edgar Bergen and his wooden dummy Charlie McCarthy opened their radio show on May 9, 1937. Charlie quickly took on his own persona and two years later Bergen added a second dummy, Mortimer Snerd. During his last year on the air, the ventriloquist often brings on his daughter, Candice.

• At the end of the year, ABC's "Press Conference" becomes the first television show to send a crew to France. The cameras record Premier Guy Mollet.

• During an on-camera "Person to Person" visit, comedian Joe E. Lewis describes interviewer Edward R. Murrow as "the only Peeping Tom in the country with a sponsor."

## TV Commercials

Pepsodent—The catchy jingle promises, "You'll wonder where the yellow went when you brush your teeth with Pepsodent."

## Memorable Radio Programs End

"Aunt Jenny's True-Life Stories" (January 18, 1937)
"The Charlie McCarthy Show" (May 9, 1937)
"Dragnet" (July 7, 1949)
"Gene Autry's Melody Ranch" (January 7, 1940)
"The Greatest Story Ever Told" (January 26, 1947)
"The Guiding Light" (January 25, 1937)
"Young Widder Brown" (September 26, 1938)

## Obituaries

**Fred Allen** (May 31, 1894–March 17, 1956). From 1932–1949, the radio comic entertained audiences with his wit and humor. "Allen's Alley" had an estimated 20 million listeners at the height of its popularity.

# SPORTS

## Winners

### Baseball

World Series—New York Yankees (AL), 4 games; Brooklyn Dodgers (NL), 3 games
Player of the Year—Mickey Mantle (New York

Yankees, AL); Don Newcombe (Brooklyn Dodgers, NL)

Rookie of the Year—Lou Aparicio (Chicago White Sox, AL); Frank Robinson (Cincinnati Redlegs, NL)

## Football

NFL Championship—New York Giants 47, Chicago Bears 7

College Bowls (January 1, 1956)—
Rose Bowl, Michigan State 17, UCLA 14
Cotton Bowl, Mississippi 14, Texas Christian 13
Orange Bowl, Oklahoma 20, Maryland 6
Sugar Bowl, Georgia Tech 7, Pittsburgh 0

Heisman Trophy—Paul Hornung (Notre Dame, QB)

Grey Cup—Edmonton Eskimos 50, Montreal Alouettes 27

## Basketball

NBA Championship—Philadelphia Warriors, 4 games; Fort Wayne Pistons, 1 game

MVP of the Year (first year)—Bob Pettit (St. Louis Hawks)

Rookie of the Year—Maurice Stokes (Rochester Royals)

NCAA Championship—San Francisco 83, Iowa 71

## Tennis

U.S. National—Men, Ken Rosewall (vs. Lew Hoad); Women, Shirley Fry (vs. Althea Gibson)

Wimbledon—Men, Lew Hoad (vs. Ken Rosewall); Women, Shirley Fry (vs. Angela Buxton)

## Golf

Masters—Jack Burke
U.S. Open—Cary Middlecoff
British Open—Peter Thomson

## Hockey

Stanley Cup—Montreal Canadiens, 4 games; Detroit Red Wings, 1 game

## Ice Skating

World Championship—Men, Hayes Alan Jenkins (U.S.); Women, Carol Heiss (U.S.)

U.S. National—Men, Hayes Alan Jenkins; Women, Tenley Albright

Canadian National—Men, Charles Snelling; Women, Carole Jane Pachl

## Kentucky Derby

Needles—Dave Erb, jockey

## Athlete of the Year

Male Athlete—Mickey Mantle (Baseball)
Female Athlete—Pat McCormick (Diving)

## Last Season

Bob Feller (Baseball)
Rocky Marciano (Boxing)
George Mikan (Basketball)
Bill Quackenbush (Hockey)
Jackie Robinson (Baseball)

# News

**January 26–February 5.** The Winter Olympics open in Italy at Cortina d'Ampezzo. The USSR, in its first appearance since 1908, places first overall with 16 medals. One of the seven Soviet golds comes in ice hockey, a sport played in the Communist nation for less than 20 years.

The United States places sixth overall, with gold medals from figure skaters Tenley Albright and Hayes Alan Jenkins. (Albright is the first American woman to win a gold medal in Olympic skating.)

**September 13.** The National Safety Council and the International Association of Police Chiefs publicly condemn drag racing. Still, some 2 million enthusiasts watch 350,000 hot-rodders at 130 legal quarter-mile strips this year. The record speed is 166.97 mph.

**October 8.** Striking out the last batter, Yankee Don Larsen pitches the first perfect major league game in 34 years and the first ever in a World Series.

The Yankees win the championship 4 games to 3, but Dodger fans never get a chance for revenge. In its next World Series, the club will no longer carry the Brooklyn name.

**October 18.** NFL owners vote against the use of on-field radio communications. Coach Paul Brown had installed receivers into Cleveland quarterback helmets, but a few days ago the Giants intercepted his defensive plays with their own technology. Owners insist the decision was made because of fan complaints over game delays.

**November 22-December 8.** The Olympic games open in Melbourne, Australia, with the smallest number of competitors since 1932. Traveling costs are a factor, but international events play a larger part: Egypt, Lebanon, and Iraq stay home over the Israeli invasion of Gaza; Communist China quits after officials mistakenly fly the Nationalist Chinese flag; and Spain, Switzerland, and the Netherlands withdraw over the invasion of Hungary.

Predictably, when the Hungarians and Soviets meet in a water-polo match, the Hungarian 4–0 victory is a bloody one; at the close of the Olympics, 46 of the 175-member Hungarian team defect.

Bobby Morrow and Patricia McCormick give Americans their greatest thrills. He is the first runner since Jesse Owens to win both the 100- and 200-meter races. McCormick, with a repeat of her 1952 double gold in platform and springboard diving, becomes the first female Olympic competitor to win two events twice and the first female swimmer to win four gold medals.

And, for the first time, the USSR places first overall in a Summer Olympics.

**November 30.** Floyd Patterson knocks out 42-year-old Archie Moore in the fifth round to win Rocky Marciano's vacated title. The 21-year-old black boxer is the youngest heavyweight champion in the history of the sport.

**December 18.** Yankee shortstop Phil Rizzuto retires and signs on as a team broadcaster. He becomes known for his characteristic exclamation, "Holy Cow!"

**More news.** Commissioner Frick, convinced that pitchers receive little recognition, creates an annual award in memory of Cy Young, baseball's winningest pitcher. He asks the Baseball Writers Association of America to choose the recipients. Brooklyn Dodger Don Newcombe is the first. After 1967, the association will make a selection from each league.

In a major rule change, the NHL permits a penalized player to return to the ice if the opposing team scores on the power play.

## Records

**May 19–28.** Pittsburgh first baseman Dale Long hits a record eight home runs in eight consecutive games.

**June 29.** Charley Dumas, age 19, breaks the 7' high-jump barrier with a leap of 7'1/2" at the U.S. Olympic trials. In competition, his straddle jump of 6'11 1/4" wins the gold.

**September 3.** Jockey Johnny Longden brings home his 4,871st career win, breaking the previous record set by England's Sir Gordon Richards.

## What They Said

Thirty-two-year-old Rocky Marciano hangs up his gloves on Apr. 27. Over a 9-year pro career, he KO'd 43 of 49 opponents, 11 of them in the first round. The only heavyweight champ to retire undefeated, Rocky tells the press, "I thought it was a mistake when Louis tried a comeback. No man can say what he will do in the future. But, barring poverty, the ring has seen the last of me."

## Obituaries

**Connie Mack** (December 23, 1862–February 8, 1956). After 10 years as a player and a stint as a manager in the Western league, Mack found his niche in 1901 with the new Philadelphia Athletics. He gradually took over sole ownership and, the best strategist of his day, captured nine league pennants and five World Series by 1931. He was among the first 13 elected to the Hall of Fame. In 1950, although the Athletics had won nothing since those glory days, the grand old man's retirement marked the end of an era.

*Babe Didrickson Zaharias is regarded as the best all-around female athlete of this century.*

**Mildred (Babe) Didrickson Zaharias** (June 26, 1914–September 27, 1956). Excelling in every sport she tried, the American athlete won the 80-meter hurdles and javelin throw at the 1932 Olympics (she lost the high jump gold for "diving" over the bar), earned the nickname 'Babe' after Babe Ruth for her baseball skills, was a three-time All-American basketball player, and won 50 major golf tournaments. Many consider Babe Didrickson Zaharias the greatest woman athlete of all time. She died after a long battle with cancer.

# 1957

The average U.S. family income has risen 50 percent in the past 10 years to $6,130, but American pride suffers a tremendous blow with the Soviet orbiting of the first man-made satellite. Washington, already expending billions on missiles and electronic detection systems, suddenly faces the added cost of a space race.

The White House receives news of Sputnik just days after the crisis in Little Rock, Arkansas. Eisenhower, following his usual policy of "not making decisions until after the event reaches you," is forced by a rebellious governor to send in federal troops. By November, Americans tell Gallup that integration is the No. 1 problem in the nation.

Other events this year include Hurricane Audrey, the worldwide Asian influenza epidemic, a Dodger move to the West Coast, and the introduction of the sack dress. Rock 'n' roll flourishes with new artists like the Crickets, Brenda Lee, Paul Anka, Ricky Nelson, the Everly Brothers, and Bobby Darin, and with Hollywood films such as April Love and Jailhouse Rock. TV capitalizes on rock's popularity with "American Bandstand" while offering the younger set "Leave It to Beaver" and parents the new "Perry Mason" and "Wagon Train."

## NEWS

**January.** A group of black Baptist ministers, including Martin Luther King, Jr., and Ralph Abernathy, form the Southern Christian Leadership Conference (SCLC).

**January 5.** In the wake of the Suez Crisis, Eisenhower asks Congress to extend the Truman Doctrine to the Middle East. The Eisenhower Doctrine signed on March 9, declares U.S. readiness to stop "overt armed aggression" by the Communists, but fails to specify the nations covered. The administration receives a $200-million congressional appropriation for military and economic projects in the area.

**January 9.** Prime Minister Sir Anthony Eden cites ill health, but the press attributes his resignation to the failure of British policy on the Suez Canal. Harold Macmillan, who also supported the Suez fiasco, replaces Eden the next day.

**February 17.** In Warrenton, Missouri, a fire in the Katie Jane Nursing Home kills 72 of 155 patients. Several elderly people jumped from the second floor as flames reached heights of 60 feet. An inquiry finds the fire was of "undetermined origin."

**March 6.** Intense negotiations and U.S. diplomatic pressure convince Prime Minister David Ben-Gurion to pull the Israeli Army back to the 1949 armistice line as a U.N. emergency force moves into Sinai and the Gaza strip. Since most Israelis opposed his decision, Ben-Gurion exacted a U.N. pledge to remain indefinitely and to safeguard Israeli security and navigational rights in the Gulf of Aqaba.

The Suez Canal will reopen on April 10 to vessels of near-maximum draft, but the Egyptians continue to refuse passage to Israeli ships or ships bound for Israel.

**March 25.** The Treaty of Rome establishes the European Economic Community (EEC), or Common Market. Over the next 12 years, Belgium, France, Italy, Luxembourg, the Netherlands, and West Germany will abolish all remaining tariff barriers and allow workers, goods, and capital to move freely across their borders. The agreement will make Europe economically competitive with the United States, but the ultimate goal of political unification turns Britain away.

**May 22.** An incorrectly placed safety device on a USAF B-36 releases a Mark 17 nuclear bomb over an uninhabited area outside Albuquerque, New Mexico. The massive weapon creates a 12-foot-deep crater on impact but fails to detonate. The public hears nothing of the accident.

**June 5.** In response to mounting public criticism and scientific dispute, Eisenhower defends atmospheric testing at today's press conference. He argues that fallout has already been reduced by "nine-tenths," and tests will continue "to see how clean we can make them" for peaceful applications.

**June 10.** Under the leadership of 61-year-old John Diefenbaker, the Progressive Conservatives win 112 seats in the Canadian federal election. The Liberals become the official opposition—after 22 years of rule—with 105 seats, the CCF collects 25 seats, the Social Credit 19, and Independents 4.

**June 17.** Reversing the contempt conviction of a UAW official, the Supreme Court limits prosecution under the Smith Act to concrete action for the forcible overthrow of the government rather than a mere belief in the abstract doctrine.

The decision frees many of the almost 100 Communist party members convicted since 1951, and gives others an opportunity for a new trial.

**June 27.** The U.S. Weather Bureau advises residents to flee to higher ground as Hurricane Audrey approaches the Gulf Coast. Since tropical storms, which usually start up in August, have never caused high-water damage, many ignore the warnings.

Audrey rips through coastal Texas and Louisiana with 105-mph winds and huge tidal waves. One of the worst disasters in U.S. history, the devastating storm kills an estimated 550 people and destroys 40,000 homes.

**July 3.** When the Presidium votes him out of office, Nikita Khrushchev demands his right to a full Central Committee vote and, with control of the majority, successfully charges the oppositionists with antiparty conspiracy. Malenkov, Molotov, and Kaganovich confess their plot and lose all high party and state offices.

**July 29.** United States ratification of the International Atomic Energy Agency makes uranium available to other nations for nuclear reactors. By the early 1960s, West Germany, Italy, South Africa, and seven other countries will have used American materials and assistance to build research reactors. France, in turn, will provide information and resources to Israel while Canada assists India.

**July 31.** Stretching across the Canadian Arctic from Alaska to Greenland, the $600-million DEW Line begins operation. Washington had hoped the electronic system, along with experimental Alaskan stations, would give the United States a six-hours advance warning of an attack. But new Soviet jets, capable of flying at 600 mph, have already cut that margin in half and, in late August, Moscow announces the successful test-firing of a long-range ICBM. The United States possesses only intermediate-range ballistic missiles.

Faced with increased Soviet capabilities, the Eisenhower administration holds to a policy of nuclear deterrence, ringing the USSR with missile bases. NATO members, in agreement, announce on December 19 the stockpiling of nuclear warheads in Western Europe. (Although a two-year timetable is indicated, Bonn reported earlier this year that the

Americans had already placed nuclear weapons in West Germany.)

**August 29.** The Senate passes the first civil rights legislation since Reconstruction. The measure establishes some federal safeguards and sets up a Commission on Civil Rights (a recommendation made by Truman's Civil Rights Committee) to investigate voting infringements because of race, religion, or national origin. The commission must report within two years and then disband.

Strom Thurmond (D., S.C.) attempted to block a Senate vote, but other opponents of the bill, fearing passage of the stronger House version, quashed his filibuster. Critics blast the bill as worse than no legislation at all, but Eisenhower signs the act on September 9.

**September 2.** To encourage U.S. utilities to invest in nuclear energy, the Price-Anderson Amendment to the Atomic Energy Act limits private liability to $60 million while guaranteeing up to $500 million in coverage. If a nuclear plant suffers a catastrophic accident, taxpayers will cover costs, currently estimated at more than $7 billion.

**September 4.** Governor Orval Faubus, looking toward a third term, orders the Arkansas National Guard to prevent the integration of Little Rock's Central High School. He talks of impending violence even though the town has successfully implemented desegregated busing, and school authorities have offered assurances.

President Eisenhower exacts a pledge from the governor to obey a court order to integrate, but another must be issued before Faubus finally removes the National Guard on the 20th. He leaves the next day for the Southern Governors Conference. On the 23rd, when nine black students approach the school, white protestors riot.

Forced to act, Eisenhower federalizes the state's National Guard the next day and dispatches 1,000 men from the 101st Airborne—the first federal troops used to protect the civil rights of Southern Negroes since Reconstruction.

In the evening, the president explains in a televised address that federal court orders must be obeyed. Many believe a reluctant Eisenhower acted to protect the sanctity of the courts and the prestige of the presidency, not the students' rights.

The black teenagers, each escorted by a soldier, accomplish integration without incident. By November, the 101st Airborne withdraws; the federalized state guard will remain until spring.

**September 11.** A major fire at the Rocky Flats nuclear plant releases plutonium into the atmosphere—at least 1 million times the maximum permitted under federal standards. Over 600,000 people live within 20 miles, but no warning is issued during the 13-hour fire, and the 30,000 gallons of water used by fire fighters escape unfiltered.

**October.** Last May, the Asian flu spread outward from Japan and Singapore to circle the globe. The first U.S. cases appeared at West Coast military installations, but once school opened the virus rapidly crossed the country. The number of cases peak this month, then rise again in January.

Although the epidemic is the most widespread in world history—80 million affected, including 20 million Americans—the death toll is much lower than the flu pandemic of 1918–1919. Antibiotics and a flu vaccine readily combat today's milder strain, and victims usually succumb to such complications as pneumonia.

**October 1.** The threat of Soviet ICBMs pushes the U.S. Strategic Air Command—the long-range nuclear strike force—to place air crews on 15-minute alerts. In November, SAC orders one-third of the force on continuous alert.

**October 7.** At the Windscale Pile, north of Liverpool, England, reactor core rods begin to burn. But with poorly placed temperature gauges, the fire burns undetected for two days as 30,000 curies of radioactive iodine escape through the smokestack. Another 30 hours pass before emergency crews risk a steam explosion and pour water into the reactor.

With local dairies contaminated, milk supplies are dumped into the sea. (No action was taken following another accident in the spring.) Still, authorities conceal radiation readings 100 times above normal, and Prime Minister Macmillan suppresses a follow-up report rather than shake public confidence in the nuclear industry. London will later attribute 39 cancer deaths to the disaster.

**October 22.** François "Papa Doc" Duvalier wins the presidential election in Haiti. When his opponent claims election fraud, the military junta declares a state of siege and Duvalier quickly establishes a regime based on voodoo magic and a brutal secret police.

The United States will end all assistance to Haiti in 1963.

**November 4.** In 1952, Security Council members and Canada formed the U.N. Disarmament Commission. The Soviets, frustrated by the disproportionate NATO membership, have demanded the establishment of a new commission with all 82 U.N. nations. But the General Assembly simply increases membership from 11 to 25 and the Soviets walk out in disgust. From this point on, Washington and Moscow will conduct arms reduction talks through normal diplomatic channels.

**November 7.** Following the *Sputnik* launchings, President Eisenhower addresses a shaken and embarrassed American people. Next day, his administration moves to enact deep policy changes.

The secretary of defense orders the army to test ballistic rockets as satellite launchers. The Pentagon, in turn, relaxes test secrecy to show Americans that their country is not second-rate. Then, in December, the president approves a $1-billion education package, with an emphasis on science subjects.

**November 25.** The president suffers a mild stroke. He returns to work on a restricted schedule just two days later, but many wonder whether Eisenhower is physically capable of meeting presidential responsibilities.

**More news.** The post-W.W.II baby boom crests with a one-year record of 4,308,000 births.

## Obituaries

**Aga Khan** (November 2, 1877–July 11, 1957). The enormously wealthy leader of 15–20 million Ismaili Moslems bypassed two sons to name his 21-year-old grandson successor, because he was brought up "in the midst of the atomic age." Shah Karim becomes Aga Khan IV.

**Grace Goodhue Coolidge** (January 3, 1879–July 8, 1957). The wife of Calvin Coolidge, the 30th president of the United States (1923–1928), was one of the nation's most popular first ladies.

**Harold Charles Gatty** (January 5, 1903–August 30, 1957). Wiley Post's navigator in their historic 1931 around-the-world flight was once described by Charles Lindbergh as the "best navigator in the country if not in the whole world."

**Haakon VII** (July 3, 1872–September 21, 1957). After Sweden and Norway dissolved their union in 1905, Prince Carl of Denmark accepted the Norwegian monarchy and took the old Norse name of Haakon. The much-loved ruler is succeeded by his 54-year-old son Olaf V.

**Joseph McCarthy** (November 14, 1908–May 2, 1957). A lawyer who served with distinction during W.W.II, McCarthy won a Senate seat in 1946, but faced likely defeat in the next election. To save himself, the Republican senator from Wisconsin launched a divisive anti-Communist witch-hunt in 1950. Televised hearings in 1954 finally exposed his unprincipled methods and resulted in Senate censure. With his political career in ruins, McCarthy drank himself to death.

**George "Bugs" Moran** (1893–February 25, 1957). The notorious gangster, who escaped the 1929 St. Valentine's Day Massacre of his gang, died in Fort Leavenworth Federal Prison.

**Elliott Ness** (April 19, 1903–May 7, 1957). Assigned a special detail to harass Al Capone, the 25-year-old Ness went through hundreds of Justice Department files to find nine honest agents. Called the "Untouchables" by the criminal world, the young men—all in their 20s—badgered the Chicago gangster while undercover revenue agents gathered evidence of income tax evasion. In 1935, Ness took over as public safety director in Cleveland and, despite great personal danger, cleaned up the city in six years. At the time of his death, he was in private business. *Note*: On August 31, Benito Mussolini's body was buried at his family tomb. The corpse had been hidden in a rural monastery since 1945, after Italian partisans had caught and killed the fleeing Dictator.

# BEGINNINGS AND ENDINGS

## News

**January 18.** Three USAF B-52 bombers complete the first nonstop jet circuit of the world (45 hours, 19 minutes). As in 1949, SAC Commander General Curtis LeMay greets the returning crews. This time, he pronounces the "capability [of Americans] to drop a hydrogen bomb anywhere in the world."

**January 29.** A West Berlin court, upholding a 1941 finding, rejects Anna Anderson's claim to be Anastasia, youngest daughter of Czar Nicholas II. The verdict follows testimony by a witness to the execution of the czar and his children.

**April 7.** In New York, at 12:32 A.M., 125 enthusiasts and regular passengers ride the city's last trolley car on its final run. (American cities once boasted some 25,000 miles of trolley tracks.)

**June 1.** With a population of 8.521 million, Tokyo replaces London (8.239 million) as the world's largest city.

**June 21.** As secretary of state, Ellen Fairclough becomes the first woman to receive a post in a Canadian cabinet.

**September 4.** Bringing in a U.N. delegation, a TU-104 jet is the first Soviet civilian aircraft to land in the United States. (A military plane flew to the West Coast in 1937.)

**More news.** The Hornet, last of the Hudson cars, sells just 1,345 of 3,876 in 1957, and American Motors discontinues the line.

---

*Statistics:* As the auto industry meets the demand for more chrome, the 1958 Buick achieves the dubious distinction of carrying the most trim ever—44 pounds.

---

## Records

**May 27.** At the age of 89 years, 7 months, and 26 days, Senator Theodore F. Green (D., R.I.) is the oldest person to serve in Congress. He will retire at the age of 93 and pass away in 1966.

## New Products and Businesses

With more Americans buying automatic clothes washers and dryers, the first antistatic agent appears on the market—Sta-Puf—for use in the wash.

An adhesive color label replaces the familiar embossed glass emblem on Coca-Cola bottles.

"Look, Mom—no cavities!"

Crest Toothpaste stops soft spots from turning into cavities—means far less decay for grownups and children.

*Crest toothpaste runs this catchy ad campaign during 1957 and 1958.*

In Massachusetts, Don Featherstone designs a unique lawn ornament—a plastic pink flamingo.

This year, in a noteworthy consumer trend, margarine outsells butter for the first time—8.6 pounds for the average American versus 8.3 pounds of butter.

The ultimate convertible, the Ford Skyliner retracts its hardtop into the trunk (leaving room for little else). Ford produces 20,766 units this year and another 14,713 in 1958, but with a tendency to rust, few Skyliners survive into the 1970s.

New Fisher-Price toys include chew-proof Snap-Lock Beads, the Pull-a-tune Xylophone, and the rolling Corn Popper.

## Fads

Fred Morrison, who joined Wham-O Manufacturing in 1955, has developed the Pluto Platter. An instant hit on college campuses, the idea likely originated with the Frisbee cookie and meat-pie tins used by Yale students in an earlier game of catch. Next year, the plastic Platter will be renamed in honor of that company.

In the first celebrity bonanza, American teens spend $25 million on Elvis Presley merchandise—hats, belts, jeans, scarves, T-shirts, charm bracelets, perfume, and "Hound Dog Orange" and "Heartbreak Pink" lipsticks.

# SCIENCE AND TECHNOLOGY

## News

**January.** The Hamilton Watch Co. in Pennsylvania brings out the first electric wristwatch. The power cell, which replaces the mainspring, is guaranteed to run for a year.

**January 31.** Columbia University Geological Observatory reports tracing a submarine fissure over a 45,000-mile meandering course around the world. It averages 20 miles in width and 2 miles in depth.

Later this year, a team will return to the United States with sedimentary evidence of a Mid-Oceanic Ridge, an interlocking formation of rifts and mountains beneath the world's oceans.

**March 22.** Research experts organized last year by the American Cancer Society and other groups report the first cause-and-effect relationship between smoking and lung cancer. An examination of 16 independent studies from five countries shows

that 1 in 10 smokers (of two packs a day) contract lung cancer while only 1 in 275 nonsmokers do.

**April.** John Backus and his group finish the FORTRAN compiler for IBM. The 25,000 lines of machine code stored on magnetic tape use algebraic notations, particularly valuable for mathematicians and scientists. FORTRAN will become the most popular high-level programming language.

**April 17.** MIT announces the development of an inertial guidance system for missiles, capable of steering the weapon without radio, compass, or radar.

**June 22.** After a five-year study, the American Red Cross replaces the back-pressure arm-lift method of artificial resuscitation for small children with the mouth-to-mouth "breath of life."

**July 19.** In Nevada, a USAF Scorpion jet fighter successfully launches the first nuclear-armed air-to-air rocket. The 1–2-kiloton detonation reportedly gives off little radiation.

**August 19–20.** To determine human adaptability to outer space, Project Man High sends USAF Major David Simons up to a record 102,000 feet in the pressurized gondola of a 20-story balloon. Later, he comments that the absolute silence of the stratosphere created a mood of forlorn loneliness.

**September 18.** Two leading manufacturers offer new computers for small- and medium-size businesses. The IBM 610—the size of a spinet piano—solves a 6-hour calculator computation in 20 minutes. It sells for $55,000. The Burrough's all-purpose computer, which fills 2,500 square feet, sells for $500,000–$600,000—the first of its type for less than $1 million.

Over this year and next, Philco and UNIVAC bring the first transistorized computers to market.

**October 4.** The Soviets use a recently tested ICBM to launch the world's first man-made satellite, *Sputnik* ("companion" in Russian). The polished 184-pound sphere reaches 18,000 mph in an elliptical orbit above Earth.

Initially, Washington presents a low-key response, but the achievement embarrasses and frightens the American people. The "backward" Soviets have surpassed them in technological know-how and apparently can deposit a missile anywhere in the world.

**October 8.** AT&T and Hawaiian Telephone open a San Francisco–Honolulu telephone connection with the world's longest (2,400 miles) and deepest (3.5 miles) transoceanic cable.

**November 3.** *Sputnik II* takes the first living creature into space, Laika the dog. She survives the launch and weightlessness in space, but with no recovery system yet in place, Laika faces certain death. Animal lovers everywhere protest in vain.

**November 10.** A two-year survey by the U.S. Office of Education confirms that the United States lags behind the USSR in scientific, technical, and other educational fields. The Soviet class ratio stands at 1:17, the American at 1:27. As well, Communist students are required to take four years of chemistry and five years of physics and biology.

**December 17.** After numerous failures, the United States successfully launches an Atlas rocket. Soviet progress in ICBMs had pushed the Americans to abandon painstaking, step-by-step testing for concurrence, the expensive simultaneous development of separate components. The Atlas will become the most widely used U.S. rocket.

**December 18.** The Shippingport station in Pennsylvania—the first atomic generator devoted to peaceful purposes—begins generating electricity. Start-up comes exactly 15 years after the Enrico Fermi group achieved the first self-sustaining chain reaction.

**More news.** For the International Geophysical Year, 1957–1958, 11 nations establish 48 scientific stations on and adjacent to Antarctica. To date, only the coastal areas and a narrow belt to the South Pole have been fully explored.

• British biochemists discover interferon, a cellular protein substance that prevents viral reproduction.

• Plasmapheresis separates plasma from red corpuscles and returns the blood to the donor in just 21 minutes. The procedure, developed by professors Joseph Smolens and Joseph Stokes, increases stocks of gamma globulin, and allows the donor to give blood once a week.

## Other Discoveries, Developments, and Inventions

The fully automatic M-14 .30-caliber rifle, for the U.S. military

Experimental 60-foot dracones, tubular floating containers for liquids

Portable resuscitator for rescue work

Air suspension in Cadillac's Eldorado Brougham model, front-end torsion bars from Chrysler, dual headlights in Lincolns and Cadillacs

Electric can opener

---

*Statistics:* The average American family eats 850 cans of food each year.

---

Electric portable typewriter weighing 19 pounds from Smith-Corona, $197

Atomic-powered surface vessel, the icebreaker *Lenin* in the USSR

## Obituaries

**Richard Byrd** (October 25, 1888–March 11, 1957). The renowned polar explorer and aviator was the first to fly over the North Pole (with Floyd Bennett, in 1926) and, with three others, the first to fly over the South Pole (1929). His fifth and last Antarctic expedition was undertaken as part of the International Geophysical Year, 1957–1958.

**Peter Freuchen** (February 20, 1886–September 2, 1957). The Danish explorer, with Knud Rasmussen, opened up Greenland. He lived among the Eskimos for seven years and, after losing a leg to frostbite, wrote several books on his experiences.

**Joseph William Kennedy** (May 30, 1916–May 5, 1957). Kennedy, Glenn T. Seaborg, Arthur C. Wahl, and Emilio Segre discovered plutonium, the essential element of the atomic bomb. The United States seized their patents as secret information during the war, but two years ago, the AEC awarded the scientists $400,000 for their discovery.

**Irving Langmuir** (January 31, 1881–August 16, 1957). One of the greatest chemists of this century, the Nobel prize winner discovered that the addition of inert gases to a light bulb reduced filament wear. As well, he invented the high-vacuum radio tube and was the first to experiment with seeding clouds.

# THE ARTS

September 26—*West Side Story*, with Carol Lawrence, Larry Kert, Chita Rivera (732 perfs.)

October 31—*Jamaica*, with Lena Horne, Ricardo Montalban (558 perfs.)

November 28—*Look Homeward, Angel*, with Jo Van Fleet, Anthony Perkins, Arthur Hill (564 perfs.)

December 5—*The Dark at the Top of the Stairs*, with Pat Hingle, Teresa Wright, Eileen Heckart (468 perfs.)

December 19—*The Music Man*, with Robert Preston, Barbara Cook, David Burns (1,375 perfs.)

## Tony Awards

Actor (Dramatic)—Fredric March, *Long Day's Journey into Night*

Actress (Dramatic)—Margaret Leighton, *Separate Tables*

Actor (Musical)—Rex Harrison, *My Fair Lady*

Actress (Musical)—Judy Holliday, *Bells Are Ringing*

Play—*Long Day's Journey into Night*

Musical—*My Fair Lady*

## News

**March 28.** Parliament creates the Canada Council to promote the study and enjoyment of the arts, humanities, and social sciences, as well as the production of related works. A $50-million endowment and yearly appropriations will fund annual grants in visual arts, music, theater, dance, and publishing.

**June 1.** In 1953, an Off-Broadway production cost as little as $500. This season, some 40 productions require an average $7,000–$15,000 each.

**July 1.** At the new Stratford Festival Theatre, a thrust stage and steeply sloped seating keep members of the audience within 65 feet. The concept will be copied by theaters around the world.

**September 10.** The Philharmonic Symphony Society of New York becomes the New York Philharmonic. On November 19, for the first time, the orchestra will name an American as sole music director—Leonard Bernstein. He will remain with the Philharmonic until 1969.

**More news.** Over the past 10 years, the Veterans Administration and Federal Housing Administration mortgaged 40–50 percent of the houses sold in the United States. Since their investments were concentrated in the suburbs, the agencies have effectively shaped the face of postwar America.

• This year, the Boston Museum of Fine Arts buys a pair of full-length, life-size portraits by Rembrandt. The $500,000 purchase price is a record sum for the 80-year-old institution.

## Obituaries

**Beniamino Gigli** (March 20, 1890–November 30, 1957). Damned by critics for his sentimental delivery, the tenor was one of the most popular operatic singers of the century.

**Ezio Pinza** (May 18, 1892–May 9, 1957). The Italian-American basso, once an opera star, is best remembered for his Broadway performance with Mary Martin, in *South Pacific*.

**Diego Rivera** (1886–November 25, 1957). His controversial murals made him a central figure in Mexico's 20th-century renaissance in art.

**Johan Julius Sibelius** (December 8, 1865–September 20, 1957). *Finlandia* (1900), the Finnish composer's best-known composition, has come to symbolize his country's nationalism.

**Arturo Toscanini** (March 25, 1867–January 16, 1957). In 1898, the young Italian conductor took over at La Scala, leading the world premieres of *Pagliacci*, *La Boheme*, and *Girl of the Golden West*. His years with the Met (1908–1915) and the Philharmonic Symphony (1928–1936) made him the world's foremost opera and orchestra conductor. But his 17 years with the NBC Symphony (1937–1954) and his countless classical recordings turned the maestro into a cult figure. A perfectionist with an awesome temper, Toscanini retired in 1954 rather than continue to work with myopia and a failing memory.

**John Van Druten** (June 1, 1901–December 19, 1957). The British-American's hit plays included *I Remember Mama* (1944) and *I Am a Camera* (1951), which will become the basis of the 1960s musical *Cabaret*.

# WORDS

James Agee, *A Death in the Family*
Ian Fleming, *From Russia, with Love*
John [Jack] Kerouac, *On the Road*
Jean Kerr, *Please Don't Eat the Daisies*
Art Linkletter, *Kids Say the Darndest Things!*
Kyle Onstott, *Mandingo*
Vance Packard, *The Hidden Persuaders*
Cyril Northcote Parkinson, *Parkinson's Law and Other Studies in Administration*
Ayn Rand, *Atlas Shrugged*
Max Shulman, *Rally Round the Flag, Boys!*
Nevil Shute, *On the Beach*

## News

**February 25.** The U.S. Supreme Court voids a Michigan law barring the sale of books, comics, and magazines "tending to incite minors to violent or depraved or immoral acts or otherwise to corrupt the morals of youth." Such restrictions, the justices argue, would reduce adults "to reading only what is fit for children."

**October 15.** President Eisenhower receives the American Bible Society's 500,000,001st bible. Over 141 years, 51 percent were given away or sold at cost in the United States and 60 foreign nations.

**More news.** In *The Hidden Persuaders*, Vance Packard exposes the manipulation behind today's sales techniques: MR, or motivation research (such as portraying a freezer as "bountiful mother"); psychological obsolescence (replacing still-working goods for newer models); and subthreshold effects (subliminal messages).

• Since 1937, Theodor Seuss Geisel has used "logical insanity" (two-headed animals need two

toothbrushes, for example) to write and illustrate children's books—*Horton Hears a Who* (1954) and *How the Grinch Stole Christmas* (1957).

This year, Dr. Seuss revolutionizes primary readers with a low-word-count book for first-graders, *The Cat in the Hat*. His cheeky feline is spectacularly successful.

## Cartoons and Comics

**This year.** Comic book publishers continue to reduce their titles. Atlas, for example, cuts back by two-thirds, to *Strange Tales* and *Journey into Mystery*.

## TIME *Man of the Year*

Nikita Khrushchev

## New Words and Phrases

Asian influenza
baby-sitter
blast-down (a rocket ship landing)
dirty, or clean, nuclear bomb (a bomb with, or without, fallout)
empty calory
escape ramp, road, route
moonlighter, moonlighting
SCUBA (self-contained underwater breathing apparatus)
special (a TV spectacular)
subliminal projection
teacher's aid
stratospheric drip (fallout)

## Obituaries

**Nikos Kazantzakís** (February 18, 1883–October 26, 1957). The Greek novelist, poet, and dramatist lost this year's Nobel prize in literature by one vote. His novels include *Zorba the Greek* (1946; English translation 1952) and *The Last Temptation of Christ* (1955; English translation 1960).

**Dorothy L. Sayers** (June 13, 1893–December 17,

1957). The British writer created the sophisticated detective Lord Peter Wimsey.

**Laura Ingalls Wilder** (February 7, 1867–February 10, 1957). At the age of 65, the American author harked back to her childhood pioneer memories to begin the *Little House* novels. (*Little House on the Prairie*, 1935, remains the most famous.) In 1954, the American Library Association created the Laura Ingalls Wilder Award for lasting contributions to children's literature.

# FASHION

## Haute Couture

Givenchy introduces the most radical new silhouette in 10 years—the sack. Described as a giant almond with sleeves, the dress puffs out from the armholes, brushes past the hipline, and tapers to a narrow hem just below the knee.

American designers produce a less drastic version, but the average woman still finds the sack impossible to iron.

## News

**This year.** Pierre Cardin, who founded a fashion house in 1950, presents his first complete collection.

• Americans are the only people in the world to purchase more than three pairs of shoes a year (an average 3.48 pairs).

• To control their designs, couture houses have long forbidden drawings or photographs for a month after presentation. This year, Givenchy permits immediate sketches of his innovative sack. Most designers follow suit next season.

• In 1948, Swiss engineer Georges de Mestral noted that thistles clung to fabric. To mimic that action, he produced one nylon strip with thousands of tiny hooks, and another with smaller loops. The fastener, dubbed Velcro ("vel" from *velours*, the French word for velvet, and "cro" from *crochet*), is patented worldwide this year.

## Colors and Materials

Designers favor yellow, orange, emerald green, and brilliant blues. Shades of brown vie with black for smart daytime wear.

A light mohair-cotton mix resists sagging. Over the last years of the decade, mohair will become one of the most fashionable fabrics.

Blends of natural fibers and new synthetics offer washability and crease resistance.

## Clothes

Most women choose a three-piece outfit or a straight-line dress with matching jacket or cardigan.

Manufacturers offer full or pencil-slim skirts.

Coat shapes widen with large stand-away collars, low shoulders, and deep armholes. Furriers, in response to the heavy use of fur trim, offer original coat designs.

Highlighting the legs, a unique evening hemline falls from a day length at the front through to the floor or into a train.

In warmer weather, college girls opt for the muu-muu.

Teenage girls love heavy and baggy sweaters, or a regular cardigan buttoned up the back.

## Accessories

Dress shoes retain their pointed toes, but the medium Louis heel replaces the ultra-high style. Some women match hats and dresses to pumps of striped or flowered fabric, but black patent leather enjoys its best season ever.

Children's styles include Ivy League saddle oxfords, saucer and bubble saddles, and Shu-Lok closures.

The popularity of fur transfers to large hats (twisted or draped to the back or side), a variety of bags, even fur jewelry.

Long pearl ropes remain popular, but a demand for "real" jewelry brings back narrow drop earrings.

## Hair and Cosmetics

The small, sleek hairstyle is gone and many women wear loose waves brushed full at the sides.

After dithering over "Is It True That Blondes Are Never Lonesome?" and "Is It True Blondes Marry Millionaires?," Lady Clairol selects "Is It True . . . Blondes Have More Fun?" Hugely successful, the ad campaign introduces a new phrase into the American vocabulary.

Under the impact of singer Elvis Presley, the very short sideburns of the early 1950s extend another 1½ inches to form a rectangle of longer, thicker hair in front of each ear.

## Obituaries

**Christian Dior** (January 21, 1905–October 24, 1957). In 1947, as New York poised to replace Paris as the center of haute couture, the little-known designer galvanized the French fashion industry with his New Look creations. A grateful government presented the shy, bald, roly-poly Dior with the Legion of Honor.

By 1953, with branches in London, Caracas, and New York, Dior's wholesale dress and perfume business pulled in a yearly $17 million. Leadership of the famous house falls to his 21-year-old protégé, Yves St. Laurent.

## POPULAR MUSIC

"All Shook Up"—Elvis Presley
"Love Letters in the Sand"—Pat Boone
"Jailhouse Rock"—Elvis Presley
"(Let Me Be Your) Teddy Bear"—Elvis Presley
"April Love"—Pat Boone
"Young Love"—Tab Hunter
"Tammy"—Debbie Reynolds
"Honeycomb"—Jimmie Rodgers
"Wake Up Little Susie"—Everly Brothers
"You Send Me"—Sam Cooke
"Too Much"—Elvis Presley
"Butterfly"—Andy Williams
"Round and Round"—Perry Como

"Chances Are"—Johnny Mathis
"Don't Forbid Me"—Pat Boone
"Diana"—Paul Anka
"That'll Be the Day"—Crickets
"Party Doll"—Buddy Knox
"Little Darlin' "—Diamonds
"So Rare"—Jimmy Dorsey, Orchestra & Chorus
"Bye Bye Love"—Everly Brothers
"Teen-Age Crush"—Tommy Sands
"A White Sport Coat (And a Pink Carnation)"—Marty Robbins
"Raunchy" (Instr.)—Bill Justis

## News

**Spring.** West Indian music becomes the rage in the United States. Radio stations give songs like "The Banana Boat Song (Day-O)" extensive air time while nightclubs switch over to a bamboo and hammock decor. (Harry Belafonte's *Calypso* album, which sparked the craze last year, will become the first LP by a solo artist to sell a million copies.)

But, despite the wishes of their parents, American teenagers remain faithful to rock 'n' roll and dance the new Stroll.

**June 15.** Paul McCartney hears the Quarrymen (named after the Quarry Bank Grammar School) at a garden fete, in Woolton, England. At a meeting the next day, group leader John Lennon is impressed by McCartney's guitar skills. John faces a decision, one he will discuss many times in the future: to keep Paul out and remain the strongest member of the group or bring him in and make the group better. McCartney is asked to join the Quarrymen. *Note:* Various sources, including a Beatle chronology, point to discrepancies over the date of their first meeting. It may have occurred on June 15, 1955 or 1956.

Late this year, Paul's friend George Harrison begins to tag along on the group's bookings and fill in on guitar.

**September 17.** Louis Armstrong confirms he has canceled a government-sponsored tour of the Soviet Union. "The way they are treating my people in the South, the government can go to hell. . . . It's getting almost so bad, a colored man hasn't got any country." The internationally known trumpeter had earlier charged that Eisenhower's handling of Little Rock proved he had "no guts" and was "two-faced." Other black artists, including Lena Horne and Marian Anderson, publicly agree with Armstrong.

**More news.** Ricky Nelson, the 17-year-old son of TV stars Ozzie and Harriet Nelson, records "I'm Walking" to impress a girlfriend who loves Elvis. Another rock 'n' roll newcomer, 15-year-old Canadian Paul Anka, writes a song about his girlfriend "Diana." Two more big songs will make him a millionaire.

• Boston bans the Everly Brothers' tune "Wake Up Little Susie."

• Buddy Holly and the Crickets, with "That'll Be the Day" and "Oh, Boy!," pioneer the use of drums, bass, and lead and rhythm guitars.

• Sonny James (Capitol) and Tab Hunter (Dot) both reach No. 1 with "Young Love"—a first for rock 'n' roll. Still, 1957 marks the final year for white cover versions of black hits. From 11 in 1955, the number dropped to 4 in 1956, and this year to 3.

• After three hits, Frankie Lymon abandons the Teenagers for a solo career. But the 15-year-old's voice breaks and success eludes him. He will die of a heroin overdose in 1968.

• More radio stations switch to the Top 40 format (see Television and Radio).

*New Recording Artists*

Paul Anka
Patsy Cline
Sam Cooke
Crickets (Buddy Holly)
Bobby Darin
Everly Brothers
Buddy Holly (solo)
Brenda Lee
Jerry Lee Lewis
Johnny Mathis
Ricky Nelson
Jimmie Rodgers
Conway Twitty
Jackie Wilson

## *Obituaries*

**Jimmy Dorsey** (February 29, 1904–June 12, 1957). Following the split with his brother Tommy in 1935, Jimmy continued with most of their musicians. His popular band scored 23 top hits in the first half of the 1940s. Just before his death from cancer, Dorsey's earlier recording of "So Rare" reached No. 2 on the "Hit Parade."

# MOVIES

*The Bridge on the River Kwai* (d. David Lean; color)—William Holden, Alec Guinness, Jack Hawkins, Sessue Hayakawa

*Desk Set* (d. Walter Lang; color)—Spencer Tracy, Katharine Hepburn, Gig Young, Joan Blondell

*Enemy Below* (d. Dick Powell; color)—Robert Mitchum, Curt Jurgens

*A Face in the Crowd* (d. Elia Kazan; bw)—Andy Griffith, Patricia Neal, Anthony Franciosa, Walter Matthau, Lee Remick

*Funny Face* (d. Stanley Donen; color)—Audrey Hepburn, Fred Astaire

*Gunfight at the OK Corral* (d. John Sturges; color)—Burt Lancaster, Kirk Douglas, Rhonda Fleming, Jo Van Fleet

*The Incredible Shrinking Man* (d. Jack Arnold; bw)—Grant Williams

*Love in the Afternoon* (d. Billy Wilder; bw)—Gary Cooper, Audrey Hepburn, Maurice Chevalier

*Man of a Thousand Faces* (d. Joseph Pevney; bw)—James Cagney, Dorothy Malone

*Old Yeller* (d. Robert Stevenson; color)—Dorothy McGuire, Fess Parker, Tommy Kirk, Kevin Corcoran

*The Pajama Game* (d. Stanley Donen; color)—Doris Day, John Raitt, Carol Haney, Eddie Foy, Jr.

*Pal Joey* (d. George Sidney; color)—Rita Hayworth, Frank Sinatra, Kim Novak

*Paths of Glory* (d. Stanley Kubrick; bw)—Kirk Douglas, Ralph Meeker, Adolphe Menjou, George Macready

*Peyton Place* (d. Mark Robson; color)—Lana Turner, Hope Lange, Arthur Kennedy, Lloyd Nolan

*Sayonara* (d. Joshua Logan; color)—Marlon Brando, Ricardo Montalban, Miiko Taka, Miyoshi Umeki, Red Buttons

*The Spirit of St. Louis* (d. Billy Wilder; color)—James Stewart

*The Three Faces of Eve* (d. Nunnally Johnson; bw)—Joanne Woodward, David Wayne, Lee J. Cobb

*12 Angry Men* (d. Sidney Lumet; bw)—Henry Fonda, Lee J. Cobb, Ed Begley, Jack Warden, E. G. Marshall, Martin Balsam, Jack Klugman

*Wild Strawberries* (Swedish, d. Ingmar Bergman; bw)—Victor Sjöström, Ingrid Thulin, Bibi Andersson

*Witness for the Prosecution* (d. Billy Wilder; bw)—Marlene Dietrich, Tyrone Power, Charles Laughton, Elsa Lanchester

## Academy Awards

**March 27.** This year, the Academy creates an annual award for the Best Foreign Language Film (previously recognized with an Honorary Oscar).

Jerry Lewis in Hollywood co-hosts with Celeste Holm in New York.

Best Picture—*Around the World in 80 Days*
Best Actor—Yul Brynner (*The King and I*)
Best Actress—Ingrid Bergman (*Anastasia*)
Best Director—George Stevens (*Giant*)
Best Supporting Actor—Anthony Quinn (*Lust for Life*)
Best Supporting Actress—Dorothy Malone (*Written on the Wind*)
Best Song—"Whatever Will Be, Will Be (Que Será, Será)" from *The Man Who Knew Too Much*
Best Foreign Film—*La Strada* (Italian)
Honorary Award—Eddie Cantor

Less than two weeks before the nominations, the Academy enacted an anti-Communist rule: "Any person who . . . shall have admitted that he is a member of the Communist party . . . or who shall have refused to answer whether or not he is . . . shall be ineligible for any Academy Award." No one appears this evening to claim Robert Rich's Oscar for his screenplay *The Brave One*.

Anthony Quinn's 8-minute performance in *Lust for Life* is probably the shortest to win an Academy Award.

## News

**April.** In a poll of American teenagers, the Gilbert Youth Research Co. finds that approximately 50 percent go to the movies at least once a week.

**August 11.** During Hollywood's most prosperous years (1938–1952) filmmakers shot 65 percent of their features from original scripts. Then producers began to choose scripts based on hit plays or best-selling novels, and over the last five years the number of original works has plummeted to 28 percent. The Writers Guild maintains that this preference for "sure-fire" hits translates to fewer films and, at least partially, explains lower box-office receipts.

**September.** A *Popular Science* photo spread looks at the 2,500-car All-Weather Drive-In Theater in Copiague, New York. Sprawling over 28 acres, the drive-in offers a children's playground and amusement park; a trackless Tally-Ho Train for transportation between areas, a simultaneous showing in a 1,200-seat indoor theater, a sky-top restaurant with an unobstructed view of the screen, and car speakers with adjustable volume controls.

**More news.** After a three-year absence from the screen, Rita Hayworth co-stars in *Pal Joey*. Her appearance concludes a 20-year contract with Columbia Pictures, described by the glamorous star as "deep slavery."

• *Island in the Sun* (1957) is the first film to portray a romance between whites and blacks. The script pairs British actor James Mason with American beauty Dorothy Dandridge and Joan Fontaine with black singer Harry Belafonte.

• Clean-cut Pat Boone makes his first appearance on screen, with Shirley Jones in *April Love* (1957). Critics describe the mediocre movie as a showcase for the popular singer's talents.

• As movie attendance continues to drop and another 1,200 theaters close, studio executives point to several factors: people abandoning cities and their big theaters for the suburbs; moviegoers' growing preference for free films on TV; and the increasing leisure time spent by Americans on sports and do-it-yourself projects.

• Actor Michael Landon, age 20, reverts to a werewolf under hypnosis, and teenagers thrill as the primal beast overpowers adults. The $150,000 *I Was a Teenage Werewolf* takes in a phenomenal $2.5 million. Several copy-cat pictures follow.

• With the shutdown of the MGM animation department this year, *Tom & Jerry* veterans Joseph Barbera and William Hanna form Hanna-Barbera Productions to create TV and theatrical cartoons. Critics deride their work's artistic quality, but the partners will sell the company to Taft Communications in 1966 for a reported $26 million.

• Dwindling returns at the ticket office end the Ma and Pa Kettle series. After their appearance in *The Egg and I* (1947), Universal brought hillbilly couple Marjorie Main and Percy Kilbride together again in the second feature comedy *Ma and Pa Kettle* (1949). That success led to a six-film run before Kilbride bowed out in 1955.

| Top Box Office Stars | Newcomers |
| --- | --- |
| Rock Hudson | Anthony Perkins |
| John Wayne | Sophia Loren |
| Pat Boone | Jayne Mansfield |
| Elvis Presley | Don Murray |
| Frank Sinatra | Carroll Baker |
| Gary Cooper | Martha Hyer |
| William Holden | Elvis Presley |
| James Stewart | Anita Ekberg |
| Jerry Lewis | Paul Newman |
| Yul Brynner | John Kerr |

## Top Money-Maker of the Year

*The Ten Commandments* (1956)

## Quote of the Year

"Answer me! You have a civil tongue in your head! I know—I sewed it in there!"

Mad scientist Whit Bissell snaps at his monster creation, Gary Conway, in *I Was a Teenage Frankenstein*. (Screenplay by Kenneth Langtry, from his short story.)

## Obituaries

**Humphrey Bogart** (December 25, 1899–January 14, 1957). In 1936, British actor Leslie Howard refused to re-create his stage role in *The Petrified Forest* unless Warner Bros. hired his Broadway co-star as mobster Duke Mantee. Bogart was a sensation in the role.

With his lisp (a lip scarred and partially paralyzed by a W.W.I shelling) and almost permanent squint, Bogey played numerous gangsters through the rest of the decade. Then his superlative performances in *High Sierra* (1941) and *The Maltese Falcon* (1941) brought better roles—Rick in *Casablanca* (1943), Charlie Allnutt in *The African Queen* (1951), for which he won an Oscar, and Captain Queeg in *The Caine Mutiny* (1954).

Not as popular in his day as Gary Cooper or Clark Gable, Bogart will attract large audiences in the mid-1960s with the rerelease of many of his 71 films. Young people, who see the tough, cynical Bogey as a modern antihero, a man who lived by his own rules, will give him a lasting place in American culture.

**Oliver Hardy** (January 18, 1892–August 7, 1957). From their first film together in 1926, the fat half of Laurel and Hardy wonderfully complemented his creative partner. Few silent comedians made the transition to talkies, but the hapless duo appeared in films until 1945. Today, critics describe them as "the greatest comedy team in the history of cinema," and young people enjoy their classics on television.

Upon the death of his partner, an inconsolable Laurel vows never to perform again.

**Louis B. Mayer** (July 4, 1885–October 29, 1957). The MGM founder (with Sam Goldwyn and Marcus Loewe in 1924) and production director created the Hollywood star system by building a movie around the special talents of each actor and actress. His abilities earned the respect of many (as well as the nation's largest salary during the 1930s and 1940s), but most insiders regarded him as ruthless, tyrannical, and paternalistic. Mayer was pushed out in 1951.

At the funeral, Sam Goldwyn reportedly says, "The only reason so many people showed up was to make sure that he was dead."

**Norma Talmadge** (May 26, 1897–December 24, 1957). The popular silent screen actress pioneered the "woman's film" long before Bette Davis and Joan Crawford. But Talmadge's Brooklyn accent finished her sound career, and she retired in 1930.

# TELEVISION AND RADIO

## New Prime-Time TV Programs

"Bachelor Father" (September 15, 1956–September 25, 1962; Situation Comedy)—John Forsythe, Noreen Corcoran, Sammee Tong

"Have Gun Will Travel" (September 14, 1957–September 21, 1963; Western)—Richard Boone, Kam Tong

"Leave It to Beaver" (October 4, 1957–September 12, 1963; Situation Comedy)—Barbara Billingsley, Hugh Beaumont, Jerry Mathers, Tony Dow

"M Squad" (September 20, 1957–September 13, 1960; Police Drama)—Lee Marvin, Paul Newlan

"The Many Loves of Dobie Gillis" (September 29, 1957–September 18, 1963; Situation Comedy)—Dwayne Hickman, Bob Denver, Frank Faylen, Florida Friebus (1957–1960)

"Maverick" (September 22, 1957–July 8, 1962; Western)—James Garner (1957–1960), Jack Kelly

"The Pat Boone–Chevy Showroom" (October 3, 1957–June 23, 1960; Musical Variety)—Pat Boone

"Perry Mason" (September 21, 1957–September 1966; Courtroom Drama)—Raymond Burr, Barbara Hale, William Hopper, William Talman

"The Price Is Right" (September 23, 1957–September 11, 1964; Quiz/Audience Participation)—Emcee: Bill Cullen

"The Real McCoys" (October 3, 1957–September 22, 1963; Situation Comedy)—Walter Brennan, Richard Crenna, Kathy Nolan (1957–1962), Lydia Reed

"Richard Diamond, Private Detective" (July 1, 1957–September 6, 1960; Detective)—David Janssen

"Sugarfoot" (September 17, 1957–July 3, 1961; Western)—Will Hutchins. *Note:* Broadcast alternate weeks 1957–1959, every three weeks 1959–1960.

"Tales of Wells Fargo" (March 18, 1957–September 8, 1962; Western)—Dale Robertson

"The Tonight Show" (July 29, 1957–March 30, 1962; Talk/Variety)—Host: Jack Paar; Regulars: Hugh Downs, Jose Melis & Orchestra

"The 20th Century" (October 20, 1957–January 4, 1970; Documentary)—Narrator: Walter Cronkite

"Wagon Train" (September 18, 1957–September 5, 1965; Western)—Ward Bond (1957–1961), John McIntire (1961–1965), Robert Horton (1957–1962)

"Zorro" (October 10, 1957–September 24, 1959; Western)—Guy Williams, George J. Lewis, Gene Sheldon, Britt Lomond, Henry Calvin

## Emmy Awards 1956 (March 16, 1957)

Best Series (one hour or more)—"Caesar's Hour" (NBC)

Best Series (half-hour)—"The Phil Silvers Show" (CBS)

Best Actor in a Series (Drama)—Robert Young ("Father Knows Best," NBC)

Best Actress in a Series (Drama)—Loretta Young ("The Loretta Young Show," NBC)

Best Comedian—Sid Caesar ("Caesar's Hour," NBC)

Best Comedienne—Nanette Fabray ("Caesar's Hour," NBC)

## News

**January 21.** NBC carries the first national video-taped broadcast, a recording of the Eisenhower–Nixon inauguration. Next day, "Truth or Consequences" becomes the first videotaped regular program. (The West Coast quiz show had found it difficult to round up an audience at 8:30 A.M. for an 11:30 live telecast to New York.) Video technology quickly makes the kinescope a relic of early television.

**May 4.** DJ Alan Freed hosts the first prime-time rock special, the "Rock 'n' Roll Show." Performers on the hour-long program, shown tonight and next week, include Edie Adams, Charles Gracie, Ivory Joe Hunter, Sal Mineo, and Andy Williams. Teens prefer Freed's guests on his four-week summer series—Frankie Avalon, Chuck Berry, Bobby Darin, the Everly Brothers, Connie Francis, and Jerry Lee Lewis.

**June 24.** CBC's "Front Page Challenge" replaces "The Denny Vaughan Show" for the summer. But viewers like the concept of hidden guests, and the show remains in the fall lineup. In the years ahead, the irascible Gordon Sinclair and other panelists will quiz prime ministers, Martin Luther King, Malcolm X, and many others. The show will still be on the air in 1975.

**July 29.** After a six-month run as a news-oriented program, "Tonight" returns to its original format for "The Jack Paar Show." The young comic, lured over from CBS game and talk shows, adopts a more relaxed pace than Steve Allen, with guest interviews and funny segments, such as attaching captions to baby pictures. Not long after Paar takes over, NBC abandons live telecasts for early-evening taping.

**August 5.** A local program in Philadelphia since 1952, "American Bandstand" and 27-year-old host Dick Clark go national on ABC. Teens in the audience dance to rock 'n' roll records or watch guest performers lip synch their songs (an acceptable practice with the present high cost of sound duplication).

**September.** Attempts by pay-TV to enter the

*Broadcast after school, "American Bandstand" draws an audience of millions. Teenagers tune in for the music, the dances, the clothes and hairstyles.*

airwaves have met stiff opposition from the networks. This month, the FCC agrees to accept applications for pay-TV tests on a limited three-year controlled basis. But none will be granted before 1958.

At this time, about 500 subscribers in Oklahoma are paying $9.50 per month for a closed-circuit telecast of films.

**September 14.** With "Gunsmoke"'s rising popularity, the networks launch 10 new Westerns this fall, including CBS's "Have Gun Will Travel." Within weeks, strangers tell crane operator Victor DeCosta how much they enjoy his new program and his sister accuses him of keeping it a secret. When he tunes in, DeCosta is stunned.

Not only does star Richard Boone look amazingly like him but "Have Gun Will Travel" has stolen his trademark character. Ten years earlier, the former rodeo rider strapped on a gun belt, dressed in black, and, with a black stallion, appeared as Paladin. He even handed out business cards—just like the TV Paladin does.

DeCosta takes his case to court. He will finally win in 1966, but the decision will be overturned.

**September 22.** Unlike the gun-for-hire in "Have Gun Will Travel," James Garner will do anything to avoid trouble in "Maverick." (He often quotes his

Pappy's advice, to run in the face of overwhelming odds.) Brother Bart, played by Jack Kelly, joins the show in November to counterbalance Bret's fun with a more serious side.

With a No. 6 rating through the 1958–1959 season, Garner will strike for a better contract. But ABC refuses to give in. Suddenly a Cousin Beauregard (Roger Moore) appears on the show and Bret disappears. The show never recovers its former popularity.

**September 23.** A daytime quiz show since last November, "The Price Is Right" appears on the fall prime-time schedule. Host Bill Cullen will stay with NBC until September 1963 when ABC will pick up both versions for one year. In 1972 Bob Barker will host a revised daytime version.

**September 29.** In 1955, hour-long drama anthologies demanded 35 plays every month while half-hour shows needed 56. Inevitably, exceptional plays gave way to lesser works and, at the end of last season, "Lux Video Theatre" and "Robert Montgomery Presents" were canceled. And tonight, after 12 years of Sunday broadcasts, NBC replaces "Television Playhouse" with a Dinah Shore musical variety.

**October.** With the continuing lack of affiliates, ABC's "Danny Thomas Show" moves over to CBS. A widower last season, his character marries Marjorie Lord, and her TV daughter Angela Cartwright joins his son Rusty Hamer and daughter Sherry Jackson.

**October 10.** Guy Williams plays the fop Don Diego de la Vega and his swashbuckling alter-ego "Zorro." The authentic swordplay (instructor Fred Cravens earlier coached Douglas Fairbanks for the original Zorro film) enthralls the bubble-gum crowd. But after two years, ABC cancels the Disney program, supposedly because a network production can make more money. Forbidden to transfer the character to CBS or NBC, Disney sues and eventually wins the right to take future characters elsewhere.

**November 6.** "I Love Lucy" was rated No. 1 in four of the last five years, but to lighten their work load, the stars switch to the irregularly scheduled "Lucille Ball–Desi Arnaz Show." The first special

flashes back to Havana of 1940 where Lucy and Ricky first met. Just two weeks later, Desilu Productions reaches a basic agreement to purchase RKO studios.

**December 25.** Queen Elizabeth broadcasts a message to the Commonwealth. She will make the Christmas Day telecast an annual tradition.

**More news.** This year, Steve Allen introduces a new character to "Tonight" fans—Kermit the Frog.

• ABC gives an up-and-coming sports commentator, Howard Cosell, his first regular network program, a daily sports wrap-up.

• When the 1953 television play *Marty* won an Oscar, Hollywood film producers enticed many New York playwrights and actors with better salaries. Lately, much of the lure has come from TV production. By the end of this year, California studios provide about 60 percent of network programming.

## TV Commercials

Allstate Insurance—For a "Playhouse 90" episode, Ed Reimers cups his hands together and says, "You're in good hands with Allstate."

## Memorable Radio Programs End

"Counterspy" (May 18, 1942)
"Fibber McGee and Molly" (April 16, 1935)
"Gang Busters" (January 15, 1936)
"Truth or Consequences" (March 23, 1940)

# SPORTS

## Winners

### Baseball

World Series—Milwaukee Braves (NL), 4 games; New York Yankees (AL), 3 games
Player of the Year—Mickey Mantle (New York Yankees, AL); Hank Aaron (Milwaukee Braves, NL)
Rookie of the Year—Tony Kubek (New York Yankees, AL); Jack Sanford (Philadelphia Phillies, NL)

## Football

NFL Championship—Detroit Lions 59, Cleveland Browns 14
College Bowls (January 1, 1957)—
Rose Bowl, Iowa 35, Oregon State 19
Cotton Bowl, Texas Christian 28, Syracuse 27
Orange Bowl, Colorado 27, Clemson 21
Sugar Bowl, Baylor 13, Tennessee 7
Heisman Trophy—John Crow (Texas A&M, HB)
Grey Cup—Hamilton Tiger-Cats 21, Winnipeg Blue Bombers 7

## Basketball

NBA Championship—Boston Celtics, 4 games; St. Louis Hawks, 3 games
MVP of the Year—Bob Cousy (Boston Celtics)
Rookie of the Year—Tom Heinsohn (Boston Celtics)
NCAA Championship—North Carolina 54, Kansas 53

## Tennis

U.S. National—Men, Malcolm Anderson (vs. Ashley Cooper); Women, Althea Gibson (vs. Louise Brough)
Wimbledon—Men, Lewis Hoad (vs. Ashley Cooper); Women, Althea Gibson (vs. Darlene Hard)

## Golf

Masters—Doug Ford
U.S. Open—Dick Mayer
British Open—Bobby Locke

## Hockey

Stanley Cup—Montreal Canadiens, 4 games; Boston Bruins, 1 game

## Ice Skating

World Championship—Men, David Jenkins (U.S.); Women, Carol Heiss (U.S.)
U.S. National—Men, David Jenkins; Women, Carol Heiss

*An avid golfer, Dwight Eisenhower draws some criticism for the amount of time spent on the links. One bumper sticker sold during his term in office reads, "Ben Hogan for President. If We're Going to Have a Golfer, Let's Have a Good One."*

Canadian National—Men, Charles Snelling; Women, Carole Jane Pachl

## Kentucky Derby

Iron Liege—Bill Hartack, jockey

## Athlete of the Year

Male—Ted Williams (Baseball)
Female—Althea Gibson (Tennis)

## Last Season

George Kell (Baseball)
Ted Kennedy (Hockey)
Sandy Saddler (Boxing)

## News

**February 25.** The Supreme Court, denying the exemption granted to baseball, places the NFL under the monopoly provisions of the Sherman and Clayton antitrust laws.

On August 1, Commissioner Bert Bell tells the House Judiciary Anti-Monopoly Subcommittee that the NFL will recognize the Players' Association as a negotiating agent. By the end of the year, NFL owners accept the organization's demands for exhibition pay, an injury protection clause, and a minimum salary of $5,000.

**March 5.** Sweden wins the World and European ice hockey championships in Moscow. The United States, Canada, and several European nations boycotted the tournament to protest Soviet repression of Hungary.

**May 4.** Thundering down the stretch at Churchill Downs, on Nerud, Willie Shoemaker stands in his stirrups—at the 16th pole. By the time the 25-year-old jockey realizes he hasn't finished, Iron Liege and Bill Hartack regain the lead and win the Kentucky Derby. Most tracks soon place bull's-eye markers at the finish line.

**June 1.** At Adelphi College in Garden City, New York, 75 paraplegics from the United States and Canada hold the first national wheelchair games. Events include table tennis, the javelin, and the 60-yard dash.

**July 6.** The first black American to win at Wimbledon, Althea Gibson defeats Darlene Hard in the final round of the women's singles. Five days later, New Yorkers honor the 29-year-old tennis star with a ticker-tape parade. In September, she becomes the first Negro to win the U.S. National Championship.

**July 9.** Since baseball's first All-Star game in 1933, player selection has rotated among fans, players, and managers. For the last 10 years, fans have held the vote.

But this year, Ford Frick angrily intervenes when Cincinnati fans, by ballot stuffing, place 7 Redlegs on the NL team. (From 1953 to 1959, Cincinnati uses the name Redlegs rather than the Reds, largely because of the Cold War.) He replaces outfielders Gus Bell and Wally Post with the Braves' Hank Aaron and the Giants' Willie Mays. Still, the AL wins 6–5.

In 1958, the commissioner will opt for a poll by players, managers, and coaches. Another 11 years will pass before fans regain the vote.

**September 29.** Following their final game in New York—a 9–1 loss to Pittsburgh—the Giants flee to the clubhouse as fans grab anything as souvenirs. The Polo Grounds, constructed in 1911, will stand empty until the Mets arrive in 1962.

**October 8.** Last May, after the Dodgers and Giants received NL permission to move out West, New York City began frantic negotiations with Dodger owner Walter O'Malley for a new stadium site. Nelson Rockefeller offered to buy into the team and participate in construction.

Today, despite promises to the contrary, the Dodger owner announces the club's relocation to Los Angeles. As anguished New Yorkers mourn the loss of another team, columnists Pete Hamill and Jack Newfield brand O'Malley one of the three most evil men of this century; the others were Hitler and Stalin.

**November 10.** Charles Sifford, with a victory at the Long Beach Open, becomes the first black American to win a major U.S. golf tournament.

## Records

**May 1.** On January 2, Sugar Ray Robinson lost his middleweight title to Gene Fullmer in a unanimous 15-round decision. Tonight, the 36-year-old Robinson knocks out Fullmer in round 5 to regain the championship for a record fourth time. Less than five months later, Carmen Basilio captures the title after a savage 15-round bout. In a 1958 rematch, Robinson will win in a 15-round decision.

**June 1.** With a time of 3:58:7, at the Pacific Amateur Athletic Union Meet in Stockton, Don Bowden becomes the first American to run a sub-4-minute mile.

**November 16.** Unbeaten since 1953, the Oklahoma football team loses 7–0 to Notre Dame. That amazing 47-game record will stand until 1975.

## What they Said

Twenty-three-year-old Milwaukee Brave Hank Aaron on his chances at the plate. "I'm up there with a bat, and all the pitcher's got is the ball. I figure that makes it all in my favor." (*Time*, July 29)

# 1958

*The United States produces the Year of the Rocket in a mad scramble to catch up with the Soviets. In the first month, an army vehicle puts the first U.S. satellite—Explorer I into orbit. Still, when highly publicized launchings end in disaster, Americans worry more about the worst recession in 20 years.*

*In foreign policy, the Eisenhower administration sends troops to Lebanon but backs down from a military confrontation with Peking. Late in the year, with Nikita Khrushchev in full control, East-West talks start on a nuclear test ban.*

*Jimmy Hoffa defies the AFL-CIO to take over the Teamsters. The government establishes NASA. For his gold medal at the Tchaikovsky International Piano Contest, Van Cliburn receives a ticker-tape parade in New York. The Hope Diamond is donated to the Smithsonian. And Los Angeles and San Francisco receive the first West Coast franchises in major league baseball.*

*Kids read the new comic strip B.C. and watch "The Rifleman" and "The Tales of Texas John Slaughter" on TV. Teenagers get Elvis back from the army, but try new singers like the Miracles and Connie Francis. Everyone tries the Hula Hoop.*

## NEWS

**Winter.** Sometime during the fall and winter of 1957–1958, a nuclear waste plant explodes in the Ural Mountains. Radiation, in a 6-mile-wide, 62-mile-long trail, forces the evacuation of 10,000 Soviets. Later, leaked eyewitness accounts will tell of hundreds, if not thousands, dying of radiation sickness.

**January 23.** Jimmy Hoffa takes over as president of the International Brotherhood of Teamsters. The AFL-CIO had demanded the expulsion of all implicated officers after former president Dave Beck was charged in 1952 with misappropriating funds. The

Teamsters refused, and the AFL-CIO expelled the union late last year.

In March, following an extensive investigation of union mismanagement, the Select Senate Committee charges Hoffa and his officers with manipulating union funds and holding close ties to organized crime. But Hoffa eludes criminal conviction and makes the Teamsters one of the nation's most powerful labor unions.

Next year, the AFL-CIO will readmit the Teamsters on a probationary basis.

**February.** Army laboratories in Maryland secretly test the effect of LSD on unwitting soldiers. One volunteer, given the hallucinogen four times,

220

will finally learn of the experiments in 1975, when army officers contact him on a follow-up study.

**February 15–20.** A severe storm strikes the northeastern and mid-Atlantic states with record snowfalls and low temperatures. The official death toll in 25 states climbs to 246.

**March 11.** The worst economic recession since W.W.II pushes U.S. unemployment to 5.1 million—almost 7 percent of the labor force—with manufacturing hit the hardest. Washington provides $10 billion for construction projects and extended unemployment benefits, but over 4 million still remain out of work in September.

**March 27.** Khrushchev ousts Nikolai Bulganin and assumes the joint leadership of party and state, roles separated since Stalin's death in 1953. Bulganin won the Soviet premiership in 1955 by supporting Khrushchev against Malenkov. Last year, he chose the wrong side. Dismissed from the Presidium, Bulganin quickly slips into obscurity.

**March 31.** Voters give John Diefenbaker and his minority Conservative government the greatest parliamentary majority in Canadian history—208 seats of 265, including an unprecedented 50 seats in Quebec. The Liberals take 49, the CCF 8, and the Social Credit are eliminated.

**April 15–22.** In Ghana, the first conference of independent African states draws three Negro and five Arab nations. The members pledge support for Algerian rebels and agree to "nonentanglement" in the struggle between East and West.

**May 13.** When Venezuelans attack Richard Nixon's motorcade during a goodwill tour of Latin America, President Eisenhower dispatches Marines to the Caribbean to guarantee the vice-president's safety.

Domestic critics condemn the administration for misjudging the state of South American relations. The people, badly hurt by the recent U.S. recession, consider Washington ignorant of their needs, particularly in its support for dictators. Nixon, while in Uruguay, claims the United States would be guilty of interference if it discriminated between governments.

**May 19.** The United States and Canada formalize the joint North American Air Defense command (NORAD), headquartered at Colorado Springs. As with previous arrangements, the 10-year agreement fails to specify whether Ottawa requires advance approval for American nuclear-armed flights over Canada.

**June 1.** Since World War II, more than 20 men have tried to form a coalition government in France. This legislative stalemate, along with strikes and a burdensome war in Algeria, has pushed the republic to the brink of civil war.

Today, the nation's politicians appoint General Charles de Gaulle premier and meet his demand for six-month rule by decree. (De Gaulle comments, "I have never been given power. I have always taken it.") Alarmists predict a dictatorship, but, in a September 28 referendum, 79.2 percent of voters choose de Gaulle and a new constitution. The general then confounds critics by relying on current systems to introduce economic reform.

In December, the people of France overwhelmingly elect de Gaulle as the first president of the Fifth Republic.

**June 4.** West German President Theodor Heuss arrives in Washington on the first official visit by a German chief of state. President Eisenhower declares the wounds of two world wars "almost wholly cured."

**June 16.** The U.S. Supreme Court narrowly (5–4) invalidates State Department regulations denying passports to Communists and others for their "beliefs and associations." (Singer Paul Robeson, who was refused a passport for eight years because of his leftist affiliations, leaves within a month on a foreign tour.)

**June 17.** Budapest announces that Imre Nagy and 276 others involved in the Hungarian Revolution were hanged yesterday. Premier at the time of the Soviet invasion in November 1956, Nagy sought refuge in the Yugoslav embassy; the Soviets tricked him into leaving. The U.S. Congress condemns the hangings as "barbarism and perfidy."

**June 23.** Concerned with the violent white response to the civil rights movement, black leaders meet with the president. Martin Luther King, Jr. (SCLC), A. Philip Randolph (AFL-CIO), Lester

Granger (National Urban League), and Roy Wilkins (NAACP) urge "a clear national policy and program of implementation" to guarantee Negroes their rights. While cordial, Eisenhower makes no commitments and offers no comment on their suggestions.

**July 14.** Pro-Nasser rebels assassinate King Faisal II and his infant son, and the next day, pull Iraq out of the federation with Jordan (Faisal and his cousin Hussein joined their two nations last February). When Egypt then provokes riots in Jordan and Lebanon, an already nervous Beirut appeals for Western assistance.

Putting the Eisenhower Doctrine into effect, the United States sends 14,000 troops to Lebanon on the 15th, while Britain complies with Hussein's request for an armed force. But in the Security Council, the Soviets veto the use of U.N. troops and threaten to intervene, bringing the world to the brink of war. Tensions hold until the Lebanese elect a neutralist government in August and the 12 Arab nations settle on a policy of noninterference. The last U.S. troops withdraw by the end of October.

The Lebanon action marks the end of the Eisenhower Doctrine, a mistaken attempt to win Arab support for the West in the Cold War. Arab nations, while individually seeking a dominant role in the Middle East, seemingly prefer neutrality on the world stage.

**July 29.** President Eisenhower signs legislation establishing the National Aeronautics and Space Administration to direct nonmilitary space activities. The separation of NASA from the Defense Department ends interservice rivalry without denying space technology to military branches for national security.

NASA's space program, announced in September, includes a manned earth satellite within 2 years, a manned landing on the moon within 6 to 10 years, and the exploration of Mars in 10 to 15 years.

**September 2.** The National Defense Education Act—the first general American education law since the mid-1800s—responds to last year's *Sputnik* launchings by encouraging the study of science, mathematics, and languages. And, to allay fears of federally controlled education, the act specifically leaves money management to the states and local communities.

**September 4.** Last month, Communist China began bombarding the Nationalist garrison on Quemoy, a small island off the mainland. The United States, in fulfillment of treaty obligations, promises the Nationalists military help, if needed, and moves the Seventh Fleet into the Formosa Strait.

The administration's decision, to protect an island unimportant in the defense of Taiwan, draws severe domestic criticism, and the Kremlin warns, "An attack on the People's Republic of China . . . is an attack on the Soviet Union." Eisenhower, in a radio-television address on the 11th, describes the Communist attack as a test of the free world's courage to resist aggression. He confirms that the United States will fight, if necessary.

But pressure continues to mount until, on September 30, Secretary of State Dulles dramatically reverses America's longstanding policy. In response, the Communists order a week-long cease-fire (afterward they shell Quemoy on alternate days). On October 23, Dulles and Chiang Kai-shek formally renounce a Nationalist use of force to regain control of the mainland.

**September 20.** As Martin Luther King, Jr., autographs copies of his book *Strike Toward Freedom: The Montgomery Story*, a Negro woman approaches, pulls out a steel letter opener, and stabs him in the chest. Rushed to the hospital, still sitting in his chair, King survives a nick to the aorta, the major blood vessel to the heart.

**September 22.** Sherman Adams, powerful assistant to the president, resigns over allegations by a congressional subcommittee. Supposedly, in return for money and gifts, he tried to influence federal investigations of industrialist Bernard Goldfine. Eisenhower has supported his friend's denials, but with early Democratic gains the party has put pressure on the president as well. Eventually Adams will be cleared.

**October 9.** Pope Pius XII dies at the age of 82. Ordained in 1899, Italian-born Eugenio Pacelli was elected pontiff on March 2, 1939. He remained a conservative on questions of Catholic doctrine and theology, but improved relations between the Vatican or various nations and increased the number of non-Italian cardinals.

Although known for his postwar relief efforts and support for arms control, Pius's failure to publicly condemn the Nazi extermination of Jews during the war casts a shadow over his good works.

On October 28, Angelo Giuseppe Cardinal Roncalli is elected pope; he takes the name Pope John XXIII.

**October 23.** In Springhill, Nova Scotia, an earthquake traps 174 miners in the No. 2 Colliery. Rescue teams, refusing to give up, find 100 survivors over the next 10 days. The nearly 400 men receive the Royal Canadian Humane Association's first group award and the Carnegie Hero Fund's second; the only other went to the heroes on the Titanic.

Since 1891, over 600 men have died at the Springhill mine, mostly in earthquakes. The owners tried to close the mine in 1956, but the economically strapped town begged for a reprieve. This time, the mine is finally shut down.

**October 30.** With the excessive fallout count, after at least 19 atmospheric tests this year, Los Angeles Mayor Norris Poulson protests yet another. The AEC and the Public Health Service deny any danger, but cancel the test nonetheless.

**November 4.** The United States, the USSR, and Britain launch talks on a formal test ban treaty. The Kremlin unilaterally suspended nuclear tests on March 31. The Eisenhower administration, under enormous pressure to match the Soviet action, suggested preliminary discussions to determine if nuclear explosions could be detected.

On August 21, technicians concluded that a network of stations would record any detonation. The next day, the White House suspended nuclear testing for one year (effective October 31) with annual renewal dependent on a detection system.

Still, this year, the two superpowers distribute their nuclear weapons to other nations, the United States to Britain, the USSR to China. As well, Washington authorizes European manufacture of tactical missiles.

**November 4.** Midterm elections give the Democrats control of the House (282 of 435 seats) and Senate (62 of 96 seats). Experts believe the overwhelming victory—the party's largest majority in 20 years—reflects voter concern and dissatisfaction with farm policies, nuclear testing, the recession and high unemployment, the White House approach to foreign affairs, and the recent Adams scandal.

**December 1.** In Chicago, just half an hour before dismissal, a fire breaks out on the ground floor of Our Lady of Angels. With smoke billowing up to the second floor, one teacher rolls her children down the stairway to safety. Another teacher barricades her classroom door until firemen arrive at the window; she loses just one child. But as flames roar up, panicked students trample and crush others or jump to their deaths. Despite heroics by the staff, firefighters and passersby, 3 nuns and 92 students die.

**December 17.** Mao Tse-tung steps down as head of the Communist Chinese government to concentrate on his role as party chairman and ideological leader. Next year, Liu Shao-Chi succeeds him.

**More news.** To overcome China's economic problems, this year's Great Leap Forward program follows the Soviet agricultural-industrial model, organizing millions of peasants into large-scale communes and setting up small steel furnaces in every village. But the overly ambitious program ends in disaster.

The government executes thousands of reluctant peasants. And, with local officials falsifying production reports to placate Peking, a failed harvest unexpectedly results in starvation; up to 20 million die.

The massive campaign will end in 1960 and the communal system will start to break up. Its failure will sow the seeds of dissension among party leaders.

## Obituaries

**Robert Cecil (Viscount Cecil of Chelwood)** (September 14, 1864–November 24, 1958). After drafting the League of Nations' covenant with Jan Smuts, Cecil served as president of the organization from 1923 to 1945. He received the 1937 Nobel peace prize for his work.

**Claire Chennault** (September 6, 1890–July 27, 1958). In late 1941, three years after the Chinese Nationalists hired him to reorganize their air force, the Texan gathered together a group of American pilots to fight the Japanese. The legendary "Flying Tigers" shot down 250 Japanese planes over China and Burma before the United States inducted them in 1942. Washington later named Chennault commander in China and promoted him to major general. He resigned in 1945, then helped the Nationalists develop a civilian airline.

**James Dole** (September 27, 1877–May 14, 1958). The founder of the Hawaiian Pineapple Co. (1903) popularized the exotic fruit on the mainland by canning it. He was pushed out of the company in 1931.

**Robert Earl Hughes** (1926–July 10, 1958). The mortuary needed a piano case and a crane to bury the carnival performer, who at 1,041 pounds was the world's heaviest human being.

**Javier Pereira** (1791?–March 30, 1958). In 1956, New York doctors estimated the Colombian Indian might be more than 150 years old. At that time, Pereira claimed to be 165.

**Pope Pius XII** (March 2, 1876–October 9, 1958). *See* News.


# BEGINNINGS AND ENDINGS

## News

**January 13.** The U.S. Communist newspaper, the *Daily Worker*, closes after 34 years. Its editor describes the 7,000-member party as "a futile and impotent political sect of no importance in our country."

**January 14.** Former prime minister Louis St. Laurent, age 75, retires at the Liberal convention in Ottawa. Two days later, delegates choose Lester B. Pearson as their new leader.

**January 20.** The first Latin American nuclear reactor starts up in Buenos Aires, Argentina.

**February 11.** Mohawk Airlines hires the nation's first black stewardess, Ruth Carol Taylor, to fly the Ithaca-New York run.

**March 8.** The decommissioning of the *Wisconsin* leaves the U.S. Navy without a battleship for the first time since 1895.

**March 19.** The inaugural session of the European Parliamentary Assembly, the governing body of the EEC and Euratom, meets in France.

**April 2.** Britain permits women to sit in the House of Lords.

**April 17.** The World's Fair—the first since 1939—opens in Brussels, Belgium. Before the gates close on October 19, some 41 million visitors marvel at the Atomium, the centerpiece 334-foot model of an iron crystal.

**May 8.** The AEC surrenders its monopoly on uranium to gain access to the growing market in nuclear fuel.

**May 30.** In ceremonies at Arlington National Cemetery, the remains of three American soldiers are buried in the Tomb of the Unknown Soldier.

President Truman authorized construction of the tomb in 1946, but work was postponed by the Korean War. Finally, this year, the military brought 13 "unknown" war dead from the Atlantic theater and 6 from the Pacific to a ship off the East Coast. Hospitalman First Class William R. Charette selected one coffin from each group to join the soldier chosen earlier from the American war dead in Korea.

**July 7.** The Automotive Information Disclosure Act requires car manufacturers to attach price stickers to new cars. Previously, dealers could charge what the market would bear.

**August 1.** The first postal increase since 1932 raises the cost of first-class U.S. mail from 3 to 4 cents per ounce.

**August 3.** The American atomic submarine *Nautilus* completes the first known voyage under the North polar ice cap.

**August 19.** Studebaker-Packard halts production of the expensive Packard line (1899).

---

*Statistics:* In the midst of a recession, the station wagon is the largest single model group—60 of 320 available styles. Still, the compact Rambler and the small, expensive Thunderbird are the year's top-sellers.

**August 25.** Former U.S. presidents receive their first pension ($25,000 a year), office space, free postage, and $50,000 for staff. (A president's widow receives $10,000 annually.) Earlier pension bills died in the House, reportedly because Republicans begrudged one to Democrat Harry S. Truman.

**September 18.** Field Marshall Bernard Montgomery, retires at the age of 70. During a distinguished military career, he led British forces to victory at Alamein in 1942, commanded Allied ground forces in the Normandy invasion of 1944, and, with peace, served as NATO deputy supreme commander.

**October 4.** The first regularly–scheduled transatlantic jet flight, a 46-passenger BOAC Comet IV, leaves New York for London. With easterly prevailing winds, the outgoing journey takes just over 6 hours; the return trip, with a refueling stop in Newfoundland, requires 10.

**November 20.** With the more efficient defense coverage provided by radar stations, the USAF discontinues the Civilian Ground Observer Corps.

**December.** Candy manufacturer Robert Welch meets with business associates to form the ultraconservative John Birch Society. (Birch was a U.S. intelligence officer killed by Chinese Communists days after the end of W.W.II.) By the early 1960s, the organization will attract some 100,000 members.

**December 10.** National Airlines inaugurates the first regular jet passenger service within the United States, a New York-Miami flight.

**More news.** Gerald Holtam bases his symbol for the British Campaign for Nuclear Disarmament on the semaphore signals for N and D. In the next decade, American activists and Vietnam War protestors will adopt the design as a peace symbol.

Former alcoholic Charles (Chuck) Dederich sets up Synanon, a storefront clinic for addiction rehabilitation. His revolutionary concept of group therapy and communal living gives birth to a network of communities in the United States and England.

## Records

**April 5.** In the world's largest nonnuclear explosion (1,375 tons of explosives), Canadian government engineers blow up Ripple Rock, a shipping hazard near Campbell River, British Columbia.

**April 26.** At the China Lake Naval Ordinance Test Station, in California, an unmanned rocket sled reaches a record ground speed of 2,827.5 mph.

## Government Departments and Agencies

**August 23.** The Federal Aviation Act establishes the Federal Aviation Agency (FAA) to control civilian and military air traffic. The CAB retains responsibility for economic matters in commercial aviation.

## New Products and Businesses

Cumberland Packing Co. of Brooklyn introduces Sweet 'n Low, a saccharin sweetener.

Pepsi-Cola switches from a straight-sided bottle to one with a distinctive swirl.

As Dan and Frank Carney ready their new pizza restaurant in Wichita, Kansas, a fixed budget limits their sign to nine letters. A family member suggests the addition of "Hut" after Pizza. The brothers open a second Pizza Hut before year's end and, by 1959, begin franchising.

For an annual fee, American Express furnishes subscribers with a credit card for air fares, hotel rooms, and car rentals.

After five years of excellent sales, French manufacturer Marcel Bich exports the disposable Bic pen to North America. By the end of the 1960s, its simple design will capture 50 percent of the U.S. pen market.

## Fads

Wham-O owners Richard Knerr and Arthur Melin opt for a new type of polyethylene in adapting the 3-foot bamboo ring used in Australian gym classes. Salespeople demonstrate the plastic Hula Hoop in California parks, and within four months Wham-O sells 25 million at $1.98 each. The fad, the first to move across country from West to East, escalates into one of the greatest national crazes in American history.

---

*Statistics:* With the population swell of baby-boomers, American households count more and more pets: Dogs are up 25 percent since 1947, parakeets 900 percent since 1951, and canaries 12 percent over the last three years. But tropical fish remain the most common pet, with 120 million in 20 million homes.

---

*Hula-Hoop contests and derbies attract enormous numbers of people across the United States.*

# SCIENCE AND TECHNOLOGY

## News

**January 31.** A Jupiter rocket, adapted by the army, takes the first U.S. satellite into orbit. Some experts believe that Wernher von Braun, who worked on the German V-2 and directed the construction of the Jupiter, could have beaten the Soviets into space if the administration had given him the go-ahead.

Instruments on board the 30.8-pound *Explorer I* measure temperature, the impact of meteorite particles, and cosmic radiation. Unexpected readings of charged particles, will later be found to follow the lines of the Earth's magnetic fields in concentrated belts of high-energy. Dubbed the Van Allen belts, after director James Van Allen, the first region will be thought to circle the Earth at an altitude of 2,000 miles and the second at 9,000–12,000 miles. But in early 1962, NASA will alter the description to a single 400-mile thick belt.

**February 26.** In closed hearings, John Foster Dulles tells the Foreign Affairs Committee that the USSR will likely be the first on the moon. The Soviets "have a good big start on us," and "spectacular things" that "use up human labor in useless ways" are "the products of despotisms." The secretary of state claims that winning the race to the moon might give the United States a psychological advantage, but the estimated $2-billion cost "is not going to put any bread in [people's] mouths or clothes on their backs."

**March 2.** In the first overland crossing of the Antarctic continent, a British Commonwealth expedition covers 2,180 miles in 99 days. Ice depth measurements taken with explosion echoes reveal above-sea-level rock along the entire route.

**March 17.** After the first navy Vanguard satellite exploded on the launching pad, and the second broke up in the air, Americans heave a collective sigh of relief when the third Vanguard reaches orbit today. Moscow laughingly calls the tiny 3¼-pound sphere a "grapefruit" (*Sputnik III*, launched in May, weighs 2,925 pounds), but its solar batteries will transmit information for 6 years.

**September 6.** An amended Food, Drug, and Cosmetic Act (1938) bars any food additive not "generally recognized as safe." A "cancer clause," inserted by Representative James J. Delaney, prohibits "any substance that tests find to induce cancer in man or animals"—no matter how large an amount or over how long a period.

Insiders believe some representatives decided to support the bill after their wives attended lectures by actress Gloria Swanson, a health-food devotee.

**September 12.** The AMA journal acknowledges for the first time that hypnosis "has a recognized place" in the practice of medicine.

**November 28.** A three-stage Atlas missile achieves the first full-range firing of an American ICBM. Early next month, Premier Khrushchev tells Senator Hubert Humphrey that the USSR has successfully fired an ICBM with an 8,700-mile range.

**December 18.** To test their first communications satellite, Project Score, the Americans transmit a recorded Christmas message from President Eisenhower and 10 minutes later relay it back to Earth—the first human voice heard from space.

**More news.** Canada's TCA pioneers the multi-channel flight recorder later dubbed the "black box."

• This year, the Pentagon introduces the first surface-to-air nuclear missile into the U.S. continental defense system. With a speed of 2,200 mph and a range of 75 miles, the Nike-Hercules marks a significant advance over the Nike-Ajax.

• In a controversial restoration, a 60-ton crane raises fallen Stonehenge blocks to their original positions. One of the heavy stones fell in 1797.

• This year, several Americans pioneer computer-assisted instruction. In Cambridge, Massachusetts, a psychologist and systems scientist use computers in math drills, graph construction, and language lessons.

## Other Discoveries, Developments, and Inventions

Temperature-resistant Corningware dishes from Corning Glass

Polyethylene bread wrappers, in place of cellophane, to extend shelf life by two days

Black polyethylene sheets for mulch cover

Auto-pilot from Chrysler, later called cruise control

Bifocal contact lenses, with distant vision in the center

## Obituaries

**Clinton Davisson** (October 22, 1881–February 1, 1958). Co-winner of the 1937 Nobel prize, the physicist perfected the electron microscope and other inventions.

**Jean Frédéric Joliot-Curie** (March 19, 1900–August 14, 1958). The French nuclear physicist was among the first to determine the principle of chain reaction. In 1940, as the Nazis threatened France, he organized the transfer of his nation's heavy water supply to Britain.

**Charles Kettering** (August 29, 1876–November 25, 1958). The American engineer was responsible for some of this century's most important and best-known inventions, including the automobile self-starter (1911–1912), the electric cash register, higher-octane gasoline, and high-compression engines. A firm believer in "pure" scientific research, he amassed a vast fortune from more than 130 patents.

**Ernest Lawrence** (August 8, 1901–August 27, 1958). The physicist received a Nobel prize in 1939 for his development of the cyclotron, or "atom smasher." It produced plutonium and uranium-235 for the first atomic bombs and enabled scientists to produce artificial radioactive elements.

## THE ARTS

January 16—*Two for the Seesaw*, with Henry Fonda, Anne Bancroft (750 perfs.)

January 30—*Sunrise at Campobello*, with Ralph Bellamy, Mary Fickett, Ann Seymour (556 perfs.)

October 14—*The World of Suzie Wong*, with France Nuyen, William Shatner (508 perfs.)

December 1—*Flower Drum Song*, with Pat Suzuki, Juanita Hall, Larry Blyden, Miyoshi Umeki (600 perfs.)

### Tony Awards

Actor (Dramatic)—Ralph Bellamy, *Sunrise at Campobello*

Actress (Dramatic)—Helen Hayes, *Time Remembered*

Actor (Musical)—Robert Preston, *The Music Man*

Actresses (Musical)—Thelma Ritter and Gwen Verdon, *New Girl in Town*

Play—*Sunrise at Campobello*

Musical—*The Music Man*

### News

**April 13.** In Moscow, Van Cliburn becomes the first American to win the coveted Tchaikovsky International Piano Contest. Upon his return to the United States, the 23-year-old Texan receives a ticker-tape parade and a contract with RCA-Victor. His recording of Tchaikovsky's *Piano Concerto No. 1* will sell a million copies by 1963—the first classical gold album.

**April 15.** A fire at the Museum of Modern Art in New York kills a worker and destroys two Monets. Authorities charge the museum with safety violations (the workers smoked near sawdust) and the building remains closed until October.

**May 12.** The Lunt-Fontanne Theatre, the first playhouse addition to Broadway in 31 years, honors the world's greatest husband-and-wife theatrical team, Alfred Lunt and Lynn Fontanne.

**June 8.** The Soviet Central Committee, admitting to previous "blatant errors," absolves Dimitri Shostakovich and other leading composers of "formalistic perversion." Prokofiev, charged as well in 1948, has since died.

**September 9.** Howls of protest greet a *Life* magazine report on the planned demolition of Carnegie Hall. Following a vocal campaign, led by violinist Isaac Stern, New York City purchases the 67-year-

old hall for $5 million. A nonprofit corporation takes over management.

**October 15.** At Sotheby and Co., in London, Cézanne's *Boy in a Red Waistcoat* sets a single-painting auction record—$616,000.

**October 16.** In her debut with the Toronto Opera, 20-year-old Teresa Stratas sings the role of Mimi. The Canadian soprano will appear on the Metropolitan Opera stage next year.

**November 6.** The difficult Maria Callas refuses to sing *La Traviata* between Met performances of *Macbeth*, and general manager Rudolf Bing revokes her contract.

**November 10.** In 1949, New York jeweler Harry Winston paid $1.2 million for the Hope Diamond. Originally 112 carats, the enormous gem was cut down in the 17th century to 67 and again in the 19th century to 45.5. Today, Winston donates the blue diamond—legendary curse and all—to the Smithsonian. He forwards it by registered mail.

**More news.** Robert Rauschenberg pioneers "pop art" by inserting an ordinary commercial product— Coca-Cola bottles—into a semiabstract painting.

### Obituaries

**Ralph Vaughan Williams** (October 12, 1872– August 26, 1958). The foremost modern English composer after Edward Elgar, Vaughan Williams founded a nationalist movement based on native folk songs.

## WORDS

Truman Capote, *Breakfast at Tiffany's*

Ian Fleming, *Dr. No*

John Kenneth Galbraith, *The Affluent Society*

John Gunther, *Inside Russia Today*

James Jones, *Some Came Running*

William J. Lederer and Eugene Burdick, *The Ugly American*

John O'Hara, *From the Terrace*

Boris Pasternak, *Doctor Zhivago*

Anya Seton, *The Winthrop Woman*

Robert Traver, *Anatomy of a Murder*

Leon Uris, *Exodus*

Abigail Van Buren, *Dear Abby*
T. H. White, *The Once and Future King*

## News

**January 23.** By dismissing the government's claim on the papers of Captain William Clark (of the Lewis and Clark expedition), the U.S. Court of Appeals reassures private collectors who feared expropriation.

**March 16–22.** The American Library Association and the National Book Committee sponsor the first National Library Week leading citizens across the country are enlisted to promote reading.

**May 24.** The 51-year-old United Press and 52-year-old Hearst International News Service merge to form United Press International (UPI).

**October 23.** Soviet writer Boris Pasternak "joyfully" accepts a Nobel prize. But, after the Soviet Writers Union expels him on the 28th, the acclaimed novelist "voluntarily" rejects the honor. Before the end of the year, his novel *Doctor Zhivago* sells over 450,000 copies in the United States alone.

## Cartoons and Comics

**August** The *Have Gun Will Travel* comic book joins *Wyatt Earp* and *Wagon Train* in a wave of TV crossovers.

**More news.** Johnny Hart debuts the comic strip *B.C.*

## TIME Man of the Year

Charles de Gaulle

## New Words and Phrases

Alaskaphobia (a Texan's fear of something bigger than his or her state)
beat, beat generation
containerization (a method of shipping merchandise on ocean freighters)
hot dog (a race driver)
overkill
parenting
sex kitten
sick joke
speakerine (a TV hostess)
wilderness park

New astronautic terms include lift-off, lunar probe, orbit, and reentry.

In October, columnist Herb Caen plays off the Soviet word *Sputnik* to coin a new name for members of the beat generation—beatnik.

## Obituaries

**(Elias) Burton Holmes** (January 8, 1870–July 22, 1958). In 1894, the American used still photographs to create the first "travelogue." He later progressed to color slides, then films.

**Mary Roberts Rinehart** (1876–September 22, 1958). The popularity of her novels and dramas during the 1920s and 1930s helped legitimize the mystery story as a form of literature. During the latter decade, Rinehart founded her own publishing firm.

**Robert Service** (January 16, 1874–September 11, 1958). The British bank clerk, who spent 18 years in Canada, won fame with his Yukon "blood and guts" verse. *Songs of a Sourdough* (1907), containing the ballad "The Shooting of Dan McGrew," sold 2 million copies by 1940.

# FASHION

## Haute Couture

Couturiers widen the tapered hem of the sack for a fuller outline and offer a slender chemise while Yves St. Laurent launches a pyramidal "trapeze" at the House of Dior.

Many women object to the looser silhouette and for the first time refuse to slavishly follow the dictates of haute couture. In response, New York designers offer more than a dozen variations of both designs.

## News

**September 2.** The U.S. Textile Fiber Content Identification Act requires manufacturers to label all garments with a percentage breakdown of fiber content (effective March 2, 1960).

**More news.** In London, small menswear boutiques on Carnaby Street sell bright "one-off" garments straight from the seamstress. The one-of-a-kind designs demand higher prices, but in less than two years this new breed of retailer will govern the street.

• Late last fall, women began buying dancers' stretch tights for everyday use. Stores report increased sales this year as girls, in turn, opt for the colorful hosiery.

• The apparel industry protests the influx of cheaply priced clothing from the Far East, particularly Japan and Hong Kong. Asian garment workers generally earn 10–15 cents per hour, while in the United States a $1.50 hourly wage drives up costs.

## Colors and Materials

Spring fashions favor paisley silks and cottons. A new finish increases their washability.

Vivid colors retain their hold while beige, in all shades, takes over as the standard neutral.

A trend toward lighter-weight fabrics reduces all-year suiting to 11 ounces or less per linear yard compared to an earlier 14.

## Clothes

For separates, women wear long bulky sweaters or hipbone-length overblouses (usually in bright satins or flowered silks) over slim skirts, skinny pants, or elasticized dancer's tights.

Coats follow the chemise and trapeze shapes in looped mohair or striking tweeds. Chinchilla appeals as a luxury fur coat.

White permanent-pleated skirts in new washable synthetics dominate summer fashions. In bathing suits, knits recall the fit of 1920s styles.

While unpopular, the sack dress nonetheless frees women from sturdy corsets. Many refuse to go back.

Nylon jackets revolutionize outdoor clothing—windproof, sturdier than cotton duck, light and warm with goose down.

Men's suits feature the "Ivy" look of natural shoulders, with the single-breasted, three-button style being the favorite.

## Accessories

Milliners succeed with fluffy fur hats and feather wigs. (Young women increasingly question the need for a different hat for every occasion.)

Shoes generally retain needle toes and thin underslung heels. A new T-strap from a low front wins acceptance. Men's shoes become more square-toed.

In these last years of the 1950s, a gold chain and heart worn on a girl's left ankle supposedly signifies a steady boyfriend; on the right, a replaceable beau.

## Hair and Cosmetics

Teasing creates fluffy "petals" of hair curving around the ears and forehead.

To proclaim their womanhood, teenagers switch from lipstick to eye shadow and false eyelashes.

## Obituaries

**Claire McCardell** (May 24, 1905–March 22, 1958). The top American designer of the forties and fifties created harem pajamas, the stretch leotard, the bareback summer dress, and the first "separates" (to extend the working girl's wardrobe). The practical McCardell, who also popularized cheap denim, was the first to franchise her designs. She died of cancer.

# POPULAR MUSIC

"At the Hop"—Danny & the Juniors
"It's All in the Game"—Tommy Edwards

"The Purple People Eater"—Sheb Wooley
"All I Have to Do Is Dream"—Everly Brothers
"Don't"—Elvis Presley
"Tequila" (Instr.)—Champs
"Nel Blu Dipinto di Blu (Volare)"—Domenico Modugno
"Sugartime"—McGuire Sisters
"He's Got the Whole World in His Hands"—Laurie London
"The Chipmunk Song"—The Chipmunks with David Seville
"Witch Doctor"—David Seville
"To Know Him Is to Love Him"—Teddy Bears
"It's Only Make Believe"—Conway Twitty
"Poor Little Fool"—Ricky Nelson
"Hard Headed Woman"—Elvis Presley
"Get a Job"—Silhouettes
"Tom Dooley"—Kingston Trio
"Patricia" (Instr.)—Perez Prado & His Orchestra
"Little Star"—Elegants
"Catch a Falling Star"—Perry Como
"Yakety Yak"—Coasters
"Bird Dog"—Everly Brothers
"Twilight Time"—Platters
"Wear My Ring Around Your Neck"—Elvis Presley
"Great Balls of Fire"—Jerry Lee Lewis
"26 Miles (Santa Catalina)"—Four Preps
"Stood Up"—Ricky Nelson
"Sweet Little Sixteen"—Chuck Berry
"Rock-in' Robin"—Bobby Day
"Lollipop"—Chordettes

## Grammy Awards (1958)

The National Academy of Recording Arts and Sciences (NARAS), founded in 1957, will present its first awards for outstanding artistic and technical creativity on May 4, 1959. The statuette of an early gramophone is dubbed a Grammy.

Record of the Year—Domenico Modugno, "Nel Blu Dipinto di Blu (Volare)"
Song of the Year (songwriter)—Domenico Modugno, "Nel Blu Dipinto di Blu (Volare)"

Album of the Year—Henry Mancini, *The Music from* Peter Gunn
Best Vocal Performance (Male)—Perry Como, "Catch a Falling Star"
Best Vocal Performance (Female)—Ella Fitzgerald, *Ella Fitzgerald Sings the Irving Berlin Song Book*

## News

**January 27.** Little Richard announces his enrollment in a Negro Alabama college run by Seventh Day Adventists. He explains that a fire on board his plane during a tour to Australia convinced him to give up rock 'n' roll to serve God.

**February 14.** Walter Cronkite reports to TV viewers that Iran has banned rock 'n' roll because dancers performing "extreme gyrations" to the music have suffered hip injuries.

**March 24.** The U.S. Army hands out draft No. 53310761 to 23-year-old Elvis Presley. Magazine and newspaper photographers cover the Big Event—a military haircut. (He puns, "Hair today, gone tomorrow.")

Unlike other singers and actors drafted in earlier years, Elvis receives no special treatment. Supposedly to give the singing idol a more wholesome image, the army deliberately sends him to Germany. Life in an armored division proves difficult for a young man who has led a relatively sheltered life. He is shattered when his mother Gladys dies in August.

**May 27.** Jerry Lee Lewis flies home after boos and catcalls forced an English theater chain to cancel his tour. The 22-year-old rock 'n' roller has outraged public morality by marrying his 13-year-old cousin Myra Brown. All but blacklisted in the United States, Lewis must wait until the sixties before changing social attitudes will give him back some of his former popularity. The marriage will last 13 years.

**September 20.** Madame Tussaud's finally immortalizes a rock 'n' roller, Tommy Steele. But England's first rock star soon switches his focus to musicals.

**More news.** The British firm Electric and Musical Industries (EMI) produced the first stereo recording in 1933, but manufacturers were unable to construct a pick-up arm for the two distinct stereo channels. (Companies continued to experiment while backlogging stereo discs for future production.) Finally, this year, a monaural-stereo cartridge and stylus allows the music industry to release the first stereo LP's. The term *hi-fi* will quickly disappear.

> *Statistics:* As the teenagers' share of record sales reaches 70 percent, the number of independent-label hits reaches 31. And from 1959–1970, an average of these hits 37 reach the top each year.

• Extending his idea from "Witch Doctor," Ross Bagdasarian—a.k.a. David Seville—records at half speed then plays the voices back at normal speed. The Chipmunks—named Alvin, Simon, and Theodore after chiefs at Liberty Records—score big with their debut novelty song, but this is one group that will never tour.

• Paramount Pictures bought out Dot Records in 1957. This year, Warner Bros., 20th Century-Fox, Columbia Pictures, and United Artists all start record companies.

• Tommy Edwards, with just one session left on his MGM contract, updates his 1951 single "It's All in the Game" as a rock 'n' roll ballad. Just six weeks after its chart entry, the Sigman-Dawes composition reaches No. 1. (Later versions by Cliff Richard in 1964, and the Four Tops in 1970, will make it one of the few singles to break the top 30 on three separate occasions.)

• The Kingston Trio hit "Tom Dooley" sets off a folk revival.

• Mitch Miller produces his first album of standards and sing-along lyrics.

• The nonprofit Record Industry Associates of America (RIAA) proposes a gold-record award for those companies willing to surrender certified sales figures. To qualify, a single must sell at least 1 million units and an LP album must post $1 million in factory billing.

This first year, RIAA certifies four singles:

"Catch a Falling Star" by Perry Como, "Patricia" by Perez Prado, "He's Got the Whole World in His Hands" by Laurie London, and the only rock 'n' roll tune, "Hard Headed Woman" by Elvis Presley. The only LP to gross $1 million is the cast recording of "Oklahoma!"

Since the awards recognize financial value, not artistic merit, and some companies keep their figures secret, many big hits (including Motown's through the 1960s) never go "gold."

• Singer Bobby Darin writes "Splish Splash" in 10 minutes. His song sells over 100,000 copies in less than a month and reaches No. 3 on the music charts.

## New Recording Artists

Frankie Avalon
Dion & the Belmonts
Duane Eddy
Connie Francis
Impressions
Kingston Trio
Little Anthony & the Imperials
Miracles
Neil Sedaka
Shirelles
Ritchie Valens

## *Obituaries*

**Lew Brown** (December 10, 1893–February 5, 1958). His estimated 7,000 song collaborations included "Sonny Boy" (1928) and "Beer Barrel Polka" (1939, English words).

**W(illiam) C(hristopher) Handy** (November 16, 1873–March 28, 1958). One of the great exponents of jazz, his compositions included the famous blues trio, "Memphis Blues" (1910), "St. Louis Blues" (1914), and "Beale Street Blues" (1916). An estimated 150,000 watch his funeral procession through the streets of Harlem.

**Harry Revel** (December 21, 1905–November 3, 1958). The British-American composer wrote such hits as "Did You Ever See a Dream Walking?" (1933) and he scored all of Shirley Temple's films.

# MOVIES

*Auntie Mame* (d. Morton Da Costa; color)—Rosalind Russell, Forrest Tucker, Coral Browne, Fred Clark

*The Big Country* (d. William Wyler; color)—Gregory Peck, Jean Simmons, Charlton Heston, Carroll Baker, Burl Ives, Charles Bickford

*Cat on a Hot Tin Roof* (d. Richard Brooks; color)—Elizabeth Taylor, Paul Newman, Burl Ives

*The Hollywood Production Code deletes all references to homosexuality in* Cat on a Hot Tin Roof, *but 33-year-old Paul Newman and 26-year-old Elizabeth Taylor carry the essence of Tennessee Williams' play to the screen.*

*Curse of the Demon* (d. Jacques Tourneur; bw)—Dana Andrews, Peggy Cummins, Niall MacGinnis

*Damn Yankees* (d. George Abbott; color)—Tab Hunter, Gwen Verdon, Ray Walston

*The Defiant Ones* (d. Stanley Kramer; bw)—Tony Curtis, Sidney Poitier

*Gigi* (d. Vincente Minnelli; color)—Leslie Caron, Maurice Chevalier, Louis Jordan, Hermione Gingold

*I Want to Live!* (d. Robert Wise; bw)—Susan Hayward, Simon Oakland

*The Last Hurrah* (d. John Ford; bw)—Spencer Tracy, Jeffrey Hunter, Diane Foster, Pat O'Brien

*A Night to Remember* (d. Roy Baker; bw)—Kenneth More (and many others in small roles)

*Separate Tables* (d. Delbert Mann; bw)—Burt Lancaster, Rita Hayworth, David Niven, Deborah Kerr, Wendy Hiller

*The Seventh Voyage of Sinbad* (d. Nathan Juran; color)—Kerwin Mathews, Kathryn Grant (Crosby), Richard Eyer, Torin Thatcher

*South Pacific* (d. Joshua Logan; color)—Rossano Brazzi, Mitzi Gaynor, John Kerr, Ray Walston, Juanita Hall, France Nuyen

*Vertigo* (d. Alfred Hitchcock; color)—James Stewart, Kim Novak

*The Young Lions* (d. Edward Dmytryk; bw)—Marlon Brando, Montgomery Clift, Dean Martin, Hope Lange, Barbara Rush, May Britt

## Academy Awards

**March 26.** This year, film companies, independent producers, and theater owners wholly finance a single Hollywood broadcast to promote new films. With industry backing, big-name stars flock to the ceremonies and many, like Clark Gable, appear on TV for the first time.

The five co-hosts are James Stewart, David Niven, Jack Lemmon, Rosalind Russell, and Bob Hope.

Best Picture—*The Bridge on the River Kwai*

Best Actor—Alec Guinness (*The Bridge on the River Kwai*)

Best Actress—Joanne Woodward (*The Three Faces of Eve*)

Best Director—David Lean (*The Bridge on the River Kwai*)

Best Supporting Actor—Red Buttons (*Sayonara*)

Best Supporting Actress—Miyoshi Umeki (*Sayonara*)

Best Song—"All the Way" from *The Joker Is Wild*

Best Foreign Film—*The Nights of Cabiria* (Italian)

With last year's awards mushrooming to 31, the Academy streamlines the total to 23.

The Communist ineligibility rule introduced in 1957 proves impossible to enforce, and the Academy revokes the clause.

Last year, actress Ingrid Bergman topped her Hollywood comeback with the best actress Oscar, but failed to attend the ceremonies. This year, she triumphantly returns from European exile to present an award.

## News

**April 4.** Lana Turner's daughter, Cheryl Crane, fatally stabs her mother's boyfriend in their Beverly Hills mansion. A coroner's jury finds Johnny Stompanato, who had threatened to scar Turner, died accidentally, but the Hollywood scandal changes the 14-year-old's life. During her teens, she will run away from home, attempt suicide, and eventually enter an institution.

**July.** After a brief shutdown, financially strapped Universal Pictures—the last major studio exclusively producing its own movies—arranges to deal with independents. In December, Universal sells its studios to Music Corporation of America for $11 million, then leases them back.

**More news.** Following Hammer Films' first big hit in 1954, *The Quatermass Experiment*, the British studio decided to resurrect the popular movie monsters of the 1930s.

In 1957, American audiences loved the gory color and melodramatic plot of *The Curse of Frankenstein* and, this year, flock to see *Horror of Dracula*. With several sequels, actors Peter Cushing and Christopher Lee become stars.

After their first appearance on screen in the Humphrey Bogart film *Dead End* (1937), the Dead End Kids starred in other Warner Bros. features. But a couple of the young toughs moved over to Universal and, in 1940, Monogram hired others to become the East Side Kids. Six years later, Monogram consolidated the remaining "kids," including Leo Gorcey and Bobby Jordan, into the Bowery Boys. This year, their 48th and final film ends the long series.

• Film companies and theaters experiment with the "hard ticket" sale—higher-priced reserved seats for two showings a day. Movies exhibited on this basis include *Gigi*, *South Pacific*, and *The Bridge on the River Kwai*. The system continues into the sixties.

• Just 10 years ago, Hollywood averaged 445 pictures a year. Then the Justice Department banned block bookings (linking good and bad films) and forced studios to sell their theater chains. Attendance figures dropped as well, and studio executives planned fewer, more costly films to lure audiences back.

• This year, for the first time, foreign films outnumber American pictures at home. The industry blames the current interest in European pornographic pictures, but the number of U.S. releases will drop below 200 before American film companies regain the edge in 1969.

| Top Box Office Stars | Newcomers |
| --- | --- |
| Glenn Ford | Joanne Woodward |
| Elizabeth Taylor | Red Buttons |
| Jerry Lewis | Diane Varsi |
| Marlon Brando | Andy Griffith |
| Rock Hudson | Anthony Franciosa |
| William Holden | Hope Lange |
| Brigitte Bardot | Brigitte Bardot |
| Yul Brynner | Burl Ives |
| James Stewart | Mickey Shaughnessy |
| Frank Sinatra | Russ Tamblyn |

## Top Money-Maker of the Year

*The Bridge on the River Kwai* (1957)

## Quote of the Year

"Teenagers—we never had 'em when I was a kid!"

An adult bemoans the criminal element in *The Cry Baby Killer*. Jack Nicholson, 21, debuts in the lead role. (Screenplay by Leo Vincent Gordon and Melvin Levy, from a story by Leo Vincent Gordon)

## Obituaries

**Harry Cohn** (July 23, 1891–February 27, 1958). The ruthless movie mogul—nicknamed "White Fang"—built Columbia Pictures.

**Ronald Colman** (February 9, 1891–May 19, 1958). One of the few silent leading men to become a bigger star with sound, the British actor typified the gentleman hero for generations of moviegoers. He won an Oscar for *A Double Life* (1947), but his best-remembered movies remain *The Prisoner of Zenda* (1937) and *Lost Horizon* (1937).

**Robert Donat** (March 18, 1905–June 9, 1958). Internationally famous and highly respected by his peers, the British stage and screen actor was limited by chronic asthma. His films included *The Thirty-Nine Steps* (1935) and *Goodbye, Mr. Chips* (1939).

**Tyrone Power** (May 5, 1914–November 15, 1958). Throughout the 1940s, the handsome actor was one of America's most popular stars, particularly in such swashbuckler pictures as *The Mark of Zorro* (1940) and *Captain from Castile* (1947). Power died of a heart attack while filming *Solomon and Sheba* in Spain.

**Mike Todd** (June 22, 1909–March 22, 1958). The American showman and producer who won fame with *Around the World in Eighty Days* (1956), left his mark on the industry by co-founding the Cinerama process and later developing Todd-AO. He was killed in a plane crash with three others while his young wife, Elizabeth Taylor, stayed home with a cold.

## TELEVISION AND RADIO

### New Prime-Time TV Programs

"The Andy Williams Show" (July 3, 1958–September 1959; September 1962–May 1967; September 1969–July 17, 1971; Musical Variety)—Andy Williams

"Bronco" (September 23, 1958–August 20, 1962; Western)—Ty Hardin (*Note:* Alternated with "Sugarfoot," 1958–1960, then every two or three weeks, 1960–1962.)

"The Donna Reed Show" (September 24, 1958–September 3, 1966; (Situation Comedy)—Donna Reed, Carl Betz, Shelley Fabares, Paul Petersen

"The Garry Moore Show" (September 1958–June 1964; September 1966–January 1967; Variety)—Garry Moore, Durwood Kirby, Marion Lorne (1958–1962), Carol Burnett (1959–1962)

"Naked City" (September 1958–September 1959; October 1960–September 1963; Police Drama)—John McIntire (1958–1959), James Franciscus (1959–1959), Paul Burke (1960–1963), Horace McMahon (1959–1963)

"Peter Gunn" (September 22, 1958–September 25, 1961; Detective)—Craig Stevens, Lola Albright, Herschel Bernardi

"The Rifleman" (September 30, 1958–July 1, 1963; Western)—Chuck Connors, Johnny Crawford, Paul Fix

"77 Sunset Strip" (October 10, 1958–September 9, 1964; Detective)—Efrem Zimbalist, Jr., Roger Smith (1958–1963), Edd Byrnes (1958–1963)

"Wanted: Dead Or Alive" (September 6, 1958–March 29, 1961; Western)—Steve McQueen

### Emmy Awards 1957 (April 15, 1958)

Best Dramatic Series—"Gunsmoke" (CBS)

Best Musical, Variety, or Quiz Series—"The Dinah Shore Chevy Show" (NBC)

Best Comedy Series—"Phil Silvers Show" (CBS)

Best Actor in a Series—Robert Young ("Father Knows Best," NBC)

Best Actress in a Series—Jane Wyatt ("Father Knows Best," NBC)

Best Continuing Performance (Male) in a Series by a Comedian, Singer, Host, etc.—Jack Benny ("The Jack Benny Show," CBS)

Best Continuing Performance (Female) in a Series by a Comedian, Singer, Host, etc.—Dinah Shore ("The Dinah Shore Chevy Show," NBC)

## News

**January 18.** Basically a music appreciation show, "CBS Young People's Concerts" will become the longest-running special series for children. Each season, conductor-composer Leonard Bernstein and guest artists like Yehudi Menuhin present four theme programs to an auditorium full of young people. Bernstein will leave the award-winning program in 1972, and Michael Tilson Thomas will take over.

**February 17.** ABC purchased the rights to 30 Three Stooges films in 1949, too early for the baby-boom generation. This month, Screen Gems releases another 78 first-run Stooges pictures for syndication. A revitalized Moe, Larry, and Curly guest on "Ed Sullivan," "Steve Allen," and other prime-time shows, and draw capacity crowds at their personal appearances.

**July 1.** A microwave relay system links Canada from coast to coast.

**August 4.** DuMont, television's first network, comes to an end with the final telecast of "Monday Night Fights." Only five stations still carry the feed.

**August 25.** New York District Attorney Frank Hogan announces an investigation into possible illegal activities on the quiz show "Dotto." One contestant supposedly discovered another with the answers. When Hogan promises to follow up any leads, contestants from other programs come forth.

By November, the scandal pushes most quiz shows off the air. The networks, in an attempt to salvage their dignity, promote a return to TV's classic comics. But the Jackie Gleason show is gone by January and Milton Berle barely lasts the season. Once again, Westerns dominate.

**August 26.** The Canadian House of Commons transfers regulatory authority to a Board of Broadcast Governors. Previously, the government-funded CBC controlled all network operations, including nongovernment broadcasters.

**October.** This fall, CBS's surefire Saturday night lineup includes "Perry Mason," "Wanted: Dead or Alive," "Have Gun Will Travel," and "Gunsmoke."

**October 1.** TV's oldest show and one of the last to broadcast live, "Kraft Television Theatre" leaves the air. According to *TV Guide*, the program presented 650 plays with 3,955 actors and actresses, such as E. G. Marshall, Joanne Woodward, Jack Lemmon, Anthony Perkins, and James Dean. But script editor Ed Rice points out that the cost per episode had risen from $3,000 to $165,000, and studio facilities in 1947 were half the area now devoted to today's commercials.

With the flexibility videotaping offers, live telecasts all but disappear. And with major production studios on the West Coast, the percentage of prime-time programs originating in California jumps this year from 40 percent to 71 percent.

**October 2.** "The Huckleberry Hound Show," a Hanna-Barbera series, enters syndication. The noble-hearted, stoic hound takes on the guise of the Purple Pumpernickel, a French Legionnaire, an American fireman, and others; Daws Butler provides his rustic twang.

This first all-new cartoon series (and the first to receive an Emmy (1959)) will draw an estimated 16 million American kids by the fall of 1960. Huckleberry's enormous success will push other cartoonists to imitate the fantasy-adventure element.

Early in 1961, Yogi the Bear, introduced in early Huck episodes, will receive his own Hanna-Barbera show.

**October 17.** In his first live broadcast before an American audience, the *New York Times* claims 59-year-old Fred Astaire "did more for the cause of dancing . . . than anyone else in the decade of television."

**October 31.** Based on the life of a real Civil War officer, "Tales of Texas John Slaughter," starring 32-year-old Tom Tryon, becomes one of the most popular series on "Walt Disney Presents." But after 17 episodes Disney moves from ABC to NBC and the agreement calls for no programming carryovers.

**More news.** Portable radios replace the turn-knob with a push on/off and volume control, allowing listeners to leave the volume at the same level.

• Kenny Rossi has 301 fan clubs. The 19-year-old is a regular audience member on "American Bandstand."

*With his joints moved slightly for each new frame of film, Speedy Alka-Seltzer plays a toy piano and bongo drums and waves his magic wand for the television audience.*

## TV Commercials

Maypo Oat Cereal—Character Marky Maypo begins his Western adventures.

Mr. Clean—The music behind the jingle, "Mr. Clean, Mr. Clean, Mr. Clean . . ." haunts Americans.

Sugar Pops—An animated squirrel with an out-sized 10-gallon hat, Sugar Pops Pete uses his

"Pop Gun" with "sparkling sugar dust" to shoot bad guys like Billy the Kidder.

### Memorable Radio Programs End

"The Bell Telephone Hour" (April 29, 1940)
"The FBI in Peace and War" (November 25, 1944)
"The Great Gildersleeve" (August 31, 1941)
"The Kate Smith Show" (May 1, 1931)
"When a Girl Marries" (May 29, 1939)
"X-Minus One" (April 24, 1955)

### Obituaries

**Harry R. (Tim) Moore** (1888?–December 13, 1958). A vaudeville star before joining the "Amos 'n' Andy" show on radio, the Negro comedian played Kingfish in the TV series.

## SPORTS

### Winners

#### Baseball

World Series—New York Yankees (AL), 4 games; Milwaukee Braves (NL), 3 games
Player of the Year—Jackie Jensen (Boston Red Sox, AL); Ernie Banks (Chicago Cubs, NL)
Rookie of the Year—Albie Pearson (Washington Senators; AL); Orlando Cepeda (San Francisco Giants; NL)

#### Football

NFL Championship—Baltimore Colts 23, New York Giants 17
College Bowls (January 1, 1958)—
  Rose Bowl, Ohio State 10, Oregon 7
  Cotton Bowl, Navy 20, Rice 7
  Orange Bowl, Oklahoma 48, Duke 21
  Sugar Bowl, Mississippi 39, Texas 7
Heisman Trophy—Pete Dawkins (U.S. Military Academy, HB)
Grey Cup—Winnipeg Blue Bombers 35, Hamilton Tiger-Cats 28

## Basketball

NBA Championship—St. Louis Hawks, 4
   games; Boston Celtics, 2 games
MVP of the Year—Bill Russell (Boston Celtics)
Rookie of the Year—Woody Sauldsberry (Philadelphia Warriors)
NCAA Championship—Kentucky 84, Seattle
   72

## Tennis

U.S. National—Men, Ashley Cooper (vs. Mal-
   colm Anderson); Women, Althea Gibson
   (vs. Darlene Hard)
Wimbledon—Men, Ashley Cooper (vs. Neale
   Fraser); Women, Althea Gibson (vs. Angela
   Mortimer)

## Golf

Masters—Arnold Palmer
U.S. Open—Tommy Bolt
British Open—Peter Thomson

## Hockey

Stanley Cup—Montreal Canadiens, 4 games;
   Boston Bruins, 2 games

## Ice Skating

World Championship—Men, David Jenkins
   (U.S.); Women, Carol Heiss (U.S.)
U.S. National—Men, David Jenkins; Women,
   Carol Heiss
Canadian National—Men, Charles Snelling;
   Women, Margaret Crosland

## Kentucky Derby

Tim Tam—Ismael Valenzuela, jockey

## Athlete of the Year

Male—Herb Elliott (Track & Field)
Female—Althea Gibson (Tennis)

## Last Season

(Gerardo Gonzalez) Kid Gavilan (Boxing)
Bob Lemon (Baseball)
Harold (Pee Wee) Reese (Baseball)

## News

**January.** Two years ago, two interprovincial football
unions loosely merged as the nine-team Canadian
Football Council. This month, the CFC becomes
the Canadian Football League (CFL).

**January 12.** In the first major rule change since
1912, U.S. intercollegiate football allows an optional two-point conversion after a TD. The team
must run the ball into the end zone.

**January 28.** Dodger Roy Campanella is paralyzed
from the neck down in a car crash. The major
league's first black catcher was a three-time MVP
and an eight-time All-Star during his 10-year career. He will stay with the team, working in community relations.

**April 6.** Arnold Palmer captures his first major
tournament with a win at Augusta. The charismatic
golfer gives the game a needed shot in the arm,
attacking each course and drawing a band of loyal
supporters along behind him. Over the next six
years, Arnie's Army will be rewarded with seven
wins in 25 major events.

**April 15.** For the first time, the major league baseball season opens with teams on the West Coast.
Some 23,000 watch the San Francisco Giants beat
the Dodgers, 8–0, at Seals Stadium. Three days
later, 78,672 crowd into Los Angeles Memorial Coli-
seum to cheer for a 6–5 Dodger victory.

**September 11.** At the Candidates Chess Tournament in Yugoslavia, 15-year-old U.S. champion
Bobby Fischer finishes fifth. He is the youngest
player to earn international grand master rating.

**September 26.** In 1851, the schooner *America*
won a British yachting cup. Subsequently donated
to the New York Yacht Club, the trophy became
known as America's Cup. From the first defense in
1857, U.S. yachts have fended off every challenger.
This year, in the first America's Cup since 1937, the
United States wins once again.

*Arnold Palmer studies his final shot at the Masters in Augusta, Georgia.*

**October 9.** With a 6–2 win over the Braves, in the seventh and final game of the World Series, the Yankees become the first club since the 1925 Pittsburgh Pirates to fight back from a 3–1 deficit.

**December 28.** The Baltimore Colts win the NFL championship with a TD in overtime. Football's first "sudden death" game turns millions of Americans into instant fans.

**More news.** The Philadelphia Eagles draft 22-year-old tackle John Madden in the 21st round. A knee injury this fall ends his playing career.

## Records

**March 6.** Detroit Piston George Yardley, with two games left in the season, breaks two NBA single-season records—George Mikan's 1,932 point total and Dolph Schayes' 625 converted free throws. In the final game, Yardley finishes with 2,001 points.

**October 18.** Romanian Iolanda Balas is the first female high jumper to clear 6 feet. She will dominate the event until 1966.

**This year.** In his second year as a pro, Cleveland Browns' fullback Jim Brown amasses 1,527 yards, shattering the previous NFL rushing record of 1,146 yards set by Steven Van Buren in 1949.

## What They Said

With a tie for 14th at this year's Masters, golfing great Ben Hogan collects a much smaller prize than usual—$1,050. "I'm glad I don't have to play this game for a living." ('Sports Illustrated' Apr. 21)

## Obituaries

**Mel Ott** (March 2, 1909–November 21, 1958). Judged the complete ball player in his era, "Master Melvin" played 22 years in the New York Giants outfield before chronic leg problems forced him to retire in 1947. He finished his career with 511 home runs—third only to Babe Ruth and Jimmie Foxx. Ott died in a head-on collision with a drunken driver.

**Tris(tram) Speaker** (April 4, 1888–December 8, 1958). Part of the famous Boston outfield with Duffy Lewis and Harry Hooper, Speaker was the greatest center fielder of his day. But Boston traded him to Cleveland when his batting average fell to .338 and he refused a pay cut. During his 11 years as an Indian, Speaker averaged .354, and as player-manager (1919–1926) he led the club to its first World Series title in 1920. After single seasons with two other teams, he finished his career in the minors.

# 1959

*"Nixon Meets Khrushchev" holds all the promise of a horror film, but the vice-president outscores the premier in a heated off-the-cuff debate in Moscow. The administration wins more positive media coverage with the opening of the St. Lawrence Seaway, the naming of the first astronauts, the proclamation of the 49th and 50th states, and a December presidential trip abroad. But while the people of Asia, Africa, and Europe welcome Eisenhower almost as a father figure, they no longer answer his call to fight Communism.*

*Other national and international headlines include the Cuban revolution and the riot in the Panama Canal Zone. Britain inaugurates the first transcontinental jet passenger service while the Soviets launch Luna 1, the first satellite to escape Earth's gravity. Liz Taylor marries Eddie Fisher and quiz shows plunge into a scandal. George C. Marshall passes away as do Frank Lloyd Wright, Buddy Holly, Billie Holiday, and the last surviving veteran of the Civil War.*

*The move by young couples to the suburbs, during the 1950s, has changed the face of America forever. Bedroom communities have spread out along transportation routes and shopping centers have sprouted everywhere. But the transition has cost more than hectic rush hours. Urban centers, left with a smaller tax base, can no longer help the largely poor and uneducated, and crime rates increase across the nation.*

## NEWS

**January 1.** Following a two-year guerrilla campaign, Fidel Castro's revolutionaries overthrow the dictatorship of Fulgencio Batista. Washington extends recognition on January 7, after Cuba honors international agreements.

During an April visit to Washington, Premier Castro describes his revolutionaries as "humanistic," not Communist. But firing squads eliminate 621 "war criminals" by mid-May. Worldwide criticism brings a halt, but by the end of the year, the executions will begin again.

**January 3.** President Eisenhower proclaims Alaska the 49th state of the Union. Purchased from Russia in 1867 and a U.S. territory since 1912, the enormous state—nearly 20 percent the area of the other 48 together—is the least populous. To encourage development, Washington grants Alaska an endowment of 102.5 million acres from vacant public lands and another 800,000 acres adjacent to communities.

**February 2.** The registration of Negro children at Norfolk and Arlington schools—a civil rights milestone—proceeds without serious resistance. Last month, the Virginia Supreme Court invalidated state laws designed to prevent school integration.

**February 20.** In light of the growing importance of missiles, Ottawa cancels production of the Avro Arrow. Although unparalleled in speed and performance, each jet now cost nearly $12.5 million each.

The controversial decision virtually destroys the Canadian aircraft industry. A stricken A. V. Roe lays off the 2,000-member design team and 12,000 manufacturing employees, and many emigrate south. The Conservative government turns to the United States for Bomarc missiles.

**March 5.** Despite a commitment to the Baghdad Pact, following last year's action in Lebanon, Washington signs separate defense agreements with the three remaining members, Iran, Pakistan, and Turkey. A last effort by the Eisenhower administration to stabilize the Middle East, the Central Treaty Organization (CENTO), fails in the end. Over the next decade, the area will become increasingly anti-American.

**March 13.** In response to Soviet submarine-launched and intercontinental missiles, Washington announces the construction of a Ballistic Missile Early Warning System. Eventually costing $1 billion, the three radar screens at Clear, Alaska, and the four at Thule, Greenland, cover the USSR in a 3,000-mile line of sight. Older warning systems will be phased out after 1965.

**March 21.** Under pressure from Democrats, the Defense Department admits that the concentration of strontium-90 is "greater in the United States than in any other area of the world." With these figures in hand, the Democrats accuse the AEC of downplaying the risks from radioactive fallout to retain control of the weapons program.

Supporting evidence continues to mount. On April 27, the Weather Bureau reports that 70 percent of radioactive debris in the atmosphere comes from U.S. tests. Just six days later, independent scientists testify that a resumption of atmospheric tests would raise fallout levels beyond the danger point.

Driven to respond, the president issues an executive order on August 14, establishing a Federal Radiation Council to set fallout and nuclear industry safety standards, and transferring safeguard regulation from the AEC to individual states.

**March 23.** The peacetime draft is extended to June 1, 1963.

**March 31.** The Dalai Lama flees after Tibetans fail to overthrow the Communist Chinese occupation. India offers religious sanctuary but no recognition of a government-in-exile.

**April 15.** John Foster Dulles, on leave and known to have cancer, resigns as secretary of state. Allowed to more or less set foreign policy under Eisenhower, Dulles threatened massive nuclear retaliation from widespread American missile bases in order to block Communist aggression. He also expanded U.S. treaty obligations in Asia (SEATO) and in the Middle East (CENTO). But in the process, the secretary committed the United States to propping up weak and corrupt governments in Vietnam, South America, and elsewhere.

When new Secretary of State Christian Herter shows limited capabilities, Eisenhower gradually takes over many of the diplomatic functions previously delegated to Dulles.

**April 26.** Queen Elizabeth, President Eisenhower, and Prime Minister Diefenbaker formally open the St. Lawrence Seaway. One of the decade's greatest engineering feats, the deep-water channel extends the North Atlantic shipping route through the Great Lakes to Midwest industrial and agricultural areas. An associated hydroelectric project will provide up to 1.8 million kilowatts of power for Canada and the United States.

Canada, which paid 70 percent of the $470 million cost, signed the St. Lawrence Agreement with the United States in 1941. Congress ratified the pact 10 years later, when the need for speedier mobilization became evident.

**May.** This month, Hanoi takes control of the growing Communist rebellion in South Vietnam, readying supply lines on the Ho Chi Minh Trail, sending another 4,500 Communist southerners back into South Vietnam, and stepping up terrorist attacks. Gunfire kills two American servicemen in their base compound on July 8—the first U.S. fatalities—and, in September, the Vietminh attack

South Vietnamese troops for the first time. As the conflict escalates into a civil war, North Vietnamese Premier Pham Van Dong declares in November, "We will drive the Americans into the sea."

**May 21.** Since 1945, according to a White House Conference on Refugees, the United States has admitted 750,000 refugees and 2.5 million under regular immigration visas.

**June 3.** In 1956, South Africa removed all coloreds from the common electoral roll. Under new prime minister Hendrik Verwoerd, the Promotion of Bantu Self Government Bill further entrenches apartheid. The seven white representatives who could use their parliamentary votes for black South African interests are eliminated and the voting age is reduced to 18 to increase the number of white voters.

In turn, the legislation supposedly transfers political power to eight homeland authorities, or "Bantustans," created out of hundreds of native reserves. In reality, Parliament retains control over homeland defense, external affairs, and much of the economy and justice system. Except for one-third of elected officials at the lowest levels, the minister of Bantu affairs can approve, veto, or dismiss any chieftain.

Worse still, when the government keeps out private capital and offers little funding to develop the poor land, most of the blacks must depend on the earnings of those family members employed in European areas.

**June 27.** In the first rejection of a cabinet nominee since 1925, the Senate votes 49–46 against confirming Lewis L. Strauss as secretary of commerce. Opposition centered on the possibility that Strauss, while chairman of the AEC, withheld the true story of radiation fallout in the United States.

**June 28.** West Germany accepts responsibility for Communist East Germany in compensating victims of Nazi persecution. With 900,000 cases settled, at a cost of $1.43 billion, Bonn promises to speed up the remaining 1.6 million claims.

**July 24.** On his first visit to Moscow and his first meeting with Nikita Khrushchev, Vice-President

Richard Nixon engages the premier in a day-long political debate. When the two visit a U.S. exhibit, a boastful Nixon asks, "Would it not be better to compete in the relative merits of washing machines than in the strength of rockets?" Khrushchev, in turn, charges, "You don't know anything about Communism except fear."

After American TV networks broadcast the taped exchange two days later, the vice-president's popularity soars. (The Soviet version, televised on the 27th, reportedly offers an inadequate translation of Nixon's remarks.)

**August 12.** Governor Faubus of Arkansas submits to a federal court ruling, and local police maintain order as five black students enroll in Little Rock public schools. Last year, the governor closed city high schools to prevent integration, then reopened them as state-funded private institutions.

**August 18.** Foreign ministers of 21 American states condemn any attempt to overthrow a legitimate government, even a dictatorship, in the Declaration of Santiago de Chile.

**August 21.** President Eisenhower proclaims Hawaii the 50th state. Since 1903, islanders had petitioned for statehood at least 17 times. Congressional opposition arose from the Southerners' fear of a largely nonwhite population, concerns with admitting a state so far from the mainland (overcome by improvements in air travel), and, more recently, misgivings about Communist influence in Hawaii's longshore and plantation unions.

Although Hawaii brings just 6,345 square miles into the nation, the islands add 585,000 people. Two senators and one representative for Hawaii raise Senate membership to 100 and that of the House to 437.

**September 8.** The Civil Rights Commission reports on Negro housing, education, and, particularly, voting rights. With 11 Southern states registering a mere 24 percent of eligible black voters (compared to 64.5 percent of whites), the 668-page document recommends corrective legislative measures, including the controversial appointment of temporary federal registrars. When Southern newspapers bitterly attack the "leaked" report, the commission—due for disbandment—receives a two-year extension.

**September 14.** Eisenhower signs the Landrum-Griffin Act, the first major labor law since 1947. Demands for new legislation arose after a two-year investigation uncovered corruption in the Teamsters and other unions.

The act includes a workers' bill of rights and eliminates the Taft-Hartley non-Communist affidavit, but unions must file annual financial reports and restrict their picketing. The AFL-CIO vows to work against the reelection of any member of Congress who voted for the act.

**September 15.** Premier Khrushchev and his wife visit the United States at the invitation of President Eisenhower, who hopes to break the impasse over Berlin. After a 10-day tour of the country and talks at Camp David, the leaders announce the withdrawal of Khrushchev's 1958 Berlin ultimatum. But, like the "Spirit of Geneva" in 1955, the "Spirit of Camp David" will be short-lived.

For Americans, the most memorable moment of Khrushchev's visit was his loud disappointment when the Secret Service overruled a trip to Disneyland as too risky.

**October 12.** The Supreme Court sustains the decision of a Mississippi Circuit Appeals Court to void the murder conviction of a Negro. Half the county population is Negro yet the list of registered voters includes only whites.

**October 19.** In a major policy change, the U.S. Development Loan Fund announces that in the future underdeveloped countries must spend grants on American goods. Critics complain that the policy will damage world trade.

**October 19.** President Eisenhower invokes the Taft-Hartley Act on the 116th day of a steel workers' strike. The Supreme Court upholds the law, ordering the men back to the mills during negotiations. The strike—one of the longest and most damaging in American history—ends in January, with the union winning major concessions. (Even before the strike, the Bureau of Labor listed the steel workers' average $3.11 per hour as one of the highest industrial wages.)

**November 3.** On the anniversary of their independence, nationalists try to parade the Panamanian flag into the canal zone. (Extending five miles on each side of the canal, the zone was granted to the U.S. in 1903 for aiding the revolution against Columbia. Still, Washington pays an annual fee, some $1.9 million since 1955.) When the Americans refuse access, the demonstrators riot.

To ease the resulting ill will, Eisenhower orders officials to fly the Panamanian and American flags together in a canal zone plaza (effective September 7, 1960). In Washington, many view this concession as the first step in the surrender of U.S. treaty rights.

**November 9.** Just before Thanksgiving Day, Americans learn that a weed-killer capable of causing cancer in rats has contaminated Oregon and Washington cranberries. But, after examination, authorities impound just 250,000 pounds of affected berries, while 20 million pounds clear in time for the holiday.

**November 17.** The National Defense Education Act requires applicants for student loans to sign an affidavit denying they are subversives. Today, Harvard and Yale withdraw from the program in protest. Another 22 institutions will withdraw in whole or part and 82 state their disapproval by the end of the academic year.

**December 1.** A 12-nation treaty sets the Antarctic aside as a scientific preserve after Britain, Chile, Argentina, and other nations had come close to war over rival territorial claims. (The United States and the USSR make no claims and recognize none.) Following ratification, the treaty will become effective in 1961. Alterable only by unanimous consent, the agreement will be subject to review in 30 years.

## Obituaries

**Henry Brittain** (circa 1874–August 14, 1959). The engineer-shipbuilder, in his youth, invented the ice cream cone. While selling ice cream at the St. Louis World's Fair in 1898, Brittain noticed that sweet pancakes in the next concession booth had curled into cones on a cold griddle. He grabbed some and inverted them over his frozen treat. Several others laid claim to the idea, including ice cream and candy manufacturer Italo Marchiony (circa 1868–July 27, 1954).

**John Foster Dulles** (February 25, 1888–May 24, 1959). As Eisenhower's secretary of state (1953–1959), the career diplomat followed an anti–Communist policy of "brinkmanship"—the preparation for and willingness to go to the brink of war. American politicians and world leaders pilloried Dulles for his inflexibility, but many conceded the stubborn secretary likely prevented the expansion of Soviet and Chinese Communism.

**Maurice Duplessis** (April 20, 1890–September 7, 1959). The French-Canadian premier of Quebec (1936–1939, 1944–1959) championed provincial autonomy, but an enormous patronage system made him one of the country's most controversial political figures.

**William "Bull" Halsey** (October 30, 1882–August 16, 1959). During W.W.II, as commander of U.S. naval forces in the South Pacific and later as commander of the Third Fleet, Halsey was a leading contributor to the defeat of Japan. Promoted to a five-star fleet admiral at the end of the war, he retired in 1947.

**George C. Marshall** (December 31, 1880–October 16, 1959). As army chief of staff, Marshall directed U.S. strategy in W.W.II. He resigned in 1945, but answered Truman's quick call to negotiate in the Chinese Civil War. Two years later, the president appointed him secretary of state, in which capacity he developed the Marshall Plan to rebuild war-torn Europe. He resigned again in January 1949, then returned to Washington in 1950 to serve one year as secretary of defense. In 1953, Marshall received the Nobel peace prize for his economic program.

**Walter Williams** (November 14, 1842?–December 19, 1959). The man reported to be the last survivor of the Civil War (1861–1865) dies at the age of 117, and President Eisenhower orders flags flown at half mast to honor all Civil War veterans. Investigators failed to find Williams' Confederate service record and suggested that he was only five years old when the war broke out; if this is

true, William A. Lundy, who died in September 1957, was the last surviving Civil War veteran.

# BEGINNINGS AND ENDINGS

## News

**January 1.** As revolutionaries gain control in Cuba, the oldest U.S. military post on foreign soil closes its gates. Guantanamo, at the eastern end of the island's south coast, was leased by the Americans in 1903—in perpetuity. Washington will continue to pay $4,085 annual rent, but Castro never cashes the checks.

**January 25.** American Airlines inaugurates the first regularly scheduled transcontinental jet passenger service, from Los Angeles to New York. The Boeing 707 cuts 2 hours, 7 minutes off the 1954 propeller-plane record of 6 hours, 10 minutes.

**February 12.** A redesigned Lincoln-head penny replaces the stylized wheat stalks on the "tails" side with the Lincoln Memorial. (The coin first circulated in 1909, the centenary of the president's birth.)

**February 20.** After a 37-percent gain over the past year, the Dow Jones Average tops the 600 mark for the first time.

**April 10.** The first member of the Japanese royal family to marry a commoner, Crown Prince Akihito weds Michiko Shoda.

**April 16.** In the first hijacking of a Cuba-U.S. flight, four supporters of ex-dictator Batista seize a Havana-Miami flight to escape Castro's firing squads.

**April 19.** Ida Pidoux is the first woman in Switzerland to vote in a canton (district) election. (The all-male electorate has refused to grant women the vote in federal elections.)

**May 22.** President Eisenhower promotes USAF General Benjamin Davis, age 46, to major general, making him the first black to attain a comparable rank in any of the Armed Forces.

**September 15.** George P. Vanier succeeds Vincent Massey as governor general of Canada.

**October 28.** The Australian airline Qantas inaugurates the first regularly scheduled round-the-world jet passenger service. (Pan Am's New York-Los Angeles route excludes the continental United States.)

**December 26.** In the first walk for charity, 21 entrants in Wiltshire, England, raise about $56 for the World Refugee Fund.

**More news.** This year, Thailand outlaws opium and closes some 900 licensed smoking dens.

• Egyptian-born Yasir Arafat and others form a movement to liberate Palestine. Naming their group Al-Fatah, or "conquest," the revolutionary leaders take noms de guerre, based on Abu, or "father of," to conceal their identities (Arafat becomes Abu Ammar).

### New Products and Businesses

The Mead Johnson Co. of Evansville, Indiana, launches the diet drink Metrecal. Its enormous success spawns the diet-food industry.

General Mills offers another sugar-coated breakfast cereal, Frosty O's.

Coca-Cola Ltd. debuts a new soft drink, Fanta. In response to Volkswagen's ever-growing pop-ularity, U.S. automakers bring out several new compact cars—the Falcon from Ford, the Corvair from Chevrolet, the Lark from Studebaker, and the Valiant from Chrysler. (Ford registered the name Falcon just 20 minutes before Chrysler.)

*Note:* The battle of the fins climaxes with the Cadillac 42-inch rise from the ground.

---

*Statistics:* This year, Japan manufactures 79,000 cars (mostly Toyotas and Datsuns) compared to 110 in 1947.

---

At the New York Toy Fair, Mattel Inc. introduces an 11½ inch doll with an adult figure and a passel of miniature clothes. Other manufacturers mock the concept, but, in the next decade, every little girl will clamor for a Barbie (Ruth and Elliott Handler named the doll after their daughter).

### Fads

The last in a decade of goofy stunts, telephone-booth stuffing spreads from South Africa to London, then skips across to the American Midwest and California this spring. Rules vary; in London someone must make or receive a phone call whereas at MIT, mathematicians simply cram in 19 bodies.

## SCIENCE AND TECHNOLOGY

### News

**January 2.** *Luna 1* is the first spacecraft to escape the Earth's gravitational pull. The Soviet satellite passes within 4,660 miles of the moon before hurtling on to orbit the sun.

**February.** Los Angeles detective Hugh C. McDonald has produced 500 master foils of lips, eyes, chins, hairlines, and other facial features from some 50,000 photos. This month, the first Identikit likeness results in an arrest.

*Ford tries for "road recognition" with the Edsel, but with over $450 million invested and only 11,000 cars sold, the name becomes synonymous with colossal failure in American culture.*

**February 6.** In his patent application, Jack Kilby of Texas Instruments proposes placing transistor, resistors, capacitor, and distributed capacitor on a single slice of silicon to simplify computer circuitry and connections. But he offers no solution for interconnections.

On July 30, Robert Noyce files a patent for Fairchild Semiconductor. Last year, coworker Jean Hoerni suggested layering silicon on top of a negative-positive-negative chip to keep off contaminants. (The application is called to the "planar process" after the flat plane of oxide.) Noyce, extending that concept, puts transistors, circuit components, and interconnections onto a chip—an integrated circuit.

Texas Instruments and Fairchild agree to call the men coinventors and proceed with manufacturing. (Noyce will be granted the patent on April 26, 1961.) Initially, the simplified circuit arouses little interest; at the beginning of the next decade, the price stands at $120. Then the military picks up the technology. To meet the demands of the Apollo program, manufacturers will etch 1,000 circuits onto a chip by 1969; six years later, that figure will pass 30,000.

**February 17.** After six failed attempts, the U.S. Navy successfully launches the first weather satellite, *Vanguard II.*

**March 4.** Just 13 months after the launching of their first satellite, the Americans send *Pioneer 4* past the moon into solar orbit. But the craft bypasses the moon by 37,300 miles rather than by the programmed 15,000. Henceforth, Pioneers will carry out planetary missions.

**March 19.** The MIT Lincoln Lab reports the first known radar contact with Venus. The signals, sent in February 1958, made the 28.2-million-mile round-trip in 295–302 seconds. Preliminary calculations show the solar system to be somewhat smaller than expected.

**April 8.** Faced with the possibility of more than one business programming language, a group of six manufacturers, academics, and users meet today, and again on May 28, to discuss computer specifications. Grace Hopper's Flow-matic (the first English-language data-processing compiler) serves as a reference point, and a working group completes COBOL

(common business-oriented language) in a year. With no ties to a specific manufacturer, and with syntax and terms much like spoken English, CO-BOL will be readily adopted by both industry and the government.

**April 9.** At a press conference, NASA introduces the seven test pilots chosen to be the first astronauts: Scott Carpenter, Gordon Cooper, John Glenn, Gus Grissom, Wally Schirra, Alan Shepard, and Deke Slayton. The American public, desperate to catch up with the Soviets, turns the men into instant heroes.

**May 28.** Monkeys Able and Baker ride a Jupiter rocket 300 miles up and 1,600 miles down range from Cape Canaveral. (Rumors persist that animals have traveled into the stratosphere for the United States before—a monkey and some mice in 1951.)

**June 11.** Traveling on a 9-inch cushion of air, Christopher Cockerell steers his experimental hovercraft across the English Channel. Modifications increase the speed from 25 mph to 68 mph, and rubber skirts allow the craft to clear the water by up to 7 feet.

**August 7.** *Explorer VI*, the first satellite developed completely by NASA, reaches orbit. A week later, the "paddlewheel" transmits the first crude TV images of earth. The satellite will fall into the atmosphere and burn up in late October.

**August 21.** Mercury test flights get under way. The program intends to put a man into orbit, test his ability to function in space, and bring him back safely. Craft will use existing technology, with the simplest and most reliable systems design.

**August 23.** British anthropologist Louis S. B. Leakey announces the discovery of fossils 600,000–1 million years old. The man-ape skull fragments, found in Tanganyika's Olduvai Gorge, are named *Zinjanthropus boisei*, but anthropologists later refer to the species as *Australopithecus.*

**August 26.** Designed by Alexander Issigonis during the 1956 oil crisis, the new Morris Mini-Minor uses a transversely mounted engine for front-wheel drive. Many deride the car's styling, but auto manufacturers around the world copy a concept that increases maneuverability.

**September 7.** Geologist Rhodes Fairbridge reports that ocean levels slowly rose 45 feet some 6,000 years ago, wiping out many early communities. He speculates that the Great Flood of the Old Testament and other ancient writings may have described this event.

**September 14.** *Luna 2* makes man's first contact with the moon, an undignified crash onto the surface. Before impact, instruments on board show that no significant magnetic field exists.

On October 4, the second anniversary of *Sputnik*, the USSR launches *Luna 3*, the first satellite to orbit the moon. Before the end of the month, Moscow newspapers release photographs of the far side with several named features, including the "Soviet" Mountains. But after a promising beginning, the USSR moon program grinds to an unexplained halt.

**September 17.** The closest yet to a winged spacecraft, the X-15 completes its first powered flight. The rocket-planes will train NASA pilots at extreme speeds and high altitudes through to 1968.

---

*Statistics*: About 94 percent of U.S. telephones are dial-operated, but only 15 million Americans can dial long-distance calls.

---

**November 13.** In West Virginia, the National Radio Astronomy Observatory plans to listen for radio signals from intelligent life in other solar systems. Early next year, Project Ozma—named after the queen of the Land of Oz—will aim parabolic antenna at stars 12 light-years from earth.

**More news.** The Xerox 914, the first production-line photocopying machine, makes six copies a minute.

• Earl C. Thom, a researcher at the Office of Climatology, invents the temperature-humidity index (THI) to measure the comfort level of hot summer days.

### Other Discoveries, Developments, and Inventions

Ski-Doo snowmobile from Joseph-Armand Bombardier in Quebec

Telescoped jetway for deplaning passengers

First U.S.-produced rear-engine car, the Chevrolet Corvair

USS *Long Beach*, the first nuclear-powered merchant ship

Telephone cable between North America and Europe

*Savannah*, the first U.S. nuclear-powered merchant ship

### Obituaries

**Sidney Baruch** (March 14, 1895–September 22, 1959). The American engineer's 200 inventions included the depth charge.

**Ross Harrison** (January 13, 1870–September 30, 1959). His simple method of transplantation, which allowed cells to grow outside the host body, galvanized scientific research.

## THE ARTS

March 11—*A Raisin in the Sun*, with Sidney Poitier, Claudia McNeil (530 perfs.)

May 21—*Gypsy*, with Ethel Merman, Jack Klugman (702 perfs.)

October 19—*The Miracle Worker*, with Anne Bancroft, Patty Duke (719 perfs.)

November 16—*The Sound of Music*, with Mary Martin, Theodore Bikel (1,443 perfs.)

November 23—*Fiorello!*, with Tom Bosley, Ellen Hanley, Howard Da Silva (795 perfs.)

### Tony Awards

Actor (Dramatic)—Jason Robards, Jr., *The Disenchanted*

Actress (Dramatic)—Gertrude Berg, *A Majority of One*

Actor (Musical)—Richard Kiley, *Redhead*

Actress (Musical)—Gwen Verdon, *Redhead*

Play—*J. B.*

Musical—*Redhead*

## News

**February 17.** In her Covent Garden debut, Joan Sutherland sings "Lucia di Lammermour." (She performs the same role at the Met in 1961.) Critics praise the Australian soprano as one of the greatest coloratura technicians in operatic history.

**April 16.** During a tour of the United States—the company's fourth trip out of the USSR in 200 years—the Bolshoi Ballet premieres *Romeo and Juliet* in New York. American reviewers praise the dancers' vitality, but criticize the conventional choreography and dated sets and costumes.

**June 24.** An anonymous British collector pays $770,000 for Ruben's *Adoration of the Magi*—a record auction price for a single painting. As well, this year, sales of individual artists reach new highs—$255,000 for a Renoir, $180,000 for a Degas.

**August 5.** The New York Philharmonic launches an official European tour with a concert in Athens. The 18 performances in the Soviet Union mark the first appearance of an American symphony there since the Russian Revolution.

**October 17.** *The Drunkard*, a 19th-century melodrama, ends an epic run at the Theatre Mart in Los Angeles. It opened July 6, 1933.

**October 21.** In 1943, Solomon R. Guggenheim commissioned Frank Lloyd Wright to design a museum for his collection of modern art. The architect's inverted white cone floats paintings out from the wall and down the length of a six-story spiral ramp. Some liken the Guggenheim Museum, which opens today in New York, to a Jell-O mold.

**December 18.** Birgit Nilsson makes her Met debut in *Tristan und Isolde*. The 41-year-old Swede is regarded as the finest Wagnerian soprano of her time.

**More news.** This year, in London, violinist Neville Marriner organizes several string players into the Academy of St. Martin-in-the-Fields. The chamber orchestra quickly gains an international reputation.

## Obituaries

**Maxwell Anderson** (December 15, 1888–February 28, 1959). His several plays included *What Price Glory?* (1924) and *Key Largo* (1939).

**Heitor Villa-Lobos** (March 5, 1884–November 17, 1959). Widely regarded as the foremost South American composer of his era, the Brazilian produced every conceivable type of music in 1,300 compositions.

**Frank Lloyd Wright** (June 8, 1869–April 9, 1959). One of the world's greatest architects, "he sought an architecture that kept life whole without keeping it back" (Edgar Kaufmann, Jr.). Prairie homes conformed to the terrain, the Imperial Hotel in Tokyo survived the 1922 earthquake, and a house at Bear Run, Pennsylvania (1936), stands over a waterfall.

## WORDS

Saul Bellow, *Henderson the Rain King*
Taylor Caldwell, *Dear and Glorious Physician*
Allen Drury, *Advise and Consent*
Ian Fleming, *Goldfinger*
Errol Flynn, *My Wicked, Wicked Ways*
Paul Gallico, *Mrs. 'Arrís Goes to Paris*
Moss Hart, *Act One: An Autobiography*
Shirley Jackson, *The Haunting of Hill House*
James A. Michener, *Hawaii*
Vance Packard, *The Status Seekers*
Mordecai Richler, *The Apprenticeship of Duddy Kravitz*
Philip Roth, *Goodbye, Columbus*
William Strunk, Jr., *Elements of Style*

## News

**February 23.** In London, a manuscript of *Canterbury Tales* fetches $42,560. Experts believe the copy was penned shortly after Chaucer's death in 1400.

**July 21.** Last month, the U.S. Postmaster General banned *Lady Chatterley's Lover*. Today, District Judge Frederick vanPelt Bryan holds that postal officials possess no special competence to evaluate morality and finds D. H. Lawrence's book is not obscene.

The first unexpurgated editions of the infamous novel shoot onto the best-seller list. In later years, sociologists will point to the Lady Chatterley decision as the dawn of a more permissive attitude toward sexuality.

**November 18.** The Vatican announces an intended revision of the 1929 Catholic index of forbidden books.

### Cartoons and Comics

**This year**—In France, writer René Goscinny and artist Albert Uderzo create the comic strip *Astérix*. The little Gaul, in his exploits against Caesar's legions, wins fans around the world.

### TIME *Man of the Year*

Dwight D. Eisenhower

### New Words and Phrases

backup (a substitute)
Beer-B-Q (a barbecue with beer as the main beverage)
bubble bug (a helicopter)
corridor (a traffic freeway or throughway in a built-up area)
denuclearization zone
go-karting
silo (a concrete ICBM "nest")
valet parking

### Obituaries

**Raymond Chandler** (July 23, 1888–March 26, 1959). A journalist first, Chandler found instant success with his first mystery, *The Big Sleep* (1939). Other literate crime novels followed—*Farewell My Lovely* (1940), *The Lady in the Lake* (1943)—and several screenplays, including *Double Indemnity* (1944).

**Sax Rohmer (Arthur Sarsfield Ward)** (February 15, 1883–June 1, 1959). The prolific British writer was best known for some 30 Dr. Fu Manchu novels. In 1955, Rohmer sold all rights to his villainous character for a reported $4 million.

# FASHION

## Haute Couture

Large-scale rejection of the sack and chemise marks the end of an era for French haute couture. In the fall, critics ruthlessly denounce St. Laurent's hobbled skirt, and Paris must now compete with the United States.

This year's softer silhouette cuts full sleeves in one piece with the bodice, redefines the waistline (some styles wrap a wide sash or cummerbund from bosom to hip), adds blousing at the back, and slims down the skirt line.

## News

**This year.** With sedate colors (black, brown, gray, dark blue) still garnering 70–90 percent of hose's highest sales, mills tone down lurid shades of red, pink, green, and orange to improve their share of the market. (Catalogs advertise full-fashioned anklet sheers for 79 cents.)

*For the company's first bikini, Cole of California adds side-ties to adjust the width of the bottom half.*

• Ignoring an unwritten rule of high fashion, Pierre Cardin presents the first collection of designer ready-to-wear clothing for women. The prestigious Chambre syndicale Couture Parisienne expels Cardin, but when others follow his lead he will be readmitted in 1963.

• Lady Dowding founds Beauty Without Cruelty Cosmetics, a line made from the natural oils of nuts, fruits, plants, and the essence of flowers. The cosmetics contain no animal products and no animals are used in clinical tests.

## Colors and Materials

Greens predominate in the spring. Muted fall colors make brown a favorite in every shade.

In June, at her second marriage, Brigitte Bardot wears a short dress of pink-and-white gingham. By summer, the plain-weave cotton—striped and checked—becomes a fad fabric.

Sportswear emphasizes gold and olive green.

Unusual weaves create a double-exposure effect with one color peeking through another.

## Clothes

Below-the-knee hemlines and three-quarter-length sleeves remain popular.

Short suit jackets lengthen and slim into a soft, natural line with unpadded shoulders.

A long, narrow evening dress replaces the bouffant line. This year, women choose a matching silk coat rather than a stole or fur cape.

The cropped jacket in various fabrics tops all casual wear. Pants just skim the ankle.

In menswear, retailers remark on the more brightly colored sportswear and note increased sales in blazer sports coats and light-colored formal clothes.

## Accessories

New shoes display rounded toes and more moderate heels, but the popular stiletto narrows to a ¼-inch width. (When Italians strengthen their heels with long steel nails, pockmarks suddenly appear on rugs, wooden floors, and other surfaces.) Leather shoes display an eggshell finish in beige, cream, oyster, and white.

The wide leather belt returns by the end of the year.

Fashionable since early in the century, bathing caps start to disappear after reaching their most extravagant form during this decade—ribbons, attached flowers, contrasting fabric bands.

Milliners reintroduce pillboxes. Turbans frequently match dress patterns.

Bead necklaces—the jewelry highlight of the year—combine crystals and pastel gems.

## Hair and Cosmetics

A revival of the Garbo and Carole Lombard look—polo coats, blond materials, deep swagger hats—brings back softer hair.

A department store in New York sells wigs in 15 different shades including "orange ice."

In a short-lived fad, some 30 cosmetic companies offer white lipstick.

# POPULAR MUSIC

"Mack the Knife"—Bobby Darin
"The Battle of New Orleans"—Johnny Horton
"Venus"—Frankie Avalon
"Stagger Lee"—Lloyd Price
"Lonely Boy"—Paul Anka
"The Three Bells"—Browns
"Come Softly to Me"—Fleetwoods
"Smoke Gets in Your Eyes"—Platters
"Heartaches by the Number"—Guy Mitchell
"Sleep Walk" (Instr.)—Santo & Johnny
"Kansas City"—Wilbert Harrison
"A Big Hunk O' Love"—Elvis Presley
"The Happy Organ" (Instr.)—Dave "Baby" Cortez
"Mr. Blue"—Fleetwoods
"Why"—Frankie Avalon
"Put Your Head on My Shoulder"—Paul Anka
"Personality"—Lloyd Price
"Charlie Brown"—Coasters

"Donna"—Ritchie Valens
"16 Candles"—Crests
"Sea of Love"—Phil Phillips with the Twilights
"My Happiness"—Connie Francis
"Don't You Know"—Della Reese
"There Goes My Baby"—Drifters
"Dream Lover"—Bobby Darin
"(Now and Then There's) A Fool Such As I"—
Elvis Presley

## Grammy Awards (1959)

Record of the Year—Bobby Darin, "Mack the Knife"
Song of the Year (songwriter)—Jimmy Driftwood, "The Battle of New Orleans"
Album of the Year—Frank Sinatra, *Come Dance With Me*
Best Vocal Performance (Male)—Frank Sinatra, *Come Dance With Me*
Best Vocal Performance (Female)—Ella Fitzgerald, "But Not for Me"
Best New Artist of the Year—Bobby Darin

## News

**February.** The first album with no outside evidence of the artist's name, *For LP Fans Only* includes previously released Presley songs such as "Lawdy, Miss Clawdy" and "Shake, Rattle and Roll."

**February 3.** On their way to North Dakota in a small plane after a concert, Buddy Holly, J. P. Richardson, and Ritchie Valens die in a crash outside Mason City, Iowa. (Guitarist Tommy Allsup lost a coin toss with Valens and took the tour bus.) Tributes pour in from other musicians, particularly for Holly. Yet the newspaper in his hometown of Lubbock, Texas, carries just a few short paragraphs and teenagers make up a large part of the 1,000 people at his funeral. Much of Holly's rock 'n' roll legend will follow as his former manager releases demos, with dubbed backings, through the next decade.

**June 17.** A British court awards Wladziu Valentino Liberace $22,400 in a libel suit against the *London Daily Mirror.* The newspaper had implied in a 1956 editorial that the 40-year-old popular pianist was a homosexual.

**October 4.** *The New York Times* compares the new RCA four-track tape cartridge with the relatively new Ampex four-track reel. At 7 inches per second (ips), the open reel produces excellent quality sound on any standard stereo recorder. The cartridge sound is also good, despite the 3³/₄ ips, but buyers need a special machine ($299 and $10 for a second speaker) for the paperback-size plastic case. Still, the cartridge requires no threading and its $4.95 price tag compares favorably with $6.95–$9.95 for a reel.

**More news.** Chuck Berry brought a 14-year-old girl up from Mexico to work in his St. Louis nightclub. Later fired, she complains to the police and the black singer is charged with transporting a minor across state lines for immoral purposes. He eventually will go to jail in 1962 and serve two years.

With Berry in trouble, Jerry Lee Lewis all but ostracized, Elvis in the army, and Holly dead, clean-cut stars and newcomers take over the pop music scene. Radio stations and "American Bandstand" give air time to Pat Boone, Frankie Avalon, Bobby Rydell, James Darren, as well as singer personalities such as Fabian and Edd "Kookie" Byrnes. And several new dances—the Dog, the Shag, and the Alligator—are banned as too sexy.

• Last year when Connie Francis scored a hit with "Stupid Cupid," would-be songwriter Neil Sedaka abandoned his training as a concert pianist to collaborate with lyricist Howard Greenfield. Sedaka's high-pitched voice puts their tune "Oh! Carol" into the top 10.

• For his live *Caravan of Stars* stage shows, Dick Clark acts as MC while artists perform two or three songs, all backed by the same band. With the enormous popularity of "American Bandstand," the shows attract capacity crowds across the country.

• Fans pick Jan Berry and Dean Torrance as the most significant new group.

• Cliff Richard becomes the first British teen idol.

• The Philadelphia Symphony Orchestra and the Mormon Tabernacle Choir amaze the pop music industry with their best-selling rendition of "The Battle Hymn of the Republic."

• Joan Baez gains recognition with her appearance at the Newport Folk Festival.

• One of the top hit makers of the decade, Guy Mitchell once again reaches No. 1, but "Heartaches by the Number" marks his last appearance on the pop charts. Columbia will drop Mitchell two years later, and he will fail to break through with other labels.

• Stereo LP's increase their share of the market to 20 percent while importers introduce or bring back long-established European labels such as Deutsche Grammophon and Telefunken.

• With mail-order clubs handling a large share of record sales, more and more dealers offer discounts.

• Songwriter Berry Gordy, Jr., borrows $800 from a family savings club to open Tamla Records in a house he dubs Hitsville, USA. Next year, Gordy adapts Detroit's nickname—Motor City—to incorporate as Motown Record Corp. His company becomes the prime outlet for talented black singles and groups.

*New Recording Artists*

Annette (Funicello)
Brook Benton
Chubby Checker
James Darren
Fabian
Isley Brothers
Jan & Dean
Cliff Richard
Bobby Rydell
Bobby Vee

## Obituaries

**Mack Gordon** (June 21, 1904–March 1, 1959). The lyricist teamed with Harry Revel in the 1930s and Harry Warren in the 1940s to produce such hits as "Did You Ever See a Dream Walking?" (1933) and "Chattanooga Choo Choo" (1941).

**Billy Holiday** (April 7, 1915–July 17, 1959). Soon after her first professional appearance at the age of 15, the young black singer caught Benny Goodman's attention. She sang with his orchestra and the Count Basie and Artie Shaw bands. Jazz fans and critics recognized one of the great jazz vocalists of all time, but Lady Day never won broad public acceptance. Always insecure, she fought alcoholism and a narcotics addiction for much of her

adult life. As the unique timbre of her voice deteriorated, Holiday's career declined.

**Buddy Holly** (September 7, 1936–February 3, 1959). In just two years, the American singer and songwriter recorded some of rock 'n' roll's best: "That'll Be the Day" (1957), "Oh, Boy!" (1957), "Maybe Baby" (1958), "Think It Over" (1958) with the Crickets; "Peggy Sue" (1957), "Rave On" (1958), "Early in the Morning" (1958) alone.

His guitar-based band, with their drums and R&B back beat, set the mold for white rock groups. And Holly, with his interest in production techniques, pioneered double-tracking and overdubbing. His vocal style (often described as "hiccuping") will influence countless rock artists including Bobby Vee and Paul McCartney.

After the split with the Crickets at the end of last year, Holly took up a heavy touring schedule for financial reasons. He was 22 years old at the time of the fatal plane crash.

**Samuel M. Lewis** (October 25, 1885–November 22, 1959). The U.S. lyricist collaborated on several hits, including "Five Foot Two, Eyes of Blue" (1925) and "I'm Sitting on Top of the World" (1925).

**Jack Norworth** (January 5, 1879–September 1, 1959). The composer and lyricist wrote an estimated 3,000 popular songs. His best-known words remain "Take Me Out to the Ball Game," written with Albert Von Tilzer in 1908.

**J. P. Richardson** (October 24, 1930 or October 29, 1932–February 3, 1959). Another victim of the plane crash in Iowa, the DJ moonlighted as the Big Bopper. His "Chantilly Lace" was one of last year's international hits.

**Ritchie Valens** (May 13, 1941–February 3, 1959). The first Chicano rock star reached No. 2 with a song written for his girlfriend, "Donna." But the flip side, "La Bamba," emerges as the longer lasting hit.

# MOVIES

*Anatomy of a Murder* (d. Otto Preminger; bw)—
    James Stewart, Lee Remick, Ben Gazzara, Eve
    Arden, Arthur O'Connell, George C. Scott
*Ben-Hur* (d. William Wyler; color)—Charlton

Heston, Stephen Boyd, Jack Hawkins, Hugh Griffith, Martha Scott

*Compulsion* (d. Richard Fleischer; bw)—Orson Welles, Diane Varsi, Dean Stockwell, Bradford Dillman

*Darby O'Gill and the Little People* (Disney, d. Robert Stevenson; color)—Albert Sharpe, Janet Munro, Sean Connery, Jimmy O'Dea

*Devil's Disciple* (d. Guy Hamilton; bw)—Burt Lancaster, Kirk Douglas, Laurence Olivier

*Hiroshima, Mon Amour* (French, d. Alain Resnais; bw)—Emmanuele Riva, Eiji Okada

*Journey to the Center of the Earth* (d. Henry Levin; color)—James Mason, Pat Boone, Arlene Dahl

*The Mouse That Roared* (British, d. Jack Arnold; color)—Peter Sellers, Jean Seberg

*North by Northwest* (d. Alfred Hitchcock; color)—Cary Grant, Eva Marie Saint, James Mason

*The Nun's Story* (d. Fred Zinnemann; color)—Audrey Hepburn, Peter Finch, Edith Evans, Peggy Ashcroft

*On the Beach* (d. Stanley Kramer; bw)—Gregory Peck, Ava Gardner, Fred Astaire, Anthony Perkins

*Operation Petticoat* (d. Blake Edwards; color)—Cary Grant, Tony Curtis, Joan O'Brien, Dina Merrill

*Pillow Talk* (d. Michael Gordon; color)—Doris Day, Rock Hudson, Tony Randall, Thelma Ritter

*Porgy and Bess* (d. Otto Preminger; color)—Sidney Poitier, Dorothy Dandridge, Sammy Davis, Jr., Pearl Bailey

*Rio Bravo* (d. Howard Hawks; color)—John Wayne, Dean Martin, Ricky Nelson, Angie Dickinson, Walter Brennan

*Room at the Top* (British, d. Jack Clayton; bw)—Laurence Harvey, Simone Signoret, Heather Sears

*Shake Hands With the Devil* (d. Michael Anderson; bw)—James Cagney, Don Murray, Dana Wynter

*Sleeping Beauty* (Disney; color; animated)—Voices: Mary Costa (Princess Aurora); Bill

*John Wayne, gunslinger Ricky Nelson, and alluring Angie Dickinson in Howard Hawks' Rio Bravo.*

Shirley (Prince Phillip); Eleanor Audley (Maleficent)

*Some Like It Hot* (d. Billy Wilder; bw)—Jack Lemmon, Tony Curtis, Marilyn Monroe, Joe E. Brown, George Raft

### Academy Awards

**April 6.** This year's co-hosts include Bob Hope, David Niven, Tony Randall, Mort Sahl, Laurence Olivier, and Jerry Lewis.

Best Picture—*Gigi*

Best Actor—David Niven (*Separate Tables*)

Best Actress—Susan Hayward (*I Want to Live!*)

Best Director—Vincente Minnelli (*Gigi*)

Best Supporting Actor—Burl Ives (*The Big Country*)

Best Supporting Actress—Wendy Hiller (*Separate Tables*)

Best Song—"Gigi" from the film of the same name

Best Foreign Film—*My Uncle* (French)

Honorary Award—Maurice Chevalier

With nine Academy Awards, *Gigi* sets a single-film Oscar record. At the same time, the smash movie achieves a less noteworthy distinction—one of just seven best pictures in the Academy's 50-year history to be denied an acting nomination.

As winners and presenters gather on stage for the big finale—"There's No Business Like Show Business"—co-host Jerry Lewis learns the show is finishing 22 minutes ahead of schedule. To fill in time, the comic asks the audience to applaud Susan Hayward again. But after a few minutes the stage begins to empty and a desperate NBC switches to a short film.

*The New York Times* pans Lewis's entire performance as "a tour de force of uncompromising ineptitude."

## News

**May 12.** Actress Elizabeth Taylor and singer Eddie Fisher marry in Las Vegas, 3½ hours after his divorce from actress Debbie Reynolds. Last year, as Fisher and Reynolds consoled the recent widow, Eddie's concern blossomed into romance.

The press casts Taylor as a home-wrecker (Reynolds is left with two children), but Fisher suffers the full brunt of public indignation. He terminates an RCA recording contract in November and his career takes a nosedive.

**June 7.** *The New York Times* reports comedian Jerry Lewis has signed a seven-year deal with Paramount for $10 million, which is likely the biggest individual contract in Hollywood history.

**June 29.** The U.S. Supreme Court unanimously upsets a New York State judgment banning *Lady Chatterley's Lover* for depicting sexual immorality, perversion, and lewdness as desirable. The Supreme Court justices hold that the lower court, in attempting to prevent the French film's advocacy of an idea, "struck at the very heart of constitutionally protected liberty."

**More news.** In an inevitable concession to the power of the small screen, every Hollywood studio except Paramount produces movies this year for half-hour or one-hour broadcasts.

• Seven years in the making, *Sleeping Beauty* is Walt Disney's most ambitious animated film. But when initial box-office receipts fail to recover the

$6-million production costs, the technically outstanding film is seen as the last of an era.

• The mediocre Italian movie *Hercules*, starring former Mr. Universe Steve Reeves, strikes gold at the box office with a massive ad campaign and multi-theater bookings. Inevitably, foreign "spears and sandals" pictures flood the U.S. market.

• Sandra Dee plays *Gidget*—short for "girl midget"—and James Darren and Cliff Robertson provide the love interest in this popular teenage movie. (Gidget's philosophy of life hangs on her bedroom wall: "To be a real woman is to bring out the best in a man.") A 1961 sequel will star Deborah Walley, but Cindy Carol will replace her in the third film two years later.

• Tyronne Power's fatal heart attack last year forced *Solomon and Sheba* producers to start over again with Yul Brynner. On location in Spain, a filming error adds further costs to the budget. Rushes of a huge Old Testament battle scene clearly show an airplane flying overhead.

• The British comedy *Carry on Sergeant* becomes just the first in a series. An average two *Carry on* films will appear each year until the 1970s.

| Top Box Office Stars | Newcomers |
|---|---|
| Rock Hudson | Sandra Dee |
| Cary Grant | Ricky Nelson |
| James Stewart | James Garner |
| Doris Day | Curt Jurgens |
| Debbie Reynolds | Lee Remick |
| Glenn Ford | John Saxon |
| Frank Sinatra | Sidney Poitier |
| John Wayne | Ernie Kovacs |
| Jerry Lewis | Kathryn Grant |
| Susan Hayward | Carolyn Jones |

## Top Money-Maker of the Year

*Auntie Mame* (1958)

## Quote of the Year

"Look at that! Look how she moves! That's just like Jello on springs. She's got some sort of built-in motor or something, huh? I tell you it's a whole different sex."

Jack Lemmon drooling at his first glimpse of Marilyn Monroe in *Some Like It Hot.* (Screenplay by Billy Wilder and I. A. L. Diamond; suggested by a story by R. Thoeren and M. Logan)

## Obituaries

**Ethel Barrymore** (August 15, 1879–June 18, 1959). Another of the famous Barrymores, she first appeared on Broadway in 1900 and on the silent screen in 1914. The veteran actress won the 1944 Oscar for her supporting role in *None But the Lonely Heart.*

**Lou Costello** (March 6, 1908–March 3, 1959). The pudgy comic played the slapstick foil to straight-man Bud Abbott for 27 years. Immensely popular on radio and stage through the 1930s, the comedy team debuted on screen in 1940. Top box-office stars from 1948 to 1951, their humor proved less appealing in the 1950s, and the partnership ended in 1957 after 37 films. Still, their classic "Who's on First?" routine will keep audiences laughing forever.

**Cecil B. DeMille** (August 12, 1881–January 21, 1959). In 1913, DeMille, Samuel Goldfish (later Goldwyn), and Jessy Lasky chose the little Los Angeles suburb of Hollywood to set up an improvised movie studio. DeMille co-directed the first American feature film, *The Squaw Man*, in 1914. Then, as the studio grew into Paramount Pictures, his name became a household word when most fans knew only the big stars.

Many critics panned the director's 70 pictures—mainly spectaculars like *Cleopatra* (1934) and *The Ten Commandments* (1956)—calling them vulgar and unrealistic. Yet DeMille's creativity pushed the industry from two- and three-reelers to feature films and made Hollywood the film center of the world.

**Errol Flynn** (June 20, 1909–October 14, 1959). The handsome devil-may-care swashbuckler caught the public's fancy during the Depression (his marital and extramarital adventures produced the phrase "In like Flynn"), and he became one of the

highest-paid actors of his era. Today, Flynn is largely remembered for one of his earliest films, *Captain Blood* (1935)—and another made as his popularity waned—*Adventures of Don Juan* (1948). He died of a heart attack likely brought on by heavy drinking.

**Edmund Gwenn** (September 26, 1877–September 6, 1959). The British actor won an Oscar for his supporting role as the department store Santa Claus in *Miracle on 34th Street* (1947).

**Mario Lanza** (January 31, 1921–October 7, 1959). Although music critics described his voice as "untrained," the American tenor's eight films in 10 years (including *The Toast of New Orleans* [1950] and *The Great Caruso* [1951]) exposed moviegoers to operatic music as never before. But extreme weight changes and alcohol and barbiturate abuse eventually made him impossible to work with. His career in ruins, Lanza suffered a heart attack in Rome.

## TELEVISION AND RADIO

### New Prime-Time TV Programs

"Adventures in Paradise" (October 5, 1959–April 1, 1962; Adventure)—Gardner McKay, Weaver Levy

"Bat Masterson" (October 8, 1959–September 21, 1961; Western)—Gene Barry

"The Bell Telephone Hour" (October 9, 1959–April 26, 1968; Music)—Featuring the Bell Telephone Orchestra conducted by Donald Voorhees

"Bonanza" (September 12, 1959—January 16, 1973; Western)—Lorne Greene, Michael Landon, Dan Blocker, Pernell Roberts, Victor Sen Yung

"Dennis the Menace" (October 4, 1959–September 22, 1963; Situation Comedy)—Jay North, Herbert Anderson, Gloria Henry, Joseph Kearns (1959–1962)

"Hawaiian Eye" (October 7, 1959–September 10, 1963; Detective)—Bob (Robert) Conrad, Anthony Eisley (1959–1962), Connie Stevens, Poncie Ponce

"Laramie" (September 15, 1959–September 17, 1963; Western)—John Smith, Robert Fuller

"The Many Loves of Dobie Gillis" (September 29, 1959–September 18, 1963; Situation Comedy)—Dwayne Hickman, Bob Denver, Frank Faylen, Florida Fiebus

"Rawhide" (January 9, 1959–January 4, 1966; Western)—Eric Fleming (1959–1965), Clint Eastwood, Sheb Wooley (1959–1965)

"Riverboat" (September 13, 1959–January 16, 1961; Adventure)—Darren McGavin, Burt Reynolds (1959–1960)

"The Twilight Zone" (October 2, 1959–September 1964; Science Fiction Anthology)—Host: Rod Serling

"The Untouchables" (October 15, 1959–September 10, 1963; Police Drama)—Robert Stack

## Emmy Awards 1958–1959 (May 6, 1959)

Best Dramatic Series—"Playhouse 90" (CBS)

Best Musical or Variety Series—"The Dinah Shore Chevy Show" (NBC)

Best Comedy Series—"The Jack Benny Show" (CBS)

Best Actor in a Series—Raymond Burr ("Perry Mason," CBS)

Best Actress in a Series—Loretta Young ("The Loretta Young Show," NBC)

Best Comedian in a Series—Jack Benny ("The Jack Benny Show," CBS)

Best Comedienne in a Series—Jane Wyatt ("Father Knows Best," CBS and NBC)

## News

**March 8.** On "General Electric Theater" tonight, Harpo and Chico Marx perform a pantomime comedy while Groucho Marx, in a cameo spot, delivers the only line of dialogue. The program marks the last joint appearance of their careers.

**April 24.** With no DJs in 1935, the weekly radio program "Your Hit Parade" became America's authority on popular music. Each week, the Hit Paraders and the Lucky Strike Orchestra performed the top 15 songs, with Nos. 1, 2, and 3 kept for last.

Television picked up the program in 1950. But by mid-decade, rock 'n' roll had begun to edge out the ballad. Since younger viewers reject cover versions, the show ends tonight.

**Fall.** The last of the regularly scheduled, large-scale drama anthologies, "Playhouse 90," is reduced from biweekly appearances to a floating special.

**September 12.** This season, 27 Westerns completely dominate network television. "Bonanza" is the first Western broadcast in color.

**September 29.** With their problems and crazy way of talking, Dobie Gillis and his friends become TV's first real teens. Fans remember his "Thinker" pose in the park long after Dobie joins the army, attends college, and finally leaves the air.

**October 2.** The opening words of the first program forever alter America's concept of reality: "There is a sixth dimension beyond that which is known to man. It is a dimension as vast as space and as timeless as infinity. It is the middle ground between light and shadow—between science and superstition; between the pit of man's fears and the sunlight of his knowledge. It is the dimension of the imagination. It is an area that we call the Twilight Zone."

Narrator, producer, and chief writer, Rod Serling exercises nearly full control over his program. His scripts turn on a twist—the bookworm who survives nuclear war and his nagging wife only to break his eyeglasses—and stars and newcomers alike line up for parts—David Wayne, Agnes Moorehead, Ed Wynn, Robert Redford, Lee Marvin.

In the second season, the man behind the voice appears before the camera. Extremely nervous, Serling nonetheless enjoys his role.

**October 6.** The House Subcommittee on Legislative Oversight begins an investigation into TV quiz shows. The scandal finishes the big-money programs. CBS cancels its remaining three after the first witness swears he was given the answers.

Most of the producers, who too often picked champions on the basis of personal appeal, cop pleas. And 18 to 20 contestants who lied during the New York district attorney's investigation plead guilty to perjury. The former winners will receive suspended sentences, punishment enough in the eyes of the court for their humiliation. None of the sponsors involved will face any form of penalty.

**More news.** One blameless quiz show inadvertently helps the law this year. A winner on "The Price is Right," one of the season's top-rated programs, walks out of the theater into the arms of the police. He had been AWOL for 1½ years and a member of the Shore Patrol happened to watch the show. The contestant picks up his car—seven years later.

• Edd Byrnes plays the young assistant on the detective show "77 Sunset Strip." With his surfer good looks and slang ("squaresville" for dull and "antsville" for too many people), Kookie becomes this year's cool guy. Teenage boys imitate his slick movements with a pocket comb while girls snap up his record "Kookie, Kookie, Lend Me Your Comb." The novelty wanes at the beginning of the next decade.

• Over the last five years, phonograph record sales nearly tripled from $213 million to $613 million. Industry observers credit the enormous increase to rock radio stations broadcasting the latest hits.

• Since their introduction in 1955, RCA has sold color TVs at a loss. This year, with sales up 30 percent over 1958, the company finally turns a profit.

---

*Statistics:* Through the 1950s, U.S. television ownership rose by an astounding 5 million per year. Radio at its height of popularity sold 2 million annually.

---

• Ampex Corp., which introduced the first successful video recorder in 1956, brings out color video.

## TV Commercials

Jell-O—A Chinese-American baby tries to eat grape Jell-O with chopsticks.

Good & Plenty—The cartoon character Choo-Choo Charlie advertises the candy for the first time this year.

## Memorable Radio Programs End

"Backstage Wife" (August 5, 1935)
"One Man's Family" (May 17, 1933)
"Our Gal Sunday" (March 29, 1937)
"People are Funny" (April 3, 1942)
"Pepper Young's Family" (June, 1936)
"Road of Life" (September 13, 1937)
"You Bet Your Life" (October 27, 1947)

## Obituaries

**George Reeves** (April 6, 1914–June 16, 1959). The actor appeared in Hollywood movies such as *Gone With the Wind* during his 28-year career, but remained Superman to the millions who had watched the television show. Despondent over his typecasting, Reeves died of a self-inflicted gunshot wound.

# SPORTS

## Winners

### Baseball

World Series—Los Angeles Dodgers (NL), 4 games; Chicago White Sox (AL), 2 games
Player of the Year—Nellie Fox (Chicago White Sox, AL); Ernie Banks (Chicago Cubs, NL)
Rookie of the Year—Bob Allison (Washington Senators, AL); Willie McCovey (San Francisco Giants, NL)

### Football

NFL Championship—Baltimore Colts 31, New York Giants 16

College Bowls (January 1, 1959)—
  Rose Bowl, Iowa 38, California 12
  Cotton Bowl, Air Force 0, Texas Christian 0
  Orange Bowl, Oklahoma 21, Syracuse 6
  Sugar Bowl, LSU 7, Clemson 0
Heisman Trophy—Billy Cannon (LSU, HB)
Grey Cup—Winnipeg Blue Bombers 21,
  Hamilton Tiger-Cats 7

*Basketball*

NBA Championship—Boston Celtics, 4
  games; Minneapolis Lakers, 0 games
MVP of the Year—Bob Pettit (St. Louis
  Hawks)
Rookie of the Year—Elgin Baylor (Minneapolis
  Lakers)
NCAA Championship—California 71, West
  Virginia 70

*Tennis*

U.S. National—Men, Neale Fraser (vs. Ale-
  jandro Olmedo); Women, Maria Bueno (vs.
  Christine Truman)
Wimbledon—Men, Alejandro Olmedo (vs.
  Rod Laver); Women, Maria Bueno (vs. Dar-
  lene Hard)

*Golf*

Masters—Art Wall, Jr.
U.S. Open—Billy Casper
British Open—Gary Player

*Hockey*

Stanley Cup—Montreal Canadiens, 4 games;
  Toronto Maple Leafs, 1 game

*Ice Skating*

World Championship—Men, David Jenkins
  (U.S.); Women, Carol Heiss (U.S.)
U.S. National—Men, David Jenkins; Women,
  Carol Heiss
Canadian National—Men, Donald Jackson;
  Women, Margaret Crosland

*Kentucky Derby*

Tomy Lee—Willie Shoemaker, jockey

*Athlete of the Year*

Male—Ingemar Johansson (Boxing)
Female—Maria Bueno (Tennis)

*Last Season*

Ed Macauley (Basketball)
Enos Slaughter (Baseball)

## News

**January.** When a Charleston hotel turns away Negro members of the Minneapolis Lakers, star Elgin
Baylor sits out the game in protest. With one-
quarter of the league's 80 players black, the association quickly adopts a protective policy. In the future, a city hosting two NBA teams must guarantee
in advance that players will not be subjected to
segregation.

**May 25.** The Supreme Court finds a Louisiana
ban on white-black boxing matches unconstitutional.

**June 26.** Over the past three years, Floyd Patterson has successfully defended his heavyweight title
four times. But tonight, Ingemar Johansson knocks
down Patterson seven times before the referee halts
the fight in the third round. The Swede—the first
non-American to capture the title since Primo
Canera in 1934—receives a hero's welcome back
home.

**July 27.** The Continental League is established
as the third major baseball league in the United
States; Branch Rickey is named president in Au-
gust. Franchises are established in Denver,
Houston, New York, Minneapolis-St. Paul, and
Toronto; Fort Worth and Buffalo are added later.
The league plans to open in 1961.

**October 6.** Down three games to one in the
World Series, the White Sox rally to defeat the
Dodgers in front of a record Los Angeles crowd of
92,706. But Chicago, the first White Sox team to
win a pennant since the scandal of 1919, loses the

sixth game. The winning Dodgers each receive $11,231; the losers get $7,275.

**November 1.** A puck shot by Ranger forward Andy Bathgate hits Jacques Plante in the face. After four broken noses, two broken cheekbones, a fractured skull, and 200 stitches, the Montreal Canadiens' goalie has had enough. He refuses to return to the ice without the plastic mask he wears during practice. Coach Tom Blake believes the device, similar to a catcher's mask, prevents a clear line of vision. But with no backup goalie (standard practice at this time), Blake is forced to give in.

The Canadiens win 3–1 and Plante allows just 13 goals over the next 11 games. His mask revolutionizes NHL goaltending.

**More news.** As the last major league team to break the color barrier, the Boston Red Sox sign Pumpsie Green. The team once turned down another black player after a tryout—Jackie Robinson.

## Records

**May 16.** At the Sam Snead Festival in West Virginia, Snead posts a record 18-hole score of 59. He is the first golfer to break 60 in a PGA-sanctioned tournament.

**August 31.** Sandy Koufax strikes out 18 Giants to tie Bob Feller's single-game record. Added to the 13 in his last appearance, the Dodgers pitcher sets a new two-game strikeout record.

**November 8.** In a 136–115 Minneapolis victory over the Celtics, Elgin Baylor scores a one-game record 64 points. Next year, he raises this NBA standard to 71.

## What They Said

Reporters constantly complain that the Yankees are not playing on their toes this season. Manager Casey Stengel, driven to distraction, snaps, "What 'a ya want me to do? Raise the wash basins in the lock room 6 inches?" (*Sports Illustrated* July 20)

38-year-old outfielder Stan Musial meets 42-year-old presidential hopeful John F. Kennedy. "They tell me I'm too old to play baseball and you're too young to be president. Maybe we should get together on this." (*Sports Illustrated* Aug. 10)

## Obituaries

**Max Baer** (February 11, 1909–November 21, 1959). The U.S. prizefighter won the heavyweight title from Primo Carnera in 1934, but lost it the following year to James Braddock.

**Bert Bell** (February 25, 1894–October 11, 1959). During his tenure as commissioner of the NFL (1946–1959), football grew into a major spectator sport due in part to his profitable television policies.

**Tony Canzoneri** (November 6, 1908–December 8, 1959). The 5″ 4′ fighter held world championships in three weight divisions—unofficial junior welterweight twice, featherweight (1928), and lightweight (1930–1933 and 1935–1936).

**Nap(oleon) (Larry) Lajoie** (September 5, 1875–February 7, 1959). The greatest second baseman in the history of the game was elected to the Baseball Hall of Fame in 1937. He rejuvenated the weak Cleveland franchise and while he was manager (1905–1909) the Indians were called the "Naps" in his honor. He retired in 1916 with 3,251 hits and a lifetime batting average of .339.

**Molla Bjurstedt Mallory** (1892–November 22, 1959). Between 1916 and 1926, the Norwegian-born tennis player won the U.S. women's singles championship a record eight times.

# *1960*

The Swinging Sixties. The Pill, the mini skirt, rock concerts, the Summer of Love, hippie clothes, drugs, communes, protest marches. Propelled by millions of baby-boomers, the material and social changes of this decade transform American society.

In this first year, the country reels under disaster after disaster—the U-2 incident and the subsequent collapse of détente, riots in Japan over Eisenhower's upcoming visit, deteriorating relations with Cuba, and a record peacetime deficit of $12.4 billion. Americans, concerned with a loss of prestige, question their national purpose.

Vice-President Nixon carries that diplomatic burden into television debates with John F. Kennedy. The articulate senator impresses viewers and, with his refusal to ignore questions about religion, collects enough votes to narrowly win the presidency.

Black Americans, many of whom vote for Kennedy, turn to the sit-in. The Supreme Court further supports civil rights with decisions on bus terminal segregation and voter exclusion through altered municipal boundaries.

International stories include civil war in the Belgian Congo—Africa's first—a devastating earthquake in Morocco, and independence for 17 African nations. The establishment of the Vietcong draws little attention.

This year witnesses the Twist, the first Playboy Club, and the Pill. The AFL is formed, the maser is patented, and the first transistorized TVs reach the market. But the untold story remains the growing number of baby-boomers. A comparison of 1950 and 1960 statistics shows school and college enrollment up 53 percent, bicycle sales nearly doubled, and Little League team membership up more than 700%.

## NEWS

**January 2.** Senator John F. Kennedy (D., Mass.) announces his candidacy for the Democratic presidential nomination. He is the first serious Catholic nominee since 1928. Within days, Richard Nixon announces his candidacy for the Republican nomination.

*Statistics*: In a December Gallup poll, 69 percent said they would accept a "well-qualified" Roman Catholic as president.

**January 4.** Britain, Austria, Denmark, Norway, Portugal, Sweden, and Switzerland establish a European Free Trade Association. But EFTA provides little economic stimulus and members continue to trade largely with the EEC. Iceland will join the group in 1970; Denmark and Britain will leave in 1972.

**February 1.** A black student who was refused service yesterday at Woolworth's lunch counter in Greensboro, North Carolina, returns with three friends to hold a sit-in. Although unsuccessful, their attempt to integrate a public facility through passive resistance marks a turning point in the emerging civil rights movement.

The sit-ins quickly spread to five other states. A month later, San Antonio, Texas, becomes the first major Southern city to desegregate variety-store lunch counters. Tennessee, North Carolina, and Virginia follow suit.

Elsewhere in the deep South, resistance to integration remains strong. Klansmen revive rallies and cross-burnings, and on February 28, form a single unified body called the Knights of the Ku Klux Klan. While seeking 10 million members in 30 states, the Knights' membership will reportedly reach just 17,000 at the height of the civil rights movement.

**February 3.** British Prime Minister Harold Macmillan tells the South African Parliament that London can no longer support white domination of black Africans. "The wind of change is blowing through the continent. Whether we like it or not, this growth of national consciousness is a political fact. We must all accept it as a fact." He receives 30 seconds of polite applause.

In the last half of the 1950s, Britain granted independence to two African nations. By the end of this decade, more than 15 will become self-governing.

**February 13.** In southwestern Algeria, France explodes its first nuclear bomb. President de Gaulle believes an independent atomic force will reduce Europe's reliance on the United States and reestablish France as a major power. His program will become law in December without the direct approval of either the Senate or the Assembly.

**February 29.** Just before midnight, an earthquake strikes Agadir, Morocco. While not severe

(5.8 on the Richter scale), the tremors crumble poorly constructed houses, killing 12,000 people in just 15 seconds. A tidal wave and a second shock, an hour later, devastate the city.

**March 14.** In New York, at the first meeting between an Israeli and a West German leader, Premier David Ben Gurion tells Chancellor Konrad Adenauer, "My people cannot forget its past. But we remember the past not in order to brood upon it but in order that it shall never reoccur. . . . The Germany of today is not the Germany of yesterday."

**March 21.** Answering a Pan-Africanist call, some 20,000 men, women, and children leave their racial identification passes at home and surrender at a police station in Sharpeville. But the white officers open fire with submachine guns, shooting nearly 300 blacks in 40 seconds; at least 67 die.

By the end of the month, under the nation's first state of emergency, the government arrests hundreds of blacks and bans the African National Congress (ANC) and the Pan-Africanist Congress. In response, the ANC organizes Umkhonto we Sizwe (the Spear of the Nation) for armed operations.

**April 15.** In Raleigh, North Carolina, young black students who participated in recent sit-ins form the Temporary Student Nonviolent Coordinating Committee (the "Temporary" is later dropped). Through the early part of the decade, SNCC, or "Snick," will spearhead various civil rights actions.

**April 27.** After Syngman Rhee won a fourth term of office in mid-March, charges of election fraud produced massive demonstrations. With civil strife spreading, South Korea's first and only president buckles under U.S. pressure and resigns.

A constitutional amendment in June introduces a parliamentary form of government. But after a series of weak administrations, a military junta will take power on May 16, 1961; General Park Chung-hee will assume control on July 3.

**May 2.** In 1948, four-time loser Caryl Chessman received the death penalty for kidnapping and sexually assaulting two women. Since then, numerous stays of execution and his autobiography have placed him at the center of the capital punishment debate. Billy Graham, Eleanor Roosevelt, Albert

Schweitzer, and thousands of others have pleaded for his life, but the courts have denied him clemency. Following Chessman's execution today, protestors attack U.S. embassies in Europe and South America.

> *Statistics:* The U.S. federal prison population rises for the 11th consecutive year to a record total of 23,160 inmates.

**May 5.** In a major shake-up, Alexei N. Kosygin becomes first deputy premier in the Soviet government. Two days later, Khrushchev names 54-year-old Leonid I. Brezhnev chairman of the presidium. The promotions strengthen Khrushchev's position as premier and first secretary of the Communist party.

**May 5.** Nikita Khrushchev announces the capture of an American U-2 reconnaissance plane. U.S. spy missions began in 1955, after Moscow rejected Eisenhower's "open skies" proposal, but Washington, confident the U-2 pilot is dead, maintains that the "weather plane" never deliberately violated Soviet airspace. With the American denial in hand, a triumphant Khrushchev reveals on May 7 that the CIA pilot, Gary Powers, is alive.

Denying at first that the flight was authorized, the U.S. State Department finally concedes on May 9 that the reconnaissance program was sanctioned by the White House. Eisenhower, with a secret congressional agreement to withhold criticism, leaves for a previously arranged summit conference in Paris.

At the opening on May 16, Khrushchev withdraws his invitation for a presidential visit and demands that the Americans formally apologize for "past acts of aggression." A furious Eisenhower, in an unprecedented admission by a world leader, publicly cancels all flights over the USSR. (Years later he says, "When you get your fingers caught in the cookie jar, there's no use of pretending that you were out in the stable somewhere.") But he refuses to apologize.

Khrushchev cancels the summit. Analysts theor-

ize that the Soviets, knowing the West would never back down over Berlin, manipulated the U-2 incident to get out of the discussions.

On August 19, the Soviets sentence Gary Powers to 10 years in prison.

**May 6.** Strengthening the voting rights provisions legislated in 1957, the Civil Rights Act of 1960 authorizes voting referees in districts with proven racial discrimination, requires the preservation of voting and registration records, sets penalties for the violent obstruction of a federal court order, and authorizes federal searches for bombing suspects.

The Southern-dominated House Rules Committee released the long bottled-up bill only after Senator Lyndon Johnson tacked stronger civil rights measures onto a completely unrelated House bill. To prevent passage, Eisenhower convinced Republican senators to join with Northern Democrats in releasing the weaker bill from committee.

The Justice Department first applies the new act against voting registrars in Bienville Parish, Louisiana, charging them with systematic racial discrimination.

> *Statistics:* Over the past 10 years, a record 1,457,000 blacks left the South for the North and West. The Negro population of New York—the largest of any state—increased by 54.4 percent, while California rose by 91.2 percent.

**May 10.** Last month, in the first significant primary, John F. Kennedy easily defeated Hubert Humphrey in Wisconsin, but lost the state's four Protestant districts. Today, Kennedy scores a resounding victory in the Protestant state of West Virginia.

With only 16 states holding presidential primaries, Kennedy can never accumulate enough delegate votes to win the Democratic nomination. Yet exposure might overcome American resistance to a Catholic president and convince the party he can win the election.

A few hours after Kennedy's win in Virginia,

Humphrey withdraws from the race. The immediacy of the primary in American politics has forever changed.

**May 21–30.** In Chile, the first in a series of earthquakes kills at least 5,700 and destroys over 100,000 homes and 20 percent of the country's industries. Tidal waves sweeping across the Pacific take another 400 lives. On Hilo, in Hawaii, at least 61 die—many at the beach watching the incoming waves.

**June 16.** After leftist students attack his advance men, President Eisenhower reluctantly omits his stopover in Japan during a goodwill tour of the Far East. In January, the United States returned full sovereignty to Japan under a mutual security treaty. But students have protested those continued ties in three weeks of anti-American demonstrations.

The incident humiliates the United States, which has carefully nurtured the alliance, and forces the Japanese premier who negotiated the treaty to resign. Nonetheless, the Diet proceeds with ratification.

**June 21.** At a Communist summit meeting in Romania, Khrushchev declares the non-inevitability of war with capitalist countries and calls for a flexible interpretation of Marxist-Leninist theory. His statements deepen the ideological differences between Soviet and Chinese Communism.

**June 27.** The U.S. Supreme Court, in a narrow 5–4 decision, abolishes the "silver platter" doctrine that allowed state officers to give illegally seized evidence to federal authorities for prosecution. Henceforth, any evidence used in a federal court must meet the tests of the Constitution.

**June 30.** The Belgian Congo receives its independence, but the coalition government of Joseph Kasavubu and Patrice Lumumba faces tribal warfare, civil strife, and a military mutiny against the remaining Belgian officers.

In mineral-rich Katanga province, President Moise Tshombe cunningly calls on Brussels for assistance. With support from Belgian mining companies, fearful of Lumumba's socialism, Tshombe declares the province's independence as Belgian troops enter key areas.

When the fledgling Congolese government seeks help from the United Nations, peacekeeping troops move in. Lumumba falls from power as the country descends into a bloody civil war.

**July 9.** Premier Khrushchev threatens to use Soviet rockets if the United States intervenes in Cuba. He denounces the Monroe Doctrine, which asserts American protection over the hemisphere, but President Eisenhower retorts that the United States will never permit a regime "dominated by international Communism in the Western hemisphere."

U.S.-Cuban relations have spiraled downward since Batista's ouster. When Havana carried out political executions, signed a Soviet aid agreement, and supported other rebel groups, Washington terminated economic aid and refused to deal in arms. Castro then seized American and British oil companies; Eisenhower suspended the sugar quota.

In retaliation, Cuba nationalizes banks and all remaining industries on October 14 and seizes nearly $1.5 billion worth of U.S. property. Days later, Washington embargoes all exports to Cuba, with the exception of medical supplies and most food.

This year, well over 1,000 Cuban refugees flee to the United States each week.

**July 13.** At the Democratic convention in Los Angeles, last-minute efforts to draft Adlai Stevenson for a third attempt at the presidency fail to draw liberal support away from John F. Kennedy. The young senator from Massachusetts wins the presidential nomination on the first ballot, then stuns delegates by choosing second-place Lyndon Johnson as his running mate. Analysts theorize that Kennedy wanted to increase his chances in the South, particularly in Johnson's native Texas.

The convention has adopted the strongest civil rights platform in party history, with a commitment to support Negro voting rights, accelerate school desegregation, and prevent racial discrimination in the workplace. On July 15, when he accepts the nomination, Kennedy tells delegates, "We stand today on the edge of a new frontier—the frontier of the 1960s—a frontier of unknown opportunities and perils—the frontier of unfulfilled hopes and threats."

**July 27.** In Chicago, Richard Nixon becomes the Republican nominee by acclamation. (He is the first vice-president in the history of the modern two-party system to win a presidential nomination.) He selects U.N. Ambassador Henry Cabot Lodge as his vice-presidential nominee.

Eisenhower, as a steadfast Republican, offers his considerable popularity and prestige to the campaign.

**July 31.** At a New York rally, Muslim leader Elijah Muhammed calls for an American Negro state in the United States or Africa. His appealing image makes the Temple of Islam a focal point for blacks seeking power in the white man's world.

**August 4.** The Canadian Bill of Rights confirms fundamental freedoms and rights under federal law. Although a future Parliament could modify it or set it aside, the legislation pushes some provinces into enacting separate human rights acts.

**August 16.** Cyprus, long a bone of contention among Turkey, Britain, and Greece gains its independence.

Turkey lost the Mediterranean island at the end of W.W.I but has continued to fight for a role in negotiations. Britain assumed control and, in 1924, made Cyprus a crown colony. Athens all along has supported demands by the island's majority Greek population for union with Greece.

A political solution became possible only after Archbishop Makarios, the spiritual leader of the Greek community, agreed to compromise. In February 1959, the three nations guaranteed British military bases, gave the Turkish minority a privileged status, and installed Makarios as first president of the Cypriot Republic. Greek extremists remain opposed to the settlement.

**August 28.** OAS foreign ministers adopt the Declaration of San José, condemning Communist intervention in Latin American affairs. Cuba is never named, but delegates understand that the statement supports Washington in its dispute with Havana. The Cubans walk out.

**September 6.** Hurricane Donna—the most destructive storm in the history of the U.S. Weather Bureau—hits the Caribbean and the East Coast. Only accurate weather forecasting and bureau warnings keep the death toll at 148.

**September 7.** A group of Protestant ministers

and laypeople question whether presidential nominee John F. Kennedy could remain free of the Catholic Church's influence. Kennedy, who has confronted the issue against the advice of his family, pledges he would make all decisions "without regard to outside religious pressures or dictates." Several non-Catholic religious groups disavow the charges, and candidate Richard Nixon maintains that the senator's statement should be accepted and the matter dropped. But the controversy continues.

**September 10.** Saudi Arabia, Iran, Iraq, Kuwait, and Venezuela establish the Organization of Petroleum Exporting Countries (OPEC) for a unified response to price changes mandated by foreign-owned oil companies. OPEC succeeds in forcing Standard Oil to retract its latest cut.

**September 24.** The admission of 16 newly independent African nations during the current session ends Western domination of the United Nations. Today, Soviet Premier Khrushchev calls for the resignation of Secretary-General Dag Hammarskjöld and the appointment of a three-bloc directorate. Fidel Castro, during a 4½-hour speech on the 26th, charges the United States with aggression against Cuba.

*Soviet Premier Khrushchev (right) and Cuban leader Fidel Castro, visiting the United Nations as delegates, use the media to maintain a high profile. Castro and his delegation bunk in Harlem.*

**September 26.** Remembering the positive impact of his "Checkers" speech in 1952, Nixon has accepted Kennedy's challenge to four televised debates. In the first tonight, neither man is a clear winner, but 80 million viewers see a very different Kennedy from the inexperienced Democrat portrayed by the Republicans. Looking poised and intelligent, the young senator clearly lays out his theme of national purpose. The vice-president, on the other hand, appears tired and unshaven, the result of pain from a recently injured knee and inappropriate makeup. Kennedy's campaign takes off.

**October 19.** The Alfred Smith Memorial Dinner in New York marks the only informal meeting of the presidential nominees during the campaign. Senator Kennedy wryly comments on Republican criticism of Harry S. Truman's "damning to hell" those who would vote for Nixon. "I would not want to give the impression that I am taking former President Truman's use of language lightly. I have sent him the following wire: 'Dear Mr. President: I have noted with interest your suggestion as to where those who vote for my opponent should go. While I understand and sympathize with your deep motivation, I think it is important that our side try to refrain from raising the religious issue.'"

**October 26.** All John F. Kennedy's campaign promises probably win fewer voters than a single telephone call made at his request today. Rev. Martin Luther King, Jr., arrested on October 22 during mass sit-in demonstrations in Atlanta, received a four-month prison term for violating an earlier probated traffic sentence. Kennedy, who has already called Mrs. King and promised to intervene, asks his brother Bobby to telephone the judge. King is released the next day. Nixon has remained silent on the case.

On the Sunday before the election, black ministers across America endorse John F. Kennedy for president.

**November 8.** In the closest presidential election since 1884, Massachusetts Senator John F. Kennedy wins by just over 100,000 popular votes out of a record 68.8 million cast. But, with Lyndon Johnson's strength in the South and the committed Negro vote, Kennedy collects ample electoral votes: 303 to Nixon's 217 (Virginia's Senator Harry Byrd wins 15).

The Democrats retain control of Congress, but the addition of a few more Republicans strengthens the conservative Republican-Democrat coalition, once again denying the White House a working majority.

**November 12.** In South Vietnam, troops loyal to President Ngo Dinh Diem crush an attempted military coup. Described variously as inflexible, authoritarian, and suspicious, Diem has alienated elements of the military and the peasant class by refusing to allow any organized opposition and by returning farmland to landlords. He has retained control by vesting power in the hands of family members and Catholic refugees from the North.

With the Diem regime still in power, Ho Chi Minh, on December 20, organizes Communists in the South into the National Liberation Front of South Vietnam. Formerly called the Vietminh, the guerrillas become known as the Vietcong. Within a year, NLF membership will quadruple to 300,000.

**November 14.** The Supreme Court returns the *Gomillion v. Lightfoot* gerrymander case to an Alabama court for retrial. The state, in changing city boundaries to exclude Negro voters, had violated the 15th Amendment's guarantee of voting rights regardless of race.

**November 14.** For the first time since the Brown decision in 1954, a federal district court orders the desegregation of a school in the deep South. But when four first-graders register in two all-white New Orleans schools, a near riot follows.

White parents boycott the schools and the Louisiana legislature moves to stop the integration. Federal courts quickly strike down each new piece of legislation, and the Supreme Court upholds the rulings.

*Statistics:* With no school desegregation in Alabama, Georgia, Mississippi, or South Carolina, and just token integration in Florida, Virginia, Louisiana, and North Carolina, only 6.3 percent of Southern black students attend integrated classes.

**December 11.** At 9:50 A.M., 73-year-old Richard P. Pavlick waits with seven sticks of dynamite outside the home of John F. Kennedy. But when the president-elect comes to the door with his family, the would-be assassin changes his mind.

Arrested four days later on a traffic violation, Pavlick is committed to a mental institution; he will be released in 1966. (The Secret Service claims he never got near Kennedy.)

**December 14.** The U.N. Declaration on Colonialism proclaims the rights of all peoples to self-determination and calls for a "speedy and unconditional end" to colonialism. The United States abstains, but, with the changeover in administrations, Washington later associates itself with the declaration.

**December 14.** With the addition of the United States and Canada to the 18-member body, the Organization for Economic Cooperation and Development (OECD) supersedes the OEEC, set up in 1948 to coordinate the Marshall Plan. Effective September 30, 1961, the OECD intends to stimulate world trade and encourage economic progress in developing nations.

**December 16.** In the worst civilian air crash in U.S. history, two commercial airliners collide over Staten Island during a heavy snowstorm. The TWA plane crashes on the island; the five survivors die within hours. The crippled United flight tries to make La Guardia but breaks up over Brooklyn. The lone survivor, an 11-year-old boy found sitting on a snow bank, dies a day later. The final death toll reaches 131—126 passengers and crew and 5 on the ground. An inquiry determines that a failed electronic device put the TWA plane 11 miles off course.

**December 19.** A fire breaks out at the Brooklyn naval shipyard on the nearly completed aircraft carrier *Constellation.* Feeding on wooden scaffolding, the flames quickly spread below deck. There are 49 deaths, more than 150 injuries, and damages totaling $75 million.

When an inquiry determines that a welding torch ignited gasoline leaking down a bomb elevator, some question whether safety standards were bypassed in the rush to finish the ship. Over 40 smaller fires broke out on the *Constellation* last year.

**December 24.** In a Gallup poll, Dwight D. Eisenhower and Eleanor Roosevelt are chosen as the nation's most admired man and woman. President Eisenhower has topped the list for 9 years and Mrs. Roosevelt for 12.

## Obituaries

**Norris Brown** (1874–January 5, 1960). In 1909, the Republican senator from Nebraska introduced a tax resolution to meet the expanding federal budget. The 16th Amendment, establishing the income tax, was proclaimed on February 25, 1913.

**Arthur Meighen** (June 16, 1874–August 5, 1960). The eloquent Conservative was prime minister of Canada twice—1920–1921 and for a few months in 1926—before losing popular support.

**Ruth Rowland Nichols** (February 23, 1901–September 25, 1960). In 1932 the aviation pioneer became the first female airline pilot in the United States. In 1958, she flew an air force jet at a record speed of more than 1,000 mph.

**Max Pruss** (circa 1891–November 28, 1960). Pruss captained the German dirigible *Hindenburg* in the fateful 1937 crash that killed 36. While he never recovered from his injuries, the veteran pilot of 170 Atlantic crossings believed in the practicality of the zeppelin until his death.

**Melvin Purvis** (October 24, 1903–February 29, 1960). The FBI agent in charge at the 1934 shootouts with John Dillinger and Pretty Boy Floyd later pursued a career in law and broadcasting.

**John D(avison) Rockefeller, Jr.** (January 29, 1874–May 11, 1960). The only son of the world's richest man rivaled his father in giving away the family wealth. Together, the Rockefellers donated more than $3 billion to education, medical and social research, and historical restoration.

# BEGINNINGS AND ENDINGS

## News

**January 19.** The Brotherhood of Railroad Trainmen votes to eliminate racial qualifications for membership.

**February 19.** Queen Elizabeth II gives birth to her third child, Andrew. He is the first child born to a reigning British monarch since 1857.

*Statistics:* An average American baby born in 1960 will live 69.7 years, up from 47.3 years in 1900.

**February 29.** Chicago men line up around the block to join the first Playboy Club. By next year, 106,000 members carry club keys (city residents pay $50, out-of-towners $25).

**April.** New York City installs its first outdoor telephone booths. (Surveys show 50 percent of phone calls are made on impulse.)

**April 1.** The introduction of the DC-8 cuts the TCA Montreal-Vancouver flight from just over 9 hours to about 5.

**May 6.** Queen Elizabeth's sister Princess Margaret marries Anthony Armstrong-Jones in Westminster Abbey. (Soon after the marriage, the queen gives the groom the title Earl of Snowden.)

For the first time, Buckingham Palace permits the filming of a royal wedding (with some restrictions).

**May 10.** The U.S. nuclear submarine *Triton* completes the first underwater circumnavigation of the world—in 84 days.

**July 1.** Amendments to the Canadian Election Act and the Indian Act grant natives the right to vote in federal elections. Many Indians resisted the change, fearing enfranchisement would bring responsibilities such as taxes.

**July 4.** Marking Independence Day, Americans fly the 50-star flag for the first time.

**July 10.** Seven-year-old Roger Woodward is the first person to survive an accidental plunge over Niagara's Horseshoe Falls. His sister was pulled from the river after their boat capsized.

**July 21.** The Sri Lanka (Freedom) party wins the Ceylon federal election, and Sirimavo Bandaranaike becomes the first female prime minister of a modern state. The previous prime minister, her husband, Solomon Bandaranaike, was assassinated last year.

**August 1.** For the first time, the American Dental Association endorses a commercial product, Crest toothpaste, for proven reduction of cavities. Within a year, Crest sales nearly double.

**November 25.** Jacqueline Kennedy, wife of president-elect John F. Kennedy, gives birth to a son, John Fitzgerald Kennedy, Jr.

**December 2.** At the first Interprovincial Conference, Canadian premiers discuss national cooperation. The gathering will become an annual event.

**December 2.** The Archbishop of Canterbury, the Most Reverend Geoffrey Fisher, visits Pope John XXIII at the Vatican, the first meeting between leaders of the Anglican and Roman Catholic churches since 1534, the year Henry VIII left the Catholic Church to found the Church of England.

**December 6.** Under pressure from the House Subcommittee on Government Secrecy, the U.S. Defense Department releases the first pictures of Little Boy and Fat Man, the atom bombs dropped on Japan in 1945. Reportedly, the department had withheld the photographs to avoid unfavorable international reaction.

**December 31.** President Kennedy chooses NAACP chairman Robert Weaver to administer the Housing and Home Finance Agency; it is the highest federal administrative post held by a Negro to date.

**More news.** Richard Nixon is the first presidential nominee to campaign in all 50 states.

• Tourism surpasses sugar as Hawaii's major industry.

• In 1958, France offered all overseas territories sovereignty or autonomy within a new French community. This year, 14 choose independence, including Chad, Mali, and Upper Volta.

## Records

**August 4.** In a test of the X-15, NASA pilot Joseph Walker sets a new record for manned flight—2,196 mph. A week later, the plane sets an altitude record of 131,000 feet.

**August 24.** A Soviet research station in the Antarctic experiences the lowest temperature ever recorded, −126.9 degrees Fahrenheit or −88.3 degrees Celcius.

**October 14.** On his 70th birthday, Dwight D. Eisenhower becomes the oldest man to serve as president of the United States. The previous oldest occupant of the White House, Andrew Jackson, was 69 when he left office in 1837.

### New Products and Businesses

The Toyo Kogyo Co. in Hiroshima, Japan, produces its first car, an R-360 Mazda coupe.

This year, *canned* Coca-Cola appears on the domestic market for the first time.

### Memorable Ad Campaigns

Ads target war-baby teenagers and the millions of baby-boomers entering their teens. Pepsi brags, "Now It's Pepsi, for Those Who Think Young."

### Fads

Trampolining sweeps California. Entrepreneurs set up 200 centers in the Los Angeles area alone, charging 40 cents for a half hour of jumping and flipping. But the number of injured customers grows and interest fades by August.

## SCIENCE AND TECHNOLOGY

### News

**January 23.** The navy bathyscaphe *Trieste* breaks all previous depth records with a seven-mile dive in the Pacific Marianas Trench. Lt. Donald Walsh and Jacques Piccard, son of inventor August Piccard, find that life exists on the seabed despite the cold temperature. Their discovery means the United States must abandon the idea of depositing radioactive wastes in the ocean.

**February 24.** The USAF announces the first successful launching of a Titan ICBM.

**March 11.** NASA launches *Pioneer 5.* In a three-month solar orbit between Venus and Earth, the radio-equipped satellite collects data on solar flares and solar wind. The United States puts 17 probes and satellites into space this year.

**March 22.** Arthur Schawlow and Charles Townes receive a patent for masers and a maser communication system (microwave amplification by stimulated emission of radiation). Townes has predicted that a similar high-frequency amplifier could operate in the visible light spectrum, creating an optical maser, or laser (*l* for "light"). In July, Dr. Theodore Maiman at the Hughes Research Lab in Malibu, California, displays the first working model of a laser. Next year, Bell Labs will surpass the pulsed action of the early laser to build a continuously operating solid-state device. Townes will receive the 1964 Nobel prize in physics for his fundamental research.

> *Statistics:* 72 percent of American households own a washing machine, about one in nine have a clothes dryer, and about one in six own a food freezer.

**March 23.** It is likely that Los Alamos scientists achieved brief, controlled thermonuclear fusion over the last two years, but proof was obtained only recently. Today's announcement states that the small egg-shaped fireball—8/10 inch in diameter—reached a temperature of 13 million degrees Fahrenheit over seven-millionths of a second—a long way from controlled thermonuclear energy.

**April 1.** NASA places *Tiros I* into orbit, the first U.S. satellite designed to take detailed weather photos. Later in the year, NASA promises to make the pictures available to meteorologists in other countries.

With increased polar coverage, Tiros satellites will transmit over 500,000 photos by the middle of the decade. Prior to this enormously successful series, weather forecasting was limited to less than 20 percent of the world's surface.

**April 6.** California approves a bill to control air pollution from automobile exhaust. The chief of the Los Angeles air-pollution district claims that this unique state legislation will eliminate smog in Southern California within six years.

**April 15.** The navy places *Transit 1B* into orbit, an experimental "lighthouse" for military ships and planes. Transit satellites will become available for commercial use only toward the end of the decade.

**April 19.** The U.S. Army displays an aircraft radar system capable of taking detailed pictures of troop movements from miles away, by day or night, and in any kind of weather.

**May 9.** Following extensive field tests, the FDA approves the first oral contraceptive. On the market for several years, Enovid 10 had previously been prescribed only for "female disorders." The medical committee of the Planned Parenthood Federation quickly approves the Pill and urges 170 affiliated centers to offer the prescription with other forms of birth control.

**May 24.** *The New York Times* reports the placement of the first successful reconnaissance satellite, *Midas II.* The program will become classified after *Midas IV.*

**June 20.** A five-year study of dolphins sponsored by the U.S. Navy reports that it found the mammals as intelligent as humans, and perhaps superior. The dolphins talk to each other, mimic human sounds, and seem to have a sense of humor about people.

---

*Statistics:* This year, whaling countries kill 14,676 whales; Japan accounts for over 5,000.

---

**July 20.** The *U.S.S. George Washington* completes the first submerged firing of a Polaris missile. (For its first patrol in November, the sophisticated vessel carries 16 missiles.) A 1958 navy memorandum noted that submarine missiles, with their reduced vulnerability, eliminate the need for foreign missile sites.

**July 28.** NASA announces that the advanced space program will be named Project Apollo. Its goal will be to put a man on the moon by 1970.

**August 11.** The navy carries out the first known recovery of a U.S. payload from space. *Discoverer XIII* ejects a capsule by radio command, and the 300-pound object descends by parachute to the ocean.

**August 12.** NASA launches the first passive telecommunications satellite, *Echo I.* Although the 100-foot aluminum-coated balloon neither amplifies nor directs, it successfully relays voice and TV signals from one ground station to another. The design is quickly abandoned in favor of an active satellite.

**August 13.** The completion of a one-year lunar geological survey offers NASA a choice of landing sites. The study has allayed fears that deep layers of dust cover the moon's surface. Still, experts predict that, with the extreme temperatures, an Apollo landing party will have to "dig in like moles to stay alive."

**August 16.** USAF parachutist Captain Joseph Kittinger, Jr., while conducting tests for the U.S. space program, ascends in a balloon to 102,800 feet. More amazingly, Kittinger then leaps from the open gondola and free-falls 16 miles, attaining a speed of 450 mph, before opening his parachute at 17,500 feet.

**August 19.** Following three Luna shots last year, the USSR returns to Sputniks. A satellite takes two dogs, Belka and Trelka, four mice, and a rat into orbit and the next day an ejected capsule descends by parachute to dry land. This is the first live payload to return to Earth.

Over this year and next, the Soviets launch five Sputniks as test vehicles for the manned Vostok program.

**August 19.** The Mercury Project acknowledges that Jerrie Cobb successfully passed rigorous astronaut tests (reportedly, scoring above John Glenn on some). But NASA has no definite project planned for the holder of several world records for women fliers.

**October 12.** Fifty miles southwest of Chicago, Commonwealth Edison dedicates the Dresden atomic energy reactor, the first to be commercially operated.

**October 24.** The Soviet space program suffers a disaster when a missile explodes on the launching pad. At least 165 soldiers and workers are burned alive. Apparently, the Soviets had ignored safety precautions in their hurry to develop an ICBM.

**November 20.** Moscow announces that a comet caused the explosion felt round the world on the night of June 30, 1908. The air blast, when the comet entered the Earth's atmosphere, leveled miles of forest.

**More news.** Dr. C. W. Lillehei and his associates at the University of Minnesota Medical School report on the success of a transistorized electronic pacemaker. About the size of a pack of cigarettes, and worn in a light sling from the shoulder, the device corrects a faltering rhythm through tiny electrodes surgically implanted in the heart muscle.

---

*Statistics:* In New York City, a doctor's house call costs about $4.83.

---

• With beer and motor oil available in aluminum cans, and sardines, cheese, and frozen foods picking up on the trend, the aluminum industry expects production to more than triple this year, to a total of 50 million pounds.

• IBM currently controls 80 percent of the market, but Digital Equipment Corp. (DEC) puts out the first minicomputer. Contained in just four 6-foot cabinets, the program data processor, or PDP-1, weighs a fraction of what most computers weigh yet still handles a wide range of tasks.

---

*Statistics:* Railroads cut back on commuter service, and more and more workers turn to their automobiles for transportation. The total number of car registrations reaches 75,958,200 this year, double the 37,841,400 of 1947.

---

• The U.S. census reveals several trends and developments over the past 10 years: The urban population increased by 29.3 percent, while the rural population decreased only slightly, so that 7 out of every 10 people in the United States now

live in urban areas. The West (including Hawaii and Alaska) led the country in growth with a population increase of 38.9 percent. For the first time, females outnumber males, possibly because of the increasing gender gap in life expectancy, the number of men posted overseas, and the dying off of an earlier immigrant generation that was largely male; and the highest level of home ownership since 1890 is recorded, with 61.9 percent of homes owner-occupied.

## Other Discoveries, Developments, and Inventions

> Antianxiety drug Librium
> Solar car from International Rectifier Corp. which needs 8–10 hours of sunlight for 1 hour of power
> Independent synthesis of chlorophyll by American Robert Woodward and German Martin Strell
> U.S.S. *Enterprise*, the first nuclear-powered aircraft carrier
> Western Electric device that, held to the throat, enables a person without a larynx to speak
> Automated post office, two football fields in size, at Providence, Rhode Island

## Obituaries

**Giuseppe Mario Bellanca** (March 19, 1886–December 26, 1960). The Italian-American designer's aircraft included the first monoplane with an enclosed cabin.

**Georges Claude** (September 24, 1870–May 23, 1960). Between 1896 and 1910, the French inventor discovered the principles of neon lighting.

**Arthur Fleming** (January 1, 1881–September 14, 1960). Early research by the British electrical engineer led to the development of radar.

**Ernest W. Goodpasture** (October 17, 1886–September 20, 1960). The physician and scientist developed a mass-production technique for vaccines that proved important during W.W.II. He refused to patent the procedure.

**Emil Grubbe** (January 1, 1875–March 26, 1960). The American radiologist pioneered the application of x-rays in the treatment of disease and the use of lead to protect operators from radiation.

# THE ARTS

February 25—*Toys in the Attic*, with Maureen Stapleton, Jason Robards, Jr., Anne Revere (556 perfs.)

March 31—*The Best Man*, with Melvyn Douglas, Lee Tracy, Frank Lovejoy (520 perfs.)

April 14—*Bye, Bye Birdie*, with Dick Van Dyke, Chita Rivera, Kay Medford, Dick Gautier (607 perfs.)

May 3—*The Fantasticks*, with Jerry Orbach, Rita Gardner, Kenneth Nelson (7,400+ perfs.)

September 29—*Irma La Douce*, with Elizabeth Seal, Clive Revill, Keith Michell (524 perfs.)

November 3—*The Unsinkable Molly Brown*, with Tammy Grimes, Harve Presnell (532 perfs.)

December 3—*Camelot*, with Richard Burton, Julie Andrews, Robert Goulet (873 perfs.)

December 26—*Do Re Mi*, with Phil Silvers, Nancy Walker (400 perfs.)

## Tony Awards

Actor (Dramatic)—Melvyn Douglas, *The Best Man*

Actress (Dramatic)—Anne Bancroft, *The Miracle Worker*

Actor (Musical)—Jackie Gleason, *Take Me Along*

Actress (Musical)—Mary Martin, *The Sound of Music*

Play—*The Miracle Worker*

Musical—*Fiorello!*; *The Sound of Music*

## News

**January 17.** In his debut at the Met, 33-year-old Canadian tenor Jon Vickers sings the lead in *Pagliacci*.

**June 2.** A contractual dispute between the actors' union and theater management shuts down Broad-

way for the first time since the great flu epidemic of 1919. The groups settle on June 12.

**July 12.** Queen Elizabeth installs Australian actress Judith Anderson as a dame commander.

**October 1.** A Broadway tryout of *Camelot* opens the new O'Keefe Centre in Toronto. The $12-million theater seats 3,200, none more than 120 feet from the stage.

## Obituaries

**Jussi Björling** (February 2, 1911–September 9, 1960). The Swedish tenor was regarded by many as the greatest in operatic history.

**Oscar Hammerstein II** (July 12, 1895–August 23, 1960). After early collaborations with Jerome Kern (*Show Boat*, 1927) and others, the lyricist worked exclusively with composer Richard Rodgers. Enormously successful, their simple tunes and thoughtful plots—*Carousel* (1945), *South Pacific* (1949), *The King and I* (1951), *The Sound of Music* (1959)—influenced the development of the American musical.

**Lawrence Tibbett** (November 16, 1896–July 15, 1960). One of the most popular baritones in the history of the Met, Tibbett sang at the Opera House from 1923 to 1950. He last appeared in the Broadway musical *Fanny* (1956).

**Leonard Warren** (April 21, 1911–March 4, 1960). At the height of his career, the baritone suffered a stroke during a Met performance.

# WORDS

Joy Adamson, *Born Free*
Ian Fleming, *For Your Eyes Only*
Nikos Kazantzakís, *The Last Temptation of Christ*
John Knowles, *A Separate Peace*
Giuseppe Tomasi di Lampedusa, *The Leopard*
Harper Lee, *To Kill a Mockingbird*
Maxwell Maltz, *Psycho-cybernetics*
Walter M. Miller, *A Canticle for Leibowitz*
William L. Shirer, *The Rise and Fall of the Third Reich*
John Updike, *Rabbit, Run*
Irving Wallace, *The Chapman Report*

## News

**November 2.** In Britain, the first major test of a new obscenity law finds *Lady Chatterley's Lover* (1928) neither obscene nor detrimental to the public good. The next day, Penguin Books ships out 200,000 copies of the unexpurgated version.

**More news.** With the wartime population spurt and the enormous postwar baby boom, U.S. schools and colleges enroll 46 million this year—a 53-percent increase over 1950.

• Since the American Book Publishers Council began keeping statistics in 1952, U.S. book sales have risen 91.8 percent. This year, for the first time, the publishing industry passes the $1-billion mark. Observers believe recent mergers, such as Holt, Rinehart & Winston, and 20 new paperback lines point the way for future growth.

• The $18,000 paid for E. M. Forster's manuscript of *A Passage to India* sets a record auction price for a living author's personal copy.

## Cartoons and Comics

**February 19.** Cartoonist Bill Keane debuts *The Family Circus*. He will add a third baby to his comic panel in 1962.

## TIME *Man of the Year*

15 Top U.S. Scientists

## New Words and Phrases

anchorman
area rug
beatnikoid (a college student attempting to be a beatnik)
bluegrass (music)
chain-drinking
compact car
docudrama
fee-vee (paid TV)
gawkocracy (TV audience)
sit-in
squirch (combination of squirm and wince)

## Obituaries

**Albert Camus** (November 7, 1913–January 4, 1960). His existentialist novels brought the French writer the 1957 Nobel prize in literature.

**Boris Pasternak** (February 10, 1890–May 30, 1960). In 1956, when his Soviet publisher decided against printing *Doctor Zhivago*, the Italian copublisher refused to surrender the manuscript. Released in 1957, the classic novel helped bring Pasternak a Nobel prize in literature.

**Emily Post** (October 3, 1873–September 25, 1960). Some 89 printings of *Etiquette* (1922), a radio program, and a syndicated column made "Emily Post" synonymous with good manners.

**Nevil Shute** (January 17, 1899–January 12, 1960). The British novelist wrote several best-sellers, including *On the Beach* (1957).

**Richard Wright** (September 4, 1908–November 28, 1960). His universally acclaimed *Native Son* (1940) chronicled the black American experience.

# FASHION

## The 1960s

In the first years of the decade, American women emulate the sophisticated style of Jacqueline Kennedy. But some 46 million baby-boomers, entering their teens through the sixties, demand more youthful fashions. The clothing industry, surrendering to their overwhelming buying power, abandons Chanel suits and pillboxes for the revealing mini-skirt and bra-less look.

## Haute Couture

The bloused silhouette of the late 1950's and the high-waisted princess style create a slender, slightly oval shape. To emphasize the graceful line, designers shorten skirts (17.5–19″ from the floor) and create a long-necked effect with cowl backs and collarless suits, dresses, and coats.

# News

**This year.** Pierre Cardin suffers the barbs of other couturiers when he presents the first major collection of men's clothing. Yet within five years Cardin will make almost as much from menswear as from women's fashions.

• During W.W.II, American chemists sought a man-made replacement for scarce rubber. DuPont continued experimentation until 1958, when it submitted the first synthetic elastic—stronger and longer-lasting than the natural product— for trade evaluation. This year, the company introduces Lycra, the first of the spandex fibers.

# Colors and Materials

Rich, dark colors—purples, bottle green— dominate, but women love hot pink coats and evening wear. Gray proves an all-year favorite.

Manufacturers feature patterns and plaids.

Evening wear emphasizes sequins or beads and embroidery.

Fake fur is in style.

With new processing methods, flat knits retain their shape and designers expand their use beyond pants to suits and sheaths.

Through the 1960s, polyester and polyester blends become the fastest-growing fibers.

# Clothes

Norman Norell popularizes divided skirts with the first culotte suit.

Two- and three-piece costumes with matched linings appear in all price ranges for both day and evening wear. Sleeveless garments are the standard.

For young girls, bras remain a symbol of womanhood and stores advertise size 28AA. Women continue to draw away from sculpted foundations.

With the steady growth in population since the war, fashion observers note the increased significance of children's clothing. Designers adapt adult trends and revive styles from earlier periods, particularly the American Revolution, the Civil War, and the Victorian era.

*White Levi's 501 jeans, in an off-white color, get their name from the customers.*

# Accessories

For the "hatted" look, millinery bars sell cloches, high-pointed styles, and deep turbans of tulle.

Low-heeled shoes heighten the "leggy" look of shorter skirts.

Cut velvet and tapestry bags prove favorites.

## Hair and Cosmetics

Hairdressers report women generally want either a high bouffant—full and back combed with a long wispy fringe—or a short bob with points on the cheeks.

Wig sales rise when partially machine-made pieces arrive on the market.

Product-line beauty bars become more common.

# POPULAR MUSIC

"Theme from *A Summer Place*" (Instr.)—Percy Faith

"Are You Lonesome Tonight?"—Elvis Presley

"It's Now or Never"—Elvis Presley

"Cathy's Clown"—Everly Brothers

"Stuck on You"—Elvis Presley

"Wonderland by Night"—Bert Kaempfert

"Running Bear"—Johnny Preston

"Save the Last Dance for Me"—Drifters

"El Paso"—Marty Robbins

"Everybody's Somebody's Fool"—Connie Francis

"Teen Angel"—Mark Dinning

"My Heart Has a Mind of Its Own"—Connie Francis

"The Twist"—Chubby Checker

"Stay"—Maurice Williams & the Zodiacs

"I'm Sorry"—Brenda Lee

"I Want to Be Wanted"—Brenda Lee

"Itsy Bitsy Teenie Weenie Yellow Polkadot Bikini"—Brian Hyland

"Alley-Oop"—Hollywood Argyles

"Mr. Custer"—Larry Verne

"Georgia on My Mind"—Ray Charles

"Greenfields"—Brothers Four

"Last Date" (Instr.)—Floyd Cramer

"He'll Have to Go"—Jim Reeves

"Chain Gang"—Sam Cooke

"Puppy Love"—Paul Anka

"Handy Man"—Jimmy Jones

"Only the Lonely (Know How I Feel)"—Roy Orbison

"Walk—Don't Run" (Instr.)—Ventures

"Wild One"—Bobby Rydell

"Poetry in Motion"—Johnny Tillotson

## Grammy Awards (1960)

Record of the Year—Percy Faith, "Theme from *A Summer Place*"

Song of the Year (songwriter)—Ernest Gold, "Theme from *Exodus*"

Album of the Year—Bob Newhart, *Button Down Mind*

Best Vocal Performance (Male)—Ray Charles, "Georgia On My Mind" (single) and Ray Charles, *Genius of Ray Charles* (album)

Best Vocal Performance (Female)—Ella Fitzgerald, "Mack the Knife" (single) and Ella Fitzgerald, *Mack the Knife—Ella in Berlin* (album)

Best New Artist—Bob Newhart

## News

**January 4.** Rejecting a five-minute single, Columbia Records agreed to put "El Paso" on an album. After weeks of heavy requests, the company sensibly released Marty Robbins' cowboy number as a 45 rpm. The first No. 1 single of the decade, "El Paso" is the first CW song to win a Grammy.

**March.** The U.S. Army discharges Elvis Presley. Capitalizing on fan anticipation, RCA has taken 1,275,077 advance orders for his first new song—the greatest advance for any single record to date. "Stuck on You" jumps to No. 1 within a month and Elvis scores three more hits before the end of the year.

**May 10.** The Moondogs rename themselves the Beatles while waiting for an audition as back-up. (John Lennon suggested a play on the word "beat.") Current manager Allan Williams dislikes the name and the British rock group tries several variations before settling with the Beatles at the end of the summer.

**August 30.** The House passes a bill to outlaw payola and rigged TV quiz shows. The legislation provides for fines of $1,000 a day for broadcasting violations (to a maximum of $10,000) and a possible one-year prison term for persistent violators.

A subcommittee investigation found that DJs had received payments from record companies to play their discs on the air. The inquiry looked at over 200 disc jockeys, but focused on Alan Freed and television DJ Dick Clark. Allegedly in a conflict of interest 50 percent of the records available through Clark's companies had played on his show "American Bandstand." Told by ABC to choose between "American Bandstand" and his businesses, Clark divested himself of outside interests before testifying. Freed's radio and TV bosses fired him in November.

**October 31.** Newcomer Ernest "Chubby Checker" Evans, age 19, creates an international dance with "The Twist." The song reaches No. 1 this week and stays in the top 40 for 15 weeks. Looking back, Checker will attribute its popularity to the fact that the "steps were so easy that anyone could do it."

**More news.** After manager George Treadwell

*To dance the Twist, singer Chubby Checker first uses an invisible towel to dry his backside, then moves his hands and hips in opposite directions, and finishes by ad-libbing the last step.*

fired the Drifters, he needed another group to fulfill contract obligations. The Five Crowns changed their name and lead singer Benjamin Nelson became Ben E. King. Following their first No. 1 hit this year, King leaves for a solo career. His "Spanish Harlem"—No. 10 on the pop charts and No. 15 on R&B—opens the way for soul ballads.

As well, this year, Dion leaves the Belmonts, and Tony Williams, in an ill-fated move, breaks with the Platters. He will never achieve any measure of success, and the Platters, after two No. 1 hits in 1958, never again break the top 10.

• Some radio stations refuse to play the morbid "Teen Angel." Britain bans the song.

• Decca executives delayed the release of "I'm Sorry" for several months, concerned the public would react negatively to a 15-year-old singing about unrequited love.

• Paul Vance and Lee Pockriss write a song about Vance's two-year-old daughter playing at the beach. "Itsy Bitsy Teenie Weenie Yellow Polkadot Bikini" scores a hit for 16-year-old Brian Hyland.

• Bridging the gap to adult listeners, Presley's "It's Now or Never" and "Are You Lonesome Tonight?" receive airtime on easy-listening stations.

• Greenwich Village folk singers move out from the coffee houses to college campuses.

• Although few spoken-word albums have previously sold well, this year comedians Bob Newhart, Shelley Berman, Mort Sahl, and Jonathan Winters find a solid audience among record buyers.

• Hank Ballard and the Midnighters are the first group to chart three records on the hot 100 at the same time—"Finger Poppin' Time," "The Twist," and "Let's Go, Let's Go, Let's Go."

• The Shirelles become the first girl group to score a No. 1 single—"Will You Love Me Tomorrow."

## New Recording Artists

Joan Baez
Gary "U.S." Bonds
Jerry Butler
Dion
Ferrante & Teicher

Brian Hyland
Henry Mancini
Charlie Rich
Ike & Tina Turner
Ventures

### *Obituaries*

**Al Hoffman** (September 25, 1902–July 21, 1960).
His hit compositions included "Hot Diggity" (1955)
and "Hawaiian Wedding Song" (1958). Hoffman
also wrote the score for the 1949 film *Cinderella*.

**Johnny Horton** (April 30, 1927–November 5,
1960). His recording of "The Battle of New Orleans" was the No. 2 song of 1959. He died in an
auto crash.

## MOVIES

*The Alamo* (d. John Wayne; color)—John
Wayne, Richard Widmark, Laurence Harvey,
Richard Boone, Frankie Avalon

*In director John Sturges' version of Akira Kurosawa's* The
Seven Samurai *(1954), American gunfighters save a
Mexican village from banditos in* The Magnificent Seven.

*The Apartment* (d. Billy Wilder; bw)—Jack Lemmon, Shirley MacLaine, Fred MacMurray

*La Dolce Vita* (Italian, d. Federico Fellini; bw)—
Marcello Mastroianni, Anita Ekberg, Anouk
Aimée (bw)

*Elmer Gantry* (d. Richard Brooks; color)—Burt
Lancaster, Jean Simmons, Arthur Kennedy,
Shirley Jones

*The Entertainer* (British, d. Tony Richardson;
bw)—Laurence Olivier, Joan Plowright

*Flaming Star* (d. Don Siegel; color)—Elvis Presley, Dolores Del Rio, Steve Forrest, Barbara
Eden

*House of Usher* (d. Roger Corman; color)—
Vincent Price, Mark Damon, Myrna Fahey

*I'm All Right, Jack* (British, d. John Boulting;
bw)—Ian Carmichael, Peter Sellers, Terry-
Thomas, Richard Attenborough

*Inherit the Wind* (d. Stanley Kramer; bw)—
Spencer Tracy, Fredric March, Gene Kelly,
Dick York

*The Magnificent Seven* (d. John Sturges; color)—
Yul Brynner, Steve McQueen, Eli Wallach,
Horst Buchholz, James Coburn, Charles Bron-
son, Robert Vaughn

*Never on Sunday* (Greek, d. Jules Dassin; bw)—
Melina Mercouri, Jules Dassin

*North to Alaska* (d. Henry Hathaway; color)—
John Wayne, Stewart Granger, Ernie Kovacs,
Fabian, Capucine

*Pollyanna* (Disney, d. David Swift; color)—
Hayley Mills, Jane Wyman, Richard Egan,
Karl Malden

*Psycho* (d. Alfred Hitchcock; bw)—Anthony
Perkins, Janet Leigh, Vera Miles, John Gavin

*Saturday Night and Sunday Morning* (British, d.
Karel Reisz; bw)—Albert Finney, Shirley
Anne Field, Rachel Roberts

*Sons and Lovers* (British, d. Jack Cardiff; bw)—
Trevor Howard, Dean Stockwell, Wendy
Hiller

*Spartacus* (d. Stanley Kubrick; color)—Kirk
Douglas, Laurence Olivier, Jean Simmons,
Tony Curtis, Charles Laughton, Peter Ustinov

*The Sundowners* (d. Fred Zinnemann; color)—
Deborah Kerr, Robert Mitchum, Peter
Ustinov, Glynis Johns

*Swiss Family Robinson* (Disney, d. Ken Annakin;
color)—John Mills, Dorothy McGuire, James
MacArthur, Janet Munro, Tommy Kirk, Kevin
Corcoran, Sessue Hayakawa

*The Time Machine* (d. George Pal; color)—Rod Taylor, Yvette Mimieux, Alan Young, Sebastian Cabot

*Tunes of Glory* (British, d. Ronald Neame; color)—Alec Guinness, John Mills, Susannah York

## Academy Awards

**April 4.** With recent one-picture sweeps of the Academy Awards, Hollywood studios terminate their Oscar funding rather than risk spotlighting a competitor's film.

Bob Hope hosts.

Best Picture—*Ben-Hur*

Best Actor—Charlton Heston (*Ben-Hur*)

Best Actress—Simone Signoret (*Room at the Top*)

Best Director—William Wyler (*Ben-Hur*)

Best Supporting Actor—Hugh Griffith (*Ben-Hur*)

Best Supporting Actress—Shelley Winters (*The Diary of Anne Frank*)

Best Song—"High Hopes" from *A Hole in the Head*

Best Foreign Film—*Black Orpheus* (French)

Honorary Award—Buster Keaton

Nominated for 12 Oscars, *Ben-Hur* collects a record 11.

French actress Simone Signoret becomes the first actress to win an Academy Award for a performance in a foreign-made film. (The first actor was Charles Laughton in 1933, for the British film *The Private Life of Henry VIII.*)

## News

**January 12.** Michael Todd, Jr., produces the first feature "smellie," a 70-mm film called *A Scent of Mystery*. Cues on the soundtrack send odors through piping to each theater seat—tobacco, garlic, wood shavings—to enhance a scene or occasionally provide a clue. Shown in Chicago, New York, and Los Angeles, the picture is a financial failure.

**January 16.** Hollywood writers strike for a share of television income for post-1948 movies. Universal-International and 40 independents have settled the issue, but the seven major studios continue to hold out.

The Actors Guild walks out in March, temporarily forcing the studios to close. They stay out 33 days; the writers 22 weeks. In the end, neither union wins its demands, but the writers will receive a percentage of television income for pictures made after 1960.

**August 7.** Since the 1947 HUAC investigation of Communism in Hollywood, producers have continued to use screenplays from blacklisted writers by crediting an assumed name. Actor Kirk Douglas pushes Universal-International into openly employing Dalton Trumbo, one of the Hollywood Ten. He receives credit for his *Spartacus* script.

**October 15.** Newspapers describe a new RCA stereophonic sound system for drive-in theaters—one speaker on each front door.

**November 20.** *The New York Times* Sunday supplement spotlights young actors and actresses being groomed for stardom: Warren Beatty, Horst Buchholz, James Darren, Sandra Dee, Troy Donahue, Dolores Hart, Nancy Kwan, and Juliet Prowse.

**More news.** Alfred Hitchcock shoots *Psycho* on a Paramount back lot in a little over a month. The legendary director chooses Anthony Perkins, who owes the studio a picture, for the lead. But when Hitchcock announces the names of those under consideration for the mother—an attempt to throw a smokescreen around the plot—actresses deluge him with requests for the role. Hitchcock shoots the film in black and white to downplay the gore, and uses chocolate sauce for the blood. The famous shower scene takes a full week from the short schedule. (Perkins must leave for a play rehearsal in New York, and a stand-in takes his part.)

*Psycho* breaks all attendance records and makes Hitchcock a wealthy man; Paramount, wanting no part of a horror film, had offered the director 60 percent of the profits if he financed the movie himself.

• *The Magnificent Seven*, this year's hit Western, launches the Hollywood careers of Steve McQueen,

Horst Buchholz, Charles Bronson, Robert Vaughn, and James Coburn. Yul Brynner already has an Oscar.

Disney signs the daughter of actor John Mills after seeing her in the British film *Tiger Bay*. Young Hayley will make six films for the studio during the early 1960s.

The financial success of *Where the Boys Are* (1960), starring Dolores Hart, George Hamilton, Yvette Mimieux, and Jim Hutton, prompts a flood of pictures focusing on teenagers.

| Top Box Office Stars | Newcomers |
|---|---|
| Doris Day | Jane Fonda |
| Rock Hudson | Stephen Boyd |
| Cary Grant | John Gavin |
| Elizabeth Taylor | Susan Kohner |
| Debbie Reynolds | Troy Donahue |
| Tony Curtis | Angie Dickinson |
| Sandra Dee | Tuesday Weld |
| Frank Sinatra | Fabian |
| Jack Lemmon | James Darren |
| John Wayne | George Hamilton |

## Top Money-Maker of the Year

*Ben-Hur* (1959)

## Flop of the Year

*The Alamo*
John Wayne's epic earns back just half of the $13–15 million production costs.

## Quote of the Year

"A boy's best friend is his mother."
Anthony Perkins explaining his philosophy to Janet Leigh in *Psycho*. (Screenplay by Joseph Stefano; based on the novel by Robert Bloch)

## Obituaries

**Ward Bond** (April 9, 1905–November 5, 1960). The popular supporting actor appeared in countless films—mostly Westerns—before finding stardom with the TV series "Wagon Train."

**Clark Gable** (February 1, 1901–November 16, 1960). The Hollywood star died of a heart attack after completing *The Misfits*. During filming, the 59-year-old actor performed many of his own stunts, and insiders believe the physical strain, plus the constant waiting around in desert heat for an unreliable Marilyn Monroe, contributed to his death.

Film critics never considered Gable a notable actor, and he appeared in many mediocre, lightweight films. Yet his remarkable charisma and rugged good looks appealed to men and women alike, and, for much of his 30-year career, the "King" remained a top box-office star. His best remembered films are *It Happened One Night* (1934), which brought him his only Oscar, *Mutiny on the Bounty* (1935), *San Francisco* (1936), and *Gone With the Wind* (1939).

Gable is survived by his fifth wife, Kay Spreckels, who is pregnant with the actor's first and only child.

**Frank Lloyd** (February 12, 1887–August 10, 1960). The motion-picture director received Oscars for *Divine Lady* (1929), *Cavalcade* (1933), and *Mutiny on the Bounty* (1935). He retired in 1945.

**Dudley Nichols** (April 6, 1895–January 4, 1960). The screenwriter's several memorable scripts and adaptations included *The Informer* (1935), for which he won an Oscar, and *For Whom the Bell Tolls* (1943).

**Mack Sennett** (January 17, 1884–November 5, 1960). With some 1,000 silent movies to his credit, the producer and director played an important part in the early development of motion pictures. Most of his films featured the Keystone Cops and the Mack Sennett Bathing Beauties in slapstick comedy, but he also developed stars like Charlie Chaplin, Gloria Swanson, Mabel Normand, and Marie Dressler. In 1937, with a special award, Hollywood acknowledged "the master of fun, discoverer of stars, sympathetic, kindly, understanding comic genius. . . ."

# TELEVISION AND RADIO

## New Prime-Time TV Programs

"The Andy Griffith Show" (October 3, 1960–September 16, 1968; Situation Comedy)—Andy Griffith, Ronny Howard, Don Knotts, (1960–1965) Frances Bavier

"The Bugs Bunny Show" (October 11, 1960–September 25, 1962; Cartoon)—Voices: Mel Blanc

"Checkmate" (September 17, 1960–September 19, 1962; Detective)—Anthony George, Doug McClure, Sebastian Cabot

"The Flintstones" (September 30, 1960–September 2, 1966); Cartoon)—Voices: Alan Reed (Fred Flintstone); Jean Vander Pyl (Wilma Flintstone); Mel Blanc (Barney Rubble) Bea Benaderet (Betty Rubble) *Note:* The program continues on Saturday morning 1966–1970.

"Matty's Funday Funnies" (September 30, 1960–December 29, 1962; Cartoon) *Note:* Following its prime-time run, the program will be shown during the day to 1967.

"My Three Sons" (September 29, 1960–August 24, 1972; Situation Comedy)—Fred MacMurray, Tim Considine (1960–1965), Don Grady, Stanley Livingston, William Frawley (1960–1964), William Demarest (1965–1972)

"Route 66" (October 7, 1960–September 18, 1964; Adventure)—Martin Milner, George Maharis (1960–1963), Glenn Corbett (1963–1964)

"Surfside Six" (October 3, 1960–September 24, 1962; Detective)—Van Williams, Lee Patterson, Troy Donahue, Diane McBain

"The Tall Man" (September 10, 1960–September 1, 1962; Western)—Clu Gulager, Barry Sullivan

## Emmy Awards 1959–1960 (June 20, 1960)

For the next several years, single programs compete for one award in each category.

Drama—"Playhouse 90" (CBS)
Variety—"The Fabulous Fifties" (CBS)
Humor—"Art Carney Special" (NBC)
Children's Programming—"The Huckleberry Hound Show"
Best Actor in a Series—Robert Stack ("The Untouchables," ABC)
Best Actress in a Series—Jane Wyatt ("Father Knows Best," CBS)

## News

**February 11.** During taping a disgruntled Jack Paar complains to his audience that NBC censored last night's joke about a "water closet." Then he walks off the stage. The network needs five weeks to reach an agreement with the talk-show host.

**February 28.** When ABC failed to get the Summer Olympics in Rome, the network withdrew its bid for the Winter Olympics. CBS steps in and broadcasts 10 unsponsored days. The games draw unexpectedly high ratings, astounding both network executives and advertisers.

**April 1.** Last month, Lucille Ball and Desi Arnaz announced their separation and pending divorce. Tonight, TV's most well-known couple make their final appearance together. Arnaz sells his share of the studio to Lucy for $3 million.

**May 12.** Just out of the army, Elvis appears on a Frank Sinatra special. The rock star receives $125,000 for a six-minute spot, the highest fee yet for a single TV guest appearance.

*Statistics:* CBS and NBC transmitted only 68 hours of color programming in all of 1954. This year, color programming averages 32 hours *per week.*

**June 17.** Television writers end their five-month strike. While the new contract brings a 10-percent pay increase, their biggest gain is the 4 percent of gross receipts for reruns into perpetuity; previously, writers received royalties only on the first five reruns.

**July 1.** Effective today, the Canadian Broadcast Board of Governors requires TV stations to raise their Canadian programming content to 45 percent.

**September 3.** Image conscious after the quiz show scandal, CBS suddenly turned the gambling casino on "Mr. Lucky" into a restaurant. The popular show quickly lost its audience and the last episode is televised tonight.

**September 24.** In 1956, with a switch from a daytime slot to Saturday morning, the zany antics of earlier "Howdy Doody" years gave way to a puppet–fairy-tale format. Today, Clarabell carries a "Surprise" sign. At the end of the show, the silent clown finally speaks after 13 years: "Goodbye, kids." (Lew Anderson has played the character since 1955.) The show has been canceled.

**September 29.** "My Three Sons" debuts today. Since Fred MacMurray will work just 65 days a year, the director must break the programs down into sequence shots—such as all front-hall scenes—to squeeze everything in. Apparently William Frawley, accustomed to an orderly sequence on "I Love Lucy," finds it difficult to cope with the MacMurray method.

**September 30.** Prime-time's first animated sitcom, "The Flintstones" gives Fred and Wilma Flintstone and Barney and Betty Rubble all the modern problems and conveniences, just at a stone-age level (starved buzzards under the sink for a kitchen garbage disposal). The show will leave the air in 1966, but with some 3,000 merchandise tie-ins, CBS will bring the Hanna-Barbera series back on Saturday morning in January 1967.

**October 11.** The complete Warner Brothers post-1948 inventory of theatrical cartoon characters—including Bugs Bunny, Daffy Duck, Tweety and Sylvester, and Porky Pig—appear in a prime-time television series beginning tonight. Host Dick Coughlan also chats with animal puppets in a hollow tree.

**November 25.** CBS, the last radio network to broadcast soap operas, wraps up its remaining few today. At the height of their popularity, soaps dominated the airwaves from 10 A.M. to 5 P.M. each day, with 28 separate 15-minute story lines. Virginia Payne, who played "Ma Perkins" for 28 years and never missed a performance, wishes the radio audience well.

Victims of television and local DJs, the soaps will be replaced with entertainment shows, 10 minutes of news on the hour, and 5 minutes of information on the half-hour.

---

*Statistics:* Since 1950, the number of commercial television stations has grown from 104 to 579.

---

**December 7.** WABC in New York adopts the top 40 format. By 1962, the radio station takes over the city's No. 1 spot. Its undeniable success boosts countrywide adoption of Formula Radio. Some stations use DJs, but most insist on a minimum of palaver, to squeeze in extra commercials.

**More news.** Last year, stores stocked the first transistorized TV sets, but most shoppers found the screens too small. This year, a 19-inch picture tube enters the market and manufacturers predict an almost complete transition from tubes to transistors over the next four to five years. The technological revolution turns the TV repairman, an all-too-familiar person in many households, into an endangered species.

## TV Commercials

Hawaiian Punch—The Oaf and Punchie commercial firsts runs on the bargain airtime of "The Jack Paar Show." The host likes the cartoon characters so much, he shows the ad again. Within three days, New York stores sell out of the fruit juice. Before long, school kids across the country ask their friends, "How about a nice Hawaiian Punch?"

Malt-O-Meal—When his nameless big brother attempts some feat, Little Freddie gobbles up his Malt-O-Meal and, with newfound strength and speed, outdoes the older boy.

Muriel Cigars—Edie Adams sings, "Hey, big Spender, spend a little dime on me."

## Memorable Radio Programs End

"Ma Perkins" (December 4, 1933)
"The Romance of Helen Trent" (July 24, 1933)

## Obituaries

**John Hogan** (February 14, 1890–December 29, 1960). The American radio pioneer invented single-dial radio tuning.

# SPORTS

## Winners

### Baseball

World Series—Pittsburgh Pirates (NL), 4 games; New York Yankees (AL), 3 games

Player of the Year—Roger Maris (New York Yankees, AL); Dick Groat (Pittsburgh Pirates, NL)

Rookie of the Year—Ron Hansen (Baltimore Orioles, AL); Frank Howard (Los Angeles Dodgers, NL)

### Football

NFL Championship—Philadelphia Eagles 17, Green Bay Packers 13

AFL Championship—Houston Oilers 24, Los Angeles Chargers 16

College Bowls (January 1, 1960)—
Rose Bowl, Washington 44, Wisconsin 8
Cotton Bowl, Syracuse 23, Texas 14
Orange Bowl, Georgia 14, Missouri 0
Sugar Bowl, Mississippi 21, LSU 0

Heisman Trophy—Joe Bellino (U.S. Naval Academy, HB)

Grey Cup—Ottawa Rough Riders 16, Edmonton Eskimos 6

### Basketball

NBA Championship—Boston Celtics, 4 games; St. Louis Hawks, 3 games

MVP of the Year—Wilt Chamberlain (Philadelphia Warriors)

Rookie of the Year—Wilt Chamberlain (Philadelphia Warriors)

NCAA Championship—Ohio State 75, California 55

### Tennis

U.S. National—Men, Neale Fraser (vs. Rod Laver); Women, Darlene Hard (vs. Maria Bueno)

Wimbledon—Men, Neale Fraser (vs. Rod Laver); Women, Maria Bueno (vs. Sandra Reynolds)

### Golf

Masters—Arnold Palmer
U.S. Open—Arnold Palmer
British Open—Kel Nagle

### Hockey

Stanley Cup—Montreal Canadiens, 4 games; Toronto Maple Leafs, 0 games

### Ice Skating

World Championship—Men, Alain Giletti (France); Women, Carol Heiss (U.S.)

U.S. National—Men, David Jenkins; Women, Carol Heiss

Canadian National—Men, Donald Jackson; Women, Wendy Griner

### Kentucky Derby

Venetian Way—Bill Hartack, jockey

### Athlete of the Year

Male—Rafer Johnson (Track & Field)
Female—Wilma Rudolph (Track & Field)

### Last Season

Alvin Dark (Baseball)
Maurice Richard (Hockey)
Norman Van Brocklin (Football)
Ted Williams (Baseball)

**News**

**February 8.** Named in January to succeed the late Bert Bell, Commissioner Pete Rozelle announces an NFL agreement with the new American Football League (AFL) prohibiting raids on the other league. Still several college athletes sign with both to hedge their bets and find themselves the center of a court-room battle.

**February 18–28.** At the Winter Olympics in Squaw Valley, California, the United States wins three events. David Jenkins and Carol Heiss each capture the individual figure skating titles and the hockey team scores an upset victory over the favored Soviets and Canadians. For Canada, Ann Heggtveit wins her country's first gold medal in skiing.

With a strong performance in speed skating, the USSR wins the unofficial team championship. The United States places third behind Sweden.

**February 23.** Former fans and players watch bulldozers move in to demolish Ebbets Field, home to the Brooklyn Dodgers from 1913 to 1957. Souvenirs not given away will be auctioned off.

**March 13.** Wilt Chamberlain is the first NBA Rookie of the Year to also win the MVP. Just 12 days later, the talented Philadelphia center retires, citing racial tensions and rough tactics on the court. Fortunately, he reverses his decision and signs a new three-year contract with the Warriors.

**May 17.** The NBA approves the transfer of the Minneapolis Lakers to Los Angeles next season.

**June 14.** In testimony before the Senate Antitrust Subcommittee, Jake LaMotta admits he threw a 1947 fight with an unknown light heavyweight for a crack at the middleweight championship of the world. The "Bronx Bull" did win the title in 1949, but fans booed and jeered his every defense until Sugar Ray Robinson took it away 13 months later.

**June 20.** Floyd Patterson knocks out Ingemar Johansson with a left hook at 1:51 of the fifth round, and becomes the first prize-fighter to regain the heavyweight crown. Next March, in their third match, Johansson will go down in the sixth.

**August 3.** In the first known manager trade, Detroit swaps Jimmy Dykes for Cleveland's Joe Gor-

don. Gordon leaves Detroit for the Kansas City Athletics near the end of the season.

**August 25–September 11.** Some 5,900 athletes from 84 nations attend the Summer Olympics in Rome. Outstanding performances include Wilma Rudolph, the first American woman to collect 3 gold medals in track and field, and American Rafer Johnson, who scores a record 8,392 points to win the decathlon. But Abebe Bikila is the big story of the games. The first black African to win a gold medal, he runs the marathon barefoot and breaks the record by almost 15 minutes. Again the Soviets dominate the Olympics, with 103 medals, 43 gold. The United States places second overall with 71 medals, 34 gold.

**September 9.** The first AFL games kick off in the United States. The Eastern Division consists of Boston, Buffalo, Houston, and New York, while the West includes Dallas, Denver, Los Angeles, and Oakland.

In an attempt to block the rival league, the NFL has placed a franchise in Dallas and next year starts up another in Minnesota. But the AFL signs a lucrative TV contract with ABC and introduces several innovations: the two-point conversion, players' names on their jerseys, official time on the scoreboard, and, most importantly, a wide-open offense which generates plenty of excitement.

Still, inadequate facilities and a general lack of top stars keeps attendance down to an average 16,500 over the first season. It is not until 1962 that the figures begin to climb.

**September 28.** Ted Williams slams his 521st HR and retires. The 42-year-old played his entire career with the Boston Red Sox (1939–1942, 1946–1960). Experts rank him second only to Ruth for power and batting average. And despite five prime years spent in a jet fighter (1943–1945, 1952–1953) he finishes third in all-time home runs, behind Babe Ruth (714) and Jimmie Foxx (534). But the Splendid Splinter will probably be best remembered as the last player to hit above .400 in a season (.406 in 1941).

**October 18.** Casey Stengel, manager of the New York Yankees since 1949, is dismissed after reaching the mandatory retirement age of 70. The legendary

Casey, who just set a record with his 10th World Series, claims he was fired for demanding sole authority over player policy.

**October 26.** Since a direct confrontation with the Continental League would raise antitrust concerns in Washington, the AL acts to preempt prime franchise areas. The Washington Senators move to Minneapolis-St. Paul next season to make way for a new Senators team, and a Los Angeles franchise will be set up for 1962. The NL will expand to 10 teams as well in 1962 with clubs in Houston and New York. Ironically, Continental League President Branch Rickey had advocated major league expansion for years.

**More news.** Maurice Richard retires from hockey at the age of 39. A right winger with the Montreal Canadiens for his entire 18-year career, Richard racked up a league-leading 544 regular season goals and 1,091 total points. But most hockey fans will remember the Rocket as the first player in NHL history to score 50 goals in 50 games.

• The last segregated association in baseball, the Negro American League, disbands. The first Negro league, the National, was established in 1920. Teams often played non-league games against white semi-pros, but, until 1947, the Negro circuit gave black Americans their only opportunity to play ball.

## Records

**April 14.** The Montreal Canadiens win a record fifth consecutive Stanley Cup.

**June 21.** German track star Armin Hary runs the 100 meters in 10 seconds flat. Accused of jumping the gun, the 23-year-old requests a second race, then posts the same time. Next month, Canada's Harry Jerome ties the historic record.

**September 2.** American Ralph Boston leaps 26' 3/4" in the long jump at the Olympics. Jesse Owens set the previous mark of 26'5⁵/₁₆" in 1936—the longest-standing record in Olympic history.

**October 13.** Yankee Bobby Richardson drives in a record 12 runs in the World Series, but Bill Mazeroski homers in the ninth inning of the seventh game to give the Pirates their first championship since 1925. Many describe the series as baseball's most exciting ever.

**December 1.** With an assist in a game against Boston, the Detroit Red Wings' Gordie Howe breaks Rocket Richard's all-time NHL scoring record. Richard retired earlier this year after 18 years with the Montreal Canadiens; this is Howe's 15th season.

## What They Said

When LSU quarterback Jimmy Field loses his wristband, with the complete offensive and defensive blueprint, in the first quarter, coach Paul Dietzel reports the loss to game officials.

At half-time, the referee brings the wristband to the LSU dressing room. "Where did you find it?" asks the relieved Dietzel. "In the Florida dressing room." Shut out in the second half, LSU loses 13–10. (*Sports Illustrated* November 7)

## Obituaries

**John Kelly** (October 4, 1889–June 20, 1960). The former U.S. athlete won the sculling singles and doubles in the 1920 and 1924 Olympics, a feat never duplicated. His daughter is Princess Grace of Monaco.

**Lester Patrick** (December 30, 1883–June 1, 1960). The "Silver Fox" steered the New York Rangers to three Stanley Cups (their only cups) and with his brother Frank introduced innovations that changed the game of hockey: an assist on a goal, the penalty shot, and a rule change that allowed a goalie to fall to the ice to make a save. Lester, who played from 1908 to 1920, was also the first defenseman to carry the puck out of his own end.

# *1961*

A new, young president promises to restore prestige to the United States. Despite the fallout from the Bay of Pigs, many Americans like his vibrancy, evident in live press conferences, and his commitment to placing a man on the moon. Just weeks before, the Soviets sent up cosmonaut Yuri Gagarin.

Other headlines include the deaths of Dag Hammarskjöld, Carl Jung, Ernest Hemingway, and Grandma Moses. A plane crash decimates the U.S. skating team, Moscow and Peking tiff over ideology, Amnesty International is established, and Rudolf Nureyev defects. Roger Maris breaks Babe Ruth's home-run record. And the beautiful Jacqueline Kennedy almost single-handedly revives the fashion industry.

For kids, 1961 brings the new "Bullwinkle Show" to TV, different kinds of comic superheros with the "Fantastic Four," and fun movies like The Absent Minded Professor, One Hundred and One Dalmatians, and The Parent Trap. Adults prefer The Guns of Navarone and The Hustler. Teens love the music of West Side Story and new recording artists like Aretha Franklin, Del Shannon, and Gladys Knight and the Pips. Hit songs include "Big Bad John," "The Lion Sleeps Tonight," "Crying," and "Will You Love Me Tomorrow."

## NEWS

**January 3.** Washington finally breaks diplomatic relations with Cuba after Castro demands the removal of all American spies from the United States embassy. Meanwhile, the island nation makes well-publicized preparations for a U.S. invasion.

**January 17.** In his farewell address, President Eisenhower reminds Americans that in the past U.S. industry geared up for war only when the battle had begun. Now, in the Cold War, "a permanent armaments industry of vast proportions" employs 3.5 million Americans. The old soldier acknowledges its importance to national security,

but surprisingly warns, "We must guard against the acquisition of unwarranted influence, whether sought or unsought, by the military-industrial complex. The potential for the disastrous rise of misplaced power exists and will persist."

**January 20.** The youngest chief executive in American history succeeds the oldest when 43-year-old John F. Kennedy is sworn in as the 35th president of the United States. Former presidents Truman and Eisenhower both attend, but last night's heavy snowfall keeps Herbert Hoover's plane from landing. This is the first time since 1885 that three ex-presidents have been alive as the next president takes office.

Kennedy unexpectedly sheds his coat in the icy cold to make his inaugural address, one of the most memorable in U.S. history. He pledges that the United States will "pay any price, bear any burden" to defend the free world, and he exhorts his fellow Americans, "Ask not what your country can do for you; ask what you can do for your country."

President Kennedy, already a wealthy man, donates his salary to charity. He began this practice when first elected to the House in 1947.

## JOHN F. KENNEDY

Born: May 29, 1917, Brookline, Massachusetts, 2nd of 9 children
Education: Harvard University, B.A., 1940
Military Service: U.S. Navy in W.W.II
Marriage: Jacqueline Bouvier, Sept. 12, 1953
Children: Caroline (b.1957), John (b. 1960), Patrick (d. 1963)
Previous Occupations: representative, senator, author
Position Before Taking Office: senator
Legal Residence When Elected: Massachusetts

**January 24.** During a mission alert, a B-52 bomber breaks up near Goldsboro, North Carolina. One atomic bomb descends by parachute, but the plane's other 24-megaton bomb plummets to the ground and breaks apart. The impact triggers five of the six interlocking safety mechanisms; only one switch prevents a nuclear explosion. Three of the eight crew members are killed.

**February.** The 1961 gross national product is up 60 percent since W.W.II (measured in constant dollars), yet with the United States in the midst of a recession, February unemployment stands at 6.8 percent, the highest level since 1941.

**February 6–7.** Convicted of fixing prices and rigging bids from 1955 to 1959, 29 major manufacturers and 44 of their executives receive fines totaling $1.92 million, seven men get 30-day jail terms, and 23 others receive 30-day suspended terms and 5 years probation. Philadelphia District Judge J. Cullen Ganey claims the biggest trade conspiracy trial in American history "destroyed

the model which we offer today as a free world alternative to state control and eventual dictatorship."

**February 17.** After talks with the United States, West Germany agrees to assume a share of the Western aid program. A $1-billion-a-year foreign aid program of loans and grants will help ease the American foreign payments deficit. In June, Tokyo agrees to repay a $490-million debt from the past 15 years of American occupation.

**March 1.** Last fall, presidential candidate John F. Kennedy suggested that American aid to underdeveloped nations be supplemented with a volunteer "peace corps." Young Americans would offer technical assistance and act as goodwill ambassadors while living "at the same level as the citizens of the [host] countries."

*President Kennedy establishes the Peace Corps. Sargent Shriver, on the far left, is the first director.*

With an executive order today, the president establishes his proposed Peace Corps. The *New York Times* reports tremendous public response and some 13,000 young Americans apply by the time the agency receives permanent status in September.

**March 29.** The 23rd Amendment to the Constitution becomes effective, giving Washington, D.C., residents the right to vote in presidential elections and three members in the Electoral College.

**April 17.** Some 1,500 Cuban refugees invade their homeland to overthrow the government of Fidel Castro. But when U.S. air support fails to arrive, Castro's forces overwhelm the poorly prepared expatriates; 400 die during the three-day battle at the Bay of Pigs.

President Eisenhower had strongly recommended the CIA-hatched scheme. The president-elect, concerned not to appear soft on Communism and convinced by guarantees of success, agreed but vetoed air support. On the 24th, President Kennedy issues a statement accepting full responsibility for U.S. participation in the failed invasion.

Misconceived and underplanned, the unilateral military action badly damages American prestige and strains relations with Latin America. For Castro, success brings increased popularity at home and aid from Moscow.

Over the next few months, those who advised the abortive invasion—CIA director Allen Dulles, top planner Richard Bissell, and Joint Chiefs Chairman General Lyman Lemnitzer—all retire.

**April 29.** At an NSC meeting, Kennedy secretly expands the role of the United States in the Vietnam conflict by sending another 100 American military advisors, along with 400 Special Forces troops, to South Vietnam; ordering CIA-directed South Vietnamese agents and Special Forces troops to carry out "sabotage and light harassment" against North Vietnam; and authorizing South Vietnamese forces to attack Communist bases and supply lines in Laos. Within weeks, the North Vietnamese report territorial and airspace violations to the International Commission of Control and Supervision (ICC).

Vice President Johnson, in South Vietnam at the end of May, announces a $40-million increase in U.S. military and economic aid while Saigon undertakes extensive domestic reforms. (The government's unpopularity was underscored in last month's election by the large number of abstentions and the substantial vote for the opposition.) On June 16, the White House agrees that Americans will instruct the Vietnamese Army directly rather than just training instructors.

Kennedy and many of his advisors fought fascism in W.W.II, only to see Eastern Europe swallowed by the Soviets. They intend to block Communism in Southeast Asia. Vice President Johnson, in his follow-up report, typically states that the United States must decide "whether to help these countries to the best of our ability or throw in the towel in the area and pull back our defenses to San Francisco and a 'Fortress America' concept."

**May 4.** To push the Kennedy administration into enforcing Supreme Court rulings on segregated bus facilities, the Congress of Racial Equality (CORE) sends two busloads of blacks and whites on a Freedom Ride from Washington to New Orleans. CORE, founded at the University of Chicago in 1942, counts on Southern reaction to desegregation to supply the needed pressure.

The Freedom Riders meet their first serious opposition in Anniston, Alabama. An incendiary bomb sends 12 passengers to the hospital, and several people on the second bus are beaten. When another mob greets them in Birmingham on May 14 and no police appear, the bus driver refuses to carry on, and the riders disband. But their grit and determination has inspired the rights movement, and leaders from SNCC, SCLC, and the Nashville Student Movement join the campaign.

A white mob attacks the new group in Montgomery on the 20th. When Alabama Governor Patterson fails to answer telephone calls from Washington, Attorney General Robert Kennedy dispatches some 500 federal marshalls to restore order. The next day, marshalls disperse a violent mob at the Montgomery First Baptist Church, where Martin Luther King, Jr., is preaching to a packed audience.

Yet federal support is withheld when the Freedom Riders move on to Jackson, Mississippi. Bobby Kennedy promised not to enforce the integration law if Mississippi prevented further violence. No violence occurs, but authorities arrest CORE director James Farmer and 26 others for attempting to use the all-white facilities.

By the end of the 12 freedom rides, Southern authorities have arrested and sentenced some 300 people. The campaign has succeeded in uniting the various civil rights groups, pulling young blacks into the movement, and focusing national attention on the cause.

---

*Statistics*: 1960 voter registration drives increased Negro political activity by 95 percent and the sit-in movement, which began last year, spreads to 20 states by September. Still, the Southern Regional Council claims that the civil rights movement has had no visible impact in Alabama, Louisiana, Mississippi, and South Carolina.

---

**May 29.** In West Virginia, Secretary of Agriculture Orville Freeman dispenses the first food stamps. The administration program grew out of President Kennedy's concern for the poverty he saw in that state during the election campaign.

**May 30.** Assassins gun down President Rafael Trujillo y Molina of the Dominican Republic. A ruthless dictator for the past 30 years, Trujillo served as president only from 1930 to 1938 and 1942 to 1952, but he maintained his power through various family members placed in high office.

**May 31.** When South African Prime Minister Strydom died in office in 1958, his replacement, Hendrik Verwoerd, a strong supporter of apartheid, quickly moved to create a republic. Last fall, whites voted 850,000 to 775,000 for a republican form of government, on the understanding that a new constitution would change little and that every effort would be made to remain within the British Commonwealth.

But South Africa must obtain a unanimous vote of support at the Commonwealth Conference to continue membership as a republic. When Canada, Malaya, Ghana, and Nigeria severely criticize its policy of apartheid, South Africa severs all ties, setting a course of increasing isolationism.

**July 12.** Some 1,000 delegates to the 52nd annual NAACP convention take a Freedom Train from Philadelphia to Washington, where representatives meet with the president. The delegation praises Kennedy's executive actions—a two-year extension of

the U.S. Civil Rights Commission and the creation of the President's Committee on Equal Employment Opportunity—but expresses dismay over "the absence of a clear call" for civil rights legislation.

**July 25.** When John F. Kennedy met with Nikita Khrushchev in June, the Soviet premier, perhaps believing the Bay of Pigs had exposed a weak president, threatened war over Berlin. Tonight, in an address to the nation, Kennedy tells the American people that the German city has become "the great testing place of Western courage and will." He outlines a program to increase U.S. Armed Forces manpower and weaponry and asks for an additional $3.25 billion for defense. As well, the president emphasizes the need for private fallout shelters in case of war. Within a week, he transfers responsibility for national civil defense to the Department of Defense.

His speech creates a national mania for bomb shelters. In the months ahead, civil defense officials distribute 31 million copies of "Fallout Protection: What to Know and Do About Nuclear Attack."

**August 3.** At an Ottawa convention, the Socialist farmers' CCF amalgamates with affiliated unions of the Canadian Labour Congress and New Party clubs to form the New Democratic party (NDP). (The convention rejects a motion to permit Communist-dominated unions to join.) The members elect Saskatchewan Premier Tommy Douglas as their first national leader.

**August 13.** Since 1949, over 3 million people have fled to West Berlin to escape East Germany's political and economic restrictions. But as the building superpower crisis threatens that access route, the steady flow has become an embarrassing flood. Over the past two weeks, some 16,000 East German refugees have crossed over, many of them skilled technicians.

Last night, a Warsaw Pact communiqué proclaimed that "temporary" measures must be taken to protect East Berlin from the espionage and subversive activity in West Berlin. Today, East German police and troops erect a wooden and barbed-wire fence along the 25-mile border. Within three days, they begin building a wall of prefabricated concrete blocks.

Western powers protest the Soviet isolation of West Berlin, but make no effort to tear down the wall. President Kennedy sends an additional 1,500 soldiers to reinforce U.S. warnings against a blockade, and Vice President Johnson visits the city on the 19th to reassure West Germany of American support.

By the end of the year, border guards will kill 8 and wound 69, yet some 10,000 East Germans will escape to the West.

**August 17.** The United States and all Latin American nations (except Cuba) formally proclaim the Alliance for Progress, a $10-billion aid package for member countries who undertake agrarian and tax reform and resist the spread of Communism. But in the last part of the decade, Washington will give the alliance little attention and it will become just another U.S. foreign aid program.

**September 1.** In Belgrade, delegates from Yugoslavia, Indonesia, the UAR, and 22 other nonaligned nations deny the inevitability of war and issue a strong denunciation of colonialism. At their second meeting, in Cairo, in 1964, 47 nations will attend.

**September 1.** Citing increased tensions between the United States and the Soviet Union, Moscow breaks the three-year voluntary moratorium on nuclear testing. Four days later, President Kennedy reluctantly orders the resumption of underground tests.

**September 5.** An amendment to the Federal Aviation Act of 1958 makes hijacking punishable by death and authorizes federal penalties for other crimes committed on commercial aircraft.

**September 18.** An airplane carrying U.N. Secretary-General Dag Hammarskjöld to the Congo crashes in northern Rhodesia, killing the six-man crew and seven of his U.N. staff. The impact throws Hammarskjöld and one aide clear, but the 56-year-old Swedish diplomat dies before help arrives; his assistant survives five days.

Under Hammarskjöld's stewardship (1953–1961), the United Nations created an impartial peacekeeping force that has successfully intervened in several international trouble spots. An outstanding negotiator himself, the Secretary-General was

to mediate between the U.N. force and the breakaway province of Katanga. Soviet opposition to Hammarskjöld and his mission along with the circumstances of the crash, to many, suggest assassination. Postmortems find bullet wounds in two of the dead, and the aide, before dying, spoke deliriously of explosions and sparks in the sky. Although a coroner rules the crash accidental—the bullets officially came from a box of ammunition—the rumor never dies.

**September 22.** The ICC reinforces a 1955 ruling against segregation in interstate travel and terminals by requiring a bus driver to report any interference with a black passenger and by establishing fines for those carriers in violation (effective November 1). Attorney General Robert Kennedy had petitioned the ICC, after the violent Southern response to the Freedom Rides, for a means of implementing the six-year-old ruling.

Justice follows up with an order to remove all segregating signs from waiting rooms, as well as a campaign to integrate 15 airports; 13 comply voluntarily, and the department files suits against the remaining 2.

**September 24.** U.S. public schools open without violence for the second successive year. Three major cities in the South—Dallas, Atlanta, and Memphis—open their first desegregated public schools, while in Georgia, Texas, North Carolina, and Florida, six public institutions of higher education admit black students.

Yet just 44 school districts have initiated desegregation plans since 1959; prior to that, 733 of 2,839 segregated school districts had taken steps toward integration. And while President Kennedy stated in February that "all students should be given the opportunity to attend public schools regardless of their race, and that's in accordance with the Constitution," he has yet to send Congress a special message to that effect.

**September 29.** In 1958, Egypt and Syria united politically as the United Arab Republic. Today, Syrian army officers rebel against Egyptian domination, dissolving the four-year union. When Yemen formally withdraws in December, leaving Egypt as the sole remaining UAR state, Nasser sees an end to his dream of creating a representative state for the Arab world.

**October 17.** With American and Soviet tanks facing each other across the border, the Berlin crisis has threatened to turn the Cold War into a hot one. After building the wall in August, the Warsaw Pact sent 300,000 troops into East Germany. The White House, in turn, dispatched an additional 40,000 troops and four fighter plane squadrons to Europe. As well, on September 7, Assistant Defense Secretary Nitze clearly stated U.S. determination to defend Berlin, with nuclear weapons if necessary.

Today, Premier Khrushchev tells the 22nd Congress of the Soviet Communist Party that Western powers have shown an inclination to resolve the German problem. (Khrushchev actually denies having made an ultimatum on the issue.) A propaganda triumph for the West, the Americans have stood firmly behind their German ally and regained much of the prestige lost earlier this year during the Cuban fiasco. Both superpowers withdraw their tanks from the wall in January.

**October 17.** At the Soviet Congress in Moscow, Khrushchev severely criticizes the Albanians. The tiny nation is boycotting the meeting over the Communist reconciliation with Yugoslavia, the policy of peaceful coexistence with the West, and de-Stalinization. China refuses to join the premier in his attack, and Chou En-lai stalks out, further widening the Sino-Soviet ideological rift.

Already cut off from Soviet aid, Albania nonetheless continues to attack USSR policy. Moscow breaks diplomatic relations in December. Albania, in turn, develops closer ties with Peking, giving the Chinese Communists a foothold in Europe. But their economic promises to Albania remain largely unfulfilled.

**November 1.** Women Strike for Peace demonstrates against the arms race. From a small group set up last year by Dagmar Wilson in Washington, D.C., WSP membership has grown to approximately 50,000 in 60 communities. The women march (signs include "Clean milk and dirty bombs don't mix"), lobby local governments, and send letters and telegrams to Washington, particularly to

Jacqueline Kennedy. The 1,500 demonstrating in the nation's capital deliver petitions to American and Soviet officials.

**November 3.** Conflicting advice on U.S. intervention in Vietnam prompts Kennedy to send General Maxwell Taylor, his military advisor, and Walt Rostow, from National Security Affairs, to survey the military and political situation in Saigon. Their report recommends increased military aid, an initial commitment of 6,000–8,000 troops, and political reforms by the South Vietnamese government.

Although intelligence reports predict that Hanoi will match American escalation, Defense Secretary McNamara and the Joint Chiefs of Staff are "inclined to recommend" Taylor's proposals. But they warn that if North Vietnam or China overtly intervenes, greater U.S. troop commitments will likely be needed in the future, up to an estimated maximum of 205,000.

Kennedy accepts all major recommendations, including a demand for reforms in the Diem government. Yet when the South Vietnamese premier resists prodding, Washington backs down. After all, they reason, the United States can rely on American spirit and drive to repel the Communists and, as Taylor suggests, if all else fails, North Vietnam would be extremely vulnerable to bombing.

The United States provides the first direct military support to South Vietnam on December 11: 33 army helicopters and an estimated 400 air and ground crew.

**November 3.** U Thant of Burma is unanimously elected as acting U.N. Secretary-General, ending a superpower dispute that has left the position vacant since Hammarskjöld's death on September 18.

**December 10.** Project Gnome, the first atoms-for-peace nuclear test under the Plowshare Program, experiments with the generation of power through trapped heat. But scientists miscalculate the force of the 5-kiloton detonation 1,216 feet underground, and highly radioactive steam vents into the atmosphere, near Carlsbad, New Mexico. The AEC later announces that the concept "does not appear feasible at this time."

With the release of radiation, opposition grows against the planned nuclear excavation of a harbor

in Alaska. Despite official endorsement by the legislature, Project Chariot will be scrapped next year.

**December 14.** Kennedy establishes the President's Commission on the Status of Women. He
tells commission head Eleanor Roosevelt that he
will back a drive to prevent "discrimination by law
or implication" against working women. Next year,
the president issues an executive order to bar sexual
discrimination in all federal agencies and executive
departments.

**December 17.** During the afternoon performance of a circus, near Rio de Janeiro, a disgruntled
employee sets a fire in the main tent. At least 323
die, burned to death or crushed in the panic-
stricken stampede to escape, and another 800 are
injured.

**More news.** The postwar baby-boom crests with
a record 4,282,000 births.

## Obituaries

**Tom Dooley** (January 17, 1927–January 18, 1961).
The American medical missionary lectured and
wrote three books on his Asian experiences to finance MEDICO, his international health organization. He died of cancer.

**Dag Hammarskjöld** (July 29, 1905–September
18, 1961). Elected in 1953 as the United Nation's
second Secretary-General, the Swedish diplomat
became the architect of the office.

Hammarskjöld deemphasized superpower concerns and, with impartiality and outstanding skills
in negotiation, actively intervened in international
crises, most notably in the Suez and Lebanon. This
year, the Swedish Academy acknowledges his work
with the first posthumous Nobel prize, the peace
award.

**John McCurdy** (August 2, 1886–June 25,
1961). The first person in the British Empire to fly
an airplane, on February 23, 1909, the Canadian
became the first pilot to send and receive wireless
messages while airborne two years later.

**Mohammed V** (August 10, 1909–February 26,
1961). The ruler of Morocco (1927–1961) was
largely responsible for his nation winning independence in 1956. (He adopted the title of king in

1957.) His son, Crown Prince Moulay Hassan, succeeds him.

**Sam Rayburn** (January 6, 1882–November 16,
1961). Generally acknowledged as the second
most powerful man in Washington, the Texas
Democrat served as speaker of the House twice as
long as any other man in U.S. history—17 years
since 1940.

**Edith Bolling Wilson** (October 15, 1872–
December 28, 1961). In 1919, after a stroke left
President Woodrow Wilson (in office 1913–1921)
partially paralyzed and almost blind, the first lady
took an active role in leading the government. After her husband's death in 1924, Mrs. Wilson faithfully attended all dedications in his honor.

**Zog (Ahmed Bey Zogu)** (October 8, 1895–
April 9, 1961). The president and virtual dictator
of Albania (1928–1939) fled when Italy invaded in
1939. The postwar Communist government barred
his return.

# BEGINNINGS AND ENDINGS

## News

**January 8.** A five-year celebration of the American Civil War officially opens with ceremonies at
the tombs of Ulysses S. Grant in the North and
Robert E. Lee in the South. The centennial comes
just two years after the death of the last Civil War
veteran.

**January 26.** President Kennedy chooses J. G.
Travell, age 59, as his personal physician—the first
woman appointed to the position and the first civilian physician since the Harding administration
(1921–1923). A grateful Kennedy credits her with
earlier diagnosing the source of much of his back
pain.

**February 20.** In New York the First National
City Bank offers a fixed-term certificate of deposit.
The marketable CD is redeemable at maturity.

**February 27.** President Kennedy names Harvard
professor Henry Kissinger, age 37, as a part-time
consultant on national security affairs.

**May 28.** British lawyer Peter Benenson, who has
defended political prisoners in Spain, Hungary, and

South Africa, protests human rights violations in his article "The Forgotten Prisoners" in *The Observer*. When more than 1,000 readers respond with offers of practical help, the human rights watchdog Amnesty International is born.

**August 9.** President Kennedy appoints James B. Parsons, age 50, judge for the Northern Illinois District, the first Negro granted a federal judgeship in the continental United States.

**November 11.** Under de-Stalinization, the Soviet city of Stalingrad is renamed Volgograd. (Last month, authorities moved Stalin's body from Red Square to a plain grave beside the Kremlin Wall.)

**More news.** A few months after the Bay of Pigs, anti-Somoza groups in Nicaragua join together in a left-wing front. Taking their name from Augosto César Sandino, a revolutionary leader who fought the Nicaraguan government and American Marines between 1927 and 1933, the guerrillas become the National Liberation Front (Frente San de Liberación Nacional, FSLN), or Sandinistas.

### New Products and Businesses

Instead of another sugar-coated cereal, General Mills promotes the nutritional value of Total.

*This year, the Danish toy manufacturer begins exporting LEGO Bricks to the United States.*

Other new products this year include Carnation non-dairy creamer Coffee-Mate, and Trommer's Red Letter Beer, the first low-calorie brew.

Aurora Plastics, a Long Island company, offers make-your-own-monster kits. Within three years, kids and their parents will buy millions of the 10 different creatures, including the 28-inch Frankenstein.

Coca-Cola brings out the no-return glass bottle, later modified for twist-top.

*The living area of the Volkswagen Camper converts into sleeping quarters and contains built-in units for cooking, washing, and refrigeration. The German automaker's success prompts American manufacturers to produce similar recreational vehicles.*

The McDonald brothers sell out to Ray Kroc for $2.7 million. By the end of the year, 323 McDonald's restaurants will have sold over 500 million hamburgers in total.

After babysitting his newborn grandchild, a Procter & Gamble researcher looked into the practicality of a disposable diaper. The company conducts a full market test of Pampers this December, but several years will pass before the diaper is distributed nationally.

## Fads

When students at the University of British Columbia push an old hospital bed 40 miles, other Canadian campuses challenge with greater distances. (McMaster's puts bicycle wheels on their model.) USC takes up the fad, but bed racing never catches on in the United States.

In 1929, businessman Thomas Duncan introduced a Filipino weapon into the U.S. toy market and called it a "yo-yo." When son Donald puts a crack Filipino team on kiddy TV shows, his sales skyrocket.

One minor fad comes from dependable Wham-O and another from the White House. The toy manufacturer creates Slip 'n Slide, a 25-foot watered-down plastic sheet for backyard summer fun. The president, in relieving his back pain, rejuvenates sales of the old-fashioned rocking chair.

# SCIENCE AND TECHNOLOGY

## News

**January 13.** The Associated Press reports that over the past five years an Italian research team has repeatedly fertilized a human egg in the laboratory. One embryo lived for 29 days. (Dr. John Rock of Harvard achieved in vitro fertilization in 1944, but failed to keep the embryo alive for more than six days.) The scientific community, on the whole, ignores the well-documented evidence.

**January 31.** In preparation for manned orbital flight, a Mercury capsule takes Ham, a male chimpanzee, on a 16-minute, 39-second flight. The program will also send up dummy astronauts.

**January 31.** Placed in orbit today, the *Samos II*

satellite is the first of a USAF reconnaissance series scheduled to replace U-2 planes by 1963.

**February 1.** In the first test firing, a Minuteman ICBM lands on target 4,500 miles down-range. Solid fuel eliminates the complicated system of loading and unloading liquid propellants.

**February 24.** American automakers announce the standardization of seat-belt hardware (in front seats) in 1962 models.

---

*Statistics*: At Cornell University, an automotive crash-injury research program concludes that seat belts would reduce accident injuries by 50 percent.

---

**March 11.** An AMA journal article theorizes that the overuse of antibiotics has eliminated sensitive strains and allowed resistant germs to survive and spread.

**April 12.** *Vostok 1* carries Yuri Gagarin on a single orbit of the Earth. From a height of 203 miles, at a maximum speed of 17,398 mph, the first man in space picks out lakes, large rivers, and coastlines, and enjoys the sensation of weightlessness.

Gagarin ejects from the capsule at 21,000 feet to land by parachute. Before he removes his helmet, the 5'2" cosmonaut frightens a young peasant woman.

Joyous news for the Soviet people, the successful flight creates an uproar in the United States. The next day, the *New York Herald-Tribune*, in a fit of pique, repeats Communist Chinese charges that two earlier Soviet cosmonauts died in flight.

Nonetheless, Gagarin receives a tumultuous welcome in Britain this July. (Prime Minister Harold Macmillan reportedly says, "It would have been twice as bad if they had sent the dog.")

**May 5.** Less than a month after Gagarin's historic circuit, U.S. Navy Commander Alan Shepard tests the integrity of the Mercury capsule in a 15-minute flight. The 2,300-pound craft reaches an altitude of 116.5 miles in a 302-mile suborbital arc.

Unlike his Soviet counterpart, the 37-year-old

astronaut fires his retro rockets to return to Earth. America's first man in space later says he had "about 30 seconds to look out the window."

**May 25.** In a special joint session, President Kennedy tells Congress, "I believe that this nation should commit itself to achieving the goal, before this decade is out, of landing a man on the moon and returning him safely to Earth." At this point, no rocket exists to launch a moon expedition.

A Gallup poll released on the 30th shows just 33 percent of Americans favor spending an estimated $40 billion to put a man on the moon.

**May 28.** American astronomers Roland L. Carpenter and Richard M. Goldstein used microwaves, at the tracking station in the Mohave Desert, to determine that Venus rotates just once in 250 days (later refined to 243.09). And, unlike other planets in the solar system, Venus turns from east to west.

**June 17.** According to *The New York Times*, Vice-Admiral Hyman Rickover last year told the Joint Atomic Energy Subcommittee that Moscow needs just $2.98 to acquire millions of dollars worth of information on the *Polaris* submarine. He claimed that U.S. toy companies based their plastic models on official navy blueprints, released in an interservice rivalry for public approval. "I certainly would like to have similar information on their submarines," he said. The Pentagon denies releasing the data.

**June 29.** *Transit IV-A* carries the first nuclear-powered device into orbit, an atomic-powered SNAP battery (Systems for Nuclear Auxiliary Power) designed to produce 2.7 watts of electricity for five years.

**July 21.** The *Liberty Bell 7* splashes down successfully after a 16-minute suborbital flight, but the hatch cover blows off prematurely, and Virgil Grissom must swim for his life. Sinking under the weight of his spacesuit, the astronaut manages to grasp a helicopter sling. The capsule and its valuable photographic record disappear beneath the waves.

Still, the Mercury suborbital flights offered NASA an opportunity to test the craft's controls and evaluate astronaut response to space.

**July 22.** A ceremonial phone call between Prime Minister Diefenbaker in the Yukon and President Kennedy in Massachusetts completes the microwave telecommunications network linking the United States to Alaska through Canada.

**August 6–7.** With 17 orbits of the Earth, 26-year-old cosmonaut Gherman Titov becomes the first man to spend a whole day in space. He eats and sleeps as *Vostok 2* travels 435,000 miles—the equivalent of a trip to the moon.

**September 8.** In a study of 3,000 men, an AMA journal article reports a clear statistical link between heart disease and smoking. Subjects who smoked more than 40 cigarettes a day suffered twice as much heart disease as light smokers or non-smokers.

**September 19.** NASA selects a 1,000-acre site near Houston, Texas, for the $60-million Apollo research and command center.

**November 29.** Following two unmanned orbital flights, in April and September, Cape Canaveral launches a 37-pound chimpanzee in a Mercury-Atlas 5 satellite. Enos circles the Earth twice before splashing down safely south of Bermuda.

**December 19.** A transatlantic voice, picture, and teletype cable between Britain and Canada establishes the first link of a Commonwealth communications network.

**December 21.** The army announces the first successful interception of an in-flight rocket, by a Nike-Zeus antimissile.

**More news.** Johns Hopkins Hospital in Baltimore demonstrates a combination of mouth-to-mouth resuscitation and external cardiac massage for heart attack victims.

• Overloaded with deck guns, the wooden ship *Vasa* sank in the Stockholm harbor just minutes after launching in 1628. This year, the Swedes raise the 198-foot vessel and recover some 3,500 objects on board.

• The AMA Council on Drugs finds that the estrogen cancer scare "does not seem justified on the basis of available evidence." Discovered by a team of doctors in 1929, synthetic estrogen was quickly recognized as a means of regulating menopause. But early research found cancer in mice, and physicians have since refused to prescribe the hormone for extended periods. By the middle of this decade, estrogen will assume a major role in preventing osteoporosis.

• In 1929 Ernst Gräfenberg introduced a coiled ring as an intrauterine contraceptive device. But the IUD subsequently gained a reputation for perforation and tubal infection. This year, U.S. physician Jack Lippes introduces a loop of inert plastic. By the mid-1960s, his device, along with the Birnberg bow and the Margulies spiral, will be widely accepted.

• Over-the-counter thalidomide, in the 1950's, won a large following throughout Europe and the British Commonwealth. People took it for sleeplessness, asthma, and early pregnancy nausea. Last year, a U.S. pharmaceutical company applied for approval to market the drug, but FDA researcher Frances Kelsey has waffled over reported side effects.

A British journal has registered complaints of numb feet and fingers, and West Germany has experienced an alarming number of phocomelic births (infants with malformed legs and arms). Kelsey will resist the pressure until April 1962, when Dr. Helen Taussig returns from Europe and, in a press conference, warns physicians about a drug already withdrawn from the European market.

By that time, thalidomide-related birth defects will number 10,000 worldwide; the United States will count just 10. Kelsey will receive a gold medal for distinguished public service.

## Other Discoveries, Developments, and Inventions

Underwater loudspeaker
Wireless microphone, from Sony, which uses a battery-operated, pocket-size transmitter
Bonnet hair dryer (3 million sales this year)
Electric toothbrush from Squibb
Kodachrome II color film with thinner emulsion for sharper images
Immunosuppressant azathioprine for organ transplantation

World's First seawater conversion plant, at Freeport, Texas

*The IBM Selectric types from a moving golf-ball-size cluster of letters rather than separate keys and a moving carriage. Other revolutionary features include plastic ribbon cartridges and an automatic feed for the paper.*

## Obituaries

**Jules Bordet** (June 13, 1870–April 6, 1961). The Belgian bacteriologist developed a new method for detecting bacteria and in 1906, with O. Gengou, identified the whooping cough bacillus. He won a Nobel prize in 1919.

**Alfred Gilbert** (February 15, 1884–January 24, 1961). In 1912, after watching construction workers replace girders, the U.S. toy inventor created the Erector set.

**Carl Jung** (July 26, 1875–June 6, 1961). One of the pioneers of modern psychiatry, along with Sigmund Freud and Alfred Adler, Jung based his theories on mythology and the unconscious. He believed, for instance, that an individual tries to reconcile the tension of complementary opposites such as feeling and thinking. Critics described Jung as obscure and too often a mystic, but his ideas appealed to the general public.

**Richard Lewisohn** (1875–August 11, 1961). His discovery of a blood preservative in 1915 made blood banks possible.

# THE ARTS

February 22—*Come Blow Your Horn*, with Lou Jacobi, Hal March, Warren Berlinger (677 perfs.)

March 8—*Mary, Mary*, with Barbara Bel Geddes, Barry Nelson (1,572 perfs.)

April 13—*Carnival!*, with Anna Maria Alberghetti, Jerry Orbach, James Mitchell, Kaye Ballard (719 perfs.)

May 4—*The Blacks*, with James Earl Jones, Cicely Tyson (1,408 perfs.)

October 14—*How to Succeed in Business Without Really Trying*, with Robert Morse, Rudy Vallee, Virginia Martin (1,416 perfs.)

November 22—*A Man for All Seasons*, with Paul Scofield (637 perfs.)

## Tony Awards

Actor (Dramatic)—Zero Mostel, *Rhinoceros*

Actress (Dramatic)—Joan Plowright, *A Taste of Honey*

Actor (Musical)—Richard Burton, *Camelot*

Actress (Musical)—Elizabeth Seal, *Irma la Douce*

Play—*Becket* by Jean Anouilh

Musical—*Bye, Bye Birdie*

## News

**January 27.** Leontyne Price—the first black American to star at the Met on opening night—debuts in *Il Trovatore*. *Saturday Review* praises her "glistening sound and warm artistry."

**March 19.** The 97-year-old Shakespeare Memorial Company, based in Stratford-upon-Avon, becomes the Royal Shakespeare Company.

**June 16.** Rudolf Nureyev asks for political asylum in Paris, as the Kirov Ballet boards a plane for London. The 23-year-old Soviet ballet star had learned he was to be sent home.

**October 8.** The Actors' Equity Association announces that, after June 1, 1962, members will no longer perform in segregated theaters.

**October 18.** A new show opens at the Museum of Modern Art in New York. Some 116,000 visitors walk past a Matisse abstract titled *The Boat* before Genevieve Habert notices it is hanging upside-down.

**November 13.** Pablo Casals plays a return engagement at the White House. The 84-year-old cellist performed for President Theodore Roosevelt in 1904.

**November 15.** New York's Metropolitan Museum of Art pays $2.3 million—triple the auction record for a single painting—for Rembrandt's *Aristotle Contemplating the Bust of Homer.*

**December.** Frustrated with negative theater critics, producer David Merrick finds average Americans with the same names as the critics and prints their rave reviews of his new show in the *Herald-Tribune.* (The individual's photograph accompanies each comment.)

**More news.** An art dealer advised Andy Warhol to paint what was important to him. Since the 31-year-old artist eats soup every day, he stencils rows of Campbell's soup cans. The piece becomes one of his most successful. When Warhol turns to silk-screen reproduction, his pioneering work propels the Pop Art movement.

## Obituaries

**Thomas Beecham** (April 29, 1879–March 8, 1961). Renowned for both his elegant interpretations and unpredictable temper, the British conductor was a legend in his own time.

**Percy Grainger** (July 8, 1882–February 20, 1961). The Australian-American classical pianist made important contributions to English folk melody with piano and instrumental arrangements.

**Moss Hart** (October 24, 1904–December 20, 1961). His Broadway plays, written with George S. Kaufman, included *The Man Who Came to Dinner* (1939). Hart, as well, wrote screenplays and won a Tony for direction.

**George S. Kaufman** (November 16, 1889–June 2, 1961). His best-known plays included *The Solid Gold Cadillac* (1953), written with Howard Teichmann.

**Grandma Moses** (Anna Mary Robertson

Moses) (September 7, 1860–December 13, 1961). Grandma Moses first picked up a brush in 1918, but won recognition only after she retired from the farm 20 years later. Critics judge her scenes of everyday life as lacking in aesthetic merit, but most agree with President Kennedy that "the directness and vividness of her paintings restored a primitive freshness to our perception of the American scene."

**Max Weber** (April 18, 1881–October 4, 1961). In 1909, an art critic described his first one-man show as "a brutal, vulgar, and unnecessary display of art license." By the 1940s, Weber was regarded as the dean of American modern art.

## WORDS

James Baldwin, *Nobody Knows My Name*
Ian Fleming, *Thunderball*
John H. Griffin, *Black Like Me*
Robert A. Heinlein, *Stranger in a Strange Land*
Joseph Heller, *Catch-22*
Gavin Maxwell, *Ring of Bright Water*
Henry Miller, *Tropic of Cancer*
Harold Robbins, *The Carpetbaggers*
J. D. Salinger, *Franny and Zooey*
Muriel Spark, *The Prime of Miss Jean Brodie*
John Steinbeck, *The Winter of Our Discontent*
Irving Stone, *The Agony and the Ecstasy*
Leon Uris, *Mila 18*
Theodore H. White, *The Making of the President, 1960*

### News

**February 1.** A poll of 276 U.S. dailies picks *The New York Times* as the country's best newspaper.

**April 27.** Police use tear gas to quell 2,000 students rioting over Harvard's decision to replace Latin with English on future diplomas. The university describes the 325-year tradition as "hypocritical" since Latin is no longer a required subject.

**May.** Grove Press releases the first American edition of Henry Miller's *Tropic of Cancer*, 27 years after its publication in Europe. The most banned

book of its day, the work will continue to be censored by communities across the nation.

**May 9.** President Kennedy recently suggested that newspapers practice voluntary restraint on items affecting national security. Former vice-president Richard Nixon tells the Detroit Press Club today that such an approach could become a "cloak for [the] errors, misjudgments, and failings of government."

**September.** Language purists bitterly object to the inclusion of slang and colloquial terms in the *Third New International Dictionary (Unabridged)*. The Merriam editors retort that the Webster update neither endorses nor prescribes words, but merely reports their usage.

**October 30.** For 30 years, American schools have preferred the "look-say" or "whole-word" method of reading instruction. But a close examination of results, sponsored by the Council of Basic Education, finds the system measurably less effective than the old "phonics" method, in which students learn to associate letters with sounds.

**More news.** To experience firsthand the prejudices endured by black Americans in the deep South, writer John Howard Griffin took a pigmentation drug, further darkened his skin with vegetable dye, and concealed his hazel eyes behind glasses. Originally published as a series of articles in the Negro magazine *Sepia*, Griffin's account in *Black Like Me* receives national and international acclaim.

### Cartoons and Comics

**November.** Marvel Comics launches a new era of fantasy superheroes with the *Fantastic Four*—Mr. Fantastic, the Human Torch, the Thing, and the Invisible Girl.

### TIME Man of the Year

John F. Kennedy

### New Words and Phrases

A-Okay
controller (a woman's corset)

high rise (a multistoried building)
knee-jerk
megalopolis
microelectronics
muscle shirt
nano-second
neutron bomb
plane-cheater (a woman's large handbag)
soul (jazz with an earthy, swinging blues feeling)

## Obituaries

**Whittaker Chambers** (April 1, 1901–July 9, 1961). The Time-Life editor retired in 1948 after accusing Alger Hiss of spying for the Soviets.

**Mazo de la Roche** (January 15, 1879–July 12, 1961). The Canadian novelist attained considerable popularity between 1925 and 1950 with her 16-volume saga of the Whiteoak family of Jalna.

**Dashiell Hammett** (May 27, 1894–January 10, 1961). *The Maltese Falcon* (1930) with cynical Sam Spade—the original hard-boiled PI—marked the apex of Hammett's writing career. His sophisticated detectives Nick and Nora Charles became better known through *The Thin Man* film series with William Powell and Myrna Loy. Hammett died of lung cancer.

**Ernest Hemingway** (July 21, 1899–July 2, 1961). His first major novel, *The Sun Also Rises* (1926), epitomized the Hemingway style (sparse, short sentences with few adverbs or adjectives) and revealed the Hemingway code (survive a complex, often painful, life with dignity and strength). That story of an aimless postwar generation made the American writer famous.

The following years produced *A Farewell to Arms* (1929), *Death in the Afternoon* (1932), *To Have and Have Not* (1937), *For Whom the Bell Tolls* (1940), and *The Old Man and the Sea* (1952), his last published work. He won the Nobel prize for literature two years later.

In poor health and subject to depression, Hemingway died of a self-inflicted gunshot wound.

**James Thurber** (December 8, 1894–November 2, 1961). The noted humorist and cartoonist was a long-time contributor to the *New Yorker*. He also produced comic stage sketches, such as *The Thurber Carnival*.

# FASHION

## Haute Couture

Rather than introduce new silhouettes, couturiers spotlight the complete costume with accessorized hats, shoes, even hair and makeup. Skirts rise to midknee, but drop again by the end of the year.

## News

**January 20.** With the inauguration of the nation's youngest president, fashion attention focuses on his wife Jacqueline. For day wear, the first lady favors a two-piece dress or suit, sleeveless or with three-quarter sleeves. The skirt, generally A-line, falls to midknee or just below, the overblouse follows simple lines, and the semifitted jacket (often collarless) touches the hipbone. Accessories include low-heeled, comfortable pumps, short white gloves, and a pillbox hat. For evening, Jackie—as Americans soon refer to her—prefers empire-line gowns.

Fashion critics describe her solid-colored silhouettes as conservative, but women admire her classic taste. The clothing industry quickly capitalizes on public admiration (even producing Jack and Jackie mannequins for store displays).

**More news.** In the United States, shoe distribution expands to nontraditional outlets—discount houses, self-service department stores, even food and drugstores.

• The American company Wolverine Shoe and Tanning Corp. registers the shoe name Hush Puppies.

• To help fur ranchers compete against dyed-skin garments, an amendment to the Fur Products Labeling Act requires unaltered skins to bear a "natural" label.

## Colors and Materials

Spring fashions feature pink; autumn styles emphasize green, berry tones, and browns; and year-round clothes use fresh shades of blue, orange, coral red, evergreen, and paler shades of green. In menswear, olive green is a brighter color.

Textured fabrics dominate—puffed, ridged, layered, blistered.

To meet the demand for dyed soft leathers during the early sixties, manufacturers introduce less expensive, shiny treated leather and synthetics. Fashion magazines dub them the "wet look."

## Clothes

New to stores this year, stretch pants use a stirrup strap to tighten the line even further. Stitched-down creases present a polished crispness, but the pants tend to bag at the knees.

In the summer, casual clothes follow the line of the Hawaiian muumuu and the pyramid or A-shape.

Women like the "little nothing" evening dress, a sleeveless loose chemise in rich velvet, silk chiffon, or brocade with beading or embroidery.

Telecasts of old movies brings back the glamorous bias cut of the 1930s. Fabrics cling without tightness, softening this year's silhouette with upper body molding and gracefully flared skirts.

Mail-order catalogs carry a one-piece nylon stocking and brief called "panti-hose." Uncertain of their appeal, some distributors list the $1.99 item with leotards rather than regular hosiery.

The double-breasted suit reappears and more men wear vests.

## Accessories

Day or evening, fashionable women prefer simple square-toed pumps of medium height, in crepe, satin, calf, or alligator. In men's shoes, slip-ons account for an estimated 35–50 percent of sales.

High, round shapes dominate women's hats. Men buy brightly colored cloth hats.

Stores note a demand for jet jewelry (a compact black coal).

## Hair and Cosmetics

According to *Britannica Yearbook*, "Hair has not had as much notice in fashion since the days of the French courts." Many credit Mrs. Kennedy, film star Brigitte Bardot, and other newsworthy women with making the bouffant the standard. Women often heighten the basic "beehive" ("bird's nest" to some) with a topknot or group of curls.

# POPULAR MUSIC

"Tossin' & Turnin' "—Bobby Lewis
"Big Bad John"—Jimmy Dean
"Runaway"—Del Shannon
"Pony Time"—Chubby Checker
"The Lion Sleeps Tonight"—Tokens
"Take Good Care of My Baby"—Bobby Vee
"Blue Moon"—Marcels
"Will You Love Me Tomorrow"—Shirelles
"Travelin' Man"—Ricky Nelson
"Calcutta" (Instr.)—Lawrence Welk
"Runaround Sue"—Dion & the Belmonts
"Quarter to Three"—Gary "U.S." Bonds
"Hit the Road, Jack"—Ray Charles
"Surrender"—Elvis Presley
"Michael"—Highwaymen
"Running Scared"—Roy Orbison
"Please Mr. Postman"—Marvelettes
"Moody River"—Pat Boone
"Wooden Heart (Muss I Denn)"—Joe Dowell
"Mother-in-law"—Ernie K-Doe
"I Like It Like That, Part 1"—Chris Kenner
"The Boll Weevil Song"—Brook Benton
"Apache" (Instr.)—Jorgen Ingmann & His Guitar
"Exodus" (Instr.)—Ferrante & Teicher
"Crying"—Roy Orbison
"Shop Around"—Miracles

## Grammy Awards (1961)

Record of the Year—Henry Mancini, "Moon River"

Song of the Year (songwriter)—Henry Mancini and Johnny Mercer, "Moon River"

Album of the Year—Judy Garland, *Judy at Carnegie Hall*

Best Vocal Performance (Male)—Jack Jones, "Lollipops and Roses" (single)

Best Vocal Performance (Female)—Judy Garland, *Judy at Carnegie Hall* (album)

Best New Artist—Peter Nero

## News

**January 30.** The Shirelles are the first female, rock 'n' roll group to reach No. 1. Their song "Will You Love Me Tomorrow" was cowritten by Gerry Goffin and 17-year-old Carole King.

**May.** The two-disc *Judy Garland at Carnegie Hall* tops the LP charts for 13 weeks. Next year, Garland will become the first woman to receive a certified gold record.

**November.** Just 15 months after "The Twist" topped the charts, the first rock 'n' roll dance craze pushes the song to No. 1 again. (Manufacturers respond with Twist shoes, chairs, hats, and other products.) Checker's innovation lasts to nearly mid-decade with adults, but teenagers turn to related dances such as the Fish, the Pony, the Hucklebuck, and the Fly.

**More news.** The Miracles score Motown's first million-seller with "Shop Around," cowritten by company owner Berry Gordy and singer Smokey Robinson. Before the end of the year, the Marvelettes give Gordy his first No. 1 hit with "Please Mr. Postman."

• Manufacturers introduce a 7-inch 33⅓, called a "little LP" or "compact six" (with three selections on each side). But this attempt to establish a single industry speed fails.

• "Those Oldies But Goodies" by Little Caesar & the Romans sets off a 1950s nostalgia craze. Doo-wop groups find renewed success, the Regents with "Barbara Ann," the Capris with "There's a Moon Out Tonight," and the Cleftones with "Heart and Soul." The Marcels reach No. 1 with "Blue Moon."

• Le Club, the first U.S. disco, opens in New York City.

• Songwriter-producer Phil Spector and partner Lester Sill launch the Philles label. Their first release, "There's No Other (Like My Baby)," with the Crystals, reaches No. 20 and sets the style for other Philles groups such as the Ronettes and the Righteous Brothers.

Folk music thrives on American campuses. New performers include 20-year-old Joan Baez.

### New Recording Artists

Glen Campbell
Judy Collins
Aretha Franklin
Ben E. King
Gladys Knight & the Pips
Lettermen
Tony Orlando (solo)
Gene Pitney
Paul Revere & the Raiders
Del Shannon
Spinners
Ray Stevens
Tokens
Mary Wells

## Obituaries

**Joe E. Howard** (February 12, 1878–May 19, 1961). A vaudeville and radio star, Howard also composed some 500 songs, including "I Wonder Who's Kissing Her Now" (1909).

**Dominick James La Rocca** (April 11, 1889–February 22, 1961). The jazz cornetist won fame as the creator of the first Dixieland jazz band in 1916.

## MOVIES

*The Absent Minded Professor* (Disney, d. Robert Stevenson; bw)—Fred MacMurray, Nancy Olson, Keenan Wynn, Tommy Kirk

*Breakfast at Tiffany's* (d. Blake Edwards; color)— Audrey Hepburn, George Peppard, Patricia Neal, Buddy Ebsen, Mickey Rooney

*The Guns of Navarone* (d. J. Lee Thompson; color)—Gregory Peck, David Niven, Anthony Quinn, Stanley Baker, Anthony Quayle, James Darren, Irene Papas

*The Hustler* (d. Robert Rossen; bw)—Paul Newman, Jackie Gleason, Piper Laurie, George C. Scott

*Judgment at Nuremberg* (d. Stanley Kramer; bw)—Spencer Tracy, Burt Lancaster, Richard Widmark, Marlene Dietrich, Maximilian Schell, Judy Garland, Montgomery Clift

*Jules and Jim* (French, d. François Truffaut; bw)—Jeanne Moreau, Oskar Werner

*Lover Come Back* (d. Delbert Mann; color)— Rock Hudson, Doris Day, Tony Randall, Edie Adams

*Nikki, Wild Dog of the North* (Disney, d. Jack Couffer; color)—Jean Coutu, Emile Genest, Nikki the dog, Neewa the bear

*One Hundred and One Dalmatians* (Disney; color; animated)—Voices: Rod Taylor (Pongo); Cate Bauer (Perdita); Betty Lou Gerson (Cruella De Vil); Lisa David (Anita)

*One, Two, Three* (d. Billy Wilder; bw)—James Cagney, Horst Buchholz, Arlene Francis, Pamela Tiffin

*The Pit and the Pendulum* (d. Roger Corman; color)—Vincent Price, John Kerr, Barbara Steele

*The Pleasure of His Company* (d. George Seaton; color)—Fred Astaire, Debbie Reynolds, Lilli Palmer, Tab Hunter

*The Roman Spring of Mrs. Stone* (d. Jose Quintero; color)—Vivien Leigh, Warren Beatty, Lotte Lenya, Jill St. John

*A Taste of Honey* (British, d. Tony Richardson; bw)—Rita Tushingham, Dora Bryan, Robert Stephens, Murray Melvin

*Two Women* (Italian, d. Victoria De Sica; bw)— Sophia Loren, Eleanora Brown, Jean-Paul Belmondo, Raf Vallone

*West Side Story* (d. Robert Wise, Jerome Robbins; color)—Natalie Wood, Richard Beymer, Rita Moreno, George Chakiris, Russ Tamblyn

*Whistle Down the Wind* (British, d. Bryan Forbes; bw)—Hayley Mills, Bernard Lee, Alan Bates

### Academy Awards

**April 17.** After 11 years at Hollywood's Pantages Theatre, Oscar moves to the larger Civic Auditorium in Santa Monica, miles from the nearest film studio. ABC broadcasts the ceremonies for the first time, under a new five-year contract, and Bob Hope welcomes an estimated 70 million viewers.

Best Picture—*The Apartment*
Best Actor—Burt Lancaster (*Elmer Gantry*)
Best Actress—Elizabeth Taylor (*Butterfield 8*)
Best Director—Billy Wilder (*The Apartment*)
Best Supporting Actor—Peter Ustinov (*Spartacus*)
Best Supporting Actress—Shirley Jones (*Elmer Gantry*)
Best Song—"Never on Sunday" from the film of the same name
Best Foreign Film—*The Virgin Spring* (Swedish)
Honorary Awards—Gary Cooper; Stan Laurel

Audience and media attention focuses on Elizabeth Taylor, just recovering from a near fatal bout of pneumonia. In later years, the actress will often remark, "I won the Oscar because I almost died— pure and simple."

Gary Cooper receives an Honorary Oscar in recognition of his "many memorable performances." Supposedly a pinched nerve kept the actor at home, but many suspect much worse when Jimmy Stewart, accepting on Coop's behalf, offers his friend an emotional tribute. One month later Gary Cooper will die of cancer.

### News

**January 23.** In a sharp reversal of recent permissive rulings, the U.S. Supreme Court holds, 5–4, that state and local motion picture censorship is not unconstitutional. (The court warns that this decision addresses movies alone and only with regard to the Chicago Municipal code.) Next month, the media industries—film, book, radio, and television—agree to form a united front against censorship.

**More news.** This year, the major studios make about 12 percent of their movies outside the United States and the independents film 63 percent overseas. Foreign countries offer authentic locales, some subsidies, and always cheaper labor. In a congressional hearing on the issue, actor Charlton Heston points out that, while MGM spent $14.5 million making *Ben-Hur* in Italy, the film's $50-million gross increased union employment and saved the studio.

• In *Blue Hawaii*, soldier Elvis Presley returns to the islands to work in a tourist agency. Joan Blackman provides the romantic interest and Angela Lansbury—just 10 years older than the star—plays his mother. With tunes such as "The Hawaiian Wedding Song" and "Can't Help Falling in Love," the movie becomes Elvis's most popular. But like his other pictures, *Blue Hawaii* receives scant critical attention.

• For the first time, Walt Disney animators photocopy drawings onto acetate cels rather than tracing each one by hand. Critics give *One Hundred and One Dalmatians* mixed reviews.

• In a sequel to the popular *Tammy and the Bachelor* (1957), Sandra Dee replaces Debbie Reynolds. The younger actress follows *Tammy and the Doctor* (1961) with a second film in 1963, *Tammy Tell Me True*.

• Mel Blanc, the voice of Bugs Bunny, Daffy Duck, and dozens of other cartoon characters, is critically injured in a car accident. The mimic lies unconscious for three weeks until a neurosurgeon asks, "How are you feeling today, Bugs Bunny?" A faint voice responds from the swathe of bandages, "Eh, just fine, Doc. How're you?"

## Top Money-Maker of the Year

*The Guns of Navarone*

| Top Box Office Stars | Newcomers |
| --- | --- |
| Elizabeth Taylor | Hayley Mills |
| Rock Hudson | Nancy Kwan |
| Doris Day | Horst Buchholz |
| John Wayne | Carol Lynley |
| Cary Grant | Dolores Hart |
| Sandra Dee | Paula Prentiss |
| Jerry Lewis | Jim Hutton |
| William Holden | Juliet Prowse |
| Tony Curtis | Connie Stevens |
| Elvis Presley | Warren Beatty |

## Quote of the Year

Marilyn Monroe: "How do you find your way back in the dark?"
Clark Gable: "Just head for the big star straight on. The highway's under it, and it'll take us right home."
—The last lines in *The Misfits* and the last words ever spoken on screen by the two superstars. (Screenplay by Arthur Miller, based on his story)

## Obituaries

**Leo Carillo** (August 6, 1880–September 10, 1961). The character actor portrayed Pancho in the TV series "The Cisco Kid."

**Jeff Chandler** (December 15, 1918–June 17, 1961). Ruggedly handsome with prematurely gray hair, Chandler played the romantic lead in several films. He died of blood poisoning following surgery.

**Charles Coburn** (June 19, 1877–August 30, 1961). The veteran stage actor, already 60 years old in his film debut, patented the role of the crusty but kind old gent. In 1944, he won the best supporting Oscar for *The More the Merrier*.

**Gary Cooper** (May 7, 1901–May 13, 1961). Never once a villain in his 35-year career, the tall, handsome actor personified the strong, silent man of integrity.

From a $5-a-day trick rider in 1925, Cooper moved up to a starring role by 1929 in *The Virginian*.

His shy manner and terse speech made him a natural for Westerns, and his enormous screen presence gave the genre new stature.

Cooper won two best actor Oscars, for his portrayal of the W.W.I hero in *Sergeant York* (1941) and the quietly brave marshal in *High Noon* (1953). Earlier this year, the Academy presented him with a special award for his contributions to the industry.

**Marion Davies** (circa 1897–September 22, 1961). While many considered her a brilliant film comedienne, Davies is remembered as the mistress of newspaper magnate William Randolph Hearst, as depicted in *Citizen Kane* (1941). She retired in 1937.

**Barry Fitzgerald** (March 10, 1888–January 4, 1961). With his heavy brogue, the cocky little stage actor became Hollywood's Irishman. His most memorable roles included *How Green Was My Valley* (1941) and *Going My Way* (1944), for which he received a best supporting Oscar.

**Chico Marx** (March 22, 1891–October 11, 1961). The oldest of the five Marx Brothers led Harpo and Groucho after Zeppo retired in 1933. Wearing a pointed hat and too-small velvet jacket, Chico used a heavy Italian accent to explain Harpo's voiceless actions. *Love Happy* (1950) was their last of 10 films together.

**Joseph Schenck** (December 25, 1878–October 22, 1961). The pioneer motion-picture executive founded 20th Century Pictures in 1933 with William Goetz and Darryl F. Zanuck. The company merged with Fox in 1935.

**Ann May Wong** (January 3, 1907–February 3, 1961). One of the first successful Chinese actresses, the American-born beauty appeared in her first movie at the age of 12. She retired in 1942.

## TELEVISION AND RADIO

### New Prime-Time TV Programs

"Ben Casey" (October 2, 1961–March 21, 1966; Medical Drama)—Vince Edwards, Sam Jaffe (1961–1965), Bettye Ackerman

"The Bullwinkle Show" (September 24, 1961–September 16, 1962; Cartoon)—Voices: Bill Scott (Bullwinkle J. Moose, Dudley Do-right, and Mr. Peabody); June Foray (Rocky Squirrel and Natasha Fatale) *Note:* The program continues in the early evening 1962–1963, Saturday morning 1963–1964, and in syndication 1964–1973.

"CBS Reports" (January 5, 1961–September 7, 1971; Documentary)

"Car 54, Where Are You?" (September 17, 1961–September 8, 1963; Situation Comedy)—Joe E. Ross, Fred Gwynne, Bea Pons, Paul Reed

"The Defenders" (September 16, 1961–September 9, 1965; Courtroom Drama)—E. G. Marshall, Robert Reed

"The Dick Van Dyke Show" (October 3, 1961–September 7, 1966; Situation Comedy)—Dick Van Dyke, Mary Tyler Moore, Rose Marie, Morey Amsterdam, Carl Reiner

"Dr. Kildare" (September 28, 1961–August 30, 1966; Medical Drama)—Richard Chamberlain, Raymond Massey

"Hazel" (September 28, 1961–September 5, 1966; Situation Comedy)—Shirley Booth, Don DeFore (1961–1965), Whitney Blake (1961–1965), Bobby Buntrock

"The Joey Bishop Show" (September 20, 1961–September 7, 1965; Situation Comedy)—Joey Bishop, Abby Dalton (1962–1965)

"Mr. Ed" (October 1, 1961–September 8, 1965; Situation Comedy)—Alan Young, Connie Hines, Larry Keating (1961–1963)

"Sing Along with Mitch" (January 27, 1961–September 1964; Musical Variety)—Mitch Miller, The Sing Along Gang, Leslie Uggams

### Emmy Awards 1960–1961 (May 16, 1961)

Drama—*Macbeth* ("Hallmark Hall of Fame," NBC)

Variety—"Astaire Time" (NBC)

Humor—"The Jack Benny Show" (CBS)

Children's Programming—"Young People's Concert" ("Aaron Copland's Birthday Party," CBS)

Best Actor in a Series—Raymond Burr ("Perry Mason," CBS)

Best Actress in a Series—Barbara Stanwyck ("The Barbara Stanwyck Show," NBC)

## News

**January 25.** President John F. Kennedy conducts the first live televised press conference. He insists on a 6:00 P.M. telecast to reach a wider audience.

**April.** The first Saturday-afternoon "Wide World of Sports," with Jim McKay, revolutionizes TV sportscasts. Rather than slot specific events one at a time, ABC offers live and pretaped segments of as many different sports as possible. The innovative, quick pacing is an unqualified success.

**May 5.** Alan Shepard's suborbital flight, at 9:34 A.M. EST, draws television's largest audience ever, an estimated 30 million.

**May 9.** At an NAB meeting, FCC chairman Newton Minow tells network executives, "It is not enough to cater to the nation's whims—you must also serve the nation's needs." But while he describes TV as "a vast wasteland," this fall's lineup signals an upswing, with "The Defenders" and "The Dick Van Dyke Show."

**June 1.** The FCC authorizes FM conversion to stereophonic broadcasting. By December, the total number of FM stations will jump from last year's 819 to 961.

**July 27.** The country's first private network, Canadian Television Network (CTV) announces that a microwave relay system will be completed by mid-1963.

**September 23.** NBC's "Saturday Night at the Movies" is the first movie series to carry post-1948 Hollywood films and the first to be aired in color. Showcasing current movie stars, the 20th Century-Fox titles draw enormous audiences. Next year, ABC follows suit and NBC adds "Monday Night." By the end of the decade, the networks will schedule a combined nine movies per week.

**September 24.** The Saturday-morning success of "Rocky and His Friends" (1959–1961) brings "The Bullwinkle Show" to prime time. Animated up-home boys Rocket J. Squirrel and Bullwinkle B.

Moose—now the star—continue to match wits with old-fashioned spies Boris Badenov and Natasha Fatale. Other animated segments carry over and, in a new component, "Dudley Do-Right of the Mounties" unendingly attempts to retrieve his girlfriend Nell from the clutches of Snidely K. Whiplash.

With excellent voices from Hans Conreid, Charles Ruggles, narrator William Conrad, and others, the irreverent, hilarious takeoffs capture adult fans as well as children. Switched back to weekends in 1963, the program will return in 1964 for nine years on ABC.

(Initially, a puppet moose introduced the show, but when he told kids to pull the knobs off their TV sets—"In that way, we'll be sure to be with you next week"—he quickly disappeared.)

**September 24.** As ABC continues to resist color broadcasts, Walt Disney switches to NBC and renames his program "Walt Disney's Wonderful World of Color." For the first time, the studio can draw on its full backlog of shows.

**October 3.** The *New York Post* describes tonight's debut episode as "flimsy." The sponsor nearly drops the program. But "The Dick Van Dyke Show" will move up into the top 10 in next season's ratings then remain in the top 20 until it leaves the air.

**December 11.** In Cleveland, KYW broadcasts a 90-minute afternoon talk show with a former big band singer. By 1963, "The Mike Douglas Show" is syndicated nationally.

**More news.** The postwar baby boom, the growing number of two-TV homes, and the time slot's cheaper costs prompt networks to give more attention to Saturday-morning programming in the early years of this decade.

Still, commercials on children's programs increasingly glamorize toys and often misrepresent them through animation. In response to consumer complaints, the NAB adopts a series of guidelines.

• ABC inaugurates a 40-second local station break for extra commercials. In 1948, the networks allotted just 10 seconds. Both CBS and NBC follow suit.

• This year, puppeteers Jim Henson and Frank Oz create Miss Piggy.

• "Car 54" producers, to avoid confusion with Bronx police cars, choose a bright red Plymouth Belvedere. TV viewers see no difference on their black and white sets.

## TV Commercials

Kodak—Using still photos, the two-minute "Turn Around" commercial follows the life of Judy Ellis from a naked baby outside her front door to a grown woman posing with her own child. Her dad, Dr. Irving Ellis, took the pictures.

Star Kist Tuna—Beatnik Charlie the Tuna, with his beret and dark glasses, insists on good-tasting tuna.

## Memorable Radio Programs End

"Gunsmoke" (April 26, 1952)

## Obituaries

**Lee De Forest** (August 26, 1873–June 30, 1961). His invention of the audio tube in 1906 made him "the father of radio." He presented the first live musical broadcast in 1909, with Enrico Caruso at the Metropolitan Opera, and the first radio news broadcast in 1916. In all, the inventor held 300 patents.

**Marian Jordan** (April 16, 1898–April 7, 1961). The radio actress played opposite her husband Jim Jordan on "Fibber McGee and Molly" (1935–1957).

# SPORTS

## Winners

### Baseball

World Series—New York Yankees (AL), 4 games; Cincinnati Reds (NL), 1 game
Player of the Year—Roger Maris (New York Yankees, AL); Frank Robinson (Cincinnati Reds, NL)

Rookie of the Year—Don Schwall (Boston Red Sox, AL); Billy Williams (Chicago Cubs, NL)

### Football

NFL Championship—Green Bay Packers 37, New York Giants 0
AFL Championship—Houston Oilers 10, San Diego Chargers 3
College Bowls (January 1, 1961)—
    Rose Bowl, Washington 17, Minnesota 7
    Cotton Bowl, Duke 7, Arkansas 6
    Orange Bowl, Missouri 21, Navy 14
    Sugar Bowl, Mississippi 14, Rice 6
Heisman Trophy—Ernie Davis (Syracuse, HB)
Grey Cup—Winnipeg Blue Bombers 21, Hamilton Tiger-Cats 14

### Basketball

NBA Championship—Boston Celtics, 4 games; St. Louis Hawks, 1 game
MVP of the Year—Bill Russell (Boston Celtics)
Rookie of the Year—Oscar Robertson (Cincinnati Royals)
NCAA Championship—Cincinnati 70, Ohio State 65

### Tennis

U.S. National—Men, Roy Emerson (vs. Rod Laver); Women, Darlene Hard (vs. Ann Haydon)
Wimbledon—Men, Rod Laver (vs. Charles McKinley); Women, Angela Mortimer (vs. Christine Truman)

### Golf

Masters—Gary Player
U.S. Open—Gene Littler
British Open—Arnold Palmer

### Hockey

Stanley Cup—Chicago Blackhawks, 4 games; Detroit Red Wings, 2 games

*Ice Skating*

World Championship—Canceled (See below)
U.S. National—Men, Bradley Lord; Women, Laurence Owen
Canadian National—Men, Donald Jackson; Women, Wendy Griner

*Kentucky Derby*

Carry Back—Johnny Sellers, jockey

*Athlete of the Year*

Male—Roger Maris (Baseball)
Female—Wilma Rudolph (Track & Field)

*Last Season*

Bill Sharman (Basketball)

## News

**February 15.** An airplane crash outside Brussels decimates the U.S. figure-skating team. The 72 fatalities include U.S. men's champion Bradley Lord, women's champion Laurence Owen, the pairs team, the dance team, all the silver and bronze medal winners of the U.S. senior championships, their coaches, officials, and friends of the team. The group was en route to Prague for the World Championships; the competition is canceled out of respect.

**April 10.** At the Masters in Augusta, 26-year-old South African Gary Player beats defending champion Arnold Palmer and amateur Charlie Coe by one stroke. He is the first foreigner to win the prestigious event.

**August 26.** The Hockey Hall of Fame opens at the Canadian National Exhibition in Toronto. Players become eligible five years after retirement.

**September 10.** Auto racer Count Wolfgang von Trips dies with 15 spectators in a terrible accident at the Italian Grand Prix in Monza. His teammate Phil Hill of Santa Monica wins the race to clinch the 1961 world drivers' championship.

**September 20–21.** Antonio Abertondo swims from England to France in 18 hours, 50 minutes, and, after a 4-minute rest, steps back into the water. A little over 24 hours later, the 42-year-old Argentinian completes the first round-trip crossing of the English Channel.

**November 9.** The PGA, 45 years after its founding, eliminates a "Caucasians only" clause in its constitution. (California had refused to allow the 1962 championship in Los Angeles because of the racial restriction.) But the ruling leaves control of tournament applications with local sponsors, and, in the end, black Americans continue to be denied admittance.

**November 28.** Syracuse halfback Ernie Davis becomes the first black to win the Heisman Trophy, football's highest honor. The Cleveland Browns sign him for $80,000, an enormous sum for an NFL rookie. But just before the 1962 College All-Star game, Davis is stricken with leukemia. He will die 16 months later.

**More news.** The first new NBA franchise since 1949, the Chicago Packers place a distant last in their division. Next season, the team becomes the Zephyrs, then in 1963 will relocate to Baltimore as the Bullets.

## Records

**March 10.** With a 32-point game against the Pistons, Wilt Chamberlain becomes the first NBA player to accumulate more than 3,000 points in a single season (3,033). Next year, the Philadelphia center will score an incredible 4,029 points.

**October 1.** As Mickey Mantle and teammate Roger Maris hit homer after homer this season, fans realize Babe Ruth's single-season record of 60 HR could be broken. When an injury sidelines Mantle, attention focuses on Maris. To add to the pressure, Commissioner Ford Frick—a personal friend of the Babe—declares that the record must be broken within 154 games, the same number Ruth played in 1927. If not, the new record would be marked with an asterisk.

Today, in the 162nd and last game of the AL season, 27-year-old Roger Maris hits his 61st HR in Yankee Stadium, "The House That Ruth Built."

**October 8.** Yankee pitcher Whitey Ford completes 32 consecutive scoreless innings of World Series play. (A toe injury forces him to leave in the sixth inning of game 4.) Babe Ruth set the previous record—29²/₃ innings—as a White Sox pitcher during 1916 and 1918.

**This year.** America's largest bowling alley opens in Willow Grove, Pennsylvania—116 lanes.

## Obituaries

**Ty(rus) Cobb** (December 18, 1886–July 17, 1961). After 21 years with the Tigers (1905–1926) and 2 years with the Athletics, the great Ty Cobb retired.

At one time, the Georgia Peach held 90 major league records, including highest career batting average (.367), runs scored (2,244), runs batted in (1,901), and career stolen bases (892) (a veteran player reportedly told a young catcher, when Cobb breaks for second, "throw to third"). The famous outfielder taught himself to hit left-handed to be closer to first base. But that same fierce competitiveness drove him to regularly spike opponents while running the bases.

The first player elected to the new Baseball Hall of Fame, in 1936, Cobb held 16 records at his death, including an enormous 4,191 career hits.

# *1962*

Without a doubt, most Americans believe the Cuban missile crisis will escalate into nuclear war. But with the hard-earned lesson from the Bay of Pigs—never trust military advisors—John F. Kennedy holds back from the fatal step. Still, to ensure a larger range of responses, he authorizes an enormous military buildup. And to demonstrate the U.S. commitment to Vietnam, he increases economic and military aid and pushes the number of American advisors to 11,000.

At home, the administration advances the black cause through existing laws and executive orders until a riot at the University of Mississippi convinces the president and his younger brother of the urgency and desperation of the civil rights movement.

This year, the United States makes great strides in space technology. John Glenn becomes the first American astronaut, a Ranger capsule reaches the moon, an interplanetary probe travels past Venus, and NASA places the first active communications satellite in orbit.

As well, 1962 witnesses the Seattle World's Fair. Sonny Liston wins the heavyweight championship, and the Mets play their first game. Johnny Carson takes over "The Tonight Show," Sean Connery stars in the first James Bond film, protest songs break into the top 40, and bouffant hair reigns supreme.

## NEWS

**January 10.** In Peru, a huge block of ice and snow falls from the north summit of Mt. Huascaran, roars down the canyon, and bursts into the river valley below. The vast expanse of snow spreads outward and buries the small agricultural community of Ranrahirca; only 97 of 2,700 townspeople escape death. Altogether the avalanche kills nearly 4,000 people and 10,000 animals.

**January 13.** USAF pilots, in C-123 transports modified for crop dusting, spray pesticide along the 70-mile route connecting Saigon with a popular sea

resort. President Kennedy, in November of last year, approved "Operation Ranch Hand" to destroy VC food supplies and to defoliate their jungle cover. Pamphlets dropped afterward tell South Vietnamese farmers that the chemicals are harmless.

**January 19.** The Canadian federal government abolishes all racially and religiously based immigration rules. Now immigrants must simply be "personally suitable and . . . have the required background and training to become worthwhile citizens."

**January 25.** Drafted by the Justice Department, the administration's first civil rights bill would safeguard black and Puerto Rican voting rights by substituting a sixth-grade education for voter literacy tests. The NAACP criticizes the measure as a "token offering" and urges Congress to supervise enrollment and management of federal elections. Still, Southern senators successfully block the bill with a three-week filibuster.

Meanwhile, the administration continues with executive action to promote equality, including a Labor Department ban on apprentice training programs barring black applicants.

**February 8.** A Pentagon spokesman announces that the United States is establishing a Military Assistance Command in South Vietnam (MACV) because "this is a war we can't afford to lose." The new group assumes responsibility for all military activities, while the Military Assistance and Advisory Group (MAAG) (in South Vietnam since 1955) will continue to advise the Vietnamese Army.

Since the Geneva Accords limit American personnel, officials decline to release a tally of U.S. "advisors" in Vietnam. Nonetheless, by the end of the year, informed sources estimate the number has jumped to 11,000. Aid reaches some $200 million this year, totaling over $2 billion since 1954.

As questions arise over the U.S. role in Indochina, Kennedy states in a February 14 press conference that he has sent no combat troops to Vietnam "in the generally understood sense of the word." But Defense Secretary McNamara confirms, on March 15, that U.S. military training personnel have returned the fire of Communist guerrilla forces.

**February 10.** In the first spy exchange of the Cold War, the United States secretly trades Rudolf Abel for Gary Powers, the pilot whose U-2 spy plane was shot down in 1960. Abel, who operated a Soviet spy network out of New York for nine years, was caught in 1957 and sentenced to 30 years in prison. The Soviets announce the release of Powers "as an act of clemency," but make no mention of Abel.

**March.** The South Vietnamese government begins moving peasants from their scattered villages into more secure hamlets, surrounded by fences and moats and protected by troops. Saigon hopes to win the farmers' allegiance with land reform and U.S.-funded schools and medical facilities.

By September, Diem claims to have relocated a third of the rural population, but the Strategic Hamlet Program fails from the outset. He never initiates the promised land reform. American funds disappear into the pockets of corrupt South Vietnamese officials, and the VC easily eliminate any strategic advantage by joining forces and overrunning single hamlets.

The peasants, removed from their ancestral lands to no advantage, become even more alienated from the government. When the Diem regime falls next year, the program will disintegrate.

**March 2.** In a nationwide address, President Kennedy announces that Soviet nuclear advances in recent months force the United States to resume atmospheric testing. (A massive blast on October 30, 1961, ranged between 58 and 90 megatons; until then, the largest man-made explosion was a 30-megaton Soviet bomb.) The ongoing nuclear test-ban conference adjourned in Geneva on January 29, as the East and West remained deadlocked over a test monitoring system.

Congressional leaders and other high administration officials respond favorably to the decision. On April 25, the AEC conducts the first U.S. atmospheric test since 1958, above Christmas Island in the central Pacific, and then detonates a low-yield device above Nevada on July 7.

**March 2.** As the hill people gain the upper hand in their fight for independence, General Ne Win seizes power in Rangoon. His military junta drives the guerrillas back, abolishes the parliamentary system, and sets up a Socialist Republic of the Union of Burma, with Ne Win as president. But the politically naive soldier, adopting a policy of neutrality and isolating Burma from all foreign contact, economically ruins the once prosperous nation.

**March 9.** In a widely criticized decision, the U.S. Labor Department sets a minimum wage of $.60–$1 for migratory Mexican workers.

As well this year, 35-year-old Cesar Chavez establishes the National Farm Workers Association (NFWA) to represent stoop labor in parts of California. A child of the migrant labor camps, Chavez resigned as director of San José's Community Service Organization after it refused to create a farm-workers union.

---

*Statistics*: The U.S. Census Bureau reports that during the 1950s the number of agricultural workers dropped 37 percent while the number of manufacturing workers rose 21 percent.

---

**March 18.** Algerian nationalist leaders sign an agreement with France ending the 7½-year colonial war and conceding full independence to Algeria following referendums. Some 172,000 people died during the war—145,000 rebels, 13,000 French soldiers, and 14,000 Moslem and European civilians.

The people of France approve the settlement, while 99 percent of Algerian voters, bitter over the French Army's brutality during the war, choose independence. On July 3, France ends 132 years of rule in Algeria. Hundreds of thousands of European settlers flee the new Moslem nation in panic as government factions fight a brief civil war. The Algerian National Assembly asks Mohammed Ben Bella to become president, and he will hold the position until overthrown by a bloodless coup in 1965.

**March 26.** The Supreme Court (6–2) reverses a well-established doctrine to give federal courts jurisdiction in the apportionment of state legislative seats.

In *Baker v. Carr*, city dwellers in Tennessee argued that the state's constitution mandated legislative reapportionment, on the basis of population growth, every 10 years. Yet the state government last made changes in 1901. As a result, a rural county of 3,454 people currently elects one house member while 627,019 urban voters elect just eight.

Earl Warren later describes the Baker decision as one of the most important cases in the history of the Supreme Court, "the parent case of the one man, one vote doctrine."

**April 11.** Six major steel companies raise the cost of steel by $6 a ton. The next day at his press conference, a furious President Kennedy points out that the government recently assisted in negotiating a noninflationary steel-worker contract to prevent just such an increase. He accuses the steel executives of "a wholly unjustifiable and irresponsible defiance of the public interest," since other unions will likely now refuse to moderate their demands.

The Federal Trade Commission and the Justice Department immediately begin to investigate possible price fixing and to inquire into possible antitrust and tax violations. Inland Steel and Kaiser, understanding the implications, refuse to match the rise. The original six rescind their increase on the 13th.

Over the following weeks, newspapers and businesspeople accuse the Kennedy administration of hostility toward business, and the Republicans describe the president's methods as heavy-handed. But Kennedy refutes the charges, stating that competition and public interest brought down the prices.

---

*Statistics*: For the 5.7 million American workers under union contract, the average 1961 wage increase was 7½ cents an hour.

---

**May 28.** The New York Stock Exchange takes its worst tumble since 1929. Shares lose $20.8 billion in value, dropping 34.95 points to close at 576.93, but rally sharply the next day to recover an estimated 60 percent. The recent steel dispute, high unemployment, a slowly expanding economy, and a lack of investment all likely contributed to a loss of confidence in the American marketplace.

**May 31.** Israel hangs Adolf Eichmann, the man who organized the transportation of Jews to Nazi extermination camps. The S.S. commander eluded capture following W.W.II and eventually settled in Argentina. Israeli agents found him there in 1960 and spirited him out of the country. At the end of a well-publicized eight-month trial, the former German S.S. officer was found guilty of crimes against the Jewish people, crimes against humanity, and

*Asked May 9 to comment on press treatment of his administration, President Kennedy responds, "Well, I'm reading it more and enjoying it less."*

other war crimes. Eichmann, who claimed, "I have never killed anyone," denied legal or moral responsibility for the atrocities right to the end.

In September, the West German Justice Ministry tallies 10,551 Nazi war criminal convictions since the end of W.W.II; 489 have been executed.

**June 3.** An Air France Boeing 707 chartered by the Atlanta Art Association crashes during takeoff at Orly Airport in Paris, killing 130. Only two stewardesses seated in the rear of the plane survive the worst single-plane disaster to date. With the larger jets in service, air disasters now take at least 100 lives.

**June 11.** Combatants in the Laotian civil war sign a cease-fire and agree to form a coalition government.

Since Laos won independence from France in 1954, three groups have fought for control of the country—royalist neutralists under Prince Sou-

vanna Phouma, Communist Pathet Lao under his half-brother Prince Souphanouvong, and pro-American rightists under a series of army officers. The United States and the Soviet Union, well aware of the country's strategic position, have aided opposing factions. At the same time, in an attempt to remove the Southeast Asian nation from the Cold War, Moscow and Washington have applied considerable pressure for negotiations.

On July 23 in Geneva, fourteen nations, including the United States, the Soviet Union, China, and North and South Vietnam, guarantee Laotian neutrality, agreeing to end all aid and withdraw all troops. The Laos Communist spokesman declares that there are no Chinese or North Vietnamese forces in Laos.

**June 15.** With a growing number of attempted escapes and an almost daily exchange of gunfire between opposing guards, East Berlin police begin constructing military-style trenches and barricades on their side of the wall. West Berlin police accuse the Communists of turning the border into a "fortified national frontier," but within days start building their own fortifications.

**June 18.** In Canada, the Conservative party loses a stunning 92 ridings, to hang on with a minority government of 116 seats. The Liberals carry 100 ridings, and the NDP, in their first national election, win 19.

The government's popularity had plummeted over the past two years, with the controversial cancellation of the Avro airplane, the placement of U.S. missiles in Canada, and the economic uncertainty created this year by pegging the Canadian dollar at $.925 U.S. (The Liberals reaped the benefits of the government's decision by printing up "Diefenbucks," green 92.5-cent bills.)

**June 25.** In a second landmark decision this year, the Supreme Court finds (6–1) that the 22-word nondenominational prayer in New York schools violates the First Amendment guarantee against state establishment of religion.

President Kennedy welcomes the ruling as "a reminder of the need for more prayer in American homes and greater church participation." But former president Eisenhower criticizes the ACLU-supported case, and several members of Congress move to introduce constitutional amendments.

**July 1.** Britain uses the Commonwealth Immigration Act to slam the door on black immigrants. Previously, any citizen of the Commonwealth could emigrate; now they must have a job waiting or possess a "special skill."

In 1971, Parliament will eliminate even those concessions in favor of a single immigration system that limits preference to applicants whose parents or grandparents were born in Britain.

**July 23.** Arriving in Hawaii for South Vietnam strategy talks, Defense Secretary Robert McNamara reaffirms his belief that a victory over the Communists may take years. *New York Times* correspondent H. Bigart, just ending a six-month assignment in Vietnam, concludes that victory appears remote. He maintains that Saigon, despite massive U.S. aid, is not trying to "win people's loyalty."

During the year, U.S. Special Forces train their South Vietnamese counterparts in guerrilla and counterinsurgency warfare. (The president reinstates the distinctive Special Forces headgear and the men become known as Green Berets.) North Vietnamese leader Ho Chi Minh has reportedly vowed to outlast American aid and fight for another 10 years if necessary.

**August 14.** At 8:00 P.M. on an isolated road near Plymouth, Massachusetts, a man dressed as a police officer stops a mail van. Quickly, four more men and a woman, all masked and armed, overpower the guards and remove $1,551,277 in small, worn bills. No one will ever be indicted for the robbery.

*Statistics:* The 1960 U.S. crime rate is up 14 percent over 1959 and an astounding 98 percent over 1950.

**August 20.** The U.S. national debt passes the $300-billion mark for the first time.

**August 31.** A controversial administration-backed bill provides for "the establishment, ownership, operation, and regulation of a U.S. commer-

cial communications satellite system." Some legislative opponents had expressed fears that, in planning and operating the system, Comsat negotiations with foreign governments could influence foreign policy.

**September 1.** A severe earthquake, measuring 7.1 on the Richter scale, strikes northwestern Iran at 10:52 P.M. The tremors crumble the traditional mud-brick houses, totally destroying over 200 villages and seriously damaging all towns in the affected 8,000-square-mile area. Over 12,000 die, another 10,000 are injured, and 25,000 are left homeless.

**September 10.** In a landmark decision, the U.S. Supreme Court gives the federal government control over a state institution by upholding an appeals court order that black air force veteran James Meredith be admitted to the University of Mississippi without further delay.

On September 20, the young man, accompanied by U.S. justice officials, makes the first of four unsuccessful attempts to enroll. Governor Ross Barnett personally bars Meredith twice, but the U.S. Fifth Circuit Court of Appeals, on the 28th, finds Barnett guilty of civil contempt and orders him to admit Meredith by October 2 or face arrest and fines.

President Kennedy, upholding the U.S. Constitution in this crisis between state and federal authority, federalizes the Mississippi National Guard on the 29th and sends in hundreds of U.S. deputy marshals. The next day on nationwide television he explains the need for federal intervention and appeals for peaceful desegregation. But large-scale rioting breaks out when hundreds of students and other segregationists, who have traveled to the area, attack the marshals on campus.

At the height of the riot, state patrolmen withdraw, and before federal troops arrive to restore order, 35 marshals are shot, hundreds of others are injured, and two men are shot to death, including French journalist Paul Guildhard.

Meredith finally registers on October 1 and begins attending classes under federal guard. Mississippi's inflexible system of segregation has been broken.

**September 13.** Following recent church burnings

in Georgia, Kennedy promises federal protection for voter registration workers. The NAACP, SCLC, and SNCC have worked hard this year to register 90,000 Southern blacks, but white resistance holds strong: In rural Mississippi and Georgia, whites have burned churches used for voter meetings; snipers have fired into the homes of blacks identified with registration activity; police have arrested registration workers on minor charges; and a new Mississippi law requires registrants to answer a subjective questionnaire, open to interpretation and easy failure.

The Justice Department has used its legal authority to assist registration and curb reprisals: initiating investigations and court actions in 100 counties, under the Civil Rights Acts of 1957 and 1960; filing 32 voting suits, 22 since Kennedy came to office; and requesting the invalidation of Mississippi laws and constitutional provisions discriminating against blacks.

**September 17.** The Justice Department files suit to end racial segregation in Richmond, Virginia, schools for the children of military personnel. Commenting on the first federal action of its kind, Attorney General Robert Kennedy declares, "It makes no sense that we should ask military personnel to make sacrifices and serve away from home and at the same time see their children treated as inferiors by local requirements that they attend segregated schools."

**September 26.** The U.S. agrees to sell defensive missiles to Israel. With the Soviets shipping missiles and jet aircraft to Arab nations, Washington reversed its policy against supplying large amounts of military equipment to the Middle East. By late 1963, Israel will become the first non-Western nation to receive American-made missiles.

**October 10.** A congressional resolution emphatically declares the readiness of the United States to defend Allied rights in Berlin "by whatever means may be necessary." The vote follows a September 28 statement by Defense Secretary McNamara that America was ready to use nuclear arms, if necessary, to protect its vital interests in Berlin.

Last month, another resolution reaffirmed U.S. policy toward aggressive Communism, that the United States would use "whatever means may be necessary, including the use of arms" to prevent Cuba from extending its "subversive activities to any part of this hemisphere." Earlier this year, the OAS excluded the Castro regime for its Marxist-Leninist philosophy and President Kennedy embargoed nearly all U.S. trade with the island.

**October 16.** U.S. surveillance photos of Cuba reveal missile bases capable of carrying half the USSR's missiles. A stunned White House fabricates a bad cold for President Kennedy and he cuts short a campaign swing through the West. *The New York Times* uncovers the crisis but accedes to a presidential request to hold the story.

President Kennedy speaks to the nation on the 22nd, and the American people quickly realize the seriousness of the situation. The next day, the OAS authorizes the use of armed force to prevent the shipment of arms into Cuba, and the United States sets up a blockade to search incoming ships. On the 25th, American representatives at the United Nations display photographic evidence of the bases to allay international skepticism.

Premier Khrushchev, his authority and prestige fading in Moscow and within the Communist bloc, secretly authorized the bases to achieve a strategic advantage in superpower negotiations. He sends Kennedy a letter on the 27th promising to remove the missiles if Washington withdraws U.S. missiles from Turkey and pledges not to invade Cuba.

Even though the American missiles are obsolete and likely will soon be removed, the Joint Chiefs of Staff, Cabinet members, including Robert Kennedy, and presidential advisors all argue against any compromise that could weaken the U.S. position in the world and let down their allies. They all favor invading Cuba on the 29th.

American children practice air raid drills, some adults hurriedly build bomb shelters and stockpile food, and authorities cordon off Key West, Florida, beaches with barbed wire as the president continues to pursue negotiations. Kennedy secretly sends his brother Bobby to Soviet Ambassador Anatoly Dobrynin with a proposal: Washington will accept the offer if Moscow never publicly reveals the connection between the dismantling of the two systems. Khrushchev, realizing the Americans will fight, accepts on the 28th.

Since Cuba rejects on-site inspections, the U.S. Navy pulls alongside outgoing Soviet ships to verify withdrawal of the missiles. Dismantling is completed on November 8, and the United States lifts the blockade on the 20th.

MEDIUM RANGE BALLISTIC MISSILE BASE IN CUBA

SAGUA LA GRANDE

*U.S. intelligence photos, carried in newspapers on October 20, clearly show the buildup of Soviet missiles in Cuba.*

During the crisis, President Kennedy, who believed there was a 33–50 percent chance of going to war, appeared tough and uncompromising. Yet it was his resolve to settle the issue peacefully that saved the nation from a possible nuclear war. For, unknown to the Pentagon, the USSR already had missiles in place and could have targeted major U.S. cities within hours. As well, convinced that recent movements of U.S. air and land forces to southeastern bases signaled an imminent invasion of Cuba, Moscow had stationed 40,000 Soviet troops on the island to augment the 270,000 Cuban soldiers already in place.

The two leaders, badly scared by how close their countries had come to war, will install an emergency hot line in the months ahead to help finalize a test ban treaty. But an intensified arms race will prove to be a less fortunate consequence of the Cuban Missile Crisis. The USSR, humiliated in the eyes of the world, resolve to achieve real military power.

**October 20.** Communist China uses military force to establish a new border between India and Tibet, then declares a cease-fire. The boundary was established by Britain and Tibet under a 1914 treaty, but China, now occupying Tibet, has contested Indian possession of some 48,000 square miles along the 2,500-mile frontier. The territorial dispute remains unresolved.

**November 6.** The Democrats show surprising strength in midterm congressional elections, losing just six seats from their heavy House majority and gaining four in the Senate. (Since the turn of the century, the president's party at midterm elections has lost an average of 44 seats in the House and 5 in the Senate.) Freshmen in the Senate include Edward Kennedy, George McGovern, and Daniel Inouye.

The Republicans fail to make big gains in gubernatorial elections, and their former presidential candidate, Richard Nixon, loses by a large margin in California to Edmund G. "Pat" Brown. The next day, Nixon appears at a press conference, haggard and worn. He ends a 15-minute tirade by bitterly denouncing the news media and apparently retiring from politics: "You won't have Nixon to kick around anymore, because, gentlemen, this is my last press conference."

**November 6.** With the addition of Uganda on October 25, the African-Asian bloc reached exactly half of the U.N. membership. Today, those 55 nations form the bulk of a 67–16 vote (with 23 abstentions) to condemn South Africa for apartheid. The United States, Great Britain, and other Western nations vote against the motion, maintaining that condemnation should be reserved for cases of obvious aggression.

**November 7.** Former First Lady Eleanor Roosevelt dies at age 78. Married to Franklin D. Roosevelt in 1905, she had six children in 10 years. After he was struck by polio in 1921, she became more active outside the home, serving as her husband's emissary during his four years as governor of New York. And when he was elected to the White House in 1932, Mrs. Roosevelt expanded the supporting role of first lady to a position of influence.

Already controversial for her interest in race relations, women's rights, education, and world peace, she began a newspaper column, "My Day," in 1936, made radio broadcasts, held press conferences, and actively participated in civil defense during W.W.II. When President Roosevelt died in 1945, Truman appointed her as a delegate to the United Nations. During a seven-year stint, she worked on the draft of the Declaration of Human Rights, then used her influence to ensure its adoption. She returned to the United Nations for President Kennedy in 1961.

For many years, the American people chose Eleanor Roosevelt as the woman they most admired. She is buried beside her husband on the grounds of the family estate at Hyde Park, New York, in ceremonies attended by President Kennedy and former presidents Truman and Eisenhower.

**November 20.** President Kennedy, acting on a 1960 campaign promise, signs an executive order barring racial and religious discrimination in new housing built or purchased with federal aid (about 50 percent of future residential construction in the suburbs and 25 percent in the cities). Civil rights leaders hail the long-awaited order, Southern conservatives denounce it, and analysts describe the action as one of the most significant moves ever by an executive to end discrimination in the United States.

**November 30.** U Thant, acting Secretary-General of the United Nations, is unanimously elected to a full four-year term. The Soviet "yes" vote for U Thant ends Moscow's demand that the U.N. Secretariat be reorganized into a tripartite.

**December 24.** Following months of negotiations between Havana and the American-based Cuban Families Committee, the Castro government frees the first of the prisoners captured in the disastrous 1961 Bay of Pigs invasion. For $50 million worth of food and medical supplies raised privately, Cuba will eventually release 9,703 people—the 1,113 invasion prisoners, U.S. prisoners, Americans living in Cuba, and about 1,500 Cuban-born U.S. citizens.

## *Obituaries*

**Warren Austin** (November 12, 1877–December 25, 1962). The first American ambassador to the United Nations served from 1946 to 1953.

**Stanley Lord** (1878–January 1962). For 50 years, the British sea captain lived under public condemnation for his role in the sinking of the *Titanic*. Survivors accused Lord of deliberately turning his ship, the *Californian*, away from their stricken vessel. He vehemently denied the charges, but a court of inquiry severely censured him.

**Charles "Lucky" Luciano** (November 11, 1896–January 26, 1962). One of the most influential figures in U.S. organized crime, Luciano died of a heart attack in Naples. In 1946, his 10-year vice sentence was commuted for guaranteeing Mafia wartime cooperation on the New York waterfront and in Italy during the Allied invasion. Deported, the Mafia don ran the mob from Italy until rivals eliminated his strongest supporters in 1957.

**(Anna) Eleanor Roosevelt** (October 11, 1884–November 7, 1962). *See* News.

**Wilhelmina** (August 31, 1880–November 28, 1962). The queen of the Netherlands fled to Canada with her family in 1940 rather than appear to collaborate with the invading Nazis. She returned home in 1945, but three years later abdicated (1890–1948) in favor of her daughter Juliana.

## BEGINNINGS AND ENDINGS

### *News*

**January 16.** An armored unit since W.W.II, the 101-year-old U.S. Sixth Cavalry officially disbands.

**February 20.** A U.S. stamp of the *Mercury* spaceship—placed on sale immediately after John Glenn's safe return—is the first stamp issued on the date it commemorates.

**April 3.** The Defense Department orders the racial integration of all military reserve units (excluding the National Guard). The program will take 15 months to complete.

**April 13.** Alaska becomes the first state to pass legislation prohibiting discrimination in both public and private housing.

**April 21.** The Seattle World's Fair (officially Century 21 Exposition) previews scientific advances of the next century. Over 9.5 million visitors pass through the gates before October 21. The first world's fair to achieve financial success also leaves behind several permanent structures, including the 607-foot-tall Space Needle, with the world's first revolving restaurant.

**August 2.** Fulfilling former premier Tommy Douglas's dream, the Saskatchewan CCF government brings in a universal medical insurance plan. Doctors immediately walk out, but the provincial government holds firm. The success of the CCF program spurs Ottawa to offer medicare to the nation.

**September 3.** The Trans-Canada Highway officially opens at Roger's Pass in the Rockies. The 4,860-mile roadway, stretching from the Atlantic to the Pacific, took 12 years to build.

**November 17.** The John Foster Dulles International Airport opens outside Washington, D.C., the first civilian airport built specifically for jet planes.

**More news.** Grossinger's Hotel in the Catskills holds America's first recorded singles-only weekend.

### New Products and Businesses

Royal Crown Cola is the first to sell a sugar-free cola nationally, cyclamate-sweetened Diet-Rite Cola.

Orange juice appears in a powdered form.

The Easy-Bake Oven, from Kenner Products, uses a light bulb to bake miniature cakes and cookies. The toy is a smash hit.

Coca-Cola launches Sprite. (The company begins replacing cork cap liners with plastic. With no cork circles to press from the underside of their shirts, kids have to give up their bottle-top badges.)

### Memorable Ad Campaigns

When Honda Motorcycles tells Americans, "You Meet the Nicest People on a Honda," motorcycle sales take off.

*Statistics*: Americans buy 339,160 imported vehicles this year, and the Volkswagen Beetle accounts for 192,570 purchases.

### Fads

Teenage boys grate on adult nerves with toe and heel taps (usually worn on black, sharply pointed shoes). Never a widespread fad, some school administrators hear enough taps to forbid them.

## SCIENCE AND TECHNOLOGY

### News

**February 20.** An Atlas rocket blasts Colonel John Glenn, Jr., into orbit. In 4 hours, 55 minutes, on board *Friendship 7*, Glenn sees four Earth sunsets. (During the first "night," Australians create a beacon by turning on all the lights of Perth.)

During reentry, the automatic control malfunctions and heat disrupts communications for seven anxious minutes, but the astronaut manually fires the retrorockets to make a successful landing.

Back home, the first American to orbit the Earth receives a tumultuous welcome. Washington celebrates John Glenn Day on the 26th, and on March 1, an estimated 4 million New Yorkers turn out for his ticker-tape parade.

Appearing before a House Committee on February 27, the celebrated astronaut states that the Soviet Union will lead in space for some time, but the United States will reach the moon first. Glenn warns against the risks of a manned space program. "There will be failures," he says. "There will be sacrifices."

**March 16.** The first Kosmos satellite enters orbit. Although Moscow releases little information about the series, most experts believe two-thirds fulfill a military purpose. Some 300 will be launched by the end of the decade.

**April.** In 1954, French engineer Louis Hartmann succeeded in bonding polytetrafluorethylene to metal. His colleague Marc Gregoire then attached a thin layer to an aluminum frying pan. But rumors have persisted in the United States that nonstick PTFE gives off poisonous fumes during cooking. Still, once du Pont places Teflon frying pans on the market, customer satisfaction quickly ends all speculation.

**April 26.** Like the Soviets' earlier mission, the first U.S. craft to reach the moon crashes into the surface—at 5,400 mph. Designed simply to photograph the lunar surface for the Apollo Project, *Rangers* lack the mechanics for a soft landing. The first two never reached deep space, the third missed the moon by nearly 23,000 miles, and when this craft fails to transmit any data and the fifth again misses the moon, NASA puts off further launches to reorganize the program.

**May 6.** In the first launching of a nuclear-armed long-range missile, a U.S. submarine detonates a Polaris missile near Christmas Island in the Pacific.

**May 10.** MIT engineers bounce a laser off the surface of the moon. This first round trip takes 2½ seconds.

**May 23.** Surgeons at the Massachusetts General Hospital are the first to successfully reattach a severed limb. The 12-year-old patient lost his arm to a freight train accident.

**May 24.** Scott Carpenter, on board *Aurora 7*, repeats John Glenn's flight. But a 3-second delay of retrofire causes the craft to overshoot splashdown by some 250 miles. A frantic navy search ends 39 minutes later when a pilot sights Carpenter signaling with a mirror.

**July.** For a year and a half, NASA has examined alternate Apollo systems. Direct flight to the moon would require the costly development of a powerful carrier, an impossibility before the end-of-the-decade deadline.

The second alternative calls for two Saturn launches to orbit a refueling tanker and an Apollo craft, and an enormous 150,000-pound payload to lift the space vehicle up from the surface of the moon.

In the third plan, a three-module spacecraft and a 7,000-pound payload would travel directly from Earth to lunar orbit. A two-stage module would take the astronauts to the surface and a third ascent stage would return them to the command module, then be jettisoned.

Today, after some million hours of study and a long, drawn-out battle, NASA decides to go with the lunar module design.

**July 9.** The AEC detonates a megaton-range device over Johnson Island to test the effect on radio communications and incoming missiles. In Hawaii, some 800 miles away, the night skies light up, radios black out for up to 3½ minutes, circuit breakers trip, burglar alarms ring, and street lights fail. Years will pass before physicists learn that a near-space explosion blankets huge areas of the planet with an electromagnetic pulse of some 50,000 volts, effectively shutting down all communication systems.

**July 10.** NASA, under contract to AT&T, launches the first active communications satellite. In low orbit, *Telstar I* receives, amplifies, and transmits telephone conversations and TV signals between the United States, Britain, and France for 20-minute periods. *Telstar II*, launched in May 1963, will reach a higher orbit and exchange signals for up to three hours.

**August 9.** After reviewing some 125 reported cases, the FDA and pharmaceutical companies find no evidence that birth control pills cause blood clotting.

**August 11–15.** Andrian Nikolayev orbits the Earth in *Vostok 3* for a record 94 hours. At one point, Pavel Popovich and *Vostok 4* travel beside Nikolayev in an adjacent orbit. The two cosmonauts talk by radio telephone while Soviets back on Earth watch the first TV relay from space.

**August 22.** At a news conference, President Kennedy reveals that U.S. nuclear-powered subs made a "historic rendezvous" under the polar ice pack on July 31, then surfaced near the North Pole on August 2. The *Skate* traveled from London and the *Seadragon* came up from Hawaii on an anti-sub exercise.

**September 16.** WHO reports that smallpox deaths between 1950 and 1960 dropped from 358,456 worldwide to 59,950.

**September 17.** NASA names new Apollo astronauts: Frank Borman, James McDivitt, Thomas Stafford, and Edward White II from the air force, Charles Conrad, James Lovell, Jr., and John Young from the navy, and civilians Neil Armstrong and Elliott See, Jr.

On October 4, President Kennedy signs a 1963 fiscal NASA appropriation of $3.67 billion, more than double the amount allotted for 1962.

**September 28.** Canada enters the space age with *Alouette*, the first satellite designed and built by a nation other than the United States or the USSR. Ionospheric and cosmic radiation readings over the next few years give *Alouette* the best test and flight record of any satellite.

**October 3.** During six orbits in *Sigma 7*, astronaut Walter Schirra completes the first U.S. telecast from space. The craft lands on target in the Pacific.

**October 10.** In response to the thalidomide scare, Congress approves the Drug Industry Act, requiring the registration of drug manufacturers, the addition of generic names on brand labels and in advertisements, and documentation of drug effectiveness.

As well, the act gives HEW authority to prohibit drug testing in humans, if preclinical testing proves unsatisfactory, and to withdraw any drug that constitutes a potential health hazard.

**November 6.** The British Navy reports a record oceanic depth of 37,782 feet in the Mindanao Trench east of the Philippines. The survey ship *Cook* established the depth through echo sounding.

**December 14.** After nearly five months in space, the first interplanetary probe passes within 22,000 miles of Venus. *Mariner 2*, with 40 pounds of scientific equipment, records the planet's surface temperature (700 degrees Fahrenheit) and transmits other valuable data over a 42-minute flyby. (Earlier in the year, *Mariner 1* veered off course and was destroyed.)

A major coup for the United States, *Mariner* continues to transmit information until almost 54 million miles from Earth.

**More news.** This year, Rachel Carson's best-selling book *Silent Spring* alerts the nation to the dangers of pesticides. The industry describes her as "emotional and ignorant," but a presidential committee will refer to Carson's study next year in calling for further research into related health hazards. Later, her exposé will be honored as the beginning of the environmental movement.

• Columbia-Presbyterian Medical Center in New York City reports the first use of a laser in eye surgery.

• At the University of London, Jacques F. A. F. Miller determines that the thymus, which withers away in adult animals and humans, is essential to the immune system in early life.

• With a hydraulic pump, a 10-horsepower motor, and magnetized strips to store commands, Unimate carries out repetitive motions with two opposed metal fingers. The 3,000-pound machine is the first all-purpose industrial robot.

• In his paper "History of Ocean Basins," American Harry Hess theorizes that molten magma constantly renews the ocean floors by flowing up through rifts then spreading them out laterally. His hypothesis, later modified by others, supports the concept of continental drift. First proposed in 1912 by Alfred Wegener, the controversial theory holds that heavier rock plates, which overlay the magma, move the great land masses. Seafloor spreading explains how the oceans widen and the continents split apart.

## Other Discoveries, Developments, and Inventions

Color film from Polaroid with 1-minute developing time

Driverless commuter train in New York City

Titan ICBM, the first missile housed in a protective silo

*Ariel 1*, on April 26, the first international satellite

Abortion vacuum for early pregnancies, in the USSR

## Obituaries

**Niels Bohr** (October 7, 1885–November 18, 1962). Winner of the 1922 Nobel prize and dubbed "the father of atomic energy," the Danish physicist developed the modern concept of the atom—a nucleus with electrons circling in restricted orbits. Although Bohr assisted at the Manhattan Project, he worked for international control of atomic energy.

**Andrew Douglass** (July 5, 1867–March 20, 1962). A study of solar effects on weather and subsequently on trees led Douglass to develop dentrochronology, or the science of tree rings.

**Garnett Dye** (1892–January 29, 1962). The United States accepted his radio-controlled aerial torpedo in 1918, but never compensated the inventor.

**George Papanicolaou** (May 13, 1883–February 19, 1962). The Greek-born researcher developed the Pap smear in 1928, but the uterine cancer test only gained clinical acceptance following a joint medical publication in 1943.

**Auguste Piccard** (January 28, 1884–March 24, 1962). The Swiss scientific explorer long held the records for ascent into the stratosphere (53,152 feet in 1932) and descent into the ocean (10,330 feet in 1953).

**Vilhjalmur Stefansson** (November 3, 1879–August 26, 1962). One of the foremost authorities on the far North, the Canadian-American explorer discovered blond Eskimos (1908–1912), surveyed newly discovered islands (1913–1918), trained U.S. troops in Arctic survival, and wrote 24 books and hundreds of monographs. One 1920s title predicted that Canada would eventually discover valuable mineral resources in the far North.

## THE ARTS

May 8—*A Funny Thing Happened on the Way to the Forum*, with Zero Mostel, Jack Gilford, David Burns (964 perfs.)

October 3—*Stop the World—I Want to Get Off*, with Anthony Newley (556 perfs.)

October 13—*Who's Afraid of Virginia Woolf?*, with Uta Hagen, Arthur Hill, George Grizzard, Melinda Dillon (664 perfs.)

November 27—*Never Too Late*, with Paul Ford, Maureen O'Sullivan, Orson Bean (1,007 perfs.)

### Tony Awards

Actor (Dramatic)—Paul Scofield, *A Man for All Seasons*

Actress (Dramatic)—Margaret Leighton, *Night of the Iguana*

Actor (Musical)—Robert Morse, *How to Succeed in Business Without Really Trying*

Actress (Musical)—Anna Maria Alberghetti, *Carnival!*; Diahann Carroll, *No Strings*

Play—*A Man for All Seasons*

Musical—*How to Succeed in Business Without Really Trying*

### News

**February 21.** In London, Rudolf Nureyev partners Dame Margot Fonteyn in *Giselle*. (A prima ballerina since 1934, she later says, "Rudolf brought me a second career, like an Indian Summer.") The Soviet becomes the first "permanent guest artist" at the Royal Ballet, and, within five years, will be described as the most exciting male dancer since Nijinsky.

**April 10.** Pablo Picasso's two-sided *Death of a Harlequin/Woman Sitting in a Garden* sells for $224,000 in a London auction—a record sum for a painting by a living artist.

**June 29.** In Canada, at Niagara-on-the-Lake, the first Shaw Festival opens in a modified 19th-century courthouse. Founder Brian Doherty—

lawyer, producer, playwright—offers eight amateur performances. Next year, professional actors will present the plays of George Bernard Shaw.

**August 6.** President Kennedy tells a White House Youth Concert, "Last year, more Americans went to symphonies than went to baseball games. This may be viewed as an alarming statistic, but I think that both baseball and the country will endure."

**September 21.** Igor Stravinsky returns to his native Soviet Union for the first time in nearly 50 years. Invited to conduct two concerts, the composer presents his *Rite of Spring* (1913) and *Orpheus* ballet suite (1947). Soviet reviews call him "a great master," but express doubts about his musical innovations.

**September 23.** After 69 years at Carnegie Hall, the New York Philharmonic moves to the Lincoln Center for the Performing Arts for an inaugural concert in the new Philharmonic Hall. But the acoustics prove disappointing. Engineers will continue to make adjustments.

**September 29.** *My Fair Lady*—the longest-running Broadway musical—closes after 2,717 performances.

## Obituaries

**Kirsten Flagstad** (July 12, 1895–December 7, 1962). After the war, the world's most famous Wagnerian soprano was initially booed for her Nazi associations in occupied Norway. She retired in 1960.

**Fritz Kreisler** (February 2, 1875–January 29, 1962). A great violinist, the Austrian-born Kreisler also composed violin and popular pieces. A car accident ended his concert career in 1950.

**Bruno Walter** (September 15, 1876–February 17, 1962). The eminent conductor excelled at the classic Viennese repertoire.

## WORDS

James Baldwin, *Another Country*
Helen Gurley Brown, *Sex and the Single Girl*
Eugene Burdick and Harvey Wheeler, *Fail-Safe*
Anthony Burgess, *A Clockwork Orange*

Rachel Carson, *Silent Spring*
Heloise Cruse, *Heloise's Housekeeping Hints*
William Faulkner, *The Reivers*
Günter Grass, *The Tin Drum*
Ken Kesey, *One Flew Over the Cuckoo's Nest*
Anne Morrow Lindbergh, *Dearly Beloved*
Richard McKenna, *The Sand Pebbles*
Katherine Ann Porter, *Ship of Fools*
Charles Schulz, *Happiness Is a Warm Puppy*
John Steinbeck, *Travels with Charley*
Barbara Tuchman, *The Guns of August*
Irving Wallace, *The Prize*
Herman Wouk, *Youngblood Hawke*

## News

**March 16.** Inspiration for *Pinocchio*, Giovanna Ragionieri dies at age 93. In the 1870s, outside Florence, Italy, apprentice maid Giovanna shared imaginative stories with a member of the family, Carlo Lorenzini. Writing as Collodi, he published *Pinocchio* (1880), one of the world's best-loved children's books. He died in 1890.

**December 10.** American novelist John Steinbeck wins the Nobel prize in literature for his realistic and imaginative writings, which combine "sympathetic humor and keen social perception."

**More news.** Experimenting with the Telstar communications satellite, a New York newspaper sends 5,000 words to Paris at a rate 16½ times faster than radio or cable.

• *The JFK Coloring Book*, one of several 1962 novelty books, devotes a section to the presidential rocking chair. The text ends, "Daddy doesn't like to be off his rocker."

## Cartoons and Comics

**August.** Unlike the invincible superheroes of the past, new Marvel Comics characters display a variety of neuroses and weaknesses. The *Hulk* was introduced in May. This month, *Thor* debuts and "Spider-Man" makes his first appearance in *Amazing Fantasy Comics No. 15*.

**More news.** Classics Illustrated folds this year

with *Faust*, the 167th issue. Sales, which numbered 25 million per week into the 1950s, had eroded under the volume of mass market paperbacks and the popularity of television. Then Gilberton lost its second-class mailing permit. (The company will sell out in 1969, but a Classics revival fails.)

## TIME *Man of the Year*

Pope John XXIII

## *New Words and Phrases*

antimatter
blockbusting (inciting property owners to sell when a member of an "undesirable" group readies to become a neighbor)
circadian (biological cycle recurring at 24 hours)
computer revolution
conventional weapons (not involving nuclear weapons)
disadvantaged
to eyeball
fail-safe (method of positive control and communication in airborne alerts)
fastback (a type of sports car with a sloping back)
flight recorder
freeze-drying
genetic code
hairy (dangerous or menacing)
hard [facts and information]
hovercraft
module (a standard structural component used repeatedly, as in a building, computer, etc.)
ombudsman
phase out
probe (into outer space)
swinging (joyful and up-to-date)
track (a separate school curriculum, based either on a pupil's desire—academic, commercial, etc.—or relative tested ability—fast, average, slow, etc.)
voiceprint

Charles Schulz's *Happiness Is a Warm Puppy* inspires sloganeers to produce endless variations of "Happiness Is . . ." over the next few years.

## *Obituaries*

**Ludwig Bemelmans** (April 27, 1898–October 1, 1962). His little French schoolgirl "Madeline" (1939) became a popular children's series.

**E. E. Cummings** (October 14, 1894–September 3, 1962). Noted for technical innovation, the American poet and author often dispensed with capitals and punctuation.

**Isak Dinesen (Baroness Blixen-Finecke)** (October 17, 1885–September 7, 1962). The Danish writer's best-known work, *Out of Africa*, was a memoir of life on an African coffee plantation. She returned home in 1931 to spend the remainder of her life in seclusion.

**William Faulkner** (September 25, 1897–July 6, 1962). His short stories and novels used multiple streams of consciousness and other narrative innovations. His most acclaimed works include *The Sound and the Fury* (1929), *As I Lay Dying* (1930), *Light in August* (1932), and his masterpiece, *Absalom, Absalom!* (1936).

Faulkner's experimentation with form and the power and intensity of his language made him one of the most important figures in 20th-century literature. Recognition came late, but within his lifetime he won the Nobel prize (1949) and a Pulitzer (a second will be awarded posthumously in 1963).

**Herman Hesse** (July 2, 1877–August 9, 1962). Winner of the 1946 Nobel prize in literature, the Swiss writer's spirituality and disdainful view of the world make his novels *Siddhartha* (1922) and *Steppenwolf* (1927) popular choices for American students throughout the decade.

## FASHION

### *Haute Couture*

Couturiers hold to a slender, straight line with Jacqueline Kennedy's slim, high-bosomed silhouette dominating this year's styles.

Fashion observers note as well the continuing influence of the 1930s and the introduction of black accents and color contrasts following the Picasso exhibit in New York.

Several leading designers respond to the growing

*First lady Jacqueline Kennedy at the Congressional Club Luncheon in Washington.*

• Marking a continuing trend, 8 percent of U.S. apparel firms close down this year.

• American Geoffrey Beene, age 35, forms a business and next year his first collection offers a line of simple, easy-to-wear clothing. Beene will expand his boutique line into the 1970s, adding menswear, jewelry, and furs.

• Shoe sales over the past eight years have reflected the increased emphasis on informal clothing —the share for all-leather uppers has dropped from 82.8 percent to 76.3 percent, while nonleather sales have risen from 11.6 percent to 17.7 percent.

• With his friend Armand Orustein, Daniel Hechter establishes a line of women's clothing. The Hechter group will add children's clothes in 1965, menswear in 1968, and in the early 1970s, the company will move into other areas of fashion including shoes and sunglasses.

interest in children's wear, adding little girls' clothes to their collections.

## News

**March 12.** To achieve the bouffant hairdo, *Newsweek* instructs teenagers, "Hold the hair straight out, tease it with a comb until it gets frizzled, then comb some of the outside hair over this big mess of frizzled-up hair and set it in place with a cloud of hair spray." One Detroit school counselor grumbled to the magazine's journalist, "We have tenth graders who find it hard to get through the doorway," but another teacher only remembered one problem—a girl's beehive prevented a boy sitting behind her from seeing the teacher.

**More news.** Two months after the French Army drafted couturier Yves St. Laurent in 1960, he was discharged with a nervous disorder. Meanwhile, the House of Dior acted on their strained relations and replaced him.

This year, the 26-year-old St. Laurent opens his own house and presents a spring collection to mixed reviews. But critics judge his autumn designs a success and within a decade St. Laurent's expression of form and sense of color will establish him as the leader of French couture.

## Colors and Materials

Favorite colors include neutrals and mellow pinks, greens, and yellows. In prints, black-and-white combinations and tones of green dominate.

Designers pair unusual patterns, like dots and stripes.

Mohair, brushed wools, and similar fabrics give bulky year-round styles an airy look.

## Clothes

In mail-order catalogs, skirts just cover the knee, tapered pants end above the ankle, and cardigans button up alone.

Rivaling the slender look, skirts fall in pleats or in a slight flare to midcalf.

Sportswear manufacturers use suede for all types of coordinates. Trendsetter Jackie Kennedy boosts the industry with her choice of casual slacks and chic T-shirts.

Givenchy creations for the movie *Breakfast at Tiffany's* promote the sleeveless, high-bosomed princess dress. Irene Sharaff's costumes for the upcoming *Cleopatra* inspire Egyptian-style gowns and jewelry.

The Twist creates an interest in ruffled and fringed dresses.

Composer sweatshirts succeed as a novelty item, with the likenesses of Bach, Brahms, or Beethoven.

Men favor President Kennedy's two-button suit with its ease through the chest and its greater exposure of tie and shirt.

### Accessories

With the revived interest in hats (the simple lines of Mrs. Kennedy's pillbox suit the bouffant), some women opt for the swagger style popularized years ago by Greta Garbo.

Kid gloves are worn day and night.

Jackie's preference for sweep-around sunglasses creates a unisex fad, but for once a craze settles into a lasting demand. By 1964, manufacturers produce an annual 134 million sun spectacles, compared with 60 million in 1956.

Low- and stacked-heel shoes appear in a range of colors with a new rounded toe and exposed sides and back. Mail-order catalogs still offer pointed toes. (Shoe imports reach an estimated 70,000–75,000, double the 1961 total. The leading export nations are Italy and Japan.)

### Hair and Cosmetics

The increasingly popular bouffant adds C-shaped curls over each cheek. Some young women use cellotape or clear nail polish to hold the curls overnight.

Along with wigs, department stores and hairdressers sell postiches, or "falls," to attach to the crown of the head.

For the first time, Americans can buy a tan. The new product, in a spray or lotion, changes skin color within a few hours. Next year, companies will move away from astringent alcohol-based tanning agents toward oil-based preparations.

# POPULAR MUSIC

"I Can't Stop Loving You"—Ray Charles

"Big Girls Don't Cry"—Four Seasons

"Sherry"—Four Seasons

"Roses Are Red (My Love)"—Bobby Vinton

"Peppermint Twist, Part 1"—Joey Dee & the Starliters

"Telstar" (Instr.)—Tornadoes

"Soldier Boy"—Shirelles

"Hey! Baby"—Bruce Channel

"Duke of Earl"—Gene Chandler

"The Twist"—Chubby Checker

"Johnny Angel"—Shelley Fabares

"Breaking Up Is Hard to Do"—Neil Sedaka

"Monster Mash"—Bobby "Boris" Pickett & the Crypt-Kickers

"He's a Rebel"—Crystals

"Sheila"—Tommy Roe

"Good Luck Charm"—Elvis Presley

"Stranger on the Shore" (Instr.)—Acker Bilk

"The Stripper" (Instr.)—David Rose & His Orchestra

"The Loco-Motion"—Little Eva

"Don't Break the Heart That Loves You"—Connie Francis

"Return to Sender"—Elvis Presley

"Limbo Rock"—Chubby Checker

"Mashed Potato Time"—Dee Dee Sharp

"Ramblin' Rose"—Nat King Cole

"The Wah Watusi"—Orlons

"The Wanderer"—Dion

"Midnight in Moscow" (Instr.)—Kenny Ball & His Jazzmen

"Can't Help Falling in Love"—Elvis Presley

"Only Love Can Break a Heart"—Gene Pitney

### Grammy Awards (1962)

Record of the Year—Tony Bennett, "I Left My Heart in San Francisco"

Song of the Year (songwriter)—Leslie Bricusse and Anthony Newley, "What Kind of Fool Am I"

Album of the Year—Vaughn Meader, *The First Family*

Best Vocal Performance (Male)—Tony Bennett, *I Left My Heart in San Francisco* (album)

Best Vocal Performance (Female)—Ella Fitzgerald, *Ella Swings Brightly with Nelson Riddle* (album)

Best New Artist—Robert Goulet

## News

**May 18.** The U.S. Court of Appeals reverses Pete Seeger's 1955 contempt conviction for refusing to answer HUAC questions. The indictment had failed to properly identify the subcommittee's authority to conduct the hearing.

**July 23.** In honor of the first satellite telecast from England, the Tornadoes record the instrumental "Telstar." The number becomes the first British rock song to reach No. 1 in America.

**August 18.** Ringo Starr debuts with the Beatles and drummer Pete Best is asked to leave. New manager Brian Epstein convinces the four young men (John is 22, Paul 20, George 19, and Ringo 23) to adopt collarless suits. Earlier this year, Decca released their first EMI single—"My Bonnie"/"The Saints"—in the United States.

**December 17.** Alan Freed, broken by the payola scandal, pleads guilty to two counts of commercial bribery. The former DJ had alienated many in the radio and music industries by refusing to play white cover versions of black hits. He receives a $300 fine and a six-month suspended sentence.

**More news.** In his garage, trumpeter Herb Alpert adds a mariachi background and crowd noises from a Tijuana bullfight to create "The Lonely Bull." The song reaches No. 6 and within three years Alpert will put together a real Tijuana Brass.

• After 15 Twist songs, the dance craze finally dies out. Teens try out the Watusi, the Mashed Potato, the Locomotion, the Bird, and the Hitch Hike.

• Adults take up the Bossa Nova after saxophonist Stan Getz introduces the jazzy tempo at the White House in November. But unlike other new steps, the Latin American rhythm requires more skill and the dance quickly dies out.

• *West Side Story* captures the musical LP market, but comedy albums are the top sellers this year. Vaughn Meader, in a hilarious takeoff on the Kennedys, sells 4 million copies of *The First Family.* And 1 million Americans buy Allan Sherman's brilliant parodies on *My Son, the Folk Singer.*

• With industry volume nearing an all-time high of $560 million, more discs receive gold certification than ever before—5 singles and 37 LPs. (Last year, only 2 singles and 15 LPs qualified.) At this time, stores generally charge 98 cents for 45's, $3.98 for mono albums, and $4.98 for stereo.

• Peter, Paul & Mary reach No. 10 with "If I Had a Hammer" while the Kingston Trio takes "Where Have All the Flowers Gone?" to No. 21, the first protest songs to break the top 40.

• Carole King and Gerry Goffin ask their 18-year-old baby-sitter to try out a new song. She does such a good job that the songwriting duo ask Eva Boyd to record "The Loco-Motion."

• Female voices dominate the airwaves this year: Patsy Cline, Little Eva, Shelley Fabares, Connie Francis, Brenda Lee, Timi Yuro, Sue Thompson, Mary Wells, the Crystals, the Marvelettes, the Orlons, the Shirelles.

### New Recording Artists

Herb Alpert & the Tijuana Brass
Beach Boys
Booker T. & the MG's
Gene Chandler
Bob Dylan
Four Seasons
Marvin Gaye
Bobby Goldsboro
Jay & the Americans
Jack Jones
Carole King
Willie Nelson
Peter, Paul & Mary
Tommy Roe
Supremes
Bobby Vinton
Dionne Warwick

## Obituaries

**Harry Carroll** (November 28, 1892–December 26, 1962). The U.S. composer's songs included "I'm Always Chasing Rainbows" (1918).

**Maceo Pinkard** (June 27, 1897–July 19, 1962). The music publisher and composer collaborated on such hits as "Sweet Georgia Brown" (1925) and "Them There Eyes" (1930), as well as his most famous, "Gimme a Little Kiss, Will Ya, Huh?" (1926).

# MOVIES

*Birdman of Alcatraz* (d. John Frankenheimer; bw)—Burt Lancaster, Karl Malden, Thelma Ritter, Betty Field, Neville Brand, Edmond O'Brien

*Days of Wine and Roses* (d. Blake Edwards; bw)—Jack Lemmon, Lee Remick, Charles Bickford, Jack Klugman

*Divorce—Italian Style* (Italian, d. Pietro Germi; bw)—Marcello Mastroianni, Daniela Rocca

*Dr. No* (British, d. Terence Young; color)—Sean Connery, Ursula Andress, Joseph Wiseman, Jack Lord, Bernard Lee, Lois Maxwell

*Hell Is for Heroes* (d. Don Siegel; bw)—Steve McQueen, Bobby Darin, Fess Parker

*Lawrence of Arabia* (d. David Lean; color)—Peter O'Toole, Alec Guinness, Jack Hawkins, Anthony Quinn, José Ferrer, Anthony Quayle, Omar Sharif, Arthur Kennedy

*Light in the Piazza* (d. Guy Green; color)—Olivia de Havilland, Rossano Brazzi, Yvette Mimieux, George Hamilton

*The Loneliness of the Long Distance Runner* (British, d. Tony Richardson; bw)—Tom Courtenay, Michael Redgrave

*Lonely Are the Brave* (d. David Miller; bw)—Kirk Douglas, Gena Rowlands, Walter Matthau

*Long Day's Journey into Night* (d. Sidney Lumet; bw)—Katharine Hepburn, Ralph Richardson, Jason Robards, Jr., Dean Stockwell

*The Longest Day* (d. Andrew Marton, Ken Annakin, Bernhard Wicki; bw)—John Wayne, Robert Mitchum, Henry Fonda, Robert Ryan, Paul Anka, Sal Mineo, Red Buttons, Richard Burton

*Lover Come Back* (d. Delbert Mann; color)—Rock Hudson, Doris Day, Tony Randall, Edie Adams

*The Man Who Shot Liberty Valance* (d. John Ford; bw)—James Stewart, John Wayne, Vera Miles, Lee Marvin

*The Manchurian Candidate* (d. John Frankenheimer; bw)—Frank Sinatra, Laurence Harvey, Janet Leigh, Angela Lansbury

*The Miracle Worker* (d. Arthur Penn; bw)—Anne Bancroft, Patty Duke

*The Music Man* (d. Morton Da Costa; color)—Robert Preston, Shirley Jones, Buddy Hackett, Hermione Gingold

*Requiem for a Heavyweight* (d. Ralph Nelson; bw)—Anthony Quinn, Jackie Gleason, Mickey Rooney, Julie Harris

*Ride the High Country* (d. Sam Peckinpah; color)—Randolph Scott, Joel McCrea, Mariette Hartley

*Sweet Bird of Youth* (d. Richard Brooks; color)—Paul Newman, Geraldine Page, Shirley Knight, Ed Begley, Rip Torn

*To Kill a Mockingbird* (d. Robert Mulligan; bw)—Gregory Peck, Mary Badham, Philip Alford, Robert Duvall

*What Ever Happened to Baby Jane?* (d. Robert Aldrich; bw)—Bette Davis, Joan Crawford, Victor Buono

*The Wrong Arm of the Law* (British, d. Cliff Owen; bw)—Peter Sellers, Lionel Jeffries, Bernard Cribbins

## Academy Awards

**April 9.** For the first time in Academy history, an actor has declined an award in advance. George C. Scott, nominated as best supporting actor for his role in *The Hustler*, requested his name be removed from the polling.

Bob Hope hosts as usual.

Best Picture—*West Side Story*

Best Actor—Maximilian Schell (*Judgment at Nuremberg*)

Best Actress—Sophia Loren (*Two Women*)
Best Director—Robert Wise and Jerome Robbins (*West Side Story*)
Best Supporting Actor—George Chakiris (*West Side Story*)
Best Supporting Actress—Rita Moreno (*West Side Story*)
Best Song—"Moon River" from *Breakfast at Tiffany's*
Best Foreign Film—*Through a Glass Darkly* (Swedish)
Honorary Award—Jerome Robbins

Two other firsts this year: the first double Oscar for best director and the first regular Oscar to an actress in a foreign-language film.

A relatively unknown Ann-Margret dazzles the audience with her performance of the nominated song "Bachelor in Paradise."

## News

**January 26.** In 1952, the British Film Institute's *Sight and Sound* magazine polled European film critics for the 10 best films in the history of cinema. Vittorio De Sica's *The Bicycle Thief* (1949) placed first, and two Charlie Chaplin films—*The Gold Rush* (1925) and *City Lights* (1931)—tied for second.

Now, ten years later, in a poll of 70 critics, *The Bicycle Thief* falls to sixth and Chaplin's films fail to place. The No. 1 position goes to a film that just missed the 1952 list—Orson Welle's *Citizen Kane* (1941).

**February 6.** Warner Bros. pays a record $5.5 million for movie rights to the Broadway musical *My Fair Lady*.

**November 5.** With the exceptions of Universal and Paramount, all the major studios have now sold or leased some post-1948 films to TV. MPAA President Eric Johnston explains Hollywood's changed attitude: "We are no longer a feature motion picture industry. We are a television *and* movies industry."

But the networks complain that the studios force them to take unwanted pictures along with the top

films. This month, in a Justice Department suit, the U.S. Supreme Court rules against package sales.

*For his first James Bond film, Dr. No, 32-year-old Sean Connery receives a reported $16,500. By 1966, his salary will rise to $750,000.*

**More news.** Western star Randolph Scott ends his 33-year film career with *Ride the High Country*. His portrayal of aging cowboys, in these latter years, remain his most memorable roles.

• With moviegoers ignoring big city theaters for smaller suburban theaters and drive-ins, Canadian and American "palaces" of yesteryear are converted into bowling alleys or supermarkets. Recognizing the trend, U.S. film companies abandon exclusive first-run showings for "saturation bookings"—simultaneous openings in several city and suburban movie houses. This approach works particularly well, this year, with *The Manchurian Candidate* and *What Ever Happened to Baby Jane?*

• *The Children's Hour* breaks new ground with the depiction of a lesbian relationship. Audrey Hepburn and Shirley MacLaine fight against the suspicions of their community until MacLaine, realizing she loves Hepburn, kills herself in remorse.

• Graphics designer Saul Bass creates a 1930s New Orleans atmosphere for *Walk on the Wild Side* with a classic titles sequence—a black tomcat, filmed from shoulder level, stalking through the streets, then battling with a white tom. Two uncooperative cats produced just a few seconds of action, but Bass's technicians reversed and reprinted the precious frames in every conceivable fashion—including backward and in slow motion—to "build" to the climactic fight.

| Top Box Office Stars | Newcomers |
| --- | --- |
| Doris Day | Bobby Darin |
| Rock Hudson | Ann-Margret |
| Cary Grant | Richard Beymer |
| John Wayne | Suzanne Pleshette |
| Elvis Presley | Capucine |
| Elizabeth Taylor | George Peppard |
| Jerry Lewis | James MacArthur |
| Frank Sinatra | Peter Falk |
| Sandra Dee | Michael Callan |
| Burt Lancaster | Yvette Mimieux |

## Top Money-Maker of the Year

*Spartacus* (1960)

## Flop of the Year

*Mutiny on the Bounty*
—With the budget skyrocketing to $24 million and star Marlon Brando gaining an obvious 40 lbs during shooting, this overlong and uninteresting adaptation sinks out of sight.

## Obituaries

**Frank Borzage** (April 23, 1893–June 19, 1962). In 1929, Borzage received the first director's award from the Motion Picture Academy of Arts and Sciences, for *Seventh Heaven* (1927). He also won the 1931–1932 Oscar for *Bad Girl*.

**Michael Curtiz** (December 24, 1888?–April 10, 1962). The Hungarian-born director immigrated to the United States in 1927. With a reputation as a tyrant, Curtiz directed such notable films as *Captain Blood* (1935), *Yankee Doodle Dandy* (1942), and *Casablanca* (1943), which brought him an Oscar.

**Hoot (Edmund Richard) Gibson** (August 6, 1892–August 23, 1962). Reportedly nicknamed for his boyhood hobby of hunting owls, the 1912 World Champion Cowboy turned to movies three years later. He began as a stunt man, then, in 1920, signed with Universal Pictures to star in a series of Westerns. An unusual cowboy who emphasized comedy over gunplay, Gibson made only occasional appearances after 1944.

**Charles Laughton** (July 1, 1899–December 15, 1962). Many film critics consider the heavyset Englishman, who won a best actor Oscar for *The Private Life of Henry VIII* (1933), the greatest character actor in the history of cinema. Two of his most well-known roles were the implacable Captain Bligh opposite Clark Gable in *Mutiny on the Bounty* (1935) and Tyrone Power's wily defense attorney in *Witness for the Prosecution* (1957).

A career shift to directing unfortunately ended with his first film, the stunning black-and-white *Night of the Hunter* (1955).

Laughton, who died of cancer, is survived by his wife of 33 years, actress Elsa Lanchester.

**Thomas Mitchell** (July 11, 1892–December 17, 1962). Already an accomplished stage actor in 1934 when he turned to films, the character actor became a movie star in his own right. In 1939, he appeared in *Mr. Smith Goes to Washington*, played Gerald O'Hara in *Gone With the Wind*, and won a best supporting Oscar as the drunken Doc Boone in *Stagecoach*. He later won an Emmy and a Tony as well.

**Marilyn Monroe** (June 1, 1926–August 5, 1962). A childhood spent in foster homes, suffering neglect and rape, pushed Norma Jean Baker into marriage at age 16. Divorced by age 20, she readily turned her back on the past to become Marilyn Monroe for 20th Century-Fox.

Her first bit part, in *Scudda Hoo! Scudda Hay!* (1948), fell to the cutting-room floor, and the following four years of roles proved less than memorable, except for small showy parts in *All About Eve* (1950) and *The Asphalt Jungle* (1950). Then, in 1952, the public learned Marilyn had once posed nude, and her career took off. Another 12 films followed, including *The Seven Year Itch* (1955), *Bus Stop* (1956), and *Some Like It Hot* (1959).

Movie fans demanded nothing more from their sex goddess than the pout, the breathless husky voice, and the spectacular figure combined with an irresistible, vulnerable innocence. But Marilyn yearned to be taken seriously as an actress. That unfulfilled ambition and her troubled personal life lead many to believe her overdose was not accidental.

In his tribute at the funeral, drama coach and friend Lee Strasberg describes Marilyn Monroe as a legend. "For the entire world she became a symbol of the eternal feminine."

**Jerry Wald** (September 16, 1912–July 13, 1962). The motion-picture producer counted among his most memorable films *Key Largo* (1948), *From Here to Eternity* (1953), and *Picnic* (1955).

## TELEVISION AND RADIO

### New Prime-Time TV Programs

"The Beverly Hillbillies" (September 26, 1962–September 7, 1971; Situation Comedy)—Buddy Ebsen, Irene Ryan, Donna Douglas, Max Baer, Jr., Raymond Bailey, Nancy Kulp

"Combat" (October 2, 1962–August 29, 1967; War Drama)—Rick Jason, Vic Morrow, Pierre Jalbert

"The Jack Paar Program" (September 21, 1962–September 10, 1965; Variety)—Host: Jack Paar

"The Jackie Gleason Show" (September 1962–September 1970; Comedy Variety)—Jackie Gleason, Frank Fontaine (1962–1966), Art Carney (1966–1970), Sheila MacRae (1966–1970), The June Taylor Dancers

"The Jetsons" (September 23, 1962–September 8, 1963; Cartoon)—Voices: George O'Hanlon (George Jetson); Penny Singleton

(Jane Jetson); Janet Waldo (Judy); Don Messick (Astro) *Note:* The program continues in syndication on Saturday morning.

"The Lucy Show" (October 1, 1962–September 2, 1974; Situation Comedy)—Lucille Ball, Vivian Vance (1962–1965), Gale Gordon (1963–1974). *Note:* In September 1968, the show will become "Here's Lucy" and the star's children, Lucie Arnaz and Desi Arnaz, Jr., will join the cast.

"McHale's Navy" (October 11, 1962–August 30, 1966; Situation Comedy)—Ernest Borgnine, Joe Flynn, Tim Conway, Carl Ballantine

"The Nurses" (September 27, 1962–September 7, 1965; Medical Drama)—Shirl Conway, Zina Bethune

"Password" (January 2, 1962–September 1965; April–May 1967; Quiz/Audience Participation)—Emcee: Allen Ludden. *Note:* A daytime program as well, the quiz show will return to a day telecast from 1971–1975.

"The Tonight Show Starring Johnny Carson" (October 2, 1962–; Talk/Variety)—Host: Johnny Carson Regulars: Ed McMahon, Skitch Henderson (1962–1966), Doc Severinson (1967–1992)

"The Virginian" (September 19, 1962–September 8, 1971; Western)—James Drury, Doug McClure, Lee J. Cobb (1962–1966). *Note:* In its last season, the show will be retitled "The Men from Shiloh."

### Emmy Awards 1961–1962 (May 22, 1962)

Drama—"The Defenders" (CBS)

Variety or Music—"The Garry Moore Show" (CBS)

Humor—"The Bob Newhart Show" (NBC)

Children's Programming—"New York Philharmonic Young People's Concerts with Leonard Bernstein" (CBS)

Best Actor in a Series—E. G. Marshall ("The Defenders," CBS)

Best Actress in a Series—Shirley Booth ("Hazel," NBC)

*With a strong lead-in from "Ed Sullivan," the Cartwrights take "Bonanza" to No. 2 in the Nielsen ratings in the shows third season.*

## News

**February 14.** Millions of Americans tour the White House with Jacqueline Kennedy (the president appears briefly at the end). The CBS program is shown simultaneously by NBC.

**February 20.** Media observers describe John Glenn's orbital flight as the most emotionally gripping news story of the year. TV networks provide 12 hours of coverage.

**March 17.** ABC's "Fight of the Week" uses special replay equipment to rerun in slow motion—over and over—the fatal blows to Kid Paret in a Madison Square Garden boxing match.

**April.** At the end of last year, CBS will establish four additional domestic news bureaus and shift the nightly news to a roving-reporter format. Douglas Edwards, anchor for 16 years, is eased out this month, and Walter Cronkite takes over.

**April 7.** ABC premieres a Saturday-morning "Bugs Bunny" program.

**April 24.** The two-year-old *Echo I* transmits the first satellite-relay TV pictures, from the MIT Lincoln Lab in California to the Millstone Hill Lab in Massachusetts. The announcement on May 3 admits the weak signal produced unclear pictures.

**June 28.** In 1955, radio humorist John Henry Faulk and others were elected as officers of the New York branch of AFTRA (American Federation of TV and Radio Artists) on an antiblacklisting slate. Immediately afterward, he and comic Orson Bean were targeted by the anti-Communist organization Aware in an intense smear campaign.

With Cold War hysteria abating somewhat, Faulk finally receives his day in court. Credible testimony to the continued existence of industry blacklisting brings him reported damages of $3.5 million. In August, he makes his first television appearance in five years.

**July 11.** Since the creation of over 1,400 UHF television stations in 1952, manufacturers have made little effort to adapt their sets to the technology. As a result, only 48 of the more than 140 UHF educational allocations have been assigned. (All but four are associated with the fledgling National Educational Television [NET] network, which schedules a mere eight hours per week.)

Today, President Kennedy signs the All-Channel Law giving the FCC authority to require manufacturers to build in reception for 70 UHF channels by April 30, 1964. Expansion of the UHF band through this decade will give the ABC network the needed affiliates to reach every American city.

**July 23.** Following tests on the 10th, the Telstar communications satellite completes the first formal exchange of broadcasts between the United States and the Eurovision network. The Americans receive a 20-minute mix of scenes such as Big Ben in London and reindeer in Sweden; hours later, Europeans watch a Kennedy news conference, a baseball game, and the Statue of Liberty. The reception is generally clear.

**Fall.** This season, in evaluating new series, some critics point to the influence of John F. Kennedy. On "The Defenders," for instance, the father and son lawyers deal with difficult issues such as abortion. Still, 25 affiliates decline to carry that episode.

• In Canada, CBC inaugurates a revitalized 79-station English-language radio network. The 55 independently owned affiliates must carry a minimum 26 of the week's 112 hours.

**September 19.** "The Virginian," starring James Drury and Doug McClure, is TV's first 90-minute regular series.

**September 23.** ABC refused for years to broadcast in color and lost the Walt Disney show as a result. This year, the network's first color program is an abysmal prime-time failure. Only 24 episodes of "The Jetsons" are broadcast. Moved to Saturday next September, however, the animated space family will become a children's favorite.

**September 26.** "The Beverly Hillbillies" debuts on CBS. In five weeks, the sitcom jumps to No. 1 and remains there through this season and next. UPI's Rick Du Brow says, "The series aimed low and hits target," but fans love the jokes: "Do you know Shaw's *Pygmalion?* I don't even know Shaw, let alone his pig." Success spawns a number of rural-based sitcoms.

**October 1.** When Jack Paar left late-night NBC in March, Hugh Downs remained on hand over the summer to provide continuity with guest hosts.

Tonight, Groucho Marx flies in to introduce previous part-time host Johnny Carson and his game-show buddy Ed McMahon on "The Tonight Show." Guests include Tony Bennett, Mel Brooks, Joan Crawford, and Rudy Vallee. Carson quickly shifts the show's emphasis from variety to light talk. Soon regular viewers anticipate Ed's introduction, "Hee-e-e-re's Johnny!"

**October 1.** Lucille Ball returns to CBS without Desi. With "The Lucy Show," she reestablishes herself as the first lady of American television.

**November 11.** Just five days after his loss in California, ABC airs "The Political Obituary of Richard Nixon." The program provokes a national controversy, with Nixon supporters denouncing the appearance of Alger Hiss. On the 18th, an ABC vice-president defends the network's right to present the news as it sees fit. Nixon was asked to appear and he refused.

**More news.** Lorenzo Milam organizes KRAB in Seattle. Described as "community," "alternative," or "public access" radio, the broadcast style adds an interesting element to noncommercial stations.

## TV Commercials

Brylcreem—In one of the most erotic commercials to date, a woman wriggles out of the product tube and asks, "Brylcreem. Are you man enough to try it?"

## Memorable Radio Programs End

"Suspense" (June 17, 1942)
"Yours Truly, Johnny Dollar" (February 18, 1949)

## Obituaries

**Ernie Kovacs** (January 23, 1919–January 13, 1962). The actor, writer, and producer remains best known as a cigar-chomping TV comic. He died in a car accident, leaving his wife of eight years, actress Edie Adams, with a pile of debts.

# SPORTS

## Winners

### Baseball

World Series—New York Yankees (AL), 4 games; San Francisco Giants (NL), 3 games
Player of the Year—Mickey Mantle (New York Yankees, AL); Maury Wills (Los Angeles Dodgers, NL)
Rookie of the Year—Tom Tresh (New York Yankees, AL); Ken Hubbs (Chicago Cubs, NL)

### Football

NFL Championship—Green Bay Packers 16, New York Giants 7
AFL Championship—Dallas Texans 20, Houston Oilers 17
College Bowls (January 1, 1962)—
Rose Bowl, Minnesota 21, UCLA 3
Cotton Bowl, Texas 12, Mississippi 7

*Complaining about Jim Brown's ball-carrying skill, New York Giants' end Kyle Rote says, "It's reached the point where our best defensive men run off the field, waving and shouting for joy, 'I touched him, I touched him' " (Sports Illustrated, March 12, 1962).*

Orange Bowl, LSU 25, Colorado 7
Sugar Bowl, Alabama 10, Arkansas 3
Heisman Trophy—Terry Baker (Oregon State, QB)
Grey Cup—Winnipeg Blue Bombers 28, Hamilton Tiger-Cats 27

## Basketball

NBA Championship—Boston Celtics, 4 games; Los Angeles Lakers, 3 games
MVP of the Year—Bill Russell (Boston Celtics)
Rookie of the Year—Walt Bellamy (Chicago Packers)
NCAA Championship—Cincinnati 71, Ohio State 59

## Tennis

U.S. National—Men, Rod Laver (vs. Roy Emerson); Women, Margaret Smith (vs. Darlene Hard)
Wimbledon—Men, Rod Laver (vs. Martin Mulligan); Women, Karen Hantzesusman (vs. Vera Suková)

## Golf

Masters—Arnold Palmer
U.S. Open—Jack Nicklaus
British Open—Arnold Palmer

## Hockey

Stanley Cup—Toronto Maple Leafs, 4 games; Chicago Blackhawks, 2 games

## Ice Skating

World Championship—Men, Donald Jackson (Canada); Women, Sjoukje Dijkstra (Netherlands)
U.S. National—Men, Monty Hoyt; Women, Barbara Roles Pursley
Canadian National—Men, Donald Jackson; Women, Wendy Griner

## Kentucky Derby

Decidedly—Bill Hartack, jockey

## Athlete of the Year

Male—Maury Wills (Baseball)
Female—Dawn Fraser (Swimming)

## Last Season

Eddie Arcaro (Horse Racing)

## News

**February 9.** Archie Moore loses his light-heavyweight title for refusing to fight recognized challengers. He took the crown from Joey Maxim in December 1952. Moore retires next year (at the estimated age of 40, no one knows for sure) with 143 KOs in 231 matches.

**March 24.** Emile Griffith wins the welterweight championship with a technical knockout (TKO) in Madison Square Garden. Benny "Kid" Paret, knocked out just four months earlier by Gene Fulmer, dies of his injuries on April 3.

**April.** Contest entrants suggested the Avengers, Burros, and Skyliners. New York's new baseball team picked the Metropolitans, soon shortened to the Mets.

Eager fans crowd into the old Polo Grounds, but the Mets lose their first nine games (their first run comes on a balk) and mathematically eliminate themselves from the pennant race before the end of August. With their final 40–120 record, everyone knows the answer to the question, "What has 18 legs and lives in the cellar?" Next year's 111 losses will indicate little improvement.

**April 23.** British driver Stirling Moss breaks nearly every bone on the left side of his body in a race at Greenwood, England. One of the best-known sports figures on the international scene, the 33-year-old has won 194 races. He recovers, but will never race again.

**May 21.** In Baltimore, U.S. District Judge Roscel Thomsen acquits the NFL in a $10-million AFL antitrust suit. When the NFL moved into Dallas and Minneapolis, AFL gate receipts dropped forcing the league to cancel its Minneapolis franchise.

**May 29.** John (Buck) O'Neil signs with the Chicago Cubs. He is the first officially recognized black coach in major league history.

**June 17.** Jack Nicklaus beats Arnold Palmer in an 18-hole play-off to capture the U.S. Open. The first rookie winner of the prestigious event, Nicklaus says, "I'm just so elated, I just can't say anything." He first played at the age of 10 when his father Charles took up golf to strengthen an injured ankle.

**July 22.** Soviet high jumper Valery Brumel is named international sportsman for the second straight year. A pioneer in track-and-field weight training, he uses the straddle jump to clear 7' 5¼" in an autumn competition.

**September 10.** Rod Laver wins the men's singles at the U.S. National Tennis Championship. With earlier victories at Wimbledon and the Australian and French Opens, he becomes the second man (after American Don Budge) to win a Grand Slam. Oddly enough, the 23 year old faced fellow Australians in the four final matches.

**September 25.** Sonny Liston knocks out heavyweight champion Floyd Patterson at 2:06 of the first round. In their rematch next July 22, the 28-year-old title holder needs just 4 seconds more to knock out Patterson a second time.

**December 1–2.** With just under 10 minutes left on the clock, Grey Cup referees call the game. Mist rolling in off Lake Ontario has enveloped the ball past midfield (fans in the upper stands can see nothing on the opposite side). The "Fog Bowl" resumes the next day and the Winnipeg Blue Bombers win the Cup almost 25 hours after kickoff.

**December 31.** With only a handful of NBA players to draw fans, the eight-team American Basketball League collapses in the middle of its second season. The league introduced one interesting feature—baskets from 25 feet out earned 3 points.

**More news.** Wimbledon decrees that women tennis players must wear all white outfits, including their panties.

• This year, the Washington Redskins trade a No. 1 draft choice for Bobby Mitchell and Leroy Jackson. Mitchell is the team's first black player.

## Records

**February 2.** Pole vaulter John Uelses breaks the magic 16-foot barrier at Madison Square Garden. But excited fans knock the standards askew and officials discount the mark. Next day, the 24-year-old marine corporal tops 16'3¾". By August of next year, the new fiber-glass poles will push athletes over 17 feet.

**March 2.** In a game against the New York Knickerbockers, Wilt Chamberlain scores an astounding 100 points—36 goals and 28 foul shots. Unfortunately, overzealous fans force the referees to call the game with 46 seconds left on the clock. With no TV coverage, only 4,000 or so people witness the Philadelphia center's remarkable feat. Still, his box-office appeal fails to solve the team's financial woes and the Warriors move to San Francisco at the end of the season.

**June 22.** Veteran outfielder Stan Musial hits a HR and two singles in a twilight doubleheader to break Ty Cobb's major league record of 5,863 career bases.

**September 26.** By August, baseball fans were calling Dodger shortstop Maury Wills the "diamond burglar." Today, in a game against the Houston Colts, the 30 year old breaks Ty Cobb's single-season record of 96 stolen bases. Cobb was caught 38 times in a 156-game season; Wills, in the same number of games, has been nabbed just 13 times. He collects 104 by the end of the season.

## What They Said

As Jack Nicklaus approached his golf ball, nestling beside a tree, an official asked if he wanted the crowd moved back. "Never mind the people. Just move this tree a few feet to the left." (*Sports Illustrated*, July 16, 1962)

## Obituaries

**Juan Belmonte y García** (April 14, 1892–April 8, 1962). The Spanish matador originated the modern bullfighting stance—in close to the bull, head erect, hands low, elbows tight. Apparently the youthful Belmonte, slipping out at night to challenge the bulls, had to get in close to see the animals in the dark.

**Mickey Cochrane** (April 6, 1903–June 28, 1962). His .320 lifetime batting average, established with the Athletics (1927–1933) and the Tigers (1934–1937), remains the best of any major league catcher. Cochrane's playing career ended in 1937 when a pitched ball fractured his skull. In 1952, "Black Mike" and former Yankee Bill Dickey were voted the best catchers of the half century.

**Clem McCarthy** (September 9, 1882–June 4, 1962). From his first radio broadcast in 1928 until 1957, McCarthy covered nearly every major sporting event with his rapid-fire delivery.

# 1963

*"President Kennedy has been shot." His traumatic death shatters the nation, then draws Americans together in grief. Those of us old enough to understand the significance of the event will always remember the exact moment we heard the terrible news.*

*In his last year in office, Kennedy's tough inaugural pledges gave way to an early Cold War thaw—a Partial Test Ban Treaty, a Moscow-Washington hot line, and negotiations for a U.S.-USSR wheat deal. On the 100th anniversary of the Emancipation Proclamation, the president offered far-reaching civil rights legislation. But White House appeals, a massive March on Washington, and even the brutalities of Birmingham failed to push the bill through Congress.*

*Years later, 1963 will remain defined by the stark images surrounding the assassination: the funeral, the little boy saluting his father, the murder of Lee Harvey Oswald before the eyes of the nation, and the formation of the Warren Commission.*

## NEWS

**January 2.** Since late 1961, when the United States began openly sending large numbers of advisory, support, and training units to bolster the Diem government, 21 Americans have been killed in action in South Vietnam and 31 have died from other causes. (UPI disputes today's figures, giving 30 combat fatalities and 19 in service accidents.)

**January 17.** President Kennedy submits a $98.8-billion budget, the largest in American history. The projected $10-billion deficit exceeds the total U.S. budget for 1940, the last full year before U.S. entry into W.W.II.

**January 29.** Concerned that a U.S.-oriented Atlantic community would absorb Europe, President Charles de Gaulle vetoes the British application for membership in the EEC. As proof, he points to last's month London-Washington agreement to provide Britain with U.S. Polaris missiles.

**February 5.** A nonconfidence motion on Canada's defense policy brings down the minority Conservative government—only the second time a government has fallen on a House of Commons vote.

The Diefenbaker government agreed to adopt U.S. nuclear weapons systems for Canadian NATO squadrons, but dragged out negotiations through the 1950s in the hope that the superpowers would reach a disarmament agreement. As a result, late last year, the Canadian squadrons received their Bomarc missiles without warheads.

Still, Ottawa held firm, maintaining that the recent U.S.-British Polaris agreement along with U.S. Secretary McNamara's concern for Bomarc obsolescence called for a reevaluation of Western defense strategy. Then a U.S. State Department memo, released in late January, criticized the Diefenbaker policy, and Parliament rose in an uproar over American interference.

Forced to resign or seek a mandate from the voters, Diefenbaker dissolves Parliament on the 6th and calls for an election.

On April 8, the government goes down to defeat. The Liberals, led by Lester Pearson, win 129 seats, just 3 short of a majority. Diefenbaker's Conservatives hold onto 95 seats, the Social Credit win 24, and the NDP, 17.

Prime Minister Pearson meets with President Kennedy in Washington next month and confirms Canada's intention to accept nuclear warheads. The new Liberal government, in turn, survives a Conservative-sponsored nonconfidence motion in late May, and the Americans deliver the Bomarc missiles on December 31.

**February 24.** In response to a White House request, a four-man investigative panel headed by Senator Mike Mansfield (D., Montana) reports to the Senate Foreign Relations Committee on U.S. aid to Southeast Asia. The members question the high level of funding, suggest the South Vietnamese expend "further effort," and conclude "there is no interest of the United States in Vietnam which would justify in present circumstances the conversion of the war . . . primarily into an American war to be fought primarily with American lives."

In Vietnam today, VC groundfire downs two of three U.S. helicopters airlifting South Vietnamese soldiers. Two days later, Americans receive authorization to shoot immediately upon sighting enemy soldiers; previously the crews had orders to shoot only when fired upon.

**March 18.** In a historic decision, the U.S. Supreme Court rules that state courts must supply free counsel to all indigents facing serious criminal charges.

Last year, Clarence Earl Gideon sat in his jail cell and wrote out a crude petition. Florida had refused his request for a lawyer; he represented himself, lost, and received a five-year sentence. The Supreme Court pulled his plea from a mass of mail; Abe Fortas was appointed to argue *Gideon v. Wainwright* (Florida director of corrections).

Previously, the *Betts v. Brady* ruling (1942) required state courts to appoint counsel only in cases carrying a death penalty. Florida and four others meet the minimum requirement.

Over the next year, 321 prisoners in Florida will get new trials and 232 will receive shorter sentences. At his retrial, Gideon will be acquitted.

**April 3.** The SCLC, under Martin Luther King, Jr., has chosen to make a symbolic stand in Birmingham, Alabama, a city known for strict segregation and frequent racist violence. Campaign goals include desegregating lunch counters, water fountains, and other facilities, gaining amnesty for demonstrators, increasing job opportunities for blacks, and establishing a biracial committee to schedule desegregation for the entire city.

Mass demonstrations begin, with protesters carefully screened to resist violence. After days of arrests, Eugene "Bull" Connor, Birmingham's commissioner of public safety seeks an injunction. For the first time, King defies a court order and tells the protesters to continue. Police arrest him, Abernathy, and about 50 others on the 12th. Before their release on the 20th, King writes a "Letter from a Birmingham Jail" to a group of unsympathetic white clergymen: "For years now I have heard the word *wait.* It rings in the ear of every Negro with piercing familiarity. This wait has almost always meant *never.* We must come to see . . . that justice too long delayed is justice denied." The letter has tremendous impact on the movement across the nation.

The demonstrations grow larger and more focused as the weeks go by, then students join on May 2. The next day, when the young people ignore an order to halt, Connor makes a strategic error that turns the tide. Newspapers around the world carry photographs of American policemen turning their dogs and fire hoses—carrying 700 pounds of pressure, enough to strip the bark off a tree—on black protestors, many of them just children. Negroes

*Black demonstrators join hands against the tremendous force of Birmingham fire hoses.*

unite in anger, the protesters swell to 3,000, and Assistant Attorney General Burke Marshall arrives in Birmingham to negotiate for the president.

With Marshall working between them, the two sides reach an agreement on the full list of demands on May 10, 38 days after the beginning of the campaign. But the next night, two bombs shatter the hard-won peace. No one suffers serious injury at the home of Rev. A. D. King, Martin's brother, or at the SCLC motel headquarters, but thousands of blacks take to the streets. Police reestablish order early in the morning, as the president stations 3,000 federal troops nearby.

Mobilizing an entire community for the first time, the movement has won an important victory in the South. On May 20, the Supreme Court finds unconstitutional those state ordinances calling for segregated facilities. In the 10 weeks following the truce, the Justice Department will count 758 civil rights demonstrations nationwide.

**April 3.** Upholding his agreement not to invade Cuba, President Kennedy reaffirms U.S. opposition to raids on Cuba by U.S.-based exiles. Noting the continued presence of approximately 4,000 Soviet troops in Cuba, he states at today's press conference that American forces will continue air and sea surveillance to intercept any guerrilla actions.

On April 30, the administration ends financial aid to the Miami-based anti-Castro Cuban Revolutionary Council. As a result, refugee groups shift to infiltration, setting up communications with dissidents in Cuba and smuggling in weapons.

**April 10.** The nuclear-powered submarine *U.S.S. Thresher* sinks in 8,400 feet of water 200 miles off the East Coast, killing all 129 men aboard. Apparently the sub sank after a loss of power, and pressure ruptured the hull.

Officially the reactor did not cause the accident (pieces of debris show low amounts of radioactivity). The three-year-old vessel, the first of an advanced model and built at a cost of $45 million, had been plagued with problems, spending one-third of its short life in dry dock.

**April 20.** At an army recruiting center in Montreal, a bomb blast kills 65-year-old night watchman Wilfred O'Neill. The Front de libération du Québec, a recently formed group of young radicals seeking the separation of Quebec from Canada, admits responsibility but maintains that his death was an accident. Despite the disclaimer, the FLQ next month plants bombs in 10 mailboxes, seriously injuring an army bomb expert.

The Montreal police form an antiterrorist unit, and by October, eight captured FLQ members receive sentences of 6–12 years for O'Neill's death. The separatist group continues with underground activities.

**May 20.** In six cases, the Supreme Court finds that cities in Alabama, Louisiana, North Carolina, and South Carolina can no longer use municipal ordinances to prosecute black Americans seeking service in privately owned stores. The rulings, in effect, sustain their right to integrate through peaceful sit-ins.

**May 28–29.** A powerful cyclone with winds reaching 150 mph hits a heavily populated strip along the East Pakistan coastline, destroying a million mud homes. Two tidal waves sweep 10,000 people into the sea; altogether an estimated 22,000 die.

**June 3.** Pope John XXIII dies at age 81. Considered a "caretaker" upon his election in 1958, John became the most influential pope of this century. He made unprecedented attempts to improve communications with non-Catholic churches, convened the second Vatican council (the first since 1870) to consider church reform, made himself accessible to the people, and took a 400-mile trip within Italy, the farthest a pope had journeyed from the Vatican in 100 years.

Through his simplicity and charm, John became a popular figure with Catholics and non-Catholics alike. Cardinal John Heenan comments, "He was not a great scholar or diplomat. He was just a loving shepherd." His death is deeply mourned.

The church elects Cardinal Giovanni Battista Montini as his successor. As the 262nd pope of the Roman Catholic Church, he assumes the name of Pope Paul VI.

**June 4.** British War Secretary John Profumo tenders his resignation with an admission that he lied last March in denying a sexual relationship with call girl Christine Keeler. His indiscretion has escalated into an international sex-and-spy scandal because another Keeler client, Soviet spy Yevgeni Ivanov, had asked her to discover from Profumo when West Germany would receive nuclear warheads.

The British government survives a confidence vote in June but remains badly shaken. A commission of inquiry reports in September that the incident was moral misbehavior by a minister, not a security risk, and clears the government, police, and security services. The report sells 100,000 copies on its first day.

**June 11.** When Governor George Wallace of Alabama pledged "segregation now, segregation tomorrow, and segregation forever" at his January swearing-in ceremony, he became the symbol of Southern resistance to integration. Today he defies a court order and personally stops two black students from enrolling at the State university.

President Kennedy signs a prepared executive order federalizing the Alabama National Guard and in the evening goes on television to describe the crisis facing the nation: "The heart of the question is whether all Americans are to be afforded equal rights and equal opportunities; whether we are going to treat our fellow Americans as we want to be treated. If an American, because his skin is dark, cannot . . . enjoy the full and free life which all of us want, then who among us would be content to have the color of his skin changed and stand in his place?" He will ask Congress for new civil rights legislation.

Next day, Wallace steps aside when the Guard arrives at the university.

**June 12.** Medgar Evers, Mississippi field secretary for the NAACP, is shot to death in front of his home in Jackson. The 37-year-old civil rights leader had supported Meredith and organized the boycott of city stores.

Mass demonstrations follow his assassination, and rioting breaks out at the funeral when police arrest some of the 3,000 in attendance. Roy Wilkins, executive director of the NAACP, cries out at the service that "the Southern political system put that man behind the rifle." A white man will be charged with Evers' murder, but two successive juries will fail to convict him.

**June 16.** A 60,000-word letter in the Peking press strongly attacks the Soviets for pursuing peaceful coexistence at the expense of world Communist revolutionary aims. Accusations and counteraccusations fly, and in July, the two powers announce the failure of ideological discussions. In December, Communist delegates to the international People's Council seemingly back Moscow with an overwhelming rejection of a Chinese resolution supporting anti-Western policies. But in practice, Communist parties around the world split over the Sino-Soviet controversy.

**June 19.** Acting on last week's promise, President Kennedy requests far-reaching civil rights legislation: ban discrimination in public accommodations, jobs, schools, and voting; provide equal access to public businesses in inter-state commerce; enable the Justice Department to initiate school desegregation suits; and expand job-training programs (the president opposes job quotas based on race).

In putting forward his program, the president asks Congress to stay in session until the laws are enacted. No civil rights bill passes before the end of the year.

---

*Statistics:* The Census Bureau reports that the same-job distribution between blacks and whites has remained constant for 20 years—60 percent of black high school graduates are laborers compared to 30 percent of white graduates, and 80 percent of black men with grade school educations hold unskilled jobs compared to 50 percent of whites. Yet, the average working black male in 1962 earned only 51 percent of the average white male's earnings, a decrease of 11 percent since 1951.

---

**June 26.** Almost a quarter of Berlin's 2.5 million citizens turn out to greet President Kennedy during his four-day trip to West Germany. Later in the day, he addresses 150,000 in an open square and promises U.S. support against the Soviets. The crowd reacts tumultuously when he declares, "As a free man I take pride in the words, 'Ich bin ein Berliner' [I am a Berliner]."

**July 1.** London reveals that former British intelligence officer Kim Philby was "the third man" in the 1950s Burgess-MacLean spy scandal. When the two men defected to the USSR in 1951, Philby himself fell under suspicion. He was relieved of his intelligence duties and then dismissed from MI-6 in 1955. Until his disappearance in January, he had worked as a journalist in Beirut.

A Soviet agent since W.W.II, Philby had revealed a great deal of sensitive information to Moscow before his warning to double agents Burgess and MacLean made him suspect. Moscow announces at the end of the month that Philby has requested and been granted Soviet citizenship and political asylum.

**July 18.** The U.S. Labor Department reports

that, for the first time the average factory wage passed $100 per week in June. This economic milestone represents a two-thirds increase over the $10.92 weekly pay of 1914 (in 1963 dollars). Yet, in the last 16 years, growing taxes have taken away much of that gain. In 1947, a worker paid just 3 percent on weekly earnings of $49.17; on a 1963 check of $100.61, taxes amount to 12 percent.

**August 5.** The foreign ministers of the United States, the USSR, and Britain sign a Partial Test Ban Treaty in Moscow, banning nuclear tests in the atmosphere, ocean, and space, where radioactive debris could extend beyond territorial limits. The Soviets had sought a total ban, but after nearly 20 years of negotiations, finally agreed to exempt underground testing.

The incentive to reach a consensus likely came from recent superpower confrontations over Berlin and Cuba, concern about the spread of nuclear arms, the continued presence of atmospheric radiation, and an awareness that recently developed satellites will be able to detect test violations.

The treaty becomes effective October 10, and by the end of the year almost 100 nations commit to signing the widely acclaimed agreement. France and China refuse and continue to carry out atmospheric tests. To date, the nuclear powers have conducted approximately 380 atmospheric tests.

**August 7.** Jacqueline Kennedy gives birth to a boy, Patrick Bouvier Kennedy. The tiny baby, just under five pounds and five and a half weeks early, dies two days later of a lung disease common in premature infants. His death marks the third loss for the Kennedys, after a miscarriage in 1955 and a stillbirth in 1956.

**August 8.** At 3:00 A.M., armed men stop a mail train between Glasgow and London, and with precise timing, remove 120 mailbags containing over $7 million in used banknotes. The police, quickly discovering the robbers' hideout and plenty of fingerprints, capture 12 of the 15 identified.

The courts sentence 11 of the men to surprisingly long terms of 24–30 years; one man, whose prints were found only on some playing cards and a game,

was discharged. The police will catch three other gang members by 1969 but will recover just $2 million. Some law enforcement experts believe as many as three more men may have escaped with money from "The Great Train Robbery."

**August 28.** Over 200,000 blacks and whites gather in Washington, D.C., to dramatize the need for civil rights legislation. Fearing violence, Attorney General Robert Kennedy had tried to prevent the march to the Lincoln Memorial, but organizers carefully monitor security.

Civil rights activists, labor leaders, and clergy meet with congressional leaders then with President Kennedy to urge the passage of the current civil rights bill.

A. Philip Randolph, the 75-year-old president of the Negro American Labor Council, first proposed such a march in 1941. Coming this year, after the success in Birmingham, the gathering underscores the momentum of the civil rights movement and the force of its leader, Martin Luther King, Jr. His spellbinding "I Have a Dream" speech late in the day draws attention to the movement as never before.

**August 30.** Washington and Moscow install a hot line to provide direct emergency communication. (During the Cuban Missile Crisis, slow diplomatic channels forced Kennedy and Khrushchev to broadcast their proposals over the radio.) The series of teleprinters can forward encoded messages in the sender's own language. To reduce the risk of error, the system is to be continuously staffed and routinely tested. In 1971, the hot line will switch to satellites.

**September 9.** Alabama district court judges issue a restraining order prohibiting Governor Wallace from blocking school integration in Birmingham, Mobile, and Tuskegee. The governor has used state troopers to bar black students from entering the schools. Many local school boards and officials have opposed his actions, perhaps in part because Kennedy sent out thousands of letters asking for their help. On the 10th, President Kennedy federalizes the National Guard to forestall Wallace from using them in place of troopers.

*Statistics:* Although 92 of every 100 black students in the South attended segregated schools during the 1962–1963 school year, a July 18 Gallup poll offers hope for greater integration. Three out of four Southern voters questioned believe widespread integration will come within 10 years.

**September 15.** Just before Sunday-morning service at Birmingham's 16th Street Baptist Church, a bomb explodes, killing 4 black schoolchildren and injuring 19. Race riots break out within hours. Two white youths shoot a 13-year-old black boy, and a policeman kills another 16-year-old black, reportedly as the boys threw rocks at passing cars. This sudden violence against children devastates the rights movement, fresh from the triumphs of Birmingham and the march on Washington. The bomber will never be caught.

**September 16.** After a severe winter and summer drought in the Soviet Union, Moscow turns to Canada for $500 million worth of wheat and flour, the largest one-year grain sale ever contracted. Next month, President Kennedy approves the sale of 4 million metric tons of wheat to the Soviets through private commercial channels.

**October 3–4.** One of the worst recorded storms to hit the Caribbean, Flora savages Haiti, killing at least 5,000 and leaving 100,000 homeless, then rages over Cuba for five days, killing 1,000, leaving 175,000 homeless, and destroying 90 percent of the coffee crop.

**October 9.** In Italy, a massive landslide down Mt. Toc plunges into the reservoir behind Vaiont Dam. A 200-foot-high wave of water roars down the narrow Piave Valley, drowning 2,000–4,000 people. The dam suffers minor damage.

**October 10.** Joseph Valachi, age 60, describes the inner workings of the American Mafia before the Senate Permanent Investigations Subcommittee. Given the kiss of death by his cellmate, Mafia boss Vito Genovese, for supposedly informing, the terrified Valachi turned to the FBI for federal protection.

During his 10 days of televised testimony, the rough-voiced mobster names the crime families and their 12 U.S. centers, but describes Miami and Las Vegas as "open cities." Reportedly, his testimony sets off a power struggle within the Cosa Nostra.

**October 11.** At the end of a 22-month study, the President's Commission on the Status of Women makes 24 proposals to curb bias against women, including paid maternity leave, child-care services, and equal-pay laws. The members suggest the best way to fight discrimination would be to obtain "definitive" Supreme Court decisions through test cases. By the beginning of November, Kennedy creates a Cabinet committee to aid in raising the status of women.

**October 15.** General Park Chung Hee is elected to a four-year term as president. Only relentless pressure from the people of South Korea and the United States forced Park last spring to agree to hold elections. But once the vote was called, the general set about eliminating most opponents.

His December 17 inauguration marks the beginning of the Third Republic of Korea. A constitutional amendment in 1971 will give him a third term, while a new constitution in 1972 will permit unlimited terms as president.

**October 18.** At age 69, British Prime Minister Harold Macmillan resigns for health reasons. Queen Elizabeth asks Sir Alexander Douglas-Home, the Earl of Home, to form a new cabinet. He resigns his peerage to assume the position, becoming the first prime minister to have no seat in either House; he wins a by-election in November.

Two other members of the old guard also leave politics this year. David Ben Gurion, prime minister of Israel since its formation in 1948, resigned on June 16 at age 76, for personal reasons; Levi Eshkol succeeded him. Konrad Adenauer, chancellor of West Germany since 1949 and the man largely responsible for bringing about West Germany's economic recovery, retired at age 87 on October 15; Ludwig Erhard succeeded him.

**November 1.** South Vietnamese Army officers overthrow the regime of Ngo Dinh Diem, murdering the president and his brother Ngo Dinh Nhu, head of the secret police. An increasingly violent suppression of Buddhist opposition had undermined any remaining government support. Then, on August 21, brutal midnight raids against Buddhist pagodas and the arrest of some 1,400 produced a flash point. Students took up the protests, and military factions already discontented with government corruption prepared to remove the Catholic leader.

President Kennedy and Henry Cabot Lodge, the ambassador to Vietnam, faced with a possible civil war and defeat before the Communists, approved a coup. The dissatisfied South Vietnamese generals received CIA intelligence on pro-Diem military forces and last month Washington cut off aid.

The Kennedy administration, ignoring an opportunity to reevaluate its commitment to Vietnam, extends recognition to the new military government and pledges continued aid.

**November 20.** The U.N. General Assembly, with the exception of South Africa, unanimously adopts a declaration stating that all discrimination on the basis of race, color, or ethnic origin "is an offense to human dignity," to be condemned as a denial of the principles of the U.N. charter.

**November 22.** President and Mrs. Kennedy arrive in Dallas, Texas, for a two-day tour, reportedly to mend a bitter dispute among Texas Democrats and to improve his standing in a pivotal state. From the airport, the Kennedys, with Governor John Connally and his wife, head for the Dallas World Trade Center and a scheduled speech. With the lovely weather, the president asks agents to remove the bubble top on the Lincoln Continental.

At 12:30 P.M., as the motorcade approaches an underpass to the freeway, shots ring out and the president slumps forward in his seat. The Secret Service rush him to the Dallas hospital, but John F. Kennedy is pronounced dead at 1:00 P.M.

Bystanders at the assassination site report seeing a rifle at the sixth-floor window of the nearby Texas School Book Depository. Police find the weapon, and questioning reveals that stockman Lee Harvey Oswald went up to the top floor while everyone else waited outside for the motorcade. Shortly after

the fatal shots were fired, Oswald was seen leaving the building.

Police release his description, and within the hour, Patrolman J. D. Tippitt sights the suspect. But the man pulls out a revolver and guns him down. At 2:15 P.M., police find Oswald in a movie theater—carrying a gun later shown to have killed Tippitt—and charge him with the murder of President Kennedy. The 24-year-old former marine is an admitted Marxist who lived in the USSR from 1959 to 1962 and married a Soviet woman.

*Judge Sarah T. Hughes swears in Lyndon Baines Johnson 99 minutes after the assassination of John F. Kennedy. Jackie Kennedy stands at his side as some 20–30 people crowd into the rear cabin of Air Force One.*

The president's grieving widow refuses to leave Dallas without his body, and Lyndon Johnson will not return to Washington without her. Accordingly, aides and Secret Service men seize the corpse from Parkland Hospital before an autopsy is performed. And so the controversy begins. Experts later conclude that the body, so badly handled, could never have provided verifiable evidence.

LYNDON BAINES JOHNSON
Born: Aug. 27, 1908, near Johnson City, Texas, eldest of 2 boys and 3 girls
Education: Southwest Texas State Teachers College, B.S., 1930

Military Service: U.S. Navy in W.W.II

Marriage: Lady Bird (Claudia Alta) Taylor, Nov. 17, 1934

Children: Lynda Bird (b. 1944), Luci Baines (b. 1947)

Previous Occupations: Teacher, rancher, senator

Position Before Taking Office: Vice-President

Legal Residence When Elected: Texas

**November 23.** The American people struggle to deal with their shock and grief as heartfelt condolences pour in from around the world. President Johnson confers with former presidents Truman and Eisenhower, members of the Cabinet, who pledge to serve him as long as needed, and other administration officials.

In one of many memorial addresses given in Congress, Senator Hubert Humphrey says of Kennedy, "He was, perhaps, a step or two ahead of the people at times. But as an American who understood America, who brought form to its amorphous yearnings, who gave direction to its efforts, John Kennedy walked with the people."

**November 24.** As millions of television viewers watch Dallas city police move Lee Harvey Oswald through the basement of the municipal building to safer quarters, Jack Ruby rushes forward and shoots the alleged assassin in the stomach. Oswald dies less than two hours later.

Ruby, a Dallas nightclub operator, later claims he thought of killing Oswald on the 22nd and then found himself in the area at the right time; he always had a gun on hand.

**November 24.** Six gray horses, followed by the traditional saddled but riderless black horse, bear the president's casket from the White House to the Capitol along streets lined with hundreds of thousands of people. All through the night, mourners file past the closed coffin to pay their last respects.

The next day, the Kennedy family and officials from almost 100 countries walk behind the casket from the White House to a requiem Mass at St. Matthew's Cathedral. A million mourners, many weeping openly, stand along the funeral route, while millions more watch on television. The 35th president of the United States is then buried with full military honors in Arlington National Cemetery. At the grave site, his wife Jacqueline lights an eternal flame; just one other burns in the United States, at the Gettysburg battlefield.

**November 27.** President Johnson, in an effort to reassure government and world leaders, addresses a joint session of Congress. He pledges to continue Kennedy's administrative programs and foreign policies but emphasizes the need for legislative action. Johnson tells Congress, "No memorial oration or eulogy could more eloquently honor President Kennedy's memory than the earliest possible passage of the civil rights bill for which he fought so long."

The next day, in a nationally televised Thanksgiving address, President Johnson urges his countrymen to new dedication: "Let us pray for His Divine wisdom in banishing from our land any injustice or intolerance or oppression to any of our fellow Americans, whatever their opinion, whatever the color of their skins, for God made all of us, not some of us, in His image."

In response to the president's plea, House GOP leader Charles Halleck on December 5 announces support for the civil rights bill and states that Republicans will work for quick floor action. House Rules Committee Chairman Howard Smith indicates he has abandoned a previously declared intention to stall the bill in committee.

**November 29.** President Johnson names Chief Justice Earl Warren to head a commission of inquiry into the Kennedy assassination. Johnson has already ordered the Justice Department and the FBI to carry out prompt investigations of the Kennedy shooting and the murder of Lee Harvey Oswald.

The only film of the assassination was shot from some 72 feet away by bystander Abraham Zapruder on his 8-millimeter Bell & Howell movie camera. Inexplicably, reporters who usually ride at the front of a motorcade to photograph the president, that day ended up last in the procession.

But on the 30th, the Warren Commission receives assistance from an unprecedented source, the Soviet Union. Moscow hands over consular files on Oswald, covering his stay in the USSR and his efforts to return there.

On December 9, the FBI's report to the commission names Oswald as the lone assassin and concludes that no link existed between Oswald and his killer, Jack Ruby.

**December 21.** The political situation in South Vietnam deteriorated rapidly following the November coup. Defense Secretary McNamara, returning from a brief fact-finding mission, reports that the VC have capitalized on an unstable Saigon government, and unless the current trend is reversed, South Vietnam will likely become a Communist-controlled state.

After the secretary's briefing, the administration confirms that a previously announced plan to withdraw U.S. personnel by the end of 1965 has been abandoned.

**December 22.** The 30-day period of national mourning for President Kennedy ends with a candlelight service at the Lincoln Memorial. Fire brought from the eternal flame at his graveside lights the first candle and each newly-lit candle starts the next. President Johnson and some 14,000 people attend the service sponsored by the Interreligious Committee on Race Relations.

## Obituaries

**William E. B. DuBois** (February 23, 1868–August 27, 1963). A major Negro leader of this century, DuBois published several important books on the black American experience, and cofounded the NAACP in 1909. He broke with the organization from 1932 to 1944, then returned for four years before resigning to become increasingly involved in Communist affairs. DuBois finally joined the party in 1961, when he also took up residency and citizenship in Ghana.

**Medgar Evers** (July 2, 1925–June 12, 1963). *See* News.

**Pope John XXIII** (November 25, 1881–June 3, 1963). *See* News.

**Estes Kefauver** (July 26, 1903–August 10, 1963). In 1952, the Tennessee senator (1949–

1963) grabbed national headlines with his Senate crime committee.

**John F. Kennedy** (May 29, 1917–November 22, 1963). Young Jack, although pushed into politics by his father, brought his family spirit of competitiveness to the House in 1946 and the Senate in 1952. And, to a tough presidential election, Kennedy brought his refreshing mix of wit, sex appeal, and courage. A fierce campaigner, he understood that overwhelming voter support would move him one step closer to the White House.

Summary attempts to evaluate the presidency of John F. Kennedy will remain, at best, uncertain. He faced the fiasco at the Bay of Pigs, near war over Berlin, the thorny issue of U.S. commitment in Vietnam, and the emergence of the American civil rights movement. Many of his decisions on those issues will have long-range implications for the United States. But death, coming part way through his first term, ended any sure chance for greatness. Instead, Americans will remember Kennedy for his grace, his style, and the promise of his future.

In a prepared speech that was never delivered, he wrote, "We in this country, in this generation are—by destiny rather than choice—the watchmen on the walls of world freedom. We ask, therefore, that we may be worthy of our power and responsibility, that we may exercise our strength with wisdom and restraint, and that we may achieve in our time and for all time the ancient vision of peace on earth, goodwill toward men."

**Lee Harvey Oswald** (October 18, 1939–November 24, 1963). *See* News.

**Robert Stroud** (1890–November 21, 1963). When he killed a Leavenworth prison guard in 1916, Stroud's mother pleaded for clemency on his behalf and President Wilson commuted a death penalty to life in solitary confinement. Alone in the yard one day, Stroud retrieved four baby sparrows from a storm-swept branch. His care for the tiny creatures expanded into research, then into authoritative volumes on bird diseases. Leavenworth prisoners dubbed him "Birdman."

Stroud was transferred to Alcatraz in 1942.

When the warden denied permission for pets, the lifer turned to other studies, including one on the American prison system. (The bureau refused to publish his massive history.) Ill in 1959, the Birdman of Alcatraz was moved to another prison, where he died.

# BEGINNINGS AND ENDINGS

## News

**January 28.** The last Southern state to desegregate, South Carolina obeys court orders and opens state colleges to black students. There are no reported incidents of opposition.

**February 14.** The British Labor party elects Harold Wilson as leader following the death of Hugh Gaitskell. The 46-year-old Wilson entered public service during W.W.II.

**March 21.** Alcatraz closes down. Built by the army in 1909, the prison was converted to a federal, maximum-security facility in 1934. Dillinger gang member James Henry "Blackie" Audett is the last inmate to leave the "Rock."

**April 12.** In Canada, Trans-Canada Airlines retires its last propeller plane and becomes the first major airline with an all-turbine fleet. This October, TCA will introduce the DC-8, the first jet freighter. (The airline name will change to a bilingual Air Canada in 1965.)

**May 25.** In Addis Ababa, 30 African heads of state establish the Organization of African Unity. Over 1964 and 1965, the association will successfully mediate in a Morocco-Algeria border dispute.

**July 1.** The U.S. Post Office adopts five-digit zip codes to speed up mail sorting. Over the past 20 years, the volume of mail has mushroomed from an annual 50.9 billion pieces to 70 billion.

**August 28.** The House imposes arbitration—the first in a peacetime labor dispute—to resolve a threatened railroad strike. Critics call the action a poor precedent for collective bargaining.

**September 14.** In South Dakota, Mary Ann Fischer gives birth to quintuplets. The four girls and a boy are the first American quints to survive infancy.

**December 10.** In memory of the slain president, New York City renames Idlewild the John F. Kennedy (JFK) International Airport.

**More news.** While touring Australia, Queen Elizabeth startles then thrills cheering onlookers when she approaches to talk. In the coming years, her subjects throughout the Commonwealth will savor these informal "walkabouts."

• With the signing of a nuclear test ban treaty, the vocal Campaign for Nuclear Disarmament fades from public view.

• This year, women in Iran get the vote.

## New Products and Businesses

Coca-Cola debuts Tab, a cyclamate-sweetened soft drink while Pepsi launches Teem and Tropic Surf.

Green Giant brings out boil-in-the-bag frozen vegetables.

On September 13, Mary Kay Ash opens a 500-square-foot retail shop in Dallas. With healthy commissions for her representatives, Mary Kay Cosmetics will post an annual $800,000 in sales within three years.

After 39-year-old housewife Jean Nidetch lost 72 pounds in 1962, she helped others with their diets. This year, Nidetch and some of those friends founded Weight Watchers. The organized club offers a balanced, nutritious diet and supportive, informal group therapy. Within five years, Weight Watchers will count 81 U.S. franchises and 10 franchises abroad.

## Memorable Ad Campaigns

Coca-Cola tells young people, "Things Go Better With Coke."

Ignoring advertising traditions, Doyle, Dane, Bernbach makes Avis Rent-A-Car the underdog. "When You're Only No. 2, You Try Harder. Or Else." The revolutionary campaign pulls the company out of the red.

## Fads

New homes on the East Coast feature Finnish dry heat baths, or saunas.

With long wool hair, cute grins, and paunchy little bodies, Troll good luck charms endear themselves to millions. The 3-inch version sells for $1.95.

During the early sixties, young people scrounge for "Woodies" (1940s station wagons with wood paneling), then tear out seats, take off doors, and sacrifice windows to make room for their surfboards. When demand for the cars outstrips supply, vans and pickup trucks suddenly appear with wood panels.

## SCIENCE AND TECHNOLOGY

### News

**February 9.** Boeing tests the prototype of the short–medium-range 727. By 1972, the company will become the first to sell 1,000 of a jetliner model.

**February 22.** Norwegian explorer Helge Ingstand reports positive proof of a Viking settlement in North America 500 years before Columbus. Artifacts and the remains of large buildings found in Lance Aux Meadows, Newfoundland, date to around A.D. 1000. The settlement might have been the "rich country" southwest of Greenland described by Viking Leif Erikson.

**March 1.** After a balloon carries a telescope to 77,000 feet, the National Center for Atmospheric Research confirms the presence of water vapor in the Martian atmosphere. Still, scientists believe life on Mars would be "marginal at best."

**March 21.** The federal government licenses two measles vaccines: a "killed" and a "live" strain. Both stem from the work of John Enders and Thomas Peebles, who first isolated the virus in 1954.

Since 90 percent of American children catch the measles, the first vaccinations will be given to infants. The surgeon general expects a drop in the number of cases by next year.

**March 28.** The California Medical Association is the first state medical society to declare cigarette smoking a health hazard. On June 8, the American Heart Association becomes the first voluntary agency to open a major drive against the habit.

**April 8.** French authorities close Lascaux Cave after discovering that condensation from human breath has produced microscopic vegetation in the cave's ancient paintings. Treatment halts deterioration, but public access will remain limited.

**April 13.** Americans Don Piccard and Ed Yost are the first to cross the English Channel in a hot air balloon (rather than a gas balloon). U.S. Navy research early in the last decade revived interest in touring balloons. (The first balloon flight was made on November 21, 1783, in France, by the Montgolfier brothers.)

**April 18.** *The New York Times* reports the first successful nerve transplant from one person to another. Drs. James B. Campbell and C. Andrew L. Bassett produced compatibility by freezing the cadaver nerves, exposing them to radiation, and sheathing each in porous plastic. The pieces, up to $5^1/3$ inches long, supply a growth superstructure for the broken ends.

**May 5.** At the Veterans Administration Hospital in Denver, doctors perform the first successful liver transplant. The patient dies of pneumonia 22 days later, but the survival rate for the procedure will slowly lengthen in the years ahead.

**May 12.** MIT's Lincoln Lab reveals that three days ago a USAF capsule released 400 million copper dipoles to form an orbiting belt of passive communications satellites. The initial test proves successful, but critics argue that Washington should have obtained an international agreement before releasing the needles (one-third the thickness of human hair and $3/4$ inch long).

**May 15–16.** In the last Mercury flight, Gordon Cooper becomes the first American to spend more than 24 hours in space and the first astronaut to launch a satellite (a strobe light deployed during the third orbit). During reentry, the automatic control system fails and Cooper must skillfully guide *Faith 7* to splashdown, 4.5 miles from target.

Since the beginning, the veteran NASA pilots

have fought against the notion of the "astronaut as passenger." They demanded a window, manual override on automatic systems, and a manually controlled escape hatch. This flight alone proves them right.

The $384-million Mercury program sent six craft aloft—two suborbital and four orbital flights. The next step is Project Gemini, designed to orbit two men in the same spacecraft.

**June 11.** Serving life in prison, a man refuses radiation treatment for his lung cancer, but agrees to a revolutionary lung transplant. Surgeons at the University of Mississippi Hospital successfully complete the operation in three hours. (The man dies of kidney failure 18 days later.) With the procedure report, in December the AMA journal concludes that medicine can now technically transplant any organ in the human body.

**June 14.** In a twin-orbit mission, the Soviets send up *Vostok 5* with Valery Bykovsky and, two days later, *Vostok 6* with 25-year-old Valentina Tereshkova—the first woman in space. Bykovsky's endurance record (both return on the 19th) signals a continuing Soviet emphasis on length of time in space. (Tereshkova marries Andrian Nikolayev, pilot of *Vostok 3*, and their healthy daughter will dispel fears that space travel might cause hereditary damage.)

**June 25.** After seven years of testing, the surgeon general's office licenses the three-in-one oral polio vaccine developed by Albert Sabin and Herald R. Cox. The first dose immediately activates immunity and, with a total of two doses rather than the three Salk inoculations, the oral form simplifies record keeping.

---

*Statistics:* Over the last half of the 1950s, the reported world incidence of polio dropped an estimated 65 percent.

---

**July.** Early in the month, 46-year-old engineer Ermal C. Fraze receives a patent for tab-opening aluminum cans. (He has already developed teartop cans.) With exclusive rights, Alcoa authorizes production with 40 can manufacturers. By the end of the decade, almost 90 percent of beer cans will use tabs.

**July 26.** NASA launches *Syncom II*, the first communications satellite placed into synchronous orbit (the radio equipment on *Syncom I* failed early in the year). By matching the Earth's rotational speed, the satellite remains fixed above a given point on the planet. Until now, communications satellites could transmit signals only when their orbits approached either of two ground stations.

With *Syncom II* maneuvered over Brazil, the United States will launch *Syncom III* in August 1964. It will settle over the international date line and transmit the Olympics from Japan.

**August 16.** Washington and Moscow finalize a cooperative agreement for weather communications and magnetic satellite programs. Next year, with *Echo 2*, the superpowers exchange cloud pictures and other data.

**September 4.** At the International Conference of Genetics, Dr. Jerome K. Sherman reports the birth of two babies conceived from sperm kept at -320 degrees Fahrenheit for two months. The current storage method, on dry ice at -108 degrees Fahrenheit loses sperm over a period of time. Using this new technique, sperm banks will open in 1964 in Tokyo and Iowa City.

**September 20.** Edna McLeod had lost three babies to the Rh factor, a biological process through which the mother produces antibodies against the blood type the baby has inherited from the father. Following her delivery today in New Zealand, the hospital reveals that an intrauterine transfusion saved the infant during pregnancy.

**October 15.** AT&T and the British post office inaugurate the first direct transatlantic submarine telephone cable between the United States and England. Just two months later, the media reports that AT&T will rely on satellites for future transatlantic communication needs.

**October 18.** NASA adds 14 men to the astronaut training program, bringing the total to 30. The jet pilots include USAF Major Edwin Aldrin and U.S. Navy Lieutenants Alan Bean, Eugene Cernan, and Roger Chaffee.

**October 25.** Premier Khrushchev announces that the USSR will not participate in a race to the moon: "Let's wish them success. And we will see how they will fly there, and how they will land there. . . . And most important, how they will get up and come back." Some Americans fear a trick; others suggest NASA should adopt a slower pace.

**November 14.** Off the south coast of Iceland, pilots sight evidence of a submarine volcano. By the end of the year, the cone reaches 415 feet above sea level; within three months, the brand-new island of Surtsey measures some 5,600 feet long. Eruptions will cease on May 5, 1967.

**November 27.** An Atlas-Centaur test marks the first known flight of a rocket propelled by liquid hydrogen. The two-stage vehicle will be used in the upper stages of the Apollo rockets.

**December.** Following FDA approval, Roche labs introduces Valium. The antianxiety drug—5 to 10 times more potent than Librium—becomes one of the most commonly prescribed medications.

**December 29.** In the Soviet Union, the Institute of Radio Engineering and Electronics reveals that through September and October scientists bounced a radio signal off the planet Jupiter. The 745-million-mile round-trip took 1 hour, 6 minutes.

**More news.** Skin overlying bruises, inflammation, fractures, and malignancies is hotter than surrounding tissue and emits more light. Barnes Engineering, with that principle in mind, produces the thermogram, a singular camera that will detect cancerous hot spots.

• The AMA suggests that people with conditions requiring special treatment wear the association's new symbol to alert medical personnel.

• This year, USAF-sponsored rocket shots confirm the existence of x-rays in the direction of the Crab nebula and the Scorpio constellation.

• Juris Upatnieks and Emmett Leith use the newly discovered laser to produce the first hologram. When Dennis Gabor presented his theory of holography in 1947, no suitable source of light existed.

## Other Discoveries, Developments, and Inventions

Dry-print reproduction of a microfilm page
First film cartridge, for the new Kodak Instamatic
Touch-tone phones
FDA approval for the first irradiated food, bacon

## Obituaries

**Ugo Cerletti** (circa 1878–July 25, 1963). The Italian psychiatrist introduced electroshock treatments in the 1930s.

**Theodore von Kármán** (May 11, 1881–May 6, 1963). During his 20 years at the California Institute of Technology, the "father of the supersonic age" formulated the designs and theories that led to the Bell X-1.

# THE ARTS

January 6—*Oliver!*, with Bruce Prochnik, Clive Revill, Georgia Brown (774 perfs.)
March 13—*Enter Laughing*, with Alan Arkin (419 perfs.)
October 23—*Barefoot in the Park*, with Elizabeth Ashley, Robert Redford, Mildred Natwick, Kurt Kaszner (1,532 perfs.)

## Tony Awards

Actor (Dramatic)—Arthur Hill, *Who's Afraid of Virginia Woolf?*
Actress (Dramatic)—Uta Hagen, *Who's Afraid of Virginia Woolf?*
Actor (Musical)—Zero Mostel, *A Funny Thing Happened on the Way to the Forum*
Actress (Musical)—Vivien Leigh, *Tovarich*
Play—*Who's Afraid of Virginia Woolf?*
Musical—*A Funny Thing Happened on the Way to the Forum*

## News

**January 8.** The National Gallery unveils Leonardo da Vinci's *Mona Lisa*, on loan from the Louvre.

Next month, the famous 450-year-old painting travels to the Metropolitan Museum in New York.

**March 20.** The Guggenheim Museum presents the first large exhibition of Pop Art, *Six Painters and the Object*. *The New York Times* review maintains that if asked, "What is art?" Andy Warhol, Robert Rauschenberg, and the others would likely answer, "What isn't?"

**September.** The Vivian Beaumont is the first New York theater to install an electronically controlled lighting system.

**October 12.** The William A. Farnsworth Library and Art Museum in Maine reports the purchase of an Andrew Wyeth painting, *Her Room*, for $65,000—a record price for the work of a living American artist.

**October 22.** Last year, the British government established the National Theatre with Laurence Olivier as director. Tonight, with the Old Vic as a temporary residence, the National Theatre presents its first production, *Hamlet*, with Peter O'Toole, Rosemary Harris, and Michael Redgrave. Olivier will remain at the helm until 1973.

**December 23.** In 1949, HUAC branded Paul Robeson a Communist. With public opinion against him, the renowned singer-actor fled to Europe once passport restrictions eased in 1958. Today, in ill health with his politics "behind him," the famous black American returns home.

## Obituaries

**George Braque** (May 13, 1882–August 31, 1963). After W.W.I military service, the cofounder of the Cubist School assumed a more serene style.

**Jean Cocteau** (July 5, 1889–October 11, 1963). The versatile French writer, painter, designer, critic, and film director transferred the techniques of one art form to another.

**Otto Harbach** (August 18, 1873–January 24, 1963). The lyricist produced more than 1,000 songs—among them, "Smoke Gets in Your Eyes" (1933)—and collaborated on the books or lyrics of some 50 musical comedies.

**Clifford Odets** (July 18, 1906–August 14, 1963). His plays included *Golden Boy* (1937) and *The Country Girl* (1950).

## WORDS

James Baldwin, *The Fire Next Time*
Ian Fleming, *On Her Majesty's Secret Service*
Betty Friedan, *The Feminine Mystique*
Rumer Godden, *The Battle of the Villa Fiorita*
Bob Hope, *I Owe Russia $1,200*
Victor Lasky, *JFK: The Man and the Myth*
John Le Carre, *The Spy Who Came in from the Cold*
Mary McCarthy, *The Group*
James A. Michener, *Caravans*
Sylvia Plath, *The Bell Jar* (first published under the pseudonym Victoria Lucas.)
Thomas Pynchon, *V*
Aleksandr Solzhenitsyn, *One Day in the Life of Ivan Denisovich*
Kurt Vonnegut, Jr., *Cat's Cradle*
Morris L. West, *The Shoes of the Fisherman*

### News

**March.** The *Oklahoma City Times* and the *Daily Oklahoman* become the first U.S. dailies written and typeset entirely by computer. At this time, 58 newspapers use photocomposition for display advertising.

**March 31.** Printers and photo-engravers settle New York City's longest newspaper strike, but the 114-day shutdown has crippled the *Mirror*. In October, despite the second largest circulation in the country, the city daily ceases publication.

**December 7.** In an obscenity trial involving *Playboy*, the jury (11 women, 1 man) votes 7–5 against convicting Hugh Hefner for publishing boudoir photographs of actress Jayne Mansfield.

**More news.** *The Feminine Mystique* catalyzes the women's movement by challenging societal attitudes that lead a woman to abandon personal fulfillment for the roles of housewife and mother.

• This year, Norman Rockwell paints the last of 317 covers for the *Saturday Evening Post*.

> *Statistics:* While U.S. publishing production rose 18 percent in the past two years, the paperback share skyrocketed from 14 percent to 33 percent.

## Cartoons and Comics

**March.** Spidey's origin is retold in the first issue of his own comic book, *The Amazing Spider-Man.*

**March.** Jerry Marcus creates the cartoon panel *Trudy.*

**September.** After canceling *The Hulk* earlier this year, Marvel Comics brings him back with Thor, Iron Man, and Ant-Man in the first issue of the *Avengers.*

In November, *Marvel's X-Men* begins a successful seven-year run. The series will return in 1975 to renewed popularity.

## TIME *Man of the Year*

Martin Luther King, Jr.

## New Words and Phrases

biodegradable
brain drain
Cosa Nostra
found object (a piece of junk used in a sculpture)
jet set
nonevent
peacenik
Pop Art
psychedelic
software
solid-state
spin-off
surfer
tokenism

## Obituaries

**Robert Frost** (March 26, 1874–January 29, 1963). With the belief that verse should "begin in delight and end in wisdom," the poet celebrated the virtues of his rugged New England. Four Pulitzers, a congressional medal, and a prominent role in the inauguration of John F. Kennedy made Frost America's unofficial poet laureate.

**Aldous Huxley** (July 26, 1894–November 22, 1963). The British novelist and essayist was best known for his satirical novel *Brave New World* (1932).

**C(live) S(taples) Lewis** (November 29, 1898–November 22, 1963). *The Lion, the Witch and the Wardrobe* (1950) was the first volume of his beloved children's series, the *Chronicles of Narnia.*

**Sylvia Plath** (October 27, 1932–February 11, 1963). The rebellious heroines of Plath's poetry and semiautobiographical novel (published after her suicide) will continue to speak to young women through the turbulent sixties and seventies.

**William Carlos Williams** (September 17, 1883–March 4, 1963). While practicing medicine, this prolific poet, author, and critic earned a place at the forefront of 20th-century American literature. As a nativist, he relied on people's speech to form the rhythm of his work.

# FASHION

## Haute Couture

Rather than change the silhouette, most collections this year introduce shaping, decorative touches, or a mood such as the "casual" look.

## News

**This year.** One of the first designers to recognize young women's styling needs, Mary Quant begins exporting her fashions to the United States—coats, mix-and-match separates, and accessories. Later, observers will credit Quant's shorter skirts and textured tights with inspiring the mini.

• Levi Strauss & Co. introduces stretch and corduroy Levi's® jeans.

• The Syndicat National de la Perfumerie Française reports a 73-percent increase in the production of French perfume over the past 10 years.

## Colors and Materials

White, pink, and yellow dominate in the spring while fall colors emphasize wine shades, all variations of green, red with white, and yellow with black. Pastels sell all year.

The industry promotes cotton and wool knits, mixes of natural and synthetic fibers, and for the evening, mohair and jersey. In menswear, sharkskin prevails in every season.

All-year patterns include plaids, classic checks, and the black-and-white combinations of last year. Spring clothes vibrate with zoo prints, blended stripes, and geometric designs.

Manufacturers make heavy use of fur and fake fur for trim and coats.

## Clothes

The simple waistless shift commands attention during the summer.

Trouser sales climb with the introduction of new shapes and styles. The narrow, tapered pant remains popular while some stores display flared bell-bottoms as an alternative. The fashion conscious prefer fit through the hip rather than the waist.

As pantyhose begin to find a market, mail-order catalogs list them with other hosiery rather than alongside leotards.

Coats feature dropped shoulders and caped fullness in the back. In catalogs, teen car coats fall to the top of the thigh.

Overblouses appear in all lengths.

Evening fashions spotlight the brocade theater suit and dresses matched with tailored full-length coats.

Designers offer a greater variety of at-home clothes—pant outfits, jeweled hostess gowns, shorts in rich velvets.

With millions of baby-boomers entering their adolescence, mail-order catalogs establish a separate teen section for girls, with a greater selection of panty girdles. (The women's listing still centers on full-control foundations.)

Sportswear enthusiasts applaud the appearance of the Husky jacket, a nylon waterproof shell with thermo-insulated polyester filling.

Menswear retailers note that gray, brown, and light blue suits outsell black and darker colors.

## Accessories

The high domed hat—fur, fabric, leather—and the brimmed casual felt hat permit just a few pieces of hair to escape.

Fashion focuses on leather boots of varying heel heights. But, with increased attention to shoes, the standard pump is replaced by gillies, sporty oxfords, and low-heeled lizard or alligator styles. As well, open-back and T-strap sandals regain their popularity.

The saddle shoe, long the badge of adolescence, surrenders to the onslaught of white sneakers.

More women choose an evening stole rather than the inevitable cardigan.

Scarves are substituted for broaches and necklaces while earrings tend toward fullness and length. Men pick up extravagant cuff links.

## Hair and Cosmetics

To create a natural look, cosmetic companies bring back paler rouges in a tube, liquid wash, and cake form with a brush. The cake blusher sells best.

A new mascara uses minute particles of fabric to lengthen lashes.

Revlon and Max Factor introduce protein-enriched products to condition hair.

The short-lived "Cleopatra look" relies on dramatic eye makeup and long, straight hair with a fringe.

Reportedly, women in high society employ makeup techniques of stage and screen to highlight good features, correct contours, and mask signs of age.

Toy manufacturers offer play cosmetics for little girls, such as creams and colorless lipsticks.

The jewelry company Swank buys out an exotic cologne, renames it Jade East, and sells $700,000 worth in the first six months.

## POPULAR MUSIC

"Sugarshack"—Jimmy Gilmer & the Fireballs
"Dominique"—Singing Nun
"He's So Fine"—Chiffons
"Hey Paula"—Paul & Paula
"Blue Velvet"—Bobby Vinton
"Fingertips (Part II)"—Little Stevie Wonder
"My Boyfriend's Back"—Angels
"Walk Like a Man"—Four Seasons
"Sukiyaki"—Kyu Sakamoto
"I Will Follow Him"—Little Peggy March
"Go Away Little Girl"—Steve Lawrence
"I'm Leaving It Up to You"—Dale & Grace
"Walk Right In"—Rooftop Singers
"If You Wanna Be Happy"—Jimmy Soul
"It's My Party"—Lesley Gore
"Surf City"—Jan & Dean
"Easier Said Than Done"—Essex
"So Much in Love"—Tymes
"Deep Purple"—Nino Tempo & April Stevens
"Our Day Will Come"—Ruby & the Romantics
"Louie Louie"—Kingsmen
"Can't Get Used to Losing You"—Andy Williams
"Be My Baby"—Ronettes
"Hello Mudduh, Hello Fadduh! (A Letter From Camp)"—Allan Sherman
"Sally, Go 'Round the Roses"—Jaynetts
"The End of the World"—Skeeter Davis
"Blowin' in the Wind"—Peter, Paul & Mary
"Puff the Magic Dragon"—Peter, Paul & Mary
"Wipeout" (Instr.)—Surfaris

## Grammys (1963)

Record of the Year—Henry Mancini, "The Days of Wine and Roses"
Song of the Year (songwriter)—Henry Mancini

and Johnny Mercer, "The Days of Wine and Roses"
Album of the Year—Barbra Streisand, *The Barbra Streisand Album*
Best Vocal Performance (Male)—Jack Jones, "Wives and Lovers" (single)
Best Vocal Performance (Female)—Barbra Streisand, *The Barbra Streisand Album*
Best New Artist—Swingle Singers

### News

**January.** Charlie Watts joins Bill Wyman, Brian Jones, Keith Richards, and Mick Jagger to form the Rolling Stones.

**February.** Vee Jay releases the Beatles single "Please Please Me"/"Ask Me Why" in the United States. Later in the year, American teens find the Beatles single "From Me to You"/"Thank You Girl" and the LP *Introducing the Beatles*. Its 12 cuts include "I Saw Her Standing There," "Do You Want to Know a Secret," and "Twist and Shout."

**November.** A Belgian nun becomes an overnight sensation with her single "Dominique." (Sister Luc-Gabrielle wrote and sang the tune under the pseudonym Soeur Sourire.) Her album *The Singing Nun* sells 750,000 in the first three months.

**December.** The death of President Kennedy finishes Vaughn Meader's career, but opens up a market for documentary recordings. More than half a dozen different titles present his inaugural address, memorable speeches, press conference excerpts, and snippets of the tributes that followed his assassination. The discs sell an estimated 5 million copies by the end of the year.

**More news.** U.S. record producers report increased sales in soul (propelled by Motown's Detroit Sound), surf music (with car songs, such as "Little Deuce Coupe" and "Drag City," as a minor variation) and folk. The popularity of informal hootenanny and coffeehouse performances prompts the industry to put out "Green Green," "If I Had a Hammer," "I'm Just a Country Boy," and many others. Teenage acceptance bridges the age gap to produce the first universal music in the United States in almost a decade.

• Newcomers include a number of youngsters: 17-year-old Lesley Gore holds the No. 1 position for two weeks with "It's My Party"; 15-year-old Little Peggy March, with "I Will Follow Him," becomes the youngest female singer to top the charts; and Motown's 12-year-old Little Stevie Wonder, with "Fingertips (Part II)," becomes the first rock artist to reach No. 1 in the singles and album charts (same title) simultaneously and the first to score a hit with a live number.

• A newcomer in 1962, with his first album Bob Dylan attracts attention when the Peter, Paul & Mary rendition of his composition "Blowin' in the Wind" reaches No. 2. The 22-year-old Minnesotan (who changed his name from Zimmerman in honor of Dylan Thomas) deliberately turned his back on rock for the deeper emotions and complexities of folk music. "Blowin' in the Wind" becomes the anthem of the protest movement and Dylan emerges as the voice of his generation.

• Although some 3,000 recording firms operate in the United States, 27 account for 96 percent of the royalties and the big four—Capitol, Columbia, Decca, and RCA Victor—continue to split 50 percent of the market. With most major companies establishing branches in Nashville, that city has taken over from Hollywood as the second largest popular music center, behind New York. (Insiders dub Nashville "Tin Pan Valley.")

• Dancers imitate the motions of climbing or shaking a tree for the Monkey, but the Limbo offers a more interesting challenge. To do the West Indies dance (introduced to teens in the 1960 film Where the Boys Are), you bend over backward from the knees, and belly under a crossbar. The question becomes, "How low can you go?"

• In 1901, C. Albert Tindley turned a religious folk song into a formal Baptist hymn, "I'll Overcome Some Day." (The music was based on the early hymn "O Sanctissima" [1774].) In the mid-1940s, Zilphia Horton learned the song from striking black tobacco workers in Charleston. She taught it to Pete Seeger and Frank Hamilton, who added a verse. This year, schoolteacher Guy Carawan copyrights a more rhythmic version as "We Shall Overcome." The song is destined to become the rallying cry of the civil rights movement.

• In Japan, Kyu Sakamoto scores a big hit with "Ue O Muite Aruko," or "I Look Up When I Walk." British Pye Records changes the title for the Western market and it becomes the first foreign-language song to top the charts. But, as Newsweek points out, the "Sukiyaki" song title is equivalent to renaming "Moon River" "Beef Stew" in Japanese.

## New Recording Artists

Beatles (in North America)
Lou Christie
Jackie DeShannon
Lesley Gore
Merle Haggard
Trini Lopez
Martha & the Vandellas
Wayne Newton
O'Jays
Wilson Pickett
Lou Rawls
Otis Redding
Righteous Brothers
Barbra Streisand
Little Stevie Wonder

## Obituaries

**Patsy Cline** (September 8, 1932–March 5, 1963). The Grand Ole Opry's featured vocalist, Cline was the first CW singer to cross over onto the pop charts. With hits such as "I Fall to Pieces" (1961) and "Crazy" (1961), Cline was named Billboard's 1962 "female artist of the year." Returning from a benefit concert, she died in a plane crash along with her manager, Hawkshaw Hawkins, Cowboy Copans, and Randy Hughes.

**Edith Piaf** (December 19, 1915–October 11, 1963). Edith Gassion left the factory at the age of 15 to sing in the streets of Paris. Named "le môme Piaf," or the waif sparrow, by her first employer, Piaf quickly found success in vaudeville, then on radio in 1936. A dance hall performer by 1939, she would sing only for POWs during the Nazi occupation.

France's best-loved singer, Piaf was known to North Americans through her 1950 hit "La Vie en Rose" and appearances on "Ed Sullivan." She retained her husky, powerful voice throughout her career.

**Dinah Washington** (August 29, 1924–December 14, 1963). With her gospel background, singular phrasing, and penetrating voice, critics found it impossible to place Washington in a single category. She was equally effective in jazz, blues, and straight pop, and she was the most popular black female singer of the 1950s. Her hits included "What a Diff'rence a Day Makes" (1959), "Unforgettable" (1959), and "September in the Rain" (1961).

## MOVIES

*All the Way Home* (d. Alex Segal; bw)—Jean Simmons, Robert Preston, Aline MacMahon, Pat Hingle, Michael Kearney

*Billy Liar* (British, d. John Schlesinger; bw)—Tom Courtenay, Julie Christie

*The Birds* (d. Alfred Hitchcock; color)—Rod Taylor, Tippi Hedren, Suzanne Pleshette, Jessica Tandy

*Charade* (d. Stanley Donen; color)—Cary Grant, Audrey Hepburn, Walter Matthau, James Coburn, George Kennedy, Ned Glass

*8½* (Italian, d. Federico Fellini; bw)—Marcello Mastroianni, Claudia Cardinale, Anouk Aimée

*From Russia with Love* (British, d. Terence Young; color)—Sean Connery, Robert Shaw, Pedro Armendariz, Daniela Bianchi

*The Great Escape* (d. John Sturges; color)—Steve McQueen, James Garner, Richard Attenborough, Charles Bronson, James Coburn, Donald Pleasance, James Donald, David McCallum

*The Haunting* (d. Robert Wise; bw)—Julie Harris, Claire Bloom, Richard Johnson

*How the West Was Won* (d. John Ford; color)—Spencer Tracy (narrator), James Stewart, Debbie Reynolds, Carroll Baker, Karl Malden, Gregory Peck, George Peppard, John Wayne, Henry Fonda

*Hud* (d. Martin Ritt; bw)—Paul Newman, Patricia Neal, Melvyn Douglas, Brandon de Wilde

*It's a Mad, Mad, Mad, Mad World* (d. Stanley Kramer; color)—Spencer Tracy, Edie Adams, Milton Berle, Sid Caesar, Phil Silvers, Buddy Hackett

*Jason and the Argonauts* (British, d. Don Chaffey; color)—Todd Armstrong, Nancy Kovack, Gary Raymond, Honor Blackman

*The Leopard* (French-Italian, d. Luchino Visconti; color)—Burt Lancaster, Alain Delon, Claudia Cardinale

*Lilies of the Field* (d. Ralph Nelson; bw)—Sidney Poitier, Lilia Skala

*Love With the Proper Stranger* (d. Robert Mulligan; bw)—Steve McQueen, Natalie Wood, Edie Adams, Herschel Bernardi

*Murder at the Gallop* (British, d. George Pollock; bw)—Margaret Rutherford, Robert Morley, Flora Robson, Charles Tingwell

*The Nutty Professor* (d. Jerry Lewis; color)—Jerry Lewis, Stella Stevens

*Sunday in New York* (d. Peter Tewksbury; color)—Cliff Robertson, Jane Fonda, Rod Taylor, Robert Culp

*The Sword in the Stone* (Disney; color; animated)—Voices: Ricky Sorenson (Wart); Sebastian Cabot (Sir Ector); Karl Swenson (Merlin); Junius Matthews (Archimedes)

*This Sporting Life* (British, d. Lindsay Anderson; bw)—Richard Harris, Rachel Roberts, Alan Badel

*Tom Jones* (British, d. Tony Richardson; color)—Albert Finney, Susannah York, Hugh Griffith, Edith Evans, Joan Greenwood, Diane Cilento

### Academy Awards

**April 8.** For the first time, Oscar presents the five nominated songs in a medley. With two large musical numbers scheduled, the producer wanted to eliminate the nominees altogether, but Academy members protested—loudly.

Frank Sinatra replaces the perennial Bob Hope as host when the comedian's regular TV sponsors conflict with the Academy's.

Best Picture—*Lawrence of Arabia*

Best Actor—Gregory Peck (*To Kill a Mockingbird*)

Best Actress—Anne Bancroft (*The Miracle Worker*)

Best Director—David Lean (*Lawrence of Arabia*)

Best Supporting Actor—Ed Begley (*Sweet Bird of Youth*)

Best Supporting Actress—Patty Duke (*The Miracle Worker*)

Best Song—"Days of Wine and Roses" from the film of the same name

Best Foreign Film—*Sundays and Cybele* (French)

Patty Duke, at age 16, becomes the first performer under 18 to win a competitive Oscar (previously the Academy honored child actors in Special Categories).

An exuberant Gregory Peck, finally winning an Oscar on his fifth nomination, tells reporters, "I hate to give it back to the Academy, even if it's only to have my name engraved on it."

## News

**January 16.** Noting Hollywood's continuing decline, the *Wall Street Journal* reports that independent motion picture companies accounted for 80 percent of U.S. releases last year. Yet, because the studios finance or release many of the independent productions, Hollywood still takes in two thirds of world box-office receipts.

**June 6.** The Cinerama projection system introduced in 1952 used three films and three projectors simultaneously. After years of technical development, the first single-lens, single-camera Cinerama commercial film reaches the theaters—*It's a Mad, Mad, Mad, Mad World.*

**December 20.** A *Life* magazine "Special Double Issue on the Movies" gives extensive coverage to new and established directors. Alfred Hitchcock tells the magazine, "Cinema is the only new medium of art invented for many centuries. It has its own rules, which are based on its own characteristics, and the first is this: pure cinema is the art of selection and arranging bits of film to create a cumulative series of calculated effects on the audience."

**More news.** The Italian documentary *Mondo Cane* uses some 30 separate episodes to show the cruelty, inhumanity, and blood thirstiness of people around the world. The film becomes an international smash hit.

• In the special *Life* issue, an article on Western stunts reveals that just 20 years ago handlers rode horses at breakneck speeds into trip wires to achieve a spectacular spill. When the ASPCA stepped in, specialists trained their horses to "lie down" at a full gallop.

• American International Pictures (AIP) capitalizes on the growing surf craze with *Beach Party*, starring Annette Funicello, Frankie Avalon, Bob Cummings, and Dorothy Malone. Following the company's advertising blitz, thousands of teenagers flock to opening day, breaking records across the country. No parents, no problems, and no end to summer—youngsters want more. AIP will put out four more beach movies over the next two years:

*Annette Funicello and Frankie Avalon set off a surf-and-sand craze with* Beach Party.

starring Annette Funicello, Frankie Avalon, Bob Cummings, and Dorothy Malone. Following the company's advertising blitz, thousands of teenagers flock to opening day, breaking records across the country. No parents, no problems, and no end to summer—youngsters want more. AIP will put out four more beach movies over the next two years: Muscle Beach Party, *Bikini Beach*, *Beach Blanket Bingo*, and *How to Stuff a Wild Bikini* (actors shiver through cold weather to complete films for the next season). But by 1966, with the emerging counterculture, the sexual innocence of the series (Funicello covered her navel to maintain a squeaky-clean Disney image).

• After viewing several screen tests, President Kennedy chooses actor Cliff Robertson to portray him in the movie *PT 109*. (During W.W.II, a Japanese destroyer rammed and sank Kennedy's torpedo boat. He organized his men and, despite a back injury, towed a wounded man three miles to a nearby island. The future president received the Purple Heart and the Navy and Marine Corps Medal for his bravery.)

• With fewer new releases and weekly attendance figures holding steady, studios reissue old classics to meet exhibitors' demands. Titles include *Wuthering Heights* (1939), and *Show Boat* (1951).

• Disney produces *Son of Flubber*, with Fred MacMurray and Tommy Kirk, follows *The Absent Minded Professor* (1961). Other than series, such as Ma and Pa Kettle, sequels have consisted of TV episodes patched together (usually for release abroad). *Flubber* is the first all-new sequel to a major feature film.

| Top Box Office Stars | Newcomers |
| --- | --- |
| Doris Day | George Chakiris |
| John Wayne | Peter Fonda |
| Rock Hudson | Stella Stevens |
| Jack Lemmon | Diane McBain |
| Cary Grant | Pamela Tiffin |
| Elizabeth Taylor | Pat Wayne |
| Elvis Presley | Dorothy Provine |
| Sandra Dee | Barbara Eden |
| Paul Newman | Ursula Andress |
| Jerry Lewis | Tony Bill |

## Top Money-Maker of the Year

*Cleopatra* (1963) (d. Joseph L. Mankiewicz, and others; color) Elizabeth Taylor, Richard Burton, Rex Harrison

## Flop of the Year

*Cleopatra*

—Tickets priced up to $5.50 (three times the normal admission) and a record budget of $37 million make *Cleopatra* the year's top grosser and the biggest money loser. Mammoth production costs, due in part to Taylor's illness, closed down 20th Century-Fox for much of 1962.

## Obituaries

**Richard Barthelmess** (May 9, 1897–August 17, 1963). A silent-screen idol and one of Hollywood's leading stars in the early years of sound, Barthelmess retired in 1941. Of his 76 films, the best known remain *Broken Blossoms* (1919) and *Dawn Patrol* (1930).

**Jack Carson** (October 27, 1910–January 2, 1963). Although a fine actor, the comedian usually played second banana to the star. His films included *Arsenic and Old Lace* (1944).

**Tom London** (August 24, 1883–December 5, 1963). His more than 2,000 appearances—beginning with *The Great Train Robbery* (1903)—far surpass the total performances of any other American actor.

**Adolphe Menjou** (February 18, 1890–October 29, 1963). A waxed black mustache and impeccable clothing typecast the dapper actor as a sophisticated man-of-the-world. He retired in 1960.

**ZaSu Pitts** 4(January 3, 1900–June 7, 1963). When the advent of sound pushed the thin-voiced actress into comedy, she found her forte. Pitts made over 100 films, and appeared on Broadway and television.

**Dick Powell** (November 14, 1904–January 2, 1963). In the 1930s, the boyish tenor starred in all Warner Brother's ensemble musicals, including the memorable *42nd Street* (1933). In the 1940s, Powell turned to dramatic roles, then, over the last decade, he mainly directed or starred on television. The actor, who died of cancer, is survived by his wife, actress June Allyson.

**Sabu** (January 27, 1924–December 2, 1963). The son of an Indian elephant driver, Sabu starred in several British pictures before moving to Hollywood in 1941. After serving in the U.S. Army during W.W.II, he returned to films, but the Arabian Nights genre was no longer popular.

**Willard Van der Veer** (1895–June 16, 1963). A member of the Byrd Arctic and Antarctic expeditions during the 1920s, he was the first to photograph the North and South Poles. His 1930 documentary won an Oscar.

## TELEVISION AND RADIO

### New Prime-Time TV Programs

"Bob Hope Presents The Chrysler Theatre" (September 27, 1963–September 6, 1967; Drama/Variety)—Host: Bob Hope

"Burke's Law" (September 20, 1963–January 12, 1966; Police/Detective Drama)—Gene Barry, Gary Conway, Regis Toomey. *Note:* In its last season, the show will become "Amos Burke—Secret Agent."

"The Danny Kaye Show" (September 25, 1963–June 7, 1967; Musical Variety)—Danny Kaye, Harvey Korman, Joyce Van Patten

"The Farmer's Daughter" (September 20, 1963–September 2, 1966; Situation Comedy)—Inger Stevens, William Windom, Cathleen Nesbitt

"The Fugitive" (September 17, 1963–August 29, 1967; Drama)—David Janssen, Barry Morse, Jacqueline Scott, Bill Raisch (One-Armed Man)

"The Jimmy Dean Show" (September 19, 1963–April 1, 1966; Musical Variety)—Host: Jimmy Dean

"Mr. Novak" (September 24, 1963–August 31, 1965; Drama)—James Franciscus, Dean Jagger

"My Favorite Martian" (September 29, 1963–September 4, 1966; Situation Comedy)—Ray Walston, Bill Bixby, Pamela Britton

"The Outer Limits" (September 16, 1963–January 16, 1965; Science Fiction Anthology)

"The Patty Duke Show" (September 18, 1963–August 31, 1966; Situation Comedy)—Patty Duke, William Schallert, Jean Byron

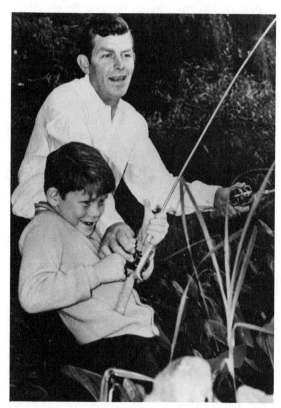

*Reportedly, scripts for "The Andy Griffith Show" take one third fewer pages than the average sitcom because the characters speak more slowly in their comfortable Southern drawl. The show opens with Andy and Ron Howard going fishing.*

"Petticoat Junction" (September 24, 1963–September 12, 1970; Situation Comedy)—Bea Benaderet, Edgar Buchanan, Linda Kaye

### Emmy Awards 1962–1963 (May 26, 1963)

Drama—"The Defenders" (CBS)
Variety—"The Andy Williams Show" (NBC)

Humor—"The Dick Van Dyke Show" (CBS)

Music—"Julie and Carol at Carnegie Hall" (CBS)

Children's Programming—"Walt Disney's Wonderful World of Color" (NBC)

Best Actor in a Series—E. G. Marshall ("The Defenders," CBS)

Best Actress in a Series—Shirley Booth ("Hazel," NBC)

## News

**April 15.** ABC launches the folk program "Hootenanny," taped weekly on college campuses. At a Rutgers University performance in September, some 400 students protest network refusal to hire Pete Seeger. In 1961, the singer was convicted of contempt for refusing to answer HUAC questions. Although the court decision was reversed in 1962, ABC would only bring him on the show if he signed an affidavit on past and present affiliations. Once again, he refused.

**August 30.** Dick Clark completes the final weekday telecast of "American Bandstand." Beginning in September, the program will be limited to Saturday afternoon.

**September.** To accommodate advertisers, CBS daytime programmer Fred Silverman dumps Saturday-morning reruns and slots in two solid hours of cartoons. He will add another hour next year, and with a doubling to six hours by 1969–1970, CBS will pull in some $65 million from sponsors.

**September 2.** CBS, with double the number of news bureaus, finds 15 minutes too short for the nightly broadcast. This evening, Walter Cronkite sits in the newsroom for the network's first 30-minute coverage. Eric Sevareid joins him with an analysis and commentary. A week later, NBC follows suit and presents the half-hour "Huntley-Brinkley Report." When Chet Huntley retires in 1970, Brinkley will rotate on the newscast with Frank McGee and John Chancellor. In August 1971, Chancellor will become sole anchor.

**September 15–21.** In a novel experiment, ABC presents all its new shows in a "sneak preview" week. The network gains a distinctive early lead over CBS and NBC.

**November 22.** Walter Cronkite interrupts the Friday broadcast of "As the World Turns" with this news bulletin: "In Dallas, Texas, three shots were fired at President Kennedy's motorcade in downtown Dallas. The first reports say that President Kennedy has been seriously wounded by this shooting."

All three networks cancel regular weekend programming and through the long hours ahead Americans lean heavily on Cronkite and other newscasters. (When President Roosevelt died in 1945, Americans relied on newspapers over the four days it took to bring his body home by train.) Dan Rather, who gave CBS their scoop, steps into the spotlight for the first time as an unofficial anchor in Dallas, and veteran reporters Roger Mudd and Harry Reasoner finally come to public attention in Washington.

In focusing national grief on the ongoing events, television finally comes into its own. And two days later when Jack Ruby shoots Lee Harvey Oswald in front of the cameras, a technology developed primarily for sports allows the networks to replay the killing again and again. With this immediacy, news coverage switches overnight from strict interpreting events to witnessing history.

**November 23.** Japanese television viewers, up early to catch the first transpacific satellite telecast, learn of the assassination when the president's taped greeting is deleted.

**December 1.** For the next three Sundays, kids across the country sit in front of their sets from 7:30 to 8:30 P.M. to watch Hayley Mills in the Walt Disney film *Pollyanna* (1960).

**December 10.** One day after his sixth birthday, Donny joins his brothers in a song on "The Andy Williams Show." Last year, the host's father, Jay Williams, discovered the Osmond Brothers performing at Disneyland.

**December 30.** "Let's Make a Deal," with host Monty Hall, becomes one of the most popular game shows of the decade. The daytime program will switch from NBC to ABC in December 1968.

**More news.** While RCA still receives royalty payments for the basic patents, Zenith and Sylvania begin producing their own color picture tubes.

• The U.S. Army's electronic research and development lab offers the infantry a hand-held radio receiver-transmitter.

• In 1946, about 33 percent of automobiles had radios. Today, that percentage has risen to nearly 70 percent. The increase has shifted radio prime time to commuting hours: 6:00–9:00 A.M. and 4:00–7:00 P.M. This year, some automakers offer an AM/FM radio.

## TV Commercials

Chevrolet—To create one of the decade's most memorable commercials, a helicopter airlifts a 1964 Chevrolet in sections to the top of a 1,500-foot pinnacle in Utah. An engineer assembles the parts then hides under the car for filming. Commercial pilots reportedly swamp air traffic controllers with questions during the day of the shoot.

Folger's Coffee—Later one of TV's most recognizable faces, Virginia Christine as Mrs. Olsen offers her first jar of "mountain-grown" coffee.

Volkswagen—Taking another but equally effective tack, Volkswagen asks, "Did you ever wonder how the man who drives a snowplow drives *to* the snowplow?" The automaker continues with the self-deprecating series until 1970 when, in the final ad, rich Uncle Max leaves his millions to the practical nephew who bought a Volkswagen.

## Obituaries

**Isaac Shoenberg** (March 1, 1880–January 25, 1963). The British inventor produced the first high-definition television system. The BBC followed his 405-line technical standard until 1964.

**Arthur R. Vinton** (February 26, 1963). The

U.S. actor played "The Shadow" in the popular 1940s radio program of the same name.

## SPORTS
### Winners
#### Baseball

World Series—Los Angeles Dodgers (NL), 4 games; New York Yankees (AL), 0 games

Player of the Year—Elston Howard (New York Yankees, AL); Sandy Koufax (Los Angeles Dodgers, NL)

Rookie of the Year—Gary Peters (Chicago White Sox, AL); Pete Rose (Cincinnati Reds, NL)

#### Football

NFL Championship—Chicago Bears 14, New York Giants 10

AFL Championship—San Diego Chargers 51, Boston Patriots 10

College Bowls (January 1, 1963)—
Rose Bowl, USC 42, Wisconsin 37
Cotton Bowl, LSU 13, Texas 0
Orange Bowl, Alabama 17, Oklahoma 0
Sugar Bowl, Mississippi 17, Arkansas 13

Heisman Trophy—Roger Staubach (U.S. Naval Academy, QB)

Grey Cup—Hamilton Tiger-Cats 21, British Columbia (BC) Lions 10

#### Basketball

NBA Championship—Boston Celtics, 4 games; LA Lakers, 2 games

MVP of the Year—Bill Russell (Boston Celtics)

Rookie of the Year—Terry Dischinger (Chicago Zephyrs)

NCAA Championship—Loyola 60, Cincinnati 58

#### Tennis

U.S. National—Men, Rafael Osuna (vs. Frank Froehling); Women, Maria Bueno (vs. Margaret Smith)

Wimbledon—Men, Charles McKinley (vs. Fred Stolle); Women, Margaret Smith (vs. Billie Jean Moffitt [King])

## Golf

Masters—Jack Nicklaus
U.S. Open—Julius Boros
British Open—Bob Charles

## Hockey

Stanley Cup—Toronto Maple Leafs, 4 games; Detroit Red Wings, 1 game

## Ice Skating

World Championship—Men, Donald McPherson (Canada); Women, Sjoukje Dijkstra (Netherlands)
U.S. National—Men, Thomas Litz; Women, Lorraine Hanlor
Canadian National—Men, Donald McPherson; Women, Wendy Griner

## Kentucky Derby

Chateaugay—Braulio Baeza, jockey

## Athlete of the Year

Male—Sandy Koufax (Baseball)
Female—Mickey Wright (Golf)

## Last Season

Yogi Berra (Baseball)
Bob Cousy (Basketball)
Bobby Layne (Football)
Stan Musial (Baseball)
Early Wynn (Baseball)

# News

**February 22.** This week, former French tennis champion René Lacoste patents a steel-framed racquet. With rings mounted on a spring-steel ring, his design, unlike wood, needs no grooving or perforating and allows for any shape.

**March 21.** Featherweight champion Davey Moore collapses after a TKO by challenger Sugar Ramos. Moore dies four days later.

*Statistics*: After an April death in Australia, *Ring* magazine tallies the number of boxing fatalities last year at 14, and the number since 1946—an estimated 217.

**April 17.** NFL Commissioner Pete Rozelle suspends Packer halfback Paul Hornung for giving out betting information, and Lion tackle Alex Karras for six significant bets over the past five years. Rozelle fines five other players as well for wagering on the 1962 championship game, and the Detroit club for ignoring reports of gambling. Hornung and Karras are reinstated in May 1964.

**May.** Perhaps to compensate for this year's wider strike zone, NL umpires have enforced the existent rule requiring a pitcher to pause one second between windup and delivery. But fans and players alike have protested and the Rules Committee drops the one-second rule early this month.

**September 7.** The NFL Hall of Fame is dedicated in Canton, Ohio. The first 11 members chosen last January include Jim Thorpe and 6 officials.

**October 6.** With a win at the Whitemarsh Open golf tournament in Pennsylvania, Arnold Palmer collects $26,000—the largest prize ever offered in a PGA-sponsored event. By the end of the year, his $128,230 in winnings make him the first golfer to earn over $100,000 in a single year.

# Records

**August 5.** At the Salt Flats in Utah, Craig Breedlove reaches a record 407.45 mph in his 35-foot jet-powered *Spirit of America*. He is the first U.S. racer in 35 years to hold the land speed record.

**August 24.** With a time of 1:58.4, at Osaka, Japan, U.S. swimmer Don Schollander becomes the first to break the 2-minute mark in the 200-meter freestyle.

**November 10.** Red Wing Gordie Howe scores his 545th goal. Ironically, he breaks Maurice Richard's record while playing the Montreal Canadiens. Next year, when Howe tops Richard's all-time total of 626 goals, the Rocket concedes from retirement that "Gordie could do everything."

## What They Said

Rookie Bob Uecker, who rooms with Braves third baseman Eddie Mathews, says, "Between me and my roommate we've hit 400 major league home runs." Uecker has hit only 1. (*Sports Illustrated*, March 18)

Jack McMahon, coach of the Cincinnati Royals, comments on Celtic defensive genius Bill Russell. "The minute you make a move, you have to assume he's coming from some place; he borders on ruining the game." (*Sports Illustrated*, November 18)

## Obituaries

**Rogers Hornsby** (April 27, 1896–January 5, 1963). Stepping forward from the back of the batter's box with a perfectly level swing, the right-handed power hitter set a .424 batting average in 1924 (a record unequaled in modern play) and a lifetime average of .358 (exceeded only by Ty Cobb). And at second base for most of his career, Hornsby established a .957 fielding average. But his cold, belligerent personality pushed him from team to team in the late 1920s and ended most of his attempts at managing.

**Davey Moore** (November 1, 1933–March 25, 1963). The four-year featherweight champion died following a title bout on March 21. The loss marked only the second time he had been stopped in 66 bouts.

**Jack Root** (May 26, 1876–June 9, 1963). The first recognized light-heavyweight of the world won his title in a 1903 bout with Kid McCoy.

# 1964

---

A master tactician, Lyndon Baines Johnson uses national grief to free much of the dead president's stalled legislative program. For black Americans, the Civil Rights Act is the most important piece of legislation, but within days of enactment, frustrated young people in Harlem bring America its first "long, hot summer."

In foreign policy, Johnson authorizes a retaliatory air strike against North Vietnam for an alleged attack in the Gulf of Tonkin. Still, the extreme rhetoric of Barry Goldwater allows the president to run as the peace candidate. Swept to victory in November, Johnson and his advisors plan a bombing campaign while experts argue that Saigon will never acquire enough popular support to defeat the Communists.

Alaska suffers a devastating earthquake, three civil rights activists are murdered in Mississippi, Jimmy Hoffa is finally convicted, a Ranger spacecraft returns photos from the moon, Cassius Clay wins the world heavyweight championship, and Martin Luther King, Jr., receives the Nobel peace prize.

Internationally, South Africa sends activist Nelson Mandela to prison, Premier Nikita Khrushchev is overthrown, Winston Churchill retires, and Palestinians establish the PLO.

Kids love the Barbie doll and G.I. Joe, the Wizard of Id, and TV spoofs like "The Munsters." Teens succumb to Beatlemania and flock to see "Hard Day's Night."

## NEWS

**January 8.** In his first State of the Union address, President Johnson carries forward John F. Kennedy's social programs and repeats administration demands for quick action on tax cuts and civil rights. As well, the president announces his own war on poverty, calling for more housing for the elderly and poor, the modernization of unemployment insurance, and the extension of minimum wage coverage.

**January 9.** To avoid inflaming nationalist tensions in Panama, Washington has ordered that no flags be flown outside schools and other public places in the canal zone. When American students attempt to raise the U.S. flag over their school, outraged Panamanians clash with U.S. troops. Anti-American attacks spread throughout the zone and into Panama City, where mobs burn and loot U.S. buildings, homes, and automobiles—20 Panamanians and 4 U.S. soldiers die.

Describing the attack as unprovoked, Panama

breaks diplomatic relations with the United States and demands a complete revision of the 1903 treaty under which the United States administers the canal zone. President Johnson opts for negotiation, rather than sending in the marines. The two nations resume relations in April.

In December, Johnson will announce that the United States will negotiate a new canal treaty while proceeding with plans to build a modern sea-level canal across Central America or Colombia.

**February 1.** Secretary of State McNamara reported in December that the Vietcong, taking advantage of the Diem coup, had widened their area of control in South Vietnam. He recommended that "progressively escalating pressure" might force Hanoi to halt VC and Pathet Lao insurrections. The Johnson administration then authorized an elaborate program of covert military operations against North Vietnam.

"Operation Plan 34A," which begins today, marks a significant turning point for American entanglement in Vietnam. Unlike previous CIA operations, these attacks are run by the U.S. military and directed by McNamara for the president: commando raids against North Vietnamese highway and railroad bridges and PT bombardment of coastal installations; CIA-piloted bombing attacks over Laos, striking ever closer to North Vietnam; and destroyer patrols in the Gulf of Tonkin. The U.S. intelligence community gives the secret program little chance of success, but Johnson and his advisors reject the analysis.

The operations quickly create an expectation for still greater efforts, and while concealing political deterioration in Saigon, the administration initiates plans to openly bomb North Vietnam and obtain a congressional resolution legitimizing American involvement. Military and economic aid are increased on March 17.

**February 3.** About 45 percent of New York City's 1 million students stay home to protest de facto segregation. The students repeat their boycott in March. By June city schools launch a 1964–1965 pilot plan—busing students from eight schools to improve the racial balance.

During the year, students in other northern cities, including Chicago, Boston, Cleveland, and Cincinnati, also hold boycotts, strikes, and demonstrations.

**February 4.** Following ratification last week by the 38th state, the 24th Amendment to the Constitution forbids poll taxes in federal elections. Southern states had used the tax to disenfranchise poor blacks since the Civil War. In fall elections, the amendment adds thousands to voter rolls in Alabama, Arkansas, Mississippi, Texas, and Virginia. But since "literacy" tests continue to keep blacks off many registration lists, the civil rights movement regards the amendment as merely symbolic.

**February 17.** In a historic decision, the Supreme Court rules (6–3) that congressional districts must be substantially equal in population. (In 37 states, the most populous district exceeds the least populous by at least 100,000.) Justice Harlan, in dissenting, charges the court with intruding "into matters

*The controversial Malcolm X.*

which the Constitution very wisely left to the political process."

The court extends the one-man, one-vote doctrine to state legislatures on June 15. (Chief Justice Earl Warren declares, "Legislators represent people, not trees or acres.") Four years later, the concept will be applied to local governments.

**March 8.** Malcolm X breaks with the Black Muslim movement of Elijah Muhammed to establish a nonsectarian, politically oriented black nationalist party. A young Malcolm Little adopted the Islam faith while serving a six-year prison sentence for armed robbery. Following his release in the early 1950s, he joined Muhammed and changed his name to "X" to represent an ancestral name lost in slavery. A charismatic speaker, Malcolm quickly advanced in the Nation of Islam to become its first national minister in 1963. He tells reporters there can be no revolution without bloodshed.

**March 13.** A man attacks Kitty Genovese, a 28-year-old bar manager, outside her Queens, New York, apartment late at night. Her wild cries for help raise over 30 neighbors, but no one comes to her aid or calls the police. At one point, someone shouts down from a window, and the attacker moves away. But he returns, assaulting her in three separate attacks over 35 minutes. Finally one neighbor, after calling a friend for advice, telephones the police. Kitty Genovese is already dead.

The killer, 29-year-old factory worker Winton Moseley, confesses to two other murders and is sentenced to life in prison. Genovese's murder forces Americans to recognize the growing isolation of their society.

**March 14.** A Dallas jury convicts Jack Ruby of the murder of Lee Harvey Oswald. Ruby was apparently in the area only by happenstance—purchasing a money order at Western Union just four minutes before he shot Oswald—but the jurors find him guilty of "murder with malice" and assess the death penalty.

**March 14.** U.N. peacekeepers arrive in Cyprus. Late last year, President Archbishop Makarios presented the Turkish minority population with a plan for constitutional revision. He claimed their constant use of the veto had paralyzed the government,

*The first U.N. peacekeeping contingent arrives in Cyprus. Canadian soldiers accept a bouquet of flowers from a woman before patrolling a nearby village.*

but the Turkish Cypriots protested that the veto protected their minority rights.

On December 16, Turkey rejected the plan on their behalf, and violence broke out in Cyprus five days later. Makarios refused to resolve the issue within NATO but accepted a U.N. peacekeeping force. The crisis remains unresolved at the end of the year.

**March 27.** The worst earthquake in U.S. history, and one of the most violent in recorded history, hits southern Alaska at 5:36 P.M. on Good Friday. Anchorage, closest to the epicenter and built on unstable clay, suffers the most damage during the four to five minutes of upheaval. Over three-quarters of the city is destroyed as the ground rises and sinks by as much as 12 feet, and slides toward the sea.

Everywhere, dozens of fissures open and close again; a man and his two children, picnicking in Valdez, disappear into one huge crack. A 17-foot tidal wave destroys much of downtown Kodiak, while in Seward waves rupture oil storage tanks, setting the town on fire. Tsunami sweep down the coastline, drowning four people in Oregon and 10 on the beach at Crescent City, California.

Despite the severity of the quake (8.4 on the Richter scale), only 118 people die in Alaska. Several factors saved lives: the state's sparse population, the Good Friday holiday, and the late-afternoon hour. But the enormous devastation wrought by the tremors on modern construction materials sobers earthquake experts. An 8+ quake in California could kill a million people.

Damage estimates in Alaska reach $500 million, but government financing allows the communities to rebuild on the same unstable ground.

**April 21.** Republican congressional leaders Senator Everett Dirksen and Representative Charles Halleck issue a joint statement accusing the Johnson administration of concealing the extent of U.S. involvement in the Vietnamese War.

The two men read from the personal letters of U.S. Air Force Captain Edwin Shank, killed in Vietnam in March, in which he tells his wife of the bad morale among Americans: "I'll bet you that anyone you talk to does not know that American pilots fight this war. . . . The Vietnamese 'students' we have on board are airmen basics. . . . The only reason they are on board is, in case we crash, there is one American 'advisor' and one Vietnamese 'student.' " Halleck states, "If we are going to war, let us prepare the American people for it," while Dirkensen declares, "Let's have the whole brutal thing out on the table and let the American people see it for what it is."

Earlier today, President Johnson described American involvement in South Vietnam as at the same level that it was a decade before under President Eisenhower. Yet, three days later, Defense Secretary McNamara reaffirms that the administration no longer plans to withdraw most military personnel by the end of 1965; U.S. armed strength in Vietnam now stands at about 15,500.

---

*Statistics:* On July 8, a U.S. military spokesman in Saigon reports that, since December 1961, American casualties have totaled 1,387: 152 killed in combat, 151 killed in noncombat accidents, 96 dead of noncombat causes, 17 missing in action, and 971 wounded in action.

---

**April 25.** President Johnson announces the appointment of Lt. General William Westmoreland, age 50, to replace retiring General Paul Harkins as head of the U.S. MACV.

**May 1.** Labor leader Hal Banks skips bail in Canada and flees to the United States. In 1949, Canadian shipping companies asked Banks to guide the Seafarers' International Union in ousting the Communist-controlled Canadian Seamen's Union. He quickly won collective bargaining rights for most sailors, but when he tried to expand the Seafarers' jurisdiction, other unions took him on. Battles broke out, shipping was disrupted, and Ottawa appointed a commission of inquiry. Banks was given a five-year sentence for conspiring to beat up a rival union organizer. The United States refuses to extradite him.

**May 19.** Acting on a tip from a Soviet defector, American wrecking crews uncover some 40 microphones embedded in the walls of the U.S. Embassy in Moscow. The embassy staff has always assumed the Soviets were eavesdropping, but investigators will determine if any sensitive information has been revealed. Since 1949, the U.S. State Department has found over 130 listening devices in American embassies in Communist countries.

**May 24.** Senator Barry Goldwater, appearing on ABC radio-TV program "Issues and Answers," proposes that "low-yield atomic weapons" be used in South Vietnam. The Democrats make full use of his radical statements during the election campaign. Robert Kennedy facetiously tells one crowd of New Yorkers that Goldwater "came up with a solution for crime in Central Park. He would use conventional nuclear weapons and defoliate it."

**May 27.** Jawaharlal Nehru, India's first prime minister, dies of a heart attack at age 74. A devoted follower of Gandhi's philosophy of nonviolence, Nehru was a leading figure in the Indian nationalist movement and spent a total of nine years in colonial prisons. With independence in 1947, he became prime minister and, with Gandhi's death a year later, the father figure of the nation.

During his years in office, Nehru failed in his attempt to eliminate poverty through industrialization and met with only partial success in developing a bloc of nonaligned nations. Yet, he pulled India into the 20th century and, through his work for world peace, established a place for his country at the head of Third World nations.

Some 1.5 million people crowd the streets of New Delhi during the funeral procession and more than 100,000 witness the cremation.

**May 25.** To prevent desegregation, Virginia shut down Prince Edward County schools (one of the original 1954 cases), and channeled state and local funds to "private" institutions. In a unanimous decision barring such closures, Justice Hugo Black writes, "The time for mere 'deliberate speed' has run out. . . . There has been entirely too much deliberation and not enough speed in enforcing the constitutional rights which we held had been denied." The county obeys the order, but white students simply switch to private schools.

**June 10.** On February 10, the House passed a civil rights bill surprisingly stronger and broader than the legislation proposed by John F. Kennedy in 1963, but over the past 4 months, the bill has stalled in Senate under hundreds of proposed amendments and a 75-day Southern filibuster. Minority leader Everett Dirksen has worked with Hubert Humphrey and Northern Democrats to marshall support and today the Senate successfully invokes cloture—the first use in American history to pass a civil rights measure.

The bill receives Senate approval, 73–27, on June 19 and the House votes, 289–126, on July 2 to complete congressional action. Five hours later, in televised ceremonies, President Johnson signs the bill into law.

The Civil Rights Act of 1964 bans racial segregation in public facilities, such as restaurants, hotels, theaters, and any other place of business connected with interstate commerce (Congress believed such a connection would be fairly easy to prove); extends suffrage by prohibiting the unequal application of registration procedures, by requiring that voter tests be written, and by setting a sixth-grade education as the level for literacy; gives the attorney general power to file suits against school segregation, the denial of voting rights, and segregated public facilities; and includes the nation's first federal fair employment practices law, prohibiting discrimination by employers, employment agencies, and unions on the basis of race, color, religion, national origin, or sex (effective July 3, 1965, for employers or unions with 100 or more employees, although the number will be reduced to 25 over the next four years), and establishes the Equal Employment Opportunity Commission (EEOC) to investigate and judge complaints.

The next day throughout the South, formerly segregated restaurants and hotels accept blacks as customers for the first time. But critics argue that the act fails to give blacks the vote, the true source of power in a democratic society.

**June 11.** Destined to succeed his father as a powerful South African tribal chief, 26-year-old Nelson Mandela instead chose to fight apartheid. Along with Oliver Tambo and Walter Sisulu, he established the African National Congress Youth League in 1944. Eight years later, Mandela and Tambo set up the first black law firm in the country. When Mandela led a group in violating apartheid laws that year, he was banned by the government.

The ANC was outlawed in 1960, following the massacre at Sharpeville, and Mandela set up a military branch to attack such targets as power lines. A police informer exposed him in 1962, and he was sentenced to five years for incitement. Today, he receives a life sentence for sabotage and conspiracy to overthrow the government of South Africa.

At his trial, Mandela said, "I have cherished the ideal of a democratic and free society in which all persons live together in harmony with equal opportunities. It is an ideal I hope to live for and to achieve. But, if needs be, it is an ideal for which I am prepared to die." Even though he spoke in an open courtroom, the South African government forbids publication of his speech.

**June 21.** The civil rights movement has planned a Freedom Summer in Mississippi to focus national attention on state segregation laws. Volunteers from the North—university students, teachers, lawyers, and ministers—will work with local SNCC groups to register black voters and set up alternative schools, free from racial bias. State newspapers warn of "an invasion."

Preparing for the campaign, three civil rights workers drive to a burned-out Negro church.

Andrew Goodman, age 21, Michael Schwerner, age 24, and James E. Chaney, age 21, never return. The next day Attorney General Kennedy orders a full-scale FBI investigation. The burnt wreckage of theircar is discovered on the 23rd, and President Johnson orders 200 sailors to join FBI agents in the search.

Meanwhile, some 1,000 workers arrive in Mississippi from the North and, with SNCC, open 41 Freedom schools and a system of community centers to provide legal and medical advice. At night, organizers use the sites for political meetings, explaining to blacks the goals of the newly formed Mississippi Freedom Democratic party and signing up members; some 60,000 join over the summer months. But white resistance mounts, and by the end of July, segregationists have burned down 15 Negro churches and beaten up 80 workers, while authorities have arrested hundreds.

On August 4, a tip from an informant leads searchers to the bodies of the three civil rights workers, hidden in an earthen dam. Chaney, a young black, had been beaten with chains until virtually every bone in his body was broken, then he was shot three times. The other two men, both white, were shot through the heart. Although relatives of Chaney and Schwerner want them buried side by side, Mississippi law requires segregated cemeteries.

The FBI will arrest 21 white men in December for the murders, and a grand jury will later indict 18.

**July 15.** Delegates at the Republican convention nominate Barry Goldwater on the first ballot. His principal opponent, Nelson Rockefeller, politically handicapped by a recent divorce and remarriage, withdrew on June 15 following several Goldwater primary victories. Representative William E. Miller becomes the Republican candidate for vice-president.

The pro-Goldwater conservative element adopts a party platform with no limits on the Vietnam war effort, a stronger world stand against Communism, support for a prayer-in-schools amendment, and a $5-billion reduction in federal spending. Goldwater's right-wing stance, a radical departure from the moderate party candidates of the past 20–30 years, divides Republicans into two opposing camps.

**July 16.** The first of America's "long, hot summers" is set off in New York City when an off-duty white policeman kills a 15-year-old black boy who allegedly threatened him with a knife. Under the pressure of existing racial tensions, protest demonstrations quickly spread to the Yorkville section of the city, and by the 18th, rioting breaks out in Harlem.

Before the police regain control on the 21st, another black dies, over 100 people are injured, including 35 policemen; some 200 people are arrested; and over 100 businesses are damaged. Riots follow in nine other northern cities over the next few weeks.

An FBI investigation, submitted to the president in late September concludes that the summer riots were spontaneous—not "race riots" in the usual sense of the phrase—and general attacks on authority. The policeman who shot the black teenager will later be cleared by a grand jury.

**July 19.** George Wallace withdraws his independent candidacy for president. The segregationist governor of Alabama claims to have accomplished his mission of "conservatizing" both parties; he denies having made a deal with Barry Goldwater.

**July 22.** In the first legal test of the 1964 Civil Rights Act, a three-judge court in Atlanta upholds the prohibition against discrimination in public accommodations and orders restaurant owner Lester Maddox to admit blacks. (The militant segregationist will close his restaurant next month, win the Georgia governorship through a 1967 legislature vote, and in 1970, be elected lieutenant governor.)

The next day, FBI agents make the first arrests under the act—three Mississippi whites who had beaten a black man for attempting to integrate a theater in Greenwood.

**July 26.** After obtaining proof that Cuba supplied Venezuelan guerrillas last year, the OAS imposes mandatory sanctions against the Communist nation. Since Cuba was excluded from the organization in 1962, suspension of trade will likely have little effect on the Cuban economy. But the members, led by the United States, want to discourage new acts of subversion. After signing the document,

U.S. State Secretary Dean Rusk declares, "Castro has no future in Cuba or this hemisphere."

---

*Statistics*: The Cuban Refugee Center in Miami reported in May that 171,606 Cuban refugees had registered in the United States since June 1961.

---

**July 26.** In his second conviction, the court finds Jimmy Hoffa guilty of fraud and conspiracy in misappropriating $1.7 million in union funds. Hoffa took over the presidency of the Teamsters in 1957, then made the union one of the most powerful in the country by bringing all American truckers under a single Teamsters contract.

Under Senate and criminal investigation for some time, Hoffa was brought to trial in 1962 for demanding and receiving illegal payments from a firm using teamsters. That case ended in a hung jury, but he was later found guilty of attempting to bribe one of the jurors and was sentenced to eight years. After exhausting the appeal process, the former Teamsters' president will enter federal prison in 1967.

**August 4.** President Johnson announces on nationwide television that two days ago North Vietnamese PT boats launched an attack on U.S. destroyers in the international waters of the Gulf of Tonkin and, despite a strong U.S. protest to Hanoi, have attacked again today. In turn, the president has ordered a retaliatory air strike against North Vietnamese gunboat bases and an oil storage depot.

Hanoi denounces the U.S. bombing and refutes the charges. During closed hearings on the attacks, Senator Wayne Morse (D., Oregon) learns that the South Vietnamese, under the command of General Westmoreland, carried out two amphibious raids on North Vietnamese islands, on July 30 and August 3. But when Morse questions McNamara, the defense secretary denies any connection between that event and the Tonkin incident.

In fact, the president approved a bombing program in March. And, after a secret strategy confer-

ence in Honolulu last June, Robert McNamara, General Westmoreland, State Secretary Dean Rusk, and others focused on preparing a U.S. air war, obtaining congressional authorization, and readying the American people for escalation.

On August 7, an outraged Congress, eager to demonstrate national unity in the face of enemy attack, adopts a joint resolution that approves "all necessary measures by the president to repel any armed attack against U.S. forces" and sanctions "all necessary steps of the president to aid any nation covered by SEATO that requested aid in defense of its freedom." House approval is unanimous, while in the Senate only two senators refuse to vote for the escalation of the war—Senator Morse and Senator Ernest Gruening (D., Alaska). Earlier Morse said, "We're going to be bogged down in Southeast Asia for years to come if we follow this course of action and we're going to kill thousands of American boys until, finally, let me say, the American people are going to say what the French people finally said: they've had enough."

President Johnson uses the Tonkin Gulf resolution—in lieu of a congressional declaration of war—to set policy in Vietnam and begin a massive military buildup, shifting the focus of the war from the ground to the air.

**August 14.** In Biloxi, 17 Negro first-graders integrate the first public schools in Mississippi.

**August 20.** The president signs the Economic Opportunity Act, authorizing appropriations of $947.5 million for antipoverty programs, such as the Job Corps (to give young people basic education and job experience), community projects, loans to low-income farmers and businesspeople, and a domestic Peace Corps.

Johnson holds great hope for this first piece of legislation to originate solely from his administration, but the growing financial demands of the war in Vietnam will eventually cut the five-year $3.5-billion budget by almost $2 billion.

**August 25.** At the Democratic convention in Atlantic City, the mixed-race Mississippi Freedom Democratic party, created during Freedom Summer, demands recognition; the current state delegation excludes blacks. The Credentials Committee refuses to seat the Freedom party, but calls for non-discriminatory selection at the 1968 convention. Freedom delegates have forced the Democratic party to open up to black influence, yet by pushing the issue, they widen the gap between moderate and militant advocates of civil rights.

**August 26.** The Democratic Convention nominates Lyndon Baines Johnson as its presidential candidate. Johnson chooses Senator Hubert Humphrey from Minnesota as his running mate.

Robert Kennedy, appearing at the convention to introduce a memorial film of his brother, John F. Kennedy, receives a 16-minute ovation. Johnson has refused to give Bobby the vice-presidency, but the younger Kennedy loyally tells delegates not to look to the past but to give that same dedication to this year's ticket.

**August 31.** President Johnson signs the Food Stamp Act to expand the pilot food stamp program established by President Kennedy in 1961 into a permanent federal-state program.

**September 16.** In ceremonies at the U.S.-Canada border between Washington State and British Columbia, President Johnson and Prime Minister Pearson sign a treaty for the joint development of the Columbia River basin. But many Canadians will become unhappy when the dams cause environmental damage and the irrigation and hydroelectric power mainly benefit the United States.

**September 27.** Three months late, the Warren Commission issues its report on the assassination of John F. Kennedy. The seven members unanimously conclude that Lee Harvey Oswald—his motives unclear—acted alone, that neither Oswald nor Ruby was "part of any conspiracy, domestic or foreign," and that no evidence exists of any "direct or indirect relationship between Oswald or Ruby." The report also dispenses with various myths surrounding the killing, including the claim that shots came from somewhere other than the book depository.

The report criticizes the Secret Service and the FBI for inadequate presidential protection and recommends thorough improvements. The commission also censures members of the Dallas police department and the press for creating a climate that would have made it difficult to conduct a fair trial for Oswald and that made his murder possible.

The commission, with the assistance of a 27-member staff, examined all investigations conducted by the FBI and other federal, state, and local agencies (the FBI alone conducted 25,000 interviews producing over 25,000 pages of documentation), as well as the testimony of 552 witnesses. The final report is 888 pages, but an additional 20 volumes, about 500 pages each, remain for possible publication at a later date.

The American people greet the Warren Commission Report with some skepticism. Numerous books will dispute the findings, claiming a conspiracy did exist, or at the very least, an effort was made to cover up the facts.

**October 11.** The current economic prosperity in the United States boosts Lyndon Johnson's campaign, but Barry Goldwater's extremism, particularly in foreign policy, gives the president his greatest advantage.

Many Americans strongly oppose Goldwater. A number of daily newspapers that have consistently supported the Republican party in the past endorse Johnson's candidacy. Martin Luther King, Jr., speaking in Brooklyn today, breaks his rule of not taking sides and urges all registered blacks to vote against the senator. King describes Goldwaterism as "destructive of all the values on which the United States was founded and which this country has always defended."

Compared to Goldwater's rhetoric, the president appears a moderate (despite a social reform program many consider radical) and a peace candidate (despite the recent escalation in Vietnam). After all, Johnson promises in an October 21 campaign speech, "We are not going to send American boys nine or ten thousand miles away from home to do what Asian boys ought to be doing for themselves."

As the election draws near, the question is not whether Johnson will win, but by how much.

**October 14–15.** The Soviets stun the world with the announcement that Nikita Khrushchev, first secretary of the Communist party, has been replaced by 57-year-old Leonid Brezhnev. The next day, Khrushchev loses his position as chairman of the USSR Council of Ministers (equivalent to premier) to 60-year-old Aleksei Kosygin. Moscow merely comments that the USSR has returned to "collective rule" and will pursue its goals with greater stability than was possible under one, often emotional, leader.

During his seven years as first secretary and premier, the pragmatic Khrushchev moved his nation away from the dictatorial limits of Stalinism. His reforms and successes met criticism and resistance from party hard-liners, but it was his alienation of Communist China and the failure of his foreign and agricultural policies that brought about his downfall.

**October 15.** The 13-year rule of the British Labour party ends as the Conservatives win a narrow majority in Parliament. Harold Wilson, at 48 years old, becomes the youngest prime minister of Britain in this century.

**October 16.** China explodes its first atomic bomb and becomes the fifth nuclear power. Peking claims that the test was necessary to break the U.S.-USSR nuclear monopoly and to open the way for genuine nuclear disarmament.

**November 3.** Lyndon Baines Johnson wins the presidential election with the largest popular vote in U.S. history—43 million votes to 27 million for the Republicans. The Johnson ticket takes 44 states and the District of Columbia, with 486 electoral votes, while Goldwater wins his own state, Arizona, and five deep South states, with a total of 52 electoral votes.

Political analysts conjecture that the uncompromising stand of the Goldwater platform alienated too many GOP voters. As well, the predicted white "backlash" to civil rights achievements proved significant only in the South, while some 90 percent of the black vote went to the Democrats, providing the margin of victory in some states.

The Democrats retain control of Congress, adding 38 seats to their majority in the House (295–140) and 2 in the Senate (68–32). A number of conservative candidates are dragged down with Goldwater, ending the Conservative coalition, which has plagued incumbents since 1938, and giving the president a solid majority for his social programs.

**November 4.** From mid-1962 to January of this year, the Boston Strangler sexually assaulted and murdered 13 women in their homes. With the city reduced to near panic, the police are no nearer a solution when Albert DeSalvo is arrested.

Once in custody, DeSalvo confesses to hundreds of assaults and, later at a mental institution, fully describes events and demonstrates the bow used by the killer to tie off his strangulation weapon. But other than his confession, the police have no substantiating evidence—the Strangler never left a fingerprint.

Since DeSalvo's lawyer would forbid him to repeat his confession in court, authorities must settle for convictions on crimes predating the serial killings. DeSalvo, described by some as a modern-day Jack the Ripper, is never tried as the Boston Strangler. He will be sentenced to prison in 1967 and will die at the hands of a fellow inmate in 1973.

**December 1.** Since the Johnson administration has already carried out covert operations and retaliatory bombings against North Vietnam, it has little latitude in increasing the U.S. commitment to South Vietnam. The intelligence community maintains that bombing will have little effect on a country with a largely agricultural and decentralized economy, but today the president secretly approves reprisal air strikes against North Vietnam, the resumption of destroyer patrols in the gulf, and increased air strikes against Communist infiltration routes and facilities in the Laotian panhandle. (The NSC advises that no public statements be released unless a plane is lost and advise then to "insist that we were merely escorting reconnaisance flights.")

By the end of the month, pilots fly 77 sorties over the panhandle. But the bombing of North Vietnam is delayed when Marshall Ky announces the overthrow of the South Vietnamese High National Council. With yet another coup in Saigon, Washington begins to perceive South Vietnam less as a partner and more as a base for American operations.

**December 3.** In September, students at the University of California organized a Free Speech Movement to challenge a ban on campus political rallies. With administrators threatening to expel leader Mario Savio, students conduct a sit-down protest in Sproul Hall on the Berkeley campus. Police, acting on orders from Governor Edmund G. "Pat" Brown, arrest 796 demonstrators in the largest mass arrest in American history. This attempt to suppress campus protest marks the beginning of U.S. student activism.

**December 10.** Martin Luther King, Jr., receives the Nobel peace prize for his leadership in the American civil rights movement and his advocacy of nonviolence. King, at age 35 the youngest person to receive the Nobel, donates the $53,000 to the movement.

## Obituaries

**Nancy Astor** (May 19, 1879–May 2, 1964). The first woman to sit in the British House of Commons (1919–1945), the American-born socialite used her wit and intelligence to support the rights of British women and children.

**Harold H. Burton** (June 22, 1888–October 28, 1964). The Supreme Court justice served from 1945 to 1958. Although he wrote the forerunner of the historic Brown decision, outlawing segregation on railroad dining cars, Burton generally advocated judicial restraint, voting to uphold the Taft-Hartley non-Communist oath and the government's right to dismiss employees suspected of disloyalty.

**Herbert Hoover** (August 10, 1874–October 20, 1964). After heading Allied relief efforts during W.W.I, the wealthy businessman served as secretary of commerce through the 1920s, under Warren Harding and Calvin Coolidge. In 1928, Hoover secured the Democratic presidential nomination and, in his first try for public office, won by a landslide.

Just eight months later, the stock market crashed and the president received much of the blame for permitting wild stock speculation while at Commerce. With the Great Depression firmly entrenched by 1932, Franklin Delano Roosevelt easily defeated him at the Democratic convention.

Hoover retired to private life, but returned to relief work at the end of W.W.II. In 1947, he accepted Truman's request to address the structure of the executive branch. His two commissions (a second sat 1953–1955) strongly influenced the reorganization of the American government. (*See* 1949 News)

During his lifetime, Hoover wrote 30 books and received two congressional resolutions of appreciation, as well as countless awards and honors from around the world. Upon his death, President Johnson declares a 30-day period of national mourning.

**Henry Larsen** (September 30, 1899–October 29, 1964). The Royal Canadian Mounted Police officer skippered the *St. Roch*—a wooden sailing ship with an auxiliary engine—on the first successful journey through the Northwest Passage (1940–1942), a return voyage (1944), and the first circumnavigation of North America (1950). He retired from the RCMP in 1961.

**Douglas MacArthur** (January 26, 1880–April 5, 1964). In the spring of 1942, when the Japanese pushed the Americans back to Corregidor, President Roosevelt ordered the general to leave his men and escape to Australia. MacArthur launched the Pacific counteroffensive in late 1942 and won back the Philippines in 1945. As general of the U.S. Army, he received the Japanese surrender at war's end. As supreme commander of occupation forces, he introduced democratic reforms in Japan and oversaw economic reconstruction.

Ordered from Japan to Korea in 1950, to take charge of U.N. forces, the general urged the White House to broaden the war into China. When he continued to air his views in public, Truman fired him. The old soldier retired. (*See* 1951 News) In 1962, Congress presented MacArthur with a resolution of appreciation for his devotion to duty.

**Jawaharlal Nehru** (November 14, 1889–May 27, 1964). *See* News.

**Paul I** (December 14, 1901–March 6, 1964). The grandson of the founder of the Greek monarchy,

Paul was a popular king during his 17-year reign. His 23-year-old son Constantine succeeds him.

**Alvin York** (December 13, 1887–September 2, 1964). During W.W.I, the one-time conscientious objector attacked a German machine-gun battalion and, using his sharp-shooting skills and ingenuity, killed 25 men and single-handedly captured 132. When asked to describe his actions, Sergeant York replied, "I surrounded 'em."

Awarded the Congressional Medal of Honor and some 50 other decorations, the American hero refused to capitalize on the public's adulation and returned to farming. In 1940, York gave Hollywood permission to film his story; Gary Cooper played the part.

# BEGINNINGS AND ENDINGS

## News

**January 6.** With a visit to Israel and Jordan, Pope Paul VI becomes the first pontiff to ride in an airplane and to travel to the Holy Land.

**January 13.** The Supreme Court invalidates a Louisiana law requiring that a candidate's race be listed on election ballots.

**February 1.** To cut processing time, the U.S. Post Office deletes the time of day from postmarks, but retains the A.M./P.M. designation.

**April 1.** To ease bureaucratic record keeping, Ottawa issues social insurance numbers to every employed Canadian. The nine-digit SIN card quickly turns into the primary means of identification.

**April 17.** Jerrie Mock, a 38-year-old aviator from Columbus, Ohio, is the first woman to fly solo around the world, taking 29 days in a Cessna-180.

**April 22.** President Johnson opens the New York World's Fair in Flushing Meadows. Attendance remains well below the predicted 70 million and the exhibition closes early, on October 17, 1965. Investors lose 61 cents on the dollar and blame high prices, lack of interesting displays, and fears of racial violence.

**May 29.** In an attempt at reconciliation, various groups at the Palestine National Congress establish the Palestine Liberation Organization (PLO).

**July 1.** California supplants New York as the most populous state—18,293,000 to 18,029,000 (revised figures).

**July 28.** Sir Winston Churchill retires 64 years after his first session in Parliament (sitting for all but 3 years). Members extend a rare official motion of gratitude for his services to Parliament, the nation, and the world.

**August 24.** At the opening of the 25th annual Liturgical Week in St. Louis, Rev. Frederick Richard McManus conducts the first mass in English in the United States. (Pope Paul authorized the use of the vernacular on December 4, 1963.) Catholic churches across the country convert to English on November 29.

**November 3.** The people of Hawaii elect Japanese-American Patsy Mink, the first woman from a racial or ethnic minority to sit in the House.

**November 12.** After 45 years on the throne, 68-year-old Grand Duchess Charlotte of Luxembourg abdicates in favor of her 43-year-old son. Prince Jean becomes grand duke.

**December 5.** Army Captain Roger H. C. Donlon, wounded four times in South Vietnam last July, receives the Congressional Medal of Honor for "conspicuous gallantry" during battle. He is the first soldier to receive the nation's highest military honor since the Korean War.

**December 15.** Earlier this year, Prime Minister Pearson proposed replacing the British Union Jack with a flag symbolizing a new Canada. Traditionalists, bitterly opposed, have dragged out the debate through more than 300 speeches. Yesterday, the government invoked closure, and this morning, at 2:13 A.M., discussion ends. By a vote of 163–78, Parliament adopts a design preselected from 2,000 submissions—a red maple leaf on a white background with vertical red bars at both ends. The new flag, first raised on Parliament Hill in February, will gradually replace the Union Jack, which will be raised only to honor the Queen or a Commonwealth occasion.

**More news.** The U.S. Mint issues a Kennedy

half-dollar to replace the Franklin coin, in use since 1948. But Americans put the new 50-cent piece away in remembrance of their late president, and few remain in circulation.

• Progressive educators institute noncompetitive pass/fail grading in some public schools this year. Through the latter half of the decade, the marking system will spread under the impact of the protest movement and Selective Service emphasis on academic standing. Only when the war winds down, in the 1970s, will most institutions return to traditional assessment.

## New Products and Businesses

Kellogg introduces Pop Tarts.

Pepsi-Cola debuts low-cal Diet Pepsi. (This year, Coca-Cola brings out the industry's first lift-top cans and crowns for bottles.)

General Foods announces the development of a freeze-dried instant coffee—Maxim.

Colonel Sanders, age 74, sells Kentucky Fried Chicken for $2 million and a lifetime endorsement salary of $40,000 per annum.

Forrest and Leroy Raffel open a restaurant in

*The brainchild of Lee Iacocca, the Ford Mustang attracts enormous media attention at a World's Fair unveiling in April. Americans subsequently buy a record 1 million in the first 12 months.*

Boardman, Ohio. As the business prospers, the two pick "Big Tex" for a chain, but the Akron restaurant with that name refuses to cooperate. The Raffel brothers (R.B.) opt for Arby's.

Statistics: Paralleling the meteoric growth in snack and convenience food sales over the past 10 years (79 percent for soft drinks), the percentage of American families reporting a deficiency in at least one major food group rose from 40 percent to 50 percent.

First-year sales for the 11½-inch G.I. Joe doll and his equipment reach an estimated $10 million.

## Memorable Ad Campaigns

The Esso cartoon tiger (launched regionally in 1959) urges drivers to "Put a Tiger in Your Tank." The campaign sets off a small fad with tiger caps, badges, stickers, and toys, while comedians and cartoonists play off the fierce big cat.

Pepsi tells young Americans, "Come Alive—You're in the Pepsi Generation." The German version produces slightly different advice—"Come Alive Out of the Grave"—as does the Chinese—"Pepsi Brings Your Ancestors Back from the Dead."

## Fads

In Britain, the Mods and Rockers have co-existed for about a year. But this spring the stylish Moderns scooter into resort areas to do battle with the leather-jacketed bikers. The *London Daily Telegraph*, in a pun on "spare the rod and spoil the child," declares, "With more rods there would be fewer mockers," but the fad continues throughout 1964.

Developed years ago for dry-land surfing practice, skateboards soar in popularity with their new ability to change direction. Prices range from $1.98 to $50 for a motorized one. Sales will die down in 1966, then take off again in 1973 with the appearance of urethane wheels.

# SCIENCE AND TECHNOLOGY

## News

**January 24.** A surgical team at the University of Mississippi performs the first human heart transplant, but the operation fails. The next day, the medical center reveals that the donor heart came from a chimpanzee.

**January 25.** The United States sends up the passive communications satellite *Echo 2*. Large enough to be seen from Earth with the naked eye, the 135-foot plastic and aluminum foil balloon broadcasts a radio signal on February 21 that the Soviets pick up near Gorki. The transmission marks the first joint U.S.-British-Soviet space venture.

**January 29.** Americans watch on TV as the first complete, fully fueled *Saturn 1* blasts off into space. In May and September launches, the experimental rocket will take dummy Apollo capsules into orbit.

Six years ago, the first American satellite weighed 31 pounds; the second stage of the Saturn weighs 37,700 pounds.

**April 3.** Dr. Louis Leakey announces the discovery of *Homo habilis*, individuals who inhabited the sub-Sahara near the end of the Pliocene, 1.8–1 million years ago. This earliest member of the *Homo* genus stood 3½–4½ feet tall, walked erect, showed an increased brain volume, possessed a well-opposed thumb, and made tools.

Other anthropologists and paleontologists question the validity of Leakey's evidence, but later specimens found at Lake Turkana will date to 2 million years.

**April 8.** In a significant step toward manned space flight, NASA places a Gemini capsule in orbit above the Earth. The two-man craft—heavier and 50 percent roomier—replaces the simple man-

ual override in the Mercury capsules with 16 thrusters of varying power. Eventually, Gemini astronauts will remain in space for up to two weeks, rendezvous and dock, and refine capsule reentries and landings.

**April 16.** Heart specialist Walter Gamble reports the first known film taken from inside the organ. Optical glass fibers, passed through an artery, captured a dog's aortic valve opening and closing.

**April 24.** Bell inaugurates the Picturephone with a conversation between Lady Bird Johnson, in Washington, and Dr. Elizabeth A. Wood, at the New York labs. General service begins the next day, but at $16 for three minutes, usage remains limited. In the years ahead, technical variations will appear, but none will catch on.

**May.** Dr. Muriel Roger at the Rockefeller Institute announces that she has successfully transplanted a single gene. The receiving cell subsequently displayed the specific hereditary trait.

**May 1.** At Dartmouth College, John Kemeny and Thomas Kurtz finish an easy programming language to maximize costly time-sharing. After their first run at 4:00 A.M., the mathematics professors put BASIC (Beginner's All-purpose Symbolic Instruction Code) into the public domain.

**June 19.** President Johnson and Premier Hayato Ikeda inaugurate the first undersea cable connection between the United States and Japan.

---

*Statistics*: This year, for the first time, the number of phones in the rest of the world equals the estimated 89 million in the United States. Experts anticipate that the current 43 phones per 100 people will swell to 150 per 100 people by the end of the century.

---

**July 21–30.** Sealab, the first human habitat tested by the Naval Deep Submergence Systems Project, lies 192 feet down, on the ocean floor off the coast of Bermuda. The underwater research station houses four men, and to facilitate movement to the outside, it maintains a constant 86-pound pressure. (The men need 2 of their 10 days to adjust to a slower pace and their high-pitched voices—a result of an 80-percent helium atmosphere.)

**July 31.** After a dismal beginning, the Ranger program finally produces some hard data. Today, as the craft hurtles toward the moon, *Ranger 7* transmits some 4,300 photos. Next March, *Rangers 8* and 9 take another 13,000 pictures. But, while their resolution is 2,000 times better than telescope photos, U.S. scientists will remain unconvinced that the lunar surface can support a landing vehicle.

**August.** Psychiatrist Marie Nyswander and researcher Vincent Dole report, in the AMA journal, that the synthetic opiate methadone successfully detoxified 22 heroin addicts. Use will become widespread, despite methadone's addictive properties.

**October 7.** In a presentation to the American Public Health Association, Dr. Seymour Rinzler reports that middle-age men who replaced the animal fats and dairy products in their diets with vegetable oils and fish suffered a significantly lower incidence of heart disease.

**October 12.** *Voskhod 1*—the first spacecraft to carry more than one person—takes three Soviets through 16 orbits before returning safely to Earth. The cosmonaut, scientist, and physician all wore gray sport suits and helmets rather than the usual spacesuits.

**November 2.** *The New York Times* reports the introduction of home dialysis for kidney patients. Although the blood-cleansing machine was invented some 20 years ago, a lack of funds and dialysis time at U.S. hospitals has resulted in an estimated 2,000 deaths per year.

**November 27.** At the United Nations, the Scientific Committee on Radiation notes a 33-percent drop in nuclear fallout worldwide. Members attribute the continuing decrease to the nuclear test ban.

**More news.** Plastic surgeons introduce silicone gel sacs for breast implants.

• Heart-lung machines substitute sugar-water solutions for blood, allowing surgeons to proceed without a large number of donors.

• J. M. O'Lane, at the Naval Hospital in San Diego, reports a higher incidence of natural abortions and premature deliveries among women who smoke.

## Other Discoveries, Developments, and Inventions

World's first nuclear-powered lighthouse, on Chesapeake Bay in Maryland

Electric knife, from GE for $27.95

Fully automatic car air-conditioning system, Cadillac's "Climate Control"

Photochromic lenses, from Corning Glass, that darken in the sun

Bullet train in Japan, designed to average 100 mph

## Obituaries

**Armand Bombardier** (April 16, 1907–February 19, 1964). Using skis to steer a tracked drive, the Canadian inventor manufactured the first snowmobile in 1937. His company also produces the Ski-Doo.

**Rachel Carson** (May 27, 1907–April 14, 1964). The American biologist alerted the nation to the dangers of pesticides in 1962 with her controversial book *Silent Spring.*

**A(lphonse) Raymond Dochez** (April 21, 1882–June 30, 1964). The American physician discovered a serum for scarlet fever.

**Gerhard Domagk** (October 30, 1895–April 24, 1964). The German pathologist and bacteriologist developed the first of the sulfa drugs in 1935. His work earned him a Nobel prize four years later.

**J(ohn) B(urdon) S(anderson) Haldane** (November 5, 1892–December 1, 1964). Along with a simple treatment for tetanus, the British geneticist contributed to the mathematical analysis of evolution and population genetics.

**Victor Francis Hess** (June 24, 1883–December 17, 1964). His discovery, at first named in his honor, was renamed "cosmic rays" in 1925. The naturalized American physicist received the Nobel prize in 1936 for his work.

**Leo Szilard** (February 11, 1898–May 30, 1964). Born in Budapest, the nuclear physicist joined the U.S. Advisory Committee on Uranium in 1939. At the University of Chicago, on December 2, 1942, he and Fermi produced the first atomic chain reaction. Szilard then spent the remainder of his life campaigning against the use of atomic weapons.

**Henry W. Walden** (1884–September 13, 1964). The inventor built and flew the first American monoplane in 1909 and patented the Times Square electric news sign in 1917.

**Norbert Wiener** (November 26, 1894–March 18, 1964). For his widely read book *Cybernetics* (1948), the mathematician was dubbed "the father of automation."

## THE ARTS

January 16—*Hello Dolly!*, with Carol Channing, David Burns, Charles Nelson Reilly (2,844 perfs.)

February 18—*Any Wednesday*, with Don Porter, Sandy Dennis, Gene Hackman, Rosemary Murphy (982 perfs.)

March 26—*Funny Girl*, with Barbra Streisand, Sydney Chaplin, Kay Medford (1,348 perfs.)

May 25—*The Subject Was Roses*, with Martin Sheen, Jack Albertson, Irene Dailey (832 perfs.)

September 22—*Fiddler on the Roof*, with Zero Mostel, Maria Karnilova, Joanna Merlin, Julia Migenes, Tanya Everett (3,242 perfs.)

October 20—*Golden Boy*, with Sammy Davis, Jr. (568 perfs.)

November 11—*Luv*, with Alan Arkin, Eli Wallach, Anne Jackson (901 perfs.)

### Tony Awards

Actor (Dramatic)—Alec Guinness, *Dylan*

Actress (Dramatic)—Sandy Dennis, *Any Wednesday*

Actor (Musical)—Bert Lahr, *Foxy*

Actress (Musical)—Carol Channing, *Hello, Dolly!*

Play—*Luther*

Musical—*Hello, Dolly!*

## News

**January 19.** Since 1941, the cost of a Broadway production has risen from $20,000 to $100,000–$150,000. Yet, over the same period, ticket prices have increased just over 50 percent, from $3.30 to $6.90.

**April 19.** The Vatican pavilion at the New York World's Fair unveils St. Peter's *Pietà*, and Michelangelo's magnificent marble sculpture.

**April 23.** At Stratford-upon-Avon, Prince Philip officially opens the 400th anniversary celebration of William Shakespeare's birth. A message from Queen Elizabeth notes that in his day the Bard was frowned upon by many. "But not by the ordinary working folk, nor by the great men of the time, and never by my predecessor, Queen Elizabeth I."

**April 24.** During the year, Americans honor Shakespeare with over 400 productions. Tonight, in one of the first, the New York City Ballet premieres *A Midsummer Night's Dream* to launch the new State Theater at Lincoln Center.

**November 6.** The Department of the Interior designates Carnegie Hall a National Historic Landmark to protect the concert hall from demolition.

---

*Statistics:* From 1900 to 1939, the number of U.S. symphonies mushroomed from 10 to 600. This year, the figure reaches 1,200—more than half the 2,000 symphonies in the world.

---

**More news.** The Episcopal Cathedral Church of St. Peter and St. Paul (commonly known as the Washington Cathedral) adds a 301-foot gothic spire.

### Obituaries

**Cedric Hardwicke** (February 19, 1893–August 6, 1964). The British star of London and Broadway stage received a knighthood in 1934. His appearances on screen were in supporting roles.

**Albert Hay Malotte** (May 19, 1895–November

16, 1964). The American composer set "The Lord's Prayer" to music.

**Sean O'Casey** (March 30, 1880–September 18, 1964). A giant of the modern theater, the playwright was best known for works set in the Irish Troubles of 1916–1923. In the late 1920s, controversy forced the Abbey Theatre to refuse his most recent work; O'Casey left Ireland and never returned.

# WORDS

Saul Bellow, *Herzog*
Thomas Berger, *Little Big Man*
Eric Berne, *Games People Play*
Ian Fleming, *You Only Live Twice*
Joanne Greenberg, *I Never Promised You a Rose Garden*
Ernest Hemingway, *A Moveable Feast*
Bel Kaufman, *Up the Down Staircase*
Timothy Leary, *The Psychedelic Experience*
Martin Luther King, Jr., *Why We Can't Wait*
Marshall McLuhan, *Understanding Media*
Irving Wallace, *The Man*

## News

**March 9.** In the landmark *New York Times Co. v. Sullivan* decision, the U.S. Supreme Court rules that a public official can recover libel damages only by proving deliberate malice. The suit in question involved a Montgomery city commissioner and a *New York Times* reference to the "official" terrorizing of young black demonstrators.

**May 23.** The *Los Angeles Free Press* (later called the "Freep") is founded, sparking a wave of underground newspapers.

**June 22.** The Supreme Court, finding *Tropic of Cancer* not legally obscene, narrowly reverses a Florida ban against the sale of Henry Miller's autobiographical novel.

**September 27.** Released today, the Warren Commission Report appears as a Bantam paperback within 80 hours. All published versions enjoy excellent sales.

**December 10.** Jean Paul Sartre wins the Nobel prize for literature. Concerned that the award will transform him into "an institution," the French dramatist and philosopher becomes the first laureate to turn down the honor of his own free will.

---

*Statistics*: A worldwide count of daily newspapers places the United States first with 1,758, and Germany a distant second with 473.

---

**More news.** In an attempt to avert dog-ears, Avon experiments with rounded corners on its paperbacks.

• William Golding's *Lord of the Flies* tops all softbound sales.

## Cartoons and Comics

**March.** Created in 1941, superpatriotic Captain America failed to make the transition to a postwar world. This month, *Avengers* No. 4 revives the superhero after his 15 years trapped on an iceberg. Captain America will receive his own title in April 1968.

**More news.** Johnny Hart and Brant Parker create the comic strip *The Wizard of Id.*

## TIME **Man of the Year**

Lyndon Baines Johnson

## New Words and Phrases

Appalachia
aquaplaning
au pair girl
balloon bread (a 1-pound loaf inflated to look like 1½ pounds)
Good Samaritan law (legal protection for medical personnel who treat people in on-the-scene emergencies)
isometrics

kinetic sculpture
metrona (a young grandmother)
nuke (a nuclear weapon)
WASP (White Anglo-Saxon Protestant)
white backlash (white resentment and hostility toward presumably overzealous civil rights advocates)

## Obituaries

**Brendan Behan** (February 9, 1923–March 20, 1964). Imprisoned several times for revolutionary activities, the Irish writer related his experiences in books and plays.

**Phil Davis** (March 4, 1906–December 16, 1964). After 30 years of syndication, his comic strip, *Mandrake the Magician*, appears in 253 newspapers at the time of his death.

**Ian Fleming** (May 28, 1908–August 12, 1964). The British novelist drew on his W.W.II training in naval intelligence to create superspy James Bond. (Fleming drew 007's name from his personal collection of books—*Birds of the West Indies* by James Bond.) His 10 tongue-in-cheek novels have thus far sold 18 million copies and 3 have transferred successfully to the motion picture screen.

**Grace Metalious** (September 8, 1924–February 25, 1964). The American writer catapulted to fame in 1956 with her novel *Peyton Place*. She died of chronic liver disease.

**Edward John (Ned) Pratt** (February 4, 1882–April 26, 1964). Canada's leading poet in the first half of the century wrote of maritime life in his native Newfoundland.

**Edith Sitwell** (September 7, 1887–December 9, 1964). One of the finest English poets of the 20th century, Dame Sitwell justified her eccentricity as "the ordinary carried to a high degree of pictorial perfection."

**T(erence) H(ansbury) White** (May 29, 1906–January 17, 1964). The British novelist's King Arthur novels were combined and condensed as *The Once and Future King* (1958), the basis for the Broadway musical *Camelot*.

# FASHION

## Haute Couture

Under the growing influence of youth, fashion collections present a high-busted, leggier silhouette and straight unfitted back.

## News

**June.** In an amusing look at the styles of tomorrow, California designer Rudi Gernreich offers the monokini—wool-knit shorts held up by a narrow halter strap. Stores stock the topless swimsuit, but most refuse to display or promote it. Even though women can never wear the suit in public, 3,000 sales make the monokini the fashion story of the year. (An astounded Gernreich remembers how, just 10 years ago, he was criticized for omitting an inner bra in a wool-knit one-piece.)

**More news.** The International Wool Secretariat, based in London, commissions Francesco Seraglio to create a logo. The Woolmark establishes the natural fiber as a quality fabric.

• Levi Strauss introduces the first wash-and-wear pants under the Sta-Prest label. In a unique demonstration, sales reps pull off their sample slacks, throw them in the washer and dryer, then put them right back on.

## Colors and Materials

With the emphasis on slim, graceful lines, bulky fabrics give way to thinner, more porous textures.

Couturiers spotlight pink, white, and browns. The industry uses pale tones and pastels for city and country wear.

## Clothes

For the first time in years, observers note the widespread use of trim and decorative touches. The monokini propels the trend toward nudity— transparent blouses, bare evening dresses with fullness at the hem for steamy discothèques. Others are made of sheer lace over "nude" chiffon; necklines plunge open to the navel and the tip of the spine.

To match the bare look, lingerie companies enter a period of drastic revision. In October, Warner's introduces the brief nylon Body Stocking, to veil rather than control.

The short, tight toreadors yield to narrow pipestem slacks while Chanel and Norell reintroduce tailored trousers. For the first time, some styles replace the side zipper with a zip fly.

Injecting touches of Asia and Africa, collections adapt the sari, Persian tunic, and North African burnoose.

Hosiery mills turn out colored and textured stockings for the new legginess.

The sporty look dominates menswear with slip-on shoes and a turtleneck bib tucked inside a V-neck sweater. Some young men, emulating their idols the Beatles, wear stovepipe pants and suit jackets buttoned to the neck.

## Accessories

During Lyndon Johnson's first full year as president, his Texas 10-gallon hat becomes the new status symbol in the Eastern United States. Prices range from $17.50 to $250 for a mink-trimmed model.

Women carry the popular shoulder bag high under the arm.

Mail-order boot styles lengthen to just below the calf.

## Hair and Cosmetics

Most teenage girls opt for long, straight hair while some boys copy the Prince Valiant haircut worn by the Beatles.

With mascara lengtheners and false eyelashes (up to $80 for a pair of mink, seal, sable, or human hair), facial interest focuses on the eye. (A *Seventeen* survey reports 90 percent of teenage girls use mascara, compared with 20 percent in 1948.)

Cosmetic firms emphasize a fragile, young look with "barely there" lipsticks. Some lines sell in flavors of cherry, orange, caramel, or peppermint.

New face masks form a transparent film that peels off.

Capitalizing on Jade East sales, some 40 new colognes appear on the market, including Brut from Fabergé and Aramis from Estée Lauder. Over the next four years, most department stores will set up specialty counters for men's toiletries.

# MUSIC

"I Want to Hold Your Hand"—Beatles
"Can't Buy Me Love"—Beatles
"There! I've Said It Again"—Bobby Vinton
"Baby Love"—Supremes
"Oh, Pretty Woman"—Roy Orbison
"I Feel Fine"—Beatles
"Chapel of Love"—Dixie Cups
"House of the Rising Sun"—Animals
"She Loves You"—Beatles
"Where Did Our Love Go"—Supremes
"My Guy"—Mary Wells
"I Get Around"—Beach Boys
"Come See About Me"—Supremes
"A Hard Day's Night"—Beatles
"Do Wah Diddy Diddy"—Manfred Mann
"Rag Doll"—Four Seasons
"Hello, Dolly!"—Louis Armstrong
"Mr. Lonely"—Bobby Vinton
"Everybody Loves Somebody"—Dean Martin
"Love Me Do"—Beatles
"A World Without Love"—Peter & Gordon
"Leader of the Pack"—Shangri-Las
"Ringo"—Lorne Greene
"Twist and Shout"—Beatles
"You Don't Own Me"—Lesley Gore
"Dancing in the Street"—Martha & the Vandellas
"Memphis"—Johnny Rivers

"Last Kiss"—J. Frank Wilson & the Cavaliers
"She's Not There"—Zombies
"Do You Want to Know a Secret"—Beatles

## Grammys (1964)

Record of the Year—Stan Getz and Astrud Gilberto, "The Girl from Ipanema"
Song of the Year (songwriter)—Jerry Herman, "Hello, Dolly!"
Album of the Year—Stan Getz and Joao Gilberto, *Getz/Gilberto*
Best Vocal Performance (Male)—Louis Armstrong, "Hello, Dolly!" (single)
Best Vocal Performance (Female)—Barbra Streisand, "People" (single)
Best New Artist—Beatles

## News

**February 7–21.** The Beatles arrive in New York for their U.S. tour. The 3,000–5,000 screaming girls waiting at JFK Airport stun everyone including the young rockers. Their first concert, in Washington on the 11th, draws 7,000.

Previously uninterested in the British phenomenon, Capitol Records finally released a Beatles single in late 1963, "I Want to Hold Your Hand." Its overnight success made the company sit up and take notice. And now "Can't Buy Me Love" has collected 2.1 million orders, an all-time high for a single.

**April 4.** Already big business, with four American labels manufacturing their records, the Beatles hold an unprecedented five spots on *Billboard's* top 40 with "Can't Buy Me Love," "Twist and Shout," "She Loves You," "I Want to Hold Your Hand," and "Please Please Me."

**April 8.** Friends Diana Ross, Mary Wilson, and Florence Ballard twice formed a quartet, but the other girls left to get married. As the Primettes, the trio cut three numbers for Motown before their first single, "I Want a Guy," appeared at the end of 1960. (Berry Gordy insisted on a name change and Florence Ballard, the only one in the office at the time, horrified Diana and Mary by choosing the Supremes.) Their song failed to break the top 100 as did the follow-up "Buttered Popcorn." Four songs later, their best showing has been a No. 75 position.

Early this year, the Marvelettes reject a tune written for them by house composers. Against their wishes, the unsuccessful Supremes today record "Where Did Our Love Go." Touring with Dick Clark's Caravan of Stars at the time of its release, the 20-year-olds sing their number to increasingly enthusiastic audiences. By the end of the summer, the Supremes headline the Caravan and their song reaches No. 1.

**August 18.** The Beatles land in San Francisco in the first stop on this year's second North American tour. Their 24 appearances wind up with a charity concert on September 20 at the Paramount Theater in Brooklyn. (Jackie DeShannon and the Righteous Brothers back up the tour.) Reportedly, Bob Dylan meets the Beatles in New York and introduces them to marijuana. His most recent album, *Another Side of Bob Dylan*, leaves protest songs behind for more personal lyrics.

**December 23.** Beach Boy Brian Wilson suffers a nervous breakdown during a plane flight to Houston. Glen Campbell fills in for six months until illness forces him to drop out. Brian Johnston then steps in as a recovering Wilson turns his attention to the production end.

**More news.** From 1955 to 1963, just five non-Americans reached No. 1 on the pop charts. That number doubles in the first six months of this year. The Animals and Peter & Gordon score hits and the Rolling Stones, the Dave Clark Five, Gerry & the Pacemakers, Chad & Jeremy, and the Searchers place in the top 10.

These multiple-label issues revitalize the 45-rpm industry, but the British invasion spells the end for many American careers. The groups from across the Atlantic shift the beat and singers such as Pat Boone, Chubby Checker, and Connie Francis, and groups such as the Shirelles never again break the top 20. Elvis, the one singer who might have challenged the British dominance, continues to cut a succession of weak movie numbers and will remain out of the top 10 until 1969.

• With a degree in electronic engineering and a Ph.D. in engineering physics, Robert A. Moog adapts features of three devices to make the first commercial music synthesizer. His voltage-controlled modules produce a variety of sounds, including animal noises, sound effects, and virtually any musical instrument. Moog developed his machine for experimental composers, but Walter Carlos's album *Switched on Bach*, in 1968, will attract attention, particularly from rock groups.

• The Four Tops, after seven years of flops with a series of labels, sign with Motown. Their contemporary soul sound in "Baby I Need Your Loving," reaches No. 11. Up until 1972, the group will make some 30 appearances on the charts, then switches to the ABC/Dunhill label. Unlike most groups in the business, the Four Tops will remain together.

• Discothèques spread from London to New York, then westward, offering the older generation the Watusi, the Swim, the Frug, and the Hully Gully. Young people also try the Jerk.

• The Animals, with their No. 1 hit "House of the Rising Sun," electrify folk music to create folk-rock. The group will split in 1966.

• Prior to 1964, Elvis and Ricky Nelson were the only rock 'n' roll artists to reach No. 1 on the LP chart. But after the Beatles hold that position for three weeks this year, most No. 1 albums will be rock.

• The first show tune to top the popular music charts in nearly a decade, Louis Armstrong's "Hello, Dolly!" is one of the few since the war to appeal to all age levels.

The James Bond film *Goldfinger* gives 27-year-old British singer Shirley Bassey international exposure and her first big U.S. hit.

### New Recording Artists

Animals
Dave Clark Five
Petula Clark (in North America)
Herman's Hermits
Al Hirt
Roger Miller
Peter & Gordon
Johnny Rivers
Rolling Stones (in North America)
Dusty Springfield
Temptations

### Obituaries

**Johnny Burnette** (March 25, 1934–August 14, 1964). A rockabilly pioneer in the 1950s, Burnette died in a boating accident.

**Sam Cooke** (January 22, 1935–December 10, 1964). With 29 top 40 hits between 1957 and 1965, the black soul singer was a major influence in the evolution of pop. Cooke is shot to death by the proprietor of a Los Angeles motel who claims he appeared to be an intruder. The courts will return a verdict of justifiable homicide.

**Cole Porter** (June 9, 1892–October 15, 1964). Born into wealth, Porter pursued a career in music against the wishes of his family and became one of the greatest songwriters of this century. His clever lyrics and brilliant melodies produced a string of hits, including "Just One of Those Things," "Night and Day," "You Do Something to Me," and "I've Got You Under My Skin." A riding accident in 1937 shattered his legs and during the remainder of his life Porter endured countless operations.

**Jim Reeves** (August 20, 1924–July 31, 1964). By eliminating fiddles and the steel guitar, the country singer became one of the first to successfully cross over into pop music. Although Reeves died this year in a plane crash, his popularity will build under the able direction of his widow Mary. Previously unreleased recordings will reach the airwaves, and by the 1970s, the singer will score more CW top 10 hits than any other artist except Webb Pierce and Eddy Arnold.

**Jack Teagarden** (August 20, 1905–January 15, 1964). One of the first white musicians to popularize the blues in the South, the trombonist and bandleader was one of the all-time jazz greats.

# MOVIES

*Becket* (d. Peter Glenville; color)—Richard Burton, Peter O'Toole, John Gielgud, Donald Wolfit

*Dr. Strangelove* or *How I Learned to Stop Worrying and Love the Bomb* (d. Stanley Kubrick; bw)—Peter Sellers, George C. Scott, Sterling Hayden, Keenan Wynn, Slim Pickens

*Fail Safe* (d. Sidney Lumet; bw)—Henry Fonda, Dan O'Herlihy, Walter Matthau, Fritz Weaver

*The Fall of the Roman Empire* (d. Anthony Mann; color)—Sophia Loren, Stephen Boyd, Alec Guinness, James Mason, Christopher Plummer

*Father Goose* (d. Ralph Nelson; color)—Cary Grant, Leslie Caron, Trevor Howard

*Goldfinger* (British, d. Guy Hamilton; color)—Sean Connery, Gert Fröbe, Honor Blackman

*A Hard Day's Night* (British, d. Richard Lester; bw)—John Lennon, Paul McCartney, George Harrison, Ringo Starr

*Hush . . . Hush, Sweet Charlotte* (d. Robert Aldrich; bw)—Bette Davis, Olivia de Havilland, Joseph Cotten, Agnes Moorehead

*Mary Poppins* (Disney, d. Robert Stevenson; color)—Julie Andrews, Dick Van Dyke, David Tomlinson, Glynis Johns, Ed Wynn, Hermione Baddeley, Karen Dotrice, Matthew Garber

*The Masque of the Red Death* (d. Roger Corman; color)—Vincent Price, Hazel Court, Jane Asher, David Weston

*My Fair Lady* (d. George Cukor; color)—Rex Harrison, Audrey Hepburn, Stanley Holloway, Wildrid Hyde-White, Gladys Cooper

*The Pink Panther* (d. Blake Edwards; color)—Peter Sellers, David Niven, Capucine, Robert Wagner, Claudia Cardinale

*Seance on a Wet Afternoon* (British, d. Bryan Forbes; bw)—Kim Stanley, Richard Attenborough

*Seven Days in May* (d. John Frankenheimer; bw)—Burt Lancaster, Kirk Douglas, Fredric March, Ava Gardner

*A Shot in the Dark* (d. Blake Edwards; color)—Peter Sellers, Elke Sommer, George Sanders, Herbert Lom

*Those Magnificent Men in Their Flying Machines* (d. Ken Annakin; color)—Stuart Whitman, Sarah Miles, James Fox, Alberto Sordi, Robert Morley

*A Thousand Clowns* (d. Fred Coe; bw)—Jason Robards, Barbara Harris, Martin Balsam, Barry Gordon

*Topkapi* (d. Jules Dassin; color)—Melina Mercouri, Peter Ustinov, Maximilian Schell, Robert Morley, Akim Tamiroff

*Umbrellas of Cherbourg* (French, d. Jacques Demy; color)—Catherine Deneuve, Nino Castelnuovo

*Von Ryan's Express* (d. Mark Robson; color)—Frank Sinatra, Trevor Howard, Raffaella Carra

*Yesterday, Today and Tomorrow* (Italian, d. Vittorio De Sica; color)—Sophia Loren, Marcello Mastroianni

*Zorba the Greek* (d. Michael Cacoyannis; bw)—Anthony Quinn, Alan Bates, Irene Papas, Lila Kedrova

### Academy Awards

**April 13.** This year, 10 of the 20 acting nominees are British-born or appear in British films. Jack Lemmon hosts the show.

Best Picture—*Tom Jones*
Best Actor—Sidney Poitier (*Lilies of the Field*)
Best Actress—Patricia Neal (*Hud*)
Best Director—Tony Richardson (*Tom Jones*)
Best Supporting Actor—Melvyn Douglas (*Hud*)
Best Supporting Actress—Margaret Rutherford (*The V.I.P.s*)
Best Song—"Call Me Irresponsible" from *Papa's Delicate Condition*
Best Foreign Film—*8½* (Italian)
   *Tom Jones* is the second British-made film to

win best picture; the first was Laurence Olivier's *Hamlet* in 1948.)

Sidney Poitier—the only acting winner present at the ceremonies—is just the second black American to collect an Oscar. Hattie McDaniel won as best supporting actress in 1939 for her portrayal of Mammy in *Gone With the Wind*.

Entertainer Sammy Davis, Jr., collects the biggest laugh of the evening when, upon receiving the wrong envelope for the music awards, he ad-libs, "Wait until the NAACP hears about this."

## News

**March 7.** *The New York Times* reports that 58 percent of the 240 U.S. movie theaters planned or finished last year are located in suburban shopping centers.

**March 15.** Just 10 days after getting a divorce from singer Eddie Fisher, 32-year-old actress Elizabeth Taylor marries her fifth husband, Richard Burton, in Montreal. This is the 38-year-old actor's second marriage. The couple met while filming *Cleopatra*, and their affair has kept the tabloids very busy.

**July 4.** Universal Studios opens to public tours. Some 6 million people will pass through the gates in the first 7 years.

**September 8.** In a feature article, *Look* magazine reports that the current popularity of horror movies stems from two events in 1957: British Hammer Films released the first of its horror films and Universal Pictures released 52 vintage monster movies to television.

Dracula, the Mummy, Wolf Man, and Frankenstein—terrifyingly different from postwar blobs, giant insects, and other atomic creatures—enthralled a new generation. When a Philadelphia TV station held a horror open house, some 13,000 kids turned up.

The original Frankenstein, Boris Karloff, remarks, "It's astonishing to me at my time of life [77 years old] to have this much work."

**October 2.** Announcing an end to the Great Girl Drought in Hollywood, *Life* features starlets Jocelyn Lane, Mia Farrow, Gila Golan, Rosemary Forsyth, and Raquel Welch.

**October 12.** *The New York Times* notes the increasing role played by movie stars in Californian and presidential election campaigns. Established actors such as Gregory Peck and Burt Lancaster, as well as young performers such as Connie Stevens and Marlo Thomas, openly support the party of their choice. Commenting on the recent change, Ruth Berle says, "Older stars used to be worried about disapproval from sponsors or studios, and many wouldn't lift a finger."

This year, a business group suggests to Ronald Reagan that he run for the governorship of California, and the 53-year-old actor agrees. His performance as a tough old gangster in *The Killers* (1964) proves to be the last of his 27-year career.

**More news.** American Airlines introduces feature films on Astrovision—small TV sets placed every three rows in tourist-class and between first-class seats. Trans World Airlines brought movies on board in 1963, but American Airlines waited for this less expensive system to reduce in-flight projection problems.

• The U.S. motion picture industry reports its biggest profits since TV became a major competitor. Filmmakers attribute the boom to profitable TV ventures, the appeal of new and renovated theaters, franker pictures, and the growth in foreign markets. (Export box-office receipts moved ahead of domestic by 1956.) With the potential of pay TV, airline in-flight movies, and TV rights for unsold post-1948 films, studio executives predict more stable and consistent earnings in the future.

• The British film *Zulu* depicts the 1879 battle at Rorke's Drift where, overwhelmingly outnumbered, British soldiers successfully defended a fort against Zulu warriors. But today's Zulu extras have never seen a movie and fail to understand a cinema "battle." Absolutely desperate, director Cy Endfield sends for an old Gene Autry Western. Once the Zulu stop laughing, production proceeds.

• Riding on the popularity of AIP's *Beach* series, other producers churn out *Ride the Wild Surf*, *Surf Party*, *Pajama Party*, and 10 more films in a similar vein, almost 9 percent of U.S. production. Ten years ago, teenage movies accounted for less than 1 percent of output.

| Top Box Office Stars | Newcomers |
| --- | --- |
| Doris Day | Elke Sommer |
| Jack Lemmon | Annette Funicello |
| Rock Hudson | Susannah York |
| John Wayne | Elizabeth Ashley |
| Cary Grant | Stefanie Powers |
| Elvis Presley | Harve Presnell |
| Shirley MacLaine | Dean Jones |
| Ann-Margret | Keir Dullea |
| Paul Newman | Nancy Sinatra |
| Jerry Lewis | Joey Heatherton |

## Top Money-Maker of the Year

*The Carpetbaggers* (1964) (d. Edward Dmytryk color)—George Peppard, Carroll Baker, Alan Ladd, Elizabeth Ashley

## Flop of the Year

*The Fall of the Roman Empire*, whose production costs reached an astronomical $18–20 million.

## Quotes of the Year

"I like you too much not to say it: You've got everything, except one thing—madness. A man needs a little madness, or else . . . he never dares cut the rope and be free."
–Anthony Quinn, the Greek, advising Alan Bates, the Englishman, in *Zorba the Greek*. (Screenplay by Michael Cacoyannis, based on the novel by Nikos Kazantzakis)

"I'm not saying we wouldn't get our hair mussed, but I do say no more than 10 to 20 million killed, tops—that is, depending on the break."
–U.S. Gen. George C. Scott contemplating nuclear war in *Dr. Strangelove. . . .*' (Screenplay by Stanley Kubrick, Terry Southern and Peter George; based on the novel *Red Alert* by Peter George)

## Obituaries

**Nacio Herb Brown** (February 22, 1896–September 28, 1964). The first composer to find success in talking pictures wrote "Singin' in the Rain" (1929), "You Are My Lucky Star" (1935), and others.

**Johnny Burke** (October 3, 1908–February 25, 1964). The lyricist for the Crosby-Hope "Road" films, Burke won a 1944 Oscar, with Jimmy Van Heusen, for "Swinging on a Star."

**Ben Hecht** (February 28, 1894–April 18, 1964). The American author and dramatist wrote or collaborated on some 70 Hollywood screenplays, including *Gunga Din* (1939), *Wuthering Heights* (1939), and *Notorious* (1946).

**Percy Kilbride** (1888–December 11, 1964). He and Marjorie Main starred in seven Ma and Pa Kettle features between 1949 and 1955.

**Alan Ladd** (September 3, 1913–January 29, 1964). In Hollywood, a short co-star stands on a box; a short star stands on level ground. For years, leading ladies stood in ditches for this handsome 5′5″ blond, best remembered as the gunfighter in *Shane* (1953).

His big break came with the role of the psychopathic killer in *This Gun for Hire* (1941). Then, after the war, Ladd made the 1947, 1953, and 1954 list of top motion picture stars. But a career built on good looks fades with age, and insiders believe the actor's alcohol and sedative overdose was suicide.

**Peter Lorre** (June 26, 1904–March 23, 1964). Virtually unknown before his starring role in the German film *M* (1931), Lorre moved to Hollywood in 1934. This fine actor, with the protuberant eyes and heavily accented nasal voice, created unforgettable screen bad guys, most notably in *The Maltese Falcon* (1941) and *Casablanca* (1943).

**Harpo Marx** (November 23, 1893–September 28, 1964). The fuzzy-wigged member of the Marx Brothers never uttered a line throughout his entire career. Beginning in vaudeville in 1918, Harpo produced his mischievous, childlike smile while pulling various props out of oversize clothes or punctuating pantomimed actions with an old-fashioned taxi horn. The self-taught musician sometimes enchanted audiences with his beautiful harp playing. He and brothers Groucho and Chico appeared together in 10 comedies.

**Joseph Schildkraut** (March 22, 1895–January 21, 1964). During his long and distinguished career, the accomplished stage and screen actor won Oscars for supporting roles in *The Life of Emile Zola* (1938) and *The Tell-Tale Heart* (1942).

# TELEVISION AND RADIO

## New Prime-Time TV Programs

"The Addams Family" (September 18, 1964–September 2, 1966; Situation Comedy)—Carolyn Jones, John Astin, Jackie Coogan, Ted Cassidy

"Bewitched" (September 17, 1964–July 1, 1972; Situation Comedy)—Elizabeth Montgomery, Dick York (1964–1969), Dick Sargent (1969–1972), Agnes Moorehead

"Daniel Boone" (September 24, 1964–August 27, 1970; Western)—Fess Parker, Patricia Blair

"Flipper" (September 19, 1964–September 1, 1968; Adventure—Brian Kelly, Luke Halpin, Tommy Norden, Suzy the Dolphin

"Gilligan's Island" (September 26, 1964–September 4, 1967; Situation Comedy)—Bob Denver, Alan Hale, Jr., Jim Backus, Natalie Schafer, Tina Louise, Russell Johnson, Dawn Wells

"Gomer Pyle USMC" (September 25, 1964–September 1969; Situation Comedy)—Jim Nabors, Frank Sutton, Ronnie Schell

"The Hollywood Palace" (January 4, 1964–February 7, 1970; Variety)—Orchestra: Mitchell Ayres

"The Man from U.N.C.L.E." (September 22, 1964–January 15, 1968; Spy Comedy)—Robert Vaughn, David McCallum, Leo G. Carroll

"The Munsters" (September 24, 1964–September 1, 1966; Situation Comedy)—Fred Gwynne, Yvonne De Carlo, Al Lewis

"Peyton Place" (September 15, 1964–June 2, 1969; Drama)—Dorothy Malone (1964–1968), Ed Nelson, Ryan O'Neal, Barbara Parkins, Mia Farrow (1964–1966), Christopher Connelly

"Voyage to the Bottom of the Sea" (September 14, 1964–September 15, 1968; Science Fiction)—Richard Basehart, David Hedison, Robert Dowdell

## Emmy Awards 1963–1964 (May 25, 1964)

Drama—"The Defenders" (CBS)
Variety—"The Danny Kaye Show" (CBS)
Comedy—"The Dick Van Dyke Show" (CBS)
Music—"The Bell Telephone Hour" (NBC)
Children's Programming—"Discovery '63–'64" (ABC)
Best Actor in a Series—Dick Van Dyke ("The Dick Van Dyke Show," CBS)
Best Actress in a Series—Mary Tyler Moore ("The Dick Van Dyke Show," CBS)

## News

**January 22.** The FCC renounces any right to censor sexually or politically "provocative" radio or television programs that may offend some listeners. Otherwise, "only the wholly inoffensive, the bland, could gain access to the radio microphone or TV camera."

**February 9.** Amazed and intrigued by the media coverage of the Beatles in Britain, Ed Sullivan agreed to headline the rock group in the New Year. His decision, in light of the response to late-year releases, appears absolutely prophetic. Tonight, an estimated 60–75 percent of all U.S. television viewers tune in to catch the Beatles. The Fab Four, with their mop-top hairstyles, set the girls screaming. Beatlemania has reached America.

**March 30.** Merv Griffin Productions finds success with the new daytime quiz show "Jeopardy,"

*During their appearance on "Ed Sullivan," the Beatles perform "Till There Was You," "She Loves You," "I Saw Her Standing There," and "I Want to Hold Your Hand."*

hosted by Art Fleming. The program will leave the air on January 3, 1975.

**August 4.** In an 8-minute address, President Johnson tells the American people that he has ordered an air strike against North Vietnamese gunboat bases in the Gulf of Tonkin. CBS gives a five-minute wrap-up and returns to regular programming.

**September 11.** Don Dunphy calls the ABC "Fight of the Week" between Dick Tiger and Don Fullmer. Tiger's 10-round victory marks the end of 20 years of weekly fight broadcasts.

**September 15.** Based on the novel by Grace Metalious and the Lana Turner film, "Peyton Place" draws an estimated audience of 60 million. Jack Paar describes TV's first prime-time soap as "television's first situation orgy," but the twice-weekly show is a smash hit, making stars of Mia Farrow and Ryan O'Neal.

**September 16.** When surveys by "hard rock" radio stations discovered a fair percentage of adult listeners, ABC scheduled "Shindig" for prime time. Jimmy O'Neill hosts the Shindig dancers and regular guests Bobby Sherman, the Righteous Brothers, the Everly Brothers, Glen Campbell, and Sonny & Cher. Other guests include the Beatles, the Rolling Stones (opening the second season), Chuck Berry, and the Beach Boys. (NBC brings out a similar show, "Hullabaloo," in January.) But ABC will cancel "Shindig" in January 1966 to make room for "Batman."

**September 18.** Within a week of each other, ABC debuts "The Addams Family" and CBS introduces "The Munsters." Sitcoms of a very different type, each relies on monster appeal and special makeup effects. The identity of Thing—the human right hand that serves the Addams family—is never revealed. Strangely, both shows will be canceled in the same week in 1966.

**September 19–25.** Copying ABC's 1963 strategy, NBC launches its fall schedule in a single week and heavily promotes the first prime-time lineup to offer more than half the shows in color.

**September 22.** While it capitalizes on the James Bond spy craze, "The Man from U.N.C.L.E." is a spoof. Superagents Napoleon Solo and Illya Kuryakin fight the evil organization THRUSH. After a slow start, the show jumps to 13th at the beginning of the second season. But the plots get sillier, and heartthrob David McCallum (Illya) is not enough to sustain interest. The show will be replaced in January 1968 by "Laugh-in."

**September 26.** Producer Sherwood Schwartz, looking for a lovable heavy to play opposite Bob Denver (Gilligan), tests Alan Hale, Jr. The second-generation Hollywood actor, about to abandon his career, wins the role as the Skipper on "Gilligan's Island."

**October.** In the past year, the number of TV stations worldwide has risen by an enormous 830 to a total 4,200 built or planned. Radio stations, on the other hand, have only increased by 350 to 10,515.

**October 7.** While some TV historians point to "High Tor" (1956) as the first feature-length TV movie, most date the birth of the modern telemovie from tonight's broadcast of "See How They Run" with John Forsythe and Jane Wyatt. Yet the two-hour program, along with others later this season, receives little promotion.

**October 10.** The satellite *Syncom 3*, although built for code and voice transmissions, uses its wideband channels to relay good-quality pictures of the opening-day ceremonies at the Olympic Games in Tokyo. (The audio feeds through an undersea cable.) But with the midnight timing of the U.S. telecast, the networks will fly in tape recordings of the athletic events.

**November 3.** With the anticipated millions of dollars needed to cover this year's elections, the radio-TV networks and the wire services agree to cooperate in collecting vote returns.

**November 3.** For TV networks, cable television initially offered a means to reach a broader audience. A hookup with cable could give a small town several big-city channels or give a rural area better reception. But early in this decade, CATV looked beyond simple retransmission of network broadcasts to specialized programming like first-run films and baseball games.

Subscription TV has been offering just such a service to 2,500 homes in the San Francisco and Los Angeles areas. But today in a statewide referendum, California voters outlaw cable TV by a 2–1 margin. A Hartford, Connecticut, experiment, now in the last year of three, claims to have proven the economic feasibility of cable, but the West Coast vote and network resistance will slow development.

**December 27.** The Supremes make their first appearance on "The Ed Sullivan Show." The three singers will become regulars on the prime-time variety program, with 19 more guest spots by 1969.

**More news.** During the first Beatles tour in the United States, Dick Clark asks road manager Ira Sidelle, a former associate, to collect odds and ends—sheets, pillowcases, pop bottles—for "American Bandstand." In the TV show's last really big contest, fans write in to win the memorabilia—the result is a million pieces of mail in a single week.

## TV Commercials

Alka-Seltzer—Speedy retires this year and the company begins a series of commercials that become classics. The first shows a pair of businessmen, from the shoulders down, poking each other's large stomachs while the T-Bones sing "No Matter What Shape Your Stomach's In."

Clairol—Nice 'n' Easy Shampoo-In Hair Color creates an American cliche, with a young man and woman running in slow motion through a field toward each other. The announcer promises women, "The closer you get . . . the better you look."

## Obituaries

**Grace Allen** (July 26, 1906–August 27, 1964). Known to one and all as Gracie, the comedienne retired in 1958 after 36 years partnering her husband, George Burns, in vaudeville, radio, movies, and television. The master of the malapropism, Allen once explained, "The reason I put the salt in the pepper shaker and the pepper in the salt shaker is that people are always getting them mixed up. Now when they get mixed up, they'll be all right."

**William Bendix** (January 14, 1906–December 14, 1964). The actor was known to millions as Chester Riley in the TV series "The Life of Riley."

**Eddie Cantor** (January 31, 1892–October 10, 1964). The talented Cantor began in vaudeville, moved on to radio and films, and ended his career in TV. Known for an ability to pop his eyes, the comedian delivered old jokes in staccato fashion and jumped around singing the songs he had introduced or popularized—"If You Knew Susie," "Yes Sir, That's My Baby," and others. One of entertainment's biggest stars for 20 years, he was forced into retirement in the early 1950s by a heart condition.

**Maurice Gosfield** (1913–October 19, 1964). Gosfield was best known for his television role as Private Doberman to Phil Silver's Sergeant Bilko.

# SPORTS

## *Winners*

### *Baseball*

World Series—St. Louis Cardinals (NL), 4 games; New York Yankees (AL), 3 games
Player of the Year—Brooks Robinson (Baltimore Orioles, AL); Ken Boyer (St. Louis Cardinals, NL)
Rookie of the Year—Tony Oliva (Minnesota Twins, AL); Richie Allen (Philadelphia Phillies, NL)

### *Football*

NFL Championship—Cleveland Browns 27, Baltimore Colts 0
AFL Championship—Buffalo Bills 20, San Diego Chargers 7

College Bowls (January 1, 1964)—
Rose Bowl, Illinois 17, Washington 7
Cotton Bowl, Texas 28, Navy 6
Orange Bowl, Nebraska 13, Auburn 7
Sugar Bowl, Alabama 12, Mississippi 7
Heisman Trophy—John Huarte (Notre Dame, QB)
Grey Cup—BC Lions 34, Hamilton Tiger-Cats 24

### *Basketball*

NBA Championship—Boston Celtics, 4 games; San Francisco Warriors, 1 game
MVP of the Year—Oscar Robertson (Cincinnati Royals)
Rookie of the Year—Jerry Lucas (Cincinnati Royals)
NCAA Championship—UCLA 98, Duke 83

### *Tennis*

U.S. National—Men, Roy Emerson (vs. Fred Stolle); Women, Maria Bueno (vs. Carole Graebner)
Wimbledon—Men, Roy Emerson (vs. Fred Stolle); Women, Maria Bueno (vs. Margaret Smith)

### *Golf*

Masters—Arnold Palmer
U.S. Open—Ken Venturi
British Open—Tony Lema

### *Hockey*

Stanley Cup—Toronto Maple Leafs, 4 games; Detroit Red Wings, 3 games

### *Ice Skating*

World Championship—Men, Manfred Schnelldorfer (West Germany); Women, Sjoukje Dijkstra (Netherlands)
U.S. National—Men, Scott Allen; Women, Peggy Fleming
Canadian National—Men, Charles Snelling; Women, Petra Burka

*Kentucky Derby*

Northern Dancer—Bill Hartack, jockey

*Athlete of the Year*

Male—Don Schollander (Swimming)
Female—Mickey Wright (Golf)

*Last Season*

Frank Gifford (Football)
Dolph Schayes (Basketball)
Duke Snider (Baseball)
Y. A. Tittle (Football)

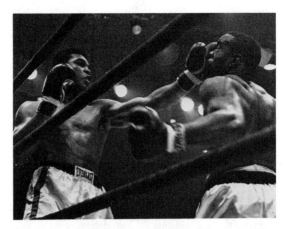

*In his defense of the heavyweight championship, Sonny Liston takes a brutal left jab to the eye from Muhammad Ali.*

# News

**January 29–February 9.** Thirty-six nations send 1,186 athletes to the Winter Olympics in Innsbruck, Austria. The USSR places first overall with 25 medals, and Soviet speed-skater Lydia Skoblikova turns in the performance of the games, with a record four Olympic gold medals.

Americans Billy Kidd and Jimmy Heuga give their nation its first medals in men's Alpine skiing, but the United States collects only five more for eighth place overall. In one of the major upsets, Canada wins gold in the four-man bobsled.

Tragically, two athletes die at Innsbruck, a British tobogganer and a 19-year-old Australian downhill skier.

**February 25.** After a hard-fought six rounds, an injured Sonny Liston throws in the towel. The boxing world is stunned. Cassius Clay had predicted, "They all must fall/In the round I call," but only 3 out of 46 sportswriters anticipated the 22-year-old would beat the heavyweight champion of the world.

Shortly after the bout, Clay reveals his membership in the Black Muslim sect and changes his name to Muhammad Ali. When he announces plans for a rematch, the World Boxing Association withdraws recognition of his title. The WBA has a rule against return bouts.

**April 17.** Some 50,000 join the New York Mets for the first game in their new home, Shea Stadium. Lawyer William Shea reportedly obtained the new baseball franchise by threatening NL owners with a rival league and restraint-of-trade hearings.

**May 24.** Near the end of the Olympic elimination soccer match in Lima, the referee disallows Peru's tying goal. Two outraged fans attack the official, and he suspends the game. Angry thousands break through the barriers and rush onto the field. Players and officials escape to the safety of the locker room, but the few policemen on duty panic and kill four with their warning shots. Fans break every window, overturn benches, and set fires in the stands. Trying to escape the pandemonium, many are trampled underfoot. When the mob surges out into the streets to loot and burn, the government declares a state of emergency. In the end, at least 298 die.

**May 30.** A fiery seven-car pileup at the Indianapolis-500 Speedway kills two drivers and delays the Memorial Day race for the first time ever. A. J. Foyt wins with an average speed of 147.3 mph.

**June 21.** Phillie Jim Bunning pitches a perfect game against the Mets in Shea Stadium—the first since 1922, the first in the NL since 1880, and only the eighth perfect game in major league history.

**October 10–24.** Scheduled to host the 1940 Olympics, Japan spends nearly $2 billion dollars on the first Asian Olympiad. For the first time, Americans at home gain an immediate sense of international competition with a satellite telecast of the opening ceremonies.

Many of the 5,140 athletes from 93 nations give outstanding performances: Soviet gymnast Larisa Latynina, in her third Olympics, sets a record medal total with nine gold, five silver, and four bronze; 18-year-old American Don Schollander becomes the first swimmer to win four gold; Australian Dawn Fraser is the first swimmer to win the same event—100-meter freestyle—in three consecutive Olympics; and Ethiopian Abebe Bikila betters his 1960 marathon time by three minutes, then performs calisthenics—five weeks after undergoing an appendectomy.

The Soviet Union places first overall with 96 medals; the second-place United States wins 90. With so many Americans stepping to the podium in track and field, the Japanese try to speed up the ceremonies by playing an abbreviated version of the "Star-Spangled Banner." An irate U.S. fan finishes the anthem on his trumpet.

**October 31.** Kelso wins his 36th race in 56 starts, with a record two-mile run in the Jockey Club Gold Cup. Next month, the seven-year-old gelding is named Horse of the Year for an unprecedented fifth consecutive time.

## Records

**April 12.** Arnold Palmer wins a record fourth Masters title. By the end of the year, he becomes the first professional golfer to win over $500,000 in career PGA competition.

**April 24.** Houston capitalizes on two walks and two errors to beat Cincinnati 1–0. Ken Johnson then becomes the only major league pitcher to toss a no-hitter in regular nine-inning play, and lose the game.

**October 10.** In another baseball record, Yankee Mickey Mantle hits a ninth-inning homer to win the third game of the World Series. His 16th World Series HR breaks the previous mark set by Babe Ruth.

## What They Said

New York Giant Y.A. Tittle on the distinct difference between pitchers and quarterbacks. "[Warren] Spahn throws a baseball and some other guy hits it with a bat. I throw a football and right after that a lot of guys weighing 250 lbs hit me." (*Sports Illustrated* October 5)

Master of the malaprop, Yankee manager Yogi Berra comments on the AL situation. "The other teams could make trouble for us if they win." (*Sports Illustrated* June 12)

# 1965

---

Unlike Kennedy, who faced several international crises, Lyndon Johnson is able to concentrate on South Vietnam. Planned air attacks begin in February, the first combat troops land in March, and by the end of the year, 180,000 U.S. soldiers turn a guerrilla war into a major conflict. When the baby-boomer bulge, moving onto college campuses, protests the escalation, Congress responds by outlawing the burning of draft cards.

At the same time, the president asks the 89th Congress to support his "Great Society." The first session, propelled by the civil rights movement and riots in Watts and other ghettos, passes a record number of bills in the most significant legislative program since Roosevelt's New Deal.

As well, this year, Cyclones in the Ganges delta kill 65,000, Rhodesia's white minority government declares unilateral independence, the northeastern United States suffers a massive power failure, Malcolm X is shot to death, NASA receives photos of Mars, and the Soviets conduct the first space walk.

The Astrodome opens, Bob Dylan goes electric, Sugar Ray Robinson retires, Sandy Koufax pitches a perfect game, Nat King Cole and Edward R. Murrow pass away, teenage girls wear mini skirts, and elementary schools teach "new math".

## NEWS

**January 1.** The Bantu Laws Amendment Act, the most rigid South African apartheid law thus far, strips almost all rights from the 7 million blacks living in white areas and on farms outside the black reservations.

**January 4.** In his State of the Union address, President Johnson asks Congress for legislation to realize the "Great Society, a place where men are more concerned with the quality of their goals than the quantity of their goods."

His plan would keep the economy growing and open to all the opportunities now enjoyed by most Americans and would improve the quality of life for all. Specific programs include Medicare for the aged, a doubling of the War on Poverty, $1.5 billion in aid to education, enforcement of the Civil Rights Act, and attainment of full voting rights for all Americans.

Before the end of the month, Johnson submits a budget with the greatest expansion of domestic welfare programs since Roosevelt's New Deal. But he allots $49 billion from the $99.7-billion budget for defense and estimates a $5.3-billion shortfall, his second consecutive deficit budget.

**January 20.** Elaborate security measures protect Lyndon Johnson at his inauguration—a newly armored limousine, a stand protected by bulletproof glass, and massive security forces, including Metro police, National Guardsmen, regular troops, and Secret Service and FBI agents.

Chief Justice Earl Warren administers the oath of office, and President Johnson, in his inaugural speech, calls for a unity of purpose in the nation and "progress without strife." He promises that in this world of fantastic change, "I will lead and I will do the best I can."

**January 24.** Winston Churchill, British statesman and author, dies at the age of 90. From 1900 when he entered Parliament as a Conservative, until 1964 when he retired, Churchill was out of politics only for a short army stint during W.W.I and for two years in the early 1920s.

First lord of the admiralty in 1911 and then again in 1939, he became prime minister on May 10, 1940. Through the long years of W.W.II, Churchill's leadership inspired his country and the entire Western world. But in 1945, the tired people of Britain elected a Labour government; Churchill led the opposition until the Conservatives won again in 1951. Knighted in 1953, he served as prime minister until 1955 when, at the age of 81, he resigned to sit as a member.

A scholar as well, he published a six-volume history, *The Second World War* and the four-volume *History of the English-Speaking Peoples*. In 1953, he received the Nobel prize for literature.

Sir Winston's coffin lies in state at Westminster Hall for three days, and an estimated 320,000 people file past. His five-hour funeral procession and service—the first British state funeral for a commoner in 50 years—is watched on television by some 350 million people worldwide. For many, especially those who lived through the war, Churchill's passing marks the end of an era.

**February 7.** The VC attack U.S. military barracks at Pleiku, and then at Qui Nhon on the 10th, killing 32 Americans and wounding more than 70. Johnson orders retaliatory bombing on the 11th. Two days later, he authorizes Operation Rolling Thunder.

After various delays, the long-planned air war against North Vietnam finally begins on March 2. In less than two weeks, U.S. planes are dropping napalm. By mid-March, Johnson regularizes the campaign, approving the selection of targets in weekly lots, but leaves the timing to commanders in the field.

**February 21.** Malcolm X is shot to death at a Harlem rally. The 39-year-old black nationalist left the Nation of Islam in 1964 to form his own religious sect, Muslim Mosque, and the politically oriented Organization of Afro-American Unity. But following a trip to Mecca late last year, he took a new name—El-Hajj Malik El-Shabazz—and spoke of the need for blacks and whites to coexist in peace. Murdered before he can spread his new message, Malcolm will be remembered as an extremist.

Many question whether the police have conducted a thorough investigation and whether the three killers, associates of Elijah Muhammad, acted on behalf of the black Muslims. Next year, the courts will sentence the assassins to life in prison.

**February 25.** In 1963, Ottawa responded to growing unrest in Quebec with the formation of a Royal Commission on Bilingualism and Biculturalism. After 18 months of inquiry and research, the commission shocks the nation with its preliminary conclusions.

A provincial crisis has become a national crisis as French-Canadians reject the existing relationship of a minority to a majority. The commission calls for an "equal partnership" of the two cultures.

The report's first volume will appear in 1967, and over the following three years, the commission will make specific recommendations for language change.

**March 4.** "Intolerable" harassment in Indonesia forces the U.S. Information Agency to withdraw aid for the first time in its history. Washington wants to underline the consequences of attacking American staff and facilities.

**March 7.** Some 200 state troopers and sheriff's deputies attack a group of 525 blacks moving toward Edmund Pettus Bridge, leading out of Selma, Alabama. The group had just begun a march to the state capital in Montgomery. Using tear gas, whips, and nightsticks, police hospitalize 17 and send over 60 for emergency treatment. The nation is outraged at the scenes of violence shown on TV. When Martin Luther King, Jr., calls to religious leaders and "people of good will" for help, hundreds flood into Selma from all over the country.

Organizers gather a second march for the 9th, but the 1,500 blacks and whites turn back at the bridge; newspapers report a prearranged retreat, mediated by the federal government, to avoid violence. The movement asks out-of-staters to stay as Governor Wallace continues to refuse them protection.

The president, aware of rising sympathy in the country, goes before a joint session of the Congress on the 15th. Stunning the nation with his use of the movement's own words, "We shall overcome," he asks for a comprehensive voting rights bill.

On the 17th, a District Court judge in Montgomery approves an SCLC petition for the Selma-Montgomery march, but Wallace claims Alabama lacks the manpower to protect the marchers. The president summons the press to his office and tells them that if Wallace is unable or unwilling to call up 10,000 National Guardsmen, he will. On March 20, Johnson signs the order to mobilize nearly 4,000 troops.

Next day, some 3,200 people begin a five-day march to protest the denial of voting rights to black Americans. On the final day of the 62-day campaign, 25,000 people join for the last 3½ miles to the Montgomery Capitol steps.

*On March 25, Dr. Martin Luther King, Jr., and his wife Coretta lead thousands of black and white Americans on the last leg of the Selma-to-Montgomery march.*

During the campaign, a Boston minister, the Rev. James Reeb, died of a beating by segregationists, but the march itself has been free of violence. On this last day, Viola Gregg Liuzzo, a volunteer from Detroit, is run off the road and shot to death; her black passenger survives by playing dead. Authorities arrest three Klansmen, and President Johnson denounces the killing, promising stringent supervision of Klan activities. (Three men accused of killing Reeb are found not guilty. The Klansmen accused of Liuzzo's murder are tried twice by state courts, but each trial ends in a hung jury. In December, a federal court finds them guilty of conspiring to deprive a citizen of her constitutional rights; they receive 10-year sentences.)

The Selma march, attracting large numbers of whites into the campaign for the first time and generating substantial government support for a strong voting rights bill, appears to herald a new era for civil rights. Yet the march marks the zenith of the movement. Next year, the SCLC-SNCC coalition will crumble when young SNCC militants proclaim Black Power.

**March 8.** In a broad interpretation of the draft law, the U.S. Supreme Court unanimously holds that conscientious objector status must be granted when "[a] belief that is sincere and meaningful occupies a place in the life of its possessor parallel to that filled by the orthodox belief in God."

**March 8.** The official "advisory" role of the United States in Vietnam ends as the first American combat troops land in South Vietnam. The Pentagon assigns the 3,500 men to guard the strategic U.S. Air Force base in Danang, the point of origin for American air strikes.

**March 23.** The Central Committee of the Romanian Communist party names Nicolae Ceauşescu to replace Geheorghe Gheorghiu-Dej, the 20-year party leader who died four days ago. As first secretary, the 47-year-old Ceauşescu quickly embarks on a vast program of industrial development. Romania will experience an economic spurt in the 1970s but at the expense of agriculture.

**April 1.** A month of bombing has had little effect on the Communist infiltration of men and supplies into South Vietnam. The president now approves a large U.S. manpower increase—18,000–20,000 men in addition to the 27,000 already in Vietnam—and switches the role of the marines at Danang from defense to offense.

A concerned Johnson wants no premature publicity and orders his decisions carried out in such a way as to "minimize any appearance of sudden changes in policy."

**April 11.** A series of tornadoes in the Midwest— the worst since 1936—kills 271 and injures thousands. Over a 12-hour period, at least 35 twisters, some appearing in clusters, and 50 thunderstorms batter Indiana, Iowa, Michigan, Wisconsin, Ohio, and Illinois; Indiana is the worst hit, with 130 dead. More die in the damaging floods that follow.

**April 11.** President Johnson signs the landmark Elementary and Secondary Education Act. To surmount concerns over federal control and funding for parochial schools, the act allots monies directly to the states and requires agencies to give aid to all students in public and private schools.

On November 8, the president signs the Higher Education Act, setting up the first federal scholarships intended for general undergraduate education. Some $200 million over three years will provide about 140,000 scholarships annually. The act, despite considerable opposition, also authorizes a Teacher Corps to work in low-income areas.

**April 15.** Israel receives the last installment of war reparations from West Germany and a month later establishes diplomatic relations with Bonn. Seven Arab nations immediately break off all contact with the Germans.

**April 17.** Students for a Democratic Society (SDS) organizes some 15,000 students and others to picket the White House over U.S. participation in the Vietnam War. Established in 1961, SDS has been active in the civil rights movement and community projects in urban ghettos. Now, with chapters on 63 campuses, the group moves to the forefront of the student antiwar movement. WSP and several civil rights organizations join the demonstration, with many marching for the first time.

The escalation of the war prompts a number of campuses to study U.S. policy in Vietnam. On May 15 in Washington, a 15½-hour televised "teach-in" draws 5,000 people; another 100,000 at over 100 colleges hear the discussions via radio hookup. But as active protest increases, the teach-in movement fades.

**April 28.** President Johnson sends 400 marines to the Dominican Republic to protect the lives of U.S. citizens. Revolutionaries are fighting to return former President Juan Bosch to power; he was ousted in a 1963 rightist coup after less than a year in office. By May 2, when Johnson announces on TV that the United States "will not permit the establishment of another Communist government in the Western Hemisphere," American troops number in the thousands.

The president's action meets wide criticism at home and abroad as both the rebels and impartial observers dispute the "Communist" tag. Still, on May 6, the OAS backs the United States by a narrow margin and representative units from several nations join the U.S. force, supposedly to maintain order.

Approximately 2,000 Dominicans die and the country suffers massive economic damage before the junta and rebels sign an accord in August. A moderate U.S.-supported government will be elected next year, and American troops will withdraw by September 1966. But Johnson's unilateral action severely damages U.S.–Latin American relations.

**May 4.** With the administration admitting annual costs at $1.5 billion for U.S. involvement in Vietnam, President Johnson urges Congress to approve an additional $700 million. On May 5, the House votes 408–7 for the budget, and the Senate concurs 88–3 the day after. By granting the funding request, Congress in effect approves the White House war policy. During the three days, over 10,000 U.S. troops land in Vietnam.

**May 11–12.** A cyclone hits the low-lying lands of the Ganges River delta in East Pakistan. The winds and tidal wave kill over 12,000, but a second storm on June 1–2, and a third on December 15, drive the death toll up to 45,000–65,000.

**June 5.** For the first time, the State Department publicly acknowledges that American ground troops are engaging in combat in defense of key installations. Three days later, the White House confirms U.S. troops have been authorized to support South Vietnamese forces when requested, but insists their primary defensive mission remains unchanged. U.S. military command in Saigon will finally announce on June 29, almost three months after Johnson ordered a switch to offense, that Americans have joined South Vietnamese troops for the first time in a search-and-destroy action.

**June 18.** Since the assassination of President Ngo Dinh Diem in November 1963, a number of military officers have shuffled through the presidential office in a series of coups and leadership realignments. In desperation, South Vietnamese military leaders ask 34-year-old Air Vice Marshal Nguyen Cao Ky to become premier.

Known only to the Americans as a fighter pilot, Ky soon announces a program of land reform and moves to build hospitals and schools in the countryside. But the politically inexperienced premier finds it almost impossible to strike a balance between the corruption in the South Vietnamese government and the expectations of the U.S. military command.

**June 30.** President Johnson launches the Head Start Program. Part of his War on Poverty, the summer project gives some 560,000 culturally deprived children close personal attention to prepare them for kindergarten or first grade in the fall. Phenomenally successful, Head Start becomes a permanent year-round program.

**July 15.** The president bars all wiretapping by federal employees, except in matters of national security and then only when approved by the attorney general. The order follows disclosures at Senate subcommittee hearings that IRS agents had used wiretapping in at least four investigations in Pittsburgh.

**July 28.** Johnson announces that the United States is increasing its military strength in Vietnam from 75,000 to 125,000 immediately and will double monthly draft calls. Congress expresses approval, as do former President Eisenhower and former Vice-President Nixon.

**July 30.** President Johnson signs a bill establishing the first U.S. government–operated health insurance program for the aged. Medicare, financed through Social Security payments, covers most people over the age of 65, and Medicaid provides a similar health program for those requiring public assistance.

To honor Harry Truman's early efforts to introduce a federal program, Johnson flies to the former president's hometown of Independence, Missouri, to affix his signature. Medicare, which many consider a move toward socialized medicine, becomes effective on July 1, 1966.

**August 6.** In the same Capitol room where Abraham Lincoln signed the Emancipation Proclamation, President Johnson signs the Voting Rights Act of 1965.

In the 11 Southern states over the past year, the number of registered black voters has increased to 44 percent of those eligible to vote. Yet in Mississippi, where blacks compose 42 percent of the population, only 6 percent of those eligible have registered, and in Alabama, only 13.7 percent.

The bipartisan bill eliminates literacy tests in those states and counties where less than 50 percent of the voting age population was registered to vote in 1964, and authorizes the attorney general to initiate lawsuits to bar discriminatory state poll taxes and to use federal examiners to register voters and supervise voting procedures.

Within 25 hours, the Justice Department files suit in Jackson, Mississippi, to abolish the state poll tax.

**August 9.** At a Titan missile silo in Searcy, Arkansas, a fire and explosion kill 53 men working under contract to modify and improve the silo facility. Although the unarmed missile remains undamaged, the military delays similar work at the other 53 Titan sites.

**August 11.** During a California heat wave, onlookers gather when white policemen attempt to arrest a drunken driver in the predominantly black Watts area of Los Angeles. The officers call for backup, but the minor incident quickly escalates into a full-scale riot.

The violence overwhelms city police, and the state government calls out the National Guard. The first guardsmen arrive on the 13th, the worst night of violence, and by the next day 12,000 supplement the 2,500 city cops, county sheriff's deputies, and highway patrolmen.

Mobs of up to 10,000 people loot, burn, throw

rocks, cut fire hoses, and snipe in a 50-square-mile area of southwestern Los Angeles. Authorities finally regain control over the 15th and 16th, but not before 34 people die, over 1,000 are injured, some 3,950 are arrested, and property damage reaches $200 million, with 209 buildings destroyed and 787 damaged. In the midst of the violence, the 21-year-old black man stopped for reckless driving pleads guilty.

The McCone Commission, appointed to investigate the six-day riot, warns of a possible recurrence and recommends massive employment and welfare efforts to offset black poverty in the area. (Watts had 30 percent unemployment before the outbreak.) But the most destructive race riot in American history to date, in this second summer of unrest, increases racial tensions across the land.

**August 18.** Governor John A. Volpe signs an act to withhold funds from any Massachusetts school board refusing to take immediate, effective steps to correct de facto segregation (defined as nonwhite enrollment exceeding 50 percent). The legislation is believed to be the first of its kind in the nation.

**August 31.** In response to student protest against Selective Service and the Vietnam War, Congress makes it a crime to burn draft cards.

In October, David J. Miller, age 22, becomes the first person arrested under the new law. In February 1966, the court will give him a three-year suspended sentence and a two-year probation, and order him to carry his draft card at all times. The sentence will be upheld later that year.

**September 21.** Great Britain announces the discovery of natural gas in the British license area of the North Sea. After extensive drilling, a 45-mile pipeline will bring the first gas ashore in 1967.

**September 26.** The Civil Rights Act of 1964 specifies that to share in federal funds for the 1965–1966 academic year, a school district must state its intention to integrate at least four grades this school year and the rest by 1967. Under this pressure, all but 77 of the 5,044 school districts in the Southern and border states have submitted plans for desegregation.

The number of black students enrolled with whites jumps this month in Alabama from 101 to more than 1,000, in South Carolina from 265 to

3,000, and in North Carolina from 4,900 to 8,000. (Judge James McMillan in April ordered crosstown busing in the Charlotte-Mecklenburg County of North Carolina, establishing a desegregation pattern to be copied across the nation.) And almost every school district in Arkansas, Florida, Tennessee, Texas, and Virginia has desegregated. Still, critics describe the desegregation as token, since most black children continue to attend all-black schools.

**October 2.** Only one river near a major U.S. urban area remains unpolluted, the St. Croix between Minnesota and Wisconsin. The Water Quality Act, signed into law today, requires all states to set antipollution standards by July 1, 1967, or HEW will do it for them. The president considers this bill one of the most important conservation measures of his administration.

**October 3.** A new U.S. immigration law replaces the racially discriminatory system of national-origins quotas with a Western Hemisphere quota of 120,000 (with no one-country limit) and a world quota of 170,000 (with no more than 20,000 to come from any one nation). An immigrant application will now be judged solely on the basis of skills and of family relationship to those already in the United States.

At a special signing ceremony at the Statue of Liberty, President Johnson also announces Havanna's acceptance of an offer to permit Cuban citizens with relatives in the United States to emigrate.

**October 4.** The first pontiff to visit the Western Hemisphere, Pope Paul spends one day in New York. In the afternoon, he appeals to U.N. delegates for peace (becoming the first person with no national ties to address the General Assembly), then celebrates a mass at Yankee Stadium before returning to Rome. During his full day, an estimated 1 million Americans caught a glimpse of the pope, while another 100 million watched him on television.

**October 8.** President Johnson undergoes a successful gallbladder operation. The event receives considerable press coverage, and some criticize the president for lack of decorum. But Johnson remains the most accessible of all presidents, and a Gallup poll taken at the end of the month shows that 66 percent of Americans like the way he is handling his job, a rise of 3 percent since September.

**October 15–16.** Antiwar protests grow, as some 70,000–100,000 demonstrate nationwide against American involvement in Vietnam; the largest rally, in New York City, draws 10,000.

The next day, the Justice Department announces an investigation of antidraft groups, including SDS. Initially, President Johnson approves, stating that the enemy could misread the protests as representative of the nation. But on November 26, he publicly backs the right to dissent. The next day, 20,000 Americans from some 140 antiwar groups march in the capital.

**October 28.** The British House of Commons abolishes capital punishment for five years. The only prisoner facing the gallows, a 19-year-old man, receives a commuted life sentence. The legislation will be extended.

**November 8.** In an attempt to obtain a ruling majority, the Liberals call another national election in Canada. The party gains two seats but again falls short. The NDP cements its position as the country's third party, adding 4 seats, for a total of 21. The Social Credit loses 19 of 24 seats and will never regains its former standing.

**November 9.** A massive power failure blacks out seven American states and the Canadian provinces of Ontario and Quebec. Originating in Ontario at 5:17 P.M., the blackout reaches New York City 10 minutes later at the height of rush hour, stranding an estimated 800,000 in stalled subways and thousands more in elevators.

Governor Rockefeller dispatches more than 5,000 National Guardsmen to the beleaguered city; their presence helps keep the crime rate even lower than usual. Brooklyn regains power at 2:00 A.M., but full power is not restored to Manhattan until 6:58 A.M.

**November 9.** Following a bitter and violent election campaign, Senator Ferdinand Marcos is elected president of the Philippines.

**November 11.** Rhodesia shocks the world with a unilateral declaration of independence; its the first British colony to do so since the American colonies in 1776.

During this decade, as more African colonies won their independence in this decade, white Rhodesians foresaw a future where London would give majority rule to the nation's 4 million blacks. Increasingly conservative governments culminated in the 1964 election of Ian Smith as prime minister, on an independence platform. Last year's referendum and the national election this past May fully supported Smith's agenda.

With the declaration, the white minority seizes control, banning all African political parties and detaining their leaders. London denounces the action as illegal and treasonable, and immediately imposes economic sanctions; other nations follow. The unorganized Rhodesian blacks put up little resistance, but British Prime Minister Wilson refuses to take military action. African nations severely criticize his decision and 10 break off diplomatic relations.

**November 15.** Since registering as a member of the Communist party can lead to prosecution (under the Subversive Activities Control Act of 1950), the Supreme Court rules (8–0) that party members may invoke their Fifth Amendment privilege against self-incrimination and may refuse to register with the government.

Communist party spokesman Gus Hallat hails the decision as "a blow against the longest political-legal vendetta in our history."

**November 15.** *Look* magazine reports that in September 1964 the United States rejected Vietnam peace talks secretly arranged by U.N. Secretary-General U Thant. The State Department confirms the story, but declares the government had doubted the sincerity of the North Vietnamese offer.

Over the winter, Prime Minister Lester Pearson of Canada, who won the 1956 Nobel peace prize for his role in forming a U.N. peacekeeping force, sends Chester Ronning to Hanoi. The retired diplomat served in China and speaks fluent Mandarin. He returns to Ottawa with an unconditional offer. If the Americans stop bombing the North, the Communists will enter peace negotiations. Washington refuses to take Hanoi seriously and soon extends the air campaign to Hanoi and Haipong.

**November 26.** The first U.S. Cavalry Division returns to base at An Khe at the end of the war's first major battle. Since October 19, Communist soldiers had engaged the Allies in the Ia Drang Valley. During the worst of the fighting, in the middle of this month, the Americans lost more than 240 soldiers; only U.S. helicopters and planes prevented a complete disaster. The North Vietnamese, with their willingness to suffer huge casualties, lost almost 1,800 men. (North Vietnamese General Giap reportedly once said that if he could keep his losses to 10 Vietminh for each French soldier, he would win the war.)

The Communists, in response to the first U.S. manpower increase, have added 7 regiments, bringing their total strength to 200,000, with some 15,000 fighting in South Vietnam alongside an estimated 63,000 VC. American forces have risen from 20,000 to 185,000, with about half combat troops. General Westmoreland now asks for more men. On the 30th, Defense Secretary McNamara recommends to the president that the United States send some 400,000 soldiers to Vietnam by the end of next year.

**December 5.** In the French presidential election, Charles de Gaulle captures just 31.7 percent of the vote. But in a run-off against François Mitterand on the 19th, the 75-year-old president takes 54.7 percent to win another seven-year presidency. De Gaulle becomes the first president of France to be popularly elected since Louis Napoleon Bonaparte won the office in 1848.

**December 20.** Each month, an estimated 4,500 VC and their war materiel travel down the Ho Chi Minh Trail, through the jungles of Cambodia and Laos, into South Vietnam. The United States earlier reached an agreement with Laos to strafe and bomb that part of the trail running through Laotian territory. Today, Washington gives field commanders permission to pursue enemy troops into Cambodia when the failure to do so would jeopardize the lives of their troops; this order includes permission to order air strikes and artillery barrages. (Cambodia severed diplomatic relations with the United States in May; Prince Norodom Sihanouk, the chief of state, seemingly decided the Communists would win the war.)

**December 24.** U.S. sorties in the Vietnam War have gradually increased from 900 to 1,500 a week, yet the Defense Intelligence Agency evaluates the air strikes as unsuccessful. The North Vietnamese economy continues to function and the Communists continue to move in supplies on foot.

Yet when President Johnson halts the bombing today as "a major peace offensive." Yet, the conditions offered to the Communists—tantamount to virtual surrender—guarantee a refusal. The Johnson administration is simply easing tensions before upping the tempo of the air war.

On January 31, the White House announces the resumption of bombing. World governments express their regrets, and some congressional leaders begin to question U.S. involvement in the war.

**More news.** The post-W.W.II baby-boom, which has produced over 4 million babies per year in the United States since 1954, ends as the birthrate falls below 20 per 1,000 (19.4 live births per 1,000 women aged 15–44 years old) for the first time since 1940.


## Obituaries

**Winston Churchill** (November 30, 1874–January 24, 1965). *See* News.

**Farouk** (February 11, 1920–March 18, 1965). Initially popular after assuming the throne in 1936, the Egyptian king soon took up a debauched lifestyle, which led to his overthrow in 1952. He died in exile.

**Father Divine (George Baker?)** (1877?–September 10, 1965). The name and age of this son of a former slave remain a mystery. In 1919, he established the Kingdom of Heaven, an interracial, nondenominational peace movement that reached a membership of 1.5 million in the 1930s and 1940s. Today, the organization holds property worth $10 million.

**Felix Frankfurter** (November 15, 1882–February 22, 1965). The former Supreme Court justice served from 1939 to 1962. A founder of the ACLU and close advisor to President Roosevelt, Frankfurter's appointment met with opposition from those who considered him too liberal. Yet, in later years, the justice argued that judges provide a poor substitute for government by the people. Typically, he submitted a 64-page dissent to the 1962 state apportionment ruling.

**Malcolm X (El-Hajj Malik El-Shabazz)** (May 19, 1925–February 21, 1965). *See* News.

**Frances Perkins** (April 10, 1882–May 14, 1965). The first woman Cabinet member was appointed secretary of labor by President Roosevelt on March 4, 1933. During her 12-year term, she introduced many New Deal reforms.

**Syngman Rhee** (April 26, 1875–July 19, 1965). In 1948, his election as the first president of Korea culminated a 35-year struggle to win independence from Japan. But, through the years, his government became increasingly dictatorial. Following a fraudulent fourth-term victory in 1960, student demonstrations forced him into exile.

**Albert Schweitzer** (January 14, 1875–September 5, 1965). At the age of 30, the renowned theologian, philosopher, gifted organist, and expert on Bach began seven years of medical training to become a missionary. Since 1925, Schweitzer had devoted his life to his hospital in Gabon, Africa. While considered paternalistic by many, his humanitarian work brought him the Nobel peace prize in 1952.

**Adlai Stevenson** (February 5, 1900–July 14, 1965). After entering government, in 1933, Stevenson rose steadily to navy secretary during W.W.I, secretary of state in 1945, U.N. delegate from 1946 to 1947, and governor of Illinois from 1948 to 1953. He captured the Democratic presidential nomination in 1952 and 1956, but Eisenhower's popularity proved insurmountable.

Stevenson returned to the United Nations in 1960 as ambassador for the president-elect. (The next year, Kennedy said of him, "In this job, he's got the nerve of a burglar.") He served at the United Nations until his sudden heart attack.

**Henry A. Wallace** (October 7, 1888–November 18, 1965). One of Roosevelt's vice-presidents (1941–1945), he ran unsuccessfully for the presidency in 1948 on the Progressive party ticket.

# BEGINNINGS AND ENDINGS

## News

**January 25.** *The New York Times* reports that "new math" is replacing traditional arithmetic in elementary schools. The system tries to help children understand, as well as perform, mathematical tasks.

**January 26.** Hindi replaces English as the official language of India. When Tamil-speaking Indians riot in the state of Madras, the government agrees to retain English as an associate language.

**April 13.** Congress hires its first Negro pages— 15-year-old Frank Mitchell for the House and 16-year-old Lawrence Bradford for the Senate.

**July 23.** Congress reduces the silver content in half-dollars from 90 percent to 40 percent and eliminates silver in dimes and quarters ("cladding" places cupro-nickel faces over a copper center). The coinage changes—the first since 1792—release silver for industry and ensure that Americans will no longer hoard coins.

**July 28.** Edward Heath, age 49, succeeds Sir Alec Douglas-Home, who resigned last week, as leader of the British Conservative party.

**October 3.** With his appointment as auxiliary bishop in New Orleans, Harold Robert Perry, age 48, becomes the first Negro bishop in a U.S. archdiocese. (The first black American bishop, Joseph Bowers, was consecrated in 1953, then assigned to Accra, West Africa.)

**October 28.** In St. Louis, builders complete the 630-foot Gateway Arch, part of the Jefferson National Expansion Memorial. Finnish-American architect Eero Saarinen, who included a gondola and observation deck in the arc, died in 1961.

**December 7.** Meeting in Istanbul, Pope Paul and Athenagoras I, patriarch of the Eastern Orthodox Church, end the 900-year schism between their churches. Their joint declaration of reconciliation expresses the hope that some day the churches "may be one."

**More news.** In Torrance, California, the first apartment building for singles rents its last unit— during construction. By the end of the decade, an entire singles subculture will emerge in the United States.

• Canadian senators, appointed by the governor general on the advice of the prime minister, previously received a lifetime appointment. Henceforth, newly appointed senators will be required to retire at age 75.

• In New York, Sanskrit scholar A. C. Bhaktivedanta, age 59, founds the International Society for Krishna Consciousness. His conservative form of Hinduism, which centers on the practice of yoga, will hold a strong appeal for hippies. A Krishna center will open within a year, followed by a second in San Francisco in 1967. Soon hundreds of young people will don saffron robes for their guru Swami Prabhupada, shave their heads, and stand on street corners chanting the "Hare Krishna" mantra to the clash of cymbals.

• About nine years ago, the nonprofit West Foundation in Brant, New York, brought in a Mongolian rodent for use in medical research. This fall, Creative Playthings, which encourages "self-discovery and experimentation," lists the little desert animal in its catalog. Some 2,000 orders flood in for a gerbil.

## Records

**August 17.** Robert Manry completes a west-east solo transatlantic crossing in the smallest sailing vessel on record—the 13½-foot *Tinkerbelle*. His journey took 78 days.

## Government Departments and Agencies

**September 9.** The president signs a bill establishing the Department of Housing and Urban Affairs (HUD).

## New Products and Businesses

University of Florida urologists develop Gatorade, a special rehydrating drink.

Campbell Soup Co. introduces circular pasta in tomato sauce—SpaghettiOs.

In competition with Volkswagen, Toyota from

Japan brings the four-door Corona sports sedan into the United States.

---

*Statistics:* American production of the soft-top convertible peaks at 507,000. By 1975, only GM will be manufacturing a soft-top—the Cadillac Eldorado, at $11,049.

---

## Fads

When chemist Norman Stingley accidentally discovered a plastic with incredible bounce, he offered the formula to Wham-O. This summer, the toy manufacturer brings out the 98-cent Super Ball. About the size and color of a plum, the ball snaps back—almost all the way to the top of a three-story building! By Christmas, Wham-O sells 7 million.

With the popularity of James Bond books and movies, a merchandise bonanza inevitably spreads from Europe to the United States this year—007 toys, raincoats, men's toiletries.

Tabletop slot-cars, which arrived from Britain in 1959, overtook electric trains in popularity by 1963. The small vehicles "slot" into grooves on a track and a hand control sets the speed. This year, an estimated 3.5 million American teens spend $3–$8 per car and $1.50 per hour to rent space on 4–8-lane tracks in stores. The craze will wane by 1967.

Recommended Christmas toys include the $4.95 Logo Gear Set, the $4.95 Sonic Mystery Gun (blast of air), $5.00 Fisher Price Dump Truckers, the $8.66 Erector Set No. 3 (battery-powered motor, gear train), and a $2.00 compact Color Drawing Set (72 Crayola crayons). For parents on the lookout for war toys, Mattel offers a "Sonic Blaster" (a 4-pound, 35-inch bazooka-like "jungle weapon" with a loud wham) for $10.99.

## SCIENCE AND TECHNOLOGY

### News

**March 18.** Tethered with a nylon cord, Soviet cosmonaut Alexei Leonov leaves *Voskhod 2* for the first walk in space. During his 12 minutes, 9 seconds outside, the craft travels approximately 3,000 miles.

**March 23.** Astronauts Virgil Grissom and John Young, in a flawless test of spacecraft maneuverability, change the size and shape of their orbit twice and the orbital plane once. This first two-man Gemini flight comes 22 months after the finish of the Mercury program.

Grissom dubbed *Gemini 3* the Molly Brown after the 1960 Broadway musical *The Unsinkable Molly Brown*. (His Mercury capsule sank beneath him in the Atlantic.) Reportedly, NASA agreed only after hearing Grissom's second choice—the *Titanic*. Following this flight, NASA announces that all succeeding missions will use an official designation. (As well, the congressional hubbub over a corned beef sandwich smuggled on board for Grissom means more stringent rules for future flights.)

**March 24.** NASA feeds some of the 5,814 *Ranger 9* photos directly to commercial TV. Precisely on target, the craft crashes onto the lunar surface.

**April.** At $18,000, the PDP-8 offers industry an alternative to largely inaccessible mainframe computers. And, despite a limited 4K memory and single-program capacity, this DEC product becomes the first mass-produced minicomputer.

**April 6.** Last year, 18 nations including the United States formed the International Telecommunications Satellite Organization (Intelsat). Today, NASA launches *Early Bird* (later *Intelsat 1*) over the Atlantic. President Johnson will use one of the 240 telephone voice circuits to exchange greetings with other national leaders on June 28.

Over the next few years, other Intelsat satellites placed over the Indian and Pacific oceans will establish a worldwide commercial system for some 1 billion people.

**April 20.** Astronomers in Puerto Rico announce

*Ed White leaves* Gemini 4 *to become the first American astronaut to walk in space. Told to return to the craft after 21 minutes, he says, "It's the saddest moment of my life."*

that Mercury, previously believed to rotate once in 88 days, actually takes only 54–64 days. As well, the planet has not been in orbit long. These last measurements revive the theory that Mercury once orbited Venus.

**May 21.** *The New York Times* reports a remarkable discovery by American radio astronomer Robert W. Wilson and German-American physicist Arno Penzias: Radio waves come from all directions in space. Since an expanding universe would stretch light waves to radio-wavelength, scientists regard these findings as "fossil" evidence of the "big bang" that theoretically created the universe.

**May 30.** In the first step of their conversion program, Bell Telephone replaces electromechanical switching in Succasunna, New Jersey, with an electronic system.

**June 3.** Ed White and Jim McDivitt pilot *Gemini*

4 into a four-day orbit above Earth, the first flight handled by the new Mission Control Center in Houston. When White leaves the craft for his historic walk in space, a thermal glove follows him out the hatch and disappears.

**July 15.** Since November 28, 1964, *Mariner 4* has traveled some 134 million miles across the solar system. The unmanned probe sends 22 detailed photos of Mars on microwave signals as a series of dots. The desolate surface, pocked with craters, shows no evidence of the famous "canals" and ends any last hope of life there.

> *Statistics:* Between 1958 and 1965, the United States moved from a 71-percent launching failure rate to a 91-percent success rate.

**August 29.** Gordon Cooper and Charles Conrad return to Earth after nearly eight days on board *Gemini 5.* During the longest U.S. space mission thus far, the astronauts tested the craft's navigational and guidance systems for space docking. Cooper, who flew in the last flight of Project Mercury, is the first astronaut to make two journeys into space.

**October 8.** This week, Bell Labs receive a patent for the first solid-state continuous-wave laser. The elimination of pulsing bursts promises countless laser applications.

**October 20.** For the first time in U.S. history, Congress mandates changes in automobile manufacturing. Amendments to the Clean Air Act of 1963 bar the sale of cars (including foreign makes) that fail to meet exhaust-emission standards.

**November 17.** While denying a cause-and-effect relationship, the FDA acknowledges asking manufacturers of the birth-control pill to add a printed warning of possible health risks. Evidence continues to mount that oral contraceptives increase the danger of blood clots.

**December 5.** The Federal Aviation Administration, referring to medical tests, states that jet travel through a number of time zones disrupts physiological and psychological functions for a three- to five-day period.

**December 15.** In the first U.S. space rendezvous, Walter Schirra and Thomas Stafford bring *Gemini 6* within 6 feet of Frank Borman and James Lovell on board *Gemini 7*. The spacecraft remain in close formation for nearly 8 hours. *Gemini 6* returns to Earth the next day, after 24 hours in orbit, but Borman and Lovell remain aloft until the 18th for a record 14-day flight.

**More news.** Gerald Stanley Hawkins, in *Stonehenge Decoded*, argues that neolithic man used the ancient structure to determine the time of astronomical events.

• Public Health Service investigator Edward Weiss finds evidence that people living in southern Utah, downwind from the nuclear test site, show a higher incidence of leukemia—28 cases rather than a predicted 19. His study remains secret.

• T. D. Lysenko is stripped of his administrative posts in the Soviet Union. During the 1930s, Lysenko branded genetics as a bourgeois science. His theory of acquired characteristics—cut off enough cat tails and cats will be born tailless—promised greater crop yields and found favor with Stalin during rapid industrialization. Geneticists, on the other hand, faced prison or death. Last year, the discrediting of Lysenko's theory contributed to the downfall of Nikita Khrushchev.

• The major obstacle in kidney transplants remains the body's rejection of the organ. When the donor and recipient are identical twins the success rate stands at 88 percent, but with siblings and other relatives it drops to 50 percent, and with plummets to 16 percent.

## Other Discoveries, Developments, and Inventions

Super 8 oversize film and cartridges from Eastman Kodak and 4-bulb Flashcube from Sylvania

MIG-25 fighter plane, code-named "Foxbat," in the USSR

Trimline phone with the dial in the handset

## Obituaries

**Geoffrey de Havilland** (July 27, 1882–May 27, 1965). The founder and technical director of de Havilland Aircraft in Britain developed a W.W.I single-seater fighter, the W.W.II Mosquito bomber, and the Comet.

**Paul Müller** (January 12, 1899–October 12, 1965). The Swiss chemist won a Nobel prize in 1948 for his development of DDT. The pesticide was first used in 1939.

**George Nasmith** (January 31, 1877–November 28, 1965). The Canadian chemist invented the gas mask while serving in France during W.W.I.

**Carl Norden** (April 23, 1880–June 14, 1965). In W.W.II, his bombsight allowed Americans to carry out precision aerial bombing.

## THE ARTS

March 10—*The Odd Couple*, with Walter Matthau, Art Carney (964 perfs.)

April 25—*Half-a-Sixpence*, with Tommy Steele, Polly James, Carrie Nye (511 perfs.)

November 22—*Man of La Mancha*, with Richard Kiley, Irving Jacobson, Joan Diener (2,328 perfs.)

December 8—*Cactus Flower*, with Lauren Bacall, Barry Nelson, Brenda Vaccaro (1,234 perfs.)

### Tony Awards

Actor (Dramatic)—Walter Matthau, *The Odd Couple*

Actress (Dramatic)—Irene Worth, *Tiny Alice*

Actor (Musical)—Zero Mostel, *Fiddler on the Roof*

Actress (Musical)—Liza Minelli, *Flora, the Red Menace*

Play—*The Subject Was Roses*

Musical—*Fiddler on The Roof*

### News

**April 18.** Tonight at Carnegie Hall, 63-year-old contralto Marian Anderson gives her last concert.

**May 9.** Vladimir Horowitz returns to the concert stage after a 12-year absence. Nervous disorders in the early 1950s forced the pianist to remain in the recording studio. Rave reviews describe his Carnegie Hall performance as virtuosic.

**May 22.** An unknown thief deposits Goya's portrait of the Duke of Wellington in a railway baggage office. The National Gallery refused to ransom the painting four years ago when it was stolen during a rash of art thefts.

**June 1.** This past season, Broadway's top-seat price reached $9.90.

**August 10.** Seiji Ozawa conducts the New York Philharmonic in Central Park's new Fiberglas concert shell. The musicians are astounded when more than 70,000 people turn out.

**September 29.** Congress creates the National Foundation for the Arts and Humanities to promote a national arts policy. The two endowments will directly benefit avant-garde groups and regional theaters.

**More news.** Breaking all auction records for a modern painting, Cézanne's *House at L'Estaque* sells to a private collector for $800,000.

• When the Museum of Modern Art presents an exhibit of optical art, fashion designers and advertisers capitalize on public interest. Yet perception studies are hardly new; Josef Albers and Victor Vasarely have worked with optical illusion and color interaction for years.

# WORDS

Giorgio Bassani, *The Garden of the Finzi-Continis*
Ian Fleming, *The Man with the Golden Gun*
Haim G. Ginott, *Between Parent and Child*
Arthur Hailey, *Hotel*
Frank Herbert, *Dune*
*Low Carbohydrate Diet*
Malcolm X, with the assistance of Alex Haley, *The Autobiography of Malcolm X*
James A. Michener, *The Source*
Robin Moore, *The Green Berets*
Arthur M. Schlesinger, Jr., *A Thousand Days*
Theodore Sorensen, *Kennedy*
Morris L. West, *The Ambassador*

## News

**This year.** *Reader's Digest* joins the *New Yorker* and *Saturday Review* in refusing cigarette ads.

**More news.** Last year, when the Warren Commission censured the press for prejudging Lee Harvey Oswald and crowding the Dallas Police Station on the day of his murder, the American Society of Newspaper Editors discussed pooling reporters for some news events. But this year, an editorial committee finds the 1963 assassination coverage accurate and complete and rejects the notion of a press code of conduct to protect criminal suspects.

A first edition of Lewis J. Carroll's *Alice in Wonderland* brings $11,760 at auction.

## Cartoons and Comics

**This year.** Charles Schulz shows Linus's blanket attacking Lucy, but United Syndicate rejects the *Peanuts* sequence as "monster stuff." The disgruntled cartoonist sends president Laurence Rutman a baby blanket with a drawn monster saying "Boo!"

• Tremendously popular on American campuses, Marvel's teenage *Spider-Man* is now distributed in 36 countries (Italians call him the Nembo Kid).

• Comic books published in the 1930s and 1940s fetch up to $80. Collectors tend to be people who have lived through that era.

### TIME **Man of the Year**

General William C. Westmoreland

### New Words and Phrases

antigravity
biological clock
bomb (a long pass in football)
camp (gesture, style, or form)
degradable (capable of chemical decomposition)
escalation (an increase in extent, volume, or scope, as in the escalation of bombing)
isolated camera (a TV camera for sports close-ups)
kook

mono (sound transmission, recording, or reproduction)

neocolonialism

omnifocal (a bifocal eyeglass ground for a smooth transition)

parameter

the pill (oral contraceptive)

residual (royalty on TV reruns)

skateboard

skydiving

solar cell

teach-in

town house

New computer terms included computerize, descriptor, hardware, to program, and readout.

New astronautic terms included burnout, to dock, payload, pod, and splashdown.

The TV show "Get Smart" gives birth to the phrase, "Would you believe. . . ."

Already a common word for Mexican-Americans in the 1930s, *Chicano* comes into prominence with the grape-pickers' strike.

David Wise titles his newspaper article "The Credibility Gap" and defines the term as "the increasing public suspicion of official optimism and versions of events in the [Vietnam] war."

## Obituaries

**Thornton Waldo Burgess** (January 14, 1874–June 5, 1965). Begun as bedtime tales for his son, Burgess's *Peter Rabbit* stories have entertained generations of children.

**Thomas B. Costain** (May 8, 1885–October 8, 1965). His popular historical novels included *The Black Rose* (1945; 2 million copies sold).

**T(homas) S(tearns) Eliot** (September 26, 1888–January 4, 1965). Perhaps the most influential poet and critic of the first half of the century, Eliot received the 1948 Nobel prize in literature. He was born in the United States, but became a British subject in 1927.

**Shirley Jackson** (b. December 14, 1919–d. August 8, 1965) Her dark tales of horror and witchcraft included the short story "The Lottery" and the novel "The Haunting of Hill House" (1959).

**W(illiam) Somerset Maugham** (January 25, 1874–December 16, 1965). Although his prolific output of plays, short stories, and novels attracted a huge contemporary audience, the British writer will remain best remembered for four novels: *Of Human Bondage* (1915), *The Moon and Sixpence* (1919), *Cakes and Ale* (1930), and *The Razor's Edge* (1944).

## FASHION

### Haute Couture

In January, couturier Andre Courrèges unveils his "space-age" collection—a formless shift falling in geometric lines to just above the knee, helmetlike headgear, huge round goggles, and white kid boots.

Intended as an asexual glimpse into the future, the French designer's dramatic, sexy look of ultra-short hemlines thrills the fashion world and reestablishes Paris as the center of haute couture. More importantly for the average woman, his sanction of the mini length mends the growing rift between high fashion and the wilder trends of ready-to-wear.

### News

**February 10.** J. C. Penney tells *Women's Wear Daily*, "About 50 percent of the women in this country are under the age of 25. We're going after that group." The company signs three European designers with demonstrated appeal to younger women.

**More news.** French designer Emanuel Ungaro presents his first collection.

### Colors and Materials

Manufacturers abandon the textured, fussy fabrics of recent years for the op-art prints of the Courrèges and St. Laurent collections—harsh bicolor contrasts, predominantly white geometric designs, swirls, and sculpted raised patterns.

Important fabrics include whipcords, gabardines,

and flannels, and designers reflect the renewed interest in suede.

The near-nude trend popularizes lace (particularly coarser cotton varieties) for everything from coats to swimwear.

## Clothes

While adopting the basic Courrèges trapeze shape and constructed line, the ready-to-wear industry ends hemlines at the top of the knee.

In the early 1960s, hosiery mills introduced an all-in-one brief and stockings called panty-hose. Sizing and shaping problems persist, but with the arrival of the mini, women give panty-hose another look. Meanwhile, lace leotards and tapestry-design stockings—new arrivals late last year—flatter the new legginess.

In keeping with the see-through look, department stores carry garments with transparent fabric over the midriff and cutouts over ribs and armholes. Lingerie companies, to create the illusion of nothing underneath, introduce "invisible underwear"

The swimwear hit of the summer, a black Lycra one-piece from Cole of California, plunges from shoulder to navel with a mesh V-inset.

Furriers go after the younger market with medium-priced jackets and "pop" coats, mainly in dyed rabbit.

In a short-lived fad, girls sew up calico granny dresses, long-sleeved, high-waisted, ankle-length with a ruffle, and finished with a choker or round neckline.

Slim-line pantsuits (slacks and matching jacket) win approval for the city.

Young women prefer straight or A-line shifts and jumpers for school and daywear, or hipster pants with moderate bell-bottoms. The favorite sweater is a close-fitting, narrow-ribbed "poor boy."

## Accessories

Courrèges uses kid-leather boots to adjust the eye to his radical new hemline. Zipped up the inside, squared off at the top, go-go boots (from the French) look like loose-fitting rubbers. Yet the already popular style sells phenomenally well in white, black, a black-white combination, bright colors, and patterns, with or without fur-edging or fringe. The craze peaks next year, but the fashion boot is here to stay.

Shoe stores offer flat-heeled pumps with chains or silver buckles. Peek-a-boo casual shoes follow the nude look.

During the summer, huge sunglasses and cutout hats crowd the beaches.

## Hair and Cosmetics

To achieve the popular straight style, young girls lay their curly hair on an ironing board, cover the tresses with a towel (to prevent burning), then iron them on the wash-and-wear setting. The hour-long procedure must be repeated with every shampooing.

According to *Time* magazine, society no longer frowns on hair rollers outside the home. (Many women still wear the lacquered bouffant.)

In London, hairstylist Vidal Sassoon makes headlines with a short, easy-to-keep cut, softly shaped and layered with deep bangs.

## Obituaries

**Helena Rubinstein** (1871–April 1, 1965). The head of Helena Rubinstein cosmetics started out 63 years ago in Europe with a beauty cream. With profits from that venture, she opened a salon in London then one in Paris before setting up a third in New York in 1915. Rubinstein remained in the United States and quickly built up a chain. At the time of her death, the huge firm counts some 110 products bearing her name.

# MUSIC

"(I Can't Get No) Satisfaction"—Rolling Stones
"Yesterday"—Beatles
"Help!"—Beatles

"Mrs. Brown You've Got a Lovely Daughter"—
Herman's Hermits
"Turn! Turn! Turn!"—Byrds
"I Got You Babe"—Sonny & Cher
"Downtown"—Petula Clark
"I Can't Help Myself"—Four Tops
"You've Lost That Lovin' Feeling"—Righteous
Brothers
"This Diamond Ring"—Gary Lewis & the Play-
boys
"Help Me, Rhonda"—Beach Boys
"Get Off My Cloud"—Rolling Stones
"Stop! In the Name of Love"—Supremes
"I Hear a Symphony"—Supremes
"Eight Days a Week"—Beatles
"I'm Telling You Now"—Freddie & the Dreamers
"My Girl"—Temptations
"Hang on Sloopy"—McCoys
"Over and Over"—Dave Clark Five
"Back in My Arms Again"—Supremes
"Game of Love"—Wayne Fontana & the Mind-
benders
"Mr. Tambourine Man"—Byrds
"Eve of Destruction"—Barry McGuire
"Ticket to Ride"—Beatles
"I'm Henry VIII, I Am"—Herman's Hermits
"A Lover's Concerto"—Toys
"Wooly Bully"—Sam the Sham & the Pharaohs
"Can't You Hear My Heartbeat"—Herman's Her-
mits
"Like a Rolling Stone"—Bob Dylan
"1-2-3"—Len Barry
Note: *Soul* replaces the term *R&B* on the hit
charts.

## Grammys (1965)

Record of the Year—Herb Alpert & the Tijuana
Brass, "A Taste of Honey"
Song of the Year (songwriter)—Paul Francis
Webster and Johnny Mandel, "The Shadow of
Your Smile"
Album of the Year—Frank Sinatra, *September of
My Years*
Best Vocal Performance (Male)—Frank Sinatra,
"It Was a Very Good Year" (single)

*Already an established "protest" singer in the early 1960s,
Joan Baez promoted Bob Dylan by recording his songs and
sharing concert bills. Photographed together in London this
year, the 24-year-olds soon end their romantic involvement.*

Best Vocal Performance (Female)—Barbra Streisand, *My Name Is Barbra* (album)
Best New Artist—Tom Jones

## News

**July 25.** In his album *Bringing It All Back Home*
released earlier this year, folk singer Bob Dylan
backed half his cuts with a rock 'n' roll band. Today,
the audience at the Newport Folk Festival boos his
use of electric instruments. But Dylan ignores the
criticism, and *Highway 61 Revisited*, his next LP,
revolutionizes white music with a rock-beat fusion
of protest songs, folk music, and the blues. In the
process, he becomes an American cultural hero.

**August 15.** At the start of their third U.S. tour,
the Beatles sing 12 songs in 35 minutes before
56,000 screaming fans at New York's Shea Stadium.

The group receives $160,000. By the end of 1965, their record sales top 140 million.

---

*Statistics:* The registry of the Beatles Fan Clubs International shows more Canadian members than any other nationality.

---

**August 27.** The Beatles hold a jukebox jam session with Elvis Presley in his Bel Air mansion. No photographs or recordings exist of the historic meeting.

**October 26.** Queen Elizabeth invests the Beatles as members of the Order of the British Empire. In June, when Buckingham Palace announced the upcoming MBEs, many previous recipients returnedtheir medals in protest. John Lennon later reveals the quartet smoked marijuana in a palace bathroom.

**More news.** "Back in My Arms Again" gives the Supremes an unprecedented fifth consecutive No. 1 hit.

• With Dylan's "Mr. Tambourine Man," the Byrds become the first group to play folk music with electric instruments. Many critics regard this decade's most innovative group as a serious threat to the dominance of the Beatles.

But the emergence of folk-rock in the United States fails to break the British stranglehold. The Rolling Stones, with their enormously successful "(I Can't Get No) Satisfaction," take over as the world's No. 2 group. Petula Clark becomes the first British female to top U.S. charts, and the Yardbirds place two songs in the top 10 this year. (Eric Clapton left the superstar quintet and Jeff Beck took his place before their first hit, "For Your Love.")

---

*Statistics:* Each year through 1950–1956, 20 records held the top three positions for an average eight weeks. Now, 34 songs make the top 3 for an average five weeks.

---

• With the Frug, partnerless dancing becomes the norm. Other new steps this year include the Boogaloo and the Shaggy Dog.

For adults, platform go-go dancing becomes all the rage in discos (from the French "au go go"). Hired performers dance on platforms or in cages above the dance floor. Customers soon climb up there to dance themselves. The idea will lose its vogue next year.

• Over the past 15 years, the number of singers who play instruments has increased 85 percent. In the last half of this decade, many guitarists experiment with electronic feedback and other technical variations. The Who, led by Pete Townshend, smash instruments on stage while Jimi Hendrix will burn some of his.

• Very late one night, Barry McGuire lays down some rough vocals over an instrumental track. When the tape receives a positive response at a local station, the vice-president of the Dunhill label releases that early mix as the final version. Some radio stations ban McGuire's protest song, but "Eve of Destruction" shoots to No. 1.

• The soundtrack of *The Sound of Music* places in the top 10 albums through to 1967.

• In the late fifties, the Primes and the Distants merged as the Elgins. Before Berry Gordy released their first cut in 1961, the group was renamed the Temptations. In 1964, "The Way You Do the Things You Do" reached No. 11. This year's "My Girl," by Smokey Robinson, shoots to the top.

In the first solo by a Beatle, Paul McCartney is backed by a string quartet (the label still reads the Beatles). He awoke one morning with the melody complete in his head. Fortunately his first lyrics, "Scrambled eggs, I love your legs," gave way to haunting phrases. The most successful ballad of the rock era, "Yesterday" will also become the most recorded song in the history of popular music.

---

*New Recording Artists*

Shirley Bassey (in North America)
Byrds
Donovan
Guess Who
Tom Jones

Gary Lewis & the Playboys
Simon & Garfunkel
Sonny & Cher
Turtles
Who
Yardbirds
Young Rascals

## Obituaries

**Bill Black** (September 17, 1926–October 21, 1965). The bass player, who toured with Elvis Presley from 1954 to 1959, retired from his Bill Black Combo in 1962. He died of a brain tumor.

**Nat King Cole** (March 17, 1919–February 15, 1965). An important jazz pianist in his early days, Cole found fame as a ballad singer. His early hits included "Mona Lisa" (1950) and, in the year the Nat King Cole Trio dissolved, "Unforgettable" (1951). His smooth voice has influenced other black singers, including Sam Cooke and Otis Redding. (Reportedly, Chuck Berry has said, "If I had only one artist to listen to through eternity, it would be Nat Cole.") Later hits included "Ramblin' Rose" (1962) and "Those Lazy-Hazy-Crazy Days of Summer" (1963). He died of lung cancer.

**Alan Freed** (December 15, 1922–January 20, 1965). The self-proclaimed father of rock 'n' roll— "Anyone who says rock and roll is a passing fad or a flash in the pan has rocks in his head, dad!"—earned his title as the first major DJ and the first to promote black artists to white teenagers. But his large role in the growth of rock made him a prime target in the payola scandal at the end of the last decade. Recently indicted for tax evasion, he died of uremia.

**Spike (Lindley Armstrong) Jones** (December 14, 1911–May 1, 1965). The U.S. bandleader formed his slapstick musical group, City Slickers, in the 1930s. Their records emphasized comedy, with pistol shots, bells, whistles, and other sound effects, but Jones always produced quality musicianship.

**Ted Snyder** (August 15, 1881–July 16, 1965). A founder of the American Society of Composers, Authors, and Publishers (ASCAP) in 1914, the composer wrote "The Sheik of Araby" (1921) and "Who's Sorry Now?" (1923), among others.

# MOVIES

*The Bedford Incident* (d. James B. Harris; bw)— Richard Widmark, Sidney Poitier, James MacArthur

*Cat Ballou* (d. Eliot Silverstein; color)—Jane Fonda, Lee Marvin, Michael Callan, Dwayne Hickman

*The Cincinnati Kid* (d. Norman Jewison; color)— Steve McQueen, Edward G. Robinson, Ann-Margret, Karl Malden

*Darling* (British, d. John Schlesinger; bw)—Julie Christie, Dirk Bogarde, Laurence Harvey

*Doctor Zhivago* (d. David Lean; color)—Omar Sharif, Julie Christie, Rod Steiger, Alec Guinness, Tom Courtenay, Geraldine Chaplin

*Help!* (British, d. Dick Lester; color)—John Lennon, Paul McCartney, George Harrison, Ringo Starr, Leo McKern

*How to Murder Your Wife* (d. Richard Quine; color)—Jack Lemmon, Virna Lisi, Terry-Thomas

*The Ipcress File* (British, d. Sidney J. Furie; color)—Michael Caine, Nigel Green

*Juliet of the Spirits* (Italian, d. Federico Fellini; color)—Giulietta Masina, Sandra Milo, Mario Pisu, Valentina Cortese

*The Knack* (British, d. Richard Lester; bw)— Rita Tushingham, Michael Crawford, Ray Brooks

*Othello* (British, d. Stuart Burge; color)— Laurence Olivier, Frank Finlay, Maggie Smith

*A Patch of Blue* (d. Guy Green; bw)—Sidney Poitier, Elizabeth Hartman, Shelley Winters

*The Pawnbroker* (d. Sidney Lumet; bw)—Rod Steiger, Geraldine Fitzgerald, Brock Peters

*Repulsion* (British, d. Roman Polanski; bw)— Catherine Deneuve, Ian Hendry, John Fraser

*Shenandoah* (d. Andrew V. McLaglen; color)— James Stewart, Doug McClure, Glenn Corbett, Patrick Wayne, Rosemary Forsyth, Katharine Ross

*Ship of Fools* (d. Stanley Kramer; bw)—Vivien Leigh, Simone Signoret, Oskar Werner, José

Ferrer, Lee Marvin, Elizabeth Ashley, George Segal

*The Shop on the High Street* (U.S.: *The Shop on Main Street*; Czechoslovakian, d. Jan Kadar; bw)—Jožef Kroner, Ida Kaminska

*The Sound of Music* (d. Robert Wise; color)—Julie Andrews, Christopher Plummer, Eleanor Parker, Richard Haydn, Peggy Wood

*The Spy Who Came in from the Cold* (British, d. Martin Ritt; bw)—Richard Burton, Claire Bloom, Oskar Werner

*That Darn Cat!* (Disney, d. Robert Stevenson; color)—Hayley Mills, Dean Jones, Dorothy Provine, Roddy McDowall

*The Train* (d. John Frankenheimer; bw)—Burt Lancaster, Paul Scofield, Michel Simon, Jeanne Moreau

## Academy Awards

**April 5.** During the evening, TV cameras switch back and forth from Julie Andrews to Audrey Hepburn. In casting *My Fair Lady*, Jack Warner chose Hepburn, a big name, over Andrews, the singer-actress who created Eliza Doolittle on stage. His controversial decision split the industry and cost Hepburn an acting nomination.

Bob Hope hosts. This year's ceremonies mark the last Oscar telecast in black and white.

Best Picture—*My Fair Lady*
Best Actor—Rex Harrison (*My Fair Lady*)
Best Actress—Julie Andrews (*Mary Poppins*)
Best Supporting Actor—Peter Ustinov (*Topkapi*)
Best Supporting Actress—Lila Kedrova (*Zorba the Greek*)
Best Director—George Cukor (*My Fair Lady*)
Best Song—"Chim Chim Cher-ee" from *Mary Poppins*
Best Foreign Film—*Yesterday, Today and Tomorrow* (Italian)

And, after 35 years of directing Oscar-winning films and actors, George Cukor wins his first Oscar—*My Fair Lady*.

## News

**March 9.** In a *Look* magazine interview, the legendary Bette Davis says of Hollywood, "Out here, women are dumped all the time. Only, I refused to be dumped." When producers described her box-office success in *What Ever Happened to Baby Jane?* (1962) as a fluke, she placed an ad in a Hollywood trade paper: "Mother of three . . . divorcée, American. Thirty years experience as an actress . . . wants steady employment in Hollywood."

**June 1.** Twelve Hollywood actors, writers, and directors filed suit on December 30, 1960, against the MPAA and its major corporate members for maintaining a blacklist. The plaintiffs, including four of the original Hollywood Ten, demanded treble damages for $2.5 million in lost income. Today, the twelve settle out of court for $80,000.

**June 22.** Low-budget "sand and sex" pictures from independents continue to reap enormous profits. (AIP's latest and most successful is *Beach Blanket Bingo*.)

A nameless Hollywood executive complains to *The New York Times*, "Teenage tastes are exerting a tyranny over our industry. It's getting so show business is one big puberty rite." Nonetheless, the major studios announce plans to increase their output of teen-oriented films.

**October 29.** Director Steve Binder shoots the Teenage Awards Music International at the Santa Monica Civic Auditorium. The revue includes the Rolling Stones, the Beach Boys (their sequence is cut), Chuck Berry, Marvin Gaye, Gerry & the Pacemakers, the Supremes, James Brown, Smokey Robinson and the Miracles, Leslie Gore, and Billy J. Kramer & the Dakotas. Fans will later describe "The TAMI Show"—the first rock concert film—as the greatest single gathering of rock musicians.

**November.** The Council of Motion Picture Organizations conducts an audience poll—the first of its kind—in 6,500 American theaters. Moviegoers select the late James Dean in *East of Eden* as best actor, Jennifer Jones in *Love Is a Many-Splendored Thing* as best actress, *Mister Roberts* as best picture, and Tab Hunter and Peggy Lee as most promising new personalities.

**November 17.** After 40 years on the Hollywood beat, ailing Louella Parsons retires. In earlier, more moralistic days, the syndicated gossip columnist could make or break a star or a movie. But in recent years, a growing number of big names—Frank Sinatra, Elvis Presley, Doris Day—refused to grant Lolly an interview. Parsons will die in 1972 at the estimated age of 90.

**More news.** Breaking its 34-year prohibition against nudity, the MPAA approves a scene of a woman naked to the waist as essential to the plot of *The Pawnbroker.* Filmmakers believe the decision opens the way for more explicit sex scenes in commercial films.

Over the past eight years, the average theater admission has increased 100 percent, from $.505 to $1.01.

| Top Box Office Stars | Newcomers |
| --- | --- |
| Sean Connery | Rosemary Forsyth |
| John Wayne | Michael Anderson, Jr. |
| Doris Day | Michael Caine |
| Julie Andrews | Michael Parks |
| Jack Lemmon | Mary Ann Mobley |
| Elvis Presley | Jocelyn Lane |
| Cary Grant | Mia Farrow |
| James Stewart | Julie Christie |
| Elizabeth Taylor | Richard Johnson |
| Richard Burton | Senta Berger |

## Top Money-Maker of the Year

*Mary Poppins* (1964)

## Flop of the Year

*The Greatest Story Ever Told*
Costs soar over $20 million, with director George Stevens' $1-million salary, countless cameos (John Wayne, the Roman centurion, speaks just one line), and expensive studio filming (after snow ruins location shots). Premiering at 4 hours 20 minutes, the biblical epic bombs. The length is

cut, again and again, in a desperate attempt to draw audiences, but the picture fails to break even.

## Quote of the Year

"What the hell! Rock Hudson's been asking Doris Day the same question for years—only here the virgin isn't turning 40."
—Creator-director Bill Asher, comments on his AIP Beach series, starring almost-lovers Frankie Avalon, 25, and Annette Funicello, 22. (*Look*, March 9, 1965)

## Obituaries

**Constance Bennett** (October 22, 1905–July 24, 1965). The sophisticated comedienne is best remembered as the beautiful ghost in the Topper films of the late 1930s.

**Clara Bow** (1905–September 26, 1965). The modern "It" girl (from the 1927 film of the same name) became one of cinema's first sex goddesses. But with her fragile mental health and disappointing talkies, Bow retired at age 26.

**Dorothy Dandridge** (1924–September 8, 1965). Leading roles in *Carmen Jones* (1954) and *Porgy and Bess* (1959) made the singer-actress one of America's first black movie stars. She died from a barbiturate overdose.

**Linda Darnell** (October 17, 1923–April 10, 1965). Among the most popular motion-picture stars of the 1940s, the retired actress died in a fire.

**Judy Holliday** (June 21, 1922–June 7, 1965). Hollywood's most famous dumb blond, the comedienne made only 11 films before her death from cancer. Her credits include *Adam's Rib* (1949), *Born Yesterday* (1950)—for which she won an Oscar—and *The Solid Gold Cadillac* (1956).

**Stan Laurel** (June 16, 1890–February 23, 1965). The creative mind behind the hilarious Laurel and Hardy routines, the thin half of the comedy duo wrote most of the gags in their 200 films and also improvised before the camera. The English-born comic would blink in confusion, scratch the top of his head, then blubber as Hardy berated him for creating "another fine mess."

**Jeanette MacDonald** (June 18, 1907–January 14, 1965). The beautiful singer and comedienne is best remembered for her eight musicals with Nelson Eddy. At the height of their popularity in the 1930s, moviegoers called the couple "America's sweethearts." But movie tastes changed with the war, and when MacDonald completed her contract in 1942, she switched to the concert stage.

**David O. Selznick** (May 10, 1902–June 22, 1965). The motion-picture producer, famous for his hundreds of memos, was among the top five Hollywood producers for 22 consecutive years (1936–1957). His films included *Little Women* (1933), *The Prisoner of Zenda* (1937), and his greatest work, *Gone With the Wind* (1939).

# TELEVISION AND RADIO

## New Prime-Time TV Programs

"The Big Valley" (September 15, 1965–May 19, 1969; Western)—Barbara Stanwyck, Richard Long, Peter Breck, Lee Majors, Linda Evans

"The Dean Martin Show" (September 16, 1965–May 24, 1974; Comedy Variety)—Dean Martin *Note:* In the last year, the title will change to "The Dean Martin Comedy Hour."

"F Troop" (September 14, 1965–August 31, 1967; Situation Comedy)—Ken Berry, Forrest Tucker, Larry Storch

"The F.B.I." (September 19, 1965–September 8, 1974; Police Drama)—Efrem Zimbalist, Jr., Philip Abbot

"Get Smart" (September 18, 1965–September 11, 1970; Situation Comedy)—Don Adams, Barbara Feldon, Edward Platt

"Green Acres" (September 15, 1965–September 7, 1971; Situation Comedy)—Eddie Albert, Eva Gabor, Pat Buttram, Tom Lester

"Hogan's Heroes" (September 17, 1965–July 4, 1971; Situation Comedy)—Bob Crane, Werner Klemperer, John Banner, Robert Clary

"I Dream of Jeannie" (September 18, 1965–September 1, 1970; Situation Comedy)—Barbara Eden, Larry Hagman, Bill Daily, Hayden Rorke

"I Spy" (September 15, 1965–September 2, 1968; Adventure/Spy)—Robert Culp, Bill Cosby

"Lost In Space" (September 15, 1965–September 1, 1968; Science Fiction)—Guy Williams, June Lockhart, Mark Goddard, Bill Mumy, Jonathan Harris

"Run For Your Life" (September 13, 1965–September 11, 1968; Adventure)—Ben Gazzara

"The Wild Wild West" (September 17, 1965–September 1969; Western)—Robert Conrad, Ross Martin

## Emmy Awards 1964–1965 (September 12, 1965)

This year's Emmys are awarded under the broad categories of "Outstanding Program Achievement in Entertainment" and "Outstanding Individual Achievement in Entertainment: Actors and Performers." Some of the recipients follow.

"The Dick Van Dyke Show" (CBS)

"My Name Is Barbra" (CBS)

Leonard Bernstein ("New York Philharmonic Young People's Concerts with Leonard Bernstein," CBS)

Barbra Streisand ("My Name Is Barbra," CBS)

Dick Van Dyke ("The Dick Van Dyke Show," CBS)

## News

**January.** Generally, the networks stay with a poorly-rated program until the summer, the time for tinkering. But this year, under a barrage of new ABC and NBC programs, CBS president James Aubrey undertakes a midseason overhaul.

**February 1.** ABC replaces their nightly news anchor with Canadian Peter Jennings.

**April 7.** The first commercial satellite, *Early Bird*, relays television signals the day after launching. On May 2, the Comsat satellite links a global audience of 300 million in the United States, Canada, Mexico, and 17 European nations. Long-distance shots lack some distinction, but the program "Out of This World" clearly shows a heart-operation in Houston, a bullfight from Barcelona, Martin Luther King, Jr., speaking from Philadelphia, and other excerpts including a Canadian file photo of criminal Georges Lemay; he is subsequently arrested.

**April 18.** In 1958, according to *The New York Times*, TV technicians balanced their color using female stand-ins with red hair and green eyes. Today, with finer tuning, the women must have brown hair and olive complexions.

**April 19.** WINS becomes the first radio station with round-the-clock news programming. Previously, the New York City station broadcast rock 'n' roll.

**July 3.** Trigger, the famous palomino, dies at age 33. Using his teeth, the horse could sign an X in a hotel register, pull a pistol out of a holster, take a rope off a saddle, and untie a hobble—his and any other horse's at hand. Unable to faceputting his friend in the ground, cowboy star Roy Rogers has Trigger stuffed and mounted.

**August.** A few months ago, during the U.S. intervention in the Dominican Republic, Harry Reasoner stated on the CBS evening news that the White House had experienced "an apparent shortage of candor." Already the administration's least favorite network, CBS presents a controversial report on Vietnam this month.

Morley Safer shows American soldiers torching the village of Cam Ne because of Vietcong activity. The powerful images of marines setting fire to thatch roofs as villagers beg for a reprieve disturbs many viewers.

Although the Johnson administration pressures the networks to fall in line, the press generally is still granted easy access to the growing war front. Coverage of Vietnam drops off during 1966 simply because the programs consistently post a poor audience share.

**Fall.** CBS and NBC become virtually all-color networks with this season's schedule. ABC will join them next year.

> *Statistics:* A GE 11-inch color TV costs $249.95.

**September 8.** Wilbur moaned when "Mr. Ed" threatened to leave, but the horse shot back, "Why not just get a dog or a cat? Everybody's going in for compacts these days." After the last show tonight, the program enters reruns. Years will pass before fans learn the identity of that wonderful voice—Allan "Rocky" Lane—or that peanut butter was placed under Mr. Ed's upper lip to make him "talk."

**September 12.** A simultaneous premiere week by all three networks presents viewers with a mind-boggling schedule of 35 new programs and new episodes of 60 returning shows.

**September 25.** While not the first animated real-life figures, "The Beatles" nonetheless sets a trend for Saturday-morning cartoons. With high ratings over four years, the show will establish a comedy and rock-music style that other networks will emulate for years to come.

**October 15.** Effective today, AM radio stations with FM affiliates in cities with over 100,000 people must broadcast a minimum 50 percent original programming on the FM station. Simulcasting will no longer be acceptable.

This year, the first FM antenna in the United States is mounted on the Empire State Building.

**October 24.** NBC is the first network to televise the evening news seven days a week.

**November 9.** While the worst blackout in history shuts down every New York City television station, about half the radio stations remain on the air with auxiliary power. In their greatest hour since the advent of TV, radio announcers earn much of the credit for preventing city-wide panic.

**December 9.** CBS presents the first *Peanuts* special, "A Charlie Brown Christmas." Its success prompts Bill Melendez Productions to produce other Schulz animation specials. The specials becomes the longest-running in television history.

**More news.** Finally bowing to pressure, CBS removes "Amos 'n' Andy" from syndication. Black Americans had continued to protest against the racial stereotypes in the 1950s comedy.

## TV Commercials

Charmin—Mr. Whipple, played by Dick Wilson, tells shoppers not to squeeze the toilet paper.

Comet—Child star Jane Withers appears as Josephine the Plumber.

Marlboro—Introduced as a woman's brand in the 1950s, Marlboro is promoted as a masculine cigarette in this decade.

## Obituaries

**Brace Beemer** (1903–March 1, 1965). The radio actor played the Lone Ranger from 1941 until the last broadcast in 1955. After some 70,000 kids turned out for a single appearance, the network kept him under wraps to maintain his heroic credibility.

**Dorothy Kilgallen** (July 3, 1913–November 8, 1965). The New York newspaper columnist was best known to Americans as a regular on the quiz show "What's My Line?"

**Edward R. Murrow** (April 25, 1908–April 27, 1965). Generally regarded as the greatest newscaster in radio and television, Murrow first came to public attention with a series of dramatic wartime broadcasts from London. During the 1950s, he was seen regularly on TV with "See It Now" and "Person to Person." Murrow won four Peabody's for excellence in broadcasting, one Emmy, and in 1964, the Medal of Freedom—the nation's highest civilian honor—from President Johnson. Eric Sevareid of CBS comments, "He was a shooting star and we will live in his afterglow a very long time." A chain-smoker, Murrow died of lung cancer.

# SPORTS

## Winners

### Baseball

World Series—Los Angeles Dodgers (NL), 4 games; Minnesota Twins (AL), 3 games;

Player of the Year—Zoilo Versalles (Minnesota Twins, AL); Willie Mays (San Francisco Giants, NL)

Rookie of the Year—Curt Blefary (Baltimore Orioles, AL); Jim Lefebvre (Los Angeles Dodgers, NL)

### Football

NFL Championship—Green Bay Packers 23, Cleveland Browns 12

AFL Championship—Buffalo Bills 23, San Diego Chargers 0

College Bowls (January 1, 1965)—
Rose Bowl, Michigan 34, Oregon State 7
Cotton Bowl, Arkansas 10, Nebraska 7
Orange Bowl, Texas 21, Alabama 17
Sugar Bowl, LSU 13, Syracuse 10

Heisman Trophy—Mike Garrett (USC, HB)

Grey Cup—Hamilton Tiger-Cats 22, Winnipeg Blue Bombers 16

### Basketball

NBA Championship—Boston Celtics, 4 games; LA Lakers, 1 game

MVP of the Year—Bill Russell (Boston Celtics)

Rookie of the Year—Willis Reed (New York Knickerbockers)

NCAA Championship—UCLA 91, Michigan 80

### Tennis

U.S. National—Men, Manuel Santana (vs. Clifford Drysdale); Women, Margaret Smith (vs. Billie Jean Moffitt [King])

Wimbledon—Men, Roy Emerson (vs. Fred

Stolle); Women, Margaret Smith (vs. Maria Bueno)

## Golf

Masters—Jack Nicklaus
U.S. Open—Gary Player
British Open—Peter Thomson

## Hockey

Stanley Cup—Montreal Canadiens, 4 games; Chicago Blackhawks, 3 games

## Ice Skating

World Championship—Men, Alain Calmat (France); Women, Petra Burka (Canada)
U.S. National—Men, Gary Visconti; Women, Peggy Fleming
Canadian National—Men, Donald Knight; Women, Petra Burka

## Kentucky Derby

Lucky Debonair—Willie Shoemaker, jockey

## Athlete of the Year

Male—Sandy Koufax (Baseball)
Female—Kathy Whitworth (Golf)
*Last Season*

Jim Brown (Football)
Tom Heinsohn (Basketball)
Tom Johnson (Hockey)
Dick Lane (Football)
Ted Lindsay (Hockey)
Bob Pettit (Basketball)
Sugar Ray Robinson (Boxing)
Warren Spahn (Baseball)

# News

**April 9.** To avoid the Texas heat, the Houston Sports Association built the Astrodome—the world's largest clear-span structure—above an air-conditioned playing field and 45,000 plush seats. Today, in the facility's inaugural exhibition game, the newly renamed Houston Astros beat the New York Yankees 2–1. Almost immediately, players complain that fly balls disappear in the glaring light. The club paints over the dome panels and turns to Monsanto for plastic grass. It quickly becomes known as Astro-Turf.

**May 25.** Last year's Liston-Clay fight shocked boxing fans; tonight's rematch produces outrage. Still the underdog, Muhammad Ali throws a seemingly harmless punch in the first round and Liston collapses. In the *Los Angeles Herald Examiner*, Melvin Durslag writes, "In my opinion, Liston either took money to go down or the Muslims had him scared to death."

Rumor suggested that the Muslims had promised dire consequences if Ali lost the title. But the champ's followers declare that Liston simply went down under a flash right hand. The controversy spurs the U.S. Senate to investigate the need for a federal boxing commission. No decision is reached.

On November 22, Ali scores a 12th-round TKO over former heavyweight champion Floyd Patterson.

**October.** During the 1964–1965 play-offs, the NHL required teams to dress a standby goalie. Previously when a goalie was injured, fans waited up to half an hour while the backup pulled on his layers of equipment. The experiment proved so successful that this season teams must dress a second goalie for every game.

**November 17.** Ford Frick retires after 13 years and Will Eckert becomes commissioner of major league baseball. Widely regarded as honest and intelligent, the retired USAF general nonetheless possesses no special aptitude for the job (he attended his last game 10 years ago). His negotiating skills prove unequal to the task and in 1968 he will offend fans by refusing to cancel games after the King and Kennedy assassinations. At the end of that year, club owners will vote him out.

**December 10.** Sugar Ray Robinson hangs up his gloves at age 45. During his 25-year career, the black boxer won 174 bouts (109 knockouts),

*Teammates mob Dodger pitcher Sandy Koufax after his perfect game against the Chicago Cubs. Shown left to right are Willie Davis, Wes Parker, Ron Fairly, Sandy Koufax, and Don LeJohn.*

including an unprecedented 5 victories over middleweight title holders. With his amazing footwork and superior hand speed, Robinson actually knocked out opponents while moving backward. He lost just 19 fights (5 over the last 6 months).

Generations of fighters have patterned themselves after Sugar Ray, but his retirement marks the end of an era. With each championship bout now worth hundreds of thousands of dollars, no boxer needs to fight more than a few times a year; Robinson stepped into the ring 201 times.

**More news.** Next year, prior to the start of the football season, Jim Brown retires. For eight of his nine years with the Cleveland Browns, the durable fullback led the NFL in rushing. And in amassing 12,312 yards, he scored 126 touchdowns for 756 points, the highest career total by a nonkicker. Brown leaves at the top of his game to pursue an acting career.

## Records

**September 9.** Sandy Koufax throws a perfect game against the Chicago Cubs and becomes the first major league pitcher to win 4 no-hitters (along with June 30, 1962, against the Mets; May 11, 1963, against the Giants; and June 4, 1964, against the Phillies).

Before the season ends, Koufax chalks up a record 382 strikeouts, smashing Bob Feller's 1946 mark of 348, and pitches 9 more shutouts (7 during the regular season, 2 in the World Series). He is the obvious choice for the Cy Young Award, but loses the MVP award to Willie Mays.

**December 12.** Gale Sayers' six touchdowns for the Chicago Bears ties the record held by Ernie Nevers (1929) and Dub Jones (1951). By the end of the season, the rookie halfback scores a record 22 touchdowns and equals or breaks six other NFL marks.

## What They Said

During the doubleheader break, on March 8, some 2,500 fans parade their homemade banners around the field at Shea Stadium. The winning entry, emblazoned on a bed sheet, reads, "To error is human, to forgive is a Mets' fan."

## Obituaries

**Branch Rickey** (December 20, 1881–December 9, 1965). During his 25 years with the St. Louis Cardinals, Rickey turned his team into a powerhouse by developing baseball's primitive farm system into a network of minor league clubs. With the Dodgers, he signed the first black player in modern baseball, then drew on Negro League talent to build a Brooklyn dynasty. Always an innovator, Rickey supported pitching machines and batting helmets and backed the Continental League. He returned to the Cardinals before retiring in 1964.

**Amos Alonzo Stagg** (August 16, 1862–March 17, 1965). Stagg remains the only member of the college Football Hall of Fame to be honored as both a player and a coach. Over 41 years at the University of Chicago (1891–1933), the coach won 7 titles. He spent 14 years at the College of the Pacific, joined his son to coach in Pennsylvania, then returned to California as an advisor. The "Grand Old Man" of football retired at the age of 98 with a record 314 wins, 181 losses, and 35 ties.

# 1966

Johnson believes America can fight a war on two fronts—against poverty at home and against the Communists in Southeast Asia. After all, the United States just marked its 59th month of continuous economic expansion. But by the end of the year, the Vietnam War begins to inflate the economy and pare funds from many of the president's Great Society programs. And with thousands of protesters gathering at each antiwar demonstration, the first divisive cracks become evident.

For black Americans, the promise of the 1965 Voting Rights Act stalls under white resistance while Congress refuses to act on open housing. Frustrated young militants support the birth of Black Power and the Black Panther party.

Elsewhere in the world, de Gaulle kicks NATO out of France, Indira Gandhi becomes prime minister of India, 116 children die in Aberfan, a nuclear bomb disappears off Spain, and floods in Florence damage hundreds of art treasures.

A number of remarkable space achievements include soft moon landings by both superpowers. The Supreme Court rules on the Miranda case and the motion picture code finally approves "blue" language. Walt Disney dies, Cary Grant makes his last movie, and the Beatles give their last concert. Hemlines rise further and paper clothes are a brief fad. The Milwaukee Braves move to Atlanta and Bobby Hull breaks the 50-goal mark. And TV offers unusual fare with "Batman," "The Monkees," and "Star Trek."

## NEWS

**January 12.** In its sixth year, the severest U.S. drought of this century affects some 5 million people in 14 northeastern states. Water levels have dropped in some areas to record lows. Conditions will return to normal with heavy snowfalls in the 1966–1967 winter.

**January 17.** During refueling, a U.S. B-52 bomber collides with a K-135 air tanker over the Spanish Mediterranean coast. All but four of the crewmen die, and four hydrogen bombs plummet to Earth. Three land near the village of Palomares, releasing some radioactive material on impact, but the fourth disappears into the sea.

Washington withholds news of the missing bomb from the public until March 2. After an extensive search involving some 100 divers, a bathyscaphe, and two miniature subs, the weapon is finally recovered on April 7. The Americans eventually remove 1,500 tons of topsoil from the village for storage in the United States.

The Palomares disaster was the 13th American "broken arrow," or airplane accident, involving nuclear weapons; none have exploded.

**January 19.** The ruling Indian Congress party elects Indira Gandhi as prime minister, replacing Lal Bahadur Shastri who died of a heart attack last week. The 48-year-old Gandhi is the daughter of Jawaharlal Nehru, who was prime minister of India from independence until his death in 1964.

**January 24.** In submitting the first $100-billion budget in U.S. history, Johnson admits that the cost of increased commitments in Vietnam has hindered Great Society programs.

**January 29–31.** The worst blizzard in 70 years hits the Eastern Seaboard of the United States, from New England to North Carolina. At least 166 people die. More severe storms will follow through the winter months.

**February 8.** With rising troop requests and an administration request for $12.3 billion in additional funding, the Senate Foreign Relations Committee holds hearings on U.S. policy in Vietnam.

During two days of televised coverage on the 8th and 10th, George Kennan of the Institute for Advanced Study states, "There is more respect to be won in the opinion of the world by a resolute and courageous liquidation of unsound positions than in the most stubborn pursuit of extravagant or unpromising objectives." Mail to the committee opposes the escalation of the war 31–1.

Defense Secretary McNamara has admitted to the president that the United States is in "an escalating military stalemate," yet he continues to urge more troops and more bombing. South Vietnamese officials, for their part, steadfastly refuse to participate in any peace talks with the NLF.

At the beginning of March, Congress passes a $4.8-billion military authorization bill (392–4 in the House, 93–2 in the Senate).

*President Lyndon Baines Johnson and Defense Secretary Robert McNamara confer in the Cabinet Room of the White House on the military situation in Vietnam.*

*Statistics:* By the end of 1965, the Americans had lost a total of 1,643 men in hostile action in Vietnam—1,404 of them died in 1965, most in the last four months of that year. Yet with helicopters providing almost immediate medical evacuation, fatalities represent less than 2 percent of the wounded. An increasing number of soldiers who previously would have died now survive, although some have permanent disabilities.

**March 5.** A BOAC flight crashes on Mt. Fuji, the third aviation disaster in Japan over the past month. On February 4, a crash in Tokyo Bay killed 133. The second plane, a Canadian Pacific airliner, crashed and exploded just 19 hours ago at the Tokyo airport, killing 64. The BOAC 707, with 124 on board, taxied past the Canadian wreckage upon takeoff.

**March 9.** In hearings before the Senate Commerce Subcommittee, GM admits to investigating consumer advocate Ralph Nader, age 31, following last year's publication of *Unsafe at Any Speed.* An indictment of the auto industry, for sacrificing safety to style, Nader's book calls for legislation to establish safety standards.

GM president James Roche apologizes on the 22nd. Nader accepts, but he sues the company and the two detectives. (The suit will be settled out of court in 1970). The scandal places Nader in the media spotlight and provides the dramatic impetus for safety legislation. In September, President Johnson signs the National Traffic and Motor Vehicle Safety Act, setting production standards for all motor vehicles from 1968 on, establishing a coordinated national safety program, and requiring manufacturers to recall all defective models.

**March 9.** President de Gaulle announces that France is withdrawing its troops from NATO and will assume control of all foreign military bases on French soil by April 1969. With Europe no longer threatened as it was after W.W.II, France has no wish to remain subordinate to an unnecessary defense organization. But Paris views the NATO military organization as separate from the North Atlantic Defense Treaty of 1949 and insists on continued participation in the alliance. The 14 NATO partners rebuke de Gaulle's decision but accede to his wishes.

**March 10.** Canadian Liberal Justice Minister Lucien Cardin reveals that cabinet members in the defeated Conservative government were involved with Gerda Munsinger, an East German woman with Communist connections. Pierre Sevigny, then deputy minister of national defense, had an affair with Munsinger but broke it off after Conservative Prime Minister Diefenbaker reprimanded him in 1960; Munsinger returned to Germany.

Canada's first major government sex scandal monopolizes the headlines as the Liberal government appoints a Royal Commission to investigate the allegations. The final report criticizes former prime minister Diefenbaker for retaining Sevigny, since his affair constituted a security risk. But the one-man commission concludes that no disloyalty was involved.

**March 12.** As a full-scale bloodbath tears the country apart President Sukarno of Indonesia yields to an army ultimatum and surrenders authority to General Suharto.

Last September, the military crushed an attempted coup by the Indonesian Communist Party (PKI). In the months since, the military has encouraged Muslim youth groups and local militia in the systematic elimination of party members. At least 250,000 have died, and perhaps as many as 1 million, in one of the worst mass murders of the century. The staunchly anti-Communist Suharto bans the remnants of the PKI and moves to stabilize the nation.

**March 24.** The U.S. Selective Service announces that college deferments will now be based on scholastic performance. When a similar test used during the Korean War was discontinued in 1961, local draft boards began deferring those college students who pursued a full-time program leading to a degree.

**March 25.** In a Justice Department case, the U.S. Supreme Court finds (6–3) the Virginia poll tax an unconstitutional barrier to voting. The ruling, in effect, contravenes all state poll taxes, and on April 8, a Mississippi federal court outlaws the last poll tax in America.

**May.** News of China's Cultural Revolution reaches the West this month. Reportedly Mao Tse-tung had expressed his concern with the lack of revolutionary zeal and the increasing number of dissenters, who had taken "the capitalist road." First he reasserted control over the party and the army, then asked young people to search out those disloyal to the worker-peasant revolution.

Militant teenagers have formed the Red Guards to zealously attack all aspects of bourgeois or foreign life, destroying private property, renaming well-known streets, and trumpeting proletariat dogma in huge parades. But what began as a leftist purge of intellectuals has quickly degenerated into a massive social struggle. Few die (some during interrogation), but by 1967 the youthful terrorist squads—the only students to carry out a successful revolution in the 1960s—will threaten anarchy, and Mao will be forced to call out the army to reestablish order.

Still, in the end, the Cultural Revolution will reaffirm Maoism in China and, through Mao's *Little Red Book* of essays and thoughts, establish the

Communist leader as a cult figure in the Western world.

**May 5.** The influential Senator J. William Fulbright, chairman of the Foreign Relations Committee since 1959, speaks out against U.S. involvement in Vietnam. In the last of three lectures at Johns Hopkins University, he attacks the administration for a foreign policy that presumes Americans can "go into a small, alien, undeveloped Asian nation and create stability where there is chaos, the will to fight where there is defeatism, democracy where there is no tradition of it, and honest government where corruption is almost a way of life." He describes Americans as "still acting like boy scouts dragging reluctant old ladies across streets they do not want to cross."

**May 16.** SNCC elects 25-year-old Stokely Carmichael as chairman and within a month shifts its focus from civil rights to Black Power, excluding white people from any position of influence within the organization.

At the CORE national convention on July 4, members adopt the concept of Black Power as well, denouncing integration as "irrelevant." CORE national director Floyd McKissick states, "As long as the white man has all the power and money, nothing will happen, because we have nothing. The only way to achieve meaningful change is to take power." (During the convention, the term *black* rather than *Negro* is increasingly used.)

On July 5, the NAACP disassociates itself from Black Power, underscoring the rift between the moderate faction of the civil rights movement, led by King and the SCLC, and the militants, headed by Carmichael and McKissick.

**May 18.** In the first incidence of violence in the 99-year history of the Canadian House of Commons, an explosion in a third-floor washroom kills a would-be terrorist. An examination of his personal effects reveals that Paul Chartier blamed the politicians for the country's problems. He had strapped dynamite to his body, but the short fuse burned down before he reached the Commons chamber.

**June 6.** Since the enactment of the 1965 Voting Rights Act, the number of registered black voters in

the United States has increased from 687,000 to 1.1 million. But white resistance in the South remains strong.

James Meredith, beginning a Memphis to Jackson march to encourage voter registration, is shot. As he writhes on the ground, the sheriff on the scene makes no attempt to stop or pursue the shooter. With news of the attack, civil rights activists quickly unite to continue the march.

The police harass them, beating several, but the activists remain nonviolent. The march, which registers some 4,000 new voters, ends on the 26th with a rally of some 15,000 in front of the Mississippi state capitol in Jackson.

But when Martin Luther King, Jr., and Stokely Carmichael speak before the crowd, the growing philosophical division within the movement becomes painfully clear. King speaks of his dream, that one day in Mississippi "justice will become reality for all of God's children." But young blacks listen more closely to Carmichael who argues, "The last thing we have to do is build a power base so strong in this country that we'll bring 'em to their knees every time they mess with us."

Never again will the two civil rights groups come together for a great march.

**June 13.** A deeply divided U.S. Supreme Court rules (5–4) that the Fifth Amendment guarantee against self-incrimination must prevail unless law officers clearly notify a suspect prior to interrogation of the right to remain silent, to be informed that anything said could and would be used in a court of law, to have a lawyer present during questioning, and if unable to afford one, to acquire court-appointed counsel on request. And if a suspect indicates a wish to remain silent or consult a lawyer, questioning must end. The decision is intended to eliminate a case-by-case examination of confessions.

Three years ago, Phoenix police officers failed to inform 22-year-old rape suspect Ernesto Miranda of his rights, and he confessed during interrogation. Next year, at his retrial, Miranda will receive a 20–30-year term; he will win parole in 1972.

**June 22.** After months of pressure from the Joint

Chiefs of Staff, Robert McNamara in March recommended air strikes against oil depots in North Vietnam. The president gives the go-ahead today.

Bad weather delays the campaign until the 29th, when U.S. bombers hit storage areas near the two major North Vietnamese cities, Hanoi and Haiphong. Johnson defends this major escalation of the war as a justified response to the increasing Communist use of motor vehicles to infiltrate the South.

But the North Vietnamese simply switch to smaller, dispersed areas that are difficult to bomb, and the infiltration of men and supplies into South Vietnam continues unabated. An extremely disappointed McNamara begins to reevaluate the American war effort.

> *Statistics:* The heavy strategic B-52 bombers, carrying 84 500-pound bombs inside and 24 750-pound bombs on racks under the wings, are extremely effective, flying too high to be heard on the ground. American soldiers call the aircraft "the Devil's freight train."

**July 10.** Martin Luther King, Jr., addresses a crowd of 30,000–45,000 at a Chicago rally. Since January, the SCLC and a city coalition of 45 groups have campaigned to end discrimination against blacks in jobs and housing. (Blacks make up a quarter of the city's population.) But after six months, this first sustained civil rights action in the North has failed to produce any tangible results. The SCLC decides to move the demonstrations to white neighborhoods.

Chicago whites respond with such violence that police are unable to protect the activists from assault. On August 5, after five hours of near-rioting by some 4,000 whites, King states he has "never seen such hate—not in Mississippi or Alabama—as I see here in Chicago."

City officials and realtors agree on August 26 to a 10-point compromise program to end de facto seg-

regation in housing. With the campaign's failure to win governmental or white-liberal support, still more young blacks question the success of nonviolence.

A riot this month on the predominantly black West Side of Chicago is mirrored in other American cities throughout the summer, including Cleveland, Jacksonville, Baltimore, Los Angeles, and Atlanta. Serious disturbances break out in 38 U.S. cities this year.

**July 13.** In the early hours of the morning, a man pushes his way into a Chicago apartment shared by nine nurses. He holds some of the women at knifepoint until their roommates return, corrals them all in a bedroom, and one at a time, takes them back into the living room. Corazon Amurao pleads with the other women to attack the intruder until, in desperation, she hides under one of the beds. Later, emerging into the quiet apartment, she finds all her friends dead—stabbed and strangled.

Amurao describes the murderer, with the tattoo "Born to Raise Hell" on his arm, and police pick up Richard Speck after an intensive three-day manhunt. The courts sentence him to 600 years in prison. Speck, who was in the areas at the time of other mass murders, may have killed before.

**July 19.** Two North Vietnamese ambassadors declare that all captured American pilots will be tried as "war criminals" for their indiscriminate bombing. Following a warning from the United States and international appeals from U Thant, Pope Paul, and others, Ho Chi Minh announces on the 23rd that there is "no trial in view."

**August 1.** Ex-marine Charles Whitman takes three rifles and two pistols to the top of the 27-story tower at the University of Texas. With phenomenal accuracy, he picks off 44 people during a 90-minute siege, killing 13 of them. The shooting finally ends when an off-duty policeman climbs the tower and kills him.

Police later find the bodies of Whitman's mother and wife in their homes and Whitman's note saying he killed them to "save them the embarrassment" of what he planned to do.

**September 6.** Prime Minister Henrik Verwoerd

is stabbed to death in the South African Parliament. His assassin, a temporary messenger, charges that Verwoerd was doing too much for blacks and not enough for poor whites. A week later, the Nationalist party elects Balthazar Johannes Vorster as leader.

**September 19.** A Senate filibuster kills the 1966 Civil Rights Bill, whose measures included a ban on racial discrimination in the sale or rental of all housing. Political analysts believe recent extremist statements by CORE and SNCC have cost blacks some support in Congress.

**October 14.** Returning from another trip to Saigon, Defense Secretary McNamara reports to President Johnson that the pacification program, inaugurated in midyear, is failing and air strikes have not "either significantly affected infiltration or cracked the morale of Hanoi."

In a radical departure from U.S. policy, McNamara for the first time recommends that the administration sharply cut back troop buildup. And he suggests that, rather than trying to kill enemy soldiers more quickly than they can be replaced, the United States should consider alternative strategies such as a pacification program based on drastic South Vietnamese reforms or cutting back the air war to increase the credibility of U.S. peace gestures.

The president listens to his secretary despite continuing claims from the Joint Chiefs that the military situation has "improved substantially over the past year." For the first time, Johnson denies General Westmoreland's troop request.

**October 15.** Black militants Huey Newton and Bobby Seale form the Black Panther party in Oakland, California. Their manifesto calls for "power to determine the destiny of our black community," with immediate emphasis on "organizing black defense groups" to "end police brutality." (Their panther symbol comes from a Loundes County, Alabama, political organization.)

Wearing leather jackets and berets, blacks recruited from the Oakland ghetto carry arms and question police procedures with law books. In their national newspaper, the Panthers describe their social program, and to overcome a common fear of law officers, portray policemen as "pigs" in uniforms.

The Panthers' style soon attracts the attention of young blacks. In 1967, Eldridge Cleaver joins the group as its minister of information.

**October 17.** Approximately 100,000 members of Housewives for Lower Food Prices boycott five Denver supermarket chains. The grocery industry has blamed price increases on general inflation, but under the boycott one chain lowers most prices the first day and the others soon follow. Within two weeks, the boycott spreads to 100 other cities in 21 states.

**October 21.** Since the late 1800s, coal mine owners in Wales have dumped waste from the diggings above ground on huge tips. Over the past few days town residents in Aberfan have reported Tip No. 7 moving slightly (a natural spring beneath the 100-foot pile has weakened the tons of rock). But authorities do nothing, and the massive slag heap finally collapses, burying the town school and 16 homes.

Miners stream in from nearby valleys to join frantic parents in digging through the rubble—116 of the 250 children in the school die along with 28 adults. At the inquest, outraged villagers insist that the coroner write "Buried alive by the National Coal Board" on the death certificates.

The government initially refuses to remove the other six tips looming over Aberfan, but will relent in 1968. It will take another six years to finish the job.

**October 25.** During a tour of Southeast Asia, President Johnson meets in Manila with representatives from Australia, New Zealand, the Philippines, Thailand, South Korea, and South Vietnam. Their four-point "Declaration of Peace" pledges to remove Allied forces from South Vietnam within six months once "the other side withdraws its forces to the North." North Vietnam, the Soviet Union, and China denounce the offer as worthless.

**October 27.** Communist China announces its first successful firing of a guided missile with a nuclear warhead. Three days later, President Johnson assures Asian allies that the United States will protect any nonnuclear nation from "the threat of nuclear blackmail."

**October 27.** The U.N. General Assembly votes to terminate the South African mandate over South-West Africa, but the Cape Town government rejects the resolution. The League of Nations awarded the mandate after W.W.I, but with the dissolution of that body in 1946, the newly formed United Nations recommended South-West Africa be placed under a U.N. trusteeship agreement.

Again in 1969 and 1970, the United Nations will vainly adopt resolutions calling for South African withdrawal from renamed Namibia, and in 1971, the International Court of Justice will find the South African presence to be illegal. Cape Town will continue to defy the international bodies.

**November 3.** The Fair Packaging and Labeling Act requires a listing of ingredients, their amounts, and net weight, while controlling package size, including deceptively large containers.

**November 4–5.** Severe flooding kills over 175 people throughout Italy, Austria, Switzerland, and Yugoslavia. In Florence, the rising Arno River reaches 15 feet in some sections, pushing tons of debris and cars along submerged streets. Despite centuries of major flooding in the river valley, the Renaissance city remains virtually unprepared for the devastation.

Volunteers save what they can, but museums and galleries have stored artwork in basements well below water level, and the flood waters destroy hundreds of paintings and manuscripts, and damage thousands of others. The disaster compels art experts to develop new restoration techniques.

**November 8.** Republicans make moderate gains in midterm elections as voters express dissatisfaction with the lack of progress in Vietnam and rising prices at home under an inflationary economy. While the Democrats retain control of Congress, analysts predict that a renewed conservative coalition will slow down Johnson's Great Society program.

Movie actor Ronald Reagan, in his first race for public office, is elected governor of California by almost 1 million votes over incumbent Edmund G. "Pat" Brown.

**November 25.** With a temperature inversion, smog conditions in the New York-New Jersey area reach a critical level over the Thanksgiving weekend. New York City officials shut down the incinerators and implore people to curb their driving.

More than 400 people die of heart attacks and respiratory failure before the alert ends on the 26th.

**December 1.** The West German Bundestag elects Kurt Kiesinger of the Christian Democratic Party (CDU) to succeed Ludwig Erhard as chancellor. Erhard had lost the confidence of his coalition partner, the Free Democratic party (FDP), while Kiesinger had worked out a coalition with the opposition Social Democratic party (SDP). Willy Brandt of the SDP becomes vice-chancellor and foreign minister.

**December 16.** The U.N. Security Council votes unanimously to impose selective mandatory economic sanctions against the rebellious white government of Rhodesia. The Smith regime will fall back on a tightly controlled economy, and trade with Portugal and South Africa which refuse to follow the sanctions. Black guerrilla groups, at first disorganized and poorly equipped, soon launch attacks against the white government.

## Obituaries

**Lenny Bruce** (October 13, 1926–August 3, 1966). With his ongoing legal battle against charges of obscenity, the controversial comedian had achieved a kind of cult status with the American counterculture. A drug addict, he died of a heroin overdose.

**Robert Fowler** (1885–June 15, 1966). In 1912, the American aviator completed the first flight from California to Florida. With the time needed to rebuild the plane after several crashes, the trip took 106 days.

**Chester William Nimitz** (February 24, 1885–February 20, 1966). Named commander-in-chief of the U.S. Pacific Fleet three weeks after Pearl Harbor, Nimitz rebuilt the American force to a strength of 2 million men and 1,000 ships. Beginning with the Battle of the Coral Sea in 1942, the fleet slowly pushed the Japanese back to home port. At the end of the war, Nimitz achieved the newly created rank of admiral of the fleet. He never retired.

**Margaret Sanger** (September 14, 1883–September 6, 1966). In 1914, moved by desperate women trying to end unwanted pregnancies, the young American nurse issued a newsletter on *birth* *control* (a new term). When authorities banned the publication and moved to arrest her, Sanger fled to Britain. She returned to the United States in 1916 and opened a birth control clinic. Subsequent court rulings cleared the way for this pioneer of planned parenthood. In 1921, she organized the first American Birth Control Conference and founded the American Birth Control League (renamed the Planned Parenthood Federation of America in 1946). Then, in 1927, Sanger convened a World Population Conference in Geneva. By 1930, the United States counted 55 birth control clinics.

# BEGINNINGS AND ENDINGS

### News

**January 1.** The Canada Pension Plan gives retirees a minimum income. Employers match worker contributions (1.8 percent of earnings) and payout begins at age 65.

**January 1.** On his first day in office, Mayor John Lindsay faces New York City's first official transit strike. Until the job action ends on the 13th, an estimated 850,000 cars jam the streets every day.

**January 18.** Robert Weaver, the first black Cabinet member, is sworn in as secretary of the newly created Department of Housing and Urban Development.

**February 14.** Australians convert their currency of pounds, shillings, and pence to a dollar-and-cents decimal system.

**April 8.** A county court judge ends Prohibition in Mississippi—the last dry state in the union—when he rules that state legislation passed in 1944 had repealed the 1908 law.

**April 14.** With the growing controversy over widespread use, Sandoz Pharmaceutical recalls and discontinues production of the hallucinogen lysergic acid diethylamide, or LSD. A spokesperson for the Swiss company—the sole LSD distributor for medical research—claims, "I should not be surprised if at any one of a number of campuses there is more LSD than we have ever made."

**May 10.** Massachusetts repeals the last state law barring the dissemination of contraceptives and birth control information. Cardinal Cushing of Boston, who actively opposed suspension in 1948, this time made no effort to impose his beliefs.

**June 30.** In 1961, the creation of the President's Commission on the Status of Women encouraged the formation of parallel groups at state levels. This year, at their third Washington conference, officials refuse to floor a resolution urging the enforcement of the Civil Rights Act provision against sexual discrimination. In frustration, a few delegates led by Betty Friedan form the National Organization for Women (NOW). Members dedicate themselves to changing "the false image of women now prevalent in the mass media, and in the texts, ceremonies, laws, and practices of our major social institutions." By fall, NOW membership numbers 300; by the end of the decade, 8,000.

**August.** The U.S. Treasury discontinues $2 bills, a currency long associated with bad luck.

**August 6.** Luci Baines Johnson, the 19-year-old daughter of the president, weds Patrick John Nugent, age 23, in Washington. All three TV networks broadcast the ceremony live.

**November 1.** With a Montreal-Moscow flight, Air Canada becomes the first North American carrier to operate regularly in the USSR.

**November 8.** Massachusetts Senator Edward Brooke becomes the first popularly elected black senator in American history. (Two black senators were elected by the Mississippi legislature following the Civil War.)

**November 18.** Ending a 1,000-year tradition, the Vatican allows American Catholics to eat meat on Fridays. (Other nations receive permission as well this year.)

• **More news.** San Francisco State College offers lectures on Black Nationalism, the first black studies course in the nation. Next year, the program will expand. Other colleges will follow suit, but the concept meets with broad resistance. Some civil rights leaders, for instance, will insist the courses do not include the skills blacks need to solve today's problems.

• The RCMP discontinues equestrian training for recruits.

## Records

**May 3.** In one of the largest stock transactions in history, Howard Hughes sells his 6.5 million shares of TWA. (He uses the $546 million to buy a large chunk of Nevada, including mining properties, a regional airline, and Las Vegas hotels and casinos.)

**June 4.** The Ad Hoc Universities Committee for the Statement on Vietnam along with the Committee of the Professions to End the War in Vietnam take out the largest political ad in newspaper history. Some 3,900 instructors and administrators, from 180 colleges and universities across the country, each sign an appeal to "evaluate seriously whether self-determination for the Vietnamese as well as our own national interest would not be best served by the termination of our military presence in Vietnam."

## Government Departments and Agencies

**October 15.** The new Department of Transportation—the 12th at cabinet level—absorbs 30 government agencies. (The department's first official day will be April 1, 1967.)

## New Products and Businesses

Nestlé Alimentana introduces Taster's Choice freeze-dried instant coffee.

General Mills brings out Bac*Os, bacon-flavored bits of soy protein isolate.

British aviation pioneer Freddie Laker establishes Laker Airways for European charter flights and cheap package tours.

## Fads

From an "experience" just for "heads" (psychedelic drug users), day-glo fluorescent paint becomes the vogue element in posters.

Originally a symbol of rebellion against the Establishment—first taken up by bikers—the Nazi iron cross has evolved into a fad. With the heavy demand, manufacturers offer the military decoration in other materials, including wood and silver.

More and more young people drop out of straight society and turn to secular and religiously oriented communes. Members of the small communities gather in old farmhouses, grow food, and make or share clothing. Many use drugs, and some practice free love. But the Manson murders in 1969 will rob the communes of their Utopian innocence and many of the estimated 2,000 communities will start to break up.

## SCIENCE AND TECHNOLOGY

### News

**January 1.** Legislation passed on July 27, 1965, and effective today, requires that tobacco manufacturers print a warning from the U.S. Surgeon General on cigarette packages: "Caution: Cigarette smoke may be hazardous to your health."

**February 3.** *Luna 9* accomplishes the first soft landing on the moon. Ejected from the craft, an egg-shaped capsule extends stabilizing legs and an antenna. Over the next three days, a TV camera transmits the first clear close-ups of the lunar surface. This brilliant success underlines the previous failures in the Soviet program. *Luna 5, 7,* and 8 crashed, while 6 missed the moon entirely.

**February 26.** A Saturn 1B launches an unmanned Apollo spacecraft just 43 months after the rocket program was authorized.

**March 1.** *Venera 1*, sent aloft in 1961, missed Venus by thousands of miles. A few days ago, *Venera 2* flew to within 15,000 miles. Today, in another Soviet triumph, *Venera 3* becomes the first Earth spacecraft to touch down on another planet. But transmission abruptly ends after the capsule lands.

**March 16.** Following orbital manuevers, Neil Armstrong and David Scott bring *Gemini 8* up to a target rocket for docking. Inexplicably, the spacecraft and the Agena begin to whirl.

NASA orders the astronauts to separate, but the spinning worsens. Close to losing consciousness, Armstrong shuts down the thruster system and activates reentry. The hand controls soon respond, and the men make an emergency landing.

While nearly disastrous (a thruster had stuck open) by docking successfully, *Gemini 8* achieved one of the major goals of the program.

**April 3.** *Luna 10* is the first craft to orbit the moon. Instruments on board study the lunar magnetic field, solar plasma, gamma radiation, and micrometeorite particles. Later this year, *Luna 11* and *12* will reach orbit and *Luna 13* will land.

**April 21.** At a Houston hospital, Dr. Michael DeBakey implants a one-pound exterior bypass pump into a 65-year-old man. By taking over the work of the left ventricle, the machine should give the heart time to heal. (The scientific community criticizes the hospital's description of an "artificial heart.") The patient dies of a ruptured lung, but later this year a 37-year-old Mexico City woman becomes the first heart patient to survive the procedure.

**May 15.** With an advanced camera system and automatic picture transmission, *Nimbus 2* feeds into 400 meteorological stations around the world. This second-generation weather satellite provides invaluable information on the life history of storms.

**June 2.** *Surveyor 1* is the first American probe to make a soft landing on the moon. A chemical analysis and some 11,000 photos of the Sea of Tranquility finally prove the lunar surface will safely bear the weight of a human.

**June 3.** During their three-day Gemini mission, Eugene Cernan and Thomas Stafford learn firsthand about the potential dangers of space: a stuck nose cover prevents a space rendezvous; a failed computer necessitates exhausting hand calculations; and the exertion of a record 2-hour, 7-minute, space walk fogs up Cernan's faceplate.

Sadly, Elliott See and Charles Bassett, the scheduled *Gemini 9* astronauts, were killed in a T-38 trainer crash on February 28.

*Statistics:* From 1920 to 1926, 1 in every 4 commercial pilots was killed in an accident. By 1932, the average dropped to 1 in 50. This year, it stands at 1 in 1,600.

**July 18.** In *Gemini 10*, John Young and Michael Collins successfully rendezvous with two Agena tar-

get vehicles. During one operation, Collins propels over to the rocket to remove microfilm and replace an instrument package, an important space first.

On September 12, *Gemini 11* takes Charles Conrad and Richard Gordon up for an unprecedented first-orbit docking. The spacecraft returns safely to Earth on the 15th.

**August 14.** Despite last year's cautionary note, the FDA reports that on the basis of available information the Pill presents no health hazard to women. The agency recommends that all prescription time limitations be removed.

*Statistics:* Today, an estimated one third of American women in their early twenties take oral contraceptives.

**August 14.** *Lunar Orbiter 1*, the first U.S. probe to orbit the moon, sends back photos of primary Apollo landing sites. By August of next year, five Orbiters will have photographed 99 percent of the lunar surface.

*Statistics:* 1966 is the peak year for U.S. satellite launches in the period 1957–1969: 70 successes out of 72 attempts. Many of the launches orbit several satellites.

**September 11.** Moscow sends Washington the first satellite photos under an agreed exchange of meteorological data. Unfortunately, in this early link, pictures lack clarity.

**October 26.** Extending research done in 1955, Drs. James A. Bassham and R. G. Jensen publish their duplication of the process of photosynthesis.

**November 11–15.** On the last voyage of the Gemini program, James Lovell, Jr. and Buzz Aldrin dock and undock four times with an Agena target and remain attached overnight.

In 20 months, 10 Gemini missions conducted purely scientific experiments (some with military application), collected data on prolonged weightlessness, developed rendezvous and docking procedures and landing techniques, and demonstrated the ability of an astronaut to move in space. (Underwater training allowed Aldrin to conserve energy with more deliberate movements.) The program cost $1.4 billion.

Prior to launching, Aldrin and Lovell each sported a handwritten sign on the back of his bulky spacesuit. Together, the words read THE END.

**More news.** The Douglas Point Nuclear Power Station opens on the Canadian shores of Lake Huron. The CANDU reactor (Canada deuterium uranium) is safer and more efficient than other types, yet few will be built outside the province of Ontario.

• In its first commercial application, Westinghouse uses a laser to pierce diamond dies. Until 1965, the only companies capitalizing on lasers were the ones producing them.

## Other Discoveries, Developments, and Inventions

Ice radar that maps snow-covered Antarctic hills and valleys
Methane gas safety monitor from the Bureau of Mines
Remote-controlled outside mirror on the Ford
Tide-powered electrical plant in France
Telephone cable link between North and South America

## Obituaries

**Sydney Camm** (1893–March 12, 1966). The British aircraft designer developed the Hurricane fighter, used in the Battle of Britain, and the vertical-takeoff Kestrel fighter.

**Norman McAlister Gregg** (March 7, 1892–July 27, 1966). The Australian surgeon discovered in 1941 that German measles contracted during early pregnancy could harm the unborn child.

**Sergei Korolev** (December 30, 1906–January 14, 1966). The rocket pioneer designed the first Soviet satellite systems as well as those later sent to the moon. Manned spacecraft were also developed under his direction.

# THE ARTS

January 29—*Sweet Charity*, with Gwen Verdon, John McMartin (608 perfs.)
May 24—*Mame*, with Angela Lansbury, Beatrice Arthur, Frankie Michaels (1,508 perfs.)
November 20—*Cabaret*, with Jill Haworth, Bert Convy, Joel Grey, Jack Gilford, Lotte Lenya (1,165 perfs.)
December 5—*I Do! I Do!*, with Mary Martin, Robert Preston (560 perfs.)

## Tony Awards

Actor (Dramatic)—Hal Holbrook, *Mark Twain Tonight!*
Actress (Dramatic)—Rosemary Harris, *The Lion in Winter*
Actor (Musical)—Richard Kiley, *Man of La Mancha*
Actress (Musical)—Angela Lansbury, *Mame*
Play—*Marat/Sade*
Musical—*Man of La Mancha*

## News

**April 16.** A five-hour gala performance closes the 83-year-old Metropolitan Opera House. At the end of the evening, the leading singers of yesterday and today join with the audience in a tearful rendition of "Auld Lang Syne." (A later recording includes a scrap of the house's fabulous gold curtain.)

On September 16, a premiere of Samuel Barber's *Antony and Cleopatra* opens the new Met, the focal point of the Lincoln Center complex. The $45-million theater features Marc Chagall murals and crystal chandeliers from the Austrian government.

**More news.** Sotheby's collects a record price for a Van Gogh—$441,000 for *Mademoiselle Ravoux*.

• Since Allan Kaprow staged the first "happening" in 1958, the concept of conventional art has broken down under an increasing mix of media—TV, film, dance, painting, technical devices. This year, psychedelic art involves the audience in re-creating the hallucinatory effects of drugs.

• Candirus de Scranage receives a U.S. patent for a snow machine—a perforated cylinder that turns slowly to release artificial flakes in a natural manner.

• In 1954, Robert Joffrey organized dancers from his school into the Robert Joffrey Ballet Concert. This year, after several incarnations, the choreographer's Joffrey Ballet is invited to become the resident company at New York City Center.

• The 1965–1966 Broadway season grossed nearly $54 million. The top ticket price was $12 for the musical *Superman.*

## Obituaries

**Russel M. Crouse** (February 20, 1893–April 3, 1966). His play *Life With Father* (1939; coauthored with Howard Lindsay) ran on Broadway for seven and a half years.

**Billy Rose** (September 6, 1899–February 10, 1966). Known as a composer in the 1920s—"Me and My Shadow" (1927), "There's a Rainbow 'Round My Shoulder" (1928)—Rose later produced such Broadway hits as *Jumbo* (1935) and *Carmen Jones* (1943).

## WORDS

Truman Capote, *In Cold Blood*
James Clavell, *Tai-Pan*
Robert Crichton, *The Secret of Santa Vittoria*
John Fowles, *The Magus*
Graham Greene, *The Comedians*
Konrad Lorenz, *On Aggression*
Bernard Malamud, *The Fixer*
William H. Masters and Virginia E. Johnson, *Human Sexual Response*
Jean Nidetch, *Weight Watcher's Cookbook*
Harold Robbins, *The Adventurers*
Cornelius Ryan, *The Last Battle*
Jacqueline Susann, *The Valley of the Dolls*

## News

**February 8.** The Vatican abolishes the centuries-old agency responsible for book censorship.
**March 21.** The U.S. Supreme Court lifts a Mas-

sachusetts ban on the sale of *Fanny Hill.* Literary experts testified that the sexually explicit story, written by John Cleland in 1750, contributed to the development of the novel.

Today the court also upholds Ralph Ginzburg's obscenity conviction for "titillating advertising" in his magazine *Eros.* Fined $28,000 and sentenced to 5 years, Ginzburg will exhaust the appeal process in 1972; he will win parole 10 months later.

**May 2.** The last British newspaper to abandon an 18th-century format, the *Times* of London replaces front-page classified ads with news. (American dailies made the change after the Civil War.) *Times* circulation will rise 25 percent over the next 18 months.

**September 12.** The *World-Telegram* and *The Sun* unite as the *World Journal Tribune.* When the three New York dailies announced their merger last April, the Newspaper Guild went on strike. The 139-day shutdown—the longest in U.S. history—finished the *Herald-Tribune,* but the two survivors unite. Within a year, the paper will cease publication, and New York will be left with just three dailies; in 1950, the city had eight.

**October 30.** At Columbia College, a comparison of the reading tastes of freshmen in 1958 and 1966 reveals that Shakespeare has fallen from first to ninth place, while Jane Austen, D. H. Lawrence, Plato, and Eugene O'Neill have dropped off the list altogether.

Instead, today's students choose (in order) John Steinbeck, Albert Camus, Ernest Hemingway, J. D. Salinger, Fyodor Dostoyevsky, James Joyce, and Sinclair Lewis. (Camus shows the most dramatic increase in popularity, rising from 2 percent to 18 percent.)

*Statistics:* From 1955 to 1965, U.S. publishers more than doubled their annual production, from 12,589 book titles to 28,595. This year, for the first time, the figure jumps over 30,000, to 30,050.

**More news.** Fulfilling the $1.25-million bequest

of Canadian businessman James Nicholson, who died in 1952, the University of Toronto releases the first volume of the *Dictionary of Canadian Biography, A. D. 1000–1700.*

• *Publishers Weekly* lists J. R. R. Tolkien's *The Hobbit* and *The Fellowship of the Ring* as the year's leading mass-market paperbacks.

• *Playboy* is the first 75-cent-plus magazine to ring up more than 4 million sales in a single month.

## Cartoons and Comics

**This year.** The soaring popularity of the "Batman" TV series renews interest in superhero back-issue comics. A rare copy of *Action Comics No. 1* (1939), with the origins of Superman, Zatara, and Lois Lane, sells for $2,000.

## TIME *Man of the Year*

Youth, 25 years and under

## New Words and Phrases

acid (LSD)
beach bunny
bowser bag (restaurant bag for leftovers)
disco
dove, hawk
fertility pill
flashcube
folk-rock
glitch
go-go [dancer]
in [crowd, place]
integrated circuit or chip
interface
Mod (a style of men's clothing)
out (not "in")
playbook (a notebook of diagrammed football plays)
rapture of the deep (a confused mental state resulting when nitrogen enters a scuba diver's bloodstream)
slurbs (a residential area of monotonous, often cheaply constructed houses on the outskirts of a large city)
streaming (school children grouped by their abilities)
Third World
vanity plate (distinctive license plate)

In his May 29 speech at Howard University, Representative Adam Clayton Powell, Jr. tells black students, "Our life must be purposed to implement human rights. . . . To demand these God-given rights is to seek *black power*—what I call audacious power—the power to build black institutions of splendid achievement." Next month, as civil rights leaders complete James Meredith's march, a more militant SNCC takes up Powell's expression. The media further popularizes the slogan.

## Obituaries

**Kathryn McLean Forbes** (March 10, 1909–May 15, 1966). Her best-seller *Mama's Bank Account* (1943) became a Broadway hit, a movie, and a TV program under the name *I Remember Mama*.

**C(ecil) S(cott) Forester** (August 27, 1899–April 2, 1966). The British novelist wrote the Horatio Hornblower series.

**Evelyn Waugh** (October 28, 1903–April 10, 1966). Five novels written between 1928 and 1938 established the British writer as the century's outstanding satirist. Slightly more serious postwar novels included *Brideshead Revisited* (1945).

# FASHION

## Haute Couture

Following Courrèges' example, fashion designers abandon the older woman for her daughter and raise hemlines 4 to 5 inches above the knee. To balance this new erogenous zone, couturiers cover up the neck, arms, even clothing fasteners. (Former Miss America and TV personality Bess Meyerson reportedly complains, "We used to dress like Jackie Kennedy; now we're dressing like Caroline.")

## News

**March 28.** When a woman sits down, her mini skirt rides up to reveal the darker garter band of her stocking—a mere 4 to 5 inches above the knee. *Newsweek* reports that hosiery mills, finally conceding the permanence of short hemlines, have introduced a longer stocking with a narrower band.

**More news.** Scott Paper packages a disposable paper dress as a publicity stunt, but enormous consumer demand gives birth to a new industry. Within a year, at least 60 manufacturers jump on the $100-million bandwagon. Dresses cost as little as $1 and evening gowns $4, but paper disintegrates in water, sometimes catches on fire, and always proves uncomfortable. Nonetheless, before the fad wanes in 1968, Scott will sell some 500,000 dresses.

## Colors and Materials

Stark colors give way to summer fruit shades, especially green and yellow, and winter reds, greens, and purples.

Coats and knitwear emphasize camel-hair color and cloth.

Patent leather, glitter fabrics, plastic rainwear, and vinyl swimsuits all contribute to the "wet" or shiny look.

With the new fun fashions, furriers dye unusual skins (badger, wolverine) and old favorites in offbeat colors (mauve, bright green, shocking pink) for pea jackets and double-breasted mini coats.

Manufacturers point to the growth in knits (from $462 million to $807 million over 1958–1964) in predicting stretch-fabric production will rise from 15 percent to 50 percent by 1972.

## Clothes

Further abbreviating the mini, skirt waistlines drop to the hipbone.

A looser T-shape dress proves popular in plain colors or stripes, with contrasting open neck and collar.

Coats adjust to skirt lengths, ending at the hemline or just above. The military style, with brass buttons and epaulette shoulders, is the most sought after.

With the availability of new colors and textures, more women opt for pantyhose.

The popularity of *Dr. Zhivago* (1965) creates a market for Russian muffs, fur hats, tunics, and a calf-length, belted coat. This first large-scale culling from a single hit film marks the beginning of a yearly ritual.

The industry increasingly uses a zip-fly front on women's slacks.

Lingerie companies bring out a combination bra-slip.

In vogue through the late sixties, crocheted dresses appear in cream or soft pastels. The more daring shed their bra or slip underneath.

Young men team a polo sweater with hipster trousers, flared slightly from the knee.

Encouraged by the androgynous Courrèges collection, young women in London wear boyish, checkered trouser suits, fitted pea jackets, and peaked gamin or yachting caps. Long-haired guys sport fancy shoes, leather vests, flowered shirts, and pants with stitch and seam detail. Americans who take up these trends generally live in the larger cities.

## Accessories

Wide, slotted leather belts accessorize hipster pants and skirts.

To avoid exaggerating the mini look, this year's shoe styles keep toes squared or broadly rounded and heels low and chunky. Colorful patent leathers sell best.

Op art is "out" and plastic, solid-colored bangles and large earrings are "in." The new vibrant jewelry encourages girls to get their ears pierced.

Handbags remain small.

As millions more baby-boomers enter adolescence, their demands produce one fashion craze after another. This year, small, wire-rimmed granny glasses flood the market—many tinted blue, pink, or green. (Supposedly

Roger McGuinn, lead singer of the Byrds, first wore dark granny glasses to protect his eyes from stage lights, then began wearing them offstage.)

## Hair and Cosmetics

Hair continues to lose fullness and height as girls and young women adopt a natural, shoulder-length line with a brow fringe. A side part hides one eye while a center part brings hair forward on both sides. Teenage boys often clash with those in authority over their long-haired Beatles look.

Eyeliner, lash-building mascara, and/or false eyelashes make eyes heavier. (American stores now carry strikingly packaged Mary Quant eye shadows.)

In tune with shorter skirts, cosmetic companies offer leg makeup in tan or beige. Revlon promotes a kit of colors and brushes, but many girls simply decorate their legs with stick-ons or a felt-tipped pen.

## Obituaries

**Elizabeth Arden** (December 31, 1882–October 18, 1966). Canadian-born Florence Nightingale Graham, who took a business name upon opening her first salon in 1910, helped develop the first nongreasy skin cream. Arden's wholly owned beauty empire grossed $60 million in annual sales before she sold out to Eli Lilly & Co.

# MUSIC

"The Ballad of the Green Berets"—Sgt. Barry Sadler

"Winchester Cathedral"—New Vaudeville Band

"Cherish"—Association

"We Can Work It Out"—Beatles

"You're My Soul & Inspiration"—Righteous Brothers

"Monday, Monday"—Mamas & the Papas

"Summer in the City"—Lovin' Spoonful

"The Sounds of Silence"—Simon & Garfunkel

"Reach Out, I'll Be There"—Four Tops

"You Can't Hurry Love"—Supremes

"My Love"—Petula Clark

"When a Man Loves a Woman"—Percy Sledge

"Paint It, Black"—Rolling Stones

"Hanky Panky"—Tommy James & the Shondells

"Paperback Writer"—Beatles

"You Keep Me Hangin' On"—Supremes

"Wild Thing"—Troggs

"Good Vibrations"—Beach Boys

"96 Tears"—? (Question Mark) & the Mysterians

"Last Train to Clarksville"—Monkees

"These Boots Are Made for Walkin' "—Nancy Sinatra

"Good Lovin' "—Young Rascals

"Poor Side of Town"—Johnny Rivers

"Strangers in the Night"—Frank Sinatra

"Lightnin' Strikes"—Lou Christie

"Sunshine Superman"—Donovan

"Mellow Yellow"—Donovan

"19th Nervous Breakdown"—Rolling Stones

"Sunny"—Bobby Hebb

"Lil' Red Riding Hood"—Sam the Sham & the Pharaohs

"Daydream"—Lovin' Spoonful

"A Groovy Kind of Love"—Mindbenders

"Barbara Ann"—Beach Boys

"Red Rubber Ball"—Cyrkle

"Rainy Day Women No. 12 and 35"—Bob Dylan

"Yellow Submarine"—Beatles

## Grammys (1966)

Record of the Year—Frank Sinatra, "Strangers in the Night"

Song of the Year (songwriter)—John Lennon and Paul McCartney, "Michelle"

Album of the Year—Frank Sinatra, *Sinatra: A Man and His Music*

Best Vocal Performance (Male)—Frank Sinatra, "Strangers in the Night" (single)

Best Vocal Performance (Female)—Eydie Gorme, "If He Walked into My Life" (single)

Best New Artist—not voted on

## News

**April 19.** Jan Berry suffers extensive brain damage when he accidentally drives his car into a parked truck, killing his three passengers. Since 1958, surf music duo Jan & Dean have charted 13 top 30 singles and sold more than 10 million records worldwide. After lengthy rehabilitation, Berry will attempt a comeback with Dean in 1973; it will be unsuccessful.

**June 11.** In San Francisco, Big Brother & the Holding Company introduce a new singer, Janis Joplin.

**July 19.** Earlier this year, Frank Sinatra broke rock's monopoly of the No. 1 chart position with "Strangers in the Night." Today, the 50-year-old singer stuns his fans by marrying 21-year-old Mia Farrow, star of the TV series "Peyton Place." The daughter of actress Maureen O'Sullivan and director John Farrow recently changed her youthful image by cutting off her waist-length blond hair.

**July 29.** While riding near his home in Woodstock, New York, Bob Dylan crashes his Triumph 55 motorcycle. Critically injured, with several broken neck vertebrae and a concussion, he suffers amnesia and some paralysis. His total record sales will reach 10 million this year.

**August 12.** In a March interview with the *Evening Standard*, John Lennon said, "Christianity will go. It will vanish and shrink. I needn't argue about that. I'm right and I will be proved right. We're more popular than Jesus now. I don't know which will go first—rock 'n' roll or Christianity." At the beginning of this month, just before the Beatles arrived for another tour, U.S. newspapers reprinted his fifth sentence out of context. Lennon has received hate mail and Beatles' tunes have been taken off the air. Under enormous pressure, John faces the press today in Chicago and apologizes.

**August 29.** The Beatles end their tour of the United States with a concert at Candlestick Park in San Francisco. Bounding on stage at 9:27 P.M., the four launch into their rendition of Chuck Berry's "Rock and Roll Music." After nine more songs, barely distinguishable over the din of 25,000 screaming fans, the Beatles finish with Little Richard's "Long Tall Sally."

The adoration of fans has frustrated the four at their concerts. And now, with their studio experimentation in recorded feedback, distortion, and tape looping (on the LP *Revolver*), Ringo believes, "We can't do a tour like before because it would be soft us going on stage, the four of us, and trying to do records we've made with orchestras and bands. We'd have to have a whole line of men behind us if we were to perform." The concert at Candlestick Park was the Beatles' last public performance.

**More news.** This year, the Brits finally give way to American performers. Still, groups rather than singles continue to dominate the pop charts.

> *Statistics:* The ever-increasing number of gold records reflects the industry's phenomenal growth—58 albums and 23 singles in 1966 compared with 38 albums and 11 singles in 1965.

• Signe Anderson leaves to have a baby and former model Grace Slick joins the Jefferson Airplane.

• Record companies hold rock singles at $2\frac{1}{2}$–3 minutes simply to receive more air time. But as FM radio expansion offers greater coverage to LPs, composers produce longer and more complex numbers. Bob Dylan pioneered the concept in 1965 with the 11-minute "Desolation Row." This year, the Stones record another 11-minute number, "Going Home." In 1967, the popularity of a Doors' hit will break the final barriers.

• Sgt. Barry Sadler, recuperating at home from injuries received in Vietnam, writes a song to honor his Special Forces group, then works on the tune with author Robin Moore. The No. 1 song of the year, "The Ballad of the Green Berets" sells 1 million copies in the first two weeks. Moore's book on the military outfit later features Sadler on the cover.

• The NAB instructs DJs to screen records for obscene or hidden (drug) meanings. (LPs have started to include the lyrics on the liner sleeve.) Some album covers have proven controversial as well. The assortment of bloodied dolls on the

Beatles' *Yesterday . . . and Today*, for instance, was pulled and more conventional artwork substituted.

• With a style that defies description, Mrs. Elva Miller sells 250,000 copies of her excruciating rendition of "Downtown."

• A Boston radio station airs selections from the album *Wednesday Morning*. Positive listener response prompts Columbia Records to redub one of the tracks with bass, drums, and electric guitar. And two years after the initial release, Simon & Garfunkel score a No. 1 hit with "Sounds of Silence." The 24-year-olds have given up the business, at least temporarily; Paul Simon has gone to work in England and Art Garfunkel has returned to graduate school. By the end of the year, four of their singles and three LPs place in the top 30.

• Lead singer ? (Question Mark), a.k.a. Rudy Martinez, and the other members of the Mysterians were born in Mexico and raised in the United States. The unusual acoustics of their hit, "96 Tears," resulted from recording in their manager's living room. Later, the song will be recognized as the forerunner of punk rock.

• New dances include the Skate, the Philly Dog, and the Boston Monkey.

• Frank Zappa & the Mothers of Invention produce the first two-disc LP, *Freak Out*.

• Songwriter Neil Diamond, who will give the Monkees their smash hit "I'm a Believer," tries singing himself this year. His second record, "Cherry, Cherry," breaks into the top 10.

• "Michelle," written by John Lennon and Paul McCartney, appears on the Beatles' album *Rubber Soul*. The David and Jonathan single reaches No. 18.

---

*New Recording Artists*

Association
Cream
Neil Diamond
Grass Roots
Hollies
Tommy James & the Shondells
Jefferson Airplane
Gordon Lightfoot

Mamas & the Papas
Sergio Mendes & Brasil '66
Monkees
B. J. Thomas
Frankie Valli

### Obituaries

**Helen Kane** (August 4, 1904?–September 26, 1966). The singer was known as the Boop-Boop-de-Doop Girl for her rendition of "I Wanna Be Loved by You." The Betty Boop cartoons imitated her squeaky style.

**Sophie Tucker** (January 13, 1884–February 9, 1966). The Last of the Red Hot Mamas belted out songs for almost 60 years. The younger TV audience remembers her as the stout lady on "Ed Sullivan" who always spoke her lyrics and carried a scarf.

## MOVIES

*Alfie* (British, d. Lewis Gilbert; color)—Michael Caine, Shelley Winters, Julia Foster

*Blow-Up* (British-Italian, d. Michelangelo Antonioni; color)—David Hemmings, Vanessa Redgrave, Sarah Miles

*Born Free* (British, d. James Hill; color)—Virginia McKenna, Bill Travers

*Closely Observed Trains* (U.S.: *Closely Watched Trains*; Czechoslovakian, d. Jiří Menzel; bw)—Vaclav Neckar, Jitka Bendova

*Endless Summer* (d. Bruce Brown; color)

*Fantastic Voyage* (d. Richard Fleischer; color)—Stephen Boyd, Raquel Welch, Edmond O'Brien, Donald Pleasence, Arthur O'Connell

*The Fortune Cookie* (d. Billy Wilder; bw)—Jack Lemmon, Walter Matthau

*Georgy Girl* (British, d. Silvio Narizzano; bw)—James Mason, Lynn Redgrave, Alan Bates, Charlotte Rampling

*The Group* (d. Sidney Lumet; color)—Candice Bergen, Joan Hackett, Elizabeth Hartman, Shirley Knight, Joanna Pettet

*How to Steal a Million* (d. William Wyler;

color)—Audrey Hepburn, Peter O'Toole, Eli Wallach, Hugh Griffith, Charles Boyer

*A Man and a Woman* (French, d. Claude Lelouch; color)—Anouk Aimée, Jean-Louis Trintignant

*A Man For All Seasons* (British, d. Fred Zinnemann; color)—Paul Scofield, Wendy Hiller, Leo McKern, Robert Shaw, Orson Welles, Susannah York

*Morgan!* (British, d. Karel Reisz; bw)—Vanessa Redgrave, David Warner

*The Naked Prey* (d. Cornel Wilde; color)—Cornel Wilde, Gert van den Berg, Ken Gampu

*Nevada Smith* (d. Henry Hathaway; color)—Steve McQueen, Karl Malden, Brian Keith, Arthur Kennedy, Suzanne Pleshette

*The Professionals* (d. Richard Brooks; color)—Burt Lancaster, Lee Marvin, Robert Ryan, Jack Palance, Claudia Cardinale

*The Sand Pebbles* (d. Robert Wise; color)—Steve McQueen, Richard Attenborough, Richard Crenna, Candice Bergen, Mako

*Seconds* (d. John Frankenheimer; bw)—Rock Hudson, Salome Jens, John Randolph, Will Geer

*Who's Afraid of Virginia Woolf?* (d. Mike Nichols; bw)—Elizabeth Taylor, Richard Burton, George Segal, Sandy Dennis

*Winnie the Pooh and the Honey Tree* (Disney; color; animated)—Voices: Sterling Holloway (Pooh); Sebastian Cabot (Narrator)

*The Wrong Box* (British, d. Bryan Forbes; color)—John Mills, Ralph Richardson, Michael Caine, Peter Cook, Dudley Moore

## Academy Awards

**April 18.** When few stars appear at this year's ceremonies, an unusual couple steals the spotlight—Lynda Bird Johnson, the president's daughter, and her escort, actor George Hamilton.

Oscar producer Joe Pasternak celebrates the Academy's first color telecast with a spectacular backdrop of 42 fountains.

As usual, Bob Hope hosts.

Best Picture—*The Sound of Music*

Best Actor—Lee Marvin (*Cat Ballou*)

Best Actress—Julie Christie (*Darling*)

Best Director—Robert Wise (*The Sound of Music*)

Best Supporting Actor—Martin Balsam (*A Thousand Clowns*)

Best Supporting Actress—Shelley Winters (*A Patch of Blue*) (first actress to win two Oscars in this category)

Best Song—"The Shadow of Your Smile" from *The Sandpiper*

Best Foreign Film—*The Shop on Main Street* (Czechoslovakian)

Honorary Award—Bob Hope

Since the first televised Oscars in 1953, the networks have relied on fashion designer Edith Head to censor women's gowns. This year, when Julie Christie breezes past Head in her booth, the fashion supervisor approves the visible high neckline (always the center of concern), but misses the length of the dress. The British actress walks on stage in a gold lamé mini and the Oscar dress code collapses.

Upon receiving his Oscar for playing a drunken cowboy on an equally sodden mount, Lee Marvin says, "I think half of this belongs to a horse somewhere out in the valley."

## News

**March 9.** With old-movie stocks depleted and TV executives balking at huge fees for recent releases, Universal Pictures begins production on the first movie made directly for television. In November, NBC broadcasts *Fame Is the Name of the Game*, starring Tony Franciosa, Jill St. John, and Jack Klugman, before the film's theatrical release. Other studios prepare similar agreements.

**June 10.** The MPAA finally sanctions "blue language," approving the shocking dialogue of *Who's Afraid of Virginia Woolf?* as reflective of "the tragic realism of life." The association creates a new seal of approval—"Recommended for Mature Audiences"—but a *Variety* editorial proclaims, "The Code Is Dead."

**July 14.** The U.S. Court of Appeals invalidates the American Directors Guild's loyalty oath after finding it "inherently vague." The organization instituted a non-Communist affidavit in 1949 as a condition of membership. But when the 2,600-member guild merged last year with the 400-member Screen Directors Guild, six directors from the smaller group sued for its removal. The ACLU hails this first overturning of a loyalty provision, and the Supreme Court refuses to review the case.

**August.** *The Sound of Music* (1965) overtakes *Gone With the Wind* (1939), which had been the top earning film since 1940.

**September 20.** Upon taking office last April, MPAA President Jack Valenti began formulating briefer guidelines to replace the 15-page Hays Code. His 10 advisory statements, released today, urge producers to use caution in dealing with sex, evil, crime, and nudity. The association also provides the first official designation for adult films—SMA, "Suggested for Mature Audiences." *Georgy Girl* and *A Funny Thing Happened on the Way to the Forum* receive the first SMA labels.

**More news.** A massive box-office hit, the low-budget, violent biker film *The Wild Angels*, starring Peter Fonda, Nancy Sinatra, and Bruce Dern, inspires a wave of biker movies through the last half of the decade.

• Hollywood sees the beginning of corporate takeovers: Gulf + Western absorbs Paramount; United Artists becomes a wholly owned subsidiary of Transamerica Corporation; and Jack Warner yields control of Warner Bros. to the independent Seven Arts Productions.

• From the mediocre *One Million Years* B.C. comes a stunning poster of a beautiful young woman clad in animal skins. The sexy photo makes a star of actress Raquel Welch.

• At age 62, the ever-youthful Cary Grant gives his last performance, in *Walk, Don't Run.* In the early 1930s, the English acrobat and comic traveled to Hollywood. After a number of supporting roles, he received a career boost with costar billing opposite Marlene Dietrich in *Blonde Venus* (1932) and Mae West in *She Done Him Wrong* (1933). (When West saw the handsome actor with the cleft chin

walking across the studio back lot, she reportedly said, "If he can talk, I'll take him.")

An established romantic lead by the late 1930s, Grant revealed a flair for screwball comedy in *Topper* (1937), *Bringing Up Baby* (1938), and similar films. With his witty, sophisticated style, the actor became a perennial favorite with moviegoers, a place of affection he held despite setbacks in his personal life. Some of his best-remembered films include *Gunga Din* (1939), *The Philadelphia Story* (1940), *Arsenic and Old Lace* (1944), *North by Northwest* (1959), and *Charade* (1963).

• With a $50,000 loan, filmmaker Bruce Brown enlarges his 16-mm documentary, rents a Manhattan theater, and pays for advertising. The unlikely chronicle of a surfer's search for the perfect wave, *The Endless Summer,* will break national attendance records over the next 18 months.

| Top Box Office Stars | Newcomers |
|---|---|
| Julie Andrews | Elizabeth Hartman |
| Sean Connery | George Segal |
| Elizabeth Taylor | Alan Arkin |
| Jack Lemmon | Raquel Welch |
| Richard Burton | Geraldine Chaplin |
| Cary Grant | Guy Stockwell |
| John Wayne | Robert Redford |
| Doris Day | Beverly Adams |
| Paul Newman | Sandy Dennis |
| Elvis Presley | Chad Everett |

### Top Money-Maker of the Year

*Thunderball* (1965) (British, d. Terence Young; color)–Sean Connery, Claudine Auger, Luciana Paluzzi, Adolfo Celi

### Flop of the Year

*The Bible,*
John Huston directs, plays Noah, and narrates, but the film fails to turn a profit.

### Obituaries

**Francis X. Bushman** (January 10, 1883–August

23, 1966). The first matinee idol, and probably the first pinup boy, debuted in films in 1911. When his career faded in the 1930s, Bushman took bit parts then turned to television. Today, his best-known role remains the villain Messala in *Ben-Hur* (1926). (Bushman refused to use a double and drove his own chariot.)

**Montgomery Clift** (October 17, 1920–July 23, 1966). Regarded as one of the new generation of "modern" actors—along with Marlon Brando and James Dean—Clift specialized in troubled, sensitive heroes. His 17 films included *The Heiress* (1949), *From Here to Eternity* (1953), and *Judgment at Nuremburg* (1962). He died of a heart attack.

**Hedda Hopper** (June 2, 1890–February 1, 1966). The queen of Hollywood gossip reigned for 30 years (a love of outrageous hats added much to Hopper's image). Her feud with Louella Parsons lasted until the rival columnist retired in 1965.

**Buster Keaton** (October 4, 1895–February 1, 1966). The accomplished vaudeville acrobat switched to movies in 1917, and within three years starred in his first feature. Using brilliant stunt work and impeccable timing, the comic brought his resourceful but restrained hero through countless adventures.

Keaton exercised complete artistic control, but with the coming of sound, his films deteriorated, and heavy drinking finished his career. In a 1950s comeback attempt, his croaky voice and deadpan expression in *The Great Stone Face* won over a whole new generation of fans.

Today, many film critics regard Keaton as the greatest of the silent-screen comedians.

**Herbert Marshall** (May 23, 1890–January 22, 1966). The British-born actor is best remembered as the older lover or husband opposite the top women stars of the 1930s and 1940s.

**Clifton Webb** (November 19, 1893 or 1896–October 13, 1966). The Broadway actor, who turned to films for a memorable role in *Laura* (1944), gave his most popular screen performance as the baby-sitter in *Sitting Pretty* (1948).

**Ed Wynn** (November 9, 1886–June 19, 1966). In one of entertainment's longest careers, the comedian began in vaudeville in 1902, moved to stage

and radio, then in the 1950s turned to dramatic acting. He won a 1956 Emmy for his performance in *Requiem for a Heavyweight* and received an Oscar nomination for his role in *The Diary of Anne Frank* (1959).

## TELEVISION AND RADIO

### New Prime-Time TV Programs

"The Avengers" (March 28, 1966–September 1969; Spy Drama)—Patrick Macnee, Diana Rigg (1966–1968), Linda Thorson (1968–1969)

"Batman" (January 12, 1966–March 14, 1968; Fantasy Adventure)—Adam West, Burt Ward, Alan Napier

*In "Get Smart!" Don Adams portrays a spy of a different caliber. Agent 86, a.k.a. Maxwell Smart, stumbles through a series of hilarious sight gags while Barbara Feldon plays his brilliant assistant, Agent 99.*

"Daktari" (January 11, 1966–January 15, 1969; Adventure)—Marshall Thompson, Cheryl Miller, Yale Summers (1965–1968), Hari Rhodes

"The Dating Game" (October 6, 1966–January 17, 1970; Quiz/Audience Participation)—Host: Jim Lange. *Note:* The show appears in the daytime from 1965 to 1973.

"Family Affair" (September 12, 1966–September 9, 1971; Situation Comedy)—Brian Keith, Sebastian Cabot, Anissa Jones, Johnnie Whitaker, Kathy Garver

"Mission: Impossible" (September 17, 1966–September 8, 1973; International Intrigue)—Peter Graves (1967–1973), Barbara Bain (1966–1969), Martin Landau (1966–1969), Greg Morris, Peter Lupus, Leonard Nimoy (1967–1971)

"The Monkees" (September 12, 1966–August 19, 1968; Situation Comedy)—David Jones, Peter Tork, Mickey Dolenz, Mike Nesmith

"Star Trek" (September 8, 1966–September 2, 1969; Science Fiction)—William Shatner, Leonard Nimoy, DeForest Kelly, George Takei, Nichelle Nichols, James Doohan, Walter Koenig

"Tarzan" (September 8, 1966–September 1968; Adventure)—Ron Ely, Manuel Padilla, Jr.

"That Girl" (September 8, 1966–September 10, 1971; Situation Comedy)—Marlo Thomas, Ted Bessell, Lew Parker

## Emmy Awards 1965–1966 (May 22, 1966)

This year's awards adopt the designations still in general use.

Drama Series—"The Fugitive" (ABC)
Variety Series—"The Andy Williams Show" (NBC)
Comedy Series—"The Dick Van Dyke Show" (CBS)
Children's Program—"A Charlie Brown Christmas" (CBS)
Best Actor in a Series—Bill Cosby ("I Spy," NBC)

*The first black hero on network television, Bill Cosby poses as an international tennis star while partner Robert Culp assumes the cover of his trainer on "I Spy." Only three NBC southern affiliates turn down the successful mix of world travel, spy adventures, and comic monologues.*

Best Actress in a Series—Barbara Stanwyck ("The Big Valley," ABC)
Best Comedian in a Series—Dick Van Dyke ("The Dick Van Dyke Show," CBS)
Best Comedienne in a Series—Mary Tyler Moore ("The Dick Van Dyke Show," CBS)

## News

**January 12.** Since CBS achieved moderate success with midseason changes last January, ABC treats the New Year like a second season. Amid great fanfare, the network introduces some new programs; "Batman" is the smash hit.

Every Wednesday night the superhero, played by 37-year-old Adam West, and Robin, 20-year-old

Burt Ward, pursue a villain right into some devilish trap. Then a "voice of doom" entices viewers back to the cliff-hanger on Thursday. Inevitably, the dynamic duo escapes the clutches of the Penguin (Burgess Meredith) or the Riddler (Frank Gorshin) or the Joker (Cesar Romero) or any other Hollywood star eager to portray an "archfiend."

Since an early time slot means limited violence, the producers opt for a campy spoof—humor for the adults and exaggerated action for the kids. Characters wear brightly colored costumes, cameras sometimes use angled framing, and during the fight scenes, written words such as "POW!," "BHAM!," and "ZAP!" replace on-screen action.

While the Soviet *Pravda* dubs Batman "a glorified FBI agent" and "a capitalist murderer," Americans love the naive, comic-book romp. The show zooms to the top of the ratings and an estimated 1,000 Bat-items flood the market by spring. When the fad wanes, the show will be yanked in 1969.

**January 29.** Robert Vaughn stands up to speak at a Democratic fund-raiser in Indianapolis. But instead of the usual enthusiastic party support, the actor lambastes Johnson and U.S. policy in Vietnam. Next day, the city newspaper reads: " 'The Man From U.N.C.L.E' (Ho Chi Minh) Speaks." TV's suave secret agent, already popular, is suddenly in demand for another reason. Well-educated, he remains vocal about the war throughout the decade.

**March 16.** When Neil Armstrong and David Scott are forced to make an emergency landing, the networks surrender $3 million in advertising to cover the splashdown of *Gemini 8*. NBC alone receives 3,000 telephone complaints about the canceled programs.

**June.** In an examination of the talk show phenomenon, *Broadcasting* reports that 80 percent of U.S. radio stations regularly broadcast some "talk" other than news.

> *Statistics:* 90 percent of Americans 18 years and older listen to the radio during the course of a week; 87 percent watch TV.

**June 27.** ABC debuts a gothic mystery as an afternoon soap. "Dark Shadows" attracts little attention until the desperate producer, near the end of his six-month contract, introduces a ghost. Ratings go up, and soon a vampire appears.

Shakespearean-trained actor Jonathan Frid, who takes the role of Barnabas Collins for some short-term money, is trapped by the program's huge success. One of the music selections breaks the top 20, spin-off books appear, and fan interest sparks an occultism fad. "Dark Shadows" will leave the air on April 2, 1971.

**July 11.** When a Robert McNamara press conference preempts "Password," millions of daytime viewers turn from CBS to ABC and catch the debut of a new quiz show, "The Newlywed Game." The rest is television history.

**September 3.** "My Friend Flicka," the first children's program shot in color, finishes a 10-year run through all three networks.

**September 8.** "Space, the final frontier. These are the voyages of the Starship Enterprise. Its five-year mission: to explore strange new worlds, to seek out new life and new civilizations, to boldly go where no man has gone before." At 8:30 on this Thursday night, Captain Kirk, Mr. Spock, and the rest of the "Star Trek" crew leave on their first journey.

**September 12.** Determined to tap into the dollars behind rock music, NBC advertises for "four insane boys, aged 17–21." Micky Dolenz, 21, Peter Thorkelson, 24, Mike Nesmith, 23, and David Jones, 20, become "The Monkees." The network fashions their half-hour show after the Beatles' film *A Hard Day's Night* (1964), with songs, visual gags, and crazy camera work.

The weekly sitcom produces a string of rock hits, but the group's music rests on a deception. Hired only for their voices, the network refuses to allow the young men to play their instruments either on TV or their records. Next year, Nesmith will reveal the bitter truth in a press conference.

**September 25.** Front-loading the new season, ABC moved its premiere week up to follow Labor Day, and tonight broadcasts *The Bridge on the River*

*Kwai* opposite TV's perennial favorites, the "Ed Sullivan Show" and "Bonanza." The Hollywood film draws an astounding 55–60 percent of the audience.

Predictably, within a week, ABC and CBS together spend some $92 million for 112 movies. NBC is conducting negotiations.

**October 6.** First broadcast on December 20, 1965, "The Dating Game" begins a concurrent broadcast in prime time. A woman or man asks questions of three unseen members of the opposite sex. The contestant and the chosen person share a night on the town or a paid trip to a fun location. Guest celebrity dates include Joe Namath (1968), Farrah Fawcett (1969), Ron Howard (1971), Michael Jackson (1972), and Arnold Schwarzenegger (1973). Both Burt Reynolds and Tom Selleck appear twice; neither is chosen.

**October 17.** In the debut segment of "Hollywood Squares," guest panelists include Morey Amsterdam, Ernest Borgnine, Agnes Moorehead, Rose Marie, and Charley Weaver. Host Peter Marshall will remain with the daytime game show through a one-year prime time scheduling and syndication in 1971.

**December 18.** Former Frankenstein Boris Karloff narrates the Chuck Jones animated version of *How the Grinch Stole Christmas*. CBS paid an unprecedented $315,000 for the special, and Dr. Seuss's tale will become a seasonal classic.

**More news.** CBC begins color television broadcasting this year.

• Since 1956, the number of prime-time series has dwindled from 123 to 97, with an increased number of 1-hour programs (from 20 to 36), the emergence of the 90-minute format, and several 2-hour slots.

• KADS in Los Angeles becomes the first all-commercial station in the United States. The FM station fills its 16 hours with real estate, help wanted, and other classified ads.

• Following last year's historic FCC order, a number of FM stations shift to jazz, or "underground" rock. This single-format programming creates a tremendous demand for special-audience records.

## TV Commercials

Noxzema—"Take it off. Take it *all* off," the sexy female voice purrs, and to the strains of "The Stripper," sports figures like Joe Namath and Carl Yazstremski stroke the shaving cream off their faces. Noxzema's business triples.

Palmolive—Jan Miner makes her first appearance as Madge the Manicurist for Palmolive Dishwashing Liquid.

Pillsbury—This year, the famous Doughboy is born.

## Obituaries

**Gertrude Berg** (October 3, 1900–September 14, 1966). The author and veteran actress of screen, stage, and television was best known for her starring role in the early 1950s sitcom "The Goldbergs."

**Walt Disney** (December 5, 1901–December 15, 1966). From his first audio cartoon, "Steamboat Willie" (1928) with Mickey Mouse, the animation pioneer and entertainment executive branched out to full-length animated features, then movies, documentaries, a TV series, and an amusement park.

His long career brought Disney some 1,000 awards and distinctions, including 29 Oscars. But for millions of young people who grew up during the 1950s and the first half of this decade, Walt Disney was like a favorite uncle who visited every week with a treasure chest of magical treats. His friendly, familiar face will be missed.

**Eric Fleming** (1925–September 28, 1966). The star of the TV Western "Rawhide" drowned during a canoe trip in Peru.

**William Frawley** (February 26, 1893–March 3, 1966). The U.S. actor was known to millions as Fred Mertz on "I Love Lucy" and Bub O'Casey on "My Three Sons." Upon his death, former co-star Desi Arnaz pays for a full-page photo of Frawley in the *Hollywood Reporter* and adds the farewell, "Buenas Noches, Amigo!"

# SPORTS

## Winners

### Baseball

World Series—Baltimore Orioles (AL), 4 games; Los Angeles Dodgers (NL), 0 games

Player of the Year—Frank Robinson (Baltimore Orioles, AL); Roberto Clemente (Pittsburgh Pirates, NL)

Rookie of the Year—Tommie Agee (Chicago White Sox, AL); Tommy Helms (Cincinnati Reds, NL)

### Football

NFL Championship—Green Bay Packers 34, Dallas Cowboys 27

AFL Championship—Kansas City Chiefs 31, Buffalo Bills 7

Super Bowl I (January 15, 1967)—Green Bay Packers 35, Kansas City Chiefs 10

College Bowls (January 1, 1966)—
Rose Bowl, UCLA 14, Michigan State 12
Cotton Bowl, LSU 14, Arkansas 7
Orange Bowl, Alabama 39, Nebraska 28
Sugar Bowl, Missouri 20, Florida 18

Heisman Trophy—Steve Spurrier (Florida, QB)

Grey Cup—Saskatchewan Roughriders 29, Ottawa Rough Riders 14

### Basketball

NBA Championship—Boston Celtics, 4 games; LA Lakers, 3 games

MVP of the Year—Wilt Chamberlain (Philadelphia 76ers)

Rookie of the Year—Rick Barry (San Francisco Warriors)

NCAA Championship—Texas Western 72, Kentucky 65

### Tennis

U.S. National—Men, Fred Stolle (vs. John Newcombe); Women, Maria Bueno (vs. Nancy Richey)

Wimbledon—Men, Manuel Santana (vs. Dennis Ralston); Women, Billie Jean King (vs. Maria Bueno)

### Golf

Masters—Jack Nicklaus
U.S. Open—Billy Casper
British Open—Jack Nicklaus

### Hockey

Stanley Cup—Montreal Canadiens, 4 games; Detroit Red Wings, 2 games

### Ice Skating

World Championship—Men, Emmerich Danzer (Austria); Women, Peggy Fleming (U.S.)

U.S. National—Men, Scott Allen; Women, Peggy Fleming

Canadian National—Men, Donald Knight; Women, Petra Burka

### Kentucky Derby

Kauai King—Don Brumfield, jockey

### Athlete of the Year

Male—Frank Robinson (Baseball)
Female—Kathy Whitworth (Golf)

### Last Season

Roosevelt (Rosey) Grier (Football)
Paul Hornung (Football)
Sandy Koufax (Baseball)
Johnny Longden (Horse Racing)
Robin Roberts (Baseball)
Jack Twyman (Basketball)

## News

**March 29.** In Toronto, heavyweight boxing champion Muhammed Ali wins a 15-round decision over Canadian title-holder George Chuvalo. Over the next seven months, Ali will defend his world title against five contenders.

**April.** The NL Milwaukee Braves move to Atlanta.

**April.** After hiding in the bushes near the starting line, Roberta Bengay jumps out just as the Boston Marathon begins. The 23-year-old beats two thirds of the male runners, but officials refuse to acknowledge her; women are not allowed to enter the race.

**April 18.** Hired by the Boston Celtics to replace retired coach Red Auerbach, player-coach Bill Russell is the first black to direct a major professional team.

**June 8.** The NFL and AFL announce a merger effective 1970 (following the completion of current TV contracts). Meanwhile, the two football leagues will meet in a 1966 championship game and, next year, hold a common draft to end cutthroat competition for college players. Reportedly, AFL owners must pay the NFL $18 million over 20 years for loss of territorial rights.

**September 26.** The Yankees fire Red Barber for telling the truth. A few days ago, the last-place team played in front of 413 people. When the veteran broadcaster requested a camera shot of the 59,000 empty seats, the producer refused. Barber told his TV audience, "This smallest crowd is the story, not the ball game."

In an interview following his dismissal, Barber contends that in the future a nonathlete will find it difficult to become a broadcaster. As evidence, he points to the remaining three members of his team, former ballplayers Phil Rizzuto, Jerry Coleman, and Joe Garagiola.

**More news.** *The New York Times* reports that television has turned spectator sports into big business. In 1956, for instance, the Green Bay Packers received $35,000 for a broadcast package; this year, networks will pay the same team $1 million.

With the lucrative TV markets, the three major sports continue to expand—4 baseball franchises added since 1959, 12 football, and 2 basketball—despite the rising cost of membership. Just six years ago, Dallas paid $600,000 for a football franchise; last year, the Miami Dolphins (the first AFL expansion team) forked over $7.5 million.

## Records

**March 12.** Chicago Blackhawk Bobby Hull breaks the single-season 50-goal record held by Montreal Canadien Boom Boom Geoffrion and retired Cana

dien Rocket Richard. Hull adds two more before the end of the season. He wins the Ross Trophy as highest scorer and the Hart Trophy as MVP.

**April 11.** Jack Nicklaus becomes the first golfer to win two consecutive Masters tournaments.

**July 30.** Geoff Hurst scores the first hat trick in a World Cup soccer final. And England's 4–2 win over West Germany at Wembley Stadium marks the first home-team victory since World Cup play began in 1930.

**September 29.** With 307 strikeouts this season, Sandy Koufax becomes the first major league pitcher to strike out more than 300 batters in three seasons (306 in 1963, 382 in 1965). Since 1961, the extraordinary southpaw has led the NL in wins and shutouts three times, complete games twice, strikeouts four times, and ERA an unprecedented five consecutive seasons. Sadly, the 30-year-old retires in November rather than permanently damage his arthritic pitching arm.

In 1972, Koufax will become the youngest inductee to the Hall of Fame and only the sixth player to be elected in his first year of eligibility.

**November 27.** The Washington Redskins and New York Giants combine to score an NFL single-game record of 16 touchdowns. The final score is 72–41 for Washington.

### What They Said

A hit ball bounces off the leg of Angeles pitcher Lou Burdette into the glove of teammate Joe Adcock. Burdette says, "This wasn't my best assist. I once started a double play with my forehead." (*Sports Illustrated* August 22)

### Obituaries

**Tony Lema** (February 25, 1934–July 24, 1966). Following his first win in 1962, golf's "bright star" captured 11 more tournaments, including the British Open. He died in a plane crash.

**Abe Saperstein** (1903–March 15, 1966). The U.S. sports promoter formed the Harlem Globetrotters in 1927. Eventually, when teams refused to play his exceptional squad, Saperstein added comedy routines. His heirs sell the Globetrotters for more than $3 million.

# 1967

As casualties mount, reporters point to a "credibility gap," antiwar demonstrations grow in size and number, a more conservative Congress balks at the prospect of a large deficit, and Martin Luther King, Jr., Robert Kennedy, and others speak out against continued involvement in Vietnam. His consensus shattered, President Johnson nonetheless refuses to believe Americans want to lose another Asian country to the Communists. He moves 19-year-olds to the top of the draft list and increases troop strength to 474,000.

Death and destruction dominate this year's headlines. In the Middle East, the Arabs and Israelis fight the Six-Day War. Britain suffers the largest oil spill in history and a department store fire kills at least 300 in Belgium. In the United States, Detroit witnesses the worst racial riot of the century, and three Apollo astronauts die on the launching pad. Canada, one of the few nations celebrating 1967, marks its centennial with Expo 67.

Across the nation, "Sgt. Pepper's Lonely Hearts Club Band" plays on the radio while young people flock to Haight-Ashbury for a Summer of Love. Elvis gets married and cinemas show Bonnie and Clyde, Fistful of Dollars, and To Sir With Love. Scientists clone frogs and transplant the first human heart. Ali loses his title and a woman enters the Boston Marathon. And most kids buy at least one Peanuts item.

## NEWS

**January 6.** The Allies enter the Iron Triangle, an area northwest of Saigon long controlled by the VC, in the biggest offensive of the war. Using a scorched-earth policy, 16,000 American and 14,000 South Vietnamese soldiers destroy 500 buildings, bunkers, and tunnels, capture large stocks of VC weapons, and resettle thousands of pro-VC civilians in camps to the south.

Operation Cedar Falls is declared a success, and in the months ahead, the Allies initiate ever larger drives. But once the troops leave, the VC return in strength, and bitter local farmers give them even greater support.

**January 10.** The House excludes Adam Clayton Powell, Jr., from his Harlem seat for the alleged improper use of government funds—only the third vote of its kind in U.S. history. Powell, who is black, calls it "lynching, Northern style."

Powell must win a special election then a 1968 election, before regaining his seat in January 1969. But the House will strip him of 22 years' seniority and fines him $25,000. The Supreme Court will vindicate Powell in June 1969, ruling the House had unconstitutionally excluded him from Congress. He will be defeated for renomination in 1970.

Later this year, the Senate votes to censure Senator Thomas Dodd (D., Conn.) for using $116,083 in campaign and testimonial funds for his own benefit. Dodd keeps his seat.

**January 16.** A French journalist reports that, in an implied understanding, China has agreed not to enter the Vietnam War if the United States refrains from invading China and North Vietnam. American officials acknowledge that representatives from the two nations exchanged "signals" in 1966 to avoid a direct clash.

Nonetheless, over this decade China sends more than 300,000 combat troops to Vietnam and grants Hanoi $20 billion. More than 4,000 Chinese soldiers will die in the war.

**January 21.** Defense acknowledges that aerial photos of North Vietnam confirm recent dispatches from *New York Times* correspondent Harrison Salisbury in Hanoi that American bombers have damaged civilian areas. (A classified CIA study this month estimates North Vietnamese casualties rose from 13,000 in 1965 to 24,000 in 1966 and 80 percent were civilians.) Yet extending the U.S. air war has not produced better results; the number of downed planes has increased from 171 to 318—and operational costs have more than doubled, from $460 million in 1965 to $1.2 billion in 1966.

**January 27.** Representatives of 60 nations, including the United States and the Soviet Union, sign a treaty banning weapons of mass destruction in outer space. Eventually, 76 nations will ratify the pact.

**February 5.** The United States and South Vietnam begin defoliating the southern part of the DMZ because of "flagrant violation" of the buffer zone by the VC. Just nine days later, three university scientists deliver a petition to the White House with the signatures of 5,000 American scientists protesting the use of chemical weapons in Vietnam. Still, the Pentagon will abandon carefully controlled defoliation missions for widespread spraying.

**February 10.** The 25th Amendment to the U.S. Constitution guarantees presidential succession.

When Harry S. Truman and Lyndon Baines Johnson stepped into the presidency, the vice-presidency remained vacant until the next election. Now, under the amendment, a president can nominate a new vice-president, subject to congressional approval. And if a president is unable to perform his duties, the vice-president becomes acting president. In the past, the president could choose whether or not to declare his disability.

**February 13.** The National Student Association confirms a *Ramparts* magazine report that over the past 15 years it has received more than $3 million in secret funding from the CIA. The money enabled American students to attend overseas youth conferences to counterbalance strong Communist representation.

In the ensuing uproar, President Johnson orders all federal agencies, including the CIA, to end secret financing of private organizations.

**February 14.** The Treaty of Tlatelolco establishes the first nuclear-free zone in an inhabited area of the world (Antarctica was designated a nuclear-free zone in 1959). Fourteen Latin American nations sign the agreement banning nuclear-weapons manufacture, storage, and testing in Central America, South America, and the Caribbean. Attached protocols prohibit the five nuclear nations who have signed the document from bringing nuclear weapons into the area or using nuclear arms against any treaty signatory.

**March 18.** The giant Liberian tanker *Torrey Canyon* founders at the western entrance of the English Channel; 100,000 tons of crude oil foul British and French beaches, killing countless sea birds and causing damage of more than $14 million.

An inquiry finds the Italian captain, Pestrego Rugiati, solely responsible for the largest oil spill to date. Still, denying liability, the ship owners will pay just $3.6 million compensation to France and England in 1969.

**March 29.** The Fifth Circuit Court of Appeals orders Texas, Alabama, Florida, Georgia, Louisiana, and Mississippi to desegregate all schools no later than this fall. On April 17, the Supreme Court refuses a postponement.

*Statistics*: Southern Education Reporting Service notes that the percentage of black students attending integrated Southern schools rose over the past year from 6 percent to 16 percent. Yet, 500,000 *more* students now attend all-black schools than in 1954, the year of the *Brown v. Board of Education* ruling.

**April 4.** For the first time, Reverend Martin Luther King, Jr., directly attacks U.S. administration policy in Vietnam. He states before the national media that a disproportionate number of blacks are dying in the war and urges young men, black and white, to declare themselves conscientious objectors. (Figures released in December will show that blacks, 11 percent of the nation's population, account for 14.1 percent of U.S. combat deaths.)

Although he realizes that a linkage of civil rights and the peace movement will likely destroy his special relationship with the president, King is stunned by the general criticism. The NAACP, for instance, claims a merger of the two movements fails to serve the cause of either. And contributions to the SCLC drop sharply.

On April 15, King joins protesters of all ages and racial and ethnic backgrounds in New York City for the largest antiwar demonstration to date. The police estimate the turnout at 100,000, but King pegs the figure at 300,000–400,000. A countermarch in mid-May draws some 70,000 in New York to support "our fighting men in Vietnam," but protest against the war continues to mount.

**April 21.** Right-wing army officers seize power in Greece, ending two years of weak government. The group, led by Colonel Georgios Papadopoulos, cancels upcoming elections, imposes censorship, and bans miniskirts and bearded tourists. King Constantine attempts a countercoup in December, but when that fails, the royal family flees into exile.

**April 24.** General Westmoreland, back home in the United States, declares that critics of the war give the enemy the "hope he can win politically that which he cannot accomplish militarily." The

next day, George McGovern and others lead a Senate attack against administration policy in Vietnam.

Fulbright accuses the White House of bringing Westmoreland home to "pave the way for escalation." McGovern claims that four administrations, including John F. Kennedy's, must share the blame for the war, and Bobby Kennedy courageously agrees with him.

When Westmoreland speaks to a joint session three days later, he refrains from criticizing dissenters and pledges, "We will prevail in Vietnam over the Communist aggressor." A majority of the Congress gives him a standing ovation.

**May 2.** The Black Panthers grab national attention when 30 members carrying rifles and shotguns storm the California State Assembly to protest a pending arms control bill. The young militants brand the legislation racist, since a ban against carrying loaded firearms in public will keep black people powerless. The group is later disarmed and arrested. Governor Reagan will sign the bill into law on July 28.

**May 8.** At today's White House meeting, Defense Secretary McNamara recommends cutting the air war in Vietnam back to the 20th parallel and concentrating on lines of communication into the South to reduce pilot and aircraft losses.

De-escalation and political compromise represent a radical departure from administration policy, but in a May 19 memo, McNamara points to the growing protest movement in arguing "the difficulties of this strategy are fewer and smaller than the difficulties of any other approach."

Although the Joint Chiefs refute his recommendations, Johnson supports McNamara with regard to the troop request, approving a 55,000-man increase rather than a 200,000-man increase. But the president, once again, ignores his secretary's advice to reduce the air war. Thoroughly disillusioned, McNamara commissions a historical study of American involvement in Vietnam, which later becomes known as the Pentagon Papers.

**May 22.** Fire sweeps through the five-story L'Innovation department store in Brussels during the busy noon hour. With no sprinkler system in the store and fire fighters delayed by the old city's narrow streets, the flames quickly spread to the roof, where hundreds of stored bottles of butane gas ignite. At least 322 people die in the worst retail-store fire on record.

**May 30.** Longstanding tribal tensions explode in Nigeria when General Odumegwu Ojukwu leads the Ibo out of the federation and proclaims the Republic of Biafra. The Lagos government, with the support of Britain and all other African states, rapidly mobilizes against the eastern secession. Slowly regaining control, the federal troops force the 8 million Biafrans into an ever-shrinking land-locked area with no access to supplies.

**June 5.** Israel launches a preemptive strike against the United Arab Republic, Syria, and Jordan. Moving with lightning speed, the Israelis destroy all three Arab air forces on the ground and take control of the Sinai Peninsula, the Golan Heights in Syria, and all the Jordanian territory west of the Jordan River. The humiliated Arabs accept a U.N.-negotiated cease-fire on June 10.

Reportedly the Arabs were preparing to invade. On May 18, Nasser had ordered the withdrawal of U.N. troops stationed in the UAR since 1956. Then, five days later, he closed the Gulf of Aqaba to Israeli shipping and, on the 30th, concluded a surprise military alliance with Jordan. Yet no proof existed of a planned Arab attack.

Some suggest the Israelis coveted new land and Washington wanted Nasser crushed. Certainly territorial gains give Israel more defensible borders, while the devastation of the UAR, the leading Arab power, provides some measure of Middle Eastern security. In September, Tel Aviv will announce plans to settle the seized territories, including the West Bank of the Jordan River, where some 600,000 Arabs already live.

Despite superpower nonintervention in the Six-Day War—ensured by Kosygin's use of the hot line—the conflict strengthens Soviet-Arab and American-Israeli alignments. U.S. support for Israel drives the Arabs closer to the Soviets, while a postwar French arms embargo forces the Americans to supply the Israelis with weapons to maintain a balance of power.

Aware of the dangerous potential for another war, Washington and Moscow strike a secret bargain. President Johnson proposes an agreement to cut the supply of the newest, most sophisticated armaments to Middle Eastern allies, and the kremlin agrees.

**June 12.** The Supreme Court finds a Virginia law barring interracial marriage to be unconstitutional. The decision invalidates similar laws in 15 other states.

**June 12.** Most states prohibit wiretapping (eavesdropping on a telephone conversation), yet 43 states permit authorized bugging (hidden microphone). The Supreme Court, citing the 14th Amendment, invalidates (6–3) a New York State law authorizing warrants for bugging.

Four days later, Attorney General Ramsey Clark prohibits all federal agencies from electronic eavesdropping except in "national security" cases.

**June 13.** Thurgood Marshall, age 59, replaces Tom C. Clark on the U.S. Supreme Court. During his 25 years as the legal director of the NAACP and then as President Johnson's solicitor general, Marshall argued 32 cases before the High Court. He won 29, including one of the four leading to the historic Brown decision. In appointing the first black American to the Supreme Court, the president declares, "I believe it is the right thing to do, the right time to do it, the right man, and the right place."

**June 19.** U.S. District Judge J. Skelly Wright charges the Washington, D.C., school board with tracking black students into blue-collar programs and whites into honor and regular curricula, and with spending less per student at black schools. The tracking system must be dismantled, teachers redistributed, and busing used to end de facto segregation by autumn.

Many consider his judgment a historic extension of Supreme Court rulings on state segregation laws, but legal opinion remains divided on the constitutionality of segregation based on population patterns.

**June 23.** In the United States to address the

United Nations, Premier Kosygin meets with President Johnson for the first time. During their two discussions in Glassboro, New Jersey, Kosygin demands that the United States withdraw from Vietnam as a precondition for improved Soviet-American relations.

**June 28.** With victory in the Middle East, Tel Aviv ignores world opinion and places the Old City of Jerusalem under Israeli control. The 1947 U.N. partition of Palestine internationalized the ancient city, but the Arab-Israeli War in 1948 split Jerusalem into Jewish and Jordanian sectors.

**June 30.** President Johnson signs a bill extending the draft to June 30, 1971, and, with an executive order, reverses the order of induction to place 19-year-olds first rather than last. Congress had barred him from instituting other suggested reforms, including a draft lottery or an end to college deferment.

---

*Statistics:* By July, the president's approval rating plunges to 39 percent, a dramatic drop from a 1964 rating of 77 percent.

---

**June 30.** In Geneva, 46 nations conclude the Kennedy Round of GATT negotiations. Three years of bargaining have reduced almost one-third of the world's industrial tariffs, liberalized agricultural trade, and created a food aid program for less-developed countries. Since 38 of the signatories account for approximately 75 percent of world commerce, analysts describe the documents as the most significant international trade liberalization in history.

**July.** A survey of 1,567 American teenage girls, published in this month's issue of *Seventeen* magazine, reports that almost 85 percent are virgins. Fewer than 5 percent of the anonymous respondents sanction premarital sex for couples with no intention of marrying.

**July 1.** The executive commissions of the EEC, European Coal and Steel Community, and Euratom merge into a single administrative body, the European Commission. The six member nations view the merger as an important step toward eventual political unification.

**July 20.** A Black Power Conference draws representatives from 197 organizations for the largest and most varied gathering of black leaders ever to assemble in the United States. The conference, which bars whites from all meetings and workshops, finishes on July 23 with a series of militant resolutions aimed at establishing a separate course for black Americans.

The discussions opened in Newark, New Jersey, just after a five-day race riot in the city left 26 dead and 1,500 injured.

**July 23.** In Puerto Rico, 66 percent of eligible voters cast their ballots in a plebiscite to decide the future course of the island: 60.5 percent of those voting reject statehood or full independence in favor of continued commonwealth status under the United States, with more of a voice for the island in internal affairs.

**July 23.** The city of Detroit is booming, but for blacks, who make up one-third of the city's population, the unemployment rate is double the national average. Their rage and frustration boils over this Saturday night when police routinely raid an illegal after-hours club and arrest over 70 people. Growing crowds start looting, and 12 hours later Governor Romney calls in the National Guard.

But the 7,000 young white Guardsmen are overwhelmed by thousands of looters, snipers, and over 1,000 separate fires. By Monday morning, 6 people are dead and hundreds injured, and Romney appeals to the White House for federal troops. (The last city to call on Washington was also Detroit, in 1943.)

Another 13 people die on Monday, and that night President Johnson orders in 4,700 soldiers. Over the next few days, an enormous law enforcement body of 17,000 arrests some 7,000 people, mostly young blacks, to put an end to the looting. The worst U.S. riot of this century leaves 43 dead, 2,000 injured, and almost 500 buildings damaged or destroyed in a 100-block area.

On July 27, Johnson appoints a Special Advisory Commission on Civil Disorders to investigate the riot in Detroit and those in 120 other cities this summer, and to recommend preventive measures.

In its first report, on August 10, the commission urges improved riot training for National Guard units and an increased number of black Guardsmen (now at 1.15 percent).

---

*Statistics:* A U.S. census report published in November pegs the nonwhite unemployment rate at 7.3 percent compared to 3.4 percent for whites, and reveals that 41 percent of nonwhites live below the poverty line of $3,300 a year, compared to 12 percent of whites.

---

**July 24.** Beginning his state visit in the French-Canadian province of Quebec, Charles de Gaulle sets off a diplomatic row with his public cry, "Vive le Quebec libre." Prime Minister Pearson publicly rebukes the French president for his unacceptable support of an independent Quebec. In response, de Gaulle cancels the remainder of his trip and returns home in a huff. The incident strains Ottawa-Paris relations, encourages Quebec separatists, and badly damages relations between English and French Canadians.

**July 29.** On the *U.S.S. Forrestal*, off North Vietnam, a 250-gallon auxiliary gas tank drops from a plane warming up for a bombing run. The fuel spreads across the flight deck and ignites. Most of the 80 sailors forced to jump into the sea drown. Altogether 134 men die in the blaze and explosions.

**August 29.** In a broadcast from Hanoi, Stokely Carmichael pledges the support of black Americans for North Vietnam. Earlier this month, over Havanna Radio, he called on black Americans to arm for "total revolution." When the SNCC chairman returns to the United States in December, authorities confiscate his passport.

**September 1.** Leaders of 13 Arab states, meeting in Khartoum, devise a joint Israeli policy: no recognition, no negotiations, no peace, and the maintenance of the rights of the Palestinian people in their nation.

**September 3.** In South Vietnamese elections, provided for by a new constitution, Nguyen Van Thieu wins a four-year term as president and Nguyen Cao Ky becomes vice-president. Ky, who has served as premier since mid-1965, was pressured by the military to run as vice-president to the 44-year-old Thieu, his superior officer and leader of the military junta.

Seven of the 10 civilian candidates charge the Thieu ticket with fraudulent voting practices, but American observers report that the elections were generally honest, although fewer than 50 percent of eligible voters turned out.

Nguyen Van Thieu is inaugurated as the first president of South Vietnam's Second Republic on October 31. U.S. Vice-President Hubert Humphrey attends the ceremonies.

**September 7.** U.S. Defense Secretary McNamara extends a Pentagon campaign to end housing discrimination against American servicemen. Calling the nationwide segregation shameful, McNamara claims that an initial drive outside military installations in Maryland and the Washington area increased the number of open housing units by over 300 percent.

**October 10.** Bolivia announces that Cuban revolutionary Che Guevara died yesterday, from wounds received during an October 8 clash with the Bolivian Army. But reporters, allowed to photograph his body, believe Guevara could never have survived a day with such severe wounds to the heart and lungs, and he was probably executed. (When his brother arrives on the 12th, Bolivian authorities claim the body has already been cremated.)

Guevara disappeared from the public eye in 1965, but reports had since linked him to guerrilla activity throughout South America. Although his latest campaign to rouse poverty-stricken Bolivian tin-miners had failed, students worldwide idealize his rejection of both capitalism and conventional Communism, turning "Che" into a cult figure.

**October 20.** After three years of investigation and litigation, a federal jury finds seven white men guilty of conspiracy in the 1964 slaying of three civil rights workers in Mississippi. Deputy Cecil Price and six others receive sentences of 3 to 10 years for denying the victims their civil rights. The jury acquits eight codefendents and fails to reach a decision on three others.

**October 21.** In Washington, 55,000–150,000 people rally at the Lincoln Memorial to protest the war in Vietnam. Afterward, many march the two miles to the Pentagon to hold a vigil.

At first, the protesters simply face the soldiers and place flowers in their rifle barrels. (A group

Hershey confirms that all draft boards received a letter from him recommending that registrants who interfere with the induction of young men into the Vietnam War be conscripted as soon as possible. Many of the 4,081 draft boards refuse to follow the order, and a coalition of some 40 antiwar groups

*Anti-Vietnam War protesters taunt the military police in front of the Pentagon.*

planning to drop the flowers into the empty center of the Pentagon was stopped at the airport.) But after two hours, radical elements try to push up the Pentagon steps. In a violent confrontation with troops and U.S. marshals, some 1,000 demonstrators are arrested. Only two will eventually come to trial and they will be acquitted.

**November 2.** Selective Service director Lewis

stage "Stop the Draft Week," December 4–8, to disrupt centers throughout the country. In New York, at the largest and most violent of the demonstrations, police arrest 585, including Dr. Benjamin Spock and poet Allen Ginsberg.

In June 1969, the District of Columbia Appeals Court will find the Hershey letter "unauthorized and contrary to the law."

**November 7.** Democrats and Republicans both claim gains in state and municipal elections. Unquestionably, blacks make significant gains: Cleveland elects its first black mayor, 40-year-old Carl Stokes; Gary, Indiana, chooses Richard Hatcher as mayor; and Virginia, Louisiana, and Mississippi send blacks to their legislatures for the first time since Reconstruction.

**November 16.** The Senate Foreign Relations Committee unanimously approves a resolution, introduced by Senator Fulbright, requiring future congressional approval to send troops abroad (except to repel an attack on the United States or to protect U.S. citizens or property). A second resolution recommends that the president ask the U.N. Security Council to take action on the Vietnam War.

The Senate unanimously adopts the U.N. resolution on November 30, but rejects committee advice to use the second resolution to reassert the congressional prerogatives of the Senate.

**November 20.** In Washington, the U.S. "population clock" officially registers the birth of the 200 millionth American, at 11:00 A.M. (many demographers believe the figure was passed earlier in the year). The country's population has doubled since 1915.

**November 22.** In a 133-page report, *A Time to Listen . . . A Time to Act*, the U.S. Civil Rights Commission urges Americans to make deterioration in big-city slums a national priority. The commission notes that the growing militancy of Northern blacks should be viewed in the context of "great frustrations, of laws and programs which promise but do not deliver, of continuing deprivation, discrimination and prejudice."

**November 23.** In Ottawa, the House of Commons approves a bill abolishing capital punishment for a five-year trial period. The ban exempts those who murder a prison guard or police officer. The last executions in Canada were carried out on December 11, 1962.

**December 10.** In an attempt to free natural gas trapped in a sandstone formation, the AEC, the Bureau of Mines, and the El Paso Natural Gas Co. detonate a 26-kiloton nuclear device east of Farmington, New Mexico. "Operation Gasbuggy," the 79th test in the Plowshare program, succeeds in releasing considerable amounts of gas, but it is all radioactive.

In 1971, the AEC will suspend the Plowshare Program (effective July 1, 1972), citing federal budget restraints, opposition from environmentalists, and lack of support from private industry.

**December 15.** President Johnson signs an act barring age discrimination against workers 40–65 years old.

**December 17.** Australian Prime Minister Harold Holt, age 59, disappears while swimming off the Victorian coast. He had succeeded Sir Robert Menzies as prime minister just last year, and in a fall election, his Liberals won a solid majority. Holt was one of the strongest foreign supporters of U.S. policy in Vietnam—in one of his first acts he increased the size of the Australian force in Vietnam by a third—and President Johnson attends his memorial service along with other world leaders. Holt's body is never recovered.

**December 20.** U.S. troop strength passes 474,300 in Vietnam, exceeding the total American troop level of 472,800 in the Korean War. U.S. bombing tonnage in Vietnam—1,630,000 tons—now exceeds the total dropped by American forces in Germany during W.W.II.

**December 21.** While in Australia, President Johnson meets with President Thieu. In an apparent effort to bridge policy differences, the two leaders proclaim the willingness of South Vietnam to talk with any individual associated with the NLF but reaffirming the non-recognition of the VC political arm.

Johnson then flies to the largest American base in Vietnam. He tells the U.S. soldiers, "We're not going to yield, and we're not going to shimmy." Reporters describe reaction to the speech as restrained.

## Obituaries

**Konrad Adenauer** (January 5, 1876–April 19, 1967). Twice imprisoned by the Nazis, Adenauer was acceptable to the Allies as the postwar leader of Germany. He founded the Christian Democratic party and, in 1949, became West Germany's first chancellor.

Following a strong anti-Communist line, Adenauer demanded and received an equal partnership in Western alliances. And, as an early advocate of European unity, he took West Germany into the EEC in 1957.

Adenauer served as chancellor until 1963 and party leader until just last year. President Johnson and other world leaders attend his funeral in tribute.

**Clement Attlee** (January 3, 1883–October 8, 1967). In 1945, the lifelong British socialist led the Labour party to its first majority government. As prime minister, Attlee oversaw the establishment of the welfare state and, by granting independence to colonies, oversaw the dismantlement of the British Empire in favor of a commonwealth of nations. The 1950 election reduced his Labour majority and a year later Churchill and the Conservatives regained power. Attlee resigned as party leader in 1955, after 20 years.

**Charles Darrow** (1889–August 28, 1967). The inventor sold Parker Brothers the rights to *Monopoly* in 1935. At the time of his death, the company has sold some 45 million games.

**Benjamin Foulois** (December 9, 1879–April 25, 1967). The first military test pilot (1910) became the first U.S. combat pilot in 1916 when he flew *Military Aircraft No. 1* in a punitive expedition against Mexico. Foulois headed American air forces during W.W.I and was first chief of the Army Air Corps from 1931 to 1935.

**John Nance Garner** (November 22, 1868–November 7, 1967). "Cactus Jack" served as vice-president during Franklin D. Roosevelt's first two terms of office (1933–1941).

**Ernest "Che" Guevara** (June 14, 1928–October 9, 1967). *See* News.

**Harold Holt** (August 5, 1908–December 17, 1967). *See* News.

**Alfried Krupp** (August 13, 1907–July 30, 1967). Found guilty in 1947 of using slave labor during W.W.II, the German industrialist was sentenced to 12 years in prison and his property was

confiscated. Four years later, he was released and given back the greater part of his family empire. Earlier this year, as the recession pushed the firm deeper into debt, Krupp was forced to offer shares to the public.

**Vincent Massey** (February 20, 1887–December 30, 1967). In 1926, Massey went to Washington as the first Canadian ambassador accredited to a foreign capital. With further diplomatic training and his wealthy, cultured background, he made the ideal choice as the first Canadian-born governor general of Canada (1952–1959).

**Frederick Morgan** (February 5, 1894–March 19, 1967). The British army officer was the chief planner of the Allied invasion of Normandy in 1944.

**Henry Pu-yi (Hsuan T'ung)** (1906–October 17, 1967). Enthroned at the age of two by the dying Dowager Empress Tzu Hsi, deposed at the age of five by the Chinese republican revolution, the Emperor of China abdicated in 1912 at the age of six.

He continued to live in a summer palace outside Peking but, with increasing unrest, fled in 1928 to the Japanese zone of Tientsin. In 1931, the Japanese occupied Manchuria and placed him at the head of a puppet government. Captured by the Soviets at the end of the war, he spent five years in a Siberian prison camp before Moscow released him to the Chinese Communists. Following years of political reeducation, the last emperor of China received a pardon and, as Henry Pu-yi, lived his remaining years as a private citizen.

**Jack Ruby** (1911–January 3, 1967). The Dallas nightclub owner shot and killed Lee Harvey Oswald on November 24, 1963, the day after the assassination of John F. Kennedy. His murder conviction was overturned in 1966 on appeal (the presiding judge ruled a confession must be voluntary and spontaneous). While awaiting a new trial, he was diagnosed with cancer and died of a blood clot in his lungs.

**Georges Vanier** (April 23, 1888–March 5, 1967). The first French-Canadian appointed to the post of governor general of Canada (1959–1967) succeeded Vincent Massey.

# BEGINNINGS AND ENDINGS

## *News*

**January 16.** In Tuskegee, Alabama, Lucius Amerson is sworn in as the first black Southern sheriff of this century.

**April 4.** Roland Michener succeeds George Vanier as governor general of Canada.

**April 12.** The House of Commons approves "O Canada" as the national anthem. Calixa Lavallée composed the music and Sir Adolphe-Basile Routhier wrote the words in the 1800's, but exactly when and why is no longer clear (the tune was performed during a mass on June 24, 1880). Parliament slightly altered the wording during debate.

**April 25.** The Canadian Forces Reorganization Act combines the Canadian Army, the Royal Canadian Navy, and the Royal Canadian Air Force into the Canadian Armed Forces—the only single unified service in the world.

*At Expo 67, visitors use walkways and escalators to move from one exhibit level to another, or take the monorail for a quick look through the huge geodesic bubble.*

**April 27.** Expo 67 opens in Montreal as part of Canada's centennial celebration. Before the gates close on October 29, some 50.3 million visit what many describe as the greatest fair ever.

**May 24.** Wisconsin is the last state to repeal the ban on yellow margarine. For years, dairies protected their interests by ensuring that margarine and its yellow coloring were packaged separately. Consumers had to mix the two at home.

**June 1.** The first Canadian McDonald's opens in Richmond, British Columbia. This year, the chain's hamburger goes up 3 cents to 18 cents.

**July 1.** Festivities on Parliament Hill, attended by the Queen and Prince Philip, mark Canada's 100th birthday.

**July 7.** For the centenary, Ottawa creates the Order of Canada to honor those who have made outstanding contributions to the country. The first 35 Companions include former governor general Vincent Massey, former prime minister Louis St. Laurent, and Montreal Mayor Jean Drapeau.

**July 31.** Some 20 prominent Americans found the Urban Coalition to confront big-city problems, the root of recent large-scale rioting. In 1970, the group will merge with Urban America (1965) to form the National Urban Coalition. Funded by donations and government contracts, the coalition will expand to 20 states.

**September 3.** The European nation with the highest car density, Sweden switches overnight from driving on the left side of the road to the right.

**September 9.** In Canada, the Progressive Conservatives replace leader John Diefenbaker (1956–1967) with Robert Stanfield. Diefenbaker had rejected the party concept of two founding nations, England and France.

**October 6.** At the beginning of the year, thousands flocked to the Haight-Ashbury district of San Francisco to attend the World's First Human Be-In. When word spread of a planned "Summer of Love," the bohemian population mushroomed again; with that influx came busloads of sightseers, reporters, and TV crews.

Today, the disenchanted flower children stage a funeral for "Hippie, devoted son of Mass Media" then turn their backs on the city. The area's population continues to grow, but within two years many storefronts will be boarded up.

**October 26.** Mohammed Reza Pahlavi, ruler of Iran for 26 years, formally crowns himself and his wife Farah in a ceremony in Tehran. His father, an army officer, overthrew the Kajar dynasty in 1921 and four years later ascended the throne.

**December 9.** Lynda Bird Johnson, the president's first daughter, weds Marine Captain Charles Robb in a White House ceremony.

## Records

**October 3.** The X15-A2 achieves a record air speed of 4,534 mph.

## New Products and Businesses

Coca-Cola launches Fresca.

Don Kracke develops Rickie Tickie Stickie. Mainly stuck on cars or in bathtubs, the paste-on vinyl daisy seems irremovable.

A Tokyo electronics firm offers a "learn as you sleep" tape-recorder and pillow speaker. Experts claim the system is useless.

Automakers bring out new models to rival Ford's incredibly successful Mustang—the Chevrolet Camaro, the Pontiac Firebird, the Plymouth Barracuda, and the Mercury Cougar. But even the most successful—the Camaro—achieves just 50 percent of Mustang sales.

## Fads

Metal buttons appeared as a form of social and political comment in 1966. This year, all sorts of buttons sell: Timothy Leary's "Turn On, Tune In, Drop Out"; antiwar declarations "Hell No We Ain't Going," "Make Love Not War," "Burn Pot, Not People"; anti-Establishment statements "Do Your Own Thing," "Tomorrow We Must Get Organized," "Don't Trust Anyone Over 30," "Stamp Out Pay Toilets"; sexual suggestions "If It Moves, Fondle It." For $.25–$1, every age group uses a button to make a statement. (In the seventies, the T-shirt will become the venue of protest.)

A small-market bonanza for Wham-O, the Shoop-Shoop Hula-Hoop produces a distinctive sound when the ball bearings move inside.

North Americans buy anything sporting a *Pea-* *nuts* character—from T-shirts to paper cups—and cartoonist Charles Schulz rakes in millions.

A college fad from 1965 to 1966, computer dating goes national this year. Subscribers feed in personal information and the computer prints out a compatible match. Dating systems will remain big business into the 1970s.

The media generally describes it as a fad, but with some 5 million runners hitting the streets, jogging is fast becoming a part of everyday life. After all, as a representative for the President's Council on Physical Fitness explains, "About all you need are some old clothes and comfortable shoes."

Rock concert posters, with their psychedelic, fluorescent swirls, became hot items late last year. Recognizing a potential market, manufacturers offer colorful Peter Max drawings and personality posters in 1967.

Teens go for David McCallum, Steve McQueen, and Spider Man while college students like Peter Fonda, Jean-Paul Belmondo, and James Dean. Surprisingly, other popular personalities include Sigmund Freud, D. H. Lawrence, W. C. Fields, and Albert Einstein.

# SCIENCE AND TECHNOLOGY

## News

**January.** A trio of Brooklyn surgeons clear clogged heart arteries with a jet of carbon dioxide. Gas endarterectomy restores normal blood flow in half the time required for conventional surgery.

**January 1.** With the nation's first fluoridation law, Connecticut requires all water companies with more than 50,000 customers to fluoridate immediately.

**January 22.** A research team at the Roswell Park Memorial Institute announces the discovery of the structure of RNA. X-ray crystallography and 16 years of hard work finally deciphered the enzyme's complex structure, more than 1,000 atoms arranged in chains of 124 amino acid units.

**January 27.** In a trial run for the first Apollo

mission, Gus Grissom, Ed White, and rookie Roger Chaffee sit in the cabin for preflight tests. Suddenly someone cries out, "I smell fire!" In seconds, the 100-percent oxygen atmosphere bursts into flames. The three men die in less than a minute.

A special review board attributes the tragedy to "some minor malfunction or failure of equipment or wire insulation." At the same time, the report criticizes "many deficiencies in design and engineering, manufacture and quality control" and condemns inadequate provision for crew escape and the slowness of rescue attempts (without fuel in the rocket no fire crew stood by). NASA knew the dangers of a 100-percent oxygen atmosphere, but had resisted any change that would result in delay.

**February.** Amana manufactures the first compact microwave oven, a $475 unit the size of an air conditioner. Litton, the biggest manufacturer of commercial microwaves, has acquired the Stouffer line of frozen foods to promote the oven to consumers.

**March 1.** On a three-month trial basis, 80 New York telephone customers can direct dial to Paris or London.

**March 6.** A U.N.-sponsored study of 12 industrial nations finds math achievement levels highest in Japan and lowest in the United States.

**April 24.** As *Soyuz 1* returns to Earth after a 24-hour orbit, the descent parachutes fail to deploy and the capsule plummets to earth. Vladimir Komarov, pilot of *Voskhod 1* in 1964, dies in the crash. As with the recent American tragedy, this terrible accident delays the Soviet space program.

**May 1.** A Public Health Service survey of 42,000 U.S. homes reveals a strong connection between smoking and heart problems, emphysema, peptic ulcers, and other diseases. Later in the year, following a review of some 2,000 research studies, the service warns that smoking is a "health hazard of sufficient importance in the United States to warrant appropriate remedial action."

**July.** In Cambridge, England, astronomer Antony Hewish has supervised the construction of some 2,000 receivers, arrayed over three acres, to detect brief microwave variations that elude conventional radio telescopes. Within a month of start-up, 24-

year-old graduate student Jocelyn Bell observes weak but precise bursts—lasting 1/30 of a second every 1.337 seconds—from a spot midway between Vega and Altair. Because of its pulsating radio energy, the neutron star is soon dubbed a pulsar.

In 1974, Hewish will receive the Nobel prize in physics. No mention will be made of the well-documented role played by Jocelyn Bell.

**July 25.** In a telephone interview with *The New York Times*, Michael Gazzinga describes his five-year study with a colleague at the California Institute of Technology. When epileptics had the two hemispheres of their brains separated to reduce convulsions, their subsequent actions revealed that the halves function independently of each other.

**July 31 and August 5.** *Mariner 6* and *Mariner 7* pass Mars at about 2,400 miles. Transmitted photos and measurements reveal a cold, dry, nearly airless environment and a surface more like that of the moon than Earth.

**September.** A study introduced at a meeting of the American Roentgen Ray Society promotes the combined use of thermography and mammography to detect breast cancers. Last year, the tests found 6 cancers in 16 total tissue biopsies. In 1967, an estimated 27,000 American women will die from breast cancer.

**September 7.** *Biosatellite II*, the first successful U.S. bioscientific research capsule, determines that bacteria reproduce 20–30 percent faster in space and that plant growth relies on gravity—in space, roots grow upward or sideways rather than down.

**October 6.** Biologists at Oxford University cloned frogs by inserting an intestinal cell into an egg from which the nucleus had been removed. But the scientific community rejected the notion that a specialized cell—one with a specific function—could produce a clone. After one last experiment, John Gurden announces that over 30 percent of intestinal cells grow into a frog.

**October 18.** During a 1-hour, 38-minute, descent to the surface of Venus, *Venera 4*'s lander records a 90–95 percent carbon dioxide atmosphere and temperatures up to 536 degrees Fahrenheit. Communications cease abruptly, and the Soviets speculate that the lander either hit a mountain peak or was crushed by atmospheric pressure 15 times that of Earth's. *Venera 4* continues on to orbit around the sun.

**October 30.** The Soviet Kosmos program performs the first automatic docking in space. The two unmanned craft remain attached for a couple of hours.

**November 9.** Last year, NASA used the Saturn 1B to launch three unmanned Apollos. This year, following a redesign of the spacecraft, *Apollo 4* lifts off on a Saturn 5.

The monster rocket, developed under the direction of Wernher von Braun, is believed to be the most powerful object put into space—363 feet tall, with a fully fueled weight of 6.4 million pounds and 180 million horsepower. The Apollo command module (CM), which reaches 25,000 mph to simulate mission velocity, breaks all records, with an orbital payload of 278,699 pounds.

*Apollo 5* will test an unmanned lunar module (LM, pronounced LEM) in January 1968, and *Apollo 6* will orbit in April.

**December 3.** In Cape Town, South Africa, Dr. Christiaan Barnard and his medical team complete the first transplant of a human heart. The medical feat makes headline news around the world, but 54-year-old Louis Washkansky, who received the heart of 24-year-old Denise Ann Darvall, succumbs to complications 18 days later.

Four days after the historic operation, New York surgeon Adrian Kantrowitz performs a transplant; the patient lives just a few hours.

**December 8.** Robert H. Lawrence, the first black astronaut, is killed in an F-104 crash at Edwards Air Force Base in California. He was chosen in June to participate in the orbiting lab program.

**December 14.** At a news conference today, Stanford University scientists announce the first artificial production of active DNA. The research team, headed by Dr. Arthur Kornberg, expects its work will open up genetic studies.

• Under the requirements of the Highway Safety Act (1966), automakers introduce major design changes to 1968 models: seat belts for every passenger, a collapsible steering column, ruptureproof and fireproof gas tanks, padded instrument panels,

dual braking, windshield washers, turning signals on the sides of vehicles. Spinner hubcaps and hood ornaments are forbidden.

• This year, Japan becomes the world's largest exporter of cameras.

• Radial ply tires, used by Europeans for years, account for a mere 2 percent of the 150 million tires sold in the United States in 1967. But major tire manufacturers are committed to increased production and marketing.

## Other Discoveries, Developments, and Inventions

World's largest hydroelectric dam, the Krasnoyarsk in Siberia, with a capacity of 6,096 megawatts compared to Grand Coulee's 2,161

First commercial tar-sand extraction plant, in Fort McMurray, Alberta, Canada

Washer-wiper in the Dodge station wagon tailgate

Chromosome breaks in the cells of LSD users, inferring inheritable abnormalities

## Obituaries

**Lester Barlow** (December 2, 1886–September 5, 1967). In W.W.I, the Americans used 500,000 of his aerial bombs, but the inventor received no compensation. Congress finally approved a payment of $529,000 in 1940. The military turned down his aerial torpedo.

**J(ames) Frank Duryea** (October 8, 1869–February 15, 1967). Duryea and his brother Charles designed and successfully road tested the first American gas-powered motor vehicle in 1893.

**Casimir Funk** (February 23, 1884–November 19, 1967). The American biochemist's "vitamine" hypothesis, proposed in 1912, gave impetus to research in nutrition.

**J. Robert Oppenheimer** (April 22, 1904–February 18, 1967). The U.S. nuclear physicist directed development and testing of the first atomic bomb at Los Alamos. He headed the AEC General Advisory Committee (1947–1952) but in 1954 was stripped of his security clearance (see 1954 News). Few in the scientific community accepted the verdict as just, and when the Kennedy administration pushed to clear his name, "the father of the atomic bomb" was honored with the Enrico Fermi Award in 1963. Oppenheimer continued his work at Princeton until retirement in 1966.

**Gregory Pincus** (April 9, 1903–August 22, 1967). With biologists M. C. Chang and John Rock, Pincus developed the birth control pill.

**Bela Schick** (July 16, 1877–December 6, 1967). His Schick test for diphtheria, developed in 1913, led to effective inoculation against the disease.

**Cyril Turner** (1898–September 24, 1967). The British aviator pioneered skywriting in 1921.

## THE ARTS

March 7—*You're a Good Man, Charlie Brown*, with Gary Burghoff, Bob Balaban, Bill Hinnant, Reva Rose (1,597 perfs.)

March 13—*You Know I Can't Hear You When the Water's Running*, with George Grizzard, Eileen Heckhart, Martin Balsam (755 perfs.)

October 16—*Rosencrantz and Guildenstern Are Dead*, with Brian Murray, John Wood (420 perfs.)

### Tony Awards

Actor (Dramatic)—Paul Rogers, *The Homecoming*

Actress (Dramatic)—Beryl Reid, *The Killing of Sister George*

Actor (Musical)—Robert Preston, *I Do!, I Do!*

Actress (Musical)—Barbara Harris, *The Apple Tree*

Play—*The Homecoming*

Musical—*Cabaret*

### News

**February 13.** Two American professors announce the accidental discovery of 700 pages of Leonardo da Vinci drawings and writings. The material was supposedly "lost" in 1892 when Spain's National Library changed its indexing system.

**February 20.** Prince Francis Joseph of Liechtenstein sells da Vinci's *Portrait of a Florentine* to the National Gallery in Washington for an astronomical $5–6 million—the highest auction price on record. As well, this year prices soar to new heights for the work of a living artist ($532,000 for Picasso's *Mother and Child*) and for an impressionist ($1.4 million for Monet's *Terrace at St. Adresse*). Rev. Theodore Pitcairn bought the Monet painting in 1926 for $11,000.

**November.** In Canada, the Stratford Festival opens an archive, the first in North America attached to a producing theater.

**More news.** In 1965, a 28-year-old graphic artist abandoned his business to prepare for a revolution in youth. He created a unique blend of natural images and abstract patterns and, with a flair for business, began selling posters, decals, scarves, and other products. This year, most young Americans recognize a Peter Max design.

• The architectural event of the year, Expo 67 presents a mirror facade, a cable-suspended roof, a monorail threaded through a geodesic dome, and other outstanding designs. In Habitat, one- and two-story prefabricated concrete boxes stacked like a Mediterranean hill town boast large terraces for a "sense of house."

### Obituaries

**Geraldine Farrar** (February 28, 1882–March 11, 1967). Thousands of adoring young women gathered outside the Met on the night of her last performance (1906–1922). The popular soprano continued with recitals for another nine years.

**Joseph Kesselring** (June 21, 1902–November 5, 1967). His *Arsenic and Old Lace* (1941) remains one of Broadway's all-time top 15 plays.

## WORDS

Sue Kaufman, *Diary of a Mad Housewife*
Elia Kazan, *The Arrangement*
Jonathan Kozol, *Death at an Early Age*
Ira Levin, *Rosemary's Baby*
William Manchester, *The Death of a President*

Catherine Marshall, *Christy*
Robert K. Massie, *Nicholas and Alexandra*
Rod McKuen, *Listen to the Warm*
Marshall McLuhan, *The Medium Is the Message*
William Paddock and Paul Paddock, *Famine—1975!*
Chaim Potok, *The Chosen*
Jess Stearn, *Edgar Cayce: The Sleeping Prophet*
Irwin Maxwell Stillman, *The Doctor's Quick Weight Loss Diet*
William Styron, *The Confessions of Nat Turner*
Irving Wallace, *The Plot*

## News

**January 16.** For his book *The Death of a President*, William Manchester interviewed Jacqueline Kennedy for 10 hours. But when she saw the manuscript, the president's widow took the author to court for his choice of personal reminiscences and "inaccurate and unfair references to other individuals" (reportedly Lyndon Johnson). Today, after considerable legal wrangling, Manchester agrees to modify or delete certain material and Mrs. Kennedy withdraws her suit.

**February 17.** Today's edition of *The New York Times* names *Mao Tse-tung's Quotations* as the world's top-selling book. Within days, Bantam acquires an English translation and churns out 250,000 paperback copies. Mao receives none of the profits, but Communist China makes no objections.

**February 20.** The New York Public Library reveals that more than 40 percent of its research collection is "in an advanced state of deterioration." Since 1870, the pulp industry has used acid in the production of paper. A residue from the treatment later eats away at the short pulp fibers until book pages disintegrate. (In the northeastern United States, the breakdown is accelerated by air pollution and wide-ranging temperatures.) Ironically, libraries find 15th-century manuscripts, with their rag content, much easier to preserve.

**November 9.** With a $7,500 investment, 21-year-old Jann Wenner publishes the first issue of *Rolling Stone*. (The cover includes a head shot of John Lennon wearing an army helmet in his recent film.) Over the next eight years, the magazine's sales will mushroom from 6,000 copies per month to 400,000.

**November 15.** *The Long Short Cut* by Andrew Garve is the first full-length book to be processed by computer and typeset by electronic photocomposition. The pages, at Videographic Systems, emerge at 10 feet per minute.

**More news.** Following Britain's lead, the United States adopts the standard book number system—10 digits identifying national geographic or language grouping and publisher, title, etc. Two years later, the U.N.-sponsored International Organization for Standardization will accept ISBNs (international standard book numbers).

• Nicolas Herman Charney raises $250,000 and, with a doctoral degree in biopsychology, puts out the first issue of *Psychology Today*.

## Cartoons and Comics

**This year.** Robert Crumb's *Zap* becomes the first underground comic book to achieve widespread popularity.

• In 1967, *Peanuts* titles account for 16 of the 58 mass-market paperbacks to sell over 600,000 copies. By next year, some 900 American and Canadian newspapers will carry the hugely popular comic strip.

• The present catches up to the future as the sci-fi comic strip *Flash Gordon* is canceled. Thirty-eight years ago, Phil Nowlan adapted his novel *Armaggedon 2419* A.D. and Dick Calkins provided the art for the strip's first panels.

## TIME *Man of the Year*

Lyndon Baines Johnson

## New Words and Phrases

body stocking
boutique

buttlegger (one who transports cigarettes for illicit sale)

colorcaster (broadcaster who adds colorful details)

dawk (an individual who takes a straddling position, as in a dispute)

fiche (from microfiche)

game ball

hippie or hippy

hipster (skirt or pants)

holography

kinky (far-out, offbeat)

micro-mini (microskirt)

mixed media (a work of art executed in more than one medium)

nark (a narcotics agent)

nitty-gritty

pantsuit (a woman's long jacket and tailored pants in the same material)

permanent press

public television

scam

skiptowner (someone who habitually leaves the city on weekends)

snowmobiling

swap meet

teeny-bopper

think tank

topless

to total (to completely wreck a car)

New drug terms included acidhead, grass head, pothead, psychedelic, ride, trip, turn on, zonked.

Counterculture figurehead Dr. Timothy Leary advises, "Turn on, tune in, drop out."

## *Obituaries*

**Langston Hughes** (February 1, 1902–May 22, 1967). The writer used every form of literature to portray the life of ordinary black Americans.

**Henry R. Luce** (April 3, 1898–February 28, 1967). In 1923, the young reporter founded, with Briton Hadden, the weekly magazine *Time*. Other periodicals followed: *Fortune* (1930), *Architectural*

*Forum* (1932; discontinued in 1964), *Life* (1936, with his wife Clare Boothe Luce), *House & Home* (1952; sold in 1964), and *Sports Illustrated* (1954). Luce served as editor-in-chief of Time, Inc., until 1964, then became editorial chairman.

**John Masefield** (June 1, 1878–May 12, 1967). With the popularity of his early sea lyrics and narrative verse, Masefield became Britain's 15th poet laureate in 1930.

**Carson McCullers** (February 17, 1917–September 29, 1967). Her works, esteemed by many writers, included the novels *The Heart Is a Lonely Hunter* (1940) and *The Member of the Wedding* (1946).

**Dorothy Parker** (August 22, 1893–June 7, 1967). A humorist ("Men seldom make passes/at girls who wear glasses"), Parker wrote short stories, pieces for *Vanity Fair* and the *New Yorker*, and a long-running syndicated book column.

**Carl Sandburg** (January 6, 1878–July 22, 1967). As a historian, Sandburg won a 1940 Pulitzer for his authoritative six-volume work on Abraham Lincoln. As a poet of the Western Prairies, he won the 1950 Pulitzer for *Complete Poems*. His other publications included a novel, an autobiography, children's books, and two collections of folk songs.

**Siegfried Sassoon** (September 8, 1886–September 1, 1967). The British writer was one of the most notable soldier-poets of W.W.I.

## FASHION

### *Haute Couture*

Last year, Dior's attempt to reintroduce length into high fashion—a calf-length "maxi" coat—failed miserably. A longer skirt this autumn fares no better and designers continue to cater to the youth market—mini skirts, long sleeves, bold-colored stockings. In the spring, Mary Quant pairs matching panties with mini-length cocktail and evening dresses.

To placate those over 25, some couturiers include classically tailored suits, shirts, and shirtwaist dresses. Yves St. Laurent presents a glamorous black velvet pantsuit.

## News

**December 14.** An amendment extends the Flammable Fabrics Act (1953) to all clothing and any house or office furnishings made of fabric or fabric-like products.

*British supermodel Twiggy wears a design from her own 1968 summer collection.*

**More news.** With her cap of blond hair, large deep-set eyes, and impossibly slim figure (92 pounds, over 5′7″), Twiggy rules the modeling world, earning $1,000 an hour. Young North American girls copy Twiggy's look—her clothes, her hair, and her makeup. The craze wanes next year and the real Leslie

Hornby, bored after three years of high-pressure modeling, quits the business at the age of 19.

**More news.** Magazines relate how the mini skirt forces women to find new ways of sitting down, bending over, and climbing stairs.

• In the early 1960s, manufacturers churned out Courrèges pencil-slim pants for everyday wear, but strict dress codes at work and in school kept women in skirts. Now those edicts begin to crumble under the onslaught of teenage baby-boomers and women demanding a fashion choice other than the dominant mini.

## Colors and Materials

The strong colors of the past two years climax with spring psychedelic pinks, greens, lemon, violet, and orange. Fall colors offer a surprisingly suppressed palate of black, winter navy, dark grays, and dark browns.

The arabesque "Liberty" and "Art Nouveau" designs prove popular.

## Clothes

Girls and young women pick the smock dress, clinging shifts, and flared, zip-up coatdresses, then team culottes and short pants with knee socks.

Furriers bridge the gap between orange rabbit and classic mink with coats in black Persian lamb (about $150) or multicolored rabbit skins stitched horizontally.

The popular gangster film *Bonnie and Clyde* sets off a brief craze for Depression-style berets and long skirts.

Designers borrow the draped caftan from Africa.

*Daily News Record* dubs 1967 "The Year of the Turtle." Mods and fashionable gentlemen alike wear the sweater everywhere while young women select the turtleneck as a longer, belted top.

Rock musicians dabbling in Eastern cultures don the Nehru jacket, a style popularized by the late prime minister of India. Collarless, single-breasted with many buttons, the jacket is worn with a pendant or love beads and a turtleneck. (Sammy Davis, Jr., lives in one.) Quickly dated, the look nonetheless marks a breakthrough in men's fashions.

College guys prefer tapered or stovepipe pants.

## Accessories

With wide capes, mufflers, and turtlenecks bunched up under the chin, the tidy peaked cap balances the fashion silhouette.

A knee-high "peel-on" boot sells in leather, imitation leather, and vinyl.

Chunky heels rise slightly and many shoes adopt the English buckle and tongue.

During the summer, girls add chains to their bags, sandals, bikini tops, and sunglasses. For men, the neck chain is a fad this year and next, then will become a standard piece of jewelry into the 1970s.

## Hair and Cosmetics

Renewed neck interest brings shorter curls into vogue by the end of the year.

No longer emphasizing their eyes, women play up or tone down facial features with contour shadowing and highlighting.

New York Yankees catcher Yogi Berra and other baseball players use their wives' hairspray in a TV commercial.

# MUSIC

"I'm a Believer"—Monkees
"To Sir With Love"—Lulu
"The Letter"—Box Tops
"Windy"—Association
"Daydream Believer"—Monkees
"Ode to Billie Joe"—Bobbie Gentry
"Groovin' "—Young Rascals
"Somethin' Stupid"—Frank & Nancy Sinatra
"Light My Fire"—Doors
"Happy Together"—Turtles
"Respect"—Aretha Franklin
"Kind of a Drag"—Buckinghams

"Incense and Peppermints"—Strawberry Alarm Clock
"Love Is Here and Now You're Gone"—Supremes
"The Happening"—Supremes
"Ruby Tuesday"—Rolling Stones
"Penny Lane"—Beatles
"All You Need Is Love"—Beatles
"Snoopy vs. the Red Baron"—Royal Guardsmen
"I Heard It Through the Grapevine"—Gladys Knight and the Pips
"Soul Man"—Sam & Dave
"Dedicated to the One I Love"—Mamas & the Papas
"The Rain, the Park & Other Things"—Cowsills
"Georgy Girl"—Seekers
"Never My Love"—Association
"Reflections"—Diana Ross & the Supremes
"Can't Take My Eyes Off You"—Frankie Valli
"A Little Bit Me, A Little Bit You"—Monkees

## Grammys (1967)

Record of the Year—5th Dimension, "Up-Up and Away"

Song of the Year (songwriter)—Jim Webb, "Up-Up and Away"

Album of the Year—The Beatles, *Sgt. Pepper's Lonely Hearts Club Band*

Best Vocal Performance (Male)—Glen Campbell, "By the Time I Get to Phoenix" (single)

Best Vocal Performance (Female)—Bobbie Gentry, "Ode to Billy Joe" (single)

Best New Artist—Bobbie Gentry

## News

**January 1.** "I'm a Believer," which reached No. 1 yesterday, will top the chart for seven weeks. With 1,051,280 advance sales, the Monkees' song went gold before copies arrived in the stores.

*Statistics:* This year, the record industry pulls in $1 billion. Since the beginning of the rock 'n' roll era, sales have jumped nearly 500 percent.

**January 14.** Some 25,000 hippies jam into Golden Gate Park in San Francisco to celebrate the birth of the Age of Aquarius. The first Be-In, with its poetry, rock music, and drugs, shocks conventional society, but the two police officers on duty make no complaints.

**May 1.** Superstar Elvis Presley marries his longtime girlfriend Priscilla Beaulieu before 14 friends in a private suite at the Aladdin Hotel in Las Vegas. He is 32; she is 21. Next February, Priscilla will give birth to their first and only child, Lisa Marie.

**June 2.** *Sgt. Pepper's Lonely Hearts Club Band* hits the record stores today. The cover—the first to express a concept—captures the essence of flower-power. The Beatles stand in the middle. In front sits an angled flower bed and a drum. Behind them, waxwork figures form the first row of a group of cutout figures. The Beatles wanted to include all their heroes, but EMI, concerned about legal problems, initially insisted on copyright release. (Gandhi was removed for fear of offending the huge market in India and Leo Gorcey, a former Bowery Boy, for insisting on a fee.) But with time running out, production went ahead without permission from many of the famous people.

In a unique moment, radio stations across the country spend much of the day playing different cuts from the Beatles album—"A Little Help From My Friends," "When I'm 64," "Lucy in the Sky With Diamonds."

---

*Statistics:* This year, only 5 British numbers place in the top 19; 3 are by the Beatles.

---

**June 16–18.** In California, some 50,000 pay $3.50–$6.00 to attend the first Monterey Pop Festival. The array of talent includes Big Brother & the Holding Co., the Grateful Dead, Country Joe & the Fish, as well as the Mamas & the Papas, Ravi Shankar, the Who, and the Byrds. Artists receive only their expenses, but Janis Joplin, Jimi Hendrix, and Otis Redding, among others, launch their careers with superlative performances at this first large-scale rock gathering. (Hendrix, for instance,

plays his Stratocaster backward and left-handed, unheard-of moves with a guitar.)

**June 17.** Barbra Streisand's free concert in Central Park, New York, draws a record crowd. But the litter left by the estimated 135,000 people creates a municipal controversy.

**June 27.** British courts convict Mick Jagger, Brian Jones, and Keith Richards of marijuana possession. Following a sympathetic outcry from the public and the London *Times*, their sentences are set aside. Meanwhile, in the United States, critics claim 16 of the top 40 songs make a positive reference to drugs or drug use. Avoiding the Stones' "Let's Spend the Night Together," DJs turn the flip side "Ruby Tuesday" into a No. 1 hit. And Billy Graham condemns Beatle Paul McCartney for his use of LSD confessed to *Life* magazine.

**August 27.** Beatles manager Brian Epstein dies of an apparent overdose of sleeping pills. The shattered Beatles, at a retreat in Wales, turn to their new acquaintance, Maharishi Mahesh Yogi. He shows them how to reduce stress and produce energy through the repetition of a mantra during 20 minutes of daily meditation. (Next year, the Maharishi's followers will introduce the techniques of Transcendental Meditation to crowds of college students in the United States.)

**December 10.** Just six months after his triumph at the Monterey Festival, soul singer Otis Redding dies in a plane crash with four members of his backup group, the Bar-Kays. Survivor Ben Cauley and Jim Alexander, who was on another plane, will form the new Bar-Kays next year.

**More news.** The audio cassette debuted in the marketplace about three years ago under the Norelco brand name. (Philips, in the Netherlands, forfeited a patent to encourage universal adoption.) Capable of playing on mono or stereo equipment and of recording on both sides, the $1.50 blank and $6 prerecorded cassettes compare favorably with the stereo 8 endless-loop cartridge. Still, few believe the 250 prerecorded tapes now available present a threat to the established record industry.

• Pink Floyd and the Who tour North America for the first time.

• With the success of folk-rock, groups experiment with country, jazz, and East Indian fusions. And several groups, such as the Righteous Brothers, Rolling Stones, Procol Harum, and the Young Rascals (who return to their original name, Rascals), make "blue-eyed" soul popular.

But with LPs outselling 45 rpm's and record companies phasing out monaural recordings, the singles-oriented groups start to disappear. Soloists also appear to be an endangered species; only Lulu, Bobbie Gentry, and Aretha Franklin score No. 1 hits this year.

• Dave Brubeck disbands his jazz quartet to concentrate on composing.

• In San Francisco, the Avalon Ballroom and Fillmore Auditorium try to replicate the effects of hallucinogenic drugs with strobe lights and light shows while groups like the Grateful Dead play LSD-inspired rock at almost unbearable decibel levels. The words *acid rock* and *psychedelic* enter the American vocabulary and the new style of poster art used to advertise the dances spreads eastward across the United States. (This summer, with the rumor circulating that dried banana-skin scrapings produce a "high," grocery stores need enormous quantities of the fruit to meet the demand.)

• The new Country Music Hall of Fame and Museum opens in Nashville, Tennessee. The first members include Jimmie Rodgers, Fred Rose, and Hank Williams as well as three living artists, Roy Acuff, Tex Ritter, and Ernest Tubb.

• Beatle George Harrison and Rolling Stone Brian Jones introduce Indian sitar musician Ravi Shankar to the West. When some performers adopt clothing from that area of the world, their increasingly outrageous fashion statements set off a Peacock Revolution.

• Returning too late to his parked car in London, Paul McCartney chats with the meter maid giving him a ticket. The famous pop composer sees her first name is Meta and remarks, "That would make a nice jingle." "Lovely Rita," the Meter Maid is born.

And at his dad's home one weekend this year, McCartney writes "The Fool on the Hill." Never released as a single, FM radio makes the track from the *Magical Mystery Tour* album one of the Beatles' best known.

• The Shing-A-Ling is the only notable new dance in 1967.

*From left to right, Mary Wilson, Cindy Birdson, and Diana Ross of the Supremes.*

• Increasingly unhappy with Diana Ross's starring role, Florence Ballard quits or is fired from the Supremes. Motown replaces her with Cindy Birdsong, a member of the Bluebelles. Ballard will record a couple of unsuccessful singles with ABC Records.

• In their first album, the Doors include a 6-minute, 50-second, number written by lead singer Jim Morrison. While their label cuts the length for a single, most rock stations play the longer version of "Light My Fire." It spends three weeks in the No. 1 position.

## New Recording Artists

Bee Gees (in North America)
Doors

5th Dimension
Grateful Dead
Jimi Hendrix Experience
Engelbert Humperdinck
Joni Mitchell
Van Morrison
Nitty Gritty Dirt Band
Gary Puckett & the Union Gap
Sly & the Family Stone

## Obituaries

**Laverne Andrews** (July 6, 1915–May 8, 1967). The biggest girl group ever, the Andrews Sisters sold some 60 million records with hits like "Rum and Coca Cola" (1944) and "Winter Wonderland" (1947). Laverne was the eldest of the three.

**John Coltrane** (September 23, 1926–July 17, 1967). The gifted musician quit drugs and alcohol in 1957 to devote himself to jazz. Switching from tenor to soprano sax, Coltrane sold unprecedented numbers of jazz albums through the sixties. He died of a liver ailment.

**David Dreyer** (September 22, 1894–March 2, 1967). Collaborating with several lyricists, the composer produced such hits as "Cecilia" (1925) and "Me and My Shadow" (1927).

**Woody (Woodrow Wilson) Guthrie** (July 14, 1912–October 3, 1967). The dean of American folk singers, Guthrie wrote the music and lyrics for more than 1,000 songs, including "So Long (It's Been Good to Know Yuh)" (1939) and "This Land Is Your Land" (1956). (His melodies often came from old folk tunes, but Guthrie opposed copyright laws on all songs, including his own.) Sympathetic to the underdog, the folk hero often entertained union and migrant workers and wrote for Communist newspapers. He was bedridden through the 1960s by the wasting disease Huntington's chorea. Frequent visitors included Bob Dylan.

**Otis Redding** (September 9, 1941–December 10, 1967). His 15 R&B hits, most in the top 10, made him one of the great soul singers of his day. A talented songwriter as well, Redding co-wrote his recent hit "(Sittin' on the) Dock of the Bay."

**Billy Strayhorn** (November 29, 1915–May 31, 1967). Working closely with Duke Ellington—neither could remember who had done what—Strayhorn contributed enormously to the development of jazz composition. One of his early works became the Ellington band theme, "Take the 'A' Train" (1941).

**Paul Whiteman** (March 28, 1890–December 29, 1967). Dubbed the "King of Jazz," the bandleader relied heavily on sidemen to score 28 No. 1 hits between 1920 and 1934, and to remain the second best-selling artist, after Bing Crosby, through to 1954.

# MOVIES

*Barefoot in the Park* (d. Gene Saks; color)—Robert Redford, Jane Fonda, Charles Boyer, Mildred Natwick

*Belle de Jour* (French-Italian, d. Luis Bunuel; color)—Catherine Deneuve, Jean Sorel, Michel Piccoli, Geneviève Page

*Depression-era gangsters Bonnie and Clyde shoot their way out of another law enforcement trap. The smash-hit movie establishes 30-year-old Warren Beatty and 26-year-old Faye Dunaway as major Hollywood stars.*

*Bonnie and Clyde* (d. Arthur Penn; color)—Warren Beatty, Faye Dunaway, Michael J. Pollard, Gene Hackman, Estelle Parsons

*Cool Hand Luke* (d. Stuart Rosenberg; color)—Paul Newman, George Kennedy, J. D. Cannon, Lou Antonio, Strother Martin, Jo Van Fleet

*The Dirty Dozen* (d. Robert Aldrich; color)—Lee Marvin, Ernest Borgnine, Charles Bronson, Jim Brown, John Cassavetes

*El Dorado* (d. Howard Hawks; color)—John Wayne, Robert Mitchum, James Caan

*A Fistful of Dollars* (Italian, d. Sergio Leone; color)—Clint Eastwood, Gian Maria Volonté, Marianne Koch (1964; released in North America this year)

*For a Few Dollars More* (Italian, d. Sergio Leone; color)—Clint Eastwood, Lee Van Cleef (1965; released in North America this year)

*Gnome Mobile* (Disney, d. Robert Stevenson; color)—Walter Brennan, Matthew Garber, Karen Dotrice

*The Graduate* (d. Mike Nichols; color)—Anne Bancroft, Dustin Hoffman, Katharine Ross

*Guess Who's Coming to Dinner* (d. Stanley Kramer; color)—Spencer Tracy, Katharine Hepburn, Sidney Poitier, Katharine Houghton

*A Guide for the Married Man* (d. Gene Kelly; color)—Walter Matthau, Inger Stevens, Robert Morse, Sue Anne Langdon

*How to Succeed in Business Without Really Trying* (d. David Swift; color)—Robert Morse, Michele Lee, Rudy Vallee

*In the Heat of the Night* (d. Norman Jewison; color)—Sidney Poitier, Rod Steiger

*The Jungle Book* (Disney; color; animated)—Voices: Phil Harris (Baloo the Bear); Sebastian Cabot (Bagheera the Panther); Sterling Holloway (Kaa the Snake); George Sanders (Shere Khan the Tiger); Bruce Reitherman (Mowgli)

*The President's Analyst* (d. Theodore J. Flicker; color)—James Coburn, Godfrey Cambridge

*The Taming of the Shrew* (U.S.-Italian, d. Franco Zeffirelli; color)—Elizabeth Taylor, Richard Burton, Cyril Cusack

*To Sir With Love* (British, d. James Clavell; color)—Sidney Poitier, Judy Geeson, Christian Roberts, Suzy Kendall, Lulu

*Wait Until Dark* (d. Terence Young; color)—Audrey Hepburn, Alan Arkin, Richard Crenna, Efrem Zimbalist, Jr.

*Who's Minding the Mint?* (d. Howard Morris; color)—Jim Hutton, Dorothy Provine, Milton Berle, Joey Bishop

## Academy Awards

**April 10.** TV technicians settle their strike just three hours before the broadcast. Bob Hope hosts the show.

Best Picture—*A Man for All Seasons*
Best Actor—Paul Scofield (*A Man for All Seasons*)
Best Actress—Elizabeth Taylor (*Who's Afraid of Virginia Woolf?*)
Best Director—Fred Zinnemann (*A Man for All Seasons*)
Best Supporting Actor—Walter Matthau (*The Fortune Cookie*)
Best Supporting Actress—Sandy Dennis (*Who's Afraid of Virginia Woolf?*)
Best Song—"Born Free" from the film of the same name
Best Foreign Film—*A Man and a Woman* (French)
Honorary Award—Yakima Canutt

Patricia Neal receives a standing ovation in her first Hollywood appearance since a series of near-fatal strokes two years ago.

In London, Elizabeth Taylor is infuriated when Burton loses the best actor award; for two weeks, she refuses to give a press conference.

## News

**February 1.** A huge hit in Western Europe, the 1964 Italian Western *A Fistful of Dollars* opens in New York. Through an interpreter, director Sergio

Leone tells reporters he picked Clint Eastwood after seeing him on the American TV show "Rawhide."

The actor, who describes the Italian version as more violent, regrets not signing for a percentage of the gross. His salary rose from $15,000 for this film, to $50,000, then $250,000 for the last. But the role of the Man With No Name makes Eastwood a star and the phrase "spaghetti western" enters the language of film.

**December 20.** *Universal Newsreel*, the only company still producing clips for American movie houses, releases its last reel. Founded as *Universal Animated Weekly* in 1913, the newsreel at one time showed regularly in some 3,300 theaters.

**More news.** Visitors to Expo 67 in Montreal are thrilled with Czech and Canadian film innovations. The Czechoslovakian pavilion accompanies some film with live action and also presents an intriguing polyvision system of multiple projection on a screen of moving shapes. In *Labyrinth*, the Canadian National Film Board offers an outstanding multiscreen presentation of two films on the exhibition's theme, Man and His World.

In a comparison of opening credits from 1930s and 1961–1966 films, *The New York Times* detects a trend toward longer and more elaborate titles. The average thirties film spent 2 percent of viewing time on the credits (1.8 minutes of 90 minutes) while sixties titles take up 5 percent (6 minutes of 2 hours).

• Chain-gang prison guards brutalize recaptured convict Paul Newman in *Cool Hand Luke* and advertisers claim, "What we've got here is a failure to communicate."

• The motion picture and television industries join with the National Endowment for the Arts to fund the nonprofit American Film Institute. With a mandate to preserve and develop "the art of film in America," the institute will encourage promising filmmakers, offer guidance through teaching activities, and rescue early films through collection and conservation measures.

• From 1957 to 1965, U.S. movie attendance averaged 42.5 million people per week. But a 1966 drop to 38 million is followed this year by a plunge to 17.8 million, a level maintained for years to come.

• After his momentous Oscar win in 1964, Sidney Poitier's next project stalled, until author James Clavell agreed to write the script for nothing and direct for a percentage of the box office. Poitier himself took no salary for the film. Columbia Pictures at first refuses to release the year-old movie, but when the frustrated actor threatens to go to the press, the studio opens the film in two theaters— one in New York and one in Los Angeles. An immediate success, *To Sir With Love* goes on to become one of the biggest hits of the year.

| Top Box Office Stars | Newcomers |
|---|---|
| Julie Andrews | Lynn Redgrave |
| Lee Marvin | Faye Dunaway |
| Paul Newman | James Caan |
| Dean Martin | John Phillip Law |
| Sean Connery | Michele Lee |
| Elizabeth Taylor | Michael Sarrazin |
| Sidney Poitier | Sharon Tate |
| John Wayne | Michael York |
| Richard Burton | Hywel Bennett |
| Steve McQueen | David Hemmings |

*Note:* Sidney Poitier is the first black American actor to appear in the annual poll of top box office stars.

## Top Money-Maker of the Year

*The Dirty Dozen*

## Flop of the Year

*Doctor Doolittle.* Production costs mushroom to $18 million, three times the original budget. (The 1,500 "talking" animals receive an average take-home pay of $750 per week.) Even with additional merchandising and a pressing of 500,000 records, 20th Century-Fox grosses just $9 million on the film over the next two years.

## Quote of the Year

"Mrs. Robinson, do you think we could say a few words to each other first this time?"–A shy Dustin

Hoffman to his older lover, Anne Bancroft, in *The Graduate.* (Screenplay by Calder Willingham and Buck Henry; based on the novel by Charles Webb)

## Obituaries

**Charles Bickford** (January 1, 1889–November 9, 1967). The gravel-voiced veteran actor appeared in dozens of films, most recently *The Big Country* (1958) and *The Unforgiven* (1960). For the past two years, he co-starred on the TV series "The Virginian."

**Smiley Burnette** (1912–February 16, 1967). Credits in 200 Westerns included 81 as Gene Autry's comic sidekick.

**Nelson Eddy** (June 29, 1901–March 6, 1967). The baritone singer enjoyed tremendous popularity with soprano Jeanette MacDonald during the 1930s. When his singing partner left MGM in 1942, Eddy moved on to a radio career and later entertained in nightclubs and at fairs across the United States and Canada.

**Bert Lahr** (August 13, 1895–December 4, 1967). From a varied career on Broadway, radio, screen, and television, the comic is best remembered as the Cowardly Lion in *The Wizard of Oz* (1939).

**Vivien Leigh** (November 5, 1913–July 7, 1967). In 1938, while visiting her lover Laurence Olivier in Hollywood, the petite British actress tested for and won the prized role of Scarlett O'Hara. Virtually unknown to Americans, Leigh won international acclaim and an Oscar for her memorable performance. (Asked once if Scarlett won Rhett back, the actress replied, "I think she probably became a much better woman, but I don't think she ever got Rhett back.")

After she married Olivier in 1940, the actress worked mainly on stage, making just eight more films. But one of those roles was as Blanche du Bois in *A Streetcar Named Desire* (1951); it brought her a second Oscar.

The famous theatrical couple divorced in 1960 under the strain of Leigh's real-life mental illness. She died of recurring tuberculosis.

**Jayne Mansfield** (April 19, 1933–June 29, 1967). The bosomy actress re-created her dizzy-blond Broadway role in *Will Success Spoil Rock Hunter?* (1957), but with only a modicum of talent, she found few parts. Mansfield died in a car accident.

**Paul Muni** (September 22, 1895–August 25, 1967). A series of biographical films, including *I Am a Fugitive from a Chain Gang* (1932), made him a top box office star in the 1930s. He received the best actor Oscar for *The Story of Louis Pasteur* (1936).

**Claude Rains** (November 10, 1889–May 30, 1967). In 1933, the English stage actor used his memorable voice to win his first screen role as *The Invisible Man*. He went on to become one of cinema's great character actors, mainly playing suave types in some 50 films. His best-remembered performances remain the police captain Louis Renault in *Casablanca* (1943) and Ingrid Bergman's fascist husband in *Notorious* (1946).

**Basil Rathbone** (June 13, 1892–July 21, 1967). Trained as a Shakespearean actor, the film veteran created some of the screen's finest villains and played the quintessential detective Sherlock Holmes in 14 films.

**Ann Sheridan** (February 21, 1915–January 21, 1967). The Hollywood star of the 1930s and 1940s made, among others, *I Was a Male War Bride* (1949) with Cary Grant. She was appearing in the TV series "Pistols 'n' Petticoats" at the time of her death.

**Spencer Tracy** (April 5, 1900–June 10, 1967). In 1930, Tracy left the stage for movies. Hardly the conventional leading man, with his stocky build and craggy features, he won over audiences with his humor, sincerity, and superlative acting.

His 73 films brought him an incredible nine Oscar nominations as best actor and two Academy Awards, for *Captains Courageous* (1937) and *Boys' Town* (1938)—the only actor to win two Oscars in a row. Throughout his career, film critics acknowledged Tracy as one of Hollywood's greatest actors.

From 1942 to 1967, he teamed with Katharine Hepburn in nine films, including *Woman of the Year* (1942), *Adam's Rib* (1949), *Pat and Mike* (1952), and his last, *Guess Who's Coming to Dinner* (1967).

Their off-screen love for each other was well known in Hollywood but, because Tracy's Catholic wife was unable to grant him a divorce, the gossip columnists gave the acting couple their privacy.

Desperately ill during the filming of his last picture, Tracy died of a heart ailment just three weeks later.

# TELEVISION AND RADIO

## New Prime-Time TV Programs

"The Carol Burnett Show" (September 11, 1967–  ; Comedy Variety)—Carol Burnett, Harvey Korman, Lyle Waggoner (1967–1974), Vicki Lawrence, Tim Conway (1975)

"The Flying Nun" (September 7, 1967–September 18, 1970; Situation Comedy)—Sally Field, Marge Redmond, Madeleine Sherwood

"Gentle Ben" (September 10, 1967–August 31, 1969; Adventure)—Dennis Weaver, Clint Howard, Beth Brickell, Ben the Bear

"The High Chaparral" (September 10, 1967–September 10, 1971; Western)—Leif Erickson, Cameron Mitchell, Henry Darrow, Linda Cristal, Mark Slade (1967–1970)

"Ironside" (September 14, 1967–January 16, 1975; Police Drama)—Raymond Burr, Don Galloway, Barbara Anderson (1967–1971), Don Mitchell

"The Jerry Lewis Show" (September 12, 1967–May 27, 1969; Comedy Variety)—Jerry Lewis

"The Kraft Music Hall" (September 13, 1967–May 12, 1971; Musical Variety)

"Mannix" (September 16, 1967–August 27, 1975; Detective)—Mike Connors, Gail Fisher (1968–1975), Robert Reed (1969–1975)

"The Mothers-In-Law" (September 10, 1967–September 7, 1969; Situation Comedy)—Eve Arden, Kaye Ballard

"N.Y.P.D." (September 5, 1967–September 16, 1969; Police Drama)—Jack Warden, Robert Hooks, Frank Converse

"The Newlywed Game" (January 7, 1967–August 30, 1971; Quiz/Audience Participation)—Emcee: Bob Eubanks

"The Smothers Brothers Comedy Hour" (February 5, 1967–June 1969; Comedy Variety)—Tom & Dick Smothers, Pat Paulsen. *Note:* The Smothers, canceled by CBS, will reappear on ABC over the summer of 1970. A third show, in 1975, will last five months.

## Emmy Awards 1966–1967 (June 4, 1967)

Drama Series—"Mission: Impossible" (CBS)

Variety Series—"The Andy Williams Show" (NBC)

Comedy Series—"The Monkees" (NBC)

Children's Program—"Jack and the Beanstalk" (NBC)

Best Actor in a Series—Bill Cosby ("I Spy," NBC)

Best Actress in a Series—Barbara Bain ("Mission: Impossible," CBS)

Best Comedian in a Series—Don Adams ("Get Smart," NBC)

Best Comedienne in a Series—Lucille Ball ("The Lucy Show," CBS)

## News

**January 2.** A trained minister who has studied child psychology and music, Fred Rogers attracts immediate attention with his simple style and happy tunes. In the years ahead, Mr. Rogers will win the affection and trust of each new batch of youngsters.

**January 15.** With CBS allegiance to the NFL, and NBC support for the AFL, the networks agree to color simulcast Super Bowl I—a television first. A. C. Nielsen later estimates a combined audience of 73 million football fans. Starting next year, the networks will take turns carrying the championship game.

**March 6.** In one of the season's highlights, Hal Holbrook repeats his interpretation of Samuel Clemens and his works for television in "Mark Twain Tonight." *The New York Times* review comments, "It has been said with some justice that Mark Twain owes as much to Hal Holbrook as Mr. Holbrook owes to Twain."

**March 9.** Today's presidential news conference from the White House is the first ever televised in color.

---

*Statistics:* An estimated 16 percent of American households possess color TV sets.

---

**June 2.** A recent formal complaint to the FCC argued that an occasional program on related health hazards could never overcome the impact of 5–10 minutes of daily cigarette commercials. Today, for the first time, the FCC extends the "fairness doctrine" to paid ads. All radio and television stations must set aside a significant amount of time for programs, news items, and spot announcements on the possible dangers of smoking.

**June 25.** As part of Expo 67, NET joins with networks in other nations to telecast "Our World." The live program shows the making of a movie in Italy, Leonard Bernstein and pianist Van Cliburn rehearsing at Lincoln Center, an opera rehearsal in Germany, and the Beatles in Britain recording "All You Need Is Love." (with friends such as Mick Jagger in the backup chorus). An estimated 200 million people in 26 countries on 5 continents watch the two-hour satellite show.

**August 29.** "The day the running stopped." For the past four seasons, suspected murderer Dr. Richard Kimble has run from Lt. Philip Gerard while looking for the one-armed man who killed his wife. Tonight, in the final episode of "The Fugitive," Kimble corners the elusive murderer on an amusement park tower. Gerard, forced into a choice, shoots the one-armed man. His alibi gone, Kimble appears doomed until a neighbor finally steps forward and admits he saw the killing. The show draws an enormous 50-percent rating.

**September 10.** CBS says that Pete Seeger is entitled to perform for the American public. Blacklisted for 17 years for his leftist connections, the singer

appears tonight on "The Smothers Brothers Comedy Hour." Still, the network avoids controversy by deleting his rendition of "Waist Deep in the Big Muddy," a song about a W.W.II soldier who drowned because his officer ordered him into a river without knowing its depth.

**November 7.** Legislation signed by President Johnson broadens the scope of noncommercial television with the establishment of the nonprofit Corporation for Public Broadcasting (CPB).

Although the FCC allocated stations for noncommercial use in 1952, the cost of building and operating a TV station were enormous. Funding remained scarce and, at the same time, manufacturers resisted the addition of UHF technology to their TV sets. NET finally received funding from Ford in 1962, and congressional legislation provided $32 million in matching grants. Within five years, the number of stations has grown from 59 to 127.

Today's act turns educational TV into public TV. The CPB will administer funds and fend off any attempts at political influence. And, in 1970, the Public Broadcasting System (PBS) will begin to function as a central programmer.

**More news.** Lucille Ball sells Desilu productions to Gulf + Western for a reported $17–$18 million. She remains president.

• Ed Sullivan says that if they want to perform the song, the Rolling Stones must change "Let's Spend the Night Together" to "Let's Spend Some Time Together." Mick Jagger sings, "Let's Spend Mumble Mumble Together."

## TV Commercials

Maytag—Jesse White takes on the loneliest, and eventually the longest, job in town as the Maytag Repairman.

McDonald's—Ronald McDonald made his first public appearance in 1963. Named official company spokesman this year, Ronald appears in his first national television commercial.

Qantas—Sad-eyed, furry, and big-eared, the koala bear says, "I hate Qantas" for bringing so many people to Australia. In the commercial's first eight years, the airline's sales will nearly triple.

# SPORTS

## *Winners*

### *Baseball*

World Series—St. Louis Cardinals (NL), 4 games;
Boston Red Sox (AL), 3 games
Player of the Year—Carl Yastrzemski (Boston Red Sox, AL); Orlando Cepeda (St. Louis Cardinals, NL)
Rookie of the Year—Rod Carew (Minnesota Twins, AL); Tom Seaver (New York Giants, NL)

### *Football*

NFL Championship—Green Bay Packers 21, Dallas Cowboys 17
AFL Championship—Oakland Raiders 40, Houston Oilers 7
Super Bowl II (January 14, 1968)—Green Bay Packers 33, Oakland Raiders 14
College Bowls (January 1, 1967)—
    Rose Bowl, Purdue 14, USC 13
    Cotton Bowl, Georgia 24, Southern Methodist 9
    Orange Bowl, Florida 27, Georgia Tech 12
    Sugar Bowl, Alabama 34, Nebraska 7
Heisman Trophy—Gary Beban (UCLA, QB)
Grey Cup—Hamilton Tiger-Cats 24, Saskatchewan Roughriders 1

### *Basketball*

NBA Championship—Philadelphia 76ers, 4 games; San Francisco Warriors, 2 games
MVP of the Year—Wilt Chamberlain (Philadelphia 76ers)
Rookie of the Year—Dave Bing (Detroit Pistons)
NCAA Championship—UCLA 79, Dayton 64

### *Tennis*

U.S. National—Men, John Newcombe (vs. Clark Edward Graebner); Women, Billie Jean King (vs. Ann Jones)
Wimbledon—Men, John Newcombe (vs. Wilhelm Bungert); Women, Billie Jean King (vs. Ann Jones)

### *Golf*

Masters—Gay Brewer
U.S. Open—Jack Nicklaus
British Open—Roberto de Vicenzo

### *Hockey*

Stanley Cup—Toronto Maple Leafs, 4 games; Montreal Canadiens, 2 games

### *Ice Skating*

World Championship—Men, Emmerich Danzer (Austria); Women, Peggy Fleming (U.S.)
U.S. National—Men, Gary Visconti; Women, Peggy Fleming
Canadian National—Men, Donald Knight; Women, Valerie Jones

### *Kentucky Derby*

Proud Clarion—Robert Ussery, jockey

### *Athlete of the Year*

Male—Carl Yastrzemski (Baseball)
Female—Billie Jean King (Tennis)

### *Last Season*

Ray Berry (Football)
(Edward Charles) Whitey Ford (Baseball)
Lou Groza (Football)
Red Kelly (Hockey)
Jim Ringo (Football)
Jim Taylor (Football)

# News

**February 2.** George Mikan heads the new 11-team American Basketball Association (ABA). Although the rival league introduces several innovations—a 30-second shot clock, a red, white, and blue ball, and 3-point field goals from 25 feet out—attendance remains sparse. And next season the NBA expands to 12 cities with teams in Seattle and San Diego.

**February 15.** In a Hollywood major league softball game, the actors put in a ringer. Legendary softball pitcher Eddie Feigner strikes out Willie Mays, Willie McCovey, Brooks Robinson, Roberto Clemente, and Harmon Killebrew—in succession.

**March 14.** In the first NFL-AFL combined draft, Charles Aaron (Bubba) Smith is the first university player chosen. The 6'8" All-American goes to the Baltimore Colts.

**April.** When K. V. Switzer convinces the Syracuse track coach she can run a marathon, he supports her entry into the annual, all-male Boston event. But when the junior college runner shows up at the starting line, at least one official suffers near apoplexy. Jock Semple tries to physically remove her official numbers until another runner intervenes. Newspapers report that the single female runner "dropped out," but an emotionally exhausted Switzer simply finished after the press had left.

Following a request from Semple and race director Will Cloney, the AAU suspends Switzer from competition for: (1) running in a men's race (the entry form carries no restriction); (2) running more than the 1½ miles permitted for women; (3) concealing her sex by using initials (her signature since the age of 10); and (4) running the marathon without a chaperone. Next year, Boston entry forms read "FOR MEN ONLY."

**April 28.** Although the army promised him a safe, home-based service with "morale-boosting" fights, Muhammed Ali stands by his Muslim religion and refuses to take the induction oath. Boxing authorities promptly strip the 25-year-old of his title. (A unanimous decision over Ernie Terrell on February 6 gave Muhammed Ali undisputed claim to the heavyweight championship.) He is indicted early next month and convicted on June 20. Requesting immediate sentencing, Ali receives a five-year prison term and a $10,000 fine, but is released pending appeal.

**September 10.** With a win at Forest Hills, New York, Billie Jean King completes her sweep of the American and British women's singles, doubles, and mixed doubles tennis championships. The last player to accomplish that feat was Alice Marble in the late 1930s.

**October.** This season the NHL doubles in size. The original six teams—Boston, Chicago, Detroit, Montreal, New York, and Toronto—form an East Division while six new franchises—Los Angeles, Minnesota, Oakland, Philadelphia, Pittsburgh, and St. Louis—make up the West.

**November 8.** Bowling alleys put in the first orders for the Brunswick Automatic Scorer.

**December 31.** Despite a −13-degree-Fahrenheit temperature and a devastating wind chill, some 50,000 fans turn out to cheer the Packers on to their third straight NFL championship. (Officials resort to hand signals when a metal whistle tears away part of a referee's lip.) Dallas unexpectedly leads with just seconds to go, but Green Bay scores a touchdown to win 21–17.

**More news.** In the first year of World Cup skiing, Nancy Greene (Canada) places first in the women's division and Jean-Claude Killy (France) takes the men's. Allotting points by placement, the series of international skiing events will give the winter circuit continuity.

• With first pick in the draft, the New York Mets choose Steve Chilcott. An amazed Kansas City club grabs collegiate star Reggie Jackson. To reduce the young slugger's strikeouts, batting instructor Joe DiMaggio tries to cut down his swing. He fails.

• In the United States, a new 12-team United Soccer Association played this year under the official sanction of the International Federation of Football Associations. At the same time, a 10-team National Professional Soccer League operated as an "outlaw" association. After a costly first season, with generally poor attendance and legal challenges before the court, the rival leagues agree to form a 17-team North American Soccer League (NASL) for 1968.

## Records

**May 28.** Last year, Francis Chichester sailed his 53-foot ketch, *Gipsy Moth IV*, from England to Australia in 107 days. Today, after another 119 days at sea, he completes his circumnavigation of the globe, returning home to a tumultuous welcome and a knighthood from the Queen. The 65-year-old sailed further and faster than any other single person in nautical history.

**September 1.** Cincinnati and San Francisco tie a 49-year record for the most scoreless innings—20. The Giants finally put a run up on the scoreboard in the 21st when Bob Lee walks Dick Groat with the bases loaded. Frank Linzy is the winning pitcher, but Gaylord Perry before him struck out 12 and yielded just 10 hits and 2 walks through 16 innings.

## What They Said

In an interview with *Life* magazine, one of the "Fearsome Foursome"—Rams defensive linesmen David Jones, Roger Brown, Merlin Olsen, and Lamar Lundy—comments on Colts quarterback Johnny Unitas:

> When he throws on third down and long yardage, he just defies you to stop it. When he sees us coming, *he* knows it's going to hurt and *we* know it's going to hurt, but he just stands there and takes it. No other quarterback has such class. (*Life*, October 13)

## Obituaries

**Jimmie Foxx** (October 22, 1907–July 21, 1967). One of baseball's greatest power hitters (one blistering shot broke a seat in the upper deck of Yankee Stadium), Foxx was home-run champion four times and finished his career (1925–1945) with a lifetime 534 home runs. In his best season, Foxx hit 58, but at least 8 shots bounced off screens put up after Babe Ruth's record 60–home run year.

**Barney Ross** (December 22, 1909–January 18, 1967). The first to hold both the world lightweight and junior welterweight championships, the U.S. fighter won the welterweight title in 1934. During his nine-year career (1929–1938), Ross was never knocked out.

# *1968*

---

On March 31, the president unilaterally halts the bombing of North Vietnam and stuns the nation with his decision not to stand for reelection. Lyndon Johnson's world has fallen apart with the capture of the U.S.S. Pueblo, the Tet Offensive, mounting dissent at home, and a surprising 42 percent showing by Eugene McCarthy in the New Hampshire primary.

Within days of the announcements, the nation reels under the assassination of Martin Luther King, Jr. Black Americans take their rage to the streets and Congress responds by quickly passing the Civil Rights Act of 1968. Just two months later, blacks and whites alike mourn the loss of Bobby Kennedy.

From a world view, the title "Year of the Student" suits 1968. West German and French students riot, 350 Mexican students die during a peaceful demonstration, and thousands in Czechoslovakia watch helplessly as Soviet tanks invade their country.

In the United States, 7 million college and university students (compared to 2.7 million in 1955) act and react against the pressures of social change. Three die at South Carolina state; 1,000 are forcibly evicted from barricaded buildings at Columbia, and others battle police in the streets outside the Democratic convention.

At the end of the year, protesters face the uncertainties of an incoming administration—Richard Nixon and Spiro Agnew.

## NEWS

**January 5.** Since January 1, 1961, the U.S. death toll in Vietnam has risen to 15,997. Last year, 9,353 Americans died, more than in all previous years combined. The troop level has reached 486,000.

**January 22.** A B-52 crashes on approach to Thule Air Force Base in Greenland, killing one airman and destroying four nuclear weapons. Amer-ican forces begin a four-month cleanup in the dark of Arctic winter, eventually sending some 237,000 cubic feet of radioactive debris, ice, and snow back to the United States for storage.

The Thule crash is the second U.S. nuclear accident on foreign soil. In one of his last acts in office, Defense Secretary McNamara cancels the dangerous and increasingly expensive nuclear-armed airborne alerts and training flights. ICBMs now form the first line of U.S. defense.

**January 23.** The *U.S.S. Pueblo*, with only two machine guns for defense, offers little resistance when North Korean gunboats move in to capture the ship. Four crewmen, attempting to destroy documents, are fired on, and one sailor is killed and three injured; 10 bags of documents are seized. The next day, North Korea broadcasts a "confession" from Commander Lloyd Bucher.

Washington demands the release of the crew, but the Communists, insisting that the ship trespassed into North Korean waters, threaten to try the 82 men as criminals. Some in Congress argue for retaliation, but the administration, fearing for the prisoners' lives, begins negotiations.

When the Tet Offensive follows just a week later, the Pentagon suspects that North Korea created the incident to draw U.S. forces and attention away from Vietnam.

**January 30.** North Vietnamese troops and the VC use the Tet truce to launch a massive offensive in South Vietnam. The Communists attack 5 of 6 major South Vietnamese cities, 36 of 44 provincial capitals, some 60 district capitals, numerous villages, and 12 American bases. Penetrating to the heart of Saigon, the attackers hold the U.S. embassy for six hours before the Americans and South Vietnamese force them to retreat.

Although the Communists fail to hold any of the targeted areas and suffer heavy casualties (some 32,000 likely decimating the VC) North Vietnamese General Giap scores a psychological victory. The widespread frontal assaults expose Allied vulnerability, the Americans lose 1,110 soldiers, the South Vietnamese some 4,000 soldiers and 7,500 civilians, and 400,000 South Vietnamese are left homeless.

Yet Giap, aware of growing antiwar sentiment in the United States, may have scored his greatest victory with the American people. Positive Pentagon reports had lulled the Johnson administration and the nation into believing victory was within reach. When the huge Allied force takes three weeks to push back the North Vietnamese, public opinion turns against U.S. involvement in the war.

**February 8.** State troopers open fire on young black students from South Carolina State College who were attempting to desegregate a local bowling alley. Three die and 37 are wounded.

In November, a federal grand jury will refuse to indict the nine officers involved. The next month, the Justice Department will charge them with violating the constitutional rights of the students—28 were shot in the side or back. But when an FBI agent testifies in a 1969 trial to hearing small gunfire beforehand and retrieving Molotov cocktails, the federal court will acquit the troopers.

The Justice Department charged the owners of the bowling alley with violating the 1964 Civil Rights Act; they will integrate their business 2½ weeks after the shootings.

**February 8.** Robert Kennedy and other major politicians sharply attack administration policy in Vietnam in the wake of the Tet Offensive. In a Chicago speech, Kennedy denies any prospect of military victory, stating, "We have misconceived the nature of the war . . . we have sought to resolve by military might a conflict whose issue depends upon the will and conviction of the South Vietnamese people. It is like sending a lion to halt an epidemic of jungle rot."

**February 29.** In a final report, the President's National Advisory Commission on Civil Disorders rejects the conspiracy theory for the 1967 race riots, pointing out that the violence often erupted following an incident of police brutality. Condemning white racism, the Kerner Commission warns that with massive black unemployment and underemployment, unfulfilled promises from early civil rights victories, and bureaucratic resistance to civil rights laws, this country is moving toward two "separate and unequal" societies.

Recommendations include major programs for housing, education, welfare, and job creation. Although critics balk at the enormous projected costs, most recognize the need to move beyond civil rights laws to break down the economic barriers confronting black Americans everywhere.

**March 12.** Peace candidate Eugene McCarthy captures an amazing 42 percent in the New Hampshire Democratic primary, to Lyndon Johnson's 48 percent. Two days ago, Americans were thoroughly disillusioned by the *New York Times* disclosure that

General Westmoreland had requested yet another 206,000 men for Vietnam. On the 22nd, the president recalls Westmoreland from Vietnam, signaling a decision against major escalation.

**March 13.** An army plane sprays 320 gallons of VX nerve gas at Dugway Proving Ground in western Utah, and a 35-mph wind carries the droplets 27 miles away toward herds of grazing sheep; within days, 6,000 animals die.

A state investigation determines the gas killed the sheep, but the army refuses to accept responsibility, even while paying out $376,000 in claims. More than a year will pass before the army finally admits that the gas killed the animals.

**March 14.** Despite death threats, the Brazilian Ministry of the Interior issues a report detailing a government campaign of genocide against the nation's Indian peoples. To clear land for development, members of the former Indian Protection Services have machine gunned, dynamited, poisoned, and deliberately infected with smallpox whole tribes of Amazonian natives under their care. The government introduces reforms, but the dispossession of Indian lands continues. Tragically, other South American nations will carry out similar campaigns.

**March 16.** Robert Kennedy announces his candidacy for the Democratic presidential nomination. Concerned that the American people might view his candidacy as a personal struggle with the president, Kennedy hesitated until the New Hampshire primary convinced him the party would never renominate Johnson.

Kennedy opens his campaign two days later with a stinging rebuke of the administration's Vietnam policy. He admits his own share of responsibility for the early military buildup, but adds that "past error is no excuse for its own perpetuation." If elected, he will actively seek a peace settlement.

**March 18.** HEW extends desegregation guidelines to Northern schools. Maintaining that every school system has an "affirmative duty" to eliminate racial segregation and discrimination, the departmental policy statement calls for an end to inferior services and facilities for black children. In 1973,

the Supreme Court will apply legal sanctions against the North.

**March 31.** In a televised broadcast, President Johnson tells the nation he is unilaterally halting U.S. air and naval bombardment of North Vietnam (except in the DMZ, where enemy buildup threatens Allied forward positions). "So tonight, in the hope that this action will lead to early talks, I am taking the first step to de-escalate the conflict."

Johnson ends his speech with the stunning announcement that he will not seek or accept another term in office. His decision may have been influenced by today's Gallup poll, showing public approval at a record low of 36 percent.

Policymakers are confounded when North Vietnam responds to Johnson's overture on April 3, declaring its readiness to meet with U.S. representatives.

**April 4.** In Memphis to support a controversial strike by sanitation workers, Dr. Martin Luther King, Jr., steps out onto the balcony of his motel at 6:00 P.M. and is struck down by an assassin's bullet. King is pronounced dead one hour later at the hospital.

President Johnson appeals to the nation "to reject the blind violence that has struck Dr. King, who lived by nonviolence," but blacks across America lash out in their rage and grief. Race riots erupt in Washington, New York, Chicago, Detroit, and 100 other communities. Local authorities call for help, and the largest military civil-emergency force in recent times—20,000 regular federal troops and 34,000 National Guardsmen—move into the troubled cities over the coming days. Altogether, 46 people die, some 2,600 are injured, 21,000 are arrested, and damage mounts to millions of dollars.

During the disturbances, Dr. King's family and friends bury him in Atlanta. At Mrs. Coretta King's request, the funeral service on the 9th includes a tape recording of her husband's last sermon:

If any of you are around when I have to meet my day, I don't want a long funeral. . . . I'd like somebody to mention that day that Martin Luther King, Jr., tried to give his life serving others. I'd like for somebody to say that day that Martin Luther King, Jr., tried to love somebody. . . . I want you to be able to say that day I did try to feed the hungry . . . that I did try in my life to clothe the naked . . . that I did try in my life to visit those who were in prison . . . that I tried to love and serve humanity. Yes, if you want to, say that I was a drum major. Say that I was a drum major for peace . . . for righteousness.

Two Georgia mules pull his coffin as 100,000 mourners march behind.

**April 5.** Rev. Ralph Abernathy succeeds Martin Luther King, Jr., at the SCLC. In tribute to the late Dr. King, he and Coretta King lead an estimated 42,000 people—30 percent whites—in the Memphis march for striking sanitation workers.

---

*Statistics:* Between June 1963 and May 1968, 15,000 people were arrested during 369 major civil rights demonstrations.

---

**April 6.** In Canada, the Liberals elect Pierre Elliott Trudeau, age 48, to succeed Lester B. Pearson as party leader. Trudeau assumes office as prime minister of the Liberal minority government on the 20th, dissolves Parliament on the 23rd, and, two days later, calls an election.

**April 8.** The U.S. Supreme Court (6–2) removes the death penalty provision from the Federal Kidnapping Law, passed in 1932 following the kidnapping and murder of Charles Lindbergh's infant son.

The justices argue that the Lindbergh law placed "an impermissible burden on the exercise of a constitutional right"—trial by jury. Rather than risk a death penalty from a jury, many defendants chose trial by judge and a maximum possible life sentence.

Today's decision also strikes down the death penalty under other laws, including the national security sections of the Atomic Energy Act.

**April 10.** In a dramatic response to the assassination of Martin Luther King, Jr., and the widespread civil disturbances that followed, the House approves a civil rights bill passed by the Senate on March 11.

The next day, President Johnson signs the Civil Rights Act of 1968, which prohibits racial discrimination in the sale or rental of about 80 percent of the nation's housing (through three stages of reduction); protects blacks or civil rights workers engaged in activities related to housing, schooling, voting, etc. from intimidation or injury through stiff federal penalties (a 10-year prison term and a $10,000 fine or, if the person dies, the death penalty); and includes anti-riot provisions.

The president describes the legislation as "a victory for every American" after "a long, tortuous and difficult road."

**April 23.** At Columbia University, some 800–1,000 students barricade themselves into five campus buildings to protest Columbia's continuing ties to the Pentagon-funded Institute for Defense Analysis and the university's plans to construct a gymnasium in an area needed for low-cost housing.

The students, including members of SDS, hold the buildings until 1,000 police officers violently eject them on the 30th, injuring at least 150 and arresting over 700. In response, the entire student body calls for a strike and, with considerable faculty support, effectively shuts down the campus until June.

In September, the Cox Commission criticizes the rebellion but condemns the police for using excessive force. While the students see little evidence of promised reform by the end of the year, their revolt triggers demonstrations around the country, as other students demand a say in the administration of their universities.

---

*Statistics:* The National Student Association reports that between January 1 and June 15 of this year, 221 major demonstrations at 101 colleges and universities involved some 39,000 students, or 2.6 percent of the enrollment.

---

**May 3.** At the Sorbonne, Paris gendarmes brutally break up a student demonstration against the antiquated state-run university system (enrollment, for instance, has tripled with no expansion of facilities). Next day, the angry students throw up barricades around the university and call for a general strike.

By May 26, an estimated 10 million striking workers paralyze the nation. Although their demands are distinct from those of the students, the May Revolt drags on. Two students die in street battles with the police, and thousands are injured.

De Gaulle calls a general election for late June, promising reform and law and order in the streets. When the strikers offer no alternative other than anarchy, voters give the Gaullists massive support at the polls. By early July, the country more or less returns to normal.

**May 3.** The South African Assembly votes to abolish the four white deputies who represent the country's 1.8 million racially mixed coloreds. To further strengthen the political separation of blacks and whites, the government bans any member of one racial group from participating in the political activities of the other. The Progressives fall in line (their only member in Parliament, Helen Suzman, strongly opposes apartheid), but the Liberals disband rather than exclude blacks.

**May 11.** Led by Reverend Ralph Abernathy, poor blacks, whites, Mexicans, and Indians arrive in Washington to illustrate their plight with the construction of a shantytown near the Lincoln Memorial. But the "Poor People's Campaign" is plagued with problems from the outset: lack of funds, black militants' attempts to dominate, and a sea of mud from unusually rainy weather. At any one time, only 2,600 protesters live in Resurrection City.

On June 19, a turnout of 50,000 for the climax Solidarity Day march falls far short of the 200,000-plus at the 1963 Washington demonstration. The government responds with $25 million for several programs and a job creation plan, but the SCLC had hoped for much more. On the 24th, police arrest the last 124 residents.

**May 13.** The United States and North Vietnam begin peace talks in Paris, with Ambassador-at-large W. Averell Harriman, age 76, leading the American delegation, and Minister of State Xuan

Thuy, age 55, leading the North Vietnamese. The United States repeatedly asks what step North Vietnam would take if Washington halted the bombing, but the negotiations will achieve little by the fall.

**May 17.** Nine antiwar protesters enter Selective Service headquarters in Catonsville, Maryland, seize almost 400 draft records, then burn them outside the building. Three of the protesters are Rev. Philip Berrigan and Thomas P. Lewis, who are already awaiting sentencing, and Rev. Daniel Berrigan.

Found guilty of destroying government property and interfering with draft procedures, the group is sentenced to 2–3½ years in prison, but Father Daniel Berrigan disappears. Before his recapture in August, 1970, the priest will give secret press interviews to publicize the peace movement. For many Americans, the Berrigans become the symbols of civil disobedience against U.S. involvement in Vietnam.

**May 21.** The nuclear-powered submarine *U.S.S. Scorpion* disappears southwest of the Azores with 99 men on board. The navy will announce the discovery of the vessel on October 31. The hull had split, likely after the sub exceeded the maximum safety depth of 1,200 feet. Safety improvements, recommended after the 1963 loss of the *U.S.S. Thresher*, had been only partially completed on the *Scorpion*.

**May 29.** The Consumer Credit Protection, or "Truth in Lending," Act requires banks and other lending institutions to inform consumers of the true interest rate and other costs on a loan agreement, restricts garnishment of wages for debt payment, and makes loan sharking a federal crime (effective July 1, 1969).

**May 30.** The Supreme Court extends the 14th Amendment guarantee of trial by jury to all but petty offenses.

**June 1.** Helen Keller, American author and leader in the education of the handicapped, dies a few weeks short of her 88th birthday. Deaf and blind from the age of 18 months, she began to learn sign language at age 7 from instructor Annie Sullivan. Keller then learned to read Braille and how to use her vocal chords. With Annie's help she graduated with honors from Radcliffe in 1904.

Helen Keller worked hard to increase public awareness of the handicapped and to support herself through writing and lectures. Her friend and helpmate Annie died in 1936. When her second companion Polly Thompson, with her since 1914, died in 1960, Keller remained alone.

Her accomplishments will continue to inspire people around the world.

**June 5.** Triumphant with his win in the California presidential primary, Robert Kennedy thanks the party faithful at the Los Angeles Ambassador Hotel and just after midnight, leaves the victory celebration. As the senator moves through the hotel kitchen, Jordanian-American Sirhan Sirhan empties his pistol into the crowd, wounding Kennedy and injuring five others. The 42-year-old junior senator from New York dies on the 6th, at 1:44 A.M.

As Bobby Kennedy clung to life, President Johnson exceeded his authority to assign Secret Service details to all major candidates. Within hours, Congress covers the security costs.

The president declares June 9 a day of mourning and, in the wake of a second assassination in just two months, appoints a commission to investigate physical violence in the United States.

> *Statistics:* In January, the Secret Service disclosed that the number of people arrested for threatening the president's life had jumped from a one-year total of 80 against John F. Kennedy to 425 against Lyndon Johnson in 1967.

**June 8.** The body of Robert Kennedy lay in state in St. Patrick's Cathedral until early this morning, as an estimated 150,000 mourners filed past. Tonight, over 2,000 attend a requiem mass. His younger brother Ted Kennedy delivers the eulogy and, at one point, in a voice choked with emotion, quotes his brother's favorite passage, from George Bernard Shaw: "Some men see things as they are and say why. I dream of things that never were and say why not." Thousands watch from railway stations and along the tracks as a 21-car funeral train travels southward to Washington for the burial.

Kennedy had entered the campaign late, but with wins in Indiana, Nebraska, and California, the Democratic nomination appeared within his grasp. He was regarded by many as the only candidate who could end the war in Vietnam and resolve the racial violence tearing at the nation, for both whites and blacks had responded to his crusader's zeal.

As with the assassination of his brother, John F. Kennedy, people consider the possibility of a conspiracy. Sirhan's gun held only 8 bullets, yet doctors reportedly found fragments from 10 bullets in the victims. Kennedy's wounds—behind the right ear, under the right arm, and in the neck—indicate the gunman stood in a different location. Yet the district attorney's office, in the early 1970s, will refuse to reopen the case.

**June 8.** Following the most intensive manhunt in police history, Scotland Yard detectives arrest James Earl Ray, the alleged assassin of Martin Luther King, Jr., at London's Heathrow Airport. The 40-year-old Ray escaped last year from Missouri State Penitentiary, where he was serving 20 years for car theft and armed robbery. The British return Ray to the United States on July 19; he is arraigned on July 27 and pleads not guilty.

**June 10.** General William Westmoreland hands over his Vietnam command to General Creighton Abrams. Westmoreland comments to reporters that "not expanding the war" made a military victory, "in a classic sense," impossible.

**June 18.** Just 10 weeks after the Civil Rights Act of 1968 barred most housing discrimination, the Supreme Court (7–2) cites an 1866 law in banning *all* racial discrimination in the sale and rental of public and private property. Legal experts believe the judgment gives Congress the authority to abolish any economic discrimination based on race.

**June 25.** Canadian voters give the Liberal party 155 seats for the first majority government since 1962. The Conservatives take 72, the NDP 22, the Credistes 14, and an Independent 1.

During the campaign, Pierre Elliott Trudeau captured the public's fancy, drawing unusually large crowds. Women of all ages responded to his debonair appearance, and he acquired the nickname PET. Last night, Trudeau also won the respect of many. At the annual St. Jean Baptiste Day parade in Montreal, an estimated 1,000 separatists rioted over his presence. Some broke to within 100 feet of the stand, throwing rocks and bottles, but Trudeau refused to leave.

**June 25.** Roy Innis, age 34, succeeds 46-year-old Floyd McKissick as national director of CORE. When the organization reconvenes in September, members adopt a new constitution advocating black nationalism, with separation as its goal, and barring white membership. This change of focus alienates many middle-of-the-road blacks and whites, who withdraw their financial support; CORE never recovers its former influence.

**June 28.** President Johnson obtains a 10-percent surcharge on income tax, but only by tying the request to a huge $6-billion cut in government spending. Congress had urged fiscal restraint to bring down interest rates, but the cut, along with other measures, only proves temporarily successful. By the end of the year, the prime lending rate reaches a record high of 6.75 percent.

**July 1.** A decade of diplomatic efforts, beginning with a basic proposal by the Irish in 1958, culminates in the Nuclear Nonproliferation Treaty. Nuclear-weapon powers (except for France and China) pledge not to transfer weapons to nonnuclear states; nonnuclear-weapon countries, with guaranteed American, Soviet, and British aid against nuclear aggression, pledge not to seek or acquire the technology or materials for weapons production. Nuclear energy for peaceful purposes will remain available.

President Nixon and President Nikolai Podgorny will affix their signatures on November 24, 1969. Another 41 nations will deposit their instruments of ratification, and the treaty will become effective March 5, 1970.

**July 1.** The Canadian Medicare system goes into effect. Only British Columbia and Saskatchewan have entered the joint federal-provincial program, but experts predict the other provinces will join by 1970. Taxes, direct premiums, and payroll deduc-

tions cover the costs, estimated at $82 million for the first year of service.

**July 5.** In response to flag burning at antiwar demonstrations, President Johnson signs a bill making it a federal offense to "cast contempt" on the U.S. flag "by publicly mutilating, defacing, or trampling upon it." The act imposes a $1,000 fine and/or one year in jail.

**July 29.** Pope Paul issues an encyclical upholding the Catholic Church's prohibition against artificial contraception. A majority papal commission report had recommended birth-control methods be left to the consciences of married couples, and many Catholic clergy openly disagree with the pope's decision. A U.S. Gallup poll shows that 54 percent of Catholics oppose the encyclical, while just 28 percent approve.

**August 8.** At the Republican Convention in Miami Beach, Richard M. Nixon wins the presidential nomination on the first ballot, easily defeating the more liberal Nelson A. Rockefeller and more conservative Ronald Reagan. Delegates appear dissatisfied with Nixon's choice of little-known Maryland Governor Spiro Agnew as his running mate.

Former president Eisenhower, who has surprisingly endorsed Nixon, suffers his sixth heart attack just hours after addressing the convention via television hookup from his hospital suite.

**August 9.** Enforcing the Civil Rights Act prohibition against discrimination by race, sex, or religion, the EEOC forbids the dismissal of airline stewardesses on the basis of age or marital status.

**August 20–21.** Under the cover of darkness, a plane lands at Prague international airport. Commandos pour out and, seizing control of the tower, guide in Soviet military aircraft loaded with tanks and troops. At the same time, 200,000 soldiers from five Warsaw Pact nations cross Czechoslovakia's borders. Realizing resistance would be bloody and futile, Prague instructs its army to stand by.

In January, student and worker demonstrations against the Stalinist regime brought down party leader Antonin Novotny. His replacement, liberal

Communist Alexander Dubček, subsequently introduced a series of reforms including an element of political democracy. Moscow had attempted to convince Dubček to halt this liberalization, but with popular support and encouragement from Tito of Yugoslavia and Ceaușescu of Romania, he had refused.

To justify the invasion, Moscow orders KGB agents in the Czech security service to seize communications and issue an official invitation to help fight "the spread of counterrevolution." But Dubček, learning of the invasion within minutes, makes a quick radio broadcast branding the Soviet troop movement illegal.

The United Nations condemns the action, but the USSR vetoes the resolution in the Security Council. Czechoslovakians watch helplessly as their leaders are forced to ban new political organizations, censor the press, limit public gatherings, and divide the state into separate Czech and Slovak "socialist republics." Initially imprisoned, Dubček assumes the position of Czech first secretary, but Slovak First Secretary Gustav Husak will replace him next year. Like 500,000 of his countrymen, Dubček will be ousted from the party and fired from his job.

**August 28.** The Democratic party meets in Chicago, in the stifling heat of a city under siege. Bus, taxi, and telephone strikes have produced near paralysis, while some 10,000–20,000 antiwar protesters are holding a "Festival of Life" in Grant and Lincoln parks. Refusing them permission to parade or sleep in the parks, Mayor Daley has brought in 5,000 National Guardsmen and 7,000 federal troops to beef up city police.

Inside the convention hall tonight, Vice-President Hubert Humphrey wins the presidential nomination on the first ballot; Senator Edmund Muskie of Maine is chosen as the vice-presidential nominee. When youthful followers of McCarthy and McGovern fail to modify the pro-Vietnam party platform, militant protest leaders—including Youth International Party, or Yippie, leaders Abbie Hoffman and Jerry Rubin, Black Panther leader Bobby Seale, and Thomas Hayden of SDS—gather their people outside convention headquarters.

As an estimated 2,000–5,000 protesters scream, "The whole world is watching," police and troops charge, using their night sticks on everyone within reach, including onlookers, passers-by, and 63 newsmen. Some 1,000 people sustain injuries and 101 need hospitalization; 192 policemen receive injuries, and 49 are hospitalized.

Television cameras film the 18-minute bloody confrontation, and the nation is shocked—but apparently not by police violence. A September Gallup poll reveals that 56 percent of respondents approve of the way authorities handled the demonstrators and only 31 percent disapprove. Even though an investigation will later describe the brutal police response as "unrestrained and indiscriminate due, at least in part, to the belief that the mayor would condone their actions," the distaste and fear of the American people make Hubert Humphrey and the Democrats the true victims of the bloody Chicago battle.

**September.** Baby-boomers flood U.S. schools, colleges, and universities. An estimated 61.4 million students and teachers—30 percent of the nation's population—attend elementary and secondary schools. Twenty-five universities register 30,000 students each, up from just 4 institutions in 1958, and 950 colleges register a total of 1.6 million students, an astounding 50 percent increase since 1963.

**September 8.** Black Panther leader Huey Newton is convicted of involuntary manslaughter and sentenced to 2 to 15 years in prison.

On October 28, 1967, police stopped Newton and a friend for a traffic check. Within minutes, one policeman was dead by his own gun, another officer was wounded, and Newton was shot in the stomach. With the notoriety of the incident, Panther membership in the San Francisco area has skyrocketed, and chapters have been established in San Diego, Los Angeles, New York, and Detroit.

In 1970, the California Court of Appeals will reverse his conviction, and Newton will be freed on bail. Two subsequent trials will end in hung juries.

**September 26.** In a belated rationalization of the invasion of Czechoslovakia, the Soviet newspaper *Pravda* claims the world socialist community has a right to intervene if socialism is under attack in a fraternal country. This ideological argument becomes known as the Brezhnev Doctrine. More likely, the Soviets will limit independent political action in satellite countries because of worsening relations with the Chinese.

**September 27.** Marcello Caetano succeeds Premier António de Oliveira Salazar, the iron-fisted ruler of Portugal since 1932. The 79-year-old dictator suffered a head injury and went into a coma 10 days ago. Perhaps believing himself indestructible, Salazar had failed to groom an heir. Initially Caetano appears more liberal, but he will later establish rigid controls.

**October.** When George Wallace polled 21-percent voter approval late last month, the Democrats and Republicans began to worry about a possible independent presidential ticket. But Wallace, an advocate of stronger police action against militants, makes a strategic error with his choice of General Curtis LeMay as a running mate. The former air force chief of staff, with a complete lack of political savvy, states in a national news conference, "[We] would use anything that we could dream up, including nuclear weapons, if it was necessary" to win the Vietnam war. The American Independence party immediately begins to lose support.

For Hubert Humphrey, a lack of funds, deep party divisions over Vietnam, and the stigma of convention violence have made the Democratic campaign an uphill battle. But, as his natural enthusiasm resurfaces, the vice-president overcomes an association with an unpopular president, stresses his commitment to working men and women, and points proudly to his record on civil rights. With a last-minute endorsement from Eugene McCarthy and the October 31 halt in bombing, Humphrey wins over some Wallace supporters and many of the undecided.

The Republican ticket has remained popular throughout the campaign despite outrageous comments by Spiro Agnew: "To some extent, if you've seen one city slum you've seen them all." Nixon has played it safe, focusing on law and order and a plan to end the Vietnam War, (which must remain se-

cret to avoid compromising peace negotiations). But as Humphrey builds momentum, the Gallup polls show Nixon's margin slowly shrinking.

**October 2.** Since Mexican students, unlike Americans and Europeans, participate in university administration, their demonstrations focus on social reform. Tonight, as the students gather in the Plaza of Three Cultures in Mexico City, police officers open fire. Blaming outside agitators, the government admits to killing fewer than 50, but newspapers report 350 deaths; many believe the toll is much higher. In 1970, 68 of the protesters will receive prison terms of 3 to 17 years.

**October 5.** In Northern Ireland, local electoral laws restrict the vote to property owners and their wives. Since the Protestant minority owns most of the land, the working-class Catholic majority lacks representation.

Catholics recently launched a civil rights campaign for one man–one vote and better housing (Protestants favor Protestants in allocating local-authority housing). During the summer, a young Catholic politician sought media attention with a squatter protest, then suggested the first Catholic march.

Today, when Londonderry authorities deny permission for a second march, 300 angry Catholic demonstrators fight with police, throw gasoline bombs, and loot stores. On the 6th, 800 Catholic youths clash with the police. Local government attempts to appease the Catholics meet with Protestant hostility—and the Irish Troubles begin.

**October 31.** In a radio and television address, President Johnson announces the complete cessation of all air, naval, and artillery bombardment in Vietnam north of the 20th parallel, at 8:00 A.M. tomorrow, to break a stalemate in negotiations. The United States has also agreed to admit the NLF to the peace talks in exchange for North Vietnam's agreement to include South Vietnam.

The Saigon government refuses to attend the talks, scheduled to begin on November 6, unless Hanoi agrees to negotiate without the NLF. U.S. Secretary of Defense Clifford, who replaced McNamara in March, warns the South Vietnamese on November 12 that if they persist in boycotting the expanded talks, Washington may proceed without them. President Thieu finally yields on the 26th.

> *Statistics:* In more than 100,000 missions over North Vietnam since February 1965, in which over 500,000 tons of bombs were dropped, the United States has lost 900 planes (most of the 1,500 plus American airmen killed, captured, or missing were casualties of those flights). Meanwhile, Communist infiltration into the South has increased from an estimated 12,000 men in 1964 to 200,000 in 1968.

**November 5.** Richard Nixon wins the presidential election by just 500,000 votes—2.3 million fewer votes than he drew in his loss to John F. Kennedy in 1960. The Republican ticket captures 43.4 percent of the popular vote, versus 43 percent for the Democrats, but 301 electoral votes to Humphrey's 191. George Wallace takes just 13.5 percent of the vote, carrying five Southern states and 46 electoral votes. Analysts believe Wallace took enough votes away from Humphrey in key industrial states, such as Ohio and Illinois, to swing those states over to Nixon.

With the Democrats retaining control of Congress (58–42 in the Senate and 243–192 in the House) Nixon becomes the first new president since Zachary Taylor in 1844 to be elected without winning a majority in at least one house of the new Congress.

In his victory speech, Nixon pledges, "This will be an open administration, open to new ideas, open to men and women of both parties, open to the critics as well as those who support us."

**November 20.** A series of explosions rip through a coal mine in James Fork, West Virginia, trapping 78 men. Over the next five days, 13 major and 12 minor explosions hamper rescuers. When they finally drill through to the cavern, air samples show a lethal level of carbon monoxide and an explosive concentration of methane gas. The mine is sealed on November 29.

*President Johnson meets with president-elect Richard Nixon at the White House.*

> *Statistics:* Federal inspection records for 1967 show that 82 percent of 5,400 U.S. underground mines were in violation of major provisions of the Safety Act. In the act's 16 years, some 5,500 miners have died.

**December 12.** The number of U.S. combat fatalities in Vietnam reaches 30,057—9,557 died in the first six months of the year, more than in all of 1967. As troop levels increased to 540,000 during the year, the conflict became the longest war in U.S. history (as dated from the first death of a U.S. soldier in 1961, rather than those killed in 1959).

**December 20.** In a letter to San Francisco newspapers, a person identifying himself as "Zodiac" takes credit for four lovers' lane murders. Witnesses describe the killer as a young male Caucasian who wears glasses. He kills two more people before the letters end on October 11, 1969. Another letter in 1974, written by the same hand, will claim a total of 37 murders, but authorities never hear from Zodiac again. The police will theorize that he died or was imprisoned or institutionalized.

**December 22.** North Korea releases the crew of the *Pueblo* after the U.S. signs a formal apology for violating Korean waters. But in a strange twist, U.S. Major General Gilbert Woodward reads a disavowal of the admission of guilt before signing the statement. Apparently, as U.S.-North Korean negotiations stalled, the wife of an American diplomat in Korea suggested the simultaneous American admission and denial of guilt to satisfy both nations.

In a navy court of inquiry next year, Commander Lloyd Bucher will testify that the *Pueblo* lacked both defensive weapons and equipment to destroy documents. Although he and his men describe the torture that forced their confessions, the court will recommend that Bucher and another officer be court-martialed. U.S. Navy Secretary John Chafee will announce in May that no disciplinary action will be taken.

Under the agreement, the Communists keep the *Pueblo*; it becomes the largest ship in the North Korean Navy.

**More news.** The Japanese government acknowledges the responsibility of Chiso Chemical Plant for the mercury pollution in Minamata Bay. Scientists traced the cause of Minamata disease to a methyl mercury compound in the bay, likely formed when mercury wastes from the plant combined with natural methyl in the water. Fish and shellfish ate the compound; seabirds, cats, and humans ate the fish. Symptoms included slurred speech, loss of muscular control, convulsions, blindness, and brain damage. Some people eventually died.

But Chiso refused inspections and the government would take no action. The villagers, overcoming their natural reticence, protested, gained wide media exposure and popular support, and through

the courts finally forced the company to shut down in 1966.

The number of cases will grow to 121 by 1971, including 47 dead, but some studies will count over 1,000 victims and 150 deaths. A long legal battle will ensue.

• Geologists discover the largest oil field in North America, on Alaska's North Slope—an estimated reserve of 5–10 billion barrels.

A consortium forms to build an 800-mile pipeline from Prudhoe Bay to the ice-free port of Valdez, but conservationists challenge a route that crosses an earthquake zone and the route of migrating caribou. Their lawsuits will successfully block legislation until 1973.

• This year, Congress acts on a 1967 Supreme Court ruling and eliminates the requirement of the Internal Security Act that members of the Communist party register with the government. The nearly defunct Subversive Activities Control Board may now maintain only a public list of organizations and individuals found to be Communist.

## Obituaries

**Helen Keller** (June 27, 1880–June 1, 1968). *See* News.

**Robert Francis Kennedy** (November 20, 1925–June 6, 1968). After his election in 1960, John F. Kennedy appointed his younger brother and campaign manager as attorney general and his leading counselor on foreign and domestic affairs. Bobby, as he was known to everyone, had served as counsel to the Democratic minority (1954–1957) and as chief counsel to the Senate committee on labor racketeering (1957–1960). Heading the Justice Department, he acted on his deep antipathy to labor corruption and worked with his older brother to establish strong federal support for civil rights.

After the president's assassination, Bobby resigned from the Cabinet to run for his first elected office, senator from New York. In the Senate, he championed social programs, and reversing his earlier stand on Vietnam, opposed the war. The charismatic young Kennedy appealed to both whites and blacks, making him a strong candidate for the party's presidential nomination. He had just won the crucial California primary when he was struck down by Sirhan Sirhan. Kennedy is survived by his pregnant wife, Ethel, and 10 children.

**Husband Edward Kimmel** (February 26, 1882–May 14, 1968). Commander of the U.S. Pacific Fleet when Japan bombed Pearl Harbor, the rear admiral resigned in 1942 under charges of dereliction of duty. After the war, a joint congressional committee charged Kimmel with "errors in judgment" only.

**Martin Luther King, Jr.** (January 15, 1929–April 4, 1968). Ordained a minister in 1947 at his father's Ebenezer Baptist Church in Atlanta, King graduated from college in 1948, then continued his education at Crozer Theological Seminary and Boston University. In 1954, the young minister accepted a pastorate in Montgomery, Alabama. At the end of the next year, he led the city's black community into a successful year-long boycott of segregated buses.

Emerging from that action as the nation's most prominent civil rights leader, King worked with others to found the SCLC in 1957. Fighting entrenched segregation throughout the South, their nonviolent protests and demonstrations expanded, along with other groups, to draw some 250,000 to the 1963 March on Washington. King's speech that day enthralled blacks and whites alike.

In 1964, Congress passed the Civil Rights Act and King received the Nobel peace prize for his leadership. Over the following four years, he focused on de facto segregation in the North, then American involvement in South Vietnam and the plight of the poor.

Recently, impatient young followers had turned from King's philosophy of nonviolence toward militancy, but the black community as a whole continued to support him. Coretta King moves to carry on her husband's work following his assassination in Memphis.

**Trygve Lie** (July 16, 1896–December 30, 1968). Elected February 1, 1946, the first Secretary General of the United Nations faced such problems as the Cold War, the first Arab-Israeli war, and Communist aggression in Korea. Although the Soviets refused to deal with him over the Korean military action—finally forcing him to resign in 1953—Secretary-General Lie was generally held in high regard.

**Arthur Mitchell** (December 22, 1883–May 9, 1968). The first Negro Democrat to serve in the House (1935–1943) was elected by the First District in Chicago.

# BEGINNINGS AND ENDINGS

## News

**January 16.** Prime Minister Harold Wilson announces the closure of Persian Gulf bases by 1971, Britain's last military presence east of the Suez. Three days later, a Colonial Office merger with the Commonwealth Relations Office (Commonwealth Office) officially brings the British Empire to an end.

**February 18.** Britain moves one hour ahead, from Greenwich Mean Time to European time.

**February 27.** For the first time, a Gallup poll reports crime as the No. 1 public concern in America. (One in five respondents say they called the police within the past 12 months.)

**April.** American oil tycoon Robert McCulloch pays $2.46 million for the slowly sinking London Bridge, then spends an additional $5.6 million to dismantle and transport the 10,000 tons of granite slabs to the United States. Rebuilt in Arizona, the 137-year-old span will open as a tourist attraction in 1971.

**April 10.** To help pay for Expo 67, Montreal Mayor Jean Drapeau sets up Canada's first lottery. When the courts find the action illegal, Quebec establishes a provincial lottery corporation (December 23, 1969).

**April 23.** The Methodist and Evangelical United Brethren churches merge as the United Methodist Church, the second largest Protestant group in the United States.

**June 27.** Ruling on the manufacture of a car phone, the FCC authorizes the connection of "foreign attachments" to a telephone system. Analysts expect the ruling will spawn a multimillion-dollar business, with the greatest activity in modems.

**June 28.** Effective January 1, 1971, the Uniform Monday Holiday Law creates five permanent three-day weekends by shifting Washington's Birthday, Memorial Day, Independence Day, and Veterans Day to Monday and by adding a new Monday holiday in October, Columbus Day.

**July 15.** Pan Am and Aeroflot inaugurate the first direct service between the United States and the Soviet Union (New York to Moscow). An economy ticket on the once-a-week flight costs $429.

**July 23.** In the first airplane hijacking for political purposes, Palestinian guerrillas force an Israeli airliner to fly to Algiers. A month later, after Tel Aviv agrees to release 16 Arab infiltrators, Algeria frees the last 5 passengers and 7 crew members, against the wishes of the terrorists.

**September 10.** Berkeley, California, becomes the first large American city with a substantial black population (approximately 41 percent) to achieve a totally desegregated school system.

**September 27.** With 80 percent of first-class mail sent to businesses, the Canadian postal service finds no further need for Saturday mail delivery (effective February 1, 1969).

**October 14.** In Quebec City, French-Canadian separatists found the Parti Québécois and choose René Lévesque as their leader.

**October 20.** Jacqueline Kennedy marries Greek tycoon Aristotle Onassis on the island of Skorpios. Americans react with anger, dismay, and indignation—almost every emotion but happiness for the bride.

Jackie is 39 years old; Ari is 62. She is Catholic; he is divorced. Rumors fly that Jackie signed a complicated financial arrangement before the ceremony.

**October 21.** The new presidential limousine arrives at the White House. Bombproof and bulletproof, the $500,000 Lincoln Continental—the most expensive car ever built—boasts an address system, a removable roof section, and a fold-down bumper for Secret Service agents.

**November 5.** New York elects the first black woman to serve in Congress, 43-year-old Shirley Chisholm. Once in the House, she will sponsor a minimum-wage bill for domestic workers, an occupation that mostly employs black women.

**November 14.** Yale University announces the admission of female undergraduate students in 1969. Other American universities, including Princeton and Sarah Lawrence, follow suit.

**December 22.** In New York City, Julie Nixon, daughter of President Richard Nixon, marries Dwight David Eisenhower II, grandson of former president Eisenhower.

**December 30.** For the first year on record, no executions took place in the United States.

**More news.** After coining the word *Yippie*, Abbie Hoffman, Jerry Rubin, Ed Sanders, and Paul Krassner form the Youth International Party (YIP) with "no leaders, no members, and no organization." Nevertheless, the quartet provides a rallying point for youthful reactionaries, particularly at the 1968 Democratic Convention.

• Authorities plan a universal 911 emergency telephone number to summon police, fire engines, and ambulances. Several cities have already set up a centralized bureau to handle such calls.

## Records

**February 1.** In the biggest consolidation in U.S. corporate history ($4 billion in assets), Pennsylvania Railroad and New York Central merge as Pennsylvania New York Central Transportation Co., or Penn Central.

**May 6.** With his decision not to seek reelection, Senator Carl Hayden (D., Ariz.) enters the record books as the longest-serving member of Congress—56 years, 10 months, 17 days. He will pass away in 1972 at the age of 94.

## New Products and Businesses

McDonald's adds the Big Mac to its menu.

## SCIENCE AND TECHNOLOGY

### News

**January 2.** South Africa's Dr. Christiaan Barnard,

in his second operation, replaces the diseased heart of a 58-year-old retired dentist with that of a 24-year-old. Philip Blaiberg lives until August 1969, making him the first successful heart transplant.

**January 9.** The last of the series, *Surveyor 7* finishes transmitting some 21,000 narrow- and wide-angle shots of the moon. Together, the five U.S. probes (*Surveyors 2* and *3* crashed) relayed 86,000 pictures, analyzed and tested the strength of the lunar surface, demonstrated remote engine start-up, and tested laser-beam communications.

**March 5.** The Whooping Crane Conservation Association announces that the endangered species has reached a modern peak of 68 birds, up from 15 in 1941–1942.

**April 20.** A USAF weather craft verifies the arrival of a ground expedition at the North Pole—the first since Robert E. Peary reached the pole in 1909. The group of four Canadians and Americans traveled 44 days on Ski-Doo snowmobiles.

**May 2.** Dr. Denton Cooley performs the first successful heart transplant in the United States. Over the coming months, the growing demand for donor organs forces the medical community to confront the issue, What is Death? In an attempt to resolve the controversy, the AMA rules in December that "brain death" signals an irreversible loss of life. A 20-percent survival rate, through to the mid-1970s, will raise questions about heart-transplant costs.

**July.** A medical journal describes the "Chinese Restaurant Syndrome"—chest pain, burning, facial pressure—brought on by the monosodium glutamate in the food. In 1969, some 20,000 tons of MSG are produced in the United States.

**September 14–21.** The USSR reactivates its lunar program with an unmanned Zond flight to the moon and back—a space first. Next month, *Soyuz 3* blasts off into Earth orbit and, in November, another Zond will reach the moon. As the U.S. suspects, the Soviets have stepped up their secret race to send a manned spacecraft to the moon. But continued problems with the booster rocket will delay then eventually cancel the Soviet program.

**September 22.** Four years ago, an enormous international effort swung into action to save Abu Simbel. Built by Ramesses II, over 3,000 years ago, the Egyptian limestone temples and giant figures were threatened by the rising waters of the Aswan Dam. Modern engineers cut the forms into huge blocks and rebuilt them higher up—to an accuracy of $1/10$ inch—inside a concrete dome. The ancient structure officially reopens today.

**September 23.** In the United States, Dr. Albert E. J. Engel reports finding the oldest remnants of life on Earth. The sea fossils, found in the South African Transvaal are 3.5 billion years old.

**October 11.** Acting on board recommendations following the tragic Apollo deaths in 1967, NASA strengthened project management, redesigned and fireproofed the spacecraft, switched to a 60–40 atmosphere mix of oxygen and nitrogen, and initiated safety features and procedures, including non-flammable glass fabric for space suits.

Today, the new capsule, *Apollo 7*, lifts off with Walter Schirra, Donn Eisele, and Ronnie Cunningham. An 11-day mission qualifies the craft for a flight to the moon.

**December 7.** Taking 11 telescopes into a nearly circular orbit, the American *OAO-2* offers astronomers their first long-term opportunity to study the universe, free of the Earth's atmosphere.

---

*Statistics:* The USSR has orbited 314 identified satellites, the United States 544, France 5, Britain 3, Canada and Italy 2 each, Australia 1, and the European Space Research Organization 3. At the end of 1968, a total of 357 remain in orbit.

---

**December 13.** The FDA warns against "unrestricted use" of artificial sweeteners, particularly cyclamates, pending further research. About 70 percent of sugar substitutes are found in soft drinks—1 part saccharine to 10 parts cyclamates.

**December 21.** A 36-story Saturn 5 rocket blasts off with *Apollo 8* (shock waves are recorded 1,000 miles away). Frank Borman, James Lovell, Jr., and William Anders—the first to leave Earth's gravitational field—reach lunar orbit 69 hours later.

During a Christmas Eve telecast, the astronauts give a moving reading from the Book of Genesis. (It is later disclosed that miniature bottles of brandy were smuggled on board.)

After 10 orbits, the Apollo capsule heads back to Earth for a flawless splashdown on the 27th. The astronauts later receive a ticker-tape parade in New York City.

**More news.** With the closure of the Suez Canal during the 1967 war, the average 138,000-ton tanker appeared woefully inadequate to supply the oil needs of the West. This year, Japan launches first one, then another 312,000-ton supertanker.

• Funded by the National Science Foundation, the 400-foot *Glomar Challenger* heads out on a Deep Sea Drilling Project. Previously, scientists gathered information on the ocean from relatively shallow samples. In the years ahead, the *Glomar* will collect invaluable data with thousands of sediment cores. One of the first, from the Gulf of Mexico, shows traces of oil below 11,000 feet.

• Men have an X and Y chromosome, but about 1 in 1,500 carries an extra Y. This year, researchers discover that a disproportionate number of males in prisons and asylums for the criminally insane possess the double-Y combination—as many as 1 in 21.

• Using radio-radar telescopes, astronomers at Cornell University map one-third of the planet Venus. Preliminary information suggests even more extreme air pressure and temperatures than Soviet data had suggested.

• In his book *The Population Bomb*, Paul Ehrlich writes, "The birth rate must be brought into line with the death rate or mankind will breed itself into oblivion." Following publication, the 36-year-old biologist appears on the Johnny Carson show and draws a record 5,000 letters in response.

## Other Discoveries, Developments, and Inventions

Eleven high-powered radar units for lightning detection at U.S. Weather Bureau

World's largest hovercraft, the SRN-4, in regular service between Britain and France—capacity of 30 cars, 254 passengers

World's first hand-held anti-aircraft missile, the Redeye, for the U.S. Army and Marine Corps

Antitheft lock in steering column, nonreflective windshields, ventless front windows in sporty cars

A 24-square-foot supertub from Britain, the Sagittarius Double Bath, for $750

Live-virus mumps vaccine, developed by Drs. Maurice Hilleman and Eugene Buynak

## Obituaries

**Hattie Alexander** (April 5, 1901–June 24, 1968). The U.S. medical researcher was world renowned for her discovery of a meningitis antibody in 1939. (Within two years, the fatality rate fell from 100 percent to about 20 percent.) As well, Alexander was one of the first to realize that resistance to serum resulted from genetic mutation.

**Hugo Benioff** (September 14, 1899–February 29, 1968). His seismology instruments were used worldwide to study and record earthquakes.

**Chester F. Carlson** (February 8, 1906–September 19, 1968). His invention of "dry writing" made Haloid—later renamed Xerox—a multimillion-dollar corporation. (*See also* Science, 1948.)

**Sanford L. Cluett** (June 6, 1874–May 18, 1968). In 1928, his preshrinking process was described as the greatest textile development since dyeing. (Lawyers left the "d" out of sanforizing.)

**Clessie L. Cummins** (1889–August 18, 1968). To prove the value of his diesel engine, Cummins entered the 1931 Indy and drove the 500 miles without a pit stop.

**Howard Florey** (September 24, 1898–February 21, 1968). In 1943, Florey and Ernst Chain made a clinical breakthrough with the antibiotic penicillin. A year later, enough of the drug existed to treat all of the severely wounded in the Allied invasion of Normandy. Florey received the Nobel prize with Chain and Fleming in 1945.

**Yuri Gagarin** (March 9, 1934–March 27, 1968). Second only to Lenin for the number of statues dedicated in his honor, the first man in space receives a full state funeral. Blocked from further space travel by inner ear damage, the former cosmonaut died during a test flight of an experimental aircraft.

**Otto Hahn** (March 8, 1879–July 28, 1968). Hahn and his team split a uranium atom in 1938. Their findings were published in a German scientific journal on January 6, 1939, and Hahn received the Nobel prize in 1944. (See Meitner below.)

**Donald A. Hall** (December 7, 1898–May 2, 1968). He designed and constructed the *Spirit of St. Louis*, the plane Charles Lindbergh flew across the Atlantic in 1927.

**Carl G. Hartman** (circa 1880–March 1, 1968). His study of the endocrine system and the reproductive process led to the development of the birth control pill.

**John McLean** (October 24, 1909–May 2, 1968). The U.S. ophthalmologist developed the closing procedure for cataract surgery. As well, he was credited with setting up the first corneal eye bank.

**Lise Meitner** (November 7, 1878–October 27, 1968). After escaping from Nazi-occupied Austria in 1938, the physicist published the findings from her work. But, unlike Otto Hahn, she realized the significance of nuclear fission and refused to join the Manhattan Project. In 1944, Meitner was denied the Nobel prize awarded to her research partner.

**Rudolf Schindler** (May 10, 1888–September 9, 1968). In 1932, the American stomach specialist invented the flexible gastroscope to view the interior of the stomach.

**William Scholl** (circa 1883–March 30, 1968). The "Doctors" more than 1,000 foot aids began with an arch support in 1904.

# THE ARTS

January 18—*Your Own Thing*, with Marian Mercer, Tom Ligon, Danny Apolinar (937 perfs.)

January 22—*Jacques Brel Is Alive and Well and Living in Paris*, with Elly Stone, Mort Shuman, Shawn Elliott, Alice Whitfield (1,847 perfs.)

February 14—*Plaza Suite*, with Maureen Stapleton, George C. Scott (1,097 perfs.)

April 10—*George M!*, with Joel Grey (427 perfs.)

April 14—*The Boys in the Band*, with Cliff Gorman, Leonard Frey, Kenneth Nelson, Robert La Tourneaux (1,000 perfs.)

April 29—*Hair* (from Off Broadway; 1,742 perfs.)

October 3—*The Great White Hope*, with James Earl Jones, Jane Alexander (556 perfs.)

December 1—*Promises, Promises*, with Jerry Orbach, Jill O'Hara (1,281 perfs.)

## Tony Awards

Actor (Dramatic)—Martin Balsam, *You Know I Can't Hear You When the Water's Running*

Actress (Dramatic)—Zoe Caldwell, *The Prime of Miss Jean Brodie*

Actor (Musical)—Robert Goulet, *The Happy Time*

Actress (Musical)—Patricia Routledge, *Darling of the Day*; Leslie Uggams, *Hallelujah, Baby!*

Play—*Rosencrantz and Guildenstern Are Dead*

Musical—*Hallelujah, Baby!*

## News

**January 21.** After $2.7 million in restorations, Ford's Theater reopens in Washington, D.C., as part of a national shrine to Abraham Lincoln. At the end of the month, the theater presents its first live production since the president's assassination in 1865.

**February 15.** With his appointment as director of the New Jersey Symphony, 36-year-old Henry Lewis becomes the first black American to head a symphony orchestra.

**April 29.** Billed as "an American tribal love-rock musical," *Hair*'s nudity, four-letter words, and hippie attitudes break every theater taboo. But with lineups at the box office, the show encourages a more permissive attitude on the American stage.

June 17. Actors' Equity shuts down 19 Broadway shows and 9 touring companies over the issue of non-American performers. Following all-night negotiations on the 19th, the association accepts a guarantee that no American will be replaced by a non-American and future appearances will be subject to arbitration.

September 26. In London, Parliament abolishes the power of censorship held by the Lord Chamberlain for 231 years. Since his office had banned the depiction of Jesus Christ until just 2 years ago, the producers of *Hair* have withheld a London premiere rather than edit the show.

October 8. Placido Domingo debuts at the Met in *Adriana Lecouvreur*. Scheduled to make his first appearance on the 12th, the 27-year-old Spanish tenor steps in for Franco Corelli.

November 23. Another great European tenor, 33-year-old Luciano Pavarotti makes his Metropolitan Opera debut in La Bohème.

## Obituaries

**Tallulah Bankhead** (January 31, 1903–December 12, 1968). The stage actress, who made "Daaahling!" a phrase, was known for her barbed wit and flamboyant personality.

**Howard Lindsay** (March 29, 1889–February 11, 1968). The colorful actor-playwright wrote *Life with Father* (1939), with Russel Crouse, *State of the Union* (1946, Pulitzer winner), and *Call Me Madam* (1950).

**Ruth St. Denis** (January 20, 1879–July 21, 1968). St. Denis pioneered modern dance with her husband Ted Shawn at the Denishawn Dance School (1915–1931); Martha Graham was their most famous student.

# WORDS

Carlos Castaneda, *The Teachings of Don Juan*
Arthur C. Clarke, *2001: A Space Odyssey*
Eldridge Cleaver, *Soul on Ice*
Arthur Hailey, *Airport*
Helen MacInnes, *The Salzburg Connection*

Peter Maas, *The Valachi Papers*
Desmond Morris, *The Naked Ape*
Aleksandr Solzhenitsyn, *Cancer Ward*
John Updike, *Couples*
Gore Vidal, *Myra Breckenridge*
Tom Wolfe, *The Electric Kool-Aid Acid Test*
Paul Zindel, *The Pigman*

## News

**March 4.** According to *Newsweek*, the American underground press has capitalized on society's new permissiveness and a general lack of youth coverage to attract some 2 million readers. (*Los Angeles Free Press* leads the pack with a circulation of 68,000.)

**July 2.** *Ramparts* magazine publishes Che Guevara's diary. (The Bolivian minister of the interior smuggled copies into Chile.)

**October.** *Ladies Home Journal* is the first of the top three women's publications to use a cover photo of a black woman, professional model Naomi Sims.

**More news.** With the burgeoning hippie culture, a store in Menlo Park, California, issues a 128-page catalog of natural foods, simple furniture, looms, and other similar items. All 2,000 copies sell by the end of the year. In 1970, a third-edition printing of the *Whole Earth Catalog* will sell 160,000 copies.

In the last years of the decade, college survey courses abandon the subject overview and textbook anthology for an examination of specific issues and problems, using 6–10 paperbacks.

## Cartoons and Comics

**This year.** *Head Comix*, an outsized Viking paperback of underground comics, showcases "Fritz the Cat." A con artist and sex maniac, the incorrigible feline is an instant hit. Success leads to an animated film, but cartoonist Robert Crumb, unhappy with negotiations, will kill off Fritz in 1972 in one last story.

## TIME Man of the Year

William Anders, Frank Borman, James Lovell, Jr.

## New Words and Phrases

acid rock

airbus

be-in (an informal public gathering, as in a park, to express love and happiness)

cassette

chicerino (one who is chic)

closet queen

crash pad (an apartment where hippies may obtain free lodging)

dime bag ($10 worth of marijuana)

to grok (to enjoy what is happening, especially among fellow hippies)

grubs (blue-jean cut-off shorts)

honkie or honky (a disparaging black term for a white person)

mace

middlescent (middle-age individual; one who has just turned 40)

mind-expanding

minibus

roll bar (in an automobile)

sanitize

speed (a synthetic drug)

spoiler (on an automobile)

wayoutitude (the state of being unconventional or extreme)

wok

In his June 23 syndicated column, Joseph Kraft describes Middle America as "the great mass of some 40 million persons who have recently moved from just above the poverty line to just below the level of affluence." Middle America emphasizes "ease of life" over economic security.

The TV program "Rowan & Martin's Laugh-in" introduces several humorous phrases, including "Sock it to me!" and "Verrrry interesting . . . but stupid!"

While war protestors shout, "Hey, hey, LBJ, how many kids did you kill today?" American soldiers in Vietnam write on their helmets, "We are the unwilling, led by the unqualified, doing the unnecessary for the ungrateful."

In August, at Miami Beach, political prankster and Rockefeller consultant Richard Tuck gives new meaning to a Nixon slogan. He hires several very pregnant women to parade up and down the street outside the Republican convention hall with signs reading, "Nixon's the One." (During the year, an administration critic greets verbose Vice-President Agnew with the sign, "Apologize now, Spiro. It will save time later.")

## Obituaries

**Rudolph Dirks** (February 26, 1877–April 20, 1968). In *Katzenjammer Kids* (1897; later *Hans and Fritz* then *The Captain and the Kids*), the cartoonist pioneered the consecutive-panel story line with ballooned dialogue. His son John plans to continue the strip.

**Edna Ferber** (August 15, 1887–April 16, 1968). The American novelist, who generally wrote about strong pioneer women, scored more than 10 best-sellers, including *So Big* (1924, Pulitzer), *Show Boat* (1926), *Cimarron* (1929), and *Giant* (1952).

**Harold Gray** (January 20, 1894–May 9, 1968). The cartoonist drew *Little Orphan Annie* from August 5, 1924, until his death. Attempts to continue the strip fail, and the syndicate reprints Gray's work in some 400 American newspapers.

**Upton Sinclair** (September 20, 1878–November 25, 1968). Sinclair's revelations about filthy Chicago meat plants, in his early novel *The Jungle* (1906), resulted in the country's first pure-food legislation. He continued to battle for social reform with another 88 books and thousands of lectures and speeches.

**John Steinbeck** (February 27, 1902–December 20, 1968). Powerful portrayals of the Depression years—*Tortilla Flat* (1935), *Of Mice and Men* (1937), *The Grapes of Wrath* (1939; Pulitzer)—formed the basis of Steinbeck's literary reputation and brought him the 1962 Nobel prize in literature. Following the war, only *The Winter of Our Discontent* (1961) equaled the rich structure and vivid language of his earlier works.

# FASHION

## Haute Couture

French and American designers bring the silhouette closer to the body and offer the trouser suit as a wardrobe alternative.

## News

**This year.** Calvin Klein, age 26, and his boyhood friend Barry Schwartz, create classic coats and dresses for the launching of Calvin Klein Ltd. Within 10 years, their business will expand into a fashion empire.

• The decade's extensive growth in polyesters finally pushes U.S. annual consumption of manmade fibers past natural fibers for the first time.

• To compete with mass-produced garments, Dior, Courrèges, Givenchy, and others have produced ready-to-wear lines and opened boutiques. Spanish-born couturier Cristóbal Balenciaga refuses to join the trend and retires.

• With no training in design, 27-year-old Ralph Lauren forms a tie company and calls it Polo. He quickly adds more menswear and, in 1971, a women's line.

• In 1853, after six years in the United States, Bavarian-born Levi Strauss made his way to San Francisco. There, using heavyweight brown canvas, he made his first pair of jeans. This year, Levi Strauss & Co. establishes a women's division.

• Japan unexpectedly changes from a large exporter of silk to an importer.

Members of the women's liberation movement hold braless days in several American cities this year, and one group protests the Miss America pageant. The women merely throw their bras, girdles, curlers, and copies of *Cosmopolitan* magazine into a "Freedom Trash Can," but stories circulate that the protesters "burned their bras." Hereafter the public will mistakenly identify the movement with that more militant action.

## Colors and Materials

Dominant colors include gray, pink, navy blue, yellow, and bright green.

Soft challis weaves in vivid prints prove popular, but leather fashions are the rage.

Colors and plaids further brighten men's fashions.

## Clothes

Reacting against the materialism of their parents, and spurred on by the antiwar movement and hippie culture, young Americans nostalgically turn to the clothing of an earlier era. They search attics and flea markets for antique or second-hand granny shawls, fur coats, and other original items, intrigued by the notion that their clothes will be different. Then, as the drug culture spreads, many pick up styles reflective of the Eastern philosophy—sandals, East Indian overblouses, loose tunics, embroidered caftans, shirts with stand-up collars, wool-lined Afghan coats with sewn-on mirrors.

Both sexes wear their hair long with a scarf or headband across the forehead and some guys sport a shaggy beard and mustache. Most don quantities of jewelry—rings, jangling bracelets, rows of Asian beads. Clothing manufacturers take from 12 to 18 months to catch up to this second fashion revolution.

Lingerie companies turn out softer bras for a more natural bust line.

Jumpers and shirtdresses regain favor. In the fall, college women adopt the hip-length version of the popular vest.

The curvaceous, rigid swimsuits of the early 1960s give way to styles with little or no padding. Over the next few years, the crocheted bikini will emerge as the top-seller.

A romantic London look tops velvet pantsuits with frilly shirts, capes, gold chains, even cavalier hats.

Men and women take to flared bell-bottoms as

the leg length drops past the ankle for the first time in years. With men's drain-pipe trousers widening out, jackets display broader lapels and more deeply flapped pockets.

Sociologists suggest the adoption of military apparel by American youths—combat boots, camouflage caps—is intended to ridicule U.S. involvement in Vietnam. Perhaps so, but by the 1970s, the craze will evolve into a commercial fashion.

The unisex look matches female suits and outfits to identical male clothing, right down to the tie. (One Carnaby clothing store displays a placard, "Please excuse us if we call you Madam, Sir.") The mood becomes less slavish into the next decade, yet the concept of sexless clothing, such as jeans, will hold.

### Accessories

Although boots remain popular, with the latest a two-toned knee or hip length, shoes make a comeback. Thickly heeled styles usually place decoration well up the foot.

The big safari handbag is this year's hit.

Wide belts flatter the new close-to-the-body silhouette, but many opt for chains at the waist.

Designers finish garments with large buttons and boldly colored, chunky zippers.

The hippie influence brings in bulky silver jewelry—long beads, enamel pendants, large rings (sometimes worn on every finger), and bracelets with semiprecious stones.

British ties in flamboyant colors and prints reach 5 to 6 inches in width.

### Hair and Cosmetics

Eyeliner disappears and false eyelashes dominate as plucked brows follow the 1930s arc.

Although long hair continues as the standard—loose or braided—the "in" cut for women is soft, short waves. Black Americans begin to wear their hair longer in an Afro.

Estée Lauder puts out the first allergy-tested, unscented line of cosmetics—Clinique.

With many workplaces barring the mod look, 1 million American men buy fake mustaches and beards for the weekend. By the end of the decade, facial hair will become more acceptable, and the fad will die out.

Mary Quant cosmetics promotes a more natural look.

## MUSIC

"Hey Jude"—Beatles
"I Heard It Through the Grapevine"—Marvin Gaye
"Love Is Blue" (Instr.)—Paul Mauriat
"People Got to Be Free"—Rascals
"Honey"—Bobby Goldsboro
"(Sittin' On) The Dock of the Bay"—Otis Redding
"This Guy's in Love with You"—Herb Alpert
"Mrs. Robinson"—Simon & Garfunkel
"Hello Goodbye"—Beatles
"Love Child"—Diana Ross & the Supremes
"Judy in Disguise (With Glasses)"—John Fred & His Playboy Band
"Tighten Up"—Archie Bell & the Drells
"Hello, I Love You"—Doors
"Grazing in the Grass"—Hugh Masekela
"Harper Valley PTA"—Jeannie C. Riley
"Green Tambourine"—Lemon Pipers
"Young Girl"—Gary Puckett & the Union Gap
"Those Were the Days"—Mary Hopkin
"Born to Be Wild"—Steppenwolf
"For Once in My Life"—Stevie Wonder
"Cry Like a Baby"—Box Tops
"Lady Willpower"—Gary Puckett & the Union Gap
"Classical Gas" (Instr.)—Mason Williams
"Chain of Fools"—Aretha Franklin
"The Good, the Bad & the Ugly" (Instr.)—Hugo Montenegro, His Orchestra & Chorus
"Little Green Apples"—O. C. Smith
"Fire"—Arthur Brown (The Crazy World of)
"MacArthur Park"—Richard Harris

## Grammys (1968)

Record of the Year—Simon & Garfunkel, "Mrs. Robinson"

Song of the Year (songwriter)—Bobby Russell, "Little Green Apples"

Album of the Year—Glen Campbell, *By the Time I Get to Phoenix*

Best Vocal Performance (Male)—José Feliciano, "Light My Fire" (single)

Best Vocal Performance (Female)—Dionne Warwick, "Do You Know the Way to San Jose?" (single)

Best New Artist—José Feliciano

## News

**July.** The Yardbirds disband in England, and Jimmy Page assembles the New Yardbirds with three relative unknowns. The group soon changes its name to Led Zeppelin, and as folk-rock gives way to hard rock, it becomes an important influence.

Another new group of British rockers takes on the name of the 1963 hit, "Deep Purple."

**August 4–5.** Some 100,000 attend this year's Newport Pop Festival at Costa Mesa, California. Performers include the Byrds, Steppenwolf, the Jefferson Airplane, the Paul Butterfield Blues Band, and Quicksilver Messenger Service.

The Miami Pop Festival, December 28–30, charges $7. The nearly 100,000 in attendance see Chuck Berry, Fleetwood Mac, Joni Mitchell, Marvin Gaye, Iron Butterfly, the Grateful Dead, Ian and Sylvia, and others.

**August 24.** "Harper Valley PTA" enters the hot 100 chart at No. 81, then in the space of a week it skyrockets to No. 7—the greatest seven-day jump in the history of pop music. The hit proves a mixed blessing for Jeannie C. Riley when fans find it difficult to separate the "sock-it-to-it" personality of the character from the singer; she never makes the top 50 again.

**August 26.** Earlier this year, Richard Harris's "MacArthur Park" simply defied cuts and its 7 minutes and 20 seconds broke the AM radio taboo

against long singles. Today, the Beatles release "Hey Jude," a 7-minute 11-second single under their new Apple label. The year's biggest hit, the song holds on to No. 1 for longer than any other Beatles tune—nine weeks. For Apple's second release, Paul McCartney writes and produces "Those Were the Days" for Mary Hopkin, her only top 10 hit.

**October 19.** In London, John Lennon and Yoko Ono appear in a magistrate court for possession of hashish. The famous Beatle pleads guilty (after the court agrees to drop charges against a pregnant Yoko) and receives a fine. The conviction will later create problems for Lennon when he tries to remain in the United States. (He will always maintain that the drugs were planted and the arrest was arranged by a police officer who had a reputation for hauling in famous people.)

On October 22, a "love-in" on the West Coast draws some 7,000, but the police report outbreaks of violence.

**More news.** Since studios first introduced tape recorders in the 1940s, background hiss had been a constant problem. Just a couple of years ago, Ray

Dolby invented a device to mask sounds at a certain level. A simplified and cheaper version appears in home tape recorders this year. By 1970, manufacturers will be selling Dolby cassettes for play on Dolby equipment.

• Paul Mauriat's hit "Love Is Blue" is the first instrumental to reach the No. 1 spot since 1962.

• Formed in 1966, Cream disbands under the strain of three creative talents. Following their farewell concerts at the end of the year, Eric Clapton and Ginger Baker form Blind Faith and Jack Bruce forms West, Bruce & Laing. A *Goodbye* album and documentary will be released in 1969.

• Well-known groups break up in the United States as well this year. The Mamas & the Papas fall apart under the disintegration of John and Michelle Phillips' marriage; Cass Elliot continues to record as a solo. John Sebastian leaves the Lovin' Spoonful for a solo career and the folk-rockers disband. Bill Medley and Bobby Hatfield split and Hatfield performs with Jimmy Walker as the Righteous Brothers. The original duo will reunite briefly in 1974.

• In his novelty hit, "Tip-Toe Through the Tulips with Me," a nearly middle-age Tiny Tim sings the old-fashioned lyrics in his unique falsetto. (He says God inspired him to sing that way.) The singer plays a left-handed ukulele, wears fuzzy hair down to his shoulders, and dresses in what later generations would call nerdy outfits. "I really believe I'm 19 and I try to stay that way." His album sells 150,000 copies in the first 15 weeks.

• Following Simon & Garfunkel's tremendous success in 1966, the duo's output slowed considerably. (Paul Simon needed three years to write the music for their first three albums.) In 1967, "At the Zoo" reached No. 16 and "Fakin' It" peaked at No. 23. This year, their *Bookends* LP produces the No. 1 hit "Mrs. Robinson."

• An essential element of the Motown sound, the Temptations change their direction in 1967, laying down the foundation for the 1970s disco sound with "Cloud 9."

• While critics maintain reel-to-reel recorders provide a better fidelity, several new cassette machines offer a high-performance sound.

## New Recording Artists

The Band
Blood, Sweat & Tears
Chi-Lites
Joe Cocker
Creedence Clearwater Revival
Tyrone Davis
First Edition (Kenny Rogers)
Fleetwood Mac
George Harrison (solo)
Mama Cass Elliot
Steppenwolf
Steve Miller Band
James Taylor

## Obituaries

**Red Foley** (June 17, 1910–September 19, 1968). Enormously influential in the early years of contemporary CW, Foley composed many of his songs and appeared regularly at Nashville's Grand Ole Opry.

**George D. Hay** (November 9, 1895–May 9, 1968). The country's top radio announcer broadcast his first "WSM Barn Dance" in 1925. One night as the program followed the NBC Symphony over the network affiliate, Hay told his listeners, "get down to Earth with us in a . . . shindig of Grand Ole Opry." The show was officially renamed in January 1926. By bringing in new talent and encouraging beginning stars, Hay established the entertainment format for CW music. He retired in 1951.

**Wes Montgomery** (March 6, 1925–June 15, 1968). The top-selling jazz artist of 1967, the self-taught guitarist was one of the most influential jazz musicians of all time.

## MOVIES

*Bullitt* (d. Peter Yates; color)—Steve McQueen, Robert Vaughn, Jacqueline Bisset, Robert Duvall

*Charly* (d. Ralph Nelson; color)—Cliff Robertson, Claire Bloom, Lilia Skala

*Countdown* (d. Robert Altman; color)—James Caan, Robert Duvall, Charles Aidman, Joanna Moore

*Faces* (d. John Cassavetes; bw)—John Marley, Gena Rowlands, Lynn Carlin, Seymour Cassel

*Funny Girl* (d. William Wyler; color)—Barbara Streisand, Omar Sharif, Kay Medford, Anne Francis, Walter Pidgeon

*The Good, the Bad and the Ugly* (Italian-Spanish, d. Sergio Leone; color)—Clint Eastwood, Lee Van Cleef, Eli Wallach (1967; released in North America in 1968)

*I Love You, Alice B. Toklas!* (d. Hy Averback; color)—Peter Sellers, Jo Van Fleet, Leigh Taylor-Young, Joyce Van Patten

*The Lion in Winter* (British, d. Anthony Harvey; color)—Katharine Hepburn, Peter O'Toole

*Madigan* (d. Donald Siegel; color)—Richard Widmark, Henry Fonda, Inger Stevens, Harry Guardino

*No Way to Treat a Lady* (d. Jack Smight; color)—Rod Steiger, Lee Remick, George Segal, Eileen Heckart

*The Odd Couple* (d. Gene Saks; color)—Jack Lemmon, Walter Matthau

*Oliver!* (British, d. Carol Reed; color)—Ron Moody, Oliver Reed, Shane Wallis, Mark Lester, Jack Wild

*Petulia* (d. Richard Lester; color)—Julie Christie, George C. Scott, Richard Chamberlain, Arthur Hill, Shirley Knight

*Planet of the Apes* (d. Franklin J. Schaffner; color)—Charlton Heston, Roddy McDowall, Kim Hunter

*The Producers* (d. Mel Brooks; color)—Zero Mostel, Gene Wilder, Kenneth Mars, Dick Shawn

*Rachel, Rachel* (d. Paul Newman; color)—Joanne Woodward, James Olson, Kate Harrington, Estelle Parsons

*Romeo and Juliet* (British-Italian, d. Franco Zeffirelli; color)—Leonard Whiting, Olivia Hussey, Michael York, John McEnery, Milo O'Shea

*Rosemary's Baby* (d. Roman Polanski; color)—Mia Farrow, John Cassavetes, Ruth Gordon, Sidney Blackmer

*The Subject Was Roses* (d. Ulu Grosbard; color)—Patricia Neal, Jack Albertson, Martin Sheen

*The Thomas Crown Affair* (d. Norman Jewison; color)—Steve McQueen, Faye Dunaway, Paul Burke

*2001: A Space Odyssey* (British, d. Stanley Kubrick; color)—Keir Dullea, Gary Lockwood, William Sylvester

*Will Penny* (d. Tom Gries; color)—Charlton Heston, Joan Hackett, Donald Pleasence

*Yellow Submarine* (British; color; animated)—Voices: John Clive (John); Geoffrey Hughes (Paul); Peter Batten (George); Paul Angelus (Ringo Chief Blue Meanie)

### Academy Awards

**April 10.** The Oscars were postponed for two days in memory of Martin Luther King, Jr. (At least five entertainers, including Louis Armstrong and Sidney Poitier, had notified the Academy they would not appear on the planned date.)

Academy president Gregory Peck reverses the no-show trend of recent years by convincing 18 of the 20 acting nominees to attend (Spencer Tracy died last year and Katharine Hepburn never appears at the Oscars).

Bob Hope hosts for the 14th year.

Best Picture—*In the Heat of the Night*
Best Actor—Rod Steiger (*In the Heat of the Night*)
Best Actress—Katharine Hepburn (*Guess Who's Coming to Dinner*)
Best Director—Mike Nichols (*The Graduate*)
Best Supporting Actor—George Kennedy (*Cool Hand Luke*)
Best Supporting Actress—Estelle Parsons (*Bonnie and Clyde*)
Best Song—"Talk to the Animals" from *Doctor Doolittle*
Best Foreign Film—*Closely Watched Trains* (Czechoslovakian)

In past years, the Academy has given two Oscars—one for black-and-white movies, the other for color—in the three categories of Costume Design, Art Direction, and Cinematography. This year, with the increasing rarity of black-and-white films, the Academy reduces the two awards to one.

John Chambers wins a Special Oscar for his *Planet of the Apes* makeup. The film's producers allotted nearly $1 million (17 percent of the total budget) for the special latex application that enabled actors to show facial expression on their ape-like features.

## News

**July 8.** *Newsweek* notes the increasing use of movie titles to set the mood, lay out the theme, or start the narrative. Techniques range from peekaboo screens within a screen (*The Thomas Crown Affair*) to a colorful animated feline and jazzy music (*The Pink Panther*).

Until *Carmen Jones* (1954), movies usually listed credits on a fabric backdrop or the turning pages of an open book. Director Otto Preminger commissioned Saul Bass to create unusual titles for the Negro opera. The graphics designer superimposed the words over a flame burning behind a rose.

**October 7.** Since the revised Production Code has failed to alleviate parental concerns over sex and violence, the MPAA creates a new classification system to keep censorship within the industry.

Regardless of theme or treatment, a movie will be assigned one of four categories: "G" for general audiences—all ages; "M" for mature audiences—parental discretion advised; "R" for restricted—children under 16 require an accompanying adult; and "X"—no one under 16 admitted.

The designation will be publicized at theater box offices, in film previews, and in all advertisements. The system remains voluntary, but a reported 90–95 percent of producers have signified their willingness to cooperate.

**More news.** With no accurate count available, the film industry estimates nearly one-third of America's 18,000 movie theaters are drive-ins. The first opened in 1934 behind R. H. Hollinshead's

machine parts shop in Camden, New Jersey (he was unable to patent his graded car ramp). Four years later, MGM sold regular-run pictures to the first-outdoor theaters. Builders have always located drive-ins on the outskirts of towns and cities, but as communities spread outward, theater owners face rising taxes. Luckily, summer business is increasing as more and more baby-boomers reach driving age.

• Capitalizing on the star's tough-guy Western image, *Coogan's Bluff* ads proclaim, "Clint Eastwood gives New York 24 hours to get out of town."

• In *Life* magazine, movie reviewer Richard Schickel bemoans the decline and fall of the Western: "As the historical West recedes from living memory, our moviemakers, naturally enough, have lost touch with its reality. All they really know about it is what they have seen at the movies, which means they are at two removes—at least—from authenticity." He further criticizes the director's tendency to add unnecessary comedy or brutality to satisfy modern audiences.

• Last year, Sean Connery quit after five James Bond films: *Dr. No* (1968), *From Russia with Love* (1963), *Goldfinger* (1964), *Thunderball* (1965), and *You Only Live Twice* (1967). Producers Cubby Broccoli and Harry Saltzman, after looking at some 400 potential replacements, narrow their search to five finalists—all 32 years old, over 6'2", and with the requisite British accent. George Lazenby wins the plum role after bloodying the nose of a stuntman in a screen-test fight.

• Doris Day's performance in *With Six You Get Eggroll* ends a 20-year film career. From 1948 through the 1950s, the freckle-faced singer played girl-next-door parts in musicals—*Calamity Jane* (1953), *Pajama Game* (1957)—and the occasional drama. Then, in 1959, the popular star made an effortless switch to sophisticated sex comedies with *Pillow Talk*, co-starring Rock Hudson. The next year, she took the coveted No. 1 spot on the annual box-office list and held that position through 1962–1964 with movies like *Lover Come Back* (1962) and *Send Me No Flowers* (1964). But the dawning of the sexual revolution has dated the "virginal" characters of her bedroom farces and Day gracefully retires from films at the age of 44 to try her hand at television.

| Top Box Office Stars | Newcomers |
|---|---|
| Sidney Poitier | Dustin Hoffman |
| Paul Newman | Katharine Ross |
| Julie Andrews | Katharine Houghton |
| John Wayne | Estelle Parsons |
| Clint Eastwood | Judy Geeson |
| Dean Martin | Robert Drivas |
| Steve McQueen | Robert Blake |
| Jack Lemmon | Jim Brown |
| Lee Marvin | Gayle Hunnicut |
| Elizabeth Taylor | Carol White |

## Top Money-Maker of the Year

The Graduate (1967)

## Flop of the Year

Star! When the Julie Andrews' musical earns back less than a quarter of its $14-million budget, 20th Century-Fox yanks the film, cuts 40 minutes, and rereleases it as Those Were the Happy Times.

## Quote of the Year

"If you've got anything on your chest besides your chin, you'd better get it off."
–Slob Walter Matthau puts it straight to neat-freak Jack Lemmon in The Odd Couple (screenplay by Neil Simon; based on his play of the same name)

## Obituaries

Wendell Corey (March 20, 1914–November 8, 1968). His best-remembered role, as James Stewart's cop friend in Rear Window (1954), typified Corey's honest, clean-cut characters.

Dan Duryea (January 23, 1907–June 7, 1968). In 60 films and some 75 television parts, the veteran actor specialized in sneering villains.

Mae Marsh (November 9, 1895–February 13, 1968). Regarded by some critics as the greatest actress of the silent screen, Marsh rose to stardom as Little Sister in D. W. Griffith's landmark film Birth of a Nation (1915). She retired in 1925 after some 60 silent pictures, but resumed her career in the 1930s and played small roles until the early years of this decade.

Ramon Novarro (February 6, 1899–October 31, 1968). One of the original Latin lovers of the silent screen, the Mexican-born actor is best remembered for his starring role in Ben-Hur (1926). Although Novarro continued to play leads until retiring in 1934, the talkies effectively ended his career. The actor was murdered.

Hunt Stromberg (July 12, 1894–August 23, 1968). Voted "Champion of Champion Producers of All Time" in 1947, Stromberg's films included The Thin Man and two sequels (1934–1939) and The Great Ziegfeld (1936), for which he received an Oscar. He retired in 1951.

Walter Wanger (July 11, 1894–November 18, 1968). During his 44-year career, Wanger produced Stage Coach (1939) and I Want to Live (1959). Unfortunately, his last movie, Cleopatra (1963), almost wrecked 20th Century-Fox with its scandal, lawsuits, and cost overruns.

# TELEVISION AND RADIO

## New Prime-Time TV Programs

"Adam 12" (September 21, 1968–August 26, 1975; Police Drama)—Martin Milner, Kent McCord, William Boyett, Gary Crosby

"The Doris Day Show" (September 24, 1968–September 10, 1973; Situation Comedy)—Doris Day

"Hawaii Five-O" (September 26, 1968–  ; Police Drama)—Jack Lord, James MacArthur, Kam Fong, Zulu (1968–1972), Richard Denning, Al Harrington (1972–1974)

"Julia" (September 17, 1968–May 25, 1971; Situation Comedy)—Diahann Carroll, Lloyd Nolan

"Land of the Giants" (September 22, 1968–

September 6, 1970; Science Fiction)—Gary
Conway, Don Matheson

"Mayberry R.F.D." (September 23, 1968–
September 6, 1971; Situation Comedy)—Ken
Berry, Frances Bavier (1968–1970), George
Lindsey

"The Mod Squad" (September 24, 1968–August
23, 1973; Police Drama)—Michael Cole,
Clarence Williams III, Peggy Lipton, Tige
Andrews

"The Name of the Game" (September 20, 1968–
September 10, 1971; Adventure)—Gene
Barry, Tony Franciosa, Robert Stack, Susan
Saint James. *Note:* Each actor star's in his own
self-contained story line every third week.

"Rowan & Martin's Laugh-In" (January 22,
1968–May 14, 1973; Comedy Variety)—Dan
Rowan, Dick Martin, Gary Owens, Ruth
Buzzi, Judy Carne (1968–1970), Goldie Hawn
(1968–1970), Arte Johnson (1968–1971),
Henry Gibson (1968–1971), Jo Anne Worley
(1968–1970), Lily Tomlin (1970–1973)

"60 Minutes" (September 24, 1968–   ; News
Magazine)—Mike Wallace, Harry Reasoner.
*Note:* For the first three years, the program
alternates weekly Tuesday broadcasts with
"CBS News Hour." Reasoner will leave in 1970
and Morley Safer will join the show.)

"Wild Kingdom" (January 7, 1968–April 11,
1971; Wildlife/Nature)—Marlin Perkins, Jim
Fowler, Stan Brock

## Emmy Awards 1967–1968
## (May 19, 1968)

Drama Series—"Mission: Impossible" (CBS)

Variety Series—"Rowan and Martin's Laugh-In"
(NBC)

Comedy Series—"Get Smart" (NBC)

Best Actor in a Series—Bill Cosby ("I Spy,"
NBC)

Best Actress in a Series—Barbara Bain ("Mission: Impossible," CBS)

Best Comedian in a Series—Don Adams ("Get
Smart," NBC)

Best Comedienne in a Series—Lucille Ball
("The Lucy Show," CBS)

## News

**January 22.** Nightclub comedians Dan Rowan and
Dick Martin introduce their first television hour of
sight gags, one-liners, cameo appearances, skits,
video snippets, and trap doors. Within weeks, millions are tuning in to catch regular slots like
"Laugh-In Looks at the News" or a spinsterish Ruth
Buzzi flattening the dirty old man with her purse.
No. 1 to 1970, the zany program will add phrases
such as "Sock it to me!," "Here come de judge,"
and "Verrrrry interesting!" to America's everyday
vocabulary.

*Walter Cronkite, shown here on his second trip to Vietnam,
reports on his return, "The only rational way out, then,
will be to negotiate, not as victors, but as honorable people
who lived up to their pledge to defend democracy and did
the best they could."*

**January 30.** Following the Tet Offensive, newscasters and reporters start questioning the long-
accepted government promise of victory in Vietnam. Their skepticism carries over into the presidential campaign.

**February 1.** The Public Health Service tells
Congress that several different makes of color TVs
leak radiation above government safety standards.

Viewers should sit 6–10 feet away and, when not watching the set, turn it off or leave the room.

---

*Statistics:* NBC estimates that the number of color televisions has risen 5 million since 1967, to 15.2 million.

---

**April 1.** Legislation replaces the Board of Broadcast Governors with the Canadian Radio-Television Commission. Less subject to political interference, the 5 full-time and 10 part-time members of the CRTC will set and enforce programming standards for the CBC and private broadcasters.

**August 28.** During their coverage of police tactics at the Democratic convention, several reporters and network newscasters are manhandled by Chicago's finest. (Mike Wallace is hustled off the floor and John Chancellor says he is "reporting from somewhere in custody.") Both the FCC and Congress call on the media to defend themselves, but an investigation will find the coverage "balanced."

**September 6.** "Search for Tomorrow" and "The Guiding Light" present their last 15-minute episodes. Three days later, the daytime soaps expand to half an hour.

**September 16.** This week's surprise guest on "Laugh-In" is presidential candidate Richard Nixon. He opens one of the small set doors and says, "Sock it to *me!*"

**September 17.** Diahann Carroll, star of the new sitcom "Julia," is the first black artist featured in a "prestigious" role (nurse) rather than as a maid like Ethel Waters in "Beulah" (1950–1953).

**October 13.** NASA has allowed live telecasts of splashdowns and recoveries since 1965, but the *Apollo 7* flight marks the first live television transmission from space.

**December 3.** A Christmas special marks Elvis Presley's first television appearance in more than eight years. He closes the program with a specially written song, "If I Can Dream." (A soundtrack single will become his first million-seller in four years.) After the live taping, the King reportedly collapses and breaks into tears in his dressing room.

**December 3.** The TV Code Review Board permits personal product advertisements in good taste with substantiated claims. Previously banned products included feminine deodorants and hemorrhoid remedies.

**December 13.** In a long-awaited ruling, the FCC restricts pay TV to one station in each market, and only in communities with four existing stations. As well, the pay station must not exceed 90 percent movie and sports programming. The conditions are intended to limit competition with commercial television.

**More news.** During the presidential campaign, a Republican television commercial superimposes the face of a smiling, laughing Hubert Humphrey over scenes of poverty, rioting, and warfare. No verbal comment is made. The Democrats protest, and the anti-Humphrey spot is removed, but the damage is done.

## TV Commercials

Raid—Faced with a dinner-hour audience, S. C. Johnson & Son decides to zap animated insects rather than real roaches. Over the next three years, the company will run a half-dozen of these memorable one-minute ads.

## Obituaries

**Bea Benaderet** (April 4, 1906–October 13, 1968). The longtime TV actress starred in "Petticoat Junction" until her death.

**William Talman** (February 4, 1917–August 30, 1968). Known to television viewers as perennial loser District Attorney Hamilton Burger on "Perry Mason," the actor made one last dramatic appearance in an antismoking message. He died of lung cancer.

**Westbrook Van Voorhis** (September 21, 1903–July 13, 1968). The announcer is best remembered as the narrator of "The March of Time" radio and film documentaries during the 1930s and 1940s.

# SPORTS

## *Winners*

### *Baseball*

World Series—Detroit Tigers (AL), 4 games; St. Louis Cardinals (NL), 3 games

Player of the Year—Denny McLain (Detroit Tigers, AL); Bob Gibson (St. Louis Cardinals, NL)

Rookie of the Year—Stan Bahnsen (New York Yankees, AL); Johnny Bench (Cincinnati Reds, NL)

### *Football*

NFL Championship—Baltimore Colts 34, Cleveland Browns 0

AFL Championship—New York Jets 27, Oakland Raiders 23

Super Bowl III (January 12, 1969)—New York Jets 16, Baltimore Colts 7

College Bowls (January 1, 1968)—
Rose Bowl, USC 14, Indiana 3
Cotton Bowl, Texas A&M 20, Alabama 16
Orange Bowl, Oklahoma 26, Tennessee 24
Sugar Bowl, LSU 20, Wyoming 13

Heisman Trophy—O. J. Simpson (USC, TB)

Grey Cup—Ottawa Rough Riders 24, Calgary Stampeders 21

### *Basketball*

NBA Championship—Boston Celtics, 4 games; LA Lakers, 2 games

MVP of the Year—Wilt Chamberlain (Philadelphia 76ers)

Rookie of the Year—Earl Monroe (Baltimore Bullets)

NCAA Championship—UCLA 78, North Carolina 55

### *Tennis*

U.S. National—Men, Arthur Ashe (vs. Robert Lutz); Women, Margaret Court (vs. Maria Bueno)

U.S. Open (first year)—Men, Arthur Ashe (vs. Tom Okker); Women, Virginia Wade (vs. Billie Jean King)

Wimbledon—Men, Rod Laver (vs. Tony Roche); Women, Billie Jean King (vs. Judy Tegart)

### *Golf*

Masters—Bob Goalby
U.S. Open—Lee Trevino
British Open—Gary Player

### *Hockey*

Stanley Cup—Montreal Canadiens, 4 games; St. Louis Blues, 0 games

### *Ice Skating*

World Championship—Men, Emmerich Danzer (Austria); Women, Peggy Fleming (U.S.)

U.S. National—Men, Tim Wood; Women, Peggy Fleming

Canadian National—Men, Jay Humphry; Women, Karen Magnussen

### *Kentucky Derby*

Dancer's Image—Robert Ussery, jockey (See below)

### *Athlete of the Year*

Male—Denny McLain (Baseball)
Female—Peggy Fleming (Figure Skating)

### *Last Season*

Bernie Geoffrion (Hockey)
Jerry Kramer (Football)
Eddie Mathews (Baseball)
Dickie Moore (Hockey)

## News

**January 15.** Minnesota North Star Bill Masterton dies of a massive brain injury suffered in a fall to the ice during a game on the 13th. His is the first fatal injury in NHL history. Later this year, the NHL Writers' Association creates the annual Bill Masterton Memorial Trophy for the player who demonstrates "the qualities of perseverance, sportsmanship, and dedication to hockey." The 29-year-old forward had come out of retirement to play this season.

**January 26.** Major league baseball clubs raise their minimum salary to $10,000. Most players continue to hold off-season jobs.

**February 6–18.** At the Winter Olympics in Grenoble, Jean-Claude Killy sweeps the Alpine events with gold in the downhill, slalom, and giant slalom. The good-looking Frenchman thrills spectators and reporters alike, but IOC president Avery Brundage fumes when Killy flashes his brand-name skis. Afterward, the committee rules that skiers must tape over all product names to retain their amateur status.

Figure skater Peggy Fleming collects the only U.S. gold and Nancy Greene captures a gold for Canada in the giant slalom.

**March 4.** In New York, 24-year-old Joe Frazier KO's Buster Mathis in the 11th round to win the heavyweight championship of the world—as recognized by that state and four others.

The WBA, which stripped Ali of his title last year, has organized an elimination tournament. In the final match on April 27, Jimmy Ellis outpoints Jerry Quarry over 15 rounds.

**April 16.** In 1891, Springfield College administrators told their physical education teacher to organize a winter game for idle athletes, so Canadian James Naismith invented basketball. Today, the Massachusetts college formally dedicates the Naismith Memorial Basketball Hall of Fame and installs four former coaches.

**May 4.** A postrace sample reveals the presence of a banned anti-inflammatory in Kentucky Derby winner Dancer's Image. Following a lengthy investigation, the state Racing Commission rules that the flashing of the "Official" sign automatically fixed the order of finish. Dancer's Image remains the winner but, in this instance, loses the purse— the first disqualification in the 94-year history of the

race. Owner Peter Fuller will appeal to the civil courts, but a 1972 decision will award the prize money to second-place finisher Forward Pass.

**May 8.** Jim "Catfish" Hunter pitches a perfect game, the first in the AL since 1922 (Oakland 4, Minnesota 0). In this "Year of the Pitcher," four others turn in no-hitters and Tiger Denny McLain posts the first plus-30 record since 1934 (31–6).

Against that kind of power, all but six regular players bat under .300. To help the hitters, the Rules Committee makes two changes at the end of the year. The pitching mound drops in height from 15 inches to 10 inches, and the strike zone narrows from shoulder-knee to armpit-top of the knee.

**June 23.** Some 90,000 Buenos Aires soccer fans crowd toward the exits at the end of a game. With thousands pressing from behind, at least 71 people are trampled to death and 40 remain in serious condition. An inquiry will later learn that Gate 12 was open, but the turnstiles were locked in place.

**July 5.** After salary negotiations reach an impasse, the Philadelphia 76ers trade Wilt Chamberlain to the LA Lakers for guard Archie Clark, forward Jerry Chambers, and center Darrall Imhoff. Chamberlain signs with the Lakers for $1 million over four years. In the 1967–1968 season, he became the first center in NBA history to lead in assists.

**September 9.** Last month, Arthur Ashe became the first black male to win the U.S. amateur tennis championship. Today, he wins the first U.S. Open. (As an amateur, the 25-year-old army lieutenant is ineligible to collect the $14,000 prize.)

This year, for the first time, amateurs compete with tennis professionals in 18 events. The mix proves so successful that the International Lawn Tennis Federation sanctions 30 open tournaments for 1969.

**October 11.** Former Yankee second baseman Billy Martin has spent seven years with Minnesota as a player, scout, and minor league manager. Today, the club hires Martin to manage the Twins. He will lead the team to an AL West championship in 1969, but will lose his job for refusing to follow front-office policy.

**October 12–27.** Mexico holds the first Latin American Olympics. The capital city's 7,500-foot altitude appears to play a part in several events, including races where Kenyans, used to higher elevations, win three gold, four silver, and a bronze.

*With a leap of 29 feet, 2½ inches, American Bob Beamon shatters the Olympic long-jump record by nearly 2 feet.*

Spectators witness several outstanding performances: Czech Vera Caslaska wins four gold medals in gymnastics (to add to three from 1964); American Al Oerter, ever the underdog, collects his record fourth consecutive gold in discus; and U.S. swimmer Deborah Heyer wins three gold medals (the U.S. dominates water events with 23 Olympic and 5 world records). American Dick Fosbury intrigues onlookers and athletes alike with his unorthodox high jumping technique, a backward head-first flip quickly dubbed the "Fosbury flop."

Innovations at this Olympiad include an excuse-proof synthetic track (in place of the usual crushed rocks and cinders) and sex tests for women. (Polish sprinter Ewa Klobukowska broke the 100-meter world record in 1965 then failed the test.)

For the first time since 1952, the United States collects more medals—95—than the Soviet Union—61. But for most Americans, black sprinters Tommie Smith and John Carlos remain the big story. On the podium, the 200-meter first- and third-place finishers bowed their heads to the U.S. national anthem and raised clenched fists in a black power salute. The two are suspended from the team and expelled from the Olympic village.

**November 17.** The Oakland Raiders are leading the New York Jets, 32–29, with 50 seconds left to go, when NBC switches over to a prescheduled children's movie. Irate New Yorkers jam the network switchboard (the system breaks down under the flood) and tie up police emergency numbers. Later in the evening, the final score runs across the bottom of the screen. The Jets came from behind to win the "*Heidi* Game" with two quick TD's, 43–32.

**More news.** To create an unusual mask for Gerry Cheevers, designer John Forristall adds mock scars and stitches on a basic white background to graphically illustrate the injuries the Boston Bruins' goalie would have received without protection.

• According to *The New York Times*, jogging is the "in" sport in the United States. But millions of joggers have just 13 different styles of running shoes to choose from.

## Records

**April 15.** A 24-inning game between Houston and New York sets three records: the longest night game, the longest game in NL history, and the greatest number of consecutive scoreless innings. The Mets, who used eight pitchers, lose 1–0 to the Astros, who used five.

**May 27.** George Halas retires as coach of the Chicago Bears. His 63 years with the team as player, coach, and owner stands as sport's longest continuous association with a single club. Over his 48-year coaching career, Papa Bear pioneered instructional techniques such as game films and assistant coaches. With his 326–150–31 record, 11 divisional titles, and 8 NFL Championships, Halas was an obvious choice as a charter member of the Pro Football Hall of Fame. In 1970, he will become the first president of the National Football Conference.

**June 8.** With a sacrifice fly, Phillie Tony Taylor scores a runner from third to end Dodger pitcher Don Drysdale's run of six consecutive shutouts. Still, his 58 scoreless innings break Walter Johnson's 1913 record of 56.

## What They Said

Earl Warren, chief justice of the U.S. Supreme Court, says: "I always turn to the sports section first. The sports page records people's accomplishments; the front page has nothing but man's failures." (*Sports Illustrated*, July 22)

## Obituaries

**Marshall Cassidy** (February 21, 1892–October 23, 1968). One of horse racing's most distinguished stewards also invented the starting gate, perfected a photo-finish camera, and installed the country's first electrical timer.

**Jim Clark** (March 4, 1936–April 7, 1968). The Scottish auto racer was killed when his Lotus-Ford spun out of control in the German Formula II championship. The youngest driver to win the Formula I (1963), Clark had chalked up a record 25 Grand Prix wins at the time of his death.

**Ray Harroun** (January 12, 1879–January 19, 1968). Winner of the first Indianapolis 500 in 1911, Harroun was one of the 10 original members of the Auto Racing Hall of Fame.

**Duke Kahanamoku** (August 26, 1890–January 22, 1968). The Hawaiian swimming champion won the 100-meter freestyle in the 1912 and 1920 Olympics, and from 1912 to 1928, he held every world record up to the $1/2$ mile. After retiring from competition, he served as sheriff of the city and county of Honolulu (1932–1961) and later as Hawaii's official greeter.

**Jess Willard** (December 29, 1881–December 15, 1968). In 1915, the U.S. boxer knocked out Jack Johnson in the 26th round to win the heavyweight championship of the world. He held the crown for four years, but lived under a cloud of suspicion for much of his life. In 1920, Johnson claimed he threw the title fight for $50,000 and relief from police harassment. Forty years passed before a long-lost film of the bout showed the 6'5" Willard to be an underrated champ.

# 1969

With a bare 0.4-percent edge in the popular vote, Richard Nixon is the first new president in 124 years without a working majority in either the House or Senate. Still, he promises to reverse the Johnson expansion of executive authority and return to a limited government. To placate critics of the war, Nixon proposes a policy of Vietnamization–to gradually replace U.S. troops with South Vietnamese.

But Vietnam continues to tear at America. Antiwar demonstrations draw hundreds of thousands and, at year's end, newspapers print the first pictures of My Lai.

Other headlines, no less sensational, include the first astronaut landing on the moon, the Charles Manson murders, the convictions of James Earl Ray and Sirhan Sirhan, Hurricane Camille, and Ted Kennedy and Chappaquiddick.

Internationally, Charles de Gaulle resigns, Golda Meir becomes prime minister of Israel, Ho Chi Minh dies, the SALT talks open, Yasir Arafat is elected chairman of the PLO, and world powers sign the Nuclear Nonproliferation Treaty.

Less weighty matters at home include a World Series win for the Mets, a new James Bond, and Woodstock. Mickey Mantle retires and the Jets beat the Colts. The media acknowledges both the counterculture and the singles subculture. And the Jackson 5, Linda Ronstandt, and Crosby, Stills & Nash hit the record stores.

## NEWS

**January 16.** After 10 weeks of discussions, American and North Vietnamese delegates agree on the table shape to be used when South Vietnamese and NLF representatives join expanded peace talks—a large round table (without nameplates, flags, or markings), to be flanked by two rectangular tables for secretarial staff.

Henry Cabot Lodge replaces W. Averell Harriman as chief U.S. negotiator. But he and his chief deputy will resign in November out of sheer frustration.

**January 17.** President Johnson tells the National Press Club in Washington that his biggest disappointment upon leaving office is the failure of his administration to achieve peace in Vietnam. On the other end of the spectrum, the Voting Rights Act of 1965—which he likens to Lincoln's Emancipation Proclamation—pleases him most. Johnson flies home to Texas on the 20th, ending a 30-year career in public office.

**January 18–26.** Nine days of torrential rainfall—up to 24 inches—cause the worst flooding in Southern California since 1938, killing at least 91 people and leaving 9,000 homeless. A second downpour from February 23–26 drives another 12,500 from their homes and 18 more people die.

Experts describe the mudslides around the hardest-hit areas of Los Angeles and Santa Barbara as a natural phenomenon and suggest legal barriers to prevent further housing construction.

**January 20.** Despite extensive security precautions, some 300–400 antiwar protesters hurl rocks and bottles at Richard Nixon's limousine, the first time a group this size has disrupted an inauguration. An estimated 250,000 watch the parade and ceremonies, far fewer than the 1.2 million in 1965.

Two days later, the Nixon Cabinet is sworn in. Members include William Rogers as secretary of state, Robert Finch as secretary of defense, Melvin Laird as secretary of the treasury, and John Mitchell as attorney general.

RICHARD NIXON

Born: Jan. 9, 1913, Yorba Linda, California, second of five sons

Education: Whittier College, B.A., 1934, Duke University Law School, LLB., 1937

Military Service: U.S. Navy in W.W.II

Marriage: (Thelma) Patricia Ryan, June 21, 1940

Children: Patricia (b. 1946), Julie (b. 1948)

Previous Occupations: lawyer, representative, senator

Position Before Taking Office: lawyer

Legal Residence When Elected: New York

**January 22.** For the first time, a government study confirms the existence of chronic hunger and malnutrition in the United States. Presented to a Senate committee, the data was drawn from complete physicals given to 12,000 people living in low-income areas of Texas, New York, Louisiana, and Kentucky.

**January 31.** The news media reports that a huge, gummy oil slick from an offshore well has contaminated at least 35 miles of California beaches. The blowout is finally plugged on February 8.

Washington will introduce strict regulations governing oil exploration within U.S. jurisdiction and, in 1974, five oil companies will agree to pay almost $9.5 million in damages.

*Statistics:* In 1968, the U.S. Coast Guard reported 714 major oil spills, up from 371 in 1966, while pollution killed an estimated 15 million fish.

**February 11.** Several Canadian campuses experience unrest this year with the worst incident in Montreal. Protesting alleged racism against West Indian students, militant students have occupied the data center at Sir George Williams University since January 29. Today, after destroying a $1.4-million computer, they set the center ablaze. Authorities arrest 97 rioters.

**February 23.** In a coordinated offensive of shellings and ground assaults, the North Vietnamese hit Saigon and more than 100 South Vietnamese towns and military targets. Some 100 Americans die in the first 15 hours of battle.

Heavy U.S. casualties continue, with 453 men killed in the first week of March, the highest American losses in nearly a year. To hinder Communist operations, President Nixon secretly authorizes intensive bombing of Cambodia.

**March 2.** Soviet and Communist Chinese forces clash on the Manchurian border, with a number killed on each side. Following a second skirmish on the 15th, the two nations deploy up to 1.5 million men with nuclear support. But anxious to prevent open warfare, both sides make conciliatory gestures, and negotiations open in October.

The border incident, while failing to escalate into war, proves a crucial turning point in Sino-Soviet relations. Now viewing the USSR as a major foe, Peking deliberately moves to end China's long-standing isolation within the world community.

**March 10.** James Earl Ray pleads guilty to the murder of Dr. Martin Luther King, Jr. Yet, when

*Fighting in the swampy northwestern corner of South Vietnam, U.S. Marines call for air cover.*

both prosecution and counsel tell the court no evidence exists of a conspiracy, the defendant refuses to concur. But after the judge questions him closely, Ray reaffirms his plea. The judge hands down a sentence of 99 years.

Three days later, Ray changes his mind, saying he was pressured by his lawyer, then later claiming the FBI threatened to jail his father and brother if he refused to sign a confession. But Ray never produces any evidence of a conspiracy and a guilty plea eliminates any possibility of a retrial.

**March 10.** Japan, with a 1968 GNP of $135 billion, tops West Germany as the third largest industrial power in the world. Reliant on technological expertise rather than raw materials, the Japanese economy posted an almost unparalleled growth rate of 17.6 percent in 1968. Economic analysts project that Japan may replace the United States as the world's greatest industrial power by the turn of the century.

**March 16.** Moments after takeoff from the Mara-

caibo airport in Venezuela, a Miami-bound DC-9 crashes into a nearby working-class district, killing 71 on the ground and all 84 on the plane, including 46 Americans. The total death toll of 155 makes this the worst aviation disaster to date.

**March 17.** Golda Meir succeeds Levi Eshkol, who died in February, as prime minister of Israel. Born in Russia in 1898, Meir emigrated to the United States with her parents in 1906, then taught school in Milwaukee before leaving for Palestine with her husband in 1921. Meir hebraized her married name of Myerson in 1956.

**March 25.** The court rules that police officers must warn suspects of their rights at the time of arrest rather than just prior to questioning.

**March 28.** Former President Dwight D. Eisenhower dies at age 78. "I Like Ike"—the Republican rallying cry in 1952—translated into enormous two-term popularity (1953–1960) for Eisenhower. Yet the 34th U.S. president remains best known for his military career.

A West Point graduate in 1915, Eisenhower rose through the ranks to commanding general of the European Theater in 1942, then supreme commander of Allied Expeditionary Forces in the invasion of Normandy. Semiretirement through 1948–1950 ended with an appointment as supreme commander of NATO.

But once in the White House, Eisenhower the general turned into a caretaker. In his eyes, the Roosevelt and Truman brawls with Congress overstepped the bounds of executive authority. For Eisenhower, consensus was the ultimate goal and he remained, to many, unprogressive and uninspiring in both domestic and foreign policies.

Still, during his years in office, the United States entered no new wars and Americans enjoyed their greatest years of prosperity. And Eisenhower never lost the trust of the people. Just months before his death, the Gallup poll once again listed the general as the most admired man in the country.

**April 3.** U.S. combat fatalities in the Vietnam War surpass the number of Americans killed in the Korean War—33,629 in Korea and 33,641 in Vietnam—making this the fourth bloodiest war in U.S. history (after the Civil War, W.W.I, and

W.W.II). At the end of the month, U.S. troop levels in Vietnam reach a peak of 543,482.

**April 17.** At the end of a four-month trial, the jury finds Sirhan Sirhan guilty of the first-degree murder of Robert Kennedy. Most people thought the case was open and shut, but Sirhan's attorney offered diminished capacity as a defense. Although the Jordanian-American claimed he was unable to remember the shooting, his diaries revealed premeditation; Sirhan hated Kennedy for his support of Israel and wrote that the senator had to die before the anniversary of the 1967 Arab-Israeli War.

While the prosecution never asked for the death penalty and Senator Edward Kennedy pleas for clemency, the jurors call for the death sentence. But like many others, Sirhan will escape execution with the Supreme Court decision in 1972.

**April 28.** French voters reject proposed government reforms, and Charles de Gaulle resigns. The former general had served as president of the Fifth Republic since January 1959. Georges Pompidou wins the presidential run-off election on June 15.

**May 4.** *Life* magazine reveals Supreme Court Justice Abe Fortas accepted and later returned $20,000 to financier Louis Wolfson, imprisoned last month for violating securities laws. But, ten days later, the *Los Angeles Times* accuses Fortas of receiving $20,000 a year for life from a Wolfson foundation.

Neither publication charges Fortas with intervention, but the appearance of impropriety is enough to bring about his resignation on May 15. He becomes the first justice in the history of the Supreme Court to give up his office under public pressure. He was appointed by Lyndon Johnson in 1965.

**May 14.** At the end of a two-week filibuster, Parliament approves (149–55) several controversial amendments to the Canadian Criminal Code: liberalizing abortion (previously granted only when the woman's life was threatened); decriminalizing homosexual acts committed by adults in private; legalizing lotteries under government, charitable, or religious auspices; requiring suspected drunk drivers to submit to breath analysis; and prohibiting the possession of firearms and ammunition if dangerous to the safety of another person.

**May 15.** Students continue to protest against the war in Vietnam and armed services' involvement on campus, and to demonstrate for the addition of black studies programs, increased acceptance of minority students, and greater student participation in university affairs. Although the radicals represent a minority of the student body, their vocal and sometimes violent demonstrations attract national attention and often provoke violence in response.

Students on the Berkeley campus, along with various street people, revolutionaries, and others, have set up a People's Park in a large vacant lot slated for dormitories. Today, hundreds of police officers eject 75 people, erect an 8-foot-high chain-link fence, and post "No Trespassing" signs. Some 2,000 demonstrators gather outside the park and a battle breaks out in the afternoon. The police use tear gas and shotguns loaded with birdshot.

Arrests continue until Governor Ronald Reagan, responding to renewed violence on the 20th, orders National Guard helicopters to spray the protesters with a skin-stinging powder, used against the VC in Vietnam. On the 23rd, the university's academic senate votes support for the park and requests an investigation of police actions. Most of the National Guardsmen leave by the next day—after 900 arrests, 1 death, some 200 injuries, and with more than $1 million expended on officer pay, equipment, and supplies.

> *Statistics:* The U.S. Census Bureau reports that 1968–1969 black enrollment in American colleges reached 434,000, or 6 percent of the college student population. This figure represents an 85-percent increase over black enrollment in 1964.

**May 20.** After 10 days of bloody battle, U.S. and South Vietnamese forces capture Dong Ap Bia, a mountain near the Laotian border deemed strategically important in holding back North Vietnamese forces from Hue. The 101st Airborne Division suffers 84 dead and 480 wounded in capturing the high ground dubbed Hamburger Hill.

As with many previous campaigns, the military

brass abandons the hill just eight days later. The cost of the "victory" creates an uproar back in the United States, and Senator Edward Kennedy speaks for many when he describes the action as "senseless and irresponsible."

**May 22.** Canada broadens its immigration guidelines to accept U.S. Army deserters along with draft dodgers. Ottawa maintains that membership in a military service is "a matter to be settled between the individual and his government."

**June 2.** During SEATO maneuvers southwest of the Philippines, the U.S. destroyer *Frank E. Evans* misinterprets an order and moves across the bow of the Australian aircraft carrier *Melbourne.* The gigantic vessel slices the *Evans* in two, lashing the back portion to its bow while the forward half sinks, with 74 American officers and enlisted men still on board.

An inquiry places the major responsibility for the tragedy on the American ship. (In 1964, the ill-fated *Melbourne* collided with the Australian destroyer *Voyager*, which sank with 82 crewmen.) The Evans is the seventh U.S. warship involved in a major accident at sea in less than three years.

**June 8.** President Nixon and President Nguyen Van Thieu meet at Midway and announce a new "Vietnamization" policy, calling for the gradual replacement of American troops by South Vietnamese forces. Nixon promises that 25,000 American soldiers will return home by the end of August.

Washington unofficially initiated the program in February, handing over 300 helicopters and 60 heavily armed river patrol boats. Then, in March, Defense Secretary Melvin Laird stated that the administration would request additional funds to modernize the ill-equipped South Vietnamese Army. Now U.S. military commanders are instructed to keep casualties to "an absolute minimum." With this strategy, the White House hopes to end American involvement in Vietnam without losing the war or abandoning an ally.

**June 10.** Almost destroyed in the Tet Offensive last year, the VC announce the formation of a Provisional Revolutionary Government of the Republic of South Vietnam. The PRG will assume responsibility for internal and foreign policy and replace the NLF at the peace talks in Paris. Communist nations offer immediate recognition.

**June 22.** At its annual meeting, the SDS splits into two rival factions. The radical splinter group will take the name Weathermen, from the lyrics of a Bob Dylan song, and carry out violent demonstrations in Chicago, in October, during the trial of the Chicago Eight. Authorities arrest 290 members; the the remaining few become the Weather Underground.

**June 23.** Earl Warren retires as chief justice after guiding the U.S. Supreme Court through nearly 16 years of the Eisenhower, Kennedy, and Johnson administrations (1953–1969).

Under Warren's leadership, the court handed down a number of historic decisions across a wide spectrum of constitutional issues, including civil rights, the rights of the accused, and reapportionment under the doctrine of one man, one vote.

The "Warren Court," as it became known, won criticism as well as praise. More than one member of Congress demanded his removal, and President Eisenhower reportedly considered his nomination of Warren "the biggest damn fool mistake I ever made."

Warren E. Burger, District of Columbia Court of Appeals judge, becomes his successor. Legal experts view Burger as a civil rights moderate and a "law and order" advocate, critical of increased rights for suspects.

**July 7.** Senator James W. Fulbright, chairman of the Senate Foreign Relations Committee, discloses that the United States signed a secret military pact with Thailand in 1965. (Thailand serves as the base for most U.S. bombing runs over North Vietnam.) The State Department acknowledges the "military contingency plan" but refuses to provide details.

In the months ahead, Americans learn that Washington agreed to assist the Thai Army in fighting Communists in Laos, before the Thai border was violated, and paid Thailand $1 billion to send an army division to fight in South Vietnam.

**July 7.** Canada amends the Official Languages Act to declare French an official language, along with English. This guarantees every Canadian the right to use either English or French when dealing with the federal government. Also, bilingual federal facilities will be maintained in any district with an English or French minority of 10 percent.

The main opposition to the amendment comes from the western provinces.

**July 8.** A welcoming crowd of 3,000 at McChord Air Force Base, near Tacoma, Washington, greets the first American soldiers to return from Vietnam under the new policy of troop reduction. While the 94 soldiers represent just a small proportion of the more than 500,000 men in South Vietnam, their arrival reverses the flow of troops to Southeast Asia for the first time since 1965.

**July 11.** The Boston Court reverses Dr. Benjamin Spock's 1968 conviction for counseling draft evasion. The famous baby doctor promises to "redouble his efforts" to free those young men imprisoned for their opposition.

**July 18.** During the night, Senator Edward Kennedy drives a car off a bridge on Chappaquiddick Island off Martha's Vineyard, Massachusetts. Unaccountably, he fails to notify the police for nearly 10 hours, even though a young campaign worker accompanying him, Mary Jo Kopechne, had drowned. Eight days later, Kennedy pleads guilty to a charge of failing to report an accident and receives a two-month suspended sentence and one year of probation.

The senator appears on television, before the people of Massachusetts, to present his version of the tragedy. He describes his efforts to save Kopechne, and how later, in shock, he swam back across the channel from the closed ferry dock. Only the next day, did he fully realize what had happened.

Telegrams of support pour in, but others wonder whether the Kennedy name will save the senator from stiffer penalties. When Edgartown authorities close the case, the Massachusetts district attorney asks for an inquest. Kennedy requests a closed inquiry, and the state Superior Court agrees.

**July 22.** H. Rap Brown took over the leadership of SNCC from Stokely Carmichael in 1967 but, a year later, chose not to stand for reelection. Today,

Brown resumes the chair, and proclaiming "All tactics must be considered," replaces the "Nonviolent" in SNCC with "National." But an ambitious program falls victim to his personal legal problems, and the organization becomes virtually defunct.

**July 25.** Beginning a diplomatic tour, President Nixon chats informally with reporters during a stopover in Guam. Asking not to be quoted directly, he states that the United States will reduce its military commitments in non-Communist Asia to avoid being enticed into another war. Americans will honor Pacific treaties, but short of a nuclear threat, Asians will have to provide their own defense. The president's off-the-cuff remarks become known as the "Nixon Doctrine." He will first use the term on November 3 during a television appeal to "the great silent majority of my fellow Americans" to support for his policy in Vietnam.

**August 3.** Israel declares its intention to retain the Gaza Strip, the Golan Heights, and large parts of the Sinai Peninsula, territories won in the 1967 Arab-Israeli War. As for the West Bank of the Jordan River, the announcement simply states that the river will remain the "eastern security border" of Israel. According to King Hussein's government, some 400,000 Arabs have fled to Jordan from the occupied territories since the war.

**August 6.** Two years ago, the Johnson administration decided to deploy an antiballistic missile system (ABM) around 17 U.S. cities for protection against nuclear attack, primarily by the Chinese. Under the Nixon administration, that $5-billion Sentinel system has become a $7-billion Safeguard system to be deployed at 14 sites away from population centers.

Over the past few weeks, the Senate has bitterly debated the proposed construction of the first two ABM bases. Many senators argue that Safeguard will escalate the arms race while others question the exorbitant cost or point to scientific doubts about the system's capability to deal with multiple-warhead missiles.

The Senate vote today splits 50–50, and Vice-President Agnew casts the deciding vote for Safeguard. But the narrowness of the victory promises a congressional battle over funding.

**August 9.** Sharon Tate, the 26-year-old pregnant wife of Hollywood director Roman Polanski, is found brutally murdered—stabbed 16 times—along with three friends and a delivery boy at her Bel-Air home. Two days later, Leno LaBianca, a supermarket chain president, and his wife are discovered slain in Los Angeles. Police arrest a group of hippies led by Charles Manson but release them for lack of evidence. But Susan Denise Atkins, jailed in October for another murder, tells her cellmate about the Tate and LaBianca killings; the cellmate tells the authorities.

Manson used sexual perversion, drugs, and religion to bind followers to him over the past two years. He sent three women and Tex Watson to murder Tate and her friends, then led the LaBianca killings himself. Linda Kasabian, who served as a lookout on the Tate killings, becomes a prosecution witness.

In January of next year, the courts will find Manson and three followers—Susan Atkins, Patricia Krenwinkel, and Leslie Van Houten—guilty of the murders of actress Sharon Tate and six others; Watson will be found guilty later in the year. All five will receive death sentences; they appeal.

**August 11.** In a special election ordered by the U.S. Supreme Court, blacks gain control of the county commission and school board of Green County, Alabama, for the first time. (The previous November, a local judge eliminated six Negro candidates for reasons of "qualification.") Rev. Ralph Abernathy describes the electoral victory as "the most significant achievement by black men since the Emancipation Proclamation."

**August 17.** Hurricane Camille slashes through Louisiana, Mississippi, and Alabama with winds up to 200 mph and a flood tide of more than 24 feet. Thousands heeded storm warnings and fled inland, but others tragically decided to ride it out. The killer hurricane takes at least 400 lives (the death toll is likely higher, since many bodies are pulled out to sea).

Heavy rains hit Virginia on the 20th, and at least another 189 die in floods and landslides before the storm dissipates over the Atlantic on the 25th.

With property damage reaching over $1.5 billion, Camille is the most expensive storm in U.S. history to date.

**August 19.** In Northern Ireland, a week of bloody clashes between Catholics and Protestants has destroyed 400 homes, 15 factories and warehouses, and hundreds of small shops, forcing more than 5,000 people to flee. Prime Minister Harold Wilson and Northern Ireland's Prime Minister James Chichester-Clark agree to send in the British Army to assume control of all security.

Protestant political leaders in Ulster and the government of Eire both denounce the action, but London dispatches 500 troops on August 23 to raise the British force to 6,600 men. The soldiers, attempting to separate the two warring factions, soon find themselves battling both sides.

**September 1.** In Libya, radical young army officers overthrow King Idris in a bloodless coup and declare a republic. The 79-year-old monarch, in Turkey for medical treatment, had faced growing opposition from the Pan-Arab officers, as well as from students and organized labor. Washington recognizes the new government on the 6th.

In January, the head of the revolutionary council, 27-year-old Colonel Muammar al-Qadhafi, assumes the posts of premier and defense minister.

**September 3.** Hanoi announces the death of Ho Chi Minh at the age of 79. Born Nguyen That Thanh (the alias Ho Chi Minh was assumed during W.W.II; *Ho* means "the Seeker of Light"), he organized a nationalist movement in the French colony during the 1920s and founded the Indochinese Communist party in 1930. When W.W.II broke out, Ho formed the Vietnamese independence movement and fought against the Japanese. With their defeat in 1945, he declared the Democratic Republic of Vietnam.

When Paris refused to grant independence, Ho led his people in a successful eight-year war. The 1954 peace settlement pledged North-South reunification, but in 1956, the American-supported South Vietnamese carried out separate elections. The Communist leader then supported the VC guerrilla war and, once the Americans began their military buildup in 1965, directly engaged them. At the time of his death, he reportedly was confident of North Vietnamese victory.

Ho Chi Minh died yesterday, but Hanoi delayed the announcement to avoid coinciding with Vietnam's national day. Although the revered Communist leader requested cremation, party leaders place Uncle Ho's embalmed body in a mausoleum.

**September 3.** Between May 11 and July 7, New York Governor Nelson Rockefeller made four fact-finding trips to Latin America for the White House. In all twenty capital cities, he met anti-American demonstrations and riots—at least seven people died—while threats of violence forced him to cancel scheduled stops in Venezuela and Chile and reduce his tour of Bolivia to a three-hour airport meeting.

Rockefeller submits two reports, one on security matters and the other on U.S.-Latin American relations. The governor urges Nixon to transform the existing paternalistic relationship into a partnership and to recognize Latin military regimes that understand the goals of their people.

**September 10.** In the largest sale of its kind in U.S. history, oil leases on 450,858 acres on Alaska's North Slope bring $900 million plus. Since last year's discovery of a vast oil field, prices have skyrocketed; a 1963–1964 auction of 960,000 acres raised only $8.5 million. The state receives $1 per acre on the lease price and rights to taxes and royalties on future production.

**September 13.** In a front-page story, *The New York Times* reports that the United States is "torn by dissent" over the issue of sex education in public schools. An estimated two-thirds of American school districts offer sex education courses, and a Gallup poll found 71-percent support for their inclusion. But opponents have placed restrictive legislation before Congress and several states. California has already passed a bill prohibiting required student attendance in sex education classes.

**September 21.** "Operation Intercept" slows traffic to a crawl along the 2,500-mile Mexican border as U.S. federal officers closely inspect all vehicles for drugs. Other points of entry are covered as well. By cutting off the source, authorities hope to make the price of marijuana too expensive for the estimated 60 percent of American students who smoke it. But, under intense pressure from the Mexican government, Intercept eases up after just three weeks.

**September 23.** Labor Secretary George Shultz orders the "Philadelphia Plan" into effect. The controversial policy sets goals for the employment of minorities in federal or federally assisted construction contracts over $500,000. The U.S. comptroller general and some members of Congress had challenged the plan as a violation of the Civil Rights Act of 1964, but the U.S. Justice Department ruled against them.

**September 24.** In the first prosecution under the antiriot provisions of the 1968 Civil Rights Act, the trial of the Chicago Eight opens before Judge Julius Hoffman. The defendants, including Abbie Hoffman, Tom Hayden, Jerry Rubin, and Bobby Seale, are charged with conspiring to incite a riot during last year's Democratic convention. In bringing the charges, the government chose to ignore the findings of the National Commission on Violence that the Chicago police were largely responsible for the confrontation.

The trial, seen by many as a test of the limits of legitimate dissent, proves controversial from the start. Judge Hoffman constantly rules against the defense; counsel enter into bitter exchanges with the bench; Seale, who has chosen to defend himself, continually interrupts, and the judge orders him gagged and shackled to his chair; and when the jury retires on February 14, 1970, Hoffman sentences seven defendants and two lawyers to jail terms for contempt.

The jurors acquit all the defendants of conspiracy, but find five guilty of seeking to incite a riot through individual acts; the judge sentences them to five years. A higher court releases the men on bail a week later. Eventually all charges will be suspended.

**September 28.** In West German elections, Chancellor Kiesinger leads the CDU to a narrow victory, but the SDP and FDP form a coalition government to end two decades of CDU rule.

On October 21, the Parliament elects SDP Willy Brandt as the nation's fourth chancellor. The coalition government, in its first major move, revaluates the West German mark.

**October 15.** Across the United States, Moratorium Day unites hundreds of thousands in protest against the Vietnam War. For the first time, many members of the middle class march and gather with students, ministers, professionals—an estimated 100,000 rally on Boston Common—sing at folk concerts, and hold seminars and teach-ins. In Washington, Coretta King leads some 45,000 in a candle-light parade past the White House, as Richard Nixon watches from behind closed curtains.

Opponents of the moratorium display the American flag and, during the day, drive with their headlights on to show support for administration policy. And Vice-President Agnew, four days later, calls the antiwar demonstrators "an effete corps of impudent snobs who characterize themselves as intellectuals." A poll reveals that 55 percent of Americans sympathize with the protesters.

**October 29.** The Nixon administration, in attempting to steer a middle course on civil rights, has met resistance from Justice Department lawyers and the Civil Rights Commission. And today, the U.S. Supreme Court unanimously rejects an administration request for delay, flatly ordering 33 school districts in Mississippi to end racial segregation "at once."

On the 30th, the administration announces full support for the court ruling.

**November 12.** Newspapers publish an unbelievable account of American troops murdering unarmed South Vietnamese men, women, and children in the village of Song My, or My Lai, on March 16, 1968. Reportedly, C Company, 1st Battalion, 20th Infantry of the 11th Infantry Brigade, led by Lt. William Calley, Jr. killed up to 109 people. (Survivors claim 567 were killed, but as the victims were buried within three days of the massacre, no official body count exists.) The army, now conducting a full-scale investigation, names the soldiers to be tried.

Following the announcement, former army photographer Ron Haeberle, who used his personal camera that day, releases grisly pictures to the *Cleveland Plain Dealer* on the 20th; *Life* magazine publishes them the following day.

According to the story that gradually emerges, Charlie Company landed in My Lai as the villagers ate their breakfast. By 11:30 A.M., with only a few of Calley's men refusing to participate, the soldiers had killed an estimated 400 people—the largest group of 102 was mown down in a roadside ditch—cutting their throats, scalping some, cutting out the tongues of others.

At the time, the U.S. military recorded the operation as "well-planned, well-executed, and successful," but Ron Ridenhour, a former GI who heard of the operation from several members of C Company, exposed the massacre a year later in 30 letters to Congress, army officials, and the White House.

Polls at the end of the year show that most Americans believe the My Lai incident never happened or there were extenuating circumstances. Yet, by 1973, U.S. Army courts will convict 278 army and marine soldiers of serious offenses against Vietnamese civilians, including murder, rape, and negligent homicide.

**November 13.** Spiro Agnew's remarks about Moratorium Day demonstrators received wide coverage on TV. Today, in a speech in Des Moines, he strikes out at the three major TV networks for distorting the news. The vice-president claims, "The views of the majority of this fraternity do not—and I repeat *not*—represent the views of America."

The vice-president extends his attack to the press just a week later, particularly criticizing *The New York Times* and the *Washington Post*.

**November 13–15.** In the largest antiwar demonstration yet, the New Mobilization Committee to End the War in Vietnam masses up to 800,000 people in Washington. The protesters—mostly young, white, and middle-class—march down Pennsylvania Avenue or attend a rally at the Washington Monument grounds. Speakers include Senator George McGovern, Coretta King, and Dr. Benjamin Spock; entertainers such as Peter, Paul & Mary and Arlo Guthrie perform.

Perhaps the most memorable part of the two days, the March Against Death, begins at 6:00 P.M. on the 13th and ends 40 hours later. Some 46,000 people each carry a placard bearing the name of an American soldier killed in Vietnam or the name of a village allegedly destroyed by U.S. troops. Marching past the White House, each calls out the name, then moves on to the Capitol to deposit the poster in one of 40 wooden coffins.

Antiwar protests are held in San Francisco and elsewhere around the world as well.

**November 17.** The United States and the USSR open the Strategic Arms Limitation Talks in Helsinki, their first formal meeting to discuss ending the nuclear arms race. SALT has evolved from the diplomatic achievements of recent years—the Test Ban Treaty and the Nuclear Nonproliferation Treaty.

In an atmosphere of cordiality, representatives pledge to avoid any agreement that would place the other side at a military disadvantage. At the end of December, the superpowers announce an accord to begin full-scale talks on April 16 in Vienna.

Meanwhile, the Stockholm International Peace Research Institute, in its first yearbook, describes the arms race as "runaway." Military outlays worldwide are doubling every 15 years—even faster in developing nations, at 7.5 percent annually—while nuclear testing has increased since the 1963 treaty.

**November 20.** In Canada, in the first appeal under the 1960 Bill of Rights, the Supreme Court finds (6–3) an Indian Act provision (making drunkenness off the reserve a criminal act) denies natives "equality before the law."

The Joseph Drybones decision marks a historic shift in Canadian law. Rather than viewing the Bill of Rights as just another act of Parliament, the Supreme Court signals its intention to invalidate any legislation infringing on individual rights.

**November 20.** The Quebec National Assembly passes Bill 63, promoting the teaching of French and establishing a French-language priority. Yet many Francophones object to the provision granting Anglophone parents the right to request English instruction for their children.

**November 20.** Citing treaty rights to unused federal lands, representatives from 20 American Indian tribes reclaim Alcatraz Island in San Francisco Bay. The island prison closed in 1963 and, with no satisfaction from the legal system, they intend to establish a cultural and educational center and to prevent the Coast Guard from mounting a lighthouse.

In June 1971, 35 U.S. marshals will remove the last 15 Native Americans from the former prison site, ending the occupation.

**November 25.** President Nixon renounces the use of chemical and biological (c&b) weapons and orders the destruction of American stocks of anthrax, Q fever, botulism, and other bacteria. The United States reserves the right to produce chemical warfare agents for defensive purposes, and the White House later clarifies that the military will continue to produce tear gas and defoliants.

Earlier this year, at a private congressional hearing, the U.S. Defense Department admitted spending $350 million a year on c&b weapons and regularly shipping lethal nerve gas by rail to and from test centers. Then an article in the *Wall Street Journal* disclosed that 25 Americans had been hospitalized in Okinawa, Japan, following the accidental discharge of nerve gas. In the resulting domestic and international furor, Defense confirmed that the United States has stored nerve-gas-loaded artillery shells and bombs at major military bases throughout the world since the 1950s.

**December.** A conflict within the Irish Republican Army over the degree of violence required against British personnel and Ulster Protestants splits the organization into "official" and "provisional" wings. The former group seeks a union through revolutionary socialism, while the Provos commit themselves to terrorism to force out the British.

The IRA was founded in 1919 to win independence from Britain through armed force. Once Eire became a republic in 1948, the IRA turned its attention to achieving unification with Protestant Northern Ireland, which remained part of the United Kingdom.

During the 1950s and 1960s, the militant organization received little support from the Catholics in the North. But Catholic marches against the Ulster government this year have created the necessary atmosphere for violence.

**December 1.** At Selective Service headquarters in Washington, officials carry out the first U.S. draft lottery since 1942. Created by executive order, the lottery uses two drawings to determine the order of eligibility for all American men between ages 19 and 26.

The first drawing randomly selects all 366 days of the year, including February 29, to establish the order of induction by birthdate. The second drawing, of the letters of the alphabet, sets the last-name order of those having the same birthdate. The first one third drawn can expect to be called.

Draws each autumn will set the order of selection for new 19-year-olds.

**December 4.** In a predawn raid on a Black Panther apartment in Chicago, police kill 21-year-old Fred Hampton, leader of the Illinois party, and another man, and wound four of the remaining seven Panthers. Authorities maintain the black militants opened fire, but the Panthers charge officers with killing Hampton in his bed.

With the discrepancies between the two accounts, public pressure leads to several investigations. A ballistics expert will state that 199 of the 200 shots fired came from police weapons. Authorities will drop all charges against the Panthers but decline to indict any of the officers.

Four days after the Chicago incident, police in Los Angeles exchange gunfire with Black Panthers for four hours before arresting 11 of them. At the end of the month, the ACLU accuses law enforcement officials of "waging a drive against the Black Panther party, resulting in serious civil liberties violations." Since the beginning of the year, police have killed 28 party leaders.

Although the Panthers count only 1,000 members out of 22 million American blacks, the party has come to represent the racial schism in the United States. A Harris poll, released May 11, 1970, reports that 66 percent of American whites view the Panthers, with their advocacy of the forceful overthrow of the government, as a serious menace. But in another survey, 64 percent of black Americans say the Panthers give their community a sense of pride; 25 percent call the revolutionary party philosophy their own.

**December 10.** The U.N. Political Committee, in a major rebuff to the United States, declares the use of any chemical in warfare, including tear gas and defoliants, prohibited by international convention. Eighteen scientists, including three Americans, had distributed a report to delegates showing that 50,000 tons of herbicide, sprayed in military operations over 3,900 square miles of Vietnam, produced a much higher intake level among residents than when used just for agriculture.

The General Assembly passes the resolution on December 16.

**December 15.** With the recent disclosures of secret U.S. military commitments to Thailand, the Senate has debated the issue in a rare closed session. A 78–11 vote, in an amendment to a defense appropriation, bars the commitment of American troops to Thailand or Laos. President Nixon approves the amendment, saying it is in keeping with administration policy.

**December 15.** Nixon announces the third U.S. troop pullout from South Vietnam—50,000 soldiers by April 15, 1970—bringing U.S. withdrawals to 115,500. Still, under this timetable, the president will not meet his promise to recall forces more quickly than suggested by Clark Clifford, former defense secretary under Lyndon Johnson.

In September, President Nguyen Van Thieu predicted the replacement of American troops by South Vietnamese would probably take "years and years" because his nation had "no ambition, no pretense to replace all U.S. troops in 1970."

**December 19.** Washington unilaterally relaxes restrictions on U.S. trade with the People's Republic of China, eliminating the $100 limit on the purchase of Chinese goods (not to be resold) and authorizing U.S. overseas affiliates and subsidiaries to trade with Communist China in nonstrategic goods.

In another indication of the shift in American-Chinese relations, the Nixon administration in

November suspended the regular two-destroyer patrol of the Taiwan Straits.

## Obituaries

**Everett Dirksen** (January 4, 1896–September 7, 1969). As Senate minority leader (1959–1969), the Republican from Illinois played a crucial role in the passage of the 1964 Civil Rights Act and the 1965 Voting Rights Act.

**Allen Dulles** (April 7, 1893–January 29, 1969). Fiercely anti-Communist, the CIA director (1953–1961) ordered covert operations against left-wing governments that opposed U.S. interests. And under his leadership, the agency began illegal surveillance of American citizens. By altering the CIA intelligence mandate, many believe Dulles pushed the United States and the Soviet Union deeper into the Cold War. After the failed Bay of Pigs invasion, an angry President Kennedy pressured him to resign.

**Dwight D. Eisenhower** (October 14, 1890–March 28, 1969). *See news.*

**Vito Genovese** (November 27, 1897–February 14, 1969). The widely publicized Mafia meeting in 1957, following the execution of Albert Anastasia, probably confirmed Genovese as the "boss of all bosses." After he led the mob into the narcotics business, rivals set him up for a drug smuggling conviction in 1959. Genovese died in prison.

**Ho Chi Minh** (May 19, 1890–September 2, 1969). *See News.*

**Joseph Kennedy** (September 6, 1888–November 18, 1969). One of America's wealthiest men served as ambassador to Britain from 1938 to 1940. He wanted his oldest son to enter politics, but Joe died in W.W.II. Jack fulfilled his father's dreams by becoming president, but he was assassinated in 1963. The patriarch lived to see Bobby, next in line, die at the hands of yet another assassin.

**John L. Lewis** (February 12, 1880–June 11, 1969). During his 40-year tenure as president of the United Mine Workers of America (1920–1960), the powerful industrial leader played a major role in implementing mining safety standards.

**Saud Ibn Abdul Aziz** (January 15, 1901–February 23, 1969). Crown Prince Faisal forced the Saudi Arabian king to abdicate in 1964 when his extravagant spending and poorly organized government threatened the country's stability.

**Moise Tshombe** (November 10, 1919–June 29, 1969). The defiant leader of secessionist Katanga province returned from exile in 1964 to assume the premiership of a united Congo. A year later, he failed in a power struggle with President Kasavubu and fled again. Tshombe was plotting yet another return, in 1967, when he was kidnapped, taken to Algiers, and imprisoned.

# BEGINNINGS AND ENDINGS

## News

**January 1.** The Boy Scouts of America permit girls to enter Explorer programs, which focus on hobbies and vocational interests.

**February 3.** The PLO elects Yasir Arafat chairman of a newly formed 11-man executive committee. The guerrilla leader, rejecting "all political settlements" with Israel, pledges to escalate Palestinian armed revolt into a war of liberation.

**May 9.** The Vatican drops 200 saints from the new calendar of feasts. The church doubts whether 46, including St. Christopher, ever existed.

**May 12.** Chevrolet discontinues the 10-year Corvair line. Sales had plummeted since Ralph Nader targeted the car's rear-engine design in his book on auto safety.

**June 10.** Pope Paul is the first pontiff to visit Geneva since the Protestant Reformation in the 16th century.

**June 23.** Under the threat of antitrust suits, IBM separates computer hardware and software costs. The rest of the industry quickly follows suit.

**July 1.** In a 60-minute ceremony at Caernarvon Castle in Wales, Queen Elizabeth invests her 20-year-old son Charles as the 21st Prince of Wales. The title, given to the heir apparent, dates back to 1284 when King Edward I presented his infant son to the Welsh people. The last Prince of Wales was Edward, later Duke of Windsor.

**July 11.** Lyman Lemnitzer is the first person to receive the Distinguished Service Medals of the

U.S. Army, Navy, and Air Force at the same time. The 51-year career soldier served as supreme allied commander in Europe (1963–1969) and commander-in-chief of the U.S. European Command (1962–1969).

**August 22.** Last year, the Pentagon returned the *New Jersey* to duty with a $22.2-million facelift. (At the end of W.W.II, the United States either scrapped or mothballed its battleships.) But the massive *New Jersey's* guns fired on North Vietnam just once before the White House declared the territory off limits. Today, the navy permanently retires America's last battleship.

**September 9.** The first U.S. postage stamp to depict a living American shows Neil Armstrong stepping onto the surface of the moon. The die used to make the printing plates accompanied the astronauts on board *Apollo 11*.

**September 21.** Led by a Canadian icebreaker, the U.S. oil tanker *Manhattan* becomes the first commercial vessel to traverse the Northwest Passage. Many believe the journey demonstrates the feasibility of shipping Alaskan oil to the East Coast, but thick ice and short Arctic summers prove to be insurmountable obstacles.

**October 31.** In the first transatlantic hijacking, AWOL Marine Lance Corporal Raffael Minichiello forces a New York-bound TWA flight to refuel twice and fly to Italy. (He had robbed a PX.) Police finally capture the hijacker after he flees into Rome with a hostage.

**December 8.** Safeway introduces unit pricing at four Washington supermarkets, for comparative shopping. Gummed computer labels attached to the shelves list costs per pint or pound.

**December 17.** The Bank of Canada announces a new series of notes with portraits of former prime ministers rather than the Queen.

**More news.** In Boston, HUD funds an experiment with simplified, color-coded traffic signs (a slashed curving arrow means no turning).

• Ralph Nader uses his settlement money to set up Nader's Center for Study of Responsive Law. Students and lawyers—Nader's Raiders—compile critical reports on industries and bureaucracies, particularly the government.

## New Products and Businesses

Campbell's Soup Co. introduces Chunky soups. Dave Thomas names his new fast-food restaurant, in Columbus, Ohio, after his daughter. Wendy's quickly expands into a chain.

*Statistics*: Americans consume more frozen foods per capita than any other nation: $70\frac{1}{2}$ pounds annually compared to 27 pounds in Sweden, $13\frac{1}{2}$ in Britain, and $7\frac{1}{2}$ in West Germany.

## Memorable Ad Campaigns

To mark the transition into the 1970s, Coca-Cola revives a slogan first used in 1942—"It's the Real Thing."

Criticized for using an American actor to promote Colombian coffee, the National Federation of Coffee Growers screens 100 Colombians. They settle on 34-year-old Carlos Sanchez, with his infectious smile and singular mustache, to play coffee grower Juan Valdez.

## Fads

Millions of Americans buy off-road minibikes (at about $150). Youngsters long to take them out on the road, but the pint-size vehicles fail to meet road safety standards. Small legal motorcycles will appear on the market by 1973.

Since the first dune buggy—fiberglass body over an old Volkswagen chassis—the industry has mushroomed to at least 40 companies. Some manufacturers predict a changeover from off-road to street vehicles.

## SCIENCE AND TECHNOLOGY

### News

**January 16.** Independent teams of scientists at Rockefeller University and Merck Labs announce the first synthesis of an enzyme, ribonuclease.

**January 16.** After a historic first docking of two manned spacecraft, *Soyuz* 4 and 5 cosmonauts transfer personnel. The result—dubbed "the world's first experimental space station" by Moscow—underlines the Soviet emphasis on living in rather than traveling in, space.

**January 20.** Astronomers at the University of Arizona, announce the first visual identification of a pulsar (previously known only from radio signals). The neutron star is found near the center of the Crab nebula.

**February.** Dr. Robert Edwards at Cambridge University reports the fertilization of a human egg outside the mother's body. He hopes the procedure will help women with damaged fallopian tubes.

**February 20.** A hospital successfully transfers a heart to another New York facility, the first time the organ has been stored for more than 20 minutes. The procedure quickly becomes common practice.

**March 2.** In its first flight, the Concorde travels 300 miles in 28 minutes. Developed jointly by Britain and France at a cost of $1.75 billion, the supersonic airliner will break the sound barrier before the end of the year. But with extensive testing and demonstration flights to some 49 countries, the craft will have yet to fly commercially by the mid-1970s.

**March 3.** During a 10-day orbit above Earth, Jim McDivitt, David Scott, and Russell Schweickart test the command and lunar modules for a flight to the moon. The *Apollo 9*, astronauts separate the two by as much as 100 miles, and successfully redock.

**April.** Dr. Ernest Sternglass, in this month's issue of *Bulletin of the Atomic Scientists*, blames nuclear atmospheric tests for the deaths of some 375,000 American children between 1951 and 1966. Reportedly, the periodical was pressured not to publish the article.

**April.** GE demonstrates an 11-foot-high, 3,000-pound cyborg (from *cybernetic* and *organism*). Unlike robots controlled from a computer keyboard, this four-legged walking machine mimics the movements of the operator seated inside.

**April 4.** When the donor heart stops beating during surgery, in desperation Houston doctors implant an artificial heart. Developed by Domingo Liotta, the four-chamber Dacron-rubber device keeps the male patient alive for 64 hours, long enough to find another donor organ. But he dies shortly after the second operation.

**April 14.** Scientists at Rockefeller University announce the discovery of the chemical structure of antibodies.

**May 16–17.** The Soviet probes *Venera 5* and *Venera 6* descend to the surface of Venus some 200 miles apart. Their instruments report temperatures of up to 750 degrees Fahrenheit and an atmosphere of 93–97 percent carbon dioxide. But both capsules soon stop operating, crushed no doubt by an atmospheric pressure 60 times that of Earth.

---

*Statistics*: In 1968, the Soviets took the lead in annual space launchings, with 74, versus 62 for the Americans. By 1972, the count will stand at 89 for the USSR versus 36 for the United States. Most Soviet satellites will remain under the Kosmos designation.

---

**May 18–26.** Thomas Stafford, John Young, and Eugene Cernan take *Apollo 10* to the moon in a full dress rehearsal. *Charlie Brown* remains in orbit while *Snoopy* descends to within nine miles of the surface, testing the propulsion system in a lunar environment and looking for a suitable landing site. But the LM begins tumbling, and the astronauts must use the abort guidance system to regain control. A switch left in the wrong position on Earth made Snoopy automatically search the skies for a rendezvous position.

**June 7.** A report presented to a Wisconsin heart association meeting describes a surgical technique developed by Dr. W. Dudley Johnson and his team. In 301 procedures over the last two years, veins or arteries from the patient's own body were used to reroute blood flow around clogged areas. Within minutes, the size of the heart decreased, and pumping and blood pressure improved. In coming years, the coronary bypass will become a common procedure.

**June 9.** Following tests in Taiwan, the U.S. government licenses a vaccine for rubella, or German measles, developed by Paul Parkman and Harry Myer earlier in the decade. Manufacturers hope to provide more than 18 million doses within a year, well ahead of the next expected epidemic in 1971–1972.

**June 24.** A U.N. advisory group on environmental pollution found that two-thirds of the world's original forest has been lost to clearance and agriculture.

---

*Statistics:* Since 1945, U.S. electrical consumption has grown from 275 billion to 1,553 billion kilowatt hours.

---

**July 19.** A two-day storm forces Thor Heyerdahl and his crew to abandon their 12-ton papyrus raft *Ra* some 600 miles short of Barbados. Heyerdahl's theory—denounced as racist by many—holds that ancient mariners from the Old World brought high culture to the Incas, Aztecs, and Mayans, before continuing on to Polynesia and Easter Island. In 1970, his second voyage from Morocco will be successful.

**July 20.** At 4:17 P.M. Eastern Daylight Time, Neil Armstrong reports, "Houston, Tranquility Base here. The *Eagle* has landed!"

The two-stage *Apollo 11* lifted off from Earth on a Saturn rocket four days ago. Today, Michael Collins remained in the CM *Columbia* while astronauts Armstrong and Edwin (Buzz) Aldrin separated in the LM *Eagle*. As the craft automatically descended toward a boulder field in the Sea of Tranquility, Armstrong took over manual controls to search for a landing site. (Reportedly, he believed the LM had a 50–50 chance of landing safely.) With just 20 seconds of descent fuel left, the craft touches down.

At the end of six hours of preparation for the ascent, mission commander Neil Armstrong opens the door of the craft. Reaching the second step of the ladder, he pulls a D-ring to deploy a TV camera. At 10:56:20 P.M. EDT, with 500 million people watching back on Earth, Armstrong places his foot on the surface of the moon: "That's one small step for man, one giant leap for mankind."

*Astronaut Edwin Aldrin's faceplate reflects photographer Neil Armstrong and the lunar module.*

Aldrin follows some 19 minutes later. The two astronauts take dozens of photos, just like tourists, and practice moving about in low gravity. Armstrong reads the inscription on the plaque signed by the astronauts and President Nixon: "Here men from the planet Earth first set foot upon the Moon July 1969 A.D. We came in peace for all mankind." The men also erect a 3- by 5-foot metallic flag.

For 2 hours and 36 minutes the astronauts familiarize themselves with the environment, evaluate equipment and clothing for future expeditions, collect some 10 pounds of moon rocks and soil, set up an aluminum sheet to trap solar-wind particles, and arrange laser reflectors for astronomers back on Earth.

On the 21st, 21 hours and 36 minutes after landing, the *Eagle* lifts off from the surface of the moon. Armstrong and Aldrin rendezvous with Collins and jettison the LM.

At 12:50 P.M. EDT, *Columbia* splashes down in the Pacific southwest of Hawaii. Navy scuba divers hand the astronauts isolation garments, and the trio move to quarantine quarters on board the *Hornet.*

On the 13th, the *Apollo 11* astronauts receive a ticker-tape parade from millions of people in New York City. Older Americans remember only two parades that were comparable: in 1927, for Charles A. Lindbergh, the first man to fly solo nonstop across the Atlantic; and in 1962, for John Glenn, the first American to orbit the Earth.

**July 29.** A British medical journal reports a possible link between birth control pills and cervical cancer. The AMA rejects the study, but in September the FDA acknowledges a direct cause-and-effect relationship between the Pill and increased blood clotting. At the end of the year, a British evaluation of clotting warns against higher dosages of estrogen.

**August 1.** American astronomers reflect the first laser beams off the equipment left on the moon, determining the LM's exact landing site.

In addition to discarded scientific equipment and miscellaneous items, *Apollo 11* left behind several commemorations: the plaque and American flag, which fell over as the LM blasted off; a micro-etched 1½-inch disk with messages of goodwill from 73 nations; a gold olive branch to symbolize peace; and an *Apollo 1* shoulder patch and medals to honor the astronauts killed in 1967 and cosmonauts Yuri Gagarin and Vladimir Komarov.

**August 8.** *The New York Times* reports on a patent issued for magnetic bubble memory. Composed of orthoferrites, the tiny bits of material form patterns of coded information for instant retrieval from computer memory.

**September 15.** Moon rocks that are 3½ billion years old surrender surprisingly high levels of chromium, titanium, yttrium, zirconium, and other rare elements. But with no evidence of water, organic material, or any of Earth's precious metals (such as gold), the samples dramatically overturn the theory that the moon was once part of the Earth.

**October 8.** HEW admits to blacklisting hundreds of prominent scientists over the years. Most were branded for their brushes with congressional committees, membership in left-wing political or-

ganizations, or opposition to the Vietnam war. Just a few months after the revelations, the department relaxes security clearance procedures.

**October 13.** Sent up in the last three days, the cosmonauts on board *Soyuz 6, 7,* and *8* experiment with remote-control welding and practice a number of rendezvous maneuvers without docking. At the end of the year, reports suggest that economic constraints forced the Soviets to cut back their space program.

**October 18.** Evidence links cyclamates to bladder cancer in rats, and HEW orders the artificial sweetener off the market by February 1, 1970. A partial exception is later made for diet foods, but the soft drink industry, which uses the sweetener extensively, fails to receive an exemption.

**November 14.** President Nixon attends the launch of *Apollo 12,* the first in a series of six additional scientific expeditions to the moon. The *Saturn 5* fires flawlessly into rain and low banks of clouds, but the craft's independent systems flash so many warning lights that the astronauts lose count. Backup batteries take over, and a few seconds later, reset circuit breakers restore the failed equipment.

Richard Gordon pilots the CM in orbit about the moon, while Charles Conrad and Alan Bean descend to the surface on November 18, just 600 feet from *Surveyor 3,* the satellite that crash landed on April 19, 1967. (Its brittle metal fragments will later help NASA design better spacecraft.) When TV cameras fail after 20 minutes, rumors spread that NASA is staging the Apollo flights in a studio somewhere.

The astronauts conduct experiments and collect another 5 pounds of soil and rock. The *Apollo 11* and *12* samples are to be made available to some 200 teams of scientists around the world.

Some 26 hours later, the pair rejoin the CM. The jettisoned LM ascent stage is deliberately crashed onto the lunar surface to test seismic reaction; instead of expected minutes, the signals last 2 hours. Splashdown occurs at 9:10 A.M. EST on the 29th.

**November 20.** The U.S. Department of Agriculture orders an end to DDT spraying in residential areas within 30 days. Other nations, including

Canada, have already taken steps to ban a pesticide that has been shown to accumulate in animals and fish.

**November 22.** A team at the Harvard Medical School reports the isolation of a single gene from common intestinal bacterium. Their accomplishment opens the way to learning how this basic unit determines hereditary traits.

**December 4.** A reptile skull from the Lower Triassic period is found within 320 miles of the South Pole. Scientists believe the 200-million-year-old skull supports the theory of continental drift.

**December 17.** In 1948, the USAF set up Project Bluebook to investigate UFO sightings. Today, after evaluating the 12,618 reports over 20 years, a scientific committee finds no evidence of extraterrestrial intervention (although 8 percent remain unexplained) and recommends the agency be disbanded.

**More news.** With developments in paper fabrics, hospitals increasingly adopt nonwoven disposables for surgical masks and gowns, bed linens, and lab coats.

## Other Discoveries, Developments, and Inventions

Childproof prescription bottle, from Eugene Treanor

Electronic fuel pumps, speedometers, and odometers in automobiles, sequential flashers, rear-window defrosters, and an air bag from Eaton Yale & Towne

Plastic roast-in-bag for frozen meat and poultry

---

*Statistics:* The average 1970-model automobile carries 100 pounds of plastic, an increase of 15 pounds over last year.

---

## Obituaries

**Harley J. Earl** (November 22, 1893–March 10, 1969). As GM styling head (1926–1940) and vice-president (1940–1958), Harley eliminated the run-

ning board and influenced such styling features as the outside luggage compartment, the wraparound windshield, the spare tire holder, two-tone paint, and fins. As well, he created the concept of "dynamic obsolescence," or annual design changes.

**William F. Friedman** (September 24, 1891–November 2, 1969). Head of the task force that broke the Japanese "purple code" shortly before U.S. entry into W.W.II, Friedman received the Congressional Medal of Honor for his cryptologic inventions and patents.

**Diamond Jenness** (February 10, 1886–November 29, 1969). Canada's most distinguished anthropologist published a number of pioneering ethnographic studies, including *The People of the Twilight* (1928) and *The Indians of Canada* (1932).

**Allan H. Lockheed** (January 20, 1889–May 27, 1969). Lockheed and his late brother Malcolm designed the first successful twin-engine 10-passenger seaplane and the first streamlined fuselage. Lockheed Aircraft is now one of the nation's largest corporations.

**Vesto Slipher** (November 11, 1875–November 8, 1969). As director of the Lowell Observatory (1926–1952), Slipher supervised the studies that led to the discovery of the planet Pluto in 1930. And his observations of space velocities and the rapid rotation of spiral nebulas formed the basis for the theory of the expanding universe.

## THE ARTS

February 12—*Play It Again, Sam,* with Woody Allen, Diane Keaton, Anthony Roberts (453 perfs.)

March 16—*1776,* with William Daniels, Howard Da Silva (1,217 perfs.)

June 17—*Oh! Calcutta!* (1,314 perfs.)

October 21—*Butterflies Are Free,* with Keir Dullea, Blythe Danner, Eileen Heckart (1,128 perfs.)

December 28—*Last of the Red Hot Lovers,* with James Coco, Linda Lavin (706 perfs.)

## Tony Awards

Actor (Dramatic)—James Earl Jones, *The Great White Hope*

Actress (Dramatic)—Julie Harris, *Forty Carats*

Actor (Musical)—Jerry Orbach, *Promises, Promises*

Actress (Musical)—Angela Lansbury, *Dear World*

Play—*The Great White Hope*

Musical—*1776*

## News

**May 31.** A two-week festival opens the National Arts Centre in Ottawa. The beautiful new complex—2,236-seat opera house, 969-seat theater, studio, and salon—cost some $46 million.

**June 17.** Kenneth Tynan cobbles together a two-act revue from pieces by Jules Feiffer, John Lennon, Sam Shepard, and others. Critics pan the faddish nudity, but *Oh, Calcutta!* sells out.

**September 25.** In New York, the Metropolitan Museum of Art announces a $100-million art bequest from Robert Lehman. His collection of nearly 3,000 works includes paintings by Renoir, Picasso, Rembrandt, and Van Gogh.

**October 26.** The official dedication of the Julliard School of Music completes the Lincoln Center for the Performing Arts. The idea for an arts community emerged in the 1950s when the Met and the Philharmonic began to look for new homes. Ground was broken on the site in 1959.

**More news.** Broadway production costs reach $500,000 for musicals and $150,000 for dramas. Standard ticket prices climb to $12.50 while top weekend seats go for $15.

## Obituaries

**Irene Castle** (April 7, 1893–January 25, 1969). Irene and Vernon Castle were internationally known ballroom dancers during the W.W.I era. Her continued popularity after his death in 1918 spurred the bobbed-hair craze of the Roaring Twenties.

**Vernon Duke** (October 10, 1903–January 17, 1969). The Broadway composer's hits included "April in Paris" (1932) and "Taking a Chance on Love" (1940).

**Frank Loesser** (June 29, 1910–July 28, 1969). The prolific lyricist and composer wrote the musicals *Guys and Dolls* (1950) and *How to Succeed in Business Without Really Trying* (1961) as well as songs such as "Bubbles in the Wine" (1939; later Lawrence Welk's theme) and "Baby, It's Cold Outside" (1948; Oscar winner).

**Giovanni Martinelli** (October 22, 1885–February 2, 1969). The Italian-American tenor was a mainstay of the Metropolitan Opera for 32 years. He retired in 1950.

**Gladys Swarthout** (December 25, 1904–July 7, 1969). Known for her interpretation of *Carmen*, the mezzo soprano sang at the Met from 1929 to 1945. A heart attack in 1954 ended her concert career.

## WORDS

William Armstrong, *Sounder*
Ray Bradbury, *I Sing the Body Electric!*
Michael Crichton, *The Andromeda Strain*
John Fowles, *The French Lieutenant's Woman*
Galloping Gourmet, *The Graham Kerr Cookbook*
Thomas A. Harris, *I'm OK—You're OK*
'J' (Joan Garrity), *The Sensuous Woman*
Elizabeth Kübler-Ross, *On Death and Dying*
Joe McGinniss, *The Selling of the President, 1968*
Rod McKuen, *In Someone's Shadow*
Laurence J. Peter and Raymond Hull, *The Peter Principle*
Chaim Potok, *The Promise*
Mario Puzo, *The Godfather*
David Reuben, *Everything You Wanted to Know About Sex; But Were Afraid to Ask, Explained*
Philip Roth, *Portnoy's Complaint*
Harrison Salisbury, *The 900 Days: The Siege of Leningrad*
Jacqueline Susann, *The Love Machine*
Kurt Vonnegut, Jr., *Slaughterhouse Five*
Irving Wallace, *The Seven Minutes*

# News

**January.** In London, 38-year-old Australian Rupert Murdoch buys *News of the World,* the largest-selling Sunday newspaper. The purchase lays the foundation of a publishing empire.

**January 10.** With $5-million losses last year, the *Saturday Evening Post* ceases publication with the February 8 issue. Over 148 years, the once highly popular and profitable magazine published such literary giants as Joseph Conrad, Jack London, and F. Scott Fitzgerald.

**April 7.** The U.S. Supreme Court finds unconstitutional all laws prohibiting the private possession of obscene material. In the unanimous decision, Thurgood Marshall writes, "Our whole constitutional heritage rebels at the thought of giving government the power to control men's minds."

**May 7.** During the four-month closeout auction of 700,000 rare and assorted books, staff at Leary's discovered a first printing of the Declaration of Independence. Today, the Philadelphia bookstore sells the historic document—1 of just 16 in existence—for $404,000.

**May 30.** Denmark legalizes the sale of visual pornography to people over the age of 16. Earlier legislation cleared obscene text.

**August.** *Sun Signs,* by Linda Goodman, is the first astrology book to make the best-seller list.

**September.** With four years of excellent sales in Britain, American publisher Robert Guccione puts *Penthouse* on New York newsstands. By the mid-1970s, his men's magazine will overtake *Playboy* in circulation.

**November 2.** The Sunday newspaper supplement "This Week" ceases publication after 34 years.

**More news.** Twenty-five *Newsday* editors and writers assume the pseudonym Penelope Ashe for their parody of bad fiction, *Naked Came the Stranger.* (Mike McGrady promised his collaborators, "Excellence in writing will be quickly blue-penciled into oblivion.") Graded "C" or worse by reviewers, the novel nonetheless sells thousands of copies—despite the authors' confession—and

brings another $127,500 for paperback rights. McGrady follows up with *Stranger Than Naked, or How to Write Dirty Books for Fun and Profit.*

In an informal survey, Herman Hesse replaces J. R. R. Tolkien as the favorite author on campus.

## Cartoons and Comics

**September.** Marvel brings out *My Love,* with "groovy chick" pinups, for a mixed audience. Next month, the company debuts *Our Love Story* just for girls.

## TIME **Man of the Year**

Middle Americans

## New Words and Phrases

ambisextrous (common to males and females)
bionics
crunch (crisis, showdown)
golden handshake (formal dismissal with a gift)
headhunter (a corporate recruiter)
in (used as an adverb-preposition [teach-in])
knockoff (a copy of a clothing design)
mind-blowing
noise pollution
pacey (up-to-date)
phase out
status symbol
telethon
unisex
wise (used as a suffix [careerwise])

Members of the Gay Liberation Front shout, "Out of the Closets and into the Streets."

General graffiti: "What do we want? Everything. When do we want it? Now!"

## Obituaries

**Jack Kerouac** (March 12, 1922–October 21, 1969). As a leader of the "beat generation," Kerouac's chronicled wanderings in *On the Road* (1957) kindled the sixties interest in drugs and Oriental mysticism.

**Frank King** (June 11, 1883–June 24, 1969). His *Gasoline Alley* (1918) comic strip was the first to show characters aging. He retired in 1951.

**Drew Pearson** (December 13, 1897–September 1, 1969). In 1932, with the avowed intention of making government "a little cleaner, a little more efficient," Pearson launched his column "Washington Merry-Go-Round." Over the years, his criticisms and disclosures sent four members of Congress to jail and brought about the defeat of others. Since 1959, the journalist had shared his byline with Jack Anderson.

# FASHION

## Haute Couture

While still emphasizing extreme youth, high fashion presents a longer silhouette—maxi coats, elongated mufflers, longer skirts, knee-length vests and pearls.

Older women continue to rely on pantsuits, now a standard element in their wardrobes (some airlines dress their employees in the trouser outfits).

## News

**This year.** When mail-order catalogs first listed pantyhose in the early 1960s, few women saw a need to put on stockings under a girdle. Then the mini arrived.

Millions of teenage baby-boomers, spurning girdles for the freedom of shorter skirts, substituted textured stockings. Last year, more women turned to pantyhose. By 1970, despite continued problems with bagging, sales will skyrocket to 624 million pairs (Hanes must farm out orders to hosiery mills in Israel).

• Couturiers may dictate lowered hemlines, but young women dither and retailers suffer one of their worst years.

## Colors and Materials

With women wearing anything and everything at the end of the decade, the concept of "seasonal color" holds little meaning. This year, furs provide the only color impact.

Patchwork fabrics prevail.

The unique color splotches of tie-dyed jeans and T-shirts—home-stewed in pots—suggest psychedelic experiences. (Popularized by rock musicians, tie-dyed clothes probably originated with San Francisco hippies in 1966–1967.) For once, the textile industry quickly takes up an innovation, but the craze will wane in the early 1970s.

## Clothes

Jumpsuits win favor, but the year's No. 1 silhouette matches pants with a sweater or long, long vest.

Young women wear the new maxi coat—the longest since 1914—over a mini, but many prefer the four-pocketed safari coat. High school girls top their old-fashioned skirts with a poncho or wool shawl.

Favorite summer fashions include a jumper-shirt combination and the new bra-dress, particularly the chemise style with low flares or pleats.

Fringe dresses are the rage.

This year's nude look bares the midriff. Some designers test the limits of the law with open-stitch crocheted bikinis and sheer chiffon tops, cut in a deep V. (In southern France, women sunbathe topless.)

Americans of every age wear jeans.

Insulated ski suits—parkas with overalls or warm-up pants—replace stretch ski pants.

Thousands of young outdoorsmen adopt the goose-down vest designed by Eddie Bauer in the late 1930s for Arctic bush pilots. In the next decade, the vest evolves into a fashion item.

Menswear highlights bell-bottom pants, colorful

shirts, wide ties, and jackets with wide lapels and double vents.

## Accessories

Chains give way to leather belts.

Magazines feature shoes with chunkier heels and thicker soles. One versatile style copies the short front section of the sling-back, adds a normal heel back, and keeps the two separate parts on with an ankle strap.

A long, narrow scarf is *the* fall and winter accessory.

With renewed interest in hats, many long lines finish off with a small neat shape. Nonetheless, the fedora dominates.

Pearls enjoy a dramatic comeback with bold strands hanging as low as the knees.

For the unisex look, some men accessorize with jewelry and a handbag (for those items impossible to squeeze into close-fitting pants) and use more toiletries, including makeup.

## Hair and Cosmetics

Makeup softens further with new peach tones.

A wig craze hits major American cities this year. With prices ranging from $15 to $300, manufacturers sell an estimated $500 million worth (compared to $35 million in 1960). By the early 1970s, wigs will become commonplace and prices will drop.

More men style their longer cuts with hair spray and hand-held blow-dryers.

# MUSIC

"Aquarius/Let the Sunshine In"—5th Dimension

"In the Year 2525"—Zager & Evans

"Get Back"—Beatles with Billy Preston

"Sugar, Sugar"—Archies

"Honky Tonk Women"—Rolling Stones

"Everyday People"—Sly & the Family Stone

"Dizzy"—Tommy Roe

"Wedding Bell Blues"—5th Dimension

"Crimson & Clover"—Tommy James & the Shondells

"I Can't Get Next to You"—Temptations

"Na Na Hey Hey Kiss Him Goodbye"—Steam

"Love Theme from *Romeo and Juliet*" (Instr.)—Henry Mancini

"Come Together"—Beatles

"Leaving on a Jet Plane"—Peter, Paul & Mary

"Someday We'll Be Together"—Diana Ross & the Supremes

"Suspicious Minds"—Elvis Presley

"Proud Mary"—Creedence Clearwater Revival

"Crystal Blue Persuasion"—Tommy James & the Shondells

"A Boy Named Sue"—Johnny Cash

"You've Made Me So Very Happy"—Blood, Sweat & Tears

"Hair"—Cowsills

"Jean"—Oliver

"I'm Gonna Make You Love Me"—Supremes & Temptations

"Love Can Make You Happy"—Mercy

"Take a Letter Maria"—R. B. Greaves

"And When I Die"—Blood, Sweat & Tears

"It's Your Thing"—Isley Brothers

"Bad Moon Rising"—Creedence Clearwater Revival

## Grammys (1969)

Record of the Year—5th Dimension, "Aquarius"/"Let the Sunshine In"

Song of the Year (songwriter)—Joe South, "Games People Play"

Album of the Year—Blood, Sweat & Tears, *Blood, Sweat & Tears*

Best Vocal Performance (Male)—Nilsson, "Everybody's Talkin' " (single)

Best Vocal Performance (Female)—Peggy Lee, "Is That All There Is" (single)

Best New Artist—Crosby, Stills & Nash

## News

**January 30.** While filming the documentary *Let It Be*, the Beatles hold an impromptu jam session on the roof of Apple studios. People hang out nearby windows and traffic stops in the street below, but with some noise complaints, London bobbies tell the four to pack it in. The Beatles will never again perform together in public.

**March.** Grand Funk Railroad play their first date. An appearance at the Atlanta Pop Festival in July, and a first album late in the year, signal the emergence of heavy metal. Next year, Grand Funk will reportedly sell more records than any other group in America.

**March 1.** At a concert in Miami, Jim Morrison of the Doors supposedly exposes his genitals and simulates masturbation and oral sex. The charges are dropped, but promoters remain leery and the band's performance schedule becomes spotty.

**March 12.** The last of the famous foursome to marry, 26-year-old Beatle Paul McCartney weds Linda Eastman. Just eight days later, 28-year-old John Lennon marries 36-year-old Yoko Ono (his second marriage, her third). On their honeymoon peace tour, the couple hold a bed-in at a Montreal hotel.

**June 20–22.** Newport '69 in California draws some 150,000 to see Creedence Clearwater Revival, Ike and Tina Turner, Jimi Hendrix, Jethro Tull, and others. For the first time, a rock festival suffers widespread damage. Gate crashers break down the fence and throw rocks at security police. At least 36 are arrested.

Other smaller festivals this year include the Atlanta Pop Festival (140,000) and the Atlantic City Festival in August (110,000).

**July 26.** In his first live appearance in almost a decade, Elvis Presley opens a month-long show in Las Vegas. He will resume a full touring schedule in 1970, and through the first half of the decade average 150 performances per year.

**August 15–17.** Denied permission by town authorities, the Woodstock Music and Art Fair sets up 55 miles away in Max Yasgur's 600-acre pasture. Through three days of incessant rain with inadequate food, water, and sanitary facilities, some 450,000 young people—the population of a small city—trip out on drugs and nonstop music: Santana, Jefferson Airplane, Ravi Shankar, Jimi Hendrix, Blood, Sweat & Tears, Joan Baez, Creedence Clearwater Revival, the Band, Arlo Guthrie, the Grateful Dead, the Who, Crosby, Stills, Nash & Young, Sly & the Family Stone, Canned Heat, and many more.

*The New York Times* pans the culture that could produce 20-mile-long traffic jams, a sea of mud, and a mountain of garbage. But following Newport, and with Altamont to come, Woodstock will become the golden moment of the nonviolent, hippie era.

**September 23.** In the first printed musings, the Illinois University newspaper questions "the present state of Beatle Paul McCartney." Over the next two months, the rumor spreads like wildfire—Paul is dead. Supposedly, McCartney died in a 1966 car crash, a double has taken his place, and the devious Beatles have left a trail of clues for their fans: The *Sergeant Pepper* album presents a grave with flowers shaped into a possible "P", or a left-handed guitar (only Paul plays one) on the back cover the others face forward while Paul stands with his back turned, and inside Paul wears a black arm patch with "OPD" (officially pronounced dead); at the end of "Strawberry Fields Forever" John sings "I buried Paul"— heard better at 45 rpm; "Revolution Number 9" played backward includes the sound of a car crash and "turn me on, dead man" and "cherish the dead"; and the *Abbey Road* album, among other things, shows Paul walking out of step with the others. And on and on. Paul tries to deal humorously with the situation, but by November he wearily tells *Life* magazine, "Can you spread it around that I am just an ordinary person and want to live in peace?"

**December 6.** Following complaints about expensive $4.50–$7.50 tickets, the Rolling Stones hold a free one-day concert for their fans at the Altamont Raceway in Livermore, California. (Additional acts include Santana, the Jefferson Airplane, and the Flying Burrito Brothers.) With little time to prepare, organizers hire the Hell's Angels to handle security (reportedly, for $500 worth of beer). Scuffles break out in the first hours between the bikers and some of the estimated 300,000 in attendance. Halfway through the concert, as the Stones sing "Sympathy for the Devil," the Angels close in on a young black man waving a gun near the stage and stab him to death.

That grisly moment, captured in the documentary *Gimme Shelter*, marks the end of the golden rock era. Local governments, backed by outraged citizens, block festival promoters or over-police events to discourage attendance. In January 1971, the courts will find the crime to have been justifiable homicide.

**More news.** For "Someday We'll Be Together"—the Supremes' 12th No. 1 hit—Maxine and Julia Walters provide backup vocals, not Mary Wilson and Cindy Birdsong (the male voice is songwriter Johnny Bristol). Diana Ross records her next disc as a solo.

• The Music Educators National Conference formally supports the addition of rock music to the curriculum of schools offering music education.

• As psychedelic music vanishes, the hottest new sound is country-rock and the new supergroup is Crosby, Stills & Nash. Their debut album places two cuts in the top 30 ("Suite: Judy Blue Eyes" and "Marrakesh Express") and brings the trio a Grammy as Best New Artist. This summer, Neil Young joins the group, but the four will split and remix in the years ahead.

• With management disagreements and under pressure to form an all-black group, superstar Jimi Hendrix leaves the Experience early in the year. The group disbands by summer.

• As well this year, Randy Bachman abandons the Guess Who. Four years later, Bachman-Turner Overdrive will release its first LP.

• Last year, the success of the Saturday-morning cartoons prompted Don Kirshner to create the Archies. The studio group, with Ron Dante and session musicians, scores an international No. 1 hit with "Sugar, Sugar." Their preteen or "bubblegum" sound is imitated by other groups such as the Ohio Express and the 1910 Fruitgum Company.

• Manufacturers recommend two speakers in front and two speakers behind for the new four-channel prerecorded tapes. In this way, listeners can duplicate the sound reflected from the back of a concert hall.

---

*Statistics*: At the end of the sixties, tape cassettes account for an estimated 40 percent of the recording business.

---

• *Let It Be* comes out later, but *Abbey Road* is the last Beatle album ("Octopus's Garden," "Here Comes the Sun," "Maxwell's Silver Hammer"). This year, John Lennon and Yoko Ono bring in Eric Clapton, Alan White, and Klaus Voorman to record as the Plastic Ono Band. Their album, *Live Peace at Toronto*, yields Lennon's first solo hit single, "Give Peace a Chance."

• The film *Monterey Pop* ignites a series of rock documentaries.

• Grammy winner Henry Mancini finally breaks the top 10 with his No. 1 single "Love Theme from *Romeo and Juliet*."

### New Recording Artists

Allman Brothers Band
David Bowie (in North America)
Bread
Chicago (Transit Authority)
Rita Coolidge
Crosby, Stills & Nash
John Denver
Roberta Flack
Grand Funk Railroad
Jackson 5
Waylon Jennings
Jethro Tull
Janis Joplin (solo)
Kool & the Gang
Led Zeppelin
Paul McCartney (solo)
Plastic Ono Band
Linda Ronstadt
Santana
Rod Stewart
Three Dog Night

## Obituaries

**Coleman Hawkins** (November 21, 1904–May 19, 1969). One of the most important musicians in the history of jazz, Hawkins was known as the father of the tenor sax. His milestone "Body and Soul" (1939), recorded as a favor to a producer, became a standard at his concerts.

*This year, 11-year-old Michael (bottom right) joins his brothers to form the Jackson 5.*

**Brian Jones** (February 28, 1944–July 3, 1969). The Rolling Stone guitarist is found dead at the bottom of his pool; an autopsy reveals high levels of alcohol and barbiturates in his bloodstream. Jones recently left the group, saying, "I no longer see eye to eye with the others over the discs we are cutting." Mick Taylor replaces him.

**James F. McHugh** (July 10, 1894–May 23, 1969). The U.S. composer wrote some 500 popular tunes, including "I'm in the Mood for Love" (1935), and 55 film and Broadway scores. Some controversy exists over whether McHugh or Fats Waller wrote the music for his most popular song "I Can't Give You Anything But Love" (1928).

**Russ Morgan** (April 29, 1904–August 7, 1969). The U.S. orchestra leader recorded 14 top-25 numbers between 1942 and 1951. His compositions included "You're Nobody 'til Somebody Loves You" (1944).

**Tony Spargo (Sbarbaro)** (June 27, 1897–October 30, 1969). The last surviving member of the Original Dixieland Jazz Band remained with the group until it disbanded in 1956.

## MOVIES

*Anne of the Thousand Days* (d. Charles Jarrott; color)—Richard Burton, Geneviève Bujold, Irene Papas, Anthony Quayle

*Butch Cassidy and the Sundance Kid* (d. George Roy Hill; color)—Paul Newman, Robert Redford, Katharine Ross

*Easy Rider* (d. Dennis Hopper; color)—Peter Fonda, Dennis Hopper, Jack Nicholson (color)

*The Love Bug* (Disney, d. Robert Stevenson; color)—Dean Jones, Michele Lee, David Tomlinson, Buddy Hackett

*Medium Cool* (d. Haskell Wexler; color)—Robert Forster, Verna Bloom

*Midnight Cowboy* (d. John Schlesinger; color)—Dustin Hoffman, Jon Voight, Sylvia Miles, Brenda Vaccaro

*Monterey Pop* (d. James Desmond and others; color)—Otis Redding, Mamas & the Papas, Jimi Hendrix, Janis Joplin, The Who, Animals, Jefferson Airplane

*On Her Majesty's Secret Service* (British, d. Peter Hunt; color)—George Lazenby, Diana Rigg, Gabriele Ferzetti, Telly Savalas

*Once Upon a Time in the West* (U.S.-Italian, d. Sergio Leone; color)—Charles Bronson, Henry Fonda, Claudia Cardinale, Jason Robards

*The Prime of Miss Jean Brodie* (British, d. Ronald Neame; color)—Maggie Smith, Robert Stephens, Pamela Franklin, Gordon Jackson

*The Sterile Cuckoo* (d. Alan J. Pakula; color)—Liza Minnelli, Tim McIntire, Wendell Burton

*Support Your Local Sheriff* (d. Burt Kennedy; color)—James Garner, Joan Hackett, Walter Brennan

*Sweet Charity* (d. Bob Fosse; color)—Shirley MacLaine, Sammy Davis, Jr., Ricardo Montalban, Chita Rivera

*Take the Money and Run* (d. Woody Allen; color)—Woody Allen, Janet Margolin

*Tell Them Willie Boy Is Here* (d. Abraham Polonsky; color)—Robert Redford, Katharine Ross, Robert Blake, Susan Clark

*They Shoot Horses, Don't They?* (d. Sydney Pollack; color)—Jane Fonda, Michael Sarrazin, Susannah York, Gig Young

*True Grit* (d. Henry Hathaway; color)—John Wayne, Glen Campbell, Kim Darby

*Where Eagles Dare* (d. Brian G. Hutton; color)—
Richard Burton, Clint Eastwood, Mary Ure
*The Wild Bunch* (d. Sam Peckinpah; color)—
William Holden, Ernest Borgnine, Robert
Ryan, Edmond O'Brien, Warren Oates, Ben
Johnson
*Z* (French-Algerian, d. Costa-Gavras; color)—
Yves Montand, Jean-Louis Trintignant,
Jacques Pérrin (color)

## Academy Awards

**April 14.** This year, Oscar moves to the Dorothy
Chandler Pavilion in the Los Angeles Music Center. And for the first time in Academy history, no
radio station broadcasts the ceremonies.

The 10 hosts include Ingrid Bergman, Burt Lancaster, Natalie Wood, Frank Sinatra, and Sidney
Poitier.

Best Picture—*Oliver!*
Best Actor—Cliff Robertson (*Charly*)
Best Actress—Katharine Hepburn (*The Lion in
Winter*) and Barbra Streisand (*Funny Girl*)
Best Director—Carol Reed (*Oliver!*)
Best Supporting Actor—Jack Albertson (*The
Subject Was Roses*)
Best Supporting Actress—Ruth Gordon (*Rose-
mary's Baby*)
Best Song—"The Windmills of Your Mind" from
*The Thomas Crown Affair*
Best Foreign Film—*War and Peace* (USSR)

For the first time, two performers receive exactly
the same number of votes—Katharine Hepburn
and Barbra Streisand. (In the Academy's early
years, two actors won if one came within three votes
of the other.) Hepburn, with previous wins in 1932,
1933 and 1967, collects her third Oscar—a record
for best actor or actress.

As usual, the older actress fails to appear, but
Streisand grabs the audience's full attention. Her
black outfit—loose top, with a high white collar,
black bow, and white-cuffed sleeves and her snug-
fitting pants, billowing below the knees—changes
from demure to transparent under the TV lights.

Viewers clearly see a second, shorter solid-black top
underneath and a bare bottom from the rear. With
millions watching tonight, the outfit inevitably
starts a see-through fashion trend.

Ruth Gordon, who bewitched Mia Farrow in
*Rosemary's Baby*, wins an Oscar with her fifth nomination. In films since 1915, the 72-year-old actress
delights the audience with her tongue-in-cheek
comment, "I can't tell you how encouraging a thing
like this is."

## News

**March.** Lawsuits protested the full frontal nudity
and simulated intercourse in *I Am Curious Yellow,*
but the Swedish film opens in New York following
a landmark court decision. Although critically
panned and barred in 10 states, the skin flick will
gross $5 million by September.

**October 24.** Elizabeth Taylor receives a 69.42-
carat diamond from her husband, Richard Burton.
Cartier in New York declines to reveal the purchase
price, but admits making a profit on its wholesale
price of $1.05 million.

**More news.** The real star of this year's big money-
maker, *The Love Bug,* is Herbie the Volkswagen.
Called upon to perform amazing stunts, the little
Beetle always comes through. But Herbie receives
expert offscreen assistance from mechanics: the
small car is fitted with a bus engine for some scenes
and a Porsche engine for others.

• A U.S. construction spurt in multitheater cinemas accounts for 62 of the 89 theaters built in Kansas City over the past 10 years. With one box office,
one refreshment stand, and a centrally located projection booth for several screens, exhibitors enjoy
low overhead, while audiences find parking plentiful
in the typical shopping center locations.

• Every actor and actress in Britain apparently
wanted to appear in *Oh! What a Lovely War,* a
musical satire of W.W.I. As a result, for the first and
only time, five Knights of the Realm appear in one
film: John Clements, John Gielgud, Laurence
Olivier, Michael Redgrave, and Ralph Richardson.
A hit in Britain, the movie fares less well in the
United States.

• Elvis Presley makes his 31st and last musical, the forgettable *Change of Habit,* co-starring Mary Tyler Moore, Barbara McNair, and Jane Elliot. Running a free clinic in a Puerto Rican neighborhood, the hip doctor performs just two songs, in a rock 'n' roll Catholic mass—"Change of Habit" and "Let Us Pray."

| Top Box Office Stars | Newcomers |
| --- | --- |
| Paul Newman | Jon Voight |
| John Wayne | Kim Darby |
| Steve McQueen | Glenn Campbell |
| Dustin Hoffman | Richard Benjamin |
| Clint Eastwood | Mark Lester |
| Sidney Poitier | Olivia Hussey |
| Lee Marvin | Leonard Whiting |
| Jack Lemmon | Ali MacGraw |
| Katharine Hepburn | Barbara Hershey |
| Barbra Streisand | Alan Alda |

## Top Money-Maker of the Year

*The Love Bug*

## Flop of the Year

*Hello Dolly!* 20th Century-Fox has squandered *Sound of Music* profits on three musical bombs—*Star, Doctor Dolittle,* and now *Hello Dolly!* The film version of Broadway's second most successful musical loses $15 million when audiences refuse to accept 26-year-old Barbra Streisand as a mature marriage maker.

## Quote of the Year

"Well, I'll tell you the truth now. I ain't a real cowboy, but I am one helluvah stud."
—Would-be gigolo Jon Voight bragging in *Midnight Cowboy* (Screenplay by Waldo Salt; based on the novel by James Leo Herlihy)

## Obituaries

**Judy Garland** (June 10, 1922–June 22, 1969). A child of stage performers, Garland scored early movie hits in the *Andy Hardy* series, with Mickey Rooney, and as Dorothy in *The Wizard of Oz* (1939). "Over the Rainbow," from that film, became her signature song.

Studio doctors put a chubby Garland on diet pills, then prescribed more drugs to counteract the chemical hyping. By age 21, the vulnerable singer-actress was making regular visits to a psychiatrist. Although increasingly unreliable, she made such classics as *Meet Me in St. Louis* (1944) and *Easter Parade* (1948) before MGM fired her in 1950.

An additional four films included the memorable *A Star Is Born* (1954), but recordings of intense performances at Carnegie Hall and the London Palladium in 1960, and other appearances, turned the singer into a cult figure.

But once again, Garland began arriving late, then missed performances completely as her mental and physical health deteriorated. The coroner rules her death as accidental barbiturate poisoning.

**Leo Gorcey** (1917–June 7, 1969). Wearing a beanie or tweed cap, he portrayed Spit in the Dead End Kids' movies between 1938 and 1942. Later, Gorcey helped create the comical Bowery Boys.

**Gabby Hayes** (May 7, 1885–February 9, 1969). The New Yorker played the grumbling, trusted sidekick to Hopalong Cassidy, and appeared alongside the likes of Roy Rogers, Gene Autry, and John Wayne in some 200 cowboy films and countless TV programs.

**Sonja Henie** (April 8, 1912–October 12, 1969). *See* Sports.

**Boris Karloff** (November 23, 1887–February 2, 1969). In 1931, Bela Lugosi turned down the role of Frankenstein and the English-born Karloff created the unforgettable character that brought him fame. But appearances in other horror masterpieces, including *The Mummy* (1932), forever typecast the actor as a monster or mad scientist.

**Thelma Ritter** (February 14, 1905–February 4, 1969). After breaking into movies at age 42, the raspy-voiced native of Brooklyn went on to become one of Hollywood's best-known character actresses. Nominated for six Oscars—an unprecedented four times in a row—Ritter never won.

**Josef von Sternberg** (1894–December 22, 1969). The Austrian-born director was best known for the German film *The Blue Angel* (1930), starring his discovery Marlene Dietrich.

**Robert Taylor** (August 5, 1911–June 8, 1969). A matinee idol during the 1930s, Taylor gradually shed his ladies'-man image after the war with films like *Quo Vadis?* (1951). Before he turned to TV in the 1960s, he set an actor's one-studio record—27 years at MGM in approximately 70 films.

# TELEVISION AND RADIO

## *New Prime-Time TV Programs*

"The Bold Ones" (September 14, 1969–June 22, 1973)—An umbrella title for rotating dramatic series: "The New Doctors," with E. G. Marshall, David Hartman, John Saxon (1969–1972); "The Lawyers," with Burl Ives, Joseph Campanella, James Farentino (1969–1972); "The Protectors," with Leslie Nielsen, Hari Rhodes (1969–1970); "The Senator," with Hal Holbrook (1970–1971)

"The Brady Bunch" (September 26, 1969–August 30, 1974; Situation Comedy)—Robert Reed, Florence Henderson, Ann B. Davis

"The Courtship of Eddie's Father" (September 17, 1969–June 14, 1972; Situation Comedy)—Bill Bixby, Brandon Cruz, Miyoshi Umeki

"The Dick Cavett Show" (May 26, 1969–December 29, 1972; Talk/Variety)—Host: Dick Cavett. *Note:* In January 1973, the show will begin appearing as part of the new "ABC Wide World of Entertainment."

"The Glen Campbell Goodtime Hour" (January 29, 1969–June 13, 1972; Musical Variety)—Glen Campbell

"Hee Haw" (June 15, 1969–July 13, 1971; Variety)—Cohosts: Buck Owens, Roy Clark

"The Jim Nabors Hour" (September 25, 1969–May 20, 1971; Comedy Variety)—Jim Nabors, Frank Sutton, Ronnie Schell

"Let's Make a Deal" (February 1969–August 30, 1971; Quiz/Audience Participation)—Emcee: Monty Hall. *Note:* The program continues as a daytime series.

"Love, American Style" (September 29, 1969–January 11, 1974; Comedy Anthology)—Repertory

"Marcus Welby, M.D." (September 23, 1969–   ; Medical Drama)—Robert Young, James Brolin, Elena Verdugo

"Medical Center" (September 24, 1969–   ; Medical Drama)—James Daly, Chad Everett

"The Merv Griffin Show" (August 18, 1969–February 11, 1972; Talk)—Host: Merv Griffin; announcer: Arthur Treacher

"Room 222" (September 17, 1969–January 11, 1974; School Drama)—Lloyd Haynes, Denise Nicholas, Michael Constantine, Karen Valentine

"This Is Tom Jones" (February 7, 1969–January 15, 1971; Musical Variety)—Tom Jones

*Comedians Dan Rowan and Dick Martin watch Goldie Hawn and Arte Johnson at the "Laugh-In" joke wall.*

## Emmy Awards 1968–1969 (June 8, 1969)

Drama Series—"NET Playhouse" (NET)
Variety Series—"Rowan & Martin's Laugh-In" (NBC)
Comedy Series—"Get Smart" (NBC)
Best Actor in a Series—Carl Betz ("Judd for the Defense," ABC)
Best Actress in a Series—Barbara Bain ("Mission: Impossible," CBS)
Best Comedian in a Series—Don Adams ("Get Smart," NBC)
Best Comedienne in a Series—Hope Lange ("The Ghost and Mrs. Muir," NBC)

## News

**April 4.** Two years ago, market research found that a variety show aimed at the 15–30 age bracket could compete against "Bonanza" in the Sunday 9:00 P.M. time slot. CBS picked the "Smothers Brothers," but Dick and particularly Tom never matched the network profile. Antiwar, pro-civil rights, their beliefs made the program a political hot potato. Network executives yanked a skit on film censorship, cut Pete Seeger's antiwar song, and blocked Pat Paulsen from appearing with his "presidential" campaign. The brothers in turn delayed submission of the finished script until just before air time.

Finally, the controversy becomes too big, and CBS, despite solid ratings, cancels the show today. The network holds firm under a barrage of protest, and the Smothers brothers launch a lawsuit.

**May 7.** Because of the health hazards connected with smoking, CBC had insisted that tobacco commercials sell the brand name rather than smoking pleasure and then only after 9:00 P.M. Today, the Canadian network terminates all radio and TV tobacco advertising (following the fulfillment of current contracts).

**May 18–26.** Dr. Peter Goldmark developed a field-sequential color TV camera for CBS 28 years ago, but his technology fell victim to RCA's all-electronic compatible system. Through these nine days, the astronauts on board *Apollo 10* use his camera for the first color transmission from space.

**July 20.** A complex series of satellite hookups transmits today's moonwalk to some 600 million viewers—one-fifth of the world's population. The linkup required the on-duty assistance of an estimated 40,000 technical and programming staff in 49 countries, and cost some $55 billion. In the United States, the Apollo mission attracts 93.9 percent of the nation's households.

**September.** With no explanation offered, either in a press release or on the program itself, Dick Sargent replaces Dick York as Darrin Stevens on the ABC sitcom "Bewitched."

**September 28.** Leonard Nimoy appears in his first episode of "Mission: Impossible"; the former Mr. Spock replaces Martin Landau, who left with wife Barbara Bain following a contract dispute. Nimoy's first series, "Star Trek," finished at the beginning of the month. Like other canceled programs, the sci-fi adventure will soon enter syndication.

**October 5.** Broadcast through to April 4, Britain's "Forsyte Saga" becomes one of the season's highlights on PBS. The 26-episode BBC dramatization of the John Galsworthy novels stars Eric Porter as Soames, Kenneth More as his cousin, Susan Hampshire as his daughter Fleur, and Nyree Dawn Porter as Irene.

**October 22.** Reports leak that the FCC will free CATV from all local curbs and allow commercials at natural program breaks. Those systems with over 3,500 subscribers must originate their own programs and honor the equal time ruling. CATV stock value rises immediately and coverage will quickly increase from 3.6 million to 4.5 million people.

**November 10.** Designed to teach disadvantaged city kids their letters and numbers, "Sesame Street" entertains as well with skits, games, songs, stories, and the Muppets. The program's goals were thoroughly researched by the nonprofit Children's Television Workshop, but some psychologists worry that children will come to expect a quick "entertainment" pace at school. Still, within two years, preschoolers in some 7.5 million American households will tune in daily. And later research will find that fans of the award-winning program enter the early grades better prepared.

**November 17.** Some 48 million Americans tune in to "The Tonight Show" for the wedding of Tiny Tim and Miss Vicky. The 40-odd-year-old ukulele-playing singer and his 17-year-old bride promise to be sweet, gentle, patient, kind, and "not puffed up." The marriage will end in early 1974.

**December 25.** In a typical attempt to avoid controversy, CBS censors cut Carol Burnett's request, made on Merv Griffin's pretaped Christmas show, for viewers to write letters to Mrs. Coretta King appealing for peace. Elke Sommer, who with Burnett belongs to "People for Peace," becomes upset when her December 29 plea is deleted as well.

**More news.** Fred Bauer debuts the first music video program. All weekend on Channel 36 in Atlanta, "The Music Connection" telecasts spliced-together tape—in several different versions–for each song. A DJ of sorts provides a voice-over, and the news, weather, and sports run across the bottom of the screen. The program will continue through next year and into 1971 before the production group disbands.

## TV Commercials

Alka-Seltzer—Movie-star gangster George Raft, sitting in a prison dining hall, disgustedly throws down his fork, grabs his tin cup, and pounding the table begins to shout, "Alka-Seltzer! Alka-Seltzer!" The commercial ends with the chants of hundreds of men echoing through the hall.

Minute Maid—Bing Crosby, who at one time advertised the product on his radio show, agrees to a television voice-over if the company will use his family instead. The singer will appear in the ads himself in 1973.

Right Guard—Bill Fiore moves into a new apartment and, on his first bleary morning, discovers he must share his pass-through medicine cabinet with jolly neighbor Chuck McCann and his Gilette deodorant. ("One shot and I'm good for the whole day.") The single episode evolves into a three-year comic opera.

Virginia Slims—"You've come a long way, baby"

first appears on TV, advertising Virginia Slims cigarettes to women.

> *Statistics:* 1950 was television's first year of profit: broadcast revenues totaled $44.5 million. This year, revenues reach $553.6 million.

# SPORTS

## Winners

### Baseball

World Series—New York Mets (NL), 4 games; Baltimore Orioles (AL), 1 game
Player of the Year—Harmon Killebrew (Minnesota Twins, AL); Willie McCovey (San Francisco Giants, NL)
Rookie of the Year—Lou Piniella (Kansas City Royals, AL); Ted Sizemore (Los Angeles Dodgers, NL)

### Football

NFL Championship—Minnesota Vikings 27, Cleveland Browns 7
AFL Championship—Kansas City Chiefs 17, Oakland Raiders 7
Super Bowl IV (January 11, 1970)—Kansas City Chiefs 23, Minnesota Vikings 7
College Bowls (January 4, 1969)—
    Rose Bowl, Ohio State 27, USC 16
    Cotton Bowl, Texas 36, Tennessee 13
    Orange Bowl, Penn State 15, Kansas 14
    Sugar Bowl, Arkansas 16, Georgia 2
Heisman Trophy—Steve Owens (Oklahoma, HB)
Grey Cup—Ottawa Rough Riders 29, Saskatchewan Roughriders 11

### Basketball

NBA Championship—Boston Celtics, 4 games; LA Lakers, 3 games
MVP of the Year—Wes Unseld (Baltimore Bullets)

Rookie of the Year—Wes Unseld (Baltimore
Bullets)
NCAA Championship—UCLA 92, Purdue 72

## Tennis

U.S. National (last year)—Men, Stan Smith
(vs. Robert Lutz); Women, Margaret Court
(vs. Virginia Wade)
U.S. Open—Men, Rod Laver (vs. Tony
Roche); Women, Margaret Court (vs. Nancy
Richey)
Wimbledon—Men, Rod Laver (vs. John New-
combe); Women, Ann Jones (vs. Billie Jean
King)

## Golf

Masters—George Archer
U.S. Open—Orville Moody
British Open—Tony Jacklin

## Hockey

Stanley Cup—Montreal Canadiens, 4 games;
St. Louis Blues, 0 games

## Ice Skating

World Championship—Men, Tim Wood
(U.S.); Women, Gabriele Seyfert (East Ger-
many)
U.S. National—Men, Tim Wood; Women,
Janet Lynn
Canadian National—Men, Jay Humphry;
Women, Linda Carbonetto

## Kentucky Derby

Majestic Prince—Bill Hartack, jockey

## Athlete of the Year

Male—Tom Seaver (Baseball)
Female—Debbie Meyer (Swimming)

## Last Season

Thomas Flores (Football)

Doug Harvey (Hockey)
Mickey Mantle (Baseball)
Roger Maris (Baseball)
Don Meredith (Football)
Pierre Pilote (Hockey)
Bill Russell (Basketball)
Allan Stanley (Hockey)

## News

**January 12.** While in training for the Super Bowl, quarterback Joe Namath guaranteed the New York Jets would beat the heavily favored Baltimore Colts. Today, his team wins in a stunning 16–7 upset— the first Super Bowl victory for the AFL.

In June, under pressure from Commissioner Rozelle, Broadway Joe retires rather than sell his restaurant, a known hangout for gamblers. But the 26-year-old changes his mind the following month, and decides to give up the eatery and stay in the game.

**February 7.** As the first woman jockey to compete against men on a major U.S. track, Diane Crump comes under enormous pressure when six male jockeys opt out of the race. But the trainer wisely puts the 19-year-old up on a 48–1 shot and she finishes 10th in a 12-horse field. (At Tropical Park this year, 11 male jockeys try to intimidate another female jockey by vandalizing her trailer; they all receive fines.) In 1970, Crump will become the first woman to ride in the Kentucky Derby.

**March 1.** "I can't hit when I want to. I can't go from first to third when I need to. There's no use trying." Mickey Mantle announces his retirement from major league baseball at age 36. An infection from a kicked shin in college football, a badly sprained knee in the 1951 World Series, the Yankee outfielder has been plagued with injuries. He played through pain in many seasons, but his aching knees have finally betrayed him.

In an 18-year career with the Yankees, the game's first power-hitting switch-hitter chalked up 536 HR to finish third in the all-time list behind Babe Ruth and Willie Mays. Still, the defensive outfielder was an all-round offensive threat with more runs scored (1,677) than driven in (1,509). A member of seven championship teams, he retires with six World Series records, including HR (18), RBI (40), and walks (43).

**March 2.** At a drag strip near Covington, Georgia, a race car hurtles off the track into a group of spectators, killing 12 and injuring another 50. The American and National Hot Rod Associations had refused to sanction the unsafe facility.

**March 28.** The Czechs defeat the Soviets in final-round play at the world championship hockey tournament in Stockholm. The victory, coming just eight months after the Warsaw Pact invasion of Czechoslovakia, sets off widespread anti-Soviet demonstrations in Prague.

**April 7.** In 1869, the Cincinnati Red Stockings became the first professional baseball team. In the game's centennial year, the major leagues expand to 24 teams.

The NL adds the Montreal Expos and San Diego Padres while the AL brings in the Kansas City Royals and Seattle Pilots. And in the first format change since 1901, the two leagues split into east and west divisions. Divisional winners will meet in a five-game championship playoff prior to the World Series.

Today, for the first time, an American team faces a baseball team from Canada. The Expos win 11–10 in New York, and a week later beat the Cards 8–7 in the first game on Canadian soil.

To increase offense this year, six ballparks shorten their outfields. As a result, average runs per game jump from 6.84 to 8.16 and the combined team batting average rises from .237 to .248.

**July 21.** On the eve of the All-Star game, American baseball writers and broadcasters announce the Greatest Team Ever (from single-team fan nominations): Lou Gehrig at first, Rogers Hornsby at second, Harold Pie Traynor at third, Honus Wagner at short, Joe DiMaggio, Babe Ruth, and Ty Cobb in the outfield, Mickey Cochrane behind home plate, and right-handed Walter Johnson and left-handed Lefty Grove on the mound. John McGraw is named manager.

Next month, temporary Baseball Commissioner Bowie Kuhn receives his formal appointment.

**October 16.** Since their first season in 1962, the

New York Mets have finished in last or second-to-last place. This year, with strong pitching from 24-year-old Tom Seaver, 25-year-old Jerry Koosman, 22-year-old Nolan Ryan, and 25-year-old Tug McGraw, manager Gil Hodges and the Mets took their division and swept the Braves in the playoff.

Today, baseball's notorious cellar-dwellers win their fourth game in five to capture the World Series. New Yorkers, still recovering from the loss of the Dodgers and the Giants, literally dance in the streets.

## Records

**March 2.** Last night, Bruin center Phil Esposito broke the single-season 97-point scoring record shared by Blackhawks Stan Mikita and Bobby Hull.

*In his NBA debut game, Lew Alcindor leverages off Piston Otto Moore. At the end of his rookie season, Alcindor (later Kareem Abdul-Jabbar) will place second in overall scoring with an average 28.8 points per game.*

Tonight, Espo becomes the first NHL player to reach the 100-point plateau. He finishes the season with an amazing 126.

**March 22.** UCLA wins an unparalleled third consecutive NCAA basketball championship and its fifth in six years. MVP for a record third time, center Lew Alcindor signs with the Milwaukee Bucks for over $1 million. The ABA offered $3.25 million.

**August 5.** Pirate Willie Stargell slams a home run over the right-field pavilion in Dodger Stadium, 506 feet from the plate. The 28-year-old is the only player ever to hit out of the Los Angeles park.

**September 8.** With a victory at the U.S. Open, Australian Rod Laver wins an unprecedented second Grand Slam. His first in 1962 was played against other amateurs; this time, tennis tournaments were open to professionals.

**September 21.** In a game against Denver, New York Jet Steve O'Neal kicks the longest punt in the history of pro football—98 yards.

## What They Said

"There is no principle involved in my holdout. Just money," says Heisman Trophy winner O. J. Simpson. On August 10, Buffalo Bills owner Ralph Wilson announces an agreement; Simpson will receive more than $80,000 a year. (*Sports Illustrated*, July 28)

## Obituaries

**Maureen Connolly** (September 17, 1934–June 21, 1969). The U.S. tennis player won three national titles, three Wimbledon championships, and a Grand Slam (the first ever by a woman) before a horseback-riding accident ended her career in 1954. She died of stomach cancer.

**Walter Hagen** (December 21, 1892–October 5, 1969). One of the giants of professional golf, "The Haig" won 2 U.S. Opens (1914 and 1919), 4 British Opens (1922, 1924, 1928, 1929), and 11 other major tournaments. A gallery favorite with his antics and elegant clothes, Hagen used his clout to gain better treatment for players, including the right to change in the clubhouse rather than the caddie shack. He retired in 1929.

**Sonja Henie** (April 8, 1912–October 12, 1969). The Norwegian figure skater held the world title from 1927 to 1936 and won gold in three consecutive Olympics. Through those years, her short costumes (rather than ankle-length skirts) and dance choreography revolutionized the sport. Spurred on by Fred Astaire's accomplishments in dance, Henie turned professional in 1936 and, over the following 12 years, skated through 11 Hollywood films.

**Edward L. Lee** (1906–May 18, 1969). The U.S. billiards player won more championships (including 20 nationals between 1931 and 1964) than any other player.

**Rocky Marciano** (September 1, 1923–August 31, 1969). The U.S. boxer turned professional in 1947. Dangerous with either hand, the 5'11" Brockton Blockbuster earned a shot at the title within five years. On September 23, 1952, he dropped Jersey Joe Walcott in the 13th round to win the heavyweight championship of the world. Marciano defended his title seven times, then retired undefeated in 1956. He died in a plane crash.

# 1970

The hope that a new decade would see Americans extricate themselves from Vietnam ends with the incursion into neutral Cambodia. Campuses across the country erupt in protest and four students die at Kent State. Nixon, in reaction, supports FBI strikes against "revolutionaries" and grants Washington police officers "no-knock" authority. With the recent rash of terrorist bombings, many Americans back stronger law enforcement.

In other news, Americans express their concern for the environment with the first Earth Day. California passes no-fault divorce law, airlines fly the first 747s, the posties strike, and women thoroughly reject the new midi. The Beatles split, as do Simon & Garfunkel, while Jimi Hendrix and Janis Joplin both die at the age of 27. Movie theaters screen Love Story, M*A*S*H, Patton, and Airport, television introduces "The Mary Tyler Moore Show" and "The Partridge Family," and newspapers offer a new comic strip by Gary Trudeau.

Elsewhere in the world, de Gaulle dies, the October Crisis tears at Canada, and the PLO hijacks several airplanes. In Peru, an earthquake kills 67,000 while in East Pakistan the worst natural disaster in history claims the lives of 1 million people.

## NEWS

**January 3.** The Gallup poll of the most admired American men ranks President Richard Nixon first, evangelist Billy Graham second, and Vice-President Spiro Agnew third.

**January 5.** Joseph "Jack" Yablonski and his wife and daughter are found murdered in their home. Last month, Yablonski lost a bitter campaign for the presidency of the United Mine Workers (UMW) to W. A. "Tony" Boyle, but had legally contested the outcome. In 1974, Boyle—already in prison for using union funds to make illegal political con-

tributions—will be found guilty of the killings and sentenced to three consecutive life terms.

**January 12.** After 31 months of civil war, Biafra capitulates to the Nigerian federal government. Lagos reorganizes the rebel nation into three states then generously applies growing petroleum revenues to rehabilitate the millions of homeless people still facing starvation.

Some 2 million Ibo died during the war. Many believe the international relief effort, while humanitarian in intent, only served to prolong the hostilities and suffering.

**January 21.** At the end of 1969, U.S. negotiators submitted a list of 1,406 Americans missing in action and asked North Vietnam for confirmation of their status as prisoners. Finally, in response, the Communist representatives refuse to publish the names saying, "We do not consider the captured pilots prisoners of war. They are criminals."

But before the end of April, Hanoi gives the names of 335 American prisoners to a U.S. antiwar group with links to the families of detained servicemen. The Defense Department declares the list to be inaccurate.

**February.** The 1967 Arab-Israeli cease-fire broke the following year when the UAR shelled Israel and the superior Israeli Air Force struck back at will, hitting deep within the Arab territory. In desperation, UAR President Nasser invited the USSR to organize his air defenses.

This month, as Cairo acknowledges Moscow's commitment, the Soviets have an estimated 4,000 military advisors in place; their number will increase to 10,000 during the year.

**February 28.** Newspapers publish a confidential memo from presidential adviser Daniel Moynihan to Nixon: "The time may have come when the issue of race could benefit from a period of benign neglect." Enraged civil rights leaders charge the administration with a "calculated, aggressive, and systematic" effort to "wipe out" two decades of civil rights gains. Moynihan later verifies the memo, but maintains he meant blacks would fare better if both ends of the political spectrum were less vocal.

**March 6.** Under congressional fire for violating the 1969 Senate resolution prohibiting the use of U.S. troops in Laos, President Nixon outlines for the first time the full extent of American involvement. U.S. assistance—close air support, equipment, training, and logistics—has risen, but he insists that no U.S. combat troops are fighting in Laos and no plans exist to introduce them.

**March 6.** A huge explosion demolishes a Greenwich Village townhouse, killing three people. When the dead are identified as Weathermen, authorities conclude that the house was a bomb factory.

The U.S. experiences modern terrorism firsthand this year by the Weathermen, Revolutionary Force 9, and other extremists. The FBI will tally 3,000 bombings and 50,000 threatened bombings across the country.

**March 16.** The State Department grants American citizens permission to visit the People's Republic of China for any legitimate purpose. Previously only doctors, scholars, newspeople, and other professionals could travel to the Communist nation.

**March 17.** The United States casts its first veto in the U.N. Security Council, blocking censure of Britain for not using force against the Rhodesian government. The next day, the council passes a compromise resolution.

**April 1.** Led by Cesar Chavez, the United Farm Workers Organizing Committee and two California Coachella Valley grape growers sign the first U.S. labor contract to cover table-grape pickers. (Chavez led the NFWA strike in 1965, then merged with another association in 1966 to form UFWOC.)

During the four-year strike, Chavez's philosophy of nonviolence made him a national figure. The farm workers won contracts with wine-grape growers early in the struggle, but table-grape growers refused to bargain. A boycott of the fruit, supported worldwide by labor and the buying public, had reduced U.S. grape sales drastically, forcing the owners to settle.

---

*Statistics:* Price comparisons between 1947 and 1970 show coffee up 44.2 cents to 91.1 cents per pound, bacon up 17.2 cents to 94.9 cents per pound, bread up 11.8 cents to 24.3 cents per loaf, and milk up 26.7 cents to 65.9 cents a half gallon (delivered). Over the same period, a dozen eggs dropped 8.2 cents to 61.4 cents and a pound of margarine, with various taxes removed, fell 11 cents to 29.8 cents.

---

**April 2.** In Massachusetts, representatives (129–29) and senators (49–3) have challenged the legality of the Vietnam War in the absence of a congressional declaration of war. Governor Francis Sargent signs the bill "to permit its sponsors to seek their day in the nation's highest court."

On November 9, the Supreme Court refuses (6–3) to hear the suit. Justice William O. Douglas, in dissenting, writes, "The question of an unconstitutional war is neither academic nor 'political' and the court should grant Massachusetts a hearing."

The state files another suit, this time against Defense Secretary Melvin Laird, but the Boston federal court will dismiss the case in 1971. Several other states undertake similar measures.

**April 7.** After hearing less than 20 minutes of testimony from four witnesses, a Massachusetts grand jury fails to indict anyone in the death of Mary Jo Kopechne. But, in closing the case the jury clears the way for the release of the January inquest transcript and the judge's report.

In extensive testimony, Ted Kennedy asserted that his swim across the channel after the accident left him in a state of confusion and exhaustion. His lawyers submitted affidavits and medical reports showing he had suffered a concussion, which caused disorientation. Kennedy was not closely cross-examined because Judge Boyle held that would be inappropriate in an inquest.

Nonetheless, in his report Boyle found neither "responsible" nor "probable" the senator's testimony that the two left the party to catch the ferry—Kopechne spoke to no one and left her purse behind—or that a wrong turn took Kennedy onto the dirt road to the bridge—both had driven over the same bridge earlier in the day. The judge concludes there is "probable cause" to believe the senator was driving negligently and such driving might have contributed to Kopechne's death.

Kennedy rejects the conclusions as "not justified," maintaining he answered all questions truthfully. He states the tragedy of the event will never end for those concerned.

The people of Massachusetts will reelect the senator by a wide margin.

**April 22.** In the largest demonstration in human history, some 30 million Americans protest against the pollution of their environment. Senator Gaylord Nelson (D., Wisc.) originally suggested an environmental teach-in to raise public awareness, but youth groups planned a much more active protest for Earth Day.

Across the nation, people attend huge rallies, clean up small communities, conduct mass phone-ins to polluters or give them special "awards," and hold mock car funerals. The NEA later estimates that 10 million school children took part.

**April 30.** President Nixon stuns the nation with the announcement of a major offensive into Cambodia. For 10 years, Chief of State Prince Sihanouk had kept his country from war by allowing the North Vietnamese to use the eastern provinces for transport, storage, and sanctuary. But last month, while Sihanouk was in Moscow, Lon Nol seized power and immediately appealed to the United States for aid in preventing a Communist takeover. On April 25, the Nixon administration began secretly shipping small arms to Cambodia, and yesterday sent in 20,000 U.S. and South Vietnamese troops.

Nixon explains that the 6- to 8-week "incursion" will drive the Communists out of Cambodia and guarantee the continued success of Vietnamization. Critics charge that, in choosing a military solution over diplomacy, the White House has widened the war in Southeast Asia.

**May 4.** President Nixon calls college radicals "bums" and soldiers in Vietnam "the greatest" when the Cambodian offensive ignites a wave of protest on campuses across the country. At Kent State University in Ohio, students rally for a noon demonstration.

Yesterday, Kent Mayor Leroy Satrom, without the knowledge of university authorities, asked Governor James Rhodes to call in the National Guard. The Guardsmen order the students to disperse, but the young people respond with taunts and rocks. The Guardsmen lob tear gas canisters and the students throw them back. The soldiers retreat to higher ground, kneel, and open fire with their M-1 rifles. In less than 15 seconds, 67 shots kill 4 students—Allison Krause, Jeff Miller, William Schroeder, and Sandra Scheuer—and wound 9 others.

Guardsmen claim sniper fire forced a response, but an FBI investigation concludes that their excuse was likely fabricated after the fatal shootings. The Presidential Commission on Campus Unrest, as well, finds no evidence of a sniper.

In October, a special grand jury—which is not given the FBI report—indicts 24 students and one faculty member but no Guardsmen. All charges will be dropped, but Attorney General Mitchell will refuse to mount an inquiry.

**May 5.** A newspaper photograph of an anguished 14-year-old Mary Ann Vecchio, kneeling over one of the wounded Kent State students, galvanizes American college and university students.

On May 9, some 60,000–100,000 peaceful demonstrators gather in Washington to protest the Cambodian incursion. A more conciliatory White House waives the required 15-day advance notice, and President Nixon makes a surprise predawn visit to talk with students at the Lincoln Memorial. By May 10, the National Student Strike Center reports 448 colleges and universities closed or on strike.

Peace protests in turn raise counterdemonstrations. One of the largest, a noontime rally in New York on May 20, draws an estimated 60,000–150,000 construction workers, longshoremen, and others supporting White House policy.

*Statistics:* With an estimated college and university enrollment of 7.8 million in the United States, at least 36 of every 100 Americans between ages 18 and 21 currently attend a school of higher learning.

**May 14.** City police and highway patrolmen fire into a crowd of students outside a women's dormitory at Jackson State College in Mississippi, killing a student and a high school senior and injuring 12.

An October report from the Commission on Campus Unrest scathingly accuses the Jackson police of "unreasonable, unjustified overreaction" and concludes that a significant cause of the tragedy was "the confidence of white officers that, if they fire weapons during a black campus disturbance, they will face neither stern departmental discipline nor criminal prosecution or conviction."

A federal grand jury in December fails to return any indictments.

**May 19.** Hosea Williams, vice president of SCLC, leads 10,000 people from Perry to Atlanta to protest deaths during May riots in Augusta, and at Kent State and Jackson State College. But the "March Against Repression"—one of the largest gatherings in the South in five years—fails to reignite the civil rights movement.

**May 31.** The most disastrous earthquake in South American history kills an estimated 67,000 in Peru. The tremors (7.75 on the Richter scale), shake loose tons of ice, rock, and mud from the slopes of Huascaran, the nation's highest mountain. The avalanche roars downward at an estimated 100 mph into the Huariles Valley and buries the entire city of Yungay and 20,000 inhabitants. (Only some 200 townspeople escape to higher ground in the cemetery.) The nearby city of Ranrahirca, rebuilt after a 1962 landslide killed 2,700 townspeople, is destroyed once again.

Because Peru is ill-equipped for rescue operations, and international relief is slow to reach inaccessible areas, thousands die from their injuries.

**June 15.** In a 5–3 vote, the U.S. Supreme Court broadens conscientious objector status to include those sincerely objecting to all wars on moral or ethical grounds. A further decision in 1971 settles the unresolved issue of draft exemption for the Vietnam War. The Court finds (8–1) that a conscientious objector must oppose "participation in war in any form." Writing the majority opinion, Thurgood Marshall argues that a military exemption not administered fairly and uniformly "might corrode the spirit of public service and the values of willing performance of a citizen's duty that are the very heart of a free government."

**June 18.** British voters turn out the Labour government of Harold Wilson, giving the Conservatives a 30-seat majority. Edward Heath, age 53, takes office as prime minister. Only one preelection poll had predicted a Conservative win.

**June 29.** U.S. forces pull out of Cambodia one day before the presidential deadline. Altogether 354 Americans were killed and 1,689 wounded.

During the offensive, the Senate for the first time moved to limit the war powers of the Oval Office. The Cooper-Church Amendment, approved on the

30th, requires congressional consent before the president can spend funds to keep U.S. forces in Cambodia, send military advisors to Cambodia, provide air combat support, or provide financial assistance to advisers or troops in countries aiding Cambodia.

Eventually the amendment will be attached to a foreign aid authorization bill, which will become law on January 5, 1971.

At the same time, the Senate attaches an important amendment to the Military Sales Act—the repeal of the 1964 Gulf of Tonkin resolution used by President Johnson as congressional authorization to escalate the war in Vietnam. Nixon will sign the act into law on January 12, 1971, but as commander-in-chief of U.S. military forces he will deny the importance of the Tonkin resolution in waging war.

**July 1.** Repealing an 1830 law, New York State makes abortion a matter between a woman and her doctor up to the 24th week of pregnancy. Governor Rockefeller credits the passage of the nation's most liberal abortion law to pressure from women's groups and sponsorship by the Republican party.

**July 29.** Three harsh anticrime bills fulfill the president's pledge to strengthen law enforcement. The District of Columbia Criminal Justice Act gives Washington officers controversial "no-knock" authority to enter private homes (with a warrant but without identifying themselves), approves up to 60 days of "preventive" detention for "dangerous" suspects, and eliminates jury trial for juveniles.

The second bill, the Organized Crime Control Act (signed October 15), eliminates witness-immunity laws and authorizes up to 25 years in prison for "dangerous and adult special offenders" and the death penalty for anyone convicted of a fatality in a college bombing.

The last bill, the Drug Abuse Control Act (signed October 27), reduces simple possession from a felony to a misdemeanor but increases the penalty for first-offense trafficking to 10 years and authorizes another no-knock provision for evidence retrieval.

**August 7.** Jonathan Jackson, the 17-year-old brother of a Soledad prisoner, smuggles guns into a San Rafael courtroom and frees a defendant and two convict witnesses. The four men take Judge Harold Haley, the prosecutor, and three women jurors hostage, to exchange for Jackson's brother and others, and bundle them into a van.

Some 100 law officers surrounding the building open fire as the vehicle pulls away. The judge, with a sawed-off shotgun taped to his head, dies immediately. The district attorney seizes a weapon and, in the ensuing gun battle, is seriously wounded; three of the convicts are killed.

The guns belong to Angela Davis, an important figure in the establishment of a Marxist collective by the Soledad Brothers. When she flees, the FBI places her on its 10 most-wanted list.

**August 12.** Under the leadership of Willy Brandt, West Germany formally acknowledges the Soviet W.W.II territorial gains in Eastern Europe. Reinforcing the Bonn-Moscow Treaty, the Treaty of Warsaw on December 7 "forever" accepts the 1945 transfer to Poland of 40,000 square miles of former German territory.

**August 18.** Despite angry public protest by Americans and a diplomatic protest by the Bahamian government, the U.S. Army sinks an old Liberty ship with 66 tons of GB nerve gas on board, just 282 miles off the Florida coast. The army acknowledges that corrosion and the extreme pressure at 16,000 feet will create leaks in the concrete and steel containers, but insists sea water will neutralize the gas within 10 hours. But the Pentagon admits that experts failed to locate and remove from the cargo a container holding 10 pounds of nerve agent VX, a far more lethal gas.

**August 26.** Acting on a suggestion by feminist Betty Friedan, a loose coalition of women's groups calls a "Women's Strike for Equality" to celebrate the 50th anniversary of American women gaining the right to vote. Thousands rally and march in East Coast cities (New York draws the largest, at 40,000), in Los Angeles, San Francisco, and numerous smaller centers, demanding equal opportunity in jobs and education, free 24-hour day-care centers, and free abortions on demand.

A week later, a *Life* magazine article underscores the unequal status of American women: 26 states deny women permission to enter certain industries or occupations, and 20 states prohibit women from working more than 8 hours a day or 48 hours a week, effectively blocking their advancement in workplaces requiring overtime.

The federal government has already begun to move against some restrictions. In June, the Labor Department announced sex bias guidelines for federal contracts. On July 20, the Justice Department filed the first suit against sexual discrimination in employment under the 1964 Civil Rights Act. That company agrees, in a December 7 settlement, to correct discriminatory practices.

**September.** During the 1969–1970 school year, civil rights leaders and the Commission on Civil Rights expressed concern that a hesitant administration was endangering nationwide school integration. But in late June, HEW announced that school districts must eliminate racial discrimination by the fall or risk losing federal aid.

With pressure from Washington, 900 Southern school districts desegregate this month. Yet because most black students in the South live in all-black neighborhoods, half continue to attend schools with few or no white students. Some districts bus white and black children to other schools to achieve a better racial balance, but busing has become a major issue in the United States. A North Carolina case has been referred to the Supreme Court.

**September 17.** Civil war breaks out between forces loyal to King Hussein and Palestinian guerrillas based in Jordan for cross-border raids on Israel. In recent months, the Palestinians have increasingly challenged the authority of the Jordanian government. And when King Hussein accepted a cease-fire with the Israelis and began peace negotiations in late August, the guerrillas struck out in fury, blowing up several hijacked airliners in the Jordanian desert.

Syrian tanks move in to support the Palestinians, but Soviet pressure and American and Israeli threats of intervention force their early withdrawal. The Jordanian Army slowly regains the upper hand, and hostilities end on September 25. Casualty estimates range from 1,500 to 5,000 dead and up to 10,000 injured.

Over the next year, the Palestinian guerrillas, with the exception of Al-Fatah under Yasir Arafat, will move their headquarters to Lebanon.

**September 21.** The first major oil strike in the British sector of the North Sea is discovered some 110 miles northeast of Aberdeen, Scotland. The North Sea Basin, divided equally in an agreement between Britain and Norway, will prove to be the largest oil field outside of the Middle East. But the region's average of 273 days of bad weather a year will make oil extraction very difficult.

**September 25–30.** Strong winds in 100-degree-Fahrenheit heat fan a suspected arsonist's blaze into the worst brushfires in California to date. Some 8,000–10,000 men, including firefighters from Montana and 2,000 convicts, battle an inferno that consumes 160,000 acres and forces more than 50,000 in San Diego County to flee their homes. Earlier fires in Los Angeles County ravaged another 100,000 acres. Altogether 14 people die.

**September 26.** The U.S. Commission on Campus Unrest reports that the unparalleled crisis on American campuses could threaten "the very survival of the nation." Blame lies equally with extremist students who bomb and burn, university administrators who handle confrontation poorly, and law officers who needlessly assault or shoot students. Commission members urge the president to provide leadership; yet, before the end of the year, observers claim that student unrest, rather than reaching a crisis point, has largely died down.

**September 28.** Gamal Abdel Nasser, president of the UAR and Arab diplomat, dies of a heart attack at age 52. Weeping millions line the streets of Cairo for the funeral procession.

A leader of the military coup that overthrew the Egyptian monarchy in 1952, Nasser initiated extensive land reform during his first years in power. The nationalization of the Suez Canal in 1956 and the subsequent international confrontation greatly enhanced his stature in the Middle East. In succeeding years, Nasser became the driving force behind the Pan-Arab movement, supporting Arab revolutionaries in other countries.

Nasser's health began to deteriorate following the stunning defeat of his country in the 1967 Arab-

Israeli War. Yet the UAR president had recently accepted an American cease-fire proposal for the canal front as an opening to negotiations. And, in light of the pact he and other Arab leaders signed just yesterday to end the Jordanian Civil War, Western powers mourn the loss of his moderating influence in the Middle East.

On October 15, Anwar Sadat, age 51, is elected president by an overwhelming majority.

**October 5.** French-Canadian FLQ revolutionaries, who have killed seven people since 1963, kidnap James Cross, the British Trade Commissioner in Montreal. When Ottawa rejects their demands for $500,000 ransom, safe conduct to Cuba for 23 convicted members, and the publication of an FLQ manifesto, the terrorists kidnap Quebec Labour Minister Pierre Laporte, on the 10th.

*Pierre Trudeau, prime minister of Canada, during the October Crisis.*

The Trudeau government orders 4,000 troops to the capital on the 12th and, at the request of the Quebec attorney general, sends forces to Montreal and Quebec City three days later. On the 16th, the governor–in–council (prime minister and cabinet) invokes the War Measures Act of 1914 (its first use in peacetime), outlawing the FLQ and giving police sweeping powers to apprehend suspects without warrants. In a predawn raid, some 465 people are arrested, mainly in Quebec.

When police discover Pierre Laporte's strangled body in the trunk of a car on the 18th, the House of Commons approves (190–16) the invocation. Parliament replaces the act on December 1 with a less severe public order strengthening civil rights: Authorities must lay charges within 3–7 days, rather than 21; and suspects retain rights to counsel, trial by jury, and the use of normal rules of evidence.

Police surround an FLQ hideout on December 3, and Cross is released after authorities grant the three terrorists and their families safe passage to Cuba. Members of the second revolutionary cell who killed Laporte—Paul Rose, Jacques Rose, and Francis Simard—are captured near Montreal on December 28. Along with Bernard Lortie, captured earlier, they receive sentences ranging from eight years to life.

As the people of Canada attempt to come to terms with the October Crisis, many argue that Prime Minister Trudeau and his cabinet, by assuming greater powers than were called for, may have damaged English-French relations beyond repair.

The federal government withdraws all troops on January 4, 1971. Two months later, the Quebec provincial government pledges to compensate those unjustly arrested and to destroy their files and fingerprints. Only 18 people will be convicted of a crime. The War Measures Act will lapse on April 30, 1971.

**October 31.** The U.S. command in South Vietnam reports 24 American fatalities for the week, the lowest total since 15 men lost their lives in October 1965.

**November 1.** In Saint-Laurent-du-Pont, near Grenoble, a discarded match starts a fire in a discothèque. Flames race through papier-mâché and plastic decorations, blocking the only accessible exit through a turnstile—146 people, ages 17 to 25, die of burns and smoke inhalation. When investigators find six serious safety violations, chastened authorities close down 806 public buildings throughout France.

**November 3.** After a bitter election campaign, both parties claim victory. The Democrats retain a majority in both houses and gain 11 governorships. The Republicans, on the other hand, gain 2 seats in the Senate and lose just 9 in the House; the party in power generally loses an average 40 House seats in midterm elections.

New representatives include Bella Abzug (D., N.Y.). Defeated senatorial candidate George Bush will be named ambassador to the United Nations.

**November 9.** In a trembling voice, President Georges Pompidou announces, "General de Gaulle is dead. France is a widow." The French soldier fought in W.W.I and, in 1940, opposed an armistice with Germany and escaped to England to lead Free French forces. Upon liberation, de Gaulle returned to France to head a provisional government but resigned in 1946. He emerged from private life only when civil war threatened his country in 1958.

Elected president of the Fifth Republic under a new constitution, Charles de Gaulle gained the broader powers more suited to his temperament. Within two years, he granted independence to French colonies. Fearing continued U.S. dominance of Europe, he created a French nuclear force during the 1960s and withdrew from NATO. His government weathered the massive workers' strike and student unrest in 1968, but when the electorate rejected his proposals for regional reform and abolition of the Senate, he resigned in 1969.

The grief-stricken nation honors de Gaulle's request to be buried near his home without a state funeral. In Paris, though, some 80 kings and heads of state, including President Nixon, attend a memorial service at Notre Dame Cathedral. The *Times of London* describes Charles de Gaulle as the "spokesman, conscience, and personification of France."

**November 13.** The worst cyclone in world history and the worst natural disaster of this century leaves up to 1 million dead in East Pakistan. Winds gusting to 150 mph drive huge waves across the mouth of the Ganges, sweeping people, houses, livestock, and crops off the low-lying land. At least 300,000 drown, many of them children. Slow and indifferent relief services provided by the federal government in West Pakistan, 2,000 miles away, cause thousands more deaths through disease and starvation.

Despite the magnitude of the disaster and the ever present threat of more storms, survivors are lured back by the rich agricultural land of the Ganges delta.

**December 8.** The U.N. General Assembly passes a resolution, 47–22, affirming the inalienable right of Palestinians to self-determination. Fifty nations abstain and the United States votes against the motion.

**December 14.** Polish workers in the Gdansk shipyards learn that the government intends to raise the price of food and other goods by up to 33 percent. Already suffering under longstanding inflation, several years of bad harvests, and the generally autocratic government of Wladyslaw Gomulka, the men march to party headquarters to protest. When police intervene, violence erupts. The rioting quickly spreads to other cities, where protesters loot and burn shops.

Brutal suppression injures hundreds and kills as many as 300. The unrest ends by December 19, and Gomulka and other members of the politburo resign the next day. Edward Gierek, party chief in Silesia, takes over as first secretary. He promises to freeze food prices for at least two years.

**December 15.** While reassuring the public, the FDA recalls nearly 1 million cans of tuna. Some 23 percent of sample tins registered unacceptable levels of mercury contamination—the first tainting discovered in ocean fish.

**December 16.** To combat the spread of terrorism, 50 nations meet in The Hague to enact an anti-hijacking law. Following ratification by 10 countries, signatories must mete out "severe punishment" to hijackers of civilian aircraft—even those seeking political asylum—and prosecute any hijacker escaping from another country.

**December 18.** At the Nevada atomic test site, an underground detonation opens a fissure 300 feet from the test hole, allowing radiation to escape into the atmosphere. By the next day, a cloud of radioactivity travels 450 miles eastward to central Utah, then disappears over Wyoming on the 21st. Environmental readings taken throughout the western United States detect radioactive material.

By conservative estimates, 32 underground tests have vented radioactivity since the first in 1958.

**December 22.** North Vietnam releases a "definitive" list of 339 American POWs; an additional 20 have reportedly died. The list fails to account for 10

U.S. airmen who the Defense Department lists as prisoners or the other 412 Americans missing in action.

**December 26.** Last April, when further laboratory tests verified that the herbicide Agent Orange causes birth defects in mice, Americans temporarily suspended spraying operations in South Vietnam. Today, the Defense Department announces an "orderly, yet rapid phase-out" of defoliation because "changed circumstances" have reduced the need for it.

Between 1965 and 1969, the United States sprayed an estimated 19 million gallons of herbicides over 5.96 million acres in South Vietnam. In addition to the health hazards, the Senate Foreign Relations Committee next year will estimate that the eight-year program cost South Vietnam food for 600,000 people a year and some 6.2 billion board feet of marketable timber.

## Obituaries

**Edouard Daladier** (June 18, 1884–October 10, 1970). In a futile attempt to appease Hitler, the premier of France agreed to the dismemberment of Czechoslovakia in 1938. He was later arrested by the collaborationist Vichy government and deported to Germany. Freed by the Allies in 1945, Daladier returned to France and served in the National Assembly until 1958.

**Benjamin O. Davis** (July 1, 1877–November 26, 1970). In 1940, Davis became the first black general in the U.S. Armed Forces. He retired in 1958 after 50 years of military service.

**Charles de Gaulle** (November 22, 1890–November 9, 1970). *See* News.

**Marie Houle (née Dionne)** (May 28, 1934–February 23, 1970). She was one of the famous Dionne quintuplets.

**Peter II** (September 6, 1923–November 5, 1970). Crowned days before Germany invaded in 1941, the Yugoslavian king fled to England to head a government-in-exile. Following the war, Britain supported the new Communist government, and the monarchy was abolished. A descendant of Queen Victoria, with the right to be buried in Westminster Abbey, Peter Karageorgevich chose burial in the U.S., where he had lived much of his life.

**Aleksandr Kerensky** (September 11, 1881–June 11, 1970). In 1917, after Russian revolutionaries forced Czar Nicholas II from the throne, Kerensky headed the provisional government for four months. A moderate socialist, he tried to introduce democratic reforms, but the Bolsheviks, led by Lenin, took control in November. Kerensky fled the country, first to France then in 1940 to the United States. From 1956 until his death, he taught at Stanford University.

**Gamal Abdel Nasser** (January 15, 1918–September 28, 1970). *See* News.

**Erik Nelson** (1889–May 9, 1970). On April 6, 1924, four U.S. Army Douglas biplanes took off on the first around-the-world flight. Each open-cockpit plane carried a single pilot and a mechanic. One aircraft crashed in Alaska, a second was forced to quit, but the remaining two—piloted by Nelson and Lowell H. Smith—flew a total of 371 hours, 11 minutes, over a period of 5 months, to complete the historic trip on September 8.

**Walter Reuther** (September 1, 1907–May 9, 1970). Traveling on union business, the president of the UAW died in a plane crash with his wife. Elected UAW president in 1946 and CIO president in 1952, he took his union into the AFL-CIO merger in 1955. But a more progressive labor leader than AFL-CIO president George Meany, Reuther pulled the UAW back out in 1968. During his tenure, he improved union wages, health benefits, and retirement plans.

**António Salazar** (April 28, 1889–July 27, 1970). The authoritarian ruler of Portugal (1932–1969) died of a heart attack.

**John T. Scopes** (August 3, 1900–October 21, 1970). In 1925, Tennessee charged the young biology teacher with breaking the law by teaching Darwin's theory of evolution. As a test case and with the famous Clarence Darrow defending against the renowned prosecutor Williams Jennings Bryan, the Scopes, or "Monkey," trial drew national attention. The state won, and Scopes left teaching for geology, but the verdict was overturned in 1927. The state law was repealed in 1967.

**Blanche Stuart Scott** (circa 1886–January 12, 1970). In 1910, the first woman to drive alone across the United States (taking 69 days) became the first American woman to fly solo. She soon turned professional, thrilling crowds with her stunt flying. But Scott grew impatient at the lack of aviation opportunities for women and retired at age 27.

**Sukarno** (June 6, 1901–June 21, 1970). Following independence in 1949, the first president of Indonesia worked to unite the nation's 3,000 islands. But through the 1950s and early 1960s, he became increasingly dictatorial while the economy deteriorated. Finally, in 1965, Sukarno was implicated in the attempted coup that led to the bloody anti-Communist purge (See News for that year). He was forced to surrender most of his powers to General Suharto in early 1966, and was officially deposed on March 12, 1967.

# BEGINNINGS AND ENDINGS

### News

**January 1.** California's no-fault divorce law, the first in the country, reduces grounds to incurable insanity and irreconcilable differences, and splits assets equally rather than awarding more to the wronged party. With one in two California marriages ending in divorce, the legislation receives widespread support.

**January 22.** A transatlantic Pan Am flight is the first commercial journey by a Boeing 747. With 94 sold in the first year, the jumbo jets all but finish the few remaining ocean liners.

**March 18.** In New York, post office employees stage the first strike in the system's 195-year history. President Nixon declares a national emergency and for the first time troops replace federal workers. The strike ends March 24, but the labor action precipitates the postal service's changeover to an independent corporation.

**May 31.** For the first time, Ottawa gives way to upward pressure on the dollar, allowing the Canadian currency to "float" against the American dollar for a more realistic rate of exchange.

**June 11.** U.S. Army officers Elizabeth P. Hoisington, age 51, and Anna Mae Hays, age 50, become the first women in American military history to reach the rank of brigadier general.

**June 14.** Her selection as Miss Iowa makes Cheryl Adrenne Browne the first black contestant in a Miss America beauty pageant.

**June 25.** Canada lowers the voting age in federal elections from 21 to 18 years.

**July 31.** The British Navy abolishes the daily rum ration, deeming the 283-year-old tradition "inappropriate" in a world of instant warfare. Canadians will follow suit in 1972.

**August 2.** The first Boeing 747 to be hijacked lands in Havana. The 379 passengers sit on the runway for 53 minutes, waiting for takeoff clearance, while the pilot answers Fidel Castro's questions on speed and capacity.

**August 2.** After a two-week legal battle, Roger Mills, a 24-year-old white civil rights law clerk, weds Berta Linson, a 21-year-old black file clerk. Theirs is the first interracial marriage in Mississippi history.

**September 1.** Computers in Texas, New Jersey, New York, and Illinois engage in the world's first computer chess tournament (averaging two minutes a move). The program was written by national chess champ Hans Berliner.

**September 22.** President Nixon signs a bill giving the District of Columbia a nonvoting delegate in the House. The district was last represented in 1871–1875, when Congress experimented with a type of territorial government.

**October 14.** An act authorizes the establishment of federal and community defender systems across the United States. The federal system will consist of salaried attorneys, under the supervision of a public defender, while community systems will receive initial federal funding, then be eligible for periodic sustaining grants.

**November 10.** The U.S. Treasury terminates the bimetal monetary standard of silver and gold by selling off its last marketable silver.

**November 12.** Admiral Elmo Zumwalt, Jr. (at age 49 the navy's youngest chief of operations) authorizes longer hair, trimmed beards, beer for enlisted men, hard liquor for officers, and more relaxed off-duty uniform regulations. Sailors call his orders "Z-grams."

**December 8.** Making several changes to attract recruits, army chief of staff General Westmoreland eliminates the use of reveille to roust soldiers out of their barracks.

**December 10.** Ford Motor Co. names Lee Iacocca president.

---

*Statistics:* In an FCC analysis of 8,800 consumer complaints, new and used car dealers rank No. 1.

---

**More news.** For the first time since aviation records were begun in 1938, regularly scheduled U.S. domestic flights record no passenger fatalities.

• United Funds, associations that coordinate charity fund-raising, reorganize this year as the United Way of America. Its cupped-hand logo will be adopted in 1972.

• In his book *The Primal Scream*, Arthur Janov tells readers to rid themselves of past traumas by crying, sobbing, and shrieking out their painful emotions. His primal theory attracts many believers, including John Lennon and Yoko Ono.

## Records

**March 2.** With Supreme Court approval, the Great Northern, the Northern Pacific, and the Chicago, Burlington & Quincy railroads merge to form the longest privately owned railway system in the world, with 25,000 miles of track.

**September 3.** Coffeyville, Kansas, recovers the largest hailstone on record—5.5 inches in diameter.

**December 23.** Topped out at 1,350 feet, the north tower of the World Trade Center, in New York, surpasses the Empire State Building as the tallest building in the world.

## Government Departments and Agencies

**July 1.** An agency of the executive branch, the U.S. Office of Management and Budget, begins operation.

**December 2.** Consolidating 15 federal pollution programs, the Environmental Protection Agency (EPA) will research the effects of pollution and establish and enforce environmental standards.

## Fads

In college dorms, hippie pads, and communes across the United States, black lights (ultraviolet) reveal phosphorescent messages on psychedelic posters. Picking up on the novelty, teenagers set off a craze for purple fluorescent paints, fabric, light bulbs, and other products.

The popularity of astrology rejuvenates tarot fortune telling. Originally a deck of 22 cards, most modern packs number 54. (Their origin is unknown.)

Manufacturers sell $15 million worth of $5 Fuzzy Foot rugs. Art Buchwald, who hangs a pair on his wall, reportedly tells guests the giant footprints are Spiro Agnew's.

Dr. Hale Dougherty of California commissions a graduate student to caricature Spiro Agnew in a takeoff on Disney's Mickey Mouse watch. Wearing stars-and-stripes shoes and shorts, the little cartoon Veep gives a peace sign at the end of each hand.

Medical authorities belittle copper bracelets as a treatment for arthritis, but wearers—overlooking skin discoloration—testify to their therapeutic powers. The jewelry grosses $400 million this year.

# SCIENCE AND TECHNOLOGY

## News

**January.** The FDA issues a warning to over 380,000 doctors about the risks associated with birth control pills. By September, manufacturers must enclose a 150-word insert about possible side effects.

**March.** By handling incoming-flight information, performing calculations, and distributing data slips, the FAA's new automated Air Space system, inaugurated in Los Angeles this month, will reduce the work load for air traffic controllers. (Last month, the first flight plan was passed automatically across the United States.)

The next step will provide radar data processing, automatic tracking, and display of vital information on the controller's radar screen. All 21 centers in the Air Route Traffic Control System should have the equipment by 1974.

**April 1.** American cigarette packages add: "The Surgeon General has determined that cigarette smoking is dangerous to your health." Since the first health warning, in 1966, the verb has changed from "may" to "is."

**April 11.** James Lovell, John Swigert, and Fred Haise blast off from Earth in *Apollo 13*. On their third day out, an oxygen tank explodes, rupturing the skin of the command module. To survive, the astronauts squeeze into the lunar module and power down all equipment to conserve electricity.

A 35-second burn puts the LM into a free-return-to-Earth trajectory, but the larger, useless CM must be towed behind because the LM lacks a heat shield for reentry. As the spacecraft loops around the moon, the men pray the LM's limited oxygen supply will last the entire voyage.

Just before reaching Earth's atmosphere, the men return to the CM and regretfully jettison the smaller craft. Splashdown proceeds without a hitch.

Investigation reveals that damaged internal wires had ignited and built up pressure. The manufacturer, Rockwell International, receives a mock $400,000 towing bill from Grumman Corp., the manufacturer of the LM. Throughout the entire Apollo program, the lunar module has never failed the NASA astronauts.

**April 24.** Two months ago, Japan became the fourth nation, after the United States, Soviet Union, and France, to launch a satellite. Today, Communist China sends up its first. The 382-pound capsule broadcasts "The East Is Red," a tune honoring Mao Tse-tung.

**April 28.** French scientists and cardiologists announce the successful implantation of the first nuclear-powered pacemaker. Unlike batteries,

which must be replaced every 22 months, the plutonium 238 should last 10 years.

**June.** The Mazda automobile, introduced to the United States this month, boasts a dual-rotor Wankel, the first new internal-combustion engine since the late 1800s.

Developed by German engineer Fritz Wankel in the 1950s, the triangular piston rotates inside a round cylinder half the size and weight of conventional motors. West Germans introduced the Wankel in 1964, but Toyo Kogyo is the first automaker to mass produce the engine.

**June 2.** Scientists at the University of Wisconsin announce the first complete synthesis of a gene, an important step toward the manipulation of hereditary traits.

**June 19.** *Soyuz* 9 returns to Earth after two cosmonauts set a new record for manned space flight—17 days, 16 hours, 59 minutes.

**June 19.** The USAF announces the successful test of a Minuteman 3 missile with multiple independently targetable reentry vehicles (MIRVs), or multiple warheads. Both are expected to be deployed early in this decade.

**July 3.** The National Communicable Disease Center reports that last year, for the first time since vaccinations began in 1955, the United States recorded no known deaths from polio.

**July 23.** Robert Choate, Jr., former consultant for the Nixon administration, tells a Senate committee that the top 60 dry cereals—including the 5 best-sellers—contain little nutritional value. He maintains that the major companies have developed highly nutritious cereals but continue to promote the better-known names.

**August 3.** The nuclear submarine *James Madison* conducts the first underwater firing of a Poseidon missile, 30 miles off Cape Kennedy. (A nearby Soviet trawler almost collides with U.S. ships trying to recover launching debris.) The missiles will replace the Polaris next January.

**September 12–24.** *Luna 16* completes the first unmanned round trip following a landing on the lunar surface. The probe brings back soil cores up to 2 feet long.

**October 3.** A U.N. committee reports that

radiation from peaceful uses of nuclear energy has surpassed the threat of bomb tests to world health.

**November 12.** In the United States, Drs. James F. Danielli, K. W. Jeon, and I. J. Lorch announce the first synthesis of a living, reproducing cell. The trio partially dismembered an amoeba, then reassembled the cell from other amoeba components. The cell reproduced and became indistinguishable from others.

**November 17.** *Luna 17* lands the first extraterrestrial robot. Controlled from Earth, the eight-wheeled, unmanned *Lunokhod I* conducts automated studies in the Mare Imbrium. And with shutdown every lunar night, the vehicle continues to operate on the moon until October 4, 1971.

**November 18.** Nobel prize winner Linus Pauling claims that large doses of vitamin C ward off the flu and the common cold. While the medical community remains skeptical, vitamin C sales skyrocket.

**December 10.** The Swedish Academy awards the Nobel peace prize to U.S. plant pathologist Norman Borlaug. During the 1960's, his improved wheat strains sparked a Green Revolution in Latin America, the Middle East, and Asia. "More than any other single person of this age, he has helped to provide bread for a hungry world."

**December 15.** A *Venera 7* lander touches down on the surface of Venus. During the first transmissions from another planet, which last more than 20 minutes, scientists learn that the surface is firm, the atmosphere consists of 97 percent carbon dioxide and 2 percent nitrogen, and the temperature at that location is 885 degrees Fahrenheit.

**December 15.** A national commission of medical experts urges Americans to halve their daily intake of cholesterol and saturated fats and to reduce their total fat intake substantially. To assist them, the members urge the FDA to require that all packaging list a food's exact fat content.

**December 18.** Detergent makers reach an agreement with the Nixon administration to remove nitrilotriacetic acid—the heralded replacement for enzymes—because of possible toxicity.

Detergents first appeared on the market in the 1930s but were little used until the more prosperous fifties. At that time, water-softening phosphates began to suds up sewer systems and waterways. Finally, in 1965, the manufacturers introduced enzymes to break down the suds. But environmentalists have discovered that phosphates remain a major source of pollution.

**More news.** This year, for the first time since the widespread introduction of penicillin, venereal diseases reach pandemic proportions in the United States; some 2 million cases of gonorrhea are reported.

• Over the last five years, the NASA budget has fallen from $5.25 billion to $4.7 billion, cutting in-house employment from 34,000 to 31,000 and contractors from 377,000 to 135,000. As the decline continues, NASA cancels three Apollo missions (scheduled between 1969 and 1972), cuts two "workshop" space stations to one *Skylab*, and abandons plans for larger stations and a nuclear rocket propulsion system for a spaceship to Mars. Programs for reusable carriers remain, but completion will take longer than originally anticipated.

• This year, American microbiologist Hamilton Othanel Smith achieves the first identification of a restriction enzyme. Because such enzymes allow the splitting of genes, his work opens the way to genetic engineering.

## Other Discoveries, Developments, and Inventions

Magicube flashes from Sylvania that fire mechanically rather than electrically

A hologram camera from Gaertner Scientific Corp., for $500

Safer bias-belted automobile tires and unleaded-fuel engines

First quartz wrist watch, from Seiko at $1,250

*Statistics:* Since 1940, the number of drivers' licenses held by American women has risen from 24.3 percent to 43.2 percent.

## Obituaries

**Max Born** (December 11, 1882–January 5, 1970). The German nuclear physicist won the 1954 Nobel prize for his earlier work on the statistical interpretation of quantum mechanics.

**William Thomas Piper** (January 8, 1881–January 15, 1970). At his death, the aircraft pioneer is credited with building more airplanes than anyone else in the world. His Piper Cub was used extensively by the army during W.W.II.

**Francis Peyton Rous** (October 5, 1879–February 16, 1970). To determine the cause of breast sarcoma, the pathologist injected hens with a cell-free solution from the diseased tissue. When the birds developed malignant growths, he concluded the cause was a filterable virus. Medical experts in 1909 rejected his theory, but later experiments vindicated his work. Rous received the Nobel prize in 1966.

## THE ARTS

March 30—*Applause*, with Lauren Bacall, Len Cariou, Penny Fuller (896 perfs.)

April 7—*The Effect of Gamma Rays on Man-in-the-Moon Marigolds*, with Sada Thompson, Pamela Payton-Wright, Amy Levitt (819 perfs.)

April 26—*Company*, with Dean Jones, Elaine Stritch (705 perfs.)

November 12—*Sleuth*, with Anthony Quayle, Keith Baxter (1,222 perfs.)

## Tony Awards

Actor (Dramatic)—Fritz Weaver, *Child's Play*
Actress (Dramatic)—Tammy Grimes, *Private Lives* (Revival)
Actor (Musical)—Cleavon Little, *Purlie*
Actress (Musical)—Lauren Bacall, *Applause*
Play—*Borstal Boy*
Musical—*Applause*

## News

**March 3.** In her debut at the Met, 36-year-old mezzo soprano Marilyn Horne sings opposite Joan Sutherland in *Norma.*

**April 10.** The producers of *Hair* close their Boston show rather than comply with a court order to remove the nudity. The Supreme Court overturns the Massachusetts decision on May 22.

**June 12.** Queen Elizabeth names Sir Laurence Olivier a baron. He is the first actor to sit in the House of Lords.

**September 4.** Britain grants political asylum to prima ballerina Natalya Makarova. Next month, the 30-year-old Soviet dancer joins the American Ballet Theater.

**December 27.** *Hello, Dolly!* closes on Broadway after a marathon 2,844 performances. (*My Fair Lady* set the previous record of 2,717.) The show returned $9 million on a $350,000 investment.

**More news.** In another year of record art sales, the Wildenstein Gallery in New York pays $5,544,000 for a Velázquez portrait.

• In 1923, Gutzon Borglum began carving Robert E. Lee, Jefferson Davis, and Stonewall Jackson on the exposed granite surface of Stone Mountain. But the sculptor soon left, following an argument with the sponsoring Daughters of the Confederacy. Augustus Lukeman worked on new designs until a 1928 deadline imposed by the property owners brought the project to an end. Thirty years passed before the state of Georgia purchased the land. A sculpting team, assigned in 1963, finally finishes the 90-foot heroic figures this year.

## Obituaries

**John Barbirolli** (December 2, 1899–July 29, 1970). The distinguished British conductor most recently held joint positions with the Houston and Manchester symphonies. He was knighted in 1949.

**Olga Hirsh Guggenheim** (September 23, 1877–February 14, 1970). The philanthropist established the Guggenheim Memorial Foundation (1925) with her husband Simon to assist artists, scholars, and scientists.

**Lawren Harris** (October 23, 1885–January 29, 1970). In the early 1910s, Harris encouraged others in eastern Canada to develop a bold new style of landscape painting. By 1920, the Group of Seven (Franklin Carmichael, A. Y. Jackson, Franz Johnston, Arthur Lismer, J. E. H. MacDonald, F. H. Varley) presented their first exhibit as a national school. Although the artists disbanded in 1933, in recognition of their own brand of conservatism, their work profoundly influenced three generations of Canadian artists. Harris was the only member and one of the first in Canada to evolve into abstraction.

# WORDS

Maya Angelou, *I Know Why the Caged Bird Sings*
Richard Bach, *Jonathan Livingston Seagull*
Henri Charrière, *Papillon*
R. F. Delderfield, *God Is an Englishman*
James Dickey, *Deliverance*
Julius Fast, *Body Language*
Graham Greene, *Travels with My Aunt*
Germaine Greer, *The Female Eunuch*
Hal Lindsey and C. C. Carlson, *The Late Great Planet Earth*
Kate Millett, *Sexual Politics*
Charles Reich, *The Greening of America*
Erich Segal, *Love Story*
Irwin Shaw, *Rich Man, Poor Man*
Albert Speer, *Inside the Third Reich*
Mary Stewart, *The Crystal Cave*
Studs Terkel, *Hard Times: An Oral History of the Great Depression*
Alvin Toffler, *Future Shock*
Robert Townsend, *Up the Organization*
Erich von Däniken, *Chariots of the Gods?*

## News

**March 16.** In translating literally from ancient sources, the *New English Bible* loses much of the rich language of the King James version.

**March 18.** When 200 women demonstrate for a liberated issue of *Ladies' Home Journal*, editor John M. Carter agrees to an eight-page supplement in the August edition. But when other magazines offer little encouragement, American women begin publishing their own periodicals.

**April.** A $50,000 grant establishes *Smithsonian* magazine. In 1846, Congress used a bequest from Englishman James Smithson (for "the increase and diffusion of knowledge among men") to found the Smithsonian Institution.

---

*Statistics:* Over the last decade, 676 new periodicals appeared in the United States while 162 merged or folded.

---

**September 29.** The *New American Bible*—the first full Catholic translation into English from original source material—replaces the Douay version in use for more than 200 years.

**September 30.** The U.S. Commission on Obscenity and Pornography releases a two-year study begun under the Johnson administration. The 12–6 majority vote finds no relationship between pornography and crime or sexual deviance and urges the legalization of all sexually explicit books, magazines, and films (intended for consenting adults). As well, members advocate a massive program of sex education.

President Nixon, who has already condemned the controversial report, promises, "So long as I am in the White House, there will be no relaxation of the national effort to control and eliminate smut from our national life."

**Fall–Winter.** "To change the world completely," Jane and John Shuttleworth quit their public relations jobs, borrow money, and publish *Mother Earth News*.

**More news.** Three sex books make this year's best-seller list: *The Sensuous Woman* by J (Joan Garrity), *Human Sexual Inadequacy* by William H. Masters and Virginia E. Johnson, and *Everything You Always Wanted to Know About Sex* by Dr. David Reuben.

• The popularity of the BBC's "Forsyte Saga" creates a huge demand for John Galsworthy's novels.

• With the growth of the feminist movement, bookstores report brisk sales in new women's-lib titles as well as classics such as *The Feminine Mystique.*

• The satirical *National Lampoon,* launched this year by former editors of *Harvard Lampoon,* is an immediate campus hit.

---

*Statistics:* In the last year, the average price for a hardcover book rose 22.7 percent, to $11.66.

---

## Cartoons and Comics

**October.** The newly established Universal Press Syndicate picks up *Bull Tales* from the *Yale Daily News.* Cartoonist Gary Trudeau, age 20, retitles the strip after central character Mike Doonesbury ("doone" is Yale slang for a good-natured fool and "bury" comes from the last name of former roommate Pillsbury). *Doonesbury* attracts a huge following, but some dailies reject Trudeau's more controversial story lines.

**October.** Marvel Comics bases *Conan the Barbarian* on "Shadow Kingdom," a Robert E. Howard story from a 1929 *Weird Tales.*

**More news.** Russell Myers creates the comic strip *Broom Hilda.*

*The Comic Book Price Guide,* compiled by Robert Overstreet, is the first publication to give current market values for back-issue and discontinued titles.

## TIME *Man of the Year*

Willy Brandt

## New Words and Phrases

AC/DC (bisexual)
all-time high, all-time low
blahs
door buster (a popular, widely advertised article)
ecosystem, ecomanagement
environmentalists

fast-food
head shop (one specializing in psychedelic accessories)
human engineering
hype
livingspace
no-no
to rip off
sexploitation
sicknik (one who is emotionally disturbed)
skinhead (British working-class youths with conservative views and very short haircuts)

## Obituaries

**John Dos Passos** (January 14, 1896–September 28, 1970). The novelist and historian wrote the celebrated *U.S.A.,* a three-volume chronicle of industrial America from 1898 to 1929.

**E(dward) M(organ) Forster** (January 1, 1879–June 7, 1970). An essayist in later life, the British novelist is best remembered for his early, important novels: *Room with a View* (1908), *Howards End* (1910), and *A Passage to India* (1924).

**Erle Stanley Gardner** (July 17, 1889–March 11, 1970). The former lawyer introduced Perry Mason in *The Case of the Velvet Claws* (1933), the first of 79 similarly titled Mason mysteries.

**John Gunther** (August 30, 1901–May 29, 1970). In his lifetime, the American writer and journalist sold over 3½ million copies of *Inside U.S.A.* (1947), *Inside Russia Today* (1958), and other *Inside* studies.

**Allen Lane** (September 21, 1902–July 7, 1970). The British publisher founded Penguin Books in 1935 and introduced the concept of quality paperbacks with *Ariel,* André Maurois' biography of the poet Shelley. Lane, who was knighted in 1952, sold 8 million Penguins in the first 10 years.

**John O'Hara** (January 31, 1905–April 11, 1970). Immensely popular, his novels depicted the moral disintegration of urban America: *Butterfield 8* (1935), *A Rage to Live* (1949), and *From the Terrace* (1958).

**Erich Maria Remarque** (June 22, 1898–September 25, 1970). The German-American author achieved international fame with his W.W.I novel *All Quiet on the Western Front* (1929).

**Bertrand Russell** (May 18, 1872–February 2, 1970). Regarded as the most distinguished philosopher of his era, the British mathematician and pacifist was governed by "the longing for love, the search for knowledge, and unbearable pity for the suffering of mankind." He received the Nobel prize in literature in 1950, campaigned over that decade for nuclear disarmament, and in the 1960s established two peace foundations and loaned his name to anti-Vietnam activities.

# FASHION

## The 1970s

Fashion remains fragmented in the early years of the decade, with some women holding fast to the mini, others experimenting with new lengths, and many simply ignoring the hemline debate and opting for pants.

This indecision gives rise to the layered look. But by 1973, the youthful explosion in fashion settles into a more conservative pattern of choice.

## Haute Couture

The Yves St. Laurent collection, running the gamut from a micro-mini to a maxi, typifies the European attitude. (The couturier says, "What is wonderful is the freedom to choose one's length.")

American designers, on the other hand, kill the mini with the first abrupt drop in hemlines since 1947. The press dubs the midcalf length "instant age."

## News

**April.** Belgian-born Diane von Furstenberg, the 23-year-old wife of a prince, presents New York buyers with clingy, lightweight jersey dresses ($24–$100) and an outfit of pants, matching tunic, and hooded cape ($80).

**August.** The national convention of the American Federation of Teachers votes to support student "freedom of speech and expression, including a choice of one's own dress and grooming."

**More news.** Refusing to heed the dictates of high fashion, American women spurn the new midi. Critics believe their unprecedented rebellion stems from the recession (abandoning a mini wardrobe would prove costly), the influence of the women's movement, and the mild autumn weather (extending the life of summer clothes). Whatever the reasons, retailers despondently dust millions of dollars worth of midi stock and some 35,000 garment workers lose their jobs.

• A survey of beauty and toiletry products finds 92 percent of women use talcum powder, 85 percent use lipstick, and 80 percent use some form of fragrance.

• After just two years, Levi's® jeans for women reach the Top 6 listing for women's apparel.

## Colors and Materials

Polyesters capture 41 percent of the textile market, knocking cotton production down to 40 percent (from 65 percent in 1960). And suede outsells leather in bags, boots, and clothes.

This year, fashion observers credit the hippie influence for the casual softness of many fabrics.

Manufacturers use exotic prints to liven up the longer midi line.

With more international laws against trafficking in endangered species, the audience at the Dior Collection greets big-cat coats with hisses—the first ever heard in the house.

## Clothes

When women choose pants rather than buy the midi, designers counter with gauchos and knickerbocker suits. Consequently, many businesses finally drop their dress restrictions against slacks.

In recent years, the impracticality of a mini winter coat promoted the sale of maxi coats.

Somewhat predictably, this fall, stores sell the double-breasted midi coat—closely fitted at the top, belted at the waist, and gently flared to midcalf. A troubled industry gratefully accepts this single success.

To vary the trouser line, young women layer a short-sleeve vest or pullover over a long-sleeve blouse.

The waist-length jacket is the newest silhouette in suits.

Nonstretch brassiere straps of earlier years have completely given way to stretch fabrics. Now lingerie companies move toward seamless bras and more daring styles—front fasteners, one-half and even one-quarter cups.

White suits attain new popularity with men this summer.

## Accessories

Dramatic accessories offset the dowdy midi profile—wide leather belts, long scarves, close-fitting headgear, shoulder bags, striking jewelry.

Manufacturers turn out shoes with an extreme 4–5-inch-thick sole. (Sprained ankles aside, the moderate platform shoe remains popular until mid-decade.) Knee-high boots, usually laced up the front, adopt a more graceful 2-inch heel.

On Earth Day in Copenhagen, yoga instructor Anna Kalso introduces the Earth Shoe. The orthopedic footwear mimics the imprint of a bare foot in wet sand—the heel below the ball of the foot.

Appliqué shapes, studs, or leather thongs decorate colorful new felt hats. Knitted and crocheted styles win approval as well through the early years of the decade. Manufacturers will begin producing matched sets of hat, scarf, and gloves in lighter wools and cottons.

Young women buy all types of chokers or "dog collars"—Indian bead designs, black velvet with a cameo or suede and an enamel ornament. In other jewelry, the butterfly is a common motif.

## Hair and Cosmetics

*Vogue* magazine photographs models with green eyebrows, forehead triangles of bright pink and yellow, and other bizarre colorings.

New eye makeup includes watercolor shadows—just add water and paint them on.

With renewed emphasis on skin care, cosmetic companies offer pH products to achieve an acid-alkaline balance.

Most young women still wear their hair long from a center part—the straighter the better—but some dry their tresses in plaits to achieve a softer, rippling effect. Hair pulled back into a chignon (sometimes covered with a crocheted snood) and a few curled tendrils over the ears creates a more sophisticated look. But the "in" cut is shaggy—short on top, longer at the sides and in the back.

This year, men sport muttonchop whiskers—narrow at the top, wide toward a shaved chin. With longer, often stylized haircuts, more than a few barbershops close down.

## Obituaries

**Nina Ricci** (January 14, 1883–November 29, 1970). The Italian-born designer founded the Paris House of Ricci in 1932. Never known for fashion innovation, she won fame with her perfumes.

# MUSIC

"Bridge Over Troubled Water"—Simon & Garfunkel

"I'll Be There"—Jackson 5

"Raindrops Keep Fallin' on My Head"—B. J. Thomas

"(They Long to Be) Close to You"—Carpenters

"I Think I Love You"—Partridge Family

"American Woman"/"No Sugar Tonight"—Guess Who

"War"—Edwin Starr

"Ain't No Mountain High Enough"—Diana Ross

"The Tears of a Clown"—Smokey Robinson & the Miracles

"Everything Is Beautiful"—Ray Stevens

"Let It Be"—Beatles

"Mama Told Me (Not to Come)"—Three Dog Night

"ABC"—Jackson 5

"The Love You Save"—Jackson 5

"Thank You (Falettinme Be Mice Elf Agin)"— Sly & the Family Stone

"The Long and Winding Road"—Beatles

"I Want You Back"—Jackson 5

"Cracklin' Rosie"—Neil Diamond

"Venus"—Shocking Blue

"Make It With You"—Bread

"We've Only Just Begun"—Carpenters

"Which Way You Goin', Billy?"—Poppy Family featuring Susan Jacks

"One Less Bell to Answer"—5th Dimension

"Lookin' Out My Back Door"—Creedence Clearwater Revival

"Hey There Lonely Girl"—Eddie Holman

"The Rapper"—Jaggerz

## Grammys (1970)

Record of the Year—Simon & Garfunkel, "Bridge Over Troubled Water"

Song of the Year (songwriter)—Paul Simon, "Bridge Over Troubled Water"

Album of the Year—Simon & Garfunkel, *Bridge Over Troubled Water*

Best Vocal Performance (Male)—Ray Stevens, "Everything Is Beautiful" (single)

Best Vocal Performance (Female)—Dionne Warwick, *I'll Never Fall in Love Again* (album)

Best New Artist—The Carpenters

## News

**January 14.** Diana Ross leaves for a solo career. Despite, or perhaps because of, changing personnel, the Supremes will never again chart a No. 1 hit.

**January 24.** Robert Moog introduces the fully portable Mini-Moog synthesizer for the concert stage (about $2,000).

**January 31.** With their debut record, "I Want You Back," the Jackson 5 grab the coveted No. 1 position. Before the end of the year, the group scores another three top hits. Michael Jackson is 11 years old.

**April 10.** Business entanglements have forced the Beatles to maintain a show of unity. Today, Paul McCartney unilaterally breaks up the group, citing artistic and personal differences. Several days later, the others confirm the headline news. By the end of the year, John, Paul, George, and Ringo all release single albums (Lennon and McCartney record only their own compositions). But fans, remembering the Beatles' unprecedented 20 hit singles in six years, call for a reunion.

**Summer.** A 23-year-old English singer, new to Los Angeles this year, wows rock fans with his voice and keyboard gymnastics. His album, *Elton John*, will break the top 10 on both sides of the Atlantic this fall.

**July 27.** At a Sly & the Family Stone free concert in Chicago's Grant Park, some of the estimated 75,000 swarm onto the stage and climb the loudspeaker towers. The band refuses to perform and police move in. Thousands swarm into the streets. Six hours later, rain finally shuts down the ongoing street battle; three people die of gunshot wounds.

**July 3–5.** This year, various city councils reject 30 of 48 proposed rock festivals. One of the biggest, Atlanta Pop, draws 200,000 over two days to see the Allman Brothers Band, Jimi Hendrix, and others.

**November 2.** The president of MGM Records, 25-year-old Mike Curb, announces his company will no longer record drug lyrics or rock groups who take drugs. ("I credit hard-drug record acts with starting hundreds of new young drug users.") Critics, who argue few current releases contain such lyrics, believe the industry's first antidrug policy was driven by economics; few of the 18 groups dropped had made any money.

**More news.** This is the year of the breakup—the Dave Clark Five, the Monkees, Peter, Paul & Mary, and the Turtles. Simon & Garfunkel, never making a major announcement, simply complete a process begun nearly two years ago. In 1969, the duo made just one appearance, a TV special. And Garfunkel, involved in his acting career, has done little more than lay down his vocal tracks for their latest album. Still, "Bridge Over Troubled Water" provides a fitting climax to their association—three Grammys (as best song, record, and album), three hit singles, and 9 million copies sold worldwide.

Most singers and musicians regard the LP as the most important aspect of their studio work. With the rising cost of 45 rpm's, record buyers tend to agree. Still, this year, only 39 percent of albums recover their investment.

---

*Statistics:* Since 1955, total retail sales of sheet music and musical instruments has risen from under $500,000 annually to about $1 billion.

---

• Observers note a distinct religious trend in rock music—"Let It Be" from the Beatles, "Spirit in the Sky" from Norman Greenbaum, and, of course, the rock musical *Jesus Christ Superstar.*

• An ill Tommy James withdraws from the music scene, reportedly because of a drug problem. To date, James and the Shondells have collected 14 gold singles and 4 gold LP's. He returns to the recording studio within a year, but as a solo act.

• Fleetwood Mac founder and leader Peter Green departs. Group membership will change continually over the next several years.

• Catchy, rhythmic reggae music, brought in by West Indian immigrants, sweeps Britain this fall.

• In a *Newsweek* feature article, jazz trumpeter Miles Davis comments, "It's a white man's world. . . . That's what makes our music different. It comes from a people who have had to learn how to make the white man move" (*Newsweek*, March 23).

## New Recording Artists

Black Sabbath
Carpenters
Eric Clapton (solo)
Mac Davis
Dawn
Al Green
Elton John
Anne Murray
Diana Ross (solo)
Ringo Starr (solo)
ZZ Top

## Obituaries

**L. Wolfe Gilbert** (August 31, 1886–July 12, 1970). The Dean of Tin Pan Alley composed some 250 popular songs, including "Waitin' for the Robert E. Lee" (1912).

**Ray Henderson** (December 1, 1896–December 31, 1970). His most successful compositions, written in four years with Lew Brown and Buddy De Sylva, included "The Birth of the Blues" (1926) and "Button Up Your Overcoat!" (1928).

**Jimi Hendrix** (November 27, 1942–September 18, 1970). After working as a sideman for Little Richard, Ike & Tina Turner, and others, Hendrix formed his own band in New York. In 1966, producer-manager Chas Chandler took him to England and helped him set up the Experience. The group traveled to the United States in 1967 and, with an appearance at the legendary Monterey Pop Festival, their name was made.

In a brief three years, Hendrix's sensual compositions ("Purple Haze," "Foxy Lady") and virtuoso performances revolutionized rock music and made him a legend in his own time. In 1969, personality conflicts forced the guitarist to disband the Experience and form the Band of Gypsies. Best-selling LP's followed.

The coroner rules Hendrix died from inhaling vomit while under the influence of barbiturates, a possible suicide but more likely an accident.

**Janis Joplin** (January 19, 1943–October 4, 1970). Joplin left her middle-class Texas home at age 17. The gutsy blues singer was performing in California bars by 1965, then a year later joined Big Brother and the Holding Company. Just one appearance, at the 1967 Monterey Pop Festival, made

Joplin a superstar. A Columbia Record deal followed and the group's *Cheap Thrills* album produced the top 20 hit "Piece of My Heart." Joplin left Big Brother within a year. Her own group released the

*Janis Joplin performing at the Festival of Peace at Shea Stadium.*

album *I Got Dem Ol' Kozmic Blues Again Mama.* The day's leading female rock vocalist, she overdosed on heroin.

**Charles Tobias** (August 15, 1897–July 7, 1970). The lyricist's several popular favorites included "Don't Sit Under the Apple Tree" (1942) and "Those Lazy-Hazy-Crazy Days of Summer" (1962).

**Harry MacGregor Woods** (November 4, 1896–January 14, 1970). His 350 popular songs, largely written in the 1920s and 1930s, included "When the Red, Red Robin Comes Bob, Bob, Bobbin' Along" (1926) and "I'm Looking Over a Four Leaf Clover" (1927).

## MOVIES

*Airport* (d. George Seaton; color)—Burt Lancaster, Dean Martin, George Kennedy, Helen Hayes, Jean Seberg, Jacqueline Bisset, Van Heflin, Maureen Stapleton

*The Aristocats* (Disney; color; animated)— Voices: Eva Gabor (Duchess); Phil Harris (Thomas O'Malley); Scatman Crothers (Scat Cat); Sterling Holloway (Rocquefort)

*The Boys in the Band* (d. William Friedkin; color)—Kenneth Nelson, Peter White, Leonard Frey, Cliff Gorman

*Cotton Comes to Harlem* (d. Ossie Davis; color)—Godfrey Cambridge, Raymond St. Jacques

*Fellini Satyricon* (Italian, d. Federico Fellini; color)—Martin Potter, Hiram Keller, Max Born, Capucine

*Five Easy Pieces* (d. Bob Rafelson; color)—Jack Nicholson, Karen Black, Billy Green Bush, Susan Anspach

*Gimme Shelter* (d. David Maysles, Albert Maysles, Charlotte Zwerin; color)—with the Rolling Stones, Jefferson Airplane and Grace Slick, Ike and Tina Turner

*Goin' Down the Road* (Canadian, d. Donald Shebib; color)—Doug McGrath, Paul Bradley, Jane Eastwood

*The Great White Hope* (d. Martin Ritt; color)— James Earl Jones, Jane Alexander

*I Never Sang for My Father* (d. Gilbert Cates; color)—Melvyn Douglas, Gene Hackman, Estelle Parsons

*The Landlord* (d. Hal Ashby; color)—Beau Bridges, Pearl Bailey, Diana Sands, Louis (Lou) Gossett, Lee Grant

*Let It Be* (British, d. Michael Lindsay-Hogg; color)—John Lennon, Paul McCartney, George Harrison, Ringo Starr

*Little Big Man* (d. Arthur Penn; color)—Dustin Hoffman, Faye Dunaway, Martin Balsam, Chief Dan George

*Love Story* (d. Arthur Hiller; color)—Ali MacGraw, Ryan O'Neal

*Lovers and Other Strangers* (d. Cy Howard; color)—Gig Young, Bea Arthur, Bonnie Bedelia

*M*A*S*H* (d. Robert Altman; color)—Donald

Sutherland, Elliott Gould, Tom Skerritt, Sally Kellerman, Robert Duvall, Jo Ann Pflug

*Patton* (d. Franklin J. Schaffner; color)—George C. Scott, Karl Malden

*The Private Life of Sherlock Holmes* (d. Billy Wilder; color)—Robert Stephens, Collin Blakely, Geneviève Page

*Scrooge* (British, d. Ronald Neame; color)—Albert Finney, Alec Guinness, Edith Evans, Kenneth More

*There Was a Crooked Man* (d. Joseph L. Mankiewicz; color)—Kirk Douglas, Henry Fonda, Hume Cronyn, Warren Oates

*Woodstock* (d. Michael Wadleigh; color)—with Joan Baez, Jimi Hendrix, The Who, Crosby, Stills & Nash, Jefferson Airplane

## Academy Awards

**April 7.** Bob Hope returns as host with 16 assistants. Legendary stars like Cary Grant, Fred Astaire, John Wayne, and Myrna Loy symbolize the Golden Days of Hollywood while new stars such as Jon Voight, Barbra Streisand, and Clint Eastwood represent the current generation.

Best Picture—*Midnight Cowboy*
Best Actor—John Wayne (*True Grit*)
Best Actress—Maggie Smith (*The Prime of Miss Jean Brodie*)
Best Director—John Schlesinger (*Midnight Cowboy*)
Best Supporting Actor—Gig Young (*They Shoot Horses, Don't They?*)
Best Supporting Actress—Goldie Hawn (*Cactus Flower*)
Best Song—"Raindrops Keep Fallin' on My Head" from *Butch Cassidy and the Sundance Kid*
Best Foreign Film—*Z* (Algerian)
Honorary Award—Cary Grant

Cary Grant never won an Oscar. Tonight, in a long-overdue tribute, the Academy presents the retired actor with a special statuette "for his unique mastery of the art of acting, with the respect and affection of his colleagues." The tumultuous ovation obviously touches the silver-haired Grant, but he appears surprised to be so well remembered.

## News

**March.** A revision of the 1968 movie classification system raises the "X" limit to 17 years and relabels the "M" category "GP." When audiences interpret "GP" to mean "General Public" (all ages admitted), rather than the intended "Parental Guidance Suggested," "GP" will become "PG" in 1972.

*Unorthodox army surgeons Elliott Gould and Donald Sutherland make an instant diagnosis in "M\*A\*S\*H."*

**March.** After a screening by two dozen officers, the U.S. Army and Air Force Motion Picture Service bans M\*A\*S\*H from military installations. The movie "succeeded in reducing the conventions and paraphernalia of war to total idiocy."

**March 24.** Movie executive Darryl F. Zanuck

says he will recommend that 20th Century-Fox transfer all movies to video cartridges five years after theatrical release.

**April 2.** EEOC public hearings and the threat of a lawsuit force 72 motion picture and television production companies to sign a Justice Department agreement to hire, train, and upgrade minorities and to set racial quotas to achieve equal employment. The terms do not cover acting jobs.

**May 3.** Auctioneers sell off 45 years' worth of MGM props and costumes, including Greta Garbo's slouch hat, Bert Lahr's Cowardly Lion suit, and Judy Garland's ruby-red slippers. In early bidding, furniture from *Marie Antoinette* (1930) goes for $1,450 while a clock from Garbo's *Ninotchka* (1939) brings $3,750. Actress Debbie Reynolds, star of 30 MGM films, bids for treasures she hopes to place in a future Hollywood hall of fame. The auctioneers, who bought the items from the studio for $1 million, take in $9 million.

**September 14.** In an apparent reference to *Easy Rider*, Vice-President Spiro Agnew tells a Republican gathering in Las Vegas that American youth is being "brainwashed" into a "drug culture" by rock movies, music, books, and underground newspapers.

**More news.** In the Fuji Group pavilion at Japan's Expo 70, a Japanese-Canadian production called *Tiger Child* introduces a dramatic new film format—Imax. The 70-mm horizontally fed film exposes an area equal to three standard 65-mm vertical frames.

• *The New York Times* reports on a unique Warner Bros.' offer. For a fee, the studio guarantees ad agencies that a client product will be "shown in a good light" in a minimum of 10 and a maximum of 40 movies. Warner notes the average film draws 15 million people.

• With a nude wrestling match between Alan Bates and Oliver Reed, *Women in Love* becomes the first commercial movie to reveal male genitalia.

• The phenomenal success of *Airport*—a $45 million return on a $10 million investment—rejuvenates the *Grand Hotel* (1932) formula of a big-name large cast. Over the coming years, Hollywood will produce several more blockbusters of this type.

| Top Box Office Stars | Newcomers |
|---|---|
| Paul Newman | Donald Sutherland |
| Clint Eastwood | Liza Minnelli |
| Steve McQueen | Goldie Hawn |
| John Wayne | Jack Nicholson |
| Elliott Gould | Geneviève Bujold |
| Dustin Hoffman | Dyan Cannon |
| Lee Marvin | Marlo Thomas |
| Jack Lemmon | Beau Bridges |
| Barbra Streisand | Sharon Farrell |
| Walter Matthau | Peter Boyle |

### Top Money-Maker of the Year

*Airport*

### Flops of the Year

*Waterloo*

Columbia Pictures goes down to defeat along with Napoleon when the picture earns back a mere $1.4 million on $25-million production costs.

*Darling Lili*

Paramount's most expensive musical, starring Julie Andrews and Rock Hudson, is a financial disaster. The budget escalates to $25 million—quadruple the original figure—and the film takes in just $5 million at the box office.

### Quote of the Year

Love means never having to say you're sorry. —After Ali MacGraw dies in *Love Story*, rich father Ray Milland apologizes to son Ryan O'Neal for never having accepted his young wife. O'Neal responds with one of the most repeated lines in cinema history. (Screenplay by Erich Segal, from his novel of the same name)

### Obituaries

**Ed Begley** (March 25, 1901–April 28, 1970). A veteran of some 12,000 radio programs, the heavyset actor switched to films in 1947. He won a Best supporting Oscar for *Sweet Bird of Youth* (1962).

**Billie Burke** (August 7, 1886–May 14, 1970). The comedienne, who specialized in feather-brained characters, created her most memorable part in *The Wizard of Oz* (1939)—Glinda, the good witch.

**Edward Everett Horton** (March 18, 1887–September 29, 1970). His fussbudget refrain "Oh, Dear Me" typified his roles in a 60-year stage, screen, and television career.

**Gypsy Rose Lee** (January 9, 1914–April 26, 1970). The best-known stripper of her day, the multi-talented "Queen of Burlesque" later became an actress, writer, and TV talk show host.

**Alfred Newman** (March 17, 1901–February 17, 1970). Associated with some 200 films, the prolific composer-conductor won eight Oscars for his scores, including "Mother Wore Tights" (1947) and "Love Is a Many-Splendored Thing" (1955).

## TELEVISION AND RADIO

### New Prime-Time TV Programs

"The Flip Wilson Show" (September 17, 1970–June 27, 1974; Comedy Variety)—Flip Wilson

"The Mary Tyler Moore Show" (September 19, 1970–  ; Situation Comedy)—Mary Tyler Moore, Edward Asner, Ted Knight, Gavin MacLeod, Valerie Harper (1970–1974), Cloris Leachman (1970–1975), Betty White (1973–  ), Georgia Engel (1973–  )

"McCloud" (September 16, 1970–  ; Police Drama)—Dennis Weaver, J. D. Cannon, Terry Carter, Diana Muldaur. *Note:* For 1971–1972, "McCloud" will leave an umbrella series to rotate with "Columbo" and "McMillan and Wife" on the "NBC Mystery Movie."

"Night Gallery" (December 16, 1970–August 12, 1973; Supernatural Anthology)—Host: Rod Serling (*Note:* The program appears on a four-week rotating basis until fall 1971.)

"The Odd Couple" (September 24, 1970–July 4,

1975; Situation Comedy)—Tony Randall, Jack Klugman

"The Partridge Family" (September 25, 1970–August 31, 1974; Situation Comedy)—Shirley Jones, David Cassidy, Susan Dey, Danny Bonnaduce, Brian Forster (1971–1974)

*Shirley Jones and her TV kids on ABC's new sitcom "The Partridge Family."*

### Emmy Awards 1969–1970 (June 7, 1970)

Drama Series—"Marcus Welby, M.D." (ABC)

Variety Series—"The David Frost Show" (syndicated)

Comedy Series—"My World and Welcome to It" (NBC)

Children's Programming—"Sesame Street" (NET)

Best Actor in a Series—Robert Young ("Marcus Welby, M.D.," ABC)

Best Actress in a Series—Susan Hampshire ("The Forsyte Saga," NET)

Best Comedian in a Series—William Windom ("My World and Welcome to It," NBC)

Best Comedienne in a Series—Hope Lange ("The Ghost and Mrs. Muir," ABC)

# News

**January 5.** ABC debuts the soap opera "All My Children." For the 1972–1973 season, cast member Mary Fickett will win the first Emmy for a daytime performance. As Ruth Martin, mother of a G.I. missing in action, she gave an emotional antiwar speech.

**May 2.** The Mississippi State Commission for Educational TV bans "Sesame Street" because the children's show is "highly integrated" and the state "was not yet ready for it." On May 24, the commission reverses its decision.

**May 22.** The CRTC has required radio and television stations to provide 55 percent Canadian content during the day and 40 percent in prime time. Effective October 1, 1971, the television percentage will alter to 50 percent throughout the day with no more than 40 percent from a single country during prime time. By 1972, that ratio must shift to 60 percent–30 percent.

Radio, on the other hand, must judge Canadian content on the basis of performance, composition, lyrics, and recording location. One qualification must be met by next January and two by January 1972.

The CRTC reassures the TV networks and radio stations that the standards are intended to help Canadians use their media to better communicate with each other.

**Fall.** The Nixon administration continues to rail against news reporting, but R. H. Bruskin and Associates find that 60 percent of Americans surveyed get most of their news from television and 50 percent find TV news to be the most believable of all media.

---

*Statistics*: A. C. Nielsen reports that the average American household watches 6.04 hours of TV per day, compared to 5.88 in 1969.

---

**Fall.** With a substantial grant from Mobil Oil, NET imports BBC dramas from Britain for "Masterpiece Theatre." Host Alistair Cooke debuts the program with "The First Churchills."

**September 1.** "I Dream of Jeannie" ends a five-year run on NBC. During the entire series, network censors never allowed genie-costumed Barbara Eden to expose her navel.

**September 12.** "Josie and the Pussycats" and "The Harlem Globetrotters" are the first network Saturday cartoon series to star minority characters.

**September 19.** "The Mary Tyler Moore Show" presents a novel character to television viewers—an unmarried woman who is neither widowed nor divorced and without a boyfriend by choice.

**September 21.** In 1959, ABC introduced professional football to network television, an 11:00 P.M. Saturday-night replay of a game played earlier that day. Tonight, in the first prime-time live broadcast, "ABC's NFL Monday Night Football" carries the game between the Cleveland Browns and the New York Jets. Keith Jackson gives the play-by-play while Don Meredith and Howard Cosell provide the color commentary. Purists resent the entertainment factor, but the game will consistently post high ratings. (Cosell was one of the commentators for the 1959 broadcast as well.)

**September 25.** Shirley Jones headlines ABC's new sitcom "The Partridge Family." In the first episode, the widow's four youngsters ask her to join them in a recording session. Their song, "I Think I Love You," becomes a smash hit and the Partridges turn to show business. In this case, life imitates art. The song reaches No. 1 on the pop charts and 20-year-old David Cassidy, Jones' stepson, becomes a teen idol. (The other kids have their voices dubbed during the numbers.)

**More news.** U.S. bus stations offer travelers a coin-operated TV chair—25 cents buys a 30-minute telecast.

• Since 1961, the number of AM country music stations has grown from 81 to 650. With 18 syndicated TV shows as well, CW receives national exposure.

## TV Commercials

Alka-Seltzer—The groom returns to the bathroom for another dose when the bride, thumbing through a cookbook, announces their second meal will be poached oysters.

Heinz—Old-time hoofer Ann Miller, a 12-foot soup can, and 4,000 fountain jets pay homage to 1930s musicals in a production number for Heinz's Great American Soups.

Kodak—"Green, Green Grass of Home" plays in the background as a real-life vet returns to his wife and hometown.

McDonald's—King Moody creates the definitive Ronald McDonald. He will appear at the opening of franchises and on TV ads.

Miller Beer—After acquiring the Miller Brewing Co. of Milwaukee, Philip Morris attempts to broaden the beverage's appeal with "If You've Got the Time, We've Got the Beer."

## *Obituaries*

**William Hopper** (January 26, 1915–March 6, 1970). With the emphasis on courtroom theatrics, Hopper's character Paul Drake usually brought Perry Mason the vital piece of evidence at the last moment.

**Inger Stevens** (October 18, 1934–April 30, 1970). The Swedish-born actress, best known for her starring role in the TV series "The Farmer's Daughter," died of acute barbiturate toxication. After her death, fans learn she had been secretly married to black musician Ike Jones since 1961.

**George Syvertsen** (March 22, 1932–1970). Captured by VC soldiers in Cambodia, the CBS correspondent was found in a ditch on June 3.

# SPORTS

## *Winners*

### *Baseball*

World Series—Baltimore Orioles (AL), 4 games; Cincinnati Reds (NL), 1 game
Player of the Year—John Powell (Baltimore Orioles, AL); Johnny Bench (Cincinnati Reds, NL)

Rookie of the Year—Thurman Munson (New York Yankees, AL); Carl Morton (Montreal Expos, NL)

### *Football*

NFL Championship—Dallas Cowboys 17, San Francisco 49ers 10
AFL Championship—Baltimore Colts 27, Oakland Raiders 17
Super Bowl V (January 17, 1971)—Baltimore Colts 16, Dallas Cowboys 13
College Bowls (January 3, 1970)—
Rose Bowl, USC 10, Michigan 3
Cotton Bowl, Texas 21, Notre Dame 17
Orange Bowl, Penn State 10, Missouri 3
Sugar Bowl, Mississippi 27, Arkansas 22
Heisman Trophy—Jim Plunkett (Stanford, QB)
Grey Cup—Montreal Alouettes 23, Calgary Stampeders 10

### *Basketball*

NBA Championship—New York Knickerbockers, 4 games; LA Lakers, 3 games
MVP of the Year—Willis Reed (New York Knickerbockers)
Rookie of the Year—Lew Alcindor (Milwaukee Bucks)
NCAA Championship—UCLA 80, Jacksonville 69

### *Tennis*

U.S. Open—Men, Ken Rosewall (vs. Tony Roche); Women, Margaret Court (vs. Rosemary Casals)
Wimbledon—Men, John Newcombe (vs. Ken Rosewall); Women, Margaret Court (vs. Billie Jean King)

### *Golf*

Masters—Billy Casper
U.S. Open—Tony Jacklin
British Open—Jack Nicklaus

*Hockey*

Stanley Cup—Boston Bruins, 4 games; St. Louis Blues, 0 games

*Ice Skating*

World Championship—Men, Tim Wood (U.S.); Women, Gabriele Seyfert (East Germany)

U.S. National—Men, Tim Wood; Women, Janet Lynn

Canadian National—Men, David McGillivray; Women, Karen Magnussen

*Kentucky Derby*

Dust Commander—Mike Manganello, jockey

*Athlete of the Year*

Male—George Blanda (Football)
Female—Chi Cheng (Track & Field)

*Last Season*

Jean Beliveau (Hockey)
Johnny Bower (Hockey)
Glenn Hall (Hockey)
Alex Karras (Football)
Marcel Pronovost (Hockey)

## News

**January 4.** Kansas City defeats Oakland, 17–7, in the last championship game of the American Football League. This fall, the AFL completes its merger with the NFL.

In the new arrangement, 13 of the old NFL teams form the National Football Conference (NFC) while the other 3 join the 10-team AFL as the American Football Conference (AFC). Divisional playoffs within each conference will send a team to the Super Bowl.

**January 21.** Boxing fans at 1,500 sites across the United States, Canada, and Europe, pay $5 to see the ultimate boxing match—Rocky Marciano versus Muhammad Ali. Last August, a movie crew filmed the two undefeated heavyweights in a series of one-minute staged rounds. Today, in the computerized result, Marciano KO's Ali in the 13th. Reportedly, Ali describes the outcome as "science fiction."

**February 16.** Joe Frazier knocks out elimination-round winner Jimmy Ellis in the fifth round of their title bout to become the undisputed heavyweight champion of the world.

**March 31.** In their first season, in 1969, the Pilots lost $1 million. Moved to Milwaukee this year, the new Brewers draw 250,000 more fans than the team did in Seattle.

**May 9.** To show their solidarity with campus demonstrations this year, many college athletes refuse to enter competitions. One of the largest protests comes today at the 36th annual Heptagonal track meet. In a five-paragraph statement, representatives from eight Ivy League schools denounce increased U.S. involvement in Asia, the deaths at Kent State, and "repression directed against political and racial minorities." West Point and Annapolis athletes were ordered to withdraw because their participation would not be appropriate.

**May 10.** Bobby Orr scores 40 seconds into overtime to give the Boston Bruins their first Stanley Cup in 29 years.

**May 15.** South Africa becomes the first nation expelled from Olympic competition since the formation of the modern Olympiad in 1896. Newly independent African states have lobbied to exclude the apartheid nation from various international sports.

**June 21.** In Mexico City, Pelé leads Brazil to a 4–1 victory over Italy in the World Cup. Back home, jubilant celebrations lead to 54 deaths and thousands of injuries.

**July 21.** For his tremendous impact on the sport of golf, sportswriters and broadcasters honor Arnold Palmer as "Athlete of the Decade." By lending his name to endorsements and franchises across the United States, Palmer has become the first athlete to parlay fame into a business empire.

**August 12.** After months of testimony by owners, players, and officials, Federal Judge Irving Ben Cooper upholds the 1922 Supreme Court decision that granted baseball immunity from prosecution under antitrust laws.

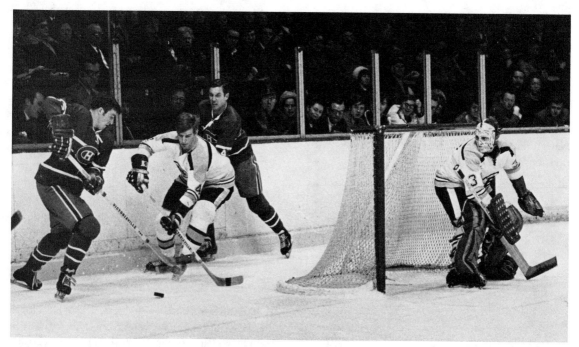

*Montreal Canadien Jean Beliveau (No. 4) battles Bobby Orr for the puck. The young Bruin defenseman becomes the first player to win all the NHL's top trophies in a single season—the Hart as MVP, the Norris as best defenseman, the Ross as top scorer, and the Smythe as playoff MVP.*

When St. Louis traded Curt Flood to Philadelphia, the outfielder took the Cardinals to court. Like every other ball player, his contract contains the reserve clause. Each year, if an athlete and his club fail to reach an agreement by a specified date, he must play with the team for an additional year. Since the same clause appears in each new contract, it effectively binds the player to a team for his entire career, unless he is traded.

Flood, who sat out the season with the support of the Players Association, will be traded to the Washington Senators. He will appear in just 13 more games before retiring.

**August 15.** Orlando Panther Steve Palinkas readies to kick for an extra point in an Atlantic Coast League game. His wife Pat will hold the ball. A bad snap forces her to run with it; 235-pound Wally Florence brings her down. (He later complains that Palinkas—the first woman to play on a professional football team—was "making folly with a man's game.") The husband and wife succeed with two other attempted conversions, but the NFL will never make her an offer.

**September 14.** Since the State Athletic Commission routinely grants boxing licenses to convicted criminals and military offenders, a New York federal court rules that it cannot deny one to Muhammad Ali. Before the end of the month, the commission restores Ali's license and the governor of Tennessee is advised that his state cannot legally bar a scheduled bout between the former heavyweight champion and Jerry Quarry. On October 26, after a 3½-year absence from the ring, Ali scores a TKO over Quarry in the third round.

**October.** For the 1970–1971 season, the NHL establishes a West division with the Blackhawks, Seals, and two new teams, the Buffalo Sabres and the Vancouver Canucks. Buffalo and Vancouver paid a record $6 million each for their franchises.

**October 1.** This season, the Reds moved into Cincinnati's Riverfront Stadium and the Pirates took possession of the new Three Rivers Stadium in

Pittsburgh. Today, the Phillies play their last game in Philadelphia's Connie Mack Stadium. But postgame ceremonies, scheduled to commemorate the end of an era, must be canceled when souvenir-crazed fans all but demolish the structure. They rip apart seats, tear down pieces of the scoreboard, and cart off such movable items as toilet bowls.

**More news.** With new franchises in Toronto and New York, the NASL splits into North and South divisions for the 1971 season.

---

*Statistics:* Over the past 10 years, attendance figures have skyrocketed in every sport: baseball—20.2 to 29.2 million; football—4.1 to 10 million; basketball—2 to 7.1 million; hockey—2.5 to 6.4 million.

---

## Records

**March.** LSU's Pete Maravich finishes his college basketball career with an enormous 3,667 points (Oscar Robertson held the previous record with 2,973). Over three years, Maravich set 11 NCAA records, including a 44.2-point game average (10.4 points better than the previous mark set by Robertson).

Many fans have berated "Pistol Pete" for hot dogging. But Press Maravich says his son, with behind-the-back and between-the-leg passes, is simply 10–15 years ahead of his time.

**March 26.** Chicago goalie Tony Esposito blanks the Toronto Maple Leafs to break the previous single-season record of 12 shutouts. Another 2 bring his goals-against-average down to 2.17 for the Vezina Trophy. As well, he collects the Calder as Rookie of the Year.

**September 7.** Jockey Willie Shoemaker brings home the 2-year-old filly Dares J, at Del Mar, for his 6,033rd winner. Former record holder Johnny Longden congratulates his successor in the winner's circle.

**November 8.** New Orleans Saint Tom Dempsey wins the game and sets a new NFL record with a 63-yard field goal. Dempsey was born without a right hand and only the back half of his right foot—the one he kicks with.

## What They Said

–"Aw, why not? I wasn't running well, anyway." Whitey Gerken on why he stopped his racing car at the Indianapolis Fairgrounds to pull an unconscious Jack Bowsher from his overturned car. Gerken is credited with saving Bowsher's life. (*Sports Illustrated*, August 3)

## Obituaries

**(Charles) Sonny Liston** (May 8, 1932–December 28, 1970?). The heavyweight boxer took the title from Floyd Patterson in 1962, then lost it to Cassius Clay two years later. In their controversial rematch, Clay (now Muhammad Ali) knocked out Liston in the first. The former champ attempted a comeback, but fought just one bout this year.

**Vince Lombardi** (June 11, 1913–September 3, 1970). Between 1959 and 1968, the U.S. football coach led the Green Bay Packers to six divisional titles, five NFL championships, and two Superbowls. He retired in 1968, but the man who reputedly said, "Winning isn't everything—it's the only thing," was unable to stay away from the game. A year later, Lombardi took on another perennial loser, the Washington Redskins; the team finished with its first winning season in 14 years. He died of cancer.

**Terry Sawchuk** (December 28, 1929–May 31, 1970). Over a 21-year career, the durable goalie recorded more than 100 shutouts and established a lifetime goals-against-average of 2.50. Sawchuk had just finished his first season with the New York Rangers when he died unexpectedly.

# 1971

Exasperated by 1970 Republican losses, Nixon virtually turns his back on Congress to rely more and more on his aides. And when The New York Times and other newspapers publish excerpts from the "Pentagon Papers," the White House establishes a policy of secrecy and containment to prevent further government leaks.

In other U.S. headlines, Washington police arrest 7,000 antiwar demonstrators, Congress kills supersonic transport, a military court convicts Lt. William Caley, the voting age drops to 18, prisoners at Attica riot, and the Supreme Court finds busing a constitutional means of integration. For the first time, American imports exceed exports as the world economic drive shifts from the United States to Germany and Japan.

Muhammad Ali has his day in court, television broadcasts the last cigarette commercials, and hot pants dominate the fashion scene. Jesus Christ Superstar premieres on Broadway, "Joy to the World" tops the year's songs, and new films include Klute, Summer of '42, The Last Picture Show, and The French Connection.

## NEWS

**January 6.** U.S. command announces a drive to combat drug abuse among American soldiers in Vietnam. Some 9,200 drug violations were recorded in the first 10 months of last year, and three days ago, a Defense Department task force reported that a policy of permissiveness had led to a breakdown in leadership and discipline at or below company command levels.

The next day, U.S. Command reports that American casualties in 1970 reached 4,204. Since January 1, 1961, 44,241 Americans have died in action in Indochina, another 9,064 from noncombat causes, and 293,529 have been wounded.

**January 22.** At the Commonwealth conference in Singapore, black African leaders bitterly oppose Britain's announced intention to resume arms sales to South Africa. Only a compromise resolution to study the embargo question prevents the breakup of the organization.

**February 4.** Washington discloses that 20,000 South Vietnamese elite forces invaded Laos on January 30 to cut Communist supply lines along the Ho Chi Minh Trail. Since congressional restrictions prevent U.S. soldiers from participating in the invasion, American advisors leave their troops at the border. The North Vietnamese, with what Defense Secretary Laird describes as "tremendously vicious and violent" resistance, overwhelm the South Vietnamese in the rough Laotian terrain. Only heavy U.S. air strikes and helicopter rescues prevent a complete annihilation.

An obvious test of Vietnamization, Nixon calls the operation successful enough to guarantee continued U.S. troop withdrawals. But at the end of the drive, on March 24, Saigon acknowledges 28 percent casualties—1,160 killed in action, 4,271 wounded, and 240 missing. Many in the South Vietnamese government and army attack their president for approving the action.

**February 9.** The worst California earthquake in 38 years (6.5 on the Richter scale) hits the San Fernando Valley at 6:00 A.M. Several freeways buckle, five major overpasses collapse, 900 buildings sustain major damage, and at least 139 buildings are judged unsafe for occupation. With few people out on the roads, the death toll remains low—62 killed, including 40 at a veterans' hospital. Aftershocks continue during the following week, and damage estimates soar to $1 billion.

**February 11.** A Sea-Bed Treaty bans the placement of nuclear weapons on or under the ocean floor. Eventually 63 nations will ratify the treaty, but France and Communist China will refuse to sign.

**February–March.** Late last year, Senator Sam Ervin of Illinois learned that 800 people in his state, including Adlai Stevenson, had been under army surveillance. True to his promise, Ervin chairs a Constitutional Rights Subcommittee investigation into military domestic spying.

Testimony reveals that U.S. Army intelligence gathering, originally undertaken to prepare for civil disturbances, has expanded to surveillance of any political dissident. The compiled dossiers—on some 25 million Americans—have circulated to every major troop center in the United States.

Following the first public disclosures last year, the army announced the discontinuation of a proposed surveillance data bank. But later inquiry reveals that a centralized file was only "abandoned" (possi-

bly meaning stored) and information continues to be collected for seven military intelligence headquarters.

**February 19.** An operator at the National Emergency Warning Center in Colorado accidentally runs the wrong tape, and radio and television stations across the United States broadcast a nuclear attack alert. Forty minutes later, the employee finally locates the countermand code word to authenticate a cancellation.

**February 21.** An estimated 40–50 tornadoes tear across Louisiana, Mississippi, and Texas, killing at least 93 people. Mississippi, the hardest hit, counts 82 dead in the delta area and 500 injured. Thousands are left homeless.

**March.** The Committee to Reelect the President (CREEP) opens offices in Washington. In the months ahead, Jeb Stuart Magruder joins as deputy director, Maurice Stans heads the Finance Committee, and next year John Mitchell will assume the directorship (although later some argue that he was in charge from the beginning). Fund-raisers "launder" checks to conceal their source, and quantities of supposedly untraceable $100 bills accumulate in CREEP coffers.

**March 24.** Ending a three-year political battle, the Senate votes 51–46 to kill the federally subsidized supersonic transport. Environmentalists had argued that the SST would produce considerable noise and pollute the stratosphere.

The British-French Concorde and the Soviet Union TU-144 continue flight trials.

**March 26.** East Pakistan breaks away from West Pakistan, declaring itself the independent republic of Bangladesh.

When Britain partitioned India in 1947, the largely Moslem province of East Bengal became part of a divided Pakistan. But the federal government in Karachi, 2,000 miles away, neglected and economically exploited the Eastern province, and the Bengalis soon sought autonomy.

Under the leadership of Mujibur Rahman (Sheik Mujib), the East Pakistani Awami League finally won a majority in the federal election this past December. But the government postponed the assembly, East Pakistan responded with a general strike, and Karachi sent in the army, mainly men from West Pakistan. Attempts at political compromise failed and fighting erupted yesterday. With the proclamation of independence, Mujib is arrested and civil war breaks out.

As the Pakistani Army brutally eliminates Awami members—students and teachers, professionals, and Hindus—more than 10 million people flee to India. Relations between Pakistan and India deteriorate until a brief war breaks out on December 3. The conflict ends on the 16th, when federal Pakistani forces surrender in Bangladesh.

President Yahya Khan of Pakistan is forced to resign, and Foreign Minister Ali Bhutto becomes the first civilian president in 13 years. Mujib will be released from prison in January 1972, and will return to Dacca to head the parliamentary government of the new Moslem nation. But the civil war has devastated the economies of both countries, and recovery will be slow.

**March 29.** U.S. Lt. William Calley, Jr., is convicted of the premeditated murder of 22 civilians in the South Vietnamese village of My Lai. Two days later, the military court sentences him to life imprisonment.

During the months of testimony and extensive news coverage, many Americans have come to view Calley as a scapegoat for those higher up or simply as a soldier doing his duty. Of the 25 officers and enlisted men originally charged with the massacre, only 6 stood trial; only Calley, the platoon leader, was found guilty.

On April 1, Nixon orders Calley released from the stockade and placed under house arrest pending his appeal. The president announces he will personally review the case, but public outcry forces him to back off.

In August, the Third Army commander reduces Calley's sentence to 20 years.

**April 6.** Last month, Washington further eased relations with Peking by ending all restrictions on American travel to China. In response, today the Communists invite the U.S. table tennis team, at championships in Japan, for a visit. The Americans spend April 10–14 in Peking, along with players from Canada and Britain, and the Chinese government admits Western newspeople, for the first time since 1949, to cover the event. The U.S. team extends a return invitation.

"Ping-pong diplomacy" helps prepare the American people for two surprise announcements from the White House. On June 10, President Nixon removes the 21-year-old U.S. embargo on trade with the People's Republic of China. Then on July 15, he promises to visit China before May 1972 "to seek the normalization of relations" between the two countries.

**April 7.** Announcing that another 100,000 U.S. troops will return home from Vietnam by December 1, Nixon states, "American involvement in this war is coming to an end." But he refrains from setting a date for complete withdrawal, claiming this would only serve the enemy's purpose. With this reduction, the number of soldiers stationed in Vietnam will drop to 184,000.

**April 20.** The Pentagon reports that in Vietnam last year the incidents of U.S. soldiers using fragmentation bombs against their own troops more than doubled. From 96 cases with 39 deaths in 1969 (the first year records were kept), the number rose to 209 incidents last year with 34 deaths. Senator Mike Mansfield describes "fragging" as "just another outgrowth of this mistaken, this tragic conflict."

**April 20.** In a series of unanimous decisions, the U.S. Supreme Court finds busing a constitutional means of integration, thus ending all efforts by the South to prevent desegregation. Still, the opinion declares schools must weigh traveling time, distance, and pupil age in considering busing.

The ruling stops short of ordering the elimination of de facto segregation in the North.

**April 22.** Haiti announces the death of President François Duvalier following a long illness. "Papa Doc," supported by his private army, the Tontons Macoutes, had brutally governed the island nation for almost 14 years. Last year, Duvalier rewrote the Haitian constitution to allow his 19-year-old son Jean-Claude to succeed him as president for life. Jean-Claude pledges to carry on the traditions of his father and soon becomes known as "Baby Doc."

**April 28.** A survey reveals that the number of

American blacks holding elective office rose 22 percent in 1970, to 1,860, with nearly three-fifths elected in the South. Yet this tremendous increase represents just 0.3 percent of all elected officials in the United States; blacks make up approximately 11 percent of the country's population.

**May 3–5.** Several weeks of antiwar demonstrations in Washington, including a gathering of some 500,000 at the Capitol on April 24, climaxes as thousands try to close down the government by disrupting city traffic. On the first day, police and federal troops arrest some 7,000 people. Lacking adequate jail facilities, authorities hold thousands on the Washington Redskins' practice field. The next day, police arrest another 2,000, and on the 5th, 1,800 more.

Attorney General Mitchell boasts that traffic is flowing again. Ted Kennedy remarks, "The city may have been safe for cars at the time, but it was a very unsafe place for citizens."

The courts dismiss most of the cases because law officers failed to include criminal charges and proper identification on field arrest forms. Just 200 will be convicted.

---

*Statistics:* The number of affirmative answers to the Gallup poll question, "Was the Vietnam War a mistake?" has steadily increased over the past five years from 35 percent to 61 percent. But a perceived generation gap concerning Vietnam is denied by a June poll, which shows more Americans *over* age 30 than *under* answered "Yes."

---

**May 4.** Heavy winter snow and spring rains have saturated the unstable clay deposits beneath the Quebec village of Saint-Jean-Vianney, but warnings from geologists have gone unheeded. At 10:45 P.M., a housing development drops 100 feet and a river of clay carries away 40 houses, cars, and a bus, killing 31 people. The Canadian government declares the area unsafe and relocates the survivors.

**May 7.** In a Gallup poll of 70 non-Communist political leaders, Prime Minister Indira Gandhi of India is chosen as the most admired person in the world.

**May 13.** The Vietnam peace talks enter their fourth year in a continued deadlock.

**June 13.** *The New York Times* excerpts a massive secret government study of the "History of the United States Decision-Making Process on Vietnam Policy" (1945–1968). The "Pentagon Papers," as they become known, were commissioned in 1967 by an increasingly disillusioned Robert McNamara, then secretary of defense under Lyndon Johnson.

From the documents and accompanying analyses, *New York Times* readers learn how each new White House administration deliberately escalated the war in Indochina while believing it could not be won, then lied about the degree of American involvement.

Although not included in the papers, the Nixon administration claims that disclosure would harm U.S. defense and diplomatic interests. *The New York Times* argues that the documents hold only historical value, but the Justice Department obtains a temporary restraining order on the 15th. The *Washington Post* prints additional passages, and when the courts issue a second restraining order, other newspapers carry on.

The issue quickly moves up to the Supreme Court. On June 30, a 6–3 vote upholds the First-Amendment right of the *Times* and *Post* to continue publication. Having failed to block the newspapers, the Justice Department goes after Daniel Ellsberg.

One of the study's authors, the 39-year-old Ellsberg leaked the highly classified Pentagon Papers to the press because he had come to believe in the immorality of the war. Along with a coworker at the Rand Institute, he is indicted in December for espionage and conspiracy.

Following the incident, Richard Nixon and his advisors establish a "special investigations unit" to prevent further leaks of confidential information. The group later becomes known as the Plumbers.

**June 30.** The states ratify the 26th Amendment to the Constitution in a record 2 months, 7 days (the old record for the 12th Amendment was 6 months, 6 days). An estimated 11 million new voters ages 18 to 20 will vote in the 1972 election.

**July 1.** The Postal Reorganization Act turns the 182-year-old U.S. Post Office into a semi-independent U.S. Postal Service. After years of unsuccessful attempts at reform, the government finally acted under the pressure of strikes and an increasing volume of mail—84.9 billion pieces last year. A board of governors, rather than the president, will now appoint the postmaster general.

**July 2.** President Nixon revives the Subversive Activities Control Board, established by Congress in 1950 to fight Communism but virtually inactive for the past 20 years. He plans to give the board new powers to investigate individuals and organizations that might be totalitarian, fascist, or subversive, or that use violence to deny rights to others.

Some members of Congress charge the administration with reviving "the spirit of McCarthyism," while Senator Sam Ervin comments, "There are some people in high position in the executive branch of the government who indicate by their recommendations that they do not like the Bill of Rights."

In 1972, the board will become the Federal Internal Security Board, with new presidential authority to investigate the character of organizations if relevant to the loyalty of federal employees.

**July 12.** Juan Vellejo Corona is indicted for the murder of 25 vagrants and migrant workers on his farm near Yuba City, California. (The Mexican immigrant fell under suspicion when authorities recovered two receipts bearing his signature from one of the first bodies found in the area.) While he may have killed the men for their small earnings, evidence suggests sex was a strong motivation.

Corona is sentenced to 25 consecutive life terms, with no chance of parole. After fellow Soledad prisoners stab him 32 times in a 1973 attack, he will be isolated for his own protection.

**July 30.** A young Japanese fighter pilot with only 21 hours of experience flies a Sabrejet into commercial air space and collides with an All-Nippon Airways Boeing 727 enroute to Tokyo. All 161 on board the airliner die. The student, who parachuted to safety, and his instructor, following in another plane, are held criminally responsible for the worst air disaster on record.

**August 2.** For the first time, the Nixon administration confirms that the CIA maintains an "irregular" army of 30,000 in Laos, mostly Thai men. A report to the Senate Foreign Relations Committee reveals that U.S. foreign aid in fiscal 1970 included $214 million in military and economic aid to the Laotian non-Communist government, and $70 million for Thai forces; in fiscal 1972, costs have risen to $374 million.

**August 9.** In an attempt to crush the IRA, Northern Ireland invokes emergency powers of internment without trial, and authorities seize over 300 people for questioning in a series of dawn raids. Another wave of rioting breaks out—reportedly the heaviest in Northern Ireland in 50 years—and within two days, at least 21 people die.

On September 6, a young girl caught in the crossfire between snipers and British troops becomes the 100th fatality in the two years of sectarian violence. In November, the Royal Ulster Constabulary announces that constables will now carry guns on patrol.

**August 24.** In 1969, Canada gave up a nuclear role in NATO and announced plans to reduce military forces in Europe from 9,800 to 5,000 men. Today, Ottawa releases a white paper further narrowing Canadian defense strategy.

Alliances will be maintained with the United States (for North American defense) and NATO (for European defense), but military resources will be directed more to the protection of Canadian sovereignty, particularly in the Arctic, and to civil and noncombatant activities.

In keeping with this policy and having judged Bomarc anti-aircraft missiles to be obsolete, the Liberal government will dismantle all nuclear weapons in Canada. Washington apparently wanted the Bomarc bases maintained.

*Statistics*: Since 1941, the population of Canada has nearly doubled from 11.5 million to 21.5 million.

**September.** Hundreds of American school districts begin the new year with court-ordered busing programs. But the Nixon administration, opposing massive busing "for the sake of busing," supports neighborhood schools instead. This official opposition appears to encourage growing resistance to the recent Supreme Court decision. In a November Gallup poll, 76 percent oppose busing, while just 18 percent believe busing will improve the quality of education for black children.

**September 9–13.** Some 1,000 prisoners riot at Attica Correctional Facility in Attica, New York, taking prison personnel hostage. The convicts release 11 injured guards, but ransom 39 others for improved conditions, including minority guards for the 60-percent black and Latino prison population. Then one of the hospitalized guards dies and the prisoners suddenly face murder charges.

The hostages plead for continued negotiations, arguing that prisoner requests are reasonable, but on Monday morning, September 13, Governor Rockefeller orders 1,500 state troopers, sheriffs' deputies, and guards to retake the prison. During the air and ground assault, 10 hostages and 29 prisoners die. Early official reports claim that the convicts slashed the guards' throats, but autopsies show all assault casualties resulted from gunshot wounds. Since no prisoner had a firearm, those killed in the attack died in the crossfire.

In a September 1972 report, the McKay Commission will strongly criticize all law enforcement officials involved in America's bloodiest prison riot: The governor should have visited the scene before giving the order; no communication lines existed between the operation leaders and police commanders; none of the troopers or deputies carried a nonlethal weapon; many indiscriminately fired shotguns loaded with buckshot; and some 89 wounded inmates received inadequate medical treatment. As well, the report notes that the prisoners had tried to air their legitimate grievances through the system.

Although a Special Congressional Subcommittee report, issued in 1973, will confirm the McKay Commission findings, charges stemming from the incident are brought against prison inmates only.

**September 11.** Nikita Khrushchev, ruler of the Soviet Union from 1958 to 1964, dies in Moscow at age 77. He rose through party ranks to become first secretary of the Communist party upon Stalin's death in 1953, the most powerful Soviet leader upon Malenkov's resignation in 1955, and premier in 1958.

Traveling extensively, Khrushchev attained a high international profile. But the jovial peasant face masked a tough leader, who in the early 1960s confronted the United States over the U-2 incident, built the Berlin Wall, and carried the world to the brink of war over the placement of Soviet missiles in Cuba.

Analysts theorize that those failed gambits, along with some domestic liberalization, an ideological rift with China, and an agricultural policy that resulted in enormous grain purchases, alienated the Soviet hard-liners who overthrew him.

Khrushchev quietly lived out his last years in Moscow and at his country dacha, and died in obscurity. The Politburo denies him a state funeral or burial in the Kremlin wall, but his son eulogizes, "There were those who loved him, there were those who hated him, but there were few who would pass him by without looking in his direction."

**September 28.** Jozsef Cardinal Mindszenty, age 79, ends a 15-year confinement in the U.S. Embassy in Budapest and accepts exile in Rome. Sentenced to life in prison in 1949 for plotting against the Communist Hungarian state, he was released in 1955 because of ill health. When the Soviets invaded the following year, the cardinal sought refuge with the Americans.

For many years a symbol to the western world of resistance to Communism, Mindszenty had become an embarrassment as the Vatican and the United States sought better relations with the Soviets.

Ordered not to speak out on his case or on Hungarian politics, the cardinal continues to criticize the Communists and Pope Paul removes him as primate. Mindszenty will die in 1975.

**October 25.** After a week of debate, the U.N.

General Assembly votes 76–35 (with 17 abstentions) to admit the People's Republic of China and expel Nationalist China from all U.N. bodies.

With the White House decision to resume limited relations with Peking, State Secretary Rogers had indicated in August that the United States would for the first time support action to seat Communist China. But American efforts to retain the Nationalist seat fail, and as the count is completed, many delegates leap to their feet and applaud wildly.

**November 6.** The Supreme Court denies a last-minute appeal for a temporary injunction against a controversial nuclear test on the Alaskan island of Amchitka. Japan, Canada, some U.S. senators, and thousands of American citizens, including environmentalists and antiwar groups, have strongly opposed the most powerful U.S. underground test ever.

Although there are no radiation leaks, a government research geophysist will report next summer that the 5-megaton detonation caused 22 minor earthquakes and hundreds of aftershocks in the succeeding three months.

**November 22.** In overturning an Idaho law favoring men as estate executors, the Supreme Court for the first time uses the 14th Amendment (enacted in 1868) to grant women equal rights and to invalidate a state law on the grounds of sex discrimination.

In past years, the court has extended the historic Brown decision on school segregation to other racial laws, but here the justices stop short of finding unconstitutional all laws drawing sexual distintions.

**November 24.** On a Northwest Orient flight, a middle-aged bespectacled man demands $200,000 or he will blow up the plane. The aircraft lands in Seattle, the 36 passengers deplane, and the hijacker—listed as D. B. Cooper—picks up his ransom. Shortly after the plane leaves for Reno, he parachutes out the rear door.

Children find some of the marked money along the Columbia River, but the hijacker and the rest of the ransom disappear. Cooper becomes a kind of folk hero, but authorities believe he probably died in his descent through the strong winds and freezing rain of a thunderstorm.

**December 9.** Nixon vetoes the Child Development Act, which would have set up a national system of day-care centers for an estimated 1–2 million children, ages 3–5 years. The president claims the bill would weaken the family structure by promoting the communal approach.

**December 18.** In August, the U.S. suspension of the convertibility of the dollar alarmed foreign governments, but President Nixon expressed a willingness to devaluate. Finance ministers from the 10 leading industrial nations meet in Washington and agree to an 8.57-percent dollar devaluation against gold—from $35 an ounce to $38—and the upward revaluation of the other currencies, including the German mark and Japanese yen. Nixon then ends the 10-percent U.S. import surtax.

**December 21.** The U.N. Security Council nominates Kurt Waldheim, a 53-year-old Austrian career diplomat, to succeed U Thant as secretary-general. The long campaign to find a successor ended when China abstained after vetoing two earlier votes. The next day, the General Assembly ratifies the nomination in a secret ballot.

## Obituaries

**Dean Acheson** (April 11, 1893–October 12, 1971). As Truman's secretary of state (1949–1953), Acheson laid the foundation for American Cold War strategy by implementing the Truman Doctrine and Marshall Plan, supporting the founding and rearmament of West Germany, defining emerging atomic and Nationalist Chinese policies, and overseeing the foundation of NATO and the conduct of the Korean War.

**Hugo L. Black** (February 27, 1886–September 25, 1971). The associate justice resigned on September 17 due to ill health, then suffered a stroke two days later. During his long career on the Supreme Court (1937–1971), Black consistently applied the Bill of Rights to state laws. His judicial philosophy often proved confrontational, yet many of his dissents—particularly on the rights of criminal defendants—later became majority rulings. Chief Justice Warren E. Burger calls Black "one of the authentic legal philosophers of our time."

**Ralph Bunche** (August 7, 1904–December 9, 1971). Following the 1948 assassination of negotiator Folke Bernadotte, the United Nations called on the experienced black American Ralph Bunche to mediate the partition of Palestine. His success with an Arab-Israeli armistice brought him the 1950 Nobel peace prize. Bunche later directed U.N. peace missions for the Suez, Congo, and Cyprus crises, then served as under-secretary-general from 1967 to his retirement in 1971.

**Thomas E. Dewey** (March 24, 1902–March 16, 1971). The Republican governor of New York (1942–1954) ran for president against Franklin Delano Roosevelt in 1944 and against Harry S. Truman in 1948.

**John M. Harlan** (May 20, 1899–December 29, 1971). Justice Harlan believed the due-process clause of the Constitution dictated legislative rather than judicial solutions to Bill of Rights violations. As a result, he often found himself with the minority on the liberal Warren Court. He retired on September 23 due to ill health, after 16 years on the Supreme Court bench.

**Nikita Khrushchev** (April 17, 1894–September 11, 1971). *See* News.

**Sylvester Magee** (May 26, 1841–October 15, 1971). Slave-trading records and a family bible supported his claim to be the last surviving American slave.

**Maurice McDonald** (1902–December 11, 1971). In 1948, he and his brother Richard cofounded McDonald's Hamburgers in California. Thirteen years later, with more than 200 restaurants franchised, the McDonalds sold out to Ray Kroc for $2.7 million.

**Lewis "Chesty" Puller** (June 26, 1898–October 11, 1971). The most decorated marine in the history of the Corps served in W.W.I, W.W.II, and the Korean War. He retired a lieutenant general.

**Elmo Roper** (July 31, 1900–April 30, 1971). The American pollster developed the first scientific method of forecasting election results. He successfully predicted, with an error rate of 1 percent,

Roosevelt's reelection in 1936, 1940, and 1944.

**Arthur Spingarn** (March 28, 1878–December 1, 1971). A leader in the long struggle to obtain equal rights for black Americans, he cofounded the NAACP and served as vice-president (1911–1940) and president (1940–1965).

**Joseph Valachi** (September 22, 1904–April 3, 1971). Under a Mafia sentence of death in 1963, he broke the code of silence to become an FBI informer. Since the bureau delays the report of his death for a week, rumors circulate that Valachi is still alive.

# BEGINNINGS AND ENDINGS

## News

**February 5.** To raise fees without hurting the needy or expanding student aid (up 904 percent in the last four years), Yale adopts the nation's first program for deferred tuition.

**February 7.** Male voters in Switzerland approve a referendum giving women the right to vote in federal elections and to hold federal office. In the fall, 11 women win seats in Parliament. (Men in Liechtenstein defeat a similar measure on February 28.)

**February 15.** Britain completes the changeover to decimal currency, ending a 1,000-year monetary tradition of shillings and pounds.

**March 1.** Secretary of Commerce Maurice Stans halts the licensing of U.S. commercial whale hunters.

**March 4.** Pierre Trudeau, age 51, weds Margaret Sinclair, age 22, in a secret ceremony. He is the first Canadian prime minister to marry while in office.

**March 31.** The first U.S. silver dollar issued since 1935 presents, on one side, the profile of Dwight D. Eisenhower, "In God We Trust," and the year. On the reverse, a bald eagle clutches an olive branch (symbolic of *Apollo 11*). This coin remains uncirculated. The dollar released to the public in the fall contains nickel and copper, like the American dime.

**April 7.** New York sets up the country's first legalized offtrack betting system to increase city revenues and take business away from organized crime.

**April 24.** In Canada, David Lewis succeeds the first leader of the NDP, Tommy Douglas.

**May 1.** Last year, Congress established the National Rail Passenger Corp. to improve rail service. Today, the first travelers ride Amtrak (originally called Railpax). Heavily subsidized, the corporation links 300 cities across the nation.

**May 12.** The Civil Service Commission rules "men only" and "women only" limitations must be dropped from nearly all federal jobs (exceptions include the position of prison matron).

**June 12.** Tricia Nixon marries Edward Cox in the Rose Garden at the White House.

**August 31.** Since December 1965, some 246,000 Cubans have left their homeland for the United States. Concerned about the number of skilled workers choosing to leave, Fidel Castro shuts down the airlift.

**September 15.** Last year, in Vancouver, three Canadians found the "Don't Make a Wave Committee" to protest nuclear testing in the Aleutian Islands. Today, Greenpeace (the trio wanted a catchier name) heads north. Although their chartered fishing boat never reaches Amchitka, their nonviolent action—"bearing witness" in the Quaker tradition—receives widespread publicity.

**September 25.** Minorities in the United States, fearing a repetition of the W.W.II internment of Japanese-Americans, finally succeed in pressuring Washington to repeal the Emergency Detention Act (Title II of the Internal Security Act). Passed in 1950, at the onset of the Cold War, the bill authorized the detention of any person suspected of sabotage or espionage during an invasion or insurrection. The government prepared six detention camps, but never used them.

**September 26.** Hirohito and Richard Nixon spend 35 minutes together in Anchorage, Alaska, in the first meeting between an American president and a Japanese emperor. Although Hirohito offers no formal apology for Japanese aggression during W.W.II, he reportedly views his trip as a form of penance.

**November 18.** Responding to a Weather Service stagnation alert, an Alabama federal judge issues the nation's first air pollution emergency (under the Clear Air Act of 1970) to shut down 23 Birmingham plants.

**November 18.** France auctions off the celebrated Maginot Line. Constructed in the 1930s as a permanent defense against German attack, the elaborate barrier—bunkers, air-conditioned living quarters, underground rail lines—proved useless in 1940. The Nazis simply rolled in behind the outward-pointing guns.

**November 20.** In Hong Kong, the Anglican Church ordains its first two women priests.

**More news.** In San Francisco, Erhard Seminars Training offers two weekends of consciousness training, a mixture of TM, Zen, Scientology, and other systems. In the early 1970s, thousands take the $300 EST workshops but, as instructed, refuse to share their "unique" personal experience. Media critics refer to Werner Erhard as a brilliant con man.

## Government Departments and Agencies

**February 24.** An executive order upgrades the seven-year-old Presidential Committee on Consumer Affairs to the Office of Consumer Affairs. The new body coordinates consumer protection agencies at the federal level.

## Memorable Ad Campaigns

McDonald's tells Americans, "You Deserve a Break Today, So Get Up and Get Away to McDonald's."

## Fads

Charles Hall, a California furniture designer, sold his first water bed last summer. King Koil Sleep Products agreed to manufacture the bed and sells about 15,000 in six months (mostly to hippies and playboys). Early models often split open, causing a flood.

In 1969, New York manufacturer N. G. Slater put out a button with small black eyes over a great big smile. Lost at first in the overloaded market, the Smile button captures the nation this year with an estimated 20 million sales. And the little grin spreads, as Americans buy Smile lighters and Smile coffee cups, waitresses draw little smiles on their bills, and graffiti artists splash them everywhere. The enormous craze—one of the biggest since the Hula Hoop—will fade next year.

Plastic Clacker Balls—available in a range of colors for $1—strike sharply together when kids swing the connecting cord up and down. But the novelty quickly wears off, and the first children's fad of the decade dies out in just a few months.

The July issue of *Popular Science* features the hottest bike in the United States. Weighing as little as 22 pounds, the 10-speed makes a 3-speed "feel like an old truck." A dealer, who sold only a dozen in 1969, can no longer keep them in stock.

# SCIENCE AND TECHNOLOGY

## *News*

**January 6.** Biochemist Choh Hao Li, at the University of California, reports the first synthesis of somatotropin, the human growth hormone produced by the pituitary gland. While the synthetic possesses just $^1/_{10}$ of the active properties of the natural hormone, it promises a simpler and cheaper procedure for promoting growth in dwarf children.

**January 10.** U.S. astronomers confirm the discovery of two "new" galaxies just 3 million light-years away. Nine years ago, Italian astronomer Paolo Maffei found two strange objects on infrared photographs of heavy interstellar dust in that region.

**January 15.** In the UAR, President Anwar Sadat and Soviet President Podgorny officially dedicate the Aswan High Dam. (The USSR contributed $1 billion and 5,000 workers to the project.) By controlling the annual flooding of the Nile, the dam brings 1.3 million acres under cultivation and provides 10 billion kilowatts of electric power. At the same time, by holding back the rich river silt, the Aswan will make riverside lands less fertile, erode

the Nile delta, and reduce the number of sardines in the eastern Mediterranean.

**January 31.** Grounded for several years due to inner ear problems, Alan Shepard sets out for the moon on *Apollo 14.* Six days later, Stuart Roosa remains in the command module while Shepard and Edgar Mitchell land on the lunar surface.

For the first time, Apollo astronauts move about in a vehicle, a four-wheel-drive Lunar Rover built by Boeing. (The cart remains on the surface for other flights.) Their total $33^1/_2$ hours on the moon include the longest surface activity to date—9 hours, 7 minutes. Just before leaving, with awkward one-armed swings, Shepard launches the first extraterrestrial tee shots.

**Early in the year.** At Intel, Marcian E. (Ted) Hoff develops the microprocessor, a complex printed electrical circuit holding all the arithmetic and logic functions of a computer. Previously, each application—keyboard, display, printer—required a different chip. With Federico Faggin's layout, Intel possesses a computer on a chip. The first appears in a Japanese calculator.

**March 24.** *The New York Times* reports the development of an effective serum hepatitis vaccine for children. The result of 15 years of ongoing research, it is regarded as an important step but not a cure.

**April 19.** *Salyut 1,* 65.6 feet long and 13 feet in diameter, reaches orbit. *Soyuz 10* docks three days later, but for some reason the crew fails to board. On June 6, *Soyuz 11* approaches, docks, and the next day, *Salyut* becomes the first manned space laboratory.

Georgi Dobrovolski, Viktor Patsayev, and Vladislav Volkov shatter all records with a 23-day stay. But the Soviets, so confident of their equipment, sent the men up without spacesuits. When *Soyuz* loses pressure during reentry, decompression kills all three cosmonauts. (U.S. astronauts journey to Moscow for the funeral.)

Devastated by the deaths, the Soviets make no further trips to the station and, six months later, the engines ignite and *Salyut* disintegrates.

**May 23.** The first American scientists allowed into China in 20 years, two U.S. biologists recount the use of acupuncture for a Shanghai news story.

Chinese physicians admit, "We know the results we will get, but we cannot explain exactly why we get them."

**July 2.** In Texas, Drs. Elizabeth S. Priori and Leon Dmochowski announce the isolation of a C-type virus from the form of cancer known as Burkitt's lymphoma. The first established link between a virus and cancer, their discovery opens up possibilities for future cancer research.

**July 26–August 7.** Better mobility (with the two-seater lunar car) as well as improved space suits and life support, allow NASA to expand the scientific knowledge of the moon through the last three Apollo flights.

*Apollo 15* astronauts Dave Scott and Jim Irwin, in three excursions, travel 5 miles, collect an 8-foot core sample, and discover a grayish rock with green glass beads (later shown to be 4 billion years old, older than any rock on Earth). As well, the men leave a plaque and small sculpture to commemorate the 14 astronauts and cosmonauts lost in the two space programs.

During the return voyage, CM pilot Alfred Worden takes the first walk in deep space. Some 197,000 miles from home, he spends 16 minutes retrieving film from outside the craft.

**September.** During the 175th anniversary of the first vaccination, the U.S. Public Health Service discontinues the smallpox shot as a routine procedure. Both PHS and WHO believe people now face greater danger from the vaccine than from the disease.

**September 29.** The FDA asserts that polychlorinated biphenyl, or PCB, is a potential, not an imminent, health hazard. But consumer advocate Ralph Nader charges the government with lulling Americans into a false sense of security by withholding information. Three years ago, 5 people died and some 1,000 more suffered a serious skin disease from PCB-contaminated cooking oil. As well, the FDA has found high levels of PCB in recycled cardboard cereal packaging.

**October 29.** Doctors at the University of Pennsylvania Medical School report the first successful use of electrical current to mend a bone fracture. A female patient with a year-old fracture healed within nine weeks of low-voltage application through a small wire cathode.

**November 13.** The first artificial satellite to orbit another planet, *Mariner 9* reaches Mars just 4.4 seconds ahead of schedule. The lifeless planet depicted in earlier fly-bys emerges as much more dynamic. Photos reveal polar regions, a huge canyon thousands of miles long, volcanic mountains, and former riverbeds.

Intended to orbit just 90 days, *Mariner 9* will remain functional until October 1972, mapping the entire planet with some 7,300 pictures.

**November 23.** The FDA warns physicians that the synthetic hormone diethylstilbestrol, or DES, taken by pregnant women to prevent spontaneous abortions, has produced a high rate of vaginal cancer in their daughters.

**December 2.** Launched on May 28, the Soviet *Mars 3* enters orbit around the planet. The capsule immediately sends a lander to the surface, but signals last a mere 20 seconds. Likely, the first object to reach the Martian surface failed under the high winds of an ongoing dust storm.

The data, transmitted by the orbiting craft over 90 days, show that the polar caps consist of frozen carbon dioxide with a core of frozen water.

None of the following probes in the Mars series achieves a successful landing.

**December 4.** In the largest voluntary recall in automotive history, GM calls back some 6.7 million Chevrolet cars and trucks. Industry observers estimate a $25-$37-million cost. Other recalls this year include 220,000 Ford Pintos; about 100 of the cars have experienced fires in their engines.

**More news.** At 2½ pounds, the Pocketronic from Texas Instruments is the first truly portable calculator. Capable of adding, subtracting, multiplying, and dividing, the all-electronic machine sells for $150.

## Other Discoveries, Developments, and Inventions

First indoor movie camera that requires no extra lighting, the Kodak XL

Home pregnancy tests in Britain

Soft contact lenses

Telephone for the deaf, in Britain, with audible signals transmitted as visible lamp signals

Commercial production of Kevlar, a strong aramid fiber, by du Pont

Auto-Train to transport automobiles between Washington, D.C., and Florida

## Obituaries

**Walter Bentley** (September 16, 1888–August 13, 1971). The British automobile designer produced the first Bentley in 1921. A win in the 1924 Le Mans endurance race established his model.

**Donald Duncan** (circa 1893–May 15, 1971). The entrepreneur, who introduced the yo-yo to North America in 1929, bought the rights to the parking meter in 1936. When his company was sold in 1959, it was producing 80 percent of the country's meters.

## THE ARTS

May 17—*Godspell*, with David Haskell (still running in 1975)

May 26—*Lenny*, with Cliff Gorman (455 perfs.)

October 12—*Jesus Christ Superstar*, with Jeff Fenholt, Ben Vereen, Yvonne Elliman (711 perfs.)

November 11—*The Prisoner of Second Avenue*, with Peter Falk, Lee Grant, Vincent Gardenia (780 perfs.)

## Tony Awards

Actor (Dramatic)—Brian Bedford, *The School for Wives*

Actress (Dramatic)—Maureen Stapleton, *Gingerbread Lady*

Actor (Musical)—Hal Linden, *The Rothchilds*

Actress (Musical)—Helen Gallagher, *No, No, Nanette*

Play—*Sleuth*

Musical—*Company*

## News

**May 31.** The 1970–71 Broadway season saw 56 productions. Only four shows repay their initial investment: *Home, Sleuth, Oh, Calcutta!, And Miss Reardon Drinks a Little.*

**September 8.** The premiere of Leonard Bernstein's *Mass* opens the John F. Kennedy Center for the Performing Arts, in Washington, D.C. An official memorial to the assassinated president, the $70-million complex houses the National Symphony Orchestra, the Washington Opera, and the American Film Institute.

**October 12.** In an unusual twist, Britain's *Jesus Christ Superstar* opens on Broadway *after* touring the United States. Various religious groups protest the rock opera's portrayal of Jesus.

**More news.** A Rembrandt print fetches $83,000 as art prices continue to escalate.

## Obituaries

**Tyrone Guthrie** (July 2, 1900–May 15, 1971). The noted British director rekindled interest in traditional theater with his original interpretations of Shakespeare and modern drama.

**Igor Stravinsky** (June 17, 1882–April 6, 1971). Compelled to compose, the young Russian abandoned the study of law and moved to Paris. His first great ballet, *The Firebird* (1910), brought him recognition; three years later, the dissonances of *The Rite of Spring* provoked a riot. Still, Stravinsky's free tonality and innovative rhythms, phrasing, and instrumentation made him one of the most influential composers of this century. He moved to the United States with the outbreak of W.W.II, and became an American citizen in 1945. Later works included the opera *The Rake's Progress* (1951).

## WORDS

Anonymous, *Go Ask Alice*

William Peter Blatty, *The Exorcist*

Dee Brown, *Bury My Heart at Wounded Knee*

Frederick Forsyth, *The Day of the Jackal*

Arthur Hailey, *Wheels*
James A. Michener, *The Drifters*
Ellen Peck, *The Baby Trap*
Harold Robbins, *The Betsy*
Gay Talese, *Honor Thy Father*
Thomas Tryon, *The Other*
John Updike, *Rabbit Redux*
Erich von Däniken, *Gods from Outer Space*
Joseph Wambaugh, *The New Centurions*
Herman Wouk, *The Winds of War*

## News

**February.** A Gallup survey reveals that 26 percent of adults read a complete book last month, the highest percentage since the question was first asked in 1958.

**June.** *New Woman* appears on the newsstands.

**October 19.** Unable to meet skyrocketing costs, the popular *Look* magazine ceases publication after 34 years.

**October 30.** The 96-year-old *Toronto Telegram* shuts down.

*Statistics:* In the United States, 157 newspaper chains control half of the 1,748 dailies and 63 percent of total circulation.

**More news.** The *Chronicle of Higher Education* lists the 10 best-sellers on campus (in order): *Everything You Always Wanted to Know About Sex*, *Love Story*, *The Greening of America*, *The Sensuous Woman*, *Future Shock*, *The Prophet*, *The French Lieutenant's Woman*, *The Godfather*, *The Population Bomb*, and *Body Language*.

• With this year's nostalgia boom, the *Saturday Evening Post* returns as a quarterly (circulation warrants a bimonthly by 1973), and a new *Liberty* uses photographic plates and stories from the original magazine.

• *Time* magazine equalizes the salaries and working conditions of male and female counterparts. *Newsweek* follows suit.

• *The Compact Edition of the Oxford English Dictionary* condenses the OED's 13 volumes into 2 (with a magnifier) at less than one third the cost of the full set.

## Cartoons and Comics

**April 15.** Publishers ease the Comics Code to allow for the portrayal of drug addiction, but only as "a vicious habit." Spider Man recently ignored the drug taboo.

**September.** The New York Cultural Center mounts the first comic-book exhibit, *75 Years of the Comics*.

*Statistics:* 81 percent of American kids spend an estimated $1.18 per week on comics.

## TIME *Man of the Year*

Richard Nixon

## New Words and Phrases

activism
ageism (prejudice or discrimination against the elderly)
body language
clean (free from drug addiction)
crazies (apolitical radicals who behave irrationally and often destructively)
creepy-bopper (a preteenage fan of monster movies)
environmental pollution
fragging (throwing a fragmentation grenade to wound or kill one's overly aggressive military leader)
gross out
guesstimate
hot line
Jesus Freak
lib (abbreviation for liberation)
no-knock (authorized police entry without announcement)

non-event
right on (interjection to express hearty approval)
sexism
shuck (deceive, swindle)
spin-off
street worker (an adult who seeks out and tries to help local teenagers)
to splurge
to trash (to vandalize, especially as an act of protest)
up front (in advance)
workaholic

## Obituaries

**Margaret Bourke-White** (June 14, 1906–August 27, 1971). The renowned *Life* photographer (1936–1969) captured some of this century's most important events, including the German attack on Moscow and the horror of Buchenwald.

**Bennett Cerf** (May 25, 1898–August 27, 1971). The head of Random House (1927–1970) published such literary giants as James Joyce, William Faulkner, and Eugene O'Neill. Cerf was also a regular panelist on TV's "What's My Line?" for 16 years.

**Manfred B. Lee** (January 11, 1905–April 2, 1971). By making their detective the "author" of 37 novels, Lee and his cousin Frederic Dannay turned Ellery Queen into a household name.

**Ogden Nash** (August 19, 1902–May 19, 1971). The American writer was best known for his humorous and satirical verse.

**Virginia O'Hanlon (Douglas)** (1890–May 13, 1971). At age 7, little Virginia wrote to the *New York Sun* to ask if Santa Claus really existed. Francis Pharcellus Church replied, "Yes, Virginia, there is a Santa Claus." His editorial appeared every Christmas until 1949.

# FASHION

## Haute Couture

After last year's disaster, spring collections offer a variety of hemlines, separates, and classic pieces. By the fall, with increasing competition from ready-to-wear, lengths stabilize at the knee.

## News

**January.** For the first time, Paris couturiers allow photographs of their creations. The London *Times* marks this concession as "the final admission that trends are not set by any one level of fashion house anymore or by any one city."

**March.** *House Beautiful* examines the influence of Hollywood glamor queens on three decades of hair and makeup styles.

Through W.W.II and the late forties, millions of working women copied the wholesome look and upswept hair of actress Betty Grable. In the 1950s, sultry Marilyn Monroe set the standard (her very initials, MM, came to symbolize beauty). Through the next decade, Audrey Hepburn and the film *Cleopatra* drew attention away from pouting lips to dramatic eyes. Today, young women emulate the California, or Natural, look of actress Ali MacGraw and others.

In concluding, the article notes a recent twist to Hollywood testimonials for cosmetics, soaps, and shampoos, actresses Polly Bergen and Zsa Zsa Gabor have developed their own cosmetic lines.

**More news.** Decorators adapt durable denim for pillows and other home fashions.

## Colors and Materials

Designers use satin (particularly nylon blends), bring back taffeta and seersucker, and introduce washable wool jerseys and new mixes of natural and synthetic fibers (such as nylon and flax).

A continuing Chinese influence popularizes quilting and highlights enamel yellow and turquoise blue. Other important colors include purple, orange, vermillion red, and strong pinks. And, once again, black is "in."

Textile manufacturers play with zodiac signs, flowers, stars, big arrows, and other vibrant patterns.

## Clothes

With most young American women still showing a preference for the mini over the midi, the hot pants fad this year is no surprise. Ranging from short-shorts to mid-thigh length, the European pants appear with a mid-length coat and high boots in the early winter months, then with platform shoes in the spring. Surprisingly, the craze dies out before summer's end.

The wrapped coat, tied with a soft belt, is a huge success.

Retailers stock three major dress silhouettes—a loose tent, the shirt dress, and the smock.

Layered separates combine and coordinate prints and patterns.

Pantsuits give way to slacks and a matched blazer with the same cut, material, and color accents as a man's jacket.

The popularity of hipster pants prompts the garment industry to bring out crotch-snap blouses and hosiery manufacturers to introduce the bodysuit in blouse and sweater styles. But next year's sales of over 12 million will plummet to 1 million by mid-decade.

The little black dress returns in a fitted, sexy styling.

The peasant look, found in most 1970 couturier collections, takes off this year—boots, flowered prints, long-fringed shawls, large shoulder bags, big earrings.

Young people personalize their faded denim jeans with badges, patches, appliqué, embroidery, paint and dye, and the favorites, rhinestone studding and an upside-down American flag. The fad begins to wane in 1974, but the method of shrinking jeans to a skintight fit remains—soak in a bathtub of warm water then wear the denims out in the sun to dry.

In menswear, with easy-care fabrics and the interest in knits and weaves, the jacket-slacks combination makes further inroads on the traditional suit. Multicolored patterns and discreet stripes replace the wilder shirt colors of recent years. For casual wear, two-piece coordinates win approval.

## Accessories

The create-your-own-style mode spotlights accessories such as the fringed shawl for the peasant look and a plumed hat for a Three Musketeers outfit.

The hosiery industry quickly responds to hot pants with sheer tights and no thigh line. Black and earthen shades predominate.

In the early 1970s, shoes promote the wet look and textured surfaces such as canvas and natural linen. (An early craze sees cut-out shapes attached or appliquéd to the end of straps.) Boot materials include canvas (one of the most popular fabrics of the decade), punched leather, and painted, silvered, or patchworked smooth leather and plastics. Purple remains the most influential color.

Young men don large "drapery" patterned ties and platform shoes or boots.

## Hair and Cosmetics

Long hair for women modifies slightly to mid-length.

For eyes, lips, and nails, cosmetic companies promote fashion colors as never before. The presence of back-to-nature products on the market owes much to an increasing concern for the environment and the growing influence of yoga.

Women pluck their eyebrows into a curve.

## Obituaries

**Gabrielle "Coco" Chanel** (August 19, 1883–January 10, 1971). In 1914, at the outbreak of war, Chanel revolutionized restrictive Victorian clothing with her comfortable, casually elegant styles.

Through the next two decades, the French couturier remained an important influence, creating the first chemise in 1920 and, five years later, introducing the classic Chanel suit, with collarless, braid-trimmed jacket. (In 1922, she chose her lucky number to name a new perfume—Chanel No. 5.)

Eclipsed by rising couturiers in the late 1930s,

Chanel retired only to make a monumental come-back in 1954. *The New York Times* calls Chanel "the fashion spirit of the 20th century."

## MUSIC

"Joy to the World"—Three Dog Night
"Maggie May"—Rod Stewart
"It's Too Late"/"I Feel the Earth Move"—Carole King
"One Bad Apple"—Osmonds
"How Can You Mend a Broken Heart"—Bee Gees
"My Sweet Lord"/"Isn't It a Pity"—George Harrison
"Knock Three Times"—Dawn
"Brand New Key"—Melanie
"Family Affair"—Sly & the Family Stone
"Go Away Little Girl"—Donny Osmond
"Gypsies, Tramps & Thieves"—Cher
"Just My Imagination (Running Away with Me)"—Temptations
"Theme from *Shaft*"—Isaac Hayes
"Me and Bobby McGee"—Janis Joplin
"Brown Sugar"—Rolling Stones
"Indian Reservation (The Lament of the Cherokee Reservation Indian)"—Raiders
"Want Ads"—Honey Cone
"You've Got a Friend"—James Taylor
"Uncle Albert/Admiral Halsey"—Paul & Linda McCartney
"What's Going On"—Marvin Gaye
"Never Can Say Goodbye"—Jackson 5
"Spanish Harlem"—Aretha Franklin
"Rainy Days and Mondays"—Carpenters
"Mama's Pearl"—Jackson 5
"Take Me Home, Country Roads"—John Denver
"She's a Lady"—Tom Jones
"Put Your Hand in the Hand"—Ocean

### Grammys (1971)

Record of the Year—Carole King, "It's Too Late"
Song of the Year (songwriter)—Carole King, "You've Got a Friend"
Album of the Year—Carole King, *Tapestry*

Best Vocal Performance (Male)—James Taylor, "You've Got a Friend" (single)
Best Vocal Performance (Female)—Carole King, *Tapestry* (album)
Best New Artist—Carly Simon

### News

**January.** At the time of her death in 1970, Janis Joplin's last album remained incomplete. Released this month, *Pearl* (her nickname) yields the No. 1 single "Me & Bobby McGee," written by Kris Kristofferson. The only previous posthumous No. 1 rock hit was Otis Redding's "Dock of the Bay."

**May 12.** Rock star Mick Jagger marries Bianca Perez Morena de Macias, the daughter of a Nicaraguan diplomat. The couple, who become parents in October, take up with the jet set.

**June 13.** At a star-studded charity concert in Los Angeles, Frank Sinatra gives his farewell appearance. The 55-year-old, who has recorded some 100 albums, sings his most famous numbers in an emotional 30-minute set. In 1973 Sinatra will return to the recording studio to make *Ol' Blue Eyes Is Back.*

**June 21–28.** With lawsuits pending and everyone from the governor down threatening violence, the Celebration of Life sets up in a 700-acre cow pasture near McCrea, Louisiana. Klansmen, worried about young blacks coming in contact with Northern whites, hassle festival personnel. (At one point state troopers lock the promoter in a police van.) Organizational and legal problems keep half the advertised performers away. And about 100 of the estimated 70,000 in attendance are arrested on drug charges, 1 person dies of an overdose, and 2 people drown. Billed as "the resurrection of the rock festival," McCrea signals its end.

**July 3.** Thousands of youths break through wooden and chain-link fences on the second evening of the nine-day Newport Jazz Festival. Police use tear gas to regain control, but as organizers announce the closure, several hundred gate crashers crowd onto the stage. With $20,000–$30,000 damage, the Folk Festival scheduled to follow is canceled. Next year, the Jazz Festival will move to New York City.

**August 1.** Over the ashes of one rock phenomenon rises another—the celebrity fund-raiser. George Harrison hosts the afternoon and evening performances of the Concert for Bangladesh at Madison Square Garden. Guests include Ringo Starr, Eric Clapton, Ravi Shankar, and an unannounced Bob Dylan at his first concert in two years. He performs a 23-minute set, then saunters off. The concerts collect $250,000, but with various problems, only a fraction of the money will be used to buy food for the fledgling nation.

**October 29.** Representatives from the U.S. and various European nations meet in Geneva to sign an international convention against record and tape piracy. Annual losses of some $200 million have made the agreement essential. Still, the most extensive copyright violations take place in the Orient and no Asian country appears as a signatory.

Within the United States, the 1960s introduction of tape cartridges and cassettes made bootlegging a relatively risk-free and extremely profitable crime—no royalties, no advertising costs, all guaranteed best-sellers. Pirates copy the original, counterfeiters sell copies as the original product, while the specialist illegally records concerts, creates a new disc with hits from different albums, or somehow lays hands on unreleased tracks such as Beatles rough cuts for "Get Back."

Since bootleggers simply move from one state to another, the American recording industry is looking to the federal government for legislation.

---

*Statistics:* Legitimate record and tape sales total $1.7 billion this year. About 60 percent of buyers are under the age of 30.

---

**More news.** As rock 'n' roll begins to splinter into jazz-rock, Latin rock, soul rock, progressive rock, and heavy metal, big-name groups demand and receive $30,000–$40,000 for a single concert. Unable to meet those prices, promoter Bill Graham closes down his Fillmore West ballroom in San Francisco and his Fillmore East in New York City.

• Last year, producers Dave Appell and Hank

Medress persuaded Tony Orlando to lay down lead vocals for a single record, then added Telma Hopkins and Joyce Vincent Wilson as backup. "Candida" was a hit and this year's "Knock Three Times" fares even better.

With several groups naming themselves Dawn, Orlando pesters Hopkins and Wilson to perform in public. Finally, just to get rid of him, Hopkins demands a first-class trip to Europe. The threesome will still be on the road in 1975.

• The Osmond brothers strike gold with their first album and the seventh son, 13-year-old Donny, goes gold with his first single. His next recording, "Go Away Little Girl," reaches No. 1, the first rock song to top the charts on two separate occasions. Steve Lawrence achieved the first hit in 1963.

• Sha Na Na cashes in on the general nostalgia craze with its renditions of fifties music. As well, this year, record buyers enjoy a still older style of music. Biograph, among other companies, issues a series of ragtime piano rolls played by Fats Waller, Jelly Roll Morton, James P. Johnson, and Scott Joplin.

• The first album to receive a gold tape award, Carole King's *Tapestry* sells a whopping 12 million copies worldwide over the next two years. The 31-year-old divorced her songwriting partner, Gerry Goffin, in 1968.

• Just two years ago, Robin Gibb split with his brother Barry and twin Maurice. Recently reunited ("If we hadn't been related," he told *Time,* "we would probably never have gotten back together"), the Bee Gees score their biggest hit yet. "How Can You Mend a Broken Heart" holds on to the No. 1 position for four weeks.

• Commissioned by Columbia Records, CBS Labs develops the stereo quadraphonic record system, four channels of sound from a two-track source. The first quadraphonic LP's will be released in 1972, but with high production costs and the incompatibility factor, the new technology will never get off the ground.

• Thirteen-year-old Michael Jackson releases his first single, "Got to be There." It reaches No. 4 on the charts.

David Cassidy
Cheech & Chong
Alice Cooper
Michael Jackson
Olivia Newton-John
Donny Osmond
Osmonds
Helen Reddy
Carly Simon
Cat Stevens (in North America)
Wings (Paul McCartney)

## Obituaries

**Duane Allman** (November 20, 1946–October 29, 1971). The lead guitarist of the Allman Brothers Band dies in a motorcycle accident.

**Louis Armstrong** (August 4, 1901–July 6, 1971). The first solo jazz star and one of the most influential musicians in this century, Armstrong learned how to play the coronet at a waif's home in New Orleans. From small groups in the early twenties, he was fronting larger bands by the end of the decade. Comfortable in the trumpet's upper register, Satchmo (shortened from Satchelmouth) would thrill his audiences with dozens of high notes. And along with those long codas, Armstrong went further than anyone in melody improvisation and almost invented scat singing.

But in the end, the jazz innovator was concerned more with entertaining his audiences. A goodwill ambassador for the United States, Armstrong always included all-time favorites like "When the Saints Go Marchin' In." And the gravelly voice, mugging, and showy white handkerchief became trademarks. His biggest pop hits included "Mack the Knife" (1956), "Blueberry Hill" (1956), and "Hello, Dolly" (1964).

**Cliff Edwards** (June 14, 1895–July 17, 1971). A popular singer in the 1920s and 1930s, Ukelele Ike sold nearly 74 million records and appeared in more than 100 movies. The younger generation knows him as the squeaky tenor voice for Jiminy Cricket in *Pinocchio.* He died an alcoholic on welfare.

**Henry D. Haynes** (July 27, 1920–August 7, 1971). Haynes and Kenneth Burns made up the bluegrass comedy team of Homer & Jethro. Their 50 albums and single hits included such butchery as "Jam-Bowl-Liar" for Hank Williams' "Jambalaya."

**Bob Hilliard** (January 28, 1918–February 1, 1971). From the mid-1940s to the 1960s, his lyrics included "Dear Hearts and Gentle People" (1949) and "Moonlight Gambler" (1956). He also wrote the score for Disney's *Alice in Wonderland* (1951).

**Ted Lewis** (June 6, 1891–August 25, 1971). The successful band leader relied on his sidemen, such as Benny Goodman and Jimmy Dorsey, in posting more than 100 hits between 1920 and 1933. Lewis wrote the words for his theme "When My Baby Smiles at Me" (1920).

**Jim Morrison** (December 8, 1943–July 3, 1971). In 1965, Morrison referred to Aldous Huxley—"If the doors of perception were cleansed every thing would appear to man as it is, infinite"—for the name of his rock group, the Doors. Just two years later, their first album produced the hit "Light My Fire" (his composition). A controversial performer, Morrison could no longer function within the band and in midyear took a year's leave in Paris. Reportedly, his heart failed, but a delayed death notice and the fact that few saw his body fuel rumors that the singer is still alive. He lies in the Poets' Corner of the Père Lachaise Cemetery.

## MOVIES

*Bananas* (d. Woody Allen; color)—Woody Allen, Louise Lasser, Carlos Montalban

*Bedknobs and Broomsticks* (Disney, d. Robert Stevenson; color)—Angela Lansbury, David Tomlinson, Roddy McDowall

*A Clockwork Orange* (d. Stanley Kubrick; color)—Malcolm McDowell, Patrick Magee, Michael Bates

*Death in Venice* (Italian, d. Luchino Visconti; color)—Dirk Bogarde, Björn Andresen, Silvana Mangano

*Diamonds Are Forever* (British, d. Guy Hamilton; color)—Sean Connery, Jill St. John, Charles Gray, Lana Wood

*Dirty Harry* (d. Don Siegel; color)—Clint Eastwood, Harry Guardino, Reni Santoni

*The Emigrants* (Swedish, d. Jan Troell; color)—Liv Ullmann, Max von Sydow

*Fiddler on the Roof* (d. Norman Jewison; color)—Topol, Norma Crane, Leonard Frey, Molly Picon, Paul Mann, Rosalind Harris

*The French Connection* (d. William Friedkin; color)—Gene Hackman, Fernando Rey, Roy Scheider, Tony LoBianco

*The Garden of the Finzi-Continis* (Italian, d. Vittorio De Sica; color)—Dominique Sanda, Lino Capolicchio, Helmut Berger

*The Go-Between* (British, d. Joseph Losey; color)—Julie Christie, Alan Bates, Dominic Guard, Margaret Leighton, Michael Redgrave

*Harold and Maude* (d. Hal Ashby; color)—Ruth Gordon, Bud Cort

*The Hospital* (d. Arthur Hiller; color)—George C. Scott, Diana Rigg, Barnard Hughes

*Klute* (d. Alan J. Pakula; color)—Jane Fonda, Donald Sutherland, Charles Cioffi, Roy Scheider

*Kotch* (d. Jack Lemmon; color)—Walter Matthau, Deborah Winters, Felicia Farr, Charles Aidman

*The Last Picture Show* (d. Peter Bogdanovich; bw)—Timothy Bottoms, Jeff Bridges, Cybill Shepherd, Ben Johnson

*Macbeth* (British, d. Roman Polanski; color)—Jon Finch, Francesca Annis, Martin Shaw, Nicholas Selby

*Play Misty For Me* (d. Clint Eastwood; color)—Clint Eastwood, Jessica Walter, Donna Mills

*The Railway Children* (British, d. Lionel Jeffries; color)—Dinah Sheridan, Bernard Cribbens, William Mervyn, Jenny Agutter

*Shaft* (d. Gordon Parks; color)—Richard Roundtree, Moses Gunn, Charles Cioffi

*Skin Game* (d. Paul Bogart; color)—James Garner, Louis (Lou) Gossett, Susan Clark, Brenda Sykes

*Summer of '42* (d. Robert Mulligan; color)—Jennifer O'Neill, Gary Grimes, Jerry Houser, Oliver Conant

*Sunday, Bloody Sunday* (British, d. John Schlesinger; color)—Glenda Jackson, Peter Finch, Murray Head

*Two-Lane Black Top* (d. Monte Hellman; color)—James Taylor, Warren Oates, Laurie Bird, Dennis Wilson

## Academy Awards

**April 15.** This year, 32 "Friends of Oscar" preside over the ceremonies, including Steve McQueen, Maggie Smith, Walter Matthau, first Oscar winner Janet Gaynor, and, of course, Bob Hope.

Best Picture—*Patton*
Best Actor—George C. Scott (*Patton*)
Best Actress—Glenda Jackson (*Women in Love*)
Best Director—Franklin J. Schaffner (*Patton*)
Best Supporting Actor—John Mills (*Ryan's Daughter*)
Best Supporting Actress—Helen Hayes (*Airport*)
Best Song—"For All We Know" from *Lovers and Other Strangers*
Best Foreign Film—*Investigation of a Citizen Above Suspicion* (Italian)
Honorary Awards—Lillian Gish; Orson Welles

Actress Helen Hayes becomes the first performer to collect Oscars for both leading (1931–1932) and supporting roles. And the Beatles receive an Oscar for their original song score in "Let It Be."

After George C. Scott again declined the Oscar nomination, president of the Academy, Daniel Taradah, responded, "Actually, Mr. Scott is not involved. It is his performance in *Patton* which is involved." When the actor wins, the award stands.

## News

**January 18.** The movie industry appears healthy, with 250 new theaters built in the last year, but *U.S. News and World Report* notes that MGM lost $8.2 million over the first nine months of 1970 and 20th Century-Fox reported a $21.3-million deficit.

Still, with the sale of huge back lots, TV profits, and the promise of technological advances, most executives look to a brighter future. As Charlton

Heston, president of the Screen Actors Guild, has said, "Video cassettes may turn out to be the biggest prize package opened in Hollywood since sound came in."

**June 28.** According to *Newsweek*, *The Godfather* producers appeased the Italian-American Civil Rights League by cutting all Mafia references from the script. Actor Robert Duvall expresses annoyance at the loss of one of his favorite lines: "A lawyer with a briefcase can steal more than a hundred men with guns."

**October.** In a Computer Cinema test run, at the Gateway Downtowner Motor Inn in Newark, New Jersey, *Business Week* found that a large number of guests paid $2–$3 to watch a movie on their in-room TV. Admittedly, 60 percent of the patrons had not seen a movie in six months, but a startling 17.6 percent chose to see the same picture a second time rather than watch free TV.

**November 24.** In disclosing European attendance figures for 1963–1970, MPAA president Jack Valenti points to the repeated link between fewer moviegoers and more TVs. But more importantly for American producers, an age breakdown of U.S. figures verifies the growing influence of baby-boomers—12- to 20-year-olds represent 22 percent of the country's population yet account for 47 percent of filmgoers.

**December 18.** *Business Week* reports a nostalgia boom as some classic films outdraw new big-budget titles. A Manhattan theater owner warns interested managers that the competition for old movies has driven up rental prices. "We played *Citizen Kane* 100 times over the years and now we can't afford it."

**More news.** Riding on the popularity of his spaghetti Westerns, Clint Eastwood convinces Universal Pictures to let him direct his next picture—*Play Misty for Me*—for a percentage of the profits. He brings the film in almost 40 percent under budget and strikes gold at the box office. With his other smash release this year, *Dirty Harry*, the 41-year-old becomes a superstar.

• A news story out of Florida claims that two packs of wild monkeys roaming a central section of the state are descendants of motion picture runaways. Reportedly, in the early 1930s, Hollywood producers brought in Asian rhesus monkeys to recreate Africa. When the company left, three of the monkeys escaped.

• Actor Tom Laughlin writes, directs, and stars in *Billy Jack*, about a half-breed karate expert who saves a "free" school from hippie-hating townspeople. A massive box office success (with a $32-million gross), this violent picture, along with *Dirty Harry*, creates a new genre for copycat Hollywood—vigilante films.

| Top Box Office Stars | Newcomers |
|---|---|
| John Wayne | Jennifer O'Neill |
| Clint Eastwood | Karen Black |
| Paul Newman | Gary Grimes |
| Steve McQueen | Sally Kellerman |
| George C. Scott | Art Garfunkel |
| Dustin Hoffman | Bruce Davison |
| Walter Matthau | Richard Roundtree |
| Ali MacGraw | Deborah Winters |
| Sean Connery | Jane Alexander |
| Lee Marvin | Rosalind Cash |

### Top Money-Maker of the Year

*Love Story* (1970)
(*Note*: Ryan O'Neal, co-star of the TV series "Peyton Place," was offered the lead role after John Voight, Beau Bridges, Michael York, Michael Douglas, and Michael Sarrazin all turned down the script.)

### Obituaries

**G(ilbert) M. "Bronco Billy" Anderson** (March 21, 1882–January 20, 1971). In 1907, the director-producer starred as Bronco Billy. With some 400 episodes over the next seven years, he became the screen's first cowboy hero.

**Gladys Cooper** (December 18, 1888–November 17, 1971). From her first Hollywood movies in 1940, the British dame of stage and screen characterized dignified British women.

**Van Heflin** (December 13, 1910–July 1971). The Oscar winner, for his supporting role in *Johnny*

*Eager* (1941), often played intelligent, determined men, like the homesteader in *Shane* (1953).

**Ub Iwerks** (March 24, 1901–July 8, 1971). The original animator for Mickey Mouse sold his partnership to the Disneys for $2,920, but returned to the studio in 1940 to develop animation techniques and supervise special effects. His multiplane camera and matte process (which blends animation and live action) brought him two Oscars.

**Harold Lloyd** (April 20, 1893–March 8, 1971). In 1917, the comic collaborated with producer Hal Roach to create his screen personna—an eternally optimistic, bespectacled young man who overcame hair-raising obstacles. In one classic sequence, the tremendously athletic Lloyd climbed a 20-story building, without harness or safety gear, then hung from a huge clock.

At the height of his career, the comedian outdrew Charlie Chaplin and Buster Keaton, but with the coming of sound his popularity waned and he retired in 1938. In 1962 and 1963, Lloyd released two compilations of his films, to worldwide acclaim.

**Audie Murphy** (June 20, 1924–May 28, 1971). The most decorated U.S. soldier in W.W.II parlayed his fame into a career in war films and Westerns.

**Max Steiner** (May 10, 1888–December 28, 1971). With 200 motion-picture scores, the three-time Oscar-winning composer strongly influenced the development of the musical score as an element of film. His most famous background music remains *Gone With the Wind* (1939).

**Paul Terry** (February 19, 1887–October 25, 1971). The cartoon pioneer, credited with perfecting cel animation, formed Terrytoons in 1931. His best-known characters—Mighty Mouse, Heckle and Jeckle, and Little Roquefort—were created after W.W.II. In 1955, Terry sold his studio and over 1,000 cartoons to CBS and retired.

## TELEVISION AND RADIO

### New Prime-Time TV Programs

"All in the Family" (January 12, 1971–   ; Situation Comedy)—Carroll O'Connor, Jean Stapleton, Sally Struthers, Rob Reiner

"Cannon" (September 14, 1971–   ; Detective)—William Conrad

"Columbo" (September 15, 1971–   ; Police Drama)—Peter Falk

"McMillan and Wife" (September 29, 1971–   ; Police Drama)—Rock Hudson, Susan Saint James, John Schuck *Note:* "Columbo," "McMillan and Wife," and "McCloud" appear in rotation on the "NBC Mystery Movie."

"The New Dick Van Dyke Show" (September 18, 1971–September 2, 1974; Situation Comedy)—Dick Van Dyke, Hope Lange, Marty Brill (1971–1973), Fannie Flagg (1971–1973), Angela Powell

"Owen Marshall, Counselor at Law" (September 16, 1971–August 24, 1974; Lawyer Drama)—Arthur Hill, Lee Majors

"The Sonny and Cher Comedy Hour" (August 1, 1971–May 1974; Musical Variety)—Sonny Bono, Cher

### Emmy Awards 1970–1971 (May 9, 1971)

Drama Series—"The Senator" ("The Bold Ones"; NBC)

Variety Series, Musical—"The Flip Wilson Show" (NBC)

Variety Series, Talk—"The David Frost Show"

Comedy Series—"All in the Family" (CBS)

Best Actor in a Series—Hal Holbrook ("The Senator" ["The Bold Ones"], NBC)

Children's Programming—"Sesame Street" (PBS)

Best Actress in a Series—Susan Hampshire ("The First Churchills," ["Masterpiece Theatre"], PBS)

Best Comedian in a Series—Jack Klugman ("The Odd Couple," ABC)

Best Comedienne in a Series—Jean Stapleton ("All in the Family," CBS)

### News

**January 2.** Cigarette advertising ends today on U.S. television. The legislation allowed an extra day so that networks could broadcast commercials during the widely watched college football games.

**January 12.** CBS warns viewers, "The program you are about to see is 'All in the Family.' It seeks to throw a humorous spotlight on our frailties, prejudices, and concerns. By making them a source of laughter, we hope to show, in a mature fashion, just how absurd they are." Producer Norman Lear agreed to delete a "goddamn it" and a scene showing the son-in-law zipping his fly on the way down the stairs, but insisted every insult and racial slur remain in the sitcom's first episode.

Extra telephone operators, hired for an expected deluge of complaints, receive about two dozen calls. Just 10 million people caught this television milestone. But with an Emmy in May, Archie, his wife Edith (a.k.a. the Dingbat), daughter Gloria, and her husband Mike (a.k.a. Meathead) capture the No. 1 spot with summer reruns. The program will remain on top through the middle of the decade.

**February 23.** "The Selling of the Pentagon" details the Defense Department's use of speakers and a variety of media to gain public support. The administration charges CBS with distortion and a congressional subcommittee subpoenas the network for "all work prints, outtakes, sound tape recordings, written scripts [and] a statement of all disbursements of money." CBS president Frank Stanton, on solid legal ground, agrees to surrender what was broadcast and nothing more. After a heated debate, the House denies the subcommittee's request for a citation for contempt.

**March.** Since the first episode, "Odd Couple" stars Jack Klugman and Tony Randall have bitterly complained about the program's atrocious laughtrack. Finally, ABC agrees to delete the canned hilarity in an experiment. At the end of the show, Randall asks viewers for written comments. Some 50,000 letters run 4–1 in favor of their decision. At the beginning of the second season, the show is filmed in front of a live audience.

**March 5.** The FCC publicly reminds radio stations of their responsibility to screen all songs for lyrics that "promote or glorify the use of illegal drugs." While the music industry and fans debate the notice, station owners receive the message loud and clear. Some DJs are told that it would be better not to play controversial numbers.

**June 6.** In the first step of a modernization plan, CBS cancels "The Ed Sullivan Show" just 2 weeks short of 23 years. Final guests include Sid Caesar, Carol Channing, and Gladys Knight & the Pips.

Some considered Sullivan a square, but a waiter at his favorite restaurant spoke for many. "He's a right guy, Ed. Listen, he's got a great variety show. He's *America.* He will never be destroyed. The way I feel about my country is the way I feel about Ed" (*Saturday Evening Post*, April 20, 1968).

**Fall.** Along with the loss of tobacco revenues this year, the networks must swallow the "access rule." Last year, to give independent producers a shot at affiliate air time, the FCC cut prime time down from $3^1/2$ hours to 3 hours for the fall of 1971. The networks filed suit, but the Supreme Court upheld the commission's authority.

As intended, affiliates turn to syndicated programs for the extra $3^1/2$ hours per week. Some successful daytime programs, like "Hollywood Squares," get their first chance at an evening slot.

**More news.** The industry estimates 50 percent of American households own a color TV set. Sales this year reach an all-time high of 7.2 million.

• Two unusual telemovies draw top ratings this year. "The Night Stalker," with wise-guy reporter Darren McGavin, brilliantly mixes comedy and horror. "Duel," a suspenseful story of an automobile driver terrorized by a trucker, brings director Steven Spielberg considerable attention.

### TV Commercials

Coca-Cola—A multinational group of teenagers stands on a hilltop outside Rome, and sings, "I'd like to buy the world a coke."

Hallmark—At the end of a difficult day, an average woman comes home to find a Hallmark

*CBS dumps "Hee Haw," "Mayberry R. F. D." "Green Acres," and "The Beverly Hillbillies" (shown here). Although the shows all have strong ratings, network executives find little advertising appeal in their audiences—rural, older or poorer.*

card waiting for her, and the concept of "social realism" revolutionizes advertising.

Levi's®—Rotoscoping—not quite human not quite animation—allows the Stranger to turn all the monochromatic denims in town into the popular, garish colors of the day.

## Obituaries

**Philo Taylor Farnsworth** (August 19, 1906–March 11, 1971). The television electronics pioneer once held more than 165 patents.

    **David Sarnoff** (February 27, 1891–December 12, 1971). For his influence on the emerging technology, the RCA president (1930–1947) and chairman (1948–1970) was dubbed the "father of American television."

# SPORTS

## *Winners*

### *Baseball*

World Series—Pittsburgh Pirates (NL), 4 games; Baltimore Orioles (AL), 3 games
Player of the Year—Vida Blue (Oakland Athletics, AL); Joe Torre (St. Louis Cardinals, NL)
Rookie of the Year—Chris Chambliss (Cleveland Indians, AL); Earl Williams (Atlanta Braves, NL)

### *Football*

NFC Championship—Dallas Cowboys 14, San Francisco 49ers 3
AFC Championship—Miami Dolphins 21, Baltimore Colts 0
Super Bowl VI (January 16, 1972) Dallas Cowboys 24, Miami Dolphins 3
College Bowls (January 2, 1971)—
    Rose Bowl, Stanford 27, Ohio State 17
    Cotton Bowl, Notre Dame 24, Texas 11
    Orange Bowl, Nebraska 17, LSU 12
    Sugar Bowl, Tennessee 34, Air Force Academy 13
Heisman Trophy—Pat Sullivan (Auburn, QB)
Grey Cup—Calgary Stampeders 14, Toronto Argonauts 11

### *Basketball*

NBA Championship—Milwaukee Bucks, 4 games; Baltimore Bullets, 0 games
MVP of the Year—Lew Alcindor (Milwaukee Bucks)
Rookie of the Year—Dave Cowens (Boston Celtics); Geoff Petrie (Portland Trail Blazers)
NCAA Championship—UCLA 68, Villanova 62

### *Tennis*

U.S. Open—Men, Stan Smith (vs. Jan Kodés); Women, Billie Jean King (vs. Rosemary Casals)

Wimbledon—Men, John Newcombe (vs. Stan Smith); Women, Evonne Goolagong (vs. Margaret Court)

## Golf

Masters—Charles Coody
U.S. Open—Lee Trevino
British Open—Lee Trevino

## Hockey

Stanley Cup—Montreal Canadiens, 4 games; Chicago Blackhawks, 3 games

## Ice Skating

World Championship—Men, Ondrej Nepela (Czechoslovakia); Women, Beatrix Schuba (Austria)
U.S. National—Men, John Petkovics; Women, Janet Lynn
Canadian National—Men, Toller Cranston; Women, Karen Magnussen

## Kentucky Derby

Canonero II—Gustavo Avila, jockey

## Athlete of the Year

Male—Lee Trevino (Golf)
Female—Evonne Goolagong (Tennis)

## Last Season

Ernie Banks (Baseball)
Andy Bathgate (Hockey)
Gale Sayers (Football)

# News

**January 2.** After a close city match, Glasgow soccer fans attempt to break through the stadium crowd barriers. In the ensuing pileup, 66 people are crushed or trampled to death.

**February 6.** On the surface of the moon, Alan Shepard pulls out a secretly prepared golf club and special heat-resistant balls. Understandably, the as-tronaut botches his first hit, but the second and third balls travel up to a half mile in the thin atmosphere. Golfers around the world sit slack-jawed in envy.

**February 9.** Satchel Paige is elected to the new Negro League wing in the Baseball Hall of Fame. The legendary pitcher, who played 20 odd years with black teams, says, "The only change is that baseball has turned Paige from a second-class citizen into a second-class immortal" (*Sports Illustrated*, February 22).

After Jackie Robinson broke the color barrier in 1947, Paige finally received a major league tryout. He played with Cleveland (1948–1949) and St. Louis (1951–1953), then returned to barnstorming. His long career ended with a three-inning appearance for the Oakland A's in 1965.

Four years earlier, the extraordinary right-hander estimated he had won 2,000 of his 2,500 games and at least 55 were no-hitters. (In the Negro Leagues, he sometimes called in the outfield to strike out the side.)

**March 8.** In his first title bout since 1967, Muhammad Ali loses on points to defending heavyweight champion Joe Frazier. (Ali took a mandatory 8-count in the 15th.) A crowd of 20,455 and closed-circuit TV coverage produces an enormous gross of $20 million; each prize-fighter receives an estimated $2.5 million.

Two days later, an exhausted Frazier enters the hospital suffering from high blood pressure.

**April 4.** The Phillies' first appearance in their new $45-million Veterans Stadium draws an NL record crowd of 56,371. Later in the season, the Giants inaugurate their new 75,000-seat Meadowlands Stadium in New Jersey.

**June 28.** The U.S. Supreme Court overturns Muhammad Ali's draft conviction. The unanimous decision notes that the Justice Department misled the Selective Service in 1967 by claiming the boxer's beliefs were neither sincere nor based on religious tenets. The former heavyweight champion, who never served any of his five-year prison term, tells reporters he will take no legal action to recover damages.

**August 26.** Bobby Orr resigns with the Boston

Bruins for $1 million over five years. Hockey's first million-dollar contract makes the young defenseman one of the highest-paid athletes.

**September.** Basketball superstar Lew Alcindor announces his conversion to the Muslim faith; he adopts the name Kareem Abdul-Jabbar.

**September 21.** Baseball owners approve the transfer of the Washington Senators to Texas for the 1972 season. The team becomes the Texas Rangers.

**October 10.** Since the first Davis Cup in 1900, the defending champion has received a bye to the final challenge round. But this year, participating nations decided, after today's final round, that the previous year's winner must henceforth play through from the beginning.

**October 13.** After 68 years, the major leagues play their first World Series night game. (NBC had recommended a prime-time start for better ratings.) The record Pittsburgh crowd of 51,378 cheers the Pirates on to a 4–3 win.

**October 24.** Detroit Lion Chuck Hughes suffers a heart attack in a game against the Chicago Bears. The 28-year-old wide receiver becomes the first professional football player to die without regaining consciousness.

**More news.** Bicycle sales boom in the United States this year—an estimated 8.5 million compared with 5.6 million in 1965 and 3.7 million in 1960.

## Records

**April.** Boston Bruin Phil Esposito finishes the NHL regular season with a record 76 goals. Teammates Bobby Orr, Johnny Bucyk, Ken Hodge, Wayne Cashman, and Johnny McKenzie place second, third, fourth, seventh, and eighth in the scoring race as Boston chalks up a record 399 goals.

**December 1.** In Yonkers, Canadian Herve Filion brings home his 500th winner of the season, a harness racing record.

**This year.** Ed Marinaro finishes his three-year football career at Cornell University with a record 4,132 yards rushing and a game average of 209 yards.

---

*Statistics:* For the first time, college football attendance reaches a yearly total of 30 million.

---

• This season, statisticians register a record 50 HBP (hit by pitch) for Montreal Expo Ron Hunt. ("Some people give their bodies to science; I give mine to baseball.") He retires in 1974 with 3 HBP records: career (243); season (this year); and game (3, tied).

## What They Said

He hit me on the head with his stick. And he didn't apologize.
–New York Ranger Rod Gilbert explains his fight with Philadelphia Flyer Bill Lesuk (*Sports Illustrated*, March 8)

## Obituaries

**Bobby Jones** (March 17, 1902–December 18, 1971). Never a professional and only a part-time player, Jones nonetheless left his mark on the game of golf. Over 14 years, he won 23 of 52 events (62 percent in his last 8 years), including four U.S. Opens, three British Opens, five U.S. Amateur titles, and, in 1930, the first Grand Slam—U.S. Open, British Open, U.S. Amateur, and British Amateur. He retired that year, but assisted with the Augusta course design and led in organizing the Masters. In later years, a spinal ailment confined him to a wheelchair.

**Dick Tiger (Dick Itehu)** (August 14, 1929–December 14, 1971). The Nigerian boxer held the middleweight and light-heavyweight titles during the 1960s.

**George Trafton** (December 6, 1896–September 5, 1971). A member of coach Knute Rockne's undefeated Notre Dame team, Trafton entered pro football with Chicago in 1920. The "iron man," one of the first centers to use the one-handed pass, never missed a game in 13 years.

# *1972*

No one believes McGovern. After all, "Tricky Dick" is the president. Even those who have heard of Watergate view opposition charges as politicking. And, in November, the Nixon-Agnew ticket wins one of the greatest popular majorities in American history.

Early in the year, the president receives praise for his trips to the People's Republic of China and the USSR. Few apparently remember that Nixon's anti-Communist leadership for years denied recognition to the Communist Chinese and labeled the Soviets as arch foes.

Troop levels in Vietnam drop to 69,000 by midyear and the last combat unit leaves in August. But a cease-fire remains elusive and, at the end of the year, Nixon orders the resumption of full-scale bombing.

In other news, Angela Davis is acquitted, J. Edgar Hoover dies, an assassin's bullet paralyzes George Wallace, and 230 drown in the Rapid City flood. The Supreme Court bars the death penalty and gives all defendants the right to a lawyer.

Apollo 17, the last of the manned flights to the moon, returns safely. Saccharine is out and pandas are in. Life magazine dies and Ms. is born. Baseball players strike, Bobby Hull jumps to the WHA, and Bobby Fischer wins the world chess title. And, sadly, the year sees the passing of Roberto Clemente, Jackie Robinson, Maurice Chevalier, and Lester Pearson.

The international story of the year is the terrorist attack on Israeli athletes at the Olympics.

# NEWS

**January 2.** In the early-morning hours, six men arrive by limousine at the Hotel Pierre in New York. Once inside, the disguised robbers handcuff 19 employees and guests, then plunder the safety deposit boxes for an estimated $4 million in cash, securities, and jewels. The greatest hotel robbery in history will remain unsolved.

**January 7.** In compliance with the 1970 Federal Aid Highway Act, the Highway Administration has inspected the 563,500 bridges in the United States, 400,000 of which were built before 1935. The first report bleakly concludes that nearly 89,000 are "critically deficient." The administration has enough money this year to replace only 50 of the most dangerous structures.

**January 13.** President Nixon announces the

withdrawal of an additional 70,000 soldiers from Vietnam by May 1, leaving U.S. troop strength at 69,000—the lowest level in almost seven years. Antiwar protests continue across the United States, but on a much smaller scale. April marches in New York, San Francisco, and Los Angeles each draw about 30,000 people.

**January 19.** The National Commission on Marijuana and Drug Abuse reveals that 24 million Americans—40 percent of 18- to 25-year-olds and 14 percent of 12- to 17-year-olds—have smoked marijuana at least once and one-third use it regularly. Commission members express surprise at the high numbers.

**January 22.** The six-nation EEC accepts Britain, Ireland, Denmark, and Norway as members, effective January 1, 1973. (Norway withdraws in September after a negative referendum.) Britain has long sought membership in the trading bloc, but French President de Gaulle vetoed two earlier bids in fear of American domination through London. His resignation from office in 1969 finally cleared the way.

**January 25.** Nixon discloses that National Security Advisor Henry Kissinger has held 12 secret talks with Le Duc Tho and/or Xuan Thuy of North Vietnam, but Hanoi has refused to continue.

The negotiators remain apart on two major points: The Communists want the United States to set a date for unconditional withdrawal from all of Indochina, while the Americans want an agreement in principle on a final settlement before withdrawing from South Vietnam only; Hanoi demands a new tripartite government with a Communist member to conduct South Vietnamese elections, while Washington wants the current government to hold a supervised election first.

**January 30.** In an interview, Black Panther leader Huey Newton claims the party has abandoned the "pick-up-the-gun-now" approach in favor of community work and voter registration. His followers blame Eldridge Cleaver, who recently resigned as head of the international section in Algiers, for the party's earlier violent philosophy. Cleaver will return from exile in 1975 to face arrest by the FBI.

**January 30.** As demonstrators march in defiance of a government ban in Londonderry, Northern Ireland, some 200 British paratroopers charge over barricades and shoot 13 civilians dead. Witnesses accuse the soldiers of firing first and directly into the crowd.

The next day, the IRA vows to retaliate for Bloody Sunday and calls for a general strike. Hundreds of shops close and the violence continues. In response, London imposes direct rule over Northern Ireland on March 30. An inquiry will absolve the army of any blame. On August 7, a Protestant militiaman will be gunned down outside his home, the 500th victim in three years of violence.

**February 7.** Nixon signs the U.S. Federal Election Campaign Act, effective April 7, limiting a candidate's media expenditures to 10 cents per constituent (with no more than 60 percent of the funds to be spent in a single medium) and requiring the disclosure of all campaign contributions. Critics suggest that Nixon, who vetoed similar legislation in 1970, delayed action to give CREEP and Republican fund-raisers more time to collect from anonymous contributors.

*Statistics:* In the 1971 election, the two parties spent an estimated $24.5 million on television campaigning (compared to $6.6 million in 1956) and $13 million on radio spots (compared to $3 million in 1956).

**February 21.** Richard Nixon arrives in Peking, the first American president to visit China. At the end of a week-long stay, he and Premier Chou En-Lai release a joint communiqué effectively ending 23 years of hostility between their nations.

The United States, in a sharp reversal of long-standing support for the Nationalist Chinese, acknowledges that "there is but one China" and that Taiwan is a part of China. The Americans agree to progressively reduce the number of troops and military installations on Taiwan, as tensions in the area diminish, and ultimately to withdraw American forces from the island.

*Mao Tse-tung greets Richard Nixon, the first American president to visit China.*

With extensive media coverage of the trip, President Nixon returns home to general acclaim.

**February 24.** Two days before Edmund Muskie's scheduled swing through New Hampshire, the *Manchester Union Leader* denounces the Democratic presidential candidate for condoning the term "Canuck" for Americans of French-Canadian descent. Right-wing publisher William Loeb bases his attack on an anonymous semiliterate letter from Florida. The next day, Loeb reprints a two-month-old *Newsweek* article accusing Mrs. Muskie of using earthy language.

On the 26th, outside the *Leader* office, Muskie tells reporters Loeb is lying. But, when the public sees his tearful reaction to the charges, the senator quickly loses ground to Democratic candidate George McGovern.

The Watergate trials will reveal that Nixon supporters masterminded the operation to deliberately destroy the senator's credibility. They believed George McGovern's left-wing platform would be easier to defeat in the presidential election.

**February 26.** Over the years, a huge artificial lake has formed behind an accumulation of coal mine wastes in the hills above Buffalo Creek Valley, West Virginia. Today, an anonymous caller warns Deputy Sheriff Mutters that recent rains have brought the 200-foot makeshift dam close to col-

lapse. Many are alerted before the waters surge through the valley, but 125 people drown and 4,000 are left homeless in 14 communities.

The mining company will eventually settle for a payment of $20,500 on each of 654 claimants.

**February 29.** Newspaper columnist Jack Anderson releases a memo, allegedly written by International Telephone and Telegraph lobbyist Dita Beard, linking a Justice Department antitrust settlement against ITT to the company's funding for the GOP national convention. In later columns, Anderson further accuses ITT officials of trying to convince the CIA to overthrow the Marxist Allende government in Chile.

Although the allegations never produce a guilty verdict, they indirectly bring down the president of the United States. During this year's election campaign, Democratic chairman Lawrence O'Brien attempts to use the accusations to discredit the Republican administration. Nixon's people, looking for information to use against O'Brien, break into Democratic headquarters in the Watergate building.

**March 22.** Congress sends the ERA to the states for ratification. First proposed in 1923, the 27th amendment states that, "equality of rights under the law shall not be denied or abridged by the United States or by any state on account of sex." Currently, lawyers must base litigation supporting women's rights on the 14th Amendment, which holds no one can be denied "the equal protection of the laws."

**March 30.** The North Vietnamese, with VC support, launch a massive offensive out of the west and south across the DMZ. At first, the Communists make impressive gains, but heavy U.S. air attacks allow the battered South Vietnamese Army to dig in.

On April 16, American planes bomb Hanoi and Haiphong for the first time since 1968. When the Communist troops continue to make advances, Nixon orders a blockade of North Vietnam on May 8, the mining of all North Vietnamese ports, and continued bombing of military targets. By midyear, the South Vietnamese gain the initiative, retaking Quang Tri province and recapturing Binh Dinh in the northeast. But with 40 percent of the country-side directly affected, the pacification program ends, creating another million refugees.

**April 10.** The Biological Weapons Convention prohibits the development, production, and stockpiling of biological weapons. Prime Minister Edward Heath calls the agreement a "true disarmament treaty" since signatories must destroy their existing stocks.

Eventually 84 countries—nearly all the industrially developed nations of the world—will ratify the convention.

**May 2.** J(ohn) Edgar Hoover, the first and only director of the FBI, dies at age 77. Appointed in 1924 under President Calvin Coolidge, Hoover introduced the latest in criminal investigation techniques. Through the next two decades the Feds built a reputation of infallibility for their director, dealing first with gangsters and organized crime figures then with dozens of German spies and fifth columnists. None of the eight presidents Hoover served under dared risk the political consequences of replacing the head of this powerful law-enforcement body.

But from uncovering Communist subversives in the 1950s, the director increasingly led his bureau, through the 1960s, into the gray area of harassment and illegal surveillance of student and antiwar activists and of black pacifists and radicals. Still, the Nixon administration pays Hoover a singular tribute. His casket lies in state in the Capitol rotunda, the first civil servant to receive such an honor.

**May 15.** After finishing a campaign speech, George Wallace is moving through the crowd in an adjacent parking lot when 22-year-old Arthur Bremer pulls a gun. The Alabama Governor is shot four times and three others are seriously injured.

The next day, Wallace wins the Democratic primaries in Michigan and Maryland, but the impressive victories mark the end of his campaign. One of the bullets has left him permanently paralyzed from the waist down. He withdraws from the Democratic presidential campaign and, in July, refuses to run as a third-party candidate.

Bremer is found guilty in August and sentenced to 63 years in prison. But as with the assassinations of the sixties, rumors abound and inconsistencies in the evidence challenge the official belief that Bremer acted alone.

In 1974, George Wallace will become the first governor of Alabama to be elected to two consecutive terms of office.

**May 22.** A deeply divided Supreme Court finds (5–4) juries in state criminal cases need not return a unanimous verdict to convict. (In one of two appeals, an armed robber in Louisiana received 35 years on a 9–3 vote.) Yet the justices fail to define "a heavy majority."

Richard Nixon, with this year's selection of Lewis F. Powell and William H. Rehnquist and his previous choices of Warren E. Burger and Harry A. Blackmun, becomes the first president since Franklin Roosevelt to make four appointments to the Supreme Court. Legal experts fully anticipate that the two new justices will complete an ideological shift from the liberal Warren Court of the 1960s to a conservative court under Burger.

**May 22–29.** In another historic first for an American president, Richard Nixon visits the Soviet Union. On May 26, he and Secretary Leonid Brezhnev sign two formal agreements, signaling a break in the Cold War.

Culminating two years of SALT negotiations, the ABM pact discourages either nation from launching a first strike by limiting defenses against nuclear attack. Each country may deploy just two protective systems of 100 missiles each, one near the capital city and the other at an ICBM site. The next day, Defense Secretary Laird halts construction on the Safeguard ABM base in Montana and terminates plans for other sites.

The second accord—an executive agreement—freezes the number of offensive ballistic missiles for up to five years. Neither permits on-site inspection to enforce the limitations.

**June 1.** Baghdad nationalizes the Iraq Petroleum Company, a consortium of American, British, Dutch, and French firms, which produces approximately 10 percent of Middle East oil. Following negotiations, the consortium agrees to pay back taxes and receives 15 million tons of Iraqi crude oil in compensation.

**June 1.** After a gun battle, Frankfurt police capture Andreas Baader, age 29, and two members of his terrorist group. Ulrike Meinhof, his 37-year-old partner, is arrested just two weeks later, on June 15.

The Baader-Meinhof Gang will come to trial in 1975 after West Germany constructs a secure courthouse—next to a prison—at a cost of approximately $4 million.

**June 3.** In the first such agreement since W.W. II, the four occupying powers—the United States, the Soviet Union, Britain, and France—ease tensions over Berlin. The stipulations will improve traffic from the West through East Germany to Berlin and make visitation between East and West Berlin easier. By accepting these terms, West Germany and the three Western allies finally acknowledge East Germany as an independent nation.

But the protocol rests on an East German and West German agreement over implementation. After months of negotiations, the two Germanies sign a general treaty on December 21, paving the way for diplomatic relations and their eventual admission into the United Nations.

**June 4.** Black militant Angela Davis is acquitted on all charges of murder-conspiracy. Her guns were used in the Marin Court House shoot-out in 1970, and a Marxist philosophy and SNCC and Panther connections immediately made her suspect. Davis ran, but was captured two months later; she has spent the last 16 months in jail.

The University of California refuses to rehire the former acting assistant professor.

**June 6.** A gigantic explosion in Rhodesia's only coal mine kills 5 on the surface and traps 427 men in the shafts. Lethal methane fumes force rescue squads to end their search, and everyone in the mining town of 20,000 loses a relative or friend.

**June 10.** Exceptionally heavy rains in the Black Hills of South Dakota have swollen Rapid Creek, flowing through the center of Rapid City, far above normal. Mayor Barnett receives an anonymous phone tip that Canyon Lake Dam, in the hills above the city, is about to burst. He frantically alerts local radio stations and sends police officers out to warn people along the creeks.

At 9:30 P.M. the flood waters hit the city of 43,000, rupturing gas lines and setting off explosions and fires everywhere. An estimated 10 percent of the buildings are destroyed and 10 feet of water covers the western section. At least 230 people die in the disaster.

**June 12.** In an extension of *Gideon v. Wainright* (1963), the Supreme Court unanimously grants all defendants the right to a lawyer—no matter how small the offense. With state courts annually processing 4–5 million misdemeanor defendants (one-third on drunk driving charges), the American judicial system reels under the implications.

**June 17.** When 24-year-old night security guard Frank Willis finds two garage doors taped open, he calls in the Washington police and changes the course of American history. The building is the Watergate hotel-office complex.

At 2:00 A.M., officers catch five well-dressed men in the sixth-floor headquarters of the Democratic party. The suspects, carrying electronic bugs, cameras, and $2,300 in consecutively numbered $100 bills, refuse to answer questions. But authorities soon discover four of the men are anti-Castro activists while the fifth is James McCord, security coordinator for CREEP and a former CIA operative.

A search of their Watergate hotel rooms uncovers more money (investigation eventually traces the bills to CREEP funds) and an address book with the entry "E. Hunt—W. H." CREEP Security chief E. Howard Hunt, another former CIA agent, was consultant to presidential counsel Charles W. Colson until March 29. The book also leads to G. Gordon Liddy, a former FBI officer and current member of the White House Domestic Council. Both Hunt and Liddy are arrested.

The day after the break-in, presidential campaign manager John Mitchell tells reporters that the burglars were not "operating either on our behalf or with our consent." But behind closed doors, the White House orders the destruction of all incriminating documents and initiates a public relations campaign to offset any damage. Jeb Magruder, deputy director of CREEP, will later testify, "I do not think there was any discussion that there would not be a cover-up."

**June 18–23.** Agnes, the first hurricane of the season, deluges the Eastern seaboard with trillions of gallons of water. The final death toll reaches 134, including 12 killed in Cuba and Florida; 125,000 are left homeless. With damages surpassing $3 billion, Agnes becomes the costliest natural disaster in the United States to date.

**June 19.** Last year, Attorney General John Mitchell claimed that the Justice Department had the right to wiretap "domestic subversives" without court warrants. (During 1969–1970, official wiretapping increased 100 percent.)

The first appellate court ruling on the issue rejected Mitchell's contention. Judge George C. Edwards, Jr., declared "not one written phrase" in the constitution justified such a claim.

Today, in a major setback for the administration, the Supreme Court unanimously finds the warrantless wiretapping of domestic radicals unconstitutional. Justice Powell writes, "History abundantly documents the tendency of government—however benevolent and benign its motives—to view with suspicion those who most fervently dispute its policies."

**June 19.** The International Federation of Air Line Pilots' Associations strikes for 24 hours to press for stronger international measures against hijacking and sabotage. American planes at home and abroad have suffered 159 hijackings since 1961, but U.S. courts bar American pilots from participating in the strike.

Washington has already begun to act. As of February, the FAA has required airlines to screen passengers and their baggage and ordered airports to send all passengers through metal detectors. In July, President Nixon will order the FAA to extend the large air-carrier security check to all commuter aircraft. In October, American Airlines and TWA will begin to inspect passengers' carry-on baggage.

No U.S. plane will be hijacked over the first eight months of 1973, as airport authorities arrest over 1,300 passengers for various offenses and seize some 900 guns.

**June 29.** A 5–4 Supreme Court ruling cites the Eighth Amendment ban on cruel and unusual punishment in setting aside the death sentences of three black men. In effect, the decision bars executions throughout the United States.

Still, legal experts believe the court will consider new capital laws. Two of the five majority opinions object to the arbitrariness of judge and jury sentencing, while Justice Douglas points to the high number of minority and lower-class defendants.

*Statistics:* At this time, in 35 states, some 600 prisoners sit on death row; at least half are black. The NAACP, with its national drive, has blocked all executions since 1967.

**July 1.** Attorney General John Mitchell left his Cabinet post in February to direct Richard Nixon's reelection campaign. But following newspaper stories about telephone calls between his wife, Martha, and UP reporter Helen Thomas, Mitchell resigns. (In a June 25 conversation, Martha explained to Thomas she still loved her husband but could no longer put up with "all those dirty things that go on.") Mitchell cites "family problems" in his resignation. The couple will legally separate in fall 1973.

**July 12.** George McGovern, age 49, wins the Democratic presidential nomination on the first ballot. Senator Thomas Eagleton of Missouri wins the vice-presidential nomination.

Dominated by young people just one year after 18-year-olds received the vote, the convention earlier today adopted a platform calling for immediate withdrawal from Vietnam, abolition of the draft, amnesty for war resisters, and a guaranteed income for those below the poverty line.

But convention euphoria evaporates when McGovern and Eagleton reveal at a July 25 press conference that between 1960 and 1968 Eagleton was hospitalized three times for depression and twice received electro-shock treatment. McGovern admits he was unaware of his running mate's medical history, but insists Eagleton will remain on the ticket. Less than a week later, the two men announce his withdrawal, to prevent further division within the party.

Ted Kennedy (approached for the second time), Edmund Muskie, and five others decline the candidacy. On August 5, McGovern names Sargent Shriver, Peace Corp director and brother-in-law to the Kennedys, as his vice presidential nominee.

**July 13.** Jane Fonda makes a radio broadcast from Hanoi, telling American soldiers of damaged dikes in civilian areas of North Vietnam. "I implore you, I beg you to reconsider what you are doing." The North Vietnamese press agency reports the broadcast on the 14th, and the U.S. State Department rebukes the actress for her antiwar speech.

**July 17.** The Census Bureau reports that the median income of U.S. families has topped $10,000 for the first time—$10,285—but, at the same time, notes that inflation has erased any gain (3.5 percent in prices in 1972). The median black family income is 60 percent of the white income, while black unemployment is 4.5 percent higher than white.

**July 18.** President Anwar Sadat announces that he has asked all Soviet personnel, an estimated 5,000 advisors and 10,000–15,000 combat personnel and pilots, to leave Egypt immediately; Soviet bases and equipment have been placed under Egyptian control. Sadat claims that Moscow's failure to meet Arab weapon needs had forced his decision.

Unknown to the Arabs or Israelis, after the 1967 war the Soviets and Americans reached a secret agreement to stabilize the Middle East by cutting arms supplies. But that pact began to unravel earlier this year when tensions increased in the area and the United States decided to sell F-4 bombers to Israel.

**July 31.** The Canadian government, while affirming the dangers of marijuana and hashish, transfers narcotics control to the Food and Drugs Act to ensure less severe penalties. The legislation abolishes jail terms for possession and gives first-time offenders the right to seek the removal of their names from court records.

**August 5.** Idi Amin, who overthrew President Obote in 1971, announces that Uganda will expel within 90 days all Asians with British or South Asian passports. Massive airlifts take the estimated 60,000 Asians to Britain, Canada, and other coun-

tries. Ironically, with the loss of most of the country's professional and business classes, native Ugandans suffer increased unemployment.

**August 12.** As the Americans conduct their heaviest bombing raids of the Vietnam War, the last U.S. ground combat unit—members of the Third Battalion of the 21st Infantry and G Battery of the 29th Field Artillery—leaves Danang without ceremony. Some 43,500 army personnel remain behind.

---

*Statistics:* From 1965 to 1972, the United States has doled out $38.3 billion in military aid to other nations.

---

**August 22.** The Republican National Convention renominates Richard Nixon by a vote of 1,347–1. The necessary dissenting vote goes to antiwar activist Paul McCloskey, Jr. With Spiro Agnew's renomination, the single dissenting vote goes to NBC television broadcaster David Brinkley.

The party platform opposes amnesty for war resisters and school busing to achieve integration. Several hundred demonstrators are arrested outside the Miami Beach convention hall.

**August 29.** Since the Watergate break-in, Nixon's people have cleaned out E. Howard Hunt's safe in the White House, destroyed documents in the offices of White House Chief of Staff H. R. Haldeman, and influenced the FBI to limit its investigation. But with the established connection between the burglars and the White House, pressure mounts and the president calls a press conference.

Nixon announces that with Justice Department, FBI, and other agency inquiries under way, he sees no need to appoint a special prosecutor. And since Chief White House Counsel John Dean has already conducted a complete investigation of Watergate, he can "state categorically" that "no one in the White House staff, no one in this administration, presently employed, was involved in this very bizarre incident. . . . What really hurts is if you try to cover it up."

**September 1.** Claiming that North Atlantic fish

stocks are depleted, Iceland unilaterally extends its 12-mile offshore boundary to 50 miles, despite a World Court interim judgment against the action. British fishermen ignore the limit, and the "Cod War" escalates as Icelandic gunboats confront the trawlers. Negotiations between the two nations continue.

**September 1.** Ejected earlier from a Montreal nightclub, two unemployed laborers throw a fire-bomb up the stairway onto the dance floor. A bolted rear door blocks escape, and 37 people die of asphyxiation. The men receive life in prison.

**September 5.** Just before dawn, eight Black September terrorists attack the Israeli men's dormitory in the Munich Olympic Village. Wrestling coach Moshe Weinberg and a weight lifter block the door, shouting to the others to get out; six escape before the Palestinians break in and kill the two at the door. The remaining nine athletes are taken hostage.

The terrorists reject offers of money or a hostage exchange, and demand that Israel release 200 Palestinian guerrillas from jail. Israel refuses to negotiate and Prime Minister Meir, with Chancellor Willy Brandt, approves a rescue attempt.

Maneuvering for an assault, the West Germans agree to transport the terrorists and their hostages to the airport. But in the ensuing shoot-out, all the Israelis die along with a German policeman and five Palestinians. In retaliation Israeli jets attack 10 Arab guerrilla bases in Lebanon and Syria on September 8.

German security precautions come under severe criticism—at least one Palestinian worked in the village—and many question the wisdom of the rescue action. Still, an official report clears all authorities of blame.

In October, Bonn releases the three surviving guerrillas when Palestinians hijack a Lufthansa aircraft.

**September 22.** From September 10–16, for the first time since March 1965, no American soldier died in action in Vietnam. Battlefield deaths stand at 45,857. The seven men who died from accidental or natural causes over the same period raised the noncombat death toll to 10,274.

**September 23.** Following several bombings in Manila and an assassination attempt on the Philippine secretary of defense, President Ferdinand Marcos declares martial law. Police arrest over 50 prominent people, including the leader of the opposition party, Senator Benigno S. Aquino, Jr.

On January 17, 1973, Marcos will permanently extend martial law and proclaim a new constitution giving him the right to rule indefinitely.

**September 24.** At a Sacramento air show, a reactivated F-86 Sabrejet fails to gain enough speed for takeoff, crosses the highway, and drags two cars in a burning fireball into Farrell's Ice Cream Parlor. With a full house of over 100 children and parents, celebrating five separate birthdays, 22 people die and 25 are seriously injured.

Pilot Richard Bingham, restricted by the FAA to longer runways, had chosen this shorter airstrip to conserve fuel. He survives the tragedy.

**September 29.** Most newspapers have dismissed the Watergate incident, but *Washington Post* reporters Bob Woodward, age 29, and Carl Bernstein, age 28, work day and night to uncover possible links to the White House. After establishing connections between the burglary and CREEP, they write today that John Mitchell personally controlled a "secret fund" at CREEP headquarters while still attorney general. Once he became campaign manager, four other people shared the responsibility in authorizing withdrawals.

Then, on October 10, Woodward and Bernstein break an even bigger story: The FBI has established that Watergate was just part of a massive political espionage and sabotage campaign conducted by CREEP and White House officials, on Nixon's behalf, during the 1972 presidential campaign. Dwight Chapin, presidential appointments secretary, hired Donald Segretti to recruit agents to discredit Democratic candidates and disrupt primary campaigns. Their "dirty tricks" included forgery, false information leaked to the press, and the Watergate break-in.

Ron Ziegler calls the report "character assassination" and shoddy journalism, but "Woodstein" accounts keep up the pressure on the White House.

**October.** By the time George McGovern settled

on a new running mate, the Eagleton issue had damaged a reputation founded on a refusal to compromise principles for political gain, and cost the Democrats nearly a month of their campaign. As well, McGovern's promise of rapid social change and his antiwar stance have alienated many voters and undermined the party's customary labor support.

This month, the Democratic candidate confronts the "most corrupt" administration in U.S. history. Charging the Republicans with espionage and with granting favors for political contributions, he places the blame directly on the president. But American voters dismiss the charges as political propaganda, and McGovern is forced once again to focus on the Vietnam War.

The Republicans, on the other hand, have prepared well. Along with the dirty tricks operations, CREEP has raised more money than Nixon can possibly use. With all the advantages of the incumbent, the president has maintained a statesmanlike image, with trips to Peking and Moscow, and avoided partisan issues. He keeps his appearances to a minimum and refuses to debate his opponent.

At the end of the month, when the administration prematurely announces, "Peace is at hand," McGovern loses his greatest base of opposition. Nixon continues to lead in the polls right up to the election.

**October 3.** After insistent Republican lobbying, the House Banking and Currency Committee rejects, 20–15, a proposal by Chairman Wright Patman (D., Tex.) to probe the Watergate break-in for possible violations of banking laws. Patman, prepared to subpoena 40 individuals and organizations, including top Nixon campaign aides, angrily declares, "The facts will come out. When they do, I am convinced they will reveal why the White House was so anxious to kill the committee's investigation. The public will fully understand why the pressure was mounted."

**October 12.** The Senate fails for a third time to end a Northern liberal filibuster against an antibusing bill. The House had approved the measure, 282–102, with the active support of President Nixon, after a June educational amendment failed to stem a flood of court orders. The defeated legislation would have barred busing for desegregation (except as a last resort), eliminated long-distance busing, and allowed the reopening of desegregation suits already settled in court (to enforce compliance).

**October 13.** A Uruguayan Air Force plane, carrying members and fans of a Montevideo rugby team, crashes on a 12,000-foot peak in the Chilean Andes. Twenty-one die on impact or shortly afterward, and an avalanche kills another 8, but 16 passengers survive. The official search ends a week later.

After a harrowing two months, with no hope of rescue, two of the young men walk for 10 days through snow to reach help. When rescuers find the others still in remarkably good condition, questions arise. The survivors soon admit to cannibalism. Their story will be told in the best-seller *Alive*.

**October 14.** A Soviet Aeroflot airliner crashes in heavy rain on its fourth attempted landing near Moscow. Reportedly, the airport's instrument landing system malfunctioned. A death toll of 176 makes this the worst air disaster to date.

**October 20.** The Local Fiscal Assistance Act establishes a $30.2-billion revenue-sharing program to strengthen state and local governments. With few spending restrictions and no matching funds required, one-third goes to state governments and two-thirds to local governments. President Nixon considers the legislation a major achievement for a Republican administration plagued by a Democratic Congress.

**October 26.** As Hanoi radio announces an agreement in principle on a peace plan, Henry Kissinger tells the Washington press that "peace is at hand" in Vietnam. He claims that one additional round of negotiations, "lasting not more than three or four days," could produce a final agreement.

Both the United States and North Vietnam have conceded key issues. The Americans, seeking better relations with the USSR and China, abandoned their condition that North Vietnamese troops withdraw before a cease-fire. In return, the Communists, with the failure of their latest offensive and under pressure from Peking and Moscow, dropped earlier demands that President Nguyen Van Thieu resign and that a coalition government be established immediately in Saigon.

But Kissinger's prediction proves optimistic, and meetings with Le Duc Tho collapse on December 13. As the South Vietnamese continue to resist any settlement requiring a coalition, Kissinger bluntly states, on December 16, that objections from Saigon will not deter the United States from signing a military agreement with Hanoi.

Meanwhile, the Americans increase armament deliveries to South Vietnam and the North Vietnamese expand operations to win more territory before the cease-fire. Communist forces in South Vietnam number 145,000 as the military stalemate continues.

**October 30.** In the closest election in Canadian history, the Liberal party wins just one more seat than the Conservatives; another added in a recount makes the final tally 109 to 107. The NDP, taking 31 seats, holds the balance of power.

With a 74-percent turnout at the polls, political analysts believe the Liberal 46-seat loss reflects strong voter dissatisfaction with inflation, unemployment, and the government's extension of French-language rights.

On January 4, 1973, the NDP announces its support for the Liberal minority government.

**October 30.** During the Chicago morning rush hour, an older, heavier commuter train crashes into the back of a new double-decker and rams through to the center section, trapping passengers above and below. Rescuers need five hours to free 320 injured passengers; most of the 44 killed were sitting in the last car.

**November 7.** Richard Nixon sweeps 49 states in one of the greatest landslides in American election history. He receives 521 electoral votes, losing just the District of Columbia and Massachusetts to George McGovern, and captures 60.7 percent of the popular vote.

Still, with the lowest voter turnout since 1948, the overwhelming presidential victory fails to translate into party gains. The Democrats retain their majority in the House and win two more seats in the Senate, making Nixon the first president to begin his second term with an opposition Congress.

**November 7.** Following the 1970 census, reapportionment gave California the largest delegation, 43 to 39 for New York.

For the first time, the people of Guam and the Virgin Islands—all American citizens—send nonvoting delegates to the House to join the resident commissioner from Puerto Rico and the delegate from the District of Columbia.

And, for the first time this century, the South elects two black members—Barbara Jordan (D., Texas) and Andrew Young, Jr. (D., Georgia)—bringing the number of blacks in the House to 16.

**November 8.** Militant American Indians end a week-long occupation of the Bureau of Indian Affairs when officials promise to study their demands. Some 500 natives had traveled to Washington to protest the government's failure to honor treaty promises and to demand a reform of natural resource policies on Indian lands.

Following the sit-in, the assistant secretary of the bureau, the Indian commissioner, and the deputy commissioner all lose their positions. But in January, the government refuses the demands, calling them a false issue, unconstructive, and "misleading to Indian people."

**November 10.** U.S. Navy Secretary John Warner and Chief of Naval Operations Admiral Elmo Zumwalt, Jr., rebuke navy admirals and Marine Corps generals for failing to act against racist behavior. Racial brawls on board the aircraft carrier *Kitty Hawk* in October left 46 injured.

A Pentagon report, released at the end of this month, confirms the existence of intentional and systematic discrimination against blacks in the armed forces. Yet little changes. The navy announces a program to recruit more blacks but raises educational standards. And early next year, a House subcommittee will find that discrimination played no part in the *Kitty Hawk* assaults.

**November 16.** At the largely black Southern University campus in Baton Rouge, Louisiana, deputies and state policemen order a large number of students—estimates vary from 300 to 2,000—to end their occupation of the administration building. The demonstrators want better food and housing and a greater voice in university decisions. Law officers shoot tear gas canisters into the crowd, one fires a shotgun, and two 20-year-old black students die.

A biracial state commission reports on December 14 that, while the students broke the law, the over-armed and underdisciplined police officers must bear responsibility for the confusion leading to two deaths. But an investigation fails to determine which officer fired his gun, and no indictments follow.

**November 21.** The second round of the U.S.-Soviet Union strategic arms limitations talks, SALT II, begins in Geneva.

**December 18.** Following the breakdown of peace talks, President Nixon personally orders the resumption of full-scale bombing and mining of North Vietnam, "until such time as a settlement is arrived at." Analysts suggest the air campaign was undertaken to appease the South Vietnamese, who continue to resist any peace settlement with the Communists.

The bombing, described as the heaviest in the history of warfare, ends on December 30, when the White House announces the resumption of peace talks on January 8. In this most recent campaign, the Americans lost at least 15 bombers and more than 80 airmen.

**December 21.** Representatives of the nine EEC countries and five EFTA members sign a pact creating a single European free trade area.

**December 23.** A strong earthquake (6.5 on the Richter scale) levels 70 percent of the buildings in Managua, Nicaragua, and touches off explosions and fires. With an estimated 10,000–12,000 dead, thousands more injured, little rescue equipment available, and some 250,000 people homeless, General Somoza orders the city evacuated to prevent the spread of disease.

As the rubble smolders and international relief pours in, the government levels and covers major portions of the city with lime.

This was the third earthquake to hit Managua in less than a century; one struck in 1885 and another in 1931.

**December 26.** Former President Harry S. Truman dies at age 88. At the end of his term in office (1945–1952), he said, "The greatest part of the president's job is to make decisions. . . . He can't pass the buck to anybody." Truman made his choices—too quickly for some—and got on with the job, with no regrets and no doubts. For him, the atomic bomb was a means to end the war. The United Nations, rearmament, the Marshall Plan, the Berlin airlift, NATO, the hydrogen bomb, and Korea were all tools to fight the Cold War. Truman's predecessors had failed to halt fascism and Nazism; he would not make the same mistake with Communism.

Winning the 1948 election in his own right gave Truman the confidence and security to present one of the most progressive legislative packages in U.S. history. But a losing battle with Congress—250 vetoes—saw his national health insurance program rejected along with the first major civil rights bill since Reconstruction.

Scrupulously honest, a champion of minority rights, and an implacable foe of McCarthyism, Truman nonetheless left the Oval Office under the shadow of administration scandals and recriminations for the loss of China. In later years, Americans came to realize the worth of their 33rd president, but Truman typically rejected a Congressional Medal: "I do not consider that I have done anything which should be the reason for any award, congressional or otherwise."

**December 29.** An Eastern Airlines flight, on approach to Miami International Airport, crashes in the Everglades. In this first fatal accident involving a jumbo jet, 75 people survive while an estimated 101 die (widely strewn wreckage and last-minute ticket changes make an accurate count impossible). The large number of survivors is credited to the jet's wide body crash-landing into mud and water.

The Transportation Safety Board later determines that the captain, first officer, second officer, and maintenance specialist were all attempting to repair a landing-gear light indicator and failed to monitor the plane's descent. The aircraft literally flew into the ground. A huge number of lawsuits are brought against the airline and the manufacturer.

## Obituaries

**Windsor, Duke of** (June 23, 1894–May 28, 1972). With the death of George V in January 1936, the popular Prince of Wales ascended the British throne as Edward VIII. His wish to make Wallis Warfield Simpson, a twice-divorced American, his queen, met with firm opposition from church and government, and on December 10, 1936, Edward abdicated in favor of his brother George, to marry the woman he loved. The duke and duchess—titles bestowed by the new king—wed on June 3, 1937. It was later discovered that Edward had lied about his finances to obtain an overly generous annual income, and the couple's relations with the royal family remained strained almost until his death.

**Frederick IX** (March 11, 1899–January 14, 1972). During his 25-year reign, Denmark passed a constitutional amendment permitting female succession. Upon his death, his eldest daughter takes the throne as Margrethe II.

**J(ohn) Edgar Hoover** (January 1, 1895–May 2, 1972). See News.

**Kwame Nkrumah** (September 21, 1909–April 27, 1972). The prime minister of the Gold Coast led his nation to independence as Ghana in 1957. Three years later, he became the first president of the new republic. Nkrumah was overthrown by a military coup in 1966, and he died in exile.

**Lester B. Pearson** (April 23, 1897–December 27, 1972). Instrumental in securing the Korean truce in 1953, the Canadian diplomat won the 1957 Nobel peace prize for his Suez peace initiative. The following year, the Liberals chose Pearson as their new leader; he led the party to victory in 1963 and served as prime minister until his retirement in 1968.

During his term, Canada completed the Columbia River Treaty, introduced a national pension plan, broadened old-age security benefits, and established a royal commission on bilingualism and

biculturalism. Yet Pearson considered the adoption of a Canadian flag and an official national anthem his two greatest accomplishments.

**Adam Clayton Powell, Jr.** (November 29, 1908–April 4, 1972). A Baptist minister and the nation's leading black politician during his 22 years in the House, Powell fought segregation, chaired the Education and Labor Committee (1960–1967), and played a major role in passing 50 important pieces of social legislation. In 1966 he fled the United States to avoid arrest for civil contempt, and the House excluded him on March 1, 1967. In 1969, Powell won two elections to regain his seat but met defeat in the 1970 primaries.

**Paul-Henri Spaak** (January 25, 1899–July 31, 1972). An important figure in Belgian politics, Spaak was known internationally as the principal architect of the EEC.

**Harry S. Truman** (May 8, 1884–December 26, 1972). See News.

# BEGINNINGS AND ENDINGS

## News

**January 24.** Found in the jungles of Guam, Sergeant Shoichi Yokoi of the Imperial Japanese Army admits he knew W.W.II was over. He hid for 27 years to escape execution at the hands of the Americans. Two fellow soldiers died in 1964; two more remain in hiding.

**April 16.** The National Zoo, in Washington, D.C., receives Hsing-hsing and Ling-ling, the first giant pandas in the United States. The Americans sent China a pair of musk oxen in exchange.

**April 28.** Oxford University admits women to five colleges (effective 1974)–after 750 years.

**May 6.** Traditionally, Eskimos of the Canadian Arctic have used just one personal name and often changed that. In 1945, to ease bureaucratic record keeping, the federal government assigned each Eskimo a number on a neck tag.

Two years ago, Ottawa agreed to a more personal system of Inuit family names, and Abraham Okpik, the first Eskimo member of the Territories' legislative council, set out to visit his people. Today,

45,000 miles later, he finishes the enormous task of recording 13,000 new names.

**May 15.** After 27 years of occupation, the United States returns Okinawa to Japan. The Americans lost 12,500 men in the 1945 invasion; about 100,000 of the 120,000-man Japanese garrison died.

**May 18.** At an assembly of churches in Philadelphia, Margaret "Maggie" Kuhn founds the non-denominational Gray Panthers to fight for senior citizens' rights. Kuhn, forced to retire two years ago at age 65, argues that ageism pervades society as deeply as sexism.

**May 22.** Ceylon becomes a republic and changes its name to Sri Lanka.

**May 31.** The last two Morse operators in Canada, working for CN-CP Telecommunications, send their final message: "What hath God wrought!" On May 24, 1844, the American Samuel Morse sent the same sentence in his first public transmission.

**June 3.** Sally Priesand, age 25, becomes the first female rabbi in the United States and only the second in Judaic history.

**June 20.** General William Westmoreland retires from the army. General Creighton Abrams, who relieved Westmoreland in Vietnam, replaces him today as chief of staff.

**July 14.** Chosen to chair the Democratic National Committee, Jean Westwood is the first woman to head either party. But her association with George McGovern and the reform element forces Westwood to resign in November.

**July 17.** The first female FBI agents are sworn in, Susan Lynn Roley, a 25-year-old former marine, and Joanne E. Pierce, a 31-year-old former nun. (Acting director Patrick Gray announced the bureau's intention to recruit women just nine days after the death of J. Edgar Hoover.)

**August 8.** Under a new electoral law, voters in Selma, Alabama, elect five blacks to the 10-member city council—the first ever.

**September 7.** Nixon nominates Major General Alexander Haig, Jr., age 47, for the second top post in the army, vice chief of staff. In choosing Henry Kissinger's former assistant security advisor, the president passes over 243 senior generals.

**September 11.** The San Francisco Bay Area Rapid Transit, the first new system in the United States since 1907, begins operating along 28 completed miles of the 75-mile line. Projected costs of $120 million have skyrocketed to $1.4 billion, yet mechanical failures plague BART from the outset.

**September 14.** Since the fifth century, the Roman Catholic Church has shaved the crown of men aspiring to the priesthood. Pope Paul, describing the ritual as empty, makes the tonsure optional.

**September 29.** Japan and China end their 35-year state of war.

**November 1.** In 1911, when the Standard Oil Group broke up under antitrust charges, members banned the Esso brand from their territories. The beleaguered company was forced to use other names—Enco, Humble—in all but 18 eastern states. Today, Esso is officially renamed Exxon.

**November 7.** House majority leader Hale Boggs (D., Louisiana) and Representative Nicholas J. Begich (D., Alaska) become the first missing persons to be elected to Congress. Their Cessna disappeared en route to Juneau on October 16. The courts will presume them dead on December 13.

**November 14.** For the first time, the Dow Jones Industrial Average closes above the 1,000 mark.

**November 22.** The Commerce Department lifts a ban established during the Korean War against American ships and planes traveling to China.

**December 7.** Rev. W. Sterling Cary, age 45, becomes the first black to be elected president of the National Council of Churches.

**More news.** United Airlines begins hiring male stewards on a regular basis, 42 years after bringing the first stewardesses on board. Their joint title becomes "flight attendant."

• Amy Vanderbilt, the authority on etiquette, says North American society now accepts unwed couples living together.

## Government Departments and Agencies

**October 28.** Legislation establishes the Consumer Product Safety Commission to regulate the manufacture and sale of a broad range of products for home, school, and recreation.

## New Businesses and Products

Celestial Seasonings Tea breaks into the booming natural-products market.

> *Statistics:* From Howard Johnson's first roadside stand in 1925, the fast-food industry has mushroomed to 35,547 outlets and $5.3 billion in annual sales.

In 1964, track coach Bill Bowerman and runner Phil Knight formed an athletic shoe company, Blue Ribbon Sports, and sold Tiger running shoes from Japan. This year, the two partners hire design student Carolyn Davidson to create a logo for their own brand of runners. She receives $35 for the Nike curved slash.

Chinese crafts and clothes pour into the United States following President Nixon's visit to Peking.

## Fads

Disillusioned with the counterculture, thousands of young Americans spurn drugs, alcohol, and extramarital sex for a mixture of old-time religion and popular culture—"Jesus" buttons, "Honk If You Love Jesus" bumper stickers, and Jesus rock music at religious meetings. Critics, pointing to high dropout rates and a fanatical right-or-wrong morality, describe Jesus freaks as a fringe group. Yet, at the same time, most observers admit that the movement's emphasis on a personal search for ultimate meanings could affect church and society in the long term.

# SCIENCE AND TECHNOLOGY

## News

**January 5.** President Nixon signs a $5.5-billion appropriation for a six-year space-shuttle program. The reusable vehicle will transport astronauts and their equipment from Earth into orbit and back.

**January 10.** In a new report, the surgeon general declares that scientists no longer disagree among themselves as to the harmful effects of smoking. And, for the first time, the office declares that high levels of smoke in a car or room can endanger the health of nonsmokers.

**January 24.** New Jersey enacts the first U.S. noise-control legislation, establishing maximum levels for machines, industries, and automobiles.

On October 28, President Nixon signs a similar bill for the nation, but the EPA retains an advisory role for aircraft noise and the FAA holds final authority.

**January 28.** Pending the outcome of further research, the FDA removes saccharine from the list of safe food additives. The artificial sweetener has produced bladder tumors in rats. The U.S. food and drink industry seeks federal compensation for business losses.

> *Statistics:* In 1962, the average American drank 16.8 gallons of soft drinks. Ten years later, Americans consume 30.3 gallons each.

**April 16.** *Apollo 16* lifts off with Charles Duke, Thomas Mattingly, and John Young. From April 20 to 23, Duke and Young spend a record 20 hours, 14 minutes on the lunar surface. The first to explore rougher terrain, the astronauts also test the Lunar Rover with skids and sharp turns and ride it over small craters.

A TV camera left behind broadcasts the lunar module's blast-off.

**June 14.** The EPA bans most remaining domestic uses of DDT. Studies have discovered the pesticide in the food chain, and scientists predict the chemical may remain in the soil for decades to come.

**July 22.** A 50-minute transmission from *Venera 8* adds considerably to the data about the planet Venus. Preliminary findings, released to the West in September, reveal a temperature of 840 degrees Fahrenheit and surface rock resembling granite (with some amounts of uranium, thorium, and potassium).

**July 23.** NASA launches the first ERTS (Earth Resources Technology Satellite), or *Landsat I.* Three TV cameras, each sensitive to a different color, send back thousands of pictures to help the United States and other nations better utilize their natural resources.

**July 25.** In 1932, the U.S. Public Health Service, with the cooperation of several health departments, began a study of 400 black men known to have contracted syphilis. Every five years, participants received a full physical and blood tests, but none received antibiotics—even after penicillin came into use in the 1950s for the treatment of venereal disease.

A health service investigator told a friend about the story, and a tip to a reporter produced today's news story. The government offers no apologies— the study was undertaken for the benefit of medical science—and a lawsuit will be settled out of court.

**August 10.** A 4,000-ton, 40-foot-wide meteor shoots across the night skies, from Utah to Alberta, at an altitude of 36 miles. Scientists later estimate that a collision with Earth would have equaled the force of the atomic bomb dropped on Hiroshima.

**August 21.** The Orbiting Astronomical Observatory, the fourth and final satellite in a series, is the heaviest and most complex unmanned craft to orbit the Earth. A 32-inch reflecting telescope, free of the Earth's atmosphere, discovers extremely hot temperatures in vast areas of space.

**November 9.** Just over a month after his father's death, Richard Leakey displaces *Homo erectus* and *Australopithecus* as the earliest representatives of human beings. With upright thigh bones and a brain case similar to modern man, the anthropologist dates the specimen to be some 2.6 million years old.

**November 9.** *Anik 1,* the first synchronous satellite orbited for domestic communications, gives Telecast Canada radio, telephone, and television communications.

**November 21.** The National Bureau of Standards lab in Colorado announces a more precise measurement of the speed of light—186,282.3960 miles per second. While earlier figures represented a margin of error up to 300 feet per second, this

research team claims an error rate of no more than 3.6 feet per second.

**November 22.** Newspapers report the navy spent $375,000 on a four-year study of the flight characteristics of the Frisbee. With a mechanical disc launcher, the Wham-O toy was tested as a vehicle for holding flares aloft over extended periods.

**December 7.** The longest of the moon flights, *Apollo 17* is also the last. The spacecraft enters orbit on the 11th; rookie Ronald Evans remains in the CM while Eugene Cernan takes Harrison Schmitt—America's first scientist in space—down to the surface.

Over the next 75 hours, the pair spend 22 hours and 5 minutes outside the LM, with a 7-hour, 37-minute stretch a record for the program. And they collect the heaviest load of samples, 249.3 pounds of rock and soil.

In a 10-minute ceremony before lift-off, the astronauts unveil a plaque fixed to the LM landing leg. Signed by President Nixon and the 17 Apollo astronauts, it reads, "Here man completed his first exploration of the Moon, December 1972 A.D. May the spirit of peace in which we came be reflected in the lives of all mankind."

The six Apollo flights translated into a total of just two weeks on the lunar surface. The last trip ends with a safe splashdown on the 19th.

**More news.** Astronomers locate Cygnus X-1, the most promising possibility for a black hole. The theory, first put forward by P. S. de Laplace in 1798, holds that a collapsed star's gravitational field is so strong that even light waves cannot escape.

• British surgeon John Charnley develops the first successful surgical procedure for hipbone replacement. He attaches a plastic socket to the head and neck of the thighbone with dental cement. Previous metal sockets always pressed on the nerves.

• The floppy disk appears this year.

## Other Discoveries, Developments, and Inventions

First single-lens instant camera, the fold-up SX-70 from Polaroid (whose other patents are about to expire)

Less flammable fabrics, sidebeams in the doors, flexible urethane front bumper to withstand five-mph impact with an immovable object (all safety standards for 1973 models)

X-ray airport baggage scanner, Saferay, for $25,000

## Obituaries

**Louis S. B. Leakey** (August 7, 1903–October 1, 1972). One of the foremost authorities in paleo-anthropology, his fossil discoveries and interpretations rewrote humankind's early history. Moreover, Leakey explained his findings to the layperson through popular journals.

**Igor Sikorsky** (May 25, 1889–October 26, 1972). His VS-300 helicopter, first flown in 1939, became the principal model for the American military.

## THE ARTS

February 14—*Grease* (On Broadway June 7), with Barry Bostwick, Carole Demas (still running in 1975)

October 23—*Pippin*, with John Rubinstein, Ben Vereen (still running in 1975)

December 20—*The Sunshine Boys*, with Jack Albertson, Sam Levene, Lewis J. Stadlen (538 perfs.)

## Tony Awards

Actor (Dramatic)—Cliff Gorman, *Lenny*
Actress (Dramatic)—Sada Thompson, *Twigs*
Actor (Musical)—Phil Silvers, *A Funny Thing Happened on the Way to the Forum* (Revival)
Actress (Musical)—Alexis Smith, *Follies*
Play—*Sticks and Bones*
Musical—*Two Gentlemen of Verona*

## News

**April 22.** In his 22 years at the Met, Rudolf Bing's aloofness and European attitudes have often put him at odds with the artists. Still, his enormous accomplishments include breaking the Met color barrier, modernizing productions, and bringing in a steady flow of international talent. Tonight, the opera house honors the outgoing general manager with a gala performance.

**May 21.** In Rome, a deranged man hammers at Michelangelo's Pietà, severing Mary's left arm and damaging her face. The next day, a reporter's mock attack on a second Michelangelo sculpture in another church underscores the continuing lack of security.

**July 2.** Last year, *Fiddler on the Roof* set a record run for a Broadway musical. Tonight, with the final show, *Fiddler* reaches 3,242 performances.

**August 11.** Environmental artist Christo hangs an orange curtain across Rifle Gap in Colorado. Just 24 hours later, the 400-foot-high, 6-ton environmental sculpture is shredded by a wind storm.

**September 30.** *The New York Times* discloses that the Metropolitan Museum has sold a Van Gogh and a Rousseau to private collectors. The museum's director claims "deaccessioning" improves the balance of the collection but, under heavy censure, he agrees to consider the public interest in the future.

**More news.** Broadway musicals collect $15 for top tickets.

• Rudolph Nureyev's $375,000 production of *Sleeping Beauty* nearly bankrupts the National Ballet of Canada. But with next year's performances at the Met, the Canadians win recognition as one of the top ballet companies of the world.

*Statistics:* Since 1965, the number of U.S. ballet and modern dance performances has risen 600 percent. Attendance has nearly kept pace with a 500 percent increase.

## Obituaries

**Richard Crooks** (June 26, 1900–October 1, 1972). The American tenor starred at the Metropolitan Opera House from 1933 to the early 1950s.

**Rudolf Friml** (December 7, 1879–November 12, 1972). After emigrating from Prague in 1906, the pianist became one of America's foremost composers of light operetta. His works included *Rose Marie* (1923) and *The Vagabond King* (1925).

**Ferde Grofe** (March 27, 1892–April 3, 1972). The American composer remains best known for his five-part *Grand Canyon Suite* (1931).

**Ted Shawn** (October 21, 1891–January 9, 1972). Too tall for ballet, the "father of modern dance" established the Denishawn School (1915), with his wife, Ruth St. Denis. He later overcame the prejudice against male dancers in the United States, by touring with his all-male group (1933), and built the Jacob's Pillow Dance Festival into the most important dance event in the country.

**Helen Traubel** (June 20, 1899–July 28, 1972). The finest American Wagnerian soprano of her generation, Traubel left the Met in 1953 rather than give up TV and nightclub appearances. She continued with that career for another decade.

# WORDS

Richard Adams, *Watership Down*
Taylor Caldwell, *Captains and the Kings*
Carlos Castaneda, *Journey to Ixtlan: The Lessons of Don Juan*
Michael Crichton, *The Terminal Man*
Frederick Forsyth, *The Odessa File*
Xaviera Hollander, *The Happy Hooker*
Dan Jenkins, *Semi-Tough*
Donella H. Meadows and others, *The Limits to Growth*
Chaim Potok, *My Name Is Asher Lev*
Aleksandr Solzhenitsyn, *August 1914*
Irving Wallace, *The Word*
Eliot Wigginston, *The Foxfire Book*

## News

**January 9.** In an extraordinary three-hour telephone conversation with Los Angeles reporters, reclusive multimillionaire Howard Hughes exposes his upcoming "autobiography" as a hoax. Author Clifford Irving forged letters and tape-recorded interviews to collect a $750,000 advance from McGraw-Hill and another $250,000 from *Life*. He will spend 17 months in jail.

**March 13.** Burt Reynolds exposes a little pubic hair in his coy *Cosmopolitan* centerfold. The 36-year-old actor, who hates *Playboy*, agreed to the parody because, "I thought it would be a kick. I have a strange sense of humor." His career takes off.

**June 29.** In *Bransburg v. Hayes*, the U.S. Supreme Court denies reporters the right to withhold an informant's name from a grand jury investigation. (Laws in 18 states offer some protection.) On October 4, the landmark decision sends the first reporter to jail, Peter Bridge of the *Newark News*.

**July 1.** *Ms.*, the first national magazine run by and for women, begins publication after a trial issue. Editor and co-founder Gloria Steinem wants a "how-to" publication, "not how to make jelly but how to seize control of your life." *Ms.* amazes critics by recovering its full investment within the first year.

**July 5.** The courts find that photographer Ron Galella "relentlessly invaded" the privacy of Jackie Onassis and her children. He is legally barred from communicating with the former first lady or approaching within 50 yards. But an appeal, next year, will cut that distance to 25 feet.

**August 22.** Avon pays a record $1.1 million for the paperback rights to *Jonathan Livingston Seagull*. Author Richard Bach, a self-professed "gypsy pilot," describes his 93-page book as an allegory, "one little sea gull's search for freedom and his striving to attain perfection."

**December 29.** With dwindling revenues, rising postal rates, and the popularity of television, *Life* magazine ceases publication after 36 years. A pioneer in photojournalism and an outlet for some of the world's finest writers, *Life* was the last mass-market magazine to use the large-photo format.

## Cartoons and Comics

**October–November.** DC introduces *The Swamp Thing* by Berni Wrightson.

**More news.** Bob Thaves brings out the cartoon strip *Frank and Ernest*.

## TIME *Man of the Year*

Richard Nixon and Henry Kissinger

## *New Words and Phrases*

alternative society (counterculture)
carnography (gory acts of violence in movies)
chick-pecked (nagged by a girlfriend)
counterproductive
crisis center
dingbat
ecocatastrophe
hatchback
house sitter
jet lag
life-style
living will
megabyte
multinational
open classroom
prequel
upfront (honest, straightforward)
windsurfing

Two new phrases this year use the verb *to get*— "get away from it all" and "get your priorities right."

In December, a new bumper sticker responds to snarled negotiations in the Vietnam War: "Don't Blame Me, I'm From Massachusetts." Massachusetts was the only state in this year's presidential election to vote for peace candidate George McGovern.

## *Obituaries*

**Ezra Pound** (October 30, 1885–November 1, 1972). A literary giant of this century, Pound influenced poets throughout the world with his innovative techniques. But his espousal of the fascist cause in Italy during W.W.II resulted in a trial back in the United States and confinement to a mental institution. In 1958, after Robert Frost and others helped to win his freedom, Pound returned to Italy.

**Edmund Wilson** (May 8, 1895–June 12, 1972).

His peers described the American critic, poet, novelist, historian, and dramatist as "the quintessential man of letters."

**Walter Winchell** (April 7, 1897–February 20, 1972). In the early 1930s, a national radio program ("Good evening, Mr. and Mrs. America and all the ships at sea, let's go to press!") and a syndicated gossip column gave Winchell an enormous audience. He remained the nation's most powerful journalist into the early fifties. (A younger generation remembers him as the narrator of "The Untouchables.")

# FASHION

## *Haute Couture*

High fashion returns to the classic silhouette with a hemline drawn just above the knee. As well, many collections add an element of the Orient.

## *News*

**This year.** Observers remark on the number of couturiers branching into other markets. In 1970, Vera, the creator of the first signature scarves, designed towels and bedding. Since then, Bill Blass, Rudi Gernreich, and others have given their names to such items as wigs, quilts, luggage, watches, wallpaper, and shopping bags.

• The monokini appears on Florida and California beaches, but police generally ignore the new bareness.

• The vice-president of McCall Patterns, Rosemary McMurty, tells a fashion audience this year that jeans are "the youth status symbol of the world." Evidently in agreement, France sets up jean factories and American Motors offers optional denim bucket seats in the Gremlin subcompact.

## *Colors and Materials*

Designers feature grass green colors in the spring, red in the summer, and yellow, eggplant, and burgundy in the fall. Year-round, white and cream shades dominate.

*Coca-Cola offer teens "the real thing" beach pants, floppy hats, and back packs.*

Manufacturers use double-knits for men's apparel.

## Clothes

Bareback evening and summer dresses are one of the biggest fashion stories of 1972. A second hot-weather favorite is the T-shirt dress (junior sizes rise to midthigh). Fall lines promote a knitted shape with wide-ribbed midsection.

Casual wear teams skintight pants with extralong, loose sweaters (like fisherman knits) or regular-cut pants with softer tops (blouson or loosely belted at the waist). For a dressier look, women match tight pants with full smocks (yoked or square-necked) or flannel slacks (wide or straight) with closer-fitting sweaters or twin sets.

With the pervasive Chinese influence, some stores carry imitation Mao jackets.

Short coats regain popularity, but for comfort over suits, women choose tent and kimono styles.

Americans buy secondhand jeans dipped in bleach.

Menswear manufacturers construct a single-breasted, more classic suit from gray, wool-synthetic blends. Shirts continue to tone down with a gray or white backing under colored stripes.

Sports trousers, wider through the bottom, present deep cuffs. Outdoor jackets, like the Hudson Bay blanket coat, follow rugged lines.

## Accessories

Wedge and platform soles thicken as heavy heels rise to $4^1/_2$ inches. In the summer, young women opt for loud-colored clogs.

Aviator glasses win favor this year.

Jeans roll up over striped, multicolored socks.

Young women often wrap a scarf around their hair.

At the end of the 1960s, members of the counterculture adopted handcrafted Indian jewelry. The chunky pieces, usually made by the Navaho in Arizona, centered around turquoise. This year, native and other outsize jewelry enters the mainstream.

Following the example of rock celebrities like Grace Slick, young women spend $15–$40 for tattoos—flowers, place names, people, sunbursts. For those who prefer to abandon their fads (and this one wanes next year), retailers offer transfer patches.

Men's ties narrow slightly while the bow tie makes a comeback.

In the early years of the decade, some homosexuals don a single gold earring to signal their preferred role in a relationship—dominant if worn in the left ear, passive in the right.

## Hair and Cosmetics

Cosmetic companies emphasize quality and safety in the growing number of natural products—herbal cleansers, protein shampoos, cucumber lotions.

Several tones of shadow and matching eyeliner halo the eyes.

The natural fall of hair remains the standard, but well-brushed, shorter cuts appeal to many. Women curl their hair for the evening only.

Men's sideburns bush out more from the cheek.

Musk takes over the perfume market.

## Obituaries

**Cristóbal Balenciaga** (1895–March 24, 1972). Regarded by many as the greatest couturier of this century, the Spaniard altered customary styling to create the standaway collar, three-quarter-length sleeve, pillbox hat, bathrobe wrap coat, semifitted jacket, and middy dress (forerunner of the sack).

A perfectionist, Balenciaga closed down his illustrious fashion house in 1968 rather than join the emerging world of designer ready-to-wear. (The only couturier with the technical ability to construct a garment from scratch, the master supposedly sewed one piece in each of his collections.)

**Norman Norell** (April 20, 1900–October 25, 1972). When W.W. II isolated haute couture in Paris, the "dean of American fashion" brought international recognition to New York. His identifiable but timeless silhouettes included trouser suits, evening sheaths (often with sequins), and the sailor look.

Coty Award judges selected Norell as the first designer in the Hall of Fame and, at the time of his stroke, the Metropolitan Museum of Art was readying a retrospective of his garments. Norell claimed his major contribution to fashion was "the simple, round, neckline . . . it did change the look of clothes."

# MUSIC

"The First Time Ever I Saw Your Face"—Roberta Flack

"Alone Again (Naturally)"—Gilbert O'Sullivan

"American Pie"—Don McLean

"Without You"—Nilsson

"I Can See Clearly Now"—Johnny Nash

"Candy Man"—Sammy Davis, Jr.

"Lean on Me"—Bill Withers

"Me & Mrs. Jones"—Billy Paul

"Baby Don't Get Hooked on Me"—Mac Davis

"A Horse with No Name"—America

"My Ding-a-Ling"—Chuck Berry

"Let's Stay Together"—Al Green

"I Am Woman"—Helen Reddy

"Brandy (You're a Fine Girl)"—Looking Glass

"Oh Girl"—Chi-Lites

"I'll Take You There"—Staple Singers

"Heart of Gold"—Neil Young

"Song Sung Blue"—Neil Diamond

"Papa Was a Rolling Stone"—Temptations

"Ben"—Michael Jackson

"Black and White"—Three Dog Night

"I Gotcha"—Joe Tex

"Clair"—Gilbert O'Sullivan

"Nights in White Satin"—Moody Blues

"Long Cool Woman (In a Black Dress)"—Hollies

"Rockin' Robin"—Michael Jackson

"Too Late to Turn Back Now"—Cornelius Brothers

"I'd Love You to Want Me"—Lobo

"Outa-Space" (Instr.)—Billy Preston

"Burning Love"—Elvis Presley

## Grammys (1972)

Record of the Year—Roberta Flack, "The First Time Ever I Saw Your Face"

Song of the Year (songwriter)—Ewan MacColl, "The First Time Ever I Saw Your Face"

Album of the Year—*The Concert for Bangladesh*, George Harrison, Ravi Shankar, etc.

Best Vocal Performance (Male)—Harry Nilsson, "Without You" (single)

Best Vocal Performance (Female)—Helen
  Reddy, "I Am Woman" (single)
Best New Artist—America

## News

**Early in the year.** The FBI opens a secret investigation into the activities of former Beatle John Lennon. Information has linked him to a series of planned antiwar concerts.

**June 4.** In their first U.S. tour since Altamont, the Rolling Stones start off in Seattle. Their performances in 30 cities draw an estimated 750,000 (a New York postcard lottery for 20,000 seats draws 550,000 requests). To prevent a recurrence of violence, the group hires T-shirted private guards.

As their warm-up act, 22-year-old Stevie Wonder receives his first widespread exposure to live audiences. He is one of the first to experiment with synthesizers.

**June 20.** The Tallahatchie Bridge, immortalized in Bobbie Gentry's "Ode to Billy Joe," collapses. Authorities believe no one was on the structure at the time.

**July 8–9.** Concert 10 at the Pocono International Raceway in Pennsylvania draws the largest rock festival crowd since Woodstock—over 200,000. For their $11 admission, fans see 10 hours of mostly hard rock: Three Dog Night, the J. Geils Band, Rod Stewart, Humble Pie, and others. But in mid-afternoon, the rain begins. When the concert resumes later in the evening, one-third of the audience has already fled the sea of mud.

**December 21.** Martha & the Vandellas give their farewell concert. Their 12 top 40 hits included some of the most popular dance records of the 1960s.

**More news.** With the nostalgia craze, Rick Nelson cracks the top 10 for the first time in 8 years. And the legendary Chuck Berry scores his first No. 1 hit in a 17-year recording career with a rather rude song titled "My Ding-a-Ling." With some 20 fifties hits on the *Billboard* hot 100, enthusiastic crowds attend concerts headlining the Penguins, Danny & the Juniors, Bill Haley & His Comets, and others.

• Bobby Sherman loses the bubble-gum set to Donny Osmond and David Cassidy, the singing star of TV's "Partridge Family."

• The Byrds, the Rascals, and Creedence Clearwater Revival break up while Smokey Robinson leaves the Miracles. Steppenwolf disbands as well, but will reunite in 1974. By that time, most of its audience has moved on; the band breaks through the top 30 just once more with "Straight Shootin' Woman."

• Don McLean's chronicle of rock 'n' roll is released as a two-sided 45-rpm, but most radio stations refuse to play it. "Buddy Holly was the first and last person I ever really idolized as a kid. . . . I like Holly because he spoke to me. He was a symbol of something deeper than the music he made. His career and the sort of group he created, the interaction between the lead singer and the three men backing him up, was a perfect metaphor for the music of the '60s and for my own youth" (*Life*, January 14). At 8 minutes, 22 seconds, "American Pie" is the longest-playing single to reach No. 1.

• Roberta Flack gives Clint Eastwood permission to use a selection from her 1969 LP in his upcoming movie *Play Misty for Me*. "The First Time Ever I Saw Your Face" brings the 33-year-old singer her first No. 1 hit.

• In 1969, Gerry Beckley, Dewey Bunnell, and Dan Peek graduated from high school in England. The offspring of U.S. military personnel, the trio named their acoustic rock group after America. They return home this year to tour as the opening act for the Everly Brothers.

• Motown moves from Detroit to Los Angeles.

• Performers place more and more emphasis on costumes and makeup. Alice Cooper and his group remain the most theatrical with their "shock-rock."

• Management conflicts, illness, and a lack of new material plague Sly & the Family Stone, but drugs remain the major problem. In 1970, Sly canceled 26 out of 80 scheduled appearances; this year, he misses 12 out of 40. And despite an estimated $1-million payment for the first LP of a new deal, "Family Affair" (1971) is the group's last No. 1 single.

Statistics: Concerts pull in an annual $150 million. Record and tape sales reach $2 billion, with LP's accounting for 86 percent of the 1972 volume.

## New Recording Artists

America
Atlanta Rhythm Section
Jackson Browne
Jim Croce
Doobie Brothers
Dr. Hook (& the Medicine Show)
Eagles
Electric Light Orchestra
Donna Fargo
Bette Midler
Seals & Crofts
Paul Simon (solo)
Steely Dan
Styx
Tanya Tucker

## Obituaries

**Mahalia Jackson** (October 26, 1911–January 27, 1972). Her powerful contralto brought gospel music to white audiences through records, concerts, and radio and television appearances. As a result, she became an important symbol for the civil rights movement during the past decade.

**Clyde McPhatter** (November 15, 1933–June 13, 1972). A lead singer with the Dominoes and the Drifters during the fifties, McPhatter scored his biggest hit solo in 1958 with "A Lover's Question." His career faded at the end of the 1960s; drugs and alcohol followed.

**David Seville (Ross Bagdasarian)** (January 27, 1919–January 16, 1972). His Chipmunk records had sold 70 million copies by 1970.

## MOVIES

*Cabaret* (d. Bob Fosse; color)—Liza Minnelli, Michael York, Joel Grey

*The Candidate* (d. Michael Ritchie; color)—Robert Redford, Peter Boyle, Don Porter

*The Concert for Bangladesh* (d. Saul Swimmer; color)—with George Harrison, Ravi Shankar, Bob Dylan, Ringo Starr

*Deliverance* (d. John Boorman; color)—Jon Voight, Burt Reynolds, Ned Beatty, Ronny Cox

*Fat City* (d. John Huston; color)—Stacy Keach, Jeff Bridges, Susan Tyrrell

*Frenzy* (British, d. Alfred Hitchcock; color)—Jon Finch, Barry Foster, Barbara Leigh-Hunt

*The Getaway* (d. Sam Peckinpah; color)—Steve McQueen, Ali MacGraw, Ben Johnson

*The Godfather* (d. Francis Ford Coppola; color)—Marlon Brando, Al Pacino, James Caan, Robert Duvall, Talia Shire

*Jeremiah Johnson* (d. Sydney Pollack; color)—Robert Redford, Will Geer

*Junior Bonner* (d. Sam Peckinpah; color)—Steve McQueen, Robert Preston, Ida Lupino

*Lady Sings the Blues* (d. Sidney J. Furie; color)—Diana Ross, Billie Dee Williams, Richard Pryor

*The Pied Piper* (British, d. Jacques Demy; color)—Donovan, Donald Pleasence, Michael Hordern, Jack Wild

*Play It Again, Sam* (d. Herbert Ross; color)—Woody Allen, Diane Keaton, Jerry Lacy

*The Poseidon Adventure* (d. Ronald Neame; color)—Gene Hackman, Ernest Borgnine, Red Buttons, Carol Lynley, Stella Stevens, Shelley Winters

*The Ruling Class* (British, d. Peter Medak; color)—Peter O'Toole, Alastair Sim, Arthur Lowe, Harry Andrews

*Sleuth* (d. Joseph L. Mankiewicz; color)—Laurence Olivier, Michael Caine

*Sounder* (d. Martin Ritt; color)—Cicely Tyson, Paul Winfield, Kevin Hooks

*Young Winston* (British, d. Richard Attenborough; color)—Simon Ward, Anne Bancroft, Robert Shaw, John Mills

## Academy Awards

**April 10.** Helen Hayes, Alan King, Jack Lemmon, and Sammy Davis, Jr., share hosting duties.

Best Picture—*The French Connection*

Best Actor—Gene Hackman (*The French Connection*)

Best Actress—Jane Fonda (*Klute*)

Best Director—William Friedkin (*The French Connection*)

Best Supporting Actor—Ben Johnson (*The Last Picture Show*)

Best Supporting Actress—Cloris Leachman (*The Last Picture Show*)

Best Song—"Theme from *Shaft*" from *Shaft*

Best Foreign Film—*The Garden of the Finzi-Continis* (Italian)

In 1929, at the first Oscar ceremonies, Charlie Chaplin received a Special Award for his 1927–1928 film achievements. But when Washington questioned his political views in 1953, the silent screen comedian left the United States.

Tonight, Chaplin returns to receive a second Honorary Award for "the incalculable effect he has had in making motion pictures the art form of this century." Out of respect, the Academy presents no other Special Oscars this year and schedules his award for the end of the evening.

A four-minute standing ovation from the audience moves the frail old man to tears.

## News

**January 24.** A *Newsweek* report on the Hollywood real-estate market notes that the lack of servants and a new fad for throwing restaurant parties have made large-scale property less appealing. Bill Cosby is selling his 18-room mansion for $495,000–$595,000, and Clark Gable's widow is asking $1 million for her ranch house and 20 acres. Still, with new construction and subdivision, the supply of large Hollywood estates is shrinking rapidly.

**Spring.** Sears Roebuck offers the first video films for rent. Such titles as *High Noon* (1952), *The Bridge on the River Kwai* (1957), and *Cactus Flower* (1969) rent for $3–$6 each. The chain is selling the video player Avco Cartavision for $1,600.

**April.** In an *Esquire* interview ("Arsenic and Old Directors"), Frank Capra blames nudity for the lack of women stars today. "A nude girl is a nude girl, and that's that—and there's no way you can make a star out of a nude girl."

In the past, stars like Claudette Colbert wanted to be known for their acting ability, not their sex appeal. In the classic *It Happened One Night* (1934), a comical but provocative clothesline curtain separated Colbert and Clark Gable in a motel room. Even though the audience saw nothing, "at the end those Walls of Jericho came down. Wheee!"

**April 19.** Senator Charles Percy reads a formal apology to Ingrid Bergman into the U.S. Congressional record. In 1950, Senator Edwin Johnson denounced the actress as a "powerful influence for evil" because of her extramarital affair. Bergman expresses surprise at the apology, but remarks she has never forgotten Johnson's abuse.

**April 28.** Hippie feline *Fritz the Cat*—the first X-rated animated feature—is a box office and critical success. Underground comic artist Robert Crumb sold the rights to his famous creation for a flat fee, but he later launches a lawsuit, claiming associates duped him.

**July 18.** Frank Sinatra appears before a House crime committee following earlier testimony, by admitted killer Joseph Barboza, that the singer-actor is a business front for the Mafia.

During his 95-minute appearance, the 56-year-old Sinatra charges the committee with listening to hearsay and denies he knew any of the other investors in an early 1960s race track venture (he withdrew his money in 1963).

A committee member suggests that the entertainer invest his money more carefully in the future.

**September 15.** *Life* magazine notes a new rash of "people-eater" horror films. Since rampaging rats in *Willard* scored a smash hit last year, Hollywood has opted for "ecological revenge": *Blood of the Pigs*, *Night of the Lepus* (men dressed as giant rabbits), *Frogs*, *Stanley* (a rattlesnake), and mad scientist *Dr. Phibes*, who uses locusts and a vampire bat as weapons.

**December.** *Mademoiselle* magazine lists 18 men who have "Movie Machismo": Marlon Brando, Raul

Julia, Clifton Davis, Jeff Bridges, Dack Rambo, Jon Voight, Frederic Forrest, Oliver Reed, Al Pacino, Jean-Pierre Léaud, Jason Miller, Mark Spitz, Ken Howard, Simon Ward, Stacy Keach, Michael York, Cliff Gorman, and Woody Allen.

**More news.** The People's Republic of China imports the first Western motion pictures: *The Sound of Music* (1965), *Tora! Tora! Tora!* (1970), *The Go-Between* (1971), and *The Tales of Beatrix Potter* (1971). Peking wanted the films for study purposes, but supposedly only select audiences viewed the second and last pictures.

• Pornographic movies find a wider audience in the United States and many reap enormous profits. *Deep Throat*, with Linda Lovelace, was filmed in six days for $40,000; it brings in some $3.2 million over the next year.

• The British *Sight and Sound* magazine polls film critics throughout the world for the 10 best titles in cinema history. The top three choices are Orson Welles' *Citizen Kane* (1941), Jean Renoir's *La Règle du Jeu* (*The Rules of the Game*) (1939), and Sergei Einstein's *The Battleship Potemkin* (1925).

• Some mini-movie houses open in America this year. Usually located in shopping centers for easy parking, the single theaters seat 200–350 and, with a fully automatic projection system, can be run by just two people.

| Top Box Office Stars | Newcomers |
|---|---|
| Clint Eastwood | Al Pacino |
| George C. Scott | Edward Albert |
| Gene Hackman | Jeff Bridges |
| John Wayne | Joel Grey |
| Barbra Streisand | Sandy Duncan |
| Marlon Brando | Timothy Bottoms |
| Paul Newman | Madeline Kahn |
| Steve McQueen | Cybill Shepherd |
| Dustin Hoffman | Malcolm McDowell |
| Goldie Hawn | Ron O'Neal |

## Top Money-Maker of the Year

*The Godfather*
(*Note:* The gangster film passes *The Sound of Music* (1965) as the top money-maker of all time.)

## Quote of the Year

"My father made him an offer he couldn't refuse."
—Al Pacino subtly comments on the strongarm tactics used by Marlon Brando, the don in *The Godfather*. (Screenplay by Mario Puzo and Francis Ford Coppola; based on the novel by Mario Puzo)

## Obituaries

**William Boyd** (June 5, 1898–September 12, 1972). A silent-screen romantic lead, the silver-haired actor turned cowboy in 1935 to play Hopalong Cassidy in "B" features. Boyd later purchased sole rights and edited the Westerns for television. The adulation of young TV fans inspired a Hopalong merchandise craze in 1950, making him a wealthy man.

**Maurice Chevalier** (September 12, 1888–January 1, 1972). A legend in his own time, the French entertainer parlayed a limited voice and an inimitable roguish air into international fame. Chevalier's early 1930s films marked the height of his 60-year career, but a role in *Gigi* (1958) signaled a comeback. That film also added "Thank Heaven for Little Girls" to his trademark songs—"Louise," "Mimi," and "Valentine." He made the last of some 40 French and American films in 1967.

**Brandon de Wilde** (April 9, 1942–July 6, 1972). The actor was best known as a child star, particularly for the Western *Shane* (1953). He died in a car accident.

**John Grierson** (April 26, 1898–February 19, 1972). Asked by Ottawa to set up a Canadian film policy, the British educator and filmmaker issued the report used to found the National Film Board in 1939. As commissioner, he almost single-handedly activated the NFB, which quickly won acclaim for its *documentaries*—a term he coined. Grierson left Canada for New York in 1945. A victim of the Communist hysteria, he moved on to UNESCO and later to television.

**Walter Lang** (August 10, 1898–February 8, 1972). Accused of pandering to popular tastes, the director nonetheless made some of the most enjoyable pictures of his day, including *There's No Business Like Show Business* (1954), *The King and I* (1956), and *Can-Can* (1960). He made his last film in 1961.

**J(oseph) Arthur Rank** (December 23, 1888–March 29, 1972). He founded the Rank Organization in 1937 and controlled the British film industry by the fifties. His movies won instant recognition with their opening clip of a well-muscled, bare-chested man striking a huge gong.

**Margaret Rutherford** (May 11, 1892–May 22, 1972). The British Dame won a best supporting Oscar for *The VIP's* (1963), but most film goers remember the stout actress as Agatha Christie's spinster detective, Miss Marple.

**George Sanders** (July 3, 1906–April 25, 1972). His Oscar-winning performance as drama critic Addison de Witt in *All About Eve* (1950) was typical of his many suave characters. Sanders committed suicide because he was "bored."

# TELEVISION AND RADIO

## New Prime-Time TV Programs

"The Bob Newhart Show" (September 16, 1972–   ; Situation Comedy)—Bob Newhart, Suzanne Pleshette, Bill Daily, Peter Bonerz

"Emergency" (January 22, 1972–   ; Drama)—Robert Fuller, Julie London, Bobby Troup, Kevin Tighe, Randolph Mantooth

"Kung Fu" (October 14, 1972–June 28, 1975; Western)—David Carradine, Keye Luke, Philip Ahn

"M*A*S*H" (September 17, 1972–   ; Situation Comedy)—Alan Alda, Wayne Rogers (1972–1975), Loretta Swit, Larry Linville, Gary Burghoff, McLean Stevenson (1972–1975), William Christopher, Jamie Farr, Harry Morgan (1975–   ), Mike Farrell (1975–   )

"Maude" (September 12, 1972–   ; Situation Comedy)—Beatrice Arthur, Bill Macy, Adrienne Barbeau

"The Rookies" (September 11, 1972–   ; Police Drama)—Georg Stanford Brown, Michael Ontkean, Sam Melville, Kate Jackson, Gerald S. O'Loughlin

"Sanford and Son" (January 14, 1972–   ; Situation Comedy)—Redd Foxx, Demond Wilson

"The Streets of San Francisco" (September 16, 1972–   ; Police Drama)—Karl Malden, Michael Douglas

"The Waltons" (September 14, 1972–   ; Drama)—Ralph Waite, Michael Learned, Will Geer, Ellen Corby, Richard Thomas

## Emmy Awards 1971–1972 (May 6, 1972)

Drama Series—"Elizabeth R" (PBS)

Variety Series, Musical—"The Carol Burnett Show" (CBS)

Variety Series, Talk—"The Dick Cavett Show" (ABC)

Comedy Series—"All in the Family" (CBS)

Children's Programming—"Sesame Street" (PBS)

Best Actor in a Series—Peter Falk ("Columbo" —[NBC Mystery Movie], NBC)

Best Actress in a Series—Glenda Jackson ("Elizabeth R," ["Masterpiece Theatre,"] PBS)

Best Comedian in a Series—Carroll O'Connor ("All in the Family," CBS)

Best Comedienne in a Series—Jean Stapleton ("All in the Family," CBS)

## News

**January 17.** Two years ago, Senator J. O. Pastore requested a study on the impact of television violence on children. Today, the surgeon general's office reports that research discovered little effect except on a small group of youngsters predisposed to aggressive behavior. In the weeks ahead, many of the researchers involved in the 43 separate studies charge their evidence clearly contradicts that conclusion.

**January 21.** The NAB board reduces the 16 minutes of commercials per hour of children's programming (7:00 A.M. to 2:00 P.M.) to 12, cuts the number of interruptions, and limits the use of hosts and cartoon characters to advertise products (effective January 1973).

**February 12.** With a full commitment to cable TV, the FCC revises its regulations to stimulate growth in smaller U.S. cities. A system must carry all stations within 35 miles and possess the capability to handle 20 signals. Still, in a controversial move, the FCC retains programming control for the broadcasting stations in the country's 50 largest markets.

During the year, cable companies start offering "pay-cable." For a second monthly charge subscribers can receive unedited first-run films, special sports events, and other similar programs.

---

*Statistics:* In 1960, 640 cable systems reached 1.4 percent of U.S. households. By the middle of this decade, 3,450 tap into 14.3 percent.

---

**April 30.** Never a singer, an actor, or even a clever ad-libber, Arthur Godfrey has nonetheless remained on CBS Radio for 27 years. His appeal comes from spontaneity—a willingness to put down advertising copy and to invite talent scout winners to remain on the show. Never canceled, he takes himself off the air today.

**May 1.** Johnny Carson and "The Tonight Show" move permanently to Burbank, California.

**May 28.** In an analysis of 1,241 TV commercials, *The New York Times* reports NOW's findings that 42.6 percent of the women shown carried out household tasks, 37.5 percent were domestic adjuncts to men, 16.7 percent were presented as sex objects, and 0.3 percent led autonomous, independent lives. Apparently, "their extraordinary incompetence [was] exceeded only by their monumental stupidity."

**July 16.** In New York, WCBS-FM becomes the city's first radio station to adopt a "solid gold" format. But with more and more stations playing oldies from the 1950s and 1960s, record companies are churning out re-recordings. Comparing the industry to the period before the Beatles invasion, Dick Clark says, "American pop music is in the doldrums now awaiting the arrival of the next musical messiah."

---

*Statistics:* From an estimated 5,000 DJ's in the United States in 1957, the number has grown to 25,000.

---

**September 9.** Comedian Bill Cosby provides most of the voices in the Saturday animated series "Fat Albert and the Cosby Kids." The CBS program is praised for its minority characters and educational message.

**September 14.** Few hold out hope for a new family drama slotted opposite the enormously popular Flip Wilson on Thursday evening. In two seasons, the comic will be gone and "The Waltons" will emerge as one of the most popular shows of the decade. Author Earl Hammer, Jr., narrates the program.

**September 17.** A slow starter, M*A*S*H is almost canceled by CBS in midseason. But for the 1973–1974 season, the network will sandwich TV's first black-humor sitcom between "All in the Family" and "The Mary Tyler Moore Show." The rest is history.

**October.** As Bob Woodward and Carl Bernstein delve further into the Watergate burglary and cover-up, the news media ignores the story—with one exception. CBS newscaster Walter Cronkite begins a nightly summary of the *Washington Post* reports.

**November 1.** "That Certain Summer," ABC's "Wednesday Movie of the Week," offers television's first sympathetic portrayal of a homosexual relationship. Hal Holbrook and Martin Sheen star.

### TV Commercials

Alka-Seltzer—This year, the company adds two new phrases to the American vocabulary—"I can't believe I ate the whole thing" and "Try it, you'll like it." The commercial's answer to the second statement is, "I tried it. Thought I was going to die."

Quaker Oats—"Let's get Mikey!" "He won't eat it. He hates everything." "He likes it! Hey, Mikey!" Three-year-old John Gilchrist (a.k.a. Mikey) eats Life Cereal despite what his real-life brothers, six-year-old Michael and eight-year-old Tommy, say.

## Obituaries

**Dan Blocker** (1929–May 13, 1972). The former teacher played Hoss Cartwright on "Bonanza." He died of a blood clot in his lung.

**Pat Brady** (December 31, 1914–February 27, 1972). The stage, screen, and television actor and musician was best known as Roy Roger's comic sidekick during the 1950s.

**Charles Correll** (February 3, 1890–September 26, 1972). He played Andy to Freeman Gosden's Amos on the long-running radio comedy series.

# SPORTS

## Winners

### Baseball

World Series—Oakland Athletics (AL), 4 games; Cincinnati Reds (NL), 3 games
Player of the Year—Richie Allen (Chicago White Sox, AL); Johnny Bench (Cincinnati Reds, NL)
Rookie of the Year—Carlton Fisk (Boston Red Sox, AL); Jon Matlack (New York Mets, NL)

### Football

NFC Championship—Washington Redskins 26, Dallas Cowboys 3
AFC Championship—Miami Dolphins 21, Pittsburgh Steelers 17
Super Bowl VII (January 14, 1973)—Miami Dolphins 14, Washington Redskins 7
College Bowls (January 1, 1972)—
   Rose Bowl, Stanford 13, Michigan 12
   Cotton Bowl, Penn State 30, Texas 6
   Orange Bowl, Nebraska 38, Alabama 6
   Sugar Bowl, Oklahoma 40, Auburn 22
Heisman Trophy—Johnny Rodgers (Nebraska, RB)
Grey Cup—Hamilton Tiger-Cats 13, Saskatchewan Roughriders 10

### Basketball

NBA Championship—LA Lakers, 4 games; New York Knickerbockers, 1 game
MVP of the Year—Kareem Abdul-Jabbar (Milwaukee Bucks)
Rookie of the Year—Sidney Wicks (Portland Trail Blazers)
NCAA Championship—UCLA 81, Florida State 76

### Tennis

U.S. Open—Men, Ilie Năstase (vs. Arthur Ashe); Women, Billie Jean King (vs. Kerry Melville)
Wimbledon—Men, Stan Smith (vs. Ilie Năstase); Women, Billie Jean King (vs. Evonne Goolagong)

### Golf

Masters—Jack Nicklaus
U.S. Open—Jack Nicklaus
British Open—Lee Trevino

### Hockey

Stanley Cup—Boston Bruins, 4 games; New York Rangers, 2 games

### Ice Skating

World Championship—Men, Ondrej Nepela (Czechoslovakia); Women, Beatrix Schuba (Austria)
U.S. National—Men, Ken Shelley; Women, Janet Lynn
Canadian National—Men, Toller Cranston; Women, Karen Magnussen

### Kentucky Derby

Riva Ridge—Ron Turcotte, jockey

### Athlete of the Year

Male—Mark Spitz (Swimming)
Female—Olga Korbut (Gymnastics)

## Last Season

Lance D. Alworth (Football)
Elgin Baylor (Basketball)
Mike Ditka (Football)
Kevin Loughery (Basketball)
Ray Nitschke (Football)
Hoyt Wilhelm (Baseball)

## News

**This year.** Contract disputes and court litigation dominate the world of sports. Basketball players tell Congress that an NBA-ABA merger would limit their bargaining prospects. NHL star Bobby Hull needs a sympathetic judge to jump to the new World Hockey Association (WHA). And, in amateur sports, the AAU says it will ask Congress to investigate NCAA efforts to control amateur athletics.

**January 8.** The NCAA allows college freshmen to compete in varsity football and basketball games (effective August 1) after a 21-year absence. Small schools already had permission.

**January 16.** After his victory in the 1971 Super Bowl, coach Tom Landry receives a call from the White House. Reporters ask if the president discussed down-and-in pass patterns. Landry replies, "He didn't mention it."

Days before the big game, Nixon phoned Miami coach Don Schula and told him to send wide receiver Paul Warfield on down-and-in pass patterns. The first three attempts failed; the fourth gained five yards.

**February 3–13.** Thirty-five nations send 1,232 athletes to the Winter Olympics in Sapporo, Japan. Outstanding performances include 17-year-old Swiss skier Marie Terese Nadig, with golds in the downhill and the giant slalom, and Ard Schenk, with three victories in speed skating for the Netherlands.

In an unusual twist, U.S. speed skater Anne Henning breaks the 500-meter record in a solo race. Already the gold-medal winner, she raced against the clock after her opponent was disqualified.

The Soviets, with twice as many gold medals as any other country, place first overall.

**February 29.** last season, Hank Aaron blasted a career-high 47 home runs and set a .327 batting average. Today, the Braves right-fielder signs baseball's first $200,000-a-year contract. During this season, Aaron hits 34 HR to pass Willie Mays and pull within 41 of Babe Ruth's record.

**April 1.** In the first universal strike since 1900, ball players demand an increased pension fund. The owners agree, on the 13th, to add $500,000 to the kitty.

The season opens on April 15, but with generally poor weather attendance figures remain low, particularly in cities with weak franchises.

**April 17.** An unofficial entrant for five years, Nina Kuscsik joins eight other women as the first recognized female runners in the 76-year history of the Boston Marathon. Although the women are scored separately, Kuscsik finishes ahead of 80 percent of the 1,081 male starters.

**June 19.** The U.S. Supreme Court upholds *Flood vs. Kuhn* (1970), which affirmed antitrust immunity for the sport of baseball. But the court describes the exemption as an "anomaly" and calls on Congress to make a final determination.

**June 23.** Title IX of the Education Amendment Act bars sex bias in athletics at colleges receiving federal assistance. In other words, the revolutionary legislation guarantees equal funding for women's sports programs and scholarships.

**June 27.** Bobby Hull stuns Chicago hockey fans by signing with Winnipeg in the WHA. NHL scoring leader in 1960, 1962, and 1966, the Golden Jet will receive $2.5 million over 10 years. His legitimization of the rival league suddenly gives NHL players leverage in their salary demands.

**July 13.** Annoyed with poor preseason attendance in Baltimore, Colts' owner Carroll Rosenbloom swaps teams with the owner of the Los Angeles Rams. All players and personnel remain in their respective cities.

**August 23.** Avery Brundage announces that Lord Michael Killanin will succeed him as president of the IOC, at the end of next month's Summer Games.

**August 26–September 10.** Following the terrorist attack on the Israeli athletes (see *News*), the

Olympics are suspended for the first time in modern history. Despite widespread objections, Brundage orders the games to resume after a memorial service on the 6th.

Mark Spitz captivates the world with a record 7 gold medals in 4 individual and 3 team swimming events. The Soviet gymnast Olga Korbut draws new interest to her sport with her daring gold-medal-winning performances.

At the other end of the spectrum, the United States records its first basketball loss since the introduction of the sport in 1936. In the gold-medal game, the Americans defeat the Soviets by 1 point, but officials twice call them back in disputes over elapsed time. The second time, Aleksandr Belov scores and the Soviets win 51–50. The outraged Americans refuse their silver medal.

At the end of the games, the USSR tallies 99 medals, for first place overall; the United States takes second with 94.

**September 1.** With a symbolic Cold War victory over the Communists, Bobby Fischer becomes the first American to win the world chess title. (Soviet grandmaster Boris Spassky trailed by four with only three matches remaining.) The 29-year-old Fischer, with his wrangling over prize money and notorious bad manners, has focused international attention on the game.

**September 28.** Sportswriter Dick Beddoes describes the first match between NHL professionals and Soviet "amateurs" as Canada's greatest adventure. Today in Moscow, tension mounts as Team Canada and the Soviets trade five goals each in the eighth and deciding game (a tie will give the Soviets the series). Then, with just 36 seconds left, Paul Henderson knocks in the winning goal. For the millions of Canadians glued to their radios and televisions back home, Henderson instantly becomes a national hero.

**October.** This season, the rival WHA establishes teams in 12 Canadian and American cities. Meanwhile, the NHL expands into Atlanta with the Flames and into New York with the Islanders. Attendance in the established league increases by 1 million over last season.

**October 1.** At the third annual New York City

Marathon, officials enter 10 women in the main race after they refuse to run in a separate competition.

**November 21.** This year, in bouts staged around the world, Muhammad Ali defeated Mac Foster, George Chuvalo, Jerry Quarry, and Floyd Patterson. Tonight, Ali puts away WBA light-heavyweight champion Bob Foster in the fifth round.

Heavyweight champion Joe Frazier, on the other hand, has remained comparatively inactive.

**December 23.** Under instructions from President Nixon, the U.S. attorney general has challenged the NFL over local-game blackouts. Today, the U.S. Appeals Court refuses to order the broadcast of the Redskin-Packer playoff game. The ruling cites the 1962 antitrust decision.

**More news.** Billie Jean King becomes the first female athlete to earn more than $100,000 in a year. But the talented tennis player needed a series of sponsored events to reach the milestone; the regular tournament circuit still offers women relatively little prize money in comparison to men. Rod Laver, on the other hand, collected $272,000 to become the first tennis player to surpass $1 million in career earnings.

## Records

**January 9.** An LA Laker loss to the Milwaukee Bucks (120–104) ends the longest winning streak in modern professional sports—33 games. Nonetheless, Laker starters Wilt Chamberlain, Happy Hairston, Jim McMillan, Jerry West, and Gail Goodrich win a record 69 games and an NBA title.

**December 16.** With a 16–0 win over the Baltimore Colts, the Miami Dolphins become the first NFL club to finish a regular season with no losses and no ties. Most fans know quarterback Bob Griese, receiver Paul Warfield, and backs Larry Csonka and Mercury Morris, but the No-Name Defense remains the heart of the team.

**This year.** In the "year of the runner," a record 10 NFL players rush for 1,000 yards or more. Buffalo's O. J. Simpson leads the pack with 1,251.

## What They Said

"I've seen better ice on the roads in Saskatchewan."
—New York Ranger coach Emile Francis on the condition of the rink in Madison Square Garden (*Sports Illustrated*, March 6)

When asked if running back Ron Bull might change his mind about retiring, Philadelphia Eagle coach Ed Khayat says, "Before ecology, you got a lot of that. Come autumn and the smell of burning leaves, a guy would decide he wanted to play again. Now, because of pollution laws, you can't burn leaves." (*Sports Illustrated*, June 26)

## Obituaries

**Charles Atlas** (October 30, 1893–December 24, 1972). Devised in 1921, his isometric system of muscle building sells an annual 70,000 courses in seven languages.

**(Walter) Turk Broda** (May 15, 1914–October 17, 1972). With just 2 years out for military service, the Turk remained in the Leaf nets for 17 years (1935–1952). A money player, who allowed just 211 goals in 101 playoff games, he led Toronto to five Stanley Cups.

**Francis Chichester** (September 17, 1901–August 26, 1972). The internationally renowned sailor circumnavigated the world in a record 226 days during 1966 and 1967.

**Roberto Clemente** (August 18, 1934–December 31, 1972). In 17 years with the Pittsburgh Pirates, the popular outfielder earned 12 Gold Gloves, led the NL in assists a record 5 times, won 4 NL batting titles, and set a lifetime average of .318 (the highest among active players) with 3,000 hits. More importantly for the game, his gymnastic fielding and determined base running influenced the style of modern play.

Honorary chairman of a Puerto Rican relief committee for earthquake victims in Nicaragua, Clemente died in a plane crash en route to the stricken nation. In 1973, the Hall of Fame will waive the usual five-year waiting period and induct Clemente immediately. The Pirates will retire his No. 21.

**Gil Hodges** (April 4, 1924–April 2, 1972). An eight-time All-Star, the Dodger first baseman collected over 100 RBI in seven consecutive seasons (1947–1961). After a single season with the Mets, he went to the Washington Senators and took over as manager. Traded back to the Mets in 1968, he steered baseball's proverbial last-place team to a pennant the very next year. Hodges died suddenly of a heart attack.

**Freddie Parent** (November 25, 1875–November 2, 1972). Parent was the last survivor of the first modern World Series in 1903. He played shortstop for the victorious Boston Red Sox against the Pittsburgh Pirates.

**Jackie Robinson** (January 31, 1919–October 24, 1972). In his eulogy, Rev. Jesse Jackson says, "This man turned a stumbling block into a stepping stone." Handpicked by Branch Rickey to break the major league color barrier in 1947, the young black overcame enormous pressure to win the first Rookie of the Year award. Two years later, the NL named him MVP. He excelled at base running, stealing home 19 times, and finished with a .311 lifetime batting average. The Dodgers, who won six NL pennants during his 10-year career, retired No. 42 earlier this year.

**George Schuster** (1873–July 4, 1972). The chief road tester of the Thomas Flyer Co. won the historic 1908 New York–Paris auto race in 169 days. The second-place car drove in from Eastern Europe 29 days later.

**(Harold J.) Pie Traynor** (November 11, 1899–March 16, 1972). Widely regarded as baseball's greatest third baseman, the durable Pirate (1920–1935) topped the .300 mark 10 times, finished with an NL record 2,288 putouts, and remains among Pittsburgh's all-time offensive leaders (except in home runs). As manager from 1934 to 1939, Traynor collected the second-most wins in team history. He finished his career as a Pirate scout.

# *1973*

---

The Vietnam peace agreement ends years of bitter division, but optimism and relief disappears in late March when Judge John Sirica receives a letter from James McCord; Watergate witnesses have lied and others are implicated. Newspaper reporters and Senate hearings uncover the Plumbers, the Enemies list, the dirty-tricks campaign, and the White House tapes.

With a court order for the recordings, Sirica seals Nixon's fate. "I am not a crook," the president protests, but his denial of access is seen by many as an admission of guilt.

The year descends in a spiral of scandal—the Ellsberg trial, the ITT memo, Spiro Agnew's resignation, the Saturday Night Massacre, the secret bombing of Cambodia. While Americans spare little thought for international events, administration support for the Israelis in the Yom Kippur War enrages OPEC nations. Their oil embargo creates an instant energy crisis and carves an Arab niche in the balance of power.

Elsewhere in the news, Roe v. Wade overturns restrictive abortion laws, NASA launches Skylab, Pioneer 10 reaches Jupiter, and Henry Kissinger and Le Duc Tho share the Nobel peace prize. Willie Mays retires, Wilt Chamberlain hits the bench, and Gordie Howe returns to the ice. Princess Anne marries a commoner, embroidered jeans are all the rage, Elvis gets a divorce, and Roger Moore becomes the new James Bond. The top tune is "Killing Me Softly with His Song" and record stores stock discs from new singers like Billy Joel, Bruce Springsteen, and Pink Floyd. Favored movies include American Graffiti, The Sting, The Exorcist, and The Way We Were. And famous obituaries include Pablo Picasso, Bobby Darin, Betty Grable, John Ford, and Bruce Lee.

## NEWS

**January 20.** Antiwar demonstrations mar the most expensive inauguration in American history. But security forces, supported by National Guardsmen and federal troops, keep the estimated 100,000 protesters away as Richard Nixon and Spiro Agnew are sworn in for a second term of office.

The day after, Senator McGovern warns at a lecture in England that the United States is "closer to one-man rule than at any time in our history."

**January 22.** Lyndon Baines Johnson dies of a heart attack in San Antonio, Texas.

Egocentric, generous, secretive, loyal, ruthless, a champion of the little guy, power hungry—all these terms and more describe the complex man who served as the 36th president of the United States (1963–1969).

After 12 years in the House, Johnson was elected to the Senate in 1948. He became Democratic whip within 3 years, minority leader in 2 more, and with midterm gains in 1955, the Senate's youngest majority leader. Placed on the 1960 Democratic ticket in a bid for Southern votes, Johnson traveled the world as vice president. His familiarity with national leaders bolstered his position in the White House following the assassination of President Kennedy.

Loyal to Kennedy's New Frontier program, Johnson skillfully exploited congressional remorse over JFK's death to enact the stalled legislation. Then, with a mandate from his 1964 election victory, Johnson requested congressional assistance in creating a "Great Society." In 1971, the former president wrote that his social program had raised annual appropriations for health care from $4.1 billion to $13.9 billion, for education from $2.3 billion to $10.8 billion, and for the poor from $12.5 billion to $24.6 billion. He worked equally hard to eliminate racial inequality, supporting the Civil Rights Acts of 1964 and 1968 and the Voting Rights Act of 1965.

For those legislative accomplishments, many historians describe Johnson as a great president. More claim his program was sacrificed on the altar of the Vietnam War. Heir to years of minimal escalation in Indochina and a victim of his Texas heritage, Johnson reneged on a 1964 campaign pledge and committed the United States to another Asian war. Ultimately, Vietnam became the tragedy of his administration. He died less than a week before the cease-fire.

**January 22.** Finding that the 14th Amendment guarantees a right of privacy "broad enough to encompass a woman's decision whether or not to terminate her pregnancy," the U.S. Supreme Court (7–2) legalizes abortion without restriction during the first trimester.

The landmark ruling in *Roe v. Wade* overturns restrictive abortion laws not only in Texas and Georgia but in 44 other states.

**January 23.** President Nixon announces over television and radio that Henry Kissinger and Le Duc Tho have initialed an agreement in Paris "to end the war and bring peace with honor in Vietnam and Southeast Asia."

Washington releases the details on the 24th: a cease-fire in place supervised by a four-nation International Commission of Control and Supervision (ICCS); the release of all POWs and civilians; the withdrawal of all U.S. forces and military personnel within 60 days; the dismantling of U.S. bases; the guaranteed right of the South Vietnamese people to determine their future without interference; and an end to military activities in Laos and Cambodia. A political section guarantees the creation of a tripartite council made up equally of members named by Saigon and the VC to implement the agreement; promote national reconciliation; and organize elections in South Vietnam.

Delegates sign the truce agreement on January 27, in two separate ceremonies. The South Vietnamese remain adamant in their refusal to recognize the PRG, and the United States meets again with North Vietnam in the afternoon, to sign papers acknowledging the political arm of the VC. The North Vietnamese give U.S. representatives a list of American POWs—555 military prisoners and 27 civilians.

The battlefield truce becomes effective at 8:00 A.M. on January 28, but the fighting continues with an estimated 870 South Vietnamese and 5,218 North Vietnamese killed by mid-February. The ICCS believes that, as long as the two sides fail to agree on territorial lines, an effective truce is impossible.

**January 30.** After less than two hours' deliberation, a jury convicts Gordon Liddy and James McCord on charges relating to the Watergate break-in; the other five defendants pleaded guilty at the beginning of the trial. Only these seven men have stood trial, despite a promise from Attorney General Richard Kleindienst that the Watergate investigation would be the "most extensive, thorough and comprehensive since the assassination of President Kennedy."

During the court case, Judge John Sirica, chief judge of the U.S. District Court in the District of

*Judge John Sirica, chief judge of the U.S. District Court in the District of Columbia, presides over the Watergate trial.*

Columbia, declared that neither the prosecution nor the defense had developed "all the facts." He personally interrogated several witnesses and uncovered the $199,000 in campaign funds paid to Liddy.

**February 12.** With the worsening U.S. trade balance, Secretary of the Treasury George Shultz announces a 10-percent devaluation of the American dollar—the second devaluation in less than 14 months.

**February 15.** The United States and Cuba sign a five-year agreement to extradite hijackers and return the planes and any ransom money. Washington insists that this "memorandum of understanding" does not signal improved relations.

**February 21.** Premier Souvanna Phouma signs a cease-fire agreement with the Communist Pathet Lao, ending the 20-year Laotian civil war. The Communists possess the military capability to win the war but have settled rather than risk increased U.S. aid to the government.

Each side retains the territories under its control, pending the installation of a permanent coalition government. The two factions must form a temporary coalition within 30 days, and all foreign troops must withdraw in 60.

**February 27.** In South Dakota, some 200 members of the radical American Indian Movement (AIM) occupy the village at Wounded Knee on the Oglala Sioux reservation—the site of the U.S. Army massacre of 300 Sioux in 1890. The armed militants demand that the government investigate the Bureau of Indian Affairs and honor hundreds of broken treaties.

Some 200 law-enforcement officers surround the town and, during constant exchanges of gunfire over the next 70 days, kill two Indians and arrest some 300 people attempting to enter or leave the community.

On May 5, government negotiators agree to investigate the Indians' charges. Three days later, the 120 or so remaining militants end their occupation. The FBI will fail to make charges stick against the leaders, but promised discussions produce no tangible results.

**February 28.** Acting FBI director L. Patrick Gray reveals during Senate confirmation hearings that he gave the White House access to the FBI Watergate investigation. In August 1972, the president's counsel, John Dean, requested bureau files on the burglary and sat in on all FBI interviews. Dean refuses to testify and President Nixon supports him, citing "executive privilege."

On April 5, Gray asks the president to withdraw his nomination for permanent director. Reports then surface that Gray, at the urging of Ehrlichman and Dean, had burned relevant files taken from the safe of E. Howard Hunt. The acting director resigns on April 27.

**March 1.** In Sudan, members of Black September seize hostages at a Saudi Arabian embassy reception and demand the release of Arab prisoners in Israel, Jordan, and the United States. The next day, when the governments refuse, the terrorists kill the U.S. ambassador and U.S. chargé d'affaires and the Belgian chargé.

The guerrillas surrender to Sudanese authorities, but after considerable foot-dragging, Khartoum allows them to leave the country. When the plane lands in Cairo, Egyptian authorities arrest the killers.

**March 2.** Representatives from 80 nations sign a treaty prohibiting commercial trade of 375 endangered wildlife species and restricting trade of another 239 animals.

**March 20.** Saying that the multinational consortium will now be only "buyers of our oil," Shah Pahlavi nationalizes the foreign-operated Iranian oil industry.

**March 23.** At the sentencing of the "Watergate Seven," Judge John Sirica reads a letter from defendant James McCord, former security coordinator for CREEP. McCord charges that others were involved in the burglary, that defendants were pressured to plead guilty, and that perjury was committed during the trial. He implicates Jeb Magruder, CREEP deputy director, and John Dean.

Magruder confesses to perjury on April 12 and accuses former Attorney General John Mitchell and presidential counsel John Dean of planning the Watergate bugging.

**March 29.** North Vietnam releases the last American POWs, and U.S. troops complete their withdrawal from South Vietnam. (The Americans had delayed one day past the terms of the agreement to obtain the release of nine Americans and one Canadian still held in Laos.) The Defense Department reports the return of 595 POWs; 1,328 remain missing in action and 1,100 were killed in action, but their bodies were never recovered. With the last Americans out of danger, POWs across the United States call news conferences to tell of the physical and mental torture inflicted on them by the Communists.

U.S. casualties for 14 years of involvement in Vietnam will eventually be revised to 46,226 combat deaths, 10,326 noncombat deaths, and 153,311 wounded (303,616, if the less seriously wounded are counted).

The much heavier Vietnamese combat casualties reach 220,357 in South Vietnam and 1 million in North Vietnam (since 1946, but the majority died during the years of American involvement). Civilian casualties in both countries are much more difficult to tally. Estimates in South Vietnam range from 250,000 to 430,000 killed and 800,000 to 1 million wounded. In North Vietnam, Communist authorities admit that they have no idea how high the numbers go.

**April 17.** President Nixon announces that a new White House inquiry into the Watergate case has produced "major developments" and that presidential aides will now be permitted to testify before the Senate committee, under certain conditions.

Presidential press secretary Ron Ziegler says Nixon's previous statements, denying the involvement of White House staff, are now "inoperative," since they were based on "investigations prior to the developments announced today."

Stinging under White House criticism of their Watergate coverage, reporters respond angrily at the press briefing on the 18th. Clark Mollenhoff, from the Des Moines (Iowa) *Register and Tribune*, tells Ziegler, "You're not entitled to any credibility at all."

**April 30.** In a nationally televised address, President Nixon accepts responsibility for the Watergate affair but states he was not personally involved in the political espionage or the attempted cover-up.

Nixon comments as well on resignations announced earlier today. White House aides John Ehrlichman and H. R. Haldeman claimed that Watergate complications had undermined their ability to perform their duties. Attorney General Kleindienst resigned because people close to him, personally and professionally, were implicated in Watergate. The president gives no reason for requesting and accepting a resignation from counsel John Dean III.

Over the next 10 days, former CIA director James Schlesinger becomes defense secretary, William Colby the CIA director, John B. Connally, Jr. a special advisor to the president, Elliot Richardson attorney general, and General Alexander Haig, Jr. a presidential aide.

**May 11.** In the Pentagon Papers trial, U.S. District Judge William Byrne drops all charges against Daniel Ellsberg and Anthony J. Russo because of government misconduct: A Justice Department memo revealed that Gordon Liddy and E. Howard Hunt, in an effort to discredit Ellsberg, had burglarized the office of his psychiatrist (the CIA has admitted assisting in the operation); Ehrlichman had introduced Byrne to the president and discussed his possible appointment as director of the FBI; and finally, the government wiretapped

Ellsberg's phone in 1969 and 1970, but the transcripts have disappeared.

Judge Byrne precludes a retrial by stating, for the record, "Bizarre events have incurably infected the prosecution of this case."

**May 12.** Overpopulation and overgrazing, the result of better health care for humans and vaccinations for livestock, have stripped the grasses from the fragile semiarid Sahel, turning an estimated 250,000 square miles into desert. Now a five-year drought tips the balance of survival.

In the six countries at this southern edge of the Sahara—Chad, Mauritania, Mali, Niger, Senegal, and Upper Volta—millions of cattle die from lack of water and an estimated 100,000 people starve or, in their weakened state, die from disease. As the nomads lose their cattle herds, social devastation follows, and up to 5 million refugees flee. Rains in fall 1974 will finally bring some relief.

**May 17.** On February 7, the Senate voted 77–0 to establish a seven-member Select Committee on Presidential Campaign Activities, chaired by Senator Sam Ervin. The Watergate Committee opens televised hearings today on the origin and aftermath of the Washington scandal.

On the second day, Watergate conspirator James McCord testifies that former White House aide John Caulfield offered him executive clemency for his silence. The hearings soon draw huge television audiences.

**May 22.** With continuing Watergate revelations and indictments, President Nixon releases a statement explaining the White House role in the affair. He acknowledges limiting the Watergate investigation, because of unrelated national security considerations of "crucial importance," but claims that he had no prior knowledge of the burglary and that aides exceeded his instructions in attempting a cover-up.

Three days later, former U.S. Solicitor General Archibald Cox is sworn in as special Watergate prosecutor.

**June 20.** With the Peronists once again in control, exiled Juan Perón returns to Argentina for the first time since being overthrown in 1955. The army had approved March elections, the first since

1964. Barred from running himself, the former dictator hand-picked Hector Campora as his stand-in. Victory brought a quick resignation from Campora, clearing the way for new elections.

On September 23, 61.8 percent of the voters choose Perón as president and his wife, Isabel, as vice-president, the first woman vice-president in Latin America.

**June 21.** Retreating from 1957 and 1966 decisions, a more conservative Supreme Court (5–4) narrows the definition of pornography from "lacking redeeming social value" to a stricter absence of serious literary, artistic, political, or scientific value. At the same time, the finding authorizes the application of local rather than national standards to questionable material.

In his dissent, Justice Brennan declares, "If a state may . . . prescribe what its citizens cannot read or cannot see, then it would seem to follow that in pursuit of the same objective a state could decree that its citizens must read certain books or must view certain films."

**June 25–29.** Senator Howard Baker, ranking Republican on the Watergate Committee, asks John Dean, "What did the president know and when did he know it?" The former White House counsel blows open the investigation with a 245-page statement. He names Ehrlichman and Haldeman as the principals, but directly accuses the president of allowing the cover-up to continue. Nixon, he says, specifically discussed hush money for the conspirators and the possibility of clemency.

During four days of testimony, Dean theorizes that "excessive concern" with political opponents and antiwar activists, plus the "do-it-yourself White House staff, regardless of the law," created the climate for Watergate. As proof, he produces the White House "Opponents List and Political Enemies Project." Initiated in 1971 and frequently updated, the dozens of names include prominent personalities in the news media, politics, organized labor, show business (Jane Fonda, Bill Cosby, and Paul Newman), and other fields.

Committee members attempt to shake Dean's credibility—he also implicates former attorney general John Mitchell, former acting director of the

FBI L. Patrick Gray, and presidential press secretary Ron Ziegler, among others—but Dean refuses to back down.

**July 1.** President Nixon signs an appropriations bill setting August 15 as the termination date for U.S. bombing of Cambodia. Last month, Nixon vetoed a congressional attempt to cut off funds, vowing to continue the bombing until Communist rebels accepted a cease-fire from President Lon Nol. But congressional leaders threatened to attach a cutoff amendment to all supplemental funding bills and Nixon was forced to compromise.

**July 10.** During three days of testimony, former attorney general John Mitchell denies he approved the Watergate break-in but admits playing a role in the cover-up. To his knowledge, the president knew nothing until long after his reelection.

**July 13.** As Watergate Committee staff privately question Alexander Butterfield about John Dean's suspicion that the Oval Office is bugged, the former presidential aide replies, "I was hoping you fellows wouldn't ask me about that."

Three days later, Butterfield publicly describes the secret taping system used since the spring of 1971 to record all Nixon's conversations and telephone calls in the White House and the Executive Office Building—without the knowledge of other participants.

The revelation stuns the nation, but the committee and special prosecutor Cox quickly move to obtain conclusive proof of presidential involvement in the Watergate affair.

**July 13.** The U.S. federal government conservatively estimates that 250,000 American servicemen and civilians participated in the 17-year atmospheric nuclear test program. Thousands viewed detonations from as close as one mile away, and hundreds marched to bomb sites afterward in military exercises.

Yet nuclear veterans must prove participation before filing a radiation disability claim. That evidence, for many, is tragically lost today when fire destroys an estimated 18 million military service records stored in St. Louis, Missouri.

**July 16.** The Senate Armed Services Committee begins an investigation into charges that the U.S.

Air Force, without congressional approval, secretly bombed Cambodia prior to the April 1970 incursion.

In a letter to the committee, Defense Secretary James Schlesinger admits that B-52s conducted "fully authorized" secret raids against Cambodia in 1969 and 1970. President Johnson had repeatedly turned down a Pentagon request to bomb North Vietnamese sanctuaries in Cambodia, but a new president in 1969 approved "Operation Menu." Schlesinger states that U.S. recognition of Cambodian neutrality necessitated "special security precautions," including falsifying records and burning mission reports. Following the 1970 invasion, the operation continued as "Freedom Deal."

At a news conference later today, the Pentagon acknowledges that Nixon and former defense secretary Melvin Laird personally authorized the raids.

**July 17.** In Afghanistan, Lt. Gen. Mohammad Daoud Khan leads a coup against his cousin and brother-in-law King Zahir Shah, age 59, now in Italy undergoing medical treatment.

The British established General Nadir Shah as king in 1929; when he was assassinated in 1933, his son Zahir took the throne. Considered a mere figurehead by most Westerners, the king nonetheless introduced constitutional government in 1964. But with the civil unrest produced by years of famine, Daoud Khan proclaims a republic and imposes martial law.

**July 23.** On July 17, following Butterfield's testimony, Watergate Committee chairman Senator Ervin sent the president a letter requesting all relevant White House documents and tapes. In his reply, Nixon states that the tapes "which have been under my sole personal control, will remain so. None has been transcribed or made public and none will be."

Later today, both the committee and special prosecutor Cox serve the president with subpoenas. When Nixon refuses on the 26th, the committee moves to resolve the issue through the courts, while Cox obtains a court order from Judge Sirica requiring the president to show cause by August 7 why the tapes should not be produced.

White House lawyers file a brief arguing that the

release of the tapes would violate the doctrine of separation of powers.

**July 24–31.** Over four days of testimony, former presidential aide John Ehrlichman admits approving the "covert operation" leading to the break-in at the office of Ellsberg's psychiatrist. But Ehrlichman says he and Nixon believed the act was well within the president's constitutional powers to protect national security. Ervin reacts sharply to this reasoning, arguing that no law gives the president authority to order an illegal act.

H. R. Haldeman—who as chief of staff to the president was fond of saying, "Every president needs an S.O.B., and I'm Nixon's"—begins his testimony on the 30th. He contradicts earlier assertions by John Dean that Nixon revealed his awareness of the cover-up on the day the Watergate Seven were indicted, September 15, 1972.

**August 7.** Fearing for his life, Elmer Wayne Henley, age 17, shoots and kills Dean Corll in Houston, Texas. Henley then leads the police to the graves of 27 young boys, tortured and murdered by Corll. The youth and his friend David Brooks had lured most of the victims to the killer's home for $200 a head, a price they seldom received.

Each denies killing anyone but accuses the other of murder. The courts will sentence Brooks to life and Henley to 594 years.

**August 15.** American combat activity in Indochina ends under the congressional order to halt the bombing of Cambodia. Contrary to White House predictions, the Lon Nol government survives the end of the 160-day air campaign. Still, the battered Communist Khmer Rouge rebels retain control over some three-quarters of the country.

**August 22.** At his first press conference in five months, President Nixon announces the resignation of William Rogers as secretary of state and the appointment of national security advisor Henry Kissinger as his replacement. Kissinger is confirmed on September 21, but continues to hold his other position as well.

**August 29.** In an unprecedented ruling, Judge John Sirica orders Richard Nixon to surrender the subpoenaed Watergate tapes for private examination. The judge explains that no reason exists "for

suspending the power of courts to get evidence and rule on questions of privilege in criminal matters simply because it is the president of the United States who holds the evidence."

The next day, the White House announces that President Nixon will appeal the order.

**September 11.** The Chilean military overthrows the Marxist government of Salvador Allende Gossens. The 65-year-old Allende reportedly died defending the presidential palace, but his wife later charges that he was murdered.

On September 4, 1970, with the support of a leftist coalition, Allende became the first elected Marxist leader in the Western Hemisphere. He worked to implement socialism within a parliamentary system, but his nationalization program had antagonized American corporations and the Nixon administration. Domestic inflation and a wave of strikes gave the military the necessary opening to end 46 years of democratic rule, the longest-lived democracy in South America.

On the 13th, the junta names Army Chief General August Pinochet Ugarte president.

**September 18.** The U.N. General Assembly admits East and West Germany, formalizing the reality of two Germanies. With U.N. membership at 135, just seven major countries remain outside the organization: Switzerland, North and South Korea, North and South Vietnam, Taiwan, and Rhodesia.

**September 24.** The Senate Watergate Committee reopens televised hearings. The second phase will examine the political sabotage, or "dirty tricks," in the 1972 presidential campaign. The first phase of 37 sessions heard 33 witnesses and compiled 7,573 pages of testimony.

**October 6.** Egypt invades the Sinai Desert and Syria moves into the Golan Heights, territories held by the Israelis since 1967. Coming on the Jewish religious holiday of Yom Kippur, the invasion surprises Israel, and the Arabs make quick gains with their Soviet missiles.

The United States and the Soviet Union, through extensive diplomacy, reach a consensus to vote in the U.N. Security Council for a cessation of hostilities. A second cease-fire holds on the 24th.

The next day, "ambiguous" Soviet signs of intervention put the United States on worldwide alert, but the USSR joins in approving a U.N. peacekeeping force. Analysts theorize that Moscow was testing the strength of the American presidency during its constitutional crisis.

The first three Arab-Israeli wars established an aura of Israeli invincibility. Even in this conflict, the Israelis gained control over some 500 square miles on the west bank of the Suez Canal, trapping 20,000 Egyptian soldiers. But by regaining some 400 square miles of the Sinai, Egypt enters the October War negotiations in a position of greater strength.

Henry Kissinger convinces the two belligerents to move their disengagement talks from the battlefront to Geneva.

**October 10.** Vice-President Spiro Agnew, advocate of law and order, astounds America with his resignation and a no-contest plea to a single federal charge of 1967 income tax evasion. Agnew is only the second U.S. vice-president to resign; John C. Calhoun resigned in 1832 to take a Senate seat.

In August, the vice-president revealed that he was under investigation for violations of criminal law. The charges concerned alleged bribes and kickbacks he received as a Baltimore County executive from 1962 to 1967, as governor of Maryland from 1967 to 1968, and, reportedly, as vice-president. He denied any wrongdoing.

In exchange for his guilty plea, the Justice Department agrees to recommend leniency and to drop all other charges. Agnew is fined $10,000 and placed on three years' unsupervised probation.

Two days later, President Nixon announces Representative Gerald R. Ford (R., Mich.) as his choice for vice-president. Under the 25th Amendment, the candidate must be confirmed by a majority in both houses of Congress.

**October 12.** Stating that the president is "not above the law's commands," the U.S. Circuit Court of Appeals upholds Judge Sirica's August 29 decision ordering President Nixon to surrender the disputed Watergate tapes.

Choosing not to appeal to the Supreme Court, Nixon offers a "compromise." Written summaries of the tapes will be made available to the courts and the committee, with Republican Senator John Stennis verifying their accuracy, but special prosecutor Cox must cease all attempts to obtain further presidential documents.

**October 17.** Negotiations between OPEC and the oil consortiums break down, and for the first time the oil nations, unilaterally increase the price of crude. Then the ministers of the Arab states, enraged at U.S. arms support for the Israelis in the recent war, flex their newfound power with an agreement to cut the oil flow 5 percent monthly until the Americans alter their Middle East policy.

But Libya, after nationalizing its industry just last month, cuts all oil exports to the United States on the 19th. Saudi Arabia follows the next day, and, on the 21st, Kuwait, Bahrain, Qatar, and Dubai complete the Arab embargo.

**October 20.** Archibald Cox explains at a press conference that he has rejected the president's compromise plan for the White House tapes. At 8:24 P.M., Ron Ziegler announces that Nixon has fired Cox.

Attorney General Elliot Richardson resigned rather than obey Nixon's order to fire the special prosecutor. When Deputy Attorney General William Ruckelhaus also refused, Nixon fired him. The president then appointed Solicitor General Robert Bork as acting attorney general; he dismissed Cox.

**October 23.** The "Saturday Night Massacre" has drawn an immediate, angry response from the American people. Some 250,000 telegrams and letters condemning the president's action have poured into the White House, while in the House today representatives introduce eight resolutions of impeachment. Amid the mounting criticism, a startled Nixon reverses himself and agrees to submit the nine disputed tapes to the courts.

The next day, White House counsel inform Judge Sirica that two of the subpoenaed tapes are nonexistent: The June 20, 1972, discussion with John Mitchell took place on a White House residential phone unconnected to the system, and the April 15, 1973, conversation with John Dean was not recorded because of a system malfunction.

Both conversations are considered crucial in determining what the president knew and when he knew it. According to John Mitchell, his conversation dealt solely with the involvement of administration officials in Watergate, while Dean maintains that his discussion covered executive clemency for a Watergate defendant.

As congressional leaders question the explanation offered for the missing tapes, the House Judiciary Committee proceeds on the 30th with preliminary investigations on the impeachment resolutions.

**November 1.** President Nixon appoints Senator William B. Saxbe as his fourth attorney general and Leon Jaworski as special Watergate prosecutor. Jaworski accepted the position only after receiving assurances of total independence.

**November 7.** Overriding Nixon's veto, Congress passes a joint resolution limiting the powers of the president to wage war. Effective immediately, the president must inform Congress within 48 hours of committing forces to a foreign conflict or "substantially" enlarging the number of combat troops in a foreign country. Congress sets a 60-day deadline for such actions, but could order an immediate withdrawal under a concurrent resolution, which could not be vetoed.

The vote marks the first time this year that Congress has mustered the necessary two-thirds majority to override a veto: 75–18 in the Senate and 284–135 in the House. Apparently, the comfortable margins reflect Nixon's loss of power because of the Watergate scandal.

**November 7.** The Watergate Committee begins its third and final phase of investigation, focusing on campaign financing. A November 3 Gallup poll gave Nixon the lowest rating of his presidency: 27-percent approval.

**November 9.** In Washington, U.S. Chief District Court Judge John Sirica sentences the Watergate defendants: 1–4 years for the anti-Castroites, 18 months to 6 years for Bernard Barker, 30 months to 8 years and a fine of $10,000 for E. Howard Hunt, and James McCord, whose letter to Sirica and subsequent testimony revealed the White House cover-up, receives 1 to 5 years. G. Gordon Liddy, who has maintained a stoic silence throughout, was sentenced at the beginning of the year to a minimum of 6 years, 8 months.

**November 17.** During a nationally televised question-and-answer session at Disney World in Florida, President Nixon tells newspaper executives, "I'm not a crook."

**November 21.** White House special counsel J. Fred Buzhardt tells Judge Sirica that a June 20, 1972, taped conversation between Nixon and Bob Haldeman, three days after the break-in, contains an 18-minute section with "an audible tone and no conversation." Sirica orders the remaining tapes turned over to him for safe keeping; the White House complies on the 26th.

On December 5, Nixon's personal secretary, Rose Mary Woods, testifies that she accidentally erased 5 minutes from one of the tapes. She expresses shock when told of an 18-minute gap.

**November 26.** In Ottawa, the House of Commons creates the Foreign Investment Review Agency (FIRA) to consider new foreign investment, determine whether it will be of "significant benefit" to Canada, and review proposed foreign takeovers of Canadian companies.

Trade Minister Alastair Gillespie comments that, because such legislation was previously lacking, Americans now control half of Canadian manufacturing.

**December 6.** Congressional reaction to the nomination of Gerald Ford has been overwhelmingly favorable, 92–3 by the Senate on November 27, and 387–35 by the House today. Most of the opposition came from black members, who dislike Ford's civil rights record.

One hour later, Ford, 60 years old, is sworn in as vice president of the United States; he is the first nonelected vice-president appointed under the 25th Amendment. (Previously, the vice-presidency remained vacant—17 times in U.S. history—until the next election.) Ford gives his support to President Nixon and announces that he has no intention after 25 years in the House of running for office in 1976. He will finish his career as vice-president and retire.

Political analysts speculate that with Ford as a

secure option for the presidency there will be renewed pressure to impeach Nixon.

**December 10.** Henry Kissinger and Le Duc Tho receive the Nobel peace prize for negotiating the Vietnam cease-fire.

The award has roused international controversy, and two of the five Nobel committee members resigned over the selection. Kissinger accepts the award in absentia, donating his share of the money to a fund for the children of servicemen killed or missing in action. Le Duc Tho refuses the prize.

**December 13.** Reeling under the oil embargo, Britain imposes a three-day workweek in most industries, effective January 1. Last month, labor disputes in the coal and electric-power industries pushed the government into instituting a state of emergency. November saw the worst monthly trade deficit in British history.

**December 23.** OPEC ministers surprise then shock the world with two announcements. The first increases the flow of oil to most countries, but the United States is not one of the lucky nations. Under the second, six OPEC nations double the price of oil, to $11.65 per barrel effective January 1.

As prices increased 300 percent in recent months, the oil-producing nations have become increasingly aware of their tremendous power. The Shah has declared, "The industrial world will have to realize that the era of their terrific progress and even more terrific income and wealth based on cheap fuel is finished. They will have to find new sources of energy and tighten their belts." Yet the embargo has hit the underdeveloped nations, which have no oil reserves, the hardest. Their crippled economies will take years to recover.

**December 24.** A Louis Harris survey reveals that 73 percent of respondents believe Richard Nixon "has lost so much credibility that it will be hard for him to be accepted as president again." A reported 44 percent think he should resign, while 45 percent want him to stay in office.

At year's end, special prosecutor Jaworski declares that a substantial number of criminal indictments can be expected over the next two months. To date, 28 individuals and 9 corporations have faced criminal charges.

## Obituaries

**Fulgencio Batista Y Zaldívar** (January 16, 1901–August 6, 1973). Denied a second presidential term by law, Batista seized control of the Cuban government in 1952. He ruled through terror and corruption until the Castro revolution forced him to flee in 1959.

**David Ben-Gurion** (October 16, 1886–December 1, 1973). The Polish Zionist emigrated to Palestine in 1906 to work for a Jewish state. As Israel's first prime minister in 1948, he directed the nation's successful defense against Arab attack. Ben-Gurion came out of a two-year retirement in 1955 to handle defense once again. Then, after three quick elections, became prime minister for a second time. Although absent from political office for 10 years, at the time of his death the tough-minded Ben-Gurion for many Israelis still symbolized their struggle in a hostile Middle East.

**Frank Costello** (1891–February 18, 1973). The mob's master of the big fix—with cops, judges, and politicians—lost his position of power following the Senate crime investigation in the 1950s. (In a futile attempt to keep a low profile, Costello refused to allow TV cameras to focus on his face.)

**Alfred Fuller** (January 13, 1885–December 4, 1973). From selling brushes door to door in 1905, the Canadian-born salesman built a company that made Fuller Brush man part of the American vocabulary. He chaired his business empire until 1968.

**Gustaf VI Adolf** (November 11, 1882–September 15, 1973). The much-loved king of Sweden was already 68 when he ascended the throne. His 27-year-old grandson, Carl XVI Gustavus, succeeds him.

**Lyndon Baines Johnson** (August 27, 1908–January 22, 1973). See *News*.

**A(lexander) S(utherland) Neill** (October 17, 1883–September 23, 1973). The Scottish educator founded the controversial Summerhill School in England. Under his free-school method, students make all the major choices, including whether or not to attend classes.

**Jeannette Rankin** (June 11, 1880–May 18,

1973). The Republican representative from Montana (1916–1919 and 1940–1943) was the first woman elected to Congress and the only member to vote against U.S. entry into both world wars. (In 1917, the House counted 50 "nay" votes, but in 1941 she stood alone.) Rankin continued her battle against warfare outside the House. In 1968, at age 87, she led some 5,000 women in a Washington march against U.S. involvement in Vietnam.

**Eddie Rickenbacker** (October 8, 1890–July 23, 1973). Rickenbacker the race-car driver won seven national championships and set a world speed record of 134 mph. The W.W.I combat pilot downed 22 enemy planes and 4 observation balloons to win 56 medals and become the most decorated American pilot of the war. The Eastern Airlines executive, during the 1930s, produced the first profits in aviation history, then bought the airline. He resigned in 1963.

**Louis St. Laurent** (February 1, 1882–July 25, 1973). In striving to unite Canada, the nation's second French-Canadian prime minister (1948–1957) brought Newfoundland into Confederation, recommended the first Canadian-born Governor general (Vincent Massey), made the Canadian Supreme Court the highest legal recourse (rather than the British Privy Council), established a role for Canada in international affairs, and initiated three massive projects—the St. Lawrence Seaway, the transcontinental natural gas pipeline, and the Trans-Canada Highway. When the Liberals lost the 1957 election, St. Laurent continued as leader of the opposition until Lester Pearson was chosen his successor the following year.

**Walter Ulbricht** (June 30, 1893–August 1, 1973). Through the 1950s and the 1960s, the East German ruler remained a steadfast ally of the USSR. His unpopular regime enforced collectivization, ruthlessly put down any internal unrest, and oversaw the building of the Berlin Wall. But as the Soviets moved toward détente, Ulbricht fell out of favor and in 1971 was forced to relinquish his party leadership. Upon his death, the East German Parliament elects Premier Willi Stoph as chief of state and Horst Sindermann as premier.

*Note:* On April 11, West German authorities announce the positive identification of a skeleton unearthed the year before in West Berlin—Martin Bormann, secretary to Adolf Hitler.

# BEGINNINGS AND ENDINGS

## News

**January 3.** House Democrats select Thomas P. (Tip) O'Neill, Jr., to replace the late Hale Boggs as majority leader.

**January 12.** Frontier Airlines hires the country's first female commercial pilot, 33-year-old Emily Howell Warner. In June, American Airlines will become the first major airline to hire a woman pilot, Bonnie Tiburzi.

**January 23.** Members of the House of Representatives cast their ballots electronically, using 44 consoles located throughout the chamber. Previously, a clerk needed 30–45 minutes to read through the roll twice; the new system takes just 15.

**January 29.** Career army officer Lt. Col. William B. Nolde, age 43, is identified as the last American killed in Vietnam. He died in an artillery attack on An Loc.

**February 22.** In a diplomatic advance, the United States and China announce that they will establish liaison offices in Peking and Washington.

**February 23.** Royal ratification of a 1972 agreement gives Saudi Arabia 25 percent of the Arabian American Oil Co. (Aramco) and the guarantee of full ownership by 1982. But the Saudi percentage will rise more quickly than that, to 60 percent in June 1974, and negotiations will begin before year's end for the remainder.

**May 1.** With the last $175 million, Japan completes repayment to the United States for post-W.W.II food assistance.

**June 1.** In Athens the cabinet abolishes the Greek monarchy (King Constantine fled into exile in 1967) and establishes a presidential republic.

**June 24.** The oldest head of state in the world, President Eamon De Valera of Ireland retires at age

90. A commander during the 1916 Easter uprising, De Valera has dominated Irish politics since 1932 (prime minister 1932–1948, 1951–1954, 1957–1959, and president since 1959). He will pass away on August 29, 1975.

**June 30.** The Military Service Act of 1971 officially ends the draft, putting U.S. Armed Forces on an all-volunteer basis for the first time since 1948.

**September 22.** Dignitaries dedicate the Dallas-Fort Worth Airport. Sprawling over 17,500 acres, with a 13-mile transit system, the world's largest airport (in 1973) cost $700 million.

**September 26.** Republican Governor Melvin Evans of the Virgin Islands is the first black elected to chair the Southern Governor's Conference. He succeeds George Wallace of Alabama.

**October 5.** The first state to decriminalize marijuana, Oregon assesses a fine of $100 for the possession of 1 ounce or less, even for repeat offenders.

**October 9.** Cape Kennedy reverts to Cape Canaveral on the unanimous recommendation of the Interior Department Committee on Domestic Geographic Names. The area was named Canaveral by a Spanish explorer.

**October 16.** With his election in Atlanta, 35-year-old Maynard Jackson becomes the first black mayor of a major Southern city.

**November 14.** Princess Anne marries commoner Captain Mark Phillips in a lavish ceremony at Westminster Abbey.

**December 24.** President Nixon signs a bill providing partial home rule for the District of Columbia, subject to voter approval. Next May 7, a charter referendum will authorize a mayor and council, the first locally elected government in 100 years. Congress retains veto power over all council legislation as well as control of the budget and the enclave containing most federal buildings and monuments.

**More news.** The first American commercial product is sold in the USSR—Pepsi.

• After receiving "a vision" 19 years ago, Korean Sun Myung Moon established the Unification Church. This year, the 53-year-old undertakes a speaking tour throughout the United States. His "Divine Principle," described by some as a mixture of puritanism, patriotism, anti-Communism, and Christian fundamentalism, attracts hundreds of young Americans. Dubbed "Moonies" by the press, they sell flowers, candles, and other items to raise money for the sect.

## Records

**May 3.** The 110-story Sears Tower in Chicago takes over the title of tallest building in the world, at 1,454 feet.

## Government Departments and Agencies

**July 1.** Consolidating three Justice Department agencies, the Drug Enforcement Agency (DEA) will implement federal laws on drug abuse and investigate drug smuggling.

## New Products and Businesses

American Gary Gigax markets his simulation game Dungeons and Dragons, with hundreds of characters inspired by magic and literary sources, such as J. R. R. Tolkien. Manufacturers initially spurned his concept.

## Fads

Backgammon, an ancient game of chance and skill, enjoys a resurgence in popularity. The best-selling model is a practical folding board resembling an attaché case.

# SCIENCE AND TECHNOLOGY

## News

**January.** Two years ago, retired electronics engineer Carl Sontheimer discovered a compact, powerful machine at the Paris housewares show. He secured distribution rights, refined the design, and this month introduces the Cuisinart food processor at the National Housewares Exposition in Chicago.

**January.** The British Interplanetary Society forms a working group to conduct the first feasibility study of a starship design for an interstellar voyage. Members name the vessel the *Daedalus*, after the mythical figure who made wings for himself and his son Icarus to escape from Crete.

**January 13.** *The New York Times* reports that MIT researchers have used x-ray scanning to determine the structure of transfer RNA. Since the chain of 76 nucleotides helps assemble proteins, the chief structural material of all living things, scientists hope to learn how the molecule works and why it is altered in cancer.

**January 16.** Another unmanned Soviet vehicle, *Lunokhod II*, starts up four days after landing on the moon. Twice as fast as the first, the robot covers 23 miles before functions cease on June 4. Apparently, that shutdown is enough to halt the Soviet lunar program. Next year, only a single Luna will enter orbit.

**January 17.** The FDA requires manufacturers to label a food product that makes a nutritional claim with the number of calories, number and size of servings, amount of fat, protein, and carbohydrate, and the percentage of recommended daily vitamins.

**March 4.** Following the first successful radar probe of Saturn, the U.S. Jet Propulsion Lab reveals that the planet's rings appear to be composed of large chunks of orbiting solid matter.

**April 1.** In the largest recall of controlled substances ever made, the FDA and the Bureau of Narcotics and Dangerous Drugs call in all diet drugs containing amphetamines. Since the stimulants compose the bulk of the diet pill market, the industry predictably opposes the order.

**May 14.** *Skylab* loses a solar panel shortly after launch and interior temperatures climb. The next day, astronauts Charles Conrad, Joseph Kerwin, and Paul Weitz reach the orbiting vehicle and put out a sun-shield parasol. The trio remains on board for a record 28 days. (With no gravity compressing the disks in their spine, the men grow $3/4$ to $1^3/4$ inches in height. They shrink again upon return to Earth.)

Approved in 1965, the first U.S. space station was developed with the idea of utilizing Apollo equipment. Weighing almost 100 tons and stretching $118^1/2$ feet in length, the vehicle gives the astronauts an unprecedented 350 cubic meters of living and working space, on two separate stories (equivalent to an average three-bedroom house).

Immensely successful, the station welcomes a second crew in July for 59 days and a third in November for 84 days. Their experiments and some 175,000 photos of the sun and 46,000 of the Earth form a solid base of data for the shuttle program and a future station. (The astronauts conduct 19 student experiments, selected by the National Science Teachers Association, including a web spun by two spiders in zero gravity.)

*Skylab* will be abandoned in February 1974.

**July 12.** Swedish researchers devise the first blood test to identify and accurately measure the chemical substance produced by marijuana. The team plans to use its process to study the drug's biochemical effects.

**August 25.** *The New York Times* reports on the computerized axial tomographic scanning machine currently under evaluation in five U.S. hospitals. Developed by Allan MacLeod Cormack and Godfrey N. Hounsfield, the revolutionary x-ray machine produces a three-dimensional image of the brain with cross sections. The health industry expects the CAT scan will reduce costs, x-ray risks, and the patient's time in the hospital.

**August 28.** WHO certifies the Western Hemisphere as free of smallpox.

---

*Statistics*: The Public Health Service, citing the failure of Americans to take advantage of immunization programs, notes a 10-percent rise in the number of measles cases over the first half of the year.

---

**December 3.** Launched March 2, 1972, *Pioneer 10* quickly reached 32,000 mph—faster than any previous space vehicle. Today, the $9^1/2$-foot probe passes within 85,000 miles of Jupiter and, with 12 scientific instruments, measures the planet and its inner moons and transmits 300 close-up photos.

*Pioneer 11*, launched April 3 of this year, will pass within 27,000 miles of the planet next December.

The Pioneer series, which began with an unsuccessful moon shot in 1958, ends with Nos. 10 and 11. Both carry a plaque with a hydrogen atom, the most common element in the universe, and basic information about the solar system, including drawings of a naked human male and female. The enormously successful *Pioneer 10*, although designed to operate for just 21 months, should leave the solar system in 1987.

**More news.** After nearly 100 years of classifying homosexuality as a mental illness, the American Psychiatric Association announces that homosexuality, by itself, "does not meet the criteria for being a psychiatric disorder."

• With more sophisticated tissue-matching techniques, the success rate for kidney transplants rises to 75 percent with nonrelatives. An estimated 2,900 procedures are performed in the United States this year.

• A study by the National Science Foundation finds the commercial exploitation of ultrasound lags in the United States. Although equipment sales are up 300 percent in the last two years, the technology continues to be used mainly in cardiology, obstetrics, neurology, and ophthalmology.

## Other Discoveries, Developments, and Inventions

Color photocopier, the Xerox 6500

World's largest aircraft, C-5A, or Galaxy, which can hold 2 helicopters or 16 ¾-ton trucks

Universal product code (UPC), adopted by grocers and manufacturers

Typewriter with electronic memory, IBM's Mag Card II, for $11,800

## Obituaries

**Robert Alexander Watson-Watt** (April 13, 1892– December 6, 1973). The Scottish scientist invented radar in 1935. His device was a major factor in the Allied victory in W.W.II.

## THE ARTS

February 25—*A Little Night Music*, with Glynis Johns, Len Cariou, Hermione Gingold (600 perfs.)

March 22—*The Hot l Baltimore*, with Judd Hirsch, Trish Hawkins (1,166 perfs.)

October 18—*Raisin*, with Virginia Capers, Joe Morton, Ernestine Jackson (874 perfs.)

### Tony Awards

Actor (Dramatic)—Alan Bates, *Butley*

Actress (Dramatic)—Julie Harris, *The Last of Mrs. Lincoln*

Actor (Musical)—Ben Vereen, *Pippin*

Actress (Musical)—Glynis Johns, *A Little Night Music*

Play—*That Championship Season*

Musical—*A Little Night Music*

### News

**June 25.** The Theatre Development Fund sets up a ticket booth in Times Square to sell same-day performances at half price. By the end of next year, the stall will handle 400,000 tickets.

**June 28.** Queen Elizabeth dedicates the Shaw Festival Theatre at Niagara-on-the-Lake. The 860-seat facility gives the popular Canadian venue a sense of permanence.

**September.** Manufacturer Avery Fisher donates $8 million worth of high-fidelity components to Philharmonic Hall. It is promptly renamed in his honor.

**October 20.** Following today's dedication, the controversial Sydney Opera House quickly becomes the recognized symbol of Australia.

**More news.** This year's art sales include a record price for a print—$160,000 for Toulouse-Lautrec's *Grand Loge*.

• Thirty-eight-year-old Seiji Ozawa's meteoric rise through the world of concert music brings him to Boston as the symphony's youngest permanent conductor.

## Obituaries

**Pablo Casals** (December 29, 1876–October 22, 1973). His expressive style and brilliant technique made him the greatest cellist of this century, possibly of all time. A distinguished pianist, composer, and conductor as well, the Spaniard refused for years to perform in any country that supported the Franco regime: "I am a man first, an artist second."

**Noel Coward** (December 16, 1899–March 26, 1973). To most Americans, the actor, playwright, novelist, composer, and director personified the cultured Englishman. His best-known works included the play *Private Lives* and the film script *Brief Encounter* (1945). Coward was knighted in 1970.

**William Inge** (May 3, 1913–June 10, 1973). His plays revealed the sexual obsessions of midwestern America: *Come Back, Little Sheba* (1950), *Picnic* (1953, Pulitzer prize winner), *Bus Stop* (1955), *Dark at the Top of the Stairs* (1957). Sadly, Inge committed suicide.

**Otto Klemperer** (May 14, 1885–July 6, 1973). The German-born conductor, although a child of the 19th century, promoted modern composers such as Schoenberg and Stravinsky.

**Ernest MacMillan** (August 18, 1893–May 6, 1973). The "statesman of Canadian music" directed the Toronto Symphony (1931–1956) while composing, guest conducting, and serving as dean of music at the University of Toronto (1927–1952) and principal at the Toronto Conservatory of Music (1926–1942). In 1935, MacMillan was the first person outside the United Kingdom to be knighted.

**Lauritz Melchior** (March 20, 1890–March 18, 1973). This century's greatest Wagnerian tenor reigned at the Met from 1926 to 1950. His career extended into radio and film.

**Pablo Picasso** (October 25, 1881–April 8, 1972). Through his artistic evolution and prolific output, the Spanish-born Picasso shaped the course of modern art. His use of a shifting viewpoint in the early 1900s gave birth to Cubism. Dislocated limbs and facial features—a radical concept in the mid-1920s—gained worldwide recognition as the mark of a "Picasso." At his death, experts value the great master's body of work—14,000 paintings and drawings, 100,000 prints, 24,000 book illustrations, 300 models and sculptures—at more than $1 billion.

**Edward Jean Steichen** (March 27, 1879–March 25, 1973). The eminent photographer who directed *The Family of Man* exhibit raised photography to the level of an art.

## WORDS

Boston Women's Health Collective, *Our Bodies, Ourselves*
Margaret Craven, *I Heard the Owl Call My Name*
Paul Erdman, *The Billion Dollar Sure Thing*
Graham Greene, *The Honorary Consul*
Erica Jong, *Fear of Flying*
Robert Ludlum, *The Matlock Paper*
Peter Maas, *Serpico*
Norman Mailer, *Marilyn*
Marabel Morgan, *The Total Woman*
Thomas Pynchon, *Gravity's Rainbow*
Flora R. Schreiber, *Sybil*
Mary Stewart, *The Hollow Hills*
Jacqueline Susann, *Once Is Not Enough*
Gore Vidal, *Burr*
Kurt Vonnegut, Jr., *Breakfast of Champions*
Joseph Wambaugh, *The Onion Field*

## News

**February 26.** According to *Time* magazine, Attorney General John Mitchell authorized FBI wiretaps on several Washington correspondents in an effort to pin down government leaks. In three years, the electronic eavesdropping has failed to uncover one source.

**March.** New American Library pays a record $1.51 million for paperback rights to *The Joy of Cooking* (1936). Author Irma S. Rombauer died in 1962, but her daughter Marion, a coauthor since the 1940s, has continued with the perennial favorite.

**May.** Catering to 6- to 12-year-olds, *Ebony Jr!* is the first national magazine for black children.

**May 7.** The *Washington Post* receives a Pulitzer for its investigation of Watergate.

May 27. Soviet analysts interpret Moscow's sudden willingness to honor the Universal Copyright convention (effective today) as an attempt to block Western publication of dissident writers.

June. *Playgirl*, the new skin magazine for women, features "Days of Our Lives" star Ryan MacDonald as a nude centerfold.

June 21. Ruling that commercial speech falls outside of First Amendment rights, the Supreme Court upholds a Pittsburgh ordinance barring male-female categorization of want ads.

August. With the opening of a new printing plant, the *Detroit News* becomes the country's largest fully automated newspaper.

October. Lenore Hershey is this century's first woman editor of *Ladies' Home Journal*.

November 4. *Time* magazine, in its first editorial in 50 years, calls for Richard Nixon's resignation.

More news. Over the first half of 1973, U.S. newspapers enjoy increased sales and a 10-percent jump in advertising. But Canadian pulp and paper mills, completely unprepared for large orders after an extended recession, suffer from summer labor disputes and a nationwide rail strike. The resulting shortages push the price of newsprint up 14 percent by the end of the year, to $200 a ton.

• With the enormous expansion in the teenage baby-boomer market, new youth magazines appear on newsstands every month. International Publishing alone launches seven new ventures.

---

*Statistics:* In anticipation of postal hikes, some 2,800 U.S. magazines raise their subscription rates an average 22 percent.

---

## Cartoons and Comics

February. DC revives Captain Marvel as *Shazam*.

September 3. George Gately Gallagher debuts the comic strip *Heathcliff*. Also this year, Dik Browne creates *Hagar the Horrible*.

## TIME *Man of the Year*

Judge John Sirica

## New Words and Phrases

biofeedback
doomster (a pessimist who forecasts ecodoom)
elint (form of electronic intelligence)
insightful
job banks
judder (blend of jump and shudder)
pedestrian mall
point in time
quadraphonic
space shuttle

## Obituaries

**Conrad Aiken** (August 5, 1889–August 17, 1973). The distinguished poet, novelist, and literary critic was one of the first American writers to use stream-of-consciousness.

**W(ystand) H(ugh) Auden** (February 21, 1907–September 28, 1973). A dominant voice in 20th-century verse, the British-American poet also wrote plays, songs, opera librettos, and film commentaries.

**Pearl S(ydenstricker) Buck** (June 26, 1892–March 6, 1973). *The Good Earth* (1931; Pulitzer), the best known of her 85 novels, typically reflected nearly half a lifetime spent in China. In 1938, Buck won the Nobel prize in literature.

**John Creasey** (September 17, 1908–June 9, 1973). One of the world's most prolific writers, the British author used his own name and 28 pseudonyms to churn out 560 books (another 14 await publication). Yet believable characters, such as Inspector West and Gideon of the Yard, brought Creasey immense success—60 million copies sold in 23 languages.

**Walt Kelly** (August 25, 1913–October 18, 1973). The American cartoonist worked at Disney Studios before launching *Pogo* in 1948. His wife Selby and son Stephen continue, but when paper shortages reduce panel size and swallow much of their detailed work, the Kellys will cancel the strip in 1975.

**J(ohn) R(onald) R(euel) Tolkien** (January 3, 1892–September 2, 1973). The British novelist's fantasies, *The Hobbit* and the *Lord of the Rings* trilogy, remain immensely popular with young people.

**Murat "Chic" Young** (January 9, 1901–March 14, 1973). The American cartoonist made *Blondie* the most popular comic strip of all time. From September 8, 1930, until his death, syndication grew to 1,623 newspapers in 60 countries.

# FASHION

## Haute Couture

With no new silhouettes from Paris or New York, women generally personalize a casual look.

## News

**October 11.** The FDA orders cosmetics manufacturers to list product ingredients on all package labels (effective March 31, 1975) and to report consumer complaints of adverse reactions.

• In the fashion capitals of the world, boutiques sell jeans at outrageous prices—patched, embroidered, bejeweled, and deliberately faded. The president of Levi Strauss & Co., Peter E. Haas, finds it "a little strange to rise from work clothes to high fashion, but we're not fighting it." The company holds a Denim Art Contest and the winning entries—culled from thousands of decorated jeans and jackets—tour museums worldwide.

• Large-scale Japanese purchases in the United States create textile shortages and push up the price of designer garments, particularly coats.

## Color and Materials

Knitwear predominates in coats, jackets, and dresses. But with bulkier autumn clothes, tweeds make a strong comeback, in discreet checks or speckles as well as the classic herringbone. Men prefer plaid.

As the enormous demand for denim reduces the supply of indigo dye, the textile industry produces more faded blues.

Manufacturers add sparkle to all types of fabrics.

Gray and brown form a standard combination, but blue is the color of the year.

## Clothes

Everyday slacks, often matched to coats, follow a straight, fairly wide line, with or without creases or cuffs. Above the waist, layered separates play up bright stripes and geometric patterns. Sportswear updates the cardigan.

The printed shirtwaist is the favorite summer silhouette, with wrapped bodice, pleated or flared skirt, and plain or matched jacket. The hem reaches just below the knee.

Jeans switch the emphasis from tight thighs to a cupped bottom. The poor look becomes passé and women dress up their denims with a halter, sweater, classic shirt, or soft blouse in a cotton crepe or Liberty print. Frilly or gathered blouses, always low-necked, drop off one shoulder. For casual wear, the tank top—new last year—displays brand names, printed front or back, on a solid-colored cotton. (The name comes from an earlier era when pools were tanks and even men wore swimming tops.)

The popularity of denim carries over to jumpsuits and ankle-skimming skirts (with spiral inserts of patchwork cotton). As an alternative, cotton skirts gather or flare, with a finishing frill at the hem.

The Welsh firm Laura Ashley, formed in 1953, offers charming, Edwardian-style dresses—full-length, with a scoop neck and short, puffed sleeves or a frilly collar and leg-of-mutton sleeves. The inexpensive prints sell well this year.

The film *The Great Gatsby* inspires jazz-age silhouettes—low-waisted white skirts, cloche hats, crepe evening dresses for women and baggy trousers, bow ties, and argyle vests for men.

More women switch from pants to dresses for the evening. The hem settles just above the ankle.

In menswear, designers return to a simpler, more elegant suit. But ready-to-wear manufacturers shorten the jacket, use bigger buttons, deepen pocket flaps, display lapels at their widest, and retain deep cuffs on the pants. Vests reappear, this time as casual wear.

## Accessories

Shoe heels rise and thin out a little, but many young women stay with their clogs. Men's styles feature thick soles, high heels, and, for younger men, bold eyelets and speckled laces.
A big, flowered hat, with a Laura Ashley dress, captures a romantic mood.
Bow ties dominate.

## Hair and Cosmetics

Makeup continues to emphasize naturalness, but women apply more in the evening, particularly iridescent eye shadow. Revlon harmonizes colors for eyes, lips, and nails.
The Gatsby look highlights short curls. In England, exotic teenagers wear a short, boyish cut with a wildly dyed front piece.

## Obituaries

**Ida Cohen Rosenthal** (January 9, 1886–March 28, 1973). In 1916, dress styles required women to tie down their breasts with a bandeau. For her fuller line, Rosenthal and husband William created a two-pocket brassiere. Demand for their undergarment skyrocketed until, in 1922, the couple formed the Maidenform Brassiere Co. When she relinquished leadership in 1966, Maidenform was marketing bras in 115 countries.

**Elsa Schiaparelli** (September 10, 1896–November 13, 1973). In 1935, the Italian-born French designer opened one of the first Parisian boutiques. Within three years, her dominance of haute couture pushed Coco Chanel into early retirement. Bold talent and daring made Schiaparelli the first designer to center a collection on a theme, the first to put zippers in dresses, the first to employ synthetics, and the first to use rough-textured fabrics for more than sportswear. Yet students of fashion remember Schiaparelli less for her vital designs than for her introduction of one color—shocking pink.

## MUSIC

"Killing Me Softly with His Song"—Roberta Flack
"Tie a Yellow Ribbon Round the Ole Oak Tree"—Dawn featuring Tony Orlando
"My Love"—Paul McCartney & Wings
"You're So Vain"—Carly Simon
"Crocodile Rock"—Elton John
"Let's Get It On"—Marvin Gaye
"The Most Beautiful Girl"—Charlie Rich
"Midnight Train to Georgia"—Gladys Knight & the Pips
"Keep on Truckin' "—Eddie Kendricks
"Top of the World"—Carpenters
"Bad, Bad Leroy Brown"—Jim Croce
"Brother Louie"—Stories
"Half-Breed"—Cher
"The Night the Lights Went Out in Georgia"—Vicki Lawrence
"Will It Go Round in Circles"—Billy Preston
"Time in a Bottle"—Jim Croce
"The Morning After"—Maureen McGovern
"Touch Me in the Morning"—Diana Ross
"The Joker"—Steve Miller Band
"Show and Tell"—Al Wilson
"Frankenstein" (Instr.)—Edgar Winter Group
"Delta Dawn"—Helen Reddy
"Angie"—Rolling Stones
"Superstition"—Stevie Wonder
"Love Train"—O'Jays
"You Are the Sunshine of My Life"—Stevie Wonder
"We're an American Band"—Grand Funk
"Photograph"—Ringo Starr
"Give Me Love (Give Me Peace on Earth)"—George Harrison
"Dueling Banjos" (Instr.)—Eric Weissberg & Steve Mandel
"Goodbye Yellow Brick Road"—Elton John
"Live and Let Die"—Paul McCartney & Wings
"Playground in My Mind"—Clint Holmes

"Neither One of Us (Wants to Be the First to Say Goodbye)"—Gladys Knight & the Pips
"The Cisco Kid"—War
"Loves Me Like a Rock"—Paul Simon
"Ramblin' Man"—Allman Brothers Band
"Yesterday Once More"—Carpenters
"Daniel"—Elton John

## Grammys (1973)

Record of the Year—Roberta Flack, "Killing Me Softly with His Song"
Song of the Year (songwriter)—Norman Gimbel and Charles Fox, "Killing Me Softly with His Song"
Album of the Year—Stevie Wonder, *Innervisions*
Best Vocal Performance (Male)—Stevie Wonder, "You Are the Sunshine of My Life" (single)
Best Vocal Performance (Female)—Roberta Flack, "Killing Me Softly with His Song" (single)
Best New Artist—Bette Midler

## News

**January 23.** In New York, Neil Young interrupts a concert to announce the signing of the U.S.-Vietnam cease-fire. Reportedly, members of the audience kissed and hugged for 10 minutes.

**March 4.** Helen Reddy receives a Grammy as best female vocalist for her rendition of "I Am Woman." Her acceptance speech outrages religious fundamentalists: "I want to thank everyone concerned at Capitol Records, my husband and manager, Jeff Wald, because he makes my success possible, and God, because She makes everything possible."

**July 10.** NARAS establishes a Hall of Fame to honor qualitatively or historically significant recordings.

**July 28.** Promoters expected 150,000, but 600,000 turn out at Watkins Glen, New York, to hear a 15-hour concert by the Allman Brothers Band, the Grateful Dead, and the Band. Unlike festivals in the 1960s, today's music lacks political overtones and concert-goers use barbiturates rather than hallucinogens. (The *Los Angeles Times* comments, "To sleep, perchance, but not to dream.") Afterward, the local county cracks down on crowds over 5,000 people.

**October 11.** Newspapers report a Presley divorce after six years of marriage. Priscilla receives a $1.5-million settlement and $8,200 a month in alimony and child support.

**November 2.** In the United States today, Apple releases the LP *Ringo*. The tracks produce a Beatle reunion of sorts: George and Ringo perform John's composition "I'm the Greatest"; Paul plays on his composition "Six O'Clock" and on "You're Sixteen"; George wrote "Sunshine Life for Me" and co-wrote "Photograph" with Ringo, and plays on both. Two cuts, "You're Sixteen" and "Photograph," top the charts.

**More news.** Country rock is big this year, with the Allman Brothers Band, ZZ Top, and others. As well, traditional CW shows renewed vitality with a large number of new singles, the first country act booked into Philharmonic Hall (Tammy Wynette and George Jones), and an all-country format on New York's WHN.

• Dawn opens the Bob Hope Show at the Cotton Bowl in Dallas before some 60,000 people. Tony Orlando laughingly tells the audience their next song has been out a little more than an hour. But when the trio starts into "Tie a Yellow Ribbon Round the Old Oak Tree," many of the 500 Vietnam POWs sitting in the front rows rise from their chairs, file up onto the stage, and join in. Orlando and Hope are astounded, but the meaning behind the lyrics will turn the song into a part of American culture.

• Bread disbands after six gold albums in three years. In a more spectacular breakup, Phil Everly throws down his guitar and storms off the stage at Knott's Berry Farm. Don tells the stunned audience that the Everly Brothers are finished.

• Carly Simon assures *Rolling Stone* magazine that husband James Taylor is not the subject of her hit "You're So Vain," but she refuses to identify the subject. Guesses range from backup vocalist Mick Jagger, to singer Kris Kristofferson, to actor Warren

Beatty. Later, Simon will claim the man was a composite of three or four individuals.

• Bette Midler wins a Grammy as Best New Artist. Critics describe the singer as the first cabaret star of the Beatles generation; she describes herself as "Trash with Flash."

• The *Schwann Record Catalogue*, which lists most available tapes and records, tallied 5,196 records last year, about the same as in 1971. Cassettes and cartridges, on the other hand, increased by 1,874 in 1971.

• In the April 15 issue of *Forbes* magazine, Steve Paley of Columbia Records says, "This business is amoral. If Hitler put together a combo, all the top executives would catch the next plane to Argentina [where many Nazis fled] to sign him up."

*New Recording Artists*

Aerosmith
Average White Band (AWB)
Bachman-Turner Overdrive (BTO)
Art Garfunkel (solo)
Billy Joel
Melissa Manchester
Pink Floyd
Pointer Sisters
Smokey Robinson (solo)
Bruce Springsteen
10cc
Barry White

## Obituaries

**Jim Croce** (January 10, 1943–September 20, 1973). A singer-guitarist since his late teens, Croce only recently found success with such hits as "Bad, Bad Leroy Brown." Following his death in a plane crash, three of Croce's albums go gold.

**Bobby Darin** (May 14, 1936–December 20, 1973). The brash singer-songwriter scored 21 top 40 hits between 1958 and 1967, but remains best remembered for his Grammy-winning rendition of "Mack the Knife." Darin branched out into acting during the sixties with film and TV appearances. Then a mystical experience at Robert Kennedy's funeral made him leave the business temporarily. He died during yet another heart operation.

**Arthur Freed** (September 9, 1894–April 12, 1973). With his chief collaborator, Nacio Herb Brown, the lyricist wrote "Singin' in the Rain" (1924), "You Are My Lucky Star" (1935), and other hits. A movie producer in later years, Freed concentrated on musicals: *Show Boat* (1951), *An American in Paris* (1951), *Gigi* (1958). He planned a screen biography of Irving Berlin, with Frank Sinatra and Julie Andrews, but MGM abandoned musicals at the end of the last decade.

**Laurens Hammond** (January 11, 1895–July 1, 1973). Hammond pioneered the electronic organ in 1935 and, 15 years later, introduced the chord organ.

**Gene Krupa** (January 15, 1909–October 16, 1973). With Benny Goodman in the 1930s, Krupa played the first drum solos. His flashy, hair-flying style made him a star and, with his own band, Krupa scored some 20 hits from 1938–1943. He died of leukemia.

**Vaughan Monroe** (October 7, 1912–May 21, 1973). The bandleader was best known for his distinctive baritone renditions typified by "Riders in the Sky" (1949). He remained semi-active in the business until his death.

**Andy Razaf** (December 16, 1895–February 3, 1973). The son of a Malagasy noble family, the lyricist wrote for Fats Waller, Eubie Blake, and others. His more than 1,000 songs included "Ain't Misbehavin' " (1929), "In the Mood" (1939), and "The Joint Is Jumpin' " (1940).

**Jack Rollins** (September 15, 1906–January 2, 1973). The songwriter's collaborations included "Frosty the Snowman" (1950) and "Peter Cottontail" (1950).

**Hugo Winterhalter** (August 15, 1909–September 17, 1973). With RCA Victor from 1950 to 1963, he provided the arrangements for 11 million-sellers.

# MOVIES

*American Graffiti* (d. George Lucas; color)—Richard Dreyfuss, Ronny Howard, Paul

LeMat, Charlie Martin Smith, Cindy Williams, Candy Clark, Mackenzie Phillips, Harrison Ford

*Bang the Drum Slowly* (d. John Hancock; color)—Robert De Niro, Michael Moriarty, Vincent Gardenia

*Charlotte's Web* (color; animated)—Voices: Debbie Reynolds (Charlotte); Henry Gibson, (Wilber); Paul Lynde (Templeton)

*Day For Night* (French, d. François Truffaut; color)—Jacqueline Bisset, Jean-Pierre Léaud, François Truffaut, Valentina Cortese

*The Day of the Jackal* (British-French, d. Fred Zinnemann; color)—Edward Fox, Alan Badel, Tony Britton

*Enter the Dragon* (d. Robert Clouse; color)—Bruce Lee, John Saxon

*The Exorcist* (d. William Friedkin; color)—Ellen Burstyn, Max von Sydow, Linda Blair, Jason Miller

*The Friends of Eddie Coyle* (d. Peter Yates; color)—Robert Mitchum, Peter Boyle, Richard Jordan

*High Plains Drifter* (d. Clint Eastwood; color)—Clint Eastwood, Verna Bloom, Marianna Hill, Mitchell Ryan

*The Hireling* (British, d. Alan Bridges; color)—Robert Shaw, Sarah Miles

*The Last Detail* (d. Hal Ashby; color)—Jack Nicholson, Otis Young, Randy Quaid

*Last Tango in Paris* (French-Italian, d. Bernardo Bertolucci; color)—Marlon Brando, Maria Schneider

*Mean Streets* (d. Martin Scorsese; color)—Robert De Niro, Harvey Keitel

*O Lucky Man!* (British, d. Lindsay Anderson; color)—Malcolm McDowell, Rachel Roberts, Ralph Richardson, Arthur Lowe

*Paper Moon* (d. Peter Bogdanovich; bw)—Ryan O'Neal, Tatum O'Neal, Madeline Kahn

*Payday* (d. Daryl Duke; color)—Rip Torn, Anna Capri, Elayne Heilveil

*Serpico* (d. Sidney Lumet; color)—Al Pacino, Tony Roberts, John Randolph, Jack Kehoe, Biff McGuire

*Sleeper* (d. Woody Allen; color)—Woody Allen, Diane Keaton, John Beck

*The Sting* (d. George Roy Hill; color)—Paul Newman, Robert Redford, Robert Shaw

*The Way We Were* (d. Sydney Pollack; color)—Barbra Streisand, Robert Redford, Bradford Dillman

*Westworld* (d. Michael Crichton; color)—Richard Benjamin, Yul Brynner, James Brolin

*The World's Greatest Athlete* (Disney, d. Robert Scheerer; color)—John Amos, Jan-Michael Vincent, Tim Conway, Roscoe Lee Browne

### Academy Awards

**March 27.** Hosts this year include Carol Burnett, Rock Hudson, Michael Caine, and Charlton Heston.

Best Picture—*The Godfather*
Best Actor—Marlon Brando (*The Godfather*)
Best Actress—Liza Minnelli (*Cabaret*)
Best Director—Bob Fosse (*Cabaret*)
Best Supporting Actor—Joel Grey (*Cabaret*)
Best Supporting Actress—Eileen Heckart (*Butterflies Are Free*)
Best Song—"The Morning After" from *The Poseidon Adventure*
Best Foreign Film—*The Discreet Charm of the Bourgeoisie* (French)
Honorary Award—Edward G. Robinson

The fourth actor to win two Oscars becomes the second actor to turn one down. In protest against the treatment of Native Americans in films and on television, Marlon Brando sends starlet Maria Cruz (who calls herself Sacheen Littlefeather) to refuse the award on his behalf. The incident creates an uproar.

### News

**January 7.** Paramount Pictures throws a birthday bash for 100-year-old Adolph Zukor. The motion picture pioneer formed Famous Players Co. in 1912, merged with Jesse Lasky in 1916, continued to absorb smaller companies, then changed the studio's corporate name to Paramount in 1930. (Gulf + Western bought the studio seven years ago.)

Early Zukor stars included some of Hollywood's biggest names—Mary Pickford, Gloria Swanson, W. C. Fields, Mae West—but in a recent interview, the centenarian stated, "Now the story is more important than any individual on the screen."

**March 31.** Director John Ford receives the American Film Institute's first annual Life Achievement Award.

**June 24.** Leaving the Western White House, Premier Leonid Brezhnev spots Chuck Connors at the helicopter pad and rushes over to envelop the TV actor in a bear hug. Connors laughingly lifts his Soviet fan off the ground, then gives him two Colt .45 six-shooters and a cowboy hat. The delighted Brezhnev pantomimes being shot dead. In July, Connors receives the return gift of a samovar.

**September 17.** Despite general Hollywood claims of financial recovery, MGM announces dramatic cutbacks and completely withdraws from motion picture distribution. Studio executives intend to place new emphasis on TV production.

In October, UA agrees to distribute 1,400 MGM films.

**October.** In 1960, some 40 foreign-language motion pictures received first-run engagements in the United States. So far this year, theaters have exhibited 18. American film critics suggest that more sophisticated moviegoers of the 1970s have lost their fascination with a non-English product.

**More news.** With this year's *Live and Let Die*, Roger Moore follows in the steps of Sean Connery, David Niven, and George Lazenby as the fourth James Bond. Moore will play the British spy again next year in *The Man with the Golden Gun*.

• In an attempt to merge the stage and silver screen, the American Film Theatre offers eight filmed plays on a subscription basis in 500 movie houses across the United States and Canada. Titles include *The Iceman Cometh* with Lee Marvin and *A*

*Delicate Balance* starring Katharine Hepburn. But the program will halt after next season when exhibitors refuse to interrupt regular scheduling for the two-day showings.

• When a ticket cost less than $1, movie houses showed ads to increase their revenues. But the expanding TV market drew advertisers away. Now, with a lack of short subjects and the newsreel gone, theater owners try to entice advertisers back—one ad for $11 per week. This year, agencies book 35,000 ads into 6,000 U.S. theaters.

• With only one commercial film to his credit, Universal demands that George Lucas find a "name" producer for *American Graffiti*. The young director brings in Francis Ford Coppola, then shoots the movie in 25 days on a $750,000 budget. After the San Francisco premiere, executives dither over "an unfinished product" and Coppola angrily offers to buy the film. The studio wisely declines and proceeds with general release.

• A $25-million box-office bonanza, *American Graffiti* boosts the careers of several young actors (Ronny Howard, Richard Dreyfuss, Cindy Williams, Harrison Ford), inspires the hit TV show "Happy Days," and gives Lucas the funds to proceed with other projects.

• Bruce Lee's last film, *Enter the Dragon*, is the first Hollywood-produced Kung Fu movie.

| *Top Box Office Stars* | *Newcomers* |
|---|---|
| Clint Eastwood | Diana Ross |
| Ryan O'Neal | Michael Moriarty |
| Steve McQueen | Marsha Mason |
| Burt Reynolds | Joe Don Baker |
| Robert Redford | Jeannie Berlin |
| Barbra Streisand | Candy Clark |
| Paul Newman | Robert De Niro |
| Charles Bronson | Jan-Michael Vincent |
| John Wayne | Roy Scheider |
| Marlon Brando | Tatum O'Neal |

### Top Money-Maker of the Year

*The Poseidon Adventure* (1972)

## Flop of the Year

*Lost Horizon*
One of the biggest bombs of the decade, the musical will make back just half of Columbia's $7-million investment.

## Quote of the Year

"I've never seen anything like this in my entire illustrious career!"
–Howard Cossell, the sports commentator, remarks on *The World's Greatest Athlete*. (Original screenplay by Gerald Gardner and Dee Caruso)

## Obituaries

**Lex Barker** (May 8, 1919–May 11, 1973). Johnny Weismuller's successor made five Tarzan films before switching to Westerns.

**Joe E. Brown** (July 28, 1892–July 6, 1973). After a 70-year career, the wide-mouthed comedian is best remembered as Jack Lemmon's millionaire boyfriend in *Some Like It Hot* (1959).

**Lon Chaney, Jr.** (February 10, 1906–July 12, 1973). The son of the famous silent screen actor mainly played in "B" monster movies.

**Merian C. Cooper** (October 24, 1895–April 21, 1973). The creator, director, and producer of the classic *King Kong* (1933) spent three years filming 18-inch models for stop action and a large mechanical head and shoulders for close-ups of the monster ape. His other productions included *Fort Apache* (1948) and *The Quiet Man* (1952).

**John Ford** (February 1, 1895–August 31, 1973). Described by the Screen Actors Guild as "one of the few giants in motion pictures," Ford directed some 130 films during his 50-year career. Through the 1930s and 1940s, his phenomenal output included such classics as *The Informer* (1935), *The Grapes of Wrath* (1940), and *How Green Was My Valley* (1941)—all of which brought him Oscars—and the Westerns *Stagecoach* (1939) and *My Darling Clementine* (1946)—a genre at which he excelled. Memorable 1950s pictures included *The Quiet Man*

(1952) (another Oscar-winner), *Mister Roberts* (1955), and *The Last Hurrah* (1958).

The cantankerous director, usually completely disinterested in film awards, accepted the first American Film Institute Life Achievement Award this year.

**Betty Grable** (December 18, 1916–July 2, 1973). A top box-office draw from 1942 to 1951, the singer-dancer recognized her limitations as a dramatic actress and stuck to light musicals like *Mother Wore Tights* (1947). Her beautiful legs (insured for $1.25 million) made Grable a favorite pinup girl during W.W.II. In one famous photo, the blond actress stands in a bathing suit and high heels looking over her shoulder; supposedly, Grable was pregnant at the time. She died of lung cancer.

**Laurence Harvey** (October 1, 1928–November 25, 1973). In his more than 40 films, the British actor often played a cad or a smoothie. His best-known works remain *Room at the Top* (1959) and *The Manchurian Candidate* (1962). He died of cancer.

**Jack Hawkins** (September 14, 1910–July 18, 1973). The craggy-faced English actor often portrayed stiff-upper-lip British soldiers as in *The Bridge on the River Kwai* (1957) and *Lawrence of Arabia* (1962). In 1966, Hawkins lost his raspy voice to cancer surgery, but continued to act with dubbing.

**Veronica Lake** (November 14, 1919–July 7, 1973). A top box-office attraction in the early 1940s, the sexy blond is mainly remembered today for her peek-a-boo hairstyle.

**Bruce Lee** (November 27, 1940–July 20, 1973). American-born, the Chinese actor returned to the United States in 1958, then played Kato in the 1960s TV series "The Green Hornet" before moving back to Hong Kong. In the last two years, Lee used his karate and kung fu expertise in four movies. Already a star in Asia, his funeral draws thousands of screaming fans. (Reportedly, he died from another person's prescription painkiller, but a recent weight loss suggests other causes.)

With the release of his pictures in North America (the last, *Return of the Dragon*, comes out in 1974), Lee's kung fu prowess will give him near cult status and create widespread interest in martial arts.

**Anna Magnani** (May 7, 1908–September 26,

1973). Her Oscar for *The Rose Tattoo* (1955) made Magnani the first Italian actress to win international recognition.

**J. Carrol Naish** (January 21, 1900–January 24, 1973). With his swarthy complexion and flair for dialect, the Irish-American played countless nationalities during his 30-year career.

**Edward G. Robinson** (December 12, 1893–January 26, 1973). Born in Bucharest, he came to the United States at age 9. His first screen success, in *Little Caesar* (1931), set the pattern for cinema gangsters and typecast the short, pug-faced actor for years afterward. During the last decade, Robinson appeared in character roles, but no matter how small the part, his powerful performances always stood out. Never the recipient of an Oscar, he is posthumously honored by the Academy this year.

**Robert Ryan** (November 11, 1913–July 11, 1973). The movie tough guy's most memorable performance was a starring role in *The Set-up* (1949). He made the last of 90 films this year.

# TELEVISION AND RADIO

## New Prime-Time TV Programs

"Barnaby Jones" (January 28, 1973– ; Detective)—Buddy Ebsen, Lee Meriwether

"Kojak" (October 24, 1973– ; Police Drama)—Telly Savalas, Dan Frazer, Kevin Dobson, George Savalas

"The Midnight Special" (February 2, 1973– ; Music)—Hostess: Helen Reddy; Announcer: Wolfman Jack

"Police Story" (September 25, 1973– ; Police Drama Anthology)

## Emmy Awards 1972–1973 (May 20, 1973)

Drama Series—"The Waltons" (CBS)

Variety Musical Series—"The Julie Andrews Hour" (ABC)

Comedy Series—"All in the Family" (CBS)

Children's Programming—"Sesame Street" (PBS); "Zoom" (PBS); "The Electric Company" (PBS)

Best Actor in a Series—Richard Thomas ("The Waltons," CBS)

Best Actress in a Series—Michael Learned ("The Waltons," CBS)

Best Comedian in a Series—Jack Klugman ("The Odd Couple," ABC)

Best Comedienne in a Series—Mary Tyler Moore ("The Mary Tyler Moore Show," CBS)

## News

**February 2.** "The Midnight Special," television's first regularly scheduled late-night program, runs on NBC from 1:00 to 2:30 A.M. on Friday night. Wolfman Jack is the announcer while guest hosts include Helen Reddy, Paul Anka, David Bowie, Ray Charles, Mac Davis, and Jerry Lee Lewis. Reddy will return on a permanent basis in 1975.

**February 19.** Nearly yanked once, "Star Trek" was saved by a letter-writing campaign. But in 1969, NBC canceled the show to go after a more attractive advertising market than teenagers and college students. Still, fans refuse to abandon the show and "Star Trek" conventions are becoming an annual event. This fall, in the first evidence of renewed network interest, the stars are reunited to provide voice-overs for the animated Saturday-morning series, "Enterprise."

**Spring.** Since its debut last September, "Bridget Loves Bernie" has received fair-to-good ratings. The sitcom revolves around the interfaith marriage of a Jewish man, played by David Birney, and an Irish Catholic woman, played by Meredith Baxter. But the Rabbinical Alliance of America has branded the show a "flagrant insult" for mocking the teachings of Judaism.

Although CBS maintains that cancellation would do a disservice to millions of viewers, by spring mounting pressure forces the network to buckle under. The Bridget-Bernie controversy is just the first of three major censorship issues this season.

**March 28.** The FCC denounces "topless" radio as trash and opens an inquiry into complaints of obscenity and suggestiveness. Two years ago, Bill Balance of KGBS in Los Angeles introduced "Feminine Forum" to talk about male-female relationships. The station's ratings went through the roof and "sex" radio was quickly syndicated into 30 markets. On the 29th, "Feminine Forum" drops the format to become "The Bill Balance Show"; other stations follow suit.

**April 6.** After a lengthy court battle, a Los Angeles jury awards Tom and Dick Smothers $776,300 in damages for the cancellation of their CBS comedy show in 1969.

**May–August.** In their first rotation agreement, the networks share live coverage of the Senate Watergate hearings. When viewing holds steady during the summer, both NBC and CBS offer nightly wrap-ups. But audience ratings for network daytime broadcasts pale in comparison to the levels for PBS prime-time coverage.

**May 29.** The U.S. Supreme Court rules (7–2), that radio and TV stations are not obligated to sell airtime for political or controversial issues as long as the FCC fairness doctrine is observed.

**August 14 and 21.** Last fall, producer Norman Lear gave Edith Bunker's cousin Maude her own series. As liberal as Archie Bunker is conservative, Beatrice Arthur's character confronts issues in her own way. A midlife pregnancy, for instance, was aborted after much soul searching.

Fully aware of the controversial nature of the two-part topic, 25 affiliates reject this month's reruns and seven major advertisers, including Pepsi-Cola, withdraw. But CBS holds tight and several groups, including NOW, boycott the former sponsors.

During this heated debate, the largest defection in network history saw 94 of 186 CBS affiliates refuse to carry the Tony award–winning drama "Sticks and Bones." Written by David Rabe, the play deals with a blind Vietnam vet and his bitter homecoming. Some stations chose to telecast the 100-minute program without advertisements. The ACLU, the National Council of Churches, and other organizations condemn the TV censorship.

**Fall.** TV writers went on strike for 3½ months in the spring. As a result, for the first time in a decade

the networks ease into the fall schedule rather than promote a single week of new programs.

**October 24.** The last of the new series to premiere and the 10th crime show, "Kojak" nonetheless becomes an immediate hit. The New York City detective introduces "Who loves ya, baby?" to the American vocabulary.

**More news.** Once again a British import wins kudos from TV viewers in the United States. "Upstairs, Downstairs" is carried by "Masterpiece Theatre" on PBS.

• CBS becomes the first network to extend its affiliate radio news feed to 24 hours a day.

## Obituaries

**Wally Cox** (December 6, 1924–February 15, 1973). Best known for his portrayal of "Mr. Peepers" during the 1950s, the comedian was recently seen on "Hollywood Squares."

**Don Messer** (May 9, 1909–March 26, 1973). Synonymous with old-time music, "Don Messer's Jubilee" was a major Saturday attraction on CBC for 10 years. When the corporation canceled the show in 1969, questions were raised in Parliament. The Canadian was known throughout North America and following his death one of his fiddles will be placed on display in Nashville.

**Irene Ryan** (October 17, 1903–April 26, 1973). After a 60-year career in vaudeville, musical comedy, movies, and the Broadway stage, the actress is remembered for her portrayal of Grannie on "The Beverly Hillbillies."

# SPORTS

## Winners

### Baseball

World Series—Oakland Athletics (AL), 4 games; New York Mets (NL), 3 games

Player of the Year—Reggie Jackson (Oakland Athletics, AL); Pete Rose (Cincinnati Reds, NL)

Rookie of the Year—Al Bumbry (Baltimore Orioles, AL); Gary Matthews (San Francisco Giants, NL)

## Football

NFC Championship—Minnesota Vikings 27, Dallas Cowboys 10

AFC Championship—Miami Dolphins 27, Oakland Raiders 10

Super Bowl VIII (January 13, 1974)—Miami Dolphins 24, Minnesota Vikings 7

College Bowls (January 1, 1973)—
Rose Bowl, USC 42, Ohio State 17
Cotton Bowl, Texas 17, Alabama 13
Orange Bowl, Nebraska 40, Notre Dame 6
Sugar Bowl, Oklahoma 14, Penn State 0

Heisman Trophy—John Cappelletti (Penn State, TB)

Grey Cup—Ottawa Rough Riders 22, Edmonton Eskimos, 18

## Basketball

NBA Championship—New York Knickerbockers, 4 games; LA Lakers, 1 game

MVP of the Year—Dave Cowens (Boston Celtics)

Rookie of the Year—Bob McAdoo (Buffalo Braves)

NCAA Championship—UCLA 87, Memphis State 66

## Tennis

U.S. Open—Men, John Newcombe (vs. Jan Kodés); Women, Margaret Court (vs. Evonne Goolagong)

Wimbledon—Men, Jan Kodés (vs. Alexander Metreveli); Women, Billie Jean King (vs. Chris Evert)

## Golf

Masters—Tommy Aaron
U.S. Open—Johnny Miller
British Open—Tom Weiskopf

## Hockey

Stanley Cup—Montreal Canadiens, 4 games; Chicago Blackhawks, 2 games

## Ice Skating

World Championship—Men, Ondrej Nepela (Czechoslovakia); Women, Karen Magnussen (Canada)

U.S. National—Men, Gordon McKellen; Women, Janet Lynn

Canadian National—Men, Toller Cranston; Women, Karen Magnussen

## Kentucky Derby

Secretariat—Ron Turcotte, jockey

## Athlete of the Year

Male—O. J. Simpson (Football)
Female—Billie Jean King (Tennis)

## Last Season

Luis Aparacio (Baseball)
Bobby Baun (Hockey)
John Brodie (Football)
Dick Butkus (Football)
Wilt Chamberlain (Basketball)
Hal Greer (Basketball)
Willie Mays (Baseball)
Jacques Plante (Hockey)
Jackie Stewart (Auto Racing)
Johnny Unitas (Football)

# News

**January 11.** The AL adds a 10th player to the roster, a designated hitter who will step to the plate for the pitcher (generally a poor batter). Team owners hope that a more offensive game will draw fans to the ball park, but the DH rule inadvertently gives the older power-hitter a second career. The three-year experiment will begin with the new season.

**January 22.** Heavyweight champion Joe Frazier, decked six times in the first two rounds, loses his crown to underdog George Foreman. The 24-year-old is a former Olympic champion.

**March 1.** Robyn Smith brings North Sea home in the Paumonok Handicap at Aqueduct Raceway. She is the first woman jockey to win a stakes race.

*On March 4, in her first pro match, Chris Evert beats Virginia Wade. In June 1974 (shown here), 19-year-old Evert will defeat 17-year-old Martina Navratilova to capture her first major tournament, the Italian Open.*

**March 5.** The first comprehensive NBA player contract grants the highest minimum salary in professional sports ($20,000) and $720 in pension benefits for each season played.

**March 31.** Little-known boxer Ken Norton breaks Muhammad Ali's jaw in a 12-round upset (Ali's second loss). In their second meeting, on September 10, the former heavyweight champion

rebounds to win a split decision. Still, many believe Norton would have won again if not for Ali's reputation.

**May 21.** At the University of Miami, swimmer Lynn Genesco receives what is believed to be the first female athletic scholarship in the United States. The university plans to select another 15 women.

**June 9.** This year, Secretariat ran the first sub-2-minute Kentucky Derby. In the Belmont Stakes today, Super Red and jockey Ron Turcotte romp home with a monumental 31-length lead. (Trainer Lucien Laurin is heard to murmur, "Don't fall off Ronnie. Just don't fall off.") The victory gives the 3-year-old chestnut the first Triple Crown in 25 years. Secretariat will be syndicated and retired to stud in November with 16 victories in 21 races and $1.3 million in earnings.

**June 19.** When the Houston Aeros asked Gordie Howe for permission to sign his underage sons, Mark and Marty, the hockey great offered to come out of retirement to make up a Howe line. Today, the WHA team signs the 45-year-old to a $1-million 4-year contract. With the father-sons combination, the Aeros take first in their division and sweep the 1973–1974 championship. Gordie, after two years away from the game, will stand third in scoring and receives the MVP award.

**September 14.** Successful in his campaign, President Nixon signs legislation barring local TV blackouts of games that sell out three days before the event. At the end of the season, football teams report 1,016,565 people failed to use purchased tickets; 656,290 of those tickets were for games telecast under the new law.

**September 20.** Promoters dub the match the "Battle of the Sexes," but Billie Jean King easily beats 55-year-old former Wimbledon champion Bobby Riggs (6–4, 6–3, 6–3) before a crowd of 30,000 at the Houston Astrodome.

**September 20.** Willie Mays retires after 21 years with the Giants and one season with the Mets. A sensational center fielder and one of the game's greatest offensive threats, the "Say Hey Kid" won four consecutive stolen-base titles (1956–1959), produced over 100 runs and RBI in eight consecutive seasons (1958–1966), and, with 660 HR, finishes third on the all-time list. Fans honor the 42 year old in a ceremony at Shea Stadium on the 25th. He says, "Just to hear you cheer like this for me and not be able to do anything about it makes me a very sad man."

**September 26.** Wilt Chamberlain jumps from the NBA to the ABA when the San Diego Conquistadors offer him $1.8 million over three years as a player-coach—a 50-percent pay raise. But when the LA Lakers sue the 37 year old for failing to play out his option, a court order benches Chamberlain for the season. He will never play basketball again. Over a 14-year career, the 7′ 1″ center established himself as the game's greatest offensive player. He had the only 100-point game, he was rebound leader in 11 seasons (13,924 career rebounds), and held records with a 4,029-point season, a single-season 50.4 scoring average, and a 30.1 career average.

**December 4.** The 1973 Players' Association contract gives those with 10 years experience in the majors the right of approval over a trade. Today, 14-year Cub veteran Ron Santo refuses a trade to the California Angels; he is the first to invoke the clause. Santo will play with the White Sox in 1974 then he will retire.

**More news.** Americans buy more bicycles than cars this year. And according to *Newsweek*, hang gliding is the fastest-growing sport in North America.

## Records

**July 15.** California Angel Nolan Ryan ties a major league record with his second no-hitter of the season. At the end of the year, his 383 strikeouts break the mark set by Sandy Koufax in 1965.

**August 12.** With a victory at the PGA, Jack Nicklaus breaks Bobby Jones' career record of 13 major tournaments. As well, this year, the Golden Bear becomes the first professional golfer to reach $2 million in lifetime earnings.

**October 21.** In a game against the Packers, Los Angeles Ram Fred Dryer sacks quarterbacks Scott

Hunter and Jim Del Gaizo in the end zone. In NFL history, only six teams have scored two safeties in a game and only four players have managed two in an entire season.

**December 16.** With 200 yards against the Jets, Buffalo Bill running back O. J. Simpson becomes the first NFL player to rush for more than 2,000 yards in a single season (2,003).

## What They Said

On January 3, a 12-man business syndicate buys the New York Yankees from CBS for $10 million. Representative George Steinbrenner, 42-year-old chairman of the American Ship Building Co., says, "We plan absent ownership as far as running the Yankees is concerned. We're not going to pretend we're something we aren't. I'll stick to building ships." *The New York Times*, January 4

Next year, on the same date, the new regime will replace manager Bill Virdon with Ralph Houk.

"It's old."–Quarterback Johnny Unitas explaining why his knee bothers him after 17 years in the NFL. The 40-year-old retires this year. (*Sports Illustrated*, August 6)

## Obituaries

**Abebe Bikila** (1927–October 25, 1973). The Ethiopian long-distance runner won the 1960 and 1964 Olympic marathons in record times. And when a 1969 car accident left him paralyzed, Bikila competed in the paraplegic Olympics.

**(Francis William) Frank Leahy** (August 27, 1908–June 21, 1973). The Notre Dame football coach led his team to an 87–11–9 record (1941–1954). He later wrote a football column.

**Paavo Nurmi** (June 13, 1897–October 2, 1973). Through the 1920s, the "Flying Finn" won 7 Olympic gold medals and set world records in 16 different running events. (In June 1924, he ran a 1,500-meter race and, a bare 60 minutes later, the 5,000-meter event—and broke the world record in both.) Just before the 1932 Olympics, Nurmi was declared a professional for allegedly padding his expenses on a European excursion. The greatest runner of all time receives a state funeral in Helsinki.

**George H. Sisler** (March 24, 1893–March 26, 1973). The St. Louis first baseman (1915–1922, 1924–1930) won accolades as the "perfect ball player." Like Ruth, his talent at the plate brought him off the pitching mound. He won the AL batting title in 1920 with a .407 batting average, and in 1922 with .420; his 257 hits in 1920 remain the single-season record. Defensively, Sisler led the league in assists seven times while his career 1,528 tops the all-time list. Sadly, Sisler lost a season to eye trouble in 1923 and his vision failed to return to normal.

# 1974

The president of the United States has covered up covert operations, lied in denying his involvement, and undermined the judicial and legislative processes of the land. In the end, he concedes only blunders in strategy, not the illegality of his actions.

A weary nation turns in relief to Gerald Ford, the third U.S. vice president to become president since W.W.II. But the honeymoon ends abruptly a month later with his pardon of Richard Nixon. Denied a public purging and faced with a recession, angry Americans turn to the Democrats in midterm elections.

Internationally, North and South Vietnam continue to jockey for territorial gains. The United States and other national forces pull out of Laos. OPEC lifts the oil embargo and Henry Kissinger creates shuttle diplomacy to jump start Middle East peace talks. India joins the nuclear club, Haile Selassie loses his throne, and Moscow expels Aleksandr Solzhenitsyn.

At home, 1974 marks the passing of Dizzy Dean, Earl Warren, Charles Lindbergh, and Duke Ellington. The Symbionese Liberation Army kidnaps heiress Patty Hearst and Boston parents fight busing. The first test-tube babies are born and women are warned about the Dalkon Shield. Mikhail Baryshnikov defects, Ali regains his title, Aaron breaks Ruth's record, and streaking takes over the nation. All the President's Men is a smash best-seller, "The Way We Were" the No. 1 song, and Death Wish, The Three Musketeers, Chinatown, and The Godfather II are all hit movies.

## NEWS

**January 4.** President Nixon refuses to comply with Watergate Committee demands for hundreds of White House tapes and documents, including his daily diary for almost four years. He argues that compliance would "irreparably impair the constitutional functions of the office of the presidency."

**January 15.** Technical experts report to Judge Sirica that the 18½-minute gap in the taped Nixon-Haldeman conversation (June 20, 1972) was caused not by a single, accidental erasure, but by five, or perhaps up to nine, deliberate erasures and rerecordings.

**January 18.** Israel and Egypt end the October War with an agreement, negotiated by Henry Kissinger, to separate their forces along the Suez Canal. Egypt will begin to clear the canal (closed since 1967) in early February and will reestablish diplomatic relations with the United States later that month.

But Syria continues to battle for the Israeli-held

Golan Heights. Only intensive negotiations, again by Kissinger, will produce a cease-fire agreement on May 31. Yet this accord, the first between the two nations since 1948, will not evolve into a general settlement, and tensions will continue along their shared border.

**February 1.** In Sao Paulo, Brazil, a fire breaks out on the 11th floor of a new 25-story office building. The blaze feeds on flammable paint and plastics, trapping hundreds on the upper floors. This city of 6 million counts just 13 poorly equipped fire stations, and firefighters watch helplessly as heat forces many people to jump to their deaths. The death total reaches 189.

**February 1.** In his annual economic report to Congress, President Nixon notes a "highly uncertain" outlook for the United States. On the 4th, he submits a fiscal 1975 budget of $304.4 billion—the first U.S. budget to surpass $300 billion. By the end of the month, consumer prices rise 1.3%, or an annual rate of 15.6%—the first double-digit inflation since the Korean War.

**February 5.** The Symbionese Liberation Army (SLA) kidnaps 19-year-old newspaper heiress Patricia Hearst from her apartment in Berkeley, California. The terrorists, linked to the 1973 slaying of an Oakland school superintendent, order her wealthy family to give food to every needy Californian. But their $2-million start barely dents the estimated $400-million cost.

On April 3, authorities receive a tape from Hearst. She has chosen "to stay and fight" for the "freedom of the oppressed people," and has taken the revolutionary name of Tanya. Just 12 days later, a bank security camera records the young heiress holding a weapon during an armed robbery. On June 6, a federal grand jury indicts Hearst for her role in that crime.

**February 6.** The House of Representatives approves, 410–4, a resolution granting the House Judiciary Committee power to determine whether grounds exist to impeach Richard Nixon. The committee will have broad powers to compel testimony and to subpoena documents from any source, including the president.

**February 7.** Truckers' representatives accept an administration proposal to impose a 6-percent surcharge on freight rates and to supply 100 percent of their fuel needs. Drivers in 42 states have staged protest strikes against fuel conservation measures established under the OPEC embargo—a reduced speed limit, higher gas prices (up 20 cents to 55 cents per gallon), and reduced fuel supplies. With up to 85 percent of American goods moved by truck, the violent strikes have hit the economy hard.

For the average American motorist, the oil embargo has meant hour-long waits at the gas pump. Many state governments, sensing a lack of leadership from Washington, have adopted their own systems of rationing, usually alternate-day gas purchases by odd-even license numbers. As commuters turn to public transportation systems, new car sales drop in the first quarter while motorcycle sales soar by 50 percent to 700,000.

**February 28.** British voters give the ruling Conservatives 296 seats and the Labour party 301. When Prime Minister Edward Heath fails to form a coalition government with 14 Liberals, he resigns and Harold Wilson, leader of the Labour party, forms a minority government.

Heath had called an election when British miners, despite the energy crisis, voted to strike for more pay. Wilson, as prime minister, settles the dispute by canceling the three-day workweek and giving the miners a raise.

On September 18, Wilson calls an October 10 general election, the first time in more than 50 years that Britain has held two elections in one year. The voters give Labour a three-seat majority and, before the end of the year, Wilson implements a mandatory energy-saving program. Measures include lower speed limits and a maximum of 68 degrees Fahrenheit in most public buildings.

**March 3.** As a Turkish DC-10 ascends to 12,000 feet enroute from Paris to London, a cargo door blows out. The sudden decompression collapses the passenger floor, cutting the flight control cables below. The plane enters a steep descent and, just 70 seconds later, hits the ground at an estimated 500 mph. Altogether 334 passengers and 12 crew members die in the worst aviation disaster to date.

An inquiry discovers that, following a similar accident two years ago (in which the pilot landed safely), an FAA airworthiness directive was issued, then withdrawn. A new directive instructs airlines to make structural changes by 1977.

**March 18.** In February, a White House statement on the legal nature of presidential impeachment maintained that a president could be impeached only for an indictable or criminal offense. During the recent grand jury hearing on the Watergate cover-up, special prosecutor Leon Jaworski quashed any attempt to indict Richard Nixon along with his seven aides. Still, when the jurors handed down indictments on March 1, they submitted a sealed report detailing the president's role.

Today, Judge Sirica rules that the secret report should be released to the House impeachment inquiry. The Court of Appeals upholds his decision three days later.

**March 18.** At an OPEC meeting in Vienna, seven oil-producing nations lift the oil embargo on the United States; Libya and Syria intend to continue the prohibition, while Iraq is absent. The members agree to maintain the embargo against the Netherlands and four other nations for failing to "make clear their position on asking for a full [Israeli] withdrawal from occupied territories." OPEC refuses to roll back prices.

The next day, President Nixon cancels some of the energy conservation measures, including a Sunday ban on gasoline sales. (Americans near the border have been scooting into Canada to fill up.) First-quarter U.S. oil company profits have risen sharply, ranging from 29 percent for Standard Oil of Ohio to 748 percent for Occidental Petroleum.

**April 3.** Separate reports issued by the Congressional Joint Committee on Internal Revenue Taxation and by the Internal Revenue Service (IRS) reveal that President Nixon owes $432,787 in back taxes ($465,000 with interest penalties). Nixon failed to report five categories of taxable income and claimed six categories of unwarranted deductions.

The IRS announces that no civil fraud penalty will be sought. The White House promptly announces that the president will pay the full amount.

**April 3–4.** An intense spring storm, pulling moist air up from the Gulf of Mexico to a cool, dry front from the east, produces the worst string of tornadoes in 49 years. An estimated 148 twisters strike across a corridor from Ontario to Georgia, killing some 350, injuring 1,200, and leaving thousands homeless. In Kentucky, the state hardest hit, one tornado nearly levels the town of Brandenburg; 71 people die out of a population of 1,600.

**April 8.** Nixon signs legislation to raise the minimum hourly wage to $2.30 by January 1976. He vetoed a similar bill last year.

**April 22.** In Israel, the ruling Labour party elects Yitzhak Rabin as prime minister to form a new cabinet. Golda Meir, who had failed to form a government since the 1973 general election, said upon resigning, "I have had enough." Critics had held the Meir government at least partially responsible for the total surprise of last October's Arab offensive, despite exoneration by a commission of inquiry.

At 52, Rabin becomes Israel's youngest and first native-born Israeli or Sabra prime minister. The previous four prime ministers were all born in Czarist Russia.

**April 25.** In Portugal, the Armed Forces Movement (MFA) ends some 40 years of dictatorial rule with a bloodless coup. A seven-man military junta led by General António Spínola receives enthusiastic popular support with a promise of elections, amnesty for political prisoners, and a plan to give up costly African colonies.

**April 28.** After four days of deliberation, a federal jury acquits former attorney general John Mitchell and former secretary of commerce Maurice Stans on charges relating to the secret Nixon campaign contribution made by financier Robert Vesco. Their acquittal encourages the White House in its continued denial of involvement in the Watergate scandal.

**April 30.** In response to a House Judiciary Committee subpoena for tapes and other materials relating to 42 White House conversations, Nixon releases 1,308 typed pages of edited transcripts. The president states that the committee's Democratic chairman and top Republican may listen to the original tapes to verify the accuracy of the text.

The committee accepts the material but votes 20–18, along party lines, to notify the president he must surrender the original tapes—11 of the conversations are missing from the pages, along with supplementary notes.

As paperback publishers and the Government Printing Office ready copies of the transcripts, newspapers begin printing excerpts the next day. Readers are dismayed by the disjointed, vindictive conversations (sprinkled with swear words—marked "expletive deleted") that cover such subjects as perjury and hush money.

Senate Republican Leader Hugh Scott denounces the conversations as "deplorable, disgusting, shabby, immoral performances." John Anderson, chairman of the House Republican Conference, declares that Nixon has "damaged himself irreparably," for the tapes show him deeply involved in Watergate before March 21, 1973, a fact he has repeatedly denied. Anderson states bluntly that Nixon will be impeached if he refuses to resign.

**May 2.** The Maryland Court of Appeals disbars Spiro Agnew, charging that the crime to which he pleaded no contest was "infested with fraud, deceit and dishonesty." The court describes the former vice-president as "morally obtuse."

**May 6.** West German Chancellor Willy Brandt resigns over the Gunter Guillaume spy affair. Intelligence had put his personal aide, known East German spy, under observation, but allowed him continued access to sensitive information.

In his five years in office, Brandt improved relations with East Germany and the rest of Eastern Europe. His efforts at détente brought him the 1971 Nobel peace prize.

On May 16, finance minister Helmut Schmidt is sworn in as the new chancellor.

**May 9.** The House Judiciary Committee begins closed formal hearings to determine whether to recommend that the full House impeach Richard Nixon.

**May 17.** When police corner six members of the SLA in their Los Angeles hideout, the two sides exchange an estimated 1,000 rounds in a one-hour gun battle. All six terrorists, including leader Donald DeFreeze, die either in the shoot-out or in the fire that consumes the building. Patty Hearst is not among the dead, and law enforcement officers issue a warrant for her arrest as "armed and very dangerous."

**May 17.** A San Francisco jury indicts the Zebra killers, four Black Muslims who murdered 12 white people at random over a five-month period last year. (The code name "Zebra" came from the radio wavelength used by the police task force.) Their trial will begin next year.

**May 18.** With an underground detonation, India becomes the sixth nuclear nation, after the United States, the Soviet Union, Great Britain, France, and China.

The Indian government describes the test as a peaceful explosion, but the United States and Canada had prohibited any military application of their nuclear energy technology. Within days, Ottawa suspends nuclear aid. And next year, the world's major exporters of nuclear materials will agree on new preventive measures.

**May 18.** Newspapers report that the Defense Department, in a secret Foreign Relations Committee hearing in March, admitted using rainmaking as a weapon during the Vietnam War. Between 1967 and 1972, 2,602 missions seeded clouds with 47,409 canisters of silver iodide and lead iodide to slow Communist infiltration to the South. The chemicals increased rainfall by an estimated 30 percent.

**May 19.** President Georges Pompidou of France died on April 2. In a runoff election to choose his successor, Valéry Giscard d'Estaing narrowly defeats François Mitterand. Mitterand was previously beaten by de Gaulle in 1965 and Pompidou in 1969.

**May 30–31.** Pressure on Richard Nixon intensifies as the House Judiciary Committee, in a 28–10 vote, informs the president that failure to comply with committee subpoenas may constitute grounds for impeachment. Special Prosecutor Jaworski, who seeks 64 tapes of presidential conversations, has petitioned the Supreme Court to hear the case immediately. On May 31, the justices agree.

Five days later, the White House acknowledges that the grand jury named Richard Nixon as an unindicted co-conspirator in the Watergate cover-up.

**June 3.** Fulfilling the terms of the 1973 Laos

peace accord, the last American military and para-military units pull out. Reportedly, the Chinese have also left, but 25,000–30,000 North Vietnamese troops remain behind. The United States lost an estimated 1,100 pilots during 10 years of military involvement in Laos.

As agreed, the Communists and anti-Communists have formed a coalition government, but the fragile alliance faces enormous difficulties. The long civil war uprooted thousands, possibly as much as one fifth of the population. And the shattered economy has forced the once self-sufficient Laotians to import rice along with other foods.

Washington continues to send economic and military aid to agencies controlled by anti-Communists.

**June 14.** One of the worst smallpox epidemics in recent history kills an estimated 10,000–30,000 people in India. Still, strict medical surveillance and inoculation have largely eradicated the disease, reducing the number of afflicted countries to 11 from 43 in 1967.

**June 30.** Inside the Atlanta Ebenezer Baptist Church, a young black man fatally shoots Alberta King, a deacon, and wounds one other person. The murderer later tells police he intended to kill Rev. King, who was preaching at the time, but Mrs. King was nearer, at the organ.

The public knows little of Alberta King, but friends and family recognized the importance of the support she gave her husband and her son, Martin Luther King, Jr.

**July 1.** President Juan Perón dies in Buenos Aires, and his wife and vice-president, Isabel, becomes the president of Argentina, the first woman head of state in the Americas. But his death throws the nation into crisis. With some 140 deaths through leftist terrorism and political assassinations by November, the widow places her country under a state of siege.

**July 8.** In Canada, NDP support for the Liberal minority government evaporated when the May 6 budget sidestepped NDP taxation measures. Two days later, the NDP and the Conservatives brought down the Liberal government with a nonconfidence vote.

But in today's election, Pierre Trudeau and the Liberals confound political analysts and pollsters by winning a majority of the seats—141 to 95 for the Conservatives and 16 for the NDP, which loses 15; the Social Credit and one Independent capture the other 12 ridings.

**July 9.** House Judiciary Committee transcripts of eight Watergate conversations released on April 30, reveal discrepancies in the White House text. In almost every instance, the committee versions show that the president was more involved in the cover-up than indicated in the White House copy.

**July 13.** After 17 months of investigation, the Senate Watergate Committee releases a 2,250-page summary with 35 recommendations for election campaign reform.

The Watergate Committee condemns the "illegal and unethical activities" of campaign officials and White House aides, but clearly states it was not the committee mandate "to determine the legal guilt or innocence of any person or whether the president should be impeached."

**July 15.** Greek-born officers in the Cyprus National Guard launch a coup in Nicosia. President Makarios narrowly escapes death and flees to London. It had become evident in recent years that the island's minority Turkish population and the government of Turkey would never sanction *enosis*, a union of Cyprus and Greece. But in seeking a political compromise, Makarios had come into conflict with the Greek officers.

In the near chaos following the coup, Turkey lands an army in northern Cyprus and, by mid-August, controls 40 percent of the island. Yet the seemingly inevitable war between Turkey and Greece is averted when the new Greek government backs down.

Makarios returns to Cyprus on December 7, but the situation remains unresolved.

**July 23.** General Dimitrios Ioannidis resigns, and President Gizikis of Greece summons former prime minister Konstantinos Karamanlis from exile.

Ioannidis led a November coup after student and army unrest forced the Papadopoulos government to promise free elections in 1974. An angry Greek people, furious also at the military's actions in Cyprus, had since placed insurmountable pressure on the junta.

Karamanlis quickly reinstates the 1952 constitution (abolished in 1967) and sanctions a November election. The new Parliament will be sworn in on December 9, the day after 69.2 percent of the Greek electorate votes against the restoration of the Greek monarchy. A new constitution will be adopted in mid-1975.

**July 24.** In a unanimous decision, the U.S. Supreme Court rules that executive privilege "cannot prevail over the fundamental demands of due process of law in the fair administration of criminal justice." President Richard Nixon must hand over 64 previously unreleased tapes to Judge John Sirica. Within a few hours of the judgment, Nixon announces in a statement read by special counsel James St. Clair that he will comply "in all respects."

**July 25.** President Nixon signs a controversial measure establishing a legal aid program for the poor (excluding criminal cases) under an independent nonprofit Legal Services Corporation.

**July 27–30.** After televised debate, the House Judiciary Committee votes on three articles of presidential impeachment. The committee approves Article I by a vote of 27–11, recommending the impeachment of Richard Nixon for obstructing the investigation of the Watergate Committee, through such activities as condoning and counseling perjury and approving the payment of hush money. On July 29, Article II passes with a vote of 28–10, charging Nixon with the abuse of his presidential powers, including the misuse of the FBI and IRS. And on July 30, members pass Article III, 21–17, citing Nixon's attempt to block impeachment by defying committee subpoenas for evidence.

**July 31.** John Ehrlichman, former domestic affairs advisor to President Nixon, is sentenced to 20 months to 5 years in prison for conspiring to violate the civil rights of Daniel Ellsberg's psychiatrist, Dr. Lewis Fielding. Co-defendant G. Gordon Liddy receives 1 to 3 years concurrent with his present sentence of 6 years, 8 months to 20 years for the Watergate break-in.

**August 5.** Unaware of the tapes' contents, presidential counsel St. Clair insists that Nixon release transcripts of three June 23, 1972, conversations. The text reveals that Bob Haldeman, then White House chief of staff, informed the president of the FBI Watergate investigation just six days after the burglary, and that Nixon instructed him to tell the FBI, "Don't go any further into this case, period!"

In a statement accompanying the transcripts, Nixon admits "a serious act of omission" in keeping the facts of the cover-up from investigators and his own counsel. But he claims this mistake does not justify "the extreme step of impeachment."

Proof of Nixon's involvement in a crime—the proverbial "smoking gun"—destroys his remaining support in Congress. Within 48 hours, the 10 Judiciary Committee members who voted against all five articles of impeachment announce that they will reverse themselves in a House vote. Senior Republican leaders advise Nixon to resign and spare the country the trauma of a presidential impeachment.

**August 6.** The Senate Foreign Relations Committee clears Henry Kissinger of responsibility in the wiretapping of 17 newsmen and officials in 1969–1971. The secretary of state had threatened to resign if he were not exonerated.

**August 8.** At 9:00 P.M., television and radio stations across the United States interrupt regular programming for a 16-minute speech by Richard M. Nixon. "I shall resign the presidency effective at noon tomorrow" because "[I] no longer [have] a strong enough political base in the Congress" to continue in office. He adds, "I would only say that if some of my judgments were wrong, and some were wrong, they were made in what I believed at the time to be the best interests of the nation."

**August 9.** Before departing the White House, Nixon meets with his Cabinet and aides in the East Room. He speaks of his pride in them, talks of his father and mother, and admonishes, "Always remember, others may hate you, but those who hate you don't win unless you hate them—and then you destroy yourself."

Nixon, his wife, and family members then board a helicopter on the south lawn as Vice-President Ford waves farewell. They will arrive in California new president quickly meets with congressional leaders, the Cabinet, the NSC, and foreign envoys to reaffirm existing foreign policy.

Ford will serve the remaining 2½ years of the second Nixon term and be eligible for another full term in office. On August 20, he nominates Nelson A. Rockefeller as vice-president.

GERALD FORD

Born: July 14, 1913, Omaha, Nebraska, Leslie Lynch King, Jr. Adopted by his stepfather, Gerald Rudolff Ford; 2 half-sisters and 1 half-brother
Education: University of Michigan, B.A., 1935, Yale University, LL.B, 1941
Military Service: U.S. Navy in W.W.II
Marriage: (Elizabeth) Betty Bloomer, Oct. 15, 1948
Children: Michael (b.1950), John (b.1952), Steven (b.1956), Susan (b.1957)
Previous Occupations: lawyer, representative
Position Before Taking Office: Vice-President
Legal Residence When Appointed: Michigan

**August 19.** Ambassador Rodger P. Davies and a secretary are shot and killed during an anti-American demonstration outside the U.S. Embassy in Cyprus. Greek Cypriots were protesting supposed American support for Turkey in the current crisis. But a coroner determines that the shots came not from the demonstrators but from a building next door. The murders will remain unsolved.

**September 8.** President Ford grants Richard Nixon a "full, free and absolute pardon" for all federal crimes he "committed or may have committed or taken part in" while in office. Nixon is given title to his presidential papers and tapes, but the documents must be kept available to the justice system for three years.

Nixon accepts the pardon and issues a statement: "One thing I can see clearly now is that I was wrong in not acting more decisively and more forthrightly in dealing with Watergate. . . . No words can describe the depths of my regret and pain at the anguish my mistakes over Watergate have caused

*Richard Nixon leaves Washington by helicopter following his resignation from the presidency.*

later in the day, to stay at their home in San Clemente.

Richard Nixon's resignation is delivered to Secretary Kissinger, at 11:35 A.M. At 12:03 P.M., in the East Room, Chief Justice Warren E. Burger swears in Gerald R. Ford as the 38th president of the United States.

In brief remarks after the ceremony, President Ford promises, "In all my public and private acts as your president, I expect to follow my instincts of openness and candor with full confidence that honesty is always the best policy in the end." He tells the American people, "Our long national nightmare is over." Congress passes a resolution expressing support for Ford as a "good and faithful friend."

To reassure Americans and the world at large, the

the nation and the presidency." Nixon makes no reference to the illegality of sanctioning the Watergate burglary and other covert operations.

The American people, who just last month offered gratitude to their new president, are shocked and outraged that Nixon should escape punishment while those who acted on his behalf are in prison or face prosecution. Ford's popularity plummets by 21 percent from August 9 to October 12, the sharpest decline of any president since the polling of White House popularity began 35 years ago.

**September 8.** Newspapers set off a major controversy with a report that the CIA spent more than $8 million from 1970 to 1973 to promote the overthrow of the Marxist government in Chile. CIA Director William Colby revealed the expenditure to a congressional committee last April and two members of Congress had discussed his appearance in a letter leaked to the press.

Both Nixon and Ford deny the activities, and Ford insists the money was used to preserve opposition parties, newspapers, and electronic media. He believes this was "[in] the best interests of the people of Chile and . . . in our best interest." Late next year, the Senate Select Committee on Intelligence will absolve the CIA of direct involvement in the 1973 coup.

**September 12.** White parents and students in Boston make international headlines with their violent opposition to school integration. On June 21, U.S. District Judge W. Arthur Garrity, Jr., charged Boston with consciously maintaining two separate school systems. Some 82 percent of black pupils attend black majority schools. He ordered the school system to achieve a racial balance in the new year through busing (18,200 of the city's 94,000 students). Boycotts will continue, and about one-third of the white students will leave the public system during the first two years.

**September 16.** President Ford offers conditional clemency to Vietnam War deserters and draft evaders in return for an oath of allegiance and up to 24 months of alternative service. Reaction is mixed: Congress approves, veterans of previous wars denounce the proposal as too lenient, while most

exiles find the offer too punitive and believe that acceptance would be an admission of guilt.

Ottawa claims that 50,000 draft dodgers fled into Canada during the war. About the same number deserted.

**September 26.** A report reaches the West that a Soviet destroyer, testing a new propulsion system and weaponry, caught fire and sank with 200–300 men on board. If true, it would be the worst peacetime naval disaster in modern times. The Soviet Union makes no response to the news story.

**October 11.** The Energy Reorganization Act abolishes the 28-year-old AEC. The basic conflict of interest in the commission's mandate— promoting nuclear energy while regulating safety within the industry—had resulted in a poor safety record. The act splits these functions, with the Energy Research and Development Administration (ERDA) promoting nuclear energy and the Nuclear Regulatory Commission (NRC) assuming the responsibilities of licensing and regulation.

**October 14.** In a 105–4 vote (with 20 abstentions), the United Nations recognizes the PLO as "the representative of the Palestinian people" and invites the organization to join in the November debate on Palestine—the first nongovernmental body to participate in the General Assembly.

On November 13, Yasir Arafat, the head of the PLO, speaks to the General Assembly with the full support of Arab heads of state. He calls for the establishment of a Palestinian state for Moslems, Christians, and Jews.

The Israelis have denounced the inclusion of an organization sworn to destroy their nation, the Jewish Defense League has threatened to assassinate Arafat, and thousands of Jews protest his visit. But on November 22, the General Assembly approves two resolutions declaring the right of the Palestinian people to independence and sovereignty, and granting the PLO observer status in U.N. affairs.

**October 14.** The Watergate cover-up trial opens in Washington before U.S. District Court Judge John Sirica. The defendants are John Mitchell, H. R. Haldeman, John Ehrlichman, Kenneth Parkinson, and Robert Mardian. Gordon Strachan has been separated from this trial, and Charles Colson has pleaded guilty to obstruction of justice.

Richard Nixon's presence is quickly felt in the courtroom when taped White House conversations are introduced as evidence. Ehrlichman wants the former president to testify, but Nixon is hospitalized on October 23 with phlebitis in his left leg. His health deteriorates, and following surgery on the 29th, his condition is listed as critical. Three court-appointed doctors conclude that a court appearance would be impossible before mid-February.

Defense counsel begin presenting their cases on November 25. On December 5, Judge Sirica rules that the former president need not testify. The decision cites Nixon's poor health and the fact that the value of his testimony to the defendants "should not be unrealistically overestimated."

**October 15.** President Ford signs a bill providing for public funding of presidential primaries and elections and imposing a ceiling on donations and spending for congressional and presidential campaigns (effective January 1). Intended to eliminate undue influence from large contributors or special-interest groups, this landmark legislation was inspired by the revelations of the Watergate scandal.

**October 17.** In probably the first formal appearance of a president before a congressional panel, Gerald Ford confronts suspicions raised by his pardon of former president Richard Nixon. Ford makes a 5,000-word opening statement and then answers five minutes of questions from each member.

The president states that the pardon was granted solely "out of my concern to serve the best interests of my country" and declares, "There was no deal, period." In his mind, Nixon's acceptance of the pardon implied an admission of guilt.

**October 21.** Employees at Chicago Purolator Security open the vault this morning to discover some $4 million replaced by 11 gasoline-filled bags. If the bags had burned, the fire likely would have covered the robbery, but only three ignited. Just $2.2 million will be recovered.

**October 28.** President Ford repeals "no-knock" drug searches authorized under 1970 legislation.

**November 5.** With the Watergate scandal and a struggling economy, American voters turn to the Democrats in midterm elections, increasing their House majority to two-thirds and giving the party three more seats in the Senate.

The large influx of newcomers to the House reduces the average member's age to under 50 for the first time in this century. New senators include Gary Hart (D., Colo.) and former astronaut John Glenn (D., Ohio).

**November 8.** The courts acquit eight former members of the Ohio National Guard of violating the rights of Kent State students killed in 1970. (Elliot Richardson, successor to John Mitchell as attorney general, had ordered an investigation, and the men were indicted in April.) The judge maintains that the prosecutors failed to prove their guilt beyond a reasonable doubt. Next year, a Federal jury will clear Ohio Governor James Rhodes and 28 Guardsmen of any personal or financial responsibility in the deaths.

**November 12.** In an unprecedented ruling, the U.N. General Assembly reduces South Africa to observer status. Arab delegates voted against the white-minority government after black African nations threatened to withdraw their support in the Palestinian debate.

**November 13.** Karen Silkwood, on her way to meet with union officials and a *New York Times* reporter, dies in a single-vehicle auto accident. The nuclear plant employee and union activist was bringing proof that Kerr-McGee in Cimarron, Oklahoma, was covering up worker health hazards. But no incriminating documents are found in the wreck and her death is ruled accidental. Early next year, an AEC report will uphold Silkwood's charges and the plant will be shut down.

**November 18.** U.S. Attorney General William Saxbe and FBI Director Clarence Kelley release details from a Department of Justice report on FBI counterintelligence operations between 1956 and 1971. The public first learned of COINTELPRO late last year, when Justice released two related FBI memos under the Freedom of Information Act.

Although the first COINTELPRO operation was undertaken against the Communist party in 1956, five of the program's seven operations were directed against domestic groups and their leaders—the two most prominent being SCLC and CORE. Other targeted organizations included SNCC, SDS, KKK, and the Black Panther party.

In May 1968, Director J. Edgar Hoover ordered a campaign against the New Left, arguing that "organizations and activists who spout revolution and unlawfully challenge society to obtain their demands must not only be contained, but must be neutralized."

COINTELPRO, which the report describes as "abhorrent in a free society," was discontinued by Hoover on April 28, 1971.

**November 21.** Congress overrides a presidential veto of 17 amendments to the Freedom of Information Act (1966), giving Americans greater access to personal government documentation (except in security and law enforcement files).

President Ford objected to the requirement for federal justification if a secrecy classification is challenged in court. Critics of the president's veto point to his earlier support for the legislation.

*U.S. President Ford and Soviet Secretary Brezhnev in Vladivostok.*

**November 23–24.** U.S. President Ford and Soviet Secretary Brezhnev sign a tentative 10-year agreement limiting strategic offensive weapons and delivery vehicles, including multiple missile systems. And, unlike the 1972 SALT agreement, this understanding establishes the principle of strategic equivalency. The final terms are to be negotiated during SALT II talks.

**November 29.** The British House of Commons approves, without opposition, legislation outlawing the IRA and giving the police broad powers to combat terrorism. Last week, in the worst anti-British attack in over two years, IRA bombings killed 21 and wounded over 100 in Birmingham.

**December 4.** When air traffic control at the Sri Lanka airport prematurely clears a chartered Dutch DC-8 for descent, the plane crashes into a hillside 44 miles from the airport. The second worst aviation disaster to date kills the crew of 9 and 182 Indonesian Moslems en route to Mecca.

**December 9.** In the heaviest fighting in almost two years, Saigon reports that government troops have suffered 3,000 casualties south of the city and in the province bordering Cambodia. The North Vietnamese now step up their attacks and, by year's end, control six district capitals.

As the Communists continue to advance, the South Vietnamese regime wrestles hopelessly with social instability, an inflationary economy, growing political opposition to government corruption, and cuts in U.S. economic and military aid.

**December 10.** In the wake of several well-publicized incidents with stripper Fanne Foxe, Representative Wilbur D. Mills (D., Ark.) resigns as chairman of the Ways and Means Committee. Since assuming the post in 1958, Mills had become one of the most powerful members of Congress. On the 30th, he confesses to alcoholism, promises to quit drinking, and affirms his intention to remain in office. Mills will leave politics in 1975.

**December 12.** Jimmy Carter announces his candidacy for the Democratic presidential nomination in 1976. The 50-year-old governor of Georgia calls for an open, efficient government free from conflict of interest, for energy conservation, reduced spending on nuclear weapons, and the rigid enforcement of desegregation: "The time for racial discrimination is over." Reporters informally refer to Carter as "Jimmy Who?"

**December 19.** Nelson A. Rockefeller is sworn in as vice-president of the United States—the first time in American history neither the president nor the vice-president has been elected to their office.

Rockefeller's nomination encountered surprising initial opposition in Congress, where some questioned whether the former governor of New York had used his wealth to improperly further his political career.

**December 25.** After the Australian weather bureau predicts that Cyclone Tracy will bypass Darwin, the storm suddenly swings around. Winds exceeding 165 mph destroy over 90 percent of the city, killing at least 50 people and injuring hundreds. Victims are airlifted from the worst natural disaster in Australian history.

**December 28.** An earthquake measuring 6.3 on the Richter scale devastates remote villages in northern Pakistan, killing an estimated 5,200 and injuring another 15,000. Hazardous winds, snow, and landslides delay relief efforts.

**December 31.** The *Los Angeles Times* claims that CIA Director William Colby has confirmed a December 22 *New York Times* story that the CIA has spied on American citizens. A recent report to President Ford supposedly confirmed that the CIA holds files on at least 9,000 citizens and has conducted clandestine operations against opponents of U.S. Vietnam policy and other dissidents.

Three major congressional committees have scheduled hearings into CIA activities in the New Year.

**December 31.** At the height of the Great Depression, President Roosevelt issued an executive order prohibiting gold ownership by private individuals. When the ban ends today, the predicted modern gold rush fails to materialize. The price of gold drops from $186 to $153 an ounce by January 6.

## Obituaries

**Dan Gerber** (May 6, 1898–March 16, 1974). In 1928, he founded the Gerber baby-food empire on an idea born while watching his wife's disgust as she strained peas for their child.

**Charles Lindbergh** (February 4, 1902–August 26, 1974). On May 21, 1927, the courageous young pilot left New York City in a single-engine plane, the "Spirit of St. Louis," and flew 33½ hours nonstop to Paris. That first solo transatlantic flight brought the Lone Eagle worldwide acclaim, a $25,000 prize, a huge ticker-tape parade in New York, and the U.S. Medal of Honor.

With his marriage to Anne Morrow in 1929, Lindbergh turned his navigational skills to plotting new airline routes and his ingenuity to constructing a series of life-sustaining mechanical pumps with Dr. Alexis Carrel of the Rockefeller Institute. But in 1932, the Lindberghs' lives were shattered when their 20-month-old son was kidnapped and murdered. The notoriety of the trial and the killer's execution in 1936 drove the distraught parents out of the country.

While in Europe, Lindbergh twice inspected the Nazi air force. Convinced of its invincibility, he later spoke out against American involvement in the European war. Rebuked by President Roosevelt for his interference, the famous pilot resigned his commission in the Air Corps Reserves. Yet once the United States entered the war, the 40-year-old made his way to the Pacific and eventually flew some 50 combat missions.

Lindbergh later worked as a consultant to Pan Am and in 1954 was promoted to brigadier general in the Air Force Reserves. That same year, he wrote the story of his historic flight; *The Spirit of St. Louis* received a Pulitzer prize.

**Wayne Morse** (October 20, 1900–July 22, 1974). A former Republican, who left the party when Richard Nixon was elected vice-president in 1952, the Oregon senator voted against the Gulf of Tonkin resolution in 1964 and afterward continued to speak out against administration policies in Vietnam. He lost his seat in 1968.

**Juan Perón** (October 8, 1895–July 1, 1974). In 1946, the charismatic Evita Perón engineered her husband's meteoric rise to the presidency of Argentina then ruled the country beside him. Perón easily won reelection in 1951, but the death of his popular wife the following year eroded much of his influence over the people. His subsequent suppression of civil liberties and political opponents, erratic economic policies, and alienation of the church eventually created the climate for a military coup. Overthrown in 1955, the dictator fled into exile. Dedicated Peronists returned the former president to power in 1973 and his new wife, Isabel, assumed the position of vice-president, a role denied to Evita by the military.

**Georges Pompidou** (July 5, 1911–April 2, 1974). A political unknown when President Charles de Gaulle appointed him premier in 1962, Pompidou gained prestige during the 1968 student riots, then won the presidency following de Gaulle's retirement in 1969. Pompidou maintained a stable government during his five years in office, strengthened the economy, and expanded the French presence on the international scene. The president was obviously ill in recent months, but his death nonetheless comes as a shock.

**Carl Spaatz** (June 28, 1891–July 14, 1974). During W.W.II, the U.S. general planned and directed the massive daylight bombing campaign over Germany. After the Nazi surrender, he assumed the Pacific command and, while opposed to the atomic bomb, ordered the Hiroshima and Nagasaki bombings upon instructions from President Truman.

**Stephen Gill Spottswood** (July 18, 1897–December 1, 1974). The bishop of the African Methodist Episcopal Zion Church chaired the NAACP from 1961 until his death. In the early part of this decade, he stirred up enormous controversy by criticizing administration policies toward blacks.

**U Thant** (January 22, 1909–November 25, 1974). The Burmese educator served as the third Secretary-General of the United Nations (1962–1971). During his tenure, the much-respected diplomat confronted such thorny issues as the Cuban missile crisis, the India-Pakistan War, and the escalation of the war in Vietnam.

**Earl Warren** (March 19, 1891–July 9, 1974). The 14th chief justice of the U.S. Supreme Court served from 1953 to 1969. (*See also* News, June 23, 1969.)

# BEGINNINGS AND ENDINGS

## News

**January 1.** In the United States, Supplementary Security Income (SSI) replaces federal and state aid to the aged, blind, and disabled.

**January 14.** Jules Leger replaces Roland Michener as the governor general of Canada.

**January 11.** In Cape Town, South Africa, Sue Rosenkowitz gives birth to sextuplets, the first to survive in modern times. The 25-year-old mother had taken a fertility drug.

**January 18.** Pauline McGibbon becomes the first woman to hold a vice-regal post in Canada, when she is named lieutenant governor of Ontario. On April 30, Albertan Ralph Steinhauer becomes the first native lieutenant governor.

**March 2.** U.S. first-class postage jumps from 8 cents to 10 cents per ounce. The postal service places ads in 323 newspapers to explain the increase.

**April 30.** Presidential authority to impose mandatory wage and price controls (under the Economic Stabilization Act of 1970) expires. Only petroleum prices remain controlled under 1973 legislation.

**May 4.** Expo 74 opens in Spokane, Washington. The first to focus on the environment, the 100-acre exposition was designed for future use as a park. It covers all expenses before closing in October.

**July 12.** A revision of the U.S. budgetary process changes the beginning of the fiscal year from July 1 to October 1 (effective 1976).

**July 16.** Along with 985 men, the U.S. Merchant Marine Academy accepts 15 women, the first female students to attend any of the nation's five service academies.

**July 29.** At the North Philadelphia Church of the Advocate, four bishops defy church law to ordain the first female Episcopalian priests. Next year, the 11 will be joined by 4 women ordained in Washington.

**July 30.** The Quebec National Assembly passes an act making French the official language of the province.

**August 8.** AT&T, the largest private employer in the United States, recommends that subsidiaries ban discrimination against homosexuals in future hiring and in the retention of jobs.

**September 2.** The Employee Retirement Income Security Act sets federal standards for private pension plans and, for those Americans with no coverage, provides a tax deduction for an individual retirement account (IRA).

**September 4.** The United States is the last Western nation to establish formal relations with East Germany. Others extended recognition after the Communist country acceded to the 1971 Berlin pact.

**September 10.** Portuguese Guinea gains independence as Guinea-Bissau. The first European nation to expand overseas, Portugal is the last to surrender its empire.

**September 17.** In Canada, the RCMP accept their first female candidates. The women, who had to meet a 5'4" height requirement rather than 5'8", will receive the same pay as their male counterparts.

**September 20.** Gail Cobb, age 24, is the first female police officer killed in the line of duty. A robbery suspect gunned her down in a Washington underground parking lot.

**October 23.** Congress creates the independent Commodity Futures Trading Commission to strengthen federal regulation.

**October 26.** President Ford signs a bill repealing the Formosa Resolution of 1955, which gave the White House authority to defend Taiwan and the nearby Pescadores.

**November 5.** In Connecticut, Ella Grasso becomes the first woman to win a governorship in her own right (not succeeding her husband).

Elected on the Democratic ticket in San Jose, Janet Gray Hayes is the first woman mayor of a large U.S. city.

---

*Statistics:* Women capture an additional 6 seats in Congress, but with 4 retirements, their number reaches only 18. (The record was 20, in 1963–1964.)

---

**November 18.** Gerald Ford travels to Japan, the first American president to visit that country.

**More news.** The completed Trans-Amazonian Highway—3,340 miles of impacted-earth roads—connects the Pacific and Atlantic coasts of South America.

### Records

**September 1.** Averaging 1,817 mph, USAF pilots James Sullivan and Noel Widdifield set a New York–London speed record of 1 hour, 55 minutes. By refueling over the Atlantic, their SR-71 jet cuts almost three hours off the previous mark.

### Government Departments and Agencies

**May 7.** The oil embargo awakened Washington to the need to consolidate U.S. energy matters. President Nixon signs a bill establishing the Federal Energy Administration (by July 1975) to be responsible for energy planning and regulation.

### New Products and Businesses

Frozen pizzas appear on the market.

---

*Statistics:* The 5-cent chocolate bar of the mid-1950s now costs 15 cents.

---

### Fads

With the end of the protest movement, university and college students turn frivolous. In late January, naked bodies (except for running shoes) dart across campuses in every state. One group of "streakers" sets a record; another group breaks it. Texas Tech claims the longest streak—five hours—and the University of Georgia the largest—1,548 students. Then streakers start to linger, encouraging others to join in the fun. Nonstudents often do. The national craze winds down with the approach of May exams.

# SCIENCE AND TECHNOLOGY

## News

**January.** Comet Kohoutek satisfies astronomers, but the media calls it a "flop." After Czech astronomer Luboš Kohoutek discovered the comet last March, predictions of daylight visibility produced a boom in telescope and binocular sales. But for the most part, city lights and pollution prevented viewing with the naked eye.

**February 22.** A study by the National Academy of Sciences found enormous damage in Vietnam from the chemical herbicides sprayed by the United States during the war. Hill-tribe children died immediately while long-term environmental effects may last up to 100 years. (Some of the 17 scientific members believe the damage was even more extensive than revealed in today's majority report.)

**March 29.** Flying past Venus on February 5, *Mariner 10* used the planet's gravitational field to swing to within 460 miles of Mercury. Today's excellent photos, broadcast on TV, show a moonlike, cratered surface.

After orbiting the sun, *Mariner 10* will pass Mercury twice more (the last time on March 16, 1975). The probe will map almost three eighths of the surface and more precisely measure diameter, mass, and surface temperatures: −280 degrees Fahrenheit on the night side and 370 degrees on the day side.

No further inner-planetary missions are anticipated until the late 1970s.

**April 13.** Following up on the FCC "open skies" policy established in 1972, NASA launches the first satellite owned and operated by U.S. industry. *Westar I* provides voice, data, TV, and Telex transmission services.

**May 29.** Planned Parenthood notifies 700 affiliated clinics to call in all patients using the Dalkon Shield. A. H. Robins has disclosed that 36 women using the IUD suffered septic abortions; 4 of the women died. Although the shield will be implicated in 219 of 287 similar cases, the FDA will simply enforce a six-month moratorium, then requires the manufacturer to keep a registry.

**June 13.** The Center for Disease Control in Atlanta links a rare and fatal liver cancer with polyvinyl chloride, a chemical used in plastic containers. Later this year, the FDA will recall over 50 brands of aerosol products containing vinyl chloride.

**June 25.** After the *Soyuz 11* tragedy in 1971, the Soviets put *Salyut 2* into orbit, but the station broke up less than two weeks later. Today, *Salyut 3* enters orbit above Earth.

Exercising caution, the Soviets wait until July 3 to send up *Soyuz 14* (*12* and *13* carried out short flights last year) and another two days before the docked crew enters the vehicle.

A two-week stay apparently reestablishes the Soviet orbital research program, but *Soyuz 15*, after several approaches in August, fails to dock before returning to Earth.

**July 12.** In the first U.S. legislation of its kind, the National Research Act establishes a committee to monitor the use of human subjects in medical research. A permanent National Advisory Council to be set up in two years will concentrate on research involving live human fetuses, children, prisoners, and the mentally ill along with those who receive brain surgery for behavior control.

**July 15.** In a report before the British Medical Association, Dr. Douglas Bevis reveals the first births from ova fertilized outside the human body. The obstetrician, who learned of his colleagues' work through correspondence, explains that the procedure was developed for women with damaged fallopian tubes. When newspapers dwell on "test-tube" babies, Bevis threatens to abandon his work.

**July 29.** Under an agreement with the FDA, 25 chemical manufacturers must inform the public of fire hazards associated with cellular plastics. Previously, the products were described as nonburning or self-extinguishing.

**September 10.** *The New York Times* reports that biochemist Har Gobind Khorana and his associates have deciphered most and perhaps all of the genetic code. Genes generally remain "turned off," but once turned on, their coded messages tell a cell what to do and what to become. With this discovery, biochemists throughout the world begin to look for the means to countermand genetic diseases such as hemophilia.

**September 10.** Analysis of data from *Pioneer 10* indicates that Jupiter largely consists of liquid hydrogen.

**September 25.** Drs. Michael B. McElroy and Steven C. Wofsy warn against the continued use of freon gases in aerosol cans. The Harvard scientists argue that atmospheric accumulations have already begun to break down the ozone layer, the component of the upper atmosphere that protects the Earth from ultraviolet radiation. Even if freon dispersal stopped today, the ozone layer will be depleted some 5 percent by 1990.

**September 29.** Yesterday, the media reported that Betty Ford had undergone a radical mastectomy for breast cancer. Today, the results of a nationwide study show that the surgical procedure offers no advantage over simple mastectomy or other techniques. The radical mastectomy, which removes the breast, the underlying chest muscle, and the lymph glands extending under the armpit, is used in 95 percent of 90,000 mastectomies carried out each year in the United States. The study also concludes that postoperative chemotherapy drastically reduces the recurrence of cancer, making radiation unnecessary.

**October 25.** An American-French-Ethiopian team led by Drs. Karl Johanson and Maurice Taieb has discovered an early hominid believed to be 1½ million years older than the earliest fossils discovered by the Leakeys. "Lucy" (after the Beatles' tune played around the campfire) is presented as 40-percent complete, but some anthropologists question the mirror-image doubling of some bones on the opposite side of the skeleton.

**November 15.** Xerox ends an FTC monopoly suit by agreeing to license competitors to use its more than 1,700 patents. Wall Street insists the giant corporation, with its current diversification, will nonetheless maintain control of 85 percent of the copier market.

**November 27.** Louis B. Russell, Jr., dies in Richmond at age 49. The longest-surviving heart transplant patient received his new organ in 1967.

**More news.** In response to the enormous rise in gasoline prices, U.S. automakers introduce catalytic converters, higher gear ratios, and other engineering innovations to achieve better mileage. But despite a 13.5-percent increase in efficiency, the best American model still ranks below 12 imported cars.

### Other Discoveries, Developments, and Inventions

Unleaded gasoline
Texas Instruments two-chip slide-rule calculator with algebraic entry for $170

### Obituaries

**James Chadwick** (October 20, 1891–July 24, 1974). The British physicist received the Nobel prize for his discovery of the neutron in 1932. During W.W. II, Chadwick traveled to the United States with other British scientists to work on the atomic bomb.

**Clyde Cowan** (December 6, 1919–May 24, 1974). The American scientist was best known as the codiscoverer of the neutrino.

**Ralph Waldo Gerard** (October 7, 1900–February 17, 1974). His work linked schizophrenia to body chemistry.

**Alfred Mirsky** (October 17, 1900–June 19, 1974). His discovery that all human and animal cells contain the same amount of DNA contributed much to the foundation of molecular biology.

**Paul Stark** (July 20, 1891–October 28, 1974). When the horticulturist received samples of a previously unknown apple, he traveled by train and horse and buggy to a mountainside in West Virginia. The fruit from that single tree were later named Golden Delicious.

## THE ARTS

May 28—*The Magic Show*, with Doug Henning, David Ogden Stiers (still running in 1975)
October 24—*Equus*, with Anthony Hopkins, Peter Firth (still running in 1975)

### Tony Awards

Actor (Dramatic)—Michael Moriarty, *Find Your Way Home*
Actress (Dramatic)—Colleen Dewhurst, *A Moon for the Misbegotten*
Actor (Musical)—Christopher Plummer, *Cyrano*
Actress (Musical)—Virginia Capers, *Raisin*
Play—*The River Niger*
Musical—*Raisin*

### News

**February 9.** With just three hours notice, lyric soprano Kiri Te Kanawa sings the role of Desdemona at the Met. Reviewers widely acclaim the 30-year-old New Zealander's debut performance.

**June 29.** On tour with the Bolshoi, Mikhail Baryshnikov defects in Toronto. Next month, the 26-year-old Soviet dancer partners Natalia Makarova in the United States. In 1975, he will achieve superstar status with cover stories in *Newsweek* and *Time*.

**September 27.** In a controversial purchase, the Australian National Gallery pays $850,000 for Willem de Kooning's *Woman V*, a record price for an American abstract expressionist (21 years ago, the painting sold for $3,000).

Museums around the world have been hit hard by inflation and the current stock-market slump. British museums charge admission for the first time. And the famous Ufizi, in Florence, opens just 20 percent of its galleries on a regular basis.

### Obituaries

**Katharine Cornell** (February 16, 1893–June 9, 1974). By the mid-1920s, Cornell was regarded as one of America's greatest dramatic actresses. She formed a company with her husband Guthrie McClintic; following his death in 1961, Cornell retired.

**Sol Hurok** (April 9, 1888–March 5, 1974). Over a 50-year career, the Russian-born impresario brought 4,000 artists and companies into the United States.

## WORDS

Peter Benchley, *Jaws*
Charles Berlitz, *The Bermuda Triangle*
Carl Bernstein and Bob Woodward, *All the President's Men*
Jacob Bronowski, *The Ascent of Man*
Vincent Bugliusi and Curt Gentry, *Helter Skelter*
Carlos Castaneda, *Tales of Power*
Frederick Forsyth, *The Dogs of War*
James Herriot, *All Things Bright and Beautiful*
John le Carré, *Tinker, Tailor, Soldier, Spy*
James A. Michener, *Centennial*
Anaïs Nin, *The Diary of Anaïs Nin*
Robert M. Pirsig, *Zen and the Art of Motorcycle Maintenance*
Piers Paul Read, *Alive: The Story of the Andes Survivors*
Robert Ringer, *Winning Through Intimidation*
Harold Robbins, *The Pirate*
Sidney Sheldon, *The Other Side of Midnight*
Aleksandr Solzhenitsyn, *The Gulag Archipelago, 1918–1956*
Irving Wallace, *The Fan Club*

### News

**February 13.** In the first political expulsion of a major dissident since 1929, the Kremlin strips writer Aleksandr Solzhenitsyn of his citizenship. Likely, the Soviet regime decided that a trial and further imprisonment would bring international condemnation.

Solzhenitsyn accepts his 1970 Nobel prize in literature at this year's ceremonies. (At the time, fearing Moscow would deny him reentry to the Soviet Union, he accepted in absentia.) The acclaimed writer declares the prize saved him from "being crushed" by persecution. Next year, he will move from Switzerland to the United States.

**March 4.** To feed the American appetite for celebrity news, Time Inc. introduces the weekly magazine *People*. The first cover features actress Mia Farrow.

**May.** The White House version of the Watergate tapes, published jointly by Bantam and *The New York Times*, immediately sells out. The Dell-*Washington Post* edition does just as well.

**June.** With William Peter Blatty, author of *The Exorcist* (1971), as guest speaker, the Seattle University program reads "Commencement Exorcises." His book will sell 11½ million copies by next year.

**June 6.** Chaucer's *Canterbury Tales* (c. 1440) fetches $216,000 at a New York auction, matching the 1966 manuscript record price set by William Caxton's *Ovid*.

**June 25.** Under a 1964 Supreme Court ruling, a public figure must prove deliberate malice to recover damages for libel. Today, in *Gertz v. Welch*, the court narrows that earlier decision, granting the press protection from libel of public figures and officials.

**More news.** With higher credit costs and continuing paper shortages, 1,050 of the country's 1,794 daily newspapers have turned to automated printing (about 500 use the video display terminal). The union battle against advanced technology finally buckles this year, when workers at *The New York Times* and the *New York Daily News* settle for guaranteed job security and incentives for early retirement. Observers expect the agreements to set an industry-wide standard.

• Faced with the same economic squeeze, book publishers trim staff, shorten publication lists, and raise prices ($12.50 for James A. Michener's *Centennial* is a record high for a novel). Just blank pages, Crown Publishers' *The Nothing Book* is the best-selling novelty of the year.

• In their best-seller *All the President's Men*, reporters Carl Bernstein and Bob Woodward reveal how an executive-branch informant—code-named Deep Throat—was instrumental in cracking Watergate. (Editor Howard Simons tied the mystery figure's "deep" background to the hit porno film.) Washington insiders speculate about Deep Throat's

identity, but Woodward has pledged never to reveal his name.

With the reporters' high profile and the public perception that the press "saved" America, journalism schools see a 15 percent rise in enrollment.

• This year, *McCall's* and *Ladies' Home Journal* introduce women's liberation columns.

---

*Statistics*: Sales of mass-market paperbacks have skyrocketed over the past decade, from $85 million to $253 million annually.

---

## Cartoons and Comics

**Spring.** DC Comics launches a *Famous First Edition* series, oversized reprints of the original Batman, Flash, Wonder Woman, Superman, and Captain Marvel comics.

**More news.** Cartoonist George Lichtenstein retires after 42 years, but *Grin and Bear It* continues to carry his byline alongside Fred Wagner's.

• Marvel Comics adapts *Planet of the Apes* and brings out *Deadly Hands of Kung Fu*, the first magazine with original martial arts heroes and film reviews.

---

*Statistics*: Comic book publishers ring up 200 million sales, at 25 cents to $1 per copy.

---

## TIME *Man of the Year*

King Faisal

## New Words and Phrases

cost-effectiveness
expletive deleted [a frequent term in Watergate transcripts]
fringe benefits
-gate (a suffix from Watergate applied to any scandal)
minibus

paranormal (abnormal, supernatural, or meta-
   physical)
petrodollars
recycling (to conserve energy and materials)
robotics
safari lodge (luxury hotels in African nature reserves)
stonewalling
stroking [used by Nixon and aides in the manipu-
   lative sense of supporting or rewarding]

Senate Watergate hearings popularize the
   phrase, "To the best of my recollection, I don't
   remember."

## Obituaries

**Georgette Heyer** (August 16, 1902–July 5, 1974).
The British novelist's popular historical romances
were set in the Regency Period (1811–1820).
   **Walter Lippmann** (September 23, 1889–
December 14, 1974). The respected journalist generally examined all sides of an issue in his widely
syndicated column and some 25 books. Numerous
awards over a long career included two Pulitzers
(1958 and 1962).
   **Jacqueline Susann** (August 20, 1921–
September 21, 1974). Panned by the critics, the
American novelist thought three successive best-
sellers proved her ability: *Valley of the Dolls* (1966;
17 million copies sold), *The Love Machine* (1969),
and *Once Is Not Enough* (1973). She died of cancer.
   **Amy Vanderbilt** (July 22, 1908–December 27,
1974). During her career, the etiquette expert produced a syndicated column, wrote several books,
and hosted radio and TV programs.

# FASHION

## Haute Couture

Other than the odd new touch, such as a profusion
of sweaters under a lightweight cape, collections
simply vary recent lines and popular pieces. With
the current state of the economy, women whole-
heartedly approve of this "wardrobe extension."

## News

**This year.** Yves St. Laurent, with his intertwined
initials stitched on every store-ready product, establishes a menswear division.
   • Soviet black marketeers rake in $90 for an $8
pair of American-made jeans.
   • Fashion observers note an increasing demand
for handmade clothes and accessories. For instance,
enthusiastic retailers snap up Dorothy Bis hand-
knit coats, sweaters, and capes. Recognizing the
trend, women's magazines insert knitting and cro-
cheting patterns for their readers.
   • Giorgio Armani's first collection includes an
unconstructed blazer. Next year, the Italian designer will add women's clothing.

## Colors and Materials

Synthetic shortages, caused by the oil embargo,
   renew interest in natural fibers.
Flowered prints dominate, with smaller patterns
   favored.
Bowing to consumer demands, manufacturers coordinate spring and fall colors.

## Clothes

The fluid line of the last few years softens and
   loosens, with the hem stabilizing at the knee
   or just below.
Spring's floral skirts (to midcalf) and matching
   jackets (with lifted shoulders) yield in the
   summer to scoop-neck T-shirts (belted or
   tucked in) and gathered skirts. For the fall,
   women wear a simply cut dress (with deep
   armholes and few seams) over a blouse or
   sweater.
The layered look gains strength with heavy
   wool skirts (mid- to lower-calf lengths) and
   full-cut blouses under knitted vests or pullovers. A fur-collared sweater substitutes for
   a blazer.
With their lace inserts, drawn-thread work, or
   embroidery, blouses of cheesecloth or un-
   bleached Indian cotton suggest lingerie.

Extending their wardrobes, women bring loungewear out of the bedroom and into the living room for at-home entertaining.

Long denim skirts, flat at the hips, grow in popularity as do printed, frilled cotton skirts, reminiscent of old-time petticoats.

The string bikini is the summer sensation—two triangular pieces, top and bottom, joined by elastic or string ties for $35–$45.

Eleven years after his topless bathing suit, Rudi Gernreich presents a bottomless thong of Lycra. The fanny-revealing creation foretells higher-cut swimwear.

Retailers stock double-breasted suits, but most men opt for patterned jackets and plain trousers. For casual wear, they choose safari or blouson-style jackets (in light tweed, linen, or cotton) and jean suits.

## Accessories

With a caped, full-skirted silhouette, the fitted, zippered boot is abandoned for a sturdier, crushed ankle. Shoe platforms thin down or disappear completely while heels become slimmer and higher.

A flower-trimmed hat and a fringed wool shawl (in an open crochet stitch) complement the longer skirts. Smart autumn accessories include a long, wool scarf and a head-hugging knit or shallow-brimmed hat.

Brightly colored men's ties measure 4–4½ inches in width.

Chic boutiques offer Hawaiian puka shell necklaces—the big jewelry fad of the year—for up to $150.

Silver jewelry approaches the status of gold.

## Hair and Cosmetics

The Gatsby look, carrying over from 1973, focuses on the eyes with black lashes and luminous shadows.

To balance this year's heavier line, long, straight hair gives way to short cuts—even 1920s and 1930s styles. Some women try a complete perm.

## Obituaries

**Anne Klein** (August 3, 1922–March, 1974). The all-American designer garnered international acclaim with her sophisticated casual clothes (generally intended for women 5'4" and under).

# MUSIC

"The Way We Were"—Barbra Streisand

"Seasons in the Sun"—Terry Jacks

"The Streak"—Ray Stevens

"(You're) Having My Baby"—Paul Anka

"TSOP (The Sound of Philadelphia)" (Instr.)—MFSB featuring the Three Degrees

"The Loco-Motion"—Grand Funk

"Kung Fu Fighting"—Carl Douglas

"I Can Help"—Billy Swann

"Billy, Don't Be a Hero"—Bo Donaldson & the Heywoods

"Annie's Song"—John Denver

"Rock Your Baby"—George McCrae

"I Honestly Love You"—Olivia Newton-John

"Can't Get Enough of Your Love Babe"—Barry White

"Bennie & the Jets"—Elton John

"Love's Theme" (Instr.)—Love Unlimited Orchestra

"Then Came You"—Dionne Warwick & Spinners

"Hooked on a Feeling"—Blue Swede

"You Haven't Done Nothin' "—Stevie Wonder

"Nothing from Nothing"—Billy Preston

"Sunshine on My Shoulders"—John Denver

"Angie Baby"—Helen Reddy

"Band on the Run"—Paul McCartney & Wings

"Feel Like Makin' Love"—Roberta Flack

"Rock Me Gently"—Andy Kim

"You're Sixteen"—Ringo Starr

"Dark Lady"—Cher

"You Ain't Seen Nothing Yet"—Bachman-Turner Overdrive (BTO)

"Cat's in the Cradle"—Harry Chapin
"The Night Chicago Died"—Paper Lace
"Sundown"—Gordon Lightfoot
"Whatever Gets You Thru the Night"—John Lennon & the Plastic Ono Nuclear Band
"Rock the Boat"—Hues Corporation
"I Shot the Sheriff"—Eric Clapton
"Dancing Machine"—Jackson 5
"You Make Me Feel Brand New"—Stylistics
"Do It ('Til You're Satisfied)"—B. T. Express
"Boogie Down"—Eddie Kendricks
"You're the First, the Last, My Everything"—Barry White
"Don't Let the Sun Go Down on Me"—Elton John
"When Will I See You Again"—Three Degrees
"Jazzman"—Carole King

## Grammys (1974)

Record of the Year—Olivia Newton-John, "I Honestly Love You"
Song of the Year (songwriter)—Marilyn and Alan Bergman and Marvin Hamlisch, "The Way We Were"
Album of the Year—Stevie Wonder, *Fulfillingness' First Finale*
Best Vocal Performance (Male)—Stevie Wonder, *Fulfillingness' First Finale* (album)
Best Vocal Performance (Female)—Olivia Newton-John, "I Honestly Love You" (single)
Best New Artist—Marvin Hamlisch

## News

**January 4.** Beginning his first concert tour in eight years, Bob Dylan appears in Chicago with the Band.

**April 6.** At California Jam I, the last big rock festival of the early seventies, some 200,000 hear Earth, Wind & Fire, Emerson, Black Sabbath, Deep Purple, Seals & Crofts, and others.

**November 28.** While recording "Whatever Gets You Thru the Night" with John Lennon, Elton John bet the former Beatle the song would reach No. 1. Tonight, Lennon pays off his debt and joins John in concert. Together, they sing the hit single "Lucy in the Sky with Diamonds" and "I Saw Her Standing There." This marks Lennon's last stage appearance.

**More news.** Blaming the oil embargo for the increased cost of vinyl, record companies raise their prices and collect some $2 billion; but for the first time in 30 years, unit sales drop. Insiders point to the absence of a new trend or commanding personality. ("Glitter rock" wanes in 1974 and modernized folk makes up one of the largest minorities.)

---

*Statistics*: The average *Rolling Stone* reader buys six LP's and 27 tapes a year.

---

• An estimated audience of 500 million watches the 1974 Eurovision Song Contest. Britain's representative, Olivia Newton-John, places fourth. Sweden's Abba takes first with the English-language song "Waterloo." (Anni-Frid, Benny, Björn, and Agnetha combined the first letters of their names.) Their song, which climbs to No. 6 on the *Billboard* chart, will sell some 5 million copies worldwide.

• After eight top 20 albums, personal problems forced Jefferson Airplane to take a break. This year, members regroup as Jefferson Starship.

• To amuse his brother Gary, a stutterer, Randy Bachman tapes "You Ain't Seen Nothing Yet." Mercury Records insists BTO include the cut in their album. Bachman finally agrees, but his attempts at rerecording fail to capture the mood. The one-take number becomes the group's first and only No. 1 hit.

• After millions of album sales, Barbra Streisand finally tops the charts with "The Way We Were"—the No. 1 single of the year.

• Between 1955 and 1960, Bill Haley's "Rock Around the Clock" sold an estimated 16 million copies and appeared in 14 different movies. This year, the new TV series "Happy Days" reintroduces the old favorite, and the song reaches No. 39.

• David Clayton-Thomas returns to Blood, Sweat & Tears after a three-year absence. Mick Taylor leaves the Rolling Stones and CW singer-songwriter Dolly Parton ends her six-year partnership with Porter Wagoner.

• The hit "Would You Lay With Me" is sung by 15-year-old Tanya Tucker.

*New Recording Artists*

Abba
Commodores (Lionel Richie)
Earth, Wind & Fire
Hall & Oates
Jefferson Starship
K. C. & the Sunshine Band
Kiss
Barry Manilow

## *Obituaries*

**Duke (Edward Kennedy) Ellington** (April 29, 1899–May 24, 1974). An American musical giant, the pianist, bandleader, and composer was largely self-taught. Nicknamed Duke for his elegant style, the black teenager led his first small jazz band in 1918. After four years at the famous Cotton Club (1927–1930), they became Duke Ellington and his Famous Orchestra.

Over the next two decades, the group played his countless compositions, including "Mood Indigo" (his first big hit), "Don't Get Around Much Anymore," and "Satin Doll." The big-band era waned, but Ellington's royalties kept them alive until an appearance at the 1956 Newport Jazz Festival reestablished his preeminence in American music.

A prolific composer, his more than 6,000 musical pieces included popular songs, symphonies, and sacred music. (He tired of the label "jazz," saying, "There are only two kinds of music: good and bad.") While many works were collaborations, with neither Ellington nor his musicians remembering who did what, his vast body of music made him an incalculable influence on 20th-century jazz.

**Cass Elliot** (February 19, 1943–July 29, 1974). A solo act since the Mamas & the Papas broke up in 1968, the overweight singer suffers a heart attack following a concert in London.

**Dorothy Fields** (July 15, 1905–March 28,

1974). The first woman elected to the Songwriter's Hall of Fame, Fields wrote the lyrics for some 400 songs, 19 Broadway shows, and over a dozen Hollywood musicals. Starting out, she faced indifferent publishers and post-W.W.I attitudes toward working women. (Her comedian father believed, "Ladies don't write lyrics.") Her best-known songs include "I Can't Give You Anything But Love, Baby" (1928), "I'm in the Mood for Love" (1935, an Oscar winner), and "If My Friends Could See Me Now" (1966).

**Ivory Joe Hunter** (October 10, 1914–November 8, 1974). The singer, pianist, and songwriter was one of the first R&B artists to interpret country music. Like many other black artists, Hunter reached a broader audience in the mid-1950s, but his popularity declined through the next decade. He died of lung cancer.

**Tex Ritter** (January 12, 1906–January 2, 1974). His accomplishments covered every field of entertainment—radio, records, Western movies, and TV. Over the years, Ritter placed dozens of singles on the CW charts, but remains best known for "Do Not Forget Me, Oh My Darling," on the soundtrack of *High Noon* (1952), and for his renditions of "You Are My Sunshine" and "Jingle, Jangle, Jingle." He was one of the first inductees to the Country Music Hall of Fame.

**Harry Ruby** (January 27, 1895–February 23, 1974). A leading popular composer through the 1930s, Ruby wrote little after his chief collaborator, lyricist Bert Kalmar, died in 1947. Ruby's best-known songs include "Who's Sorry Now" (1923).

**Tim Spencer** (July 7, 1908–April 27, 1974). Spencer, Bob Nolan, and Leonard Slye formed the Sons of the Pioneers, a leading Western group. Slye became Roy Rogers while Spencer remained with the group until 1950, then managed new personnel for another five years.

## MOVIES

*The Apprenticeship of Duddy Kravitz* (Canadian, d. Ted Kotcheff; color)—Richard Dreyfuss, Micheline Lanctot, Jack Warden

*Benji* (d. Joe Camp; color)—Higgins as Benji, Cynthia Smith, Allen Fiuzat, Peter Breck

*Blazing Saddles* (d. Mel Brooks; color)—Cleavon Little, Gene Wilder, Slim Pickens, Harvey Korman, Madeline Kahn

*Chinatown* (d. Roman Polanski; color)—Jack Nicholson, Faye Dunaway, John Huston

*The Conversation* (d. Francis Ford Coppola; color)—Gene Hackman, John Cazale

*Death Wish* (d. Michael Winner; color)— Charles Bronson, Hope Lange, Vincent Gardenia

*The Godfather, Part II* (d. Francis Ford Coppola; color)—Al Pacino, Robert Duvall, Diane Keaton, Robert De Niro, Marlon Brando

*Harry and Tonto* (d. Paul Mazursky; color)—Art Carney, Ellen Burstyn, Chief Dan George, Geraldine Fitzgerald

*Lenny* (d. Bob Fosse; bw)—Dustin Hoffman, Valerie Perrine

*The Longest Yard* (d. Robert Aldrich; color)— Burt Reynolds, Eddie Albert, Ed Lauter

*Murder on the Orient Express* (British, d. Sidney Lumet; color)—Albert Finney, Ingrid Bergman, Lauren Bacall, Wendy Hiller, Sean Connery, Vanessa Redgrave, Michael York

*The Parallax View* (d. Alan J. Pakula; color)— Warren Beatty, Paula Prentiss

*Stardust* (British, d. Michael Apted; color)— David Essex, Adam Faith, Larry Hagman

*The Sugarland Express* (d. Steven Spielberg; color)—Goldie Hawn, Ben Johnson, Michael Sacks, William Atherton

*The Taking of Pelham One Two Three* (d. Joseph Sargent; color)—Walter Matthau, Robert Shaw, Martin Balsam

*The Texas Chainsaw Massacre* (d. Tobe Hooper; color)—Marilyn Burns, Allen Danziger, Paul A. Partain, William Vail

*That's Entertainment!* (d. Jack Haley, Jr.; color and bw)—Hosts include Fred Astaire, Bing Crosby, James Stewart

*The Three Musketeers* (d. Richard Lester; color)—Oliver Reed, Raquel Welch, Richard Chamberlain, Michael York, Frank Finlay

*Thunderbolt and Lightfoot* (d. Michael Cimino; color)—Clint Eastwood, Jeff Bridges, George Kennedy

*Young Frankenstein* (d. Mel Brooks; bw)—Gene Wilder, Peter Boyle, Marty Feldman, Teri Garr, Madeline Kahn, Cloris Leachman

### Academy Awards

**April 2.** Oscar's hosts include John Huston, Diana Ross, Burt Reynolds, and David Niven.

> Best Picture—*The Sting*
> Best Actor—Jack Lemmon (*Save the Tiger*)
> Best Actress—Glenda Jackson (*A Touch of Class*)
> Best Director—George Roy Hill (*The Sting*)
> Best Supporting Actor—John Houseman (*The Paper Chase*)
> Best Supporting Actress—Tatum O'Neal (*Paper Moon*)
> Best Song—"The Way We Were," from the film of the same name
> Best Foreign Film—*Day for Night* (French)
> Honorary Award—Groucho Marx

When a naked man streaks across the stage behind David Niven, the actor quips, "Isn't it fascinating to think that probably the only laugh that man will ever get in his life is by stripping off his clothes and showing his shortcomings."

Three-time Oscar winner Katharine Hepburn makes her very first appearance at the Academy Awards to present her friend producer Lawrence Weingarten with the Thalberg Award. She tells the audience, "I'm so glad no one called out, 'It's about time!'" Hepburn delights the audience but outrages organizers by wearing a black Mao-style pantsuit rather than a glamorous evening gown.

At age 10, Tatum O'Neal becomes the youngest performer to win an Oscar. First-choice Linda Blair lost out when the industry learned veteran actress Mercedes McCambridge created Blair's demonic voice-over in *The Exorcist*, but received no official credit.

### News

**March 4.** *Newsweek* describes women movie stars as an endangered species. In 1934, 6 of the top 10 box-office attractions were female: Janet Gaynor, Joan Crawford, Mae West, Marie Dressler, Norma Shearer, and Shirley Temple. Today, one woman makes the list: Barbra Streisand.

Male speaking parts outnumber female parts 12 to 1. The few women's roles available usually support the male star—neurotic wife, girlfriend, prostitute, or kook, all losers or victims. And actresses see little possibility for change. Only 8 of 3,068 guild producers are women, only 23 of 2,366 directors, and 148 of 2,976 writers.

**March 13.** The American Film Institute honors actor James Cagney with its Lifetime Achievement Award.

**June 24.** Author Peter Benchley received $1 million for the movie rights to *Jaws*, yet director Steven Spielberg found the characters totally unsympathetic. "He put them in a situation where you were rooting for the shark to eat the people—in alphabetical order."

But after script rewrites, the director promises *Newsweek*, "It's a horror film that's going to tear your guts out. *The Exorcist* made you vomit, and this film will make you clutch your hands to your armpits."

**June 26.** A Swiss court awards Elizabeth Taylor a divorce from Richard Burton on the grounds of incompatibility. The couple will remarry next year in Botswana.

**More news.** Courts find lawyer Jerome Rosenthal liable for losses sustained by Doris Day while her finances were in his keeping; with interest and punitive damages, the verdict amounts to $22.8 million. He plans to appeal.

When Day's husband of 17 years, Marty Melcher, died in 1968, Rosenthal laid claim to 50 percent of her remaining funds. The actress then discovered that the Beverly Hills lawyer had invested $20 million of her lifetime earnings in shady deals.

• Movie fans note a growing number of actors promoting commercial products and services: Orson Welles plugs Eastern Airlines, Burgess Meredith supports United, Lee J. Cobb pushes Pan Am. The actors receive scale pay of $118 per day, but residuals push their salaries as high as $100,000. For a film role, actors receive about $250,000.

In response to changing audience tastes during the past 20 years, motion picture producers have cut the number of Westerns from 21.4 percent of total releases to 1.1 percent. Romance movies have fared little better, dropping from 19.8 percent to 2.9 percent, and musicals are down from 9.3 percent to 5.3 percent. According to the industry, moviegoers of the 1970s prefer sex films (up from 0 percent in 1954 to 17.7 percent, but with pornographic movies accounting for some of the increase), crime pictures (17.1 percent to 31.6 percent), and movies centering on black Americans (0 percent to 13.9 percent, but this total will prove to be the peak for this category).

• Genres on the rise include horror movies, concert films (usually rock festivals), and disaster movies modeled after *Airport* (1970).

The story of a 1957 Brooklyn gang, *Lords of Flatbush* introduces several young unknowns to American audiences: Sylvester Stallone, in his leading-man debut, Henry Winkler, Ray Sharkey, and Armand Assante.

• Warner Bros., with rights to the novel *The Tower*, and 20th Century-Fox, with rights to *The Glass Inferno*, agree to a collaboration, *The Towering Inferno*. Irwin Allen, producer of the box-office hit *The Poseidon Adventure*, gathers together a blockbuster cast—Steve McQueen, Paul Newman, William Holden, Faye Dunaway, Fred Astaire, Susan Blakely, Richard Chamberlain, Jennifer Jones, and Robert Wagner. Moviegoers flock to see the disaster film.

| *Top Box Office Stars* | *Newcomers* |
|---|---|
| Robert Redford | Valerie Perrine |
| Clint Eastwood | Richard Dreyfuss |
| Paul Newman | Randy Quaid |
| Barbra Streisand | Deborah Raffin |
| Steve McQueen | Joseph Bottoms |
| Burt Reynolds | Ron Howard |
| Charles Bronson | Sam Waterston |
| Jack Nicholson | Linda Blair |
| Al Pacino | Keith Carradine |
| John Wayne | Steven Warner |

## Top Money-Maker of the Year

*The Sting*

## Obituaries

**Bud Abbott** (October 2, 1895–April 24, 1974). The straight man in the Abbott and Costello comedy team split with his partner in 1957, two years before Costello's death. A gold record of their classic "Who's on First?" routine remains on permanent display at the National Baseball Hall of Fame.

**Walter Brennan** (July 25, 1894–September 21, 1974). The character actor began playing a toothless, cantankerous old man after losing his teeth at age 38. His 50-year career brought him a record three best-supporting Oscars: *Come and Get It* (1936), *Kentucky* (1938), and *The Westerner* (1940). More recently, Brennan starred in the TV series "The Real McCoys."

**Johnny Mack Brown** (September 1, 1904–November 14, 1974). In 1926 probably the first athlete to turn to movies, the good-looking All-American football player became one of Hollywood's top Western stars by the 1940s.

**Vittorio De Sica** (July 7, 1901–November 13, 1974). De Sica the actor appeared in more than 150 Italian movies. The director leaves a rich legacy of 25 films (1940–1974), including foreign-language Oscar winners *Shoeshine* (1947), *The Bicycle Thief* (1949), *Yesterday, Today and Tomorrow* (1964), and *The Garden of the Finzi-Continis* (1971).

**Samuel Goldwyn** (August 27, 1882–January 31, 1974). The pioneer filmmaker collaborated on one of Hollywood's first films, *The Squaw Man* (1914), then formed Goldwyn pictures with Edgar Selwyn and others. When their failed company merged with Metro and Mayer in 1923, the former Samuel Goldfish established Samuel Goldwyn Productions. (Apparently the public's confusion between his company and MGM tickled him.) His films included *Wuthering Heights* (1939), *The Best Years of Our Lives* (1946), and *Guys and Dolls* (1955).

**Agnes Moorehead** (December 6, 1906–April 30, 1974). Although the stage and radio actress won five Oscar nominations during her career, a younger TV generation will likely remember her as the witch Endora on the series "Bewitched."

# TELEVISION AND RADIO

## New Prime-Time TV Programs

"Chico and the Man" (September 13, 1974–  ; Situation Comedy)—Jack Albertson, Freddie Prinze, Scatman Crothers

"Good Times" (February 1, 1974–  ; Situation Comedy)—Esther Rolle, John Amos, Jimmie Walker

"Happy Days" (January 15, 1974–  ; Situation Comedy)—Ron Howard, Henry Winkler, Tom Bosley, Marion Ross, Anson Williams, Donny Most, Erin Moran

"Harry-O" (September 12, 1974– ; Detective)—David Janssen, Henry Darrow (1974–1975), Anthony Zerbe (1975–  )

"Little House on the Prairie" (September 11, 1974–  ; Adventure/Drama)—Michael Landon, Karen Grassle, Melissa Gilbert, Melissa Sue Anderson

"Police Woman" (September 13, 1974–  ; Police Drama)—Angie Dickinson, Earl Holliman, Ed Bernard

"Rhoda" (September 9, 1974–  ; Situation Comedy)—Valerie Harper, Julie Kavner, David Groh, Lorenzo Music (Carlton the Doorman)

"The Rockford Files" (September 13, 1974–  ; Detective)—James Garner, Noah Beery, Joe Santos

"The Six Million Dollar Man" (January 18, 1974–  ; Adventure)—Lee Majors, Richard Anderson

"Tony Orlando and Dawn" (July 3, 1974–  ; Musical Variety)—Tony Orlando, Telma Hopkins, Joyce Vincent Wilson

## Emmy Awards 1973–1974 (May 28, 1974)

Drama Series—"Upstairs, Downstairs" ("Masterpiece Theatre," PBS)

Music/Variety Series—"The Carol Burnett Show" (CBS)

Comedy Series—"M*A*S*H" (CBS)

Best Actor in a Series—Telly Savalas ("Kojak," CBS)

Best Actress in a Series—Michael Learned ("The Waltons," CBS)

Best Comedian in a Series—Alan Alda ("M*A*S*H," CBS)

Best Comedienne in a Series—Mary Tyler Moore ("The Mary Tyler Moore Show," CBS)

## News

**January 6.** "The CBS Radio Mystery Theatre" is an ambitious attempt to revitalize radio drama. Starting today, E. G. Marshall hosts daily dramas of the macabre. Some affiliates refuse to carry the 60-minute program while others broadcast it late in the evening.

**January 27.** Forty years old in the first episode, actor Raymond Burr is nearly 57 as "Perry Mason" ends today. In all those years the lawyer lost just one case, when his client refused to disclose the evidence that would save her. Mason discovered the culprit later anyway.

**January 31.** CBS presents a dramatic adaptation of "The Autobiography of Miss Jane Pittman." Cicely Tyson portrays the main character through 110 years of black American history. The highly praised special will win nine Emmys.

**Spring.** ABC drops 10 prime-time programs and NBC clears out half, supposedly because a Senate communications subcommittee found that TV gun and fist fights have a disturbing influence on viewers. Whether social conscience or low ratings prompted the cancellations, viewers react negatively to the fall lineup.

**April 29.** During his televised speech President Nixon shows TV viewers a stack of notebook transcripts from the White House tapes. All three networks present oral readings of pertinent excerpts.

**May 17.** KNX-TV carries a two-hour live broadcast of the shoot-out between the SLA and the Los Angeles Police Department.

**May 31.** A leader through the early years of radio

and television, RCA pulls out of manufacturing, as Japanese imports corner the market.

**July 4.** CBS launches the "Bicentennial Minute." Each night over the next two years, a celebrity will describe an event in American history on that day 200 years ago.

**July 15.** In Sarasota, Florida, Chris Chubbuck interrupts her reading of the news on the A.M. show "Suncoast Digest." She says, "In keeping with Channel 40's policy of bringing you the latest in blood and guts, and in living color, you are going to see another first—attempted suicide." Chubbuck pulls out a .38 revolver and shoots herself in the head. She succeeds.

**September 2.** After 21 years on CBS sitcoms, Lucille Ball retires from the weekly grind.

**September 9.** A "Mary Tyler Moore" spin-off, "Rhoda" offers viewers a character they know and like. That built-in appeal brings the premiere a No. 1 rating—the first ever by a debut episode. Then, on October 28, "Rhoda's wedding" becomes the top-rated one-hour special of the season.

**September 13.** While not a Norman Lear series, "Chico and the Man" demonstrates the established strength of ethnic humor in the mid-1970s. Jack Albertson portrays Ed Brown, the owner of an East Los Angeles garage, and Freddie Prinze plays his Chicano assistant.

**September 13.** Another new NBC series is "The Rockford Files." Reminiscent of his "Maverick" character, James Garner plays ex-con private investigator Jim Rockford. The program quickly draws an audience, while more violent crime shows, such as "Police Woman," need a full season to gather a following.

**Fall.** A few public television stations broadcast the British comedy series "Monty Python's Flying Circus." By mid-1975, the group's irreverent brand of humor will be carried on 120 stations.

**More news.** A 1938 Gallup poll of American leisure pursuits found 21 percent chose reading, 17 percent movies, and 9 percent radio. By 1960, TV accounted for 28 percent, reading dropped to 10 percent, movies to 6 percent, and radio fell off the chart. TV continues to hold on to No. 1, but the others have begun to recover—9 percent of respondents in 1974 choose movies, 14 percent reading, and 5 percent radio.

• During the oil crisis, truckers used their citizens band (CB) radios to keep up-to-date on gas sources and police whereabouts on the highway. Average Americans take to the idea this year and some 2 million file for a license. (In the last 15 years, a total of 1 million have been granted.) With the growing demand, the FCC opens up 23 two-way radio channels. By mid-decade, interest evolves into a fad with CB lingo, magazines, bumper stickers, lighters, and other merchandise.

## TV Commercials

Beautymist Panty Hose—A camera passes lovingly along a pair of shapely legs, reaches the body, and finds—Joe Namath? "Was that *really* Joe Namath wearing pantyhose?" Johnny Carson asks.

The Hartford—Deciding to personalize a symbol used since the 19th century, the insurance company introduces Laurence the stag to TV audiences.

Hertz—O. J. Simpson races through an airport terminal hurtling over suitcases and anything else in his way, to demonstrate Hertz's speed of service.

Wella—Looking for the continuity of a single model, the beauty products company chooses Farrah Fawcett.

## Obituaries

**Cliff Arquette** (December 28, 1905–September 23, 1974). As Charley Weaver, the entertainer told his anecdotes on a variety of radio and TV programs, including "Hollywood Squares."

**Jack Benny** (February 14, 1894–December 26, 1974). His vaudeville career took a different turn after an appearance on Ed Sullivan's radio show in 1932. Benny soon had a program of his own and, through the 1940s, was one of the biggest stars on the air. In the 1950s, still 39 years old and miserly, the comedian used his uncanny timing and delivery to draw even more laughs on the television

screen. Although he played the violin well, Benny screeched through many pieces to raise money for charity.

**Chet Huntley** (December 10, 1911–March 20, 1974). The newscaster teamed with David Brinkley on NBC from 1956 to 1970, when he retired.

**Frank McGee** (September 12, 1921–April 17, 1974). The newscaster hosted the award-winning "Today" show on NBC.

**Ed Sullivan** (September 28, 1901–October 13, 1974). To imitate Ole Stoneface, simply look serious, clasp your elbows, and say, "We have a reee-allly big shee-ee-ew for you tonight!" Yet that recognition factor says much about his place in American culture. A Broadway and Hollywood columnist until his death, Sullivan won fame with an uncanny knack for finding the best and brightest of international talent for his TV variety show. Every Sunday night for 23 years he gave viewers across the country ballet dancers, opera singers, jugglers, rock groups, famous actors, and news personalities.

# SPORTS

## Winners

### Baseball

World Series—Oakland Athletics (AL), 4 games; Los Angeles Dodgers (NL), 1 game

Player of the Year—Jeff Burroughs (Texas Rangers, AL); Steve Garvey (Los Angeles Dodgers, NL)

Rookie of the Year—Mike Hargrove (Texas Rangers, AL); Bake McBride (St. Louis Cardinals, NL)

### Football

NFC Championship—Minnesota Vikings 14, Los Angeles Rams 10

AFC Championship—Pittsburgh Steelers 24, Oakland Raiders 13

Super Bowl IX (January 12, 1975)—Pittsburgh Steelers 16, Minnesota Vikings 6

College Bowls (January 1, 1974)—
Rose Bowl, Ohio State 42, USC 21

Cotton Bowl, Nebraska 19, Texas 3
Orange Bowl, Penn State 16, LSU 9
Sugar Bowl, Notre Dame 24, Alabama 23
Heisman Trophy—Archie Griffin (Ohio State, TB)
Grey Cup—Montreal Alouettes 20, Edmonton Eskimos 7

## Basketball

NBA Championship—Boston Celtics, 4 games; Milwaukee Bucks, 3 games
MVP of the Year—Kareem Abdul-Jabbar (Milwaukee Bucks)
Rookie of the Year—Ernie Regorio (Buffalo Braves)
NCAA Championship—North Carolina State 76, Marquette 64

## Tennis

U.S. Open—Men, Jimmy Connors (vs. Ken Rosewall); Women, Billie Jean King (vs. Evonne Goolagong)
Wimbledon—Men, Jimmy Connors (vs. Ken Rosewall); Women, Chris Evert (vs. Olga Morozova)

## Golf

Masters—Gary Player
U.S. Open—Hale Irwin
British Open—Gary Player

## Hockey

Stanley Cup—Philadelphia Flyers, 4 games; Boston Bruins, 2 games

## Ice Skating

World Championship—Men, Jan Hoffmann (East Germany); Women, Christine Errath (East Germany)
U.S. National—Men, Gordon McKellen; Women, Dorothy Hamill
Canadian National—Men, Toller Cranston; Women, Lynn Nightingale

## Kentucky Derby

Cannonade—Angel Cordero, Jr., jockey

## Athlete of the Year

Male—Muhammad Ali (Boxing)
Female—Chris Evert (Tennis)

## Last Season

Bobby Bell (Football)
Dave DeBusschere (Basketball)
Alex Delvecchio (Hockey)
David (Deacon) Jones (Football)
Al Kaline (Baseball)
Frank Mahovlich (Hockey)
Willis Reed (Basketball)
Oscar Robertson (Basketball)
(Lorne) Gump Worsley (Hockey)

## News

**February 17.** At the last minute, promoters shift a soccer match between the Egyptian National team and a visiting Czechoslovakian team from a 100,000-seat stadium to a smaller 45,000-seat facility for "the comfort of the spectators." Nearly 80,000 turn up. In the ensuing stampede and riot, 47 people die.

**February 19.** The NHL and WHA end their 18-month feud with an out-of-court settlement. The NHL agrees to pay the WHA $1.75 million and to provide greater access to NHL arenas; the WHA, in turn, drops its antitrust suit. Joint terms include the recognition of the other's player contracts.

Forced to look further afield for talent, both leagues send scouts to Europe. The Maple Leafs recruit Borje Salming, one of Sweden's top defensemen, while the Winnipeg Jets put Swedes Anders Hedberg and Ulf Nilsson on a line with superstar Bobby Hull.

**March 23.** A Nielsen survey printed in *The New York Times* breaks down recreational sports in the United States: 107.9 million Americans swim, 65.6 million bicycle, 61.2 million fish, 54.4 million camp, 38.2 million bowl, and so on down the line.

A Harris survey on spectator sports reveals that only tennis and horse racing show increased interest.

**April 8.** Hank Aaron finished the 1973 baseball season just one home run shy of Babe Ruth's all-time record of 714 HR. On opening day this season, Aaron tied the record with his second at bat. He sat out the next game to appear before hometown fans today in Atlanta.

*Hank Aaron breaks Babe Ruth's longstanding record with his 715th home run.*

With his first swing, the 40-year-old power-hitter slams Al Downing's pitch out of left field. Fans cheer wildly as Aaron jogs around the bases and Dodger Tom House, who easily caught the ball in the bull pen, brings it in.

At the end of the season, Aaron signs a two-year DH contract with the Milwaukee Brewers.

**April 21.** Lee Elder is the first black professional golfer to appear in the Masters. His win in the Monsanto Open gave him automatic eligibility.

**April 25.** In the most sweeping changes in 41 years, NFL owners introduce several new rules, including 15-minute sudden-death for tied games; goal posts moved to the back of the end zone; kickoff pushed back 15 yards to the 35-yard line; ball placement, following a missed field goal, at the line of scrimmage or 20-yard line, whichever is further out; no below-the-knee blocking against wide receivers.

**May 19.** The Philadelphia Flyers, with a 1–0 victory in the sixth game of the series, become the first expansion team to win the Stanley Cup. Fans praise goalie Bernie Parent, but critics point to the team's staggering accumulation of 1,756 penalty minutes over the past season—600 more than the next most-penalized team. Speaking for his "Broad Street Bullies," Captain Bobby Clarke says, "We take the most direct route to the puck and we arrive in ill humor."

**June 4.** Seattle pays $16 million for an NFL franchise; Tampa joined earlier this year. In the coming season, most NFL tickets will cost $10–$12.

**June 4.** In one of the most harebrained promotion stunts in the history of baseball, the Cleveland Indians offer beer at 10 cents a cup. By the seventh inning, flying cups, fireworks, and smoke bombs force Texas pitchers to retreat from the bull pen to the dugout. In the bottom of the ninth—after 60,000 beers—inebriated fans jump into right field and head straight for Texas Ranger Jeff Burroughs. Both benches clear to help the hapless target. When one of the umpires comes under attack, officials award the game to the Rangers with a 9–0 score. Ironically, when the fans took control, their team had a potential winning run on third base (the game was tied, 5–5).

**August 28.** Moses Malone is the first basketball player to go straight from high school to a pro team. He had agreed to attend Maryland, but the Utah Stars' $150,000 salary offer proved irresistible. (The ABA team adds a $30,000 bonus for each year of college courses completed off season.) Next year, the Philadelphia 76ers will sign the NBA's first high school player, Darryl Dawkins, for a reported $1 million.

**September 8.** In a highly publicized event, Evel Knievel and his Sky-Cycle X-2 fall to the bottom of Snake River Canyon. America's best-known stunt-man had hoped to rocket across the 1,600-foot-wide canyon, but his tail chute opened prematurely. Knievel escapes with cuts and scrapes.

**October 30.** Muhammad Ali KO's heavyweight champion George Foreman in the eighth round of their bout in Kinshasa, Zaire. The second boxer to regain the heavyweight title (Floyd Patterson was the first), Ali never lost his in the ring.

**November 27.** Last August, George Steinbren-ner pled guilty to making illegal contributions to Richard Nixon's campaign and received a $15,000 fine. Today, in a 12-page ruling, baseball commis-sioner Bowie Kuhn declares the principal owner of the New York Yankees "ineligible and incompetent" and denies him the right to associate with major league clubs or their personnel.

**December 26.** Last year in Michigan, a 12-year-old center fielder who had beat out all others was denied the position on the team because she was a girl. Detroit courts claimed a lack of jurisdiction over Little League, but her lawsuit generated a num-ber of similar actions.

In June of this year, after most teams had picked their players, Little League headquarters an-nounced that girls could play, but any decisions would be made at the local level. Today, President Ford signs legislation guaranteeing girls that right.

**December 31.** Following an intense bidding war, Jim "Catfish" Hunter signs with the New York Yan-kees for an estimated $3.75 million over five years. (The ace pitcher was declared a free agent when Oakland A's owner Charles O. Finley defaulted on his contract.) Many believe Hunter's multimillion-dollar deal will open the floodgates for other players.

**More news.** The 12-team World Football League (WFL) ran up an enormous $10-million debt in its first season. Payrolls were missed, uniforms and equipment confiscated, two franchises failed, and two were forced to move. Still, most teams intend to hang on until some 60 NFL players can legally switch leagues in 1975.

• Tennis stars Chris Evert and Jimmy Connors titillate the American public with their on-and-off romance. Connors loses just four matches this year, while Evert wins 15 tournaments, including Wim-bledon. In April 1975, the two will announce the end of their relationship.

• Since 1967, the NHL has expanded from 6 to 16 teams. With the addition of Kansas and Wash-ington this year, the league realigns into two confer-ences of nine teams each: the Prince of Wales with the Norris and Adams Divisions and the Clarence Campbell Conference with the Smythe and Patrick Divisions. The schedule expands to 80 games.

## Records

**January 19.** A 71–70 loss to Notre Dame brings the UCLA basketball team back to earth after 88 consecutive wins. On March 25, North Carolina ends UCLA's string of 38 tournament wins and 7 straight NCAA championships. (North Carolina lost only once during the season—to UCLA.)

**August 20.** Nolan Ryan breaks Bob Feller's 28-year record of 98.6 mph with a 100.9-mph pitch. Ryan, who believes scientific scrutiny hurts his con-centration, strikes out 19 batters in the same game, against the Tigers.

**September 10.** In a home game against the Phil-lies, 35-year-old Cardinal Lou Brock breaks Maury Wills' major league record of 104 stolen bases. He finishes the year with 118.

**September 12–13.** The St. Louis Cardinals beat the New York Mets 4–3 in the longest night game in major league history—25 innings. Quitting time at Shea Stadium: 3:13 A.M.

## What They Said

When he was general manager of the struggling Houston Oilers, John Breen said, "We were tipping off our plays. Whenever we broke from the huddle, three backs were laughing and one was pale as a ghost."
—*Sports Illustrated*, January 7

## Obituaries

**James Braddock** (December 6, 1905–November 29, 1974). On June 13, 1935, the U.S. boxer upset heavyweight champion Max Baer in a unanimous decision. Two years later, in the first defense of his title, Braddock was knocked out by Joe Louis.

**(Jay Hanna) Dizzy Dean** (January 16, 1911–July 17, 1974). Dean pitched just six full seasons, between 1932 and 1941, but his crazy antics on and off the field made him a legend in his own time. Unfortunately, the 1934 MVP and four-time All-Star hurt his pitching arm when he returned to the mound too soon from a broken toe. The Cardinals traded him to the Cubs in 1938 and he had to retire three years later. In 1950, Dean began broadcasting the "Game of the Week." Despite, or perhaps because of, his butchered English, he remained a TV favorite for more than 20 years.

**(Miles Gilbert) Tim Horton** (January 12, 1930–February 21, 1974). The six-time All-Star defenseman played for the Toronto Maple Leafs from 1952 to 1970. While incredibly strong, Horton averaged just one minor penalty every two games and remained one of hockey's most popular players. He died in a single-vehicle accident.

**Agnes Geraghty McAndrews** (1907–March 1, 1974). In 1925, three years after she learned how to swim, the young American set 32 swimming records in Athletic Union competition.

**Hazel Hotchkiss Wightman** (December 20, 1886–December 5, 1974). The top U.S. female tennis player through the W.W.I era, Wightman won 45 national championships. In 1919, she donated a trophy for women's international team competition. The United States and Britain began competing for the Wightman Cup four years later.

# *1975*

---

In 1975, the world closes a number of chapters. Israel and Egypt sign an accord and the Suez Canal reopens after eight years. Portugal leaves Angola, ending colonial rule in Africa. Francisco Franco and Chiang Kai-shek, the last of the old guard, die.

At the same time, lesser and greater events signal trends for the future. Civil war breaks out in Lebanon, the United Nations resolves that Zionism is a form of racism, and the Khmer Rouge march into Phnom Penh. Indira Gandhi assumes emergency powers in India and Margaret Thatcher takes over as leader of the British Conservatives. And the world population, which doubled from 1 billion to 2 billion between 1800 and 1940, has since doubled again to 4 billion.

Americans withdraw from Saigon just hours before the North Vietnamese enter the city. With the Helsinki Agreement, Washington recognizes post–W.W.II Communist satellite nations. At home, the courts convict the Watergate defendants, the HUAC is shut down, and congressional investigations of the FBI and CIA uncover abuses of power. Jimmy Hoffa disappears and authorities arrest Patty Hearst. The FDA finally recognizes the dangers attached to the Pill and the Apollo space program ends with an international mission.

In new beginnings, legislation expands minority voting rights and admits women to the Armed Forces. Bicentennial celebrations commence. NASA launches a Viking craft and the first personal computers appear on the market. The long dormant Mt. Baker volcano vents steam and gases. U.S. airlines introduce no-frills fares. And the New York Yankees hire Billy Martin.

Yet, shattered by the agony of Vietnam and the presidential crisis, and suffering under continued high unemployment, most Americans face the second half of the decade with uncertainty and a renewed sense of isolation.

## NEWS

**January 1.** In the Watergate cover-up trial, the jury convicts the four defendants on all counts. In February, Judge John Sirica sentences former attorney general John Mitchell, and former presidential aides H. R. Haldeman and John Ehrlichman, to 2½ years to 8 years and former assistant attorney general Robert Mardian to 10 months to 3 years.

In May, former secretary of commerce Maurice

Stans pleads guilty to five misdemeanor violations of federal campaign laws and receives a fine of $5,000. Former attorney general Richard G. Kleindienst receives a suspended sentence for withholding information, and former secretary of the treasury John B. Connally, Jr., is acquitted of bribery charges.

Sirica orders the release of John Dean, Herbert Kalmbach, and Jeb Magruder on January 8, reducing their sentences to time served. All three had testified as prosecution witnesses.

**January 16.** A six-member jury awards $12 million in damages to 1,200 people arrested during the May 5, 1971, antiwar demonstration in Washington, D.C., finding the arrests improper, the punishment cruel, and the government prosecution malicious.

Reportedly, the verdict marks the first damages for the violation of constitutional rather than civil rights. And the *Los Angeles Times* describes the case as the largest civil suit not involving a corporation.

The police retain the fingerprints and photographs of those arrested.

**January 16.** With 75 freshmen entering the House, the Democrats successfully challenge the congressional seniority system. In a stunning vote, the party ousts the heads of the Agricultural, Armed Services, and Banking and Currency committees—the first time since 1925 that a majority party has unseated more than one chairperson at a time.

**January 22.** President Ford signs the 1925 Geneva Protocol banning chemical and biological weapons, and the 1972 Geneva Agreement barring the production and stockpiling of toxic weapons. The last major power to sign, the United States had stalled until the United Nations reached a compromise on the use of tear gas and herbicides. Still, the accords fail to provide a system for verification.

**February 3.** President Ford submits a $349.4-billion budget for fiscal 1976 with a $51.9-billion deficit. He forecasts a deep recession, high inflation, and the highest unemployment rate in 25 years explaining the largest peacetime deficit in U.S. history.

**February 5.** Ignoring opposition from the Oval Office, Congress responds to the continuing stalemate in Cyprus by cutting off military aid to Turkey. But Turkey refuses to knuckle under, and on February 13, Turkish Cypriots establish a separate state in the northern half of the island, forcing some 200,000 Greek Cypriots to flee.

**February 28.** A six-coach London subway train speeds through Moorgate station and hits the end wall at 40 mph. The second car telescopes the first, while the third rides over the top of the others. Only the unusually high 16-foot tunnel roof prevents further compression and a greater loss of life. Altogether, 43 people die. An inquiry determines the cause was either mechanical failure or a deliberate act by the driver, who was killed.

**March 22.** Using a candle to locate air leaks, two technicians ignite insulated cables at Brown's Ferry nuclear reactor near Decatur, Alabama. When the flames burn through to electrical strands, plant safety devices shut down and the water coolant over the reactor core drops dangerously low. Fire fighters battle the blaze with chemicals for seven hours before reluctant officials authorize the use of water to prevent meltdown.

The near disaster closes the world's largest nuclear reactor for months. A sprinkler system is installed and the NRC demands expensive design changes at other power plants. In later air-leak checks, technicians will use a feather.

---

*Statistics:* At the end of May, 175 nuclear plants are operating worldwide.

---

**March 25.** King Faisal of Saudi Arabia is assassinated. Middle East experts concede that the 70-year-old Faisal, who succeeded to the throne in 1964, had modernized his desert nation and pushed it to a position of eminence among the Arab states.

His half-brother Crown Prince Khalid ascends the throne. The assassin, a playboy nephew with a history of mental illness, is beheaded next month.

**March 30.** On the 13th, the North Vietnamese gained control of the capital of Dar Lac province, at the southern limits of the strategic Central High-

*Desperate South Vietnamese try to board the last American consulate helicopter out of Nha Trang on April 2. All other escape routes from the city are closed.*

lands. Government troops, ordered to retreat from the "indefensible" mountain region, fled to the coast, abandoning more than $1 billion worth of U.S. weapons and equipment along the way.

Sweeping down the coastline, the Communists today take Da Nang, the second largest city in South Vietnam. By the beginning of April, the North Vietnamese move to within 40 miles of Saigon.

**March 30.** Called by James Ruppert, police find the unemployed 40-year-old's mother, his brother Leonard, wife Alma, and their eight children all shot to death. The Ohio family had gathered for Easter dinner. Ruppert receives 11 consecutive life sentences for the largest mass murder of one family in American history.

**March 31.** The clemency discharge program for Vietnam War deserters and draft resisters ends in the United States. Only a fraction of those eligible have applied—22,500 of 124,000.

**April 4.** As Communist forces press forward, the USAF begins evacuating American aid workers and Amerasian orphans already adopted in the United States. One of the cargo planes, with an estimated 325 people on board, crashes today after takeoff—155 die, including 98 children. The airlift continues and, by its termination on the 14th, delivers 1,400 children to the United States (far short of a projected 2,000) and 263 to Australia and Canada.

**April 10.** President Ford asks a joint session of Congress to approve nearly $1 billion in military and "humanitarian" aid for South Vietnam, to give the country a chance to "save itself" and to fund the evacuation of Americans and South Vietnamese "should the worst come to pass." Congress rejects his request.

A bitter President Nguyen Van Thieu points to assurances given by Richard Nixon in 1973 that the United States would react vigorously to any large-scale Communist violation of the cease-fire.

**April 12.** In Cambodia, as the Khmer Rouge approach the last non-Communist stronghold in Phnom Penh, the United States closes its embassy and evacuates 276 Americans, Cambodians, and other nationals by helicopter.

President Ford had requested additional military aid for the beleaguered Lon Nol government, but with no U.S. troops in Indochina and with the North Vietnamese making steady gains, Congress refused to authorize further expenditures.

The Khmer Rouge (Communist National United Front) march triumphantly into the capital on April 17. Prince Sihanouk, who has backed the Communists from exile, is named chief of state for life; he will assume the post in September.

The five-year civil war killed one in eight and, at some point, made refugees of half the population. But a military resolution fails to bring peace.

The dozen foreign reporters who remain behind, including *New York Times* correspondent Sydney Schanberg and his Cambodian assistant Dith Pran, witness the forcible removal of the city's population to the countryside to work the land. The revolutionaries cite the threat of famine, but those who escape tell of political "reeducation" and the murder of hundreds.

**April 13.** A right-wing Christian Falange attack on Palestinian commandos plunges Lebanon into civil war.

At the end of W.W.I., the League of Nations gave France a mandate over the Turkish territories of Lebanon and Syria. Before leaving Lebanon in 1943, the French used a 1932 census, which counted the Christian population at 51%, to allot the presidency to the Christians and parliamentary leadership to the Moslems. That division of powers, in effect, institutionalized religious differences.

The Christians, a largely Western-oriented business class, have since dropped to approximately 40%, but holding tightly to their advantage, have never taken another census. The Moslems, generally a poor people who look to the Arab world, now demand a fairer share of the government.

Although the Christian attack on the Palestinian terrorist base inflames the dissatisfied Moslems, other complexities prolong the bloodshed. Rival political factions financed by other Arab nations fight for supremacy and often goad one religion to fight the other. And some private militias, like the Falangists, outnumber the national army.

By November, the conflict will destroy some 3,500 businesses in Beirut, forcing over half the foreign community to flee and turning some 300,000 Lebanese into refugees. An estimated 5,000 will die by the end of the year.

**April 21.** With military collapse imminent, South Vietnamese President Nguyen Van Thieu finally steps down. But Hanoi refuses to negotiate with his successor or any other politician tied to the former president. The National Assembly then transfers power to General Duong Van Minh who, as a leader of the 1963 coup against the hated Diem is acceptable as a transitional head of government.

On the 29th, the North Vietnamese launch a massive rocket attack on Saigon airport. President Ford orders the remaining 1,000 Americans and some 5,500 South Vietnamese evacuated to offshore ships. About 120,000 South Vietnamese have already fled to the United States, but thousands more who were promised evacuation struggle in vain to reach the helicopters. The final chopper lifts off the roof of the American embassy 19 hours later.

The next day, to avoid the devastation of a final battle, the government announces the unconditional surrender of South Vietnam at 10:02 A.M. Saigon time. The Communists raise the new government flag over the presidential palace at 12:15 P.M., ending nearly a century of Western domination.

---

*Statistics:* From 1950 to 1975, the United States granted Vietnam $15.2 billion in aid (28 percent of all U.S. arms aid) and spent $141 billion for the war effort that cost over 56,000 American lives.

**May 1.** As thousands of desperate South Vietnamese try to reach offshore American ships, the U.S. Defense Department orders the termination of all refugee operations. On May 14, Congress approves a $405-million program to resettle the refugees throughout the United States. The Ford administration has already announced plans to waive immigration restrictions for an estimated 132,000.

**May 7.** Two years after the last combat troops left South Vietnam, President Ford signs a proclamation terminating war time veterans' benefits. He states, "America is no longer at war."

**May 12.** The Cambodian Navy seizes the American cargo ship *Mayaguez* bound for Hong Kong. Calling the capture "piracy," the White House sends diplomatic notes to Cambodia and China demanding the immediate release of the ship and crew of 39. When the notes return unanswered, the president orders marines to retake the ship.

On the 14th, just before the attack, the Cambodians offer to release the *Mayaguez*, sending the captured crew out on a fishing boat. The Americans pick up the crew but continue with their mission, sinking three gunboats and bombing an air base and petroleum depot near Sihanoukville. U.S. casualties total one dead and an undetermined number missing and wounded.

Back in the United States, some question the administration's failure to exhaust all avenues of diplomacy; others, more critical, charge Ford with violating the War Powers Act of 1973. Yet overall, Congress and the American people, dismayed over South Vietnam's surrender, react favorably to the "firmness" of the operation.

Then the casualty figures start to mount. When the final tally reaches 41 dead or missing, many draw the bitter conclusion that the administration deliberately delayed an accurate accounting.

**June 5.** In the first national referendum in British history, 67.2 percent of voters choose continued membership in the EEC. The result convinces union leaders, who have boycotted the European organization, to work for its success, and Prime Minister Wilson declares an end to 14 years of national bickering.

**June 9.** The Philippines becomes the 100th nation to recognize the Communist People's Republic of China. As usual, the Taiwanese immediately cut ties with the offending nation; they now maintain relations with just 26 countries.

**June 10.** Late last year, the U.S. news media uncovered CIA domestic intelligence operations. Ford asked Vice President Rockefeller to conduct the first full-scale government inquiry into the 28-year-old agency. After five months of investigation, the Commission on CIA Activities reports that the agency has engaged in "plainly unlawful" activities that "constituted improper invasions upon the rights of Americans."

But the panel discovered that CIA domestic spying dated back much earlier than the Nixon administration. In 1953, under the directorship of Allen Dulles (1953–1961), agents began monitoring mail sent overseas. Before the program shut down in 1973, the CIA handled more than 4 million pieces and opened some 13,000 letters to the Soviet Union each year. No evidence was found that any president knew of the operation.

Operation Chaos, on the other hand, was initiated in 1967 by President Lyndon Johnson to uncover any foreign influence behind domestic dissidence, then later expanded at Richard Nixon's request. After agents and informers joined antiwar groups, the CIA assembled an estimated 13,000 files—more than half of them on American citizens—and developed a computerized index of some 300,000 people.

As well, the agency dabbled in illegal wiretaps, electronic surveillance, and LSD experiments on unwitting volunteers.

In conclusion, the panel defends the overall CIA record and finds no need to rewrite the National Security Act. Still, to prevent future excesses, members make 30 recommendations. The president must await the findings of ongoing House and Senate investigations before initiating any changes.

**June 24.** In the worst single U.S. airplane disaster to date, 113 people die when an Eastern Airlines Boeing 727 hits several light towers and crashes on approach to Kennedy Airport.

Investigation reveals that a revised weather forecast calling for thunderstorms and heavy rain was never given to the pilot nor was he informed that a DC-8 pilot, landing on the same runway just 10 minutes earlier, had encountered severe wind shear and had strongly recommended that the runway be closed down. In a follow-up flight simulation, 8 out of 10 pilots declare they would have lost control and crashed.

**June 26.** "Mere public intolerance or animosity cannot constitutionally justify the deprivation of a person's physical liberty." With these words, the U.S. Supreme Court finds that the mentally ill cannot be hospitalized against their will unless they represent a danger to themselves or to others. Officials estimate that the decision could effect the release of 250,000 patients.

**June 26.** On June 12, India's district High Court found Prime Minister Indira Gandhi guilty of 1971 electoral corruption and barred her from public office for six years.

With her appeal pending, Gandhi uses the Internal Security Act to arrest 676 political opponents. The next day, her majority government assumes emergency powers and bars the courts from declaring any law unconstitutional. Eventually the government will arrest 20,000, enforce press censorship, and ban most political organizations.

In December, Gandhi will win the approval of party leaders to postpone elections and continue the emergency indefinitely.

**July 2.** In Mexico City, some 1,300 delegates end the U.N. International Women's Year Conference with the adoption of a 10-year plan to improve the status of women. Goals include increased employment opportunities and the recognition of the value of women's work in food production and in the home. A stylized peace dove bearing the equality sign and the female symbol remains a lasting image of the conference.

**July 8.** Gerald Ford announces that he will seek the Republican nomination for the 1976 presidential election.

**July 30.** Former Teamsters' leader Jimmy Hoffa disappears from a restaurant in Bloomfield Township, Michigan. His 1967 prison sentence was com-

muted in 1971 by Richard Nixon on the condition that he stay out of union politics for 10 years. But Hoffa was challenging that stipulation in the courts and had moved to regain control of the Teamsters.

Hoffa telephoned his wife from the restaurant and said his meeting with a Detroit labor leader and an organized crime figure had fallen through, yet witnesses saw him get into a car with several men. Murder theories abound, and with over $200,000 in reward money, people start digging everywhere.

**August 1.** Culminating two years of negotiations, the United States, Canada, and 33 European nations sign the Final Act of the Conference on Security and Cooperation in Europe. Also known as the Helsinki Agreement, the document accepts as "inviolable" the boundary changes arising out of W.W.II, including the Soviet absorption of the three Baltic republics and the revision of Eastern European boundaries. A pledge of noninterference in the internal affairs of other countries, in effect, recognizes the communization of those nations.

The agreement represents a diplomatic triumph for Leonid Brezhnev. To achieve his declared policy of East-West détente, the Soviet secretary had only to affirm human rights and support free movement across European borders—in a nonbinding treaty.

**August 6.** President Ford signs a seven-year extension of the 1965 Voting Rights Act, broadening coverage to include Spanish-speaking Americans and other minority-language groups.

**August 11.** The United States vetoes U.N. admission of North and South Vietnam, the first time the Americans have blocked a membership proposal. U.S. representative Daniel Moynihan reminds the Security Council that just five days earlier it refused to even consider the admission of America's ally South Korea.

**August 15.** A jury of seven women and five men acquit Joanne Little of second-degree murder and voluntary manslaughter in Raleigh, North Carolina. The black woman, serving 7–10 years for breaking and entering, killed a white jail guard when he tried to rape her, then she escaped. A cause célèbre for women's groups and civil rights activists, the trial attracted national attention.

Little returns to prison and appeals her original

sentence, but at the end of the year the Supreme Court refuses to hear the case.

This year, a number of states revamp their prosecution of rape cases. California, for instance, no longer requires judges to instruct juries that rape is difficult to defend in court, and Indiana judges can now block defense questions about a victim's sexual past.

**August 15.** Sheikh Mujib (Mujibur Rahman), the president of Bangladesh, and his family are assassinated. Late last year, Mujib declared a state of emergency following severe flooding. Then, in January, he amended the constitution to give himself more executive power and ban all political parties but his Awami League.

Martial law is introduced, but with a second government upheaval in November, Bangladesh remains one of the world's neediest nations.

**August 31.** The House Select Committee investigating the U.S. intelligence community reveals that the NSA, with the cooperation of three international telegraphic companies, secretly monitored American overseas cable traffic for 28 years and distributed thousands of analyses to other agencies.

President Truman and his attorney general approved "Operation Shamrock" in 1949, but the program continued without the express consent of any administration until Defense Secretary James Schlesinger terminated it last May. President Ford had opposed the House disclosure as damaging to the U.S. intelligence effort.

**September.** In one of the largest surveys of its kind, *Redbook* magazine questioned the sexual attitudes and habits of middle-class, married women in the United States—74 percent were between 20 and 34 years old and 95 percent were white. An overwhelming majority of the 100,000 participants no longer hold to a sexual double standard; that is, 80 percent engaged in premarital sex (90 percent of women under age 25) and almost half had their first sexual experience by age 17.

**September 4.** In June, Middle Eastern experts interpreted the reopening of the Suez Canal as a sign that Anwar Sadat might be ready to negotiate a peace settlement. Today, Egypt signs a U.S.-mediated interim accord with Israel, providing for a further Israeli withdrawal from the Sinai Peninsula. (Israeli agreement rested on the placement of 200 American technicians in the Sinai passes, to monitor an early warning system.)

Critics claim that Secretary of State Kissinger squandered American diplomatic clout for what amounts to a truce. After all, Arab leaders have rejected Sadat's "surrender," and Egypt, promised billions in U.S. economic aid, will lack the incentive to negotiate further. But others argue that the United States has simply bought time to seek a more lasting peace.

**September 5.** In Sacramento, as Gerald Ford shakes hands with the public just 2 feet away, Lynette "Squeaky" Fromme points a loaded .45 automatic pistol at the president. A Secret Service agent grabs the gun; luckily, none of the pistol's four bullets was in the firing chamber.

A follower of Charles Manson, Fromme is charged with attempted assassination under a 1965 law, used here for the first time. The 26-year-old will be sentenced to life imprisonment in December. Reportedly, threats on the president's life increase dramatically after the incident.

**September 10.** The U.S. Army halved Lt. William Calley's 20-year sentence in 1974. But that September, the courts overturned his conviction, ruling massive publicity precluded a fair trial, and Calley was released on bail. Today, the U.S. Court of Appeals in New Orleans modifies his status to federal parole. Calley was the only soldier convicted for the My Lai massacre.

**September 10.** Teacher strikes, affecting almost 2 million students in 12 states, and antibusing demonstrations mar the beginning of the new school year.

In racially troubled Boston, authorities use an initial display of force to reduce violence. And in Louisville, Kentucky, three riots bring out 2,500 police and National Guardsmen. By the end of the second week, Louisville student attendance rises to 77.3 percent.

Still, as Congress refuses funding and black leaders charge the government with racism, busing becomes the focal point of racial tension in the United States. Whites continue to leave the inner city and, by the end of the year, 19 major urban school systems report that 50 percent or more of their student populations are black.

**September 18.** After a 19-month search, FBI agents arrest Patty Hearst in a San Francisco apartment and capture SLA members William and Emily Harris on a nearby street. When a psychiatric examination verifies Hearst's mental competency, the 21-year-old heiress is ordered to stand trial for armed robbery and use of a firearm to commit a felony. The Harrises are charged with kidnapping, robbery, and assault.

**September 22.** President Ford escapes injury in the second attempt on his life in less than three weeks. As Sara Jane Moore aims a gun from a crowd, retired marine Oliver Sipple grabs her arm and the .38 bullet ricochets some distance away, slightly injuring a cab driver.

Agents push the president to the ground then bundle him into his car and onto the floor. Once out of danger, Ford comments to the two agents piled on top, "You guys are heavy."

Moore, who has worked as a police and FBI informant, was questioned just last night as a potential threat to the president. On December 16, the 45-year-old pleads guilty to attempted assassination; she awaits sentencing at the end of the year.

**October 17.** Typical urban problems and the added drain of 1 million welfare residents have pushed New York City's deficit up steadily to $3 billion. At the last minute, the United Federation of Teachers saves the city from bankruptcy by purchasing $150 million worth of municipal bonds to complete a $2.3-billion state rescue program.

Ford says on October 29 that he will veto any federal attempt to save the city. (The next day, the *New York Daily News* headline reads, "Ford to City: Drop Dead." Yet less than a month later, the president asks Congress to approve up to $2.3 billion in annual loans. Undoubtedly advisors pointed out the possible domino effect of the big city's economic failure.

**November 2.** Newspapers report that President Ford, in a major administration reshuffle, dismissed Defense Secretary James Schlesinger and CIA Director William Colby and asked Henry

Kissinger to resign as national security advisor but to remain as secretary of state; Kissinger has agreed. The next day, Ford confirms the story and announces his nomination of Donald Rumsfeld as defense secretary and George Bush as head of the CIA.

Political analysts suggest that a lack of direction within the administration and the president's steady drop in the polls precipitated his attempt to assert leadership. But the abrupt manner of the "Halloween Massacre," with all its implications, brings Ford the greatest criticism since he pardoned Richard Nixon. Still, November elections show no clearcut pattern of voter response.

**November 4.** New York and New Jersey vote against the ERA, but supporters remain confident. In the first year following congressional approval, thirty states ratified the amendment. In five other states, ratification failed only by a very narrow margin.

**November 10.** The U.N. General Assembly approves, 72–35 (with 32 abstentions), an Arab-sponsored resolution defining Zionism as "a form of racism and racial discrimination." (Historically, Zion was another name for Jerusalem, then later it became the movement to establish a Jewish nation on the eastern shore of the Mediterranean.)

The embittered Israelis and angry Ameri-

*Daniel P. Moynihan presses the 'No' button on the proposal to invite PLO representatives to all "efforts, deliberations and conferences" on the Middle East.*

cans denounce the resolution as the legitimization of anti-Semitism. Other opponents argue that this resolution and two others, calling for PLO participation in peace talks and the creation of an independent Palestinian state, destroy any chance for lasting peace in the Middle East and contradict the founding principle of the United Nations.

---

*Statistics:* The former Dutch colony of Suriname joins the United Nations on December 4, bringing membership in the international body to 144 nations.

---

**November 11.** Portugal grants independence to Angola, ending 320 years of colonial rule. But the Angolan people are already fighting a civil war, and rival groups declare their own governments. By the end of the year, the war raises international concerns and several countries move to protect their own interests. The U.S. Senate, recognizing public fears of another Vietnam, cuts off financial support for the rightists.

**November 12.** In 1939, at age 41, William O. Douglas became one of the youngest justices ever appointed to the Supreme Court. Citing failing health following a stroke last year, he retires after serving an unprecedented 36½ years.

One of the country's staunchest defenders of individual rights, Douglas often led the court in applying the Constitution and Bill of Rights to state law. He was alone in dissent until the early 1960s when other justices joined him on this issue. Still, Douglas never convinced the court to review the legality of the Vietnam War.

**November 20.** Francisco Franco, the absolute ruler of Spain for 36 years, dies at age 83. By 1926, without influence or money, Franco had risen through the army ranks to general. Ten years later, he and others led a rightist military revolt against the Republican government, throwing the country into a three-year civil war that shattered the economy and killed almost 1 million Spaniards. Franco emerged in complete control.

The general accepted aid from the Nazis and Italian Fascists but kept Spain neutral during W.W.II. In 1947, perhaps anticipating a challenge to his authority, Franco proclaimed Spain a monarchy and himself regent. Prince Don Juan Carlos de Borbón, groomed as his successor, took over as chief of state last month. He is proclaimed king on November 22.

Only the United States, with military bases in Spain since 1953, sends a high-ranking official, Vice President Rockefeller, to attend the funeral. Western Europe refuses to forgive Franco's relationship with Hitler and Mussolini and the atrocities of the Spanish Civil War.

**November 20.** The Senate Intelligence Committee ignores strong administration opposition and publicly details its investigation of politically sensitive information omitted from the presidential commission's report on the CIA.

Operating through the agency, government officials under the Eisenhower, Kennedy, and Johnson presidencies ordered the assassinations of Fidel Castro and Patrice Lumumba and were involved in plots against Rafael Trujillo of the Dominican Republic, Ngo Dinh Diem of South Vietnam, and General René Schneider of Chile, who all died in coups. Only Castro is still alive, and not because of the CIA's lack of creative murder plots, including Mafia assistance and a poison pen (the agency stockpiled poisons even after a presidential destruct order).

The committee, unable to determine if any of the three presidents personally ordered an assassination, found the alternative—no presidential authorization—even more disturbing. Members recommend that Congress make conspiracy to assassinate and the assassination of a foreign leader federal offenses.

**November 24.** When SALT (1972) limited the superpowers to two ABM sites, Washington chose to establish just one. A successful research and developmental period followed and the first Minutemen base was declared operational at Grand Forks, North Dakota, a few weeks ago. Today, with some $5.7 billion invested in the Safeguard system, the House and Senate vote to dismantle the installation.

**December 3.** In delving into FBI political abuses

over the past 35 years, the Senate Intelligence Committee discovered that the FBI has given every president since Franklin Roosevelt information on journalists, political opponents, and administration critics.

According to the report released today, the FBI also conducted more than 238 burglaries against "domestic subversive targets" over a 26-year period, then attempted to hide or destroy records of the "clearly illegal" activities. The current director, Clarence Kelley, had maintained that such operations occurred only in national security cases, but the *Washington Post* and further committee investigation determined the bureau also targeted ordinary criminals or dissidents, such as Martin Luther King, Jr.

This year's revelations of gross misconduct in the American intelligence community have created a public demand for new investigations into the assassinations of the Kennedys, King, and the attempt against George Wallace.

**December 3.** The Pathet Lao dissolve their coalition government with the non-Communists and, abolishing the country's 600-year-old monarchy, form the Democratic People's Republic of Laos. The Communists, who already administer 75 percent of the country under the 1974 peace agreement, decided in May that American nonintervention in Cambodia and South Vietnam signaled an opportunity for a bloodless takeover.

Before the end of the year, some 700 Soviet advisors arrive and the Chinese send food. The new Communist government forces Washington to close the U.S. aid mission and to drastically cut back embassy staff, but the Americans hold tight to their single diplomatic post in Indochina.

**December 7.** Indonesia invades East Timor. A Portuguese colony since 1512, the island nation declared independence just nine days ago.

**December 8.** Three more countries nationalize their oil industries this year. Dubai assumed full ownership in July; today, Iraq takes over the remaining 23.75 percent of British, French, and Dutch assets; at the end of the month, Venezuela ends 61 years of foreign domination.

**December 10.** Andrei Sakharov receives the Nobel peace prize for his struggle "against the abuse of power and all forms of violation of human dignity." Moscow refused Sakharov, father of the Soviet hydrogen bomb, permission to travel to Oslo, citing a security risk. His wife Yelena appears in his place.

**December 15.** Columnist William Safire of the *New York Times* accuses the Senate Intelligence Committee of covering up a relationship between John F. Kennedy and Judith Katherine Campbell, a "close friend" of Mafia bosses Sam Giancana and John Roselli.

The senators, after determining that Campbell had no knowledge of the CIA-Mafia plot to kill Castro, unanimously voted to omit the details from their report rather than "wade into the personal life of the president."

The investigation discovered that Campbell made over 70 phone calls to the White House between March 29, 1961 and March 22, 1962. On the day of her last call, President Kennedy had lunch with FBI Director J. Edgar Hoover.

**December 15.** The Trudeau government sets strict wage and price controls and establishes an Anti-Inflation Board to enforce the three-year program of restraints. During the 1974 election campaign, opposition leader Robert Stanfield recommended a 90-day wage and price freeze to slow inflation, but Prime Minister Trudeau warned Canadian workers against the proposal.

**December 22.** President Ford signs a national energy policy calling for an immediate 12-percent rollback in the price of domestic crude oil, the removal of a $2-per-barrel tariff previously imposed to discourage the use of imported oil, and a price-control phaseout over 40 months. But the American consumer will see little change at the gas pump, since the October OPEC price hike and backlogged industry cost increases have yet to be implemented.

**December 27.** Following two explosions in a coal mine near Dhanbad, India, millions of gallons of water from a nearby reservoir pour into the mining tunnels, drowning an estimated 431 miners. Mine safety standards have become lax in the three years since the Indian government nationalized the coal industry.

**December 29.** A bomb explodes in the main terminal of La Guardia Airport in New York City, blowing out 10-foot-high glass windows and setting off a two-alarm fire; 11 people die and 75 are injured. Investigators trace the explosion to a coin locker and estimate that the device held 25 sticks of dynamite. No one claims responsibility for the bomb, and no one is apprehended.

## Obituaries

**Chiang Kai-shek** (October 31, 1887–April 5, 1975). During W.W.II, the Chinese Nationalist leader attained world stature and, following Japan's surrender, received Allied assistance to fight Mao Tse-tung and the Communists. But Chiang proved unable or unwilling to prevent corruption within his own forces, and the Americans eventually withdrew their support. In 1949, the Communist army forced Chiang and the Nationalists to flee the mainland for Formosa (Taiwan).

Two years later, as the West fought Communist expansion in Korea, Washington backed Chiang's government in order to keep Red China confined to the mainland. Taiwan prospered, but in the early 1970s, Chinese power shifted to Peking.

**Francisco Franco** (December 4, 1892–November 20, 1975). *See* News.

**Sam Giancana** (May 24, 1908–June 19, 1975). Unknown assailants gun down the former boss of Chicago organized crime. Since he allegedly participated in the CIA plot to kill Castro, Giancana's death sparks wild rumors.

**Haile Selassie** (July 23, 1892–August 27, 1975). Forced to flee Mussolini's invading army in 1935, the emperor of Ethiopia returned with the Allied liberation in 1941. During the following years, the diminutive leader became Africa's senior statesman, but at home his corrupt government maintained absolute control, even concealing the famine of 1973. But strikes and demonstrations over the food shortages gave the military a window of opportunity. A junta imprisoned the emperor in

September 1974 and abolished the 3,000-year-old Ethiopian monarchy earlier this year.

**Anthony McAuliffe** (July 2, 1898–August 11, 1975). The U.S. commander during the Battle of the Bulge in December 1944, he won fame by responding "Nuts!" when the Nazis called for his surrender. The 101st Airborne held throughout the month-long battle, forcing Germany to exhaust its last reserves.

**Elijah Muhammad** (October 7, 1897–February 25, 1975). When W. D. Fard, leader of the Black Muslims, disappeared in 1934, his disciple Robert Poole took the name of Muhammad and assumed spiritual leadership.

Claiming to be Allah's divinely chosen messenger, he preached a mixture of black nationalism, self-knowledge, and self-reliance and advocated total abstention from drugs, alcohol, tobacco, gambling, and extramarital sex. Thousands of black Americans accepted his beliefs and proudly watched as the Nation of Islam founded mosques, schools, and businesses.

But by urging racial separation and barring involvement in politics or the civil rights movement, Muhammad pushed some activists, such as Malcolm X, out of the sect. Reportedly, the Muslim leader modified his views in the years before his death.

**Aristotle Onassis** (January 15, 1906?–March 15, 1975). The Greek shipping tycoon won worldwide recognition in 1968 with his marriage to Jacqueline Kennedy, the widow of U.S. president John F. Kennedy.

**Charlotte Whitton** (March 8, 1896–January 25, 1975). Ottawa elected Canada's first woman mayor in 1951. The outspoken and energetic Whitton, who won reelection four times, was unintimidated by male colleagues. She once quipped, "Whatever women do, they must do it twice as well as men to be thought half as good. Luckily, this is not difficult." She retired from politics in 1972.

**Hugo Zacchini** (circa 1899–October 20, 1975). In 1922, the young Italian used his W.W.I artillery experience to create a new circus act—shooting himself out of a cannon into a net. He retired in 1961.

# BEGINNINGS AND ENDINGS

## News

**January 7.** Chrysler offers the auto industry's first rebate, $200–$400 on certain models purchased before mid-February. With more than 200,000 layoffs and a slump in new-car sales, GM and Ford quickly follow suit.

**February 11.** The first woman chosen to lead a major British political party, 49-year-old Conservative Margaret Thatcher promises "continuity and change."

**March 1.** U.S. Bicentennial celebrations officially kick off in Washington.

**March 9.** Construction gets under way on the Alaskan oil pipeline (789 miles from Prudhoe Bay to the ice-free port of Valdez). The largest private project in American history, the pipeline is scheduled for completion by fall 1978.

**March 17–20.** In the country's first major strike by doctors, 2,000 interns and resident physicians walk out of 21 New York City hospitals. A settlement limits work hours.

**March 24.** With Royal assent, the beaver becomes the official symbol of Canada, in commemoration of the trade in beaver pelts that opened up the vast nation.

**March 28.** The Civil Aeronautics Board gives National Airlines the go-ahead for the first no-frill fares, up to a 35-percent discount for waiving amenities such as meals and drinks. Other airlines win approval within two weeks.

**April 1.** Canadians switch from Fahrenheit to Celsius temperature scales, the first changeover in a gradual conversion to metric.

**April 7.** The statute of limitations runs out on illegal contributions to Richard Nixon's 1972 re-election campaign.

**April 16.** Lila Cockrell is elected mayor of San Antonio, the first woman to head one of the nation's 10 largest cities.

**May 1.** Ottawa regains control of Canadian air defense for the first time since signing the 1958 NORAD agreement with the United States.

**May 5.** After 40 years as the country's No. 1 corporation, GM gives way to Exxon in *Fortune* magazine's annual listing.

**May 16.** At 12:30 P.M., Junko Tabei stands at the top of Mt. Everest. The 36th climber to reach the 29,028-foot summit, the 35-year-old Japanese is the first woman.

**June 7.** Washington removes the last U.S. combat aircraft from Taiwan and reduces American forces to 2,800 men.

**July 1.** After surveying career-minded sailors, the U.S. Navy replaces the 100-year traditional uniform of bell-bottom trousers, white gob hats, wide-collar jumpers, and knotted neckerchiefs with officer-style blues and work clothes of blue denim pants, loose pullovers, and baseball caps.

**July 7.** In Canada the socialist NDP chooses John Edward (Ed) Broadbent, a member of the House since 1966, to lead the party. Former leader David Lewis lost his seat in last year's election.

**July 8.** Yitzhak Rabin arrives in West Germany, the first Israeli head of state to visit the nation. He pays his respects to victims of the Holocaust at the Bergen-Belsen concentration camp.

**July 11.** Parliament establishes Petro-Canada to discover, develop, refine, and market petroleum and natural gas. The government-owned company starts with $500 million in capital.

**July 22.** With his great-grandson looking on, the House restores American citizenship to Robert E. Lee, 105 years after his death.

To become eligible for public office after the Civil War, the Confederate general needed a pardon from the White House. He forwarded his request then followed with the required oath of allegiance. That second document, discovered just five years ago, never reached President Andrew Johnson.

**July 29.** The OAS lifts the 11-year trade embargo against Cuba. A month later, Washington lifts the 12-year ban on sales to Cuba by American foreign subsidiaries. But the direct U.S.-Cuba embargo remains in effect.

**August 5.** For the first time, the Massachusetts Supreme Court readmits a disbarred lawyer—Alger Hiss, who was convicted of perjury in a notorious spy trial in 1950 (he served three years in prison).

The ruling cites the 70-year-old's demonstrated "moral and intellectual fitness."

**September 14.** In Rome, Pope Paul declares Mother Elizabeth Ann Bayley Seton a saint. The first American-born woman to be canonized, Seton is acknowledged as the founder of the U.S. parochial school system.

**September 24.** With "the changing circumstances" in Southeast Asia, SEATO ministers agree to phase out the 21-year defensive alliance. Never invoked in any major incident, the treaty instead gave birth to medical, cultural, and economic projects.

**September 28.** Congress authorizes the admission of women to the three military academies—West Point (Army), Colorado Springs (Air Force), and Annapolis (Navy)—by fall 1976.

**September 30.** Hirohito, the first Japanese emperor to visit the continental United States, arrives in Washington on a goodwill tour. He expresses regret for the "tragic interlude" of W.W.II and hopes his visit will contribute to "everlasting friendship." President Ford makes no mention of the war.

**October 7.** A revised friendship treaty between East Germany and the USSR makes no reference to a unified Germany.

**October 16.** The First Women's Bank and Trust Co. opens in New York, the first full-service financial institution organized and run primarily by women. Some 350 women opening accounts describe their difficulties in obtaining credit elsewhere.

**December 5.** Britain terminates the policy of denying IRA suspects a trial. Since August 9, 1971, British forces in Northern Ireland have held 1,981 men and women without charge.

**December 19.** The last American combat planes leave Thailand.

**December 20.** The South Vietnamese resettlement program ends as the last of some 140,000 refugees leave Fort Chaffee, Arkansas.

**December 26.** The world's first supersonic airliner, the TU-144 begins a domestic schedule in the Soviet Union, taking 1 hour, 58 minutes, to fly 1,900 miles. The subsonic IL-62 takes 4 hours.

**December 31.** After considerable controversy, the U.S. Post Office receives court permission to raise the first-class rate from 10 cents to 13 cents.

**More news.** For the first time, the number of divorces in the United States surpasses 1 million— 1,026,000. (Over the past decade, the divorce rate has more than doubled.)

• McDonald's builds the first drive-thru restaurant.

## Records

**March 31.** Topped off with an antenna mast, Toronto's CN Tower becomes the world's tallest freestanding structure—1,815 feet 5 inches.

## Government Departments and Agencies

**January 15.** Known as the House Un-American Activities Committee before 1969, the Internal Security Committee has received $6.5 million in funds and produced just one major piece of legislation. Today, the House votes 259–150 to abolish the committee and shift jurisdiction to the Judiciary Committee.

## New Products and Businesses

Johnson & Johnson nationally markets the painkiller Tylenol.

Wrigley brings out nonstick chewing gum for denture wearers.

Giving up the talent agency business, Wally Amos opens a chocolate chip cookie store in Los Angeles—Famous Amos Cookies.

## Memorable Ad Campaigns

After earlier successes with a pen and a disposable razor, Bic offers a disposable lighter. And "Flick Your Bic," a line intended to reflect sophistication, enters the American vocabulary.

When Pepsi challenges Coca–Cola fans to a

taste test, the advertising world eagerly grabs at the new sales concept.

## Fads

Last summer, Joshua Reynolds invented a ring that changes color on the finger. Heat-sensitive quartz crystals encased in plastic supposedly react to a person's disposition—angry, happy, sad. Anonymously dubbed a "mood ring," Reynolds' imaginative piece of jewelry soon faces a flood of imitators. Cheaper plastic models cost as little as $2.98, while more expensive versions come with a colored mood chart. One of the biggest fads of the decade, retailers sell some 20 million before sales crest in November.

Unemployed advertising man Gary Dahl puts an ordinary rock in a box with air holes, adds a "training manual," and calls it a Pet Rock. A little zaniness in a terrible economy, his outrageous marketing idea makes him a millionaire (1.2 million pets sold) in six months.

Pie throwing is a less pervasive but more exciting craze. "Hit men" charge as much as $300 to target a VIP.

# SCIENCE AND TECHNOLOGY

## News

**January.** This month's issue of *Popular Electronics* carries an ad for the Altair microcomputer, the first personal computer. Made by a New Mexico firm, the $350 kit is based on the Intel 8080 chip.

**February 4.** Tremors measuring 7.3 on the Richter scale hit a major industrial district in China, but no widespread damage or deaths are reported. Shortly afterward, the West learns that people in the area were warned before the quake hit. In this first recorded instance of earthquake prediction, scientists reportedly relied on the radon content of deep-well water. Crystal rock under stress releases this short-lived radioactive gas.

**February 27.** In a rare scientific agreement, molecular biologists from 17 nations propose tighter standards in genetic research to prevent experimental risks. Although participants hope a collective effort will develop safer biological tools, the pact carries only the force of morality not law.

**April 18.** According to the EPA, the water supplies of 79 American cities show measurable amounts of chemical substances that might cause cancer. The study was undertaken after 66 chemicals were found in New Orleans water.

**May 30.** Replacing two earlier organizations, the European Space Agency pools the resources of member nations for the design and launching of communications and scientific satellites and space transportation systems. It is the world's only multinational space program.

**June 4.** *The New York Times* reports the discovery in North Carolina of the oldest animal fossils ever found in the United States: large marine worms some 620 million years old. At that time, during the pre-Cambrian period, no vertebrates had evolved.

**June 30.** Using infrared spectrometry to overcome the night-sky glow, astronomers have located the farthest known galaxy from Earth. Some 8 billion light-years away, Galaxy 3C123 has long been known as the source of extremely intense radio noise.

**July.** Washington state authorities close almost 10,000 acres of waterways and recreational lands as the long dormant Mt. Baker volcano shows signs of renewed life. Aware that eruptions have followed similar activity at other volcanos, scientists worry that venting steam could trigger avalanches and mud slides.

**July.** The first new land volcano since Parícutin erupted in Mexico in 1943 has risen out of level ground on the Kamchatka Peninsula in the USSR. A thousand feet high in less than six weeks, the cone has released clouds of ash and hot gases.

**July 11.** Peking announces the discovery of a pottery army dating to the reign of China's first emperor, Shih Huang-ti. The 500 figures uncovered thus far, each different from the other, hold bows, crossbows, and lances made of wood, lead, iron, and bronze; some have retained their original paint.

Archaeologists believe the soldiers re-created the symbolic battle of unification. Historical records describe a vast underground palace nearby, a work that took 36 years to build.

**July 17.** In 1972, during President Nixon's visit to Moscow, the superpowers signed a joint-flight agreement. Today, in a historic moment, *Soyuz 19* and *Apollo 18* link up 140 miles above Earth.

While the world appreciates the irony of cold-war rivals cooperating in space, few realize the technical obstacles that had to be overcome. *Apollo 18*, for instance, is considerably larger than *Soyuz 19*, and different cabin atmospheres necessitated an intermediate airlock chamber.

In the first in-space astronaut-cosmonaut meeting, the Americans visit the *Soyuz* capsule. The spacecraft separate and redock on the 19th to test a possible rescue mission. The Americans and Soviets meet four times and share meals.

With the Apollo program at an end, critics question the value for the billions of dollars spent. But supporters point to the technological achievements, including the sift-down effect (pocket calculators, personal computers) and the worldwide sense of unity that emerged from photos of an Earth with no territorial boundaries.

**July–August.** An FDA drug bulletin warns U.S. physicians that women under age 40 who take the Pill carry a risk of heart attack four times greater than that of non-users. And women over 40 should be advised to use other forms of contraception. Obesity, smoking, and other factors further increase the danger. The figures are based on two studies published in a British medical journal.

**August 11.** The Royal Victoria Hospital in Ireland announces the development of a portable defibrillator for use on heart attack victims outside the hospital. The 7-pound device (compared to 35 pounds for conventional units) is being imported into the United States for extensive testing.

---

*Statistics:* Doctors credit an 8-percent decrease in heart disease over the past decade to a reduction in the number of cigarette smokers (from 60 percent of males in 1955 to 40 percent in 1975), a less fatty diet, high blood pressure medication, and more exercise.

---

**August 20.** In a culmination of almost 14 years of Mars exploration, the United States launches the first Viking craft (the second lifts off next month). The 1,269-pound landers, meticulously designed and engineered to prevent contamination of alien life forms, are scheduled to land on Mars in 1976.

**October 7.** At the University of California, urologist Dr. Sherman Silber describes a new microscopic surgical technique to reverse a vasectomy. He has achieved a 25-percent success rate in counteracting an operation previously regarded as permanent.

---

*Statistics:* In the past five years, medical malpractice insurance has skyrocketed. An orthopedic surgeon who paid $5,000 in 1970 today needs $15,000 for a group policy and, if sued once before, $30,000 for individual coverage.

---

**October 20.** A four-year government-sponsored study has found that amniocentesis does not cause pregnant women to miscarry. During the procedure, a long needle pierces the woman's stomach and draws out a small amount of the fluid surrounding the fetus in the womb. Specimen cells grown in lab cultures will reveal certain fetal abnormalities, such as Down's syndrome, while abortion is still possible. Some 52 institutions across the United States now conduct a total of 3,000 such procedures annually.

**October 22.** In an enormous astronautical achievement, a lander from *Venera 9* transmits the first photograph of Venus. The planet's 460-degree Centigrade temperature and crushing atmosphere (equivalent to 90 Earth atmospheres) destroy the craft after the Soviets receive a single picture of a young, evolving terrain with sharp, angular rocks.

Just three days later, *Venera 10* lands about 1,400 miles away and endures the heat and wind (only two to three mph, but in that dense atmosphere, equal to an ocean wave on Earth) long enough to transmit one shot. The flat, eroded ground reveals the diversity of Venusian landscapes.

**October 26.** Each year, an estimated 2,500–3,900 Americans choke to death on food. Today's newspapers report that the AMA Emergency Medical Services Committee has approved the Heimlich maneuver to clear a blocked airway. A rescuer grabs a person from behind and, grasping the hands below the rib cage, pulls a clenched fist in a quick, upward thrust into the abdomen. The technique was introduced nine months ago by Dr. Henry J. Heimlich.

**November 21.** Concerned about high levels of PCBs in fish taken from the Hudson River, Assistant Secretary of the Interior Nathaniel Reed advocates confining the use of the chemicals to electrical transformers and capacitors. At this time, municipal and industrial wastes continue to leak the toxin into the environment.

**December.** A report in the journal *Cancer Research* suggests that nutritional factors—food additives, high-fat diet, excessive alcohol, lack of vitamins A and C—may be responsible for 50 percent of cancers in women and 30 percent in men.

**More news.** Farmers in the Los Angeles area discover an agricultural pest not indigenous to that region, the Mediterranean fruit fly.

• At the end of the year, 24 U.S. institutions are conducting tests with the whole-body CAT scanner. Already a revolutionary tool in diagnosing brain disorders, computerized axial tomography directs a thin line of x-ray photons at a narrow cross-section of the body then analyzes how much of the radiation is absorbed.

• From 650,000 sales in 1974, digital watches skyrocket to some 2 million this year. Powered by tiny cells and using quartz crystals, the pieces show the time digitally in liquid-crystal displays. While the price has dropped to $30–$70 for some makes, many in the industry consider the technology a passing gimmick.

• William Millard offers the IMSAI 8080 through the mail. A kit, the first commercial-grade personal computer weighs some 80 pounds and includes no software for the $500 price. Nonetheless, his small ad in *Popular Electronics* draws 3,500 responses.

• Interest arose when several research groups found opiate receptors in animal tissues. This year, endorphins are found in humans—a natural compound from the nervous system that alleviates pain.

### Other Discoveries, Developments, and Inventions

Electronic fuel injection in autos and dual transverse torsion bar suspension

Kuiper Airborne Observatory, a 4-engine jet with a 36-inch telescope

### Obituaries

**William Coolidge** (October 23, 1873–February 3, 1975). The U.S. inventor produced less brittle tungsten light-bulb filaments, a high-vacuum tube to emit predictable amounts of radiation (1916), portable x-ray units, and the first successful submarine-detection system.

**John Dunning** (September 24, 1907–August 25, 1975). The U.S. physicist directed the construction of the cyclotron, which on January 25, 1939, confirmed the possibility of controlled nuclear fission. He later directed the project to isolate uranium-235, essential for atomic bombs and the production of enriched uranium for nuclear reactors.

**William Kouwenhoven** (January 13, 1886–November 10, 1975). The U.S. biomedical engineer saved countless lives with his defibrillator and his method of closed-chest heart massage.

**Alfred Lee Loomis** (November 4, 1887–August 11, 1975). The physicist contributed to the development of the electroencephalograph, a long-range navigational system, and a device to measure the speed of projectiles.

## THE ARTS

January 5—*The Wiz*, with Stephanie Mills, Hinton Battle, Ted Ross, Tiger Haynes

January 7—*Shenandoah*, with John Cullum

March 13—*Same Time, Next Year*, with Ellen Burstyn, Charles Grodin

June 3—*Chicago*, with Gwen Verdon, Jerry Orbach, Chita Rivera
July 25—*Chorus Line*

## Tony Awards

Actor (Dramatic)—John Kane, *Sizwe Banzi Is Dead* and *The Island*; Winston Ntshona, *Sizwe Banzi Is Dead* and *The Island*
Actress (Dramatic)—Ellen Burstyn, *Same Time, Next Year*
Actor (Musical)—John Cullum, *Shenandoah*
Actress (Musical)—Angela Lansbury, *Gypsy*
Play—*Equus*
Musical—*The Wiz*

## News

**April 7.** After 20 years with the New York City Opera, soprano Beverly Sills debuts at the Met.

**May 3.** In 1960, reviewers offered little encouragement when *The Fantasticks* opened Off Broadway. But word-of-mouth and the growing popularity of its tune "Try to Remember" continued to fill the 150-seat theater. Tonight, the world's longest-running musical celebrates its 15th anniversary.

**August 23.** When the curtain rises at the Theatre Royal in Bath, cast members see a real ghost in an upper-circle box. The Lady in Grey, who supposedly committed suicide after her jealous husband killed her lover, trails the scent of jasmine between the theater and nearby Garrick's Head pub.

**More news.** Private dealers respond to the economic downturn by withholding Old Master paintings from this year's auctions.

## Obituaries

**Josephine Baker** (June 3, 1906–April 12, 1975). In the 1920s, the black American singer-dancer wowed Parisian audiences with her exuberant delivery and skimpy outfits. She remained in France and became a citizen in 1937. Fifty years later, during her anniversary revue, the legendary entertainer collapsed and died.

**Dmitri Shostakovich** (September 25, 1906–August 9, 1975). Despite constant government censure for offending "Socialist realism," the acclaimed Soviet composer completed operas, ballets, concertos, string quartets, and 15 symphonies.

**Richard Tucker** (August 28, 1913–January 8, 1975). For 30 years, Tucker was America's leading tenor. The Met, in a unique acknowledgment, conducts his funeral on stage.

## WORDS

Philip Agee, *Inside the Company*
Harold H. Bloomfield, *TM: Discovering Inner Energy and Overcoming Stress*
Susan Brownmiller, *Against Our Will: Men, Women and Rape*
Agatha Christie, *Curtain*
James Clavell, *Shōgun*
Michael Crichton, *The Great Train Robbery*
E. L. Doctorow, *Ragtime*
Arthur Hailey, *The Moneychangers*
Jack Higgins, *The Eagle Has Landed*
David Niven, *Bring on the Empty Horses*
Judith Rossner, *Looking for Mr. Goodbar*
Joseph Wambaugh, *The Choirboys*

## News

**January 21.** The *New York Times* reports that former White House aide John Dean has sold his version of Watergate to Simon & Schuster for $300,000. In another part of the newspaper, Russell Baker wryly comments on the rash of Watergate book deals: "The wages of sin in this affair have already swollen so succulently that we may see a revival of youth's urge to grow up and be President, or even Vice-President, or a President's flunky . . . jobs which a lad with an ineptitude for corruption may now dream of parlaying into riches ever after."

**March 6.** Pocket Books pays Agatha Christie $925,000 for paperback rights to Hercule Poirot's last case. The British novelist wrote *Curtain* in the mid-1940s to ensure that the Belgian detective would die with her.

**May 27.** Upholding government security procedures, the U.S. Supreme Court orders former operative Victor Marchetti to submit his manuscript *The CIA and the Cult of Intelligence* for agency approval. (The author had agreed not to divulge any information obtained during his employment.) The landmark decision denies Marchetti's publisher, Alfred A. Knopf, the right to restore censored material in any future edition.

**August 1.** Bantam pays a record (to date) $1.85 million for paperback rights to *Ragtime*, E. L. Doctorow's critically acclaimed novel.

**More news.** With paper costs up 44 percent since 1973, U.S. magazines raise their newsstand price an average 30 percent. As well, those with huge mailing lists, such as *McCall's* and *Ladies' Home Journal*, deliberately cut circulation to avoid overextension. Book publishers, with 2 percent fewer titles, credit higher prices for their rising dollar sales.

• With the 1975 movie tie-in, Peter Benchley's *Jaws* sells a total 9½ million copies by the end of the year.

## Cartoons and Comics

**June 9.** An estimated 100 million Americans, of all ages and socioeconomic levels, read the funnies. Yet in 1975, the number of nationally syndicated comic strips drops to an all-time low of 200.

In a two-page article on comic strips, *U.S. News & World Report* credits the dwindling number to the increased popularity of liberal cartoonists, such as Gary Trudeau. Commenting on readers' changing tastes, Al Capp remarks, "The comic page is the only page in a newspaper you can trust anymore."

**December 23.** To end a long legal battle, Warner Communications agrees to pay Jerry Siegel and Joe Shuster $20,000 a year for life and to add their byline to all *Superman* publications.

Siegel and Shuster created the invincible hero in 1933 when they were teenagers, but the Great Depression brought years of rejection slips. Finally, in 1938, Action Comics bought the story and all character rights for $135.

## TIME **Man of the Year**

Women of the Year
(Susan Brownmiller, Kathleen Byerly, Alison Cheek, Jill Ker Conway, Betty Ford, Ella Grasso, Carla Hills, Barbara Jordan, Billie Jean King, Susie Sharp, Carol Sutton, Addie Wyatt)

## New Words and Phrases

chairperson
fireperson
flyby (*Mariner 10*'s flight past Venus)
hoolifans (hooligan football fans)
hydrofoil
low profile
overview
recap
rising fives (children just under age five)
scenario
traumatic experience
walkabout

London commuters read on the subway walls, "God is not dead. He is alive and working on a much less ambitious project."

## Obituaries

**Ross McWhirter** (August 12, 1925–November 27, 1975). The coeditor of the *Guinness Book of World Records* is gunned down in the doorway of his London home. A well-known champion of individual freedoms, McWhirter had chaired an organization paying for information on terrorists.

**Bob Montana** (October 23, 1920–January 4, 1975). The cartoonist created *Archie*, the first teenage comic book, in winter 1942–1943. Four years later, an *Archie* strip was introduced under his byline. Montana never varied his artistic style or attempted to make the teens more "believable." Yet his characters remain extremely popular.

**Rex Stout** (December 1, 1886–October 27, 1975). Nero Wolfe, the American writer's fictional detective, solved 46 mysteries in 41 years.

**Arnold Toynbee** (April 14, 1889–October 22, 1975). The British historian was best known for *A Study of History*, a monumental 12-volume work that took 40 years to write in longhand. His theory, that all civilizations eventually decay and collapse, won him the epithet "prophet of doom."

**Thornton Wilder** (April 17, 1897–December 7, 1975). The American author, who believed experiences "repeat and repeat in the lives of the millions," won Pulitzer prizes for his novel *The Bridge of San Luis Rey* (1927) and his plays *Our Town* (1938) and *The Skin of Our Teeth* (1942). A less successful play, *The Matchmaker* (1954), became the hit musical *Hello, Dolly!*.

**P(elham) G(renville) Wodehouse** (October 15, 1881–February 14, 1975). A prolific writer, the British-born humorist was at his best with fictional bachelor Bertie Wooster and his superior manservant Jeeves. (Asked to explain his fascination with butlers, he responded, "Mystery hangs about them like a nimbus.") A naturalized American, Wodehouse was knighted by Queen Elizabeth just a month before his death.

# FASHION

## Haute Couture

Astoundingly similar collections in Paris and New York emphasize the full silhouette and offer a tube line. As well, many touch on the Orient or present a military theme in khaki.

## News

**This year.** Asked to select the world's most beautiful woman, visitors to Madame Tussaud's Waxwork Museum in London chose Elizabeth Taylor in 1970 and 1971, Raquel Welch in 1972, and Sophia Loren in 1973 and 1974 (repeaters in the No. 2–5 positions included Brigitte Bardot, Twiggy, and Princess Grace of Monaco). This year, once again, Elizabeth Taylor takes the No. 1 spot.

## Colors and Materials

Khaki dominates year-round.

Liberty prints, with bright colors or pastel pinks and blues laid over dark backgrounds, sweep the fashion world.

Manufacturers simulate denim with dyed or printed knits and wovens. (Since 1964, Levi Strauss's annual gross sales have skyrocketed from $100 million to $1 billion.)

The Bay City Rollers, Scottish rock group, set off a craze for tartan fabrics.

## Clothes

In the spring, women favor the smock dress and a floral skirt, gathered or flared. The fitted sheath, with hemline drawn at the top of the calf, prevails in summer.

Over a turtleneck or the more recent cowl pullover, the layered look for fall 1975 adds a loose shirt, then the new waistcoat (often shorter than the shirt) over a pencil-slim skirt or jumper. Women who prefer pants usually tuck them into boots and wear a tunic on top. To balance this slimmer silhouette, a fringed scarf or heavy rib-knit stole is knotted at the shoulder.

Overalls and jumpsuits remain popular into the fall.

The pervasive Chinese influence brings in quilted, box-shaped jackets in plain cotton or wool jersey (often with contrasting lining). Winter touches of the Orient include fastenings (frog and off-center), braid trimming, mandarin collars, and split side seams.

A romantic summer dress touches the neck with frills, covers the arms with long sleeves, then falls through a high waist to one or two flounces at the hem.

Capes are "out" and ponchos are "in" with their buttoned tabs, additional slits, and occasional hoods.

Slim-cut jeans turn up to the ankle or higher while some young people cut them off across the thigh to create shorts (a red dollar sign is the latest embroidery). Other young women tuck their jeans into high-heeled boots or, for a chic look, don cowboy boots and a velvet blazer.

The newest casual top is a kimono-sleeved T-shirt, pulled tight and knotted in front. (T's sport *Peanuts* characters, portraits of film stars, and scratch-and-sniff perfumes and foods like pizza.)

Capitalizing on the denim craze, stores stock fatigue uniforms, bib-front railroad overalls, and skirts with jean styling or stitching.

Another popular skirt is the wraparound with dye-matched Danskin leotards.

While the three-piece suit makes a strong comeback, the two-piece, single-breasted continues as the classic center of most men's wardrobes. (Gray suits account for over 80 percent of sales.) Casual wear features the pulled-together safari style in lightweight camel or biscuit-colored textiles.

## Accessories

A wide elasticized belt with three hook fasteners cinches in the sheath.

A scarf wraps the head in a peasant manner or, occasionally, in more elaborate headdresses.

A hem-length, fringed scarf accessorizes the long cotton skirt, a floppy straw hat complements the romantic dress, and a plaited pith hat with narrow leather headband finishes off jeans and a T-shirt. Still, the Chinese straw shoulder bag remains summer's biggest accessory.

Teens opt for wooden or leather clogs while young women choose espadrilles with canvas uppers and rope soles. T-strapped, thin-soled sandals and higher-heeled pumps win approval as well. The natural shoe with a lowered heel and comfortable sole is a best-seller.

As platform shoes all but disappear, more men turn to cowboy boots or moccasins.

A close-fitting bonnet in knitted or crocheted wool balances top-heavy layers.

Small clutches and enormous totes sell best.

Women's jewelry reflects the essence of China. Men slip on more pieces this year—rings, bracelets, a pendant, or a necklace of shark's teeth.

## Hair and Cosmetics

As separates and huge shawls gather at the neck, hairdressers promote bobbed or cropped cuts with softening fluff and an eye fringe.

Transparent spring makeup (laid down over beige, honey, or sand-tinted foundations) gives way in the fall to warmer tones of red and amber (in copper or brown tints). With these paler shades, facial interest focuses on lower-lid eyeliner.

## Obituaries

**Charles Haskell Revson** (October 11, 1906–August 24, 1975). In 1932, Charles and two brothers formed a cosmetics company with their total assets of $300. Revlon has since grown into one of the world's largest cosmetic empires.

**Madeleine Vionnet** (June 22, 1876–March 2, 1975). At the height of her influence (between 1919 and 1939 when she closed down her house), the French couturier used the innovative bias cut to free women from corsets and petticoats. Many rank her with Chanel and Balenciaga as one of the greatest designers of the 20th century.

# MUSIC

"Love Will Keep Us Together"—Captain & Tennille

"Fly, Robin, Fly" (Instr.)—Silver Convention

"Island Girl"—Elton John

"Bad Blood"—Neil Sedaka

"He Don't Love You (Like I Love You)"—Tony Orlando & Dawn

"Rhinestone Cowboy"—Glen Campbell

"Philadelphia Freedom"—Elton John

"Fame"—David Bowie

"That's the Way (I Like It)"—K. C. & the Sunshine Band

"Jive Talkin' "—Bee Gees

"Lucy in the Sky with Diamonds"—Elton John

"Before the Next Teardrop Falls"—Freddy Fender

"Thank God I'm a Country Boy"—John Denver

"Laughter in the Rain"—Neil Sedaka

"Best of My Love"—Eagles

"My Eyes Adored You"—Frankie Valli

"(Hey Won't You Play) Another Somebody Done Somebody Wrong Song"—B. J. Thomas

"Shining Star"—Earth, Wind & Fire

"One of These Nights"—Eagles

"Pick Up the Pieces" (Instr.)—Average White Band

"Lady Marmalade"—Labelle

"Lovin' You"—Minnie Riperton

"I'm Sorry"—John Denver

"Mandy"—Barry Manilow

"The Hustle" (Instr.)—Van McCoy & the Soul City Symphony

"Please Mr. Postman"—Carpenters

"Fire"—Ohio Players

"Black Water"—Doobie Brothers

"Sister Golden Hair"—America

"Fallin' in Love"—Hamilton, Joe Frank & Reynolds

"Let's Do It Again"—Staple Singers

"Saturday Night"—Bay City Rollers

"Have You Never Been Mellow"—Olivia Newton-John

"Listen to What the Man Said"—Paul McCartney & Wings

"You're No Good"—Linda Ronstadt

"Get Down Tonight"—K. C. & the Sunshine Band

Note: For the first time, each of the 37 songs in the year's list is a No. 1 hit. By way of explanation, insiders point to the splintering of rock in this decade and this year's arrival of disco. During the 1960s, an average 20 titles reached No. 1 each year.

## Grammys (1975)

Record of the Year—Captain & Tenille, "Love Will Keep Us Together"

Song of the Year (songwriter)—Stephen Sondheim, "Send in the Clowns"

Album of the Year—Paul Simon, *Still Crazy After All These Years*

Best Vocal Performance (Male)—Paul Simon, *Still Crazy After All These Years* (album)

Best Vocal Performance (Female)—Janis Ian, "At Seventeen" (single)

Best New Artist—Natalie Cole

## News

**March 1.** In a *New York Times* article, recording executives complain that NARAS members tend to give Grammys to older, more conservative white performers. The Beatles, for instance, never won Record of the Year despite a three-year domination of the market. Academy President Bill Lowery acknowledges a split in the early days, but maintains that the imbalance has been corrected.

**June 23.** Presidents from nine record companies and corporations are indicted in a nationwide payola scandal. Older music fans thought the illegal practice of bribing DJs for air time had all but disappeared following similar charges in 1960.

**October 7.** The New York Supreme Court, refusing to condone "selective deportation based upon secret political grounds," finds that John Lennon cannot be deported for a 1968 British conviction for marijuana possession. (The ruling alludes to evidence that the Nixon administration initiated the proceedings in 1972.) The judges add that Lennon's four-year battle to remain in the United States attests to his faith in the American dream.

**October 27.** Critics praise his new album, *Born to Run*, and compare him to Bob Dylan, Mick Jagger, and Elton John. This week, both *Time* and *Newsweek* feature 26-year-old Bruce Springsteen on their covers—a first for a rock star.

**November 6.** In London, an art school social planner literally pulls the amplifier plugs on Johnny

Rotten & the Sex Pistols after 10 minutes of their act.

**More news.** Two of the original members of the 5th Dimension, Marilyn McCoo and Billy Davis, leave to work as a duo. The Guess Who disbands after 10 years and 14 top 40 hits. Rod Stewart and the Faces split and Ron Wood joins the Stones. In a reunion this year, Paul Simon sings his composition, "My Little Town," with Art Garfunkel. The number appears on both of their solo albums.

• To meet the demand of a revitalized disco scene, the industry churns out dance music with generally forgettable lyrics. Still, discos bring back body contact with the first distinctive dance since 1967—the Hustle.

• This year, Elton John scores a hit with another John Lennon composition. When the Beatles first released the number in 1967, most fans believed the song was drug-inspired. Lennon now reveals that his son Julian drew a friend and a sky full of stars and titled it "Lucy in the Sky with Diamonds." His father followed up with images from "Alice in Wonderland."

• For gold certification, the RIAA requires that an LP collect $1 million in sales. But higher prices have given more and more low-selling albums the coveted testimonial. This year, the association establishes a new standard (effective in 1976): An album, cassette, or multiple-LP set must sell 500,000 copies and the dollar volume must total at least $1 million. Singles must still sell 1 million copies.

• In a spectacular comeback, singer-songwriter Neil Sedaka reaches No. 1 twice this year with "Laughter in the Rain" and "Bad Blood." Elton John, who brought Sedaka to his record label, sings background vocals on the second hit.

• Various artists have recorded reggae through the early 1970s. Johnny Nash broke the top 20 with the Bob Marley tune "Stir It Up" in 1973. This year, Marley & His Wailers introduce their Jamaican Rastafarian music to the United States during a tour. He remains the only reggae star.

• With record sales down and more air time given to fewer hits, industry executives subsidize road tours to give their performers more exposure. Promoters, on the other hand, need big-name attractions to fill large concert halls and auditoriums during the current recession.

• A poll conducted by *Billboard*, *Cash Box*, and *Record World* rates Olivia Newton-John and Elton John as the top recording stars of 1975, and "Love Will Keep Us Together" as the top single.

*New Recording Artists*

Bay City Rollers
Captain & Tenille
Natalie Cole
Queen (in North America)

## *Obituaries*

**Julian "Cannonball" Adderley** (September 15, 1928–August 8, 1975). The saxophonist, damned by purists for selling out, nonetheless turned many Americans into jazz fans. He played with Miles Davis, toured with George Shearing, and formed his own quintet. He later switched from alto to soprano sax. He died four weeks after suffering a stroke.

**Leroy Anderson** (June 29, 1908–May 18, 1975). The semiclassical composer was best known to pop audiences for his descriptive pieces, such as "The Syncopated Clock" (1948).

## MOVIES

*Alice Doesn't Live Here Anymore* (d. Martin Scorsese; color)—Ellen Burstyn, Alfred Lutter, Kris Kristofferson

*Barry Lyndon* (British, d. Stanley Kubrick; color)—Ryan O'Neal, Marisa Berenson, Patrick Magee

*Bite the Bullet* (d. Richard Brooks; color)—Gene Hackman, Candice Bergen, James Coburn, Ben Johnson, Ian Bannen

*The Day of the Locust* (d. John Schlesinger; color)—Donald Sutherland, Karen Black, Burgess Meredith, William Atherton

*Dog Day Afternoon* (d. Sidney Lumet; color)—
Al Pacino, John Cazale, Charles Durning

*Farewell, My Lovely* (d. Dick Richards; color)—
Robert Mitchum, Charlotte Rampling, John Ireland

*The Fortune* (d. Mike Nichols; color)—Jack Nicholson, Warren Beatty, Stockard Channing

*The Four Musketeers* (d. Richard Lester; color)—
Oliver Reed, Raquel Welch, Richard Chamberlain, Michael York, Faye Dunaway, Christopher Lee

*Give 'em Hell, Harry!* (d. Steve Binder; color)—
James Whitmore

*Hearts of the West* (d. Howard Zieff; color)—Jeff Bridges, Andy Griffith, Donald Pleasence

*Hester Street* (d. Joan Micklin Silver; bw)—
Steven Keats, Carol Kane, Dorrie Kavanaugh

*Jaws* (d. Steven Spielberg; color)—Roy Scheider, Robert Shaw, Richard Dreyfuss

*Love and Death* (d. Woody Allen; color)—
Woody Allen, Diane Keaton

*The Man Who Would Be King* (d. John Houston; color)—Sean Connery, Michael Caine, Christopher Plummer

*Nashville* (d. Robert Altman; color)—Henry Gibson, Karen Black, Ronee Blakely, Keith Carradine, Lily Tomlin, Geraldine Chaplin, Ned Beatty

*Night Moves* (d. Arthur Penn; color)—Gene Hackman, Susan Clark, Jennifer Warren

*One Flew Over the Cuckoo's Nest* (d. Milos Forman; color)—Jack Nicholson, Louise Fletcher, Will Samson

*The Prisoner of Second Avenue* (d. Neil Simon; color)—Jack Lemmon, Anne Bancroft, Gene Saks

*The Rocky Horror Picture Show* (British, d. Jim Sharman; color)—Tim Curry, Susan Sarandon, Barry Bostwick, Richard O'Brien

*The Sunshine Boys* (d. Herbert Ross; color)—
Walter Matthau, George Burns, Richard Benjamin

*Three Days of the Condor* (d. Sydney Pollack; color)—Robert Redford, Faye Dunaway, Cliff Robertson, Max von Sydow

## Academy Awards

**April 8.** Prior to the ceremonies, nominee Dustin Hoffman described the Oscars as "a beauty pageant." Comedian Bob Hope jests during the evening, "If Dustin Hoffman wins tonight, he's going to have a friend pick it up for him—George C. Scott."

Frank Sinatra, Sammy Davis, Jr., and Shirley MacLaine join Hope as hosts.

Best Picture—*The Godfather, Part II*
Best Actor—Art Carney (*Harry and Tonto*)
Best Actress—Ellen Burstyn (*Alice Doesn't Live Here Anymore*)
Best Director—Francis Ford Coppola (*The Godfather, Part II*)
Best Supporting Actor—Robert De Niro (*The Godfather, Part II*)
Best Supporting Actress—Ingrid Bergman (*Murder on the Orient Express*)
Best Song—"We May Never Love Like This Again" from *The Towering Inferno*
Honorary Awards—Jean Renoir; Howard Hawks

Best actress Ellen Burstyn signs part of her acceptance speech for her deaf parents. Ingrid Bergman tells the world Valentina Cortese deserved to win as supporting actress.

*The Godfather, Part II* is the first sequel to win best picture.

Producer Bert Schneider, in accepting an Oscar for his Vietnam War documentary, *Hearts and Minds*, reads a telegram of greetings from the VC delegation in Paris. Since Academy bylaws prohibit any consideration of labor, economic, or political issues, a furious Bob Hope writes a disclaimer and Frank Sinatra reads it to the audience. The statement gets a mixed reaction.

## News

**February 9.** This year's American Film Institute Lifetime Achievement Award goes to director Orson Welles.

**March 4.** Queen Elizabeth knights 85-year-old Charles Chaplin. The silent screen actor, who grew up in London, declares he would rather be called Sir Charles than Sir Charlie.

**April 7.** *Business Week* reports that nine major film companies have funded a new MPAA Film Security Office to guard against the theft of original prints and to investigate piracy complaints.

With the $250-cost of 16-mm prints, pirates find a ready market for $75 or $150 counterfeits. And videotape copies offer an even greater profit margin, with blanks priced at about $20. A recent New York police raid recovered illegal copies of 500 films, including *The Towering Inferno* and *The Godfather, Part II*.

**May 17.** After refusing to cooperate with HUAC in 1947, Dalton Trumbo served 10 months in prison and was blacklisted by the industry. Since the screenwriter could sell work only under a pseudonym, he dared not claim the 1957 Oscar awarded to "Robert Rich" for *The Brave One*. Trumbo admitted two years later to being Rich, but the Academy delayed giving him the award until today.

**August 25.** The Museum of Modern Art honors John Randolph Bray with a 96th birthday party and a showing of animated shorts from 1910 to 1918. The pioneer cartoonist released the first commercial cartoon in the United States: *The Dachshund and the Sausage* (1910).

Bray created movement by filming a sequence of drawings, each slightly advancing the action. But while he made no deliberate changes in the background, unavoidable variations from frame to frame produced a noticeable wobble when the film was run through a projector. To eliminate this problem, the cartoonist sketched each drawing on transparent material, placed the sheet on top of a set background, and photographed the whole as one frame. His patented cel system cut drawing time by 80 percent and laid the basis of all cartooning methods to follow.

**August 28.** On the 100th anniversary of the birth of author Edgar Rice Burroughs, four actors who portrayed his jungle character Tarzan hold a reunion in Los Angeles. Johnny Weismuller, Buster Crabbe, Jock Mahoney, and James Pierce played Tarzan in 6 movie serials, 40 films, hundreds of radio broadcasts, and 52 TV episodes.

The *New York Times* notes that Burroughs' literary heirs began to exploit Tarzan's full commercial value just eight years ago. They now collect an estimated $50 million annually.

**December 27.** According to an article in *The New Republic*, Central Casting has become "a shell of its former self." In the earliest American films, directors used few actors in a scene. Then D. W. Griffith peopled his movie backgrounds to achieve reality and created the "extra."

By the mid-1920s, Hollywood studios needed thousands of extras every day. To coordinate hiring, the major studios cooperatively established the Central Casting Corporation in 1926. Today, those same studios shoot few films in Hollywood.

**More news.** Jawsmania grips America as fake fins appear in swimming pools, stores sell spin-off products, and beach resorts lose money. A motel owner in St. Petersburg, Florida, laments to *Newsweek* magazine, "The picture premiered here last Friday. Since Saturday, people have been standing out on the beach looking out over the water for sharks. They don't go in."

• The lovable blue gnomes created in 1958 as minor characters in a Belgian cartoon series appear in their first movie—*The Flute with the Six Smurfs*.

• After a 20-year effort to get the picture off the ground, John Huston finally makes *The Man Who Would Be King* (1975). He first planned to pair Clark Gable and Humphrey Bogart, but Bogey became ill, then died in 1957. A later teaming of Richard Burton and Peter O'Toole was abandoned when Huston failed to find the necessary backing.

• Since 1949, John Wayne has failed to make the annual list of box-office stars only once—1958. This year, Duke falls off the list permanently.

• For American moviegoers, the average admission price has risen 100 percent since 1965—from $1 to $2. In 1975, the movie industry reports a second straight year of record revenues with some $2 billion.

• The 20-member Stuntwomen's Association pressures movie producers to end the traditional practice of dressing a man in women's clothing for female stars' dangerous stunts. Arguing that trained women can take a bruising fall just as well as men, the head of the association, Jeannie Epper, declares, "Audiences are getting smarter. And you know what a man looks like in drag."

• An *Esquire* article on the new gang in Hollywood profiles three rising stars: Joe Don Baker, Pamela Grier, and Robert De Niro.

| Top Box Office Stars | Newcomers |
|---|---|
| Robert Redford | Stockard Channing |
| Barbra Streisand | Bo Svenson |
| Al Pacino | Susan Blakely |
| Charles Bronson | William Atherton |
| Paul Newman | Brad Dourif |
| Clint Eastwood | Perry King |
| Burt Reynolds | Bo Hopkins |
| Woody Allen | Conny Van Dyke |
| Steve McQueen | Ronee Blakley |
| Gene Hackman | Paul LeMat |

## Top Money-Maker of the Year

*Jaws*
(Making a record $124 million in the first 80 days, the huge shark quickly knocks *The Godfather* [1972] out of first place.)

## Flop of the Year

*At Long Last Love*
The 1930s-style musical, directed by Peter Bogdanovich and starring Burt Reynolds and Cybill Shepherd, recovers less than a quarter of its $6-million production costs.

## Quote of the Year

"It's not that I'm afraid to die, I just don't want to be there when it happens."
—Actor-director Woody Allen (*Newsweek*, June 23)

## Obituaries

**Susan Hayward** (June 30, 1919–March 14, 1975). The beautiful redhead was one of Hollywood's most bankable women stars during the 1950s. At her best portraying troubled and despairing women, Hayward won an Oscar for her performance as a real-life convicted killer in *I Want to Live* (1958). She died of a brain tumor.

**Moe Howard** (June 19, 1897–May 4, 1975). The last of the original Three Stooges survived Larry Fine (October 5, 1911–January 24, 1975) by just five months. Howard and Fine formed a vaudeville trio with Moe's brother Shemp in the 1920s, but a third brother, Curly (Jerome) Howard (1906–January 18, 1952) replaced Shemp in the early 1930s.

From 1934 to 1958, the Three Stooges bopped, punched, and slapped their way through some 200 Columbia shorts, the longest-running series of two-reel comedies in cinema history.

When Curly suffered a stroke in 1946, Shemp returned. He died in 1955 (1952–November 22, 1955) and Joe Besser took over, to be replaced in turn by Joe De Rita in 1959. At that time, with the exposure of TV reruns, the comic trio finally ventured into feature films.

**Marjorie Main** (February 24, 1890–April 10,

*Larry Fine, Moe Howard and Curly Howard in a typical Three Stooges comedy scene.*

1975). During the 1950s, the veteran actress delighted moviegoers as the hillbilly Ma Kettle in a series of comedy second features.

**Fredric March** (August 31, 1897–April 14, 1975). Alternating between the stage and screen during his 50-year career, March became one of the most respected actors in the profession. He won two best actor Oscars for *Dr. Jekyll and Mr. Hyde* (1932) and *The Best Years of Our Lives* (1946).

**George Stevens** (December 8, 1904?–March 8, 1975). During his 35-year career, Stevens directed several American classics including *Gunga Din* (1939), *A Place in the Sun* (1951), for an Oscar, *Shane* (1953), and *Giant* (1956), for a second Oscar. But after *The Greatest Story Ever Told* (1965) proved to be a monumental flop, Stevens made only one more film.

**William Wellman** (February 29, 1896–December 9, 1975). The boisterous film director made many mediocre movies, but his best included *Wings* (1929)—the winner of the first best-picture Oscar—*Public Enemy* (1931), *A Star Is Born* (1937), and *The Ox-Bow Incident* (1942).

## TELEVISION AND RADIO

### New Prime-Time TV Programs

"Baretta" (January 17, 1975– ; Police Drama)—Robert Blake, Edward Grover, Tom Ewell, Michael D. Roberts

"Barney Miller" (January 23, 1975– ; Situation Comedy)—Hal Linden, Abe Vigoda, Maxwell Gail, Jack Soo, Ron Glass

"The Jeffersons" (January 18, 1975– ; Situation Comedy)—Sherman Hemsley, Isabel Sanford, Damon Evans

"NBC's Saturday Night Live" (October 11, 1975– ; Comedy/Variety)—Regulars: Gilda Radner, Garrett Morris, Jane Curtin, Laraine Newman, John Belushi, Chevy Chase, Dan Aykroyd, Albert Brooks

"One Day at a Time" (December 16, 1975– ; Situation Comedy)—Bonnie Franklin, Mackenzie Phillips, Valerie Bertinelli, Pat Harrington, Jr.

"Starsky and Hutch" (September 3, 1975– ; Police Drama)—Paul Michael Glaser, David Soul, Bernie Hamilton, Antonio Fargas

"Switch" (September 9, 1975– ; Detective)—Robert Wagner, Eddie Albert, Charlie Callas, Sharon Gless

"Welcome Back, Kotter" (September 9, 1975– ; Situation Comedy)—Gabriel Kaplan, Marcia Strassman, John Travolta, Robert Hegyes, Lawrence-Hilton Jacobs, Ron Palillo

### Emmy Awards 1974–1975 (May 19, 1975)

Drama Series—"Upstairs, Downstairs" ("Masterpiece Theatre," PBS)

Comedy/Variety or Music Series—"The Carol Burnett Show" (CBS)

Comedy Series—"The Mary Tyler Moore Show" (CBS)

Children's Series—"Star Trek" (NBC)

Best Actor in a Series—Robert Blake ("Baretta," ABC)

Best Actress in a Series—Jean Marsh ("Upstairs, Downstairs," ["Masterpiece Theatre," PBS])

Best Comedian in a Series—Tony Randall ("The Odd Couple," ABC)

Best Comedienne in a Series—Valerie Harper ("Rhoda," CBS)

### News

**January 1.** Effective today, the NAB Television Code reduces commercial time for children's programming to 10 minutes per hour on weekends. The move was largely prompted by TV's promotion of sugar-coated cereals and expensive toys during Saturday-morning programming. The revision also forbids the use of a show's character—real or animated—in advertising the product.

**January 6.** Bill Beutel and Stephanie Edwards host the first ABC morning show, "A.M. America." By the beginning of November, the network will completely overhaul the program, putting David Hartman and Nancy Dussault on "Good Morning America."

**January 6.** NBC expands the daytime soap "Another World" to a full hour. With the doubling of "Days of Our Lives" in April, the network takes six of nine daytime slots. Predictably, CBS and ABC follow suit with their soaps. Several daytime game shows stretch to an hour as well this year.

**January 6.** Chuck Woolery and Susan Stafford spin the "Wheel of Fortune," a new NBC quiz show from Merv Griffin Productions.

**January 18.** In yet another spin-off from "All in the Family," Norman Lear portrays a black American in "The Jeffersons." Pigheaded and reactionary as Archie Bunker, George Jefferson nonetheless faces the country's racial problems from a completely different angle.

**March.** During the first two weeks of the month, all three networks announce forthcoming dramatizations of classic and best-selling novels. Some will appear next season, some the year after. ABC, for instance, will use the new miniseries format for "Rich Man, Poor Man."

**Spring.** One day, Wayne Rogers fails to show up for work; he never returns. Originally intended to be the star of "M*A*S*H," his role has deteriorated into playing second fiddle to Alan Alda. The script sends him home without a goodbye, and Hawkeye meets his replacement, B. J. Hunnicut, played by Mike Farrell.

But when popular McLean Stevenson leaves "M*A*S*H" for a long-term contract with rival NBC, CBS secretly decides to kill off his character, Col. Henry Blake. Just before taping, Gary Burghoff is given the news to deliver as Radar. The stunned faces in the operating room hold that little grain of truth. In the next episode, Col. Sherman Potter arrives.

**April 8.** Under pressure from the FCC and various groups protesting TV sex and violence, the networks reluctantly agree to make 8:00–9:00 P.M. the family hour. None of the fall programs in this time slot will last past January.

**May 5.** The first South African television transmission takes place in Johannesburg. The government, which has long regarded TV as morally corrupt, authorizes a regular 35-hour weekly schedule for next January.

**May 25.** In a long article, *The New York Times* discusses the present status of the video cassette. Over the past eight years, some 10 companies have produced workable systems, but none has proved marketable. The magnetic-tape machine, for instance, resists manufacturers' efforts to bring the unit cost below $1,000 and the $1/2$-inch tape under $30.

Recently, both RCA and Philips-MCA announced plans to introduce a shallow, rectangular player with a phonograph-record-size disc; the disc will be placed on a turntable and the lid closed. But RCA takes the image from the top while MCA uses the lower surface, making the systems incompatible.

**June 1.** The NBC News and Information Service offers some two dozen radio affiliates 50 minutes of news and features per hour. The network loses millions, but the experiment introduces the all-news concept to a broader market base.

*Statistics:* In the 1960–1961 academic year, some 2,600 undergraduates enrolled in 98 broadcasting degree programs across the country. This year, the NAB estimates that 17,250 will enter 228 programs.

**July.** In one of the largest package transactions, the networks pay Paramount $76 million for the television rights to 42 recent films. NBC shells out $15 million alone for *Godfather I* and *Godfather II*. Most fees cover multiple showings, but some, like *Chinatown*, will be telecast just once.

**August 6.** NBC is the first to insert 60-second news updates into prime time.

**August 10.** First lady Betty Ford tells "60 Minutes" that all her children may have tried marijuana, that she might have tried it herself when young if it had been available, that she would not be surprised if her 18-year-old daughter Susan admitted to having an affair, and that the Supreme Court made a "great decision" in legalizing abortion. The interview creates an uproar, but the White House press secretary says President Ford "has long ceased to be perturbed or surprised by his wife's remarks."

**September 1.** "Gunsmoke" leaves the air after a 20-year run. Since Marshal Dillon and the other inhabitants of Dodge city inspired a flock of imitators through the 1950s and 1960s, it is perhaps fitting that the CBS perennial was the last Western left on network television.

---

*Statistics:* TV viewers have a choice of 20 police/private-eye series this year, up from 7 in 1969 and none in 1964.

---

**September 29.** WGPR-TV in Detroit is the first black-owned television station in the continental United States.

**September 30.** With 9–10 million subscribers (14.5 percent of U.S. televisions), cable is striving to provide more popular programming. Tonight systems in Florida and Mississippi transmit the Ali-Frazier fight from the Philippines for an extra charge. The "pay-cable" industry will likely expand more rapidly with the completion of 20 satellite-receiving stations now under construction.

**October 11.** NBC premieres "Saturday Night Live," a freewheeling comedy-variety show starring the Not Ready for Prime Time Players—Dan Ackroyd, John Belushi, Chevy Chase, Jane Curtin, Laraine Newman, and Gilda Radner. George Carlin hosts the first show and the musical guests are Janis Ian and Billy Preston. (On December 13, the 90-minute show is not quite live. Afraid host Richard Pryor might cross the censorship line, the network uses a five-second electronic delay; two deletions are made.)

**November.** The CBC inaugurates its stereo FM network, the longest system of its kind in the world.

**December.** Correspondents Mike Wallace and Morley Safer welcome Dan Rather to "60 Minutes."

**More news.** While music and news continue to dominate the air waves, the nostalgia boom introduces more and more old-time programs to radio listeners: "Fibber McGee and Molly," "The Green Hornet," "The Shadow," and others.

Since 1964, the percentage of American households with a color television set has mushroomed from 3.1 percent to 70 percent.

### TV Commercials

Pepsi-Cola—A spontaneous photo shoot provides the soft drink company with one of its most successful commercials. A litter of puppies bowl over a small boy, who thrashes around in fits of laughter.

Xerox—Brother Dominic, the monk who photocopies his manuscripts, is intended as a one-time commercial. But he becomes so popular that the company employs actor Jack Eagle on a full-time basis.

### Obituaries

**Ernst Alexanderson** (January 25, 1878–May 14, 1975). The Swedish-born electrical engineer registered over 300 patents in his lifetime. His selective tuning device made the first radio transmission possible and remains part of the modern system. He improved antennae and telephone relays, and gave the first public demonstration of a home television in 1930.

**Milton Cross** (April 16, 1897–January 3, 1975). For 43 years, Cross introduced the Saturday-afternoon broadcasts of the Metropolitan Opera. The "Voice of the Met" was one of the few left from the golden age of radio.

**James Earl Jewell** (February 20, 1906–August 5, 1975). Later a radio executive, Jewell in his early days wrote, produced, and directed the original "Green Hornet" and "Lone Ranger" radio series.

**(Jackie) Moms Mabley** (March 19, 1897–May 23, 1975). The earthy black comedienne entertained talk show audiences with her ragtag getups, raspy voice, and toothless ruminating.

**Ozzie Nelson** (March 20, 1907–June 3, 1975). Nelson and his wife, Harriet, entertained generations of Americans with their radio and television family adventures.

**Rod Serling** (December 25, 1924–June 28, 1975). One of television's finest dramatists, with five Emmys between 1955 and 1964, Serling will be best remembered for his contribution to American pop culture—the "Twilight Zone."

**Arthur Treacher** (July 23, 1894–December 14, 1975). The archetypical disdainful butler in movies, Treacher played second fiddle to talk-show host Merv Griffin through the 1960s.

# SPORTS

## *Winners*

### *Baseball*

World Series—Cincinnati Reds (NL), 4 games; Boston Red Sox (AL), 3 games

Player of the Year—Fred Lynn (Boston Red Sox, AL); Joe Morgan (Cincinnati Reds, NL)

Rookie of the Year—Fred Lynn (Boston Red Sox, AL); John Montefusco (San Francisco Giants, NL)

### *Football*

NFC Championship—Dallas Cowboys 37, Los Angeles Rams 7

AFC Championship—Pittsburgh Steelers 16, Oakland Raiders 10

Super Bowl X (January 18, 1976)—Pittsburgh Steelers 21, Dallas Cowboys 17

College Bowls (January 1, 1975)—
Rose Bowl, USC 18, Ohio State 17
Cotton Bowl, Penn State 41, Baylor 20
Orange Bowl, Notre Dame 13, Alabama 11
Sugar Bowl, Nebraska 13, Florida 10

Heisman Trophy—Archie Griffin (Ohio State, TB)

Grey Cup—Edmonton Eskimos 9, Montreal Alouettes 8

### *Basketball*

NBA Championship—Golden State Warriors, 4 games; Washington Bullets, 0 games

MVP of the Year—Bob McAdoo (Buffalo Braves)

Rookie of the Year—Keith Wilkes (Golden State Warriors)

### NCAA Championship—UCLA 92, Kentucky 85

### *Tennis*

U.S. Open—Men, Manuel Orantes (vs. Jimmy Connors); Women, Chris Evert (vs. Evonne Goolagong [Cawley])

Wimbledon—Men, Arthur Ashe (vs. Jimmy Connors); Women, Billy Jean King (vs. Evonne Goolagong [Cawley])

### *Golf*

Masters—Jack Nicklaus
U.S. Open—Lou Graham
British Open—Tom Watson

### *Hockey*

Stanley Cup—Philadelphia Flyers, 4 games; Buffalo Sabres, 2 games

### *Ice Skating*

World Championship—Men, Sergei Volkov (USSR); Women, Dianne de Leeuw (The Netherlands)

U.S. National—Men, Gordon McKellen; Women, Dorothy Hamill

Canadian National—Men, Toller Cranston; Women, Lynn Nightingale

### *Kentucky Derby*

Foolish Pleasure—Jacinto Vasquez, jockey

### *Athlete of the Year*

Male—Fred Lynn (Baseball)
Female—Chris Evert (Tennis)

### *Last Season*

George Blanda (Football)
Len Dawson (Football)
Rollie Fingers (Baseball)
Bob Gibson (Baseball)
Henri Richard (Hockey)

Chester Walker (Basketball)
Len Wilkens (Basketball)

## News

**January 12.** Pittsburgh wins the Super Bowl, the team's first NFL Championship in 42 years. Franco Harris, with 158 yards rushing, is named MVP.

**March 19.** In the first statewide ruling on the constitutionality of male-female sports competition, a Pennsylvania court rules that the Interscholastic Athletic Association must admit girls.

**April.** At a track meet in Portland, pole vaulter Steve Smith clears 18′4″. Since 1962, the standard has risen 2′4″.

**April 3.** The International Chess Federation strips American Bobby Fischer of his world title. He had refused to play unless the federation guaranteed the title would remain his in the event of a draw. Soviet challenger Anatoly Karpov becomes champion by default.

**April 5.** No. 1-ranked Chris Evert, with a win over Martina Navratilova in the Virginia Slims Championship, collects the biggest prize in the history of women's tennis—$40,000.00. The Women's Tennis Association, fed up with smaller purses, threatens Wimbledon with a boycott. The tournament reluctantly raises the female-male prize ratio from 70 percent to 80 percent and agrees to annual renegotiations.

**April 7.** Julius Erving of the New York Nets and George McGinnis of the Indiana Pacers receive an equal number of MVP votes for the 1974–1975 season. The joint ABA award marks the first MVP tie in the history of pro basketball.

---

*Statistics:* Through the 1947–1948 season, the BAA and NBL scored an average 66.5 points a game. This season, the NBA chalked up an average 108.8 points. The 24-second shot clock, introduced in the 1950s, accounts for much of the 27-year difference, but the average basketball player has grown from 6′3″ and 195 pounds to 6′6″ and 208 pounds.

---

**April 8.** Frank Robinson debuts as the first major-league black manager. The Cleveland Indians designated hitter today as well, he hits his 575th HR in his first at bat.

**April 27.** With her sixth-place finish in Spain, Lella Lombard becomes the first woman to score in a Grand Prix auto race.

**May 4.** A home run in a game against the Giants drives in Houston Astro Bob Watson—the 1 millionth run in major league baseball. Watson receives a $1,000 watch, but loses his shoes to the Baseball Hall of Fame.

**June 3.** Brazilian Edson Arantes de Nascimento comes out of retirement at age 34 to sign with the New York Cosmos. The legendary soccer star—better known as Pelé—averaged a goal a game throughout his career and set an international record with three World Cup appearances—1958, 1962, and 1970.

For $4½–$7 million, over three years, team owner Warner Communications can also use Pelé's name in publicity and product ads and will collect 50 percent of increased gate receipts at other league stadiums.

**June 3.** Many educational institutions have simply ignored Title IX of the 1972 Educational Act. The University of Nebraska, for instance, allocates women's programs a mere $45,000 of a $4-million athletic budget. Through with voluntary compliance, the Department of Health, Education, and Welfare sends funding guidelines to all public schools and colleges receiving federal aid.

**July 6.** In a match race against Kentucky Derby winner Foolish Pleasure, Ruffian pulls up with a shattered leg. Veterinarians attempt surgery, but the horse must be destroyed. The unbeatable filly had swept nine races in two seasons.

**July 18.** In a game last January, Boston Bruin Dave Forbes used the butt end of his stick against Minnesota North Star Henry Boucha. The NHL handed down a 10-game suspension, but when Boucha required eye surgery, Forbes was indicted for assault. He is the first professional athlete charged with a crime committed during play. The trial ends today in a hung jury.

**August 1.** The New York Yankees hire Billy Martin to replace Bill Virdon as manager. (Martin was just fired by the Texas Rangers.) Newspapers describe player reaction as "mixed."

**August 3.** New Orleans formally dedicates the Superdome. Finished behind schedule at a cost of $162 million, the world's largest indoor sports and entertainment center seats 97,365.

**September 6.** Martina Navratilova asks the United States for political asylum. The Czech tennis star will turn 19 on October 18.

**October 1 (September 30 in the United States).** At their last meeting in 1971 Joe Frazier won. But last night Muhammad Ali said, "If old Joe even dreams of beating me he should have to wake up and apologize." Today, in the title bout, a battered Frazier throws in the towel in the 14th round. Promoters estimate some 700 million people watched the savage "Thrilla in Manila." Ali makes about $4½ million and Frazier collects $2 million.

**October 22.** With a bloop single by second-baseman Joe Morgan in the bottom of the ninth, the Cincinnati Reds win their first World Series in 35 years.

**October 22.** The WFL ceases operations 12 weeks into its second season. The league's head office blames competition from the NFL, media skepticism, and bad weather. The lack of a lucrative TV contract undoubtedly proved a major factor as well. Two days later, NFL Commissioner Pete Rozelle tells his clubs that no WFL player may be signed during the remainder of this season. Stranded players include Larry Csonka and Paul Warfield.

---

*Statistics:* In 1947, some 1.8 million people attended 60 NFL regular season games. This year, 182 games draw 10.2 million fans.

---

**December 2.** Ohio State University running back Archie Griffin becomes the first college player to collect a second Heisman Trophy.

**December 23.** A three-member arbitration panel finds that Dodger Andy Messersmith and Expo Dave McNally may become free agents after playing out their option year. Overruling baseball's long-standing reserve clause, the decision gives the athlete the power to determine the course of his own career.

## Records

**February 16.** With a victory over Vitas Gerulaitis, Jimmy Connors becomes the first tennis player in modern times to win three consecutive National Men's Indoor Open championships.

**April 13.** Jack Nicklaus wins an unprecedented fifth Masters at Augusta. And only Ben Hogan in 1953, and Nicklaus himself in 1965, had posted better scores than this year's 276. Afterward, the 35-year-old reveals one secret of the game. Because a golf ball needs at least 10 minutes to regain its shape, he never uses the same ball two holes in a row.

**May 10.** At the professional track and field event in El Paso, American shot-putter Brian Oldfield stuns spectators with a toss of 75 feet. His distance breaks the current world record by 3 feet, 2 inches—the largest gain ever on any standing record. (Oldfield uses an unusual technique, spinning like a discus thrower.) Unfortunately, the record books recognize only amateur achievements.

**June 1.** With a 1–0 win over the Baltimore Orioles, Nolan Ryan ties the single-season four no-hitter record set by Sandy Koufax. But in September, bone chips will force Ryan to undergo elbow surgery and his future will remain uncertain. That month, in one of baseball's most interesting no-hitters, four Oakland pitchers combine to beat Ryan's Angels 5–0.

**July 30.** In her swim across the English Channel, 17-year-old Canadian Cindy Nicholas sets a new women's record of 9 hours, 46 minutes.

**August 12.** John Walker of New Zealand breaks the 3:50-mile barrier with a time of 3:49:4. The feat comes 21 years after Roger Bannister ran the first sub-4-minute mile. *Track and Field* predicts athletes will achieve a 3:40 mile by the year 2000.

## What They Said

After winning his first starting game, Dolphin third-string quarterback Don Strock tells reporters, "I don't think I've been asked this many questions since my mother caught me drinking in high school." *Sports Illustrated*, December 22–29 [double issue]

## Obituaries

**Avery Brundage** (September 28, 1887–May 8, 1975). A U.S. entrant in the 1912 Olympic pentathlon and decathlon, Brundage strove throughout his life to preserve amatuerism in sport. As president of the IOC (1952–1972), he punished athletes for minor infractions and refused to allow political events to interfere with Olympic competition. Many characterized his views as an obsession and dubbed him "Slavery Bondage."

**Ezzard Charles** (July 7, 1921–May 28, 1975). The U.S. boxer held the heavyweight championship of the world from 1949 to 1951. At his retirement he had won 96 of 122 bouts. A muscle disease later confined him to a wheelchair.

**(Robert Moses) Lefty Grove** (March 6, 1900–May 22, 1975). In nine seasons with the Athletics (1925–1933) and eight with the Red Sox (1934–1941), the left-hander led the AL in ERA nine times, chalked up 2,266 strikeouts, and posted 300 victories and 141 losses. In one of his most memorable appearances, with the tying run on third, the temperamental pitcher struck out New York Yankee greats Lou Gehrig, Babe Ruth, and Bob Meusel—with nine pitches.

**Graham Hill** (February 15, 1929–November 29, 1975). The British racing driver won 14 of his record 176 Grand Prix races. After a bad crash in 1969, he fought back and won the 1972 Le Mans. He died attempting to land his plane in the fog.

**(Charles Dillon) Casey Stengel** (July 30, 1890–September 29, 1975). After 13 years in the outfield with five major league teams, Stengel took over as manager of the 1934 Brooklyn Dodgers. He moved to the Braves in 1938 and returned to the minors (1944–1948) before joining the New York Yankees as manager in 1949.

Dismissed as a clown for his inventive language and antics (he would "faint" at an umpire's decision), Casey shocked critics and fans alike by leading the Yanks to five straight pennants and five World Series. The team won another three divisional titles and two World Series before management fired him for being too old. (He responded with typical Stengelese: "Ill never make the mistake of being 70 again.")

But the Ol' Professor refused to quit. He returned to the dugout as the Mets first manager. And while the team placed last every year, the fans still loved him. Finally a broken hip forced Stengel into retirement in 1965. The following year, he was elected to the Hall of Fame and the Yankees retired his No. 37.

# Acronyms and Abbreviations

AAU—Amateur Athletic Union
ABA—American Basketball Association
ABC—American Broadcasting Company
ABM—antiballistic missile system
ACLU—American Civil Liberties Union
AEC—Atomic Energy Commission
AFC—American Football Conference
AFL—American Federation of Labor
AFL—American Football League
AIM—American Indian Movement
AIP—American International Pictures
AL—American League (baseball)
ALA—American Library Association
AMA—American Medical Association
ANC—African National Congress
AP—Associated Press
ASCAP—American Society of Composers, Authors and Publishers
AT&T—American Telephone and Telegraph
BAA—Basketball Association of America
BASIC—Beginner's All-purpose Symbolic Instruction Code (computers)
BBC—British Broadcasting Corporation
BOAC—British Overseas Airways Corporation
CAA—Civil Aeronautics Administration
CAB—Civil Aeronautics Board

CAT—computerized axial tomography (scanning machine)
CATV—cable television
CB—Citizens Band (radio)
c&b—chemical and biological (weapons)
CBC—Canadian Broadcasting Corporation
CBS—Columbia Broadcasting System
CCF—Co-operative Commonwealth Federation (Canada)
CDU—Christian Democratic Party (West Germany)
CENTO—Central Treaty Organization
CFL—Canadian Football League
CIA—Central Intelligence Agency
CIO—Congress of Industrial Organizations
CM—command module (Apollo)
CNR—Canadian National Railway
COBOL—Common Business Oriented Language (computers)
Cominform—Communist Information Bureau
Comsat—Communications Satellite Corporation
CORE—Congress of Racial Equality
CPB—Corporation for Public Broadcasting
CPR—Canadian Pacific Railway
CREEP—Committee to Reelect the President
CRTC—Canadian Radio-Television Commission

CTV—Canadian Television Network
CW—country and western (music)
DEA—Drug Enforcement Agency
DDT—dichlorodiphenyltrichloroethane
DEC—Digital Equipment Corporation
DES—diethylstilbestrol
DEW—Distant Early Warning Line
DH—designated hitter (baseball)
DJ—disc jockey
DMZ—Demilitarized Zone
DNA—deoxyribonucleic acid
EC—Educational Comics, later Entertaining Comics
EEC—European Economic Community
EEOC—Equal Employment Opportunities Commission
EFTA—European Free Trade Association
EMI—Electric and Musical Industries
EPA—Environmental Protection Agency
ERA—earned run average (baseball)
ERA—Equal Rights Amendment
ERDA—Energy Research and Development Administration
ESRO—European Space Research Organization
FAA—Federal Aviation Administration
FBI—Federal Bureau of Investigation
FCC—Federal Communications Commission
FDA—Food and Drug Administration
FDP—Free Democratic Party (West Germany)
FLN—Front de la Libération Nationale (Algeria)
FLQ—Front de libération du Québec
FOA—Foreign Operations Administration
FTC—Federal Trade Commission
GATT—General Agreement on Tariffs and Trade
GE—General Electric
GM—General Motors
GNP—gross national product
HBP—hit by a pitch (baseball)
HEW—Department of Health, Education, and Welfare
HFFA—Housing and Home Finance Agency
HOLC—Home Owners' Loan Corporation
HR—home run
HUAC—House Un-American Activities Committee

HUD—Housing and Urban Affairs Department
IBM—International Business Machines
IC—integrated circuit
ICBM—intercontinental ballistic missile
ICC—Interstate Commerce Commission
ICCS—International Commission of Control and Supervision
ICI—Imperial Chemical Industries
IMF—International Monetary Fund
Intelsat—International Telecommunications Satellite Consortium
IOC—International Olympic Committee
IRA—individual retirement account
IRA—Irish Republican Army
IRS—Internal Revenue Service
ITT—International Telephone and Telegraph
IUD—intrauterine contraceptive device
KGB—Committee on State Security (Komitet Gosudarstvennoi Bezopasnosti)
KKK—Ku Klux Klan
KO, KO's, KO'd—to knock out, knocks out, knocked out (boxing)
LM—lunar module (Apollo)
LP—long-playing phonograph record
LPGA—Ladies Professional Golf Association
LSD—lysergic acid diethylamide
MAAG—Military Assistance and Advisory Group in South Vietnam
MACV—Military Assistance Command in South Vietnam
MASH—Mobile Army Surgical Hospital
MBS—Mutual Broadcasting System
MGM—Metro-Goldwyn-Mayer
MIRV—multiple independently targetable reentry vehicle
MP—Member of Parliament
MPAA—Motion Picture Association of America
MPPDA—Motion Picture Producers and Distributors of America
MSG—monosodium glutamate
MVP—most valuable player (athletics)
NAA—National Aeronautic Association
NAACP—National Association for the Advancement of Colored People
NAB—National Association of Broadcasting

NARAS—National Academy of Recording Arts and Sciences
NASA—National Aeronautics and Space Administration
NASL—North American Soccer League
NATO—North Atlantic Treaty Organization
NBA—National Basketball Association
NBC—National Broadcasting Company
NBL—National Basketball League
NCAA—National Collegiate Athletic Association
NDP—New Democratic Party (Canada)
NEA—National Education Association
NET—National Educational Television
NFB—National Film Board (Canada)
NFC—National Football Conference
NFL—National Football League
NFWA—National Farm Workers Association
NHL—National Hockey League
NL—National League (baseball)
NLF—National Liberation Front (South Vietnam)
NORAD—North American Air Defense
NOW—National Organization for Women
NRC—Nuclear Regulatory Commission
NSA—National Security Agency
NSC—National Security Council
OAS—Organization of American States
OECD—Organization for Economic Cooperation and Development
OEEC—Organization for European Economic Cooperation
OPEC—Organization of Petroleum Exporting Countries
PBS—Public Broadcasting System
PCB—polychlorinated biphenyl
PGA—Professional Golfers' Association
PHS—Public Health Service
PLO—Palestine Liberation Organization
PM—prime minister
POW—prisoner of war
PRG—Provisional Revolutionary Government of the Republic of South Vietnam
PT—patrol torpedo
RAF—Royal Air Force (Britain)

R&B—rhythm & blues (music)
RBI—runs batted in (baseball)
RCA—Radio Corporation of America
RCMP—Royal Canadian Mounted Police
RIAA—Record Industry Associates of America
RKO—Radio-Keith Orpheum
RNA—ribonucleic acid
rpm—revolutions per minute (records)
SAC—Strategic Air Command
SALT—Strategic Arms Limitation Talks
SAM—surface-to-air missile
SCLC—Southern Christian Leadership Conference
SDP—Social Democratic Party (West Germany)
SDS—Students for a Democratic Society
SEATO—Southeast Asia Treaty Organization
SEC—Securities and Exchange Commission
SHAPE—Supreme Headquarters Allied Powers in Europe
SLA—Symbionese Liberation Army
SNCC—Student Nonviolent Coordinating Committee
SSEC—Selective Sequence Electronic Calculator
SSI—supplementary security income
TCA—Trans-Canada Airlines
TD—touchdown (football)
3-D—three-dimensional (motion picture)
TKO—Technical Knockout (boxing)
TM—transcendental meditation
TWA—Trans World Airlines
UA—United Artists
UAR—United Arab Republic
UAW—United Auto Workers
UFO—unidentified flying object
UHF—ultra-high frequency
UN—United Nations
UNIVAC—Universal Automatic Computer
UNICEF—United Nations Children's Fund (originally United Nations International Children's Emergency Fund)
UP—United Press
UPC—universal product code
UPI—United Press International
USAF—United States Air Force
USIA—United States Information Agency

USSR—Union of Soviet Socialist Republics
VC—Vietcong
VHF—very high frequency
VOA—Voice of America
WBA—World Boxing Association
WFL—World Football League

WHA—World Hockey Association
WHO—World Health Organization
WSP—Women Strike for Peace
W.W.I—World War I
W.W.II—World War II
YIP—Youth International Party

# Bibliography

## GENERAL

*The Americana Annual: Yearbook of the Encyclopedia Americana.* Americana Corp., 1955–

*Britannica Book of the Year.* Encyclopaedia Britannica, Inc., 1948–

*Carruth, Gorton. *The Encyclopedia of American Facts and Dates*, 8th edition. Harper & Row, 1987.

*Chronicle of the 20th Century.* Chronicle Publications, 1987.

*The Fabulous Sixties* [Videorecording]. MPI Home Video, 1970. 10 videocassettes.

*Facts on File. Yearbook, 1947– .* Facts on File, Inc.

Gallup, George Horace. *The Gallup Poll, 1935–1971.* Random House, 1972. 3 volumes.

*Historical Statistics of the United States, Colonial Times to 1970.* Bureau of the Census, 1975. 2 volumes.

Kane, Joseph Nathan. *Famous First Facts*, 4th edition. H. W. Wilson, 1981.

Leonard, Thomas M. *Day by Day, the Forties.* Facts On File, 1977. (This publisher also produces *Day by Day, the Fifties*; *Day by Day, the Sixties*; and *Day by Day, the Seventies.*)

*New York Times.* 1947–

Robertson, Patrick. *The Shell Book of Firsts*, 2nd edition. Ebury Press and Michael Joseph, Ltd., 1983.

*This fabulous Century, Vol. 5 (1940–1950), vol. 6 (1950–1960), vol. 7 (1960–1970).* Time-Life Books, 1969.

*Trager, James, ed. *The People's Chronology: A Year-by-Year Record of Human Events from Prehistory to the Present.* Holt, Rinehart and Winston, 1979.

* Books for further browsing.

## NEWS

Bondy, Robert J., and William C. Mattys. *Years of Promise: Canada 1945–1963.* Prentice Hall, 1980.

Cornell, James. *The Great International Disaster Book.* Charles Scribner's Sons, 1976.

*Eyes on the Prize: America's Civil Rights Years* [Videorecording]. Blackside, Inc. Boston, Massachusetts.

Granatstein, J. L. *Canada 1957–1967: The Years of Uncertainty and Innovation.* McClelland and Stewart, 1986.

Hochman, Stanley. *Yesterday and Today: A Dictionary of Recent American History.* McGraw-Hill, 1979.

Kohn, George C. *Encyclopedia of American Scandal.* Facts on File, 1989.

*Lapping, Brian. *Apartheid: A History.* George Braziller, 1986.

*Leuchtenburg, William E. *The Age of Change. Vol. 12: Life History of the United States.* Time-Life Books, 1977.

Nash, Jay Robert. *Darkest Hours.* Nelson-Hall, 1976.

*The Nuclear Almanac; Confronting the Atom in War and Peace.* Compiled and edited by faculty members at MIT. Addison-Wesley, 1984.

Palmer, Alan. *The Facts on File Dictionary of 20th Century History.* Facts On File, 1979.

Palmer, Alan, and Veronica Palmer. *Quotations in History.* The Harvester Press, 1976.

*Quick Canadian Facts*, 35th annual edition. CanExpo Publishers, 1981.

*Quotable Woman 1800–1980.* Facts On File, 1982.

Sifakis, Carl. *Encyclopedia of American Crime.* Facts On File, 1982.

*Taylor, Derek. *It Was 20 Years Ago Today.* Simon & Schuster, 1987.

## ARTS

Bordman, Gerald. *The Oxford Companion to American Theatre*. Oxford University Press, 1984.
Burbank, Richard. *Twentieth Century Music 1900–1980*. Facts On File, 1984.
Loney, Glenn. *20th Century Theatre*. Facts On File, 1983. 2 volumes.
*The Metropolitan Opera Encyclopedia*. Simon & Schuster, 1987.

## BIOGRAPHY

*Current Biography*. H. W. Wilson Co., 1947–
*Fucini, Joseph J., and Suzy Fucini. *Entrepreneurs: The Men and Women Behind Famous Brand Names and How They Made It*. G. K. Hall & Co., 1985.
Hacker, Carlotta. *The Book of Canadians*. Hurtig, 1983.
*McCullough, Joan. *First of All*. Holt, Rinehart and Winston, 1980.
*The Negro Almanac: A Reference Work on the African American*, 5th edition. Compiled and edited by Harry A. Ploski and James Williams. Gale Research Inc., 1989.
*Nobel Prize Winners*. H. W. Wilson Co., 1987.
*Notable American Women: The Modern Period*. The Belknap Press of Harvard University Press, 1980.
Vernoff, Edward, and Rima Shore. *The International Dictionary of 20th-Century Biography*. New American Library, 1987.

## FASHION

Bond, David. *The Guinness Guide to 20th Century Fashion*. Guinness Superlatives Ltd., 1981.
Corson, Richard. *Fashions in Makeup*. Peter Owen Ltd., 1972.
Dorner, Jane. *Fashion in the Forties and Fifties*. Arlington House Publishers, 1975.
*Melinkoff, Ellen. *What We Wore: An Offbeat Social History of Women's Clothing, 1950 to 1980*. Quill, 1984.
Tyrrell, Anne V. *Changing Trends in Fashions*. B. T. Batsford Ltd., 1986.

## MOVIES

Aros, Andrew A. *A Title Guide to the Talkies, 1964 through 1974*. The Scarecrow Press, Inc., 1977.

* Books for further browsing.

Dimmitt, Richard Bertrand. *A Title Guide to the Talkies*. The Scarecrow Press, Inc., 1965.
*Haun, Harry. *The Movie Quote Book*. Lippincott & Crowell, 1980.
*Hirschhorn, Clive. *The Hollywood Musical*. Crown Publishing, 1981.
Katz, Ephraim. *The Film Encyclopedia*. Thomas Y. Crowell, 1979.
*Leonard Maltin's TV Movies and Video Guide 1990 Edition*. New American Library, 1989.
Monaco, James. *The Connoisseur's Guide to the Movies*. Facts on File, 1985.
Nash, Jay Robert, and Stanley Ralph Ross. *The Motion Picture Guide 1927–1983*. Cinebooks, Inc., 1985. 12 volumes.
*Osborne, Robert. *60 Years of the Oscar: The Official History of the Academy Awards*. Abbeville Press, 1989.
Robertson, Patrick. *Guinness Film Facts and Feats*. Guinness Superlatives Ltd., 1985.
*Stanley, John. *The Creature Features Movie Guide*. Creatures at Large, 1981.
Truitt, Evelyn Mack. *Who Was Who On Screen*, 3rd edition. R. R. Bowker, Co., 1983.
*Wiley, Mason, and Damien Bona. *Inside Oscar: The Unofficial History of the Academy Awards*. Ballantine Books, 1986.

## MUSIC

*The ASCAP Biographical Dictionary of Composers, Authors and Publishers*, 3rd edition. ASCAP, 1966.
*Bronson, Fred. *The Billboard Book of Number One Hits*. Billboard Publications, 1985.
Gilbert, Bob, and Gary Theroux. *The Top Ten: 1956–Present*. Simon & Schuster, 1982.
*Hendler, Herb. *Year by Year in the Rock Era*. Greenwood Press, 1983.
*Marsh, Dave, and Kevin Stein. *The Book of Rock Lists*. Dell, 1981.
*Nite, Norm N. *Rock on Almanac*. Harper & Row, 1989.
*The Penguin Encyclopedia of Popular Music*. Viking, 1989.
*The Rolling Stone Encyclopedia of Rock and Roll*. Rolling Stone Press, 1983.
Shapiro, Nat. *Popular Music, 1920–1979*. Gale Research Co., 1985. 3 volumes.
Tyler, Don. *Hit Parade 1920–1955*. William Morrow, 1985.
Wiener, Allen J. *The Beatles: A Recording History*. McFarland & Co., 1986.

Whitburn, Joel. *The Billboard Book of Top 40 Hits: 1955 to Present*. Billboard Publications, 1983.

## POPULAR CULTURE

*Asakawa, Gil, and Leland Rucker. *The Toy Book*. Alfred A. Knopf, 1992.

Hine, Thomas. *Populuxe*. Alfred A. Knopf, 1986.

Johnson, Richard A. *American Fads*. Beech Tree Books, 1985.

*Marum, Andrew, and Frank Parise. *Follies and Foibles: A View of 20th Century Fads*. Facts On File, 1984.

*McGrath, Molly Wade. *Top Sellers, U.S.A.: Success Stories Behind America's Best-Selling Alka-Seltzer to Zippo*. Morrow, 1983.

Skolnik, Peter L., Laura Torbet, and Nikki Smith. *Fads: America's Crazes, Fevers and Fancies from the 1890s to the 1970s*. Thomas Y. Crowell, 1978.

## SCIENCE AND TECHNOLOGY

*Asimov, Isaac. *Asimov's Chronology of Science and Discovery*. Harper & Row, 1989.

*Encyclopedia of Human Evolution and Prehistory*. Garland Publishing, 1988.

*Encyclopedia of Psychology*. John Wiley & Sons, 1984. 4 volumes.

*Giscard d'Estaing, Valérie-Anne. *The World Almanac Book of Inventions*. World Almanac Publications, 1985.

Hellemans, Alexander, and Bryan Bunch. *The Timetables of Science*. Simon & Schuster, 1988.

*Jane's Encyclopedia of Aviation*. Jane's, 1980. 5 volumes.

Magill, Frank N., ed. *Magill's Survey of Science. Space Exploration Series*. Salem Press, 1989. 5 volumes.

*McAleer, Neil. *The OMNI Space Almanac*. World Almanac, 1987.

Moloney, James H., and George H. Dammann. *Encyclopedia of American Cars 1946–1959*. Crestline Publishing, 1980.

*Slater, Robert. *Portraits in Silicon*. The MIT Press, 1987.

*The Timetable of Technology*. Hearst Books, 1982.

*Vare, Ethlie Ann, and Greg Ptacek. *Mothers of Invention*. William Morrow, 1982.

*von Braun, Wernher, and Frederick I. Ordway III. *Space Travel; A History*. Harper & Row, 1985.

* Books for further browsing.

## SPORTS

*The Ballplayers: Baseball's Ultimate Biographical Reference*. William Morrow, 1990.

*Biographical Dictionary of American Sports. Football*. Greenwood Press, 1987.

Clark, Patrick. *Sports Firsts*. Facts on File, 1981.

*The Encyclopedia of Tennis*. George Allen & Unwin, 1974.

*Fischler, Stan. *Hockey's 100*. Beaufort Books, 1984.

Frommer, Harvey. *Sports Roots*. Atheneum, 1979.

*Golesworthy, Maurice. *Encyclopaedia of Boxing*, 6th edition. Robert Hale, 1979.

*Golf in America*. Harry N. Abrams, 1988.

*Grey Cup Tradition*. E. S. P. Marketing & Communications, 1987.

Hickock, Ralph. *New Encyclopedia of Sports*. McGraw-Hill, 1977.

Hollander, Zander. *The Modern Encyclopedia of Basketball*, 2nd revised edition. Dolphin Books, 1979.

*The National Hockey League Official Guide and Record Book/1988–1989*. The National Hockey League, 1988.

*The NFL's Official Encyclopedic History of Professional Football*. Macmillan, 1977.

Reichler, Joseph L., ed. *The Baseball Encyclopedia*. Macmillan, 1988.

*The Ring: 1981 Record Book and Boxing Encyclopedia*. Atheneum, 1981.

*The Sports Encyclopedia: Pro Basketball*. Grosset & Dunlap, 1975.

*Sports Quotes: The Insider's View of the Sports World*. Facts On File, 1983.

## TELEVISION AND RADIO

Brooks, Tim, and Earle Marsh. *The Complete Directory to Prime Time Network TV Shows 1946–Present*. Ballantine Books, 1979.

*Castleman, Harry, and Walter J. Podrazik. *Harry and Wally's Favorite TV Shows*. Prentice Hall Press, 1989.

*Castleman, Harry, and Walter J. Podrazik. *Watching TV: Four Decades of American Television*. McGraw-Hill, 1982.

Diamant, Lincoln. *Television's Classic Commercials: The Golden Years, 1948–1958*. Hastings House, 1971.

*Dunning, John. *Tune in Yesterday: The Ultimate Encyclopedia of Old-Time Radio 1925–1976*. Prentice Hall, 1976.

Fornatale, Peter. *Radio in the Television Age*. The Overlook Press, 1980.

Greenfield, Jeff. *Television, the First 50 Years.* Harry N. Abrams, 1977.

Hall, Jim. *Mighty Minutes: An Illustrated History of Television's Best Commercials.* Harmony, 1984.

Schemering, Christopher. *The Soap Opera Encyclopedia.* Ballantine Books, 1985.

*Woolery, George W. *Children's Television: The First Thirty-five Years, 1946–1981.* The Scarecrow Press, Inc., 1983 (Part I: Animated cartoon series); 1985 (Part II: Live, film, and tape series).

## WORDS AND PICTURES

Hackett, Alice Payne, and James Henry Burke. *80 Years of Best Sellers, 1895–1975.* R. R. Bowker, 1977.

Overstreet, Robert M. *The Official Overstreet Comic Book Price Guide 1991–1992,* 21st edition. The House of Collectibles, 1991.

Rees, Nigel. *Slogans.* George Allen & Unwin, 1982.

*The World Encyclopedia of Comics.* Edited by Maurice Horn. Chelsea House Publishers, 1976. 6 volumes.

* Books for further browsing.

# INDEX

Due to limited space, most actors, authors, cartoonists, and singers involved with ONE WORK have not been indexed.
Please check the TITLE of the work.
*Note: italicized page numbers refer to photographs*